For Reference

Not to be Taken from Library

ECCB
The Eighteenth-Century Current Bibliography

ECCB
The Eighteenth-Century Current Bibliography

n.s. volume 27—for 2001

For Reference
Not to be Taken from Library

❧

General Editors

Kevin L. Cope & Robert C. Leitz, III

❧

WITHDRAWN

AMS PRESS, INC.
NEW YORK

ECCB
The Eighteenth-Century Current Bibliography

International Standard Book Number

series: 0-404-62200-3

n.s. volume 27: 0-404-62229-1

Copyright © 2005 by AMS Press, Inc.

ISSN: 0161-0996

MANUFACTURED IN THE UNITED STATES OF AMERICA

Field Editors

James May, *Printing and Bibliographical Studies*
Sean C. Goodlett, *Historical, Social, and Economic Studies*
David Venturo, *Philosophy, Science, and Religion*
Gloria Eive, *Fine Arts*
Megan Conway, *Foreign Literatures and Languages*
Kathryn Duncan, *British Literatures*
Robert C. Leitz, III, *New World Literatures and Languages*

Editorial Contributors

Heinz-Joachim Müllenbrock, *German Studies on English*
Henry Fulton, *Religious Studies*
Deborah Armintor, *Printing and Bibliographical Studies*
Christopher Roberson, *Philosophy*
Íñigo Sánchez-Llama, *Iberian Literatures*

Contents

Preface   xi

I: Printing and Bibliographical Studies   3

II: Historical, Social, and Economic Studies   19

III: Philosophy, Science, and Religion   99

IV: Fine Arts   217

    Art and Architecture   217
    Dance   229
    Music   231
    Music Recordings and Scores   255
    Theater   258

V: Foreign Literatures and Languages   265

    Iberian Literatures and Languages   265
    French Literature and Language   291
    Germanic and Slavic Literatures and Languages   315
    Italian Literature and Language   360

VI: British Literatures   367

VII: New World Literatures and Languages   461

    American Literature and Language   461
    Australian, New Zealand, and Adjacent Literatures and Cultures (1999)   478
    Australian, New Zealand, and Adjacent Literatures and Cultures (2000)   494
    Australian, New Zealand, and Adjacent Literatures and Cultures (2001)   508

Special Section: Late Entries and Reviews — 521

- Printing and Bibliographical Studies — 521
- Historical, Social, and Economic Studies: Europe, Africa, Asia, Central and South America — 536
- Historical, Social, and Economic Studies: North America — 567
- Philosophy, Science, and Religion — 589
- Fine Arts: Painting, Prints, Drawing, Sculpture, Architecture — 622
- Fine Arts: Theater — 633
- Foreign Literatures and Languages: Iberian — 649
- Foreign Literatures and Languages: French — 649
- Foreign Literatures and Languages: Germanic and Slavic — 661
- Foreign Literatures and Languages: Multiple Language Traditions — 662
- British Literatures — 662
- New World Literatures and Languages — 669

Index — 677

Dedication

In recognition and celebration of his pioneering work on the creation of the comprehensive and interdisciplinary bibliography and textual studies that would become the modern *ECCB*, this volume is dedicated to the memory of a great friend, colleague, eighteenth-century scholar, and bibliographer,

Paul J. Korshin

PREFACE

Expansion and consolidation have been accounted highly suspect activities since the rise, in the later twentieth century, of socially conscious schools of cultural history. Few scholars have been willing to applaud the worldwide "colonialist" extension of European power; fewer still have praised long-eighteenth-century societies for enriching their centralized various bases of operation in assorted home countries. Among bibliographers, however, expansion and consolidation are always welcome. Everyone hails the enlargement of scholarly resources; everyone favors the compacting of large information stores into convenient one-stop formats.

Volume 27 of *ECCB: The Eighteenth-Century Current Bibliography* invites its readers and users to a festival of bibliogaphical expansion and consolidation. The last several volumes of *ECCB* have gradually realigned its principle coverage areas—currently, seven major fields—with the kinds and quantities of scholarship being currently produced. As a result, the *ECCB* editorial staff expects that the shape and arrangement of the *ECCB* will now remain stable, at least until the next major revolution in scholarly interest. Within these seven main coverage areas, however, expansion, revision, refinement, and consolidation continue. This volume, for one example, institutes a promising change within the recently established "New World Literatures and Languages" section. The Field Editors and Sub-Field Editors for this section have begun rethinking and clarifying the definition of "new world," with the result that this section has been subdivided into two interest areas: the specifically "American" and the Pacific (Australia, New Zealand, and adjacent islands). As with all new developments, this expansion of the *ECCB* portfolio anticipates future adjustments and refinements as the *ECCB* attempts to cover more North American material (including Canada and Mexico) and to find appropriate ways to organize scholarly studies on that most diffuse and dispersed of spaces, the great Pacific Ocean basin. The staff of the *ECCB* nevertheless hopes that this initial foray into the western seas will not only enrich and balance the emerging interest in "transatlantic" studies—an area in which the *ECCB* already excels—but will, in the spirit of Enlightenment exploration, open new worlds yet to be defined.

Consolidation as well as expansion is essential to the continuing revitalization of the *ECCB*. During the 1990s, many of the widespread resources from which the *ECCB* draws its information made the switch over to electronic, computerized information systems, a change accomplished with sometimes more and sometimes less grace and efficiency. Some libraries or databases moved into the electronic world with nary a glitch or hiccup; others have remained barely usable, even to this day. One side-effect of this unpredictable changeover period was the inability to find many items that would be suitable for recording in the *ECCB*. Hard-pressed to make minimal computing resources go a long way in a short time, many library and database technologists of the 1990s set priorities that could push less prominent but nevertheless valuable scholarly items to the cybernetic sidelines. Today, however, computer technology has passed out of puberty if not altogether into adulthood, although occasional eruptions of the electronic equivalent of acne continue to trouble its complexion. As catalogues, web pages, journal sites, databases, search engines, and a thousand-and-one other electronic resources grow more powerful, reliable, and complete, the recovery of missed entries becomes easier and more practicable. Taking advantage of this upturn in electronic research capabilities, Co-General Editor Robert C. Leitz, III has assembled a formidable list of late entries and reviews. That list, which comprises the eighth or "special" section of this volume, attempts to recover items in any and all specialty fields that have gone missing over the last several years. Of special note within this section is Leitz's comprehensive list of materials in the "American" areas, including American literature—a keepsake-quality list that more than makes up for earlier omissions. In addition to these new-world items in the "late entries" section, Sub-Field Editor Bärbel Czennia has included entries for 1999 and 2000 and well as 2001 publications in her specialty field—Australia, New Zealand, and adjacent islands—in a designated sub-section within the "New World Literatures and Languages" section (section VII). Given that this volume marks the debut for "Pacific" studies in the *ECCB*, the editors thought it better to place all this material in one location rather than subdivide this small but growing field into "current" and "catch-up" segments. This consolidation of the oceanic material within one section should create a focal point for *ECCB* users working in this important but sometimes overlooked area.

ECCB users will also note a variety of formal improvements within this volume, the most salient of which is the introduction of subsection headers into the table of contents. For example, the table of contents includes a page location for "French Literature and Language" in particular as well as for "Foreign Languages and Literatures" generally.

Preface

This modification has been introduced with the intention of accelerating access to specialized information and of promoting quick interdisciplinary searching.

The *ECCB* is pleased to welcome back Professor James May as Field Editor for Printing and Bibliographical Studies. After a brief sabbatical from his duties, Professor May returns to the post that he manned for so many successful years, ready once again to monitor and evaluate the world of bibliographical studies. We welcome Professor May and we offer thanks and good wishes to retiring Field Editor Deborah Armintor for her service to textual studies.

It has taken time to bring the *ECCB* up to its present and back to its past vital and current form. Unfortunately, that time has also taken its toll. We affectionately but regretfully dedicate this volume to Professor Paul J. Korshin, whom we lost to a serious illness in March 2005. Professor Korshin—Paul—was not only a personal friend of most of the present *ECCB* staff but was also largely responsible for the metamorphosis of the *ECCB* into its present, world-renowned form. For many years, indeed for decades, the *ECCB* had routinely appeared as an occasional supplement to such prestigious periodicals as *Philological Quarterly*. In those earlier contexts, the bibliography did admirable service to what was then a somewhat more Eurocentric world of eighteenth-century studies. It covered all the beloved British authors and supplemented its records with references to occasional studies in assorted philosophical and philological areas. Paul, however, early on recognized what we now would call "the growth potential" of interdisciplinary eighteenth-century studies. As early as the 1970s, he saw the need for a large bibliography with a disciplined framework and a sound funding and publishing base. At the time an officer of as well as prominent figure within the American Society for Eighteenth-Century (ASECS), Paul made benevolent use of his influence to secure organizational, institutional, economic, and even governmental support for an official bibliography of what less forward-thinking scholars often depreciated as a drawing-room specialty. Paul demonstrated an uncanny prescience with regard to computer technology, attempting to devise automated, electronic, and computational solutions to humanities and bibliographical challenges at a time when even modest pocket calculators cost a month's salary and broke down more often than they reckoned up. Like most visionaries, Paul encountered occasional resistance and sometimes overwhelming technical challenges. Yet, in the long run, his vision prevailed. Technology caught up with anticipation; the *ECCB* achieved its modern identity and began to show the rudiments of its present structure. In later years, Paul moved on to other projects (such as his renowned annual journal, *The Age of Johnson*), but he never lost interest in the *ECCB*. Indeed, this volume contains what will be his two last entries. As if to commemorate his character, these entries record fascinating and diverse, obscure yet attention-grabbing items that were gathered from the far corners of the globe (please see the entries for essays by Kenneth Nyberg and Michael Keevak). As befit Paul's endearingly spontaneous modus operandi, these entries simply appeared one day, out of the blue, unsolicited, accompanied with an impeccably tasteful personal printed calling card, in the *ECCB* mailbox, as a shipment from not only a spirit, but a veritable freighter, of generosity. We thank you, Paul J. Korshin, for a monumental bibliography.

Kevin L. Cope
Robert C. Leitz, III
General Editors

Correction. The *ECCB* combined volume for 1996–1998 (volumes 22–24) contained a review of Anne B. Shteir's book, *Cultivating Women, Cultivating Science: Flora's Daughters and Botany in England, 1760–1860*. Authorship credit for that review was inadvertently admitted. The review was written by Yvonne Noble, to whom the editors apologize for the by-line omission.

ECCB
The Eighteenth-Century
Current Bibliography

I: Printing and Bibliographical Studies

Bahr, Ehrhard, and Walter K. Stewart. "North American Goethe Dissertations: 1989–99 Supplement." *Goethe Yearbook: Publications of the Goethe Society of North America*, 10 (2001), 263–75.

Bandry, Anne. "A Bibliography of Sterne in French." *Shandean: An Annual Devoted to Laurence Sterne and His Works*, 12 (2001), 91–113.

Barchas, Janine. "Before Print Culture: Mary, Lady Chudleigh, and the Assimilation of the Book." Pp. 15–35 of *Eighteenth-Century Genre and Culture: Serious Reflections on Occasional Forms: Essays in Honor of J. Paul Hunter*. Edited by Dennis Todd and Cynthia Wall. Newark: University of Delaware Press, 2001.

A welcome characteristic of J. Paul Hunter's contextualizing scholarship has been its tendency to force other scholars to reconceive their work in various fields. It is appropriate then that Janine Barchas's article, which leads off the recent collection edited by Dennis Todd and Cynthia Wall in Hunter's honor, exemplifies precisely this trend. Barchas's article seeks to refine John Brewer's notion of a "print revolution" in the eighteenth century. Using data gathered from the ESTC database, Barchas wants to argue for a more gradual emergence of "print culture" in the eighteenth century. The weight of the argument rests on a reading of Lady Mary Chudleigh's *The Ladies Defence* (1701). According to Barchas, "multiple alternative visions for the printed book are mapped out" through the main characters of the dialogue. As a result of this mapping, Chudleigh emerges as one who "displays an ambivalent attitude towards the development of…'print culture.'"

Parts of the argument don't quite work because some of the local readings of Chudleigh's poem are not entirely convincing. To take one example, lines 115–18 (spoken by Chudleigh's female stand-in, Melissa, to the bachelor rake Loveal) are glossed as an allusion to Satan's temptation of Eve in Genesis. Here are the lines:

> Then at her Feet, false Man, you flattering lay,
> And pray'd, and vow'd, and sigh'd your Hours away;
> Admir'd her Face, her Shape, her Mein, her Air,

And swore that none was so divinely fair.

It is not clear why these lines (which are meant to describe Loveall's attempt to seduce a woman) exemplify the temptation scene in Eden, since they are followed by a straightforward explanation of how Loveall's words fail to win his target, and he resorts to distinctly un-Lucifer-like silent courting.

The strength of the essay lies in its observation that Chudleigh seems to have salted away a number of terms referring to printing in the dialogue itself. So, for example, Loveall exclaims at the Parson's wish to force women to learn his rules by memory, that "You've set 'em Copies, and dare you repine, / If they transcribe each black, detested Line?" (265–66). Barchas's notion that setting copies and black lines here refers to printers' cant introduces a valuable new contextual dimension into readings of Chudleigh's poem. To that extent, the article is a fitting first essay in Todd and Wall's volume.—Michael Caldwell

Barth, Marilyn. "Exploring the Book Arts Through One Fine Copy of *The Castle of Otranto*." *The Eighteenth-Century Novel*, 1 (2001), 287–310.

Marilyn Barth explores how one copy of Horace Walpole's *The Castle of Otranto*—a copy of the 1791 Parma sixth edition held by the Smithsonian Institution—reveals aspects of the book arts in the late eighteenth century. Those aspects include illustration, bookbinding, and printing, all of which Barth not only describes but shows through twelve accompanying pictures. She alternates descriptions of these physical features with discussions of the processes and personalities involved in the creation of this book. She argues that "through this exploration, glimpses will be provided into the life and times of one of the eighteenth century's best-known authors" (289). Many of those "glimpses" will be familiar to scholars of the eighteenth-century novel and the history of the book. The information on Walpole's life, for instance, is well known. The significance of this article lies not in the originality of particular glimpses, then, but in Barth's exploration of the convergence of several arts and personalities in the creation of this book.

One personality was the author himself, Horace Walpole. Barth explains that Walpole set his novel in Otranto (in southern Italy) without realizing that it did actually have a castle. A Mr. Reveley drew this castle and showed it to Walpole. The drawing was subsequently engraved to make illustrations for copies of the 1791 edition published by the bookseller James Edwards. Barth clarifies the prominence of Edwards's family in the book trade, where they were recognized as having three specialties: hidden fore-edge painting, "Etruscan" binding, and transparent vellum bindings. The first two of these specialties appear in the Parma edition of *The Castle of Otranto*, which has an Etruscan binding and a hidden fore-edge painting of a landscape scene with a castle in the background. Edwards further enhanced this edition by commissioning the famous Giambattista Bodoni of Parma to print it. Barth notes that Bodoni "helped restore printing, typography, and page design to art forms" (292). He was renowned for the beauty of his typefaces, the precision of his presswork, and the inaccuracy of the typesetting. Indeed, Bodoni's first printing of *The Castle of Otranto* was so inaccurate that he did a second printing, which unfortunately introduced further errors.

Barth guides the reader through this wealth of material by clarifying connections among personalities, providing the reader with ample subject headings, and including well-chosen illustrations. She succeeds in showing the complexity and beauty in the creation of this exemplary copy of the 1791 Parma sixth edition. For readers unfamiliar with the eighteenth-century book arts, her article provides an engaging introduction; for scholars of this subject and the eighteenth-century novel, it offers a satisfying overview of the connections among some of this period's great figures.—Caroline Breashears

Basker, James G. (ed.). *The Critical Review, or, Annals of Literature, 1756–1763*. 16 volumes. London: Pickering & Chatto, 2001. Pp. 6400.

I: Printing and Bibliographical Studies

Beatty, John D. *Protestant Women's Narratives of the Irish Rebellion of 1798*. Dublin: Four Courts Press, 2001. Pp. 272; index.

Bell, Maureen, Shirley Chew, Simon Eliot, Lynette Hunter, and James L. W. West (eds.). *Re-Constructing the Book: Literary Texts in Transmission*. Aldershot: Ashgate Publishing Company, 2001. Pp. 231.

Rev. by Julian Warner in *Library Quarterly*, 72 (2002), 398–99.

Berg, Peter. "Eighteenth-Century Holdings at Michigan State University." *East-Central Intelligencer*, 15 (2001), 4–9.

Black, Frank Gees. *The Epistolary Novel in the Late Eighteenth Century: A Descriptive and Bibliographical Study*. Eugene: University of Oregon Press, 2001. Pp. 184; illustrations.

Cain, Robert J. (ed.). *Colonial Records of North Carolina. Second Series. Volume X: The Church of England in North Carolina: Documents, 1699–1741*. Raleigh: North Carolina Division of Archives and History, Historical Publications Section, 2001. Pp. 664.

Cope, Kevin L., and Robert C. Leitz, III (eds.).*The Eighteenth Century: A Current Bibliography*. New York: AMS Press, 2001. Pp. Xii + 600; index.

Davis, Michael T. *The London Corresponding Society: Publications, 1792–1799*. 6 volumes. London: Pickering & Chatto, 2001. Pp. 2,400.

Defoe, Daniel. *Writings on Travel, Discovery and History*. Edited by W. R. Owens, P. N. Furbank, D. W. Hayton, N.H. Keeble, John McVeagh, and Andrew Wear. London: Pickering & Chatto, 2001. Pp. 1,408.

Donoghue, Frank. "Avoiding the 'Cooler Tribunal of the Study': Richard Brinsley Sheridan's Writer's Block and Late Eighteenth-Century Print Culture." *ELH*, 68 (2001), 831–56.

Dorleijn, G. J., and Keith van Rees. "The Eighteenth-Century Literary Field in Western Europe: The Interdependence of Material and Symbolic Production and Consumption." *Poetics*, 28 (2001), 331–48.

Dussinger, John A. *Questions of Literary Property in Eighteenth-Century England*. Atlanta: Georgia State University Press, 2001. Pp. vi + 153; bibliography; illustrations.

Eddy, Donald D., and Robert J. Barry. "J. D. Fleeman and His Bibliography of the Works of Samuel Johnson." *Library: The Transactions of the Bibliographical Society*, 2 (2001), 161–78.

Eger, Elizabeth. "Representing Culture: 'The Nine Living Muses of Great Britain' (1779)." Pp. 104–32 of *Women, Writing, and the Public Sphere: 1700–1830*. Edited by Elizabeth Eger, Charlotte Grant, Clíona O Gallchoire, and Penny Warburton. Cambridge: Cambridge University Press, 2001.

Eger, Elizabeth, Charlotte Grant, Clíona O Gallchoire, and Penny Warburton (eds.). *Women, Writing, and the Public Sphere: 1700–1830*. Cambridge: Cambridge University Press, 2001. Pp. xii + 320; illustrations; index.

Includes Eger's "Representing Culture: 'The Nine Living Muses of Great Britain' (1779)" (104–32); and Ellis Markman's "Coffee-Women, *The Spectator* and the Public Sphere in the Early Eighteenth Century" (27–52).

Ellison, Julie. "News, Blues, and Cowper's Busy World." *Modern Language Quarterly*, 62 (2001), 219–37.

Ferdinand, C. Y. "The Economics of the Eighteenth-Century Provincial Book Trade: The Case of Ward and Chandler." Pp. 42–56 of *Re-Constructing the Book: Literary Texts in Transmission*. Edited by Maureen Bell, Shirley Chew, Simon Eliot, Lynette Hunter, and James L. W. West. Aldershot: Ashgate Publishing Company, 2001.

Forster, Antonia. "Review Journals and the Reading Public." Pp. 171–90 of *Books and Their Readers in Eighteenth-Century England: New Essays*. Edited by Isabel Rivers. London: Continuum, 2001.

Goldgar, Bertrand. "Imitation and Plagiarism: The Lauder Affair and Its Critical Aftermath." *Studies in the Literary Imagination*, 34 (2001), 1–16.

Goodman, Roy E. "A Selected Guide to Printed Materials Relating to the Iconography and Artifacts of Benjamin Franklin." Pp. 170–82 of *Finding Colonial Americas: Essays Honoring J. A. Leo Lemay*. Edited by Carla Mulford and David S. Shields. Newark: University of Delaware Press, 2001.

Green, James N. "Thinking about Benjamin Franklin's Library." Pp. 343–56 of *Finding Colonial Americas: Essays Honoring J. A. Leo Lemay*. Edited by Carla Mulford and David S. Shields. Newark: University of Delaware Press, 2001.

I: Printing and Bibliographical Studies

Grossman, Carol. "The Trianon Press's William Blake's Water-Colour Designs for the Poems of Thomas Gray." *Printing History*, 21 (2001), 19.

Hanley, Brian. *Samuel Johnson as Book Reviewer: A Duty to Examine the Labors of the Learned.* Newark: University of Delaware Press, 2001. Pp. 293; index.

Hughes, Derek (ed.). *Eighteenth-Century Women Playwrights.* 6 volumes. London: Pickering & Chatto, 2001. Pp. 1,864.

Isaac, Peter. "The English Provincial Book Trade: A Northern Mosaic." *Papers of the Bibliographical Society of America*, 95 (2001), 410–41.

Isaac, Peter, and Barry McKay (eds.). *The Moving Market: Continuity and Change in the Book Trade.* New Castle: Oak Knoll Press, 2001. Pp. xiv + 201; illustrations.

These essays, presented at the 2000 Seminar on the British Book Trade, explore various niches of the provincial (i.e., outside London, Oxford, or Cambridge) "book trade," very broadly defined. The essays explore, among other topics, Welsh-language publishing, the beginnings of book ownership in medieval Leicester, nineteenth-century children's "lottery" books, and circulating libraries in Melbourne. Considered singly, each essay is highly specialized, but as a group they demonstrate that answers to the questions scholars find themselves asking—Who read what? When? And, if possible, why?—are available. As collected conference papers, these essays reflect varying stages of development. In Jeffrey Smith's "Books and Culture in Late Eighteenth- and Early Nineteenth-Century Newcastle," for instance, the wealth of information threatens to overwhelm the constraints of the essay. In others, like "John Atkinson's 'Lottery' Book of 1809" by Barry McKay, a preliminary consideration of a previously unexplored topic leaves the reader eager to learn more.

The historical periods addressed in this collection range from the Middle Ages to the end of the twentieth century. Two essays are of direct interest to eighteenth-century scholars. Smith's essay, mentioned above, depicts the "rich crop of cultural personalities" in Newcastle around the turn of the nineteenth century. Concentrating on four men who were all involved in Newcastle's intellectual life, Smith argues for Newcastle as an independent center for the growth of culture, "almost a hotbed...of intellectual activity." Richard Sher and Hugh Amory's profile of "the greatest bookseller in mid-eighteenth-century Britain," Andrew Millar, uses available bibliographic evidence to trace Millar's rise to metropolitan prominence from the "highly literate Presbyterian culture" into which he was born in Scotland. Both essays demonstrate that literacy, print culture, and intellectual debate were flourishing outside London in the period.

Some essays in the collection, such as Iain Beavan's examination of nineteenth-century Scottish booksellers' societies or Philip Henry Jones's "The First World War and Welsh-language Publishing," concentrate more strictly on the "book trade" itself. These would therefore be of more use to scholars with a similar interest in bibliography. More generally useful are those like Sher and Amory's, which identify the book trade as part of a larger cultural framework. Overall, though, this anthology accomplishes the goal stated in its opening "Editorial": to show to readers "the human face of the book trade."—Laura Thomason Wood

Jacob, Margaret C. *The Enlightenment: A Brief History with Documents.* Boston: St. Martin's Press, 2001. Pp. xiii + 237; illustrations; map; index.

Kennedy, Maíre. *French Books in Eighteenth-Century Ireland.* Oxford: Voltaire Foundation, 2001. Pp. x + 253; index.

Kewes, Paulina. "'[A] Play, Which I Presume to Call Original': Appropriation, Creative Genius, and Eighteenth-Century Playwriting." *Studies in the Literary Imagination*, 34 (2001), 17–47.

Keymer, Thomas, and Peter Sabor (eds.). *The Pamela Controversy: Criticisms and Adaptations of Samuel Richardson's Pamela, 1740–1750.* 6 volumes. London: Pickering & Chatto, 2001. Illustrations; facsimiles.

Rumors surrounding *Pamela*'s birth, like those around Mark Twain's death, have been wildly exaggerated. Many of us were taught in our undergraduate literature classes that *Pamela* was the first novel, and that its composition was a felicitous accident: Richardson was trying to write a sampler pack of form letters for maids to copy out, and he got carried away with the pretext for one, seeking a new position after the mistress' son made unwelcome advances, and *voilà*, a new genre was christened. Perhaps the myth of Pamela's innovation began with Ian Watt's *Rise of the Novel* (1957); certainly Watt is the buttress in many a history of the novel class that shores up the fairy story of *Pamela*'s miraculous and unforeseen arrival on the literary scene. Yet, if one looks carefully at Watt's argument, he does not say there were no novels before *Pamela* in 1740: indeed he mentions the *Satyricon* of Petronius and Heliodorus's *Aethiopica*. But Watt unequivocally does single out *Pamela* as an unprecedented literary achievement, and dismisses the praise of a novel on grounds other than originality: "it is surely very damaging for a novel to be in any sense an imitation of another literary work (Ian Watt, *The Rise of the Novel: Studies in Defoe, Richardson and Fielding* [Berkeley: University of California Press, 1957], 13). With untutored intuition as the benchmark for the novelist, Watt then makes local claims for Richardson's originality, such as "he was very careful to locate all his events of his narrative in an unprecedently detailed time-scheme" and "In the strictest sense of course, formal realism was not discovered by Defoe and Richardson; they only applied it much more completely than had been done before" (33).

Such claims for "genius" and "originality" are no longer the fashion. Nowadays, critics do better to appear circumspect and cautious in their claims for the impact of discourse. In 1996, Margaret Anne Doody indicted critics of the novel for "parochialism" and "chauvinism" in treating the novel "as if it were somehow essentially English" ignoring the Spanish, French, and even Ancient prose examples of psychological investigation that might have a reasonable claim on that title; "English criticism of the novel," she wrote masterfully, "has by and large taken place within the sound of the parish pump (Margaret Anne Doody, *The True Story of the Novel* [New York: Harper, 1996], 1–2). I, for one, felt that I had been personally dressed down by the headmistress. After an appropriate interval during which I thought about what I had done in the quiet time-out room, I vowed to renounce all hypnotically totalizing statements that Pamela was the first novel, the first modern individual, the first maid ever to resist a handsome employer.

Is it so strange that we who study English novels should have wanted *Pamela* to be the first in line as she has been first in our affections? Primogeniture has always been important to the social world of the English novel: first-borns inherit estates, titles, and the right to walk into dinner first; like Mary Crawford in *Mansfield Park*, we feel we should like the eldest best because it is socially advantageous to do so, despite the many charms of a younger, poorer Edmund over a Tom Bertram. So, reluctantly, we've stopped asserting *Pamela*'s first-bornness in the world of novels. Yet we're left with a residue from *Pamela*: while not the first of her kind, two hundred sixty-plus years later, *Pamela* is an indelible image left in printer's ink. She'll get under your skin.

And now, into the vacuum left by investigations into novels that predate *Pamela* comes the six-volume *Pamela Controversy: Criticisms and Adaptations of Samuel Richardson's Pamela, 1740–1750. Vols. 1–6*, edited by Thomas Keymer and Peter Sabor and published by Pickering & Chatto in 2001. *The Pamela Controversy* is an exhaustive sampling of the absolute deluge of printed and illustrated reviews, responses, parodies, burlesques, dramatic and operatic adaptations all seeking to join a vibrant conversation about this novel in mid-century Britain. In Keymer and Sabor's six volumes, professors of the novel will find ample evidence to use in classrooms where Richardson's impact on printing will take precedence over his originality. Volume Two, for example, includes engravings from diverse editions of *Pamela* as well as paintings by Hayman, Gravelot, and Mercier. The latter's decidedly lurid images—he shows Pamela with bared breasts, issuing an invitation to the viewer to join her in a curtained bed where she has just been writing letters—will surely provoke lively class discussion about the nature of Pamela's virtue and its ability to be construed differently by different readers and viewers.

Many of us have long taught *Pamela* in conjunction with Fielding's *Shamela*, which appears here in Volume One. But to Fielding's misogynist dismissal of Squire Booby's ridiculous affection for a common trollop, we can now add Eliza Haywood's *Anti-Pamela*, which appears in Volume Three of the series. Haywood also warns young gentlemen against "the mischiefs that arise from a too sudden Admiration," but she also manages to add nuance and depth to her cautionary tale, never dismissing the young woman's charms as amidst crudely punning misspellings in her letters, as Fielding does. Other pieces, both prose and verse, rehearse the challenges a maid has in acclimating herself to "high life," among those of her husband's birth and wealth. Many were poems published in leading journals of the day, which spoke to the public's continued desire to think of this heroine. With these poems and reviews in hand, we can introduce our students to the central irony of *Pamela*: that the novel which determinedly equates circulation of texts with sexual violation, the impulse to probe a woman's mind with the cruel wish to take her body against her will, would itself inspire more and more publication, thus making voyeuristic Mr. Bs out of us all.

In making such a vast array of visual and textual responses available to academic libraries and private purchasers, *The Pamela Controversy* enables critics and teachers of the novel to return to an old favorite with a refreshed gaze. This scrupulous and expansive collection salvages *Pamela*'s status in novel history, proving that, while not the first, Richardson's novel was unique in its ability to move and infuriate, entertain and animate all those who love the protean nature of language.—Bonnie Blackwell

Lockwood, Thomas. "Subscription Hunters and Their Prey." *Studies in the Literary Imagination*, 34 (2001), 121–35.

Mandelbrote, Scott. "The English Bible and Its Readers in the Eighteenth Century." Pp. 35–78 of *Books and Their Readers in Eighteenth-Century England: New Essays*. Edited by Isabel Rivers. London: Continuum, 2001.

Markman, Ellis. "Coffee-Women, *The Spectator*, and the Public Sphere in the Early Eighteenth Century." Pp. 27–52 of *Women, Writing, and the Public Sphere: 1700–1830*. Edited by Elizabeth Eger, Charlotte Grant, Clíona O Gallchoire, and Penny Warburton. Cambridge: Cambridge University Press, 2001.

Maruca, Lisa. "Political Propriety and Feminine Property: Women in the Eighteenth-Century Text Trades." *Studies in the Literary Imagination*, 34 (2001), 79–99.

The fundamental intentions of Lisa Maruca's article are laudable: she wishes to put the writer into the chain of material processes of text production and distribution and to discuss women's involvement in those processes. Taking Foucault's formulation of the proprietary author as precede and defined by transgressive discourse as a given, Maruca argues that critics working on the professionalization of authorship and the novel have removed the author from the group of print workers who made up the chain targeted by government censorship in the second half of the seventeenth century. Through her examination of the language of the Licensing Act and other contemporary texts, Maruca establishes that the author was indeed considered part of the chain of persons who held legal accountability for a text. However, in practice, as the essay acknowledges, although authors were part of the cited group of print workers, it was publishers and booksellers who were most often prosecuted. The economics of the trade (principally the sellers' desire to alienate, own and, thus, profit by the text) tended to push the writer/author off the stage of ownership and the attendant legal responsibility.

Having made a convincing argument on her first point, Maruca focuses on a particular method in the panoply of ingenious ways booksellers found to circumvent and confuse the regulators. In the period after 1695 greater enforcement of the libel and sedition laws and the Stamp Act encouraged booksellers to foist the imprinting of the potentially seditious or libelous text on the lower end of the distribution chain. The eighteenth-century bookseller (closest to what we would consider publisher) gave over distribution to a variety of outlets: first in degree of social status were trade publishers who then supplied the mercuries who had only small shops or stalls, and itinerant hawkers. Often it was women who occupied the more distant end of the trade because these jobs were marginal and low-status. According to Maruca's analysis, women in these positions were named on the texts because the courts could hold these women legally responsible for the seditious or libelous text while the courts also found it difficult to overcome the various defenses including virtuous femininity that the culture permitted women. Several cases discussed in the essay show that women "performed" these gender expectations in the interests of escaping punishment. The essay highlights a most interesting contradiction in the result of this practice, that is, "the feminine part of the trade gave women responsibility as it simultaneously took it away" (89).

Having established two significant points, Maruca argues that "censorship worked to produce the authorized feminine story – a modest regulated print product" (92). As in the earlier portion of the essay, this section is compelling in its ability to discover meaningful gaps in arguments. Maruca points out that we do not understand how feminized discourse became the standard for the eighteenth-century novel, arguing that the discrepancy may be taken to imply that women possessed an inner urge to write that was somehow outside of the cultural construction of women. However, it appears that the essay's answer to this paradox is that the women who disseminated texts—the print workers—established a precedent for balancing public and private and acting the virtuous feminine in the pursuit of their occupation that enabled later feminine writing. While the rest of the essay grounds its claims in materiality, echoing its author's interest in the work of textuality, this claim is made by analogy. The interpretative leap between the two sets of events may be too great.—Doreen Alvarez Saar

Maslen, K.I.D. *Samuel Richardson of London, Printer: A Study of His Printing Based on Ornament Use and Business Accounts.* (Otago Studies in English, 7.) Dunedin: Department of English, University of Otago, 2001. Pp. xii + 317; illustrations; facsimiles.

May, James E. "Who Will Edit the ESTC? (and have you checked OCLC lately?)." *Analytical and Enumerative Bibliography*, n.s. 12 (2001), 288–304.

McKinstry, E. Richard. "Resources for Eighteenth-Century Studies at the Winterthur Library." *East-Central Intelligencer*, 15 (2001), 19–22.

McLaverty, J. *Pope, Print, and Meaning.* New York: Oxford University Press, 2001. Pp. vi + 257.

I: Printing and Bibliographical Studies

This study pursues an understanding of the works of Alexander Pope through close attention to the material circumstances of publication, arguing that Pope's interest all aspects of the printing of his works demonstrates the importance of print itself to literary meaning. McLaverty claims that Pope "loved the look of print: dropped heads, italics, black letter, caps. And smalls; fine paper, wide margins, and good ink; headpieces, tailpieces, initials, and plates" though the Pope who painstakingly tended to the minutiae of print is lesser known to the great poet constructed by literary history. Playing on Pope's familiarity with the effect that packaging had upon human experience due to his own deformity, McLaverty argues that "Pope found print an essential form of self-expression but one involving a necessary deformation." The study focuses its chapters around a particular text, beginning with attention to print, breaking up the works into subsections in order to pay particular attention to the details of publication, including revisions, notes, and illustrations. However, the study is not limited to a description and interpretation of such details. McLaverty's study presupposes our interest in determining the author's intentionality while trying to understand a literary text: "The full significance of typographical features comes from the evidence they provide for the author's intentionality in the context of the work as a whole."

Individual chapters focus upon specific works and the circumstances of their publication; for example, chapter two discusses *The Rape of the Lock*, both in its initial manuscript form and its later revised form, tracing Pope's change in reputation from "court poet" to what we think of now as a professional writer. The history of *The Rape of the Lock*'s publication reveals the competing interests that shaped the rest of Pope's career, including his attention to generic requirements, the impulse to create aesthetically beautiful books through quality publication and illustration, and the drive to make money. McLaverty posits a model of "invagination" for understanding Pope's career; he argues that the externals of publication (printing, illustration, etc.) express the poet, and enable him to sever the private circumstances of the subject matter (in this case, the rape itself, and Pope's personal relation to a circle of real people) from its original context and then present it again, "reinstated in changed form." The next stage in Pope's career, according to McLaverty's schema, was to publish a volume of his own Works, which was an unusual decision, given his youth at the time of publication. However, McLaverty sees Pope's publication of the *Works* as an early exploration of the author function; in effect, he is "building a monument" to himself as an author in an effort to gain "some control over the new public responsibility of the author." The bulk of the book argues that, from 1717 onward (the date of publication of Pope's *Works*), Pope is publishing and marketing himself as an author in equal measure to his creative work. Print allows Pope to manipulate the shaping of his own image. Later on in his career, this shaping of himself in the public sphere led to social problems with powerful personal enemies.

Overall this is a tight study, and McLaverty demonstrates a remarkable attention to detail and an impressive display and exploitation of bibliographical knowledge. McLaverty's claim for an interest in the author's intentionality sounds more essentialist than it actually is, and he provides extensive theoretical bases for his various interpretations. Though his painstaking attention to detail of print circumstances is occasionally almost too specialized, McLaverty's study is significant in that it successfully shows Pope to be actively engaged with the emerging print culture at the same time as he remained skeptical of its influence.—Anna Viele

Mooney, James E. (ed.). *Eighteenth-Century Catalogues of the Yale College Library*. New Haven: Yale University Beinecke Library, 2001. Pp. xxi + 151; index.

O'Brien, Karen. "The History Market in Eighteenth-Century England." Pp. 105–33 of *Books and Their Readers in Eighteenth-Century England: New Essays*. Edited by Isabel Rivers. London: Continuum, 2001.

Paradise, Nathaniel. "From Poet to Novelist: Women Writers and the Literary Marketplace." *Eighteenth-Century Women: Studies in Their Lives, Work, and Culture* (2001), 237–62.

Pettit, Alexander. "Rex v. Curll: Pornography and Punishment in Court and on the Page." *Studies in the Literary Imagination*, 34 (2001), 63–78.

Pooley, Julian. "The Papers of the Nichols Family and Business: New Discoveries and the Work of the Nichols Archive Project." *Library*, 2 (2001), 10–52.

Rivers, Isabel. "Biographical Dictionaries and Their Uses from Bayle to Chalmers." Pp. 135–69 of *Books and Their Readers in Eighteenth-Century England: New Essays*. Edited by Isabel Rivers. London: Continuum, 2001.

Rivers, Isabel (ed.). *Books and Their Readers in Eighteenth-Century England: New Essays*. New York: Continuum, 2001. Pp. x + 294; index.

In 1982, Ian Hilson and Isabel Rivers published *Books and Their Readers in Eighteenth-Century England*, a groundbreaking collection addressed to "the history of the book" before that was a major subject of research. The text featured now classic, highly influential essays such as Pat Rogers' on chapbooks, Thomas Preston's on Biblical criticism, G. S. Rousseau's on science books, and W. A. Speck's on the politics of subscription publication. The essays demonstrated that many apparently ordinary genres (such as chapbooks) and practices (such as subscription) only *seemed* simple and were actually involved with complex economic, cultural factors that scholars had not until then investigated. What, for example, were the iconographic, economic, and moralistic connections between "penny histories," such as abridgements of *Robinson Crusoe*, and conventional literary texts? What was the semiotic significance of a subscribers' list in class-conscious Britain? *Books and Their Readers* raised new, fascinating questions about how the market for books developed alongside demand at all levels of the reading population. Needless to say, such questions are no longer new: book history is now an academic industry, with its own societies such as SHARP, and numerous research centers in the America and Europe. Indeed, the average scholarly article must take account of this increased awareness of early modern books, and cannot, for example, confuse booksellers with publishers. Sensing an expanded "market" for book history, therefore, Rivers is now back with *Books and Their Readers in Eighteenth Century England: New Essays*, which extends the scope of the first group of essays and, in Rivers's words, reflects the "revolution in the academic study of the book" over the last twenty years. This new *Books and Their Readers*, erudite and hugely thought-provoking, demonstrates how sophisticated the study of the book has become. What emerges is that book history is wide-ranging cultural history—it just takes books as its starting point.

The first essay, "The Book Trades," is by James Raven, the dean of book historians in Britain. It focuses on financing—how were booksellers/publishers implicated in the market for credit? what were the start-up costs and overhead expenses of publishing? how were print runs calculated? what was the effect of transportation costs? the relationship between book sales and newspaper advertising? the effect on sales of auctions, second-hand dealers and libraries? were the Dublin pirates after the market in England? what were booksellers' margins? what of the mutual trading relationships among competing booksellers/publishers? By now we are accustomed to thinking of books as commodities, but Raven explores the kind of commodity that books were. He expands our accustomed focus on copyright—which involves authors, and is still of "literary" interest—to one that more nearly reflects how books were produced and sold. For traditional literary scholars, the perspective is new, but the question lurking in the wings is whether such scholars should care—where in all this is the text? The answer, of course, is that as literary and cultural studies become inextricable, it is impossible not to care. Eighteenth-century women writers, for example, refer constantly to the book market, and we need to know what so exercises them. In my own case,

I recently wrote an article about commercial speech in eighteenth-century prefaces—but what was this commercialism in actual practice? Raven's discussion, including his voluminous citations, answers the question.

Each essay in *Books and Their Readers* offers a picture of eighteenth-century book production vastly more complicated than anything a non-specialist would have imagined. For example, when I read the Authorized Version of the Bible, I see a monument to scholarship and consensus that has endured for four hundred years. But in "The English Bible and Its Readers in the Eighteenth Century," Scott Mandelbrote examines numerous intense efforts at retranslation, many fraught with religious and political contention. Disputes over the Trinity, for example, as well as claims for a Trinity foreshadowed in Old Testament Hebrew, motivated several divines to seek a new iteration. There were debates over the Psalter, and over the role of metrical psalms in worship. Linguistic archaism came under attack. Bibles with massive exegetical apparatuses raised yet more objections. The Authorized Version was a lightning rod for disputes over theology and styles of worship, and it was the irony of Tom Paine's outspoken deism that it reinforced conservatives, who raised fears of disaster from *any* new translation. The dynamic, fascinating in itself, alters how one reads a familiar text, destabilizing old assumptions. Given a text so central as the Bible, one's readings of dependent texts—devotionals, conduct books, children's primers—are destabilized as well. The possibilities are exciting.

Karen O'Brien's "The History Market in Eighteenth-Century England" is similarly engaging, raising questions that go beyond her nominal subject, broaching issues of a burgeoning national consciousness more readily associated with Benedict Anderson and Linda Colley. O'Brien's focus is on the role of the market in producing the "authoritative historian," and in the search for a "viable history" of England to follow monuments such as Clarendon's *History of the Rebellion* (1702). Her essay traces the development of "philosophical," French-style history in England, more comparative and reflective, less narrowly political than earlier types. Such history was more stylish, idiosyncratic, and abrasive than that written by statesmen, and even pop histories asserted stereotypical philosophical (that is, Voltairean) ambitions. It was often concerned with manners–the family and social life—and was as imaginatively engaging as it was moral or prudential, deploying literary techniques such as sentimentality and character development. It conveyed a sense of participation in events, and was marketed to women in a way that older types of history could not be. O'Brien's essay, like others in the collection, demonstrates how Enlightenment was marketed. What is distinctive about the essay is that it provides a handy rationale for decentering the novel, allowing other forms of narrative to occupy an important place in the English imaginary. It proves that narrative genres possessed conscious stylistic affinities—a question that raises epistemological issues which break out all over the early novel. Thus if one ever doubted that book history animates the textual study of novels, O'Brien's essay provides powerful positive evidence.

My other favorite essay in *Books and Their Readers* is Marcus Walsh's "Literary Scholarship and the Life of Editing," parallel to O'Brien's in tracing the eighteenth-century development of a new type of literary humanism, in which serious editorial modes previously confined to the Bible, the Greek and Roman classics were extended to the canon of English literature. What made possible, for example, the massive apparatus of Malone's *Shakespeare*? What assumptions mediated the relative authority of author and editor, expressed as in the case of Malone by the placement of notes on the same page as the text? Walsh points out that "the object of such editions is not display but use, more specifically use by readers who believed that understanding of Shakespeare, as of other past writers, depended on the dialectical exercise and communication of a substantial body of pertinent knowledge." The extension of serious inquiry to *vernacular* classics encouraged a series of editors, working for an evolving consortium of booksellers, to produce editions successively building on preceding editions, utilizing some or all of their techniques, adding to previous knowledge and understanding. The result was a type of editing that begins to seem modern, wherein (to quote Malone) "conjecture and emendation have given place to rational explanation." Walsh is excellent on how editorial ego comes to be submerged in cooperation and collaboration—the moral equivalent of the great variorum editions—as evidenced by "overlapping circles of scholarly friendship": correspondence, lending and borrowing, annotation, bequeathing, referring, and assisting among the likes of Samuel Johnson, Malone, Thomas Gray, the Warton brothers, even women such as Elizabeth Carter and Elizabeth Montagu. Most of these were non-academics, and many spent large portions of their resources to promote their own and others' scholarship. But to whom did the products of this domestic Republic of Letters appeal? Why did *booksellers* produce it? Walsh is again excellent in decoding subscription lists which, he suggests, evince "in a wide variety of ways the particular social and cultural positioning of works of literary scholarship, in many cases delineating a characteristic audience or even confirming an agenda." What emerges is that there was a type of Common Reader, like the scholars themselves, who was outside the academy but still passionately interested in learning—or at least in appearing so. O, for the good old days!

Other essays in *Books and Their Readers* deal with such important subjects as theological books, biographical dictionaries, review journals, and the production and consumption of poetic miscellanies. Taken together, all of the essays are a reflection of the amazing vitality of eighteenth-century book production, as well as of the complex ways in which readers, authors, and bookseller/publishers influenced each other. *Books and Their Readers* is not just for specialists. Rather, it is for anyone interested in cultural history, of which books are necessarily a part. It is a natural adjunct to the growing body of literature on "reading practices," and on how audiences were constituted. Most particularly, it poses—and helps answer—questions that you did not know you had to ask.—Sandra Sherman

Isabel Rivers explains in her introduction that *Books and Their Readers in Eighteenth-Century England: New Essays*, like her 1982 collection *Books and Their Readers in Eighteenth-Century England*, is "concerned with the writing, editing, making, distributing, reading and interpreting of books in England, with some reference to Scotland and Ireland" (ix). Like the first collection, this compilation includes eight essays, two of which center on religious texts—Scott Mandelbrote's "The English Bible and its Readers in the Eighteenth Century" and Brian Young's "Theological Books from *The Naked Gospel* to *Nemesis of Faith*"—suggesting somewhat of an intentional patterning of this recent work on its predecessor.

The new collection extends this patterning to include a "state of the field" essay, "The Book Trades" by James Raven, that serves as a kind of homage to Terry Belanger's "Publishers and Writers in Eighteenth-Century England" that appeared in the 1982 volume. But the 2001 compilation expands its scope to include such diverse works as Karen O'Brien's "The History Market in Eighteenth-Century England" and Michael F. Suarez's "The Production of Consumption of the Eighteenth-Century Poetic Miscellany." Marcus Walsh's "Literary Scholarship and the Life of Editing," Antonia Forster's "Review Journals and the Reading Public," and Isabel Rivers's "Biographical Dictionaries and their Uses from Boyle to Chalmers" round out the works in the collection.

Each article, meticulously researched and detailed in presentation, provides an interesting glimpse into a different facet of the book trade, or as Raven explains, the book "trades." Some of the works assume an audience somewhat familiar with their particular line of enquiry; for example, Young's essay deals with issues of Socianians and Trinitarians as well as the implications of Oxford's Convocation, demonstrating an assumption of previous knowledge. Other essays, such as Suarez's piece, provide enough background for even a reader only casually interested in the topic at hand. To give one illustration, Suarez helpfully distinguishes between miscellanies and anthologies to better lay the groundwork for a reader unfamiliar with the intricacies of the publishing of poetry in the eighteenth century.

The biggest drawback of the collection, while not even meriting the name of a drawback, is that the volume cannot physically contain a yet wider range of topics. Perhaps it's ironic that a review of *Books and Their Readers in Eighteenth-Century England: New Essays* must grapple with an essay centering upon review journals. Antonia Forster's "Review Journals and the Reading Public" explains that "on many occasions reviewers try to present themselves as reluctantly doing their duty to steer deluded would-be writers in another direction" (186), but the likely duty of reviewers of this collection of essays is to steer more writers in the direction of the history of the book to help expand upon the groundwork laid by Rivers both here and in her earlier collection.—Kathryn Strong

I: Printing and Bibliographical Studies

Roth, Barry. "Jane Austen Bibliography for 2000." *Persuasions: Journal of the Jane Austen Society of North America,* 23 (2001), 222–28.

Roth, Barry. "Jane Austen Works and Studies 1999." *Persuasions: The Jane Austen Journal On-Line,* 22 (2001).

Ruwe, Donelle. "Guarding the British Bible from Rousseau: Sarah Trimmer, William Godwin, and the Pedagogical Periodical." *Children's Literature: Annual of the Modern Language Association Division on Children's Literature,* 29 (2001), 1–17.

Salman, Jeroen. "Children's Books as a Commodity: The Rise of a New Literary Subsystem in the Eighteenth-Century Dutch Republic." *Poetics,* 28 (2001), 399–421.

Sambrook, James. "'A Just Balance Between Patronage and the Press': The Case of James Thomson." *Studies in the Literary Imagination,* 34 (2001), 137–53.

James Sambrook, who has been almost single-handedly keeping the name of James Thomson before us in his recent editions of the poetry (now, sadly, out of print) as well as a 1991 biography of the poet, in this essay focuses on Thomson's literary earnings. Testing Oliver Goldsmith's nostalgic comment on the reign of Queen Anne as a time when there was "a just balance between patronage and the press," Sambrook discusses the patronage, theatre receipts, subscription income, and sale of copyrights to conclude that Thomson "contrived to be about three-quarters independent" (151).

Tracing the tangle of pensions and appointments, as well as more traditional fees for dedications, Sambrook provides a short-course in Whig political fortunes and allegiances during Thomson's career in London, 1725–48. Beginning in 1726 with a dedication to the Speaker of the House of Commons (whom he had never met), Thomson's patrons provided the better part of his income in his early career, as well as the hospitality of great houses and introductions to important literary and political men and women. Never fully independent of these patrons, he complained to his friend Mallet in 1729 that he was "far from that divine Freedom, that independent Life, which the Muses love" (141). The subscription editions of *The Seasons* were eventually important in freeing him somewhat from individual patrons or booksellers, and his plays after 1730 provided an increasing, though irregular, part of his income. Thomson is now known almost totally as a poet, yet plays accounted for half his creative production and all were popular enough for author's third night proceeds.

Thomson was a founding member of the Society for the Encouragement of Learning, established in 1736 to attempt to lessen the monopoly of booksellers. Members' subscriptions were pooled to print books, with profits reinvested in the collective. He seems to have been inactive in the short-lived experiment, and continued to be dependent on booksellers, especially Andrew Millar who bought most of Thomson's copyrights. In fact, Millar's copyrights for *The Seasons* were the subject of the two important copyright cases of the eighteenth century, in 1769 and 1774.

Thomson's reliance on patrons and booksellers remained necessary, but remarkably complicated. He became friends with Millar, who often advanced money when Thomson's mismanagement ran him into debt. And his relationship with Lord Lyttelton, the ideal patron praised in *Spring*, provoked Lyttelton's substantial suggestions for revisions of the 1744 edition of *The Seasons*. Was this the "just balance between patronage and the press" that Goldsmith described? Perhaps, Sambrook concludes, but it did not provide Thomson "that divine Freedom, that independent Life" he craved.—Jan Widmayer

Sisman, Adam. *Boswell's Presumptuous Task: The Making of the Life of Dr. Johnson.* New York: Farrar, Straus, and Giroux, 2001. Pp. xxii + 351; illustrations; index.

Smith, David. *Bibliography of the Writings of Helvétius.* Ferney-Voltaire: Centre International d'étude du XVIIIe siècle, 2001. Pp. xli + 407; illustrations; index.

Smyth, Elaine. "Eclectic and Underadmired: 18th-Century Holdings in the LSU Libraries." *East-Central Intelligencer,* 15 (2001), 23–25.

Strugnell, Anthony (ed.). *From Letter to Publication: Studies on Correspondence and the History of the Book, with the Besterman Lecture 2000.* Oxford: Voltaire Foundation, 2001. Pp. v + 295; bibliography.

Includes Robert Darnton's "J.-P. Brissot et la Société typographique de Neuchâtel (1779–1787)" and Daniel Droixhe's "Signatures clandestines et autres essais sur les contrefaçons de Liège et de Maastricht au XVIII siècle."

Suarez, Michael F. "The Production and Consumption of the Eighteenth-Century Poetic Miscellany." Pp. 217–51 of *Books and Their Readers in Eighteenth-Century England: New Essays.* Edited by Isabel Rivers. London: Continuum, 2001.

Tieken-Boon van Ostade, Ingrid. "Lowth's Short Introduction to English Grammar (1762) Reprinted." *Publishing History: The Social, Economic and Literary History of Book, Newspaper and Magazine Publishing,* 49 (2001), 83–95.

Tierney, James. "Advertisements for Books in London Newspapers, 1760–1785." *Studies in Eighteenth-Century Culture,* 30 (2001), 153–64.

Todd, Dennis, and Cynthia Wall (eds.). *Eighteenth-Century Genre and Culture: Serious Reflections on Occasional Forms: Essays in Honor of J. Paul Hunter.* Newark: University of Delaware Press, 2001. Pp. 316.

Uglow, Nathan. *The Historian's Two Bodies: The Reception of Historical Texts in France, 1701–1790.* Aldershot: Ashgate Publishing Company, 2001. Pp. 272.

Voltaire Foundation. *Voltaire, Religion and Ideology, Women's Studies, History of the Book, Passion in the Eighteenth Century.* Oxford: Voltaire Foundation, 2001. Pp. vi + 476; illustrations; portraits.

Walsh, Marcus. "Literary Scholarship and the Life of Editing." Pp. 191–215 of *Books and Their Readers in Eighteenth-Century England: New Essays*. Edited by Isabel Rivers. London: Continuum, 2001.

Williams, Jerry M. (ed.). *Peralta Barnuevo and the Art of Propaganda: Politics, Poetry, and Religion in Eighteenth-Century Lima: Five Texts*. Newark: Juan de la Cuesta, 2001. Pp. xxiv + 315; illustrations; map.

Yeo, Richard R. *Encyclopaedic Visions: Scientific Dictionaries and Enlightenment Culture*. Cambridge: Cambridge University Press, 2001. Pp. xxi + 336; illustrations; index.

Historians and literary scholars have written and commented on the *Encyclopédie* of Diderot and d'Alembert extensively—on its origins, intellectual contents and scandal-ridden publishing history. While this outpouring has clearly advanced our understanding of Enlightenment thought and print culture, this book's canonical status has often overshadowed other major reference works of the period. Richard Yeo's *Encyclopaedic Visions* serves as a timely corrective to this trend. This study focuses on three major British encyclopedic projects in the period from 1700 to 1820: John Harris's *Lexicon Technicum* (1704 and 1710), Ephraim Chambers's *Cyclopaedia* (1728) and the *Encyclopaedia Britannica*, which appeared in Edinburgh from 1768. In a series of tightly organized chapters, Yeo examines the intellectual heritage, ambitions and tensions that shaped these publications.

Following a lengthy general introduction to medieval and early modern encyclopedism, the first series of chapters assesses the place of encyclopedias in the European Republic of Letters of the early 1700s. These works—known also as "scientific dictionaries" to denote their generous coverage of the physical sciences and technical subjects—sought to communicate an innovative, enduring, and accessible body of scientific knowledge to a large potential readership of specialists and non-specialists alike. Of course, such an ambitious enterprise encountered serious methodological problems. The most pressing issue was how to integrate the latest scientific advances into a relatively condensed presentation format. Encyclopedias were to be both cutting edge and concise, a Herculean task during an age of rapid growth in all matters scientific. In order to keep their dictionaries within manageable dimensions, Harris and Chambers defined the arts and sciences in a most specific way: history, biography, geography, trade and commerce were all excluded, and even the coverage of natural history was minimal. In this attempt to distill human knowledge to essentials and present it in an orderly manner, encyclopedias were responding to an acute anxiety over the multitude of books delivered by the printing press. The learned public of Enlightenment Europe saw the encyclopedia as a potential remedy to this ever-increasing knowledge burden.

In the second part of his study, Yeo further explores how the concerns of controlling and ordering knowledge shaped eighteenth-century British encyclopedias. In 1736, Chambers modestly described his two-volume *Cyclopaedia* as "the best Book in the Universe" on the grounds that it offered readers the accessibility of alphabetical arrangement while at the same time promising to show the overarching order and connection between the parts of scientific knowledge. The opening pages introduced a "View of Knowledge" which visually divided forty-seven disciplines into an elaborate classification system. Yeo explains that this scheme displayed how subjects were related epistemologically or conceptually, the order in which they were to be studied, and the relationship between a particular science or art and the terms that properly belonged to it. Chambers also cross-referenced nearly half his entries in the hope that such links would enable the reader to carefully reconstitute a science by consulting the relevant terms. To reconstruct the science of physics, for example, one would consult the entries on "element," "atom," "particle," "body," and the like.

Encyclopedias of the first half of the century followed Chambers's call for order and connection between the sciences. But with the publication of the first editions of the *Encyclopaedia Britannica*, the encyclopedic project of the Enlightenment began to transform in two significant ways. First, unlike the *Cyclopaedia* and the *Encyclopédie*, this Scottish work displayed no general map of knowledge and did not elaborate on the relations between subjects. Instead, the editors sought coherence at the level of the sciences themselves by composing long articles that were to be self-contained syntheses of subjects. Yeo explains that this change in format arose in light of what some historians now regard as a "second scientific revolution" during the last decades of the century—new disciplines such as biology, geology, and physiology emerged and subjects like chemistry and optics were becoming ever more complex and controversial. Lengthy treatises allowed the presentation of both acceptable truths and rival theories to readers without definitively endorsing one doctrine or the other. The editors duly acknowledged their intellectual debt to the *Cyclopaedia*, but felt that reliance on a cross-reference system to reconstruct a science was no longer practical in an age of extensive specialization of scientific knowledge. A second implication of the increasing complexity and debate within the sciences for the *Britannica* was that editors began to solicit expert contributors in their respective fields rather than rely on the heroic efforts of a single compiler, such as a Chambers or a Harris. This trend had important consequences for the communication of knowledge, highlighted in Yeo's final chapter. Most importantly, editors were faced with the daunting prospect of dealing with many individuals, each promoting their own theoretical views and recent findings. This produced disagreement between contributors, forcing editors to find a balance between intellectual consensus of the scientific community and coverage of the most recent, controversial hypotheses. By the early 1800s, British encyclopedias like the *Britannica* had become a critical interface between specialty knowledge and an educated lay public.

Yeo has made a significant contribution to the study of scientific knowledge and print culture in eighteenth-century Britain. His book is especially valuable because it considers the works of Chambers and Harris in their own right, and not just as mere precursors to the grand *Encyclopédie*. Yeo offers readers much more than a meticulous reconstruction of these less well-known publication ventures, however. By squarely placing the encyclopedia in its cultural and material conditions, he engages with a number of topics relevant to the cultural history of the Enlightenment, such as the development of the idea of the author, copyright debates and the public communication of knowledge. And yet this book regrettably tells us very little about the "public" to which these dictionary compilers appealed. Granted, Yeo professes not to be undertaking a study of readership—a notoriously difficult subject—but this omission weakens his arguments about the attraction of encyclopedias to potential buyers. Take, for example, the suggestion that the *Cyclopaedia* effectively advertised itself as a ready-made commonplace book to stimulate a reader's memory of prior scientific study. Yeo convincingly demonstrates that Chambers inscribed his work in the tradition of commonplaces, but it remains to be demonstrated that actual readers appropriated the encyclopedia in this manner: it is not enough to show the intellectual affinity between these two systems of knowledge classification. Fortunately, such elisions are rare. The research underlying *Encyclopaedic Visions* is broad and deep and Yeo includes a comprehensive thirty-nine page bibliography which will be a useful tool for future research. Despite the occasional typographical error, Yeo's prose is clear and highly readable. The book is also extensively illustrated with images from Enlightenment encyclopedias, not as decoration, but as a serious part of the text showing just what is being discussed. Overall, Professor Yeo has written a detailed account of a distinctive moment in the history of encyclopedias, and has also reminded us that our present age is not the first to grapple with issues of knowledge and information management.—Kenneth Loiselle

Young, Brian. "Theological Books from the Naked Gospel to Nemesis of Faith." Pp. 79–104 of *Books and Their Readers in Eighteenth-Century England: New Essays*. Edited by Isabel Rivers. London: Continuum, 2001.

II: Historical, Social, and Economic Studies

Abarca Vásquez, Carlos A. *Castigados: poder político y sanción penal en Costa Rica, 1750–1880*. San José: C.A. Abarca Vásquez, 2001. Pp. 298.

Abbattista, Guido. "The English Universal History: Publishing, Authorship and Historiography in a European Project (1736–1790)." *Storia della Storiografia*, 39 (2001), 103–08.

Abdullah, Thabit A. J. *Merchants, Mamluks, and Murder: The Political Economy of Trade in Eighteenth Century Basra*. (SUNY Series in the Social and Economic History of the Middle East.) Albany: State University of New York Press, 2001. Pp. xviii + 180.

Adler, Hans, and Carsten Zelle. *Akademien im 18. Jahrhundert*. (Das achtzehnte Jahrhundert 5.) Göttingen: Wallstein, 2001.

Ageeva, Olga Genievna. "Petrovskii Peterburg V Vospriiatii Sovremennikov." *Otechestvennaia Istoriia*, 5 (2001), 3–11.

Aguirrezabala, Marcela. "Mujeres casadas en los negocios y el comercio ultramarino entre el Río de La Plata y La Península a fines del siglo XVIII." *Anuario de Estudios Americanos*, 58 (2001), 111–33.

Ahishali, Recep. *Osmanli devlet teskilatinda Reisülküttâblik: XVIII. Yüzyil*. Istanbul: Tatav, 2001. Pp. x + 390; illustrations.

Alatorre, Antonio. *El brujo de Autlán*. (Colección La Torre inclinada.) México: Editorial Aldus, 2001. Pp. 211.

Alchon, Suzanne Austin. "Disease, Population, and Public Health in Eighteenth-Century Quito," in *Secret Judgments of God: Old World Disease in Colonial Spanish America*. (The Civilization of the American Indian Series.) Edited by Noble David Cook and W. George Lovell. Norman: University of Oklahoma Press, 2001.

Algor, Catherine. *Parlor Politics: In Which the Ladies of Washington Help Build a City and a Government*. Charlottesville: University Press of Virginia, 2001. Pp. 299; illustrations.

Allan, David. "The Age of Pericles in the Modern Athens: Greek History, Scottish Politics, and the Fading of Enlightenment." *Historical Journal*, 44 (2001), 391–417.

Allan, David. "Eighteenth-Century Private Subscription Libraries and Provincial Urban Culture: The Amicable Society of Lancaster, 1769–c. 1820." *Library History*, 17 (2001), 57–76.

Amalric, Jean-Pierre, and Lucienne Domergue. *La España de la Ilustración, 1700–1833*. (Libros de Historia.) Barcelona: Crítica, 2001. Pp. 184; illustrations.

Anderson, Fred. *Crucible of War: The Seven Years' War and the Fate of Empire in British North America, 1754–1766*. (Reissue.) New York: Vintage Books, 2001. Pp. xxvii + 862; illustrations; maps.

Andreev, Andrei IUr'evich. *Lektsii po istorii Moskovskogo universiteta, 1755–1855*. (Trudy Istoricheskogo fakul'teta MGU 16.) Moskva: Izd-vo Moskovskogo universiteta, 2001. Pp. 237.

Andrew, Donna T., and Randall McGowen. *The Perreaus and Mrs. Rudd: Forgery and Betrayal in Eighteenth-Century London*. Berkeley: University of California, 2001. Pp. xii + 346; map.

Andrews, Jonathan, and Andrew Scull. *Undertaker of the Mind: John Monro and Mad-Doctoring in Eighteenth-Century England*. (Medicine and Society 11.) Berkeley: University of California Press, 2001. Pp. xxii + 364; illustrations.

Andronov, Ilja. "Che Cosa è il Prosvescenie." *Rivista Storica Italiana*, 113 (2001), 831–42.

Anzur, Tea. "Naravoslovne Znanosti in Ustanovitev Biotehniske Fakultete." *Kronika*, 49 (2001), 231–44.

Arnheim, Arthur. "Hebrew Prints and Censorship in Altona." *Studies in Bibliography and Booklore*, 21 (2001), 3–9.

II: Historical, Social, and Economic Studies

Arntz, Katherine. "The Garrison Behind the Facades: The Development of Potsdam as the Second Residence of the Prussian Monarchy." *Planning History*, 23 (2001), 13–19.

Arru, Angiolina "The Rights of Foreigners and Access to Citizenship in Eighteenth- and Nineteenth-Century Rome." In *Family History Revisited: Comparative Perspectives*. (Historische Familienforschung.) Edited by Richard Wall, Tamara K. Hareven, Josef Ehmer, and Markus Cerman. Newark: University of Delaware Press, 2001.

Artigas-Menant, Geneviève. *Du secret des clandestins à la propagande voltairienne*. (Libre pensée et littérature clandestine 13.) Paris: Honoré Champion, 2001. Pp. 440.

Asbach, Olaf, Klaus Malettke, and Sven Externbrink (eds.). *Altes Reich, Frankreich und Europa: politische, philosophische und historische Aspekte des französischen Deutschlandbildes im 17. und 18. Jahrhundert*. (Historische Forschungen 70.) Berlin: Duncker & Humblot, 2001. Pp. 298.

Asch, Ronald G. *Der europäische Adel im Ancien Régime: von der Krise der ständischen Monarchien bis zur Revolution (ca. 1600–1789)*. Köln: Böhlau, 2001. Pp. vii + 438; illustrations.

Aubin, Anne-Marie. *Criminalité en Berry au XVIIIème siècle*. (Chroniques d'antan.) Toulouse: Royer, 2001. Pp. 155

Audisio, Gabriel. *Religion et exclusion, XIIe–XVIIIe siècle*. (Collection Le temps de l'histoire.) Aix-en-Provence: Publications de l'Université de Provence, 2001. Pp. 216.

Axtell, James. *Natives and Newcomers: The Cultural Origins of North America*. Oxford: Oxford University Press, 2001. Pp. xi + 418; illustrations; maps.

Baecque, Antoine de. *Glory and Terror: Seven Deaths Under the French Revolution*. Translated by Charlotte Mandell. New York: Routledge, 2001. Pp. 243; illustrations.

Baggerman, Arianne and Rudolf Dekker. "Sensibilité et éducation d'un enfant a l'époque batave: le journal intime d'Otto van Eck (1791–1796) (I)." Translated by Annie Jourdan. *Annales historiques de la révolution française*, 326 (2001), 129–39.

Bakewell, Sarah. *The Smart: The Story of Margaret Caroline Rudd and the Unfortunate Perreau Brothers*. London: Chatto & Windus, 2001. Pp. xiv + 321; plates; illustrations.

Balano, Randy Carol and Craig L. Symonds (eds.). *New Interpretations in Naval History: Selected Papers from the Fourteenth Naval History Symposium, Held at Annapolis, Maryland, 23–25 September 1999*. Annapolis: Naval Institute Press, 2001. Pp. xii + 430.

Barbiche, Bernard. *Les institutions de la monarchie française à l'époque moderne, XVIe–XVIIIe siècle.* 2nd edition. (Collection Premier cycle.) Paris: Presses universitaires de France, 2001. Pp. xi + 430; maps.

Bardet, Jean-Pierre. "Early Marriage in Pre-Modern France." *History of the Family*, 6 (2001), 345–63.

Barker, Hannah, and David Vincent (eds.). *Language, Print, and Electoral Politics, 1790–1832: Newcastle-Under-Lyme Broadsides.* (Parliamentary History Record Series 2.) Woodbridge: Boydell Press, 2001. Pp. xliv + 337; illustrations.

Barker, Nicolas (ed.). *A Potencie of Life. Books in Society: The Clark Lectures, 1986–1987.* (The British Library Studies in the History of the Book.) London: British Library, 2001. Pp. vi + 206; illustrations.

Barnard, Alan J. "Anthropology, Race, and Englishness: Changing Notions of Complexion and Character." *Eighteenth-Century Life*, 25 (2001), 94–102.

Barnard, T. C. "Considering the Inconsiderable: Electors, Patrons and Irish Elections 1659–1761." *Parliamentary History*, 20 (2001), 107–27.

Barnard, Timothy P. "Texts, Raja Ismail and Violence: Siak and the Transformation of Malay Identity in the Eighteenth Century." *Journal of Southeast Asian Studies*, 32 (2001), 331–42.

Barnett, S. J. "The Temporal Imperative: Criticism and Defence of Eighteenth-Century Roman Theocracy." *History of Political Thought*, 22 (2001), 472–93.

Barth-Scalmani, Gunda. "Eighteenth-Century Marriage Contracts: Linking Legal and Gender History" in *Time, Space, and Women's Lives in Early Modern Europe.* (Sixteenth Century Essays & Studies 57.) Edited by Anne Jacobson Schutte, Thomas Kuehn, and Silvana Seidel Menchi. Kirksville: Truman State University Press, 2001.

Basso, Matthew, Laura McCall, and Dee Garceau (eds.). *Across the Great Divide: Cultures of Manhood in the American West.* New York Routledge, 2001. Pp. x + 308; illustrations.

Bastien, Pascal. "Fête populaire ou cérémonial d'état? Le rituel de l'exécution publique selon deux bourgeois de Paris (1718–1789)." *French Historical Studies*, 24 (2001), 501–26.

Baten, Jörg. "Climate, Grain Production and Nutritional Status in Southern Germany during the XVIIIth Century." *Journal of European Economic History*, 30 (2001), 9–47.

II: Historical, Social, and Economic Studies

Battenberg, J. Friedrich. *Die Juden in Deutschland vom 16. bis zum Ende des 18. Jahrhunderts.* (Enzyklopädie deutscher Geschichte 60.) München: R. Oldenbourg, 2001. Pp. xii + 180.

Baumann, Annette. *Die Gesellschaft der Frühen Neuzeit im Spiegel der Reichskammergerichtsprozesse: eine sozialgeschichtliche Untersuchung zum 17. und 18. Jahrhundert.* (Quellen und Forschungen zur höchsten Gerichtsbarkeit im alten Reich 36.) Köln: Böhlau, 2001. Pp. vi + 177; illustrations.

Baumann, Ursula. *Vom Recht auf den eigenen Tod: die Geschichte des Suizids vom 18. bis zum 20. Jahrhundert.* Weimar: H. Böhlaus Nachfolger, 2001. Pp. viii + 407; illustrations.

Bauer, Joachim, Birgitt Hellmann, and Gerhard Müller (eds.). *Logenbrüder, Alchemisten und Studenten: Jena und seine geheimen Gesellschaften im 18. Jahrhundert.* Rudolstadt: Hain-Verlag, 2001. Pp. 205; illustrations.

Bayly, C.A. *Origins of Nationality in South Asia: Patriotism and Ethical Government in the Making of Modern India.* (Reissue.) Oxford: Oxford University Press, 2001. Pp. 350.

Bayly, Susan. *Caste, Society and Politics in India from the Eighteenth Century to the Modern Age.* New York: Cambridge University Press, 2001. Pp. xi + 421; illustrations; maps.

Beachy, Robert. "Business Was a Family Affair: Women of Commerce in Central Europe, 1650–1880." *Histoire sociale*, 34 (2001), 307–30.

Beattie, J. M. *Policing and Punishment in London 1660–1750: Urban Crime and the Limits of Terror.* Oxford: Oxford University Press, 2001. Pp. xiv + 491; illustrations; maps.

Beatty, John D. (ed.). *Protestant Women's Narratives of the Irish Rebellion of 1798.* Portland: Four Courts Press, 2001. Pp. 272; table; index.

Beaud-Ladoire, Paule. *Mancini Mazarin, dernier duc de Nevers, 1716–1798: une injustice de l'histoire.* Paris: Editions Christian, 2001. Pp. 243; plates; illustrations.

Beauvalet-Boutouyre, Scarlett. *Etre veuve sous l'Ancien Régime.* (Histoire et société. Essais d'histoire moderne.) Paris: Belin, 2001. Pp. 415.

Becker, Peter, and William Clark (eds.). *Little Tools of Knowledge: Historical Essays on Academic and Bureaucratic Practices.* (Social History, Popular Culture, and Politics in Germany.) Ann Arbor: University of Michigan Press, 2001. Pp. x + 322; illustrations.

Behrendt, Stephen D. "Markets, Transaction Cycles, and Profits: Merchant Decision Making in the British Slave Trade." *William and Mary Quarterly*, 58 (2001), 171–204.

Bell, David A. *The Cult of the Nation in France: Inventing Nationalism, 1680–1800.* Cambridge: Harvard University Press, 2001. Pp. xiv + 304; illustrations; map.

Bell, David A. "The Unbearable Lightness of Being French: Law, Republicanism and National Identity at the End of the Old Regime." *American Historical Review*, 106 (2001), 1215–35.

Bély, Lucien. *Les relations internationales en Europe (XVIIe–XVIIIe siècles).* 3rd edition. (Thémis. Histoire.) Paris: Presses universitaires de France, 2001. Pp. xxiii + 731; illustrations; maps.

Benedict, Barbara M. *Curiosity: A Cultural History of Early Modern Inquiry.* Chicago: University of Chicago Press, 2001. Pp. ix + 321; illustrations.

Benhamou, Reed. "Who Controls This Private Space? The Offense and Defense of the Hoop in Early Eighteenth-Century France and England." *Dress*, 28 (2001), 13–22.

Benito Aguado, María Teresa. *La sociedad vitoriana en el siglo XVIII: el clero, espectador y protagonista.* (Historia medieval y moderna.) Bilbao: Servicio Editorial de la Universidad del País Vasco, 2001. Pp. 413; illustrations.

Ben-Naeh, Yaron. "Same-Sex Relations among Ottoman Jews." *Zion*, 66 (2001), 171–200.

Benzoni, Gino. *Le metamorfosi di Venezia: da capitale di stato a città del mondo.* (Civiltà veneziana. Saggi 45.) Firenze: L.S. Olschki, 2001. Pp. vi + 321; illustrations.

Berghahn, Cord-Friedrich. *Moses Mendelssohns "Jerusalem": ein Beitrag zur Geschichte der Menschenrechte und der pluralistischen Gesellschaft in der deutschen Aufklärung.* (Studien zur deutschen Literatur 161.) Tübingen: Niemeyer, 2001. Pp. vi + 320.

Bernier, Marc André. "La question du despotisme oriental en France sous le règne du sultan Zeokinizul." *Tangence*, 65 (2001), 52–59.

Berkemer, Georg (ed.). *Explorations in History of South Asia: Essays in Honour of Dietmar Rothermund.* (South Asian Studies 36.) New Delhi: Manohar, 2001. Pp. xxx + 420; plates; color illustrations.

II: Historical, Social, and Economic Studies

Bernardi, Walter. "La controverse sur l'électricité animale dans l'Italie du XVIIIe siècle: Galvani, Volta et d'autres." *Revue d'histoire des sciences*, 54 (2001), 53–70.

Bernardini, Paolo, and Norman Fiering (eds.). *The Jews and the Expansion of Europe to the West, 1450 to 1800.* (European Expansion and Global Interaction 2.) New York: Berghahn Books, 2001. Pp. xv + 567; illustrations; maps.

Bernasconi, Robert (ed.). *Concepts of Race in the Eighteenth Century.* Vols I–VIII. Bristol: Thoemmes, 2001.

Bernasconi, Robert (ed.). *Race.* (Blackwell Readings in Continental Philosophy.) Malden: Blackwell, 2001. Pp. viii + 309.

Bernasconi, Robert. "Who Invented the Concept of Race: Kant's Role in the Enlightenment Construction of Race." in *Race.* (Blackwell Readings in Continental Philosophy.) Edited by Robert Bernasconi. Malden: Blackwell, 2001.

Berry, Helen. "Rethinking Politeness in Eighteenth-Century England: Moll King's Coffee House and the Significance of 'Flash Talk.'" *Transactions of the Royal Historical Society*, 11 (2001), 65–81.

Berteau, Pierre C. "Le Cat et l'école d'anatomie." *Histoire des sciences médicales*, 35 (2001), 141–50.

Bertomeu Sánchez, José R., and García Belmar, Antonio. "Pedro Gutiérrez Bueno (1745–1822) y las relaciones entre la química y la farmacia durante el último tercio del siglo XVIII." *Hispania*, 61 (2001), 539–61.

Bianchi, Diana. *La ilustración española y la pobreza: debates metropolitanos y realidades coloniales.* Montevideo: Facultad de Humanidades y Ciencias de la Educación, 2001. Pp. 372.

Bicalho, Maria Fernanda Baptista. "The City of Rio de Janeiro and the Articulation of the South Atlantic World in the Seventeenth and Eighteenth Centuries." *Mediterranean Studies*, 10 (2001), 143–55.

Bieganska, Anna. "The Learned Scots in Poland (From the Mid-Sixteenth to the Close of the Eighteenth Century)." *Canadian Slavonic Papers*, 43 (2001), 1–27.

Birn, Raymond. *Forging Rousseau: Print, Commerce and Cultural Manipulation in the Late Enlightenment.* (Studies on Voltaire and the Eighteenth Century 8.) Oxford: Voltaire Foundation, 2001. Pp. ix + 281.

Black, Jeremy. *British Diplomats and Diplomacy, 1688–1800.* Exeter: University of Exeter Press, 2001. Pp. xii + 244.

Black, Jeremy. *Eighteenth-Century Britain, 1688–1783.* (Palgrave History of Britain.) New York: Palgrave, 2001. Pp. viii + 312; index.

Black, Jeremy. *The Making of Modern Britain: The Age of Empire to the New Millennium.* Stroud: Sutton, 2001. Pp. viii + 273; illustrations; maps.

Black, Jeremy. *Western Warfare, 1775–1882.* Bloomington: Indiana University Press, 2001. Pp. xiii + 210.

Blackburn, Anne M. *Buddhist Learning and Textual Practice in Eighteenth-Century Lankan Monastic Culture.* (Buddhisms.) Princeton: Princeton University Press, 2001. Pp. 241; illustrations; map.

Blanquie, Christophe. "La vérification des dettes de bordeaux (1665–1670): la fronde, quinze ans après." *Annales du Midi*, 113 (2001), 39–57.

Blay, Michel. "De l'apparition subreptice des futures formules de conservation à l'occasion de l'algorithmisation de la science du mouvement au tournant des XVIIe et XVIIIe siècles." *Revue d'histoire des sciences*, 54 (2001), 291–301.

Bödeker, Hans Erich, and Lieselotte Steinbrügge. *Conceptualiser la femme dans la pensée des Lumières.* (Concepts & symboles du dix-huitième siècle européen.) Berlin: Arno Spitz, 2001. Pp. vii + 188; illustrations.

Boer, Dick E. H. de, Gudrun Gleba, and Rudolf Holbach (eds.). *"—In guete freuntlichen nachbarlichen Verwantnus und Hantierung—": Wanderung von Personen, Verbreitung von Ideen, Austausch von Waren in den niederländischen und deutschen Küstenregionen vom 13.–18. Jahrhundert.* (Oldenburger Schriften zur Geschichtswissenschaft 6.) Oldenburg: Bibliotheks- und Informationssystem der Universität Oldenburg, 2001. Pp. 441.

Bogucka, Maria. "Fairs in Early Modern Poland." *Studia Historiæ Œconomicæ*, 24 (2001), 23–30.

II: Historical, Social, and Economic Studies

Bogucka, Maria. "Between the Ideal and Reality. Polish Women in the 16th-18th Centuries." Translated by Janina Dorosz. *Acta Poloniae Historica*, 83 (2001), 79–93.

Boisson, Didier. "La bibliothèque d'un marchand de vin protestant à la fin du XVIIIe siècle." *Bulletin de la société de l'histoire du protestantisme français*, 147 (2001), 201–24.

Boisson, Didier. "Une communauté protestante au XVIIIe siècle; les vignerons d'Asnières-les-Bourges." *Histoire et sociétés rurales*, 15 (2001), 37–66.

Bolton, Herbert Eugene. *Texas in the Middle Eighteenth Century: Studies in Spanish Colonial History and Administration*. (University of California Publications in History 3. Reissue.) La Crosse: Brookhaven Press, 2001. Pp. x + 501; plates; illustrations; maps.

Boncompain, Jacques. *La révolution des auteurs (1773–1815): naissance de la propriété intellectuelle*. Paris: Fayard, 2001. Pp. 1172; illustrations.

Bondeson, Jan. *The London Monster: A Sanguinary Tale*. Philadelphia: University of Pennsylvania Press, 2001. Pp. xv + 237; illustrations; maps.

Bonney, Richard. "France and the First European Paper Money Experiment." *French History*, 15 (2001), 254–72.

Bontemps, Alex. *The Punished Self: Surviving Slavery in the Colonial South*. Ithaca: Cornell University Press, 2001. Pp. x + 224.

Boogert, Maurits H. van den. "Redress for Ottoman Victims of European Privateering: A Case against the Dutch in the *Divan-I Hümayun* (1708–1715)." *Revue d'études turques*, 33 (2001), 91–118.

Bordo, Michael D., and Roberto Cortés-Conde (eds.). *Transferring Wealth and Power from the Old to the New World: Monetary and Fiscal Institutions in the 17th through the 19th Century*. (Studies in Macroeconomic History.) Cambridge: Cambridge University Press, 2001. Pp. x + 482; illustrations.

Bosse, David. "The Boston Map Trade of the Eighteenth Century" in *Mapping Boston*. Cambridge: MIT Press, 2001. Pp. xiv + 278; illustrations; maps.

Boucher, David. "British Idealism and the Human Rights Culture." *History of European Ideas*, 27 (2001), 61–78.

Boudreau, George W., and William A. Pencak (eds.). *Explorations in Early American Culture.* Volume 5. University Park: Pennsylvania Historical Association, 2001. Pp. 388; illustrations.

Boulinier, Georges. "Une femme anatomiste au siècle des lumières: Marie Marguerite Biheron (1719–1795)." *Histoire des Sciences médicales*, 35 (2001), 411–23.

Bourguinat, Nicolas. "Libre-commerce du blé et représentations de l'espace français: les crises frumentaires au début du XIXe siècle." *Annales: Histoire, Sciences Sociales*, 56 (2001), 125–52.

Boyce, D. George, Robert Eccleshall, and Vincent Geoghegan (eds.). *Political Discourse in Seventeenth- and Eighteenth-Century Ireland.* New York: Palgrave, 2001. Pp. xii + 309.

Braddick, M. J., and John Walter (eds.). *Negotiating Power in Early Modern Society: Order, Hierarchy, and Subordination in Britain and Ireland.* Cambridge: Cambridge University Press, 2001. Pp. x + 302.

Braden, Jutta. *Hamburger Judenpolitik im Zeitalter lutherischer Orthodoxie 1590–1710.* (Hamburger Beiträge zur Geschichte der deutschen Juden 23.) Hamburg: Christians, 2001. Pp. 606; illustrations.

Bradley, James E., and Dale K. Van Kley (eds.). *Religion and Politics in Enlightenment Europe.* (Erasmus Institute Books.) Notre Dame: University of Notre Dame Press, 2001. Pp. xiii + 409.

Brakensiek, Stefan. Erfahrungen mit der hessischen Policey- und Niedergerichtsbarkeit des 18. Jahrhunderts: Zugleich ein Plädoyer für eine Geschichte des Gerichtspersonals." *Historische Zeitschrift*, Supplement (2001), 349–68.

Branson, Susan. *These Fiery Frenchified Dames: Women and Political Culture in Early National Philadelphia.* (Early American Studies.) Philadelphia: University of Pennsylvania Press, 2001. Pp. 218; illustrations; maps.

Brech, Alison, and McConnell, Anita. "The Pigott Family: Eighteenth Century Connections with Church, Science and Law." *Recusant History*, 25 (2001), 449–60.

Breen, T. H. *Tobacco Culture: The Mentality of the Great Tidewater Planters on the Eve of Revolution.* 2nd edition. Princeton: Princeton University Press, 2001. Pp. xxx + 216; illustrations.

II: Historical, Social, and Economic Studies

Bressler, Ann Lee. *The Universalist Movement in America, 1770–1880*. New York: Oxford University Press, 2001. Pp. viii + 204.

Breuer, Dieter (ed.). *Die Aufklärung in den deutschsprachigen katholischen Ländern, 1750–1800: kulturelle Ausgleichsprozesse im Spiegel von Bibliotheken in Luzern, Eichstätt und Klosterneuburg*. Paderborn: Schöningh, 2001. Pp. 619.

Bric, Maurice J. "Patterns of Irish Emigration to America, 1783–1800." *Eire-Ireland*, 36 (2001), 10–28.

Briley, Ron. "More than Just a Slave Holder? George Washington, Adolescents, and American Culture in the 1990s." Pp. 215–37 of *George Washington in and as Culture*. Edited by Kevin L. Cope, William S. Pederson, and Frank Williams. New York: AMS Press, 2001.

Bromley, J. S. "Outlaws at Sea, 1660–1720: Liberty, Equality, and Fraternity among the Caribbean Freebooters," in *Bandits at Sea: A Pirates Reader*. Edited by C.R. Pennell. New York: New York University Press, 2001.

Brown, Gillian. *The Consent of the Governed: The Lockean Legacy in Early American Culture*. Cambridge: Harvard University Press, 2001. Pp. 237.

Brown, Kendall W. "Workers' Health and Colonial Mercury Mining at Huancavelica, Peru." *Americas: A Quarterly Review of Inter-American Cultural History*, 57 (2001), 467–96.

Brown, Laura. *Fables of Modernity: Literature and Culture in the English Eighteenth Century*. Ithaca: Cornell University Press, 2001. Pp. xii + 273.

Bruckmann, Patricia C. "Clothes of Pamela's Own: Shopping at B-Hall." *Eighteenth-Century Life*, 25 (2001), 201–13.

Brumwell, Stephen, and W. A. Speck. *Cassell's Companion to Eighteenth-Century Britain*. London: Cassell, 2001. Pp. 455.

Buczynski, Alexander. "The Development of Sericulture and the Production of Silk in Croatia." *Povijesni prilozi*, 21 (2001), 171–81.

Bulatov, Vladimir E., Catherine Delano Smith, and Francis Herbert. "Andrew Dury's *Map of the Present Seat of War between the Russians, Poles, and Turks* (1769)." *Imago Mundi*, 53 (2001), 71–82.

Burguière, André. "L'état monarchique et la famille (XVIe–XVIIIe siècle)." *Annales: Histoire, Sciences Sociales*, 56 (2001), 313–35.

Burhans, Bruce J. "The Evolution of the Family in Great Britain." *Michigan Academician*, 33 (2001), 273–86.

Burke, Tim. "Humanity Is Now the Pop'lar Cry: Laboring-Class Writers and the Liverpool Slave Trade, 1787–1789." *Eighteenth Century: Theory and Interpretation*, 42 (2001), 245–63.

Bermúdez, Isabel Cristina. *Imágenes y representaciones de la mujer en la Gobernación de Popayán.* (Serie Magíster 13.) Quito: Universidad Andina Simón Bolívar, 2001. Pp. 102.

Burnard, Trevor, and Kenneth Morgan. "The Dynamics of the Slave Market and Slave Purchasing Patterns in Jamaica, 1655–1788." *William and Mary Quarterly*, 58 (2001), 205–28.

Butterwick, Richard. *The Polish-Lithuanian Monarchy in European Context c. 1500–1795.* New York: Palgrave, 2001. Pp. xix + 249; illustrations; maps.

Byrd, Ronald. "George Washington and Wellness." Pp. 240–68 of *George Washington in and as Culture*. Edited by Kevin L. Cope, William S. Pederson, and Frank Williams. New York: AMS Press, 2001.

Caballero Espericueta, Mariano. "Las uniones estratégicas de los comerciantes e industriales Madrileños (1800–1813)." *Cuadernos de Historia Contemporánea*, 23 (2001), 217–40.

Calaça, Carlos Eduardo. "Do Reino ao Rio: Cristãos-novo, migração, mobilidade social e sociabilida de no Rio de Janeiro." *Tempo*, 6 (2001), 223–50.

Calaresu, Melissa. "Constructing an Intellectual Identity: Autobiography and Biography in Eighteenth-Century Naples." *Journal of Modern Italian Studies*, 6 (2001), 157–77.

Cameron, David Kerr. *London's Pleasures: From Restoration to Regency.* Stroud: Sutton, 2001. Pp. 234; illustrations.

Cañizares-Esguerra, Jorge. *How to Write the History of the New World: Histories, Epistemologies, and Identities in the Eighteenth-Century Atlantic World.* (Cultural Sitings.) Stanford: Stanford University Press, 2001. Pp. xviii + 450; illustrations; maps.

II: Historical, Social, and Economic Studies

Canning, Joseph, and Hermann Wellenreuther (eds.). *Britain and Germany Compared: Nationality, Society and Nobility in the Eighteenth Century*. (Göttinger Gespräche zur Geschichtswissenschaft 13.) Göttingen: Wallstein, 2001. Pp. 239.

Carswell, John. *The South Sea Bubble*. Stroud: Sutton, 2001. Pp. xvii + 293; plates; illustrations.

Carter, Philip. *Men and the Emergence of Polite Society, Britain, 1660–1800*. (Women and Men in History.) New York: Pearson Education, 2001. Pp. viii + 232; illustrations.

Carton, Fernand. "La littérature dialectale à Lille au XVIIIe siècle." *Bibliothèque de l'Ecole des Chartes*, 159 (2001), 69–91.

Casanova, Jean-Claude. "L'université française du XIXe au XXIe siècle." *Revue des sciences morales & politiques*, 4 (2001), 73–103.

Casanueva, Fernando. "Smallpox and War in Southern Chile in the Late Eighteenth Century." In *Secret Judgments of God: Old World Disease in Colonial Spanish America*. (The Civilization of the American Indian Series.) Edited by Noble David Cook and W. George Lovell. Norman: University of Oklahoma Press, 2001.

Castleman, Bruce A. "Social Climbers in a Colonial Mexican City: Individual Mobility within the Sistema de Castas in Orizaba, 1777–1791." *Colonial Latin American Review*, 10 (2001), 229–49.

Cavaliero, Roderick. *The Last of the Crusaders: The Knights of St. John and Malta in the Eighteenth Century*. (Reissue.) Valletta: Progress Press, 2001. Pp. x + 298; illustrations; maps.

Cerman, Markus. "Central Europe and the "'European Marriage Pattern': Marriage Patterns and Family Structure in Central Europe, 16th-19th Centuries." In *Family History Revisited: Comparative Perspectives*. (Historische Familienforschung.) Edited by Richard Wall, Tamara K. Hareven, Josef Ehmer, and Markus Cerman. Newark: University of Delaware Press, 2001.

Chabot, Jean-Luc. *Histoire de la pensée politique: fin XVIIIe–début XXIe siècle*. (Le politique en plus.) Grenoble: Presses universitaires de Grenoble, 2001. Pp. 307.

Chantin, Jean-Pierre. "Le Jansénisme convulsionnaire à la fin du XVIIIe siècle: permanence et diversité du mouvement port-royaliste tardif." *Cristianesimo nella Storia*, 22 (2001), 153–66.

Chatel de Brancion, Laurence (ed.). *Cambacérés: fondateur de la justice moderne: actes du colloque tenu à Montpellier*. Saint-Rémy-en-l'Eau: Monelle Hayot, 2001. Pp. 183; illustrations.

Cherkasov, Petr Petrovich. *Ekaterina II i Liudovik XVI: russko-frantsuzskie otnosheniia 1774–1792*. Moskva: "Nauka," 2001. Pp. 525; illustrations.

Chiappe, Jean-François. *Histoire des droites françaises: de 1789 au centenaire de la revolution*. Paris: Édition du Rocher, 2001.

Chisick, Harvey. "Utopia, Reform and Revolution: The Political Assumptions of L. S. Mercier's *L'An 2440*." *History of Political Thought*, 22 (2001), 648–68.

Chiu, Peng-sheng. "Shiba Shiji Diantong Shichang Zhong de Guanshang Guanxi Yu Liyi Guannian." *Zhongyang Yanjiuyuan Lishi Yuyan Yanjiusuo Jikan (Bulletin of the Institute of History and Philology, Academia Sinica)*, 72 (2001), 49–119.

Choquette, Leslie. *De Français à paysans: modernité et tradition dans le peuplement du Canada français*. Sillery: Septentrion, 2001. Pp. x + 323.

Christiansen, Palle Ove. "Lebensperspektive, Erfahrung, Arbeit: Fatalisten unter den ostdänischen Gutsbauern im 18. Jahrhundert." *Historische Zeitschrift*, Supplement (2001), 155–68.

Ciappara, Frans. "Perceptions of Marriage in Late-Eighteenth-Century Malta." *Continuity and Change*, 16 (2001), 379–98.

Cicchini, Marco. "'Sa majesté voulant pourvoir d'une manière digne de sa sagesse et de son humanité à la punition des déserteurs...': Répression de la désertion à Genève, 1760–1790." *Crime, Histoire & Sociétés*, 5 (2001), 75–91.

Ciobanu, Veniamin (ed.). *Europe and the Porte: New Documents on the Eastern Question*. Iasi: Center for Romanian Studies, 2001.

Cirakman, Asli. "From Tyranny to Despotism: The Enlightenment's Unenlightened Image of the Turks." *International Journal of Middle East Studies*, 33 (2001), 49–68.

Clark, David H., and Stephen P. H. Clark. *Newton's Tyranny: The Suppressed Scientific Discoveries of Stephen Gray and John Flamsteed*. New York: W. H. Freeman, 2001. Pp. xvi + 188.

II: Historical, Social, and Economic Studies

Clark, Gregory, and Anthony Clark. "Common Rights to Land in England, 1475–1839." *Journal of Economic History*, 61 (2001), 1009–36.

Coleman, Terry. *Nelson: The Man and the Legend*. London: Bloomsbury, 2001. Pp. xix + 424; illustrations; maps.

Collani, Claudia von. "China in the German '*Geistesgeschichte*' in the Seventeenth and Eighteenth Centuries." In *China and Christianity: Burdened Past, Hopeful Future*. Edited by Stephen Uhalley, Jr., and Xiaoxin Wu. Armonk: M.E. Sharpe, 2001.

Collette, Sophie. "Les religieuses de la visitation Sainte-Marie de la ville d'Amiens aux XVIIe et XVIIIe siècles." *Revue du Nord*, 83 (2001), 519–40.

Condette-Marcant, Anne-Sophie, and Albert Rigaudière. *Bâtir une généralité: le droit des travaux publics dans la généralité d'Amiens au XVIIIe siècle*. (Histoire économique et financière de la France.) Paris: Comité pour l'histoire économique et financière de la France, 2001. Pp. xxvi + 661; plates; illustrations.

Conermann, Stephan. "Mongolische Religiosität zwischen Islam und Lamaismus (13. bis 18. Jahrhundert)." In *Die Mongolei: Aspekte ihrer Geschichte und Kultur*. (Grazer morgenländische Studien 5.) Edited by Johannes Giessauf. Graz: Urania, 2001.

Connolly, Sean J. *Priests and People in Pre-Famine Ireland, 1780–1845*. Dublin: Four Courts, 2001. Pp. 285; map.

Conrad, Margaret, and Barry Moody (eds.). *Planter Links: Community and Culture in Colonial Nova Scotia*. (Planters Studies Series 4.) Fredericton: Acadiensis Press, 2001. Pp. iii + 236; illustrations.

Constantine, David. *Fields of Fire: A Life of Sir William Hamilton*. London: Weidenfeld & Nicolson, 2001. Pp. xxvii + 324; plates; illustrations.

Conway, Stephen. "War and National Identity in the Mid-Eighteenth-Century British Isles." *English Historical Review*, 116 (2001), 863–93.

Cook, Noble David, and W. George Lovell (eds.). *Secret Judgments of God: Old World Disease in Colonial Spanish America*. (The Civilization of the American Indian Series.). Norman: University of Oklahoma Press, 2001. Pp. xxiv + 285; illustrations; maps.

Coquard, Claude and Claudine Durand-Coquard. *Société rurale et justice de paix: deux cantons d'Allier en Révolution*. (Etudes sur le Massif Central.) Clermont-Ferrand: Presses Universitaires Blaise-Pascal, 2001. Pp. 492; illustrations.

Cordonnier, Alexis. "Une industrie fragile: le raffinage du sucre à Lille (1675–1790)." *Revue du Nord*, 83 (2001), 541–57.

Corona Páez, Sergio Antonio (ed.) *Tríptico de Santa María de las Parras: notas para su historia, geografía y política en tres documentos del siglo XVIII*. (Colección Lobo rampante 4.) Saltillo: Universidad Iberoamericana, Laguna, 2001. Pp. 68.

Cosandey, Fanny, and Isabelle Poutrin. *Monarchies espagnole et française, 1550–1714*. (Clefs concours. Histoire moderne.) Neuilly: Atlande, 2001. Pp. 640; maps.

Cossy, Valérie, and Deidre Dawson (eds.). *Progrès et violence au XVIIIe siècle*. (Etudes internationales sur le dix-huitième siècle 3.) Paris: Honoré Champion, 2001. Pp. 458.

Cottret, Bernard. *Histoire de la Réforme protestante: Luther, Calvin, Wesley, XVIè–XVIIIe siècle*. (Collection Pour l'histoire.) Paris: Perrin, 2001. Pp. 398.

Coull, James R. "Fishery Development in Scotland in the Eighteenth Century." *Scottish Economic and Social History*, 21 (2001), 1–21.

Couty, Mathieu. *Jean-Benjamin de Laborde, ou, Le bonheur d'être fermier-général*. Paris: Michel de Maule, 2001. Pp. 406.

Cowan, Brian. "What Was Masculine About the Public Sphere? Gender and the Coffeehouse Milieu in Post-Restoration England." *History Workshop Journal*, 51 (2001), 127–57.

Cowans, Jon. *To Speak for the People: Public Opinion and the Problem of Legitimacy in the French Revolution*. New York: Routledge, 2001. Pp. 249.

Cox, Michael, Tim Dunne, and Ken Booth (eds.). *Empires, Systems and States: Great Transformations in International Politics*. Cambridge: Cambridge University Press, 2001. Pp. xii + 298.

Crawford, Alan Pell. *Unwise Passions: A True Story of a Remarkable Woman – and the First Great Scandal of Eighteenth-Century America*. (Large Print Reprint Edition.) Thorndike: G.K. Hall, 2001. Pp. 296.

II: Historical, Social, and Economic Studies

Crawford, William H. *The Management of a Major Ulster Estate in the Late Eighteenth Century: The Eighth Earl of Abercorn and His Irish Agents.* (Maynooth Studies in Irish Local History 35.) Dublin: Irish Academic Press, 2001. Pp. 73; maps.

Crecelius, Daniel. "Al-Jabarti's `Aja'ib al-Athar fi al-Tarajim wa'l-Akhbar and the Arabic Histories of Ottoman Egypt in the Eighteenth Century." In *The Historiography of Islamic Egypt, c. 950–1800.* (The Medieval Mediterranean 31.) Edited by Hugh Kennedy. Leiden: Brill, 2001.

Crespí, Juan. *A Description of Distant Roads: Original Journals of the First Expedition into California, 1769–1770.* Translated by Alan K. Brown. San Diego: San Diego State University Press, 2001. Pp. xv + 848; illustrations; maps.

Crespo Solana, Ana. *El comercio marítimo entre Amsterdam y Cádiz (1713–1778).* (Estudios de historia económica 40.) Madrid: Banco de España, Servicio de Estudios, 2001. Pp. 162.

Crowston, Clare Haru. *Fabricating Women: The Seamstresses of Old Regime France, 1675–1791.* Durham: Duke University Press, 2001. Pp. xviii + 508.

This is a meticulously researched and beautifully written book that traces the history of seamstresses and their guild from the time of its creation in Paris in 1675 until its dissolution during the Revolution in 1791, along with all other corporations. While the work focuses heavily on Paris, Clare Haru Crowston also considers seamstresses in the provinces of Provence and Normandy for comparative purposes. The first section of the book looks at seamstresses as producers of clothes, examining the types of garments they made, the changing fashions over the course of the century, the techniques and commercial practices of the seamstresses, and the nature of the labor market. (This section, while fascinating, fits rather oddly with the rest of the book, and might have worked better in a separate project). The second part more closely explores the guilds, specifically how the women governed themselves and their efforts both to distance themselves from and maintain their privileges vis-à-vis the tailors' guilds. In the final section, Crowston looks at the career paths and hypothesizes about the personal lives of the seamstresses, ending with an epilogue that considers their fate as the guilds were abolished and the garment trade was radically restructured in the nineteenth century. To weave her story, Crowston consulted an impressive array of documents, including the laws and regulations of the guilds, notarial archives, the archives of the police of Paris, bankruptcy records, and a wide variety of visual and material artifacts that lend color and heft to her analysis.

Crowston's work is theoretically sophisticated. She is interested not only in reassessing the guilds and their role in Old Regime France, but also in considering the effects of gender on this particular trade, and the relationship between women and guilds. Indeed, gender is central to her analysis. Most specifically, Crowston re-examines the concept of "family economy," and its centrality for women under the ancien régime. In opposition to historians of gender who have argued that the rise of both the corporate system and the absolutist state in late medieval and early modern Europe led to a narrowing of women's economic opportunities, Crowston argues that women could and did flourish under the corporate system; authorities did not always discriminate against female labor. Further, Crowston takes on historians who date the emergence of modern gender identities to the late eighteenth century; while she acknowledges that "binary distinctions centered on an essentialized male-female opposition may indeed be a development of the late eighteenth century," in fact "the seamstresses demonstrate very clearly that cultural ideas about masculinity and femininity shaped a sexual division of labor during the seventeenth century" (11). These two separate strands of analysis do not always hold together as well as they might, and Crowston—especially in her conclusion—makes some rather sweeping challenges to historians who see the guilds with their regulations and restrictions as a less positive system for women. She makes a vigorous case for the strength of the seamstresses' guild in Paris, and for the benefits it conferred on mistresses in particular. But even though it was one of the largest guilds in Paris, these benefits reached a relatively small group of women – as Crowston herself recognizes, few seamstresses ever achieved full status within the guild system. Still, her work nuances our understanding of the guild system and its effect on women, and this richly textured book enhances our understanding of the key trade for women in the early modern, and well into the modern, era. – Christine Adams

Croxson, Bronwyn. "The Foundation and Evolution of the Middlesex Hospital's Lying-In Service, 1745–86." *Social History of Medicine*, 14 (2001), 27–57.

Crummey, Robert O., Holm Sundhaussen, and Ricarda Vulpius (eds.). *Russische und ukrainische Geschichte vom 16.–18. Jahrhundert.* (Forschungen zur osteuropäischen Geschichte 58.) Wiesbaden: Harrassowitz, 2001. Pp. 336; illustrations.

Cruz, Enrique Normando. "La nueva sociedad de frontera: Los grupos sociales en la frontera de San Ignacio de Ledesma, Chaco Occidental, finales del siglo XVIII." *Anuario de Estudios Americanos*, 58 (2001), 135–60.

Curran, Stuart. "Dynamics of Female Friendship in the Later Eighteenth Century." *Nineteenth-Century Contexts*, 23 (2001), 221–39.

Curtin, Philip. *Migration and Mortality in Africa and the Atlantic World, 1700–1900.* (Variorum Collected Studies Series.) Burlington: Ashgate/Variorum, 2001. Illustrations; maps.

Dabas, Bal Kishan. *The Political and Social History of the Jats.* Delhi: Sanjay Prakashan, 2001. Pp. 291.

Dalporto, Jeannie. "Landscape, Labor, and the Ideology of Improvement in Mary Leapor's 'Crumble-Hall.'" *Eighteenth Century: Theory and Interpretation*, 42 (2001), 228–44.

Danforth, Susan. "Cultivating Empire: Sir Joseph Banks and the (Failed) Botanical Garden at Nassau." *Terrae Incognitae*, 33 (2001), 48–58.

Danson, Edwin. *Drawing the Line: How Mason and Dixon Surveyed the Most Famous Border in America.* New York: John Wiley, 2001. Pp. viii + 232; illustrations; maps.

Darcel, Jean-Louis. "Les chemins de l'exil, 1792–1817." *Revue des études maistiennes*, 13 (2001), 35–48.

II: Historical, Social, and Economic Studies

D'arcy, Frank. *Wild Geese and Travelling Scholars.* (Compact Irish History.) Cork: Mercier Press, 2001. Pp. 112; illustrations; maps.

Darnton, Robert. "J.-P. Brissot and the société typographique de neuchâtel (1779–1787)." In *From Letter to Publication: Studies on Correspondence and the History of the Book.* (Studies on Voltaire and the Eighteenth Century 10.) Edited by Robert V. McNamee, Robert Darnton, and Daniel Droixhe. Oxford: Voltaire Foundation, 2001.

Dashkova, E. R. *O smysle slova "vospitanie": sochineniia, pis'ma, dokumenty.* Sankt-Peterburg: D. Bulanin, 2001. Pp. 459; illustrations.

Daston, Lorraine and Katharine Park. *Wonders and the Order of Nature, 1150–1750.* New York: Zone Books, 2001. Pp. 511; illustrations.

Davids, Karel. "From de la Court to Vreede. Regulation and Self-Regulation in Dutch Economic Discourse from c. 1660 to the Napoleonic Era." *Journal of European Economic History*, 30 (2001), 245–89.

Davidson, Jenny. "Swift's Servant Problem: Livery and Hypocrisy in the Project for the Advancement of Religion and the Directions to Servants." *Studies in Eighteenth-Century Culture*, 30 (2001), 105–25.

Dawson, Ruth. "'Europens Kaiserinn': Katharina II. und die Zelebrität." *L'Homme*, 12 (2001), 265–90.

Dear, Peter Robert. *Revolutionizing the Sciences: European Knowledge and its Ambitions, 1500–1700.* Princeton: Princeton University Press, 2001. Pp. viii + 208.

Delâge, Denys, and Jean-Pierre Sawaya. *Les traités des Sept-Feux avec les Britanniques: droits et pièges d'un héritage colonial au Québec.* Sillery: Septentrion, 2001. Pp. 292; maps.

Delille, Gérard. "Réflexions sur le système européen de la parenté et de l'alliance." *Annales: Histoire, Sciences Sociales*, 56 (2001), 369–80.

Delmaire, Danielle. *Les communautés juives septentrionales, 1791–1939: Naissance, croissance, épanouissement.* (Thèse à la carte.) Villeneuve d'Ascq: Presses universitaires du Septentrion, 2001.

Deol, Jeevan. "Eighteenth-Century Khalsa Identity: Discourse, Praxis and Narrative" In *Sikh Religion, Culture and Ethnicity*. Edited by Arvind-pal Singh, Christopher Shackle, and Gurharpal Singh. Richmond: Curzon, 2001.

Demel, Bernhard. "Die Bestande des 'Exercitium Militare' und 'Militaria' im Zentralarchiv des Deutschen Ordens in Wien." *Mitteilungen des österreichischen Staatsarchivs*, 49 (2001), 311–47.

Demerson, Paula de. "Muertes aparentes y socorros administrados a los ahogados y asfixiados en las postrimerías del siglo XVIII." *Asclepio*, 53 (2001), 45–68.

Demkin, A.V. *Gorodskoe predprinimatel'stvo v Rossii na rubezhe XVII–XVIII vekov*. Moskva: Institut rossiiskoi istorii RAN, 2001. Pp. 163.

Denis, Gilles. "Pratiques paysannes et théories savantes préagronomiques au XVIIIe siècle: le cas des débats sur la transmission des maladies des grains de blé." *Revue d'histoire des sciences*, 54 (2001), 451–94.

Derex, Jean-Michel. "Le décret du 14 frimaire an II sur l'assèchement des étangs: Folles espérances et piètres résultats. L'application du décret en brie." *Annales historiques de la révolution française*, 325 (2001), 77–97.

Deschênes, Gaston. *Les voyageurs d'autrefois sur la Côte-du-Sud*. Sillery, Québec: Septentrion, 2001. Pp. 322; illustrations; maps.

Desplat, Christian. *Cultures en Béarn*. (Colleccion "Radics.) [Pau]: Princi Negue, 2001. Pp. 265; illustrations.

Devine, Thomas Martin. *The Scottish Nation: 1700–2000*. New York: Penguin Books, 2001. Pp. xxiii + 695; maps.

Díez, Fernando. "El gremialismo de Antonio de Capmany (1742–1813): La idea del trabajo de un conservador ingenuo." *Historia y Política: Ideas, Procesos y Movimientos Sociales*, 1 (2001), 171–206.

Ditt, Karl, Rita Gudermann, and Norwich Rüsse (eds.). *Agrarmodernisierung und ökologische Folgen: Westfalen vom 18. bis zum 20. Jahrhundert*. (Forschungen zur Regionalgeschichte 40.) Paderborn: Schöningh, 2001. Pp. xi + 812; illustrations.

II: Historical, Social, and Economic Studies 39

Dolan, Brian. *Ladies of the Grand Tour: British Women in Pursuit of Enlightenment and Adventure in Eighteenth-Century Europe.* New York: HarperCollins, 2001. Pp. xi + 337; plates; illustrations.

Doering-Manteuffel, Sabine, Josef Mancal, and Wolfgang Wüst (eds.). *Pressewesen der Aufklärung: periodische Schriften im Alten Reich.* (Colloquia Augustana 15.) Berlin: Akademie Verlag, 2001. Pp. 558; illustrations.

Domergue, Lucienne, Antonio Risco, and Christine Bénavidès (eds.). *Justice et société en Espagne au XVIIIe siècle.* 2 volumes. Paris: Ophrys, 2001.

Dompnier, Bernard and Dominique Julia (eds.). *Visitation et visitandines aux XVIIe et XVIIIe siècles: actes du colloque d'Annecy, 3–5 juin 1999, organisé par le Centre d'histoire Espaces et cultures, Université Blaise Pascal, Clermont-Ferrand et le Centre d'anthropologie religieuse européenne, Ecole des hautes études en sciences sociales, Paris.* (Travaux et recherches 14.) Saint-Étienne: Publications de l'Université de Saint-Etienne, 2001. Pp. 603; illustrations.

Dormois, Jean-Pierre. "Etudiants montbéliardais au «Stift» évangélique de Tübingen du XVIe au XVIIIe siècle." *Revue d'histoire et de philosophie religieuses*, 81 (2001), 277–99.

Dougherty, Keith L. *Collective Action Under the Articles of Confederation.* Cambridge: Cambridge University Press, 2001. Pp. xii + 211; illustrations.

Doyle, Anthony. *Charles Powell Leslie (II)'s Estates at Glaslough, County Monaghan, 1800–41: Portrait of a Landed Estate Business and its Community in Changing Times.* (Maynooth Studies in Irish Local History 38.) Dublin: Irish Academic Press, 2001. Pp. vii + 68; illustrations; maps.

Doyle, William. *Old Regime France, 1648–1788.* (The Short Oxford History of France.) Oxford: Oxford University Press, 2001. Pp. xii + 281; maps.

Draper, Anthony J. "William Eden and Leniency in Punishment." *History of Political Thought*, 22 (2001), 106–30.

Dresser, Madge. *Slavery Obscured: The Social History of the Slave Trade in an English Provincial Port.* (The Black Atlantic.) New York: Continuum, 2001. Pp. xii + 242.

Driancourt-Girod, Janine. "L'utilisation des chapelles d'ambassade scandinaves par les marchands luthériens des 'ports de l'océan de France' au XVIIIe siècle." *Bulletin de la Société de l'Histoire du Protestantisme Français*, 147 (2001), 225–49.

Droixhe, Daniel. "Signatures clandestines et autres essais sur les contrefacons de Liège et de Maastricht au XVIII siècle." In *From Letter to Publication: Studies on Correspondence and the History of the Book*. (Studies on Voltaire and the Eighteenth Century 10.) Edited by Robert V. McNamee, Robert Darnton, and Daniel Droixhe Oxford: Voltaire Foundation, 2001.

Drury, Marjule Anne. "Anti-Catholicism in Germany, Britain, and the United States: A Review and Critique of Recent Scholarship." *Church History*, 70 (2001), 98–131.

Dubin, Lois. "Researching Port Jews and Port Jewries: Trieste and Beyond." *Jewish Culture and History*, 4 (2001), 47–58.

Duchesne, Ricardo. "Between Sinocentrism and Eurocentrism: Debating André Gunder Frank's *Re-Orient: Global Economy in the Asian Age*." *Science & Society*, 65 (2001–02), 428–63.

Dudley, William S., and Michael J. Crawford (eds.). *The Early Republic and the Sea: Essays on the Naval and Maritime History of the Early United States*. Washington, DC.: Brassey's, 2001. Pp. xv + 256; illustrations; maps.

Duffy, Michael, and Roger Morriss (eds.). *The Glorious First of June 1794: A Naval Battle and Its Aftermath*. (Exeter Maritime Studies.) Exeter: University of Exeter Press, 2001. Pp. 179; illustrations; maps.

Dufour, Hortense. *Marie-Antoinette, la mal-aimée*. Paris: Flammarion, 2001. Pp. 765.

Duhart, Frédéric. *Habiter et consommer à Bayonne au XVIIIe siècle: éléments d'une culture matérielle urbaine*. (Collection Villes et entreprises.) Paris: L'Harmattan, 2001. Pp. 286.

Dunn, Walter S., Jr. *The New Imperial Economy: The British Army and the American Frontier, 1764-1768*. Westport: Praeger, 2001. Pp. viii + 208.

The eighteenth- and early nineteenth-century Euro-Indian frontier has played a large role in the writing of American history since Fredrick Jackson Turner lamented the frontier's closing at the turn of the twentieth century. Most recently, frontier studies have focused on cross-cultural interchange and the place of American Indians in the imperial rivalry and struggle for power that punctuated the Seven Year's War and led to the American Revolution. Employing research conducted during the 1950s and 1960s, Walter S. Dunn, Jr., does not comment on this recent trend, but instead focuses his study on the British Army and its impact on the economic development of the late eighteenth-century North American frontier.

As it had in each of its previous colonial wars with France, in 1755, Parliament appropriated money, supplied ships, and sent troops to its American colonies to rid North America of their French adversaries and to establish British control over the continent. The real difference with the Seven Year's War was the unprecedented scale of the enterprise. Between 1755 and the effective end of the war in North America in 1760, Britain sent more than 30,000 troops to America and doubled their national debt to pay for them.

II: Historical, Social, and Economic Studies 41

The Seven Years' War was the largest European undertaking in North America and it consequently had an enormous impact on the American frontier. Not only was much of the war fought in those parts of Indian Country that the English and French considered their frontier precincts, but the war itself heated the frontier economy to fever pitch, just as it did everywhere else in the American colonies. With British and French money freely flowing into the coffers of frontier officials, the accounts of large merchant houses, and the larger villages of powerful Indian leaders, the frontier was awash in easy money, and new fortunes were speedily constructed while older fortunes were thoroughly supplemented.

The British victory in 1760, and the Paris peace treaty that followed in 1763, gave English frontier developers every reason to expect even greater profits in the postwar era. After all, French competitors were eliminated, Indian traders could no longer keep costs up by playing one European power against another, and hundreds of thousands of acres of western land were now available for profitable speculation.

These bright hopes quickly foundered, however, as British postwar policy turned in unexpected directions. The first sign of trouble was the British decision to maintain French control over the fur trade in Canada and the Missouri territories, albeit now under direct British supervision. This undercut the expectations of English and Anglo-American merchants, who had assumed that they would inherit the French fur trade in the backcountry. Making matters worse, British policymakers abruptly ordered most of its troops out of the frontier and stationed them in Boston, New York, and other seaport cities. Perhaps more than any other measure, the removal of British troops hobbled the frontier economy. Maintenance of these troops had brought £400,000 annually into the backcountry, making the frontier second only to the southern tobacco colonies (£900,000/annum) in regional colonial income.

The final blow to the frontier economy came with the Proclamation Line of 1763, which prohibited white settlement in Indian Country altogether. Though designed as a temporary measure, the Proclamation Line ended any hope of land speculation for the foreseeable future and further dashed hopes of frontier economic development. After 1763, the frontier would become a bad dream of unrealized expectations—expectations that, in the end, would drive most people involved in the frontier economy into the arms of the Patriot cause in the 1770s.

While there is little new in *The New Imperial Economy*, it tells an important story and it tells it well. It is a fitting capstone to the author's public history career.—Ronald Schultz

Dupas, Didier Mathias. "Un procès de magiciens au XVIIIe siècle." *Histoire, économie et société*, 20 (2001), 219–29.

Duran, Yves. *L'ordre du monde: idéal politique et valeurs sociales en France, XVIe–XVIIIe siècle*. (Regards sur l'histoire 148.) Paris: Sedes, 2001. Pp. 398.

Dussinger, John. *Questions of Literary Property in Eighteenth-Century England*. (Studies in the Literary Imagination 34.) Atlanta: Georgia State University Press, 2001. Pp. vi + 153; illustrations.

Duteil, Jean-Pierre. *L'Asie aux XVIe, XVIIe, XVIIIe siècles*. (Synthèse & histoire.) Paris: Ophrys, 2001. Pp. 160; maps.

Dykstal, Timothy. *The Luxury of Skepticism: Politics, Philosophy, and Dialogue in the English Public Sphere, 1660–1740*. Charlottesville: University Press of Virginia, 2001. Pp. x + 222.

Earle, Rebecca. "'Two Pairs of Pink Satin Shoes!!' Race, Clothing and Identity in the Americas (17th–19th Centuries)." *History Workshop Journal*, 52 (2001), 175–95.

Eddy, M. D. "The Doctrine of Salts and Rev. John Walker's Analysis of a Scottish Spa (1749–1761)." *Ambix*, 48 (2001), 137–60.

Eger, Elizabeth. *Women, Writing, and the Public Sphere: 1700–1830*. Cambridge: Cambridge University Press, 2001. Pp. xii + 320; illustrations.

Eisenbach, Ulrich and Gerd Hardach (eds.). *Reisebilder aus Hessen: Fremdenverkehr, Kur und Tourismus seit dem 18. Jahrhundert*. (Schriften zur hessischen Wirtschafts- und Unternehmensgeschichte 5.) Darmstadt: Hessisches Wirtschaftsarchiv, 2001. Pp. 413; illustrations; maps.

Elazar, Daniel J. "Religious Diversity and Federalism." *International Social Science Journal*, 53 (2001), 61–65.

Elliott, Mark C. *The Manchu Way: The Eight Banners and Ethnic Identity in Late Imperial China*. Stanford: Stanford University Press, 2001. Pp. xxiii + 580; illustrations; maps.

Elm, Veit. *Die Moderne und der Kirchenstaat: Aufklärung und römisch-katholische Staatlichkeit im Urteil der Geschichtsschreibung vom 18. Jahrhundert bis zur Postmoderne*. (Historische Forschungen 72.) Berlin: Duncker & Humblot, 2001. Pp. 317.

Elmarsafy, Ziad M. *The Histrionic Sensibility: Theatricality and Identity from Corneille to Rousseau*. (Biblio 17.) Tübingen: G. Narr, 2001. Pp. 243.

Endelman, Todd M. "In Defense of Jewish Social History." *Jewish Social Studies*, 7 (2001), 52–67.

Engels, Jens Ivo. "Beyond Sacral Monarchy: A New Look at the Image of the Early Modern French Monarchy." *French History*, 15 (2001), 139–58.

Engerman, Stanley L., and Kenneth L. Sokoloff. *The Evolution of Suffrage Institutions in the New World*. (NBER Working Paper Series 8512.) Cambridge: National Bureau of Economic Research, 2001. Pp. 31.

Engstrand, Iris H. W. "Spanish Naturalists in Cuba and the West Indies, 1795–1802." *Terrae Incognitae*, 33 (2001), 59–68.

II: Historical, Social, and Economic Studies

Entenmann, Robert. "The problem of Chinese Rites in Eighteenth-Century Sichuan." In *China and Christianity: Burdened Past, Hopeful Future*. Edited by Stephen Uhalley, Jr. and Xiaoxin Wu. Armonk: M.E. Sharpe, 2001.

Esquivel Triana, Ricardo. "Fuentes para la historia agraria e industrial de la provincia de Neiva 1778–1938." *Memoria y Sociedad*, 5 (2001), 61–88.

Eustace, Nicole. "Vehement Movements: Debates on Emotion, Self, and Society during the Seven Years' War in Pennsylvania." In *Explorations in Early American Culture*. Volume 5. Edited by George W. Boudreau and William A. Pencak. University Park: Pennsylvania Historical Association, 2001.

Evans, Chris. "Global Commerce and Industrial Organization in an Eighteenth-Century Welsh Enterprise: The Melingriffith Company." *Welsh History Review*, 20 (2001), 413–34.

Evans, Eric. *The Forging of the Modern State: Early Industrial Britain, 1783–1870*. (Foundations of Modern Britain.) New York: Longman, 2001. Pp. xl + 585; illustrations; maps.

Faculty of Law of the University of Zagreb. *Faculty of Law, University of Zagreb*. Zagreb: University of Zagreb Presses, 2001. Pp. 194; color and black-and-white illustrations; charts; tables.

An extensive history of both legal and, more generally, higher education in Croatia.

Fagan, Patrick. *The Diocese of Meath in the Eighteenth Century*. Dublin: Four Courts Press, 2001. Pp. 224; maps.

Falino, Jeannine, and Gerald W. R. Ward (eds.). *New England Silver & Silversmithing: 1620–1815*. (Publications of the Colonial Society of Massachusetts 70.) Boston: Colonial Society of Massachusetts, 2001. Pp. xiv + 281; illustrations.

Fallon, Peter K. "Why the Irish Speak English: The Consequences of One Culture's Resistance to Technological Change." *Printing History*, 21 (2001), 31–41.

Faus Prieto, Alfredo. "La real academia de bellas artes de San Carlos y el ejercicio de la agrimensura en la Valencia del siglo XVIII." *Asclepio*, 53 (2001), 117–42.

Farley, James J. "'To Commit Ourselves to Our Own Ingenuity and Industry': Joshua Humphreys and the Construction of the U. S. United States, 1794–1799." In *Explorations* in *Early American Culture*. Volume 5. Edited by George W. Boudreau and William A. Pencak. University Park: Pennsylvania Historical Association, 2001.

Fauve-Chamoux, Antoinette. "Continuity and Change Among the Rhemish Proletariat: Preindustrial Textile Work in Family Perspective." *History of the Family*, 6 (2001), 167–85.

Fay, Mary Ann. "Ottoman Women through the Eyes of Mary Wortley Montagu." In *Unfolding the Orient: Travellers in Egypt and the Near East*. Edited by Paul Starkey and Janet Starkey. Reading: Ithaca, 2001.

Fea, John. "Ethnicity and Congregational Life in the Eighteenth-Century Delaware Valley: The Swedish Lutherans of New Jersey." In *Explorations in Early American Culture*. Volume 5. Edited by George W. Boudreau and William A. Pencak. University Park: Pennsylvania Historical Association, 2001.

Federhofer, Marie-Theres. *Moi simple amateur: Johann Heinrich Merck und der naturwissenschaftliche Dilettantismus im 18. Jahrhundert*. Hannover: Wehrhahn, 2001. Pp. 262.

Fehrenbacher, Don E. *The Slaveholding Republic: An Account of the United States Government's Relations to Slavery*. New York: Oxford University Press, 2001. Pp. xii + 465.

Fenn, Elizabeth A. *Pox Americana: The Great Smallpox Epidemic of 1775–82*. (Variola.) New York: Hill and Wang, 2001. Pp. xiv + 370; illustrations; maps.

Fernández Albaladejo, Pablo (ed.). *Los Borbones: dinastía y memoria de nación en la España del siglo XVIII: actas del coloquio internacional celebrado en Madrid, mayo de 2000*. (Historia.) Madrid: Marcial Pons, Ediciones de Historia: Casa de Velázquez, 2001. Pp. 646.

Ferraro, Giovanni. "Analytical Symbols and Geometrical Figures in Eighteenth-Century Calculus." *Studies in History and Philosophy of Science*, 32 (2001), 535–55.

Ferrone, Vincenzo. "Il nuovo repubblicanesimo dei diritti dell'uomo nelle logge italiane alla fine del XVIII secolo." *Rivista Storica Italiana*, 113 (2001), 843–58.

Fields, Polly Stevens. "Samson Occom and/in the Missionary Position: Consideration of a Native American Preacher in 1770s Colonial America." *Wordsworth Circle*, 32 (2001), 14–20.

Figeac, Michel. *La douceur des Lumières: noblesse et art de vivre en Guyenne au XVIIIe siècle*. Bordeaux: Mollat, 2001. Pp. 311; illustrations.

II: Historical, Social, and Economic Studies 45

Fitzgerald, Patrick and Steve Ickringill (eds.). *Atlantic Crossroads: Historical Connections between Scotland, Ulster, and North America*. Newtownards: Colourpoint, 2001. Pp. 144.

Ford, Brian J. "The Royal Society and the Microscope." *Notes and Records of the Royal Society of London*, 55 (2001), 29–49.

Foreman, Amanda. *Georgiana, Duchess of Devonshire*. (Reissue.) New York: Modern Library, 2001. Pp. xx + 456; illustrations.

Forero Romero, Juan Carlos. *San Agustín de Fonseca: de pueblo de indios a parroquia de blancos, siglo XVIII*. La Guajira: Fondo Mixto para la Promoción de la Cultura y las Artes de La Guajira, 2001. Pp. 83; plates; maps.

Forster, Marc R. *Catholic Revival in the Age of the Baroque: Religious Identity in Southwest Germany, 1550–1750*. (New studies in European history.) Cambridge: Cambridge University Press, 2001. Pp. xiii + 268; maps.

Fortescue, John. *The War of Independence: The British Army in North America, 1775–1783*. (History of the British Army 3.) London: Greenhill Books, 2001. Pp. xix + 263; maps.

Francesconi, Daniele. "Periodizzazione storica e generi storiografici: lo scoppio della guerra civile nella *History of England* di Hume." *Storia della Storiografia*, 39 (2001).

Franco-Rubio, Gloria A. *La vida cotidiana en tiempos de Carlos III*. (Nuestra historia.) Madrid: Ediciones Libertarias, 2001. Pp. 265.

Frasca-Spada, Marina. "The Many Lives of Eighteenth-Century Philosophy." *British Journal for the History of Philosophy*, 9 (2001), 135–44.

Freeman, Joanne B. *Affairs of Honor: National Politics in the New Republic*. New Haven: Yale University Press, 2001. Pp. xxiv + 376; illustrations.

Frey, Manuel. "Europäer und ihre Feinde: Der Wandel des Türkenbildes von der Frühen Neuzeit bis zur Mitte des 19. Jahrhunderts." *Sozialwissenschaftliche Informationen*, 30 (2001), 14–21.

Fritzsche, Peter. "Specters of History: On Nostalgia, Exile, and Modernity." *American Historical Review*, 106 (2001), 1587–618.

Froide, Amy M. "Female Relationships in Early Modern England." *Journal of British Studies*, 40 (2001), 279–89.

Fuhrmann, Martin. " Die Politik der Volksvermehrung und Menschenveredelung. Der Bevölkerungsdiskurs in der politischen und ökonomischen Theorie der deutschen Aufklärung." *Aufklärung*, 13 (2001), 243–82.

Fumaroli, Marc. *Quand l'Europe parlait français*. Paris: Fallois, 2001. Pp. 489.

Gailus, Manfred. "Die Erfindung des 'Korn-Juden'. Zur Geschichte eines anti-jüdischen Feindbildes des 18. und frühen 19. Jahrhunderts." *Historische Zeitschrift*, 272 (2001), 597–622.

Gainot, Bernard. *1799, un nouveau Jacobinisme: la démocratie représentative, une alternative à brumaire*. Paris: Ministère de l'éducation nationale, 2001. Pp. 542.

Gandt, François de. *Cirey dans la vie intellectuelle: la réception de Newton en France*. (Studies on Voltaire and the Eighteenth Century 11.) Oxford: Voltaire Foundation, 2001. Pp. v + 253.

Gantet, Claire. *La paix de Westphalie (1648): une histoire sociale, XVIIe–XVIIIe siècles*. (Histoire et société.) Paris: Belin, 2001. Pp. 447; illustrations; maps.

García Belmar, Antonio, Bertomeu Sánchez, and José Ramón. "Pedro Gutiérrez Bueno (1745–1822), Los libros de texto y los nuevos públicos de la química en el último tercio del siglo XVIII." *Dynamis*, 21 (2001), 351–74.

García Belmar, Antonio, Bertomeu Sánchez, and José Ramón. "Viajes de cultivadores de la química españoles a Francia (1770– 1830)." *Asclepio*, 53 (2001), 95–139.

Garrioch, David. "Sacred Neighborhoods and Secular Neighborhoods: Milan and Paris in the Eighteenth Century." *Journal of Urban History*, (2001), 405–19.

Gaspar, David Barry. "With a Rod of Iron: Barbados Slave Laws as a Model for Jamaica, South Carolina, and Antigua, 1661–1697." In *Crossing Boundaries: Comparative History of Black People in Diaspora*. (Blacks in the Diaspora.) Edited by Darlene Clark Heine and Jacqueline McLeod. Bloomington: Indiana University Press, 2001.

Gavira Marquez, Maria Concepcion. "Producción de plata y comercio en Oruro afines del período colonial. Análisis a través de las fuentes fiscales." *Revista de Indias*, 61 (2001), 377–405.

II: Historical, Social, and Economic Studies 47

Geggus, David Patrick (ed.). *The Impact of the Haitian Revolution in the Atlantic World*. (The Carolina Lowcountry and the Atlantic World.) Columbia: University of South Carolina Press, 2001. Pp. xviii + 261; maps.

Gerzina, Gretchen Holbrook. "Mobility in Chains: Freedom of Movement in the Early Black Atlantic." *South Atlantic Quarterly*, 100 (2001), 41–59.

Gibbons, J. M. "Laying the Moral Foundations: Writer, Religion and Late Eighteenth-Century Society. The Case of J. M. R. Lenz." *German Life and Letters*, 54 (2001), 137–54.

Gibson, William. *The Church of England, 1688–1832: Unity and Accord*. New York: Routledge, 2001. Pp. vi + 269.

Giessauf, Johannes (ed.). *Die Mongolei: Aspekte ihrer Geschichte und Kultur*. (Grazer morgenländische Studien 5.) Graz: Urania, 2001. Pp. 146; illustrations; maps.

Gil Novales, Alberto. "Pueblo y nación en España durante la Guerra de la Independencia." *Spagna contemporanea*, 10 (2001), 169–87.

Ginio, Eyal. "Piracy and Redemption in the Aegean Sea during the First Half of the Eighteenth Century." *Turcica*, 33 (2001), 135–47.

Ginio, Eyal (Gurbuz, Emre, transl.). "Kad nlar, Yoksulluk Ve 18. Yüzy l Selanik'in de Hayatta Kalma Stratejileri." *Toplum ve Bilim*, 89 (2001), 190–204.

Gladfelder, Hal. *Criminality and Narrative in Eighteenth-Century England: Beyond the Law*. Baltimore: Johns Hopkins University Press, 2001. Pp. xiii + 281.

Göbel, Walter, Saskia Schabio, and Martin Windisch (eds.). *Engendering Images of Man in the Long Eighteenth Century*. Trier: WVT Wissenschaftlicher Verlag, 2001. Pp. xiii + 295.

Godfrey, Peter B., and G. M. Ditchfield. "The Unitarian Archives at Essex Hall." *Archives*, 26 (2001), 58–70.

Gogoleva, Alla Anatol'evna. "Rabota Voronezhskikh Arkhivistov S Knigami Deloproizvodstva Gosuchrezhdenii Serediny XVII–Nachala XVIII V." *Otechestvennye Arkhivy*, 3 (2001), 10–18.

Golay, Eric. *Quand le peuple devint roi: mouvement populaire, politique et révolution à Genève de 1789 à 1794*. (Travaux sur la Suisse des lumières 3.) Genève: Slatkine, 2001. Pp. 688; illustrations.

Goldstein, Marc A. *Social and Polticial Thought of the French Revolution, 1788–1797: An Anthology of Original Texts.* New York: Peter Lang, 2001. Pp. xiv + 367.

González y González, Enrique, and Leticia Pérez Puente (eds.). *Colegios y universidades: del antiguo régimen al liberalismo.* (La Real Universidad de México, estudios y textos 11.) México: Centro de Estudios sobre la Universidad, 2001.

Gordon, Daniel (ed.). *Postmodernism and the Enlightenment: New Perspectives in Eighteenth-Century French Intellectual History.* New York: Routledge, 2001. Pp. vi + 227.

Gordon, Felicia. "This Accursed Child: The Early Years of Marie Madeleine Jodin (1741–90), Actress, Philosophe and Feminist." *Women's History Review*, 10 (2001), 229–48.

Göse, Frank. "Zum Verhältnis von landadeliger Sozialisation zu adeliger Militärkarriere. Das Beispiel Preußen und Österreich im ausgehenden 17. und 18. Jahrhundert." *Mitteilungen des Instituts für Österreichische Geschichtsforschung*, 109 (2001), 118–53.

Gottsch, Silke. "Körpererfahrung und Soziale Schicht." *Historische Zeitschrift*, Supplement (2001), 107–13.

Goyhenetche, Manex. *Histoire générale du Pays Basque. Tome III, Evolution économique et sociale du XVIe au XVIIIe siècle.* Bayonne: Elkarlanean, 2001. Pp. 411.

Graham, Kenneth W. *William Godwin Reviewed: A Reception History, 1783–1834.* New York: AMS Press, 2001. Pp. 588; illustrations.

Graille, Patrick. *Les hermaphrodites: aux XVIIe et XVIIIe siècles.* Paris: Les Belles Lettres, 2001. Pp. 246; illustrations.

Gramain-Kibleur, Pascale. "Le rôle des prescriptions médicamenteuses dans la société française du XVIIIe siècle." *Histoire, économie et société*, 20 (2001), 321–37.

Gramberg, Gerhard Anton, Friedrich Nicolai, and Gabriele Crusius (eds.). *"Leben und wirken Sie noch lange für Wahrheit, Wissenschaft und Geschmack!": Briefe des Oldenburger Arztes und Schriftstellers Gerhard Anton Gramberg an den Berliner Buchhändler und Schriftsteller Friedrich Nicolai aus der Zeit zwischen 1789 und 1808.* (Oldenburger Forschungen 14.) Oldenburg: Isensee, 2001. Pp. 143; illustrations.

Grange, Cyril, and Jacques Renard. "Adolescent Migrants from Normandy in Paris at the End of the 18th Century." *History of the Family*, 6 (2001), 423–37.

II: Historical, Social, and Economic Studies 49

Grateau, Philippe. *Les cahiers de doléances: une relecture culturelle*. (Collection "Histoire.") Rennes: Presses Universitaires de Rennes, 2001. Pp. 384; illustrations; maps.

Graves, Rolande. *Born to Procreate: Women and Childbirth in France from the Middle Ages to the Eighteenth Century*. (Studies in the Humanities 53.) New York: Peter Lang, 2001. Pp. x + 162; illustrations.

Greene, Jack P., Rosemary Brana-Shute, and Randy J. Sparks (eds.). *Money, Trade, and Power: The Evolution of Colonial South Carolina's Plantation Society*. (The Carolina Lowcountry and the Atlantic World.) Columbia: University of South Carolina Press, 2001. Pp. xiii + 399; illustrations.

Greene, Richard. "Mary Leapor: The Problem of Personal Identity." *Eighteenth Century: Theory and Interpretation*, 42 (2001), 218–27.

Gregg, Stephen H. "A Truly Christian Hero: Religion, Effeminacy, and Nation in the Writings of the Societies for Reformation of Manners." *Eighteenth-Century Life*, 25 (2001), 17–28.

Griffith, Paddy. "Infantry Armament and the Perception of Tactical Need, 1789–1918." In *War in the Age of Technology: Myriad Faces of Modern Armed Conflict*. Edited by Geoffrey Jensen and Andrew A. Wiest. New York: New York University Press, 2001. Pp. ix + 397.

Griffin, Patrick. *The People with No Name: Ireland's Ulster Scots, America's Scots Irish, and the Creation of a British Atlantic World, 1689–1764*. Princeton: Princeton University Press, 2001. Pp. xv + 244; maps.

Grinberg, Keila. "Freedom Suits and Civil Law in Brazil and the United States." *Slavery & Abolition*, 22 (2001), 66–82.

Grise, Philippe. "Claude Nicolas Le Cat (1700–1768): un grand nom de la chirurgie et de l'urologie au XVIIIeme siècle." *Histoire des sciences médicales*, 35 (2001), 133–40.

Gronke, Horst, Thomas Meyer, and Barbara Neisser (eds.). *Antisemitische und antijudaistische Motive bei Denkern der Aufklärung: Susanne Miller zum 85. Geburtstag*. (PPA-Schriften 1.) Münster: Lit, 2001. Pp. 88.

Gross, Robert A. *The Minutemen and Their World*. (Reissue.) New York: Hill and Wang, 2001. Pp. xix + 258; map.

Grozdanova, Elena and Stefan Andreev. "Das Los der Frauen nach den Osmanischen Registerbuchern der Beschwerden vom 17. und 18. Jh." *Bulgarian Historical Review*, 29 (2001), 52–68.

Guijarro Mora, Víctor. "Petrus Van Musschenbroek y la física experimental del siglo XVIII." *Asclepio*, 53 (2001), 191–212.

Gupta, Ashin Das. "Indian Merchant and the Indian Ocean 1500–1800." In *Explorations in History of South Asia: Essays in Honour of Dietmar Rothermund*. (South Asian Studies 36.) Edited by Georg Berkemer. New Delhi: Manohar, 2001.

Gutiérrez Escudero, Antonio. "Tabaco y desarrollo económico en Santo Domingo (siglo XVIII)." *Anuario de Estudios Americanos*, 58 (2001), 713–36.

Haechler, Jean. *Le règne des femmes: 1715–1793*. Paris: B. Grasset, 2001. Pp. 488; illustrations.

Hafter, Daryl. "Women in the Underground Business of Eighteenth-Century Lyon." *Enterprise & Society: The International Journal of Business History*, 2 (2001), 11–40.

Hall, A. Rupert. "Cambridge: Newton's Legacy." *Notes and Records of the Royal Society of London*, 55 (2001), 205–26.

Hall, Douglas Gordon Hawkins. "Incalculability as a Feature of Sugar Production during the Eighteenth Century." *Journal of Caribbean History*, 35 (2001), 80–96.

Hall, Leslie. *Land & Allegiance in Revolutionary Georgia*. Athens: University of Georgia Press, 2001. Pp. xiv + 231.

Hall, Nigel. "The Emergence of the Liverpool Raw Cotton Market, 1800–1850." *Northern History*, 38 (2001), 65–81.

Hall, Richard. "Profiling the Yorkshire County Elector of the Early Eighteenth Century: New Material and Methods." *Historical Research*, 74 (2001), 172–92.

Halliday, E. M. *Understanding Thomas Jefferson*. New York: HarperCollins Publishers, 2001. Pp. xiii + 284; illustrations.

Halloran, Brian M. "Jesuits in 18th-Century Scotland." *Innes Review*, 52 (2001), 80–100.

II: Historical, Social, and Economic Studies

Handler, Jerome S., and Kenneth M. Bilby. "On the Early Use and Origin of the Term 'Obeah' in Barbados and the Anglophone Caribbean." *Slavery & Abolition*, 22 (2001), 87–100.

Harding, Vanessa. "Controlling a Complex Metropolis, 1650–1750: Politics, Parishes and Powers." *London Journal*, 26 (2001), 29–37.

Hardy, Jean-Pierre. *La vie quotidienne dans la vallée du Saint-laurent, 1790–1835*. Hull: Musée canadien des civilsations, 2001. Pp. 174; illustrations.

Harley, J. B., and Paul Laxton. *The New Nature of Maps: Essays in the History of Cartography*. Baltimore: Johns Hopkins University Press, 2001. Pp. xv + 331; illustrations; maps.

Harrison, Paul. "Rational Equity Valuation at the Time of the South Sea Bubble." *History of Political Economy*, 33 (2001), 269–81.

Hart, Edward H. *Andrew Elliot's Philadelphia Odyssey: His Early Years, 1728–1764: The Story of a Young Scottish Merchant in America on His Way to Becoming a Royal Officer*. Unionville: Royal Fireworks Press, 2001. Pp. x + 258.

Harvey, Karen. "Gender, Space and Modernity in Eighteenth-Century England: A Place Called Sex." *History Workshop Journal*, 51 (2001), 158–79.

Haslam, Thomas J. "Benjamin Franklin, David Hume, Autobiography, and the Jealousy of Empire." Pp. 292–306 of *Finding Colonial Americas: Essays Honoring J. A. Leo Lemay*. Edited by Carla Mulford and David S. Shields. Newark: University of Delaware Press, 2001.

Hautebert, Joel. "Le maintien de l'ordre en France et en Castille sous la monarchie absolue: Prévôté des maréchaux et 'hermandades.'" *Revue historique de droit français et étranger*, 79 (2001), 31–55.

Hawgood, Barbara J. "Alexander Russell (1715–1768) and Patrick Russell (1727–1805): Physicians and Natural Historians of Aleppo." *Journal of Medical Biography*, 9 (2001), 1–6.

Hayden, J. Michael, and Malcolm R. Greenshields. "Les Réformations catholiques en France: le témoignage des statuts synodaux." *Revue d'histoire moderne et contemporaine*, 48 (2001), 5–29.

Hayes, Derek. *First Crossing: Alexander Mackenzie, His Expedition Across North America, and the Opening of the Continent*. Seattle: Sasquatch Books, 2001. Pp. 320; illustrations; maps.

Hayton, David. *The Irish Parliament in the Eighteenth Century: The Long Apprenticeship*. Edinburgh: Edinburgh University Press for the Parliamentary History Yearbook Trust, 2001. Pp. 156; maps.

Heesen, Anke te, and E. C. Spary (eds.). *Sammeln als Wissen: das Sammeln und seine wissenschaftsgeschichtliche Bedeutung*. (Wissenschaftsgeschichte.) Göttingen: Wallstein, 2001. Pp. 223; illustrations.

Heilbron, John L. "Some Connections among the Heroes." *Revue d'histoire des sciences*, 54 (2001), 11–28.

Heine, Darlene Clark, and Jacqueline McLeod (eds.). *Crossing Boundaries: Comparative History of Black People in Diaspora*. (Blacks in the Diaspora.) Bloomington: Indiana University Press, 2001. Pp. xxv + 491; map.

Hejja, Julianna Erika. "Egy XVIII. Szazadi Bekes Varmegyei Kisnemes, Hrabovszky Laszlo Olvasmanyai." *Magyar Konyvszemle*, 117 (2001), 351–55.

Hellmuth, Thomas, and Ewald Hiebl (eds.). *Kulturgeschichte des Salzes: 18. bis 20. Jahrhundert*. (Verlag für Geschichte und Politik.) München: Oldenbourg, 2001. Pp. 344; illustrations.

Helmstadter, Axel. "Recharging the Battery of Life: Electricity in the Theory and Practice of Drug Treatment." *Pharmacy in History*, 43 (2001), 134–43.

Henning, Hansjoachim. "Karl Erich Born (1922–2000)." *Vierteljahrschrift für Sozial- und Wirtschaftsgeschichte*, 88 (2001), 141–44.

Henningsen, Peter. "Peasant Society and the Perception of a Moral Economy: Redistribution and Risk Aversion in Traditional Peasant Culture." *Scandinavian Journal of History*, 26 (2001), 271–96.

Hentsch, Thierry. "Penser l'histoire." *Bulletin d'histoire politique*, 10 (2001), 10–15.

Herger, Csabane. "A Rekatolizacio Eszkoztara Magyarorszagon a 16–18. Szazadban." *Szazadok*, 135 (2001), 871–87.

Herman, Bernard L. "Franklin's Houses." Pp. 249–60 of *Finding Colonial Americas: Essays Honoring J. A. Leo Lemay*. Edited by Carla Mulford and David S. Shields. Newark: University of Delaware Press, 2001.

II: Historical, Social, and Economic Studies

Herndon, Ruth Wallis. *Unwelcome Americans: Living on the Margin in Early New England.* (Early American Studies.) Philadelphia: University of Pennsylvania Press, 2001. Pp. xi + 243; illustrations.

Herzfeld, Erika. *Juden in Brandenburg-Preussen: Beiträge zu ihrer Geschichte im 17. und 18. Jahrhundert.* Teetz: Hentrich & Hentrich, 2001. Pp. 202; illustrations; maps.

Hibbert, Christopher. *The Road to Tyburn: The Story of Jack Sheppard and the Eighteenth-Century Underworld.* London: Penguin, 2001. Pp. 163; plates; illustrations.

Hicks, Carola. *Improper Pursuits: The Scandalous Life of Lady Di Beauclerk.* London: Macmillan, 2001. Pp. 403; illustrations.

Higby, Gregory J., and Elaine C. Stroud (eds.). *Apothecaries and the Drug Trade: Essays in Celebration of the Work of David L. Cowen.* (Publication—American Institute of the History of Pharmacy 19.) Madison: American Institute of the History of Pharmacy, 2001.

Hill, Jacqueline. "Convergence and Conflict in Eighteenth-Century Ireland." *Historical Journal,* 44 (2001), 1039–63.

Hille, Martin. "Mensch und Klima in der frühen Neuzeit. Die Anfänge regelmäßiger Wetterbobachtung, 'Kleine Eiszeit' und ihre Wahrnehmung bei Renward Cysat (1545–1613)." *Archiv für Kulturgeschichte,* 83 (2001), 63–91.

Hitchcock, Tim. "The Publicity of Poverty in Early Eighteenth-Century London." In *Imagining Early Modern London: Perceptions and Portrayals of the City from Stow to Strype, 1598–1720.* Edited by J. F. Merritt. Cambridge: Cambridge University Press, 2001.

Hitzel, Frédéric. *L'Empire ottoman: XVe–XVIIIe siècles.* (Guide Belles lettres des civilizations.) Paris: Belles letters, 2001. Pp. 319; illustrations; maps.

Hochedlinger, Michael. "Militärhistorisch Relevantes Archivgut im Haus-, Hof- und Staatsarchiv." *Mitteilungen des Österreichischen Staatsarchivs,* 49 (2001), 257–84.

Hofstetter, Michael. *The Romantic Idea of a University: England and Germany, 1770–1850.* (Romanticism in Perspective.) New York: Palgrave, 2001. Pp. xiv + 162.

Hogan, John, and Gary Murphy. "From Guild to Union: The Evolution of the Dublin Bricklayers' Society, 1670–1888." *Saothar,* 26 (2001), 17–24.

Holenstein, André. "'Gute Policey' und lokale Gesellschaft: Erfahrung als Kategorie im Verwaltungshandeln des 18. Jahrhunderts." *Historische Zeitschrift*, 31 (2001), 433–50.

Holmes, Richard. *Redcoat: The British Soldier in the Age of Horse and Musket*. London: HarperCollins, 2001. Pp. xxx + 466; illustrations; maps.

Horstmann, Monika. "Religious Dignitaries in the Court Protocol of Jaipur (Mid-Eighteenth to Early Nineteenth Century)." In *Explorations in History of South Asia: Essays in Honour of Dietmar Rothermund*. (South Asian Studies 36.) Edited by Georg Berkemer. New Delhi: Manohar, 2001.

Hou, Jianxin. "Gongye Geming Qian Yingguo Nongmin de Shenghuo Yu Xiaofei Shuiping." *Shijie Lishi (World History)*, 1 (2001), 29–36.

Houston, R. A. "Professions and the Identification of Mental Incapacity in Eighteenth-Century Scotland." *Journal of Historical Sociology*, 14 (2001), 441–66.

Houston, Robert. "Institutional Care for the Insane and Idiots in Scotland before 1820. Part 2." *History of Psychiatry*, 12 (2001), 177–97.

Huertas, Monique de. *Aimée de Coigny*. Paris: Pygmalion, 2001. Pp. 251.

Hung, Ho-fung. "Imperial China and Capitalist Europe in the Eighteenth-Century Global Economy." *Review (Fernand Braudel Center)*, 24 (2001), 473–513.

Hunter, Brooke. "'Prospect of Independent Americans': The Grain Trade and Economic Development during the 1780s." In *Explorations in Early American Culture*. Volume 5. Edited by George W. Boudreau and William A. Pencak. University Park: Pennsylvania Historical Association, 2001.

Hunter, James. *Culloden and the Last Clansman*. Edinburgh: Mainstream Publications, 2001. Pp. 238; map.

Hurpin, Gérard. "Claude Nicolas Le Cat ou de la notoriété médicale au XVIIIeme siècle." *Histoire des sciences médicales*, 35 (2001), 151–62.

Iakovlev, Sergei Evgen'evich. "Kazennye Mashinnye Suda Na Volge V Seredine XVIII Veka." *Voprosy Istorii*, 4 (2001), 145–51.

II: Historical, Social, and Economic Studies 55

Imbruglia, Girolamo. "'È difficile vivere in epoca di rivoluzione': Franco Venturi e la politica dello storico." *Storia della Storiografia*, 40 (2001), 67–90.

Ionov, Igor' Nikolaevich. "Women and Power in Russia: History and Prospects." *Russian Studies in History*, 40 (2001), 15–34.

Irr, Caren. "Literature as Proleptic Globalization, or a Prehistory of the New Intellectual Property." *South Atlantic Quarterly*, 100 (2001), 773–802.

Islaev, Faizulkhak Gabdulkhakovich. *Islam i pravoslavie v Povolzh'e XVIII stoletiia: ot konfrontatsii k terpimosti*. Kazan': Izd-vo Kazanskogo universiteta, 2001. Pp. 214.

Islamoglu, Huri. "Modernities Compared: State Transformations and Constitutions of Property in the Qing and Ottoman Empires." *Journal of Early Modern History*, 5 (2001), 353–86.

Jackson, Dianah Leigh. "Anatomy of Observation: From the Académie Royale de la Chirurgie to the Salons of Denis Diderot." *Canadian Journal of History*, 36 (2001), 27–49.

Jacob, Margaret, and David Reid. "Technical Knowledge and the Mental Universe of Manchester's Early Cotton Manufacturers." *Canadian Journal of History*, 36 (2001), 283–304.

Jacob, Margaret C. *The Enlightenment: A Brief History with Documents*. (Bedford Series in History and Culture.) Boston: Bedford/St. Martin's, 2001. Pp. xiii + 237; illustrations; maps.

Jacquin, Frédéric. "Un empoisonnement à Paris: l'empoisonnement du sieur de Vaux (1742)." *Histoire, Economie et Société*, 20 (2001), 23–36.

Jaffe, James A. "Commerce, Character, and Civil Society: Critiques of Capitalism during the Early Industrial Period." *European Legacy*, 6 (2001), 251–64.

Jägers, Regine. *Duisburg im 18. Jahrhundert: Sozialstruktur und Bevölkerungsbewegung einer niederrheinischen Kleinstadt im Ancien Regime (1713–1814)*. (Rheinisches Archiv 143.) Köln: Böhlau, 2001. Pp. xiii + 422; illustrations.

Jarnoux, Philippe. *Moi, Hypolite Radegonde Loz: un "divorce" au siècle des lumières*. Rennes: Apogée, 2001. Pp. 191; map.

Jensen, Geoffrey, and Andrew A. Wiest (eds.). *War in the Age of Technology: Myriad Faces of Modern Armed Conflict*. New York: New York University Press, 2001. Pp. ix + 397.

Jezierski, Andrzej, and Leszczynska, Cecylia. "Eastern Markets in Historical Perspective." *Studia Historiæ Œconomicæ*, 24 (2001), 73–86.

Jiraskova, Alena. "Die K.(U.)K. Militärakten im Militärarchiv Prag." *Mitteilungen des Österreichischen Staatsarchivs*, 49 (2001), 483–88.

Jobst, Kerstin S. "Die Taurische Reise von 1787 als Beginn der Mythisierung der Krim. Bemerkungen zum europäischen Krim-Diskurs des 18. und 19. Jahrhunderts." *Archiv für Kulturgeschichte*, 83 (2001), 121–44.

Johnson, Sherry. *The Social Transformation of Eighteenth-Century Cuba*. Gainesville: University Press of Florida, 2001. Pp. x + 267; map.

Johnston, Andrew John Bayly. *Control and Order in French Colonial Louisbourg, 1713–1758*. East Lansing: Michigan State University Press, 2001. Pp. xlv + 346; illustrations; maps.

Johnston, René. "Comercio en el mar del Sur: ciertos aspectos prácticos del intercambio comercial marítimo, siglo XVIII." *Revista de Historia*, 43 (2001), 143–66.

Jones, Dorothy. "Defining Self and Others through Textile and Text." *Women's Writing*, 8 (2001), 375–89.

Juet, Hubert. *Louis XIV à la conquête du Pérou: avec Jérôme de Ponchartrain, 1694–1715*. Paris: Sémaphore, 2001. Pp. 319; maps.

Jurdjevic, Mark. "Virtue, Commerce, and the Enduring Florentine Republican Moment: Reintegrating Italy into the Atlantic Republican Debate." *Journal of the History of Ideas*, 62 (2001), 721–43.

Jurt, Joseph. "Die Konstruktion nationaler Identitäten in Europa (18. bis 20. Jahrhundert)." *Francia*, 28 (2001), 1–14.

Kapitzke, Robert L. *Religion, Power, and Politics in Colonial St. Augustine*. (The Ripley P. Bullen Series.) Gainesville: University Press of Florida, 2001. Pp. 219; illustrations.

Kaplan, Steven L. "Un laboratoire de la doctrine corporatiste sous le régime de Vichy: l'Institut d'études corporatives et sociales." *Mouvement Social*, 195 (2001), 35–77.

Kaplan, Steven L. (Béatrice Vierne, trans.). *La fin des corporations*. Paris: Fayard, 2001. Pp. xvi + 740.

II: Historical, Social, and Economic Studies

Kardasis, Vassilis. *Diaspora Merchants in the Black Sea: The Greeks in Southern Russia, 1775–1861*. Lanham: Lexington Books, 2001. Pp. xxiv + 243.

Karp, Sergueï, and Larry Wolff (eds.). *Le mirage russe au XVIIIe siècle*. (Publications du Centre international d'étude du XVIIIe siècle 10.) Ferney-Voltaire: Centre international d'étude du XVIIIe siècle, 2001. Pp. 264; illustrations.

Kates, Gary. *Monsieur d'Eon Is a Woman: A Tale of Political Intrigue and Sexual Masquerade*. Baltimore: Johns Hopkins University Press, 2001. Pp. xxix + 368; plates; illustrations.

Kaufman, Matthew H. *Surgeons at War: Medical Arrangements for the Treatment of the Sick and Wounded in the British Army During the Late 18th and 19th Centuries*. (Contributions in Military Studiies 205.) Westport: Greenwood Press, 2001. Pp. x + 227; illustrations.

Keevak, Michael. "George Psalmanazar: Impostor, Traveler." Pp. 91–101 of *Crossings: Travel, Art, Literature, Politics*. Edited by Rudolphus Teeuwen. Taipai: Bookman Books, 2001.

Kelley, Donald R. "Grounds for Comparison." *Storia della Storiografia*, 39 (2001), 3–16.

Kelly, James. "Monitoring the Constitution: The Operation of Poynings' Law in the 1760s." *Parliamentary History*, 20 (2001), 87–106.

Kendall, Gavin. "Normality and Meaningfulness: Detailing the Child in Eighteenth-Century England." *History of Education Review*, 30 (2001), 26–36.

Kennedy, Hugh (ed.). *The Historiography of Islamic Egypt, c. 950–1800*. (The Medieval Mediterranean 31.) Leiden: Brill, 2001. Pp. vi + 269.

Kennedy, Máire. *French Books in Eighteenth-Century Ireland*. (Studies on Voltaire and the Eighteenth Century 7.) Oxford: Voltaire Foundation, 2001. Pp. x + 253.

Kennedy, Michael V., and William G. Shade (eds.). *The World Turned Upside-Down: The State of Eighteenth-Century American Studies at the Beginning of the Twenty-First Century*. Bethlehem: Lehigh University Press, 2001. Pp. 336.

Kersh, Rogan. *Dreams of a More Perfect Union*. Ithaca: Cornell University Press, 2001. Pp. xi + 358; illustrations.

Kessel, Martina. *Langeweile: zum Umgang mit Zeit und Gefühlen in Deutschland vom späten 18. bis zum frühen 20. Jahrhundert*. Göttingen: Wallstein, 2001. Pp. 411; illustrations.

Khanna, Vinod C. "The Chinese Diaspora." *China Report*, 37 (2001), 427–43.

Khoury, Dina Rizk. "Administrative Practice Between Religious Law (*Shari'a*) and State Law (*Kanun*) on the Eastern Frontiers of the Ottoman Empire." *Journal of Early Modern History*, 5 (2001), 305–30.

Khristoforova, N.V. *Rossiiskie gimnazii XVIII–XX vekov: na materiale g. Moskvy*. Moskva: Greko-latinskii kabinet IU.A. Shichalina, 2001. Pp. 192; illustrations.

King, Stewart R. *Blue Coat or Powdered Wig: Free People of Color in Pre-Revolutionary Saint Domingue*. Athens: University of Georgia Press, 2001. Pp. xxvi + 328; maps.

Kirkham, Linda M., and Anne Loft. "The Lady and the Accounts: Missing From Accounting History?" *Accounting Historians Journal*, 28 (2001), 67–90.

Klassen, Sherri. "Greying in the Cloister: The Ursuline Life Course in Eighteenth-Century France." *Journal of Women's History*, 12 (2001), 87–112.

Klein, Joachim, Simon Dixon, and Maarten Fraanje (eds.). *Reflections on Russia in the Eighteenth Century*. (Slavistische Forschungen 37.) Cologne: Böhlau Verlag, 2001. Pp. viii + 404; illustrations.

Knight, Franklin W. "Slavery and the Transformation of Society in Cuba, 1511–1760." In *Slavery, Freedom and Gender: The Dynamics of Caribbean Society*. Edited by Brian L. Moore. Kingston: University of the West Indies Press, 2001.

Kochan, James. *The United States Army 1783–1811*. Oxford: Osprey Military, 2001. Pp. 48; plates; illustrations.

Koehn, Barbara. *La crise de la modernité européenne*. (Collection "Etudes germaniques.") Rennes: Presses universitaires de Rennes, 2001. Pp. 485.

Kraus, Gerlinde. *Christiane Fürstin von der Osten-Sacken: eine frühkapitalistische Unternehmerin und ihre Erben während der Frühindustrialisierung im 18./19. Jahrhundert*. (Beiträge zur Unternehmensgeschichte 10.) Stuttgart: Franz Steiner Verlag, 2001. Pp. 340; illustrations.

Kresin, Oleksii. *Polityko-pravova spadshchyna ukraïns'koï politychnoï emihratsiï pershoï polovyny XVIII stolittia*. Kyïv: Natsional'na akademiia nauk Ukraïny, 2001. Pp. 466; illustrations.

II: Historical, Social, and Economic Studies 59

Krieger, Alex, David A. Cobb, Amy Turner, and David C. Bosse (eds.). *Mapping Boston*. Cambridge: MIT Press, 2001. Pp. xiv + 278; illustrations; maps.

Krishna, V. V. "Reflections on the Changing Status of Academic Science in India." *International Social Science Journal*, 53 (2001), 231–46.

Kronick, David A. "The Commerce of Letters: Networks and Invisible Colleges in Seventeenth- and Eighteenth-Century Europe." *Library Quarterly*, 71 (2001), 28–43.

Kushkumbaev, Aibolat Kairsliamovich. *Voennoe delo kazakhov v XVII–XVIII vekakh*. (Kazakhstanskie vostokovednye issledovaniia.) Almaty: Daik-Press, 2001. Pp. 169; illustrations.

Kylmäkoski, Merja. *The Virtue of the Citizen: Jean-Jacques Rousseau's Republicanism in the Eighteenth-Century French Context*. (Europäische Studien zur Ideen- und Wissenschaftsgeschichte 10.) Frankfurt: P. Lang, 2001. Pp. 213.

Labouvie, Eva. "Der Leib als Medium, Raum, Zeichen und Zustand. Zur kulturellen Erfahrung und Selbstwahrnehmung des schwangeren Körpers." *Historische Zeitschrift*, 31 Supplement (2001), 115–26.

Lacour, Eva. "Faces of Violence Revisited: A Typology of Violence in Early Modern Rural Germany." *Journal of Social History*, 34 (2001), 649–67.

Laffrado, Laura. "Constructing the Subaltern: White Creole Culture and Raced Captivity in Eighteenth-Century Dutch Suriname." *Studies in Eighteenth-Century Culture*, 30 (2001), 31–48.

Lafont, Jean Marie. *Chitra: Cities and Monuments of Eighteenth-Century India from French Archives*. New Delhi: Oxford University Press, 2001. Pp. xiv + 162; illustrations; maps.

Lamprecht, Oliver. *Das Streben nach Demokratie, Volkssouveränität und Menschenrechten in Deutschland am Ende des 18. Jahrhunderts: zum Staats- und Verfassungsverständnis der deutschen Jakobiner*. (Schriften zur Verfassungsgeschichte 63.) Berlin: Duncker & Humblot, 2001. Pp. 174.

Lamont, Stewart. *When Scotland Ruled the World: The Story of the Golden Age of Genius, Creativity and Exploration*. London: HarperCollins, 2001. Pp. xii + 244.

Landes, Joan B. *Visualizing the Nation: Gender, Representation, and Revolution in Eighteenth-Century France*. Ithaca: Cornell University Press, 2001. Pp. 254; illustrations.

Landsman, Ned C. (ed.). *Nation and Province in the first British Empire: Scotland and the Americas, 1600–1800*. (Studies in Eighteenth-Century Scotland.) Lewisburg: Bucknell University Press, 2001. Pp. 292; illustrations.

Laponce, J. A. "National Self-Determination and Referendums: The Case for Territorial Revisionism." *Nationalism & Ethnic Politics*, 7 (2001), 33–56.

Larguier, Gilbert, Jean-Pierre Dedieu, and Jean-Paul Le Flem (eds.). *Les monarchies espagnole et française au temps de leur affrontement: milieu XVIe siècle–1714: synthèse et documents*. (Collection de la Maison des pays ibériques 81.) Perpignan: Presses universitaires de Perpignan, 2001. Pp. 414; illustrations; maps.

Larsson, Jonas. "Behandlingstanken Inom Svensk Sinnessjukvård under Början av 1800-Talet." *Historisk Tidskrift*, 4 (2001), 511–36.

Laurence, Janet. "Notes on an Eighteenth-Century Manuscript Recipe Book" in *Food and the Memory: Proceedings of the Oxford Symposium on Food and Cookery, 2000*. Edited by Harlan Walker. Devon: Prospect Books, 2001. Pp. 318; illustrations.

Lautman, Jean-Pierre. *Paul-Louis Courier, ou, La plume indomptée*. Chambray: C.L.D., 2001. Pp. 335; illustrations.

Laux-Huetz de Lemps, Claire. "L'hénothéisme, transition essentielle dans l'évolution religieuse et politique des îles de Polynésie." *Bulletin de la Société de l'Histoire du Protestantisme Français*, 147 (2001), 251–81.

Lavroff, Dmitri Georges. *Histoire des idées politiques, de l'antiquité à la fin du XVIIIe siècle*. 4th edition. (Mémentos.) Paris: Dalloz, 2001. Pp. v + 192.

Leduc, Christophe. "Géographie paroissiale en milieu urbain: l'exemple cambrésien a l'époque moderne." *Revue du Nord*, 83 (2001), 359–79.

Lee, Haiyan. "All the Feelings That Are Fit to Print: The Community of Sentiment and the Literary Public Sphere in China, 1900–1918." *Modern China*, 27 (2001), 291–327.

Lee, Wayne E. *Crowds and Soldiers in Revolutionary North Carolina: The Culture of Violence in Riot and War*. (Southern Dissent.) Gainesville: University Press of Florida, 2001. Pp. xv + 380; illustrations; maps.

II: Historical, Social, and Economic Studies

Legay, Marie-Laure. *Les états provinciaux dans la construction de l'état moderne, aux XVIIe et XVIIIe siècles.* (Travaux du Grand Siècle 20.) Geneva: Droz, 2001. Pp. 565.

Lenman, Bruce. *Britain's Colonial Wars, 1688–1783.* (Modern Wars in Perspective.) New York: Longman, 2001. Pp. x + 284; maps.

León, Leonardo. *Los señores de las cordilleras y las pampas: los pehuenches de Malalhue, 1770–1800.* Mendoza: Universidad de Congreso, 2001. Pp. x + 315; map.

Lever, Maurice. *Louis XV: libertin malgré lui.* (Portraits intimes.) Paris: Payot, 2001. Pp. 215.

Lewis, Brian. *The Middlemost and the Milltowns: Bourgeois Culture and Politics in Early Industrial England.* Stanford: Stanford University Press, 2001. Pp. viii + 580.

Lewis, Meriwether, and William Clark. *The Journals of the Lewis and Clark Expedition.* Volume 13: Comprehensive Index. Edited by Gary E. Moulton. Lincoln: University of Nebraska Press, 2001. Pp. 174.

Li, Hsiao-t'i. "Shiba Shiji Zhongguo Shehui Zhong de Qingyu Yu Shenti: Lijiao Shijie Wai de Jianian Huahui." *Zhongyang Yanjiuyuan Lishi Yuyan Yanjiusuo Jikan (Bulletin of the Institute of History and Philology, Academia Sinica)*, 72 (2001), 543–95.

Lieburg, Fred van. "The Dutch Book Trade, Christian Enlightenment and the National Bibliography: The Catalogues of Johannes van Abkoude (1703–60) and Reinier Arrenberg (1733–1812)." *Quaerendo*, 31 (2001), 3–16.

Lincoln, Margarette (ed.). *Science and Exploration in the Pacific: European Voyages to the Southern Oceans in the Eighteenth Century.* Woodbridge: Boydell & Brewer, 2001. Pp. 248; illustrations.

Lind, William S. "Preserved in Amber: The 18th-Century Dockyard at Karlskrona, Sweden." *Sea History*, 97 (2001), 20–23.

Linton, Marisa. *The Politics of Virtue in Enlightenment France.* (Studies in Modern History.) New York: Palgrave, 2001. Pp. xi + 258.

Livesey, James. *Making Democracy in the French Revolution.* (Harvard Historical Studies 140.) Cambridge: Harvard University Press, 2001. Pp. 326.

Lockley, Timothy James. *Lines in the Sand: Race and Class in lowcountry Georgia, 1750–1860.* Athens: University of Georgia Press, 2001. Pp. xviii + 280.

Loesch, Perk. *L'art de la fortification: Festungsbau und Festungskrieg vom 16. bis zum 18. Jahrhundert.* Dresden: Sächsische Landesbibliothek, Staats- und Universitätsbibliothek Dresden, 2001. Pp. 142; illustrations; facsimiles; maps.

Lombardi, Daniela. *Matrimoni di antico regime.* (Annali dell'Istituto storico italo-germanico in Trento. Monografie 34.) Bologna: Il Mulino, 2001. Pp. 513.

Lorieux, Denis *Saint-Simon: 1675–1755.* Paris: Perrin, 2001. Pp. 426.

Louis-Courvoisier, Micheline. "Le malade et son médecin: Le cadre de la relation thérapeutique dans la deuxième moitié du XVIII siècle." *Bulletin canadien d'histoire de la médecine,* 18 (2001), 277–96.

Lovejoy, Paul E., and David Richardson. "Letters of the Old Calibar Slave Trade, 1760–1789." Pp. 88–115 of *Genius in Bondage: Literature of the Early Black Atlantic.* Edited by Vincent Carretta and Philip Gould. Lexington: University Press of Kentucky, 2001.

Loveland, Jeff. *Rhetoric and Natural History: Buffon in Polemical and Literary Context.* (Studies on Voltaire and the Eighteenth Century 3.) Oxford: Voltaire Foundation, 2001. Pp. ix + 214; illustrations.

Lowengard, Sarah. "Colour Quality and Production: Testing Colour in Eighteenth-Century France." *Journal of Design History,* 14 (2001), 91–103.

Lowerson, John. "Starting From Your Own Past? The Serious Business of Leisure History." *Journal of Contemporary History,* 36 (2001), 517–29.

Luo, Bingliang. "Ping Zhang Xuecheng de Shixueshi Guannian." *Shixueshi Yanjiu (Journal of Historiography),* 2 (2001), 50–56.

Luque Alcaide, Elisa. "¿Entre Roma y Madrid? La reforma regalista y el Sínodo de Charcas (1771–1773)." *Anuario de Estudios Americanos,* 58 (2001), 473–93.

Luria, Sarah. "George Washington's Romance: Plotting in the Federal City, 1791–1800." *Prospects,* 26 (2001), 1–34.

II: Historical, Social, and Economic Studies 63

Lushpai, Vladimir Borisovich. "Antipapskaia Propaganda Belorusskikh Iezuitov Vo Vtoroi Polovine XVIII Veka." *Voprosy Istorii*, 8 (2001), 124–33.

Lynch, John. *Latin America between Colony and Nation: Selected Essays*. (Institute of Latin American Studies Series.) New York: Palgrave, 2001. Pp. viii + 256.

Lynch, John. *América Latina, entre colonia y nación*. (Libros de historia.) Barcelona: Crítica, 2001. Pp. 342.

Lynn, John A. "The Treatment of Military Subjects in Diderot's *Encyclopédie*." *Journal of Military History*, 65 (2001), 131–65.

Lynn, Michael R. "Divining the Enlightenment: Public Opinion and Popular Science in Old Regime France." *Isis*, 92 (2001), 34–54.

Maas, David E. "The Founding Father of the American Presidency." Pp. 11–24 of of *George Washington in and as Culture*. Edited by Kevin L. Cope, William S. Pederson, and Frank Williams. New York: AMS Press, 2001.

Macaulay, John Allen. *Unitarianism in the Antebellum South: The Other Invisible Institution*. (Religion and American Culture.) Tuscaloosa: University of Alabama, 2001. Pp. xiii + 222; illustrations.

Macauley, Melissa. "A World Made Simple: Law and Property in the Ottoman and Qing Empires." *Journal of Early Modern History*, 5 (2001), 331–52.

MacGregor, Arthur. "The Ashmolean as a Museum of Natural History, 1683–1860." *Journal of the History of Collections*, 13 (2001), 125–44.

Maciulyte, Kristina. "Pamokslo Ypatybes XVIII A. Mazojoje Lietuvoje: Pietizmo Ir Svietimo Ideju Itaka." *Lituanistica*, 2 (2001), 118–27.

Maeder, Ernesto J.A. *Los bienes de los jesuitas: destino y administración de sus temporalidades en el Río de la Plata, 1767–1813*. Resistencia: Instituto de Investigaciones Geohístoricas CONICET, 2001. Pp. 390; maps.

Mahan, Alfred Thayer. *The Life of Nelson: The Embodiment of the Sea Power of Great Britain*. (Reprint of 1899 edition.) Annapolis: Naval Institute Press, 2001. Pp. xxii + 764; illustrations; maps.

Maitte, Corine. *La trame incertaine: le monde textile de Prato, XVIIIe–XIXe siècles.* (Histoire et civilizations.) Villeneuve d'Ascq: Presses universitaires du Septentrion, 2001. Pp. 494; illustrations; maps.

Malik, Iftikhar H. "Ireland, Orientalism and South Asia." *Asian Affairs*, 32 (2001), 189–94.

Malik, Zahiruddin. *Agrarian System in Medieval India: Land Revenue Arrangements in Sarkar Shahabad (Bihar), 1734–1790.* Jaipur: Rawat Publications, 2001. Pp. xvi + 207.

Mann, Alastair J. "The Anatomy of the Printed Book in Early Modern Scotland." *Scottish Historical Review*, 80 (2001), 181–200.

Mann, Michael. "German Expertise in India? Early Forest Management on the Malabar Coast, 1792–1805." In *Explorations in History of South Asia: Essays in Honour of Dietmar Rothermund.* (South Asian Studies 36.) Edited by Georg Berkemer. New Delhi: Manohar, 2001.

Mann, Michael. "Timber Trade on the Malabar Coast, c. 1780–1840." *Environment and History*, 7 (2001), 403–26.

Mansel, Philip. "Grand tour in the Ottoman Empire, 1699–1826." In *Unfolding the Orient: Travellers in Egypt and the Near East.* Edited by Paul Starkey and Janet Starkey. Reading: Ithaca, 2001.

Mapp, Paul. "French Reactions to the British Search for a Northwest Passage from Hudson Bay and the Origins of the Seven Years' War." *Terrae Incognitae*, 33 (2001), 13–32.

Marchena Fernández, Juan. *El tiempo ilustrado de Pablo de Olavide: vida, obra y sueños de un americano en la España del s. XVIII.* (Colección "El Mapa y el calendario" 14.) Sevilla: Ediciones Alfar, 2001. Pp. 227; illustrations.

Marichal, Carlos, and Daniela Marino (eds.). *De colonia a nación: impuestos y política en México, 1750–1860.* México: El Colegio de México, Centro de Estudios Históricos, 2001. Pp. 279; illustrations.

Marker, Gary. "The Ambiguities of the 18th Century." *Kritika: Explorations in Russian and Eurasian History*, 2 (2001), 241–52.

Marshall, P. J. "Britain and the World in the Eighteenth Century: IV. The Turning Outwards of Britain." *Transactions of the Royal Historical Society*, 11 (2001), 1–15.

II: Historical, Social, and Economic Studies

Marshall, P. J. (ed.). *The Oxford History of the British Empire.* Volume 2: The Eighteenth Century. Oxford: Oxford University Press, 2001. Pp. xxi + 639.

Martí, Marc. *Ciudad y campo en la España de la Ilustración.* (Colección Hispania 14.) Lleida: Editorial Milenio, 2001. Pp. 300; charts.

Martin, Jean-Clément. *La contre-révolution en Europe, XVIIIe–XIXe siècles; réalités politiques et socials. Résonances culturelles et idéologiques.* (Collections "Histoire.") Rennes: Presses Universitaires de Rennes, 2001. Pp. 312; illustrations; maps.

Martin, Olivier. "Da estatística política à sociologia estatística. Desenvolvimento e transformações da análise estatística da sociedade (séculos XVII–XIX)." Translated by Teresa Malatian. *Revista Brasileira de Historia*, 21 (2001), 13–34.

Martin, Xavier. *Human Nature and the French Revolution: From the Enlightenment to the Napoleonic Code.* (Polygons 3.) New York: Berghahn Books, 2001. Pp. viii + 292.

Martschukat, Jürgen. "'Ein Mörder aus Liebe': über Vaterschaft, Fürsorge und Verzweiflung an der Wende vom 18. zum 19. Jahrhundert." Pp. 8–26 of *Männer.* (Werkstatt Geschichte 29.) Edited by Jürgen Martschukat and Olaf Stieglitz. Hamburg: Ergebnisse, 2001.

Martschukat, Jürgen, and Olaf Stieglitz (eds). *Männer.* (WerkstattGeschichte 29.) Hamburg: Ergebnisse, 2001. Pp. 118; illustrations.

Mastrogregori, Massimo. "Liberation from the Past." *European Legacy*, 6 (2001), 37–47.

Matthieu, Jacques. *La Nouvelle-France: les français en Amérique du Nord, XVIe–XVIIIe siècle.* 2nd edition. Sainte-Foy: Presses de l'Université Laval, 2001. Pp. ix + 271; illustrations.

Matthews, Christopher N. "Political Economy and Race: Comparative Archaeologies of Annapolis and New Orleans in the Eighteenth Century." In *Race and the Archaeology of Identity.* (Foundations of Archaeological Inquiry.) Edited by Charles E. Orser, Jr. Salt Lake City: University of Utah Press, 2001.

Mauch, Christof. "Im Westen angekommen. Ideengeschichtliche Forschungen zur frühen Bundesrepublik." *Historische Zeitschrift*, 272 (2001), 107–14.

Mauerer, Esteban. *Südwestdeutscher Reichsadel im 17. und 18. Jahrhundert: Geld, Reputation, Karriere – das Haus Fürstenberg.* (Schriftenreihe der Historischen Kommission bei der Bayerischen Akademie der Wissenschaften 66.) Göttingen: Vandenhoeck & Ruprecht, 2001. Pp. 456.

Maur, Eduard (ed.). *Gutsherrschaft und "zweite Leibeigenschaft" in Böhmen: Studien zur Wirtschafts-, Sozial- und Bevölkerungsgeschichte (14.–18. Jahrhundert)*. (Sozial- und wirtschaftshistorische Studien 26.) München: R. Oldenbourg, 2001. Pp. 246; illustrations.

Mayhew, Robert J. "Where Was Enlightenment? English Problems, English Answers." *Journal of Historical Geography*, 27 (2001), 436–40.

Mazek, Dorota (Agnieszka Kreczmar, transl.). "The Wardship of the Mentally Ill in the Polish-Lithuanian Commonwealth in the Second Half of the 18th C." *Acta Poloniæ Historica*, 83 (2001), 95–122.

McCorkle, Barbara. "The Mapping of New England before 1800." In *Mapping Boston*. Edited by Alex Krieger, David A. Cobb, Amy Turner, and David C. Bosse. Cambridge: MIT Press, 2001.

McCullough, David. *John Adams*. New York: Simon & Schuster, 2001. Pp. 751; illustrations; maps; plates.

McDonald, Archie P. "George Washington, More than Man." Pp. 3–10 of *George Washington in and as Culture*. Edited by Kevin L. Cope, William S. Pederson, and Frank Williams. New York: AMS Press, 2001.

McGaw, Judith A. "'So Much Depends upon a Red Wheelbarrow': Agricultural Tool Ownership in the Eighteenth-Century Mid-Atlantic." In *American Technology*. (Blackwell Readers in American Social and Cultural History 7.) Edited by Carroll Pursell. Malden: Blackwell, 2001.

McLaren, Martha. *British India & British Scotland, 1780–1830: Career Building, Empire Building, and a Scottish School of Thought on Indian Governance*. (Series on International, Political, and Economic History.) Akron: University of Akron Press, 2001. Pp. viii + 306; map.

McMahon, Darrin M. *Enemies of the Enlightenment: The French Counter-Enlightenment and the Making of Modernity*. Oxford: Oxford University Press, 2001. Pp. xii + 262; illustrations.

McNamee, Robert V., Robert Darnton, and Daniel Droixhe (eds.). *From Letter to Publication: Studies on Correspondence and the History of the Book*. (Studies on Voltaire and the Eighteenth Century 10.). Oxford: Voltaire Foundation, 2001. Pp. v + 295; illustrations.

McNeil, David. "The Spectacle of Protest and Punishment: Newspaper Coverage of the Melksham Weavers' Riot of 1738." *Media History*, 7 (2001), 71–86.

II: Historical, Social, and Economic Studies

Mee, Bob. *Bare Fists: The History of Bare-Knuckle Prize-Fighting.* Woodstock: Overlook Press, 2001. Pp. 241 + illustrations.

Melton, James Van Horn. *The Rise of the Public in Enlightenment Europe.* (New Approaches to European History 22.) New York: Cambridge University Press, 2001. Pp. xiv + 284.

Menegus Bornemann, Margarita. *Universidad y sociedad en Hispanoamérica: grupos de poder, siglos XVIII y XIX.* (Colección historia. Serie mayor.) México: Universidad Nacional Autónoma de México, 2001. Pp. 383.

Menze, Ernest A. "Benjamin Franklin Seen with German Eyes: Selective Co-Optations By German Authors." *Yearbook of German-American Studies,* 36 (2001), 29–46.

Mercier, Gilbert. *Madame Voltaire.* Paris: Fallois, 2001. Pp. 348.

Merrick, Jeffrey, and Bryant T. Ragan, Jr. (eds.). *Homosexuality in Early Modern France: A Documentary Collection.* New York: Oxford University Press, 2001. Pp. xvi + 256.

Merritt, J. F. (ed.). *Imagining Early Modern London: Perceptions and Portrayals of the City from Stow to Strype, 1598–1720.* Cambridge: Cambridge University Press, 2001. Pp. xii + 305; illustrations.

Metayer, Christine. "Normes graphiques et pratiques de l'écriture: maîtres écrivains et écrivains publics à Paris aux XVIIe et XVIIIe siècles." *Annales: Histoire, sciences sociales,* 56 (2001), 881–901.

Metzler, Guido. "Markgraf Karl Friedrich von Baden und die französischen Physiokraten." *Francia,* 28 (2001), 35–63.

Michon, Jacques, and Jean-Yves Mollier (eds.). *Les mutations du livre et de l'édition dans le monde, du XVIIIe siècle à l'an 2000: actes du colloque international.* Sainte-Foy: Presses de l'Université Laval, 2001. Pp. 597.

Miles, M. "Including Disabled Children in Indian Schools, 1790s–1890s: Innovations of Educational Approach and Technique." *Paedagogica Historica,* 37 (2001), 291–315.

Miller, James (ed.). *American Slavery.* (The Complete History of.) San Diego: Greenhaven Press, 2001. Pp. 642; illustrations; maps.

Miller, Tim R. and Karen Fyke. "George Washington and the Art of Billiards." Pp. 279–315 of *George Washington in and as Culture*. Edited by Kevin L. Cope, William S. Pederson, and Frank Williams. New York: AMS Press, 2001.

Minart, Gérard. *Pierre Claude François Daunou, l'anti-Robespierre: de la Révolution à l'Empire, l'itinéraire d'un juste (1761–1840)*. (Bibliothèque historique Privat.) Toulouse: Privat, 2001. Pp. 205.

Mines, Mattison. "Courts of Law and Styles of Self in Eighteenth-Century Madras: From Hybrid to Colonial Self." *Modern Asian Studies*, 35 (2001), 33–74.

Minken, Anne. "Etnisk Identitet og Yrkesidentitet: En Innvandrergruppe og Etterkommerne deres 1741–1865." *Historisk Tidsskrift*, 80 (2001), 459–78.

Miño Grijalva, Manuel. *El mundo novohispano: población, ciudades y economía: siglos XVII y XVIII*. (Hacia una nueva historia de México.) México: El Colegio de México, 2001. Pp. 448; illustrations; maps.

Mohrmann, Ruth-Elisabeth (ed.). *Städtische Volkskultur im 18. Jahrhundert*. (Städteforschung 51.) Köln: Böhlau, 2001. Pp. xviii + 209; illustrations.

Molina del Villar, América. *La Nueva España y el matlazahuatl, 1736–1739*. (Colección Historias.) México: Centro de Investigaciones y Estudios Superiores en Antropología Social, 2001. Pp. 335; maps; tables.

Moller, Horst. "Jacques Droz (1909–1998)." *Francia*, 28 (2001), 195–98.

Möller, Lenelotte. *Höhere Mädchenschulen in der Kurpfalz und im fränkischen Raum im 18. Jahrhundert*. (Mainzer Studien zur Neueren Geschichte 5.) Frankfurt am Main: P. Lang, 2001. Pp. 399; illustrations; maps.

Montague, Mary Wortley, Lady. *L'Islam au péril des femmes: une Anglaise en Turquie au XVIIIe siècle*. (La Découverte 109.) Edited and translated by Anne Marie Moulin and Pierre Chuvin. Paris: Editions La Découverte, 2001. Pp. 253; maps.

Monteiro, Nuno Gonçalo F. "Identificação da política setecentista: Notas sobre Portugal no inicio do período Joanino." *Analise Social*, 35 (2001), 961–87.

II: Historical, Social, and Economic Studies 69

Montlinot, Charles-Antoine-Joseph Leclerc de, and Guy Thuillier (eds.). *Un observateur des misères sociales, Leclerc de Montlinot, 1732–1801.* Paris: Comité d'histoire de la sécurité sociale, 2001. Pp. 644.

Moody, Margaret Josephine. *The Royal Poorhouse in 18th-Century Turin, Italy: The King and the Paupers.* Lewiston: E. Mellen Press, 2001. Pp. x + 152; illustrations.

Moore, Brian L. (ed.). *Slavery, Freedom and Gender: The Dynamics of Caribbean Society.* Kingston: University of the West Indies Press, 2001. Pp. xv + 297.

Moore, Lucy (ed.). *Con Men and Cutpurses: Scenes from the Hogarthian Underworld.* (Reissue.) New York: Penguin Books, 2001. Pp. xxvii + 299; illustrations.

Morant Deusa, Isabel, and Mónica Bolufer Peruga. "Josefa Amar y Borbón. Une intellectuelle espagnole dans les débats des lumières." *Clio: Histoire, femmes et sociétés*, 13 (2001), 69–97.

Morgan, Kenneth. *Slavery and Servitude in Colonial North America: A Short History.* New York: New York University Press, 2001. Pp. 152.

Morillo, John. "John Dennis: Enthusiastic Passions, Cultural Memory, and Literary Theory." *Eighteenth-Century Studies*, 34 (2001), 21–41.

Morineau, Michel. "Quodlibet: or brésilien, macroéconomie et croissance économique en France et en Angleterre au XVIIIe siècle." *Revue d'Histoire Moderne et Contemporaine*, 48 (2001), 245–306.

Mortier, Roland. "Lumières et consorts: les avatars d'un concept historique." In *La diffusion de Locke en France, traduction au dix-huitième siècle, lectures de Rousseau.* (Studies on Voltaire and the Eighteenth Century 04.) Edited by Jørn Schløser. Oxford: Voltaire Foundation, 2001.

Moscoso, Javier. "Los efectos de la imaginación: Medicina, ciencia y sociedad en el siglo XVIII." *Asclepio*, 53 (2001), 141–71.

Mounsey, Chris (ed.). *Presenting Gender: Changing Sex in Early-Modern Culture.* (Bucknell Studies in Eighteenth-Century Literature and Culture.) Lewisburg: Bucknell University Press, 2001. Pp. 301; illustrations.

Muchembled, Robert. *Société, cultures et mentalités dans la France moderne: XVIe–XVIIIe siècle.* 3rd edition. (Collection Cursus. Histoire.) Paris: A. Colin, 2001. Pp. 192; illustrations; maps.

Muller, Michael G. "Adel und Elitenwandel in Ostmitteleuropa. Fragen an die Polnische Adelsgeschichte im Ausgehenden 18. und 19. Jahrhundert." *Zeitschrift für Ostmitteleuropa-Forschung*, 50 (2001), 497–513.

Muller, Michael. "La suppression des Jésuites dans le royaume de France en 1764 et la réorganisation du collège de Louis-le-grand par le parlement de Paris: analyse des sources manuscrites conservées dans les archives nationales et dans la bibliothèque nationale de France, Paris." *Francia*, 28 (2001), 155–61.

Munson, James. *Maria Fitzherbert: The Secret Wife of George IV*. New York: Carroll & Graf Publishers, 2001. Pp. xiii + 414; illustrations.

Murphy, John A. "A Public Voice of History." *History Ireland*, 9 (2001), 12–15.

Murphy, Thomas. *Jesuit Slaveholding in Maryland, 1717–1838*. (Studies in African American History and Culture.) New York: Routledge, 2001. Pp. xxv + 258.

Murray, Dian. "The Practice of Homosexuality among the Pirates of Late Eighteenth- and Early Nineteenth-Century China." In *Bandits at Sea: A Pirates Reader*. Edited by C. R. Pennell. New York: New York University Press, 2001.

Musa, Sulaiman. "Islam Among the Nupe People of Northern Nigeria." *Journal of the Pakistan Historical Society*, 49 (2001), 19–28.

Mussmann, Olaf. "Zwischen Verschleppung und sozialem Aufstieg – Türken im Deutschland des 17. Jahrhunderts." *Sozialwissenschaftliche Informationen*, 30 (2001), 10–13.

Naguschewski, Dirk, and Sabine Schrader (eds.). *Sehen, Lesen, Begehren: Homosexualität in französischer Literatur und Kultur*. (Gender Studies Romanistik 6.). Berlin: Edition Tanvia, 2001. Pp. 280.

Nardin, Jane. "Hannah More and the Rhetoric of Educational Reform." *Women's History Review*, 10 (2001), 211–27.

Naveda Chávez-Hita, Adriana (ed.). *Pardos, mulatos y libertos: Sexto Encuentro de Afromexicanistas*. (Biblioteca.) Xalapa: Universidad Veracruzana, 2001. Pp. 249.

Neher-Bernheim, Renée. *La vie juive en Terre sainte sous les Turcs ottomans, 1517–1918*. Paris: Calmann-Lévy, 2001. Pp. 396; map.

II: Historical, Social, and Economic Studies

Neidleman, Jason Andrew. *The General Will Is Citizenship: Inquiries into French Political Thought.* Lanham: Rowman & Littlefield Publishers, 2001. Pp. vii + 195.

Nelson, E. Charles. "Patrick Browne M.D. (c. 1720–1790), an Irish Doctor in the Caribbean: His Residence on Saint Croix (1757–1765) and His Unpublished Accounts of Volcanic Activity on Montserrat." *Archives of Natural History*, 28 (2001), 135–47.

Nelson, John K. *A Blessed Company: Parishes, Parsons, and Parishioners in Anglican Virginia, 1690–1776.* Chapel Hill: University of North Carolina Press, 2001. Pp. 477; illustrations; maps.

Neugebauer, Wolfgang. *Zentralprovinz im Absolutismus: Brandenburg im 17. und 18. Jahrhundert.* (Bibliothek der brandenburgischen und preussischen Geschichte 5.) Berlin: Berlin Verlag Arno Spitz, 2001. Pp. 222.

Nichols, David A. "'The Main Mean of their Political Management': George Washington and the Practice of Indian Trade in the Early Republic." Pp. 143–61 of *George Washington in and as Culture*. Edited by Kevin L. Cope, William S. Pederson, and Frank Williams. New York: AMS Press, 2001.

Nicolas, Gilbert, Heinz-Werner Wollersheim, Yves Defrance, and Alain Coulon (eds.). *La construction de l'identité régionale: les exemples de la Saxe et de la Bretagne, XVIIIe–XXe siècle.* (Collection Histoire.) Rennes: Presses universitaires de Rennes, 2001. Pp. 208; maps; illustrations.

Nieto-Galan, Agustí. *Colouring Textiles: A History of Natural Dyestuffs in Industrial Europe.* Dordrecht: Kluwer Academic, 2001. Pp. xxv + 246; illustrations.

Niewójt, Monika and Alessandra Minerbi. "La figura di Stanislaw August Poniatowski in un recente convegno." *Storia della Storiografia*, 40 (2001), 91–101.

Nini, Yehuda, and Nissim Benjamin Gamlieli (eds.). *Almisavadeh: pinkas bet-ha-din shel kehilat Yehude Tsan`a ba-me'ah ha-18.* (Pirsume-ha-Makhon le-heker ha-tefutsot 145.) Ramat Aviv: Universitat Tel-Aviv, 2001.

Nora, Pierre. *Rethinking France = Les lieux de mémoire.* Vol. 1: The State. Chicago: University of Chicago Press, 2001. Illustrations; maps.

Novinsky, Anita. "Ser marrano em Minas colonial." *Revista Brasileira de Historia*, 21 (2001), 161–76.

Novopashina, Lidiia Iur'evna. "Britanskaia Kolonial'naia Ekspansiia Na Malaiskom Arkhipelage Na Rubezhe XVIII–XIX Vekov." *Novaia i Noveishaia Istoriia*, 5 (2001), 59–74.

Núñez Sánchez, Jorge. "Quito y la defensa de Cartagena." *Boletín de historia y antigüedades*, 88 (2001), 567–82.

Nussbaum, Felicity. "Being a Man: Olaudah Equiano and Ignatius Sancho." Pp. 54–71 of *Genius in Bondage: Literature of the Early Black Atlantic*. Edited by Vincent Carretta and Philip Gould. Lexington: University Press of Kentucky, 2001.

O'Connor, Thomas. *The Irish in Europe, 1580–1815*. Dublin: Four Courts Press, 2001. Pp. 219.

O'Dea, Michael. "Philosophie, histoire et imagination dans le *Discours sur l'origine de l'inégalité* de Jean-Jacques Rousseau." In *La diffusion de Locke en France, traduction au dix-huitième siècle, lectures de Rousseau*. (Studies on Voltaire and the Eighteenth Century 04.) Edited by Jørn Schløser. Oxford: Voltaire Foundation, 2001.

Ogborn, Miles. "This Is London! How D'ye Like It?" *Journal of Urban History*, 27 (2001), 206–16.

Ogundiran, Akinwumi O. "Factional Competition, Sociopolitical Development, and Settlement Cycling in Ilare District (ca. 1200–1900): Oral Traditions of Historical Experience in a Yoruba Community." *History in Africa*, 28 (2001), 203–23.

Oliphant, John. *Peace and War on the Anglo-Cherokee Frontier, 1756–63*. Hampshire: Palgrave, 2001. Pp. xvii + 269; maps.

O'Loughlin, Katrina. "Having Lived Much in the World: Inhabitation, Embodiment and English Women Travellers' Representations of Russia in the Eighteenth Century." *Women's Writing*, 8 (2001), 419–39.

Orser, Charles E., Jr. (ed.). *Race and the Archaeology of Identity*. (Foundations of Archaeological Inquiry.) Salt Lake City: University of Utah Press, 2001. Pp. viii + 260; illustrations.

Osiander, Andreas. "Before Sovereignty: Society and Politics in *Ancien Régime* Europe." In *Empires, Systems and States: Great Transformations in International Politics*. Edited by Michael Cox, Tim Dunne, and Ken Booth. Cambridge: Cambridge University Press, 2001.

Pacini, Monica. *Tra acque e strade: Lastra a Signa da Pietro Leopoldo al Regno d'Italia*. Firenze: L. S. Olschki, 2001. Pp. xx + 392; plates; illustrations; maps.

II: Historical, Social, and Economic Studies

Pack, Spencer J. "Unpacking Adam Smith: Critical Theorist?" *Research in the History of Economic Thought and Methodology*, 19 (2001), 33–46.

Paiva, Eduardo França. *Escravidão e universo cultural na colônia: Minas Gerais, 1716–1789.* (Coleção Origem 5.) Belo Horizonte: Editora UFMG, 2001. Pp. 285; illustrations.

Palti, Elias Jose. "The Nation as a Problem: Historians and the National Question." *History and Theory*, 40 (2001), 324–46.

Panova, Snezhka. "The Ottoman Empire and the Great Powers during the 18th Century (Piracy and Privateering)." *Archiv Orientalni*, 69 (2001), 265–84.

Parthasarathi, Prasannan. *The Transition to a Colonial Economy in South India: Industry and Commerce in the Eighteenth Century.* (Cambridge Studies in Indian History and Society 7.) Cambridge: Cambridge University Press, 2001. Pp. 280.

Pasley, Jeffrey L. *"The Tyranny of Printers": Newspaper Politics in the early American Republic.* (Jeffersonian America.) Charlottesville: University Press of Virginia, 2001. Pp. xviii + 517.

Paton, Diana. "Punishment, Crime, and the Bodies of Slaves in Eighteenth-Century Jamaica." *Journal of Social History*, 34 (2001), 923–54.

Paxman, David. "Lancashire Spiritual Culture and the Question of Magic." *Studies in Eighteenth-Century Culture*, 30 (2001), 223–43.

Pennell, C. R. (ed.). *Bandits at Sea: A Pirates Reader.* New York: New York University Press, 2001. Pp. ix + 351; illustrations; maps.

Penskoi, Vitali Viktorovich. "Armiia Rossiiskoi Imperii V XVIII V.: Vybor Modeli Razvitiia." *Voprosy Istorii*, 7 (2001), 119–36.

Pérez González, Maria Luisa. "Los caminos reales de América en la legislación y en la historia." *Anuario de Estudios Americanos*, 58 (2001), 33–60.

Perez Romero, Emilio. "Trashumancia, comercio lanero y crédito. La Compañía de Ganaderos de las Provincias de soria y Burgos (1781–1800)." *Historia Agraria*, 23 (2001), 119–46.

Pérez Samper, María de los Ángeles. "Espacios y prácticas de sociabilidad en el siglo XVIII: tertulias, refrescos y cafés de Barcelona." *Cuadernos de Historia Moderna*, 26 (2001), 11–55.

Pérotin-Dumon, Anne. "The Pirate and the Emperor: Power and the Law on the Seas, 1450–1850." In *Bandits at Sea: A Pirates Reader*. Edited by C. R. Pennell. New York: New York University Press, 2001.

Pfeil, Tom. "La hantise de la banqueroute: les finances publiques dans la période franco-batave (1795–1810)." Translated by Annie Jourdan. *Annales historiques de la révolution française*, 326 (2001), 53–64.

Philipp, Thomas. *Acre: The Rise and Fall of a Palestinian City, 1730–1831*. (History and Society of the Modern Middle East Series.) New York: Columbia University Press, 2001. Pp. 299; illustrations; maps.

Phillips, Carla Rahn. "The Life Blood of the Navy: Recruiting Sailors in Eighteenth-Century Spain." *Mariner's Mirror*, 87 (2001), 420–45.

Philosophical Faculty of the University of Zagreb. *Nikola Škrlec Lomnicki, 1729–1799*, volume 3. Zagreb: University of Zagreb Presses, 2001. Pp. xxii + 253.

Picard, Georges. *Une terre, son passé, un témoin: du XVIIIe au XXe siècle*. Laval: 2001. Pp. 360; illustrations; maps.

Picard, Liza. *Dr. Johnson's London: Coffee-Houses and Climbing Boys, Medicine, Toothpaste and Gin, Poverty and Press-Gangs, Freakshows and Female Education*. New York: St. Martin's Press, 2001. Pp. xxi + 362; illustrations; map.

Pijning, Ernst (Cristina Meneguello, trans.). "Contrabando, ilegalidade e medidas políticas no Rio de Janeiro do século XVIII." *Revista Brasileira de Historia*, 21 (2001), 397–414.

Pingué, Danièle. *Les mouvements jacobins en Normandie orientale: les sociétés politiques dans l'Eure et la Seine-Inférieure, 1790–1795*. (Mémoires et documents 56.) Paris: CTHS, 2001. Pp. 653; illustrations; maps.

Plank, Geoffrey G. *An Unsettled Conquest: The British Campaign Against the Peoples of Acadia*. (Early American studies.) Philadelphia: University of Pennsylvania Press, 2001. Pp. 239; illustrations; maps.

Pleve, Igor R. *The German Colonies on the Volga: The Second Half of the Eighteenth Century*. Lincoln: American Historical Society of Germans from Russia, 2001. Pp. 474.

II: Historical, Social, and Economic Studies

Plummer, Marguerite R. "George Washington's Founding Vision and the American West." Pp. 25–36 of *George Washington in and as Culture*. Edited by Kevin L. Cope, William S. Pederson, and Frank Williams. New York: AMS Press, 2001.

Poirier, Roger. *Jean-François de Saint-Lambert, 1786–1803: sa vie, son oeuvre*. Sarreguemines: Pierron, 2001. Pp. 337; illustrations.

Polet, Jean. "Rendre aux peuples d'Afrique par l'histoire des arts leur place dans l'histoire." *Cahiers d'histoire: revue d'histoire Critique*, 82 (2001), 9–19.

Poole, Kenneth. "The Origins of the Local Government Service." *Historian*, 72 (2001), 12–20.

Popkin, Jeremy D. *A History of Modern France*. 2nd edition. Upper Saddle River: Prentice Hall, 2001. Pp. xii + 322; illustrations; maps.

Provizer, Norman. "In the Shadow of Washington: Golda Meir, Duty, and the Call to Power." Pp. 197–211 of *George Washington in and as Culture*. Edited by Kevin L. Cope, William S. Pederson, and Frank Williams. New York: AMS Press, 2001.

Roy Porter. *Bodies Politic: Disease, Death and Doctors in Britain, 1650–1900*. Ithaca: Cornell University Press, 2001. Pp. 328.

Bodies Politic was the last of Roy Porter's long series of books on British medicine in the "long eighteenth century" to be published in his lifetime. As the title indicates, this work focuses on the body. The body, Porter argues, is an "expressive medium." "We feel and experience through our bodies, they negotiate the boundaries and crossings of self and society, and furnish the models and metaphors ... needed to name and navigate life" (35). But the book is also a study of images. As Porter explains in the preface, this work is his first attempt seriously to grapple with the many varieties of "visual evidence" (9), the various paintings, prints, caricatures, and drawings in which death and disease, doctors and patients, are portrayed. Porter has chosen one hundred and thirty five images for reproduction in this work, many in full color (kudos to Cornell University Press for the quality of the reproductions). The book is largely structured around the elucidation of theses images.

Bodies Politic ranges from the late-Tudor period to the Victorians, but the bulk of the book centers on the eighteenth century. The central arguments can be reduced to three. In the first place, Porter argues that the print culture of this period reflects medicine's participation in the commercialization and secularization of British society. Second, and more importantly, Porter contends that this print culture was itself constitutive of medical reality. Images, Porter argues, are not simply representations or "Polaroids of the world we have lost," but rather "embodiments, in form and content alike, of discursive practices and aesthetic expectations" (12). The representations, in other words, "are reality" (12), by which Porter seems to mean such images informed the ways in which people experienced disease, illness, and death. Third, Porter maintains that before the advent of "scientific medicine" (151), medicine remained a "quasi-religious morality play" (25) and thus provided a particularly rich source for satire and social commentary.

Much of this is convincing, and one cannot help but marvel at the extraordinarily richness of the print culture of this period. Parts of the book, however, are underargued. The connection between the two themes of the book, bodies and images, remains unclear. And Porter never sufficiently develops his contention that "representations are reality." Porter treats his images more as illustrations of social reality than as constitutive elements of that reality. Somewhat typically, for instance, the chapter on "Victorian Developments," opens with a discussion of the "reality" of the nineteenth-century medical profession, and only then moves on to a discussion of how print images from the period reflected that reality. Not every chapter is so wooden in its approach, but even in the more successful and richer chapters on the eighteenth century Porter does not wholly succeed in getting beyond a simple contextual reading of his images.

I am inclined to take my cue from the jazz writer reviewing the latest release by a much admired musician. In *Bodies Politic* Porter treats the reader to his usual display of erudition, wit, and anecdote. The writing is lively and the book consistently entertaining. Those familiar with Porter's work, however, are unlikely to learn much that is new, while those new to Porter are better advised to seek out some of his earlier works. For completists only.—Alex Dracobly

Porter, Roy. *The Enlightenment*. (Studies in European History.) 2nd edition. New York: Palgrave, 2001. Pp. x + 90.

Pott, Sandra. "Gemeinwohl oder 'schöner Schein.' Staatszwecke und Staatsideen bei Christoph Martin Wieland und in der Weimarer Klassik." *Aufklärung*, 13 (2001), 211–42.

Praud, Jocelyne. "French Women and the Liberal Model of Political Citizenship: From Exclusion to Inclusion?" *Contemporary French Civilization*, 25 (2001), 250–70.

Preda, Alex. "In the Enchanted Grove: Financial Conversations and the Marketplace in England and France in the 18th Century." *Journal of Historical Sociology*, 14 (2001), 276–307.

Prüfer, Thomas. "Der Fortschritt der Menschheitsgeschichte am Ende des 18. Jahrhunderts." *Storia della Storiografia*, 39 (2001), 109–18.

Pucci, Suzanne R. *Sites of The Spectator: Emerging Literary and Cultural Practice in Eighteenth-Century France*. (Studies on Voltaire and the Eighteenth Century 9.) Oxford: Voltaire Foundation, 2001. Pp. ix + 202.

Pursell, Carroll (ed.). *American Technology*. (Blackwell Readers in American Social and Cultural History 7.) Malden: Blackwell, 2001. Pp. x + 362.

Qi, Han. "Sino-French Scientific Relations through the French Jesuits and the Académie Royale des Sciences in the Seventeenth and Eighteenth Centuries." In *China and Christianity: Burdened Past, Hopeful Future*. Edited by Stephen Uhalley, Jr., and Xiaoxin Wu. Armonk: M.E. Sharpe, 2001.

II: Historical, Social, and Economic Studies

Quadros, Eduardo Gusmao de. "A luta pela Lingua." *Historia: Questoes & Debates*, 18 (2001), 211–25.

Queneau, Jacqueline, and Jean-Yves Patte. *La France au temps des libertines*. Paris: Editions du Chêne, 2001. Pp. 187; illustrations.

Quinault, Roland. "From National to World Metropolis: Governing London, 1750–1850." *London Journal*, 26 (2001), 38–46.

Rabe, Robert. *German Professions of the Eighteenth and Nineteenth Centuries*. Bainbridge Island: Ravenhurst Castle Press, 2001. Pp. 188; illustrations.

Rabuzzi, Daniel A. "Fading Images, Fading Realities? Female Merchants in Scandinavia and the Baltic." *Histoire Sociale*, 34 (2001), 355–70.

Radford, Peter. *The Celebrated Captain Barclay: Sport, Money and Fame in Regency Britain*. London: Headline, 2001. Pp. x + 342; plates; illustrations.

Ragan, Edward D. "Brother, Destroyer, Father: George Washington's Legacy in Iriquoia." Pp. 123–41 of *George Washington in and as Culture*. Edited by Kevin L. Cope, William S. Pederson, and Frank Williams. New York: AMS Press, 2001.

Rahikainen, Marjatta. "Ageing Men and Women in the Labour Market: Continuity and Change." *Scandinavian Journal of History*, 26 (2001), 297–314.

Raj, Kapil. "Refashioning Civilities, Engineering Trust: William Jones, Indian Intermediaries and the Production of Reliable Legal Knowledge in Late 18th-Century Bengal." *Studies in History*, 17 (2001), 175–209.

Ras, Norberto. *El origen de la riqueza en una frontera ganadera: fines del siglo XVIII en el Río de la Plata*. (Serie 30.) Buenos Aires: Academia Nacional de Agronomía y Veterinaria, 2001. Pp. vii + 126.

Ray, Aniruddha (ed.). *Tipu Sultan and His Age: A Collection of Seminar Papers*. (Seminar and Public Lecture Series.) Kolkata: Asiatic Society, 2001. Pp. x + 204; illustrations.

Rebel, Hermann. "What Do the Peasants Want Now? Realists and Fundamentalists in Swiss and South German Rural Politics, 1650–1750." *Central European History*, 34 (2001), 313–56.

Reddy, William M. *The Navigation of Feeling: A Framework for the History of Emotions.* Cambridge: Cambridge University Press, 2001. Pp. xiv + 380; illustrations.

Rée, Peta. "James Silk Buckingham (1786–1855)." In *Unfolding the Orient: Travellers in Egypt and the Near East.* Edited by Paul Starkey and Janet Starkey. Reading: Ithaca, 2001.

Rees, Siân. *The Floating Brothel: The Extraordinary True Story of an Eiighteenth-Century Ship and Its Cargo of Female Convicts.* London: Headline, 2001. Pp. 248; plates; illustrations.

Reid-Maroney, Nina. *Philadelphia's Enlightenment, 1740–1800: Kingdom of Christ, Empire of Reason.* (Contributions to the Study of World History 81.) Westport: Greenwood Press, 2001. Pp. xv + 199; map.

Reilly, Robin. *Wolfe of Quebec.* London: Cassell, 2001. Pp. xiv + 366; illustrations; maps.

Reynard, Pierre Claude. "The Language of Failure: Bankruptcy in Eighteenth-Century France." *Journal of European Economic History*, 30 (2001), 355–90.

Richard, Jacques. "La bibliothèque de Jean Astruc, médecin des lumières (1684–1766)." *Histoire des sciences médicales*, 35 (2001), 99–108.

Ricuperati, Giuseppe. "Ipotesi su Carlo Denina storico e comparatista." *Rivista Storica Italiana*, 113 (2001), 107–37.

Ricuperati, Giuseppe. *Lo stato sabaudo nel Settecento: dal trionfo delle burocrazie alla crisi d'antico regime.* Torino: UTET libreria, 2001. Pp. xi + 464.

Riethmüller, Jürgen. *Die Anfänge des demokratischen Denkens in Deutschland: demokratische Staatsphilosophie, Grundlegung einer demokratischen Verfassungstradition und Ausstrahlung auf die Unterschichten im ausgehenden 18. Jahrhundert.* (Deutsche Hochschuledition 114.) Neuried: Ars Una, 2001. Pp. viii + 518.

Rigal, Laura. *The American Manufactory: Art, Labor, and the World of Things in the Early Republic.* Princeton: Princeton University Press, 2001. Pp. 272; illustrations.

Rivers, Isabel (ed.). *Books and Their Readers in Eighteenth-Century England: New Essays.* London: Continuum, 2001. Pp. x + 294.

Rizo Castellón, José (ed.). *Documentos históricos de Nicaragua, 1750–1940.* Managua: Banco Central de Nicaragua, 2001. Pp. 303.

II: Historical, Social, and Economic Studies 79

Robbins, Louise E. *Elephant Slaves and Pampered Parrots: Exotic Animals in Eighteenth-Century Paris.* Baltimore: Johns Hopkins University Press, 2001. Pp. 352; illustrations.

Roche, Daniel (Marco Platania, transl.). "Dell'illuminismo: Per una storia sociale della cultura." *Rivista Storica Italiana*, 113 (2001), 86–106.

Roche, Daniel. "Electricité et institution sociale de la science: réflexions pour une conclusion." *Revue d'histoire des sciences*, 54 (2001), 99–114.

Roche, Daniel. *Almanach parisien, en faveur des étrangers et des personnes curieuses.* (Lire le dix-huitième siècle.) Saint-Étienne: Publications de l'Université de Saint-Étienne, 2001. Pp. 176.

Roggero, Marina. "L'alphabétisation en Italie: Une conquête féminine?" Translated by Maria-Novella Borghetti. *Annales: Histoire, sciences sociales*, 56 (2001), 903–25.

Rohrbasser, Jean-Marc. *Dieu, l'ordre et le nombre: théologie physique et dénombrement au XVIIIe siècle.* (Philosophies 144.) Paris: Presses universitaires de France, 2001. Pp. 127.

Rollyson, Carl. "Samuel Johnson: Dean of Contemporary Biographers." *Biography*, 24 (2001), 442–47.

Roman, Alain. *Saint-Malo au temps des négriers.* (Collection "Hommes et sociétés".) Paris: Karthala, 2001. Pp. 357; plates; illustrations.

Romeiro, Adriana. *Um visionário na corte de D. João V: revolta e milenarismo nas Minas Gerais.* (Humanitas 57.) Belo Horizonte: Editora UFMG, 2001. Pp. 286.

Romero Jaramillo, Dolcey. "Nicolás Fester: un cimarrón barranquillero del siglo XVIII." *Memoria y Sociedad*, 5 (2001), 105–20.

Rommelt, Stefan W. "Kaiser, Papst und Vaterland. Jubiläen und die Memorialkultur in der Germania sacra. Die Jahrtausendfeiern in Fulda und Kempten." *Historisches Jahrbuch*, 121 (2001), 115–54.

Rosa, Mario. "La chiesa Toscana e la pietà illuminata." *Archivio Storico Italiano*, 159 (2001), 547–89.

Rosenfeld, Sophia. *A Revolution in Language: The Problem of Signs in Late Eighteenth-Century France.* Stanford: Stanford University Press, 2001. Pp. vi + 410; illustrations.

Rothschild, Emma. *Economic Sentiments: Adam Smith, Condorcet, and the Enlightenment.* Cambridge: Harvard University Press, 2001. Pp. ix + 353.

Rousseau, G. S. "Ingenious Pain: Fiction, History, Biography, and the Miraculous Eighteenth Century." *Eighteenth-Century Life*, 25 (2001), 47–62.

Roux, Jean Claude. "De los límites a la frontera: o los malentendidos de la geopolítica amazónica." *Revista de Indias*, 61 (2001), 513–39.

Roux, Pascal. "Education et formation des officiers militaires à Toulouse dans la deuxième moitie du XVIIIe siècle." *Histoire, économie et société*, 20 (2001), 371–83.

Rowe, William T. *Saving the World: Chen Hongmou and Elite Consciousness in Eighteenth-Century China.* Stanford: Stanford University Press, 2001. Pp. xii + 601; illustrations; map.

Rozbicki, Michal J. "To Save Them From Themselves: Proposals to Enslave the British Poor, 1698–1755." *Slavery & Abolition*, 22 (2001), 29–50.

Rudert, Thomas and Hartmut Zückert (eds.). *Gemeindeleben: Dörfer und kleine Städte im östlichen Deutschland (16.–18. Jahrhundert).* (Potsdamer Studien zu Geschichte der ländlichen Gesellschaft 1.) Köln: Böhlau, 2001. Pp. xvi + 452.

Rueda Novoa, Rocío. *Zambaje y autonomía: historia de la gente negra de la provincia de Esmeraldas, siglos XVI–XVIII.* (Colección Marejada 1.) Quito: Taller de Estudios Históricos, 2001. Pp. 195; illustrations; maps.

Ruggiu, François-Joseph. "The Urban Gentry in England, 1660–1780: A French Approach." *Historical Research*, 74 (2001), 249–70.

Ryan, Vanessa L. "The Physiological Sublime: Burke's Critique of Reason." *Journal of the History of Ideas*, 62 (2001), 265–79.

Saage, Richard. "Der Ethnologe als Utopist: Zu Lahontans Bon Sauvage-Utopie." *Paideuma*, 47 (2001), 43–60.

Safier, Neil. "Unveiling the Amazon to European Science and Society: The Reading and Reception of la Condamine's *Relation abrégée d'un voyage fait dans l'interieur de l'Amérique méridionale* (1745)." *Terrae Incognitae*, 33 (2001), 33–47.

II: Historical, Social, and Economic Studies 81

Salewski, Michael. "Preußischer Militarismus – Realität oder Mythos? Gedanken zu einem Phantom." *Zeitschrift für Religions- und Geistesgeschichte*, 53 (2001), 19–34.

Sani, Valentino. *La rivoluzione senza rivoluzione: potere e società a Ferrara dal tramonto della legazione pontificia alla nascita della Repubblica Cisalpina (1787–1797)*. (Studi e ricerche storiche 279.) Milano: F. Angeli, 2001. Pp. 441.

Sanmartín Miguez, J. Santiago. "Los boticarios del Hospital Real de Santiago de Compostela en el siglo XVIII." *Asclepio*, 53 (2001), 57–93.

Santiago Correa Restrepo, Juan. *Minería y comercio: las raíces de la elite antioqueña (1775–1810)*. (Tesis de grado 7.) Bogota, Colombia: Universidad Externado de Colombia, 2001. Pp. 125; illustrations; maps.

Sarmant, Thierry. "Mars archiviste: département de la guerre, dépôt de la guerre, archives de la guerre, 1630–1791." *Revue historique des armées*, 1 (2001), 113–22.

Sashalmi, Endre. "A Cár Akarata —Torvény: Az Abszolutizmus És Az Uralkodói Akarat a Péteri Ideológiában." *Századok*, 135 (2001), 1413–31.

Saur, Wolfgang. "Der Soldatenkönig: Friedrich Wilhelm I. in seiner Zeit. 42. Jahrestagung der Gesellschaft für Geistesgeschichte vom 26.–28. Oktober 2000 in Königs Wusterhausen." *Zeitschrift für Religions- und Geistesgeschichte*, 53 (2001), 278–81.

Schama, Simon. *A History of Britain*. Volume 2: The Wars of the British, 1603–1776. New York: Hyperion, 2001. Pp. 544; illustrations; maps.

Scharf, Claus. *Katharina II., Russland und Europa: Beiträge zur internationalen Forschung*. (Veröffentlichungen des Instituts für Europäische Geschichte Mainz. Beiheft 45.) Mainz: Philipp von Zabern, 2001. Pp. xxx + 607; illustrations.

Scher-Zembitska, Lydia. *L'aigle et le phénix: un siècle de relations franco-polonaise, 1732–1832*. (CNRS Histoire.) Paris: CNRS editions, 2001. Pp. 469.

Scheutz, Martin. "Öffentlichkeit und Politische Partizipation in einem Grundherrschaftlichen Markt des 18. Jahrhunderts: Das Beispiel der Scheibbser Taidinge und die Strategie der Amtervergabe." *Mitteilungen des Instituts für Österreichische Geschichtsforschung*, 109 (2001), 382–422.

Scheutz, Martin. *Alltag und Kriminalität: Disziplierungsversuche im steirish-österreichischen Grenzgebiet im 18. Jahrhundert.* (Mitteilungen des Instituts für Österreichische Geschichtsforschung. Ergänzungsband 38.) Wien: R. Oldenbourg, 2001. Pp. 599; illustrations.

Schløser, Jørn (ed.). *La diffusion de Locke en France, traduction au dix-huitième siècle, lectures de Rousseau.* (Studies on Voltaire and the Eighteenth Century 4.) Oxford: Voltaire Foundation, 2001. Pp. v + 364.

Schmidt, Leigh Eric. *Holy Fairs: Scotland and the Making of American Revivalism.* Grand Rapids: William B. Eerdmans, 2001. Pp. xxix + 278; illustrations.

Schmolz-Haberlein, Michaela, and Mark Haberlein. "Eighteenth-Century Anabaptists in the Margravate of Baden and Neighboring Territories." *Mennonite Quarterly Review*, 75 (2001), 471–92.

Schnegg, Brigitte. "Gleichgestimmte Seelen. Empfindsame Inszenierung und intellektueller Wettstreit von Männern und Frauen in der Freundschaftskultur der Aufklärung." *WerkstattGeschichte*, 28 (2001), 23–42.

Schneider, Konrad. "Bemerkungen zum Papiergeldumlauf in Frankfurt am Main." *Bankhistorisches Archiv*, 27 (2001), 115–28.

Schneider, Jürgen, Otto-Ernst Krawehl, and Markus A. Denzel (eds.). *Statistik des Hamburger seewärtigen Einfuhrhandels im 18. Jahrhundert: nach den Admiralitäts- und Convoygeld-Einnahmebüchern.* (Quellen und Forschungen zur historischen Statistik von Deutschland 20.) St. Katharinen: Scripta Mercaturae, 2001. Pp. 619.

Scholze, Dietrich, and Ewa Tomicka-Krumrey (eds.). *Mit Wort und Tat: deutsch-polnischer Kultur- und Wissenschaftsdialog seit dem 18. Jahrhundert.* Leipzig: Leipziger Universitätsverlag, 2001. Pp. 185; illustrations.

Schonemann, Bernd. "Die Geschichtskultur der Erlebnisgesellschaft: August der Starke in Tokio." *Sozialwissenschaftliche Informationen*, 30 (2001), 135–42.

Schönwälder, Karen, and Imke Sturm-Martin. *Die britische Gesellschaft zwischen Offenheit und Abgrenzung: Einwanderung und Integration vom 18. bis zum 20. Jahrhundert.* (Veröffentlichung 46.) Bodenheim: Philo, 2001.

Schrader, Sabine. "Nonnen, Königinnen und Voyeure: Imagologien der Lesbe im 18. Jahrhundert." Pp. 33–47 of *Sehen, Lesen, Begehren: Homosexualität in französischer Literatur und*

II: Historical, Social, and Economic Studies

Kultur. (Gender Studies Romanistik 6.) Edited by Dirk Naguschewski and Sabine Schrader. Berlin: Edition Tanvia, 2001.

Schulte, Rolf. *Hexenverfolgung in Schleswig-Holstein vom 16.–18. Jahrhundert.* Heide: Boyens, 2001. Pp. 176; illustrations.

Schutte, Anne Jacobson. *Aspiring Saints: Pretense of Holiness, Inquisition, and Gender in the Republic of Venice, 1618–1750.* Baltimore: Johns Hopkins University Press, 2001. Pp. xvi + 337; illustrations.

Schutte, Anne Jacobson, Thomas Kuehn, and Silvana Seidel Menchi (eds.). *Time, Space, and Women's Lives in Early Modern Europe.* (Sixteenth Century Essays & Studies 57. Kirksville: Truman State University Press, 2001. Pp. xvii + 336; illustrations.

Schwarz, Angela. "'Wie uns die Stunde schlägt'. Zeitbewußtsein und Zeiterfahrungen im Industriezeitalter als Gegenstand der Mentalitätsgeschichte." *Archiv für Kulturgeschichte*, 83 (2001), 451–79.

Schwarz, Anna. "Pokrovitel'stvo Sem'i Romanovykh Muzykal'noi Kul'ture Rossii V Kontse XVIII–Seredine XIX Veka." *Novaia i Noveishaia Istoriia*, 6 (2001), 190–92.

Schwerhoff, Gerd. "Justiz-Erfahrungen. Einige einleitende Gedanken." *Historische Zeitschrift*, 31 (2001), 341–48.

Scott, H. M. *The Emergence of the Eastern Powers, 1756–1775.* (Cambridge Studies in Early Modern History.) Cambridge: Cambridge University Press, 2001. Pp. xv + 285.

Scull, Andrew, and Jonathan Andrews. *Patrons and Customers of the Mad-Trade: John Monro and Mad-Doctoring in Eighteenth Century England.* London: Athlone, 2001. Pp. 160.

Scully, Randolph. "'Somewhat limited': Baptist Discourses of Race and Slavery in Nat Turner's Virginia, 1770–1840." In *Explorations in Early American Culture.* Volume 5. Edited by George W. Boudreau and William A. Pencak. University Park: Pennsylvania Historical Association, 2001. Pp. 388; illustrations.

Sebastiani, Sylvia. "Conjectural History vs. the Bible: Eighteenth-Century Scottish Historians and the Idea of History in the *Encyclopaedia Britannica*." *Storia della Storiografia*, 39 (2001).

Segala, Marco. "Electricité animale, magnétisme animal, galvanisme universel: à la recherche de l'identité entre l'homme et la nature." *Revue d'histoire des sciences*, 54 (2001), 71–84.

Seguin, Maria Susana. *Science et religion dans la pensée française du XVIIIe siècle: le mythe du Déluge universel*. Paris: Honoré Champion, 2001. Pp. 535; illustrations.

Selles, Manuel A. "El vapor en el laboratorio: Una memoria sobre la ebullición del abate Nollet." *Asclepio*, 53 (2001), 165–89.

Shamin, S. M. "Rossiia I Mir: Problemy Vzaimovospriiatiia V XVI–XX Vekakh." *Otechestvennaia Istoriia*, 6 (2001), 192–96.

Sharpe, Pamela. "Gender in the Economy: Female Merchants and Family Businesses in the British Isles, 1600–1850." *Histoire sociale*, 34 (2001), 283–306.

Shields, David S. "The World I Ate: The Prophets of Global Consumption Culture." *Eighteenth-Century Life*, 25 (2001), 214–24.

Shoemaker, Robert. "Male Honour and the Decline of Public Violence in Eighteenth-Century London." *Social History*, 26 (2001), 190–208.

Shoemaker, Robert B. "Gendered Spaces: Patterns of Mobility and Perceptions of London's Geography, 1660–1750." In *Imagining Early Modern London: Perceptions and Portrayals of the City from Stow to Strype, 1598–1720*. Edited by J. F. Merritt. Cambridge: Cambridge University Press, 2001.

Siena, Kevin P. "The Foul Disease and Privacy: The Effects of Venereal Disease and Patient Demand on the Medical Marketplace in Early Modern London." *Bulletin of the History of Medicine*, 75 (2001), 199–224.

Sigrist, René. "L'expérimentation comme rhétorique de la preuve: L'exemple du *Traité d'insectologie* de Charles Bonnet." *Revue d'histoire des sciences*, 54 (2001), 419–49.

Silva, Kalina Vanderlei. *O miserável soldo & a boa ordem da sociedade colonial: militarização e marginalidade na capitania de Pernambuco dos séculos XVII e XVIII*. Recife: Fundação de Cultura Cidade do Recife, 2001. Pp. 320.

Silverman, David. "Deposing the Sachem to Defend the Sachemship: Land Sales and Native Political Structure on Martha's Vineyard, 1680–1740." In *Explorations in Early American Culture*. Volume 5. Edited by George W. Boudreau and William A. Pencak. University Park: Pennsylvania Historical Association, 2001.

II: Historical, Social, and Economic Studies

Silverstone, Paul H. *The Sailing Navy, 1775–1854*. Annapolis: Naval Institute Press, 2001. Pp. xv + 101.

Simonetto, Michele. *I lumi nelle campagne: accademie e agricoltura nella Repubblica di Venezia, 1768–1797*. (Studi veneti 7.) Treviso: Fondazione Benetton studi ricerche, 2001. Pp. xii + 491.

Simpson, Matthew. "You Have Not Such a One in England: St Andrews University Library as an Eighteenth-Century Mission Statement." *Library History*, 17 (2001), 41–56.

Singh, Arvind-pal, Christopher Shackle, and Gurharpal Singh (eds.). *Sikh Religion, Culture and Ethnicity*. Richmond: Curzon, 2001. Pp. ix + 220.

Sirgo, Henry B. "George Washington as the Natural President." Pp. 239–47 of *George Washington in and as Culture*. Edited by Kevin L. Cope, William S. Pederson, and Frank Williams. New York: AMS Press, 2001.

Skoczylas, Anne. *Mr. Simson's Knotty Case: Divinity, Politics, and Due Process in Early Eighteenth-Century Scotland*. (McGill–Queen's Studies in the History of Ideas 31.) Montreal: McGill–Queen's University Press, 2001. Pp. x + 403.

Sloan, Herbert E. *Principle and Interest: Thomas Jefferson and the Problem of Debt*. (Reissue.) Charlottesville: University Press of Virginia, 2001. Pp. viii + 377.

Smyth, Jim. *The Making of the United Kingdom, 1660–1800: State, Religion and Identity in Britain and Ireland*. (British Isles Series.) New York: Longman, 2001. Pp. xv + 252; illustrations; maps.

Snapp, J. Russell. "An Enlightened Empire: Scottish and Irish Imperial Reformers in the Age of the American Revolution." *Albion*, 33 (2001), 388–403.

Soares, Luiz Carlos. "Ciência, religião e Ilustração: as academias de ensino dos dissentes racionalistas ingleses no século XVIII." *Revista Brasileira de Historia*, 21 (2001), 173–200.

Sofka, James R. "Eighteenth-Century International System: Parity or Primacy." In *Empires, Systems and States: Great Transformations in International Politics*. Edited by Michael Cox, Tim Dunne, and Ken Booth. Cambridge: Cambridge University Press, 2001.

Sola-Corbacho, Juan Carlos. "Urban Economies in the Spanish World: The Cases of Madrid and Mexico City at the End of the Eighteenth Century." *Journal of Urban History*, 27 (2001), 604–32.

Sordet, Yann. *L'amour des livres au siècle des Lumières: Pierre Adamoli et ses collections*. (Mémoires et documents de l'Ecole des chartes 60.) Paris: Ecole des chartes, 2001. Pp. 537; illustrations.

Souhami, Diana. *Selkirk's Island*. London: Weidenfeld & Nicolson, 2001. Pp. 246; illustrations; maps.

Soulodre-La France, Renée. "Socially Not So Dead! Slave Identities in Bourbon Nueva Granada." *Colonial Latin American Review*, 10 (2001), 87–103.

Spini, Giorgio. "Settecento protestante." *Rivista Storica Italiana*, 113 (2001), 817–30.

Stanley, Brian (ed.). *Christian Missions and the Enlightenment*. (Studies in the History of Christian Missions.) Grand Rapids:W. B. Eerdmans, 2001. Pp. xi + 246.

Stapelfeldt, Gerhard. *Der Merkantilismus: die Genese der Weltgesellschaft vom 16. bis zum 18. Jahrhundert*. Freiburg: Ça ira, 2001. Pp. 569; illustrations.

Stark, David M. "Surviving Slavery: Marriage Strategies and Family Formation Patterns Among the Eighteenth-Century Puerto Rican Slave Population." In *Crossing Boundaries: Comparative History of Black People in Diaspora*. (Blacks in the Diaspora.) Edited by Darlene Clark Heine and Jacqueline McLeod. Bloomington: Indiana University Press, 2001.

Starkey, David. "The English Historian's Role and the Place of History in English National Life." *Historian*, 71 (2001), 6–15.

Starkey, David J. "The Origins and Regulation of Eighteenth-Century British Privateering." In *Bandits at Sea: A Pirates Reader*. Edited by C. R. Pennell. New York: New York University Press, 2001.

Starkey, Paul, and Janet Starkey (eds.). *Unfolding the Orient: Travellers in Egypt and the Near East*. Reading: Ithaca, 2001. Pp. vi + 318; illustrations.

Stefanov, Svetoslav, and Robev, Nikola. "The Doomed Peninsula: Confronting National Stereotypes in the Balkans from the Enlightenment until World War II." *Nordic Notes*, 5 (2001).

II: Historical, Social, and Economic Studies

Steinberg, Arthur K. "George Washington and Slavery." Pp. 163–75 of *George Washington in and as Culture*. Edited by Kevin L. Cope, William S. Pederson, and Frank Williams. New York: AMS Press, 2001.

Stern, Selma. *Der Hofjude im Zeitalter des Absolutismus: ein Beitrag zur europäischen Geschichte im 17. und 18. Jahrhundert.* (Schriftenreihe wissenschaftlicher Abhandlungen des Leo Baeck Instituts 64.) Tübingen: Mohr Siebeck, 2001. Pp. x + 285; illustrations.

Stevenson, David. *The Beggar's Benison: Sex Clubs of Enlightenment Scotland and Their Rituals.* East Linton: Tuckwell Press, 2001. Pp. xviii + 265; plates; illustrations; maps.

Stibbert, Frederick. *European Civil and Military Clothing from the First to the Eighteenth Century.* (Dover Pictorial Archive Series.) Mineola: Dover Publications, 2001. Pp. 217; illustrations.

Stirk, Nigel. "Intellectual Property and the Role of Manufacturers: Definitions from the Late Eighteenth Century." *Journal of Historical Geography*, 27 (2001), 475–92.

Stoler, Ann Laura. "Tense and Tender Ties: The Politics of Comparison in North American History and (Post)Colonial Studies." *Journal of American History*, 88 (2001), 829–65.

Stollberg-Rilinger, Barbara. "Rang vor Gericht. Zur Verrechtlichung sozialer Rangkonflikte in der frühen Neuzeit." *Zeitschrift für Historische Forschung*, 28 (2001), 385–418.

Stollberg-Rilinger, Barbara. *Vormoderne politische Verfahren.* (Zeitschrift für historische Forschung 25.) Berlin: Duncker & Humblot, 2001. Pp. 590; illustrations.

Stone, Daniel. *The Polish-Lithuanian State, 1386–1795.* (History of East Central Europe 4.) Seattle: University of Washington Press, 2001. Pp. xii + 374; maps.

Strayer, Brian Eugene. *Huguenots and Camisards as Aliens in France, 1598–1789: The Struggle for Religious Toleration.* (Studies in Religion and Society 50.) Lewiston: E. Mellen Press, 2001. Pp. iv + 616; illustrations.

Strickrodt, Silke. "A Neglected Source for the History of Little Popo: The Thomas Miles Papers, ca. 1789–1796." *History in Africa*, 28 (2001), 293–330.

Struck, Bernhard. "De l'affinité sociale à la différence culturelle: la France vue par les voyageurs allemands au XVIIIe siècle." *Francia*, 28 (2001), 17–34.

Stukenbrock, Karin. "Der sezierte Leichnam als Objekt der (Körper-)Erfahrung in der Frühen Neuzeit." *Historische Zeitschrift*, Supplement (2001), 73–88.

Subramanian, Lakshmi. "Arms and the Merchant: The Making of the Bania Raj in Late Eighteenth-Century India." *South Asia*, 24 (2001), 1–27.

Suderman, Jeffrey M. *Orthodoxy and Enlightenment: George Campbell in the Eighteenth Century.* (McGill–Queen's Studies in the History of Ideas 32.) Montréal: McGill–Queen's University Press, 2001. Pp. xiv + 293.

Sueur, Philippe. *Histoire du droit public français, XVe–XVIIIe siècle: la genèse de l'État contemporain* Two volumes. 3rd edition. (Thémis. Droit public.) Paris: Presses Universitaires de France, 2001.

Suire, Éric. *La sainteté française de la Réforme catholique (XVIe–XVIIIe siècles): d'après les textes hagiographiques et les procès de canonization.* Pessac: Presses Universitaires de Bordeaux, 2001. Pp. 506; illustrations.

Sumner, James. "John Richardson, Saccharometry and the Pounds-Per-Barrel Extract: The Construction of a Quantity." *British Journal for the History of Science*, 34 (2001), 255–73.

Sutherland, Heather. "The Makassar Malays: Adaptation and Identity, c. 1660–1790." *Journal of Southeast Asian Studies*, 32 (2001), 397–421.

Svatos, Martin. "Patria und die patriotischen Tendenzen in der lateinischen Historiographie in den böhmischen Ländern im 17. und 18. Jahrhundert" in *Es hat sich viel ereignet, Gutes wie Böses: lateinische Geschichtsschreibung der Spät- und Nachantike.* (Beiträge zur Altertumskunde 141.) München: K.G. Saur, 2001. Pp. 213.

Sward, Ellen E. *The Decline of the Civil Jury.* Durham: Carolina Academic Press, 2001. Pp. xiii + 394.

Sweet, John Wood. "'More than tears': The Ordeal of Abolition in Revolutionary New England." In *Explorations in Early American Culture.* Volume 5. Edited by George W. Boudreau and William A. Pencak. University Park: Pennsylvania Historical Association, 2001.

Sweet, Rosemary. "Antiquaries and Antiquities in Eighteenth-Century England." *Eighteenth-Century Studies*, 34 (2001), 181–206.

II: Historical, Social, and Economic Studies

Tadmor, Naomi. *Family and Friends in Eighteenth-Century England: Household, Kinship, and Patronage*. Cambridge: Cambridge University Press, 2001. Pp. x + 312.

Tague, Ingrid H. "Love, Honor, and Obedience: Fashionable Women and the Discourse of Marriage in the Early Eighteenth Century." *Journal of British Studies*, (2001), 76–106.

Tamari, Steve. "Ottoman Madrasas: The Multiple Lives of Educational Institutions in Eighteenth-Century Syria." *Journal of Early Modern History*, 5 (2001), 99–127.

Tanck de Estrada, Dorothy. "Trips by Indians Financed by Communal Funds in Colonial Mexico." *Jahrbuch für Geschichte Lateinamerikas*, 38 (2001), 73–84.

Tarin, René. *Diderot et la Révolution française: controverses et polémique autour d'un philosophe*. (Les dix-huitièmes siècles 55.) Paris: Honoré Champion, 2001. Pp. 179; illustrations.

Tassin, Guy. *Mariages, ménages au XVIIIe siècle: alliances et parentés à Haveluy*. Paris: Harmattan, 2001. Pp. 485; illustrations; maps.

Taylor, Kay S. "The Role of Quaker Women in the Seventeenth Century, and the Experiences of the Wiltshire Friends." *Southern History*, 23 (2001), 10–29.

Tejada, Luis Coronas, José Fernández García, María Antonia Bel Bravo, and José Miguel Delgado Barrado (eds.) *El cambio dinástico y sus repercusiones en la España del siglo XVIII*. Jaén: Universidad de Jaén, 2001. Pp. 630.

Thiesse, Anne-Marie. *La création des identités nationales: Europe, XVIIIe–XXe siècle*. (Points Histoire 296.) Paris: Editions du Seuil, 2001. Pp. 307.

Thompson, Noel. "The Adventures of Peter Porcupine: William Cobbett in the United States, 1792–1800." *Historian*, 69 (2001), 4–8.

Thomson, Thomas. *Thomson's History of the Royal Society, from its Institution to the End of the Eighteenth Century*. (Reissue of 1812 Edition.) Bristol: Thoemmes, 2001. Pp. 254; facsimiles.

Tietz, Manfred, and Dietrich Briesemeister (eds.). *Los Jesuitas españoles expulsos: su imagen y su contribución al saber sobre el mundo hispánico en la Europa del siglo XVIII: actas del coloquio internacional de Berlín (7–10 de abril de 1999)*. Madrid: Iberoamericana, 2001. Pp. 710; illustrations.

Tippner, Anja. "'Wissende Unschuld': Selbstinszenierung und Repräsentation in den Memoiren Katharinas II." *Deutsche Vierteljahrsschrift für Literaturwissenschaft und Geistesgeschichte*, 75 (2001), 422–45.

Tomlins, Christopher L., and Bruce H. Mann (eds.). *The Many Legalities of Early America*. Chapel Hill: Omohundro Institute of Early American History and Culture, 2001. Pp. ix + 466.

Tonnesson, Kare. "The Norwegian Constitution of 17 May 1814—International Influences and Models." *Parliaments, Estates & Representation*, 21 (2001), 175–86.

Toohey, John. *Captain Bligh's Portable Nightmare*. New York: Perennial, 2001. Pp. vii + 211; illustrations; maps.

Torke, Hans-Joachim, Robert O Crummey, Holm Sundhaussen, and Ricarda Vulpius (eds.). *Russische und ukrainische Geschichte vom 16.–18. Jahrhundert*. (Forschungen zur osteuropäischen Geschichte 58.) Wiesbaden, Germany: Harrassowitz, 2001. Pp. 336; illustrations.

Torre Curiel, José Refugio de la. *Vicarios en entredicho: crisis y desestructuración de la provincia franciscana de Santiago de Xalisco, 1749–1860*. (Colección Investigaciones.) Zamora: El Colegio de Michoacán, 2001. Pp. 398; illustrations; maps.

Torres Sánchez, Jaime. *Haciendas y posesiones de la Compañía de Jesús en Venezuela: el Colegio de Caracas en el siglo XVIII*. Sevilla: Universidad de Sevilla, 2001. Pp. xxii + 341; illustrations.

Torrey, E. Fuller. *The Invisible Plague: The Rise of Mental Illness from 1750 to the Present*. New Brunswick: Rutgers University Press, 2001. Pp. xiv + 416; illustrations; maps.

Toth, Istvan Gyorgy. "Une société aux lisières de l'alphabet: la paysannerie hongroise aux XVIIe et XVIIIe siècles." Translated by Marie-Pierre Gaviano. *Annales: Histoire, Sciences Sociales*, 56 (2001), 863–80.

Touchard, Jean. *Histoire des idées politiques*. Tome 1: Des origines au XVIIIe siècle. (Quadrige 335.) Paris: Presses universitaires de France, 2001. Pp. xi + 382.

Touchard, Jean. *Histoire des idées politiques*. Tome 2, Du XVIIIe siècle à nos jours. (Quadrige 336.) Paris: Presses universitaires de France, 2001. Pp. 384–870.

Toulalan, Sarah. "Private Rooms and Back Doors in Abundance: The Illusion of Privacy in Pornography in Seventeenth-Century England." *Women's History Review*, 10 (2001), 701–19.

II: Historical, Social, and Economic Studies

Troost, Linda V. (ed.). *Eighteenth-Century Women: Studies in their Lives, Work, and Culture.* Volume 1. New York: AMS Press, 2001. Pp. xi + 356.

Truxes, Thomas E. (ed.). *Letterbook of Greg & Cunningham, 1756–57: Merchants of New York and Belfast.* (Records of Social and Economic History n.s. 28.) Oxford: Oxford University Press, 2001. Pp. xxxi + 430; illustrations.

Tuck, Richard. *The Rights of War and Peace: Political Thought and the International Order from Grotius to Kant.* (Reprint.) Oxford: Oxford University Press, 2001. Pp. 252.

Ulrich, Laurel Thatcher. *The Age of Homespun: Objects and Stories in the Creation of An American Myth.* New York: Knopf, 2001. Pp. 501; illustrations; maps.

Ultee, Maarten. "Defending the Honor of French Surgery, 1760–1788." *Proceedings of the Annual Meeting of the Western Society for French History*, 27 (2001), 51–62.

Umar, Muhammad. *Urban Culture in Northern India during the Eighteenth Century.* New Delhi: Munshiram Manoharlal, 2001. Pp. 393.

Underdown, David. *Start of Play: Cricket and Culture in Eighteenth-Century England.* London: Penguin, 2001. Pp. xx + 257; plates; illustrations; facsimiles; maps.

Upton, Anthony F. *Europe, 1600–1789.* (The Arnold History of Europe.) New York: Oxford University Press, 2001. Pp. x + 437; maps.

Uribe Uran, Victor (ed.). *State and Society in Spanish America during the Age of Revolution.* Wilmington: SR Books, 2001. Pp. xxi + 261.

Vahtre, Sulev. "Meie Vanema Historiograafia Uurimisseisust Ja Ülesannetest." *Ajalooline Ajakiri*, 3 (2001), 5–26.

Vallée, M. G. (ed.). *Au service de la Compagnie des Indes: lettres inédites d'une famille du Poitou au XVIIIe siècle, les Renault de Saint-Germain.* Paris: Maisonneuve et Larose, 2001. Pp. 175; illustrations.

Valle Pavon, Guillermina del. "Antagonismo entre el Consulado de México y el virrey Revillagigedo por la apertura comercial de Nueva España, 1789–1792." *Estudios de Historia Novohispana*, 24 (2001), 111–37.

VandenBerg, Richard, and Christophe Salvat. "Scottish Subtlety: Andre Morellet's Comments on *The Wealth of Nations.*" *European Journal of the History of Economic Thought*, 8 (2001), 146–85.

Vanhaute, Eric. "Rich Agriculture and Poor Farmers: Land, Landlords and Farmers in Flanders in the Eighteenth and Nineteenth Centuries." *Rural History*, 12 (2001), 19–40.

Velasquez, Melida. "El Comercio de esclavos en la alcaldía mayor de Tegucigalpa, siglos XVI al XVIII." *Mesoamérica*, 22 (2001), 199–222.

Verdun-sur-Garonne au fil de son histoire: des origines à la fin du XVIIIe siècle. (Pages d'histoire en pays de Tarn-et-Garonne.) Montauban: CDDP de Tarn-et-Garonne, 2001. Pp. 211.

Vickery, Amanda (ed.). *Women, Privilege, and Power: British Politics, 1750 to the Present.* (The Making of Modern Freedom.) Stanford: Stanford University Press, 2001. Pp. x + 413; illustrations.

Vicq, Pierre. "Recherches sur la procédure civile en Lorraine: du Code Léopold au Code de procédure civile." *Revue historique de droit français et étranger*, 79 (2001), 57–69.

Vicq, Pierre. "Une forme originale d'aide judiciaire en Lorraine dans la deuxiéme moitié du XVIII siècle: la Chambre des consultations." *Revue historique de droit français et étranger*, 79 (2001), 485–506.

Vierling-Ihrig, Heike Irma Katharina. *Schule der Vernunft: Leben und Werk des Aufklärungspädagogen Cajetan von Weiller (1762–1826).* (Miscellanea Bavarica Monacensia 176.) München: Schriftenreihe des Stadtarchivs München, 2001. Pp. 298.

Villatoux, Marie-Catherine and Degardin, Alain. "La 'folie' des ballons au XVIIIe siècle." *Revue historique des armées*, 1 (2001), 98–104.

Vlcek, Radomir. "Ruska Expanze Do Střední Asie A Jeji Vyvrcholeni V 19. Století." *Slovansky Prehled*, 87 (2001), 257–68.

Vocelka, K., and A. Traninger (eds.). *Wien: Geschichte einer Stadt.* Vol. 2: Die frühneuzeitliche Residenz (16. bis 18. Jahrhundert). Wien: Böhlau, 2001.

Vocelka, Karl. *Glanz und Untergang der höfischen Welt: Repräsentation, Reform und Reaktion im habsburgischen Vielvölkerstaat.* (Österreichische Geschichte, 1699–1815.) Wien: Ueberreuter, 2001. Pp. 542; illustrations; maps.

II: Historical, Social, and Economic Studies

Völkel, Markus. "Aufstieg und Fall der protestantischen Universalgeschichte." *Storia della Storiografia*, 39 (2001), 67–73.

Vuyst, Wout de, and Everaert, Guido. "De Handelsbeurs: De Metamorfoses van de Gentse Hoofdwacht (18de–Begin 20ste Eeuw)." *Handelingen der Maatschappij voor Geschiedenis en Oudheidkun de te Gent*, 55 (2001), 297–346.

Wadauer, Sigrid. "Il viaggio di tirocinio e la scrittura dei lavoranti artigiani. Un conflitto sistematico." Translated by Anselm Jappe. *Quaderni Storici*, 36 (2001), 91–114.

Wagstaff, Malcolm. "Family Size in the Peloponnese (Southern Greece) in 1700." *Journal of Family History*, 26 (2001), 337–49.

Wahrman, Dror. "The English Problem of Identity in the American Revolution." *American Historical Review*, 106 (2001), 1236–62.

Wakao, Yuji. "A Comparative Perspective on Rural Families in Japan from the Early Modern Period until the Middle of the Nineteenth Century" In *Family History Revisited: Comparative Perspectives*. (Historische Familienforschung.) Edited by Richard Wall, Tamara K. Hareven, Josef Ehmer, and Markus Cerman. Newark: University of Delaware Press, 2001.

Walker, Brett L. "Commercial Growth and Environmental Change in Early Modern Japan: Hachinohe's Wild Boar Famine of 1749." *Journal of Asian Studies*, (2001), 329–51.

Walker, Lesley H. "Sweet and Consoling Virtue: The Memoirs of Madame Roland." *Eighteenth-Century Studies*, 34 (2001), 403–19.

Wall, Richard, Tamara K. Hareven, Josef Ehmer, and Markus Cerman (eds.). *Family History Revisited: Comparative Perspectives*. (Historische Familienforschung.) Newark: University of Delaware Press, 2001. Pp. 403; illustrations.

Walsh, John Evangelist. *The Execution of Major Andre*. New York: Palgrave, 2001. Pp. 239; illustrations; map.

Walsh, Lorena Seebach. *From Calabar to Carter's Grove: The History of a Virginia Slave Community*. (Colonial Williamsburg Studies in Chesapeake History and Culture.) Charlottesville: University Press of Virginia, 2001. Pp. xxii + 335; illustrations; maps.

Walsh, Patrick. "Daniel Corkery's the Hidden Ireland and Revisionism." *New Hibernia Review*, 5 (2001), 27–44.

Warner, Jessica, and Carol Birchmore-Timney. "On the Vanguard of the First Drug Scare: Newspapers and Gin in London, 1736–1751." *Journalism History*, 27 (2001–02), 178–87.

Weeks, Daniel J. *Not for Filthy Lucre's Sake: Richard Saltar and the Antiproprietary Movement in East New Jersey, 1665–1707*. Bethlehem: Lehigh University Press, 2001. Pp. 342.

Weil, Sebastien. "Le marche foncier à Camembert (1752–1790)." *Annales de Normandie*, 51 (2001), 331–55.

Weinbrot, Howard D., Peter J. Schakel, and Stephen E. Karian (eds.). *Eighteenth-Century Contexts: Historical Inquiries in Honor of Phillip Harth*. Madison: University of Wisconsin Press, 2001. Pp. xvii + 305; illustrations.

Weinberger, Elisabeth. *Waldnutzung und Waldgewerbe in Altbayern im 18. und beginnnenden 19. Jahrhundert*. (Vierteljahrschrift für Sozial- und Wirtschaftsgeschichte 157.) Stuttgart: F. Steiner, 2001. Pp. 315.

Weltman-Aron, Brigitte. *On Other Grounds: Landscape Gardening and Nationalism in Eighteenth-Century England and France*. (The Margins of Literature.) Albany: State University of New York Press, 2001. Pp. x + 190.

Werkstetter, Christine. *Frauen im Augsburger Zunfthandwerk: Arbeit, Arbeitsbeziehungen und Geschlechterverhältnisse im 18. Jahrhundert*. (Colloquia Augustana 14.) Berlin: Akademie Verlag, 2001. Pp. 567; illustrations.

Wharam, Alan. *Murder in the Tower: And Other Tales from the State Trials*. Burlington: Ashgate, 2001. Pp. vi + 275; illustrations.

Wheeler, Roxann. "'Betrayed by some of my own complexion': Cugoano, Abolition, and Contemporary Language of Radicalism." Pp. 17–38 of *Genius in Bondage: Literature of the Early Black Atlantic*. Edited by Vincent Carretta and Philip Gould. Lexington: University Press of Kentucky, 2001.

Whelan, Frederick G. "Oriental Despotism: Anquetil-Duperron's Response to Montesquieu." *History of Political Thought*, 22 (2001), 619–47.

White, Clare. *William Fleming, Patriot*. Baltimore: Gateway Press, 2001. Pp. ix + 336; illustrations; maps.

II: Historical, Social, and Economic Studies

Wilkins, Roger W. *Jefferson's Pillow: The Founding Fathers and the Dilemma of Black Patriotism.* Boston: Beacon Press, 2001. Pp. 163.

Willcox, William B., and Walter L. Arnstein. *The Age of Aristocracy, 1688–1830.* (History of England 3.) Boston: Houghton Mifflin Co, 2001. Pp. xvii + 358; illustrations; maps.

Williams, Helen Maria. *Letters Written in France: In the Summer 1790, to a Friend in England, Containing Various Anecdotes Relative to the French Revolution.* (Broadview Literary Texts.) Peterborough: Broadview Press, 2001. Pp. 295; illustrations.

Williams, Roger L. *Botanophilia in Eighteenth-Century France: The Spirit of the Enlightenment.* (Archives internationales d'histoire des idées 179.) Dordrecht: Kluwer Academic Publishers, 2001. Pp. 197; illustrations.

Wilson, Renate. "Eighteenth-Century Practitioners of Medicine from Central Europe: The Pietist Connection." In *Apothecaries and the Drug Trade: Essays in Celebration of the Work of David L. Cowen.* Edited by Gregory J. Higby and Elaine C. Stroud. (Publication – American Institute of the History of Pharmacy 19.) Madison: American Institute of the History of Pharmacy, 2001. Pp. vii + 81; illustrations.

Wilson, Richard. "Novelty and Amusement? Visiting the Georgian Country House." *Historian*, 70 (2001), 4–9.

Windler, Christian. "Representing a State in a Segmentary Society: French Consuls in Tunis from the *Ancien Régime* to the Restoration." *Journal of Modern History*, 73 (2001), 233–74.

Winkelmann, Peter. *Gesundheitswesen, Gesundheitsverhältnisse und medizinische Versorgung der Bevölkerung in der kurtrierischen Amtsstadt Oberwesel im 17. und 18. Jahrhundert.* (Geschichte der Medizin 2.) Wuppertal: E. Pies, 2001. Pp. 222; illustrations; CD-ROM.

Wolff, Larry. *Venice and the Slavs: The Discovery of Dalmatia in the Age of Enlightenment.* Stanford: Stanford University Press, 2001. Pp. x + 408; illustrations.

Woodman, Richard. *The Sea Warriors: Fighting Captains and Frigate Warfare in the Age of Nelson.* New York: Carroll & Graf Publishers, 2001. Pp. xvi + 384; illustrations; maps.

Wright, Amos J. *The McGillivray and McIntosh Traders on the Old Southwest Frontier, 1716–1815.* Montgomery: New South Books, 2001. Pp. 329; illustrations; map.

Wright, Robert E. *Origins of Commercial Banking in America, 1750–1800*. Lanham: Rowman & Littlefield, 2001. Pp. xii + 219; illustrations.

Wu, Yixiong. "Guangzhou Yingyu Yu 19 Shiji Zhongye Yiqian de Zhongxi Jiaowang." *Jindaishi Yanjiu*, 3 (2001), 172–202.

Yacou, Alain. *Journaux de bord et de traite de Joseph Crassous de Médeuil: de La Rochelle à la côte de Guinée et aux Antilles, 1772–1776*. (Hommes et sociétés.) Paris: CERC, Université des Antilles et de la Guyane, 2001. Pp. 341; illustrations; maps.

Yang, Su-hsien. "Qingnian Xipeng: Yili Luoma Diguo Lishijia de Yangcheng." *Xin Shixue*, 12 (2001), 41–130.

Yeo, Richard R. *Encyclopaedic Visions: Scientific Dictionaries and Enlightenment Culture*. Cambridge: Cambridge University Press, 2001. Pp. xxi + 336; illustrations.

Zajka, Vital. "The Self-Perception of Lithuanian-Belarusian Jewry in the Eighteenth and Nineteenth Centuries." *Polin: Studies in Polish Jewry*, 14 (2001), 19–30.

Zall, Paul M. *Dolley Madison*. Huntington: Nova History Publications, 2001. Pp. xi + 114.

Zall, Paul M. "Thomas Jefferson, Protecting Privacy." Pp. 379–86 of *Finding Colonial Americas: Essays Honoring J. A. Leo Lemay*. Edited by Carla Mulford and David S. Shields. Newark: University of Delaware Press, 2001.

Zalyvskii, Nikolai. *Mikhail Vasil'evich Lomonosov i ekonomicheskaia nauka Rossii: monografiia*. Arkhangel'sk: Pomorskii gos. universitet imeni M.V. Lomonosova, 2001. Pp. 184; plates; illustrations.

Zamoyski, Adam. *Holy Madness: Romantics, Patriots, and Revolutionaries, 1776–1871*. (Reissue.) New York: Penguin Books, 2001. Pp. xii + 498; plates; illustrations.

Zarzoso, Alfons. "El pluralismo medico a través de la correspondencia privada en la Cataluna del siglo XVIII." *Dynamis*, 21 (2001), 409–33.

Zedelmaier, Helmut. "Der Beginn der Geschichte. Überlegungen zur Auflösung des Alteuropäischen Modells der Universalgeschichte." *Storia della Storiografia*, 39 (2001), 87–92.

II: Historical, Social, and Economic Studies 97

Zhang, Guangxiang. "Quan'e Tongyi Shichang Jiujing Xingcheng Yu Heshi." *Shijie Lishi (World History)*, 3 (2001), 90–101.

Zmolek, Mike. "Further Thoughts on Agrarian Capitalism: A Reply to a Britton." *Journal of Peasant Studies*, 29 (2001), 129–54.

Zorin, Andrei. *Kormia dvuglavogo orla: literatura i gosudarstvennaia ideologiia v Rossii v poslednei treti XVIII–pervoi treti XIX veka*. (Historia Rossica.) Moscow: Novoe literaturnoe obozrenie, 2001. Pp. 414; illustrations.

Zusman, Perla. "Entre el lugar y la línea: La constitución de las fronteras coloniales Patagónicas 1780–1792." *Fronteras de la Historia*, 6 (2001), 37-59.

III: Philosophy, Science, and Religion

Abbattista, Guido. "The English Universal History: Publishing, Authorship and Historiography in a European Project (1736–1790)." *Storia della Storiografia*, 39 (2001), 103–08.

Abing, Kevin. "Before Bleeding Kansas: Christian Missionaries, Slavery, and the Shawnee Indians in Pre-Territorial Kansas, 1844–1854." *Kansas History*, 24 (2001), 54–70.

Abu-Tarbush, José. "The Presence of Islam in the Canaries: A Historical Overview." *Journal of Muslim Minority Affairs,* 21 (2001), 79–92.

Acemoglu, Daron, Simon Johnson, and James A. Robinson. "The Colonial Origins of Comparative Development: An Empirical Investigation." *American Economic Review*, 91 (2001), 1369–1401.

Aceves Pastrana, Patricia. *Periodismo científico en el siglo XVIII: José Antonio de Alzate y Ramírez.* (Estudios de historia social de las ciencias químicas y biológicas 6.) México, D.F.: Universidad Autónoma Metropolitana Sociedad Química de México, 2001. Pp. 663.

Adams, Beverly. "The 'Durty Spirit' at Hertford: A Falling out of Friends." *Journal of Ecclesiastical History*, 52 (2001), 647–74.

Adamson, Christopher. "Evangelical Quakerism and the Early American Penitentiary Revisited: The Contributions of Thomas Eddy, Roberts Vaux, John Griscom, Stephen Grellet, Elisha Bates, and Isaac Hopper." *Quaker History*, 90 (2001), 35–58.

Adelman, Howard Tzvi. "Law and Love: The Jewish Family in Early Modern Italy." *Continuity and Change*, 16 (2001), 283–303.

Aftalion, Fred. *A History of the International Chemical Industry: From the "Early Days" to 2000*. 2nd edition. Philadelphia: Chemical Heritage Foundation, 2001. Pp. 442.

Agnew, Robin A. L. "Catalogue of the Library of Sir John Forbes (1787–1861), MD EDIN FRCP LOND FRS, Part 1: Some General Works." *Journal of Medical Biography*, 9 (2001), 104–08.

Agnew, Robin A. L. "Catalogue of the Library of Sir John Forbes (1787–1861), MD EDIN FRCP LOND FRS, Part 2: Works Referring to Sir John Forbes." *Journal of Medical Biography*, 9 (2001), 175–80.

Akyeampong, Emmanuel. "History, Memory, Slave-Trade and Slavery in Anlo (Ghana)." *Slavery and Abolition*, 22 (2001), 1–24.

Alatorre, Antonio. *El brujo de Autlán*. *Colección la Torre inclinada*. México, D.F.: Editorial Aldus, 2001. Pp. 211.

Albright, Carol Bonomo. "Joseph Rocchietti: Political Thinker in Literary Clothing." *Italian Americana*, 19 (2001), 142–45.

Aldini, Nicolò Nicoli. "Parola e gesto nell'insegnamento medico: le lezioni chirurgiche di Antonio Scarpa." *Gesnerus*, 58 (2001), 103–22.

Alejos-Grau, Carmen José. "La contribución de los eclesiásticos novohispanos a la formación de la conciencia nacional méxicana (siglos XVII y XVII)." *Hispania Sacra*, 53 (2001), 285–309.

Alexandre, Josette. "Les richesses de la bibliothèque de l'Observatoire de Paris." Pp. 221–28 of *Sur les traces des Cassini: Astronomes et observatoires du sud de la France*. Edited by Paul Brouzeng and Suzanne Débarbat. Paris: Comité des travaux historiques et scientifiques, 2001.

Alfonso-Goldfarb, Ana Maria. "Las concepciones sobre la materia mineral entre los siglos XVII y XVIII: ¿Tradición versus modernidad o tradición y modernidad?" Pp. 207–12 of *Periodismo científico en el siglo XVIII: José Antonio de Alzate y Ramírez*. Edited by Patricia Aceves Pastrana. Mexico: Universidad Autónoma Metropolitana Unidad Xochimilco, 2001.

III: Philosophy, Science, and Religion

Allen, Lee N. "Alabama Baptists Prompted by a Missionary Spirit in Early Days." *Alabama Baptist Historian,* 37 (2001), 19–21.

Allen, Lee N. "Anti-Missions, Church-Only Polity Disruptive to Goals." *Alabama Baptist Historian*, 37 (2001), 21–23.

Allison, Henry E. *Kant's Theory of Taste: A Reading of the Critique of Aesthetic Judgment.* (Modern European Philosophy.) Cambridge: Cambridge University Press, 2001. Pp. xvi + 424.

Almeida, Jaime de. "Religião, política e memoria no Grande Cauca, 1810–1834." *Tempo,* 6 (2001), 93–109.

Alpert, Michael. *Crypto-Judaism and the Spanish Inquisition.* New York: Palgrave, 2001. Pp. 246.

Amalvi, Christian. "Le Mythe du Général Desaix dans des littératures populaires et scolaires de la Troisième République." *Annales historiques de la Révolution française*, 324 (2001), 179–91.

Amelang, James, and G. Franzinetti (trans.). "L'Europa delle città di Marino Berengo." *Rivista Storica Italiana,* 113 (2001), 754–63.

Amerman, Richard H. "Medical Practices in New Netherland." *Halve Maen,* 74 (2001), 69–72.

Ancarani, Maria Elisabetta. *Per grazia ricevuta: Analisi storica del culto della Madonna del Bosco nei dipinti votivi.* Ravenna: Edizioni del Girasole, 2001. Pp. 126.

Ancillon, Louis Frédéric. "Dialogue between Berkeley and Hume." Translated by Charlotte Stanley. *Hume Studies*, 27 (2001), 99–128.

Anderson, Frank G., Jr., and Edith A. Wakefield. *The History of Medicine in Brazos County.* Bryan: F. G. Anderson, 2001. Pp. 179.

Anderson, Stephanie. "French Anthropology in Australia, the First Fieldwork Report: François Peron's 'Maria Island—Anthropological Observations.'" *Aboriginal History,* 25 (2001), 228–42.

Anderson, Timothy G. "The Creation of an Ethnic Culture Complex Region: Pennsylvania Germans in Central Ohio, 1790–1850." *Historical Geography*, 29 (2001), 135–57.

Anderson-Gold, Sharon. *Unnecessary Evil: History and Moral Progress in the Philosophy of Immanuel Kant.* (SUNY Series in Philosophy.) Albany: State University of New York Press, 2001. Pp. xiii + 138.

Andor, Eszter, and István György Tóth (eds.). *Frontiers of Faith: Religious Exchange and the Constitution of Religious Identities, 1400–1750.* Budapest: Central European University Press, 2001. Pp. 295.

Andrés Turrión, Maria Luisa de, and Pilar García de Yébenes Torres. "La oficina de destilación de aguas y aceites del Real sitio de Aranjuez (1564–1721)." *Asclepio,* 53 (2001), 5–25.

Andrews, Jonathan, and Andrew Scull. *Undertaker of the Mind: John Monro and Mad-Doctoring in Eighteenth-Century England.* Berkeley: University of California Press, 2001. Pp. 164.

Ansart, Guillaume. "Jansenist Themes and Influences in Prévost's *Cleveland.*" *Studies on Voltaire and the Eighteenth Century* (2001–2), pp. 47–55.

Ansart, Guillaume. *Voltaire; Religion and Ideology; Women's Studies; History of the Book; Passion in the Eighteenth Century.* SVEC: 12. Oxford: Voltaire Foundation, 2001. Pp. vi + 476.

Antognazza, Maria Rosa. "The Defence of the Mysteries of the Trinity and the Incarnation: An Example of Leibniz's 'Other' Reason." *British Journal for the History of Philosophy,* 9 (2001), 283–309.

Antognazza, Maria Rosa. "Leibniz's *de Deo Trino*: Philosophical Aspects of Leibniz's Conception of the Trinity." *Religious Studies,* 37 (2001), 1–14.

Anzur, Tea. "Naravoslovne Znanosti in Ustanovitev Biotehniske Fakultete." *Kronika,* 49 (2001), 231–44.

Appleby, John H. "Mapping Russia: Farquharson, Delisle and the Royal Society." *Notes and Records of the Royal Society of London,* 55 (2001), 191–204.

Arbell, Mordechai. "Jewish Settlements in the French Colonies in the Caribbean (Martinique, Guadaloupe, Haiti, Cayenne) and the 'Black Code'." Pp. 287–313 of *The Jews and the Expansion of Europe to the West, 1450–1800.* Edited by Paolo Bernardini and Norman Fiering. New York: Berghahn Books, 2001.

III: Philosophy, Science, and Religion

Arbour, Keith. "Solomon Stoddard's 'Addition' to the Safety of Appearing (Boston, 1729) and the Attribution of Its Printing, with a Note on 'Reilly 695.'" *Papers of the Bibliographical Society of America,* 95 (2001), 340–47.

Arias Martínez, Manuel. "Nuevos datos sobre la capilla de los Alderete en San Antolin de Tordesillas y el escultor Bartolome Hernández." *Archivo Español de Arte,* 74 (2001), 127–38.

Armillas Vicente, Jose A. "Problemas eclesiásticos de la Luisiana tras su cesión a España." *Hispania Sacra,* 53 (2001), 311–26.

Arnheim, Arthur. "Hebrew Prints and Censorship in Altona." *Studies in Bibliography and Booklore,* 21 (2001), 3–9.

Aronnica, Ferdinando. "Il Sinodo agrigentino di Mons. Ramirez (1703) e la sua normitiva." *Itinerarium* (Messina) 9 (2001), 93–112.

Arzano, Simone and Yvon Georgelin. "Premières découvertes astronomiques effectuées à Marseille: Pythéas le Massaliote." Pp. 231–42 of *Sur les traces des Cassini: Astronomes et observatoires du sud de la France.* Edited by Paul Brouzeng and Suzanne Débarbat. Paris: Comité des travaux historiques et scientifiques, 2001.

Asad, M. N. M. Kamil. "History of Muslim Women's Education in Sri Lanka." *Journal of the Pakistan Historical Society,* 49 (2001), 15–19.

Aspromourgos, Tony. "The Mind of the Oeconomist: An Overview of the 'Petty Papers' Archive." *History of Economic Ideas,* 9 (2001), 39–101.

Austern, Linda Phyllis. "'Tis Nature's Voice': Music, Natural Philosophy and the Hidden World in Seventeenth-Century England." Pp. 30–67 of *Music Theory and Natural Order from the Renaissance to the Early Twentieth Century.* Edited by Suzannah Clark and Alexander Rehding. Cambridge: Cambridge University Press, 2001.

Azevedo, Cecilia. "A santificaçao pelas obras: experiências do protestantismo nos EUA." *Tempo,* 6 (2001), 111–29.

Baader, Maria Benjamin. "When Judaism Turned Bourgeois: Gender in Jewish Associational Life and in the Synagogue, 1750–1850." *Leo Baeck Institute. Year Book,* 46 (2001), 113–23.

Bach, Jeffrey. "Ephrata and Moravian Relations: The View from Ephrata." *Communal Societies,* 21 (2001), 49–60.

Bacon, Jacqueline. "Rhetoric and Identity in Absalom Jones and Richard Allen's Narrative of the Proceedings of the Black People, During the Late Awful Calamity in Philadelphia." *Pennsylvania Magazine of History and Biography*, 125 (2001), 61–90.

Badía Cabrera, Miguel A. *Hume's Reflection on Religion*. (Archives internationales d'histoire des idées, 178.) Dordrecht: Kluwer Academic Press, 2001. Pp. xiii + 328.

Bahar, Saba. "Jane Marcet and the Limits to Public Science." *British Journal for the History of Science*, 34 (2001), 29–49.

Bahr, Ehrhard. "Goethe and the Concept of Bildung in Jewish Emancipation." Pp. 16–28 of *Goethe in German-Jewish Culture*. Edited by Klaus L. Berghahn and Jost Hermand. Rochester: Camden House, 2001.

Baitugan, Boris, and Salavat Midkhatovich Isakhov (comp.). "'Kristallizatsiia' Gorskogo Osvoboditel'nogo Dvizheniia. Razmyshleniia B. Baitugana ob Istorii Musul'man Severnogo Kavkaza i Dagestana." *Voprosy Istorii*, 5 (2001), 3–31.

Baker, Emerson W., and James Kences. "Maine, Indian Land Speculation, and the Essex County Witchcraft Outbreak of 1692." *Maine History*, 40 (2001), 158–89.

Baker, Keith Michael, and Peter Hanns Reill (eds.). *What's Left of Enlightenment?: A Postmodern Question*. Stanford: Stanford University Press, 2001. Pp. ix + 203.

Bakken, Dawn E. "Young Believers and Old Believers in the Wilderness: Narratives of Place and the Construction of Family Among Western Shakers." *Indiana Magazine of History*, 97 (2001), 278–95.

Banderier, Gilles. "Corneille et les Jésuites: Un Poème Inédit." *Dix-septième siècle*, 53 (2001), 545–49.

Bankert, Norbert R. "More on the Identity of Abigail (Graves) Dibble, and Her Tragic Death and Suspicions of Witchcraft." *New England Historical and Genealogical Register*, 155 (2001), 273–78.

Barfield, Rodney D. "Thomas and John Day and the Journey to North Carolina." *North Carolina Historical Review*, 78 (2001), 1–31.

Bari, Abdul. "Graeco-Arab Medicine in Iran During Safwi Period." *Studies in History of Medicine and Science*, 17 (2001), 39–49.

Barker, Michael. "The Proof Structure of Kant's A-Deduction." *Kant-Studien*, 92 (2001), 259–82.

Barnett, S. J. "The Temporal Imperative: Criticism and Defence of Eighteenth-Century Roman Theocracy." *History of Political Thought,* 22 (2001), 472–93.

Barquist, David L. *Myer Myers: Jewish Silversmith in Colonial New York*. New Haven: Yale University Art Gallery, 2001. Pp. 304.

Barr, William. "Harpoon Guns, the Lost Greenland Settlement, and Penal Colonies: George Manby's Arctic Obsessions." *Polar Record,* 37 (2001), 291–314.

Barth, J. Robert. *The Symbolic Imagination: Coleridge and the Romantic Tradition*, 2nd ed. (Studies in Religion and Literature 3.) New York: Fordham University Press, 2001. Pp. xv + 176.

Bartlett, Thomas. "Clemency and Compensation: The Treatment of Defeated Rebels and Suffering Loyalists after the 1798 Rebellion." Pp. 99–127 of *Revolution, Counter-Revolution and Union: Ireland in the 1790s*. Edited by Jim Smyth. Cambridge: Cambridge University Press, 2001.

Bates, A. W. "The 'De monstrorum' of Fortunio Liceti: A Landmark of Descriptive Teratology." *Journal of Medical Biography,* 9 (2001), 49–54.

Battenberg, J. Friedrich. "Fürstliche Ansiedlungspolitik und Landjudenschaft im 17/18. Jahrhundert: Merkantilistische Politik und Juden im Bereich von Sachsen-Anhalt." *Aschkenas,* 11 (2001), 59–85.

Bauer, Aaron M., and Kraig Adler. "The Dating and Correct Citation of A. F. A. Wiegmann's 'Amphibien' Section of Meyen's *Reise um die Erde*, with a Bibliography of Wiegmann's Herpetological Publications." *Archives of Natural History,* 28 (2001), 313–26.

Baverel-Croissant, Marie-Françoise. "Les devises tirées de l'Ecriture et la Passion de Mr. Fouquet, deux exercices de dtyle des partisans du surintendant." *Dix-septième siècle,* 53 (2001), 699–712.

Baverel-Croissant, Marie-Françoise. "Les devises tirées de l'Ecriture et la Passion de Mr. Fouquet, un exercice de dtyle des partisans du surintendant." *Dix-septième siècle,* 53 (2001), 213.

Baxter, Donald L. M. "Hume on Steadfast Objects and Time." *Hume Studies*, 27 (2001), 129–148.

Beavan, Iain. "'Neatness and Order': The Diaries and Papers of William Knight, Professor of Natural Philosophy, Marischal College, 1823–1844." *Northern Scotland,* 21 (2001), 129–39.

Begheyn, Paul. "The Collection of Copperplates by Members of the Wierix Family in the Jesuit Church 'De Krijtberg' in Amsterdam." *Quaerendo,* 31 (2001), 192–204.

Bek, Michael. "Die Vermittlungsleistung der reflektierenden Urteilskraft." *Kant-Studien*, 92 (2001), 296–327.

Belaubre, Christophe. "Poder y redes sociales en Centroamérica: el caso de la orden de los Dominicos, 1757–1829." *Mesoamérica,* 22 (2001), 31–76.

Bell, Martin. "The Relation between Literary Form and Philosophical Argument in Hume's Dialogues Concerning Natural Religion." *Hume Studies*, 27 (2001), 227–46.

Ben-Chaim, Michael. "The Discovery of Natural Goods: Newton's Vocation as an 'Experimental Philosopher.'" *British Journal for the History of Science,* 34 (2001), 395–416.

Benedict, Barbara M. *Curiosity: A Cultural History of Early Modern Inquiry.* Chicago: University of Chicago Press, 2001. Pp. ix + 321.

Benítez, Leonel Rodríguez. "José Antonio de Alzate: Un puente entre la ilustración Novohispana y la comunidad dico científica Mexicana." Pp. 651–63 of *Periodismo científico en el siglo XVIII: José Antonio de Alzate y Ramírez.* Edited by Patricia Aceves Pastrana. Mexico: Universidad Autónoma Metropolitana Unidad Xochimilco, 2001.

Ben-Naeh, Yaron. "Same-Sex Relations among Ottoman Jews." *Zion,* 66 (2001), 171–200.

Ben-Ur, Aviva. "The Exceptional and the Mundane: A Biographical Portrait of Rebecca Machado Phillips (1746–1831)." Pp. 46–80 of *Women and American Judaism: Historical Perspectives.* Edited by Pamela S. Nadell and Jonathan D. Sarna. Hanover: University Press of New England, 2001.

Beretta, Marco. "From Nollet to Volta: Lavoisier and Electricity." *Revue d'histoire des sciences,* 54 (2001), 29–52.

III: Philosophy, Science, and Religion 107

Beretta, Marco. *Imaging a Career in Science: The Iconography of Antoine Laurent Lavoisier.* Canton: Science History Publishing, 2001. Pp. 126.

Beretta, Marco. "Lavoisier and His Last Printed Work: The 'Memoires de physique et de chimie' (1805)." *Annals of Science,* 58 (2001), 327–56.

Berghahn, Cord-Friedrich. *Moses Mendelssohns "Jerusalem": ein Beitrag zur Geschichte der Menschenrechte und der Pluralistischen Gesellschaft in der deutschen Aufklärung.* Studien zur deutschen Literatur, Bd. 161. Tübingen: Max Niemeyer Verlag, 2001. Pp. vi + 320.

Berghahn, Klaus L. "Patterns of Childhood: Goethe and the Jews." Pp. 3–15 of *Goethe in German-Jewish Culture.* Edited by Klaus L. Berghahn and Jost Hermand. Rochester: Camden House, 2001.

Berghahn, Klaus L. and Jost Hermand (eds.). *Goethe in German-Jewish Culture.* Rochester: Camden House, 2001. Pp. 190.

Bergquist, Lars. *Swedenborg's Dream Diary. Translated by Anders Hallengren.* (Swedenborg Studies 11.) West Chester: Swedenborg Foundation, 2001. Pp. vii + 371.

Bermúdez, Isabel Cristina. *Imágenes y representaciones de la mujer en la gobernación de Popayán.* (Serie Magíster 13.) Quito: Universidad Andina Simón Bolívar, 2001. Pp. 102.

Bernal, Luz Fernanda Azuela, and José Omar Moncada Maya. "La Geografía en las *Gacetas de Literatura.*" Pp. 431–50 of *Periodismo científico en el siglo XVIII: José Antonio de Alzate y Ramírez.* Edited by Patricia Aceves Pastrana. Mexico: Universidad Autónoma Metropolitana Unidad Xochimilco, 2001.

Bernand, Carmen, Stefania Capone, Frederic Lenoir, and Françoise Champion. "Regards croisés sur le bricolage et le syncrétisme." *Archives de Sciences Sociales des Religions,* 46 (2001), 39–59.

Bernardi, Walter. "La controverse sur l'électricité animale dans l'Italie du XVIIIe siècle: Galvani, Volta et d'autres." *Revue d'histoire des sciences,* 54 (2001), 53–70.

Bernardini, Paolo, and Norman Fiering (eds.). *The Jews and the Expansion of Europe to the West, 1450–1800.* New York: Berghahn, 2001. Pp. 567.

Berteau, Pierre C. "Le Cat et l'École d'anatomie." *Histoire des Sciences médicales,* 35 (2001), 141–50.

Berthiaume, P. "Exercises spirituelles et quietisme dans *Le Confessions de comte de ** * de Charles Pinot Duclos*." *Studies on Voltaire and the Eighteenth Century* (2001), 57–68.

Bianchi, Diana. "Elementos para una tipología de los pobres asistidos en el Hospital de Caridad de Montevideo (1787–1830)." *Revista complutense de historia de América,* 27 (2001), 107–29.

Bigelow, Ann Clymer. "Columbus's Pioneer Doctor John M. Edmiston: The Fabric of His Life and Death." *Ohio History*, 110 (2001), 5–25.

Binder, Harald. "Eine multikulturelle Gesellschaft: Polen, Ukrainer und Juden in Galizien 1772–1918." *Österreichische Osthefte,* 43 (2001), 425–28.

Birnstiel, Eckart, and Chrystel Bernat (eds.). *La Diaspora des Huguenots: Les refugiés protestants de France et leur dispersion dans le monde (XVIe–XVIIIe siècles)*. Paris: Honoré Champion Éditeur, 2001. Pp. 208; illustrations; map.

Birnstiel, Eckart. "La diaspora Hugeunote dans le nouveau monde." Pp. 99–118 of *La Diaspora Des Hugeunots: Les réfugiés protestants de France et leur dispersion dans le monde (XVIe–XVIIIe siècles)*. Edited by Eckart Birnstiel and Chrystel Bernat. Paris: Honoré Champion Éditeur, 2001.

Black, J. William. "From Martin Bucer to Richard Baxter: 'Discipline' and Reformation in Sixteenth- and Seventeenth-Century England." *Church History,* 70 (2001), 644–73.

Black, Jeremy. "European Overseas Expansion and the Military Revolution." Pp. 1–30 of *Technology, Disease and Colonial Conquests, Sixteenth to Eighteenth Centuries: Essays Reappraising the Guns and Germs Theories*. Edited by George Raudzens. Boston: Brill, 2001.

Blackburn, Anne M. *Buddhist Learning and Textual Practice in Eighteenth-Century Lankan Monastic Culture*. (Buddhism Series.) Princeton: Princeton University Press, 2001. Pp. x + 241.

Blackwell, Bonnie. "Tristram Shandy and the Theater of the Mechanical Mother." *ELH,* 68 (2001), 81–133.

Blackwell, Marilyn S. "Surrogate Ministers: Women, Revivalism, and Maternal Associations in Vermont." *Vermont History,* 69 (2001), 66–78.

III: Philosophy, Science, and Religion

Blay, Michel. "De l'apparition subreptice des futures formules de conservation à l'occasion de l'algorithmisation de la science du mouvement au tournant des XVIIe et XVIIIe siècles." *Revue d'histoire des sciences,* 54 (2001), 291–301.

Blay, Michel. "Descartes: Une science déductive du monde." *Science et Avenir* (Hors-série, 2001), 61.

Blay, Michel. "La naissance de la science classique au XVIIe siecle," *Axiales* (2001), 7-18.

Blewitt, Paul, and Simon Reynolds. "The Moravian Church Archives and Library." *Journal of the Society of Archivists,* 22 (2001), 193–203.

Bluhm, Andreas, and Louise Lippincott. *Light!: The Industrial Age, 1750–1900: Art and Science, Technology and Society.* New York: Thames and Hudson, 2001. Pp. 271.

Boarini, Serge. "Deux procédures de résolution des situations morales difficiles: aux origines des conférences de consensus." *Revue d'Histoire et de Philosophie Religieuses,* 81 (2001), 171–87.

Bobrick, Benson. *Wide as the Waters: The Story of the English Bible and the Revolution It Inspired.* New York: Simon & Schuster, 2001. Pp. 379.

Boch, Julie. "L'anecdote dans les Voyages dans les Alpes de Saussure." Pp. 337–49 of *H.-B. de Saussure (1740–1799): Un Regard sur la Terre.* Edited by René Sigrist. Geneva: Georg Editeur, 2001.

Bogen, David S. "Mathias De Sousa: Maryland's First Colonist of African Descent." *Maryland Historical Magazine*, 96 (2001), 68–85.

Bogue, David, and James Bennett. *History of the Dissenters from the Revolution of 1688 to 1838.* 3 volumes. Stoke-on-Trent: Tentmaker, 2001. Pp. 400.

Böhm, Günter. "Crypto-Jews and New Christians in Colonial Peru and Chile." Pp. 203–12 of *The Jews and the Expansion of Europe to the West, 1450–1800.* Edited by Paolo Bernardini and Norman Fiering. New York: Berghahn Books, 2001.

Böhme, Katrin. "Die Gesellschaft Naturforschender Freunde zu Berlin— Bestand und Wandel einer gelehrten Gesellschaft: Ein Überblick." *Berichte zur Wissenschaftsgeschichte,* 24 (2001), 271–83.

Boisson, Didier. "La bibliothèque d'un marchand de vin protestant à la fin du XVIIIe siècle." *Bulletin de la Société de l'Histoire du Protestantisme Français,* 147 (2001), 201–24.

Boles, John B. (ed.). *Autobiographical Reflections on Southern Religious History.* Athens: University of Georgia Press, 2001. Pp. 272.

Bonincontro, Eleonora. *Il festino straordinario di sant'Agata del 1799: Politica e devozione nell'anno della Repubblica partenopea.* Catania: G. Maimone, 2001. Pp. 97.

Bonney, Richard. "The Forging and Relinquishing of Protestant Identities: Religion and Politics in Britain and Germany since the Reformation." Pp. 165–89 of *Religion und Politik in Deutschland und Großbritannien.* Edited by Richard Bonney, Franz Bosbach, and Thomas Brockmann. Munich: K. G. Saur, 2001.

Bonney, Richard, Franz Bosbach, and Thomas Brockmann (eds.). *Religion und Politik in Deutschland und Grossbritannien.* Munich: K. G. Saur, 2001. Pp. 201.

Bònoli, Fabrizio, and Alessandro Braccesi. "Bibliographie des œuvres de Cassini pendant son séjour à Bologne." Pp. 209–11 of *Sur les traces des Cassini: Astronomes et observatoires du sud de la France.* Edited by Paul Brouzeng and Suzanne Débarbat. Paris: Comité des travaux historiques et scientifiques, 2001.

Bònoli, Fabrizio, and Alessandro Braccesi. "Les recherches astronomiques de Giovanni Domenico Cassini à Bologne: 1649–1669." Pp. 101–27 of *Sur les traces des Cassini: Astronomes et observatoires du sud de la France.* Edited by Paul Brouzeng and Suzanne Débarbat. Paris: Comité des travaux historiques et scientifiques, 2001.

Borgen, Peder. "George Wolff (1736–1828): Norwegian-Born Merchant, Consul, Benevolent Methodist Layman, Close Friend of John Wesley." *Methodist History,* 40 (2001), 17–28.

Bost, Hubert. *Ces Messieurs de la R.P.R. histoires et écritures des Huguenots, XVIIe–XVIIIe siècles.* Paris: Editions Honoré Champion, 2001. Pp. 416.

Bots, Hans. "Le refuge dans les provinces-unies." Pp. 63–74 of *La Diaspora Des Hugeunots: Les réfugiés protestants de France et leur dispersion dans le monde (XVIe–XVIIIe siècles).* Edited by Eckart Birnstiel and Chrystel Bernat. Paris: Honoré Champion Éditeur, 2001.

Boulinier, Georges. "Une femme anatomiste au siècle des lumières: Marie Marguerite Biheron (1719–1795)." *Histoire des Sciences médicales,* 35 (2001), 411–23.

III: Philosophy, Science, and Religion

Bouveresse, Jacques. "Mathématiques et logique chez Leibniz." *Revue d'histoire des sciences,* 54 (2001), 223–46.

Boyajian, James C. "New Christians and Jews in the Sugar Trade, 1550–1750: Two Centuries of Development of the Atlantic Economy." Pp. 471–84 of *The Jews and the Expansion of Europe to the West, 1450–1800.* Edited by Paolo Bernardini and Norman Fiering. New York: Berghahn Books, 2001.

Boyle, Nicholas. "'Art,' Literature, Theology: Learning from Germany." Pp. 87–112 of *Higher Learning and Catholic Traditions.* Edited by Robert E. Sullivan. Notre Dame: University of Notre Dame Press, 2001.

Bracken, David. "Irish Migrants in Paris Hospitals, 1702–30: Extracts from the Registers of Bicêtre, La Charité, La Pitié and La Salpêtrière." *Archivium Hibernicum,* 55 (2001), 7–47.

Brading, D. A. *Mexican Phoenix. Our Lady of Guadalupe: Image and Tradition, 1531–2000.* New York: Cambridge University Press, 2001. Pp. 444.

Bradley, James E. "The Religious Origins of Radical Politics in England, Scotland, and Ireland, 1662–1800." Pp. 187–253 of *Religion and Politics in Enlightenment Europe.* Edited by James E. Bradley and Dale K. Van Kley. Notre Dame: University of Notre Dame Press, 2001.

Bradley, James E., and Dale K. Van Kley (eds.). *Religion and Politics in Enlightenment Europe.* Erasmus Institute Books. Notre Dame: University of Notre Dame Press, 2001. Pp. xiii + 409.

Brake, Wayne te. "Religious Identities and the Boundaries of Citizenship in the Dutch Republic." Pp. 254–93 of *Religion and Politics in Enlightenment Europe.* Edited by James E. Bradley and Dale K. Van Kley. Notre Dame: University of Notre Dame Press, 2001.

Branfoot, Crispin. "Tirumala Nayaka's 'New Hall' and the European Study of the South Indian Temple." *Journal of the Royal Asiatic Society,* 11 (2001), 191–217.

Branson, Susan. "Elizabeth Drinker: Quaker Values and Federalist Support in the 1790s." *Pennsylvania History,* 68 (2001), 465–82.

Braun, Mark. "Faith of Our Fathers." *Concordia Historical Institute Quarterly,* 74 (2001), 198–218.

Breazeale, Daniel. "Fichte's Conception of Philosophy as a 'Pragmatic History of the Human Mind' and the Contributions of Kant, Platner, and Maimon." *Journal of the History of Ideas,* 62 (2001), 685–703.

Breazeale, Daniel, and Tom Rockmore (eds.). *New Essays in Fichte's Foundation of the Entire Doctrine of Scientific Knowledge.* Amherst: Humanity Books, 2001. Pp. 257.

Brech, Alison, and Anita McConnell. "The Pigott Family: Eighteenth Century Connections with Church, Science and Law." *Recusant History,* 25 (2001), 449–60.

Breen, Louise A. *Transgressing the Bounds: Subversive Enterprises among the Puritan Elite in Massachusetts, 1630–1692* (Religion in America Series). New York: Oxford University Press, 2001. Pp. 304.

Bremer, Manuel E. "Eine Notiz zu den Argumentationsstrukturen in der 'Widerlegung des Idealismus'." *Kant-Studien,* 92 (2001), 13–18.

Bresc-Bautier, Geneviève. "Paroisse et penitents au Revest-Les-Eaux: l'espace religieux remodelé (1673–1681)." *Provençe Historique,* 51 (2001), 41–50.

Breslaw, Elaine G. "From Edinburgh to Annapolis: Dr. Alexander Hamilton's Colonial Maryland Medical Practice." *Maryland Historical Magazine,* 96 (2001), 400–20.

Bressler, Ann Lee. *The Universalist Movement in America, 1770–1880.* New York: Oxford University Press, 2001. Pp. viii + 204.

Bret, Patrice. "Alzate y Ramírez et l'Académie Royale des Sciences de Paris: La réception des travaux d'un savant du nouveau monde." Pp. 123–205 of *Periodismo científico en el siglo XVIII: José Antonio de Alzate y Ramírez.* Edited by Patricia Aceves Pastrana. Mexico: Universidad Autónoma Metropolitana Unidad Xochimilco, 2001.

Brewer, William D. *The Mental Anatomies of William Godwin and Mary Shelley.* Madison: Fairleigh Dickinson University Press, 2001. Pp. 246.

Broadie, Alexander. *The Scottish Enlightenment: The Historical Age of the Historical Nation.* Edinburgh: Birlinn, 2001. Pp. xii + 240.

Brodeur, Patrice. "The Changing Nature of Islamic Studies and American Religious History. Part 1." *Muslim World,* 91 (2001), 71–98.

III: Philosophy, Science, and Religion

Broers, Michael. "'The War against God': Napoleon, Pope Pius VII and the People of Italy, 1800–1814." *Historian,* 69 (2001), 16–21.

Brooks, Francis. "The Impact of Disease." Pp. 127–65 of *Technology, Disease and Colonial Conquests, Sixteenth to Eighteenth Centuries: Essays Reappraising the Guns and Germs Theories.* Edited by George Raudzens. Boston: Brill, 2001.

Brooks, Richard S., and David K. Himrod. *Science and Religion in the English-Speaking World, 1600–1727: A Bibliographic Guide to the Secondary Literature.* Metuchen: Scarecrow, 2001. Pp. 656.

Brosche, Peter, and Suzanne Débarbat. "Franz Xaver von Zach et l'astronomie danz la France méridionale." Pp. 279–86 of *Sur les traces des Cassini: Astronomes et observatoires du sud de la France.* Edited by Paul Brouzeng and Suzanne Débarbat. Paris: Comité des travaux historiques et scientifiques, 2001.

Brouzeng, Paul, and Suzanne Débarbat (eds.). *Sur les traces des Cassini: astronomes et observatoires du Sud de la France.* Paris: Comité des Travaux historiques et scientifiques, 2001. Pp. 370.

Brown, Callum G. "The Myth of the Established Church of Scotland." Pp. 48–74 of *The Scottish Churches and the Union Parliament 1707–1999.* Edited by James Kirk. Edinburgh: Scottish Church History Society, 2001.

Brown, Kenneth, and Reyes Bertolin Cebrian. "Spanish, Portuguese, and Neo-Latin Poetry Written and/or Published by Seventeenth-, Eighteenth-, and Nineteenth-Century Sephardim from Hamburg and Frankfurt. Part 2." *Sefarad,* 61 (2001), 3–56.

Brown, Roger L. "Welsh Freemasonry and the Church: An Historical Enquiry." *Journal of Welsh Religious History,* 1 (2001), 34–45.

Brown, Stewart J. "The End of the Old Established Church Ideal in Scotland, 1780–1850." Pp. 75–102 of *The Scottish Churches and the Union Parliament 1707–1999.* Edited by James Kirk. Edinburgh: Scottish Church History Society, 2001.

Brown, Stewart J. *The National Churches of England, Ireland, and Scotland, 1801–1846.* New York: Oxford University Press, 2001. Pp. 459.

Brown, Stuart. "The Regularization of Providence in Post-Cartesian Philosophy." Pp. 1–16 of *Religion, Reason and Nature in Early Modern Europe.* Edited by Robert Crocker. Dordrecht: Kluwer Academic Publishers, 2001.

Brown, Tracy L. "Conversion to Christianity in Eighteenth-Century New Mexico: Pedagogy and Personhood in the Pueblo–Franciscan Encounter." *Catholic Southwest: A Journal of History and Culture*, 12 (2001), 29–50.

Buchwald, Jed Z., and I. Bernard Cohen (eds.). *Isaac Newton's Natural Philosophy*. (Dibner Institute Studies in the History of Science and Technology.) Cambridge: MIT Press, 2001. Pp. xx + 354.

Buckle, Stephen. *Hume's Enlightenment Tract: The Unity and Purpose of* An Enquiry Concerning Human Understanding. Oxford: Clarendon Press of Oxford University Press, 2001. Pp. xi + 351.

Buckle, Stephen. "Tully, Locke and America." *British Journal for the History of Philosophy*, 9 (2001), 245–81.

Budd, Graham E. "Royal Fossils: The Royal Society and Progress in Palaeontology." *Notes and Records of the Royal Society of London,* 55 (2001), 51–67.

Bueno, Antonio González. "Las relaciones de José Antonio de Alzate y Ramírez con los reales gabinetes de la metrópoli." Pp. 107–21 of *Periodismo científico en el siglo XVIII: José Antonio de Alzate y Ramírez*. Edited by Patricia Aceves Pastrana. Mexico: Universidad Autónoma Metropolitana Unidad Xochimilco, 2001.

Bungener, Patrick. "Les rapports de Saussure avec la botanique." Pp. 33–49 of *H.-B. de Saussure (1740–1799): Un Regard sur la Terre*. Edited by René Sigrist. Geneva: Georg Editeur, 2001.

Burgio, Alberto. "La natura come storia. Teleologia e autodeterminazione nella «storia filosofica» di Kant." *Cromohs*, 6 (2001).

Burns, William E. *The Scientific Revolution: An Encyclopedia*. Santa Barbara: ABC-Clio, 2001. Pp. 364.

Burton, John D. "'The Awful Judgements of God Upon the Land': Smallpox in Colonial Cambridge, Massachusetts." *New England Quarterly*, 74 (2001), 495–506.

Butler, Jon. "Listening for God in America." *Reviews in American History,* 29 (2001), 497–501.

Butterfield, Kevin. "Puritans and Religious Strife in the Early Chesapeake." *Virginia Magazine of History and Biography,* 109 (2001), 5–36.

III: Philosophy, Science, and Religion

Buttner, Manfred. "Begrundung der Wissenschaftlichen Geographie durch Bernhard Varenius (1622–1650)? Gedanken zu den Defiziten der Varenius-Forschung aus Anlass des Varenius-Jahres 2000." *Berichte zur Wissenschaftsgeschichte,* 24 (2001), 237–54.

Buyssens, Danielle. "Saussure Mémorable dan les arts et les lettres." Pp. 1–22 of *H.-B. de Saussure (1740–1799): Un Regard sur la Terre.* Edited by René Sigrist. Geneva: Georg Editeur, 2001.

Caffentzis, C. George. "Hume, Money, and Civilization; or, Why Was Hume a Metalist?" *Hume Studies* 27 (2001), 301–35.

Caffort, Michel. "Sparte et Jérusalem, les davidiens et la peinture religieuse sous la Restauration." *Revue d'histoire de l'Église de France,* 87 (2001), 415–37.

Cahill, David. "The Long Conquest: Collaboration by Native Andean Elites in the Colonial System, 1532–1825." Pp. 85–126 of *Technology, Disease and Colonial Conquests, Sixteenth to Eighteenth Centuries: Essays Reappraising the Guns and Germs Theories.* Edited by George Raudzens. Boston: Brill, 2001.

Calhoon, Robert M. "Cusp of Spring." Pp. 53–72 of *Autobiographical Reflections on Southern Religious History.* Edited by John B. Boles. Athens: University of Georgia Press, 2001.

Campbell, Sabrina, and Colin D. Campbell (eds.). "Rural New York in a Woman's Hand: The 1803 Diary of Sabrina Campbell." *New York History,* 82 (2001), 336–61.

Campenhausen, Christoph von. "Eine Vorform der dreidimensionalen Farbensysteme in dem von Rubens illustrierten Lehrbuch des Franciscus Aguilonius (1613)." *Medizinhistorisches Journal,* 36 (2001), 267–307.

Canales, Jimena. "The Single Eye: Re-Evaluating Ancien Régime Science." *History of Science,* 39 (2001), 71–94.

Candaux, Jean-Daniel. "Les réseaux d'un enquêteur: Saussure et ses correspondants." Pp. 249–58 of *H.-B. de Saussure (1740–1799): Un Regard sur la Terre.* Edited by René Sigrist. Geneva: Georg Editeur, 2001.

Candaux, Jean-Daniel, and René Sigrist. "Saussure et la Société des Arts." Pp. 431–52 of *H.-B. de Saussure (1740–1799): Un Regard sur la Terre.* Edited by René Sigrist. Geneva: Georg Editeur, 2001.

Cantor, Geoffrey. "The Rise and Fall of Emanuel Mendes da Costa: A Severe Case of the 'Philosophical Dropsy'?" *English Historical Review,* 116 (2001), 584–603.

Canuel, Mark. "Coleridge's Polemic Divinity." *ELH,* 68 (2001), 929–63.

Carlebach, Elisheva. *Divided Souls: Converts from Judaism in Germany, 1500–1750.* New Haven: Yale University Press, 2001. Pp. 336.

Carlson, Andrew. *The Divine Ethic of Creation in Leibniz.* (Studies in Theoretical and Applied Ethics, 6.) New York: Peter Lang, 2001. Pp. xiii + 658.

Carlson, David J. "Edward Taylor and Puritan Entrepreneurship." *Studies in Puritan American Spirituality,* 7 (2001), 111–41.

Carneiro, Henrique Soares. "O multiplo imaginario das viagens modernas: ciencia, literatura e turismo." *Historia: Questoes e Debates,* 18 (2001), 227–47.

Carozzi, Albert V. "Du dogme Neptuniste au concept de refoulements horizontaux: Les étapes d'une réflexion Géologique." Pp. 83–108 of *H.-B. de Saussure (1740–1799): Un Regard sur la Terre.* Edited by René Sigrist. Geneva: Georg Editeur, 2001.

Carozzi, Albert V. "Saussure et la controverse sur le basalte (1772–1798)." Pp. 175–95 of *H.-B. de Saussure (1740–1799): Un Regard sur la Terre.* Edited by René Sigrist. Geneva: Georg Editeur, 2001.

Carroll-Burke, Patrick. "Tools, Instruments and Engines: Getting a Handle on the Specificity of Engine Science." *Social Studies of Science,* 31 (2001), 593–625.

Carter, Brian. "Catholic Charitable Endeavour in London, 1810–1840. Part 1." *Recusant History,* 25 (2001), 487–510.

Casanovas, Juam. "G. D. Cassini, élève de la Compagnie de Jésus." Pp. 27–32 of *Sur les traces des Cassini: Astronomes et observatoires du sud de la France.* Edited by Paul Brouzeng and Suzanne Débarbat. Paris: Comité des travaux historiques et scientifiques, 2001.

Cashin, Edward J. *Beloved Bethesda: A History of George Whitefield's Home for Boys, 1740–2000.* Macon: Mercer University Press, 2001. Pp. 278.

III: Philosophy, Science, and Religion

Cassese, Michele. "Diritti religiosi e civili dei protestanti nella politica di tolleranza di Giuseppe II in Lombardia: le ripercussioni del caso Blondel." *Cristianesimo nella storia,* 22 (2001), 65–110.

Cassini, Anna. "Perinaldo, pays d'astronomes: à la recherche des lieux cassiniens." Pp. 33–42 of *Sur les traces des Cassini: Astronomes et observatoires du sud de la France.* Edited by Paul Brouzeng and Suzanne Débarbat. Paris: Comité des travaux historiques et scientifiques, 2001.

Castillo, Benito del, and Eugenia Mazuecos. "Utillaje científico del siglo XVIII en el Museo de la Farmacia Hispana." Pp. 327–40 of *Periodismo científico en el siglo XVIII: José Antonio de Alzate y Ramírez.* Edited by Patricia Aceves Pastrana. Mexico: Universidad Autónoma Metropolitana Unidad Xochimilco, 2001.

Castro, Taurino Burón. "Colegio franciscano de misiones populares de Sahagún (1680) según in manuscrito del año 1805." *Archivo Ibero-Americano,* 61 (2001), 165–250.

Caulier, Brigitte, and Raymond Brodeur. "Des catéchismes à l'enseignement religieux: le cadre des représentations religieuses." *Études d'histoire religieuse: Société canadienne d'histoire de l'Église catholique,* 67 (2001), 143–54.

Cavallo, Sandra. "La leggerezza delle origini: rotture e stabilità nelle storie dei chirurghi torinesi tra Sei e Settecento." *Quaderni storici,* 36 (2001), 59–90.

Cesarani, David. "The Dynamics of Diaspora: The Transformation of British Jewish Identity." *Jewish Culture and History,* 4 (2001), 53–64.

Cesarani, David. "The Forgotten Port Jews of London: Court Jews Who Were Also Port Jews." *Jewish Culture and History,* 4 (2001), 111–24.

Cesareo, Francesco C. "The Complex Nature of Catholicism in the Renaissance." *Renaissance Quarterly,* 54 (2001), 1561–73.

Chàline, Olivier. "Frontières Religieuses: La Bohême Après la Montagne Blanche." Pp. 55–65 of *Frontiers of Faith: Religious Exchange and the Constitution of Religious Identities 1400–1750.* Edited by Eszter Andor and Istvan Gyorgy Toth. Budapest: Central European University European Science Foundation, 2001.

Chalmers, Mary E. "A Gendered Nation: The French Periphery in July Monarchy Social Sciences." *Proceedings of the Annual Meeting of the Western Society for French History,* 27 (2001), 63–73.

Chamayou, Fabienne. "Le refuge dans les îles Britanniques." Pp. 43–62 of *La Diaspora Des Hugeunots: Les réfugiés protestants de France et leur dispersion dans le monde (XVIe–XVIIIe siècles).* Edited by Eckart Birnstiel and Chrystel Bernat. Paris: Honoré Champion Éditeur, 2001.

Champion, J. A. I. "John Toland, the Druids, and the Politics of Celtic Scholarship." *Irish Historical Studies,* 32 (2001), 321–42.

Champion, Neil. *James Watt, Groundbreakers.* Chicago: Heinemann Library, 2001. Pp. 48.

Chan, Hok-lam. "Beijing Wai Cheng Nezha Xu Miao Tan Su" [On the Origins of Nezha Construction in the Outer City of Beijing]. *Zhongguo Wenhua Yanjiusuo Xuebao (Journal of Chinese Studies),* 10 (2001), 151–69.

Chang, Hasok. "Spirit, Air, and Quicksilver: The Search for the 'Real' Scale of Temperature." *Historical Studies in the Physical and Biological Sciences,* 31 (2001), 249–84.

Chantin, Jean-Pierre. "Le jansénisme convulsionnaire à la fin du XVIIIe siècle: Permanence et diversité du mouvement port-royaliste tardif." *Cristianesimo nella storia,* 22 (2001), 153–66.

Charles, S. J., C. Laursen, R. H. Popkin, and A. Zakatistvos. "Hume and Berkeley in the Prussian Academy: Louis Frédéric Ancillon's 'Dialogue between Berkeley and Hume' of 1796." *Hume Studies,* 27 (2001), 85–97.

Cheetham, Mark A. *Kant, Art, and Art History: Moments of Discipline.* Cambridge: Cambridge University Press, 2001. Pp. x + 222.

Cheuse, Alan. "Port of Entry." *Preservation,* 53 (2001), 28–31, 34.

China Number One Historical Archives. "Qianjia Nianjian Wutaishan Simiao Xinggong Xiushan Gongcheng Shiliao (Shang)" [Historical Information on the Construction and Building of the Temples of Mount Wutai During the Years of Qian Jia]. *Lishi Dang'an (Historical Archive),* 3 (2001), 31–44.

Chinchilla Pawling, Perla. "La composición de lugar: de la imaginación a la memorización." *Historia y Grafia,* 16 (2001), 15–44.

III: Philosophy, Science, and Religion

Chinnici, Ileana. "Le voyage scientifique de Georges Rayet en Italie et la fondation de l'observatoire de Bordeaux." Pp. 259–69 of *Sur les traces des Cassini: Astronomes et observatoires du sud de la France*. Edited by Paul Brouzeng and Suzanne Débarbat. Paris: Comité des travaux historiques et scientifiques, 2001.

Chohan, Sandeep, and Ron A. Geaves. "The Religious Dimension in the Struggle for Khalistan and Its Roots in Sikh History." *International Journal of Punjab Studies*, 8 (2001), 79–96.

Christian, Charles W., Robert Schultz and Steven Gertz. "The Leadership Team." *Christian History*, 20 (2001), 39–42.

Christie, Nancy (ed.). *Households of Faith: Family, Gender and Community in Canada, 1760–1969*. Montreal: McGill–Queen's University Press, 2001. Pp. 386.

Chung, David. *Syncretism: The Religious Context of Christian Beginnings in Korea*. Albany: State University of New York Press, 2001. Pp. 263.

Ciappara, Frans. "Perceptions of Marriage in Late-Eighteenth-Century Malta." *Continuity and Change*, 16 (2001), 379–98.

Ciardi, Marco. "Amedeo Avogadro's Concept of the Atom: Some New Remarks." *Ambix*, 48 (2001), 17–24.

Ciardi, Marco. "Forces et molécules: Amedeo Avogadro, l'électricité et l'hypothèse de 1811." *Revue d'histoire des sciences*, 54 (2001), 85–97.

Cicovacki, Predrag (ed.). *Kant's Legacy: Essays in Honor of Lewis White Beck*. (Rochester Studies in Philosophy, 2.) Rochester: University of Rochester Press, 2001. Pp. xxvi + 441.

Cislo, Waldemar. *Die Religionskritik der Französischen Enzyklopädisten*. Frankfurt am Main: Peter Lang, 2001. Pp. 202.

Clark, David H., and Stephen P. H. Clark. *Newton's Tyranny: The Suppressed Scientific Discoveries of Stephen Gray and John Flamsteed*. New York: W. H. Freeman, 2001. Pp. xvi + 188.

Clark, Stuart. *Languages of Witchcraft: Narrative, Ideology, and Meaning in Early Modern Culture*. New York: St. Martin's Press, 2001. Pp. xiii + 241.

Clark, Suzannah, and Alexander Rehding (eds.). *Music Theory and Natural Order from the Renaissance to the Early Twentieth Century*. New York: Cambridge University Press, 2001. Pp. 243.

Clayton, Lawrence. "The Iberian Advantage." Pp. 211–35 of *Technology, Disease and Colonial Conquests, Sixteenth to Eighteenth Centuries: Essays Reappraising the Guns and Germs Theories*. Edited by George Raudzens. Boston: Brill, 2001.

Cleaveland, Timothy. *Becoming Walata: A History of Saharan Social Formation and Transformation*. Portsmouth: Heinemann, 2001. Pp. 232.

Clune, John James. "Redefining the Role of Convents in Late-Eighteenth-Century Havana." *Colonial Latin American Historical Review,* 10 (2001), 127–45.

Cock, Randolph. "'The Finest Invention in the World': The Royal Navy's Early Trials of Copper Sheathing, 1708–1770." *Mariner's Mirror,* 87 (2001), 446–59.

Coffman, Elesha. "Attack of the Bible-Moths." *Christian History*, 20 (2001), 20–22.

Cohen, Charles L. "In Retrospect: Robert Middlekauff's *The Mathers*." *Reviews in American History*, 29 (2001), 635–46.

Cohen, David E. "The 'Gift of Nature': Musical 'Instinct' and Musical Cognition in Rameau." Pp. 68–92 of *Music Theory and Natural Order from the Renaissance to the Early Twentieth Century*. Edited by Suzannah Clark and Alexander Rehding. Cambridge: Cambridge University Press, 2001.

Cohon, Rachel (ed.). *Hume: Moral and Political Philosophy*. (The International Library of Critical Essays in the History of Philosophy 15.) Aldershot: Ashgate Publishing Company, 2001. Pp. xxi + 530.

Coleman, Dorothy. "Baconian Probability and Hume's Theory of Testimony." *Hume Studies*, 27 (2001), 195–225.

Coley, Noel G. "George Fordyce M.D., F.R.S. (1736–1802): Physician-Chemist and Eccentric." *Notes and Records of the Royal Society of London,* 55 (2001), 395–409.

Colin, Jacques, and Jérôme de La Nöe. "Foundation et histoire de l'onservatoire de Bordeaux à Floirac." Pp. 337–40 of *Sur les traces des Cassini: Astronomes et observatoires du sud de la France*.

III: Philosophy, Science, and Religion 121

Edited by Paul Brouzeng and Suzanne Débarbat. Paris: Comité des travaux historiques et scientifiques, 2001.

Collette, Sophie. "Les religieuses de la Visitation Sainte-Marie de la ville d'Amiens aux XVIIe et XVIIIe siècles." *Revue du Nord*, 83 (2001), 519–40.

"Colonial Lancaster County: Snippets of History, 1607–1776." *Northern Neck of Virginia Historical Magazine*, 51 (2001), 6039–50.

Come, Arnold B. "The Occasion and Contribution of the Confession of 1967." *Journal of Presbyterian History*, 79 (2001), 59–71.

Conacher, I. D. "The Enigma of Johnnie 'Notions' Williamson." *Journal of Medical Biography*, 9 (2001), 208–12.

Condillac, Etienne Bonnot de. *Essay on the Origin of Human Knowledge*. Translated and edited by Hans Aarsleff. (Cambridge Texts in the History of Philosophy.) Cambridge: Cambridge University Press, 2001. Pp. xlv + 225.

Conforti, Maria. "La medicina nel 'Giornale de' Letterati' di Roma (1668–1681)." *Medicina nei secoli,* 13 (2001), 59–91.

Conforti, Maria. "Testes alterum cerebrum: succo nerveo e succo seminale nella macchina del vivente di Giovanni Alfonso Borelli." *Medicina nei secoli,* 13 (2001), 577–95.

Connolly, William R. "Christian Johnson and Pagan Hume." *Hume Studies*, 27 (2001), 149–60.

Cook, Alan. "J.-D. Cassini et ses collègues anglais." Pp. 130–35 of *Sur les traces des Cassini: Astronomes et observatoires du sud de la France*. Edited by Paul Brouzeng and Suzanne Débarbat. Paris: Comité des travaux historiques et scientifiques, 2001.

Cook, Alan. "Edmond Halley and the Magnetic Field of the Earth." *Notes and Records of the Royal Society of London,* 55 (2001), 473–90.

Cook, Alan. "Time and the Royal Society." *Notes and Records of the Royal Society of London,* 55 (2001), 9–27.

Cook, G. C. "William Twining (1790–1835): The First Accurate Clinical Descriptions of 'Tropical Sprue' and Kala-Azar?" *Journal of Medical Biography,* 9 (2001), 125–31.

Corral, Marco Arturo Moreno. "Los conocimientos astronómicos de Alzate." Pp. 361–77 of *Periodismo científico en el siglo XVIII: José Antonio de Alzate y Ramírez*. Edited by Patricia Aceves Pastrana. Mexico: Universidad Autónoma Metropolitana Unidad Xochimilco, 2001.

Cosme, Alba Dolores Morales. "La salud de la ciudad de México en la obra de Alzate." Pp. 307–26 of *Periodismo científico en el siglo XVIII: José Antonio de Alzate y Ramírez*. Edited by Patricia Aceves Pastrana. Mexico: Universidad Autónoma Metropolitana Unidad Xochimilco, 2001.

Costilla, Nora Reyes. "El demonio entre los marginales: población negra y el pacto con le demonio en el norte de Nueva España, siglos XVII y XVIII." *Colonial Latin American Historical Review*, 10 (2001), 199–221.

Cotton, John. *The Correspondence of John Cotton*. Chapel Hill: University of North Carolina Press, for the Omohundro Institute of Early American History and Culture, 2001. Pp. 548.

Courreges, Hélène de. "La reclusion des prêtres dans les séminaires: un aspect meconnu de la mission des séminaires d'ancien régime." *Revue historique de droit francais et éranger*, 79 (2001), 511–27.

Creed, Brad. "John Leland and Sunday Mail Delivery: Religious Liberty, Evangelical Piety, and the Problem of a 'Christian Nation.'" *Fides et Historia*, 33 (2001), 1–11.

Cresswell, M. J. "An 'Ontological' Argument for the Contract-Trust Theory." *Locke Studies*, 1 (2001), 159–71.

Cresti, Federico. "Gli schiavi cristiani ad Algeri in età ottomana: considerazioni sulle fonti e questioni storiografiche." *Quaderni storici*, 36 (2001), 415–35.

Crimmins, J. E. "Bentham's Religious Radicalism Revisited: A Response to Schofield." *History of Political Thought*, 22 (2001), 494–500.

Crocker, Robert. "Henry More and the Preexistence of the Soul." Pp. 77–96 of *Religion, Reason and Nature in Early Modern Europe*. Edited by Robert Crocker. Dordrecht: Kluwer Academic Publishers, 2001.

Crocker, Robert (ed.). *Religion, Reason and Nature in Early Modern Europe*. Boston: Kluwer, 2001. Pp. 228.

III: Philosophy, Science, and Religion

Crouch, Margaret A. "Locke on Language and Reality." *Locke Studies*, 1 (2001), 87–104.

Cruse, Bernard W. *Union Churches in North Carolina During the Eighteenth and Nineteenth Centuries.* Concord: B.W. Cruse, Jr., 2001. Pp. x + 69.

Cruz, Béatriz Nates. "Reapropiación y articulación socio-cultural de santos y vírgenes caótolicos en los Andes sur colombianos." *Archives de Sciences Sociales des Religions,* 46 (2001), 27–44.

Csetri, Elek. "Körösi és az Akadémia." *Századok,* 135 (2001), 103–20.

Cullen, Fintan. "Radicals and Reactionaries: Portraits of the 1790s in Ireland." Pp. 161–94 of *Revolution, Counter-Revolution and Union: Ireland in the 1790s.* Edited by Jim Smyth. Cambridge: Cambridge University Press, 2001.

Cullen, Louis M. "The Politics of Crisis and Rebellion, 1792–1798." Pp. 21–38 of *Revolution, Counter-Revolution and Union: Ireland in the 1790s.* Edited by Jim Smyth. Cambridge: Cambridge University Press, 2001.

Cunja, Vesna. "Aspetti di cultura e vita religiosa nelle lettere di Carlo Michele d'Attems, arcivescovo di Gorizia, a Franz Xavier Taufferer, abate di Sticna (1764–1773)." *Ricerche di Storia Sociale e Religiosa,* 30 (2001), 97–133.

Cunningham, Andrew. "The End of the Sacred Ritual of Anatomy." *Canadian Bulletin of Medical History,* 18 (2001), 187–204.

Curtin, Nancy J. "The Magistracy and Counter-Revolution in Ulster, 1795–1798." Pp. 39–54 of *Revolution, Counter-Revolution and Union: Ireland in the 1790s.* Edited by Jim Smyth. Cambridge: Cambridge University Press, 2001.

Curtis, Bruce. "Irish Schools for Canada: Arthur Buller to the Bishop of Quebec, 1838." *Historical Studies in Education,* 13 (2001), 49–58.

Daliès, Nandou. "Ka debeyre des Cassini 1673–1793: éléments bibliographiques." Pp. 213–220 of *Sur les traces des Cassini: Astronomes et observatoires du sud de la France.* Edited by Paul Brouzeng and Suzanne Débarbat. Paris: Comité des travaux historiques et scientifiques, 2001.

Daly, Robert. "Lexias and Agency in Anne Bradstreet." *Studies in Puritan American Spirituality*, 7 (2001), 1–22.

Danforth, Susan. "Cultivating Empire: Sir Joseph Banks and the (Failed) Botanical Garden at Nassau." *Terrae Incognitae*, 33 (2001), 48–58.

Daniel, Stephen H. "Berkeley's Christian Neoplatonism, Archetypes, and Divine Ideas." *Journal of the History of Philosophy*, 39 (2001), 239–58.

Daniel, Stephen H. "The Ramist Context of Berkeley's Philosophy." *British Journal for the History of Philosophy*, 9 (2001), 487–505.

Darrigol, Olivier. "God, Waterwheels, and Molecules: Saint-Venant's Anticipation of Energy Conservation." *Historical Studies in the Physical and Biological Sciences*, 31 (2001), 285–353.

David, François. "Refuge Huguenot et assimilation: Le cas de la colonie Française de Berlin." Pp. 75–97 of *La Diaspora Des Hugeunots: Les réfugiés protestants de France et leur dispersion dans le monde (XVIe–XVIIIe siècles)*. Edited by Eckart Birnstiel and Chrystel Bernat. Paris: Honoré Champion Éditeur, 2001.

Davidson, Jenny. "Swift's Servant Problem: Livery and Hypocrisy in the Project for the Advancement of Religion and the Directions to Servants." *Studies in Eighteenth-Century Culture*, 30 (2001), 105–25.

Davis, Martin L. "The Business of Tolerance. David Friedländer (1750–1834) and the Civic Constitution of German-Jewish Existence." Pp. 51–61 of *Religion und Politik in Deutschland und Großbritannien*. Edited by Richard Bonney, Franz Bosbach, and Thomas Brockmann. Munich: K. G. Saur, 2001.

Davis, Robert C., and Benjamin C. I. Ravid (eds.). *The Jews of Early Modern Venice*. Baltimore: Johns Hopkins University Press, 2001. Pp. 314.

Davison, Doris M. "Bishop Enoch George." *Northern Neck of Virginia Historical Magazine*, 51 (2001), 6081–97.

D'Costa, Anthony. "The Orchards and Bazar of Agra and Royal Sport in Shah Jehan's Days." *Indica*, 38 (2001), 135–42.

de Burigny, Jean Lévesque. *Examen critique des apologists de la religion chrétienne [1730]*. Edited by Alain Niderst. Paris: Editions Honoré Champion, 2001. Pp. 336.

III: Philosophy, Science, and Religion

de Cassini, Alain. "La sélection des artistes ingénieurs patentés auprès de l'Académie des sciences 1787–1789." Pp. 97–98 of *Sur les traces des Cassini: Astronomes et observatoires du sud de la France*. Edited by Paul Brouzeng and Suzanne Débarbat. Paris: Comité des travaux historiques et scientifiques, 2001.

de Cassini, Daniel. "La statue de Cassini Ier de Jean-Guillaume Moitte." Pp. 92–96 of *Sur les traces des Cassini: Astronomes et observatoires du sud de la France*. Edited by Paul Brouzeng and Suzanne Débarbat. Paris: Comité des travaux historiques et scientifiques, 2001.

de Cassini, Patrice. "Jean-Dominique de Cassini (Cassini IV) huit mois en prison en 1794." Pp. 89–91 of *Sur les traces des Cassini: Astronomes et observatoires du sud de la France*. Edited by Paul Brouzeng and Suzanne Débarbat. Paris: Comité des travaux historiques et scientifiques, 2001.

de Gandt, Francois. "Qu'est-ce qu'être newtonien en 1740?" Pp. 126–147 of *Cirey dans la vie intellectuelle: La réception de Newton en France*. Edited by François de Gandt. Oxford: Voltaire Foundation, 2001.

De Jong, Willem R. "Bernard Bolzano, Analyticity and the Aristotelian Model of Science." *Kant-Studien*, 92 (2001), 328–49.

De Pierris, Graciela. "Hume's Pyrrhonian Skepticism and the Belief in Causal Laws." *Journal of the History of Philosophy* 39 (2001), 351–83.

Dean, Michael Emmans. "Homeopathy and the Progress of Science." *History of Science*, 39 (2001), 255–83.

Deans-Smith, Susan. "Remapping Spanish Imperialism, Colonialism, and Post-Colonialism: The Case of Cuzco, Peru." *Historical Journal*, 44 (2001), 297–306.

Delbecke, Maarten. "A Note on the Immaculist Patronage of Alexander VII: Chigi and the Pilgrimage Church of Scherpenheuvel in the Low Countries." *Bulletin de l'Institut historique belge de Rome*, 71 (2001), 167–200.

Delille, Gérard. "Réflexions sur le système européen de la parenté et de l'alliance." *Annales: histoire, sciences sociales*, 56 (2001), 369–80.

Delporte, Christophe. "Du bon usage 'de ses ors,' ou les comptes de la paroisse Sainte-Marie-Madeleine d'Arras (1669–1730)." *Revue du Nord*, 83 (2001), 341–58.

Demelas, Marie-Danielle. "Da la 'petite guerre' à la guerre populaire: genèse de la guerilla comme valeur en Amerique du Sud." *Cahiers des Amériques Latines*, 36 (2001), 17–35.

Demeulenaere-Douyère, Christiane. "La famille Cassini et l'Académie des sciences." Pp. 67–86 of *Sur les traces des Cassini: Astronomes et observatoires du sud de la France.* Edited by Paul Brouzeng and Suzanne Débarbat. Paris: Comité des travaux historiques et scientifiques, 2001.

Denis, Gilles. "Pratiques paysannes et modèles théoriques savantes pré-agronomiques au XVIIIe siècle: Le cas des débats sur la transmission des maladies des grains de blés." *Revue d'histoire des sciences,* 54 (2001), 451–94.

Deppermann, Arnulf. "Eine analytische Interpretation von Kants 'ich denke.'" *Kant-Studien*, 92 (2001), 129–52.

DeRogatis, Amy. "Models of Piety: Plan of Union Missionaries on the Western Reserve, 1800–1806." *Journal of Presbyterian History*, 79 (2001), 257–75.

DesChene, Dennis. *Spirits and Clocks: Machine and Organism in Descartes.* Ithaca: Cornell University Press, 2001. Pp. 181.

Desforges, Jane. "'Satisfaction and Improvement': A Study of Reading in a Small Quaker Community 1770–1820." *Publishing History,* 49 (2001), 5–47.

Diaz, Ramón Lourido, OFM. "El conocimiento del árabe entre franciscanos españoles de Terra Santa." *Archivum Franciscanum Historicum*, 94 (2001), 147–86.

Diaz-Trechuelo, Lourdes. "Religiosidad popular en Filipinas: Hermandades y cofradías (siglos XVI–XVIII)." *Hispania Sacra,* 53 (2001), 345–66.

Dibble, Ernest F. "Religion on Florida's Territorial Frontiers." *Florida Historical Quarterly,* 80 (2001), 1–23.

Dietl, Ralph. "Comment on Part Two: American Diplomacy: The Quest for a Global *Pax Americana*: Myths and Realities A Reply." Pp. 231–48 of *Visions of the Future in Germany and America.* Edited by Norbert Finzsch and Hermann Wellenreuther. Oxford: Berg, 2001.

Diggins, John Patrick. "Religion and the Founders." *Partisan Review*, 68 (2001), 371–78.

III: Philosophy, Science, and Religion

Dine, Sarah Blank. "Diaries and Doctors: Elizabeth Drinker and Philadelphia Medical Practice, 1760–1810." *Pennsylvania History*, 68 (2001), 413–34.

DiStefano, Roberto. "Religión y cultura: libros, bibliotecas y lecturas del clero secular rioplatense (1767–1840)." *Bulletin Hispanique,* 103 (2001), 511–41.

Djerassi, Carl, and Roald Hoffmann. *Oxygen: A Play in Two Acts.* New York: Wiley-VCH, 2001. Pp. vii + 119.

Dolan, Frances E. "Ashes and 'The Archive': The London Fire of 1666, Partisanship, and Proof." *Journal of Medieval and Early Modern Studies,* 31 (2001), 379–408.

Dominicis, Giulia de. "The Roman Theatres in the Age of Pius VI." *Theatre History Studies,* 21 (2001), 81–86.

Donat, James G. "The Rev. John Wesley's Extractions from Dr. Tissot: A Methodist Imprimatur." *History of Science,* 39 (2001), 285–98.

Dörrer, Fridolin. "Zeremoniell, Alte Praxis und "Neuer Geist": Zum Verhalten der Herrscher und Regierungen in Wien und Florenz zu den Nuntien: Beispiele aus de Jahren um 1760." *Romische Historische Mitteilungen,* 43 (2001), 587–630.

Doss, Chriss H. "Baptist Churches in Frontier Alabama." *Alabama Baptist Historian*, 37 (2001), 1–4.

Doss, Chriss H. "Early Baptist Ministers in Alabama." *Alabama Baptist Historian,* 37 (2001), 4–10.

Doss, Chriss H. "Early Baptists Find Value in Associations." *Alabama Baptist Historian,* 37 (2001), 10–12.

Doyle, Peter. "Charles Fell [1687–1753], Miracles and the Lives of the Saints. A Forgotten 18th- Century Hagiographer." *Analecta Bollandiana* (2001), 62–87.

Dreisbach, Daniel L. "Mr. Jefferson, a Mammoth Cheese, and the 'Wall of Separation between Church and State': A Bicentennial Commemoration." *Journal of Church and State,* 43 (2001), 725–45.

Drescher, Seymour. "Jews and New Christians in the Atlantic Slave Trade." Pp. 439–470 of *The Jews and the Expansion of Europe to the West, 1450–1800.* Edited by Paolo Bernardini and Norman Fiering. New York: Berghahn Books, 2001.

Driancourt-Girod, Janine. "L'utilisation des chapelles d'ambassades scandinaves per les marchands luthèriens des 'ports de l'Océan de France' au XVIIIe siècle." *Bulletin de la société de l'histoire du protestantisme français*, 147 (2001), 225– 47.

Drowne, Solomon, Jr., and Joyce D.Goodfriend (eds.). "New York City in 1772: The Journal of Solomon Drowne, Junior." *New York History*, 82 (2001), 25–52.

Drury, Marjule Anne. "Anti-Catholicism in Germany, Britain, and the United States: A Review and Critique of Recent Scholarship." *Church History*, 70 (2001), 98–131.

Du Bois Marcus, Nancy. *Vico and Plato.* (Emory Vico Studies, 8.) New York: Peter Lang, 2001. Pp. xiii + 261.

Du Halde, J. B., Dedi Zheng, Yimin Lèu, and Jian Shen. *Yesu Hui Shi Zhongguo Shu Jian Ji: Zhongguo Hui Yi Lu.* Di 1 ban. ed, *Xi Fang Zao Qi Han Xue Jing Dian Yi Cong.* Zhengzhou Shi: Da xiang chu ban she, 2001. Pp. v + 1.

Dubin, Lois. "Researching Port Jews and Port Jewries: Trieste and Beyond." *Jewish Culture and History*, 4 (2001), 47–58.

Dubois, Paul-André. "Des mondes religieux parallèles, un espace commun? Amérindiens et musique vocale européenne sous la Régime français." *Études d'histoire religieuse: Société canadienne d'histoire de l'Église catholique*, 67 (2001), 105–15.

Dubovitski, A. B. "Paisii ligarid i ego Uchastie v dele patriarkha Nikona." *Vestnik Moskovskogo Universiteta, Seriia 8: Istoriia,* 3 (2001), 88–111.

Dumaitre, Paule. "Ambroise Pare: son destin posthume, ses historiens." *Histoire des Sciences médicales,* 35 (2001), 281–98.

Dumont, Simone. "Sur quelques correspondances reçues par les Cassini et par les Maraldi (1670–1793)." Pp. 185–95 of *Sur les traces des Cassini: Astronomes et observatoires du sud de la France.* Edited by Paul Brouzeng and Suzanne Débarbat. Paris: Comité des travaux historiques et scientifiques, 2001.

III: Philosophy, Science, and Religion

Dumouchel, Paul. "The Political Problem of Religion: Hobbes's Reading of the Bible." Pp. 1–27 of *English Philosophy in the Age of Locke*. (Oxford Studies in the History of Philosophy 3.) Edited by M. A. Stewart. Oxford: Clarendon Press, 2001.

Dupas, Didier Mathias. "Un procès de magiciens au XVIIIe siècle." *Histoire, Économie et Société*, 20 (2001), 219–29.

Durey, Michael. "Marquess Cornwallis and the Fate of Irish Rebel Prisoners in the Aftermath of the 1798 Rebellion." Pp. 128–45 of *Revolution, Counter-Revolution and Union: Ireland in the 1790s*. Edited by Jim Smyth. Cambridge: Cambridge University Press, 2001.

Durnbaugh, Donald F. "Pennsylvania's Crazy Quilt of German Religious Groups." *Pennsylvania History*, 68 (2001), 8–30.

Du Toit, Alexander. "'A Species of False Religion': William Robertson, Catholic Relief and the Myth of Modern Tolerance." *Innes Review*, 52 (2001), 167–88.

Eddy, M. D. "The 'Doctrine of Salts' and Rev. John Walker's Analysis of a Scottish Spa (1749–1761)." *Ambix*, 48 (2001), 137–60.

Eddy, M. D. "Geology, Mineralogy and Time in John Walker's University of Edinburgh Natural History Lectures (1779–1803)." *History of Science*, 39 (2001), 95–119.

Edwards, Jonathan. *The Works of Jonathan Edwards*. Volume XIX: Sermons and Discourses. Edited by M. X. Lesser. New Haven: Yale University Press, 2001. Pp. 864.

Ehrenpreis, Stefan. "Catholic Minorities and School Education: The cases of Brandenburg and the Dutch Republic, 1600–1750." Pp. 177–93 of *Frontiers of Faith: Religious Exchange and the Constitution of Religious Identities 1400–1750*. Edited by Eszter Andor and Istvan Gyorgy Toth. Budapest: Central European University European Science Foundation, 2001.

Eicholz, Hans L. *Harmonizing Sentiments: The Declaration of Independence and the Jeffersonian Idea of Self Government*. (Masterworks in the Western Tradition 4.) New York: Peter Lang, 2001. Pp. ix + 245.

Elazar, Daniel J. "Religious Diversity and Federalism." *International Social Science Journal*, 53 (2001), 61–65.

Ella, George M. *William Cowper: The Man of God Stamp*. Olema: Joshua Press, 2001. Pp. 236.

Elbel, Martin. "Pilgrims on the Way of the Cross: Pilgrimage Practice and Confessional Identity in Early Modern Bohemia." Pp. 275–83 of *Frontiers of Faith: Religious Exchange and the Constitution of Religious Identities 1400–1750*. Edited by Eszter Andor and Istvan Gyorgy Toth. Budapest: Central European University European Science Foundation, 2001.

Elrod, Eileen Razzari. "Moses and the Egyptian: Religious Authority in Olaudah Equiano's Interesting Narrative." *African American Review,* 35 (2001), 409–25.

Elwell, Frank W. *A Commentary on Malthus' 1798 Essay* On Population *as Social Theory*. (Mellen Studies in Sociology 26.) Lewiston: Edwin Mellen Press, 2001. Pp. v + 303.

Emch-Deriaz, Antoinette. "De l'importance de tater le pouls." *Canadian Bulletin of Medical History,* 18 (2001), 369–80.

Engelstein, Laura. "Holy Russia in Modern Times: An Essay on Orthodoxy and Cultural Change." *Past and Present,* 173 (2001), 129–56.

Engstrand, Iris H. W. "Spanish Naturalists in Cuba and the West Indies, 1795–1802." *Terrae Incognitae,* 33 (2001), 59–68.

Erskine, Ebenezer. *The Beauties of Ebenezer Erskine*. Edited by Samuel McMillan. Belleville: Christian Focus Publications, 2001. Pp. 700.

Erskine, Ebenezer. *The Whole Works of Ebenezer Erskine*. 3 volumes. Glasgow: Free Presbyterian Publications, 2001. Pp. 1,500.

Escamilla González, Iván. "La memoria de gobierno del virrey duque de Alburquerque, 1710." *Estudios de Historia Novohispana,* 25 (2001), 157–78.

Eshet, Dan. "Rereading Priestley: Science at the Intersection of Theology and Politics." *History of Science,* 39 (2001), 127–59.

Eustace, Nicole. "Vehement Movements: Debates on Emotion, Self, and Society During the Seven Years' War in Pennsylvania." *Explorations in Early American Culture,* 5 (2001), 79–117.

Fabila, René Avilés. "Alzate, escritor, literato, traductor y periodista: Apuntes." Pp. 595–602 of *Periodismo científico en el siglo XVIII: José Antonio de Alzate y Ramírez*. Edited by Patricia Aceves Pastrana. Mexico: Universidad Autónoma Metropolitana Unidad Xochimilco, 2001.

III: Philosophy, Science, and Religion

Fagan, Patrick. *The Diocese of Meath in the Eighteenth Century*. Dublin: Four Courts Press, 2001. Pp. 224.

Faggionato, Raffaella. "From a Society of the Enlightened to the Enlightenment of Society: The Russian Bible Society and Rosicrucianism in the Age of Alexander I." *Slavic and Eastern European Review*, 79 (2001), 459–87.

Faidit, Jean-Michel. "Astronomie et astronomes en Languedoc au XVIIIe siècle." Pp. 299–309 of *Sur les traces des Cassini: Astronomes et observatoires du sud de la France*. Edited by Paul Brouzeng and Suzanne Débarbat. Paris: Comité des travaux historiques et scientifiques, 2001.

Faroqhi, Suraiya. "Quis Custodiet Custodes? Controlling Slave Identities and Slave Traders in Seventeenth- and Eighteenth-Century Istanbul." Pp. 121–36 of *Frontiers of Faith: Religious Exchange and the Constitution of Religious Identities 1400–1750*. Edited by Eszter Andor and Istvan Gyorgy Toth. Budapest: Central European University European Science Foundation, 2001.

Farr, David. "Kin, Cash, Catholics and Cavaliers: The Role of Kinship in the Financial Management of Major-General John Lambert." *Historical Research*, 74 (2001), 44–62.

Fatio, Olivier. "La spiritualité de Saussure." Pp. 487–99 of *H.-B. de Saussure (1740–1799): Un Regard sur la Terre*. Edited by René Sigrist. Geneva: Georg Editeur, 2001.

Fauchois, Yann. "La difficulté d'être libre: les droits de l'homme, l'église catholique et l'assemblée constituante, 1789–1791." *Revue d'Histoire moderne et contemporaine*, 48 (2001), 71–101.

Fauque, Danielle. "Du bon usage de l'éloge: cas de celui de Pierre Bouguer." *Revue d'histoire des sciences*, 54 (2001), 351–82.

Fea, John. "'The Chosen People of God': Presbyterians and Jeffersonian Republicanism in the New Jersey Countryside." *American Nineteenth Century History*, 2 (2001), 1–28.

Fea, John. "Ethnicity and Congregational Life in the Eighteenth-Century Delaware Valley: The Swedish Lutherans of New Jersey." *Explorations in Early American Culture*, 5 (2001), 45–78.

Feest, Christian F. "Father Lafitau as Ethnographer of the Iroquois." *European Review of Native American Studies*, 15 (2001), 19–25.

Feng, Hongqian. "Qing Benchao Ganmu Shiyi Shouyi Fang Kaozhu." *Zhongguo Nongshi (Agricultural History of China),* 20 (2001), 79–85.

Feng, Lisheng. "Cong Guan Kaohe de Leicai Zhaocha Fa Kan "Shoushi Li" Ping Li Ding San Chafa Zhi Yuan." *Ziran Kexueshi Yanjiu (Studies in the History of Natural Sciences),* 20 (2001), 132–42.

Fenn, Elizabeth A. *Pox Americana: The Great Smallpox Epidemic of 1775–82.* New York: Hill and Wang, 2001. Pp. 320.

Fenning, Hugh. "Troy to Bray: Letters from Dublin to Thurles, 1792–1817." *Archivium Hibernicum,* 55 (2001), 48–125.

Ferguson, Niall. "Metternich and the Rothschilds: 'A Dance with Torches on Powder Kegs'?" *Leo Baeck Institute. Year Book,* 46 (2001), 19–54.

Ferguson, Sally. "Lockian Teleosemantics." *Locke Studies*, 1 (2001), 105–22.

Ferm, Robert L. "Seth Storrs, Congregationalism, and the Founding of Middlebury College." *Vermont History,* 69 (2001), 253–66.

Ferraro, Giovanni. "Analytical Symbols and Geometrical Figures in Eighteenth-Century Calculus." *Studies in History and Philosophy of Science,* 32A (2001), 535–55.

Ferraz, Marcia H. M. "Un proyecto ilustrado: La reforma de la Universidad de Coimbra y el Estudio de las ciencias." Pp. 213–20 of *Periodismo científico en el siglo XVIII: José Antonio de Alzate y Ramírez.* Edited by Patricia Aceves Pastrana. Mexico: Universidad Autónoma Metropolitana Unidad Xochimilco, 2001.

Field, Clive D. "Bibliography of Methodist Historical Literature 2000." *Proceedings of the Wesley Historical Society,* Supplement (2001), 62–80.

Finzsch, Norbert, and Hermann Wellenreuther (eds.). *Visions of the Future in Germany and America.* Oxford: Berg, 2001. Pp. 580.

Firode, Alain. "Locke et les philosophes français." Pp. 57–72 of *Cirey dans la vie intellectuelle: La réception de Newton en France.* Edited by François de Gandt. Oxford: Voltaire Foundation, 2001.

III: Philosophy, Science, and Religion

Fisher, Howard J. *Faraday's Experimental Researches in Electricity: Guide to a First Reading*. Santa Fe: Green Lion, 2001. Pp. 619.

Fisher, N. R. R. "Robert Balle, Merchant of Leghorn and Fellow of the Royal Society (Ca. 1640–Ca. 1734)." *Notes and Records of the Royal Society of London,* 55 (2001), 351–71.

Flach, Werner. "Kants Lehre von der Gesetzmäßigkeit der Empirie. Zur Argumentation der Kantischen Schematismuslehre." *Kant-Studien*, 92 (2001), 464–73.

Fleuriot, Jacques. *A Combination of Geometry Theorem Proving and Nonstandard Analysis with Application to Newton's Principia*. (Distinguished Dissertations.) London: Springer Verlag, 2001. Pp. xi + 140.

Flores, Ramón Sánchez. "José Antonio de Alzate, Precursor de la Tecnología Mexicana." Pp. 341–60 of *Periodismo científico en el siglo XVIII: José Antonio de Alzate y Ramírez*. Edited by Patricia Aceves Pastrana. Mexico: Universidad Autónoma Metropolitana Unidad Xochimilco, 2001.

Flynn, James T. "Contrasting Similarities: Bishops Troy and Lisovskii in Ireland and Belorussia in the Age of the French Revolution." *Catholic Historical Review*, 87 (2001), 214–28.

Fogarty, Gerald P. *Commonwealth Catholicism: A History of the Catholic Church in Virginia*. Notre Dame: University of Notre Dame Press, 2001. Pp. 688.

Fogel, Robert W., and Fredric Smoler (interviewer). "The Fourth Great Awakening." *American Heritage,* 52 (2001), 70–75.

Fogg, G. E. "The Royal Society and the South Seas." *Notes and Records of the Royal Society of London,* 55 (2001), 81–103.

Fogleman, Aaron. "Comment on Part One: The Failure and Success of Millenarianism in American Religious Culture." Pp. 99–106 of *Visions of the Future in Germany and America*. Edited by Norbert Finzsch and Hermann Wellenreuther. Oxford: Berg, 2001.

Force, James E. "Newton's Theocentric Cosmogony and Hume's Cometary 'Seeds'." Pp. 159–79 of *Religion, Reason and Nature in Early Modern Europe*. Edited by Robert Crocker. Dordrecht: Kluwer Academic Publishers, 2001.

Ford, Brian J. "The Royal Society and the Microscope." *Notes and Records of the Royal Society of London,* 55 (2001), 29–49.

Forster, Eckart. "Goethe and the 'Auge des Geistes.'" *Deutsche Vierteljahrsschrift für Literaturwissenschaft und Geistesgeschichte,* 75 (2001), 87–101.

Forster, Marc R. *Catholic Revival in the Age of the Baroque: Religious Identity in Southwest Germany, 1550–1750.* New Studies in European History. Cambridge: Cambridge University Press, 2001. Pp. xiii + 268.

Fouilleron, Joel. "Les Jésuites châsses de la cité: violences pour un retour: Mauriac, 6–7 Septembre 1762." *Revue d'Histoire moderne et contemporaine,* 48 (2001), 50–70.

Francis, Richard. *Ann the Word: The Story of Ann Lee, Female Messiah, Mother of the Shakers, the Woman Clothed with the Sun.* New York: Arcade Publishing, 2001. Pp. 400.

Franco, Adolfo Olea. "Archivo de Sabiduría indígena: La aproximación de Alzate a la agricultura." Pp. 533–93 of *Periodismo científico en el siglo XVIII: José Antonio de Alzate y Ramírez.* Edited by Patricia Aceves Pastrana. Mexico: Universidad Autónoma Metropolitana Unidad Xochimilco, 2001.

Frank, Allen J. *Muslim Religious Institutions in Imperial Russia: The Islamic World of Novouzensk District and the Kazakh Inner Horde, 1780–1910.* Leiden: Brill, 2001. Pp. 341.

Frank, Michael. "Der rote Hahn: Wahrnehmung und Verarbeitung von Feuersbrünsten in der Frühen Neuzeit." *Historische Zeitschrift,* Supplement (2001), 229–47.

Frankel, Rachel. "Antecedents and Remnants of Jodensavanne: The Synagogues and Cemeteries of the First Permanent Plantation Settlement of New World Jews." Pp. 394–436 of *The Jews and the Expansion of Europe to the West, 1450–1800.* Edited by Paolo Bernardini and Norman Fiering. New York: Berghahn Books, 2001.

Frantz, John B. "The Religious Development of the Early German Settlers in 'Greater Pennsylvania': The Shenandoah Valley of Virginia." *Pennsylvania History,* 68 (2001), 66–100.

Frasca-Spada, Marina. "The Many Lives of Eighteenth-Century Philosophy." *British Journal for the History of Philosophy,* 9 (2001), 135–44.

Froeschlé, Michel. "Un astronome marseillais en voyage: le père Louis Feuillée dans les mers du Sud de 1707 à 1711." Pp. 243–58 of *Sur les traces des Cassini: Astronomes et observatoires du sud de la France.* Edited by Paul Brouzeng and Suzanne Débarbat. Paris: Comité des travaux historiques et scientifiques, 2001.

III: Philosophy, Science, and Religion

Frey, Manuel. "Europäer und ihre Feinde: Der Wandel des Türkenbildes von der frühen Neuzeit bis zur Mitte des 19. Jahrhunderts." *Sozialwissenschaftliche Informationen,* 30 (2001), 14–21.

Friedman, Jean E. *Ways of Wisdom: Moral Education in the Early National Period, Including the Diary of Rachel Mordecai Lazarus.* Athens: University of Georgia Press, 2001. Pp. 286.

Friesen, Ilse E. *The Female Crucifix: Images of St. Wilgefortis since the Middle Ages.* Waterloo: Wilfrid Laurier University Press, 2001. Pp. 173.

Froeschle-Chopard, Marie-Hélène, and Michel Froeschlé. "'Sciences et Arts' dans les 'Mémoires de Trevoux' (1701–1762)." *Revue d'Histoire moderne et contemporaine,* 48 (2001), 30–49.

Fu, Banghong, and Yunli Shi. "Chongzhen Lishu He Lixiang Kaocheng Houbian Zhong Suo Shu de Meng Qi Cha Xiuzheng Wenti." *Zhongguo Keji Shiliao (China Historical Materials of Science and Technology),* 22 (2001), 260–68.

Fukala, Radek. "Dansky Vpad do Slezska a Rozklad Opavske Stavovske Spolecnosti." *Slezsky Sbornik,* 99 (2001), 81–94.

Funaro, Liana Elda. "'Il criterio e la mano': Viaggi e donativi sovrani all'Imperiale e Regio Museo fiorentino." *Nuncius,* 16 (2001), 153–89.

Furdell, Elizabeth Lane. *The Royal Doctors, 1485–1714: Medical Personnel at the Tudor and Stuart Courts.* Rochester: Boydell and Brewer, 2001. Pp. 305.

Furner, Mark. "Lay Casuistry and the Survival of Later Anabaptists in Bern." *Mennonite Quarterly Review,* 75 (2001), 429–70.

Füssel, Marian. "Geschichtsschreibung als Wissenschaft vom Anderen: Michel de Certeau SJ." *Storia della Storiografia,* 39 (2001), 17–38.

Gahan, Daniel. "Class, Religion and Rebellion: Wexford in 1798." Pp. 83–98 of *Revolution, Counter-Revolution and Union: Ireland in the 1790s.* Edited by Jim Smyth. Cambridge: Cambridge University Press, 2001.

Gailus, Manfred. "Die Erfindung des "Korn-Juden": Zur Geschichte eines antijüdischen Feindbildes des 18. und Frühen 19. Jahrhunderts." *Historische Zeitschrift,* 272 (2001), 597–622.

Galley, Chris, and Nicola Shelton. "Bridging the Gap: Determining Long-Term Changes in Infant Mortality in Pre-Registration England and Wales." *Population Studies,* 55 (2001), 65–77.

Gandt, François de. *Cirey dans la vie intellectuelle: la réception de Newton en France.* SVEC: 11. Oxford: Voltaire Foundation, 2001. Pp. v + 253.

García, Alberto Saladino. "José Antonio de Alzate y Ramírez: Figura de la cultura Novohispana del siglo XVIII." Pp. 37–55 of *Periodismo científico en el siglo XVIII: José Antonio de Alzate y Ramírez.* Edited by Patricia Aceves Pastrana. Mexico: Universidad Autónoma Metropolitana Unidad Xochimilco, 2001.

García, Alberto Saladino. "José Antonio de Alzate y el periodismo ilustrado Latinoamericano." Pp. 603–16 of *Periodismo científico en el siglo XVIII: José Antonio de Alzate y Ramírez.* Edited by Patricia Aceves Pastrana. Mexico: Universidad Autónoma Metropolitana Unidad Xochimilco, 2001.

García de Leon, Porfirio. "El Axólotl: Personaje vivo de la historia de la ciencia. De Alzate a la uam-xochimilco." Pp. 451–69 of *Periodismo científico en el siglo XVIII: José Antonio de Alzate y Ramírez.* Edited by Patricia Aceves Pastrana. Mexico: Universidad Autónoma Metropolitana Unidad Xochimilco, 2001.

García-Melero, José Enrique. *Las catedrales góticas en la España de la Ilustración: la incidencia del neoclasicismo en el gótico, el dinamismo de las catedrales.* Madrid: Ediciónes Encuentro, 2001. Pp. 188.

García Belmar, Antonio, and José Ramón Bertomeu Sánchez. "Pedro Gutiérrez Bueno (1745–1822), los libros de texto y los nuevos públicos de la química en el último tercio del siglo XVIII." *Dynamis,* 21 (2001), 351–74.

García Belmar, Antonio, and José Ramón Bertomeu Sánchez. "Pedro Gutiérrez Bueno y las relaciones entre la química y la farmacia durante el último tercio del siglo XVIII." *Hispania,* 61 (2001), 539–63.

García Belmar, Antonio, and José Ramón Bertomeu Sánchez. "Viajes a Francia para el estudio de la química, 1770–1833." *Asclepio,* 53 (2001), 95–139.

Garms, Jörg. "Materialien zur Kunsttätigkeit der gegenreformatorischen Orden in Österreich and in andern Ländern der Habsburgermonarchie bis 1800: VIII. Das Archiv des Piaristenordens (Fortsetzung)." *Römische Historische Mitteilungen,* 43 (2001), 631–51.

III: Philosophy, Science, and Religion

Garrigus, John D. "New Christians/'New Whites': Sephardic Jews, Free People of Color, and Citizenship in French Saint-Domingue, 1760–1789." Pp. 314–32 of *The Jews and the Expansion of Europe to the West, 1450–1800*. Edited by Paolo Bernardini and Norman Fiering. New York: Berghahn Books, 2001.

Garrioch, David. "Sacred Neighborhoods and Secular Neighborhoods: Milan and Paris in the Eighteenth Century." *Journal of Urban History,* 27 (2001), 405–19.

Gartner, Lloyd P. *History of the Jews in Modern Times.* New York: Oxford University Press, 2001. Pp. 468.

Gassmann, Gunther, with Duane H. Larson, and W. Oldenburg Mark. *Historical Dictionary of Lutheranism.* Lanham: Scarecrow, 2001. Pp. 420.

Gaustad, Edwin S. *Roger Williams, Prophet of Liberty.* (Oxford Portraits.) New York: Oxford University Press, 2001. Pp. 144.

Gaustad, Edwin S. "U.S. Baptists and Modernity: Great Dissenters, Lousy Conformists." *Baptist History and Heritage,* 36 (2001), 101–12.

Gazzaniga, Valentina, and Paola Frati. "In venerem ignavus: impotenza, medicina e legislazione in età moderna." *Medicina nei secoli,* 13 (2001), 597–626.

Genet-Rouffiac, Nathalie. "The Wild Geese: Les regiments irlandais au service de Louis XIV (1688–1715)." *Revue historique des armées,* 1 (2001), 35–48.

Geraci, Robert P. "Going Abroad or Going to Russia? Orthodox Missionaries in the Kazakh Steppe, 1881–1917." Pp. 274–310 of *Of Religion and Empire: Missions, Conversion, and Tolerance in Tsarist Russia*. Edited by Robert P. Geraci and Michael Khodarkovsky. Ithaca: Cornell University Press, 2001.

Geraci, Robert P., and Michael Khodarkovsky (eds.). *Of Religion and Empire: Missions, Conversion, and Tolerance in Tsarist Russia.* Ithaca: Cornell University Press, 2001. Pp. 356.

Gere, Cathy. "William Harvey's Weak Experiment: The Archaeology of an Anecdote." *History Workshop Journal,* 51 (2001), 19–36.

Gevitz, Norman. "'Pray Let the Medicines Be Good': The New England Apothecary in the Seventeenth and Early Eighteenth Centuries." Pp. 5–27 of *Apothecaries and the Drug Trade:*

Essays in Celebration of the Work of David L. Cowen. Edited by Gregory J. Higby and Elaine C. Stroud. Madison: American Institute of the History of Pharmacy, 2001.

Gibbons, J. M. "Laying the Moral Foundations: Writer, Religion and Late Eighteenth-Century Society: The Case of J. M. R. Lenz." *German Life and Letters,* 54 (2001), 137–54.

Gibbons, Luke. "Republicanism and Radical Memory: The O'Conors, O'Carolan and the United Irishmen." Pp. 211–37 of *Revolution, Counter-Revolution and Union: Ireland in the 1790s.* Edited by Jim Smyth. Cambridge: Cambridge University Press, 2001.

Gibson, William. "'Be It as Prayed': A Note on a Quiet Reform of the Lord Chancellor's Ecclesiastical Patronage." *Archives,* 26 (2001), 118–22.

Gil Novales, Alberto. "Pueblo y nación en España durante la Guerra de la Independencia." *Spagna contemporanea,* 10 (2001), 169–87.

Ginio, Eyal. "'Every Soul Shall Taste Death'— Dealing with Death and the Afterlife in Eighteenth-Century Ottoman Salonica." *Studia Islamica,* 93 (2001), 113–32.

Ginio, Eyal. "Piraterie et rachat en mer Égée durant la premiére moitié du XVIII siécle. *Turcica,* 33 (2001), 135–47.

Gireau-Geneaux, Annie. "Mme Du Châtelet entre Leibniz et Newton: matière, force et substance." Pp. 173–86 of *Cirey dans la vie intellectuelle: La réception de Newton en France.* Edited by François de Gandt. Oxford: Voltaire Foundation, 2001.

Glen, Marilyn. "Launching a Clerical Career in Late Georgian England: Nathaniel K. Pugsley— from Hoxton Academy to Industrial Stockport." *Journal of the United Reformed Church History Society,* 6 (2001), 642–72.

Glover, William. "The Navigation of the Nonsuch, 1668–69." *Northern Mariner,* 11 (2001), 49–63.

Godfrey, Peter B., and G. M. Ditchfield. "The Unitarian Archives at Essex Hall." *Archives,* 26 (2001), 58–70.

Godsey, William D., Jr. "Noble Survival and Transformation at the Beginning of the Late Modern Era: The Counts Coudenhove from Rhenish Cathedral Canons to Austrian Priests, 1750–1850." *German History,* 19 (2001), 499–524.

III: Philosophy, Science, and Religion

Godwin, William. *Memoirs of the Author of A Vindication of the Rights of Woman*. Edited by Pamela Clemit and Gina Luria Walker. (Broadview Literary Texts.) Peterborough: Broadview Press, 2001. Pp. 224.

Golden, Janet. "Exhibition Review: A State of Health: New Jersey's Medical Heritage." *Journal of American History*, 88 (2001), 1036–38.

Goldstein, Jonathan. "The Sorkin and Golab Theses and Their Applicability to South, Southeast, and East Asian Port Jewry." *Jewish Culture and History*, 4 (2001), 179–96.

Goldstein, Marc Allan (ed. and trans.). *Social and Political Thought of the French Revolution, 1788-1797: An Anthology of Original Texts*. Abridged edition. New York: Peter Lang, 2001. Pp. xiv + 367.

Golinski, Jan. "'Exquisite Atmography': Theories of the World and Experiences of the Weather in a Diary of 1703." *British Journal for the History of Science*, 34 (2001), 149–71.

Goodhue, Thomas W. "The Faith of a Fossilist: Mary Anning." *Anglican and Episcopal History*, 70 (2001), 80–100.

Goodlad, Graham. "Britain and Ireland 1798–1921: An Impossible Unity?" *Modern History Review*, 13 (2001), 20–23.

Goodwin, Charles H. "The Terrors of the Thunderstorm: Medieval Popular Cosmology and Methodist Revivalism." *Methodist History*, 39 (2001), 99–107.

Gorner, Paul. "Reid, Husserl and Phenomenology." *British Journal for the History of Philosophy*, 9 (2001), 545–55.

Gouldbourne, Ruth. "'This Sad Work': Scandal in Broadmead." *Baptist Quarterly*, 39 (2001), 146–52.

Graham, Kenneth W. *William Godwin Reviewed: A Reception History, 1783-1834*. (AMS Studies in the Nineteenth Century 20.) New York: AMS Press, 2001. Pp. 588.

Graham, Tommy. "The Shift in United Irish Leadership from Belfast to Dublin, 1796–1798." Pp. 55–66 of *Revolution, Counter-Revolution and Union: Ireland in the 1790s*. Edited by Jim Smyth. Cambridge: Cambridge University Press, 2001.

Gramain-Kibleur, Pascale. "Le rôle des prescriptions médicamenteuses dans la société française du XVIIIe siècle." *Histoire, Economie et Société,* 20 (2001), 321–37.

Gramlich-Oka, Bettina. "Tadano Makuzu and Her Hitori Kangae." *Monumenta Nipponica,* 56 (2001), 1–20.

Gratton, D. J. "The Fifth Earl Fitzwilliam's Patronage in the Church and in Education: A Whig Nobleman Does His Duty." *Northern History,* 38 (2001), 275–94.

Greaves, Richard L. "Seditious Sectaries or 'Sober and Useful Inhabitants'? Changing Conceptions of the Quakers in Early Modern Britain." *Albion,* 33 (2001), 24–50.

Greenagel, Frank L. *The New Jersey Churchscape: Encountering Eighteenth and Nineteenth Century Churches.* New Brunswick: Rutgers University Press, 2001. Pp. xiv + 248.

Greenberg, Robert. *Kant's Theory of a Priori Knowledge.* University Park: Pennsylvania State University Press, 2001. Pp. ix + 278.

Gregg, Stephen H. "'A Truly Christian Hero': Religion, Effeminacy, and Nation in the Writings of the Societies for Reformation of Manners." *Eighteenth-Century Life,* 25 (2001), 17–28.

Grenberg, Jeanine M. "Feeling, Desire and Interest in Kant's Theory of Action." *Kant-Studien,* 92 (2001), 153–79.

Grenon, Michel. "Les observations météorologiques et climatiques de Saussure." Pp. 141–57 of *H.-B. de Saussure (1740–1799): Un Regard sur la Terre.* Edited by René Sigrist. Geneva: Georg Editeur, 2001.

Greve, James R. "'Long Island Has Been a School to Me': The 1825 Letter of an Instructor at Schools at Rockaway and Great Neck." *Long Island Historical Journal,* 14 (2001), 119–24.

Greyerz, Kaspar von. "Religiöse Erfahrungsräume im Reformiertentun." *Historische Zeitschrift,* Supplement (2001), 307–16.

Griffin, Mark C., Patricia M. Lambert, and Elizabeth Monahan Driscoll. "Biological Relationships and Population History of Native Peoples in Spanish Florida and the American Southeast." Pp. 226–73 of *Bioarchaeology of Spanish Florida: The Impact of Colonialism.* Edited by Clark Spencer Larsen. Gainesville: University Press of Florida, 2001.

III: Philosophy, Science, and Religion 141

Griffin, Patrick. *The People with No Name: Ireland's Ulster Scots, America's Scotch-Irish, and the Creation of a British Atlantic World, 1689-1764*. Princeton: Princeton University Press, 2001. Pp. xv + 244.

Griffin's book is a study of the first two waves of Scotch-Irish emigration to central Pennsylvania in the eighteenth-century and the role religion played in their adjustment to the severities of frontier life. This is another title in a vein similar to Linda Colley's groundbreaking book, *Britons* (1992), that attempts to define ethnic identity in the "greater Atlantic community" in terms of religious affiliation. The research in manuscript and archival collections in northern Ireland and in Philadelphia and Lancaster County, Pennsylvania, is excellent; the survey of contemporary printed materials is equally admirable. Griffin's coverage, however, may appear inadequate in range, and some assumptions seem questionable.

Early chapters describe the discouraging situation Ulster Presbyterians found themselves in at the close of the seventeenth century, as well as the selective prosperity some found in the prosecution of the linen industry, so much that many relinquished their portion of land to devote more time to spinning. Griffin maintains that settlers in northern Ireland did not see themselves as "Scottish"; while "they embraced Scottish traditions, their experiences in Ireland diverged from those of their coreligionists within the Kirk" (2)–largely because their denomination, unlike Presbyterianism in Scotland, was not "established." On the other hand, they could hardly term themselves Irish, as they could not participate in government, and few owned what land they farmed. They could be seen as "people with no name," though one questions whether this was actually the case, particularly in Pennsylvania. Their "neighbors" certainly knew who they were!

Around the time some Ulster Presbyterians were thriving in the linen trade there developed a serious doctrinal split within their denomination that parallels the growth of early Moderatism in the Scottish church. In the Ulster church, "New Lights. . . advocated theological and political ideas that they believed better spoke to a society of increased [economic] opportunities" (38). (Some of their clergy were strongly influenced by their teachers at Glasgow University, where most trained–Gershom Carmichael and the Irishman Francis Hutcheson in moral philosophy and John Simson in divinity–who was prosecuted on two occasions for "unsound teaching" and finally suspended in 1729.) Here also arose the Subscription Controversy: Old Lights in Ulster insisted that clergy "subscribe" to all the articles of the Westminster Confession (1643), the document that best embodied the tenets of traditional Reformation theology. At the same time as these people "encountered new economic possibilities within a broader Irish society, the policies of the Ascendancy [the Anglican establishment] pressed men and women to rely more heavily on church structures set apart from the institutional life of the kingdom to order their lives" (37). Rural folk, people who barely thrived, tended to support subscription. Others comparatively well off did not. By 1726, the Old Lights, the Subscribers, had driven the New Lights out of the church. ("Subscription," adds Griffin perceptively, "not the refusal to subscribe, was an unprecedented departure from the Reformed tradition" [51].)

How did this schism impact the departures of Ulster Presbyterians for the New World and their subsequent adjustment to the new freedoms and isolation they found in the wilderness of central Pennsylvania?

Religion was only one factor in the decision of Ulster Presbyterians to emigrate and not the chief one. In a period of famine when the linen industry began to decline, the primary reason, which should surprise no one, was economic, yet in keeping with Griffin's tenuous thesis that emigration only broadened these persons' consciousness that even in resettling they remained part of a larger Atlantic community, the first wave of Scotch-Irish immigrants (1718-1725) chose Pennsylvania because of its religious freedom and because heretofore they had imported their flaxseed from that colony. (Hutcheson claimed that one of the reasons to emigrate was the persistence of the Test Act.) Another reason, Griffin adds, was the population density of cities like Derry, Donegal, and Tyrone. The original settlers sold their leases in northern Ireland and were able to pay their own passage.

"Each group of migrants to the New World," Griffin states, "overcame the religious and regional divisions of their place of origin to invent markers of membership that bound the group together. Only in America, therefore, did men and women who left Scotland become Scots, as migrants from German-speaking regions of Europe discovered a semblance of German unity" (4). However, the "polite discourse" of New Light settlers did not take hold in central Pennsylvania (though how many New Light settlers were among the first wave of immigrants is not known.) The conditions of settlement were severe and rude, and the new arrivals behaved accordingly, acquiring among other ethnic groups a reputation for being "the very scum of mankind." They became known as a notoriously fractious people, civilly troublesome, sticking together clannishly, while trying to attract clergy from across the water to establish congregations. Their Presbyterian heritage provided the initial model for the little civic order they had.

The Presbytery of Donegal, between Lancaster and the Susquehanna River (not to be confused with modern Donegal in Westmoreland County), was established in 1732; soon it joined the Presbytery of New Castle, Delaware, in insisting on subscription, doubtless as a means of social control (though Griffin does not put it that way). Many objected, arguing that subscription was the sort of thing they came to the New World to escape—but "the church needed a better set of institutional structures for discipline to overrule erring presbyteries and to ensure a godly ministry" (118). Griffin adds, "Nearly every minister who out of conscience refused to subscribe in Ireland also pushed for ironclad subscription in the synod of Philadelphia" (122). Subscription did not last, needless to say: as settlements grew and became more connected to the larger world, support for post-Calvinist orthodoxy weakened (as it did in the Netherlands in the seventeenth century and in Geneva in the early eighteenth century, when economic conditions improved).

The second wave of Ulster emigration started in 1740. Its economic background was less prosperous as most could not pay their way and had to undergo indenture. As a newly arrived group, it became subject to the emotional appeal of Whitefield's "Great Awakening." They were infected with a "vital piety" and a desire for like-minded clergy, different from the religious interests of both Old and New Lights. Once their seven years were paid off, they moved further west, beyond the German settlements.

Griffin argues that at the conclusion of the Seven Years' War the immigrants from Ulster "celebrated their participation in a larger empire and confirmed their attachment to a unifying Britishness" (158). This is the kind of generalization that needs qualification. One of the regrets about this book is that it does not consider the next wave from Ulster that came in the early 1770s and settled east of Pittsburgh. It is maybe true that a new sense of "Britishness" prompted the protest of many that the taxes imposed in the 1760s did not treat the colonists like Britons living at home, but it must be remembered that the Scotch-Irish of all these waves were quick to seize arms against British occupation.

Besides Griffin's diligent research, one is grateful for the explanation of the split that occurred in northern Ireland between Old and New Lights, and his description of life in central Pennsylvania tells us much about the life of the first Scotch-Irish settlers. But the book seems oblivious to the larger context in which this movement was played out—the similar theological split occurring in Scotland, the religious tyranny among the Puritans in New England, and the role religion played in similar emigrations to the New World. In addition, Griffin never seems convincing about how great a role religion played in the movement of the settlers. The theological split in Ulster, so carefully described, has little to do with the decision to emigrate, and its relation to pressing economic factors, once folk reached the shores of the New World, can only be inferred. Were the settlers in the forests along the Susquehanna River conscious of the role assigned to them in the "greater Atlantic community"? We do not know for sure.—Henry L Fulton

Griffin, Patrick. "The People with No Name: Ulster's Migrants and Identity Formation in Eighteenth-Century Pennsylvania." *William and Mary Quarterly,* 58 (2001), 587–614.

Griffiths, Steve. *Redeem the Time: Sin in the Writings of John Owen [1616–1683].* Belleville: Spring Arbor, 2001. Pp. 316.

III: Philosophy, Science, and Religion 143

Grier, Michelle. *Kant's Doctrine of Transcendental Illusion*. (Modern European Philosophy.) Cambridge: Cambridge University Press, 2001. Pp. xiii + 315.

Grise, Philippe. "Claude-Nicolas le Cat (1700–1768): Un grand nom de la chirurgie et de l'urologie au XVIIIème siècle." *Histoire des Sciences médicales,* 35 (2001), 133–40.

Griswold, Mac. "Planting the English Landscape Garden: There Were Flowers." *Raritan,* 20 (2001), 80–106.

Groemer, Gerald. "The Creation of the Edo Outcaste Order." *Journal of Japanese Studies,* 27 (2001), 263–94.

Gronim, Sara Stidstone. "Geography and Persuasion: Maps in British Colonial New York." *William and Mary Quarterly,* 58 (2001), 373–402.

Grossi, Filipo. "Trois natifs de Perinaldo, astronomes de l'Observatoire de Paris." Pp. 13–25 of *Sur les traces des Cassini: Astronomes et observatoires du sud de la France.* Edited by Paul Brouzeng and Suzanne Débarbat. Paris: Comité des travaux historiques et scientifiques, 2001.

Grosskopf, Jan Schenk. "Family, Religion, and Disorder: The Rogerenes of New London, 1676–1726." *Connecticut History,* 40 (2001), 203–24.

Groves, Eric W. "Archibald Menzies (1754–1842), an Early Botanist on the Northwestern Seaboard of North America, 1792–1794, with Further Notes on His Life and Work." *Archives of Natural History,* 28 (2001), 71–122.

Grozdanova, Elena, and Stefan Andreev. "Das Los der Frauen nach den osmanischen 'Registerbüchern der Beschwerden' vom 17. und 18. Jh." *Bulgarian Historical Review,* 29 (2001), 52–68.

Grumet, Robert S. (ed.). *Voices from the Delaware Big House Ceremony.* Norman: University of Oklahoma Press, 2001. Pp. 240.

Guenther, Karen. "A Crisis of Allegiance: Berks County, Pennsylvania Quakers and the War for Independence." *Quaker History,* 90 (2001), 15–34.

Guijarro Mora, Víctor. "Petrus van Musschenbroek y la física experimental del siglo XVIII." *Asclepio,* 53 (2001), 191–212.

Gunnarsdóttir, Ellen. "The Convent of Santa Clara, the Elite and Social Change in Eighteenth-Century Querétaro." *Journal of Latin American Studies,* 33 (2001), 257–90.

Gunst, Peter. "Marczali Henrik es a 'Kortortenetiras.'" *Szazadok,* 135 (2001), 181–90.

Gunther-Canada, Wendy. *Rebel Writer: Mary Wollstonecraft and Enlightenment Politics.* DeKalb: Northern Illinois University Press, 2001. Pp. xi + 203.

Haakonssen, Knud. "The Character and Obligation of Natural Law According to Richard Cumberland." Pp. 29–47 of *English Philosophy in the Age of Locke.* (Oxford Studies in the History of Philosophy 3). Edited by M. A. Stewart. Oxford: Clarendon Press, 2001.

Haakonssen, Knud, and A. S. Skinner (eds.). *Index to the Works of Adam Smith.* Oxford: Clarendon Press, 2001. Pp. ix + 209.

Hafstein, Valdimar (trans.). "Biological Metaphors in Folklore Theory: An Essay in the History of Ideas." *Arv,* 57 (2001), 7–32.

Hagihara, Mamoru. "Shindai Mongoru No Infushabi Ni Taisuru Horitsu No Tekiyo: Daikatsubutsu No Ryomin to Keiji Saiban." *Shirin,* 84 (2001), 100–27.

Hague, Hope, Brenda Machosky, and Marcel Rotter. "Waiting for Goethe: Goethe Biographies from Ludwig Geiger to Friedrich Gundolf." Pp. 84–103 of *Goethe in German-Jewish Culture.* Edited by Klaus L. Berghahn and Jost Hermand. Rochester: Camden House, 2001.

Hahn, Barbara. "Demarcations and Projections: Goethe in the Berlin Salons." Pp. 31–43 of *Goethe in German-Jewish Culture.* Edited by Klaus L. Berghahn and Jost Hermand. Rochester: Camden House, 2001.

Haines, Catharine M. C., and Helen M. Stevens. *International Women in Science: A Biographical Dictionary to 1950.* Santa Barbara: ABC-Clio Inc., 2001. Pp. 383.

Hall, A. Rupert. "Cambridge: Newton's Legacy." *Notes and Records of the Royal Society of London,* 55 (2001), 205–26.

Hall, Roland. "Recent Publications on Locke." *Locke Studies*, 1 (2001), 3–13.

Hall, Roland. "The Role of Experience in Locke." *Locke Studies*, 1 (2001), 15–30.

III: Philosophy, Science, and Religion

Halleux, Robert. *Les publications de l'Académie royale des sciences de Paris (1666–1793)*. 2 volumes. Turnhout: Brepols, 2001. Pp. 850.

Halloran, Brian M. "Jesuits in 18th-Century Scotland." *Innes Review*, 52 (2001), 80–100.

Hamada, Masami. "Jihâd, hijra et 'devoir du sel' dans l'histoire du Turkestan oriental." *Turcica*, 33 (2001), 35–61.

Hamid, Ahmud Fauzi Abdul. "Sufi Undercurrents in Islamic Revivalism: Traditional, Post-Traditional and Modern Images of Islamic Activism in Malaysia." *Islamic Quarterly*, 45 (2001), 119–37.

Hamilton, Frances. "Alabama Baptist Convention Result of Great Visionary." *Alabama Baptist Historian*, 37 (2001), 17–19.

Hamilton, Frances. "Triennial Convention Inspired Baptist Support of Missions." *Alabama Baptist Historian*, 37 (2001), 12–14.

Hamm, E. P. "Of 'Histories Written by the Hand of Nature Itself.'" *Annals of Science*, 58 (2001), 311–17.

Hamm, E. P. "Unpacking Goethe's Collections: The Public and the Private in Natural-Historical Collecting." *British Journal for the History of Science*, 34 (2001), 275–300.

Hammer, Stephanie. *Schiller's Wound: The Theater of Trauma from Crisis to Commodity*. (Kritik.) Detroit: Wayne State University Press, 2001. Pp. 172.

Hammond, Christopher. "A Note on Newton's Measurements of Film Thicknesses and Their Corresponding (Interference) Colours." *Notes and Records of the Royal Society of London*, 55 (2001), 391–94.

Hamou, Philippe. "Algarotti vulgarisateur." Pp. 73–89 of *Cirey dans la vie intellectuelle: La réception de Newton en France*. Edited by François de Gandt. Oxford: Voltaire Foundation, 2001.

Handler, Jerome S., and Kenneth M. Bilby. "On the Early Use and Origin of the Term 'Obeah' in Barbados and the Anglophone Caribbean." *Slavery and Abolition*, 22 (2001), 87–100.

Haney, David P. *The Challenge of Coleridge: Ethics and Interpretation in Romanticism and Modern Philosophy*. University Park: Pennsylvania State University Press, 2001. Pp. xviii + 309.

Haney, Frank. "Pavel Florenskij und Kant—eine wichtige Seite der russischen Kant-Rezeption." *Kant-Studien*, 92 (2001), 81–103.

Hanna, Robert. *Kant and the Foundations of Analytic Philosophy*. Oxford: Clarendon Press of Oxford University Press, 2001. Pp. xv + 312.

Hansel, Joelle. "La figure du *mashal* dans l'herméneutique du XVIe au XVIIIe siècle." *Revue des Études Juives*, 160 (2001), 135–54.

Hanshaw, Mark E. "Wesley and Liberty: Embracing Poles." *Methodist History*, 40 (2001), 51–60.

Hanson, James A. "Fire Steels." *Museum of the Fur Trade Quarterly*, 37 (2001), 2–8.

Hara, Junichiro. "Kinseiki Meisho no Settoka to Fuji Oyama Sankei." *Nihon Rekishi*, 6 (2001), 34–50.

Harber, W. H. "Le Newton de Voltaire." Pp. 115–25 of *Cirey dans la vie intellectuelle: La réception de Newton en France*. Edited by François de Gandt. Oxford: Voltaire Foundation, 2001.

Harris, Cath. "Liberty of Conscience in Action: James Naylor and the Second Protectorate Parliament, 1656." *Melbourne Historical Journal*, 29 (2001), 100–06.

Haroche-Bouzinac, Geneviève. "Voltaire à Cirey, poète et philosophe, d'après sa correspondance, 1735–1738." Pp. 16–25 of *Cirey dans la vie intellectuelle: La réception de Newton en France*. Edited by François de Gandt. Oxford: Voltaire Foundation, 2001.

Harris, Ian. "Locke on Justice." Pp. 49–85 of *English Philosophy in the Age of Locke*. (Oxford Studies in the History of Philosophy 3.) Edited by M. A. Stewart. Oxford: Clarendon Press, 2001.

Hastings, Adrian. "The British Empire and the Missionary Movement." Pp. 83–93 of *Religion und Politik in Deutschland und Großbritannien*. Edited by Richard Bonney, Franz Bosbach, and Thomas Brockmann. Munich: K. G. Saur, 2001.

Hartweg, Frédéric. "Von der Entfremdung zur Annäherung: Die deutsch-französische Erbfeindschaft." *Kirchliche Zeitgeschichte*, 14 (2001), 313–72.

III: Philosophy, Science, and Religion

Harvey, Bruce A. *American Geographics: U. S. National Narratives and the Representation of the Non-European World, 1830–1865.* Stanford: Stanford University Press, 2001. Pp. 344.

Hatvany, Matthew G. "'Wedded to the Marshes': Salt Marshes and Socio-Economic Differentiation in Early Prince Edward Island." *Acadiensis,* 30 (2001), 40–55.

Hawgood, Barbara J. "Alexander Russell (1715–1768) and Patrick Russell (1727–1805): Physicians and Natural Historians of Aleppo." *Journal of Medical Biography,* 9 (2001), 1–6.

Hawkes, David. "The Politics of Character in Milton's Divorce Tracts." *Journal of the History of Ideas,* 62 (2001), 141–60.

Hayden, J. Michael, and Malcolm R. Greenshields. "Les Réformations catholiques en France: le témoignage des statuts synodaux." *Revue d'histoire moderne et contemporaine,* 48 (2001), 5–29.

Hayden, Roger. "Caleb Evans and the Anti-Slavery Question." *Baptist Quarterly,* 39 (2001), 4–14.

Hayes, Derek. *Historical Atlas of the North Pacific Ocean: Maps of Discovery and Scientific Exploration, 1500–2000.* Seattle: Sasquatch Books, 2001. Pp. 224.

Hearne, John. "Landscape with Faces." *Caribbean Quarterly,* 47 (2001), 42–68.

Heilbron, John L. "Some Connections among the Heroes." *Medicina nei secoli,* 54 (2001), 11–28.

Heitzenrater, Richard P. "A Tale of Two Brothers." *Christian History,* 20 (2001), 10–17.

Helmstadter, Axel. "Recharging the Battery of Life: Electricity in the Theory and Practice of Drug Treatment." *Pharmacy in History,* 43 (2001), 134–43.

Henriksen, Jan-Olav. *The Reconstruction of Religion: Lessing, Kierkegaard, and Nietzsche.* Grand Rapids: William B. Eerdmans Publishing Company, 2001. Pp. x + 208.

Henrikson, Alan K. "Geographical Antipathy, and the Personification of 'Place Hate.'" *Political Geography,* 20 (2001), 17–23.

Hentsch, Thierry. "Penser l'histoire." *Bulletin d'histoire politique,* 10 (2001), 10–15.

Herger, Csabane. "A Rekatolizacio Eszkoztara Magyarorszagon a 16–18. Bzazadban." *Szazadok,* 135 (2001), 871–87.

Hermand, Jost. "A View form Below: H. Heine's Relationship to Johann Wolfgang van Goethe." Pp. 44–62 of *Goethe in German-Jewish Culture.* Edited by Klaus L. Berghahn and Jost Hermand. Rochester: Camden House, 2001.

Hernandez Sáenz, Luz María, and George M. Foster. "Curers and Their Cures in Colonial New Spain and Guatemala: The Spanish Component." Pp. 19–46 of *Mesoamerican Healers.* Edited by Brad R. Huber and Alan R. Sandstrom. Austin: University of Texas Press, 2001.

Herren, Madeleine. "'Die Erweiterung des Wissens beruht Vorzugsweise auf dem Kontakt mit der Aussenwelt': Wissenschaftliche Netzwerke aus historischer Perspektive." *Zeitschrift für Geschichtswissenschaft,* 49 (2001), 197–207.

Higby, Gregory, and Elaine Condouris Stroud. *Apothecaries and the Drug Trade: Essays in Celebration of the Work of David L. Cowen.* Madison: American Institute of the History of Pharmacy, 2001. Pp. vii + 81.

Hight, Marc A. "Locke's Implicit Ontology of Ideas." *British Journal for the History of Philosophy* 9 (2001), 17–42.

Hikino, Kyosuke. "Shinshu Dangihon No Kinseiteki Tenkai." *Nihon Rekishi,* 4 (2001), 52–68.

Hill, Harvey. "The Law of Nature Revived: Christianity and Natural Religion in the Sermons of John Tillotson." *Anglican and Episcopal History,* 70 (2001), 169–89.

Hill, Lisa. "Eighteenth-Century Anticipations of the Sociology of Conflict: The Case of Adam Ferguson." *Journal of the History of Ideas,* 62 (2001), 281–99.

Hill, Lisa. "The Hidden Theology of Adam Smith." *European Journal of the History of Economic Thought,* 8 (2001), 1–29.

Hilton, Mary. "Revisioning Romanticism: Towards a Women's History of Progressive Thought 1780–1850." *History of Education,* 30 (2001), 471–87.

Hirsch, Alison Duncan. "Uncovering 'The Hidden History of Mestizo America' in Elizabeth Drinker's Diary: Interracial Relationships in Late Eighteenth-Century Philadelphia." *Pennsylvania History,* 68 (2001), 483–506.

III: Philosophy, Science, and Religion 149

Hitchcock, Edward, and Paul S. Boyer (eds.). "Geology of Martha's Vineyard and the Elizabeth Islands in 1823." *Dukes County Intelligencer,* 42 (2001), 186–91.

Hodgson, Barbara. *In the Arms of Morpheus: The Tragic History of Laudanum, Morphine, and Patent Medicines.* Willowdale: Firefly, 2001. Pp. 160.

Hodson, Christopher. "'In Praise of the Third Estate': Religious and Social Imagery in the Early French Revolution." *Eighteenth-Century Studies,* 34 (2001), 337–62.

Hoecherl-Alden, Gisela. "Upholding the Ideals of the 'Other Germany': German-Jewish Goethe Scholars in U.S. Exile." Pp. 123–45 of *Goethe in German-Jewish Culture.* Edited by Klaus L. Berghahn and Jost Hermand. Rochester: Camden House, 2001.

Hoeber, Francis W. "Drama in the Courtroom, Theater in the Streets: Philadelphia's Irish Riot of 1831." *Pennsylvania Magazine of History and Biography,* 125 (2001), 191–232.

Hollinshead, Janet E. "From Cambrai to Woolton: Lancashire's First Female Religious House." *Recusant History,* 25 (2001), 461–86.

Holmes, Paula Elizabeth. "The Narrative Repatriation of Blessed Kateri Tekakwitha." *Anthropologica,* 43 (2001), 87–103.

Holmes, Stephen R. *God of Grace and God of Glory: An Account of the Theology of Jonathan Edwards.* Grand Rapids: William B. Eerdmans Publishing Company, 2001. Pp. xiv + 289.

Holub, Robert C. "From the Pedestal to the Couch: Goethe, Freud, and Jewish Assimilation." Pp. 104–20 of *Goethe in German-Jewish Culture.* Edited by Klaus L. Berghahn and Jost Hermand. Rochester: Camden House, 2001.

Holzem, Andreas. "Bedingungen und Formen religiöser Erfahrung im Katholizismus zwischen Konfessionalisierung und Aufklärung." *Historische Zeitschrift,* Supplement (2001), 317–32.

Holzhey, Helmut, and Wilhelm Schmidt-Biggemann (eds). *Die Philosophie des 17. Jahrhunderts.* Volume 4: *Das Heilige Römische Reich Deutscher Nation, Nord- und Ostmitteleuropa.* (Grundriss der Geschichte der Philosophie). Basel: Schwabe, 2001. Pp. xxiv + 1507; bibliographies; indices.

Gottfried Wilhelm Leibniz has long overshadowed depictions of seventeenth-century German philosophy. Only recently have contributions of other important figures, such as Christian Thomasius and Samuel Pufendorf, begun slowly to edge toward the limelight. Pufendorf, for example, is enjoying a mini-renaissance in the English-speaking world with the ongoing publication of selected works by the Liberty Fund, while Ian Hunter's study *Rival Enlightenments: Civil and Metaphysical Philosophy in Early Modern Germany* (Cambridge 2001) draws attention to both Thomasius and Pufendorf as well as other philosophers of the early German Enlightenment. And now, with this volume, the variety and complexity of German philosophical culture in the seventeenth century is finally fully acknowledged. More than forty contributors demonstrate on more than 1,200 pages the richness of the philosophical discourse in the realm of the "Holy Roman Empire of German Nations" while another 200 pages describe philosophy in Scandinavia, Poland, and Hungary. In accordance with the definition of the age, philosophy is understood in the widest possible sense: Contributions from the fields of physics, astronomy, politics, law, theology, and mysticism also are covered when philosophically relevant. Naturally, philosophical relevance is a debatable claim, which becomes difficult to uphold at the margins of philosophical discourse. Nevertheless, the curious reader will welcome the inclusion of rather more than less material.

This book is also of great use to anyone interested in the philosophy of eighteenth-century Germany, Scandinavia, or Eastern Europe. It provides information about many developments in the seventeenth century that had an enormous impact on philosophical inquiry far beyond the year 1700. The relevance of Leibniz's philosophy for eighteenth-century Germany long has been established but the importance of other discourses, such as "Schulphilosophie" and esoteric thinking, for this period have only recently been explored. It is a unique characteristic of the German context that philosophy in the narrow sense survived almost exclusively in the scholastic world of the universities as "Schulphilosophie." As the subject "philosophy" was a mandatory part of the university's curriculum, the Aristotelian "Schulphilosophie" remained the most influential German philosophical discourse far into the second half of the eighteenth century–the early Kant, for example, still used a work by Alexander Gottlieb Baumgarten, one of the most important representatives of the late "Schulphilosophie" in Germany, as the basis for his lectures on metaphysics. This central aspect of seventeenth- and eighteenth-century German philosophical culture is finally given its due in this volume. More than 300 pages are devoted to the different versions of "Schulphilosophie" at the major German universities. Another interesting part of the German philosophical climate in the seventeenth and also the eighteenth century, esoteric thinking and mysticism, is also presented in a well informed discussion, including even philosophically marginalized genres such as mystical poetry. The tradition of the prisca sapientia (freshly reinvigorated by the Italian Renaissance), alchemy, esoteric texts such as the Kabbalah and hermetic writings as well as their social representations in the form of groups including the Rosicrucians and the Freemasons are still important parts of the philosophical picture in Germany well into the last third of the eighteenth century. The success of these vitalistic worldviews—as the introduction to this topic points out correctly—resulted from their ability to offer a welcome alternative to a mechanistic philosophy of nature as well as to the scholastic "Schulphilosophie." So it is no surprise that even a late figure such as Goethe was still heavily influenced in his early years by esoteric discourse.

In short, this work provides an enormous amount of new information for the specialist in seventeenth- and eighteenth-century philosophy, but it is equally suitable for the beginner. Aside from chapters on Leibniz and Thomasius, it is structured thematically according to general topics such as philosophy of nature, mysticism, and political philosophy, while each chapter is further divided into subchapters on individual philosophers. These excellent and efficient introductions to numerous thinkers provide accessible overviews of their lives and thought, as each subchapter contains a list of works, a biography, abstracts of the most important works, a summary of his (or very rarely her) philosophy, and a brief review of its reception. The rich information about their original works and the secondary literature is especially useful in enabling the reader to decide quickly which course of research he or she wants to pursue. Highly recommended!—Tino Markworth

Hood, Paxton. *Isaac Watts, His Life and Hymns.* Naples: Ambassador Publications, 2001. Pp. 348.

III: Philosophy, Science, and Religion

Hotchkiss, Gregory K. "The Revolutionary William White and Democratic Catholicity." *Anglican and Episcopal History*, 70 (2001), 40–74.

Houlbrook, Matt. "Toward a Historical Geography of Sexuality." *Journal of Urban History*, 27 (2001), 497–504.

Houlbrooke, Ralph. *Death, Religion, and the Family in England, 1480–1750* (Oxford Studies in Social History.) New York: Oxford University Press, 2001. Pp. 436.

Houston, Alan and Steve Pincus (eds.). *A Nation Transformed: England after the Restoration*. New York: Cambridge University Press, 2001. Pp. 337.

Houston, Robert. "Institutional Care for the Insane and Idiots in Scotland before 1820. Part 2." *History of Psychiatry*, 12 (2001), 177–97.

Houston, R. A. "Professions and the Identification of Mental Incapacity in Eighteenth-Century Scotland." *Journal of Historical Sociology*, 14 (2001), 441–66.

Houzawa, Naohide. "Bakuhan Kenri to Jidan Kankei: Ikka Ichiji-Sei O Megutte." *Shigaku Zasshi*, 110 (2001), 1–40.

Hov, Live. "The 'Women' of the Roman Stage: As Goethe Saw Them." *Theatre History Studies*, 21 (2001), 61–79.

Hoxsie, Russell. "Medical Tales from a Doctor's Diary (1829–1842)." *Dukes County Intelligencer*, 43 (2001), 51–74.

Hsia, Ke-chin. "De Yizhi Yu Qimeng Yundong (Aufklarung): Yige Chubu de Fansi." *Xin Shixue (New History)*, 12 (2001), 129–65.

Hsia, R. Po-chia. "Cong Tianru Huiyi Dao Dongxi Fenqi: Ouzhou Zhongguo Guan de Yanbian." *Xin Shixue (New History)*, 12 (2001), 1–18.

Hsia, Ronnie Po-Chia. "Conversion and Conversation: A Dialogical History of the Catholic Missions in China from the Sixteenth to the Eighteenth Century." Pp. 37–54 of *Frontiers of Faith: Religious Exchange and the Constitution of Religious Identities 1400–1750*. Edited by Eszter Andor and Istvan Gyorgy Toth. Budapest: Central European University European Science Foundation, 2001.

Huber, Brad R., and Alan R. Sandstrom (eds.). *Mesoamerican Healers.* Austin: University of Texas Press, 2001. Pp. 403.

Hubert, Olivier. "Construire le rite comme un objet historique: pour un usage pragmatique de l'anthropologie en histoire religieuse du Québec." *Études d'histoire religieuse: Société canadienne d'histoire de l'Église catholique,* 67 (2001), 81–91.

Hubert, Olivier. "Ritual Performance and Parish Sociability: French-Canadian Catholic Families at Mass from the seventeenth to the Nineteenth Century." Pp. 37–76 of *Households of Faith: Family, Gender, and Community in Canada, 1760–1969.* Edited by Nancy Christie. Montreal: McGill–Queen's University Press, 2001.

Hucho, Christine. "Female Writers, Women's Networks, and the Preservation of Culture: The Schwenkfelder Women of Eighteenth-Century Pennsylvania." *Pennsylvania History,* 68 (2001), 101–30.

Hudon, Christine. "Beaucoup de bruits pour rien? Rumeurs, plaintes et scandales autour du clergé dans les paroisses gaspésiennes, 1766–1900." *Revue d'histoire de l'Amérique Française,* 55 (2001), 217–40.

Hughes, Peter. "The Second Phase of the Restorationist Controversy: Disciplinary Crisis and Schism, 1824–1831." *Journal of Unitarian Universalist History,* 28 (2001), 28–91.

Hull, Gillian. "Archibald Menzies (1754–1842): A Respected Surgeon/Naturalist." *Journal of Medical Biography,* 9 (2001), 226–30.

Hullinger, David, and Charles Culpepper. *The American Intellectual Tradition.* Volume I: 1630–1865. 4th edition. Chapel Hill: University of North Carolina Press, 2001. Pp. 576.

Hulme, Hank. "Early History of Mount Olivet United Methodist Church: Arlington's Oldest Church." *Arlington Historical Magazine,* 12 (2001), 29–39.

Hunter, Ian. "Christian Thomasius' Attack on Protestant Scholasticism." *History of Education Review,* 30 (2001), 1–16.

Hunter, Michael, and Charles Littleton. "The Work-Diaries of Robert Boyle: A Newly Discovered Source and Its Internet Publication." *Notes and Records of the Royal Society of London,* 55 (2001), 373–90.

III: Philosophy, Science, and Religion

Hurpin, Gérard. "Claude-Nicolas le Cat ou de la notoriété médicale au XVIIIème siècle." *Histoire des Sciences médicales,* 35 (2001), 151–62.

Hutton, Gordon. "Archbishop King, the Bank Scheme, and Wood's Halfpence (1722–25)." *Éire–Ireland*, 35 (2000–2001), 3–4, 81–101.

Hutton, Sarah. "Ralph Cudworth, God, Mind and Nature." Pp. 61–76 of *Religion, Reason and Nature in Early Modern Europe*. Edited by Robert Crocker. Dordrecht: Kluwer Academic Publishers, 2001.

Imbruglia, Girolamo. "'É difficile vivere in epoca di rivoluzione': Franco Venturi e la politica dello storico." *Storia della Storiografia,* 40 (2001), 67–90.

"Index to the Hamilton Papers." *Archivium Hibernicum* , 55 (2001), 140–67.

Ingham, Cynthia Jo. "Set at Liberty: Virginia Presbyterianism after the Revolution." *Journal of Presbyterian History*, 79 (2001), 243–55.

Irlam, Shaun. "'Wish You Were Here': Exporting England in James Grainger's 'The Sugarcane.'" *ELH*, 68 (2001), 377–96.

Islamov, Tofik Muslimovich. "Imperiia Gabsburgov. Stanovlenie i Razvitie. XVI–XIX VV." *Novaia i Noveishaia Istoriia,* 2 (2001), 11–40.

Israel, Jonathan I. "The Jews of Dutch America." Pp. 335–49 of *The Jews and the Expansion of Europe to the West, 1450–1800*. Edited by Paolo Bernardini and Norman Fiering. New York: Berghahn Books, 2001.

Israel, Jonathan Irvine. *Radical Enlightenment: Philosophy and the Making of Modernity, 1650-1750*. Oxford: Oxford University Press, 2001. Pp. xvi + 810.

Jabour, Anya. "Resisting the Altar: A Case Study of Conversion and Courtship in the Antebellum South." *Maryland Historical Magazine,* 96 (2001), 29–51.

Jackson, Dianah Leigh. "Anatomy of Observation: From the Academie Royale de la Chirurgie to the Salons of Denis Diderot." *Canadian Journal of History,* 36 (2001), 27–49.

Jackson, Kent P. "Joseph Smith's Cooperstown Bible: The Historical Context of the Bible Used in the Joseph Smith Translation." *BYU Studies*, 40 (2001), 41–70.

Jackson, Robert H., and Camilo Hoyos (tr.). "Una frustrada evangelización: las limitaciónes del cambio social, cultural y religioso en los "Pueblos Errantes" de las misiónes del Desierto Central de baja California y la región de la costa del Golfo de Texas." *Fronteras de la Historia,* 6 (2001), 9–36.

Jacob, Margaret C. *The Enlightenment: A Brief History with Documents.* (Bedford Series in History and Culture.) Boston: St. Martin's Press, 2001. Pp. xiii + 237.

Jacob, Margaret C. "Factoring Mary Poovey's a History of the Modern Fact." *History and Theory,* 40 (2001), 280–89.

Jacob, Margaret, and David Reid. "Technical Knowledge and the Mental Universe of Manchester's Early Cotton Manufacturers." *Canadian Journal of History,* 36 (2001), 283–304.

Jacobs, Diane. *Her Own Woman: The Life of Mary Wollstonecraft.* New York: Simon & Schuster, 2001. Pp. 333.

Jacobsen, Anja Skaar. "Spirit and Unity: Orsted's Fascination by Winterl's Chemistry." *Centaurus,* 43 (2001), 184–218.

Jacobsen, Douglas. "The New Look of Mission History." *Fides et Historia,* 33 (2001), 87–91.

Jacquette, Dale. *David Hume's Critique of Infinity.* (Brill's Studies in Intellectual History 102.) Boston: Brill, 2001. Pp. xvi + 384.

Jaramillo, Ana María Hermillo. "La materia médica y la farmacia en las *Gacetas de Literatura* de Alzate." Pp. 287–305 of *Periodismo científico en el siglo XVIII: José Antonio de Alzate y Ramírez.* Edited by Patricia Aceves Pastrana. Mexico: Universidad Autónoma Metropolitana Unidad Xochimilco, 2001.

Jardine, Lisa. "Monuments and Microscopes: Scientific Thinking on a Grand Scale in the Early Royal Society." *Notes and Records of the Royal Society of London,* 55 (2001), 289–308.

Jauhiainen, Peter D. "'Reasoning out of the Scriptures': Samuel Hopkins, the Theological Enterprise, and the Deist Threat." *Journal of Presbyterian History,* 79 (2001), 119–33.

Jodziewicz, Thomas W. "'The Catholic Missionary of Boston' Fr. John Thayer: Controversialist and Ecumenist?" *American Catholic Studies,* 112 (2001), 23–47.

III: Philosophy, Science, and Religion

Jogėla, Vytautas. *Vyskupo Ignoto Jokuubo Masalskio kauno dekanato Vizitacija 1782 m.* Lietuvos Istorijos Ésaltiniai; 6 T. Vilnius: Katalikų akademija, 2001. Pp. xvi + 943.

Johnson, Maria Poggi. "Probability the Guide of Life: The Influence of Butler's Analogy on Keble and Newman." *Anglican and Episcopal History*, 70 (2001), 302–23.

Jones, George Fenwick. "Sephardim and Ashkenazim Jewish Settlers in Colonial Georgia." *Georgia Historical Quarterly*, 85 (2001), 519–37.

Joly, Bernard. "Les théories du feu de Voltaire et de Mme Du Châtelet." Pp. 212–37 of *Cirey dans la vie intellectuelle: La réception de Newton en France*. Edited by François de Gandt. Oxford: Voltaire Foundation, 2001.

Jones, Marshall B., and Elizabeth Rapley. "Behavioral Contagion and the Rise of Convent Education in France." *Journal of Interdisciplinary History*, 312 (2001), 489–521.

Jordan, David P. "Barbarism and Religion: Where Is Gibbon the Historian?" *History and Theory*, 40 (2001), 385–92.

Juengel, Scott. "Countenancing History: Mary Wollstonecraft, Samuel Stanhope Smith, and Enlightenment Racial Science." *ELH*, 68 (2001), 897–927.

Juliani, Richard N., C. Walker Gollar, Shawn Weldon, and Dale B. Light. "Review: Dale B. Light's *Rome and the New Republic: Conflict and Community in Philadelphia Catholicism between the Revolution and the Civil War*." *American Catholic Studies*, 112 (2001), 81–90.

Julien, Pascal. "Illusions et jeux d'optique dans la peinture aixoise des XVIIe et XVIIIe siècles." *Provençe Historique*, 51 (2001), 85–104.

Jung, Hans Rudolf. *Thematischer Katalog der Musikaliensammlung Grossfahner/Eschenbergen in Thüringen: Mit einer Einleitung zur Pflege der Figuralmusik in Grossfahner, Eschenbergen und dem Herzogtum Sachsen-Gotha zwischen 1640 und 1750, Catalogus Musicus, 17.* Kassel: Bärenreiter, 2001. Pp. 578.

Jutte, Robert. "Einleitung: auf den Leib Geschrieben." *Historische Zeitschrift*, Supplement (2001), 31–36.

Kaboré, Boniface. "Le formalisme est un humanisme: retour sur les fondements de la morale kantienne." *Kant-Studien*, 92 (2001), 350–58.

Kadane, Matthew. "Les bibliothèques de deux théologians reformés au XVIIe siècle, l'un puritain anglais, l'autre pasteur huguenot." *Bulletin de la société de l'histoire de protestantisme français,* 147 (2001), 67–99.

Kahn, Jean. "Une correction à apporter au texte d'une définition du beau dans la *Critique de la faculté de juger.*" *Kant-Studien,* 92 (2001), 79–80.

Kalik, Judith. "Christian Servants Employed by Jews in the Polish-Lithuanian Commonwealth in the Seventeenth and Eighteenth Centuries." *Polin: Studies in Polish Jewry,* 14 (2001), 259–70.

Kalista, Zdenek. *Česká barokní pout: K religiozite českého lidu v dobe barokní.* Žd'ár nad Sázavou: Cisterciana Sarensis, 2001. Pp. 287.

Kallen, Stuart A. *The 1700s.* San Diego: Greenhaven Press, 2001. Pp. 287.

Kampmann, Christoph. "Emacipation and Violence on the Interpretation of the Anti-Jewish Riots in the German *Vormärz.*" Pp. 63–82 of *Religion und Politik in Deutschland und Großbritannien.* Edited by Richard Bonney, Franz Bosbach, and Thomas Brockmann. Munich: K. G. Saur, 2001.

Kan, Sergei. "Russian Orthodox Missionaries at Home and Abroad: The Case of Siberian and Alaskan Indigenous Peoples." Pp. 173–200 of *Of Religion and Empire: Missions, Conversion, and Tolerance in Tsarist Russia.* Edited by Robert P. Geraci and Michael Khodarkovsky. Ithaca: Cornell University Press, 2001.

Kant, Immanuel. *Lectures on Metaphysics.* (The Cambridge Edition of the Works of Immanuel Kant.) Translated and edited by Karl Ameriks and Steve Naragon. Cambridge: Cambridge University Press, 1997. Pp. xlvii + 642.

Kanter, Douglas. "Robert Peel and the Waning of the 'Influence of the Crown' in Ireland, 1812–1818." *New Hibernia Review,* 5 (2001), 54–71.

Kapitzke, Robert L. *Religion, Power, and Politics in Colonial St. Augustine.* Ripley P. Bullen Series. Gainesville: University Press of Florida, 2001. Pp. 219.

Karhausen, L. R. "Mozart's Terminal Illness: Unravelling the Clinical Evidence." *Journal of Medical Biography,* 9 (2001), 34–48.

III: Philosophy, Science, and Religion

Kassler, Michael, and Philip Olleson (comps.). *Samuel Wesley (1766–1837): A Source Book.* Burlington: Ashgate Publishing Company, 2001. Pp. 790.

Kearns, Daniel F. "Bishop John England and the Possibilities of Catholic Republicanism." *South Carolina Historical Magazine,* 102 (2001), 47–67.

Kearns, Gerry. "Constructions of the Social." *Journal of Urban History,* 28 (2001), 98–106.

Kefeli, Agnès. "The Role of Tatar and Kriashen Women in the Transmission of Islamic Knowledge, 1800–1870." Pp. 250–73 of *Of Religion and Empire: Missions, Conversion, and Tolerance in Tsarist Russia.* Edited by Robert P. Geraci and Michael Khodarkovsky. Ithaca: Cornell University Press, 2001.

Kelley, Donald R. "Grounds for Comparison." *Storia della Storiografia,* 39 (2001), 3–16.

Kelly, Joseph. "Charleston's Bishop John England and American Slavery." *New Hibernia Review,* 5 (2001), 48–56.

Kenney, Alice P. "Patricians and Plebeians in Colonial Albany: Historical Demography and the Hudson Valley Dutch." *Halve Maen,* 74 (2001), 75–77.

Kenshur, O. "Virtue and Defilement: Moral Rationalism and Sexual Prohibitions in the *Lettres persanes.*" *Studies on Voltaire and the Eighteenth Century* (2001), 69–111.

Kerry, Paul E. *Enlightenment Thought in the Writings of Goethe: A Contribution to the History of Ideas.* (Studies in German Literature, Linguistics, and Culture.) Rochester: Camden House, 2001. Pp. x + 243.

Kerov, Valeri Vsevolodovich. "'Konfessional' no-Eticheskaia Motivatsiia Khoziastvovaniia Staroverov V XVII–XIX Vekakh." *Otechestvennaia Istoriia,* 4 (2001), 18–40.

Kertzer, David I. *The Popes Against the Jews: The Vatican's Role in the Rise of Modern Anti-Semitism.* New York: Knopf, 2001. Pp. 368.

Keynes, Milo. "A Bogus Newtonian 'Curiosity' at the Royal Society." *Notes and Records of the Royal Society of London,* 55 (2001), 247–52.

Khaleeli, Zhaleh. "Harmony or Hegemony? The Rise and Fall of the Native Medical Institution, Calcutta, 1822–35." *South Asia Research,* 21 (2001), 77–104.

Khodarkovsky, Michael. "The Conversion of Non-Christians in Early Modern Russia." Pp. 115–43 of *Of Religion and Empire: Missions, Conversion, and Tolerance in Tsarist Russia*. Edited by Robert P. Geraci and Michael Khodarkovsky. Ithaca: Cornell University Press, 2001.

Khoury, Dina Rizk. "Administrative Practice between Religious Law (Shari'a) and State Law (Kanun) on the Eastern Frontiers of the Ottoman Empire." *Journal of Early Modern History*, 5 (2001), 305–30.

Kidd, Colin C. "Constructing a Civil Religion: Scots Presbyterians and the Eighteenth-Century British State." Pp. 1–21 of *The Scottish Churches and the Union Parliament 1707–1999*. Edited by James Kirk. Edinburgh: Scottish Church History Society, 2001.

Kim, Mi Gyung. "The Analytic Ideal of Chemical Elements: Robert Boyle and the French Didactic Tradition of Chemistry." *Science in Context*, 14 (2001), 361–95.

Kinnaman, Ted. "Problems in Kant's Vindication of Pure Reason." *Journal of the History of Philosophy*, 39 (2001), 559–80.

Kinnaman, Ted. "The Task of the Critique of Judgment: Why Kant Needs a Deduction of the Principle of the Purposiveness of Nature." *American Catholic Philosophical Quarterly*, 75 (2001), 243–70.

Kiple, Kenneth F., and Sheldon Watts. "Response to Sheldon Watts: 'Yellow Fever Immunities in West Africa and the Americas in the Age of Slavery and Beyond.'" *Journal of Social History*, 34 (2001), 969–74.

Kirillov, V. V. "'Moskva Yauzskaia': K Rekonstruktsii Pervykh Gospital'nykh Zdanii Petrovskogo Vremeni i Usad'by N. Bidloo." *Vestnik Moskovskogo Universiteta, Seriia 8: Istoriia*, 1 (2001), 93–103.

Kirk, Brian. "Emmanuel Harford (c. 1641–1706): A Note." *Journal of the United Reformed Church History Society*, 6 (2001), 567–70.

Kirk, James (ed.). *The Scottish Church and the Union Parliament, 1707–1999*. Edinburgh: Scottish Church History Society, 2001. Pp. 163.

Kirkland, Trevor. "This Sad Work— The Case of Mary Smith of Broadmead: A Rejoinder." *Baptist Quarterly*, 39 (2001), 199–203.

III: Philosophy, Science, and Religion 159

Klein, Herbert S., Stanley L. Engerman, Robin Haines, and Ralph Shlomowitz. "Transoceanic Mortality: The Slave Trade in Comparative Perspective." *William and Mary Quarterly,* 58 (2001), 93–117.

Kleingeld, Pauline : "Nature or Providence? On the Theoretical and Moral Importance of Kant's Philosophy of History." *American Catholic Philosophical Quarterly* 75 (2001), 201–19.

Klieber, Rupert. "Verischerungen für Fegefeur: Bruderschaften and Liebesbünde nach Trient am Beispel Salzburg (1600–1950)." *Revue d'histoire ecclésiastique,* 96 (2001), 34–70.

Klier, John D. "State Policies and the Conversion of Jews in Imperial Russia." Pp. 92–112 of *Of Religion and Empire: Missions, Conversion, and Tolerance in Tsarist Russia.* Edited by Robert P. Geraci and Michael Khodarkovsky. Ithaca: Cornell University Press, 2001.

Klooster, Wim. "The Jews in Suriname and Curaçao." Pp. 350–68 of *The Jews and the Expansion of Europe to the West, 1450–1800.* Edited by Paolo Bernardini and Norman Fiering. New York: Berghahn Books, 2001.

Knapp, Éva. "Egy ismeretlen Magyar nyelvű orvosi nyomtatvany 1660–bol." *Magyar Könyvszemle,* 117 (2001), 301–17.

Knapp, Éva. *Pietás és Literatúra: Irodalomkínálat és MüvelOdési program a barokk kori társulati Kiadványokban.* (Historia Litteraria 9.) Budapest: Universitas Kvk., 2001. Pp. 317.

Knell, S. J., and C. L. E. Lewis (eds.). *The Age of the Earth: From 4004 BC To AD 2002.* Bath: Geological Society, 2001. Pp. 288.

Knoblauch, Hubert. "Kommentar." *Historische Zeitschrift,* Supplement (2001), 333–37.

Knoeff, Rina. "The Making of a Calvinist Chemist: Herman Boerhaave, God, Fire and Truth." *Ambix,* 48 (2001), 102–11.

Kolchinsky, Eduard I. (ed.). *Russko-nemetskie sviazi v biologii i meditsine.* St. Petersburg: Borei, 2001. Pp. 184.

Komlos, John. "On the Biological Standard of Living of Eighteenth-Century Americans: Taller, Richer, Healthier." *Research in Economic History,* 20 (2001), 223–48.

Kondakov, Jurij Evgen'evich. "Esaul E. N. Kotel'nikov." *Voprosy Istorii,* 5 (2001), 133–40.

Kontler, László. "'Mahometan Christianity': Islam and the English Deists." Pp. 107–19 of *Frontiers of Faith: Religious Exchange and the Constitution of Religious Identities 1400–1750*. Edited by Eszter Andor and Istvan Gyorgy Toth. Budapest: Central European University European Science Foundation, 2001.

Koos, Greg. "The Irish Hedge Schoolmaster in the American Backcountry." *New Hibernia Review*, 5 (2001), 9–26.

Korman, Gerd. "Jews as a Changing People of the Talmud: An American Exploration." *Modern Judaism*, 21 (2001), 23–66.

Koslofsky, Craig. "Suicide and the Secularization of the Body in Early Modern Saxony." *Continuity and Change*, 16 (2001), 45–70.

Kottman, Karl A. (ed.). *Millenarianism and Messianism in Early Modern European Culture. Volume 2: Catholic Messianism from Savonarola to the Abbe Gregoire*. Dordrecht: Kluwer, 2001. Pp. 108.

Kow, Simon. "Maistre and Hobbes on Providential History and the English Civil War." *Clio*, 30 (2001), 267–88.

Kowalská, Eva. "The Social Function of Orthodoxy: The Lutherans in Hungary, 1700–1750." Pp. 195–201 of *Frontiers of Faith: Religious Exchange and the Constitution of Religious Identities 1400–1750*. Edited by Eszter Andor and Istvan Gyorgy Toth. Budapest: Central European University European Science Foundation, 2001.

Kowalski, Waldemar. "From the Land of Diverse Sects to National Religion: Converts to Catholicism and Reformed Franciscans in Early Modern Poland." *Church History*, 70 (2001), 482–526.

Kraybill, Donald B., and Carl F. Bowman. *On the Backroad to Heaven: Old Order Hutterites, Mennonites, Amish, and Brethren*. Baltimore: Johns Hopkins University Press, 2001. Pp. 300.

Kretzschmar, Louise. "Baptist Theological Education in Africa, Particularly in South Africa." *Baptist History and Heritage*, 36 (2001), 190–212.

Kronick, David A. "The Commerce of Letters: Networks and 'Invisible Colleges' in Seventeenth- and Eighteenth-Century Europe." *Library Quarterly*, 71 (2001), 28–43.

III: Philosophy, Science, and Religion 161

Kuehn, Manfred. *Kant: A Biography*. New York: Cambridge University Press, 2001. Pp. xxii + 544.

Kugle, Scott Alan. "Framed, Blamed and Renamed: The Recasting of Islamic Jurisprudence in Colonial South Asia." *Modern Asian Studies*, 35 (2001), 257–313.

Kuklick, Bruce. "An Edwards for the Millenium." *Religion and American Culture*, 11 (2001), 109–17.

Kulenkampff, Jens. "Macht oder Überzeugung? Spinoza und Hume über die Grundlagen des Staates." 349–74.

Kuppers-Braun, Ute. "'Kinder-Abpracticirung': Kinder zwischen den Konfessionen im 18. Jahrhundert." *Zeitschrift für Geschichtswissenschaft*, 49 (2001), 208–25.

Kushner, Tony. "A Tale of Two Port Jewish Communities: Southampton and Portsmouth Compared." *Jewish Culture and History*, 4 (2001), 87–110.

Kutty, Bilal Ahmad. "Religious and Political Origins of Saudi Arabia." *Hamdard Islamicus*, 24 (2001), 51–65.

Kuzniaeva, Sofia, and Elena Filatova (comp.) and John Klier (ed. and trans.). "The National Historical Archive of Belarus." *East European Jewish Affairs*, 31 (2001), 101–04.

Kyba, Daniel A. "Duncan McGillivray's 1800 Reconnaissance of the Upper Brazeau River." *Alberta History*, 49 (2001), 17–24.

Laffey, Paul. "John Wesley on Insanity." *History of Psychiatry*, 12 (2001), 467–79.

Lagree, Jacqueline. "Grotius: Natural Law and Natural Religion." Pp. 17–39 of *Religion, Reason and Nature in Early Modern Europe*. Edited by Robert Crocker. Dordrecht: Kluwer Academic Publishers, 2001.

Lai, Whalen, and Michael von Bruck. *Christianity and Buddhism: A Multicultural History of Their Dialogue*. Maryknoll: Orbis Books, 2001. Pp. 265.

Landau, Philippe-Èfraïm. "Olry Terquem (1782–1862): Régénerer les Juifs et réformer le Judaïsme." *Revue des Études Juives*, 160 (2001), 169–87.

Laperriere, Guy. "Les Communautés religieuses au Québec: Pour une approche par familles spirituelles." *Études d'histoire religieuse: Société canadienne d'histoire de l'Église catholique,* 67 (2001), 167–82.

Lara, María de la Paz Ramos. "Alzate y Física en sus *Gacetas de Literatura.*" Pp. 403–30 of *Periodismo científico en el siglo XVIII: José Antonio de Alzate y Ramírez.* Edited by Patricia Aceves Pastrana. Mexico: Universidad Autónoma Metropolitana Unidad Xochimilco, 2001.

Larrimore, Mark. "Substitutes for Wisdom: Kant's Practical Thought and the Tradition of the Temperaments." *Journal of the History of Philosophy,* 39 (2001), 259–86.

Larsen, Clark Spencer (ed.). *Bioarchaeology of Spanish Florida: The Impact of Colonialism.* Gainesville: University Press of Florida, 2001. Pp. 324.

Larsen, Clark Spencer, Dale L. Hutchinson, Margaret J. Schoeninger, and Lynette Norr. "Food and Stable Isotopes in La Florida." Pp. 52–81 of *Bioarchaeology of Spanish Florida: The Impact of Colonialism.* Edited by Clark Spencer Larsen. Gainesville: University Press of Florida, 2001.

Larson, Edward J. *Evolution's Workshop: God and Science on the Galápagos Islands.* New York: Basic Books, 2001. Pp. 320.

Lässig, Simone, and Karl Heinrich Pohl. "Verbürgerlichung als kulturelles Phänomen: eine jüdische Quelle." *Geschichte in Wissenschaft und Unterricht,* 52 (2001), 433–44.

Latham, John, and Louis J. Pigott (comp.). "A Letter from John Latham to Thomas Pennant, 1789." *Archives of Natural History,* 28 (2001), 257–59.

Lavrov, Aleksandr. "Les gravures religieuses commes mediatrices dans les echanges culturels (Ukraine et Russie des XVIe–XVIIIe siécles)." Pp. 267–73 of *Frontiers of Faith: Religious Exchange and the Constitution of Religious Identities 1400–1750.* Edited by Eszter Andor and Istvan Gyorgy Toth. Budapest: Central European University European Science Foundation, 2001.

Lazo, Yolanda and José Manuel Espinosa. "Alzate y las matemáticas en las *Gacetas de Literatura.*" Pp. 379–401 of *Periodismo científico en el siglo XVIII: José Antonio de Alzate y Ramírez.* Edited by Patricia Aceves Pastrana. Mexico: Universidad Autónoma Metropolitana Unidad Xochimilco, 2001.

III: Philosophy, Science, and Religion

Le Rue, Véronique. "La conception sceptique de la matière au temps de Cirey." Pp. 148–58 of *Cirey dans la vie intellectuelle: La réception de Newton en France*. Edited by François de Gandt. Oxford: Voltaire Foundation, 2001.

Lecourt, Dominique. "L'idee française de la science." *Revue des Sciences Morales et Politiques*, 3 (2001), 1–18.

Leduc, Christophe. "Géographie paroissiale en milieu urbain: l'exemple Cambresien á l'epoque moderne." *Revue du Nord*, 83 (2001), 359–79.

Leech, Peter. "Musicians in the Catholic Chapel of Catherine of Braganza, 1662–92." *Early Music*, 29 (2001), 570–87.

Lefebvre, Bernard. "La Terreur et ses victimes dans une ville de la frontière du nord. L'example de Douai (juin 1793, juillet 1794)." *Revue du Nord*, 83 (2001), 777–800.

Lefèvre, Wolfgang. *Between Leibniz, Newton, and Kant: Philosophy and Science in the Eighteenth Century*. (Boston Studies in the Philosophy of Science 220.) Boston: Kluwer Academic Publishers, 2001. Pp. xvi + 281.

Lemercier, Jean-Pierre. "Claude-Nicolas le Cat et l'Académie des sciences, belles lettres et arts de Rouen." *Histoire des Sciences médicales*, 35 (2001), 163–68.

LeMinor, Jean-Marie. "Augustin Belloste (1654–1730): Aspects de la chirurgie militaire hospitalière pendant la Guerre de Piemont-Savoie (1686–96)." *Histoire des Sciences médicales*, 35 (2001), 317–27.

Lena, Alberto. "Benjamin Franklin's 'Canada Pamphlet' or 'the Ravings of a Mad Prophet': Nationalism, Ethnicity and Imperialism." *European Journal of American Culture*, 20 (2001), 36–49.

Lerner, Lawrence Scott. "Beyond Gregoire: A Third Discourse on Jews and the French." *Modern Judaism*, 21 (2001), 199–215.

Leshchilovskaia, Inna Ivanovna. "Petr II Balkany." *Voprosy Istorii*, 2 (2001), 46–57.

Levine, Neil Ann Stuckey. "A Selection of Remedies from the Reist Notebook." *Pennsylvania Mennonite Heritage*, 24 (2001), 2–22.

Levis, R. Barry. "Whig Ecclesiology and Changes in English Church Music, 1714–1760." *European Studies Journal,* 18–19 (2001), 151–68.

Lewis, Alison. "Bicentenary of Rev. James Evans, Inventor of the Syllabic Script for the Cree: 1801–1846." *Proceedings of the Wesley Historical Society,* 53 (2001), 38–41.

Lewis, Marilyn. "'The Anabaptist Washt and Washt, and Shrunk in the Washing': John Gibb's Baptismal Controversies with Richard Carpenter and Richard Davis, c. 1652 and 1691–1692." *Journal of the United Reformed Church History Society,* 6 (2001), 632–41.

Li, Liukun. "Wenbing Mingjia Wu Jutong Shengping Shukao." [A Study of the Life of Master Doctor Wu Jutong.] *Zhonghua Yishi Zazhi (Chinese Journal of Medical History),* 31 (2001), 103–05.

Libo, Kenneth, and Abigail Kursheedt Hoffman. *The Seixas-Kursheedts and the Rise of Early American Jewry.* New York: Bloch, 2001. Pp. 101.

Lieburg, Fred van. "The Dutch Book Trade, Christian Enlightenment and the National Bibliography: The Catalogues of Johannes van Abkoude (1703–60) and Reinier Arrenberg (1733–1812)." *Quaerendo,* 31 (2001), 3–16.

Liedtke, Rainer. "Germany's Door to the World: A Haven for the Jews? Hamburg, 1590–1933." *Jewish Culture and History,* 4 (2001), 75–86.

Lim, Seung-Hwi. "Mathieu de Morgues, bon Français ou bon catholique?" *Dix-septième siècle,* 53 (2001), 655–72.

Lindman, Janet Moore, and Michele Lise Tarter (eds.). *A Centre of Wonders: The Body in Early America.* Ithaca: Cornell University Press, 2001. Pp. vii + 283; illustrations.

Lindmark, Daniel. "Literature for Swedish Lutherans in Colonial America, 1696–1730." *Paedagogica Historica,* 37 (2001), 35–54.

Little, Ann M. "The Life of Mother Marie-Joseph de l'Enfant Jesus, or, How a Little English Girl from Wells Became a Big French Politician." *Maine History,* 40 (2001), 278–308.

Little, Patrick. "The Irish 'Independents' and Viscount Lisle's Lieutenancy of Ireland." *Historical Journal,* 44 (2001), 941–61.

Liu, Peng. "Meiguo de Zhengjiao Guanxi" [On the Relationship between Politics and Religion in America]. *Meiguo Yanjiu (American Studies Quarterly),* 15 (2001), 83–100.

Liu, Zhenggang. "Mingqing Aomen Nuxing Yanjiu" [A Study of Macao Women in the Ming and Qing Dynasties]. *Lishi Dang'an,* 2 (2001), 84–90.

Lobachev, S. V. "Patriarch Nikon's Rise to Power." *Slavic and Eastern European Review,* 79 (2001), 290–307. Nikon's dates: 1605–1681.

Locqueneux, Robert. "La physique expérimentale vers 1740: expériences, systèmes et hypothèses." Pp. 90–111 of *Cirey dans la vie intellectuelle: La réception de Newton en France.* Edited by François de Gandt. Oxford: Voltaire Foundation, 2001.

Lodge, Paul. "Leibniz's Notion of an Aggregate." *British Journal for the History of Philosophy,* 9 (2001), 467–86.

Loker, Zvi, and Herbert C. Zafren (collaborator). "Da Zaras in Italy and the Jewish Presence in Zadar (Zara)." *Studies in Bibliography and Booklore,* 21 (2001), 74–81.

Longstaffe-Gowan, Todd. *The London Town Garden, 1700–1840.* New Haven: Yale University Press, 2001. Pp. 289.

Loptson, Peter. "Hellenism, Freedom, and Morality in Hume and Johnson." *Hume Studies,* 27 (2001), 161.

Losonsky, Michael. *Enlightenment and Action from Descartes to Kant: Passionate Thought.* Cambridge: Cambridge University Press, 2001. Pp. xvii + 221.

Loughran, Trish. "The First American Contrasts: Region and Nation under the Articles of Confederation." *Explorations in Early American Culture,* 5 (2001), 230–59.

Louis-Courvoisier, Micheline. "Le malade et son médecin: le cadre de la relation thérapeutique dans la deuxième moitie du XVIII siècle." *Canadian Bulletin of Medical History,* 18 (2001), 277–96.

Loveland, Jeff. *Rhetoric and Natural History: Buffon in Polemical and Literary Context.* Oxford: Voltaire Foundation, 2001. Pp. 214.

Lowengard, Sarah. "Colour Quality and Production: Testing Colour in Eighteenth-Century France." *Journal of Design History,* 14 (2001), 91–103.

Ludwig, Bernd. "David Humes 'ewige Schranke' gegen den Aberglauben." *Zeitschrift für philosophische Forschung*, 55 (2001), 52–78.

Ludwig, Frieder. "Zur 'Verteidigung und Verbreitung des Glaubens': Das Wirken der Jesuiten in Ubersee und seine Rezeption in den Konfessionellen Auseinandersetzungen Europas." *Zeitschrift für Kirchengeschichte,* 112 (2001), 44–64.

Ludwin, Dawn M. *Blaise Pascal's Quest for the Ineffable.* (New Perspectives in Philosophical Scholarship, 16.) New York: Peter Lang, 2001. Pp. xi + 159.

Luque Alcaide, Elisa. "¿Entre Roma y Madrid? La reforma regalista y el Sínodo de Charcas (1771–1773)." *Anuario de Estudios Americanos,* 58 (2001), 473–93.

Lushpai, Vladimir Borisovich. "Antipapskaia Propaganda Belorusskikh Iezuitov vo Vtoroi Polovine XVIII Veka." *Voprosy Istorii,* 8 (2001), 124–33.

Lynch, William T. *Solomon's Child: Method in the Early Royal Society of London.* Stanford: Stanford University Press, 2001. Pp. 292.

Lyons, Clare A. "Single in the Quaker City." *Reviews in American History,* 29 (2001), 15–22.

Lyons, Jack C. "General Rules and the Justification of Probable Belief in Hume's Treatise." *Hume Studies*, 27 (2001), 247–77.

Macaulay, John Allen. *Unitarianism in the Antebellum South: The Other Invisible Institution.* Tuscaloosa: University of Alabama, 2001. Pp. xiii + 222.

MacDonald, Stuart. *The Witches of Fife: Witch-Hunting in a Scottish Shire, 1560–1710.* East Linton: Tuckwell Press, 2001. Pp. 232.

MacGregor, Arthur. "The Ashmolean as a Museum of Natural History, 1683–1860." *Journal of the History of Collections,* 13 (2001), 125–44.

Maciulyte, Kristina. "Pamokslo Ypatybes XVIII A. Mazojoje Lietuvoje: Pietizmo ir Svietimo Ideju Itaka." *Lituanistica,* 2 (2001), 118–27.

Maclean, Kama. "Conflicting Spaces: The Kumbh Mela and the Fort of Allahabad." *South Asia,* 24 (2001), 135–59.

Maddox, Randy L. "Be Ye Perfect?" *Christian History,* 20 (2001), 32–34.

Magnin, Charles, and Marco Marcacci. "Le projet de réforme du Collège (1774): Entre instruction publique, politique et économie." Pp. 409–29 of *H.-B. de Saussure (1740–1799): Un Regard sur la Terre.* Edited by René Sigrist. Geneva: Georg Editeur, 2001.

Mahlke, Regina. *Der Reale Nutz: Angewandte Wissenschaften in Preussen Im 18. Jahrhundert.* Berlin: Staatsbibliothek zu Berlin-Preussischer Kulturbesitz, 2001. Pp. 170.

Maimon, Salomon. *Solomon Maimon: An Autobiography.* Urbana: University of Illinois Press, 2001. Pp. xxxvii + 307.

Maio, Marcos Chor, and Carlos Eduardo Calaca. "New Christians and Jews in Brazil: Migrations and Antisemitism." *Shofar,* 19 (2001), 73–85.

Malik, Iftikhar H. "Ireland, Orientalism and South Asia." *Asian Affairs,* 32 (2001), 189–94.

Manfredi, Tommaso. "Architettura della gloria—architettura della memoria. La committenza asburgicopraghese per la testa di canonizzazione di Giovanni Nepomuceno e l'eredità del progetto di Borromini per la faccinta di San Giovanni in Laterano." *Römische Historische Mitteilungen,* 43 (2001), 561–86.

Mann, Kristin Dutcher. "Music and Popular Religiosity in Northern New Spain." *Catholic Southwest: A Journal of History and Culture,* 12 (2001), 7–27.

Mantilla, R. Luis Carlos. "Fray Francisco Florido: Un Franciscano Patriota al Servicio de Ramiriqui." *Boletin de Historia y Antiguedades,* 88 (2001), 675–714.

Manuel-Gismondi, Vincent. "Un document conservé chez les Maraldi sur « Le parfait ingénieur » de Cassini III." Pp. 155–65 of *Sur les traces des Cassini: Astronomes et observatoires du sud de la France.* Edited by Paul Brouzeng and Suzanne Débarbat. Paris: Comité des travaux historiques et scientifiques, 2001.

Mapp, Paul. "French Reactions to the British Search for a Northwest Passage from Hudson Bay and the Origins of the Seven Years' War." *Terrae Incognitae,* 33 (2001), 13–32.

Marcil, Yasmine. "Saussure, savant ou voyageur? Les Voyages dans les Alpes dans les périodiques des années 1780." Pp. 351–65 of *H.-B. de Saussure (1740–1799): Un Regard sur la Terre.* Edited by René Sigrist. Geneva: Georg Editeur, 2001.

Mariña, Jacqueline. "The Religious Significance of Kant's Ethics." *American Catholic Philosophical Quarterly*, 75 (2001), 179–200.

Marsden, William E. *The School Textbook: Geography, History, and Social Studies*. Portland: Woburn, 2001. Pp. 305.

Marshall, Patricia Phillips. "The Legendary Thomas Day: Debunking the Popular Mythology of an African American Craftsman." *North Carolina Historical Review*, 78 (2001), 32–66.

Marshall, John. "Locke, Socinianism, 'Socinianism', and Unitarianism." Pp. 111–82 of *English Philosophy in the Age of Locke*. (Oxford Studies in the History of Philosophy 3). Edited by M. A. Stewart. Oxford: Clarendon Press, 2001.

Martin, Joel W. *The Land Looks after Us: A History of Native American Religion*. New York: Oxford University Press, 2001. Pp. xiv + 156; illustrations; map.

Martin, Philippe. "Le livre de piété (1640 vers 1850). Approche méthodologique et premières conclusions." *Revue historique de l'eglise de France*, 87 (2001), 135–49.

Martin, Xavier. *Human Nature and the French Revolution: From the Enlightenment to the Napoleonic Code*. (Polygons 3.) Translated by Patrick Corcoran. Oxford: Berghahn Books, 2001. Pp. viii + 292.

Marx, William. "Le couronnement de Voltaire ou Pétrarque perverti." *Histoire, Economie et Société*, 20 (2001), 199–210.

Marzagalli, Silvia. "Atlantic Trade and Sephardim Merchants in Eighteenth-Century France: The Case of Bordeaux." Pp. 268–86 of *The Jews and the Expansion of Europe to the West, 1450–1800*. Edited by Paolo Bernardini and Norman Fiering. New York: Berghahn Books, 2001.

Mascarenhas, Vijay. "Hume's Recantation Revisited." *Hume Studies*, 27 (2001), 279–99.

Mason, J. C. S. *The Moravian Church and the Missionary Awakening in England, 1760–1800*. (Royal Historical Society Studies in History. New Series.) Woodbridge: Boydell Press, 2001. Pp. xv + 229.

Masters, Bruce. *Christians and Jews in the Ottoman Arab World: The Roots of Sectarianism*. New York: Cambridge University Press, 2001. Pp. 222.

III: Philosophy, Science, and Religion

Masui, Shitsuyo. "Joji Hoitofuirudo to Kanda Seiyo Fukuin Shugi Bunka No Seiritsu: 1738–1771." *Journal of American and Canadian Studies,* 19 (2001), 61–83.

Matar, Nabil. "Britons, Muslims, and American Indians: Gender and Power." *The Muslim World,* 91 (2001), 371–80.

Matsuura, Shigeru. "1709 Nen Iezusu Kaishi Rejisu No Enkai Chiho Chosa." *Shirin,* 84 (2001), 77–108.

Matusikova, Lenka. "Die Juden im Ersten Böhmischen Kataster, 1653–1655." *Judaica Bohemiae,* 37 (2001), 5–91.

Maurer, Trude. "Plädoyer für eine vergleichende Erforschung der jüdischen Geschichte Deutschlands und Osteuropas." *Geschichte und Gesellschaft,* 27 (2001), 308–26.

Maxwell-Stuart, P. G. *Witchcraft in Europe and the New World, 1400–1800.* London: Palgrave, 2001. Pp. 119.

Mayhew, Robert J. "'Where Was Enlightenment?' English Problems, English Answers." *Journal of Historical Geography,* 27 (2001), 436–40.

Mazek, Dorota, and Agnieszka Kreczmar (trans.). "The Wardship of the Mentally Ill in the Polish-Lithuanian Commonwealth in the Second Half of the 18th Century." *Acta Poloniae Historica,* 83 (2001), 95–122.

Mazzotti, Massimo. "Maria Gaetana Agnesi: Mathematics and the Making of the Catholic Enlightenment." *Isis,* 92 (2001), 656–83.

McCaffrey, John F. "The Catholic Chuch and Scottish Politics since 1707." Pp. 22–47 of *The Scottish Churches and the Union Parliament 1707–1999.* Edited by James Kirk. Edinburgh: Scottish Church History Society, 2001.

McCarthy, Keely. "Conversion, Identity, and the Indian Missionary." *Early American Literature,* 36 (2001), 353–69.

McClellan, Chris. "The Legacy of Georges Cuvier in Auguste Comte's Natural Philosophy." *Studies in History and Philosophy of Science,* 32A (2001), 1–29.

McCoy, Rebecca. "Religious Accommodation and Political Authority in an Alsatian Community, 1648–1715." *Journal of Ecclesiastical History,* 52 (2001), 244–81.

McDannell, Coleen (ed.). *Religions of the United States in Practice*. 2 volumes. Princeton: Princeton University Press, 2001. Pp. 528; 488.

McDermott, Rachel Fell. *Mother of My Heart, Daughter of My Dreams: Kali and Uma in the Devotional Poetry of Bengal*. New York: Oxford University Press, 2001. Pp. 437.

McDermott, Rachel Fell. *Singing to the Goddess: Poems to Kali and Uma from Bengal*. New York: Oxford University Press, 2001. Pp. 208.

McEvoy, John. "Postpositivist Interpretations of the Chemical Revolution." *Canadian Journal of History*, 36 (2001), 453–69.

McEwan, Bonnie G. "The Spiritual Conquest of La Florida." *American Anthropologist*, 103 (2001), 633–44.

McFarland, Cynthia (ed.). "A Newly Discovered Document and a Fresh View of an American Leader: Bishop William White's *An Essay on High-Church Principles.*" *Anglican and Episcopal History*, 70 (2001), 4–39.

McGrayne, Sharon Bertsch. *Prometheans in the Lab: Chemistry and the Making of the Modern World*. New York: McGraw-Hill, 2001. Pp. 243.

McHugh, Timothy J. "The Hopital General, the Parisian Elites and Crown Social Policy During the Reign of Louis XIV." *French History*, 15 (2001), 235–53.

McMahon, Darrin M. *Enemies of the Enlightenment: The French Counter-Enlightenment and the Making of Modernity*. New York: Oxford University Press, 2001. Pp. 288.

McNab, David, Bruce Hodgins, and Dale Standen. "'Black with Canoes.' Aboriginal Resistance and the Canoe: Diplomacy, Trade and Warfare in the Meeting Grounds of Northeastern North America, 1600–1821." Pp. 237–92 of *Technology, Disease and Colonial Conquests, Sixteenth to Eighteenth Centuries: Essays Reappraising the Guns and Germs Theories*. Edited by George Raudzens. Boston: Brill, 2001.

McOuat, Gordon. "Cataloguing Power: Delineating 'Competent Naturalists' and the Meaning of Species in the British Museum." *British Journal for the History of Science*, 34 (2001), 1–28.

Melton, James Van Horn. "Pietism, Politics, and the Public Sphere in Germany." Pp. 294–333 of *Religion and Politics in Enlightenment Europe*. Edited by James E. Bradley and Dale K. Van Kley. Notre Dame: University of Notre Dame Press, 2001.

III: Philosophy, Science, and Religion

Melton, James van Horn. *The Rise of the Public in Enlightenment Europe.* (New Approaches to European History.) Cambridge: Cambridge University Press, 2001. Pp. xiv + 284.

Menze, Ernest A. "Benjamin Franklin Seen with German Eyes: Selective Co-Optations by German Authors." *Yearbook of German-American Studies,* 36 (2001), 29–46.

Mercer, Christia. *Leibniz's Metaphysics: Its Origins and Development.* Cambridge: Cambridge University Press, 2001. Pp. xiii + 528.

Mercer, Matthew. "Dissenting Academies and the Education of the Laity, 1750–1850." *History of Education,* 30 (2001), 35–58.

Messmer, Marietta. "Negotiations of Cultural Identity and Poetic Agency in Anne Bradstreet's Seventeenth-Century London and Boston Editions." *Studies in Puritan American Spirituality,* 7 (2001), 51–79.

Metzger, Hans-Dieter. "Heiden, Juden oder Teufel? Milleniarismus and Indianermission in Massachusetts, 1630–1700." *Geschichte and Gesellschaft,* 27 (2001), 118–48.

Meyer, Annette. "Das Projekt einer 'Natural History of Man' in der schottischen Aufklärung." *Storia della Storiografia,* 39 (2001), 93–102.

Meyer, Jeffrey F. *Myths in Stone: Religious Dimensions of Washington, D.C.* Berkeley: University of California Press, 2001. Pp. 343.

Meyers, Robert. "Was Locke an Empiricist?" *Locke Studies,* 1 (2001), 63–85.

Meynell, Guy. "Locke as a Pupil of Peter Stahl." *Locke Studies,* 1 (2001), 221–27.

Michaels, Leon. *The Eighteenth-Century Origin of Angina Pectoris: Predisposing Causes, Recognition and Aftermath.* London: Wellcome Trust Centre for the History of Medicine at UCL, 2001. Pp. 219.

Michéa, Hubert. "Le voyage à la mer du Sud par Amédée Frézier: routines de navigation et longitudes corrigées (1711–1713)." Pp. 271–78 of *Sur les traces des Cassini: Astronomes et observatoires du sud de la France.* Edited by Paul Brouzeng and Suzanne Débarbat. Paris: Comité des travaux historiques et scientifiques, 2001.

Michels, Georg. "Rescuing the Orthodox: The Church Policies of Archbishop Afanasii of Kholmogory, 1682–1702." Pp. 19–37 of *Of Religion and Empire: Missions, Conversion, and*

Tolerance in Tsarist Russia. Edited by Robert P. Geraci and Michael Khodarkovsky. Ithaca: Cornell University Press, 2001.

Mignot, Arthur T. "'Mon Plaisir' and the Methodists of Guernsey." *Proceedings of the Wesley Historical Society,* 53 (2001), 42–45.

Milford, T. A. "J. S. J. Gardiner, Early National Letters, and the Perserverance of British-American Culture." *Anglican and Episcopal History*, 70 (2001), 407–37.

Miller, David W. "Irish Christianity and Revolution." Pp. 195–210 of *Revolution, Counter-Revolution and Union: Ireland in the 1790s*. Edited by Jim Smyth. Cambridge: Cambridge University Press, 2001.

Miller, Jacqueline C. "The Body Politic and the Body Somatic: Benjamin Rush's Fear of Social Disorder and His Treatment of Yellow Fever." Pp. 61–74 of *A Centre of Wonders: The Body in Early America*. Edited by Janet Moore Lindman and Michele Lise Tarter. Ithaca: Cornell University Press, 2001.

Miller, Jonathan. "Magnetic Mockeries." *Social Research,* 68 (2001), 717–40.

Miller, Peter N. "The 'Antiquarianization' of Biblical Scholarship and the London Polyglot Bible (1653–57)." *Journal of the History of Ideas*, 62 (2001), 463–82.

Miller, Stephen. *Three Deaths and Enlightenment Thought: Hume, Johnson, Marat*. Lewisburg: Bucknell University Press, 2001. Pp. 219.

Mills, Elizabeth Shown. "Quintanilla's Crusade, 1775–1783: 'Moral Reform' and Its Consequences on the Natchitoches Frontier." *Louisiana History,* 42 (2001), 277–302.

Mills, Randy J. "'I Wish the World to Look Upon Them as My Murderers': A Story of Cultural Violence on the Ohio Valley Frontier." *Ohio Valley History*, 1 (2001), 21–30.

Milton, J. R. "Locke and Gassendi: A Reappraisal." Pp. 87–109 of *English Philosophy in the Age of Locke*. (Oxford Studies in the History of Philosophy 3.) Edited by M. A. Stewart. Oxford: Clarendon Press, 2001.

Milton, J. R. "Locke, Medicine and the Mechanical Philosophy." *British Journal for the History of Philosophy,* 9 (2001), 221–43.

III: Philosophy, Science, and Religion

Milton, J. R. "Some Recent Additions to Locke's Correspondence." *Locke Studies*, 1 (2001), 229–33.

Minkema, Kenneth P. "Old Age and Religion in the Writings and Life of Jonathan Edwards." *Church History*, 70 (2001), 674–704.

Minken, Anne. "Etnisk identitet og yrkesidentitet: en innvandrergruppe og etterkommerne deres 1741–1865." *Historisk tidsskrift*, 80 (2001), 459–78.

Mirafuentes Galván, José Luis. "Los maleficios de Don Marcos Humuta: orden y conflicto en una comunidad Opata de Sonora (Bacerac, 1704)." *Estudios de Historia Novohispaña*, 25 (2001), 117–54.

Moore, D. T. "Some Aspects of the Work of Robert Brown and the Investigator Naturalists in Madeira During August 1801." *Archives of Natural History*, 28 (2001), 383–94.

Moral Roncal, Antonio Manuel. "La impronta religiosa en la vida del Infante Don Carlos Maria Isidro de Borbón." *Hispania Sacra*, 53 (2001), 111–31.

Moran Orti, Manuel. "El libro religioso durante la crisis del Antiguo Régimen: un estudio cuantitativo a través del Diario de Madrid." *Hispania Sacra*, 53 (2001), 133–48.

Moreno, Deborah. "'Here the Society Is United': 'Respectable' Anglos and Intercultural Marriage in Pre-Gold Rush California." *California History*, 80 (2001), 2–17.

Morgan, Kenneth. "Slavery and the Debate over Ratification of the United States Constitution." *Slavery and Abolition*, 22 (2001), 40–65.

Moscoso, Javier. "Los efectos de la imaginación: medicina, ciencia y sociedad en el siglo XVIII." *Asclepio*, 53 (2001), 141–71.

Mossner, Ernest Campbell. *The Life of David Hume*. 2nd edition. Oxford: Clarendon Press of Oxford University Press, 2001. Pp. xx + 709.

Mostashari, Firouzeh. "Colonial Dilemmas: Russian Policies in the Muslim Caucasus." Pp. 229–49 of *Of Religion and Empire: Missions, Conversion, and Tolerance in Tsarist Russia*. Edited by Robert P. Geraci and Michael Khodarkovsky. Ithaca: Cornell University Press, 2001.

Mott, Luiz. "Os filhos da dissidência: O pecado de sodomia e sua nefanda matéria." *Tempo*, 6 (2001), 189–204.

Mott, Luiz. "Meu menino lindo: cartas de amor de um frade sodomita, Lisboa (1690)." *Luso-Brazilian Review*, 38 (2001), 97–115.

Muchembled, Richard. "Introduction: Frontières vives: La naissance du sujet en Europe (XVe–XVIIe siècle)." Pp. 1–8 of *Frontiers of Faith: Religious Exchange and the Constitution of Religious Identities 1400–1750*. Edited by Eszter Andor and Istvan Gyorgy Toth. Budapest: Central European University European Science Foundation, 2001.

Muhly, Frank. "Firm Foundations in Philadelphia: The Lewis and Clark Expedition's Ties to Pennsylvania." *Pennsylvania Heritage*, 27 (2001), 14–21.

Muller, Michael. "La suppression des Jésuites dans le royaume de France en 1764 et la réorganisation du College de Louis-le-Grand par le Parlement de Paris: analyse des sources manuscrites conservées dans les Archives Nationales et dans la Bibliothèque Nationale de France, Paris." *Francia*, 28 (2001), 155–61.

Müller-Bahlke, Thomas J. (ed.). *Gott zur Ehr und zu des Landes Besten. Die Franckeschen Stiftungen und Preussen: Aspekte einer alten Allianz*. Ausstellung in den Franckeschen Stiftungen zu Halle. Vom 26. Halle: Verlag der Franckeschen Stiftungen, 2001. Pp. 383.

Mulligan, Lotte. "Robert Boyle, 'The Christian Virtuoso' and the Rhetoric of 'Reason'." Pp. 97–116 of *Religion, Reason and Nature in Early Modern Europe*. Edited by Robert Crocker. Dordrecht: Kluwer Academic Publishers, 2001.

Mungello, D. E. "Fact and Fantasy in the Sexual Seduction of Chinese Converts by Catholic Priests: The Case of the 120 Martyrs." *Sino-Western Cultural Relations Journal*, 23 (2001), 8–21.

Munson, Cheryl Ann, and Della Collins Cook. "Residential Mortuary Practices and Skeletal Biology at the Late Mississippian Hovey Lake Site, Posey County, Indiana." *Midcontinental Journal of Archaeology*, 26 (2001), 1–52.

Murphy, Larry. *Down by the Riverside: Readings in African American Religion*. New York: New York University Press, 2001. Pp. 495.

Murphy, Thomas. *Jesuit Slaveholding in Maryland, 1717–1838*. (Studies in African American History and Culture.) New York: Routledge, 2001. Pp. 258.

Murray, Laura J. "Joining Signs with Words: Missionaries, Metaphors, and the Massachusetts Language." *New England Quarterly*, 74 (2001), 62–93.

III: Philosophy, Science, and Religion

Mursell, Gordon. *English Spirituality: From 1700 to the Present Day.* Westminster John Knox Press, 2001. Pp. x + 580.

Musa, Sulaiman. "Islam among the Nupe People of Northern Nigeria." *Journal of the Pakistan Historical Society,* 49 (2001), 19–28.

Muto, Giovanni. "Sacred Places in Spanish Naples during the Counter-Reformation." Pp. 99–105 of *Frontiers of Faith: Religious Exchange and the Constitution of Religious Identities 1400–1750.* Edited by Eszter Andor and Istvan Gyorgy Toth. Budapest: Central European University European Science Foundation, 2001.

Myers, Marya C., and Donald W. James, Jr. "William James of Scituate and Boston, Shipwright and Quaker." *New England Historical and Genealogical Register,* 155 (2001), 36–68.

Myles, Anne G. "From Monster to Martyr: Re-Presenting Mary Dyer." *Early American Literature,* 36 (2001), 1–30.

Nadell, Pamela S., and Jonathan D. Sarna (eds.). *Women and American Judaism: Historical Perspectives.* Hanover: University Press of New England, 2001. Pp. 322.

Nahon, Gérard. "The Portugese Jewish Nation of Saint-Esprit-lès-Bayonne: The American Dimension." Pp. 254–67 of *The Jews and the Expansion of Europe to the West, 1450–1800.* Edited by Paolo Bernardini and Norman Fiering. New York: Berghahn Books, 2001.

Naidu, B. Narasingaraja. "Placing Christian Studies in the Right Perspective." *Indica,* 38 (2001), 301–08.

Nate, Richard. "'Plain and Vulgarly Express'd': Margaret Cavendish and the Discourse of the New Science." *Rhetorica,* 19 (2001), 403–17.

Nelson, E. Charles. "Patrick Browne M. D. (c. 1720–1790), an Irish Doctor in the Caribbean: His Residence on Saint Croix (1757–1765) and His Unpublished Accounts of Volcanic Activity on Montserrat." *Archives of Natural History,* 28 (2001), 135–47.

Nelson, John K. *A Blessed Company: Parishes, Parsons, and Parishioners in Anglican Virginia, 1690–1776.* Chapel Hill: University of North Carolina Press, 2001. Pp. 477.

Neufeld, Hermann, and John D. Thiesen (trans.). "Prussian Mennonite Sermon from 1790." *Mennonite Life,* 56 (2001).

Newberry, Paul A. "Joseph Butler on Forgiveness: A Presupposed Theory of Emotion." *Journal of the History of Ideas*, 62 (2001), 233–44.

Newson, Linda. "Pathogens, Places and Peoples: Geographical Variations in the Impact of Disease in Early Spanish America and the Philippines." Pp. 167–210 of *Technology, Disease and Colonial Conquests, Sixteenth to Eighteenth Centuries: Essays Reappraising the Guns and Germs Theories*. Edited by George Raudzens. Boston: Brill, 2001.

Ng, On-Cho. *Cheng-Zhu Confucianism in the Early Qing: Li Guangdi (1642–1718) and Qing Learning*. Albany: State University of New York Press, 2001. Pp. 267.

Ni, Peimin. *On Reid*. (Wadsworth Philosophers Series.) Belmont: Wadsworth/Thomson Learning, 2001. Pp. 84.

Nichols, Joel A. "A Man True to His Principles: John Joachim Zubly and Calvinism." *Journal of Church and State*, 43 (2001), 297–317.

Nicoletta, Julie. "The Gendering of Order and Disorder: Mother Ann Lee and Shaker Architecture." *New England Quarterly*, 74 (2001), 303–16.

Nikitin, Nikolai Ivanovich. "Semen Dezhnev." *Voprosy Istorii*, 4 (2001), 135–44.

Nikolow, Sybilla. "A. F. W. Crome's Measurements of the 'Strength of the State': Statistical Representations in Central Europe around 1800." *History of Political Economy*, 33 (2001), 23–56.

Nockles, Peter B. "A Disputed Legacy: Anglican Historiographies of the Reformation from the Era of the Caroline Divines to That of the Oxford Movement." *Bulletin of the John Rylands University Library of Manchester*, 83 (2001), 121–67.

Noel, Charles C. "Clerics and Crown in Bourbon Spain, 1700–1808: Jesuits, Jansenists, and Enlightened Reformers." Pp. 119–53 of *Religion and Politics in Enlightenment Europe*. Edited by James E. Bradley and Dale K. Van Kley. Notre Dame: University of Notre Dame Press, 2001.

Noel, Jan. "Besieged but Connected: Survival Strategies at a Quebec Convent." *Historical Studies: Canadian Catholic Historical Association*, 67 (2001), 27–41.

Noel, Jan. "Caste and Clientage in an Eighteenth-Century Quebec Convent." *Canadian Historical Review*, 82 (2001), 465–90.

III: Philosophy, Science, and Religion

Noll, Mark A. "Methodism Unbound." *Reviews in American History,* 29 (2001), 192–97.

Norris, Jim. "Franciscans Eclipsed: Church and State in Spanish New Mexico, 1750–1780." *New Mexico Historical Review,* 76 (2001),: 161–74.

Norton, David Fate. "From John Locke to Dugald Stewart." *Journal of the History of Ideas,* 62 (2001), 359–65.

Norton, Mary Beth. "George Burroughs and the Girls from Casco: The Maine Roots of Salem Witchcraft." *Maine History,* 40 (2001), 258–77.

Novinsky, Anita. "Marranos and the Inquisition: On the Gold Route in Minas Gerais, Brazil." Pp. 215–41 of *The Jews and the Expansion of Europe to the West, 1450–1800.* Edited by Paolo Bernardini and Norman Fiering. New York: Berghahn Books, 2001.

Novinsky, Anita. "Ser marrano em Minas Colonial." *Revista Brasileira de História,* 21 (2001), 161–76.

Nuchelmans, J. C. F. "Het prekenboek en het preekvademecum van Vranck Verburch, pastoor te Poeldijk 1647–1708." *Trajecta,* 10 (2001), 62–76.

Nuland, Sherwin B. "The Uncertain Art: Grave Robbing." *American Scholar,* 70 (2001), 125–28.

Nuovo, Victor. "Locke's Theology, 1694–1704." Pp. 183–215 of *English Philosophy in the Age of Locke.* (Oxford Studies in the History of Philosophy 3.) Edited by M. A. Stewart. Oxford: Clarendon Press, 2001.

Nuttall, Geoffrey F. "The Speldhurst Church Book." *Journal of the United Reformed Church History Society,* 6 (2001), 557–67.

Oden, Tom. "Weeds in the Garden." *Christian History,* 20 (2001), 43–45.

Oehler, K. Eberhard. "'Der zeigt dir einen andern Weg, als du vormal erkannt': Der Pietist and Psalmensänger Michael Miller (1673–1704)." *Blätter für württemburgische Kirchengeschichte,* 101 (2001), 49–69.

O'Fahey, R. S. "A Colonial Servant: Al-Salawi and the Sudan." *Sudanic Africa,* 12 (2001), 33–42.

OhAnnrachain, Eoghan. "Some Early Wild Geese at the Invalides." *Irish Sword*, 22 (2001), 249–64.

OhAnnrachain, Tadg. *Catholic Reformation in Ireland: The Mission of Rinuccini, 1645–1649*. New York: Oxford University Press, 2001. Pp. 324.

O'Hara, Matthew. "Politics and Piety: The Church in Colonial and Nineteenth-Century Mexico." *Mexican Studies*, 17 (2001), 213–31.

Okudaira, Ryuji, and Andrew Huxley. "A Burmese Tract on Kingship: Political Theory in the 1782 Manuscript of Manugye." *Bulletin of the School of Oriental and African Studies*, 64 (2001), 248–59.

Olden-Jørgensen, Sebastian. "Die Konversion Niels Steensens (1667) und der frühneuzeitliche Deismus." *Historisches Jahrbuch*, 121 (2001), 97–114.

Olin, Margaret. *The Nation without Art: Examining Modern Discourses on Jewish Art*. Lincoln: University of Nebraska Press, 2001. Pp. 275.

Oliveira, Rosiska Darcy de. "500 Years of Brazil: Global and Cultural Perspectives." *Luso-Brazilian Review*, 38 (2001), 5–9.

Olleson, Philip (ed.). *The Complete Professional Correspondence of Samuel Wesley (1766–1837)*. New York: Oxford University Press, 2001. Pp. 976.

Olmi, Giuseppe. "Museums on Paper in Emilia-Romagna from the Sixteenth to the Nineteenth Centuries: From Aldrovandi to Count Sanvitale." *Archives of Natural History*, 28 (2001), 157–78.

Olson, Alison G. "Huguenots and Palatines." *Historian*, 63 (2001), 269–85.

Olson, Alison Gilbert. "Pennsylvania Satire Before the Stamp Act." *Pennsylvania History*, 68 (2001), 507–32.

Opsomer, Carmélia. "Un foyer d'études sous l'Ancien Régime: le Collège des Jésuites anglais de Liège." *Académie royale de Belgique. Bulletin de la classe des Lettres et des Sciences Morales et Politiques*, 12 (2001), 11–39.

Opwis, Felicitas. "Is Smoking Permissible in Islamic Law? Answers from Arabic Manuscripts in the Beinecke Collection." *Yale University Library Gazette*, Supplement (2001), 178–84.

III: Philosophy, Science, and Religion

Orchard, Stephen. "The Wilson Family and Derbyshire." *Journal of the United Reformed Church History Society,* 6 (2001), 570–89.

Orlandi, Giuseppi. "Otto lettere inedite di S. Alfonso [1696–1787]." *Spicilegium Historicum C.SS.R.*, 49 (2001), 457–74.

Orlin, Lena Cowen. "Rewriting Stone's Renaissance." *Huntington Library Quarterly,* 64 (2001), 188–230.

Ormsby-Lennon, Hugh. "The Correspondence of Jonathan Swift." *Anglican and Episcopal History,* 70 (2001), 498–503.

Othow, Helen Chavis. *John Chavis: African American Patriot, Preacher, Teacher, and Mentor (1763–1838).* Jefferson: McFarland, 2001. Pp. 216.

Owczarski, Adam, C.SS.R. "Bibliografia hofbauriana." *Spicilegium Historicum C.SS.R.*, 49 (2001), 475–553.

Pabst-Béziat, Annette. "Les réfugiés protestants du pays castrais et leur dispersion dans le monde." Pp. 119–39 of *La Diaspora Des Hugeunots: Les réfugiés protestants de France et leur dispersion dans le monde (XVIe–XVIIIe siècles).* Edited by Eckart Birnstiel and Chrystel Bernat. Paris: Honoré Champion Éditeur, 2001.

Paiva, José Pedro. "The Portugese Secular Clergy in the Sixteenth and Seventeenth Centuries." Pp. 157–66 of *Frontiers of Faith: Religious Exchange and the Constitution of Religious Identities 1400–1750.* Edited by Eszter Andor and Istvan Gyorgy Toth. Budapest: Central European University European Science Foundation, 2001.

Paradis, Olivier. "L'encadrement médical à l'École Royale Militaire d'Effiat, 1776–1793." *Revue Historique des Armées,* 1 (2001), 87–97.

Parascandola, John. "The Contributions of David L. Cowen." Pp. 1–3 of *Apothecaries and the Drug Trade: Essays in Celebration of the Work of David L. Cowen.* Edited by Gregory J. Higby and Elaine C. Stroud. Madison: American Institute of the History of Pharmacy, 2001.

Pardoe, Elizabeth Lewis. "Poor Children and Enlightened Citizens: Lutheran Education in America, 1748–1800." *Pennsylvania History,* 68 (2001), 162–201.

Park, John Sungmin. *Theological Ethics of Friedrich Schleiermacher.* (Schleiermacher Studies and Translations, 20.) Lewiston: Edwin Mellen Press, 2001.

Parmentier, Marc. "Démonstrations et infiniment petits dans la Quadratura arithmetica de Leibniz." *Revue d'histoire des sciences,* 54 (2001), 275–89.

Parnham, David. "Politics Spun out of Theology and Prophecy: Sir Henry Vane on the Spiritual Environment of Public Power." *History of Political Thought,* 22 (2001), 53–83.

Passeron, Irène. "Muse ou élève? Sur les lettres de Clairaut à Mme Du Châtelet." Pp. 187–97 of *Cirey dans la vie intellectuelle: La réception de Newton en France.* Edited by François de Gandt. Oxford: Voltaire Foundation, 2001.

Pasternack, Lawrence. "The *ens realissimum* and Necessary Being in *The Critique of Pure Reason.*" *Religious Studies,* 37 (2001), 467–74.

Pastrana, Patricia Aceves. "Átomos y luces en los periódicos de Alzate." Pp. 221–50 of *Periodismo científico en el siglo XVIII: José Antonio de Alzate y Ramírez.* Edited by Patricia Aceves Pastrana. Mexico: Universidad Autónoma Metropolitana Unidad Xochimilco, 2001.

Patkas, Ronald D. "Conflict in the Church and in the City: The Problem of Catholic Parish Government in Boston, 1790–1865." *Historical Journal of Massachusetts,* 29 (2001), 53–76.

Paton, Bruce C. *Lewis and Clark: Doctors in the Wilderness.* Golden: Fulcrum, 2001. Pp. 228.

Patterson, Richard. "Charles Thomas Jackson M.D., Vesuvius, and the Idea of Surgical Anaesthesia." *Journal of Medical Biography,* 9 (2001), 220–25.

Paul, Michael C. "Western Negative Perceptions of Russia: 'The Cold War Mentality' over Five Hundred Years." *International Social Science Review,* 76 (2001), 103–21.

Paxman, David. "Lancashire Spiritual Culture and the Question of Magic." *Studies in Eighteenth-Century Culture,* 30 (2001), 223–43.

Payne, E. A., and Leonard J. Maguire (eds.). "The Baptist Church near the Barbican." *Baptist Quarterly,* 39 (2001), 132–45.

Pedersen, Kurt Møller. "Jacques Cassini, James Gregory, Christiaan Huygens et leurs déterminations de la distance entre Sirius et la Terre." Pp. 137–54 of *Sur les traces des*

III: Philosophy, Science, and Religion

Cassini: Astronomes et observatoires du sud de la France. Edited by Paul Brouzeng and Suzanne Débarbat. Paris: Comité des travaux historiques et scientifiques, 2001.

Pelletier, Monique. "La Carte de Cassini: lœuvre scientifique et les exigences des utilisateurs." Pp. 169–84 of *Sur les traces des Cassini: Astronomes et observatoires du sud de la France*. Edited by Paul Brouzeng and Suzanne Débarbat. Paris: Comité des travaux historiques et scientifiques, 2001.

Penslar, Derek J. *Shylock's Children: Economics and Jewish Identity in Modern Europe*. Berkeley: University of California Press, 2001. Pp. 374.

Pérez Puente, Leticia. "Dos periodos de conflicto en torno a la administración del diezmo en el arzobispado de México: 1653–1663 y 1664–1680." *Estudios de Historia Novohispaña*, 25 (2001), 15–57.

Perrin, Liese M. "Resisting Reproduction: Reconsidering Slave Contraception in the Old South." *Journal of American Studies*, 35 (2001), 255–74.

Peset, José Luis. "Símbolos e ideas en torno al comcepto de la naturaleza." Pp. 67–77 of *Periodismo científico en el siglo XVIII: José Antonio de Alzate y Ramírez*. Edited by Patricia Aceves Pastrana. Mexico: Universidad Autónoma Metropolitana Unidad Xochimilco, 2001.

Pessin, Andrew. "Malebranche's Distinction Between General and Particular Volitions." *Journal of the History of Philosophy*, 39 (2001), 77–99.

Peterson, Mark A. "Puritanism and Refinement in Early New England: Reflections on Communion Silver." *William and Mary Quarterly*, 58 (2001), 307–46.

Petzoldt, Klaus. *Der unterlegene Sieger: Valentine Ernst Löscher im absolutistischen Sachsen*. Leipzig: Evangelische Verlagsanstalt, 2001. Pp. 229.

Peumery, Jean-Jacques. "Vicq d'Azyr et la Révolution française." *Histoire des Sciences médicales*, 35 (2001), 263–70.

Pickstone, John V. *Ways of Knowing: A New History of Science, Technology, and Medicine*. Chicago: University of Chicago Press, 2001. Pp. 271.

Pietsch, Theodore W. "Charles Plumier (1646–1704) and His Drawings of French and American Fishes." *Archives of Natural History*, 28 (2001), 1–57.

Pijning, Ernst. "New Christians as Sugar Cultivators and Traders in the Portugese Atlantic, 1450–1800." Pp. 485–500 of *The Jews and the Expansion of Europe to the West, 1450–1800*. Edited by Paolo Bernardini and Norman Fiering. New York: Berghahn Books, 2001.

Pinilla Monroy, German. "El colegio mayor de Nuestra Señora del Rosario y el capitulo metropolitano de Bogota." *Boletin de Historia y Antiguedades*, 88 (2001), 885–902.

Piper, John. *The Roots of Endurance: Invincible Perseverance in the Lives of John Newton, Charles Simeon, and William Wilberforce*. Downers Grove: Intervarsity Press, 2001. Pp. 176.

Piper, John. *Tested by Fire: The Fruit of Suffering in the Lives of John Bunyan, William Cowper, and David Brainerd*. Downers Grove: Intervarsity Press, 2001. Pp. 176.

Piva, Paolo, and Maria-Rosa Simonelli. *Storia di San Benedetto Polirone: L'età della soppressione.* (Il Mondo Medievale. Sezione di Storia Medievale dell'Italia Padana 10.) Bologna: Pàtron, 2001. Pp. 235.

Polisensky, Josef. "Tschechische und Deutschböhmische Auswanderung nach Amerika." *Bohemia,* 42 (2001), 27–38.

Pomeau, René. "Voltaire et Mme Du Châtelet à Cirey: amour et travail." Pp. 9–15 of *Cirey dans la vie intellectuelle: La réception de Newton en France*. Edited by François de Gandt. Oxford: Voltaire Foundation, 2001.

Popkin, Richard H. "The Image of Judaism in Seventeenth Century Europe." Pp. 181–97 of *Religion, Reason and Nature in Early Modern Europe*. Edited by Robert Crocker. Dordrecht: Kluwer Academic Publishers, 2001.

Porret, Michel. "La voie de Paolo Zacchias: médecine et crime." *Crime, Histoire et Sociétés,* 5 (2001), 129–33.

Porter, Roy. "The Body Politic: Diseases and Discourses." *History Today,* 51 (2001), 23–29.

Porter, Roy. *Bodies Politic: Disease, Death and Doctors in Britain, 1650–1900*. Ithaca: Cornell University Press, 2001. Pp. 328.

Porter, Roy. *The Enlightenment*. 2nd edition. (Studies in European History.) New York: Palgrave, 2001. Pp. x + 90.

Porter, Roy. "Matrix of Modernity." *History Today,* 51 (2001), 24–31.

III: Philosophy, Science, and Religion 183

Porter, Roy. *Quacks: Fakers and Charlatans in English Medicine.* Stroud: Tempus, 2001. Pp. 254.

Porter, Roy S. "The Wilkins Lecture 2000. Medical Futures." *Notes and Records of the Royal Society of London,* 55 (2001), 309–23.

Potkay, Adam. "Hume's 'Supplement to Gulliver': The Medieval Volumes of the History of England." *Eighteenth-Century Life,* 25 (2001), 32–46.

Potkay, Adam. "A Response to My Critics." *Hume Studies,* 27 (2001), 173–79.

Potter, Elizabeth. *Gender and Boyle's Law of Gases.* Bloomington: Indiana University Press, 2001. Pp. xiii + 210.

Pourciau, Bruce. "A New Translation of and Guide to Newton's Principia." *Annals of Science,* 58 (2001), 85–91.

Prasmantaite, Aldona. "Del 1832 M. Kataliku Katekizmo Apie Pagarba Carui Lenku Kalba Autorystes ir jo Vertejo i Lietuviu Kalba." *Lituanistica,* 1 (2001), 27–38.

Pulsipher, Jenny Hale. "'Our Sages Are Sageles': A Letter on Massachusetts Indian Policy after King Philip's War." *William and Mary Quarterly,* 58 (2001), 431–48.

Purcell, Mark. "'A Lunatick of Unsound Mind': Edward, Lord Leigh (1742–86) and the Refounding of Oriel College Library." *Bodleian Library Record,* 17 (2001), 246–60.

"Qianlong Chunian Zhengchi Minfeng Minsu Shiliao (Shang)" [Historical Archive of the Political Customs and Folk Manners in the Early Years of Emperor Shang]. *Lishi Dang'an (Historical Archive),* 1 (2001), 28–46.

"Qianlong Chunian Zhengchi Minfeng Minsu Shiliao (Xia)" [Historical Archive of the Political Customs and Folk Manners in the Early Years of Emperor Xia]. *Lishi Dang'an (Historical Archive),* 2 (2001), 25–42.

Quadros, Eduardo Gusmao de. "A Luta Pela Lingua." *Historia: Questoes et Debates,* 18 (2001), 211–25.

Quantin, Jean-Louis. "Patristique et politique dans l'Angleterre e la Restauration." *Rivista di Storia e Litteratura Religiosa,* 36 (2001), 415–48.

Quinn, Frederick. *To Be a Pilgrim: The Anglican Ethos in History*. New York: Crossroad, 2001. Pp. 320.

Rack, Henry D. "'But, Lord, Let It Be Betsy!' Love and Marriage in Early Methodism." *Proceedings of the Wesley Historical Society*, 53 (2001), 1–13.

Raina, Dhruv. "Disciplinary Boundaries and the Civilizational Encounter: The Mathematics and Astronomy of India in Delambre's *Histoire* (1800–1820)." *Studies in History*, 17 (2001), 211–43.

Raj, Kapil. "Refashioning Civilities, Engineering Trust: William Jones, Indian Intermediaries and the Production of Reliable Legal Knowledge in Late Eighteenth-Century Bengal." *Studies in History*, 17 (2001), 175–209.

Ramati, Ayval. "The Hidden Truth of Creation: Newton's Method of Fluxions." *British Journal for the History of Science*, 34 (2001), 417–38.

Rashid, Samory. "The Islamic Origins of Spanish Florida's Ft. Musa." *Journal of Muslim Minority Affairs*, 21 (2001), 209–26.

Ratcliff, Marc J. "Pratuques, systèmes et laboratoire. Saussure et la Découverte de la division des animalcules (1765–1766)." Pp. 51–81 of *H.-B. de Saussure (1740–1799): Un Regard sur la Terre*. Edited by René Sigrist. Geneva: Georg Editeur, 2001.

Raudzens, George. "Outfighting or Outpopulating? Main Reasons for Early Colonial Conquests, 1493–1788." Pp. 31–57 of *Technology, Disease and Colonial Conquests, Sixteenth to Eighteenth Centuries: Essays Reappraising the Guns and Germs Theories*. Edited by George Raudzens. Boston: Brill, 2001.

Raudzens, George (ed.). *Technology, Disease and Colonial Conquests, Sixteenth to Eighteenth Centuries: Essays Reappraising the Guns and Germs Theories*. Boston: Brill, 2001. Pp. 304.

Rawson, Claude. *God, Gulliver, and Genocide: Barbarism and the European Imagination, 1492–1945*. New York: Oxford University Press, 2001. Pp. 418.

Ray, Mark Douglas. "Young Alabama Baptist Pastor Was a Real Pioneer, True Historian." *Alabama Baptist Historian*, 37 (2001), 15–17.

Razzell, Peter, Timothy Leunig, and Hans-Joachim Voth. "Did Smallpox Reduce Height? A Final Comment." *Economic History Review*, 54 (2001), 108–09.

III: Philosophy, Science, and Religion

Reardon, Colleen. *Holy Concord within Sacred Walls: Nuns and Music in Siena, 1575–1700.* New York: Oxford University Press, 2001. Pp. 320.

Recker, Jo Ann M. *Françoise Blin de Bourdon, Woman of Influence: The Story of the Cofoundress of the Sisters of Notre Dame.* Mahwah: Paulist, 2001. Pp. 224.

Recker, Jo Ann M. *"Tres affectueusement, votre mere en Dieu." Françoise Blin—French Aristocrat, Belgian Citizen, Co-Foundress of the Sisters of Notre Dame de Namur (1756–1838).* New York: P. Lang, 2001. Pp. 185.

Recuenco Pérez, Julian. "Religiosidad popular en Cuenca durante la Edad Moderna: El origen de las cofradías penitenciales de Semana Santa." *Hispania Sacra,* 53 (2001), 7–30.

Reedy, Gerald, S.J. "A Preface to Anglican Rationalism." Pp. 44–59 of *Eighteenth-Century Contexts: Historical Inquiries in Honor of Philip Harth.* Edited by Howard J. Weinbrot, Peter J. Schakel, and Stephen E. Karian. Madison: University of Wisconsin Press, 2001.

Reichler, Claude. "L'esthétique du paysage dans les Voyages dans les Alpes." Pp. 303–35 of *H.-B. de Saussure (1740–1799): Un Regard sur la Terre.* Edited by René Sigrist. Geneva: Georg Editeur, 2001.

Reid-Maroney, Nina. *Philadelphia's Enlightenment, 1740–1800: Kingdom of Christ, Empire of Reason.* (Contributions to the Study of World History 81.) Westport: Greenwood Press, 2001. Pp. xv + 199.

Reis, Elizabeth. "The Trouble with Angels." *Common-Place,* 1 (2001).

Rheinberger, Rudolf. "'Bemerkungen über den Sogenannten Milzbrand...': Ein Frühes Medizin-Wissenschaftliches Dokument aus Liechtenstein." *Jahrbuch des Historischen Vereins für das Fürstentum Liechtenstein,* 99 (2001), 207–16.

Richards, Peter Judson. "'A Clear Stand and Steady Channel': Isaac Backus and the Limits of Liberty." *Journal of Church and State,* 43 (2001), 447–82.

Richey, Russell E. "Denominationalism in Perspective." *Journal of Presbyterian History,* 79 (2001), 199–213.

Ricuperati, Giuseppe. *La città terrena di Pietro Giannone: Un itinerario tra "crisi della coscienza europea' e illuminismo radicale.* Studi e testi per la storia della tolleranza in Europa nei secoli XVI–XVIII, 4. Firenze: L.S. Olschki, 2001. Pp. xvi + 196.

Ricuperati, Giuseppe. "Ipotesi su Carlo Denina storico e comparatista." *Rivista Storica Italiana,* 113 (2001), 107–37.

Ricuperati, Giuseppe. "Per Marino Berengo." *Rivista Storica Italiana,* 113 (2001), 746–53.

Rieder, Philip and Vincent Barras. "Santé et maladie chez Saussure." Pp. 501–24 of *H.-B. de Saussure (1740–1799): Un Regard sur la Terre.* Edited by René Sigrist. Geneva: Georg Editeur, 2001.

Rigal, Laura. "The Electric Books of 1747." *Common-Place,* 1 (2001).

Ritzmann, Iris. "Leidenserfahrung in der historischen Betrachtung: ein Seiltanz zwischen sozialem Konstrukt und humanbiologischer Konstanz." *Historische Zeitschrift,* Supplement (2001), 59–72.

Rivers, Isabel. "Responses to Hume on Religion by Anglicans and Dissenters." *Journal of Ecclesiastical History,* 52 (2001), 675–95.

Robertson, John Kent. "Friends near the Frontier: An Account of the Development of the Hunting Creek Friends Meeting, 1794–1828." *Southern Friend,* 23 (2001), 7–42.

Roche, Daniel. "Electricité et institution sociale de la science: réflexions pour une conclusion." *Revue d'histoire des sciences,* 54 (2001), 99–114.

Rodén, Marie-Louise. "Fabio Chigi and the World beyond the Alps." Pp. 245–54 of *Frontiers of Faith: Religious Exchange and the Constitution of Religious Identities 1400–1750.* Edited by Eszter Andor and Istvan Gyorgy Toth. Budapest: Central European University European Science Foundation, 2001.

Rodríguez López-Brea, Carlos M. "¿Alianza entre trono y altar? la iglesia y la politica fiscal de Fernando VII en la Diócesis de Toledo (1814–1820)." *Spagna Contemporanea,* 10 (2001), 29–46.

Rodríguez López-Brea, Carlos M. "La crisis de la economía eclesiástica en tiempos de Carlos IV: Algunos apuntes sobre las Diócesis de Toledo y Sevilla." *Hispania Sacra,* 53 (2001), 193–211.

Roeber, A. Gregg. "The Migration of the Pious: Methodists, Pietists, and the Antinomian Character of North American Religious History." Pp. 25–47 of *Visions of the Future in*

III: Philosophy, Science, and Religion

Germany and America. Edited by Norbert Finzsch and Hermann Wellenreuther. Oxford: Berg, 2001.

Roeber, A. G. "What the Law Requires Is Written on Their Hearts: Noachic and Natural Law among German-Speakers in Early Modern North America." *William and Mary Quarterly,* 58 (2001), 883–912.

Roffidal-Motte, Emilie. "Dessins et prix-faits à Marseille et à Aix 1685–1785." *Provençe Historique,* 51 (2001), 3–12.

Rogal, Samuel J. *Susanna Annesley Wesley (1669–1742): A Biography of Strength and Love.* Bristol: Wyndham Hall, 2001. Pp. 212.

Rogal, Samuel J. *The Wesleyan Connection in Shelburne and Birchtown, Nova Scotia: Saving Souls or Catching Whales.* (Studies in the History of Missions 20.) Lewiston: Edwin Mellen Press, 2001. Pp. xiii + 200.

Rogers, G. A. J. "Nature, Man and God in the English Enlightenment." Pp. 139–58 of *Religion, Reason and Nature in Early Modern Europe.* Edited by Robert Crocker. Dordrecht: Kluwer Academic Publishers, 2001.

Rogoff, Leonard. *Homelands: Southern Jewish Identity in Durham and Chapel Hill, North Carolina.* Tuscaloosa: University of Alabama Press, 2001. Pp. 398.

Rohrer, S. Scott. "Evangelism and Acculturation in the Backcountry: The Case of Wachovia, North Carolina, 1753–1830." *Journal of the Early Republic,* 21 (2001), 199–229.

Rosa, Mario. "La Chiesa Toscana e la Pieta Illuminata." *Archivio Storico Italiano,* 159 (2001), 547–89.

Rose, Emily C. *Portraits of Our Past: Jews of the German Countryside.* Philadelphia: Jewish Publishing Society, 2001. Pp. 372.

Ross, D. Reid. "Joris and Catalina Rapalje: The First Colonists in New Netherland." *Long Island Historical Journal,* 13 (2001), 205–18.

Ross, Richard J. "Jews and Pietists in Early America. Introduction: Intersecting Diasporas." *William and Mary Quarterly,* 58 (2001), 849–54.

Rossi, Philip J. "Autonomy: Toward the Social Self–Governance of Reason." *American Catholic Philosophical Quarterly*, 75 (2001), 171–78.

Roth, Randolph. "Can Faith Change the World? Religion and Society in Vermont's Age of Reform." *Vermont History,* 69 (2001), 7–18.

Roth, Randolph. "Child Murder in New England." *Social Science History,* 25 (2001), 101–47.

Roth-Lochner, Barbara. "Comment Saussure perdit sa fortune." Pp. 471–85 of *H.-B. de Saussure (1740–1799): Un Regard sur la Terre*. Edited by René Sigrist. Geneva: Georg Editeur, 2001.

Round, Phillip H. "Anne Bradstreet's Several Poems and the Rise of Christian Belletrism in Eighteenth-Century New England." *Studies in Puritan American Spirituality,* 7 (2001), 23–50.

Rousseau, G. S. "Ingenious Pain: Fiction, History, Biography, and the Miraculous Eighteenth Century." *Eighteenth-Century Life*, 25 (2001), 47–62.

Rowland, Robert. "New Christian, Marrano, Jew." Pp. 125–48 of *The Jews and the Expansion of Europe to the West, 1450–1800*. Edited by Paolo Bernardini and Norman Fiering. New York: Berghahn Books, 2001.

Rowlands, Alison. "Witchcraft and Old Women in Early Modern Germany." *Past and Present*, 173 (2001), 50–89.

Rubin, Rehav. "Historical Geography in Israel: Ideas, Themes and Perspectives." *Cathedra*, 100 (2001), 339–60.

Rucker, Walter. "Conjure, Magic, and Power: The Influence of Afro-Atlantic Religious Practices on Slave Resistance and Rebellion." *Journal of Black Studies*, 32 (2001), 84–103.

Ruffing, Margit. "Kant-Bibliographie 1999." *Kant-Studien*, 92 (2001), 474–517.

Ruisinger, Marion M. "Auf Messers Schneide: Patientperspektiven aus der Chirurgischen Praxis Lorenz Heisters (1683–1758)." *Medizinhistorisches Journal,* 36 (2001), 309–33.

Ruiz, Roberto Gallegos. "El ilustrado José Antonio de Alzate: Sus aportaciones al conocimiento arqueológico y al reconocimiento del hombre Precolombino." Pp. 471–533 of *Periodismo científico en el siglo XVIII: José Antonio de Alzate y Ramírez*. Edited by Patricia Aceves Pastrana. Mexico: Universidad Autónoma Metropolitana Unidad Xochimilco, 2001.

III: Philosophy, Science, and Religion

Rush, Fred L. Jr. "The Harmony of the Faculties." *Kant-Studien*, 92 (2001), 38–61.

Russett, Bruce. "Not All the Nations Furiously Rage Together." Pp. 61–85 of *Higher Learning and Catholic Traditions*. Edited by Robert E. Sullivan. Notre Dame: University of Notre Dame Press, 2001.

Rutz, Michael A. "The Politicizing of Evangelical Dissent, 1811–1813." *Parliamentary History*, 20 (2001), 187–207.

Ryan, Vanessa L. "The Physiological Sublime: Burke's Critique of Reason." *Journal of the History of Ideas* 62 (2001), 265–79.

Ryden, David. "Running the Numbers: An Overview of the Trans-Atlantic Slave Trade CD-ROM." *Slavery and Abolition*, 22 (2001), 141–49.

Sacks, David Harris. "Iniquity and Regeneration: Urban Life and the Reformation in England." *Journal of British Studies*, 40 (2001), 268–79.

Safier, Neil. "Unveiling the Amazon to European Science and Society: The Reading and Reception of la Condamine's *Relation Abrégée d'un voyage fait dans l'Interieur de l'Amérique méridionale (1745)*." *Terrae Incognitae*, 33 (2001), 33–47.

Saka, Paul. "Pascal's Wager and the Many Gods Objection." *Religious Studies*, 37 (2001), 323–42.

Sakula, Alex. "Dr. John Arbuthnot (1667–1735): Royal Physician and Political Satirist." *Journal of Medical Biography*, 9 (2001), 20–22.

Salamanca Lopez, Manuel. "La Iglesia Extremeña durante la Guerra de la Independencia: Acercamiento al auto de arreglo y plan beneficial de las parroquias de Olivenza de 1810." *Hispania Sacra*, 53 (2001), 229–49.

Salls, Timothy G. X. (transcriber). "Account Book and Family Record of Robert Cook of Needham, Massachusetts." *New England Historical and Genealogical Register*, 155 (2001), 391–96.

Salomon, Ronald. "Being Good: An Abolitionist Family Attempts to Live up to Its Own Standards." *Vermont History*, 69 (2001), 32–47.

Sánchez-Albornoz, Nicolas. "De las lenguas amerindias al castellano: Ley o interaccióon en el periodo colonial." *Colonial Latin American Review,* 10 (2001), 49–67.

Sandkühler, Hans Jörg. "Die Geschichte, das Recht und der Staat als 'zweite Natur'. Zu Schellings politischer Philosophie." *Zeitschrift für philosophische Forschung* 55 (2001), 196–220.

Sankey, Margaret. "The Paradoxes of Modernity: Rational Religion and Mythical Science in the Novels of Cyrano de Bergerac." Pp. 41–59 of *Religion, Reason and Nature in Early Modern Europe.* Edited by Robert Crocker. Dordrecht: Kluwer Academic Publishers, 2001.

Sarjeant, William A. S., and Trent A. Mitchell. "A Forgotten Theory on the Origin of Fossils: Daines Barrington's Concept (1781)." *Archives of Natural History,* 28 (2001), 123–33.

Sanmartín Miguez, J. Santiago. "Los boticarios del hospital Real de Santiago de Compostela en el siglo XVIII." *Asclepio,* 53 (2001), 57–93.

Sarmiento, Francisco Javier Puerto. "José Antonio de Alzate y Ramírez ante la ciencia Española ilustrada." Pp. 79–105 of *Periodismo científico en el siglo XVIII: José Antonio de Alzate y Ramírez.* Edited by Patricia Aceves Pastrana. Mexico: Universidad Autónoma Metropolitana Unidad Xochimilco, 2001.

Sarna, Jonathan D. "The Jews in British America." Pp. 519–31 of *The Jews and the Expansion of Europe to the West, 1450–1800.* Edited by Paolo Bernardini and Norman Fiering. New York: Berghahn Books, 2001.

Sarti, Raffaella. "Bolognesi schiavi dei "Turchi" e schiavi "turchi" a Bologna tra Cinque e Settecento: alterità etnico-religiosa e riduzione in schiavitù." *Quaderni storici,* 36 (2001), 437–73.

Sassi, Jonathan D. "The First Party Competition and Southern New England's Public Christianity." *Journal of the Early Republic,* 21 (2001), 261–99.

Sassi, Jonathan D. *A Republic of Righteousness: The Public Christianity of the Post-Revolutionary New England Clergy.* (Religion in America Series.) New York: Oxford University Press, 2001. Pp. 320.

Savonius, S.-J. "The Swedish Translation of John Locke's 'Second Treatise.'" *Locke Studies,* 1 (2001), 191–219.

III: Philosophy, Science, and Religion 191

Schabas, Margaret. "David Hume on Experimental Natural Philosophy, Money, and Fluids." *History of Political Economy,* 33 (2001), 411–35.

Schafer, Daniel L. "St. Augustine's British Years 1763–1784." *Escribano,* 38 (2001), 1–283.

Scheffel, Michael (ed.). *Erschriebene Natur: Internationale Perspektiven auf Texte des 18. Jahrhunderts. Jahrbuch für Internationale Germanistik, Reihe A, Bd. 66.* New York: P. Lang, 2001. Pp. 333.

Scheick, William J. "'The Captive Exile Hasteth': Increase Mather, Meditation, and Authority." *Early American Literature,* 36 (2001), 183–200.

Scheutz, Martin. "'…im Rauben und Saufen allzu gierig': Soldatenbilder in ausgewählten Selbstzeugnissen katholischer Geistlicher aus der Zeit des Dreissigjährigen Krieges." *L'homme,* 12 (2001), 51–72.

Schickore, Jutta. "Ever-Present Impediments: Exploring Instruments and Methods of Microscopy." *Perspectives on Science,* 9 (2001), 126–46.

Schilling, Heinz. "Confessionalisation and the Rise of Religious and Cultural Frontiers in Early Modern Europe." Pp. 21–35 of *Frontiers of Faith: Religious Exchange and the Constitution of Religious Identities 1400–1750.* Edited by Eszter Andor and Istvan Gyorgy Toth. Budapest: Central European University European Science Foundation, 2001.

Schlumbohm, Jürgen. "'The Pregnant Women Are Here for the Sake of the Teaching Institution': The Lying-in Hospital of Gottingen University, 1751 to c. 1830." *Social History of Medicine,* 14 (2001), 59–78.

Schlup, Michel. "Les voyages dans les Alpes (1779–1796): Une édition disputée entre libraires Neuchâtelois et Genevois." Pp. 367–83 of *H.-B. de Saussure (1740–1799): Un Regard sur la Terre.* Edited by René Sigrist. Geneva: Georg Editeur, 2001.

Schmal, Kerstin. *Die Pietas Maria Theresias im Spannungsfeld von Barock und Aufklärung: Religiöse Praxis und Sendungsbewusstsein gegenüber Familie, Untertanen und Dynastie.* (Mainzer Studien zur Neueren Geschichte, Bd. 7.) Frankfurt: Lang, 2001. Pp. 287.

Schmidt, Dennis J. *On Germans and Other Greeks: Tragedy and Ethical Life.* (Studies in Continental Thought.) Bloomington: Indiana University Press, 2001. Pp. xviii + 337.

Schmolz-Haberlein, Michaela, and Mark Haberlein. "Eighteenth-Century Anabaptists in the Margravate of Baden and Neighboring Territories." *Mennonite Quarterly Review,* 75 (2001), 471–92.

Schneider, Gerhard. "Medikalisierung und Professionalisierung: Die Verdrängung der "Quacksalber" aus dem Gesundheitswesen am Beispiel des Kurfürstentums Hannover um 1800." *Geschichte in Wissenschaft und Unterricht,* 52 (2001), 415–32.

Schnurmann, Claudia. "Das Erdbeben von Jamaika (Juni 1692) im zeitgenössischen Verständnis der englischen Kolonialreichs: Katastrophen als Mittel der Weltdeutung." *Historische Zeitschrift,* Supplement (2001), 249–59.

Schoeps, Julius H. "Chevrat Chinuch Nearim. Die jüdische Freischule in Berlin." *Zeitschrift fur Religions- und Geistesgeschichte,* 53 (2001), 274–77.

Scholz, Sally J. *On Rousseau.* (Wadsworth Philosophers Series.) Belmont: Wadsworth/ Thomson Learning, 2001. Pp. 92.

Schorsch, Jonathan. "Portmanteau Jews: Sephardim and Race in the Early Modern Atlantic World." *Jewish Culture and History,* 4 (2001), 59–74.

Schosler, J. "Sensualisme et apologétique: l'enjeu métaphysique de'sourd et muet' de Chartres." *Studies on Voltaire and the Eighteenth Century* (2001), 113–20.

Schulte, Anja. "Gerontocide in Science-Fiction and Fact: A Critical Review of Sources on Native North America." *European Review of Native American Studies,* 15 (2001), 31–36.

Schultz, Karla L. "The Insufficient as Event: Goethe Lesson at the Frankfurt School." Pp. 165–80 of *Goethe in German-Jewish Culture.* Edited by Klaus L. Berghahn and Jost Hermand. Rochester: Camden House, 2001.

Schumacher, John N. "Blessed Pedro Calungsod, Martyr: An Historian's Comments on His Philippine Background." *Philippine Studies,* 49 (2001), 287–336.

Schumacher, John N. "Blessed Pedro Calungsod, Martyr: An Historian's Comments on the Mission in the Marianas." *Philippine Studies,* 49 (2001), 455–87.

Schuurman, Paul. "Locke's Logic of Ideas in Context: Content and Structure." *British Journal for the History of Philosophy,* 9 (2001), 439–65.

Schuurman, Paul. "Locke's *Of the Conduct of the Understanding.*" *Locke Studies*, 1 (2001), 123–57.

Schutte, Anne Jacobson. *Aspiring Saints: Pretense of Holiness, Inquisition, and Gender in the Republic of Venice, 1618–1750.* Baltimore: Johns Hopkins University Press, 2001. Pp. xvi + 337.

Schwarz, Philip J. *Migrants against Slavery: Virginians and the Nation.* Charlottesville: University Press of Virginia, 2001. Pp. 250.

Schwarzbach, Bertram Eugene. "Les études bibliques à Cirey." Pp. 26–54 of *Cirey dans la vie intellectuelle: La réception de Newton en France.* Edited by François de Gandt. Oxford: Voltaire Foundation, 2001.

Schwerhoff, Gerd. "Justiz-Erfahrungen: Einige einleitende Gedanken." *Historische Zeitschrift,* Supplement (2001), 341–48.

Scully, Randolph. "'Somewhat Liberated': Baptist Discourses of Race and Slavery in Nat Turner's Virginia, 1770–1840." *Explorations in Early American Culture,* 5 (2001), 328–71.

Sebastiani, Silvia. "Conjectural History vs. The Bible: Eighteenth-Century Scottish Historians and the Idea of History in the Encyclopedia Britannica." *Cromohs: Cyber Review of Modern Historiography*, 6 (2001).

Seeman, Erik R. "Reading Indians' Deathbed Scenes: Ethnohistorical and Representational Approaches." *Journal of American History,* 88 (2001), 17–47.

Ségal, Alain. "Claude-Nicolas le Cat et Reims." *Histoire des Sciences médicales,* 35 (2001), 127–31.

Segala, Marco. "Électricité animale, magnétisme animal, galvanisme universel: à la recherche de l'identité entre l'homme et la nature." *Revue d'histoire des sciences,* 54 (2001), 71–84.

Seguin, Maria Susana. Science *et religion dans la pensée française de XVIIIe siècle: Le mythe de déluge universel*. Paris: Editions Honoré Champion, 2001. Pp. 528.

Sellés, Manuel A. "El vapor en el laboratorio: una memoria sobre la ebullición del abate Nollet." *Asclepio,* 53 (2001), 165–89.

Semler, L. E. "The Creed of Eliza's Babes (1652): Nakedness, Adam, and Divinity." *Albion,* 33 (2001), 185–217.

Serarcangeli, Carla, and Gennaro Rispoli. "'Ars mingendi cum instrumentis': sonde, candelette, minugie, cateteri." *Medicina nei secoli,* 13 (2001), 689–706.

Sesso, Gloria. "The Common School: 'The Lion's Den': Teaching About Slavery." *Common-place,* 1 (2001), www.common-place.org/vol-01/no-04/school.

Shaker Collection (Library of Congress). "Shaker Collection of Records Concerning the United Society of Believers in Christ's Second Appearing, 1676–1937 (Bulk 1792–1937)," 500.

Shapiro, Lionel Stefan. "'The Transition from Sensibility to Reason In Regressu': Indeterminism in Kant's *Reflexionen.*" *Kant-Studien,* 92 (2001), 3–12.

Shcheblygina, I. V. "Tema Nravstvennogo Vospitaniia i Obrazovaniia Dvorianstva v Trudakh A. T. Bolotova." *Vestnik Moskovskogo Universiteta, Seriia 8: Istoriia,* 5 (2001), 46–61.

Short, Colin C. "Robert Winfield and the Revivalists." *Proceedings of the Wesley Historical Society,* 53 (2001), 93–102.

Sicker, Martin. *The Islamic World in Decline: From the Treaty of Karlowitz to the Disintegration of the Ottoman Empire.* Westport: Praeger, 2001. Pp. 249.

Sider, Sandra. "New Resources for Emblem Studies." *Renaissance Quarterly,* 54 (2001), 1574–80.

Sieben, Hermann-Josef, S.J. "Die Schannat-Hartzheimische Sammlung der Deutschen Konzilien (1759–1790). Geschichte einer Schwer- und Spätgeburt." *Theologie and Philosophic,* 76 (2001), 1–30.

Sieber, Patricia. "Getting at It in a Single Genuine Invocation: Tang Anthologies, Buddhist Rhetorical Practices, and Jin Shengtan's (1608–1661) Conception of Poetry." *Monumenta Serica,* 49 (2001), 33–56.

Siena, Kevin P. "The 'Foul Disease' and Privacy: The Effects of Venereal Disease and Patient Demand on the Medical Marketplace in Early Modern London." *Bulletin of the History of Medicine,* 75 (2001), 199–224.

Sievers, Julie. "Awakening the Inner Light: Elizabeth Ashbridge and the Transformation of Quaker Community." *Early American Literature,* 36 (2001), 235–62.

III: Philosophy, Science, and Religion

Sigrist, René. "L'expérimentation comme rhétorique de la preuve: l'exemple du *Traité d'insectologie* de Charles Bonnet." *Revue d'histoire des sciences*, 54 (2001), 419–49.

Sigrist, René. "Les essais sur l'hydrométrie (1783) ou l'art de la mesure précise." Pp. 109–40 of *H.-B. de Saussure (1740–1799): Un Regard sur la Terre*. Edited by René Sigrist. Geneva: Georg Editeur, 2001.

Sigrist, René. "La géographie de Saussure à l'horizon des savoirs du XVIIIe siècle." Pp. 215–248 of *H.-B. de Saussure (1740–1799): Un Regard sur la Terre*. Edited by René Sigrist. Geneva: Georg Editeur, 2001.

Sigrist, René (ed.). *H.-B. De Saussure (1740–1799): Un Regard Sur la Terre*. Geneva: Georg Editeur, 2001. Pp. 541.

Sigrist, René. "Les itinéraires du chercheur." Pp. 23–31 of *H.-B. de Saussure (1740–1799): Un Regard sur la Terre*. Edited by René Sigrist. Geneva: Georg Editeur, 2001.

Sigrist, René. "Le souffle des voyages." Pp. 259–68 of *H.-B. de Saussure (1740–1799): Un Regard sur la Terre*. Edited by René Sigrist. Geneva: Georg Editeur, 2001.

Sigrist, René. "Une figure de l'Honnete homme." Pp. 385–93 of *H.-B. de Saussure (1740–1799): Un Regard sur la Terre*. Edited by René Sigrist. Geneva: Georg Editeur, 2001.

Simmons, A. John. "The Conjugal and the Political in Locke." *Locke Studies*, 1 (2001), 173–89.

Simon, Julia. *Beyond Contractual Morality: Ethics, Law, and Literature in Eighteenth-Century France*. Rochester: University of Rochester Press, 2001. Pp. x + 233.

Simonutti, Luisa. "Spinoza and Boyle: Rational Religion and Natural Philosophy." Pp. 117–38 of *Religion, Reason and Nature in Early Modern Europe*. Edited by Robert Crocker. Dordrecht: Kluwer Academic Publishers, 2001.

Simpson, Robert Drew (ed.). "The Lost Letters of Bishop Asbury." *Methodist History*, 39 (2001), 201–06.

Skoczylas, Anne. *Mr. Simson's Knotty Case: Divinity, Politics, and Due Process in Early Eighteenth-Century Scotland*. (McGill–Queen's Studies in the History of Ideas 31.) Montreal: McGill–Queen's University Press, 2001. Pp. x + 403.

Smallwood, Philip (ed.). *Johnson Re-Visioned: Looking Before and After.* (The Bucknell Studies in Eighteenth-Century Literature and Culture.) Lewisburg: Bucknell University Press, 2001. Pp. 179.

Smet, Rudolf de and Karin Verelst. "Newton's Scholium Generale: The Platonic and Stoic Legacy— Philo, Justus Lipsius and the Cambridge Platonists." *History of Science,* 39 (2001), 1–30.

Smith, Carl. "The Far Side of Paradise: California, Florida, and the Landscape of Catastrophe." *American Literary History,* 13 (2001), 354–75.

Smith, Jonathan Z. "A Twice-Told Tale: The History of the History of Religions' History." *Numen: International Review for the History of Religions,* 48 (2001), 131–46.

Smith, Mark M. "Remembering Mary, Shaping Revolt: Reconsidering the Stono Rebellion." *Journal of Southern History*, 67 (2001), 513–34.

Smyth, Elizabeth M. "Writing the History of Women Religious in Canada (1996–2001)." *International Journal of Canadian Studies,* 23 (2001), 205–11.

Smyth, Jim. "The Act of Union and 'Public Opinion'." Pp. 146–60 of *Revolution, Counter-Revolution and Union: Ireland in the 1790s.* Edited by Jim Smyth. Cambridge: Cambridge University Press, 2001.

Smyth, Jim. "Introduction: The 1798 Rebellion in its Eighteenth-Century Contexts." Pp. 1–20 of *Revolution, Counter-Revolution and Union: Ireland in the 1790s.* Edited by Jim Smyth. Cambridge: Cambridge University Press, 2001.

Smyth, Jim. *The Making of the United Kingdom, 1660–1800: State, Religion and Identity in Britain and Ireland.* (The Four Nations Series.) New York: Longman, 2001. Pp. xxii + 252.

Snobelen, Stephen D. "Mathematics, Historians and Newton's Principia." *Annals of Science,* 58 (2001), 75–84.

Snyder, Holly. "Queens of the Household: The Jewish Women of British America, 1700–1800." Pp. 15–45 of *Women and American Judaism: Historical Perspectives.* Edited by Pamela S. Nadell and Jonathan D. Sarna. Hanover: University Press of New England, 2001.

Snyder, Holly. "A Tree with Two Different Fruits: The Jewish Encounter with German Pietists in the Eighteenth-Century Atlantic World." *William and Mary Quarterly*, 58 (2001), 855–82.

Soares, Luiz Carlos. "Ciência, religião e Ilustração: as academias de ensino dos dissentes racionalistas ingleses no século XVIII." *Revista Brasileira de Historia,* 21 (2001), 173–200.

Soghayroun, Ibrahim E. "The Arab and Swahili Culture in Historical Perspective: Some Important Links in *The History of the Mazru`is in East Africa* by Shaykh Al-Amin B. `Ali Al-Mazru`I.`" *Sudanic Africa,* 12 (2001), 15–32.

Sokol, David. "Portrayals of Childhood and Race in Sunday School Conversion Narratives, 1827–1852." *Methodist History,* 40 (2001), 3–16.

Soles, David, and Katherine Bradfield. "Some Remarks on Locke's Use of Thought Experiments." *Locke Studies,* 1 (2001), 31–62.

Sommer, Andreas Urs. "Weltgeschichte und Heilslogik: Jonathan Edwards' *History of the Work of Redemption.*" *Zeitschrift für Religions- und Geistesgeschichte,* 53 (2001), 115–44.

Sorkin, David. "The Emigre Synthesis: German-Jewish History in Modern Times." *Central European History*, 34 (2001), 531–59.

Sorkin, David. "Port Jews and the Three Regions of Emancipation." *Jewish Culture and History,* 4 (2001), 31–46.

Sorrenson, Richard. "Dollond & Son's Pursuit of Achromaticity, 1758–1789." *History of Science,* 39 (2001), 31–55.

Soto, Rosalba Cruz. "El nacionalismo de José Antonio de Alzate en el periódico cientifico *Gaceta de Literatura.*" Pp. 618–49 of *Periodismo científico en el siglo XVIII: José Antonio de Alzate y Ramírez.* Edited by Patricia Aceves Pastrana. Mexico: Universidad Autónoma Metropolitana Unidad Xochimilco, 2001.

Sousa Araújo, António de. "Vida Christã em Carnide no periódo áureo da Luz—1600–1749 (na perspectiva dos visitadores diocesanos)." *Itinerarium,* 47 (2001), 281–331.

Southgate, Beverley C. "'Beating Down Scepticism': The Solid Philosophy of John Sergeant, 1623–1707." Pp. 281–315 of *English Philosophy in the Age of Locke.* (Oxford Studies in the History of Philosophy 3.) Edited by M. A. Stewart. Oxford: Clarendon Press, 2001.

Souza, Juliana Beatriz Almeida de. "Virgem mestiça: devoção a Nossa Senhora na colonização do Novo Mundo." *Tempo*, 6 (2001), 77–92.

Spaans, Joke (ed.). *Een golf van beroering: De omstreden religieuze opwekking in Nederland in het midden van de achttiende eeuw.* Amsterdamse Historische Reeks. (Grote Serie 25.) Hilversum: Verloren, 2001. Pp. 176.

Spaeth, Donald A. *The Church in an Age of Danger: Parsons and Parishioners, 1660–1740.* New York: Cambridge University Press, 2001. Pp. 304.

Spalding, Matthew. *The Enduring Principles of the American Founding.* Washington, D.C.: The Heritage Foundation, 2001. Pp. xiv + 87.

Spangler, Jewel L. "Becoming Baptists: Conversion in Colonial and Early National Virginia." *Journal of Southern History*, 67 (2001), 243–86.

Sparks, John. *The Roots of Appalachian Christianity: The Life and Legacy of Elder Shubal Stearns.* Lexington: University Press of Kentucky, 2001. Pp. xx + 327.

Spector, Sheila A. *Wonders Divine: The Development of Blake's Kabbalistic Myth.* Lewisburg: Bucknell University Press, 2001. Pp. 213.

Spini, Giorgio. "Settecento protestante." *Rivista Storica Italiana*, 113 (2001), 817–30.

Sproule, Anna. *James Watt: Master of the Steam Engine.* (Giants of Science.) Woodbridge: Blackbirch Press, 2001. Pp. 64.

Spurr, John. "The Profane History of Early Modern Oaths." *Transactions of the Royal Historical Society*, 11 (2001), 37–63.

Spyra, Janusz, and Gwido Zlatkes (trans.). "Jewish Rights of Residence in Cieszyn Silesia, 1742–1848." *Polin: Studies in Polish Jewry*, 14 (2001), 31–48.

Standaert, Nicolas. "European Astrology in Early Qing China: Xue Fengzuo's and Smogulecki's Translation of Cardano's Commentaries on Ptolemy's *Tetrabiblos*." *Sino-Western Cultural Relations Journal*, 23 (2001), 50–79.

Stanley, Brian (ed.). *Christian Missions and the Enlightenment.* Grand Rapids: William B. Eerdmans Publishing Company, 2001. Pp. 246.

III: Philosophy, Science, and Religion

Stanley, J. Ford. "The Glasite–Sandemanian Movement in the Eighteenth-Century Atlantic World." *Eighteenth-Century Scotland*, 25 (2001), 8–11.

Starkey, Armstrong. "Conflict and Synthesis: Frontier Warfare in North America, 1513–1815." Pp. 59–84 of *Technology, Disease and Colonial Conquests, Sixteenth to Eighteenth Centuries: Essays Reappraising the Guns and Germs Theories*. Edited by George Raudzens. Boston: Brill, 2001.

Stavinschi, Magdalena. "Notara, un élève de Cassini." Pp. 197–200 of *Sur les traces des Cassini: Astronomes et observatoires du sud de la France*. Edited by Paul Brouzeng and Suzanne Débarbat. Paris: Comité des travaux historiques et scientifiques, 2001.

Steele, Volney. "Lewis and Clark: Military Explorers, Scientists, and Physicians." *Military History of the West*, 31 (2001), 51–65.

Stein, Craig C. *Schleiermacher's Construction of the Subject in the Introduction to The Christian Faith: In Light of M. Foucault's Critique of Modern Knowledge*. (Schleiermacher Studies and Translations 19.) Lewiston: Edwin Mellen Press, 2001. Pp. x + 201.

Stein, K. James. "Unsectarian Preachers and Uncertain Beginnings: The First Annual Conference of the Church of the United Brethren in Christ, September 25–26, 1800." *Methodist History*, 39 (2001), 211–25.

Stevenson, Christine. *Medicine and Magnificence: British Hospital and Asylum Architecture, 1660–1815*. New Haven: Yale University Press, 2001. Pp. 320.

Stewart, M. A. (ed.). *English Philosophy in the Age of Locke*. (Oxford Studies in the History of Philosophy 3.) New York: Oxford University Press, 2001. Pp. 336.

Stewart, M. A. "Stillingfleet and the Way of Ideas." Pp. 245–80 of *English Philosophy in the Age of Locke*. (Oxford Studies in the History of Philosophy 3). Edited by M. A. Stewart. Oxford: Clarendon Press, 2001.

Stewart, Tony K. "In Search of Equivalence: Conceiving Muslim-Hindu Encounter through Translation Theory." *History of Religions*, 40 (2001), 260–87.

Stirk, Nigel. "Intellectual Property and the Role of Manufacturers: Definitions from the Late Eighteenth Century." *Journal of Historical Geography*, 27 (2001), 475–92.

Stolberg, Michael. "Der gesunde Leib: Zur Geschichtlichkeit frühneuzeitlicher Körpererfahrung." *Historische Zeitschrift,* Supplement (2001), 37–57.

Storey, Geoffrey O. "John Yelloly (1774–1842)." *Journal of Medical Biography,* 9 (2001), 63–69.

Strayer, Brian Eugene. *Huguenots and Camisards as Aliens in France, 1598–1789: The Struggle for Religious Toleration.* Lewiston: Edwin Mellen Press, 2001. Pp. iv + 616.

Streiff, Patrick. *Reluctant Saint? A Theological Biography of Fletcher of Madeley.* Manchester: Epworth, 2001. Pp. 406.

Strickland, Michael. "Some Selected Internet Resources for Novice Researchers of Christian History." *Journal of Religious and Theological Information,* 3 (2001), 151–60.

Strickland, Trent. "The Forgotten Quaker Meeting of Richmond County, N.C." *Southern Friend,* 23 (2001), 3–15.

Stroumsa, Guy G. "John Spencer and the Roots of Idolatry." *History of Religions,* 41 (2001), 1–23.

Stukenbrock, Karin. "Der sezierte Leichnam als Objekt der (Körper-)Erfahrung in der Frühen Neuzeit." *Historische Zeitschrift,* Supplement (2001), 73–88.

Sturgeon, Nicholas. "Moral Skepticism and Moral Naturalism in Hume's *Treatise.*" *Hume Studies,* 27 (2001), 3–83.

Sturkenboom, Dorothée, and A. Kost. "Une société savante exclusivement feminine: présage des temps modernes ou vestige de l'Ancien Régime? (I)." *Annales historiques de la Révolution française,* 326 (2001), 117–27.

Subramanian, Lakshmi. "Arms and the Merchant: The Making of the Bania Raj in Late Eighteenth-Century India." *South Asia,* 24 (2001), 1–27.

Sullivan, Heather I. "Ruins and the Construction of Time: Geological and Literary Perspectives in the Age of Goethe." *Studies in Eighteenth-Century Culture,* 30 (2001), 1–30.

Sullivan, Robert. "Rethinking Christianity in Enlightened Europe." *Eighteenth-Century Studies,* 34 (2001), 298–309.

III: Philosophy, Science, and Religion

Sullivan, Robert E. (ed.). *Higher Learning and Catholic Traditions.* Notre Dame: University of Notre Dame Press, 2001. Pp. 160.

Sumner, James. "John Richardson, Saccharometry and the Pounds-Per-Barrel Extract: The Construction of a Quantity." *British Journal for the History of Science,* 34 (2001), 255–73.

Šumrada, Janez. "Ziga Zois in Deodat de Dolomieu." *Kronika,* 49 (2001), 65–72.

Sutherland, Heather. "The Makassar Malays: Adaptation and Identity, C. 1660–1790." *Journal of Southeast Asian Studies,* 32 (2001), 397–421.

Sweet, John Wood. "'More Than Tears': The Ordeal of Abolition in Revolutionary New England." *Explorations in Early American Culture,* 5 (2001), 118–72.

Symons, John. "'A Most Hideous Object': John Davies (1796–1872) and Plastic Surgery." *Medical History,* 45 (2001), 395–402.

Szechi, Daniel. "A Blueprint for Tyranny? Sir Edward Hales and the Catholic Jacobite Response to the Revolution of 1688." *English Historical Review,* 116 (2001), 342–67.

Tackett, Timothy. "Interpreting the Terror." *French Historical Studies,* 24 (2001), 569–78.

Tait, L. Gordon. *The Piety of John Witherspoon: Pew, Pulpit, and Public Forum.* Louisville: Geneva Press, 2001. Pp. xxiii + 256; illustrations.

Talha, Naureen. "Rise of New Capitalist Classes in India under the British." *Asian Profile,* 29 (2001), 255–61.

Tamari, Steve. "Ottoman Madrasas: The Multiple Lives of Educational Institutions in Eighteenth-Century Syria." *Journal of Early Modern History,* 5 (2001), 99–127.

Tammiksaar, Erki. "Mathias von Hedenstrom: New Lands Appear on the Map of the Northern Coast of Siberia." *Polar Record,* 37 (2001), 67–69.

Tanturri, Alberto. "Gli Scolopi nel Mezzogiorno d'Italia in età moderna." *Archivum Scholorum Piarum,* 25 (2001), 1–221.

Taylor, Alan. "The Free Seekers: Religious Culture in Upstate New York, 1790–1835." *Journal of Mormon History,* 27 (2001), 42–66.

Taylor, E. Derek. "Mary Astell's Ironic Assault on John Locke's Theory of Thinking Matter." *Journal of the History of Ideas,* 62 (2001), 505–22.

Taylor, Kenneth L. "The Beginnings of a Geological Naturalist: Desmarest, the Printed Word, and Nature." *Earth Sciences History,* 20 (2001), 44–61.

Teillet, Claude. "Jean-Dominique, Cassini IV (1748–1845), le dernier directeur de l'Observatoire de Paris, sous l'Ancien Régime, raconté par lui-même." Pp. 43–65 of *Sur les traces des Cassini: Astronomes et observatoires du sud de la France.* Edited by Paul Brouzeng and Suzanne Débarbat. Paris: Comité des travaux historiques et scientifiques, 2001.

Teja, Jesus F. de la. "St. James at the Fair: Religious Ceremony, Civic Boosterism, and Commercial Development on the Colonial Mexican Frontier." *Americas: A Quarterly Review of Inter-American Cultural History,* 57 (2001), 395–416.

Teulon, F. "Fiasco théorique de *l'Ideologie* chez Destutt de Tracy." *Studies on Voltaire and the Eighteenth Century* (2001), pp. 121–31.

Thale, Mary. "Deists, Papists and Methodists at London Debating Societies, 1749–1799." *History,* 86 (2001), 328–47.

Thiel, Udo. "The Trinity and Human Personal Identity." Pp. 217–43 of *English Philosophy in the Age of Locke.* (Oxford Studies in the History of Philosophy 3). Edited by M. A. Stewart. Oxford: Clarendon Press, 2001.

Thielke, Peter. "Discursivity and Causality: Maimon's Challenge to the Second Analogy." *Kant-Studien* 92 (2001), 440–463.

Thiesen, Barbara A. (comp.). "Mennonite Bibliography, 2000." *Mennonite Life,* 56 (2001).

Thomas, David C. "To Seek, Suffer, and Trust: Ascetic Devotion in a Modern Church on the Frontier." *Oregon Historical Quarterly,* 102 (2001), 48–71.

Thompson, Kevin. "Kant's Transcendental Deduction of Political Authority." *Kant-Studien,* 92 (2001), 62–78.

Thuente, Mary Helen. "'The Belfast Laugh': The Context and Significance of United Irish Satires." Pp. 67–82 of *Revolution, Counter-Revolution and Union: Ireland in the 1790s.* Edited by Jim Smyth. Cambridge: Cambridge University Press, 2001.

III: Philosophy, Science, and Religion

Tierney, Brian. "Kant on Property: The Problem of Permissive Law." *Journal of the History of Ideas*, 62 (2001), 301–12.

Tierney, Brian. "Permissive Natural Law and Property: Gratian to Kant." *Journal of the History of Ideas*, 62 (2001), 381–99.

Timms, Edward. "The Pernicious Rift: Metternich and the Debate About Jewish Emancipation at the Congress of Vienna." *Leo Baeck Institute Year Book,* 46 (2001), 3–18.

Tinsley, Barbara Sher. *Pierre Bayle's Reformation: Conscience and Criticism on the Eve of the Enlightenment.* Selinsgrove: Susquehanna University Press, 2001. Pp. 476.

Tobin, Robert D. *Doctor's Orders: Goethe and Enlightenment Thought.* Lewisburg: Bucknell University Press, 2001. Pp. 255.

Todes, Samuel. *Body and World.* Cambridge: MIT Press, 2001. Revised edition of *The Human Body as Material Subject of the World.* (New York: Garland, 1990.) Pp. xlvi + 337.

Todorov, Tzvetan. *Frail Happiness: An Essay on Rousseau.* Translated by John T. Scott and Robert D. Zaretsky. University Park: Pennsylvania State University Press, 2001. Pp. xxxii + 70.

Tollet, Daniel. "Cohabitation, concurrence et conversion dan la Confédération Plono-Lituanienne au tournant des XVe et XVIIe siècles." Pp. 67–78 of *Frontiers of Faith: Religious Exchange and the Constitution of Religious Identities 1400–1750*. Edited by Eszter Andor and Istvan Gyorgy Toth. Budapest: Central European University European Science Foundation, 2001.

Toman, Cynthia. "George Spence: Surgeon and Servant of the Hudson's Bay Company, 1738–41." *Canadian Bulletin of Medical History,* 18 (2001), 17–42.

Tomes, Nancy. "The History of Shit: An Essay Review." *Journal of the History of Medicine and Allied Sciences,* 56 (2001), 400–04.

Tomic, Sacha. "L'Analyse chimique des végétaux: le cas du quinquina." *Annals of Science,* 58 (2001), 287–309.

Tongiorgi, Tomasi Lucia. "The Study of the Natural Sciences and Botanical and Zoological Illustration in Tuscany under the Medicis from the Sixteenth to the Eighteenth Centuries." *Archives of Natural History,* 28 (2001), 179–93.

Torres, Maria Amparo Ros. "El Testamento de José Antonio de Alzate y Ramírez." Pp. 57–77 of *Periodismo científico en el siglo XVIII: José Antonio de Alzate y Ramírez*. Edited by Patricia Aceves Pastrana. Mexico: Universidad Autónoma Metropolitana Unidad Xochimilco, 2001.

Torrey, E. Fuller, and Judy Miller. *The Invisible Plague: The Rise of Mental Illness from 1750 to the Present*. New Brunswick: Rutgers University Press, 2001. Pp. 416.

Tosti, Osvaldo, Sch.P. "Gli Scolopi a Cortonia dal 1706 al 1880." *Archivum Scholarum Piarum*, 25 (2001), 3–107.

Toth, Istvan Gyorgy. "The Missionary and the Devil: Ways of Conversion in Catholic Missions in Hungary." Pp. 79–87 of *Frontiers of Faith: Religious Exchange and the Constitution of Religious Identities 1400–1750*. Edited by Eszter Andor and Istvan Gyorgy Toth. Budapest: Central European University European Science Foundation, 2001.

Trabulse, Elías. "La ciencia de la ilustración Mexicana: Alcances y límites de una tradición historiográfica." Pp. 19–35 of *Periodismo científico en el siglo XVIII: José Antonio de Alzate y Ramírez*. Edited by Patricia Aceves Pastrana. Mexico: Universidad Autónoma Metropolitana Unidad Xochimilco, 2001.

Trappes-Lomax, John. "Chaplain and Steward: Francis Blakiston, S.J. (1617–93) at Linton-on-Ouse." *Recusant History*, 25 (2001), 423–33.

Treloar, John L. "Kant on Philosophy and Being a Philosopher." *American Catholic Philosophical Quarterly*, 75 (2001), 297–312.

Treviño, Carlos Viesca. "Curanderismo in Mexico and Guatemala." Pp. 47–65 of *Mesoamerican Healers*. Edited by Brad R. Huber and Alan R. Sandstrom. Austin: University of Texas Press, 2001.

Troost, Linda V. (ed.). *Religion in the Eighteenth Century*. (Topic: A Journal of the Liberal Arts 51.) Washington: Washington and Jefferson College, 2001. Pp. 69.

Tsapina, Olga A. "Secularization and Opposition in the Time of Catherine the Great." Pp. 334–89 of *Religion and Politics in Enlightenment Europe*. Edited by James E. Bradley and Dale K. Van Kley. Notre Dame: University of Notre Dame Press, 2001.

Tuomey, Michael. *The Papers of Michael Tuomey*. Spartanburg: Reprint Company, 2001. Pp. 364.

III: Philosophy, Science, and Religion

Tüskes, Gábor, and Éva Knapp. *Népi Vallásosság Magyarországon a 17–18. Században: Források, Formák, Közvetítők*. Budapest: Osiris, 2001. Pp. 410.

Tusseau, Guillaume. *Jeremy Bentham et le droit constitutionnel: Une approche de l'utilitarisme juridique.* (Logiques juridiques.) Paris: Harmattan, 2001. Pp. 320.

Tyrsenko, Andreï Vladimirovich. "Ot Prosveshcheniia k Revoliutsii. Obshchestvenno-Politicheskie Vzgliady Siiesa." *Novaia i Noveishaia Istoriia,* 5 (2001), 137–60.

Uhalley, Stephen, Jr., and Xiaoxin Wu (eds.). *China and Christianity: Burdened Past, Hopeful Future.* Armonk: M.E. Sharpe, 2001. Pp. xiii + 499.

Ullmann, Helen Schatvet, and Kathryn Smith Black. "Some Marriages from Records of the First Congregational Church in Thompson, Connecticut, 1796–1850, Including Some Corrections to the Barbour Collection of Connecticut Vital Records." *New England Historical and Genealogical Register,* 155 (2001), 295–317.

Ulrich, Laurel Thatcher. "John Winthrop's City of Women." *Massachusetts Historical Review,* 3 (2001), 19–48.

Ultee, Maarten. "Defending the Honor of French Surgery, 1760–1788." *Proceedings of the Annual Meeting of the Western Society for French History,* 27 (2001), 51–62.

Urban, Hugh B. "The Marketplace and the Temple: Economic Metaphors and Religious Meanings in the Folk Songs of Colonial Bengal." *Journal of Asian Studies,* 60 (2001), 1085–114.

Urban, Hugh B. *Songs of Ecstasy: Tantric and Devotional Songs from Colonial Bengal.* New York: Oxford University Press, 2001. Pp. 208.

Vaccari, Ezio. "Les Voyages dans les Alpes et la géologie Italienne." Pp. 197–213 of *H.-B. de Saussure (1740–1799): Un Regard sur la Terre.* Edited by René Sigrist. Geneva: Georg Editeur, 2001.

Vaj, Daniela. "Saussure à la découverte de l'Italie (1772–1773)." Pp. 269–301 of *H.-B. de Saussure (1740–1799): Un Regard sur la Terre.* Edited by René Sigrist. Geneva: Georg Editeur, 2001.

Valasek, Hubert, Rudolf Brazdil, and Zbynek Svitak. "František Alois Mag z Maggu a Jeho Nejstarsi Pristrojova Meteorologická Mereni na Morave." *Časopis Matice Moravské,* 120 (2001), 37–65.

Valiance, Edward. "'An Holy and Sacramentall Paction': Federal Thought and the Solemn League and Covenant in England." *English Historical Review,* 116 (2001), 50–75.

Valiance, Edward. "Oaths, Casuistry, and Equivocation: Anglican Responses to the Engagement Controversy." *Historical Journal,* 44 (2001), 59–78.

Valone, David A. "Hugh James Rose's Anglican Critique of Cambridge: Science, Antirationalism, and Coleridgean Idealism in Late Georgian England." *Albion,* 33 (2001), 218–42.

Vamboulis, Epaminondas. "La discussion de l'attraction chez Voltaire." Pp. 159–70 of *Cirey dans la vie intellectuelle: La réception de Newton en France.* Edited by François de Gandt. Oxford: Voltaire Foundation, 2001.

Van Kley, Dale K. "Catholic Conciliar Reform in an Age of Anti-Catholic Revolution: France, Italy, and the Netherlands, 1758–1801." Pp. 46–118 of *Religion and Politics in Enlightenment Europe.* Edited by James E. Bradley and Dale K. Van Kley. Notre Dame: University of Notre Dame Press, 2001.

Van Mill, David. *Liberty, Rationality, and Agency in Hobbes's Leviathan.* Albany: State University of New York Press, 2001. Pp. xii + 253.

Vandenabeele, Bart. "On the Notion of 'Disinterestedness': Kant, Lyotard, and Schopenhauer." *Journal of the History of Ideas,* 62 (2001), 705–20.

VanDeusen, Nancy E. *Between the Sacred and the Worldly: The Institutional and Cultural Practice of Recogimiento in Colonial Lima.* Stanford: Stanford University Press, 2001. Pp. 319.

Vanysacker, Dries. "L'homme derrière le cardinal. Les lettres originales de Giuseppe Garampi à son frère aîné Francesco (1752–1788) conservées dans le Fondo *Eredi Garampi* à la Biblioteca Gambalunghiana de Rimini." *Bulletin de l'Institut historique belge de Rome,* 71 (2001), 201–41.

Varma, Lalima. "State and Religion in Japan." *China Report,* 37 (2001), 41–50.

Vater, Michael. "F. W. J. Schelling: Further Presentations from the System of Philosophy (1802)." *The Philosophical Forum,* 32 (2001), 373–97.

III: Philosophy, Science, and Religion

Vater, Michael. "F. W. J. Schelling: Presentation of My System of Philosophy (1801)." *The Philosophical Forum*, 32 (2001), 339–71.

Velagic, Zoran. "The Croation Author at the Frontier of Catholicism and Orthodoxy in Croatia." Pp. 89–97 of *Frontiers of Faith: Religious Exchange and the Constitution of Religious Identities 1400–1750*. Edited by Eszter Andor and Istvan Gyorgy Toth. Budapest: Central European University European Science Foundation, 2001.

Velkley, Richard L. "Metaphysics, Freedom and History: Kant and the End of Reason." *American Catholic Philosophical Quarterly* 75 (2001), 153–70.

Vera, Eugenia Roldan. "Reading in Questions and Answers: The Catechism as an Educational Genre in Early Independent Spanish America." *Book History,* 4 (2001), 17–48.

Viesca, Carlos and José Sanfilippo. "La medicina en las *Gacetas de Literatura*." Pp. 251–85 of *Periodismo científico en el siglo XVIII: José Antonio de Alzate y Ramírez*. Edited by Patricia Aceves Pastrana. Mexico: Universidad Autónoma Metropolitana Unidad Xochimilco, 2001.

Villacañas, Beatriz. "De doctores y monstruos: la ciencia como transgresión en *Dr. Faustus*, *Frankenstein* y *Dr. Jekyll and Mr. Hyde*." *Asclepio,* 53 (2001), 197–211.

Villatoux, Marie-Catherine, and Alain Degardin. "La 'folie' des ballons au XVIIIe siècle." *Revue Historique des Armées,* 1 (2001), 98–104.

Vlastuin, W. van. *De geest van opwekking: een onderzoek naar de leer van de Heilige Geest in de opwekkingstheologie van Jonathan Edwards (1703–1758)*. Heerenveen: Groen, 2001. Pp. 389.

Vogt, Peter. "'Ehereligion': The Moravian Theory and Practice of Marriage as Point of Contention in the Conflict between Ephrata and Bethlehem." *Communal Societies,* 21 (2001), 37–48.

Völkel, Markus. "Aufstieg und Fall der protestantischen Universalgeschichte." *Storia della Storiografia,* 39 (2001), 67–73.

Volwahsen, Andreas. *Cosmic Architecture in India: The Astronomical Monuments of Maharaja Jai Singh II*. New York: Prestel, 2001. Pp. 158.

Vondraskova, Iveta. "'The Events of Times' by Abraham Trebitsch of Mikulov (Nikolsburg): The Chronicle and Its Relationship to the Development of Modern Historiography." *Judaica Bohemiae,* 37 (2001), 92–144.

Voorhees, David William. "In the Republic's Tradition: The Persistence of Dutch Culture in the Mid-Atlantic Colonies after the 1664 English Conquest." *Halve Maen,* 74 (2001), 49–54.

Voros, Kati. "How Jewish is Jewish Budapest?" *Jewish Social Studies,* 8 (2001), 88–125.

Vroede, M. de. "Parochiale clerus en lager onderwijs in het zuiden van het koninkrijk der Nederlanden, 1815–1830." *Trajecta,* 10 (2001), 3–15.

Wade, Nicholas, Josef Brozek, and Jiri Hoskovec. *Purkinje's Vision: The Dawning of Neuroscience.* Hillsdale: L. Erlbaum Association, 2001. Pp. 159.

Walford, David. "Kant's 1768 *Gegenden im Raume* Essay." *Kant-Studien,* 92 (2001), 407–39.

Walker, Anita M., and Edmund H. Dickerman. "A Notorious Woman: Possession, Witchcraft and Sexuality in Seventeenth-Century Provence." *Historical Reflections,* 27 (2001), 1–26.

Walker, Corinne, and Anastazja Winiger-Labuda. "Saussure et l'Architecture: Entre goût et nécessité." Pp. 453–70 of *H.-B. de Saussure (1740–1799): Un Regard sur la Terre.* Edited by René Sigrist. Geneva: Georg Editeur, 2001.

Walker, Phillip L. "A Spanish Borderlands Perspective on La Florida Bioarchaeology." Pp. 274–307 of *Bioarchaeology of Spanish Florida: The Impact of Colonialism.* Edited by Clark Spencer Larsen. Gainesville: University Press of Florida, 2001.

Waller, Ralph. "Converging and Diverging Lines: Aspects of the Relationship between Methodism and Rational Dissent." *Proceedings of the Wesley Historical Society,* 53 (2001), 81–92.

Walters, Robert L. "La querelle des forces vives et la rôle de Mme Du Châtelet." Pp. 198–211 of *Cirey dans la vie intellectuelle: La réception de Newton en France.* Edited by François de Gandt. Oxford: Voltaire Foundation, 2001.

Wang, Rongbin. "Guanyu Guankaohe Dui 'Shoushi Li' Jiao Shi Suanfa de Jidian Yanjiu." *Ziran Kexueshi Yanjiu (Studies in the History of Natural Sciences),* 20 (2001), 143–50.

Ward, Andrew. "Kant's First Analogy of Experience." *Kant-Studien,* 92 (2001), 387–406.

III: Philosophy, Science, and Religion

Ward, W. R. "Late Jansenism and the Habsburgs." Pp. 154–186 of *Religion and Politics in Enlightenment Europe*. Edited by James E. Bradley and Dale K. Van Kley. Notre Dame: University of Notre Dame Press, 2001.

Warner, John Harley, and Janet A. Tighe (eds.). *Major Problems in the History of American Medicine and Public Health*. Boston: Houghton Mifflin, 2001. Pp 539.

Wasserstein, Bernard. *Divided Jerusalem: The Struggle for the Holy City*. New Haven: Yale University Press, 2001. Pp. 412.

Wätjer, Jürgen. *Das katholische Domkapitel zu Hamburg von den anfängen bis zur Reformation und seine Wiedererrichtung 1996: Eine kanonistische Untersuchung*. Frankfurt: P. Lang Europaischer Verlag der Wissenschaften, 2001. Pp. 283.

Watkins, Eric (ed.). *Kant and the Sciences*. Oxford: Oxford University Press, 2001. Pp. xiii + 289.

Watson, William C. "Rethinking the Late Stuart Church: The Extent of Liberal Anglicanism, 1688–1715." *Anglican and Episcopal History,* 70 (2001), 143–68.

Weaver, John C. "Exploitation by Design: The Dismal Science, Land Reform, and the Cape Boers, 1805–22." *Journal of Imperial and Commonwealth History,* 29 (2001), 1–32.

Weber, Christoph. *Genealogien zur Papstgeschichte*. 2 volumes. Stuttgart: Anton Hiersemann, 2001. Pp. cxxxii + 980.

Weber, Francis J. *Encyclopedia of California's Catholic Heritage: 1769–1999*. Mission Hills: Saint Francis Historical Society, 2001. Pp. 1148.

Weddle, Meredith Baldwin. *Walking in the Way of Peace: Quaker Pacifism in the Seventeenth Century*. New York: Oxford University Press, 2001. Pp. 368.

Weder, Christine. "Moral Interest and Religious Truth: On the Relationship between Morality and Religion in Novalis." *German Life and Letters,* 54 (2001), 291–309.

Weidemann, Hermann. "Kants Kritik am Eudämonismus und die Platonische Ethik." *Kant-Studien*, 92 (2001), 19–37.

Weinberg, Bennett Alan, and Bonnie K. Bealer. *The World of Caffeine: The Science and Culture of the World's Most Popular Drug*. New York: Routledge, 2001. Pp. 394.

Weinberg, Robert. "Urban Life and Modernity among Europe's Jews: Two Case Studies." *Journal of Urban History*, 27 (2001), 505–10.

Weingrad, Michael. "Parisian Messianism: Catholicism, Decadence, and the Transgressions of Georges Bataille." *History and Memory,* 13 (2001), 113–33.

Weinstein, Jack Russell. *On Adam Smith*. Belmont: Wadsworth/Thompson Learning, 2001. (Wadsworth Philosophers Series.) Pp. 97.

Weiss, Holger. "European Images of Islam in the Northern Hinterlands of the Gold Coast through the Early Colonial Period." *Sudanic Africa,* 12 (2001), 83–110.

Weiss, Otto. "Das Hofbauerbild im Wandel." *Spicilegium Historicum C.S.S.R.*, 49 (2001), 315–48.

Wesley, Charles. *The Sermons of Charles Wesley: A Critical Edition with Introduction and Notes*. Edited by Kenneth G. C. Newport. New York: Oxford University Press, 2001. Pp. 500.

Wesselius, Allen Doc. "A Lasting Legacy: The Lewis and Clark Place Names of the Pacific Northwest. Part 2." *Columbia*, 15 (2001), 23–30.

Westerfield Tucker, Karen B. "The Liturgical Ministries of the United Methodist Deacon: Continuity and Change." *Methodist History,* 39 (2001), 82–98.

Whelan, Timothy. "A Glance at the 1795 Catalogue of Books in the Library of the Bristol Baptist Academy and Museum." *Baptist Quarterly,* 39 (2001), 35–38.

White, Charles Edward. "Spare the Rod and Spoil the Church." *Christian History,* 20 (2001), 28–31.

White, Eryn M. "'The People Called Methodists': Early Welsh Methodism and the Question of Identity." *Journal of Welsh Religious History,* 1 (2001), 1–14.

White, Heather Rachelle. "'The Glory of Southern Christianity': Methodism and the Mission to the Slaves." *Methodist History,* 39 (2001), 108–21.

White, William, and Cynthia McFarland (eds.). "Bishop William White's *An Essay on High-Church Principles.*" *Anglican and Episcopal History*, 70 (2001), 4–39.

III: Philosophy, Science, and Religion

Wielema, M. R. "Ongeloof en atheîsme in vroegmodern Europa." *Tijdschrift voor geschiedenis*, 114 (2001), 332–53.

Wigger, John H. *Taking Heaven by Storm: Methodism and the Rise of Popular Christianity in America*. Urbana: University of Illinois Press, 2001. Pp. 288.

Wiggins, Rosalind C. "Paul and Stephen, Unlikely Friends." *Quaker History*, 90 (2001), 8–27.

Wilcher, Robert. *The Writings of Regalism, 1628–1660*. Cambridge: Cambridge University Press, 2001. Pp. 415.

Wilde, Guillermo. "Los guaraníes después de la expulsión de los jesuitas: dinámicas políticas y transacciones simbólicas." *Revista complutense de historia de América*, 27 (2001), 69–106.

Will de Chaparro, Martina E. "Parceling Out Their Salvation: The Good Death in New Mexican Wills, 1760–1850." *Catholic Southwest: A Journal of History and Culture*, 12 (2001), 51–74.

Williams, Carolyn. "'Inhumanly Brought Back to Life and Misery': Mary Wollstonecraft, 'Frankenstein,' and the Royal Humane Society." *Women's Writing*, 8 (2001), 213–34.

Williams, Howard. "Metamorphosis or Palingenesis? Political Change in Kant." *Review of Politics*, 63 (2001), 693–722.

Williams, James Homer. "An Atlantic Perspective on the Jewish Struggle for Rights and Opportunities in Brazil, New Netherland, and New York." Pp. 369–93 of *The Jews and the Expansion of Europe to the West, 1450–1800*. Edited by Paolo Bernardini and Norman Fiering. New York: Berghahn Books, 2001.

Williams, John Alexander. "Appalachian History: Regional History in the Post-Modern Zone." *Appalachian Journal*, 28 (2001), 168–87.

Williams, Peter W. *America's Religions: From Their Origins to the Twenty-First Century*. Urbana: University of Illinois Press, 2001. Pp. 601.

Williams, Vernon J., Jr. "Racial Essentialism: A Case of Historical Continuity and Discontinuity in the Social Sciences." *Western Journal of Black Studies*, 25 (2001), 202–10.

Williamson, Arthur. "Edward Gibbon, Edmund Burke, and John Pocock: The Appeals of Whigs Old and New." *Canadian Journal of History*, 36 (2001), 517–22.

Wills, Garry. *Venice: Lion City. The Religion of Empire*. New York: Simon & Schuster, 2001. Pp. 420.

Wilson, Anna. *Persuasive Fictions: Feminist Narrative and Critical Myth*. Lewisburg.: Bucknell University Press, 2001. Pp. 161.

Wilson, Brian. "The Spirit of the Motor City: Three Hundred Years of Religious History in Detroit." *Michigan Historical Review,* 27 (2001), 21–56.

Wilson, Catherine (ed.). *Leibniz*. (International Library of Critical Essays in the History of Philosophy 12.) Aldershot: Ashgate Publishing Company, 2001. Pp. xx + 486.

Wilson, Jeffrey. "Incommensurable, Supersensible, Sublime." *American Catholic Philosophical Quarterly* 75 (2001), 221–42.

Wilson, Renate. "Eighteenth-Century Practitioners of Medicine from Central Europe: The Pietist Connection." Pp. 29–49 of *Apothecaries and the Drug Trade: Essays in Celebration of the Work of David L. Cowen*. Edited by Gregory J. Higby and Elaine C. Stroud. Madison: American Institute of the History of Pharmacy, 2001.

Wilson, Renate, and J. Woodrow Savacool. "The Theory and Practice of Pharmacy in Pennsylvania: Observations on Two Colonial Country Doctors." *Pennsylvania History*, 68 (2001), 31–65.

Wilson, Stephen A. "The Possibility of a Habituation Model of Moral Development in Jonathan Edwards's Conception of the Will's Freedom." *Journal of Religion,* 81 (2001), 49–77.

Wilson, W. Daniel. "'Humanitätssalbader': Goethe's Distaste for Jewish Emancipation, and Jewish Responses." Pp. 146–64 of *Goethe in German-Jewish Culture*. Edited by Klaus L. Berghahn and Jost Hermand. Rochester: Camden House, 2001.

Wimmer, Andreas, and Isabelle Schulte-Tenckhoff (trans.). "Globalizations Avant la Lettre: A Comparative View of Isomorphization and Heteromorphization in an Inter-Connecting World." *Comparative Studies in Society and History,* 43 (2001), 435–66.

Winchester, Simon. *The Map That Changed the World: William Smith and the Birth of Modern Geology*. New York: HarperCollins, 2001. Pp. 336.

III: Philosophy, Science, and Religion 213

Windler, Christian. "Diplomatic History as a Field for Cultural Analysis: Muslim-Christian Relations in Tunis, 1700–1840." *Historical Journal,* 44 (2001), 79–106.

Winship, Michael P. "Were There Any Puritans in New England?" *New England Quarterly,* 74 (2001), 118–38.

Wittwer, Hector. "Über Kants Verbot der Selbsttötung." *Kant-Studien*, 92 (2001), 180–209.

Wolterstorff, Nicholas. *Thomas Reid and the Story of Epistemology.* (Modern European Philosophy.) Cambridge: Cambridge University Press, 2001. Pp. xiii + 265.

Wood, Craig D. "The Welsh Response to the Glorious Revolution of 1688." *Journal of Welsh Religious History,* 1 (2001), 15–33.

Wood, David. "Novalis: Kant Studies (1797)." *The Philosophical Forum*, 32 (2001), 323–38.

Wood, Robert E. "Kant's 'Antinomic' Aesthetics." *American Catholic Philosophical Quarterly* 75 (2001), 271–96.

Woolston, Thomas. *Six discourses sur les Miracles de Notre Sauveur [1727–1729]: Deux Traductions de manuscripts du XVIIIe siècle dont une de Mme du Châtelet.* Edited by William Trapnell. Paris: Editions Honoré Champion, 2001. Pp. 432.

Worth, John E. "The Ethnohistorical Context of Bioarchaeology in Spanish Florida." Pp. 1–21 of *Bioarchaeology of Spanish Florida: The Impact of Colonialism.* Edited by Clark Spencer Larsen. Gainesville: University Press of Florida, 2001.

Wyller, Truls. "Wahrnehmung, Substanz und Kausalität bei Kant." *Kant-Studien*, 92 (2001), 283–95.

Yardeni, Myriam. "La France protestant et le refuge Huguenot." Pp. 27–42 of *La Diaspora des Hugeunots: Les réfugiés protestants de France et leur dispersion dans le monde (XVIe–XVIIIe siècles).* Edited by Eckart Birnstiel and Chrystel Bernat. Paris: Honoré Champion Éditeur, 2001.

Yeo, Richard R. *Encyclopaedic Visions: Scientific Dictionaries and Enlightenment Culture.* Cambridge: Cambridge University Press, 2001. Pp. xxi + 336.

Yildrum, Onur. "Transformation of the Craft Guilds in Istanbul (1650–1860)." *Islamic Studies,* 40 (2001), 49–66.

Yokota, Kariann. "'To Pursue the Stream to Its Fountain': Race, Inequality, and the Post-Colonial Exchange of Knowledge across the Atlantic." *Explorations in Early American Culture,* 5 (2001), 173–229.

Yolton, John W. "Locke's Man." *Journal of the History of Ideas,* 62 (2001), 665–83.

Young, Amy L., Michael Tuma, and Cliff Jenkins. "The Role of Hunting to Cope with Risk at Saragossa Plantation, Natchez, Mississippi." *American Anthropologist,* 103 (2001), 692–704.

Young, John R. "The Scottish Parliament and the War for the Three Kingdoms, 1639–1651." *Parliaments, Estates and Representation,* 21 (2001), 103–23.

Yousef, Nancy. "Savage or Solitary? The Wild Child and Rousseau's Man of Nature." *Journal of the History of Ideas,* 62 (2001), 245–63.

Yrigoyen, Charles, Jr. "Start the Presses." *Christian History,* 20 (2001), 36–38.

Yu, Xinzhong. "Jiadao Zhiji Jiangnan Da Yi de Qianqian Houhou." *Qing Shi Yanjiu,* 2 (2001), 1–18.

Yu, Xinzhong. "Lanhousha Chuxian Niandai Chutan" [An Initial Study on the Emergence of "Lanhousha"]. *Zhonghua Yishi Zazhi (Chinese Journal of Medical History),* 31 (2001), 81–85.

Zajka, Vital. "The Self-Perception of Lithuanian-Belarusian Jewry in the Eighteenth and Nineteenth Centuries." *Polin: Studies in Polish Jewry,* 14 (2001), 19–30.

Zarka, Yves Charles. "Liberty, Necessity and Chance: Hobbes's General Theory of Events." *British Journal for the History of Philosophy* 9 (2001), 425–37.

Zarzoso, Alfons. "El pluralismo médico a través de la correspondencia privada en la Cataluña del siglo XVIII." *Dynamis ,* 21 (2001), 409–33.

Zayas, Concepción. "La escritora Ana de Zayas y el obispo poblano Manuel Fernández de Santa Cruz." *Anuario de Estudios Americanos,* 58 (2001), 61–81.

Zbirkova, Viera. *Kapitoly o posobeni ceskych exulantov na zapadnom Slovensku koncom 17. A Zaciatkom 18. Storocia.* Vyd. 1. Nitra: Univerzita Konstantina Filozofa v Nitre, Filozoficka fakulta, 2001. Pp. 174.

III: Philosophy, Science, and Religion

Zedelmaier, Helmut. "Der Beginn der Geschichte. Überlegungen zur Auflösung des Alteuropäischen Modells der Universalgeschichte." *Storia della Storiografia*, 39 (2001), 87–92.

Zenuch, Peter. "K Dejinam Podkarpatskych a Vychodoslovenskych Rusinov." *Historický Časopis*, 49 (2001), 501–14.

Zhao, Shiyu, and Qingping Deng. "Lu Ban Hui: Qing Zhi Minguo Chunian Beijing de Jisi Zuzhi Yu Hangye Zuzhi." *Qing Shi Yanjiu*, 1 (2001), 1–12.

Zhou, Xun. *Chinese Perceptions of the "Jews" and Judaism: A History of the Youtai*. Richmond: Curzon, 2001. Pp. 202.

Zimmerman, Robert. "Escape from the Iroquois." *American History*, 36 (2001), 30–36.

Zinsser, Judith P. "Translating Newton's *Principia*: The Marquise du Chatelet's Revisions and Additions for a French Audience." *Notes and Records of the Royal Society of London*, 55 (2001), 227–45.

Znamenskij, Petr Vasilevich. *Dukhovnye shkoly v Rossii do reformy 1808 Goda*. Sankt-Peterburg: Letnij sad; Kolo, 2001. Pp. 798.

Zucchi, Luca. "Linneo e Parkinson: il botanico e le scimmie nel giardino dell'Eden." *Nuncius*, 16 (2001), 85–152.

Zryd, Amédée. "Saussure «Glaciologue»." Pp. 159–73 of *H.-B. de Saussure (1740–1799): Un Regard sur la Terre*. Edited by René Sigrist. Geneva: Georg Editeur, 2001.

Zumkeller, Dominique. "Un père Agronome: Nicolas de Saussure (1709–1791)." Pp. 395–408 of *H.-B. de Saussure (1740–1799): Un Regard sur la Terre*. Edited by René Sigrist. Geneva: Georg Editeur, 2001.

Zweig, Arnulf. "I. Kant: Letter to Carl Leonhard Reinhold (1789)." *The Philosophical Forum*, 32 (2001), 283–84.

Zweig, Arnulf. "I. Kant: Letter to Friedrich August Nitsch (1794)." *The Philosophical Forum*, 32 (2001), 285–88.

Zytaruk, Maria. "'Occasional Specimens, Not Compleate Systemes': John Evelyn's Culture of Collecting." *Bodleian Library Record*, 17 (2001), 185–212.

IV: Fine Arts

Art and Architecture

Acanfora, Elisa. "L'arredo e la decorazione d'interni: Casa Bujonarroti." Pp. 134–37 of *Il Seicento*. (Storia delle arti in Toscana.) Edited by Mina Gregori. Firenze: Edifir, 2001.

Acanfora, Elisa. "L'arredo e la decorazione d'interni: il gusto tardobarocco." Pp. 262–66 of *Il Seicento*. (Storia delle arti in Toscana.) Edited by Mina Gregori. Firenze: Edifir, 2001.

Acanfora, Elisa. "La decorazione di Palazzo Pitti da Giovanni da San Giovanni a Jacopo Chiavistelli." Pp. 147–54 of *Il Seicento*. (Storia delle Arti in Toscana.) Edited by Mina Gregori. Firenze: Edifir, 2001.

Acanfora, Elisa. "La pittura ad affresco fino a Giovanni da San Giovanni." Pp. 45–60 of *Il Seicento*. (Storia delle arti in Toscana.) Edited by Mina Gregori. Firenze: Edifir, 2001.

Alvarez, J. "Fama temprana de Cano en Europa." *Cuadernos de Arte de la Universidad de Granada*, 32 (2001), 17–43.

Asleson, Robyn, Shelley M. Bennett (eds.). *British Paintings at the Huntington*. Catalogue. Catalogue researched and written by Robyn Asleson; Shelly M. Bennett, General Editor and project supervisor; Technical notes by Rosamond Westmoreland and Shelley Svoboda; Additional contributions by Melinda McCurdy and Elizabeth Pergam. San Marino: Henry E. Huntington Library, Art Collections, and Botanical Gardens in association with Yale University Press, New Haven, 2001. Pp. vii + 568; 200 black and white plates; 185 colour plates.

Athanassoglou-Kallmeyer, Nina. "Blemished Physiologies: Delacroix, Paganini, and the Cholera Epidemic of 1832." *The Art Bulletin,* 84 (2001), 686–710.

Baarsen, Reinier J., Bart Cornelis, Jan Piet Filedt Kok, Wouter Theodore Kloek, Guido Jansen, and Frits Scholten. *Netherlandish Art 1600-1700.* New Haven: Yale University Press; Published in association with Waanders Publishers and the Rijksmuseum, Amsterdam. 2001. Pp. 288; 150 black-and-white plates; 190 colour plates.

Baarsen, Reinier, et al. (eds.). *Rococo in Nederland.* Zwolle: Waanders Uitgevers, 2001. (Published in conjunction with an exhibition held at the Rijksmuseum, Amsterdam, November 2, 2001–February 3, 2002.) Pp. 330; bibliography; coloured illustrations; index.

Barbolani di Montauto, Novella. "La natura morte da Cosimo II a Cosimo III." Pp. 119–25 of *Il Seicento.* (Storia delle arti in Toscana.) Edited by Mina Gregori. Firenze, Edifir, 2001.

Barbolani di Montauto, Novella. "Il paesaggio e il ritratto nella seconda metà del secolo. Pp. 253–61 of *Il Seicento.* (Storia delle arti in Toscana.) Edited by Mina Gregori. Firenze: Edifir, 2001.

Bareau, Juliet Wilson. *Goya: Drawings from His Private Albums.* Essay by Tom Lubbock. London: Hayward Gallery; Lund Humphries, 2001. Pp. 206; black-and-white and colored illustrations.

Published by the Hayward Gallery in association with Lund Humphries on the occasion of the exhibition "Goya: Drawings from his Private Albums," organized by the Hayward Gallery, London, February 22–May 13, 2001.

Bellesi, Sandro. "La scultura tra il tardomanierismo e il barocco." Pp. 29–44 of *Il Seicento.* (Storia delle arti in Toscana.) Edited by Mina Gregori. Firenze: Edifir, 2001.

Beneš, Mirka, and Dianne Harris. *Villas and Gardens in Early Modern Italy and France.* (Cambridge Studies in New Art History and Criticism.) Cambridge: Cambridge University Press, 2001. Pp. xx + 428; 104 line diagrams; 62 halftone illustrations.

Bentley, G. E., Jr. *The Stranger from Paradise. A Biography of William Blake.* New Haven: Published for the Paul Mellon Centre for Studies in British Art by Yale University Press, 2001. Pp. xv + 532; appendices (including list of works); endnotes; 40 figures; index; 136 black and white, and color plates; tables.

Berkel, Klaas van. "Vermeer and the representation of science." Pp. 131–39 of *The Cambridge Companion to Vermeer.* (Cambridge Companions to the History of Art.) Edited by Wayne E. Franits. Cambridge: Cambridge University Press, 2001.

IV: Fine Arts

Bertini, Giuseppe. "Giacomo Gaufrido's Collection of Paintings Confiscated in 1650 by the Farnese." *The Burlington Magazine.* CXLIII: 1174 (January 2001), Online edition: http://www.burlington.org.uk/issues/1174.asp.

Biermann, Veronica. "The Virtue of a King and the Desire of a Woman? Mythological Representations in the Collection of Queen Christina." *Art History,* 24 (2001), 213–30.

Blasio, Silvia, "Il paesaggio." Pp. 126–33 of *Il Seicento.* (Storia delle arti in Toscana.) Edited by Mina Gregori. Firenze: Edifir, 2001.

Bowron, Edgar Peters (ed.). *Bernardo Bellotto and the Capitals of Europe.* New Haven: Yale University Press, 2001. Pp. xiii + 280; bibliography; genealogical table; colored plates.

Catalog of an exhibition held at the Museo correr, Venice, February 10–June 27, 2001, and at the Museum of Fine Arts, Houston, Texas, July 29–October 21, 2001.

Botteri, Lauro, and Francesco Mati. "Un alloriano minore tra impegni granducali e committenze nel territorio in Il Seicento in Casentino. Dalla Controriforma al Tardo Barocco." *Quaderni della Rilliana,* XXIII (2001), 109–14.

Bullen, J. B. "Sara Losh: Architect, Romantic, Mythologist." *The Burlington Magazine,* 143 (2001). Online edition: http://www.burlington.org.uk/issues/1184.asp/.

Caffort, Michel. "Sparte et Jérusalem les Davidiens et la peinture religieuse sous la restauration." *Revue d'Histoire de l'Eglise de France,* 87 (2001), 415–37.

Carofano, Pierluigi, and Franco Pallaga. *Pittura e collezionismo a Pisa nel Seicento.* Pisa: Edizioni ETS, 2001. Pp. 278; bibliography; indices; 52 black and white and coloured plates.

Carroll, Noël. *Beyond Aesthetics: Philosophical Essays.* Cambridge: Cambridge University Press, 2001. Pp. xiv + 450; bibliography; index.

Cheetham, Mark A. *Kant, Art, and Art History: Moments of Discipline.* Cambridge: Cambridge University Press, 2001. Pp. x + 222; bibliography; index; illustrations.

Christiansen, Keith, and Judith W. Mann (eds.). *Orazio and Artemisia Gentileschi.* New Haven: Published for the Metropolitan Museum of Art by Yale University Press, 2001. Pp. xx + 476; appendices; bibliography; chronology; index; 146 black-and-white plates; 85 color plates.

In 1976, Ann Sutherland Harris and Linda Nochlin curated a seminal exhibition entitled "Women Artists: 1550–1950" (*Exhibition catalogue.* New York: Alfred A. Knopf, 1976). This traveling exhibition brought to the American viewing public six paintings by the Roman-born artist Artemisia Gentileschi (1593–1652). In 1989, Mary Garrard wrote a compelling monograph of the artist who had, at that point, gone from virtual anonymity to the forefront of feminist culture studies (Mary D. Garrard, *Artemisia Gentileschi: The Image of the Female Hero in Italian Baroque Art*. Princeton: Princeton University Press, 1989). The present voluminous study by Keith Christiansen and Judith W. Mann seeks to expand the discourse on Artemisia by looking equally hard at the work of her father and teacher Orazio (c. 1563–1639). The two painters, father and daughter, were followers of Caravaggio and as artists, their work looks forward, anticipating the century to come. Their use of the model and an almost scientific observation of nature anticipate the artistic characteristics of the Enlightenment. According to Judith Mann, "Although Artemisia does not seek the accuracy of surface and texture that engaged her father, early on she evinced an interest in rendering narrative in a believable manner. Orazio rarely demonstrates such attunement to the dramatic details of his stories. His protagonists often assumed masterful poses that further the narrative" (256).

Artemisia Gentileschi was the most important and influential female painter of her time, even becoming a member of the academy in 1616. She was married to a Florentine painter named Pietro Stiattesi, and together they had a daughter, Prudentia (named after Artemisia's mother), who was born in 1618. A few years later, perhaps while separated from her husband, Artemisia had a second daughter. Both daughters continued in the family business, becoming third-generation painters and their mother's students.

The popularity of Artemisia's work, which was fueled by R. Ward Bissell's catalogue *raisonné* (*Artemisia Gentileschi and the Authority of Art: Critical Reading and Catalogue Raisonné* (University Park: Penn State University Press, 1998), has caused confusion in the attribution of much of Orazio's work. The similarities of their styles and parallel uses of biblical and classical themes has created an academic tug-of-war, much of which revolves around issues of gender. The present study, an exhibition catalogue produced jointly by the Museo del Palazzo di Venezia, Rome, the Metropolitan Museum of Art, New York, and the Saint Louis Art Museum, is valuable for its efforts to clarify the provenance of these disputed paintings. There are several works in particular that remain controversial in terms of attribution and a focus of scholarship: *Danae in St. Louis*, *Cleopatra in Milan*, and *The Pentitent Madgalena in London*. This book puts forth documentation that goes beyond feminist analysis and looks objectively at the influence of father on daughter. In order to do this, the authors have focused on patronage and the patronage infrastructure that supported them both.

Artemisia and Orazio were part of a wide-spread circle of well-known artists in Europe and these connections gave them access to international network of patronage. Artemisia was friends with Michaelangelo Buonarroti in Florence, and in Genoa, where they moved in 1620, they became friends with the painter Anthony Van Dyke. In Naples Artemisia enjoyed the company of the Spanish artist Diego Velasquez, who as "painter to Philip IV of Spain, had arrived in [Naples, in 1631] ... in the retinue of the Spanish Infanta [Maria, Philip's sister]" (381). Unfortunately, Orazio was also friends with Agostino Tassi, who raped the nineteen-year-old Artemisia while she was under his tutelage, in 1612. The rape led to Tassi's sensational seven-month trial that followed at the heels of his other trial for murdering his wife and having what was regarded at the time as an incestuous relationship with her sister.

Until her death in 1633 at the age of sixty-one, Artemisia exercised a decided influence on younger artists. This was particularly evident in Naples where the work of Francesco Guarino, Pacecco de Rosa, Massimo Stansione, and her pupil Onofrio Palumbo show a clear stylistic relationship to Artemisia's late paintings. "In the Saint Cecilia, Guarino makes an elaborate study of the saint's white, blue, and yellow drapery—a veritable homage to Artemisia's masterly rendering of color"(387). The Neapolitan painter Pacecco de Rosa also "shows a perhaps not coincidental similarity with Artemisia's most successful works" (188).

Private patronage for Artemisia came from was provided by many influential collectors. As a young artist in Florence, she was awarded numerous commissions from her admirer Cosimo II de Medici. She worked for King Charles I in England, and Orazio also worked for the court until the end of his life, dying in England in 1639. Artemisia also had numerous Spanish and Neapolitan patrons who promoted her work. "Artemisia's ability to find support throughout her career perhaps explains the confidence with which she worked" (382).

This handsome and informative volume concludes with several appendices of note and an annotated bibliography that illuminates the scholarship pertaining to both artists. This book is both a significant contribution to the history of the Gentileschi's work and the history of artistic patronage in seventeenth-century Europe. It is evidenced by this study that Artemisia was not merely a follower of her father, working in isolation imposed at the time by her gender, rather she was an active member of artistic circles that stimulated her work and contributed to "the intensity with which [she] measured herself against her male colleagues" (390)—Anna Novakov

Ciampolini, M. "L'independenza di Siena." Pp. 219–27 of *Il Seicento*. (Storia delle arti in Toscana.) Edited by Mina Gregori. Firenze: Edifir, 2001.

Cole, Michael. "The Figura Sforzata: Modelling, Power and the Mannerist Body." *Art History*, 24 (2001), 520–51.

Cowart, G. "Watteau's Pilgrimage to Cythera and the Subversive Utopia of the Opera-Ballet." *The Art Bulletin*, 83 (2001), 461–78.

D'Afflitto, Chiara. "'Naturale' e tradizione nella pittura religiosa a Firenze, da Cigoli a Carlo Dolci." Pp. 81–98 of *Il Seicento*. (Storia delle arti in Toscana.) Edited by Mina Gregori. Firenze: Edifir, 2001.

Davis, Whitney. "Homoerotic Art Collection from 1750 to 1920. *Art History*, 24 (2001), 247–77.

DeTurk, Sabrina. "Illicit Arousal: The Erotic Subtext of Tintoretto's *Tarquin and Lucretia*." *Aurora,* II (2001). Online edition: http:/www.arthistory.rutgers.edu.

Feo, Roberto de. "The 'Omaggio delle Provincie Venete': A Venetian Table Made for the Empress of Austria Rediscovered." *The Burlington Magazine*, 143 (2001). Online edition: http://www.burlington.org.uk/issues/1179.asp/.

Fornasari, Liletta, "Arezzo e provincia tra Firenze." Pp. 242–50 of *Il Seicento*. (Storia delle arti in Toscana.) Edited by Mina Gregori. Firenze: Edifir, 2001.

Fort, Bernadette, and Angela Rosenthal (eds,). *The Other Hogarth: Aesthetics of Difference*. Princeton: Princeton University Press, 2001. Pp. viii + 320; bibliography; 26 duotone illustrations; 129 halftone illustrations; index.

Franits, Wayne. "Johannes Vermeer: An Overview of his Life and Stylistic Development." Pp. 8–26 of *The Cambridge Companion to Vermeer*. Edited by Wayne E. Franits. Cambridge: Cambridge University Press, 2001.

Franits, Wayne E. (ed.). *The Cambridge Companion to Vermeer*. Cambridge: Cambridge University Press, 2001. Pp. xxiv + 241; bibliography; chronology; endnotes; geographical index; name index; map; black-and-white plates.

Johannes Vermeer of Delft (1632-1675), with other Netherlands painters, glorified the Dutch art of the seventeenth century, usually known as the "Golden Age" of Dutch paintings. Of the many paintings attributed to Vermeer, only thirty-six are now considered "authentic" and these, considered the most precious pieces in their respective collections, are exhibited in museums and galleries as well as in private collections. Although his pictures seemed to be painted vigorously and easily, as if at one breath, Vermeer worked slowly and carefully. Rich colours, the play of pearl and red-brown in combination with intensive blues and yellows serve as his "pictorial signature". His idiosyncratic style of painting distinguished his pictures from those of other Dutch masters, but despite Vermeer's works traveled from one famous collection to another and were widely viewed during the seventeenth and eighteenth centuries, they were not in great demand by art-collectors and connoisseurs until the second half of the nineteenth century, and collectors of the twentieth century only took a keen interest in his paintings when they became topical examples of the "Golden Age".

A number of important monographs and studies of Vermeer's paintings were published during the twentieth century, and these were followed by the monumental Vermeer exhibition which was held in Washington, D.C. and The Hague during 1995-1996, The overwhelming response to this exhibition was based on Vermeer's "modern" qualities, and almost continuous revaluation of his works has accompanied him since the eighteenth century. Notwithstanding all the attention he has received, this "master of light" is still very enigmatic.

The focal points of this edition of *The Cambridge Companion to Vermeer* are the varied aspects of Vermeer's works and the different ways in which they have been understood and interpreted since the seventeenth century. As editor Franits explains in his introduction, this volume is "meant to bridge the gap between experts on one hand, and students and general art lovers on the other"(2), and the following ten essays contributed by scholars of Dutch art are indeed addressed to readers of many different backgrounds. Franits' biography of Vermeer and his overview of his stylistic development (1–20), with essays by Walter Liedtke on Vermeer's self-taught techniques (28–40), and Arthur Wheelock on Vermeer's 'craft' (41–53), provide a general survey of Vermeer's life, education, and artistic development. They also furnish the reader with a comprehensive background for the following essays, which explore Vermeer's art within the broader context of contemporary Dutch culture. These essays trace a broad trajectory, offering perspectives such as Lisa Vergara's on "women" (54–72), Elise Goodman's on Vermeer's "landscapes" (73–88), H. Rodney Nevitt's discussion of Vermeer's representations of "love and courtship" (89–110), Valerie Hedquist's analysis of the role of "religion" in Vermeer's art (111–30), and Klaas van Berkel's discussion of Vermeer's representation of "science" (131–39).

The volume concludes with two studies of the growing interest in Vermeer's paintings. Christiane Hertel charts Vermeer's neglect in previous centuries (140–60), and Arthur K. Wheelock and Marguerite Glass address the rediscovery of his works, which began in the decade after his death and gained increasing momentum in the nineteenth and twentieth centuries (161–82). Each chapter is accompanied by a profusion of black-and-white plates and figures, and the reader will also find, at the beginning of the volume, a separate album of all Vermeer's works and a map of the town of Delft where he worked. Since these, too, are only black-and-white plates, they can provide only an approximation of Vermeer's paintings in which colour plays such an important role.

As Franits intended, this *Companion to Vermeer* does indeed "examine the art and life of Vermeer from a variety of perspectives" (2), and students and laypersons, alike, will find a wealth of general facts and documented material, systematized and prepared for easy acceptance. Scholars considering Vermeer in the context of the "long" eighteenth century will find here a sampling of the wide range of methodologies and interpretations applied to his art during this period. Since Vermeer was not a popular artist in the seventeenth and eighteenth centuries, however, eighteenth-century scholars will find the data and contextual documentation of greatest value. Of particular interest are the accounts of collections in which Vermeer's work was exhibited during the eighteenth century, the names of contemporary art lovers who were interested in his work, and very detailed comparisons between the sales of Vermeer's paintings "to wealthy burghers in the early 1800s and their sales, in the years around 1900, again to wealthy collectors from the world of business and commerce" (144). Also of interest to eighteenth-century researchers are the aesthetic standards revealed in contemporary critiques of Vermeer.

As "the art of Vermeer continues to fascinate art historians" (2) and art lovers, this volume provides a significant contribution to Vermeer scholarship and commemoration of his work. For the contributors to *The Cambridge Companion to Vermeer,* as for Vermeer, himself, the "task is not to solve enigmas, but to be aware of them, to bow our heads before them" (Z. Herbert, "Letter of Vermeer to Van Leeuwenhoek," 156). As their essays make abundantly clear, they have successfully fulfilled this task.—Olga Roussinova.

Frischer, Bernard D., and Iain Gordon Brown (eds.). *Allan Ramsay and the Search for Horace's Villa.* Contributions by Patricia R. Andrew, John Dixon Hunt, Martin Goalen. (Reinterpreting classicism.) Brookfield: Ashgate Publishing Company, 2001. Pp. xx + 183; bibliography; index; maps; black-and-white plates; color plates.

Gainsborough, Thomas. *The Letters of Thomas Gainsborough.* Edited by John Hayes. New Haven: Published for the Paul Mellon Centre for Studies in British Art by Yale University Press, 2001. Pp xxx + 209; bibliography; illustrations; index.

Georgopoulou, Maria. *Venice's Mediterranean Colonies: Architecture and Urbanism.* Cambridge: Cambridge University Press, 2001. Pp. xv + 383; bibliography; index; illustrations.

Geraghty, Anthony. "Edward Woodroofe: Sir Christopher Wren's First Draughtsman." *The Burlington Magazine*, 143 (2001). Online edition: http://www.burlington.org.uk/issues/1181.asp/.

Gill, Miriam, and Richard K. Morris. "A Wall Painting of the Apocalypse in Coventry Rediscovered." *The Burlington Magazine*, 143 (2001). Online edition: http://www.burlington.org.uk/issues/1180.asp/.

Giusti, A. M. "I fasti delle pietre dure." Pp. 138–42 of *Il Seicento.* (Storia delle arti in Toscana.) Edited by Mina Gregori. Firenze: Edifir, 2001.

Giusti Maccari, Patrizia. "Influenze fiorentine a Lucca." Pp. 228–33 of *Il Seicento.* (Storia delle arti in Toscana.) Edited by Mina Gregori. Firenze: Edifir, 2001.

Goodman, Elise. "The Landscape on the Wall in Vermeer." Pp. 73–88 of *The Cambridge Companion to Vermeer.* (Cambridge Companions to the History of Art.) Edited by Wayne E. Franits. Cambridge: Cambridge University Press, 2001.

Gregori, Mina. "I decenni centrali del secolo. 'Maxima et minima': Volterrano, Stefano della Bella e oltre." Pp. 155–64 of *Il Seicento.* (Storia delle arti in Toscana.) Edited by Mina Gregori. Firenze: Edifir, 2001.

Gregori, Mina. "I pittori fiorentini tra Venezia, Parma e Roma." Pp. 9–20 of *Il Seicento.* (Storia delle arti in Toscana.) Edited by Mina Gregori. Firenze: Edifir, 2001.

Gregori, Mina (ed.). *Il Seicento.* (Storia delle arti in Toscana.) Firenze: Edifir, 2001. Pp. 300; bibliography; index; 285 black-and-white and colored plates.

Hamon, Etienne. "Evaluer la peine des hommes. La mesure de l'architecture à Paris à la fin du moyen age (XVe-début XVIe siècle)." *Histoire & Mesure*, 16 (2001), 283–307.

Harbison, P. "'Irish Artists on Irish Subjects'—The Cooper Collection in the National Library." *Irish Arts Review Yearbook*, 17 (2001), 61–69.

Hedin, Thomas F. "The Petite Commande of 1664: Burlesque in the Gardens of Versailles." *The Art Bulletin*, 83 (2001), 651–87.

Hedquist, Valerie. "Religion in the Art and Life of Vermeer." Pp. 111–30 of *The Cambridge Companion to Vermeer*. (Cambridge Companions to the History of Art.) Edited by Wayne E. Franits. Cambridge: Cambridge University Press, 2001.

Hertel, Christiane. "Seven Vermeers: Collection, Reception, Response." Pp. 140–60 of *The Cambridge Companion to Vermeer*. (Cambridge Companions to the History of Art.) Edited by Wayne E. Franits. Cambridge: Cambridge University Press, 2001.

Honer, John. "The Genius of Soane." *Notes and Records of the Royal Society of London*, 55 (2001), 325–29.

Hsu, Ginger Cheng-chi. *A Bushel of Pearls: Painting for Sale in Eighteenth-Century Yangchow*. Stanford: Stanford University Press, 2001. Pp. xiii + 314.

Hughes, Christopher G. "Embarrassment and Disconvenance in Poussin's *Rebecca and Eliezar at the Well.*" *Art History*, 24 (2001), 493–519.

Ingamells, John and John Edgcumbe (eds.). *The Letters of Sir Joshua Reynolds*. New Haven: Yale University Press for the Paul Mellon Centre for Studies in British Art, 2001. Pp. xxix + 290; illustrations; indices.

Jeffares, N. "L'abbe Pommyer, honoraire amateur de l'Academie royale de peinture." *Gazette des Beaux-Arts*, 137 (2001), 237–56.

Johnson, Lee. "Some sketches made by Delacroix in Dieppe." *The Burlington Magazine*. CXLIII: 1177 (April, 2001), Online edition: http://www.burlington.org.uk/issues/1177.asp.

Jones, Alun R. "Adaptations by a Proud Hot Welshman." *National Library of Wales Journal*, 31 (2001), 61–72.

Kaldenbach, Kees. "Vermeer Geography: Homes of Artists and Patrons in the Age of Vermeer" (with foldout map). Pp. xxi–xxiv of *The Cambridge Companion to Vermeer*.

IV: Fine Arts

(Cambridge Companions to the History of Art.) Edited by Wayne E. Franits. Cambridge: Cambridge University Press, 2001.

Katz, Melissa R. (ed.). *Divine Mirrors. The Virgin Mary in the Visual Arts.* With Essays by Melissa R. Katz and Robert A. Orsi. Oxford: Catalog of an exhibition held at the Davis Museum and Cultural Center, Wellesley College, Wellesley, MA. Oxford University Press, 2001. Pp. xxi + 297; bibliography; index; monochrome and colored plates.

Kieven, Elisabeth and Pinto, John. *Pietro Bracci and Eighteenth-Century Rome: Drawings for Architecture and Sculpture in the Canadian Centre for Architecture and Other Collections.* Montreal: Canadian Centre for Architecture, 2001. Pp. xi + 296; plates; illustrations.

Lenzi Iacomelli, Carlotta. "I casi di Prato, Pistoia e Pisa. Pp. 234–41 of *Il Seicento*. (Storia delle arti in Toscana.) Edited by Mina Gregori. Firenze: Edifir, 2001.

Leonard, Mark, Narayan Khandekar, and Dawson W. Carr. "'Amber varnish' and Orazio Gentileschi's 'Lot and His Daughters.'" *The Burlington Magazine.* CXLIII: 1174 (January 2001), Online edition: http://www.burlington.org.uk/issues/1174.asp.

Liedtke, Walter. *A View of Delft. Vermeer and his Contemporaries.* Zwolle: Yale University Press, 2001. Distributed for Wanders Publishers. Pp. 320; bibliography; index; black and white plates; color plates.

Liedtke, Walter. "Vermeer Teaching Himself." Pp. 27–40 of *The Cambridge Companion to Vermeer.* (Cambridge Companions to the History of Art.) Edited by Wayne E. Franits. Cambridge: Cambridge University Press, 2001.

Longstaffe-Gowan, Todd. *The London Town Garden, 1700-1840.* New Haven: Yale University Press for the Paul Mellon Centre for Studies in British Art, 2001. Pp. xiii + 289; bibliography; index; black-and-white plates; color plates.

Lorizzo, Loredana. "Cardinal Ascanio Filomarino's Purchases of Works of Art in Rome: Poussin, Caravaggio, Vouet and Valentin." *The Burlington Magazine*, 143 (2001). Online edition: http://www.burlington.org.uk/issues/1180.asp/.

Lowrey, John. "From Caesarea to Athens: Greek Revival Edinburgh and the Question of Scottish Identity within the Unionist State." *Journal of the Society of Architectural Historians*, 60 (2001), 136–57.

Maffeis, Rodolfo. "La pittura da stanza." Pp. 61–80 of *Il Seicento*. (Storia delle arti in Toscana.) Edited by Mina Gregori. Firenze: Edifir, 2001.

Mcevansoneya, Philip. "Lord Egremont and Flaxman's 'St. Michael Overcoming Satan.'" *The Burlington Magazine*, 143 (2001). Online edition: http://www.burlington.org.uk/issues/1179.asp/.

Meoni, L. "L'arazzeria medicea." Pp. 107–18 of *Il Seicento*. (Storia delle arti in Toscana.) Edited by Mina Gregori. Firenze: Edifir, 2001.

Meslay, Olivier. "Murillo and 'smoking mirrors.'" *The Burlington Magazine*, 143 (2001). Online edition: http://www.burlington.org.uk/issues/1175.asp/.

Millington, Jon. "Engravings of Fonthill." *The Beckford Journal*, 7 (2001), 47–59.

Minor, Heather Hyde. "Rejecting Piranesi." *The Burlington Magazine*. CXLIII: 1180 (July, 2001), Online edition: http://www.burlington.org.uk/issues/ 1180.asp.

Mongeig Goguel, Catherine. "'Sul bianco del foglio' colla matita, la penna, i pastelli." Pp. 95–106 of *Il Seicento*. (Storia delle arti in Toscana.) Edited by Mina Gregori. Firenze: Edifir, 2001.

Myrone, Martin. *Henry Fuseli*. (British Artists.) Princeton: Princeton University Press, 2001. Pp. 80; bibliography; chronology; end notes; index; 62 halftone and colored plates.

Nevitt, H. Rodney. "Vermeer on the Question of Love." Pp. 89–110 of *The Cambridge Companion to Vermeer*. (Cambridge Companions to the History of Art.) Edited b Wayne E. Franits. Cambridge: Cambridge University Press, 2001.

Ogata, Amy F. *Art Nouveau and the Social Vision of Modern Living: Belgian Artists in a European Context*. (Modern Architecture and Cultural Identity.) Cambridge: Cambridge University Press, 2001. Pp. xvi + 239; bibliography; index; black and white and colored plates.

Ostergard, Derek E. (ed.). "William Beckford, 1760–1844: An Eye for the Magnificent." Catalogue published in conjunction with exhibitions "William Beckford, 1760–1844: An Eye for the Magnificent" held at Bard Graduate Center for Studies in the Decorative Arts, Design, and Culture, October 18, 2001–January 6, 2002 and Dulwich Picture Gallery, London, February 5–April 14, 2002. New Haven: Yale University Press, 2001. Pp. 448; black-and-white and colored illustrations; plans.

Pacini, Piero. *Le sedi del Accademia del Disegno al "Cestello" e alla "Crocetta."* (Accademia delle arti e del disegno 8.) Firenze: Leo S. Olschki, 2001. Pp. xv + 287; bibliography; illustrations; indices.

IV: Fine Arts

Pellicari, Medardo. "Scagliole a Firenze nel Seicento." Pp. 143–46 of *Il Seicento*. (Storia delle arti in Toscana.) Edited by Mina Gregori. Firenze: Edifir, 2001.

Phillips, Michael. *Wiliam Blake. The Creation of the Songs from Manuscript to Illuminated Printing.* Princeton: Princeton University Press, 2001. Pp. xi + 180; bibliography; endnotes; Blake index; general index; 36 black and white plates; 72 color plates.

Pointon, Marcia. "Surrounded with Brilliants: Miniature Portraits in Eighteenth-Century England." *The Art Bulletin,* 83 (2001), 48–71.

Poke, Christopher. "Jacques Androuet Ducerceau's 'Petites Grotesques' as a Source for Urbino maiolica decoration." *The Burlington Magazine*, 143 (2001). Online edition: http://www.burlington.org.uk/issues/1179.asp/.

Rijk, Michel Nuss de, Robert Schmedding, Clemens Steinbicker, and Guy Leclerc. *The Genealogy of the Family Schmedding*. Veneux-les Sablons: Helioservice, 2001, Volume II: 51–89.

Rosenberg, Pierre, and Colin B. Bailey. "Not Greuze, but Bernard d'Agesci." *The Burlington Magazine*, 143 (2002). Online edition: http://www.burlington.org.uk/issues/1175.asp/.

Roworth, Wendy Wassyng. "Re-thinking Eighteenth-Century Rome." Exhibition Review: *The Splendor of Eighteenth-Century Rome*, Philadelphia Museum of Art and Museum of Fine Arts, Houston, March, 2001. *The Art Bulletin*, 83 (2001), 135–44.

Rudolf, C., and S. F. Ostrow. "*Isaac Laughing*: Caravaggio, Non-traditional Imagery and Traditional Identification." *Art History,* 24 (2001), 646–81.

Rüger, Axel. "Vermeer and Painting in Delft." Published to accompany an exhibition held at the National Gallery, London, June 20–September 16, 2001. London: National Gallery Company, 2001. Pp. 72; bibliography; colored plates; maps.

Russell, Terence M. (ed.) *The Napoleonic Survey of Egypt: Description de l'Égypte. The Monuments and Customs of Egypt: Selected Engravings and Ttexts.* Two volumes. Aldershot: Ashgate Publishing Company, 2001. Pp. xvi + 296, 328; bibliography; 200 black-and-white plates; index.

Sánchez-Jáuregui, Maria Dolores. "Two portraits of Francis Basset by Pompeo Batoni in Madrid." *The Burlington Magazine*, 143 (2001). Online edition: http://www.burlington.org.uk/issues/1180.asp./

Schnapp, Alain. "Archéologie, histoire de l'art. Aux origines de la différenciation." *Cahiers d'Histoire: Revue d'Histoire Critique*, 82 (2001), 31–35.

Schraven, Minou. "Giovanni Battista Borghese's funeral 'apparato' of 1650 in Santa Maria Maggiore, Rome." *The Burlington Magazine*. CXLIII: 1174 (January 2001), Online edition: http://www.burlington.org.uk/issues/ 1174.asp.

Shelton, Andrew Carrington Shelton. "Art, Politics, and the Politics of Art: Ingres's *Saint Symphorien* at the 1834 Salon." *The Art Bulletin*, 83 (2001), 711–39.

Shiner, Larry *The Invention of Art: A Cultural History*. Chicago: University of Chicago Press, 2001. Pp. xix + 362; bibliography; figures; index; black-and-white plates; tables.

Sickel, Lothar. "Remarks on the patronage of Caravaggio's 'Entombment of Christ'." *The Burlington Magazine*. CXLIII: 1180 (July, 2001), Online edition: http://www.burlington. org.uk/issues/1180.asp.

Smalls, James. "Stepping Out on a Limb: Questioning Masculinity in Girodet's 'Scene of a Deluge' (1806)." *Aurora. The Journal of the History of Art*. II (2001), Online edition: http://arthistory.rutgers.edu/aurora.

Smith, Nicola. *The Royal Image and the English People*. Aldershot: Ashgate Publishing Company, 2001. Pp. xii + 234; bibliography; 73 black-and-white illustrations; index.

Sohm, Philip L. *Style in the Art Theory of Early Modern Italy*. Cambridge: Cambridge University Press, 2001. Pp. xii + 315; bibliography; index; illustrations.

Sørensen, Bent. "Two overlooked drawings by Piranesi for San Giovanni in Laterano in Rome." *The Burlington Magazine*. CXLIII: 1180 (July, 2001), Online edition: http://www.burlington.org.uk/issues/ 1180.asp.

Spinelli, Riccardo. "La grande decorazione murale (1675–1700)." Pp. 181–200 of *Il Seicento*. (Storia delle arti in Toscana.) Edited by Mina Gregori. Firenze: Edifir, 2001.

Thistlethwaite, Mark. "*Washington Crossing the Delaware*: Navigating the Image(s) of the Hero." Pp. 39–63 of *George Washington in and as Culture*. Edited by Kevin L. Cope, William S. Pederson, and Frank Williams. New York: AMS Press, 2001.

Vergara, Lisa. "Perspectives on women in the art of Vermeer." Pp. 54–72 of *The Cambridge Companion to Vermeer*. (Cambridge Companions to the History of Art.) Edited by Wayne E. Franits. Cambridge: Cambridge University Press, 2001.

IV: Fine Arts

Visonà, Mara, "L'Accademia di Cosimo III a Roma (1763–1686)." Pp. 165–80 of *Il Seicento*. (Storia delle arti in Toscana.) Edited by Mina Gregori. Firenze: Edifir, 2001.

Visonà, Mara. "La scultura a Firenze alla fine del secolo." Pp. 201–17 of *Il Seicento*. (Storia delle arti in Toscana.) Edited by Mina Gregori. Firenze: Edifir, 2001.

Vogtherr, Christope Martin. "Absent Love in Pleasure Houses. Frederick II of Prussia as Art Collector and Patron." *Art History,* 24 (2001), 231–46.

Wallen, Gerard de. "Corot as a copyist at the Louvre, and new evidence on his technique." *The Burlington Magazine*. CXLIII: 1184 (November, 2001), Online edition: http://www.burlington.org.uk/issues/1184.asp

Webb, J. "The Reign in Spain." *Art & Antiques*, 24 (2001), 76–83.

Wheelock, Arthur K., Jr. "Vermeer's Craft and Artistry." Pp. 41–53 of *The Cambridge Companion to Vermeer*. (Cambridge Companions to the History of Art.) Edited by Wayne E. Franits. Cambridge: Cambridge University Press, 2001.

Wheelock, Arthur K. and Marguerite Glass. "The Appreciation of Vermeer in Twentieth-century America." Pp. 161–82 of *The Cambridge Companion to Vermeer*. (Cambridge Companions to the History of Art.) Edited by Wayne E. Franits. Cambridge: Cambridge University Press, 2001, 161–82.

Wright, Beth S. *The Cambridge Companion to Delacroix*. Pp. xvi + 240; bibliography; chronology; end notes; 58 black-and-white illustrations; index; 11 half-tone plates.

Wunder, Amanda. "Murillo and the Canonisation Case of San Fernando, 1649–52." *The Burlington Magazine*, 143 (2001). Online edition: http://www.burlington.org.uk/issues/1184.asp/.

Dance

Albright, Ann Cooper, and Ann Dils (eds.). *Moving History—Dancing Cultures: A Dance History Reader*. Middletown: Wesleyan University Press, 2001. Pp. xviii + 492 pp; bibliography; index.

Desmond, Jane C. (ed.). *Dancing Desires: Choreographing Sexualities on and off the Stage*. (Studies in Dance History 18.) Madison: University of Wisconsin Press, 2001. Pp. x + 475; bibliography; index; black-and-white illustrations.

Guest, Ivor Forbes. *Le Ballet de l'Opéra de Paris.* Paris: Groupe Flammarion, 2001. Pp. 336; bibliography; illustrations; index.

Little, Meredith, and Natalie Jenne. *Dance and the Music of J. S. Bach. Expanded Edition.* (Music Scholarship and Performance.) Bloomington: Indiana University Press, 1991/2001. Pp. xii + 337; appendices; bibliography; diagrams; index; musical examples; notes; black-and-white plates; tables.

Revisions offer the opportunity to reevaluate. The 2001 edition of Little and Jenne's monograph on Bach's dance music adds a new chapter, "Dance Rhythms in Bach's Larger Work" (204–59), and a revised Appendix B which identifies *circa* 180 of Bach's pieces incorporating dance characteristics (299–306). Apart from this appendix, the 2001 edition is not a revision, but, rather, adheres closely to the earlier 1991 publication, and all new material—including further reflections on "Gigas" (260–85)— is in the same vein as the authors' previous work.

The opening chapter identifies French influences in places where Bach lived. "Terms and Procedures" entabulates the metric hierarchies for each generic dance, while revealing that each is shaped by a distinct energy (arsis) and repose (thesis) profile. Michel L'Affilard's concept of "dance models" in characteristic rhythms, shapes and phrase structures (25) and Marpurg's construct that a rhythmical hierarchy comprises "paragraphs, periods, and phrases" (25–30) are the declared theoretical foundations of this study. The authors' claim that they are "applying new...analytical tools" to Bach's music (xi) is not supported by a detailed explanation of their methodology. We are told that "the arsic and thetic quality of the harmony" is a contributing factor to "deriv[ing] the dance models and the characteristics of the dance types" (25), but there is neither discussion of what makes a harmonic progression arsic or thetic nor justification of a selective system which does not count every harmonic progression when determining most dances' energy profiles. Moreover, the place of Johann Kirnberger's theories— particularly as interpreted by the authors' doctoral supervisor, Putnam Aldrich—in the development of Little and Jenne's work, are not clear. See, for example, Aldrich's *festschrift* essay "'Rhythmic Harmony' as Taught by Johann Philipp Kirnberger" in *Studies in Eighteenth-Century Music, A Tribute to Karl Geiringer...* (London: George Allen and Unwin, 1970, 37–51).

Ultimately, this work is performer oriented, and the authors declare "the core of our approach to Baroque dance music is that rhythm and articulation grow from the performer's conception of phrases" (20). Chapters dedicated to individual dance types consider their affect or character, review temporal and rhythmic characteristics, present evidence about *tempi*, and detail the generic metric structures, rhythmic patterns, and energy profiles of the respective dances. As a consequence of considering each piece within Bach's titled dance repertory, the authors are unable to provide detailed analyses. Discussion of the *courante* from the *Overture in the French Style* (BWV 831) is characteristic: "[This piece] is fairly balanced in phrase structure, cast in strains of equal length (12 + 12), internally organised as 4 + 8 and 6 + 6. But at the same time it is a magnificent example of Bach's complete understanding of the French *courante* style, embellished with touches unique to his own genius. The opening measures have a pedal point on B with figuration which reaches to the low register of the harpsichord. The bass-line rhythms here accentuate arsic places in the *courante* rhythmic pattern, an idea which returns in measures 20–21. Shortening of eighth notes (or sixteenths) preceding beats 1 and 3 of the measure will lend a *courante* "feeling" in this piece. Arpeggiation, where indicated, is usually most successful from the top note down in order to preserve proper voice-leading" (128).

Little and Jenne's chapter on "Dance Rhythms in Bach's Larger Works" includes a checklist for each dance type which outlines its typical meter, affect, tempo, phrase structure, rhythmic patterns, and degree of harmonic complexity. A brief description of many of the "dance-like" pieces follows, including some preliminary considerations of the connections between texted works and the "characteristic" affect (a controversial concept) of the appropriate dance.

The authors' particular interest in the relevance of dance to music performance is reflected in several American Doctor of Musical Arts. dissertations written in the past two decades, and in the long tradition in German scholarship of engaging with these aspects of Bach's compositional style. Scholars worldwide are engaged in identifying dance rhythms in Bach's oeuvre, with some considering the symbolic functions of these figures. Although its lack of transparency reduces the present study's potential to serve as a foundation for parallel investigations into the work of other composers, the reader does develop a heightened appreciation of how dances of the time were shaped. Little and Jenne's most original contribution to scholarship is their detailed application of the rhythms and phrasing of baroque dance towards understanding the phrasing and gestures of distinctly "undanceable" music. It is unfortunate that their voyage of discovery is not presented in a sufficiently transparent, and therefore transferable, manner—Sarah McCleave

Mansfield, William. "Play of A Fiddle: Traditional Music, Dance and Folklore in West Virginia." *Oral History Review,* 28 (2001), 162–64.

Music

Adkins, Cecil. "Oboes Beyond Compare: The Instruments of Hendrik and Fredrik Richters." *The Double Reed,* 24 (2001), 69–98.

Allihn, Ingeborg (ed.). *Führer Barokmusic. Instrumentalmusik 1550-1770.* Stuttgart: J. B. Metzler–Bärenreiter, 2001. Pp. xx + 551; indices.

Andrews, R. "From Beaumarchais to Da Ponte: A New View of the Sexual Politics of "Figaro.'" *Music and Letters,* 82 (2001), 214–33.

Arce, Daniel Mendoza de. *Music in Ibero-America to 1850. A Historical Survey.* Lanham: Scarecrow Press, 2001. Pp. xviii + 722; bibliography; end notes; indices.

Arbo, Alessandro. "Gli uccelli cantano davvero?" *De Musica,* V (2001), Online edition: http://users.unimi.it/~gpiana/dm5idxrd.htm/.

Ashbee, Andrew, Robert Thompson, and Jonathan Wainwright (eds.). *The Viola da Gamba Society Index of Manuscripts containing consort Music.* Volume 1. Brookfield: Ashgate Publishing Company, 2001 Pp. v + 418; bibliography; illustrations; index.

Bar-Shany, Michael. "Beethoven in the Eyes of *The Harmonicon* (1823-1833): The Reviews of the Philharmonic Society Concerts." *Beethoven Journal.* 16 (2001), 12–19.

Beahrs, Virginia. "Kantian Concepts in the Life and Music of Beethoven: Reassessing Beethoven's Moral Imperatives." *Beethoven Journal,* 16 (2001), 54–61.

Beckage, Donna. "Evoking Beethoven on the Stage: Peter Ustinov, Stanley Freiberg, and Adrienne Kennedy." *Beethoven Journal,* 16 (2001), 2–11.

Berggren, Ulf. "Kognitiva strukturer i Olof Åhlströms sonater: Nutida teorier för analys av satstekniska konventioner i komposition av wienklassisk musik." *STM-Online,* 4 (2001). Online edition: http://www.musik.uu.se/ssm/stmonline/index.html.

Berke, Dietrich. "Mozart-Forschung und Mozart-Edition. Zur Erinnerung an Wolfgang Plath (1930–1995)." *Mozart-Jahrbuch* (2001), 1-12.

Biba, Otto. "Recalling Mozart." *Mozart Society of America Newsletter,* 1 (2001), 1–2, 4–5.

Birkett, Stephen, and William Jurgenson. "Why Didn't Historical Makers Need Drawings:" *The Galpin Society Journal,* liv (2001), 242–84.

Bockholdt, Rudolf. "Liebe zu einer unterschätzten Komposition Joseph Haydns. Die Finalsätze von Haydns 'Russischem' Quartett in G-Dur und Mozarts 'Haydn'—Quartett in d-Moll." Pp. 61–70 of *Studien zur Musik der Wiener Klassiker. Eine Aufsatzsammlung zum 70. Geburtstag des Autors.* Edited by Rudolf Bockholdt. Bonn: Verlag Beethoven-Haus, 2001.

Bongiovanni, Carmela. "Le fonti della musica vocale da camera di Ferdinando Paer." *Fonti Musicali Italiane,* 6 (2001), 21–104.

Boxall, Maria. "The Origins and Evolution of Diatonic Fretting." *The Galpin Society Journal,* 54 (2001), 143–99.

Boyd, Malcolm. *Bach.* (The Master Musicians Series.) Oxford: Oxford University Press, 2000. Pp. xvi + 312; appendices; bibliography; calendar of events; indices; list of works; map; musical examples; black-and-white and color plates; tables.

Since the death of Johann Sebastian Bach in 1750 our understanding of his life and music has grown exponentially, proceeding in tidy 50-year increments. In the latter half of the eighteenth century his reputation as an unsurpassed contrapuntist and composer of keyboard works spread from Thuringia to the rest of Europe as manuscript copies passed from hand to hand among musicians. The period from 1800 to 1850 saw the publication of Johann Nikolaus Forkel's critical biography (*Über Johann Sebastian Bachs leben, kunst und kunstwerke,* 1802/Reprint edited by Walther Vetter. Berlin: Henschel, 1982), and the growing popularity, among a wider public audience, of Bach's previously unknown choral works. The *Bach-Gesellschaft,* founded in 1850, undertook the monumental task of identifying and publishing Bach's complete works. The *Neue Bach-Gesellschaft* which replaced it (1900) expanded the society's music-publishing activities to promote the performance of Bach's music, and encouraged the exchange of information through its publication of *Bach-Jahrbuch,* an annual, scholarly journal. A comprehensive index of Bach's works, however, was not published until 1950 (Schmieder, Wolfgang, editor, *Thematisch-systematisches Verzeichnis der musikalischen Werke von Johann Sebastian Bach [Bach-Werke-Verzeichnis (BWV)]*). Wiesbaden: Breitkopf und Härtel, 1950/Reprint: 1990). The increasing number of discoveries and publications in Bach scholarship after 1950 were inspired, in part, by Georg von Dadelsen's handwriting analyses of Bach's manuscripts (Dadelsen, Georg von. *Beiträge zur Chronologie der Werke Johann Sebastian Bachs.* Trossingen: Hohner, 1958) and Alfred Dürr's studies of Bach's manuscripts and his revised chronology of Bach's works (Dürr, Alfred. *Johann Sebastian Bach: seine Handschrift, Abbild seines Schaffens.* Wiesbaden: Breitkopf und Härtel, 1984). The result of their work was a virtual revolution in Bach scholarship, accompanied by a reevaluation of Bach's biography and demands for new, improved editorial standards for publications by the *Neue Bach-Ausgabe.*

This third edition of Boyd's biography of Bach, which commemorates the 250th anniversary of the composer's death, represents a significant revision and enlargement of the publication's earlier editions of 1983 and 1990. Boyd summarizes recent Bach scholarship in both his narrative and in the appendices which have been extensively revised. These include a useful Calendar of events in Bach's life, with a corresponding column for activities of contemporary musicians (247–54), a List of Works which reflects the revised dating and chronology of Bach's compositions (255–82), a Personalia—an index of personal details in Bach's life—which includes results of recent archival studies (283–94), and a Select Bibliography, which has been updated to include several important studies published in the 1990s (295–300).

Topics expanded upon or newly introduced in this edition include a discussion of performance practices for Bach's music, such as articulation and the disposition of singers and instrumentalists in performance, tonal allegory and musical rhetoric, and number symbolism, which Boyd explains then dismisses (193–7; 234–7). Bach's youthful compositions receive particular attention, especially in the light of his chorale preludes found in the "Neumeister" chorale collection which was re-discovered at Yale University Library in 1984 (*LM 4708*; 29–32). Boyd also addresses Bach's use of parody technique, an unnecessarily contentious topic, although it is given a balanced treatment here (178–92). The 1999 discovery of the Alt-Bachisches Archiv in Kiev—Bach's personal collection of organ works by his musical forefathers, thought to have been lost since World War II—receives only brief mention in Boyd's text (177–78), perhaps in anticipation of new publications summarizing recent research on the collection. It would have been helpful, however, if Boyd had provided more information about the circumstances and musical "detective work" that led to this spectacular find (See Daniel Melamed's discussion in his monograph, *J. S. Bach and the German Motet*. Cambridge: Cambridge University Press, 1995; 161–88. Reviewed by Warwick Cole in *ECCB*, n.s. 20/21 [1994–95], 32–33).

The most illuminating additions in this new edition are Boyd's examinations of style and meaning in Bach's late instrumental works, particularly in *Clavier-Übung III* (194–97), *Well-Tempered Clavier II* (210–11), *Musical Offering* (203–04; 213–20), and *Art of Fugue* (220–27). These are part of a larger discussion of Bach's last works "Canons and Counterpoints" (Chapter 12) and his musical legacy, "The Bach Heritage" (Chapter 13). Boyd concludes with a moment of poetry, startling in a work as concise and factual as this. To one who thoughtfully ponders the score, he suggests, the augmentation canons in *Musical Offering* and *Art of Fugue* "offer an insight into the mysteries of infinity every bit as teasing in its mathematical beauty as Zeno's paradox of Achilles and the tortoise. [Only through the study of this music can we] "hope to arrive at a complete perception of it, and after study, contemplation; for it exists in a world far removed from the *musica humana* of our own, where music, mathematics, and philosophy are one" (227)—Jean M. Widaman.

Braunschweig, Karl. "Genealogy and Musica Poetica in Seventeenth- and Eighteenth-Century Theory." *Acta Musicologica*, 73 (2001), 25–50.

Brügge, Joachim. "Ausgesuchte Aspekte zu den Werkautographen, am Beispiel von *KV 458* I, und den Skizzen und Fragmenten im Umfeld der *Haydn-Quartette* Mozarts." *Mozart-Jahrbuch*, (2001), 345–54.

Brügge, Joachim. "Perspektiven und Grenzen von 'Typus und Modell' für die Mozart-Forschung." *Mozart-Jahrbuch*, (2001), 19–32.

Byrt, John. "Alteration in Handel: A Fresh Approach." *The Musical Quarterly*, 85 (2001), 194–219.

Caplin, William E. "The Classical Sonata Exposition: Cadential Goals and Form-Functional Plans." *Tijdschrift voor Muziektheorie* 3 (2001) (Online edition). http://cva.ahk.nl/tvm/tvm-e.html.

Carew, Derek. *The Piano and Its Music 1770–1850*. Aldershot: Ashgate Publishing Company, 2001. 2 volumes. Pp. 350 and 150; biographies; glossary; indices.

Carman, Judith E., William K. Gaeddert, and Rita M. Resch (eds.). *Art Song in the United States, 1759--1999: An Annotated Bibliography*. 3rd edition. Lanham: Scarecrow Press, 2001. Pp. xxiv + 475; chronological list of composers; indices: composers. poets, publishers, special characters, titles; with accompanying CD.

Casler, Lawrence. *Symphonic Program Music and Its Literary Sources*. (Studies in History and Interpretation of Music 75a-b.) 2 volumes. Lewiston: Edwin Mellen Press, 2001. Pp. 404 and 448; bibliography; indices.

Cerruti, Solbiati, and Silvio Cerruti. "I Luoghi della Mente: L'acqua in Schubert." *De Musica: Annuario in divenire,* V (2001). Online edition: http://users.unimi.it/ ~gpiana/dm5idxrd.htm/.

Charack, André. *Raison et perception: fonder l'harmonie au xviiie siècle*. Paris: Librarie Philosophique, J. Vrin, 2001. Pp. 319; bibliography; index.

Charteris, Richard. "Theophilus Hawney: A Little-Known Composer and His Much Travelled Works." *Early Music*, 29 (2001), 626–33.

Clark, Suzannah, and Alexander Rehding (eds.). *Music Theory and Natural Order from the Renaissance to the Early Twentieth Century*. Cambridge: Cambridge University Press, 2001. Pp. xi + 243; illustrations.

Collins, Dennis, and W. Andrew Schloss. "Unusual Effect in the Canon Per Tonos from J. S. Bach's *Musical Offering*." *Music Perception,* 19 (2001), 141–53.

Cooper, Barry. "Beethoven's 'Abendlied' and the 'Wiener Zeitschrift.'" *Music and Letters*, 82 (2001), 234–50.

Cooper, Barry. "The Cramer Anecdote about Beethoven: A Reassessment." *Beethoven Journal*, 16 (2001), 20–23.

Corp, E. "Handel, Scarlatti and the Stuarts: A Response to David Hunter." *Music and Letters*, 82 (2001), 556–58.

Crawford, Richard. *America's Musical Life: A History*. New York: W. W. Norton, 2001. Pp. xv + 976; bibliography; credits; index; musical examples; notes; black-and-white plates.

IV: Fine Arts

America's Musical Life is a much lighter "read" than the tome's three-pound weight and forty chapters would portend. Using a more journalistic than academic style, with minimal footnotes and lacking musical examples, Richard Crawford's survey covers five hundred years of musical activity in North America. Despite his attempts, in the early chapters, to discuss the music of Spanish and French settlements in California and Canada, and notwithstanding a chapter devoted to Native American music (a subject which receives a post-1820 update in Chapter 20), the "America" in the title of this book can rightly be viewed as synonymous with "United States" as the country makes its westward expansion from the Atlantic coast. Hence, after less than two dozen pages, Crawford's chronological account settles on the New England settlements (Chapter 2:20), moves to New Orleans and Chicago with the nationalization of jazz in the early twentieth century (Chapter 30), and then to southern California in the mid-twentieth century, where the Broadway musical takes to film (Chapter 32). A Los Angeles concert series of 1947 (Chapter 33) serves as a paradigm for the place of classical music in American life during the remainder of the century. The final six chapters and 150 pages of text treat a variety of popular and commercial musics that have emerged since 1965.

Eighteenth-century music, limited to only 100 pages in the text proper (Chapters 3 through 7), makes an unexpected reappearance in the Epilogue. Here, the author enters the narrative, describing a concert in the Upper Peninsula of Michigan that he attended in 1995. This program, sponsored by an amateur, modern-instrument orchestra, featured Mozart's concerto for two pianos (*K*.375) performed on replicas of eighteenth-century *fortepianos*. The program also included a work by a living American composer composer—discussed in detail by Crawford— in which the performers, ironically, chose to perform the piano part on the eighteenth-century-style instrument, having gone so far as to select the work because of its perceived adaptability to the unusual instrument. Crawford uses this journalistic device of a concert review (or report) to reflect on the challenges and rewards of writing historical narrative and also to recapitulate his intention, stated on the first page of the introduction (i), to use performance rather than composition as the focus of *America's Musical Life*.

The narrative chapters devoted to the eighteenth century are divided by function: church music (Chapter 3), song, dance, and domestic music (Chapter 4), military, concert, and theater music (Chapter 5), oral traditions and African music (Chapter 6), and church music--again (Chapter 7). With lack of patronage from state, church, or court, the musicians, themselves, created the support basis for eighteenth-century American music, by drawing on the resources provided by European settlers and their descendants. The result was a clear need for self-promotion and a growing dependence on imported repertory from England. In contrast, African slaves recreated the oral culture of Africa from memory, drawing on remembered traditions, even as regional differences developed between blacks in the north, in Louisiana, in Virginia, and in South Carolina. Crawford concludes this chapter on oral traditions and African music (Chapter 6) with a description of the Evangelical Camp Meeting, a unique occasion in eighteenth-century life where blacks and whites experienced some social intermingling. As a result, white participants, were influenced by black singing practices and developed a style of hymnody that was both emotional and formulaic, thus providing an early example of black musical influence and white adaptation that later formed the basis for much of the music that is uniquely "American".

Under the umbrella of the nineteenth century, Crawford begins Chapter 8 with a discussion of the long life and career of Lowell Mason (1792–1872). Mason's contributions to America's music in the fields of religion and education, well established by mid-century, fit well with Crawford's emphasis on musical function as a determining criterion. Mason, who was also a musical entrepreneur, published his first collection of church music, the *Boston Handel and Haydn Society Collection of Church Music* in 1822, and a textbook for singing teachers, the *Manual of the Boston Academy of Music* in 1834. Prior to the publications noted above, Lowell Mason studied composition with Frederick L. Abel, a German who had lived in London before immigrating to Savannah, Georgia, and thus was thoroughly schooled in European musical traditions.

Moving south, Crawford discusses shape-note singing (Chapter 9). He devotes another chapter to musical theater and opera (Chapter 10), and the role of new immigration in American life reveals itself in these chapters. The first performance of an opera in America (*The Barber of Seville* in New York, 1825) was arranged, in part, by Lorenzo Da Ponte, Mozart's librettist, who had emigrated to the United States in 1805.

As Crawford discloses in his introduction, *America's Musical Life* extends and updates the methodologies of two earlier surveys of American music: Gilbert Chase's, *America's Music, from the Pilgrims to the Present* (New

York: McGraw-Hill, 1955), and Wiley Hitchcock's, *Music in the United States: A Historical Introduction* (Englewood Cliffs: Prentice-Hall, 1969). In this new edition, which supplants the earlier volumes, Crawford intertwines narratives of folk, popular, and classical music, and while we might wish that he had not avoided controversy as carefully and as successfully as he did in tracing musical currents in the United States, this seminal study of *America's Musical Life* will serve as the preeminent treatment of the subject for the next generation of students and teachers—JoAnn Udovich

Croll, Gerhard. "Das *Andantino* für Klavier *KV* 236 (588b)—eine Gluck-Bearbeitung als Variationen-Thema. Bemerkungen zur autographen Überlieferung, zu Zweckbestimmung und Datierung." *Mozart-Jahrbuch* (2001), 245–56.

Dellaborra, Maria Teresa. "Il sacro sconosciuto: inediti sammartiniani a Vimercate," *Fonti Musicali Italiane,* 6 (2001), 7–19.

Durante, Sergio. "Considerations on Mozart's Changing Approach to Recitatives and on Other Choices of Dramaturgical Significance." *Mozart-Jahrbuch* (2001), 231–44.

Danckwardt, Marianne. "Nochmals zu den beiden *Lambacher Sinfonien.*" *Mozart-Jahrbuch,* (2001), 163–80.

Davies, Benjamin. "The Historiography of the Reformation, or the Reformation of Historiography." *Early Music,* 29 (2001), 263–74.

Eby, Jack. "A Requiem Mass for Louis XV: Charles d'Helfer, François Giroust and the *Missa pro defunctis* of 1775." *Early Music*, 29 (2001), 218–33.

Edgecombe, Rodney Stenning. "On the Limits of Genre: Some Nineteenth-Century Barcaroles." *19th-Century Music,* 24 (2001), 252–67.

Ellison, Paul M. "Beethoven and Schenker: Unraveling those Graphs, with an Explanation of Schenker's Analysis of the 'Ode to Joy.'" *Beethoven Journal,* 16 (2001), 69–73.

Ellison, Paul M. "Beethoven News 2001–2002." *Beethoven Journal*, 16 (2001), 79–80.

Etter, Brian. *From Classicism to Modernism: Western Musical Culture and the Metaphysics of Order.* Aldershot: Ashgate Publishing Company, 2001. Pp. 320; bibliography; index; musical examples.

Ewell, Terry B. "Proportional Tempos in the Concertos of Antonio Vivaldi." *The Double Reed,* 24 (2001), 113–21.

Fisk, Charles. *Returning Cycles. Contexts for the Interpretation of Schubert's Impromptus and Last Sonatas.* (Studies in 19th-Century Music.) Berkeley: University of California Press, 2001. Pp. xi + 307; index; musical examples; notes; tables.

Following the completion of the song cycle *Winterreise* in 1827, the year before his premature death, Schubert composed a remarkable series of cyclic works, including the last three sonatas for the piano and the two sets of impromptus, Opp. 90 and 142. In *Returning Cycles*, Fisk puts forth the theory that *Winterreise* and these piano works are related in a substantive, biographical way. His theory may be summarized as follows.

The author believes that Schubert, in composing *Winterreise*, came to identify himself palpably with the wanderer protagonist—with his sense of alienation, of loneliness (the wanderer's very first line in the song cycle is "A stranger I came, a stranger I depart"). The reasons for the composer's feeling this way were apparently his contraction of syphilis (he was already ill by January, 1823) and his purported homosexuality. To be sure, Schubert's allegorical tale "Mein Traum," dated July 23, 1822, but discovered only after his death, already conveys to us the composer's acute sense of alienation and rejection. In that fantastic tale—its origins as an actual dream is uncertain, although there is no doubt that the tale speaks of deep pain—he is twice banished from home by his father for rejecting the food served at the feasting table. Father and son are later reconciled, however, but inexplicably at the tomb of an unspecified (and hence mysterious) dead maiden where "heavenly thoughts" and "the most wondrous lovely sound" is heard" (9).

In contrast to "Mein Traum," *Winterreise* does not conclude with a reconciliation. By the end of the work, the wanderer, having trudged in the snow all night in a state of deep mental anguish, has become psychologically shattered and unable to engage with the world around him. Fisk contends that Schubert regretted the fate of the wanderer, and that in the major instrumental and chamber works composed after *Winterreise*, he sought to counter the song cycle's terrible ending by means of a "redemption or rebirth" (11) that cyclic procedures symbolically afford through the recall of previously heard music. To this purpose, the composer looked to his *Wanderer Fantasy* of 1822 (the year of "Mein Traum") as his model. As is well known, this work appropriates in a striking manner a melody from the 1816 song "Der Wanderer" which, like *Winterreise*, embodies a dejected wanderer as protagonist. Fisk claims that in pitting C-sharp minor, the key of the song melody, against C major, the key of the fantasy, in the slow movement, and thereafter bringing the tonal conflict to a resolution, Schubert has brought the wanderer home from his estrangement, just as the composer himself reconciles with his father at the end of "Mein Traum."

It is rare indeed that a critic would use biography to explain in this manner musical procedures that may yet be construed in purely musical terms. Implicit in Fisk's contention is that the story of the wanderer in the song is incomplete, and that its continuation, engendered by the composer instead of the poet, is contained in a genre where the agency of the voice, the protagonist, is no longer present or relevant. Rather, the genre of song, where the text tells a story, is replaced—indeed usurped—by one informed by reminiscences that are represented in purely technical terms. It is this mode of operation that Fisk believes the impromptus and the last three piano sonatas to embody vis-à-vis *Winterreise*, even though one may not claim that these piano works continue the specific story of the song cycle in a similar way. As the author puts it, it is through cyclic procedures in these pieces that "a *Winterreise*-haunted self, threatened with annihilation, in intensified doubt over its own unity and persistence, can seem gradually to regain continuity and integration" (12). If we accept Fisk's formulation, we may say further that Schubert tried to achieve in his music the "continuity and integration" that he knew he could not have while he was alive.

The analyses that form much of the rest of the book reveal cyclic features and procedures in the impromptus and late sonatas that one suspects often go unnoticed. They are informed not only by the sort of critical insights that a performer sensitive to what he plays and hears can give, but also by an acute musical memory. The cyclic reminiscences and connections in the music that Fisk—a performer, himself—uncovers are many and significant. They refer not only to recurring tonal relationships but also to specific thematic and other gestures, harmonic juxtapositions, cadential formulas, and so on. Thus, although the Opp. 90 and 142 impromptus are not normally thought of as cyclic works, Fisk is yet able to argue that they indeed are cyclic by pointing out the ways in which Schubert has infused the four *impromptus* of each set with interlocking features that are either similar or identical. The arguments here and elsewhere in the book make one listen to the music with new ears. This alone is a difficult goal for any author to achieve, but Fisk has accomplished still more. He has given us plausible and deeply human reasons for why Schubert fashioned these works as "returning cycles" and he has also taught us to understand Schubert in an important new way.—Seow-Chin Ong

Fitch, Donald. "Lake Set to Music: Supplement 2001." *Blake: An Illustrated Quarterly*, 35 (2001), 40–60.

Flothuis, Marius. "Autograph—Abschrift—Erstdruck. Eine kritische Bewertung." *Mozart-Jahrbuch* (2001), 13–18.

Flothuis, Marius. "Lernen aus Mozarts Autographen." *Mozart-Jahrbuch* (2001), 295–304.

Flotzinger, Rudolf, "Mozart, Tanz und Stubenmädchen." *Mozart-Jahrbuch,* (2001), 191–204.

Freemanova, Michaela. "The Two Haydns and the Brothers Hospitallers (Barmherzige Brüder, Fatabene Fratelli, O.S.I): The Four Pupils, the Less Known Sources." *Hudebni Veda*, 38 (2001). 333–41.

Freitas, R."Singing and Playing: the Italian Cantata and the Rage for Wit." *Music and Letters*, 82 (2001), 509–42.

Frisch, Walter. "Reger's Bach and Historicist Modernism." *19th-Century Music*, 25 (2001), 196–312.

Frolich, Martha. "Beethoven's Piano Sonata in F major, Op. 54, Second Movement: The Final Version and Sketches." *Journal of Musicology,* 18 (2001). 98–128.

Getz, Christine. "Simon Boyleau and the Church of the 'Madonna of Miracles': Educating and Cultivating the Aristocratic Audience in Post-Tridentine Milan." *Journal of the Royal Music Association,* 126 (2001), 145–68.

Giglberger, Veronika. "'Man hört drei vernünftige Leute sich untereinander unterhalten.' Beobachtungen zur Satztechnik im Divertimento *KV 563*." *Mozart-Jahrbuch* (2001), 61–70.

Grave, Floyd K. "Concerto Style in Haydn's String Quartets." *Journal of Musicology,* 18 (2001), 76–97.

Gross, Suzanne, and Wesley Berg. "'Singing It 'Our Way': Pennsylvania-German Mennonite Notenbüchlein (1780–1835)." *American Music*, 19 (2001), 190–209.

Grout, Donald J., and Claude V. Palisca (eds.). *A History of Western Music, Sixth Edition*. New York: W. W. Norton, 2001. Pp. xvi + 843; bibliography; illustrations; index. Companion sound recording (compact disc).

Haeffli, Anton. "Nichts ist teurer als ein Anfang: Joseph Haydn's Anfangen und Beenden von Musikwerken als kompositorische Herausforderung." *Dissonanz,* 67 (2001), 6–13.

Harris, Ellen T. *Handel as Orpheus: Voice and Desire in the Chamber Cantatas.* Cambridge: Harvard University Press, 2001. Pp. [415] + xi; title index of Handel's cantatas; general index; musical examples.

In *Handel as Orpheus* Ellen Harris sets out to provide "the first comprehensive study of all the [Handel] cantatas, both continuo and instrumental, set within the parameters of private aristocratic patronage and the eighteenth-century context of same-sex love" (2). In addressing these issues her work successfully rectifies several major gaps in Handel scholarship and provides one of the most important contextual studies of this major composer to date.

In addition to exploring Handel's cantatas, a relatively unstudied aspect of his oeuvre, the underlying theme of Harris's book is the continual identification of Handel by his contemporaries with the mythical figure of Orpheus. Orpheus is the prototype of both the power of music and homosexuality and, as such, Harris also believes that a close reading of the cantata texts "in terms of their literary heritage and social environment confirmed a consistent homoerotic subtext." (1). Though ultimately ambivalent about Handel's sexuality she nonetheless adds a large amount of empirical information that significantly builds upon Gary C. Thomas's controversial essay "Was George Frideric Handel Gay?"("'Was George Frideric Handel Gay?': On Closet Questions and Cultural Politics." Pp. 155–203 of *Queering the Pitch: The New Gay and Lesbian Musicology.* Edited by P. Brett, E. Wood, and G. C. Thomas. [New York: Routledge, 1994]).

The book takes the form of six chapters and an Epilogue all organized by topic. The first chapter focuses on an early cantata, *Hendel, non può mia musa,* on a text written by Cardinal Pamphili which compares Handel to Orpheus. Harris analyses this work and the Orpheus myth to demonstrate that the image of Orpheus functioned as a double emblem of the musician and homosexual in the eighteenth century. Chapters 2, 3, and 4 examine the different types of cantatas that Handel composed in Italy: solo instrumental cantatas, solo continuo cantatas, and multi-voice instrumental cantatas. In Chapter 2, Harris concentrates on solo instrumental cantatas, written largely during the year 1707. She specifically contrasts Handel's cantatas that are dominated by women, who speak largely in their own voices and concentrate on themes of love, condemnation, abandonment, and suicide, with those centered on male characters which, notably, are narrated in the third person and are typically more concerned with fortune and ambition than love. Chapter Three studies the continuo cantatas, contextualizing textual codes and same-sex attraction in the Arcadian Academy in 1707 and 1708, while Chapter 4 explores the instrumental duet and trio cantatas to show how their classical and mythological texts are concerned with transformation or sublimation of desire.

Chapter Five focuses on the pervasive references to silence and the increasing presence of tacit pauses in Handel's cantatas after 1710. Harris persuasively argues that such silences "preview the growing use of silence in literary texts—where notated blanks and sashes leave gaping holes— and more particularly the naturalistic stage acting represented especially by [David] Garrick" (207). Chapter 6 presents allegorical interpretations of Handel's large-scale works produced at the end of his cantata period, such as *Acis and Galatea,* and *Esther.* Based on classical precedence and eighteenth-century contextual evidence, Harris provides a particularly thought provoking homosexual reading of *Acis and Galatea.* The Epilogue surveys the revival and alteration of several of Handel's cantatas with particular focus on three different homosexually implicit images—legal, classical, and exotic—that were assigned to Handel during his life.

Among the most outstanding aspects of Harris's study are the two exhaustive appendices. The first presents a tabular summary of the documentary evidence that supports a "chronological understanding of the cantatas" (3). Appendix 2 provides complete texts and translations of the continuo cantatas. Taken by themselves these appendices represent an important contribution to and resource for Handel studies that, among other issues, establish that all the cantatas were written between 1706 and 1723.

Handel as Orpheus must rank as one of the most significant books on the composer in recent times. Harris has managed an outstanding feat—balancing traditional archival research against critical theory and interpretive study to provide a well balanced picture of both Handel and his cantatas, and their sociopolitical meaning. Her work provides a model of what musicology should be doing today, successfully knitting together both positivistic archival study with meaningful interpretive and contextual study—Kenneth McLeod

Harvey, Brian W. *The Violin Family and its Makers in the British Isles: An Illustrated History and Directory.* Oxford: Clarendon Press, 1995. Pp. x + 307; appendices; figures; illustrations; select bibliography; tables.

This exhaustive volume is a labor of love by a member of the faculty of Law at the University of Birmingham. It will be one of the authorities on its subject for many years to come, and the reading public will be most grateful for Mr. Harvey's abiding interest in British violin makers and the thoroughness of his research.

Of particular note is the richness of detail in revealing the lives, circumstances and attitudes of individual makers. Some ten pages are devoted to the life of Edward Heron-Allen, a renaissance man of the Victorian Era whose book *Violin-Making as it Was and Is* (London: Ward, Lock,1884/R Ottawa: Algrove Publishers, 2000), is, according to Harvey, "probably the most important and comprehensive book on violin-making and its history ever to have been written" (269). An entire chapter, including a family tree, is given to the Hill family whose reputation as violin makers, dealers, and restorers is not only of the very highest standard in the violin world, but also represents British commercial achievement at its best. In this chapter Harvey also describes the rise of bow making in England beginning with Dodd, who was a contemporary of the French bow maker Tourte, and continuing with Tubbs and the Hill bows. Harvey provides a complete listing of the bow makers who worked in the Hill studios, with dates where available, and an additional table showing the identifying marks that Hill bow makers placed on their work.

Harvey takes pains to place each aspect of British violin making in its proper historical setting, starting with the transition from madrigal singing to a growing demand for viols in the seventeenth century, and continuing through the burgeoning demand, in the nineteenth century, both for high quality instruments and for improved commercial skills. Three chapters are devoted to a discussion of the beginnings of the craft in England, and Harvey provides a wealth of information on the earliest makers, their materials and techniques, and their established customs and procedures in the seventeenth century. In the following chapters, Harvey describes in fascinating detail the somewhat backward nature of retail business models in London at the beginning of the eighteenth century, the rise of new violin makers, the changing economic values and the position of English instruments vis-à-vis German and French products, pricing and fraudulent practices, and the rising demand, in the nineteenth century, for higher quality violins, violas and cellos.

The work of violin makers in other parts of the British Isles is addressed also, and a chapter is dedicated to craftsmen of Wales, Scotland, and Ireland, such as Thomas Perry of Dublin. The work of Walter Mayson and other Victorians leads to a discussion of the great exhibitions and the appearance of collectors who drew attention to the fact that quality British instruments had become excellent buys in view of the inflated prices of old Italian instruments—a situation that prevails in a similar way to this day. A full chapter is devoted to a discussion of books and periodicals on violin making. We are brought up to date, in the final chapter, on British violin making in the twentieth century. This chapter also contains an interesting survey of the number of British instruments in use by members of three different orchestras in London, in the provinces, and in Scotland.

Harvey's very complete directory of British violin and bow makers runs to some ninety pages, and this is clearly the new reference of choice on the subject. Illustrations of facsimile labels referred to in the directory are followed by 109 annotated plates, showing representative violins of British make from front, back, and scroll views. It is here that the only shortcoming of this outstanding book is evident: the plates illustrating the instruments would have been much more valuable in full color, showing the grain of the wood and the color of the varnish more clearly. An extensive bibliography rounds out this remarkable volume.

Although most of the information about violin playing, composition for strings, and violin making in England during the eighteenth century can be found in existing publications, Harvey's survey and his treatment of the many complex aspects of his subject are unique. Representative examples are his detailed discussions of the effect of such momentous events as the arrival of Händel in London in 1710, his founding of the Royal Society of Musicians in 1738, and the impact, on British violin makers, of Geminiani's treatise on "The Art

IV: Fine Arts

of Playing on the Violin" (London, in 1751). Combining a conversational style with a wealth of precise information, Harvey's investigation into the work of each violin maker reads with the fascination of a mystery novel. His discussion of the violins of William Pryor of Gateside, for example, with comments on their style and authenticity by such authorities as John Dilworth and Arthur E. Hill, complete with a facsimile label from the Hill Archive (Appendix 2), will leave the reader avidly turning the pages in search of more such research and discoveries (107).

In spite of its lack of color plates, this is a remarkable work that will be found indispensable as a reference in libraries, and of enormous assistance to collectors. The depth of historical material also makes this study of great educational value to all interested readers—Roy Bogas

Harvey. Ross. "A Music Publisher's Response to Competition: Henry Playford, 1690–1702." *Bibliographical Society of Australia and New Zealand Bulletin,* 25 (2001), 121–34.

Hepokoski, James. "Back and Forth from Egmont: Beethoven, Mozart, and the Nonresolving Recapitulation." *19th-Century Music,* 25 (2001), 127–54.

Hiller, Johann Adam. *Treatise on Vocal Performance and ornamentation by Johann Adam Hiller.* [Anweisung zum musikalisch-zierlichen Gesänge.] Translated and edited by Suzanne J. Beicken. (Cambridge Musical Texts and Monographs.) Cambridge: Cambridge University Press, 2001. Pp. ix + 199; bibliography; index; musical examples.

Hochreiter, Martina. "Die Geistlichen Oden und Lieder nach Texten von Christian Fürchtegott Gellert: *KV Anhang* 270-283 (*KV* 6, *Anhang* C 8.32-46). *Mozart-Jahrbuch,* (2001), 87–100.

Holman, Peter. "Compositional Choices in Henry Purcell's *Three Parts upon a Ground.*" *Early Music,* 29 (2001), 250–62.

Hunter, D. "Handel Among the Jacobites." *Music and Letters,* 82 (2001), 543–56.

Hurley, David Ross. *Handel's Music: Patterns of Creation in His Oratorios and Musical Dramas, 1743-1751.* (Oxford Monographs on Music.) Oxford: Oxford University Press, 2001. Pp. ix + [291]; bibliography; diagrams; general index; index of Handel's works; musical examples, black-and-white plates; tables.

David Ross Hurley's stated aim in *Handel's Muse...* is to address "Handel's compositional process as a purely musical phenomenon" (7). In addressing this issue Hurley rectifies a long overlooked aspect of Handel scholarship and brings it into conformity with well known studies devoted to the compositional procedures of other composers such as Bach, Mozart, and Beethoven.

The work is organized into three large sections, each devoted to a different aspect of Handel's compositional process. The first three chapters deal with the nuts and bolts of Handel's compositional procedures and the "pre-compositional" concerns reflected in surviving sketches and drafts. In the second section of the work (Chapters 4 through 8), Hurley concentrates on the different types of revisions that are found repeatedly in Handel's autographs. Hurley particularly focuses here on revisions made for musical reasons, rather than in response to extra-musical concerns such as venue or availability of performers. Handel's changes in musical form and the related issues of his approach to text-setting and his librettos are discussed in detail (Chapter 8), and three chapters (Chapters 4 through 7) are devoted to details of Handel's composition techniques: issues of thematic repetition and thematic diversity; revisions of harmonic goals and formal proportion; revisions to texture; and revisions "that achieve a more seamless musical texture" (7). In this section Hurley is openly indebted to Robert Marshall's influential study of Bach's autographs (*The compositional process of J.S. Bach; A Study of the Autograph Scores of the Vocal Works*. [Princeton: Princeton University Press, 1972]).

In the final section (Chapters 9–11), Hurley explores issues of text and word setting, and the role of certain singers in Handel's compositional process. Chapter Ten is particularly effective in elucidating Handel's efforts to balance musical expression with the particular capabilities of his singers. Concentrating on revisions for three singers, Giulia Frasi, Thomas Lowe, and Signora Sibilla, the chapter outlines the way in which Handel managed the problems of transferring musical material from one singer to another for different performances, and the effect these changes wrought on the overall composition. Hurley concludes that, in contrast to commonly held belief, by Jens Peter Larsen, among others, the "needs of the singers do not always clash with the 'higher aim' of oratorio; very often revisions made to suit a soloist also enhance both music and drama" (251).

Hurley focuses on six of Handel's major works composed between 1743 and 1751 (*Semele, Hercules, Belshazzar, Solomon, Susanna*, and *Jeptha*), and addresses, in *Handel's Muse...*, one of the fundamental issues in the Handel literature: "Was Handel predominantly a spontaneous, "improvisatory" composer or did he plan his compositions before the event" (7)? The issue is never answered definitively, however, and Hurley merely concludes that "Handel utilized an enormous variety of techniques and formal designs" when approaching a composition (83). Hurley returns to this thread in the conclusion of the book, though with the more specific observation that, particularly in regards to composing a ritornello, "Handel seems often to have decided first upon his melodic material and maintained it through the process of composition while improvising the form…" (281).

Hurley's work is solidly argued, well grounded, and is generally well written and presented. The work is somewhat narrow in its focus, naturally enough, given that this is an expansion of the author's doctoral dissertation, and would therefore be of interest largely to post graduate scholars with a particular interest in Handel. Hurley's introduction to *Handel's Muse...* is somewhat apologetic because he does not address aspects of postmodern musicology such as "feminism, gender and other elements of social contextualiztion" (1). Indeed, though Hurley's work lacks something of the interpretive flair and insights of Ellen Harris's more recent study of Handel's Cantatas (*Handel as Orpheus* [Cambridge: Harvard University Press, 2002]), it is, nevertheless, an important work of Handel scholarship. It seems clear that musicology, both traditional or "new," benefits both from the availability of interpretive contextual studies such as Harris's, and more positivistic studies such as Hurley's—Ken McLeod

Huron, David. "Tone and Voice: A Derivation of the Rules of Voice-Leading from Perceptual Principles." *Music Perception*, 19 (2001), 1–64.

Ianne, Antonia. "Le risorse Internet per la musicologia: strategie di ricerca e criteri di valutazione. *Fonti Musicali Italiane,* 6 (2001), 119–43.

Jander, Owen. "In Defense of the Cramer Narrative." *Beethoven Journal* 16 (2001), 24–25.

Janitzek, Martina. *Studien zur Editionsgeschichte der Palestrina-Werke vom späten 18. Jahrhundert bis um 1900*. Tutzing: Schneider, 2001. Pp. 438; music.

Jenkins, Jennifer R. "Why Doesn't the Whole World Love Chamber Music?" *American Music*, 19 (2001), 315–39.

IV: Fine Arts

Jones, Simon. "The Legacy of the 'stupendious' Nicola Matteis." *Early Music,* 29 (2001), 553–68.

Johnstone, H. Diack. "A Flourish for Handel." *Early Music*, 29 (2001), 619–25.

Jost, Peter. "Mozarts Instrumentation anhand autographer Quellen." *Mozart-Jahrbuch,* (2001), 133–50.

Kagan, Susan and Thomas Wendel. "Beethoven on CD." *Beethoven Journal*, 16 (2001), 88–90.

Kassler, Jamie C. *Music, Science, Philosophy. Models in the Universe of Thought.* (Vafiorum Collected Studies, Series CS713.) Brookfield: Ashgate Publishing Company, 2001. Pp. xvi + 301; bibliography; illustrations; index.

Kassler, Michael, and Philip Olleson. *Samuel Wesley (1766–1837): A Source Book.* Aldershot: Ashgate Publishing Company, 2001. Pp. xxiii + 765; calendars of correspondence; index to correspondence; 2 facsimiles; iconography; table; works lists.

Kramer, Lawrence. *Musical Meaning: Toward a Critical History.* Berkeley: University of California Press, 2001. Pp ix + 335; bibliography; index; musical examples; black-and-white plates. Companion sound recording: Compact disc (contains computer realization of the author's musical composition "Revenants: 32 Variations in C Minor").

Keefe, Simon P. "'An entirely special manne': Mozart's *Piano Concerto No. 14* in E flat, *KV* 449, and the Stylistic Implications of Confrontation." *Music and Letters,* 82 (2001), 559–81.

Keefe, Simon P. *Mozart's Piano Concertos: Dramatic Dialogue in the Age of Enlightenment.* Woodbridge: Boydell Press. 2001. Pp. x + 205; bibliography; indices; musical examples.

It is difficult not to greet the appearance of yet another book on Mozart's piano concertos with some skepticism: there have been so many books, to say nothing of articles, about these pieces over the last fifty or sixty years that there seems little new to say. Yet, like the works of Shakespeare or Goethe, these icons of European music history continue to fascinate musicians of all kinds, and each new generation has found new paths to understanding them. Simon Keefe's study, which grew out of his doctoral dissertation, focuses on a single aspect of these concertos, one that in fact has frequently been a factor their analysis—the interactions between the solo piano and the orchestral *tutti*. He proposes to found his own observations on what he terms "dramatic dialogue," not simply on an analysis of the score itself, however, but more fundamentally, on ideas he finds in contemporaneous critical and theoretical musical commentaries. Especially because he does begin his study with an informative tour of those literary sources, his work will be of use to any scholar of the later eighteenth century who is interested in its music.

Keefe has divided his book into two unequal parts. The first, "Theories and Contexts" (which comprises almost a quarter of the whole), focuses on the writings of Heinrich Christoph Koch (1749–1816) in the late eighteenth century, and those of Antoine Reicha (1770–1836) in the early nineteenth (Koch, *Versuch einer*

Einleitung zur Composition [1782-93]; Reicha, *Traité de mélodie* [1814], *Traité de haute composition musicale* [1824-26], *Art du compositeur dramatique* [1833]). In the longer second part, "Style," Keefe analyzes what he identifies as dramatic dialogue in the concertos themselves. The text on which he most depends is a passage written by Koch in 1793 that has become known as the definitive assertion of a parallel between the solo concerto and a staged drama (in this case, an ancient Greek tragedy). In a concerto, Koch explains, "There is a passionate dialogue [*leidenschaftliche Unterhaltung*] between the concerto player and the accompanying orchestra. He expresses his feelings to the orchestra, and it signals him through short interspersed phrases sometimes approval, sometimes acceptance of his expression, as it were. Now in the allegro it tries to stimulate his noble feelings still more; now it commiserates, now it comforts him in the adagio (17)....In short, by a concerto I imagine something similar to the tragedy of the ancients, where the actor expressed his feelings not towards the pit, but to the chorus. The chorus was involved most closely with the action and was at the same time justified in participating in the expression of feelings" (18; translated by N. K. Baker, *Introductory Essay on Composition The Mechanical Rules of Melody. Sections 3 and 4/Von den mechanischen Regeln der Melodie. 3. Von der Beschaffenheit der melodischen Theile*.4. [New Haven: Yale University Press, 1983]).

Koch's metaphorical view of the concerto recognizes a kind of meaning in the interaction of solo and orchestra. This perspective has been extremely attractive to music historians searching for appropriate alternative modes of analysis that can produce more broadly meaningful interpretations than purely formalistic analysis has generally afforded. Although Keefe has been only partially successful in achieving his goal of integrating a metaphorical and a more traditional musical analysis of Mozart's concertos, his work affords a glimpse of how such an integration might be worked out, and lays out some convincing arguments about the concertos themselves.

In the two chapters of Part I, Keefe works to lay out the ways in which music theorists and critics in the late eighteenth and early nineteenth centuries used the notions of dialogue and drama to describe particular pieces. These chapters, and the opening part of Chapter 3—which is also devoted to literary sources (this time about solo-orchestra relationships in the concerto)—offer a wealth of textual fragments relevant to dialogue and (rather less) to drama in music. Unfortunately, however, these brief extracts are neither put in the context of the works from which they are drawn, nor are they integrated into a single coherent exposition. (It is symptomatic of the fragmentation of his discussion that Koch's well known passage is split in two, the first part in the section on "Dialogue" and the second within "Drama.") The musical analyses that make up the bulk of Part II, although not easily accessible to the musically non-literate or even to the non-specialist, suffer no such fragmentation. The argument here is clearly directed toward establishing the nature and importance of various kinds of dialogue between piano and orchestra in the concertos, taking Reicha's specific classifications as a basis, but otherwise following rather traditional lines. It is here, interestingly, that Keefe finally succeeds in justifying his interpretation of this dialogue as "dramatic": by analyzing the explicitly dramatic dialogue in Mozart's operas contemporaneous with the concertos, he demonstrates that the procedures governing staged drama are directly comparable to those of the piano concerto. In the end, the contribution of this study lies less in its metaphorical, subjective interpretations of musical events than in its analysis of a particular group of musical procedures convincingly shown to be shared with a distinctly non-metaphorical genre—Jane R. Stevens

Kerman, Joseph. "Beethoven's Opus 131 and the Uncanny." *19th-Century Music*, 25:2–3 (November, 2001), 155–64.

Kierkegaard, Søren. "Una fugace osservazione su un particolare nel Don Giovanni." Commentary: Gallucci, Marcello. "Nota su Kierkegaard recensore." *De Musica: Annuario in divenire*, V (2001), Online edition: http://users.unimi.it/~gpiana/dm5idxrd.htm/.

Kim, Jin-Ah. "Tradition und Innovation im Finale von W. A. Mozarts *Jupiter-Sinfonie KV 551*." *Mozart-Jahrbuch*, (2001), 151–62.

IV: Fine Arts 245

Kivy, Peter *The Possessor and the Possessed: Handel, Mozart, Beethoven, and the Idea of Musical Genius.* New Haven: Yale University Press, 2001. Pp. xiv + 287. bibliigraphy; index

Koch, Heinrich Christoph. *Musikalisches Lexikon. Faksimile-Reprint der Ausgabe Frankfurt/Main 1802.* Herausgegeben und mit einer Einführung versehen von Nicole Schwindt. Kassel: Bärenreiter-Verlag, 2001. German text. Pp. xiv + [510] + [903]; Columns I:1019; II: [1805]; diagrams; musical examples.

Reviewed with Johann Gottfried Walther, *Musicalisches Lexicon oder Musicalische Bibliotheck. Studienausgabe im Neusatz des Textes und der Noten.*

LaRue, Jan. "Bifocal Tonality: An Explanation for Ambiguous Baroque Cadences." *Journal of Musicology*, 18 (2001), 283–94.

LaRue, Jan. "Fundamental Considerations in Style Analysis." *Journal of Musicology*, 18 (2001), 295–312.

LaRue, Jan. "Major and Minor Mysteries of Identification in the 18th-Century Symphony." *Journal of Musicology*, 18 (2001), 249–67.

Leclerc, Guy. " Das Haus Verona-Blesson ‚ein Jahrhundert italienisch-französischer Familiengeschiche 17/18 unter den Linden, heute 47." *Monatsschrift* (2001), 64–75.

Leclerc, Guy. "Tassaert et Sarti." *Tournefeuille,* 10 (2001), 8–9.

Ledbetter, David. "On the Manner of Playing the Adagio: Neglected Features of a Genre." *Early Music* 29 (2001), 15–28.

Lederer, Josef-Horst. "Wenn der Bruch im Satzgefüge auf Überraschung basiert. Zur Konzeption dramatischer Wendepunkte in Mozarts Seria-Opern." *Mozart-Jahrbuch,* (2001), 221–30.

Leech, Peter. "Musicians in the Catholic Chapel of Catherine of Braganza, 1662–92." *Early Music,* 29 (2001), 570–87.

Levy, Janet M. "The Power of the Performer: Interpreting Beethoven." *Journal of Musicology,* 18 (2001) 31–56.

Letzter, Jacqueline, and Robert Adelson. *Women Writing Opera. Creativity and Controversy in the Age of the French Revolution.* (Studies on the History of Society and Culture 43.) Berkeley: University of California Press, 2001. Pp. xvii + 341; appendix; bibliography; endnotes; index; 3 black-and-white plates; tables.

Libin, Laurence. "Robert Adam's Instruments for Catherine the Great." *Early Music*, 29 (2001), 355–67.

Lister, W. "In Brief. Wilhelm Cramer and the Opera Concert Orchestra: 'Damnatio Memoriae'?" *Music and Letters*, 82 (2001), 78.

Lütteken, Laurenz. "Konversation als Spiel. Überlegungen zur Textur von Mozarts Divertimento KV 563." *Mozart-Jahrbuch*, (2001), 71–86.

Lühning, Helga. "Mozarts Auseinandersetzung mit der *Da capo-Arie* in Mitridate, *re di Ponto.*" *Mozart-Jahrbuch*, (2001), 427–62.

Mahling, Christoph-Hellmut. "Nochmals Bemerkungen zum *Violinkonzert* D-Dur *KV* 271a (271i)."*Mozart-Jahrbuch*, (2001), 101–8.

Mancal, Josef. "Historische Quellen: Faktum und Interpretation." *Mozart-Jahrbuch*, (2001), 33–46.

Marco, Guy. *Opera: A Research and Information Guide.* New York: Garland Publishing, 2001. Pp. xx + 632; annotated bibliographies; indices.

Marco's *Opera: A Research and Information Guide,* one of the numerous series of useful Garland reference works in the humanities, this second edition updates his original work, which is now expanded from 714 numbered entries in the first edition to over 2,800 here. The guide is divided into broad sections including many standard reference works and collections of source materials. The biographical section on singers and performers of opera is regrettably brief, however, the section on opera production features a more expansive list of titles. Music students and those seeking to incorporate opera as part of a larger course or project will doubtless turn to the final sections, "Composers and Their Operas" (Abbatini to Zumsteeg), and "Countries" (Latin America to Yugoslavia). This is a relatively accessible text for the inexperienced researcher, student, enthusiast, or scholar from other fields and Marco's annotations usually provide good hints toward what will or will not be found once a book or article is in hand. His opinions, however, are occasionally more acerbic than helpful—the late Donald Jay Grout's and Hermine Weigel's *A Short History of Opera* (New York: Columbia University Press, c2003), for example, is relegated, with some feminist and queer studies titles, to the section on "Philosophy and Theory of Opera."

Among the sections of particular interest to eighteenth-century studies, the bibliographies for specific composers are quite comprehensive for major figures such as George Frederic Handel, Christoph Willibald Gluck, or Wolfgang Amadeus Mozart. Extensive composer bibliographies, such as that for Handel, are usefully subdivided into categories such as "Letters and documents" and scholarship on individual works, for example, articles on Mozart's *The Magic Flute*. Lesser-known composers, however, such as Elisabeth Claude Jacquet de la Guerre, are often represented with only a single publication, which does not always reflect current levels of interest or scholarship.

While some dissertations are listed (a few of those for "high profile" composers such as Giuseppe Verdi), none is annotated, nor are annotations provided for any of opera handbooks or guides listed. While Marco explains that this is done for reasons of practicality, this is regrettable in the case of the Cambridge opera handbooks, since they are a very varied lot and are precisely where a neophyte opera lover or scholar might benefit from some guidance. Overall, Marco's work is a useful starting point for the student and a helpful bibliographic survey for the scholar interested in opera—Kathryn Lowerre

Marx, Hans Joachim. "A Newly Discovered Gloria by Handel." *Early Music,* 29 (2001), 342–52.

McMullin, B. J. "A New Bibliography of John Crowne." *Harvard Library Bulletin*, 12 (2001), 3–101.

Meredith, William. "Beethoven Papers Read at the 2001 Meeting of the American Musicological Society." *Beethoven Journal,* 16 (2001), 91–95.

Miller, Malcolm. "Conference Report. 'Beethoven's String Quartets: A Classic or Modernistic Legacy?' School of Music, University of Victoria, Canada, March 24–26, 2000." *Beethoven Journal*, 16 (2001), 26–29.

Mitchell, Robert W., and Matthew C. Gallaher. "Embodying Music: Matching Music and Dance in Memory." *Music Perception,* 19 (2001), 65–85.

Moore, A. F. "Categorical Conventions in Music Discourse: Style and Genre." *Music and Letters,* 82 (2001), 432–42.

Myers, Herbert W. "The Sizes and Tunings of Early Viols: Some Questions (and a Few Answers)." *Journal of the Viola da Gamba Society of America,* 38 (2001), 5–26.

Oleskiewicz, Mary. "The Hole Truth and Nothing but the Truth: The Resolution of a Problem in Flute Iconography." *Early Music,* 29 (2001), 56–59.

Ophälders, Markus. "Der Weltgeist am Klavier: Adorno interpreta Beethoven. Note per una critica." *De Musica: Annuario in divenire,* V (2001), online edition: http://users.unimi.it/~gpiana/ dm5idxrd .htm/.

Owens, Samantha. "Professional Women Musicians in Early Eighteenth-Century Württemberg." *Music and Letters*, 82 (2001), 32–50.

Pesic, Peter. "The Child and the Daemon: Mozart and Deep Play." *19th-Century Music,* 25 (2001), 91–107.

Pike, L. "Purcell's 'Rejoice in the Lord,' all ways."*Music and Letters,* 82 (2001), 391–420.

Portowitz, Adena. "Art and Taste in Mozart's Sonata-Rondo Finales: Two Case Studies." *Journal of Musicology,* 18 (2001), 129–49.

Price, Charles Gower. "Free Ornamentation in the Solo Sonatas of William Babell: Defining a Personal Style of Improvised Embellishment." *Early Music*, 29 (2001), 29–55.

Pulkert, Oldrich. "Almerie Esterházy Revisted: Defining Celeda's 'Immortal Beloved' Theory." *Beethoven Journal,* 16 (2001), 62–68.

Raab, Michael. "Mozart und die Kadenz. Zu den 'Solo-Kadenzen' im *Konzert für zwei Klaviere Es-Dur KV* 365." *Mozart-Jahrbuch,* (2001), 287–94.

Reijen, Paul van. "Zur Frage der Autorschaft der unechten 'Mozart'-Messen *KV Anh*ang, 185 und *Anhang* 186." *Mozart-Jahrbuch,* (2001), 109–32.

Raab, Armin. "Haydn-Bibliographie 1991–2001." *Haydn-Studien,* 7 (2001), 79–214.

Ratner, Leonard G. "Mozart's Parting Gifts." *Journal of Musicology,* 18 (2001), 189–211.

Rehm, Wolfgang. "1956–1991–2006: Milestones in the *Neue Mozart-Ausgabe.*" *Mozart Society of America Newsletter,* 2 (2001), 1–2, 4–5.

Richards, Annette. *The Free Fantasia and the Musical Picturesque.* (New Perspectives in Music, History and Criticism.) Cambridge: Cambridge University Press, 2001. Pp. xiii + 256; bibliography; illustrations; index.

Renwick, William. *The Langloz Manuscript. Fugal Improvisation through Figured Bass.* With introductory essay and performance notes by William Renwick. (Oxford Early Music Series). Oxford: Oxford University Press, 2001. Pp. xvi + 190; facsimiles; musical examples.

Roglieri, Maria Ann. *Dante and Music: Musical Adaptations of the 'Commedia' from the Sixteenth Century to the Present.* Aldershot: Ashgate Publishing Company, 2001. Pp. xii + 317; bibliography; illustrations; index.

Rohr, Deborah Adams. *The Careers of British Musicians, 1750–1850: A Profession of Artisans.* Cambridge: Cambridge University Press, 2001. Pp. xi + 233; bibliography; index.

Rosand, Ellen. "Vivaldi's Stage." *Journal of Musicology,* 18 (2001), 8–30.

Rose, Stephen. "Heinrich Albert's *Arien* in Print and Performance." *Early Music,* 29 (2001), 588–605.

Rowland, David. *Early Keyboard Instruments: A Practical Guide.* (Cambridge Handbooks to the Historical Performance of Music.) Cambridge: Cambridge University Press, 2001. Pp. xi + 154; bibliography; illustrations; index.

IV: Fine Arts

Russakovsky, Lubov. "The Altered Recapitulation in the First Movements of Haydn's String Quartets." *Tijdschrift voor Muziektheorie*, 6 (2001), online edition: http://cva.ahk. nl/ tvm/ tvm-e..html.

Schmalfeldt, Janet. "In Search of Dido." *Journal of Musicology*, 18 (2001), 584–615.

Schick, Hartmut. "Originalkomposition oder Bearbeitung? Zur Quellenlage und musikalischen Faktur von Mozarts *Klaviertrio KV 564.*" *Mozart-Jahrbuch* (2001), 273–86.

Schmidt-Beste, Thomas. Vom Streichquartett im Streichquintett. Zu Mozarts letzten Kammermusikwerken," *Mozart-Jahrbuch* (2001), 47–60.

Schneider, Herbert, and Reinhard Wiesend (eds.). *Die Oper im 18 Jahrhundert*. (Handbuch der musikalischen Gattungen, 12.) Laaber: Laaber-Verlag, 2001. Pp. 349; bibliography; illustrations; index; musical examples.

Schwab-Felisch, Oliver. "Functions of the Unclear: Chromaticism in Beethoven's String Quartet in E^b major, op. 74." *Tijdschrift voor Muziektheorie*, 3 (2001), online edition: http://cva.ahk.nl/tvm/tvm-e.html.

Schwartz, Judith L. "Conceptions of Musical Unity in the 18th Century." *Journal of Musicology*, 18 (2001), 56–75.

Seiffert, Wolf-Dieter. "Die Untersuchung autographer Korrekturen als Chance 'authentischer' Werkinterpretation. Dargestellt anhand von Mozarts *Haydn-Quartetten,*" *Mozart-Jahrbuch* (2001), 305–44.

Shambar, Beth. "Schubert's Classic Legacy: Some Thoughts on Exposition-Recap. Form." *Journal of Musicology*, 18 (2001), 150–69.

Sheer, Miriam. "The Godard–Beethoven Connection: On the Use of Beethoven's Quartets in Godard's Films." *Journal of Musicology*, 18 (2001), 170–88.

Sherr, David. "Four Town Pipers, Three Professional Fiddlers, and One Apprentice." *The Double Reed*, 24 (2001), 124–26.

Slonimsky, Nicolas, and Laura Kuhn (eds.). *Baker's Biographical Dictionary of Musicians*. Centennial Edition. New York: Schirmer Books, 2001. 6 volumes. Pp. lxiv + 4,220; bibliography; discography; indices.

Spring, Matthew. *The Lute in Britain: A History of the Instrument and its Music*. Oxford: Oxford University Press, 2001. Pp. xxxii + 536; bibliography; illustrations; index.

Stanley, Glenn. "Einzelwerk als Gattungskritik. Mozarts *Klavierrondo* in a-Moll KV 511."*Mozart-Jahrbuch,* (2001), 257–72.

Steiner, Stefanie. "Zwischen Kirche, Bühne und Konzertsaal. Vokalmusik von Haydns 'Schöpfung' bis zu Beethovens 'Neunter.' Dissertation: Universität Dresden, 1999–2000. Kassel: Bärenreiter, 2001. Pp. 250. bibliography; musical examples.

Stevens, Jane R. *The Bach Family and the Keyboard Concerto. The Evolution of a Genre.* Warren: Harmonie Park Press, 2001. Pp. [xx] + 269; appendix; bibliography; diagrams; musical examples; black-and-white plates; tables.

This rich study challenges the traditional view of a rupture in the history of the keyboard concerto between J. S. Bach and Mozart by demonstrating that the genre had a continuous, if gradually changing, identity across the eighteenth century. At the outset, Jane Stevens admits that "any replacement of [the traditional and] simplistic formulation of concerto history...must unravel a complex fabric of interactions and interrelationships among a truly daunting number of composers and musical centers over a period of several decades, many of which have never been seriously investigated.... The desire for an alternative view has been frustrated by our relative lack of knowledge about keyboard concertos during the middle of the eighteenth century" (3–4). Stevens' contribution to this alternative view lies in reevaluating the keyboard concertos of J. S. Bach's three best-known sons, Wilhelm Friedemann, Carl Philipp Emanuel, and Johann Christian, who together produced nearly ninety works of this type (Carl Philipp Emanuel, alone, accounts for more than half of this number). In understanding their pieces not simply as stepping-stones that do not quite measure up against the yardsticks of later times, but rather, in their own terms, her results offer both specific insight into the works considered, as well as a means of approaching other mid-eighteenth-century keyboard concertos that lay outside the scope of the study.

The book is ordered chronologically, with main chapters devoted to J. S. Bach and his three abovementioned sons, in turn. These are punctuated by short interlude-chapters providing some wider contextual perspectives. A concise overview of the repertory, sources, and, where discernible, chronology, is given at the beginning of the discussion of each composer's output. Analyses then follow, either of individual movements or of patterns and characteristics shared by groups of works. The focus, somewhat inevitably, is on the relationship of *solo* to *tutti*, and of part to whole in first-movement *ritornello* structures. The continuities that Stevens seeks to demonstrate emerge from reassessing modern analytical preconceptions of what these entail against both the actual events in the music and in eighteenth-century theory. In her discussion of J. S. Bach's arrangement for four harpsichords and strings of Vivaldi's concerto for four violins (Op. 3, No. 10), for example, Stevens repositions the form in terms of harmonic structure rather than timbral opposition, which she shows to have only become conventional at a later date (36–48). It is then through this same tonal model that shared generic concerns can be seen among the expansively broad concertos of Johann Christian, on the one hand, and the more discursive concertos of Carl Philipp Emanuel and Wilhelm Friedemann, on the other. Clear diagrammatic representations of all the discussed pieces make it easy to follow the details of the arguments.

Current debates and future research-avenues pepper the text (and, more frequently, the provocative and extensive footnotes). A brief challenge is mounted on the currently accepted view that all of J. S. Bach's keyboard concertos are arrangements of concertos for other instruments (27). The important suggestion that all of J. S. Bach's multi-keyboard concertos could have begun life without accompanying strings is inspired by the all-too-overlooked practice of playing concertos at the keyboard alone, a practice evident not just in J. S. Bach's arrangements of Vivaldi's concertos for the organ, but also in C. P. E. Bach's concertos, as well as in the published versions of Handel's organ concertos (48). More suggestive still are the scattered references to other experiments with keyboard concertos more or less contemporaneously with those of J. S. Bach: by "Graun" in Dresden (the source does not specify which), Handel in England, Seixas in Portugal, and Pergolesi in Italy. These surely point to performance practices in the 1720s and 1730s that wait to be uncovered. As

IV: Fine Arts 251

both a stimulus for further work and a guide to a much-misunderstood repertory, this book is a significant addition to the literature—D. J. Burn

Stone, A. "A Singer at the Fountain: Homage and Irony in Ciconia's 'Sus une Fontayne.'" *Music and Letters,* 82 (2001), 361–90.

Stowell, Robin. *The Early Violin and Viola: A Practical Guide.* (Cambridge Handbooks to the Historical Performance of Music.) Cambridge: Cambridge University Press, 2001. Pp. xv + 234; bibliography; 10 figures; index; 49 musical examples; 2 tables

Stroh, Patricia. "Recent Beethoven and Beethoven-Related Books and Music Editions (1998–2001)." *Beethoven Journal*, 16 (2001), 34–39.

Stroh, Patricia. "Recent Beethoven and Beethoven-Related Books and Music Editions (1999–2001)." *Beethoven Journal*, 16 (2001), 96–100.

Stroh, Patricia "Selected Special Acquisitions (2000–2001) at the Beethoven Center." *Beethoven Journal*, 16 (2001), 101–02.

Strohm, Richard (ed.). *The Eighteenth-Century Diaspora of Italian Music and Musicians.* (Speculum musicae 8.) Turnhout: Brepols, 2001. Pp. xix + 345; bibliography; facsimiles; illustrations; index; musical examples.

Sutcliffe, Richard. "Re-examining the Pardessus de Viole and its Literature, Part II: Repertoire from 1722 to c. 1790." *Journal of the Viola da Gamba Society of America,* 38 (2001), 27–77.

Talbot, Michael. "How Recitatives End and Arias Begin in the Solo Cantatas of Antonio Vivaldi." *Journal of the Royal Music Association,* 126 (2001), 161–92.

Thompson, Shirley, "Reflections on Four Charpentier Chronologies." *Journal for Seventeenth-Century Music*, 7 (2001). Online edition: http://www.sscm-jscm.org/jscm/v7/no1/Thompson.html.

Tolley, Thomas. "Haydn, the Engraver Thomas Park, and Maria Hester Park's 'Little Sonata.'" *Music and Letters,* 82 (2001), 421–31.

Toscani, Claudio. "Una nuova acquisizione belliniana: fonti sconosciute per Adelson e Salvini, *Fonti Musicali Italiane,* 6 (2001), 105–117.

Tusa, Michael C. "Music as drama: structure, style, and process in *Fidelio.*" Pp. 101–31 of *Ludwig van Beethoven, "Fidelio.".* (Cambridge Opera Handbooks.) Edited by Paul Robinson. Cambridge: Cambridge University Press, 1996.

Waeber, J. "'Cette Horrible Innovation': The First Version of the Recitative Parts of Rousseau's *'Le Devin du Village.'*" *Music and Letters,* 82 (2001), 177–213.

Walther, Johann Gottfried. *Musicalisches Lexicon oder Musicalische Bibliothec. Studienausgabe im Neusatz des Textes und der Noten.* Herausgegeben von Friedericke Ramm. Kassel: Bärenreiter-Verlag, 2001. German text. Pp. ix + 601; Korrekturverzeichnis; musical examples.

Also reviewed is Heinrich Christoph Koch, *Musikalisches Lexikon. Faksimile-Reprint der Ausgabe Frankfurt/Main 1802.*

These two music dictionaries, one by Johann Gottfrried Walther (1684–1748) and the other by Heinrich Christoph Koch (1749–1816), are by far the best known works of their kind written in German during the eighteenth century, and their republication is a welcome event for anyone interested in the music and musical thought of the period. Originally published just seventy years apart, in 1732 and 1802, respectively, these two dictionaries have been recognized both in their day and in our own as monumental works that sum up the musical knowledge of their times. For the present-day scholar they provide two rather different compendia of knowledge, based in both cases not just on their authors' impressively wide reading, but on the practical experience of their professional lives. Both writers earned their livelihoods as practicing musicians, Walther as a church organist in Weimar from 1707 onward, and Koch as a violinist (and briefly *Kapellmeister*) at the court in Rudolstadt. Both were also composers as well as performers and writers. Non-scholars of music may be familiar with Walther's name in connection with Johann Sebastian Bach, with whom he had a close association between 1708 and 1717, while Bach was employed at the ducal court in Weimar. The broad learning and serious intellect evident in Walther's dictionary are reminiscent of Bach's wide reading and lively intelligence, and it is not hard to understand why the two men would have formed a friendship in this small town.

Walther's is the first significant music dictionary in German, and the first in any language to include biographical entries alongside definitions and discussions of musical terms. It has been widely available in facsimile since 1953, a testament to its long recognized importance. The new publication has been reset "in modern type and notation" as one of a series of "study editions" issued by Bärenreiter, intended to make the text more easily accessible to a younger generation of scholars that too often has not mastered the subtleties of the C clefs and Fraktur type of the original. The resulting text is admirable in every way, offering a meticulously faithful transcription of the layout, the varieties of type, and even (in marginal notations) the pagination of the original. In its 593 pages (contracted from the 659 of the 1732 edition), the modern reader can find, for example, biographies of Orlando Lassus and a number of Bachs (among them Johann Sebastian), side by side with a definition and discussion of the term *largo* and a thorough explanation of *b* (the flat sign). Walther's sources, cited with admirable precision, range from texts of classical antiquity and the Renaissance to more recent and numerous treatises of the seventeenth century, together with the works of his prolific contemporary Johann Mattheson, from whom he draws most often. In addition to the biographical information about contemporary musicians, for which he solicited the subjects themselves, perhaps the most notable feature of the dictionary is Walther's extensive coverage of both ancient and modern music theory, a pursuit that had deeply interested him through much of his life.

Although Koch's dictionary was probably his best known work before the mid-twentieth century, unlike Walther's, it was not recognized until recently as an important resource for the study of music history. Partly because it does not include biographies of contemporary musicians, a function that had been filled a few years earlier by Ernst Gerber's biographical dictionary, which was based, importantly, on Walther's work (Gerber, Ernst Ludwig, 1746–1819, *Historisch-biographisches Lexicon der Tonkunstler* [Leipzig: J. G. I. Breitkopf, 1790–92]), and partly because of a traditional scholarly focus on the ideal "classicism" of late-eighteenth-century music without reference to contemporaneous theory, historians were largely ignorant of Koch's works before the middle of the last century. Even then, it was his exhaustive treatise on music composition, published in three volumes between 1782 and 1793, that was most often read and cited by a younger generation of scholars

(*Versuch einer Anleitung zur Composition* [Leipzig: Bey A.F. Böhme, 1782–93]). A much shortened version of the dictionary "for practical composers and dilettants," published in 1807, was published in facsimile in 1981 (*Kurzgefasstes Handwörterbuch der Musik für praktische Tonkünstler und für Dilettanten*, Hildesheim: G. Olms, 1981), and is available in many libraries, but it has been over forty years since the appearance (also in facsimile) of the much longer primary work, which has been more difficult to find. This new facsimile edition will thus be a welcome addition to many collections. The new publication is especially valuable, furthermore, in its addition of an extended and informative Introduction (in modern type) explaining the history of Koch's *Lexikon*, its precedents, and the nature of his sources.

Even upon a cursory review, the differences between Koch's and Walther's dictionaries are remarkably apparent. Only the last twenty of Koch's 1802 columns are devoted to biographical information, and this is limited to brief identifications of writers and composers mentioned importantly in the dictionary entries. Those entries, moreover, include not just definitions of terms and theoretical explanations, but also many articles on what are now understood as aesthetic ideas. Entries on theoretical terms and principles strikingly reflect the changes in musical thinking over the eighteenth century: *Dur*, for instance, which appears in Walther only in connection with *B Dur* ("hard B"), as a characteristic melodic pitch, is discussed at length by Koch, exclusively within the context of triads and keys and in the modern sense of "major" (a meaning not mentioned in Walther's brief definition). Similar differences appear in their entries on "Rhythmus" which refers not to simple note rhythms, but, rather, to some kind of higher rhythmic organization. Predictably, Walther's brief definition is limited to theoretical explanations of some ancient authors. Koch, on the other hand, begins with a definition (that might be translated as "the measure of the movement"), provided by his contemporary Johann Nicolaus Forkel. Koch then proceeds to relate this definition to the ideas about phrasing he had worked out in detail in his earlier compositional treatise, ideas based firmly in the modern style of the late eighteenth century.

Koch's intended audience is also decidedly broader than Walther's readers—or perhaps merely less classically or professionally educated— and may be interested less in theoretical knowledge and their own playing ability than in listening to the performances of more professional musicians. Particularly evident in Koch's dictionary is his deep interest in issues of musical expression, in connection with which he includes lengthy quotations from J. G. Sulzer's *Allgemeine Theorie der schönen Künste* (1771–74). The four-column article on "Leidenschaft (*Affect*) for instance, states at the outset that "the expression of passionate feelings is the principal object of music"; yet neither of these terms is even listed by Walther. The only comparable term included in his earlier dictionary is "*Affetto (ital.)*...an affect, or a movement of the feelings," with a list of typical passions including love, sorrow, joy, and anger, but no elaboration of ways these might be translated into music Similarly, *Ausdruck*, the usual term for expression in music, whether of the composer or of the music itself, takes up three columns of Koch's dictionary, whereas Walther rather unsurprisingly makes no mention of it at all. In addition to helping us better understand the terms used by other eighteenth-century writers, then, these two apparently straightforward collections of simple information demonstrate in a remarkably compact form the enormous changes that took place in musical thought during the eighteenth century, and dictionary lovers may be expected to learn much from them—Jane R. Stevens

Weber-Bockholdt, Petra. "F-Dur in Mozarts Opern." *Mozart-Jahrbuch,* (2001), 181–90.

Webster, James. "Between Enlightenment and Romanticism in Music History:' First Viennese Modernism' and the Delayed Nineteenth Century." *19th-Century Music,* 25 (2001), 108–6.

Weiner, Howard. "The Soprano Trombone Hoax." *Historic Brass Society Journal,* 13 (2001), 138–60.

Williams, Alastair. *Constructing Musicology.* Burlington: Ashgate Publishing Company, 2001. Pp. xi + 164; bibliography; illustrations; index.

Wilson, David K. (ed. and tr.). *Georg Muffat on Performance Practice: The Texts from Florilegium Primum, Florilegium Secundum, and Auserlesene Instrumentalmusik. A New Translation with Commentary.* Edited and translated by David K. Wilson from a collation prepared by Ingeborg Harer, Yvonne Luisi-Weichsel, Ernest Hoetzl, and Thomas Binkley. Bloomington: Indiana University Press, 2001. Pp. xvi + 123; bibliography; list of source materials and editions; musical examples.

Georg Muffat's instructions to players concerning bowing, ornamentation and other aspects of the "Lullist" orchestral style remain among the most important documents for performance practice of late seventeenth- and early eighteenth-century music. These instructions were aimed particularly at transalpine performers to familiarize them with the newest styles and techniques of the time. Written originally in Latin, German, French, and Italian (one language in each of several part-books), these documents first appeared as prefaces to the original editions of Muffat's suites and concerti published in 1695, 1698, and 1701. In the music itself, Muffat combines French, German, and Italian styles, in order, as he said, to craft a musical "peace" during a time of warfare.

Facsimile editions and reprints of the original versions of the prefaces are readily accessible to modern performers either in *Denkmäler der Tonkunst in Österreich* (Graz: Akademische Druck- und Verlagsanstalt, 1953–1959. Jahrgang 1/2, Band 2; Jahrgang 2/2, Band. 4; Jahrgang 11/2, Band 23, Band. 89), or in a four-column format in Walter Kolneder's *Georg Muffat zur Aufführungspraxis* (Sammlung musikwissenschaftlicher Abhandlungen, Band 50. Strasbourg: P. H. Heitz, 1970). English-speaking players, however, have hitherto been limited only to scattered and incomplete translations: Muffat's dedication to his sponsor is reproduced in Oliver W. Strunk's *Source Readings in Music History* (New York: W. W. Norton, 1950/1965/1998); the remarks on bowing are published in Carol MacClintock's *Readings in the History of Music in Performance* (Bloomington: Indiana University Press, 1979); and almost all of the performance instructions are published in a translation by Kenneth Cooper and Julius Zsako in the *Musical Quarterly* ("Georg Muffat's Observations on the Lully style of performance." *Musical Quarterly.* 53 [1967], 220–45).

David Wilson, editor and translator of the present edition, is a baroque violinist with extensive experience, and has done a great service to English and American performers by bringing together in this new translation, all of Muffat's writings on string instrument performance. Wilson has supplemented them with his own brief but cogent essays on Muffat's intentions, the instruments of the period, performance techniques, the differences between French and German performance practice, and performance settings. Although they are not quite as idiomatic for our own language as MacClintock's (which, strangely, he does not include in his bibliography), Wilson's translations read well. They are not only more accurate than previous translations in interpreting Muffat's technical terms and concepts, but Wilson's use of appropriate modern terminology should also prove more helpful to modern players.

Instead of presenting a composite translation of Muffat's four original versions, Wilson has based his translation on the German version, augmenting it with notes on significant differences in the French, Italian, and Latin versions. The two-column layout, with the main text in a wide column and variant readings in a narrow column to the right, works very well with the exception of a few pages, where the many variants create large blank areas which disrupt the main text. Wilson's in-line placement of Muffat's musical examples is also an improvement over their original placement at the end of the Italian text. Wilson does retain Muffat's alphabetic designations of the examples, however, thus making it easy for anyone who wants to consult the original versions. The use of more up-to-date music software would have made the musical examples even clearer.

Some small problems with Wilson's book should be mentioned: Muffat's horizontal brackets corresponding to "notes marked in the following way" (the modern "first ending" brackets) are inadvertently omitted. There is also an inaccuracy in translation: the French *toucher juste* means "to play in tune" (the main point in all the original versions), not "exact fingering" as Wilson has rendered it. These inconsistencies could be a consequence of having used an intermediate translation and collation in modern German rather than the original, for other than a bibliographic reference, no mention is made of Kolneder's edition which so conveniently lays out the original texts side-by-side. There are similar inconsistencies in Wilson's translation of Muffat's performance practices. Wilson alerts us that in the musical examples he has (wisely) translated Muffat's signs for up- and down-bows into their modern equivalents. He does not make it clear, however, that his modern "grace note" notation for *appoggiaturas* is quite different from the slanting lines prominent in all the other editions cited, although his other markings for ornaments are close to Muffat's.

Since this book is intended primarily for performers, one important bibliographic omission should be pointed out, namely the comparatively recent performing editions of Muffat's music by Les Editions Doblinger (Vienna) and Editio Musica Budapest (Budapest). These include separate parts for the players but lack just that guidance for ornamentation and other performance details that Muffat intended to provide. It is precisely in such cases that the benefits of Wilson's edition are most evident. He provides a much needed and admirable resource for the preparation of stylistically correct performances—Michael and Edith Kimbel

Winkler, Gerhard J. "Marionettenoper: *Die Feuerbrunst*, Joseph Haydn zugeschrieben." *Osterreichische Musikzeitschrift*, 56 (2001), 8–14.

Woodfield, Ian. "Recent Research on the Viol." *Journal of the Viola da Gamba Society of America*, 38 (2001), 78–80.

Wolff, Christoph. "Defining Genius: Early Reflections of J. S. Bach's Self-Image." *Proceedings of the American Philosophical Society*, 145 (2001), 474–81.

Music Recordings and Scores

Graziani, Carlo. *Sonatas for Violoncello and Basso*. Mara E. Parker, editor. Madison: A-R Editions, Inc., 1997, Musical Score. Pp. [xviii] + 100; appendix; cadenzas; editorial note; musical examples; 4 black-and-white plates; table.

This critical score by A-R Editions adds to our knowledge of the violoncello repertoire from the second half of the eighteenth century, when the Baroque period was making its transition into the Classical era, and the cello was slowly acquiring its modern *persona* as a solo virtuoso instrument. Carlo Graziani (d. 1787) was one of the best cellist-composers of the time who carried that trend, and took part in creating that repertory. Graziani was an Italian who followed a well-trodden path by many of his compatriots who crossed the border seeking employment in Northern European courts and civic centers with an emerging urban musical life. There is a host of names who undertook this journey, and their work and compositions, even if little known today, provide the basic material of the rich musical life of eighteenth-century Europe and its subsequent musical inheritance to us.

Graziani toured Europe as a cellist before finally establishing himself in Germany in the position of royal teacher to the young prince of Prussia, Friedrich Wilhelm II. After his pupil's ascension to the crown as King of Prussia, in 1786, Graziani followed him to Berlin where he died a year later, in 1787. Works for cello are central to Graziani's musical output and include three volumes of sonatas published during his lifetime (Opp. 1–3, c1760–80), plus another nineteen works which survive in manuscript. These manuscripts are of particular interest as they stem from Graziani's later years and exemplify cello composition and technique in the late eighteenth century. From these works, Mara E. Parker has selected nine sonatas for the present edition.

The main interest of this music is the glimpse it affords us of the level of contemporary cello playing and composition, but it is also reveals an image of the rich musical establishment surrounding Friedrich Wilhelm, who was a keen amateur musician and an accomplished cellist himself. Parker, who has written a doctoral dissertation on music in the court of Friedrich Wilhelm, believes that many of these pieces were written for the musical instruction and pleasure of the prince and later king. Indeed, an added bonus of these manuscripts is the inclusion of pencilled-in fingerings believed to have been added to facilitate their performance at court. Echoes of that court environment can also be found in that, apart from the traditional harpsichord accompaniment from the bass, these sonatas can also be performed by two cellists as duets, prompting us to visualize master and pupil playing together.

Parker is in an excellent position to provide an authoritative edition of these pieces both because of her academic research and her expertise as a cellist. As a result, the prefatory material and instructions strike an excellent balance, making happy both the general reader, the specialist, and the cellist performer—Vassilis Vavoulis

Over the Hills and Far Away. Being a Collection of Music from 18th-century Annapolis. [*A collection of songs with instrumental accompaniment, and instrumental pieces.*] David and Ginger Hildebrand, musical arrangements and sound recordings. Performers: David Hildebrand, Ginger Hildebrand, Robert Gallagher, John Barry Talley, Thomas Mosser, Nancy Almquist. Arnold: David and Ginger Hildebrand (BMI); Albany: Albany Music Distributors, 1990. Compact Disc.

Reviewed with

Music of the Charles Carroll Family, from 1785 to 1832. David and Ginger Hildebrand. [*A collection of songs with instrumental accompaniment and instrumental pieces.*] David and Ginger Hildebrand, musical arrangements and sound recordings. Performers: David Hildebrand, Ginger Hildebrand, Robert Gallagher, Thomas Mosser, Peggy Haas Howell. Arnold: David & Ginger Hildebrand (BMI); Albany: Albany Music Distributors, 1991. Compact Disc.

The music played in the Maryland state capital of Annapolis before the American Revolution has been the focus of David Hildebrand's research and performance since the mid-1980s. *Over the Hills and Far Away* is the first of two CDs presenting the practical result of this work, and serves as a summary of the variety of music as it might have sounded in eighteenth-century Annapolis. The twenty selections on the recording are organized by venue and type: four songs represent "The Scottish vogue." The other songs present a selection of music from the theater, the Tuesday Club of Annapolis (a social organization that met from 1745 to 1756), selections with topical reference to Maryland, and music for the tavern. Because of the paucity of source material, the final selection, representing "The Church," offers a more speculative interpretation of psalm verses set to the tune "St. Anne"—a clever choice since the Episcopal church of Annapolis is named for St. Anne and is known to have had an organ after 1761.

As the title suggests, *Music of the Charles Carroll Family, from 1785 to 1832* is devoted to compositions from the family library of Charles Carroll of Carrollton, a signer of the Declaration of Independence, representing Maryland. The sixteen selections on the CD are taken from music books published in London and Edinburgh between 1762 and 1829, and thereby serve as both a complement and a sequel to "Over the Hills." The musical library of the Catholic Carroll family included a variety of songs, keyboard pieces, operas, and theater works. One of the most unusual works in the family collection was a volume of ten voluntaries for organ or harpsichord by the Anglican composer John Stanley (1712–1783) of London. Voluntaries are generally considered "sacred music", but in its American context, the genre acquires a more prosaic character and function. Although a selection from Stanley's volume is played on an eighteenth-century church organ in this recording, the music preserved in the Carroll library were intended for domestic consumption, and the otherwise sacred voluntary should be understood here in its household role.

Most of the vocals on the two recordings feature the natural, untrained voice of David Hildebrand. The accompanying instruments include harpsichord, violin, hammered dulcimer, guitar and recorders—all instruments that would have been played in eighteenth-century America. The result is a sound that synthesizes acoustic folk music with a more historically-informed, early-music approach. The recordings themselves were made at historic locations in Annapolis, and although the authentic locations add little to the aural ambiance of the CDs, they do point to the care for historical contexts that the producers have lavished on these recordings. Intriguingly, the CD booklet reports the original harpsichord owned by the Carroll family still survives at the Groton School in Groton, Massachusetts, but for unstated reasons, that instrument is not used in the recordings.

The organization of the selections on these two CDs corresponds to their functional genre (songs, theater, tavern, church) and follows the synthesis established by Richard Crawford in *America's Musical Life* (reviewed elsewhere in this volume). These two CDs are particularly valuable for their carefully researched and footnoted liner notes, bibliographies, and source identifications and represent a significant addition to a little-known field—JoAnn Udovich.

Telemann, Georg Philipp [1681-1767]. *Noveaux Quatuors en Six Suites (Paris 1738).* 'Pariser Quartette'/'Paris Quartets.' *A une Flûte Traversière, un Violon, une Basse de Viole, ou Violoncelle, et Basse continue.* Urtext der Telemann-Ausgabe/Urtext of the Telemann Edition (taken from Georg Philipp Telemann, *Musikalische Werke*, issued on behalf of the Gesellschaft ür Musikforschung, Volume XIX: *Nouveaux Quatuors en Six Suites* (BA 2944), edited by Walter Bergmann; [1950].) Kassel: Bärenreiter-Verlag, [1950] / 2001. 2 volumes: BA 5881 (Band 1); BA 5882 (Band 2), Music Score (2 volumes) + 6 parts (2 volumes) ; German and English texts.

Band 1:*1er quatuor* TWV 43:D3; *2e quatuor* TWV 43:a2; *3e quatuor* TWV 43:G4;

Band 2:*4e quatuor* TWV 43:h2; *5e quatuor* TWV 43:A3; *6e quatuor* TWV 43:e4;

Partitur /Score: Vol. I: Pp. ix + 89; Vol. II: Pp. ix + 74. Vol. I and II [same text, German and English]: bibliography; notes; preface.

Parts: *Flute traversière*: Vol. I: Pp. 23; Vol. II: Pp. 22; *Violon*: Vol. I: Pp. 22; Vol. II: Pp. 22; *Basse de Viole*: Vol. I: Pp. 21; Vol. II: Pp. 20; *Violoncelle*: Vol. I: Pp. 21; Vol. II: Pp. 20; *Basse continue* [figured; unrealized]: Vol. I: Pp. 17; Vol. II: Pp. 19; *Basse continue* [figured; realization for keyboard instrument by Walter Bergmann, 1950]: Vol I: Pp. 31; Vol. II: Pp. 28.

Bärenreiter's new edition of Telemann's Quartets for flute, violin, *viola da gamba* or cello, and *continuo* is beautifully produced. It is divided into two sections, easily identified by their reference numbers. The bars are laid out with enough space, so that the eye is not confused, and the printing is strong and clear. Bar numbers are placed at the beginning of every line, and each section has the scores of its other three trios bound together. Awkward page turns have been carefully avoided in almost every part, although there is an exception to this in the sixth quartet. Here, the flute and violin are expected to turn while playing. The violin does have four bars rest just before the turn, so it seems a little unfortunate that the two following bars could not be fitted on to the next page.

The scores have been scrupulously edited, and great care has been taken to keep all dynamic markings as accurate as possible. There has long been controversy amongst musicologists concerning the length and articulation of staccato dots and heavy strokes over notes. Some editors, including Walter Bergman in his earlier edition of the quartets, think that these two dynamic indications have the same meaning. In this new edition, the present editor believes that there is, indeed, a slight difference of articulation in performance between the staccato dot and the heavy stroke: the staccato sign means that the note is very short, while the stroke means it is accented. By keeping both signs, the editor makes Telemann's intentions perfectly clear and easy to follow. As the editor observes, in the preface, there are very few added editorial signs, and those that appear are in small type. The editor has used French for the names of the instruments and dynamic markings as Telemann did, rather than Italian.

Cues are usually included for those instruments that do not start the movement, unless the rhythm and speed are very obvious. A problem for players who are sight-reading, especially if they are not very experienced, is how to know who enters after a pause. A case in point is the first movement of the fourth quartet, which has a 3/8 section in the middle, following a pause. The third beat of the pause bar is played by the cello and continuo, but there is no indication of this in either the violin or flute parts, a feature which would not be helpful for sight-readers.

These are all small criticisms, however, and this edition of Telemann's "Paris Quartets" is a pleasure to study and perform. The quartets have been edited with care and reveal the editor's detailed knowledge of the performance practices of the time. The preface, written in German, but also translated into English, is interesting to read and emphasizes Telemann's understanding and appreciation of the French style of composition in the first half of the eighteenth century.

Both amateur and professional performers will welcome this excellent new edition. Telemann's unflagging invention and his mastery of the French style, his richly varied rhythms and his elegant scoring are allowed full expression—Martha Kingdon-Ward

Theater

Bideaux, Michel (ed.). *Le Théâtre à Montpellier, 1755-1851. Pierre Jourda.* (SVEC, 2001:02.) Oxford: Voltaire Foundation, 2001. Pp. xi + 267; bibliography; illustrations; indices.

Charlton, David. "The French theatrical origins of *Fidelio.*" Pp. 51–67 of *Ludwig van Beethoven, "Fidelio."* (Cambridge Opera Handbooks.) Edited by Paul Robinson. Cambridge: Cambridge University Press, 1996.

Cotticelli, Francesco, Anne Goodrich Heck, and Thomas F. Heck (eds. and trans.). *The Commedia dell'Arte in Naples: A Bilingual Edition of the 176 Casamarciano Scenarios. Volume 1: English Edition.* Lanham: Scarecrow Press, Inc., 2001. Pp. xxvi + 563; facsimiles; indices; table of concordances.

Reviewed with

Cotticelli, Francesco (ed.). *La Commedia dell'Arte a Napoli: Edizione Bilingue dei 176 Scenari Casamarciano. Volume 2: Edizione Italiana.* Lanham: Scarecrow Press, Inc., 2001. Pp. xv + 569; bibliography; indices; notes; color plate.

Francesco Cotticelli's interest in the *Commedia dell'Arte* in general and the Casamarciano Scenarios in particular dates back over a decade. His long-standing commitment comes to full fruition in the present bilingual edition of 176 of the original 183 scenarios, made possible with the collaboration of Thomas Heck and Anne Goodrich Heck, who translated and edited the English language volume.

The scenarios, otherwise known as *canovacci*, are the basic stage directions for *Commedia dell'Arte* comedies. Generally organized in three acts, the scenarios do not contain dialogues, but rather outlines, simple cues for speeches, comic actions, or routines (otherwise known as *lazzi*), entrances, exits, scenery, and staging details. They constitute the basic framework of the story, which the actors would be able to enrich freely with dialogues and *lazzi* of their own creation. The practice of recording scenarios came late in the history of the *Commedia dell'Arte*, one might say almost at its twilight, possibly born of an awareness of the fragility of an art based on oral, rather than written traditions. The present edition is based on the *zibaldone*, or collection of scenarios by Annibale Sersale, Count of Casamarciano, dating from the late 1600s and early 1700s.

The essentially non-dialogical nature of the texts positions the scenarios at the margin of literature, pointing to a paraliterary function which Cotticelli questions and examines in the introduction. In a felicitous twist of fate, the document was acquired by Italy's most famous historian and literary critic, Benedetto Croce. Recognizing their importance within the history of the *Commedia* in general and Neapolitan cultural tradition in particular, Croce donated them to the *Biblioteca Nazionale* of Naples in 1896.

Cotticelli's edition represents the largest compilation of scenarios published so far, the others being the 50 *Scenari Correr* edited by Carmelo Alberti (*Gli scenari Correr. La Commedia dell'Arte a Venezia*, Roma, Bulzoni, 1996) and Delia Gambelli's edition of 80 scenarios by Domenico Biancolelli (Gambelli, Delia [ed.], *Arlecchino a Parigi. II. Lo scenario di Domenico Biancolelli*. Roma, Bulzoni, 1997). With 183 scenarios, this edition of the Casamarciano manuscript is an invaluable historical and anthological record documenting the development of the *Commedia dell'Arte*. Some of the recorded *canovacci* reveal their sources in earlier collections, while others clearly point to the influence of Spanish plays, demonstrating a continuity of the subject matter and its transformation through time.

Cotticelli discusses the difficulty in defining the scenarios as literary artifacts, and explains their importance in the process of crystallization of the *maschere*. The vulnerability and the genius of a theater based on the improvisational skills of individual actors naturally led to the desire to fix the ever changing nature of the *Commedia dell'Arte*, which by its nature always lives in the present moment, while still creating a performative continuity between different episodes and times. As Cotticelli explains "The problem is that a *canovaccio* does not just [bear] witness to the skill of professional actors; rather it mediates between abstract intention and concrete action. It is the image of a reality that has already taken place between an audience and the performers, and at the same time, [it is also] a subtle prefiguration of future performances, repeated and renewed. It [a *canovaccio*] determines the timing and the limits of an otherwise unbounded creativity" (I,13; II, 5).

The bilingual edition is arranged in two volumes. Volume I contains the English translation of the scenarios and a summary of Cotticelli's introduction, facsimiles of two scenarios (i/91 and ii/57), a Table of Concordances, and a very valuable introduction to the English edition by Thomas Heck. Volume II contains the original Italian transcription of the scenarios, the full text of Cotticelli's introduction in Italian and a very detailed bibliography. Readers and scholars who are not native speakers of Italian should be cautioned that the complex style of Cotticelli's introduction is characteristic of Italian academic writing. Those who are familiar with the language will appreciate the subtleties of Cotticelli's analysis of the genre and his excellent notes.

The edition is an erudite, fundamental work that will be of interest to "scholars and students of dramatic literature, linguists, humanists and theater practitioners" (I, xv). In order to fully appreciate its valuable contents, the non-specialist could benefit from familiarizing themselves with the present scholarship on the *Commedia dell'Arte* and its relationship to Cotticelli's work. Some details should be noted. Volume I includes facsimiles of two individual scenarios. Although the editors do not provide a formal explanation as to why these were chosen for inclusion, their inclusion is a valuable feature which illustrates graphically the condition of the original texts and the difficulties in transcribing them (seven of the original scenarios could not be deciphered). There is also a change in the handwriting styles illustrated by the facsimiles (i/91 and ii/57), which was taken into account by the editors in the present grouping of the scenarios in this edition. Finally, the scenarios reproduced in the facsimiles are among the several examples quoted by Cotticelli in his Introduction: i/91, *Pulcinella, Mad in Spite of Himself* (quoted in I,14–15 and II,7, respectively) illustrates the gradual marginalization of Pulcinella, while ii/57, *The Seven Princes of Ara* (quoted in I,18 and II,12, respectively) exemplifies the complex staging of the scenarios.

Volume I also contains a very comprehensive table of concordances but its usefulness would have been significantly enhanced with the addition of a brief paragraph explaining the nature and use of concordances and the significance of the concordances noted in the table. Readers new to the history and traditions of the *Commedia dell'Arte* should not overlook the foreword by Nancy D'Antuono—included in both the Italian and the English volumes—which provides a brief but very clear and salient introduction to the *Commedia dell'Arte* and a discussion of its evolution from the sixteenth to the eighteenth century.

The relevance and importance of the bilingual edition is twofold: on the one hand it offers an unprecedented wealth of scenarios, meticulously deciphered and transcribed for the use of native Italian specialists; on the other, this bilingual edition opens the study of the *Commedia dell'Arte* and its *canovacci* to a much larger public thanks to the thorough and expert translation, which not only transfers the meaning of the Italian texts into English, but also translates and develops the often cryptic cues into comprehensible sentences. Analyzed side by side, the translations of the scenarios maintains the condensed and naked feeling of the original dramas, while also conveying the dynamism and extemporaneity of texts that were subject to constant transformation and interpretation. Anne Goodrich Heck and Thomas Heck merit special praise for their impeccable translations, their attention to detail, and their respect for the integrity of the original texts—Costanza Gislon Dopfel

Dean, Winton. "Beethoven and opera." Pp. 22–50 of *Ludwig van Beethoven, "Fidelio"*. (Cambridge Opera Handbooks.) Edited by Paul Robinson. Cambridge: Cambridge University Press, 1996.

Everist, Mark. "Enshrining Mozart: *Don Giovanni* and the Viardot Circle." *19th-Century Music*, 25 (2001) 165–89.

Gordon, Felicia and P. N. Furbank. *Marie Madeleine Jodin 1741–1790 Actress, Philosophe and Feminist*. (Women and Gender in the Early Modern World.) Brookfield: Ashgate Publishing Company, 2001. Pp xii + 224; bibliography; index; black-and-white plates.

Kerman, Joseph. "Augenblicke in *Fidelio*." Pp. 132–44 of *Ludwig van Beethoven, "Fidelio"*. (Cambridge Opera Handbooks.) Cambridge: Cambridge University Press, 1996.

Milhous, Judith, Gabriella Dideriksen, and Robert D. Hume. *Italian Opera in Late Eighteenth-Century London*. Volume II: The Pantheon Opera and its Aftermath, 1789–1795. Oxford: Clarendon Press, 2001. Pp. xxvii + 883; 8 appendices; bibliography; index; 18 musical examples; 32 black-and-white plates; 22 tables.

"This book would never have been conceived" if Milhous and Hume had not discovered a "massive cache" of Pantheon Opera documents in the Bedford Estates Office in 1985. Those that pre-date the conflagration which destroyed the theater on January 14, 1792, may have been "deliberately removed" before it began. "The likelihood of arson is extremely high," because "the fire was enormously convenient for the Pantheon's secret backers" (the Duke of Bedford and the Earl of Salisbury, who served as Lord Chamberlain). They had already lost £35,000 and were committed to pay £3,500 annually for their twelve-year lease on the building (II: viii, 146–47, 260, 392, 620, 654).

In Part 1, the authors proceed chronologically, proceeding from the fiery destruction of the old King's Theatre on June 17, 1789, to the managerial chicaneries of William Taylor at the new one in 1793–96. At the outset, they evaluate various rebuilding plans of 1789–90, and thus supplement the discussion found in the penultimate chapter of *Volume I: The King's Theatre, Haymarket, 1778–1791* (Curtis Price, Judith Milhous, and Robert D. Hume, *Italian Opera in Late Eighteenth-Century London. Volume I. The King's Theatre, Haymarket 1778–1791* [Oxford: Clarendon Press, 1995]. Reviewed by Lowell E. Lindgren in *Il Saggiatore Musicale*, III [1996], 183–92; by Pauline M. Minevich in *ECCB*. Volumes 20–21, for 1994 and 1995, 378–79). In chapter 2, they discuss the Pantheon's first season (February 17– July 19, 1791), which presented captivating singers, dancers, and repertory, but detrimental acoustics, stage size, and stage settings. Attendance was poor, partly because vocal pieces and ballets were also being performed (23 February 23– July 5) at the new King's Theatre. Such competition and the "disorganization and administrative incompetence" of the manager, Robert

Bray O'Reilly, led to expenses that far exceeded income. O'Reilly had to flee to Paris in order to escape debtor's prison, even though he was "in fact merely a cat's-paw" (I: 557) and "the financial fall-guy" (II: 110–11) for the secret backers. He prospered in Paris, however, and surely merits a less harsh treatment by the authors (II: 253–55) They are well aware, however, that readers might contest their "broader conclusions," which are based on their "factually ambitious and interpretively bold" treatment of "a vast heap of particulars and nitty-gritty details." They present such particulars iridescently rather than dryly, and they link details by reasoning, for example, "as we understand the rather tortuous complexities of a succession of deals," or by speculation, for example, although "we have found not a scintilla of hard evidence" (II: x, 179, 181).

The managers, singers, dancers, and repertory of the next four seasons are discussed in the final two chapters of Part 1. The rival companies signed a secret treaty in October 1791. After the Pantheon's suspicious fire in January 1792, its company moved to the Little Haymarket Theatre, which was often "woefully empty," as shown in the record of nightly attendance and cash receipts (II: Table 2.159–63). Accordingly, its losses continued, and its legal agent, William Sheldon, was held liable in case after case filed by creditors (II: 166–67). A settlement in August, 1792 united the rival companies at the King's Theatre and should have terminated the managerial career of Taylor, who was "a supremely slippery scoundrel." Instead, "a loophole" allowed him to regain power in 1793. This was disastrous for the company, since he possessed "great aptitude for financial jiggery-pokery" (I: 66) and "had no interest whatever in trying to pay off the debts" of the two companies (II: 178–81, 205). The authors conjecture that the Prince of Wales blocked any scheme that could have terminated Taylor's management. They then speculate that the person who "got at" the Prince was the dramatist and manager Richard Brinsley Sheridan, who thus became "the evil genius of opera" in late eighteenth-century London (I: 55, 115; II: 181. 256). When they declare rather than speculate that the Prince stood in the way, however, the reader may well wonder whether any strong evidence supports their declarations (II: 205, 240, 250).

The first three chapters of Part 2 concern the architectural design that converted the Pantheon into an opera house, the large staff employed by the house, and six components of each production: scenes and related machines, costumes, properties, lighting, prompting, and rehearsals. The design was revealed by two plans that came to light in 1988. These plans, two other eighteenth-century drawings, and four recent reconstructions constitute eight of the thirty-two plates. The employees (more than 200 in 1790–91 and about 150 in 1791–92) are categorized in the text and partly represented on four of the twenty-two tables. The masters in charge of staging in 1790–92 are each evaluated. With solemn wit, the authors then admit that they "cannot document the cat," yet "presume its presence. Like the British Museum of today, the Pantheon would have been overrun with undesirable little creatures had it not kept a cat or cats on its payroll" (II: 372).

The final three chapters provide extended descriptions of the operas and ballets staged in 1790–92, then summarize the finances of these disastrous seasons. Music for both genres was given ample discussion in volume I, which includes twenty-four excerpts by twelve composers who worked in London. It receives relatively short shrift in volume II, which includes eighteen excerpts by four composers, only one of whom—Joseph Mazzinghi—worked in London for the Pantheon. The Pantheon's backers expected to focus on ballets that told a tale (*ballets d'action*), and on serious operas, but comic works accounted for 40 of the 55 performances given during the first season, and for all of the forty-eight performances given during the second. Three comic operas received their London premieres during each season. The only opera written for the Pantheon was Paisiello's *La locanda;* it ended the first season, dominated the second, and virtually all of its arias and small ensembles were published. The only known manuscript score for a Pantheon production preserves act I of Paisiello's *La discordia conjugale*. Many were drawn to each performance by the two ballets rather than the opera. Jean Bercher Dauberval choreographed all thirteen ballets, hired the dancers and the scenic designer, danced, and supplied much of the music. The authors' vivid descriptions of ballets are derived from the four published scenarios, the five published keyboard scores, and most notably from the detailed wardrobe book preserved in the Bedford Estates Office.

The eight appendices present in an orderly manner "a vast heap of particulars and nitty-gritty details." For example, Appendix 1 lists each employee during 1790–92 and her/his salary; Appendix 4 is an edited version of the wardrobe book; Appendix 6 lists the subscribers alphabetically; and Appendix 8 is a short catalogue of the Bedford Opera Papers. The ensuing bibliography (omitted in volume I) encompasses both volumes I and II. The closing index is as detailed and therefore as helpful as can be.

The authors' "factually ambitious and interpretively bold" treatment of their wealth of material is spectacular. Each of the two volumes is similarly structured and indomitably documented. Each thus serves as a glorious monument to a great theatrical fire, and to the fascinating lives and works that encircled it—Lowell E. Lindgren

Norman, Larry F. *The Book in the Age of Theater: 1550–1750.* Chicago: University of Chicago Library, 2001. Pp. 72; illustrations.

Pucci, Suzanne R. *Sites of the Spectator. Emerging Literary and Cultural Practice in Eighteenth-Century France.* (Studies on Voltaire and the Eighteenth Century 9.) Oxford: Voltaire Foundation, 2001. Pp. ix + 201; bibliography; index.

Robinson, Paul (ed.). "An Interpretive History." Pp. 145–64 of *Ludwig van Beethoven, "Fidelio."* (Cambridge Opera Handbooks.) Edited by Paul Robinson. Cambridge: Cambridge University Press, 1996, 145–64.

Robinson, Paul. *Ludwig von Beethoven. "Fidelio".* (Cambridge Opera Handbooks.) Cambridge. Cambridge University Press. 1996. Pp xi + 191; bibliography; end notes; index; musical examples; monochrome and color plates.

This is a very comprehensive, detailed, and well written account of the history of Beethoven's *Fidelio*, from the French origins of the libretto to the final version by a young lawyer, Jean-Nicolas Bouilly (1763–1842) which he entitled *Léonore, ou l'amour conjugal*. The opera was written at a time of great political torment in France, during the period of the dictatorial five-man Directory (1795–99). It was first performed in Paris in 1798, as *Léonore*, in a setting by Pierre Gaveaux, a singer who took the part of Florestan in the performance.

The opera underwent various transformations until, perhaps rather reluctantly, it was used by Beethoven in 1805. As Beethoven himself said in 1824, "My *Fidelio* was not understood by the public…[for] the symphony is my true element. When sounds stir within me, I always hear the full orchestra…but with vocal compositions I must always be asking myself, can this be sung" (Beethoven, *Letters, Journals and Conversations*. Edited and translated by Michael Hamburger [New York: Pantheon, 1952], 212). Robinson provides a full synopsis of the libretto (Chapter 2), not in dialogue form, however, but rather explaining the thoughts as well as the character of the participants as the plot unfolds.

It is a pleasure to re-read Winton Dean's chapter "Beethoven and Opera" (22–50), originally published in *The Beethoven Companion*, edited by Denis Arnold and Nigel Fortune (London: Faber and Faber, 1971), 331–86. Dean gives a wonderfully lucid account of other contemporary operas, and the gloomy details of *Fidelio*'s first performance in Vienna on November 20, 1805. The production, at the Kärntnerthor Theatre, had only three performances and was a disaster for the opera. The city had been occupied for several days by the French army, and most of Beethoven's friends and the nobility had fled to the country. The first performance was full of French troops; the other two were empty.

A fascinating chapter [by Paul Robinson], entitled "An Interpretive History" (145–64) concludes the book. Here we have discussions of the singers, the conductors, the scenery, the productions, and the many alterations to the opera from the early nineteenth century to the end of the twentieth century, via Gustave Mahler and Herbert von Karajan to Jonathan Miller and Roger Norrington. The discussion here, and in other chapters throughout the book, is enhanced with illustrations of early singers and scenery used in later productions, and beautifully clear musical examples. This is altogether a book to be treasured by anyone wanting to have all the information possible to enjoy the opera. Cambridge University Press and Paul Robinson are certainly to be congratulated on the production of this illuminating "Handbook"—Elsie Arnold.

IV: Fine Arts

Robinson, Paul. "*Fidelio* and the French Revolution." Pp. 68–100 of *Ludwig van Beethoven, "Fidelio"*. (Cambridge Opera Handbooks.) Edited by Paul Robinson. Cambridge: Cambridge University Press, 1996, 68–100.

Rudlin, John, and Olly Crick. *Commedia dell'Arte, a Handbook for Troupes*. London: Routledge, 2001. Pp. xiii + 251; bibliography; illustrations; index; map; musical examples.

Stallknecht, Fabian A. *Dramenmodell und ideologische Entwicklung der italienischen Oper im frühen Ottocento*. (Metzler-Poeschel Schriftenreihe für Wissenschafgt und Forschung. Stuttgart: Metzler, 2001. Pp. 611; bibliography.

Taylor, Nancy. "John Weaver and the Origins of English Pantomime: A Neoclassical Theory and Practice for Uniting Dance and Theatre." *Theatre Survey: The Journal of the American Society for Theatre Research*, 42 (2001), 191–214.

Wagner, Marie-France and Claire Le Brun-Gouanvic (eds.). *Les arts du spectacle au théâtre (1550-1700)*. (Colloques, congrès et conférences sur la Renaissance, 23) Paris: H. Champion, 2001. Pp. 273; bibliography; index. French text.

Wagner, Marie-France and Claire Le Brun-Gouanvic (eds.). *Les arts du spectacle dans la ville (1404-1721)*. (Colloques, congrès et conférences sur la Renaissance, 24.) Paris: H. Champion, 2001. Pp. 288; bibliography; illustrations; index. French text.

Woodfield, Ian. *Opera and Drama in Eighteenth-Century London. The King's Theatre, Garrick, and the Business of Performance*. Cambridge: Cambridge University Press, 2001. Pp. xii + 339; appendices; index; musical examples; notes.

Woodfield's *Opera and Drama in Eighteenth-Century London*, a recent addition to the Cambridge Studies in Opera series, follows earlier volumes in providing a closely-researched examination of a rarely studied passage in opera history. He gives close attention to "the politics and economics of opera, the operatic representation of women or the singers who portrayed them, the history of opera as theatre, and the evolution of the opera house" (series overview). Unlike many conventional opera histories, the Cambridge series publishes studies such as Woodfield's, which is neither a narrative of a composer's musical development nor is it centered on the musical score.

Despite the inclusive-sounding title, however, Woodfield's book focuses on a single decade, the 1770s, although it is an eventful, exciting, and under-researched period. Woodfield's introduction sets the stage, describing the precarious state of opera during the 1750s and 1760s, and its continued reliance on Italian *castrati* and French dancers assembled for a motley assortment of productions. By the 1780s, the managed combination of comic and serious opera with ballet had become a successful practice, as documented by the extensive research of Judith Milhous and Robert Hume, working with musicologist Curtis Price. Woodfield's account covers the period immediately preceeding their study of The King's Theatre and Haymarket (Curtis Price, Judith Milhous, and Robert D. Hume, editors. *Italian Opera in Late Eighteenth-Century London*, Vol. 1, *The King's Theatre, Haymarket, 1778–1791* [Oxford: Clarendon Press, 1995]).

Woodfield argues that 1773 was "in retrospect, a critical turning point for Italian opera in London" (9), and that novelist-critic Frances Brooke, who became the leading manager of the King's Theatre, was "a much more influential figure in the history of Italian opera in London than has hitherto been recognized" (3). Woodfield's introduction concludes with a section on sources which includes both new and familiar materials, many in manuscript, that are invaluable to those evaluating Woodfield's work and to those working (or planning to work) in this area. Of particular interest are the opera accounts for the King's Theatre from 1773 to 1777 at Henry Hoare & Co.. These are transcribed in Appendix 1A, which also includes useful details pertaining to receipts and expenditures.

Brooke was a novice at theater management and Woodfield argues from the available evidence that Dr. Charles Burney functioned as Frances Brooke's "artistic advisor" (58) in recruiting singers and selecting repertoire. While Burney is best remembered today for his *History of Music*. (*A General History of Music from the Earliest Ages to the Present Period*, edited by Frank Mercer (London: Dover, 1935/1957, 2 volumes), he was intensely involved in the contemporary music scene in London and maintained contacts throughout Europe. While Burney's expertise was doubtless important to Brooke's success, her own negotiating skills and financial acumen are also applauded by Woodfield. Several of Burney's daughters were also keen opera enthusiasts and observers of the London musical scene, and Woodfield draws on their letters and diaries as well as on their father's published accounts of musicians and music-making.

The opening chapters deal with Brooke and her co-managers (actors Mary Ann and Richard Yates) and their struggle to establish the new company established in the face of its formidable competition. Central chapters address the recruitment and employment of Italian singers, particularly Giovanni Lovattini and Caterina Gabrielli, and their competition with singers engaged at the Pantheon, especially Lucrezia Agujari. The closing chapters deal with the final flare-up of the famous feud between David Garrick and the King's Theatre managers, the artistic and financial success of the King's Theatre management, and events leading to the sale of the theater in 1778.

Woodfield writes concisely and handles his documentary material gracefully. Nonetheless, readers who are not familiar with the librettists, singers, and composers of the 1770s may feel they need to read this work with supplementary biographical texts in hand, such as *A Biographical Dictionary of Actors, Actresses, Musicians, Dancers, Managers and Other Stage Personnel in London 1600–1800*, edited by Philip H. Highfill, Jr, Kalman A. Burnim, and Edward A. Langhans (Carbondale, 1973–93). Although Woodfield avoids the literary trap of inserting summary biographies or asides which would interrupt the flow of his argument, this can sometimes leave the reader without needed guidance, and one has to turn to the index often to find someone's full name. The scenery and special effects wizard "Colomba" (152), for example, Giovanni Colomba, and the composer "Gasman" (163), whose comic opera is mentioned in Antoine Le Textier's *Journal Etranger* is cited in the index as Florian Leopold Gassman. A sharper editorial eye would have found and corrected these minor infelicities.

Woodfield's work provides an important addition to our understanding of the mechanics of producing opera in London during the late eighteenth century. His account of Frances Brooke and her co-managers and singers at the King's Theatre weaves together important figures from the history of opera and theater, and charts "the resurrection of one of Europe's leading opera houses, [and] the transformation over the course of a single decade of an enterprise precariously balanced on the edge of viability, into one of London's leading cultural institutions" (18)—Kathryn Lowerre

V: Foreign Literatures and Languages

Iberian Literatures and Languages

Aguilar Piñal, Francisco. *Bibliografía de autores españoles del siglo XVIII*. Madrid: Consejo Superior de Investigaciones Científicas, 2001. Pp. 736; index.

Álvarez Barrientos, Joaquín. "*La Celestina*, del siglo XVIII a Menéndez Pelayo." Pp. 73–96 of *"Celestina": recepción y herencia de un mito literario*. Edited by Gregorio Torres Nebrera. Cáceres: Universidad de Extremadura, 2001.

Álvarez Barrientos, Joaquín. "Los judíos y su cultura en la producción literaria española del siglo XVIII: la construcción del tópico "judeo-masón-liberal" durante la Ilustración y el Romanticismo." Pp. 267–300 of *Judíos en la literatura española*. Edited by Iacob M. Hassán and Ricardo Izquierdo Benito. Cuenca: Universidad de Castilla–La Mancha, 2001.

Angulo Egea, María. "Cadalso en la obra de Comella. Con la edición de *El violeto universal o El Café*." *Dieciocho*, 24 (2001), 33–84.

Animan Akassi, Clément. "La figure du 'vieux chrétien' lascasien comme fondement idéologique de la pratique d'exclusion des Noirs à Cuba." Pp. 243–63 of *Las Casas face à l'esclavage des Noirs: vision critique du "Onzième Remède" (1516)/Las Casas frente a la esclavitud de los negros: visión crítica del "Undécimo Remedio" (1516)*. Edited by Victorien Lavou Zoungbo. Perpignan: Université de Perpignan, 2001.

Arellano, Ignacio. "*La Celestina* en la comedia del siglo XVII." Pp. 51–72 of *"Celestina": recepción y herencia de un mito literario*. Edited by Gregorio Torres Nebrera. Cáceres: Universidad de Extremadura, 2001.

Aymes, Jean-René. "La familia en el *Semanario Pintoresco Español* (1836–1857) y en otros textos costumbristas contemporáneos." Pp. 193–208 of *Historia social y literatura. Familia y clases populares en España (siglos XVIII–XIX)*. Edited by Roberto Fernández and Jacques Soubeyroux. Lérida: Milenio, 2001.

Baker, Edward. "Nuestras antigüedades: La formación del canon poético medieval en el siglo XVIII." *Hispania*, 61 (2001), 813–29.

Bidima, Jean-Godefroy. "Du droit des gens: la tolerance et l'expérience chez Las Casas (1474–1556) et Benito J. Feijoo (1676–1764)." Pp. 215–41 of *Las Casas face à l'esclavage des Noirs: vision critique du "Onzième Remède" (1516)/Las Casas frente a la esclavitud de los negros: Visión crítica del " Undécimo Remedio" (1516)*. Edited by Victorien Lavou Zoungbo. Perpignan: Université de Perpignan, 2001.

Bittoun-Debruyne, Nathalie. "*Los menestrales* de Trigueros, entre la realidad y el deseo." Pp. 85–111 of *Historia social y literatura. Familia y clases populares en España (siglos XVIII–XIX)*. Edited by Roberto Fernández and Jacques Soubeyroux. Lérida: Milenio, 2001.

Blanco, Emilio. "Algunas notas sobre la recepción de *Celestina* en los siglos XVI y XVII." Pp. 17–49 of *"Celestina": recepción y herencia de un mito literario*. Edited by Gregorio Torres Nebrera. Cáceres: Universidad de Extremadura, 2001.

Bombi, Andrea. "*. . . Imitar las cadenas italianas*. El recitativo en Valencia antes de la ópera." Pp. 131–74 of *La ópera en España e Hispanoamérica. Actas del Congreso Internacional, "La ópera en España y en Hispanoamérica. Una creación propia." Madrid, 29.XI/3.XII de 1999*. Edited by Emilio Casares Rodicio and Álvaro Torrente. Madrid: ICCMU, 2001.

Bueno, Eva Paulino. "Filhos de Coré: Vieira e a escrivadão negra no Brasil." Pp. 139–56 of *Las Casas face à l'esclavage des Noirs: vision critique du "Onzième Remède" (1516)/Las Casas frente a la esclavitud de los negros: visión crítica del "Undécimo Remedio" (1516)*. Edited by Victorien Lavou Zoungbo. Perpignan: Université de Perpignan, 2001.

Caballero Fernández-Rufete, Carmelo. "*En trova de lo humano a lo divino*: las óperas de Calderón de la Barca y los villancicos de Miguel Gómez Camargo." Pp. 95–115 of *La ópera en España e Hispanoamérica. Actas del Congreso Internacional, "La ópera en España y en Hispanoamérica. Una creación propia." Madrid, 29.XI/3.XII de 1999*. Edited by Emilio Casares Rodicio and Álvaro Torrente. Madrid: ICCMU, 2001.

Cadalso, José. *Anales de cinco días*. Edited by Francisco Alonso. Madrid: Comunidad de Madrid, 2001. Pp. 163; illustrations, maps (some folded).

After falling into disfavor and being considered a second-rate writer since early in the nineteenth century, José de Cadalso (1741–82) has slowly been regaining the literary prestige he enjoyed among his contemporaries. The number of editions and critical studies of his works in the last forty years surpasses that of any other Spanish writer of the long eighteenth century, perhaps with the exception of Leandro Fernández de Moratín. By far his most studied and edited work is *Cartas Marruecas* [*Moroccan Letters*], followed by *Noches lúgubres* [*Mournful Nights*] and *Los eruditos a la violeta* [*The Pseudo-Intellectuals*]. Only the latter work was published during Cadalso's lifetime, but all three have seen several editions from the late eighteenth century up to our days. Lesser-known writings, such as much of Cadalso's poetry, his correspondence, the satirical *Calendario manual* [*Handy Calendar*], the neoclassical tragedies *Don Sancho García* and *Solaya*, his autobiographical sketches, the *Suplemento* and other continuations to *The Pseudo-Intellectuals*, the *Defensa de la nación española contra la Carta persiana LXXVIII de Montesquieu* [*Defense of the Spanish Nation against Montesquieu's Persian Letter LXXVIII*], have all been published in the last thiry-plus years for the first time ever or for the first since the few decades after Cadalso's death. *Annals of Five Days*, first published in volume 17 of the *Semanario Erudito* [*Erudite Weekly*] (1789) and then not since 1818, now joins the list with this attractively printed and illustrated edition by Francisco Alonso.

The *Annals* were written during a period—1778 or 1779—when Cadalso was at the height of his welcome among the highest social circles of the court, held in good opinion, as he himself writes, by the Prince and Princess—the future Carlos IV and Queen María Luisa—a friend of their favorites, and a frequent escort of ladies of the high aristocracy, such as the Countess-Duchess of Benavente. In the second edition of the text, included in a four-volume collection of *Works by Don Joseph Cadalso* (1803), the title is followed by a description of its content: *Anales de Cinco Días, o Carta de un amigo a otro. Es una invectiva contra el lujo, modas y usos del siglo ilustrado* [*Annals of Five Days, or Letter from One Friend to Another. Being an Invective Against the Luxury, Fashions, and Ways of the Enlightened Century*]. The work is a narrative with interpolated dialogue in the form of a satyrical and pun-filled letter sent by the narrator to a friend, organized in eighty-eight numbered paragraphs. The narrator recounts his five-day visit to Madrid from the provinces, as he reacts to the novelties he encounters at the levée and toilette of a lady of the high aristocracy, in a series of urban gathering spaces and public spectacles, in the lifestyles and linguistic usages of the Madrid high society. The work contrasts urban vice and rural virtue, defends linguistic purism and ridicules Gallicizers; makes fun of foppish guests of fashionable salons and generally of the frivolous and unproductive life of the aristocracy; denounces the fashion-craze that has given rise to a new but also socially useless aristocracy of tailors, hairdressers, and shoemakers; and casts a critical eye on public entertainments, such as bullfights and the theater.

The edition has three parts of roughly equal size: An introductory study by Alonso, the text of the *Annals*, and a section of appendices. Alonso opens his introduction highlighting the importance of Cadalso as a signal figure in the frontier zone between neoclassicism and romanticism, and arbitrates in the polemic between the two most eminent students of Cadalso, Nigel Glendinning and Russell Sebold, whose early books on the writer were surely the decisive spur to his rise in critical esteem. A short biography of Cadalso follows, and then a survey of the themes of *Annals of Five Days*, many of them already present in better-known texts, such as the *Moroccan Letters* and *The Pseudo-Intellectuals*. The next section is a defense of the attribution of the work to Cadalso, based on external evidence (it was attributed to him in all five early editions; Cadalso's friends filtered several of his confirmed works to periodical publications in the years after his death) and internal evidence (coincidence in themes and narrative strategies with other works of Cadalso). Surprisingly, Alonso does not mention other evidence suggested by Russell Sebold in his *Colonel Don José Cadalso* (New York: Twayne, 1971): That allusions would indicate that the great lady whose levee the narrator attends is modeled on Cadalso's friend, the Countess-Duchess of Benavente; that the description of one of the bystanders to the narrator during an afternoon promenade along the Paseo del Prado [Prado Avenue] (paragraph 55) is actually a self-portrait of the author; and the constant ridiculing of "the Enlightened century," a recurring motif in Cadalso's work. The attribution of the *Annals* to Cadalso, in any case, has not been seriously questioned by scholars. The final section of the introductory study is a very partial bibliography of works on Cadalso. Only texts in Spanish are listed.

Appendix I is an excerpt from the *Carta de un amigo* [*Letter from a Friend*], an anonymous text which first appeared in an 1822 edition of *Mournful Nights*, and which claims that the disinterment of the cadaver of a woman by her lover, described in the first part of the *Nights*, in fact describes a real attempt by a grieving Cadalso to disinter his beloved María Ignacia Ibáñez, a talented young actress who had succumbed to typhoid fever. Appendix II is a "Memorial to the king" dated March 18, 1781, in which Cadalso summarizes his military career and merits and requests the rank of colonel. It is pertinent to the *Annals of Five Days* in that it makes clear that Cadalso was in a military mission in the south of Spain during the Holy Week of 1789, and that the *Annals* must therefore be the product of his 1788 six month stay in Madrid. Appendix III includes excerpts from two recent essays on urban planning and reform in Madrid during the reign of Carlos III. Appendix IV is Cadalso's 1775 letter to his friend the poet Juan Meléndez Valdés, in which he entrusts him with his manuscripts, which he lists, and gives him indications on what to do with them in the eventuality of his death in battle. The letter is the source of our knowledge of some of Cadalso's lost works. Appendix V are two odes "Sobre un nuevo amor" ["On a New Love"] in Sapphic and Adonic verses, sent by Cadalso to his friend the poet Nicolás Fernández de Moratín around March 1774. Appendix VI is a letter from Cadalso to a friend dated March 25, 1775, on poetic matters, specifically against the use of Pindaric odes for trivial subjects. Appendix VII reproduces number LXXXVIII of the *Moroccan Letters*, where Cadalso argues—through the character Ben-Beley—the role of luxury and frivolous self-indulgence in the decay of nations, and laments that his times are of such decay. These are themes central to the *Annals*. Appendix VIII is Cadalso's poem to the Countess-Duchess of Benavente, recognizing in her a fellow philosophical soul and inviting her to escape the cunning, flattery and pretense of the Court and to join him for a simple, true and joyful life in the countryside. Appendix IX reproduces number XXXV of the *Moroccan Letters*, a critique of ridiculous Gallicisms and of their promoters, the purveyors of luxury and self-indulgence: tailors, shoemakers, valets, dressmakers, cooks and pastrycooks, hairdressers, and "other individuals equally useful to the vigor and glory of nations." Finally the book includes a foldout reproduction of a map of Madrid, published in London in 1831, over half of a century after the writing of the *Annals*.

Overall, this final section provides a hodgepodge of materials that are not without interest in themselves, put that with a couple of exceptions have only a tangential relation to *Annals of Five Days*. The rationale for the inclusion of the texts in Appendices V and VI, for example, is that they were filtered by friends of Cadalso after his death to the periodical where they were first published, a fact which could suggest that the same occurred with the *Annals*, therefore reinforcing the certainty of Cadalso's authorship. The texts in appendices II, IV, V, VI and VIII were already published by Nigel Glendinning in his *Cadalso: Escritos autobiográficos y epistolario* [*Cadalso: Autobiographical Writings and Letters*] (London: Támesis, 1979).

We can be grateful to Francisco Alonso for making the *Annals* easily accessible to students of Cadalso. But the text is screaming for notes, and the annotation by Alonso is rather negligible, when not odd: Note 15 explains a reference to a mule carriage as an allusion to a 1783 (!) law limiting the number of mules or horses per carriage. What other scholars have said of the text is barely incorporated, and Alonso's few notes—a meager total of nineteen—do little to clarify the multiple allusions to Madrid social mores and to Cadalso's circles in particular, the constant but not always obvious puns, and the many references, Gallicized or not, to the world of fashion and the trappings of luxury. *Anales de cinco días*, then, is still waiting for a scholarly edition.—José A. Valero

Cadé, Michel. "Le jeu du passé et du présent dans *La controverse de Valladolid*." Pp. 305–12 of
    Las Casas face à l'esclavage des Noirs: vision critique du "Onzième Remède" (1516)/Las Casas frente

a la esclavitud de los negros: visión crítica del "Undécimo Remedio" (1516). Edited by Victorien Lavou Zoungbo. Perpignan: Université de Perpignan, 2001.

Campos, José Antonio. "A manera de prólogo." Pp. 13–19 of *La ópera en España e Hispanoamérica. Actas del Congreso Internacional, "La ópera en España y en Hispanoamérica. Una creación propia." Madrid, 29.XI/3.XII de 1999*. Madrid: ICCMU, 2001.

Camplani, Clara. "La defensa de los negros en Bartolomé de las Casas." Pp. 95–107 of *Las Casas face à l'esclavage des Noirs: vision critique du "Onzième Remède" (1516)/Las Casas frente a la esclavitud de los negros: visión crítica del "Undécimo Remedio" (1516)*. Edited by Victorien Lavou Zoungbo. Perpignan: Université de Perpignan, 2001.

Cañizares, José. *La ilustre fregona*. Edited by Marco Presotto. Rimini: Panozzo. 2001. Pp. 252; bibliography; illustrations.

Capdevila, Néstor. "Las Casas et les Noirs: quels problèmes?" Pp. 191–214 of *Las Casas face à l'esclavage des Noirs: vision critique du "Onzième Remède" (1516)/Las Casas frente a la esclavitud de los negros: visión crítica del "Undécimo Remedio" (1516)*. Edited by Victorien Lavou Zoungbo. Perpignan: Université de Perpignan, 2001.

Carneiro, Henrique Soares. "O múltiplo imaginário das viagens modernas: Ciência, literatura e turismo." *Historia: Questões & Debates*, 18 (2001), 227–47.

Carreras, Juan José. "Amores difíciles: la ópera de corte en la España del siglo XVIII." Pp. 205–30 of *La ópera en España e Hispanoamérica. Actas del Congreso Internacional, "La ópera en España y en Hispanoamérica. Una creación propia". Madrid, 29.XI/3.XII de 1999*. Edited by Emilio Casares Rodicio and Álvaro Torrente. Madrid: ICCMU, 2001.

Casares Rodicio, Emilio. "La creación artística en España. Premisas para la interpretación de un patrimonio." Pp. 21–57 of *La ópera en España e Hispanoamérica. Actas del Congreso Internacional, "La ópera en España y en Hispanoamérica. Una creación propia." Madrid, 29.XI/3.XII de 1999*. Edited by Emilio Casares Rodicio and Álvaro Torrente. Madrid: ICCMU, 2001.

Casares Rodicio, Emilio, and Álvaro Torrente (eds.). *La ópera en España e Hispanoamérica. Actas del Congreso Internacional, "La ópera en España e Hispanoamérica. Una creación propia." Madrid, 29.XI/3.XII de 1999*. Madrid: ICCMU, 2001. Pp. 500; illustrations; index.

Cedeño, Aristófanes. "La función teatral de la reforma social en *El delincuente honrado*." *Dieciocho*, 24 (2001), 279–95.

Cid, Jesús-Antonio. "Judíos en la prosa española del siglo XVII (imperfecta síntesis y antología mínima)." Pp. 213–65 of *Judíos en la literatura española*. Edited by Iacob M. Hassán and Ricardo Izquierdo Benito. Cuenca: Universidad de Castilla–La Mancha, 2001.

Cortés, Rocío. "Los estudios coloniales hispanoamericanos: reconsideraciones y aperturas." *Revista de Estudios Hispánicos*, 35 (2001), 577–83.

Díaz Esteban, Fernando. "La primitiva poesía española y los judíos." Pp. 9–27 of *Judíos en la literatura española*. Edited by Iacob M. Hassán and Ricardo Izquierdo Benito. Cuenca: Universidad de Castilla–La Mancha, 2001.

Díaz-Mas, Paloma. "Poesía medieval judía." Pp. 29–55 of *Judíos en la literatura española*. Edited by Iacob M. Hassán and Ricardo Izquierdo Benito. Cuenca: Universidad de Castilla–La Mancha, 2001.

Dubuis, Michel. "La poesía popular frente a la familia ilustrada en *La vida de don Guindo Cerezo*." Pp. 57–65 of *Historia social y literatura. Familia y clases populares en España (siglos XVIII–XIX)*. Edited by Roberto Fernández and Jacques Soubeyroux. Lérida: Milenio, 2001.

Espido Freire, Mila. "La diversidad de fuentes para la música en las fiestas de zarzuela. *Alfeo y Aretusa* (1672), de J.B. Diamante (1625–1687)." Pp. 175–92 of *La ópera en España e Hispanoamérica. Actas del Congreso Internacional, "La ópera en España y en Hispanoamérica. Una creación propia." Madrid, 29.XI/3.XII de 1999*. Edited by Emilio Casares Rodicio and Álvaro Torrente. Madrid: ICCMU, 2001.

Fabris, Dinko. "Nápoles y España en la ópera napolitana del siglo XVII." Pp. 117–30 of *La ópera en España e Hispanoamérica. Actas del Congreso Internacional, "La ópera en España y en Hispanoamérica. Una creación propia." Madrid, 29.XI/3.XII de 1999*. Edited by Emilio Casares Rodicio and Álvaro Torrente. Madrid: ICCMU, 2001.

Feliú de San Pedro, Benito de. *Arte del romance castellano*. Edited by Eulalia Hernández Sánchez and María Isabel López Martínez. Murcia: Universidad, 2001. Pp. 125; CD-ROM.

Fernández, Pura. "La literatura del siglo XIX y los orígenes del contubernio judeo-masónico-comunista." Pp. 301–51 of *Judíos en la literatura española*. Edited by Iacob M. Hassán and Ricardo Izquierdo Benito. Cuenca: Universidad de Castilla–La Mancha, 2001.

Fernández, Roberto. "Las clases populares en *Los enredos de un lugar*, de Fernando Gutiérrez de Vegas." Pp. 67–84 of *Historia social y literatura. Familia y clases populares en España (siglos XVIII–XIX)*. Edited by Roberto Fernández and Jacques Soubeyroux. Lérida: Milenio, 2001.

Fernández, Roberto, and Jacques Soubeyroux (eds.). *Historia social y literatura. Familia y clases populares en España (siglos XVIII–XIX)*. Lérida: Milenio, 2001. Pp. 353; index.

Recent work on the Spanish nobility and middle classes of the eighteenth century has resulted in a wealth of social histories and critical studies on the living conditions and working relations of a sizeable segment of Spain's population. However, as the introduction to this volume points out, there is a paucity of recent research on the Spanish working classes, which have not been subject to similar academic attention. The editors of this collection offer two reasons for their absence: a long-standing lack of interest in the lower classes (and in the project of writing a history of the peoples without history) and the very real lack of documentation regarding non-propertied people in the principal Spanish historical archives (judicial, administrative, and notarial), which were organized during the eighteenth century according to the principles of ownership and social power. The eighteen authors in this collection tackle the problem of limited official documentation of the social history of working-class Spaniards of the eighteenth century by turning to contemporary literary works. The scholars in this volume propose to analyze literary representations of the popular classes not as equivalents to the historical archives or as a means to recover faithful depictions of the general populace but rather in order to examine the dominant contemporary attitudes towards the lower-classes by writers and other middle and upper-class individuals with social power.

This volume of essays is the result of a multi-year, international cooperative research project between the Université Jean Monnet de Saint-Étienne and the Universidad de Lérida on Social History and Literature of the eighteenth and nineteenth centuries. The pieces included in this volume present the work of a number of French and Spanish scholars originally delivered at a colloquium at Saint-Étienne in September 2000.

While grounded in the social history of the period between 1700 and 1800, the studies move beyond the eighteenth century to include the important nineteenth century, when Spain experienced its greatest political and social upheaval. Nine essays are devoted to eighteenth-century texts and nine essays deal with nineteenth-century texts. While the first set will likely be of more immediate interest to the readers of the *ECCB*, the articles covering the nineteenth century are a crucial complement to the questions and themes raised in the first half of the volume. Among the key themes to develop are the initial distinctions between rural and urban populations in terms of literary representations and a historically documented separation of social and political power during the eighteenth century. The authors' analyses of literary representations of the general populace in class-based Spanish society demonstrate that during the eighteenth century, the long-established models of the urban and rural poor as lazy and vice-ridden began to undergo challenges and modifications. However, whereas bourgeois ideologies of the family were reflected in an increase in literary representations of upper and middle class families, literary representations of domesticity among the lower classes throughout the eighteenth and nineteenth centuries developed much more slowly.

One limitation to the discussion of eighteenth- and nineteenth-century representations of family life is the restricted definition of a modern family used by most, but not all, of the authors in this volume. By expressly favoring a narrow bourgeois view of a nuclear family, widows, servants, orphans and extended family members are, to a great extent, excluded from consideration. As a result, while the most salient themes are significant and several essays make important contributions, much of the discussion of the modern Spanish working-class confirms or develops concepts already generally established. In addition, a few of the essays are only loosely connected to the main thrust of the project.

Among the essays on eighteenth-century themes, the studies by Céline Gilard (27–53) and Josep Maria Sala Valldaura (113–29) are excellent examples of the interdisciplinary objectives of this volume. Gilard examines literary representations of the working classes in the brief piece "El cortante de Cádiz" [The butcher of Cadiz] written for a working class readership and discusses its codification of contemporary attitudes towards family, economic class and, particularly, members of the "lesser" guilds (such as butchers). Sala Valldaura studies the non-verbal gestures of affection between a servant and her mistress in Leandro Fernández de Moratín's important neoclassical play *El sí de las niñas* [The Maiden's Consent] as emblematic of Enlightenment desires for greater communication between social classes in addition to good manners and measured sentiments in late eighteenth-century Spain.

Antonio Risco (37–56) and Jacques Soubeyroux (141–56) successfully test the limits of the methods proposed in this volume to read fiction, drama and popular fiction not for their artistic value, but rather in an attempt to approximate the data of archival documentation that does not exist for the Spanish lower classes. Risco examines "pliego de cordel" [popular] literature alongside a contemporary housekeeping manual in order to compare the data on domestic budgets that can be gleaned from works of fiction with the archival-based statistical data published by David Ringrose. Using Ringrose's data as an authoritative yardstick, Risco demonstrates that a surprising degree of accuracy in terms of specific expenses and budgets can be found in fictional representations of family life in eighteenth-century Madrid. Turning from economics to social policy, Soubeyroux analyzes the persistence of traditional depictions of the poor in the late eighteenth century and traces a slow, but marked evolution in the literary representations of Spain's lowest economic classes in light of specific political and social policies implemented by the government ministers under Spain's enlightened despots.

Among the essays focusing on nineteenth-century topics, several pieces trace the themes of family, domesticity and representations of the working class through extremely well-known, canonical texts, a method that is particularly profitable, given the close ties between history and fiction present in the representational modes of *costumbrismo* [literary genre of (local) customs and manners] and realism. Jean-René Aymes (193–208) examines the changing depictions of the lower- and middle-class families in the works of Mariano José de Larra early in the nineteenth century. Colette Rabaté (209–29) follows the growing protagonism of the working class through the immensely popular "María" trilogy of the socialist-leaning writer and editor Wenceslao Ayguals de Izco during the mid-nineteenth century and finds that while the previous paradigm (virtuous aristocracy and vice-ridden poor) was not completely inverted, honorable and admirable working class families did serve an didactic function, much like their middle or upper-class counterparts. A fervent faith in the bourgeois ideals of family and domesticity led Ayguals to impart an evangelical view of society and his trilogy represents an important turning point in the literary representations of lower classes and families. Jaume Pont (231–53) is one of the few scholars in this collection to depart from the bourgeois-defined family and address orphans and abandoned children in his study of the prose works of Antonio Ros de Olano (a contemporary of the more well known Romantic poet José de Espronceda). Pont reads Romantic orphans and abandoned children as poetic symbols of a break in the natural balance between Mothers and Sons, or as a reflection of the social deficiencies of a State government that fails to provide for its citizens. That is, Pont argues that the fictional family transcends its role a more or less realist depiction of a historically accurate event and becomes a powerful political metaphor. Antoni Jové's contribution (267–86) reassesses the canonical author who has traditionally been characterized as the chronicler of Madrid's middle and lower classes: Benito Pérez Galdós. While readers might expect an essay on Galdós to confirm the final ascendance of the lower classes in Spanish literature as representatives of modern Spanish life, Jové rejects the definition of Galdós as the "buen burgués" and argues that the author was fundamentally an admirer of the aristocracy who truly disdained the general populace. Examining the relationship between literature and political and social policy beyond the borders of the literary text, Jové suggests that Galdós's acclaim as the novelist of the Spanish people was tied to the literary politics of the end of the nineteenth century rather than to any heart-felt populist sentiment.

While the practice of mining literature for historical data is certainly not new, this volume as a whole does reveal several important trends in the evolving modern attitudes towards the Spanish working classes. Given the wide and heterogeneous range of authors and texts covered in this volume, the consistent recurrence of these themes is significant. By reading across all eighteen essays in this volume, scholars of social history and modern Spanish literature will easily be able to trace the uneven development of the working class as appropriate protagonists of Spanish literature and, consequently, representatives of Spanish life. Also of relevance are the sometimes surprising ways that the political, social and literary intersect, such as in the persistence of traditional stereotypes about the lower classes, even by writers considered to be progressive. Readers of this volume will note the slow but steady rise of the family as the representative demographic for the lower classes, as bourgeois ideology allowed even the anonymous masses to individuate over the course of the nineteenth century.

The second volume of essays to result from this collaborative project is programmed to showcase work on The Family and The Bourgeoisie presented at the University of Lérida in October 2001. Given the breadth of topics and approaches of the first volume, the second promises to be useful for anyone studying modern Spanish literature and culture.—Lisa Surwillo

Fernández Álvarez, Manuel. *Jovellanos, el patriota*. Madrid: Espasa, 2001. Pp. 207; bibliography; index.

Fernández Fernández, Olga. "*La clemencia de Tito* de Metastasio en la traducción de Luzán y la visión de la ópera a través de los neoclásicos españoles del siglo XVIII." *Dieciocho*, 24 (2001), 217–44.

Fernández Retamar, Roberto. "Contra la Leyenda Negra." Pp. 109–38 of *Las Casas face à l'esclavage des Noirs: vision critique du "Onzième Remède (1516)/Las Casas frente a la esclavitud de los negros: visión crítica del "Undécimo Remedio" (1516)*. Edited by Victorien Lavou Zoungbo. Perpignan: Université de Perpignan, 2001.

Flesler, Daniela. "El *Rodrigo* de Pedro Montegón y la leyenda de la pérdida de España entre la Ilustración y el Romanticismo." *Dieciocho*, 24 (2001), 85–98.

Fuentes, Yvonne. "Two Endings to a Same Deception: The Stories of Federica and Cœlia." *Hispanófila*, 131 (2001), 21–30.

Gabaldón, Rodrigo. *Comedias*. Edited by Alfredo Rojas Navarro. Murcia: Real Academia Alfonso X el sabio; Murcia: Universidad, 2001. Pp. 126.

This reproduction of the 1757 *Comedias* [*Comedies*] is an example of the recent contributions to the rediscovery and reevaluation of the long forgotten Hispanic eighteenth century, hence consolidating the argument that the Spanish cultural and literary paradigm was rich in its plurality as opposed to the monolithic and homogeneous formation/manifestation that critics have attributed to it. Vilar and Rojas Navarro begin the introduction tracing the bibliographical references to *Comedias* to a 1953 article by José María Soler which appeared in the local journal *Villena*. The article sought to inform the readers of an early edition of *Comedias* found among the papers and books of Don Salvador Avellán, former presbyter of the locality of Villena. Besides announcing this finding, Soler recommended the publication of a new edition of the text for its relevance to the town and its rarity as it was absent from journals, catalogues, and the standard bibliographies.

The editors of the edition we review in this essay reiterate Soler's assertion that the value of the *Comedias* is twofold: literary and sociological/historical. Though published in 1757, *Comedias* retained many of the literary tropes of the Spanish Golden Age. Consequently, numerous mythological and religious references, subordination of character to plot, stock figures such as the servant, the lover, the abandoned maiden, and intricate situations abound in *Comedias* as in many of the dramatic productions of the eighteenth century. However, the news and information about the Shrine to María de Las Virtudes (Our Lady of Virtue) and the Marian devotion of Villena after the accidental finding of the statue of the Blessed Mother in 1474, may have valuable historical and sociological significance to the researcher of cultural studies, folklore, history, and so forth. Moreover, the references to the origin of the Festivities of Moros y Cristianos (Moors and Christians) in Villena and in neighboring towns contribute to the historical and cultural appeal of the book since these festivities are still today the celebration par excellence. The events to which they refer evoke the days when Christians battled Moors during the re-conquest of Spain, and more specifically the Christian victory in the thirteenth century over the troops of Al-Azraq in the region, and are especially pertinent in the second part of *Comedias* (10).

The critical introduction justifies the plural form of the title, *Comedias*, arguing that though the book is in fact two plays, they share and form a thematic unity and purpose, that is, to extol the blessings of Our Lady of Virtue has bestowed on the town of Villena. As stated earlier, this new edition is re-publication and reproduction of the 1757 editions preceded by a critical introduction.

The *Comedias* consists of two parts, each containing a three-act play. The first play takes place in the countryside to where the townspeople have fled from the terrible epidemic that has afflicted their beloved Villena. Having tried all earthly remedies to reduce the spread of the disease, the people in their desperation decide to choose a heavenly patron who will protect them. Each person is asked to write the name of a saint on a piece of paper, and an angel, guised as a child, chooses the paper bearing the name of Our Lady of Virtue, not once but thrice, thus convincing all that she is to become their intercessor and protector in such a time of need. Parallel to this story is a novelesque plot that resembles many others of the latter seventeenth century: a woman believes her lover, Don Félix, is dead while he is convinced she has abandoned him. All is clarified at the end and love/virtue prevails. What is interesting about both plots is that the villain is indeed the epitome of villainy, that is to say, Lucifer himself. He is the cause of the epidemic, and by impersonating her lover, he leads the woman to believe Don Felix is dead. His dialogue portrays him as arrogant; resentful that the Archangel Michel interferes with all his machinations; and truly bewildered by the piety and faith of the town folks.

The last scene of the third act ends with an almost comical Lucifer: the villain is so furious that his plans to destroy Villena and humanity did not come to fruition that he decides to go "home" (dare we say, slamming the door on his way out?) "I cannot control my fury // ... // I'll return back to hell" and leaves "with great noise" (36). In the second part/play we encounter the same couple, married, and Lucifer again up to no good. By now, the sanctuary to Our Lady of Virtue has been erected and its care trusted to an Augustinian order. The abundance of miracles attributed to Our Lady of Virtue seems to reinforce the theological premise that when faced with adversity man's only option is to pray for divine interference and deliverance. Thus, she is credited for interceding in more than ten occasions in various towns, cities and even countries such as Villena, Alicante, Murcia, Almansa and Malta. Here again the two forces, good and evil, vie for man's soul though we never doubt the outcome since they are under the protection of Our Lady of Virtue.

Once more, the playwright has introduced two parallel plots: that of a husband who in a jealous rage stabs the wife to death (we later find her alive in the Shrine); and the miracle performed by Our Lady of Virtue when captives (the husband among them) are "flown" from Algeria back to Villena along with the Moor who enslaved them. Not only does Our Lady of Virtue release and transport the Christian captives back to safety, she also brings the Muslim Zaide along. The miracle reveals the truth to Zaide who immediately falls on his knees abjuring his false faith, and embraces the "truth". It is precisely the episode of the conversion which serves as the basis for many re-enactments during the Festivities of Moors and Christians.

The parallel story of the jealous husband, who in a fit of rage attempts to murder his virtuous wife, is also resolved thanks to the divine intervention. However, there is a comment made by the servant Aloque at the beginning of the third act that is noteworthy. Concerned after learning that Don Felix has returned to Villena (also miraculously released and flown-back from captivity) and on his way to his house, the servant exclaims: "Big mistake, they will surely hang him for his crime" (25). While the issue of uxoricide in defense of honor (the act of murdering one's wife) had not been an uncommon one in the plays of the Spanish Golden Age and in other European dramatic traditions of the seventeenth century, the legal punishments were rarely mentioned. The murder was, from a dramatic and perhaps societal perspective, excused (throughout the long history of the Spanish penal code one can find occasions when the punishment for uxoricide was merely banishment). What is not so frequent is to ponder the legal ramifications and consequences of such an "honorable" act that if not legally condoned, at least was accepted as a mitigating factor. This exception may lead one to speculate that the author of *Comedias* shared a more enlightened perhaps modern view on what constituted honor. On the other hand, the revelation that the wife survived the brutal attack is also attributed to divine intervention. As expected, once again Lucifer is defeated and the people of Villena reaffirm their faith in Our Lady of Virtue.

In conclusion, this edition of the *Comedias* represents another small piece of the rich tableau that is slowly emerging and configuring the Spanish eighteenth century as a dynamic and plural expression of aesthetics, world views and traditions.—Yvonne Fuentes

Gálvez, María Rosa. *La familia a la moda: Comedia en tres actos y en verso*. Edited by René Andioc. Salamanca: Universidad, 2001. Pp. 256; index.

In 1804 the dramatist/poet María Rosa de Gálvez (1768–1806) requested permission to publish and stage a new satire of Spanish customs, titled *La familia a la moda* [*The Fashionable Family*]. Gálvez, who arrived in Madrid from Málaga in 1800, had already successfully staged several plays in the capital, and her *Obras poéticas* [*Poetic Works*] had been approved for publication in 1804. This new comedy seemed to be perfectly suited to the audiences' interests. It pilloried the disturbing ways of a gambler (Canuto), his clotheshorse wife (Madama), their wastrel son (Faustino), and their convent-educated daughter (Inés). The parody is developed from the perspective of Guiomar, a childless widow who upholds the standards of the "old" Spain while her brother's family fritters away money and time on certifiably frivolous (that is, French) pastimes. Rich (naturally) and thereby in control of the family's future (they hope to inherit), Guiomar offers lessons in moral rectitude, good education, conservative values, and sensible budgeting. Surprisingly, the play was banned by the ecclesiastical censors, who thought it "immoral" and representative of the "school of corruption and licentiousness." Such were the times.

One of the most intriguing aspects of this comedy is Gálvez's depiction of role of women. The dramatic tension in the work stems from conflict among the women characters; the men are in essence secondary characters, reflecting the needs, opinions, and desires of their sister, sister-in-law, wife, daughter, aunt, and others. The men are seen as blockheads, individuals whose self-absorption reaches such lows that in one scene Faustino, the rude son, treats the women as mere furniture: wanting to go over his dance lessons but unable to find an appropriate partner, he picks up a chair and dances with it. Inés refuses to rebel outright against her mother's wishes—when her mother opposes her proposed marriage to Carlos rather than the more socially prestigious, but foolish, marqués), Inés states: "Nunca usaré yo del mío/si mi madre no quisiese" ["I will never use my free will/if it contradicts my mother's wish"]— even when Guiomar insists. Still, Gálvez manipulates the plot to allow Inés not only to recognize her duty as a daughter (to care for her parents as they age) and inherit her aunt Guiomar's money, but also to marry the man of her dreams. Inés succeeds because she is the virtuous child, the very paradigm of the "mujer virtuosa" [virtuous woman] which would come to dominate the discourse on women throughout the nineteenth century. Guiomar succeeds because she is smart, rich, and determined. And it is Guiomar who has the last word, literally, in the play:

> Espero
> que te pongan donde aprendas
> la crianza y buenas prendas
> que adornan a un caballero.
> Yo, a pagar lo que tú debas,
> hermano, y tú a gobernar
> tu casa sin malgastar,
> que ya un escarmiento llevas,
> puesto que a nadie acomoda
> imitar en sus sandeces

todas las ridiculeces
de una familia a la moda.

[I hope
you will be taught
the good manners and virtues
which befit a gentleman.
I will pay what you owe,
my brother, and you will govern
your household without wasting money,
you learned your lesson
since it is now clear nobody
should imitate the foolishness
and absurdity
of a fashionable family.]

René Andioc, the leading scholar of Spanish eighteenth-century theater, now brings us a new edition of Gálvez's play (Fernando Doménech produced a good edition of this play along with *Safo* and *Zinda* in Cádiz in 1995), replete with scholarly apparatus and a superb introduction to Gálvez's life and works. His introduction contains valuable biographical information, a useful section on the Spanish theater in the years immediately preceding the debut of *La familia a la moda* in 1805 (yes, after some cuts, the ecclesiastical censors relented), and a careful study of the characters, context, and plot of the play. The text of the play itself is amply footnoted, and the notes help the reader sort out obscure references, Gallicisms, linguistic mysteries, and cultural material.

This is an ideal play to study with students of Spanish literature, particularly those interested in the history of theater, women's issues, the Enlightenment, or the development of women's writing in the eighteenth and nineteenth centuries. The editor's work is clear, helpful, and informative, and the play itself, while hardly an undiscovered treasure of dramaturgy, provides a lot of laughs, much to contemplate, and a further piece in the enormous puzzle that is Spanish eighteenth- and nineteenth-century play writing.—David Thatcher Gies

García Fraile, Dámaso. "Reivindicación del idioma castellano en la ópera española de finales del siglo XVIII." Pp. 455–75 of *La ópera en España e Hispanoamérica. Actas del Congreso Internacional, "La ópera en España y en Hispanoamérica. Una creación propia." Madrid, 29.XI/3.XII de 1999*. Edited by Emilio Casares Rodicio and Álvaro Torrente. Madrid: ICCMU, 2001.

Gilard, Céline. "Luces, familia y reivindicación social en la literatura de cordel: *El Cortante de Cádiz*." Pp. 27–35 of *Historia social y literatura. Familia y clases populares en España (siglos XVIII–XIX)*. Edited by Roberto Fernández and Jacques Soubeyroux. Lérida: Milenio, 2001.

Giné Janer, Marta. "El rol de la mujer en los relatos fantásticos del romanticismo español." Pp. 177–91 of *Historia social y literatura. Familia y clases populares en España (siglos XVIII–XIX)*. Edited by Roberto Fernández and Jacques Soubeyroux. Lérida: Milenio, 2001.

Gómez Moreno, Ángel. "Judíos y conversos en la prosa castellana medieval (con un excurso sobre el círculo cultural del marqués de Santillana)." Pp. 57–86 of *Judíos en la literatura española*. Edited by Iacob M. Hassán and Ricardo Izquierdo Benito. Cuenca: Universidad de Castilla–La Mancha, 2001.

González de Garay, María Teresa. "Ignacio de Luzán y el *Poema heroico de la invención de la Cruz*, de Francisco González de Zárate." *Dieciocho,* 24 (2001), 99–120.

González Marín, Luis Antonio. "Recuperación o restauración del teatro musical español del siglo XVII." Pp. 59–78 of *La ópera en España e Hispanoamérica. Actas del Congreso Internacional, "La ópera en España y en Hispanoamérica. Una creación propia." Madrid, 29.XI/3.XII de 1999.* Edited by Emilio Casares Rodicio and Álvaro Torrente. Madrid: ICCMU, 2001.

Graf, E. C. "Necrophilia and Materialist Thoughts in Jose Cadalso's *Noches lúgubres*: Romanticism's Anxious Adornment of Political Economy." *Journal of Spanish Cultural Studies*, 2 (2001)), 211–30.

Guereña, Jean-Louis. "Literatura y prostitución en el siglo XIX. De la novela folletinesca a la literatura clandestina." Pp. 157–75 of *Historia social y literatura. Familia y clases populares en España (siglos XVIII–XIX)*. Edited by Roberto Fernández and Jacques Soubeyroux. Lérida: Milenio, 2001.

Gembero Ustárroz, María. "El repertorio operístico en una corte nobiliaria española del siglo XVIII: la obra de Girolamo Sertori al servicio de los marqueses de Castelfuerte." Pp. 403–53 of *La ópera en España e Hispanoamérica. Actas del Congreso Internacional, "La ópera en España y en Hispanoamérica. Una creación propia." Madrid, 29.XI/3.XII de 1999.* Edited by Emilio Casares Rodicio and Álvaro Torrente. Madrid: ICCMU, 2001.

Guicharnaud–Tollis, Michèle. "L'introduction des esclaves noirs dans le *Memorial de catorce remedios* (1516) de Bartolomé de las Casas: une *aberration*?" Pp. 23–40 of *Las Casas face à l'esclavage des Noirs: vision critique du "Onzième Remède (1516)/Las Casas frente a la esclavitud de los negros: visión crítica del "Undécimo Remedio" (1516)*. Edited by Victorien Lavou Zoungbo. Perpignan: Université de Perpignan, 2001.

Hassán, Iacob M. "Judíos en la literatura española (un curso sobre)." Pp. 489–510 of *Judíos en la literatura española*. Edited by Iacob M. Hassán and Ricardo Izquierdo Benito. Cuenca: Universidad de Castilla–La Mancha, 2001.

Hassán, Iacob M., and Ricardo Izquierdo Benito (eds.). *Judíos en la literatura española*. Cuenca: Universidad de Castilla–La Mancha, 2001. Pp. 510; index.

The present volume gathers the proceedings of the *IX Curso Cultural Hispanojudía y Sefardí de la Universidad de Castilla la Mancha* [Analysis on Jewish and Sephardic Culture at the University of Castilla La Mancha]. Organized in 1999 by the Association of Friends of the Sephardic Museum, the conference saw the participation of an exclusive number of philologists—specialists in different literary ages—who were all determined to yield some light to the always thorny question of the Jews in the Spanish literature. The thirteen articles—plus a bibliographical repertory contributed by Uriel Macías Kapón (437–87)—are a comprehensive coverage of the period that goes from the first medieval literary manifestations to the first part of the twentieth century, and always with a methodology which emphasizes the fact that literature by the Jewish and the Semite theme is a long-standing topic in Spanish literature. The chapter, "La primitiva poesía española y los judíos" [Ancient Spanish Poetry and the Jews], by Fernando Díaz Esteban (9–27), offers remarkable insights. The basis for Díaz Esteban's research stresses the modernity that pervades Semitic creativity in medieval times: from the translators who worked with Alphonsus X to Sem Tob in the field of sapiential poetry, and concluding with Diego de San Pedro and his definitive contribution to the sentimental novel, *Cárcel de amor* [Prison of Love]. However, and tiptoeing on the brief study on the *jarchas* [kharja] contained in the Hebrew *moaxajas*, the main virtue of his work is the exploration of the Jewish people as a literary topic through a thorough review that dwells on Raquel and Vidas (*Poema del Mio Cid* [Poem of the Cid]), as representatives of a society that considered them an essential piece of their social and artistic fabric, and also in the Semites that—sparsely—appear in the works by Gonzalo de Berceo (*Lores de Nuestra Señora* [Praises of Our Lady] and *Los Milagros de Nuestra Señora* [Miracles of Our Lady]). In this respect, Díaz Esteban has a point when he affirms that the consideration of Berceo as anti-Semite would be simplistic, since the poorly edifying behavior exhibited by the Jews in their works runs parallel—and even behind—that shown by Catholic clerics and nuns. This is also the case of the Alphonsian *Cantigas* [Songs] which offer an remarkable example of the anti-Semite agitation that had swept Europe in hardly half a century—since the earliest Bercian testimonies. Nonetheless, the ill will against all Hebraic to be felt in the *Cantigas* can be blamed on the French texts that acted as mediators, since it is common knowledge that the Castilian king surrounded himself by a great number of Jews and converts as Gómez Moreno remembers in his chapter on the important cultural role developed in Medieval Spain by *conversos* [converted Jews] (57–84).

The chapter by Paloma Díaz-Mas, "Poesía medieval judía" [Medieval Jewish Poetry] (29–55), offers illuminating perspective on this topic. Equally relevant, especially from a sociological point of view, is the chapter by Julio Rodríguez Puértolas, "La poesía de la Baja Edad Media" [Poetry of the Low Middle Age] (29–55). The chapter by Felipe B. Pedraza Jiménez (153–211) offers an interesting travel around the Semitic theme in Spanish Golden Age theatre, paying special attention to the works by Lope de Vega. Pedraza Jiménez argues for an alternative reading of Lope's comedies which emphasizes the respect of this Golden Age Spanish dramatist toward respect to the Jewish population. The author discusses Lope de Vega's dramas, *Las paces de los reyes y judía de Toledo* [The Peace Settled by the Kings and the Jewess from Toledo] and *El niño inocente from La Guardia* [The Child of La Guardia]. The latter drama is a clear example of how the extreme perversity shown by the Jews is attenuated, and even justified, by virtue of a prejudiced policy that put them on the verge of the abyss.

Joaquín Álvarez Barrientos develops an analysis of the change of attitude—common all around Europe—with regards to the Jewish people that is experienced after the French *Encyclopédie*, a turn based on an interest towards their culture and relative respect for their religion (267–300). Paradoxically, 1700's literature is very scant in the treatment of the Jewish question. Isolated examples are the adaptation of the mentioned play by Lope, *El niño inocente de La Guardia*, carried out by Juan de la Hoz and José de Cañizares, a proposal calling for the desideologization of the plot while fomenting the love theme and the spectacular component and, of course, *Raquel*, by Vicente García de la Huerta, whose main character—the Jewish *Femosa* [Famous]—has been seen by most critics as a staged image of Esquilache, royal favorite of Carlos III. The Jew character seems to embody in this drama the pressure exerted on the royal will. A larger presence of the Jewish theme can be noticed in the cultural field of history and scholarship, as recorded in *Biblioteca Española* [Spanih Library], by José Rodríguez.

The ample chronological spectrum comprehended in this magnificent volume culminates with "Los judíos en la literatura española del siglo XX" [The Jews in Contemporary Spanish Literature], by José-Carlos Mainer (374–402). Mainer points out the widespread bias against Hebraic culture in right-wing contemporary Spanish writing which identifies the Jews with modernity, rationalism, and secularization. Mainer selects the example of Pío Baroja's prejudices. This Spanish writer goes too far against the Jews especially in his miscellaneous *Comunistas, judíos y demás ralea* [*Communist, Jews, and Other Evil Groups*]. Baroja seems to justify his 1492 expulsion from Spain because of their association with the "evils" of bureaucratic socialism. As opposed to Baroja's intolerant prejudices there are two favorable representations of Jewish culture in pre-Civil War Spanish literature: Vicente Blasco Ibáñez (*Los muertos mandan*) [*The Deads Rule*] and Rafael Cansinos-Asséns, whose fascination for the Jewish culture is practically an aesthetic conversion similar to Valle Inclán's Carlist attachment. Mainer concludes his survey describing favorable representations of the Jewish in literary works written by the exiled Spanish liberal writers Max Aub and Máximo José Kalm.—Emilo Peral Vega

Higgins, Antony. "Colonia e imperio: algunas reflexiones sobre la trayectoria de los estudios sobre la cultura y la literatura virreinales." *Revista de Estudios Hispánicos*, 35 (2001), 601–14.

Hill, Ruth. "Modern Science as Emergent Culture: Luzán's *Juicio de Paris renovado: fábula épica*." *Hispanófila*, 132 (2001), 53–68.

Illari, Bernardo. "Metastasio nell'Indie: de óperas ausentes y arias presentes en América colonial." Pp. 343–74 of *La ópera en España e Hispanoamérica. Actas del Congreso Internacional, "La ópera en España y en Hispanoamérica. Una creación propia."* Madrid, 29.XI/3.XII de 1999. Edited by Emilio Casares Rodicio and Álvaro Torrente. Madrid: ICCMU, 2001.

Jacobs, Helmut C. *Belleza y buen gusto: las teorías de las artes en la literatura española del siglo XVIII*. Madrid: Iberoamericana, 2001. Pp. 372; bibliography; index.

Jaffe, Catherine. "From *Précieuses Ridicules* to *Preciosas ridículas*: Ramón de la Cruz's Translation of Molière and the Problems of Cultural Adaptation." *Dieciocho*, 24 (2001), 147–68.

Jones, Joseph. "Recreating Eighteenth–Century Musical Theater: The Collaborations of the Composer Enrique Granados (1867–1916) and the Librettist Fernando Periquet y Zuaznábar (1873–1940)." *Dieciocho*, 24 (2001), 121–46.

Jové, Antoni. "Historia, clases populares y familia en Galdós: la segunda serie de los *Episodios Nacionales*." Pp. 267–86 of *Historia social y literatura. Familia y clases populares en España (siglos XVIII–XIX)*. Edited by Roberto Fernández and Jacques Soubeyroux. Lérida: Milenio, 2001.

Kapón, Uriel Macías. "Bibliografía sobre judíos en la literatura española." Pp. 437–87 of *Judíos en la literatura española*. Edited by Iacob M. Hassán and Ricardo Izquierdo Benito. Cuenca: Universidad de Castilla–La Mancha, 2001.

Kossigan, Patrice. "Fray Bartolomé de Las Casas: de defensor de los indios a *defensor de los negros y guanches*." Pp. 287–304 of *Las Casas face à l'esclavage des Noirs: vision critique du "Onzième*

Remède" (1516)/Las Casas frente a la esclavitud de los negros: visión crítica del "Undécimo Remedio" (1516). Edited by Victorien Lavou Zoungbo. Perpignan: Université de Perpignan, 2001.

Lavou Zoungbo, Victorien. "Du Nègre comme un Hercule doublé d'un Saint–Phallus: una humanité différée." Pp. 59–93 of *Las Casas face à l'esclavage des Noirs: vision critique du "Onzième Remède" (1516)/Las Casas frente a la esclavitud de los negros: visión crítica del "Undécimo Remedio" (1516)*. Edited by Victorien Lavou Zoungbo. Perpignan: Université de Perpignan, 2001.

Lavou Zoungbo, Victorien (ed.). *Las Casas face à l'esclavage des Noirs: vision critique du "Onzième Remède" (1516)/Las Casas frente a la esclavitud de los negros: visión crítica del "Undécimo Remedio" (1516)*. Perpignan: Université de Perpignan, 2001. Pp. 389; index.

Lavou Zoungbo, Victorien. "Présentation générale." Pp. 7–14 of *Las Casas face à l'esclavage des Noirs: vision critique du "Onzième Remède" (1516)/Las Casas frente a la esclavitud de los negros: visión crítica del "Undécimo Remedio" (1516)*. Edited by Victorien Lavou Zoungbo. Perpignan: Université de Perpignan, 2001.

Lesage, Alano René. *Aventuras de Gil Blas de Santillana*. Translated by José Francisco de Isla. Sevilla: Alfar, 2001. Pp. 612; illustrations; index.

Leza, José Máximo. "Aspectos productivos de la ópera en los teatros públicos de Madrid (1730–1799)." Pp. 231–62 of *La ópera en España e Hispanoamérica. Actas del Congreso Internacional, "La ópera en España y en Hispanoamérica. Una creación propia." Madrid, 29.XI/3.XII de 1999*. Edited by Emilio Casares Rodicio and Álvaro Torrente. Madrid: ICCMU, 2001.

López Cano, Rubén. "Tonos humanos y análisis musical: una asignatura pendiente." Pp. 193–203 of *La ópera en España e Hispanoamérica. Actas del Congreso Internacional, "La ópera en España y en Hispanoamérica. Una creación propia." Madrid, 29.XI/3.XII de 1999*. Edited by Emilio Casares Rodicio and Álvaro Torrente. Madrid: ICCMU, 2001.

Lucena Salmoral, Manuel. "Planteamiento de la 'Duda Indiana' (1534–1549). Crisis de la conciencia nacional: las dudas de Carlos V." Pp. 157–89 of *Las Casas face à l'esclavage des Noirs: vision critique du "Onzième Remède" (1516)/Las Casas frente a la esclavitud de los negros: visión crítica del "Undécimo Remedio" (1516)*. Edited by Victorien Lavou Zoungbo. Perpignan: Université de Perpignan, 2001.

Mainer, José–Carlos. "Los judíos en la literatura española de la primera mitad del siglo XX: notas sobre un tema." Pp. 375–402 of *Judíos en la literatura española*. Edited by Iacob M. Hassán and Ricardo Izquierdo Benito. Cuenca: Universidad de Castilla–La Mancha, 2001.

Marcos Marín, Francisco. "La tragicomedia de Calixto y Melibea como conflicto de comunidades." Pp. 135–52 of *Judíos en la literatura española*. Edited by Iacob M. Hassán and Ricardo Izquierdo Benito. Cuenca: Universidad de Castilla–La Mancha, 2001.

Marín, Miguel Ángel. "Arias de ópera en ciudades provincianas: las arias italianas conservadas en la Catedral de Jaca." Pp. 375–401 of *La ópera en España e Hispanoamérica. Actas del Congreso Internacional, "La ópera en España y en Hispanoamérica. Una creación propia." Madrid, 29.XI/3.XII de 1999*. Edited by Emilio Casares Rodicio and Álvaro Torrente. Madrid: ICCMU, 2001.

Martí, Marc, and Jacques Soubeyroux (eds.). *Ciudad y campo en la España de la Ilustración*. Lérida: Milenio, 2001. Pp. 300; bibliography; index.

This monograph analyzes the aesthetic and economic foundations of the rise of pastoral plots in eighteenth-century Spanish literature and culture. *Ciudad y campo en la España de la Ilustración* [*The Countryside and the City in Spain during the Enlightenment*] is not a revision of file documentation but rather an explanatory synthesis of the most distinguished scholarly works on the interaction of ideology, economy, and culture in eighteenth-century Spain (15).

The author gives us the structural base of the text discussed at the same time that he demonstrates the importance of the combination of national and local data, of microhistory with the global historical vision. The countryside appears to be in eighteenth-century Spain as the exploited periphery, while the city absorbs capital because of the collection of tithes, leasings and rights into the hands of the urban elites. The control of the farmer economy by the city is absolute. City and countryside are antagonistic and complementary spaces, not only in economic aspects but also in the social ones. During the eighteenth century the Spanish rural areas maintained similar structures to those of the "Antiguo Régimen" [Old Regime] and experienced subsistence problems, while the city improved at expenses of the countryside. This fact would be the explanation of the multiplication of projects to reform the agriculture system and the countryside. In addition Martí also stresses the growing rise of economic literature because of the foundation of Economic Societies in Spain.

The author emphasizes the extremely important cultural role developed by Economic Societies in the shaping of a Spanish Enlightenment. Economic Societies are defined as institutions in which enlightened nobility produces a language which justifies the modernization of Spain. The analysis of the mottos and emblems of this language allows Marc Martí to rescue a lot of constants that help us to understand the Spanish Enlightenment. He reads under this historical framework not only the vindication of classical pastoral plots but also the emergence a reformist ideology shaped by the faith in Reason, Science, Progress or Education (145).

Chronological limits of Marc Martí's analysis are marked by the social and economic reality. Pastoral themes surfaced in literature between 1770 and 1790. At this time the countryside is idealized as a manifestation of love in its original purity. Pastoral poetry was a magnificent vehicle of expression for this topic, although strongly codified by classical tradition. Agrarian ideology filters in the literary utopia. Utility, abundance and happiness are the values embraced by aristocracy, while the bourgeois ideology adds "virtues" like humbleness and "aureas mediocritas" [praise of the mediocrity]. Meléndez Valdés, Jovellanos, Cienfuegos, Tomás de Carvajal are some of the Spanish poets discussed by Martí.

Martí argues for a different reading of pastoral themes developed in eighteenth-century Spanish theatre. First of all, the genre seems to be less codified by classicism than poetry. Staged *sainetes* [one-act Farces] by Ramon de la Cruz textualize the opposition of the village and the city, and reveal a cultural conflict developed in Spanish eighteenth-century economic literature and poetry . The ambivalence of Cruz's comic "payos" [rustic characters] demonstrates not only the complex balance that requires the classical aspiration of "enseñar deleitando"[teaching and entertaining], but also the result of the paradoxical thought adopted by the Spanish Enlightenment toward the countryside.

The genre of the novel, with its formal flexibility, appears like the privileged receiver to develop thematics in which the proprietary classes construct their cultural and social arena. The reading of *Mirtilo o los pastores transhumantes* [*Mirtilo and the Nomadic Shepherd*] by Pedro Montegón and *Aventuras de Juan Luis* [*Adventures of Juan Luis*] by Diego Ventura Rexón y Lucas, shows the development of classical topics such as the *locus amoenus* [pleasant countryside] or the *alabanza de corte y menosprecio de aldea* [praise of Court and rejection of countryside]. The author is very forceful in stating the purpose of his research: "Más allá de la explicación del resurgimiento de algunos temas literarios, este trabajo nos permitió esbozar los mecanismos que pueden regir las relaciones entre el mundo de las ideas y la organización económica y social" [This work shows how the mechanisms that mediate ideology, culture and economy can function altogether in the development and rise of some Enlightenment topics] (287).

This jargon-free book is very successful in the development of its interdisciplinary approach. Each chapter includes a conclusion, and each part a compilation of conclusions. The greater findings of the author, however, reveal its main defect since each section leaves us with a desire to "know more," no matter whether we are economists, sociologists, or historians of Literature. The bibliography that accompanies the book, and which includes a few specialized works by the same author, invites us to go beyond the introductory nature of the book and to follow deeper in different itineraries that it proposes.—Beatriz Ferrús Antón

Martí, Marc. "La familia popular en la reflexión económica del final del siglo XVIII." Pp. 131–40 of *Historia social y literatura. Familia y clases populares en España (siglos XVIII–XIX)*. Edited by Roberto Fernández and Jacques Soubeyroux. Lérida: Milenio, 2001.

Meléndez, Mariselle. "Eighteenth-Century Spanish America: Historical Dimensions and New Theoretical Approaches." *Revista de Estudios Hispánicos*, 35 (2001), 615–32.

Meléndez, Mariselle."Inconstancia en la mujer: Espacio y cuerpo femenino en el *Mercurio peruano*, 179–94." *Revista Iberoamericana*, 67 (2001), 79–88.

Miampica, Wilfrid. "Détours caribéens: résistance, mémoire et créolisation." Pp. 265–86 of *Las Casas face à l'esclavage des Noirs: vision critique du "Onzième Remède" (1516)/Las Casas frente a la esclavitud de los negros: visión crítica del "Undécimo Remedio" (1516)*. Edited by Victorien Lavou Zoungbo. Perpignan: Université de Perpignan, 2001.

Nebrera, Gregorio Torres (ed.). *"Celestina": recepción y herencia de un mito literario*. Cáceres: Universidad de Extremadura, 2001. Pp. 207.

Ogoula, Landry, and Danielle Ada Ondo. "Lecture et interprétation du *Onzième Remède* (1516) de Las Casas par des universitaires européens et latino–américains: une synthèse critique." Pp. 369–81 of *Las Casas face à l'esclavage des Noirs: vision critique du "Onzième Remède" (1516)/Las Casas frente a la esclavitud de los negros: visión crítica del "Undécimo Remedio" (1516)*. Edited by Victorien Lavou Zoungbo. Perpignan: Université de Perpignan, 2001.

Pajares Infantes, Eterio. "La primera traducción española de *Tom Jones*: análisis crítico." *Dieciocho,* 24 (2001), 245–60.

Passola i Tejedor, Antoni. "Las clases populares en la literatura costumbrista del Setecientos: el ejemplo de *Morir viviendo en la aldea y vivir muriendo en la corte*, de Antonio Muñoz." Pp. 13–26 of *Historia social y literatura. Familia y clases populares en España (siglos XVIII–XIX).* Edited by Roberto Fernández and Jacques Soubeyroux. Lérida: Milenio, 2001.

Pedraza Jiménez, Felipe B. "*La Celestina* en las tablas: sistemas dramáticos y técnicas escénicas." Pp. 97–124 of *"Celestina": recepción y herencia de un mito literario.* Edited by Gregorio Torres Nebrera. Cáceres: Universidad de Extremadura, 2001.

Pedraza Jiménez, Felipe B. "Los judíos en el teatro del siglo XVII: la comedia y el entremés." Pp. 153–211 of *Judíos en la literatura española.* Edited by Iacob M. Hassán and Ricardo Izquierdo Benito. Cuenca: Universidad de Castilla–La Mancha, 2001.

Pedrosa, José Manuel. "Los judíos en la literatura tradicional española." Pp. 403–36 of *Judíos en la literatura española.* Edited by Iacob M. Hassán and Ricardo Izquierdo Benito. Cuenca: Universidad de Castilla–La Mancha, 2001.

Pérez Magallón, Jesús. *El teatro neoclásico.* Madrid: Ediciones del Laberinto, 2001. Pp. 319.

Until the decade of the 1960s Spanish neoclassicism was little more than a disdainful footnote in Spanish literary histories, reduced usually to a listing of a few authors and titles and promptly dismissed as a servile imitation of French forms and doctrines. Russell P. Sebold, mentor of the author under review and an eighteenth-century specialist who did much to remedy that situation, denounced what he called the "mitos antineoclásicos españoles" [Spanish antineoclassical myths] erected by a conservative nationalist criticism hostile to the Enlightenment and interested in identifying the Catholic and tradition-oriented dominant culture of the previous centuries with a presumed genuinely Spanish character. Given the prevalence of those myths, it is no surprise that the few early monographic works devoted to neoclassical drama originated outside of Spain. After Robert Pellisier's brief *The Neo-Classic Movement in Spain during the Eighteenth Century* (1918), nothing of substance appeared until John A. Cook's *Neoclassic Drama in Spain. Theory and Practice* (1959; reedited in 1974), an extensively researched book providing information on play content, performances, theory and critical polemics, journalistic criticism, literary influences, and institutional contexts. Although somewhat moralistic and too dependent on the critical parameters of the object of study itself, Cook's book helped promote inquiry in the field among English-speaking hispanism. Unfortunately, its usefulness was marred by the author's decision to translate all citations and titles into English, without including their originals.

    The next milestone was Ivy McClelland's two-volume *Spanish Drama of Pathos, 1750–1808* (1970), still a necessary reference point for scholars investigating neoclassical tragedy or sentimental drama. To this day, there is still no comprehensive study of Spanish neoclassical comedy. The book that laid the groundwork for a sociohistorical consideration of eighteenth-century theater, and which remains the richest study to date to take that approach, is René Andioc's *Teatro y Sociedad en el Madrid del Siglo XVIII* [*Theatre and Society in Eighteenth-century Madrid*] (1976; corrected and expanded 1987), which subsumed matters of poetics and theatrical polemics within a sociological framework based on solid quantitative research on class-differentiated consumption of plays, not only neoclassical but also of the more popular varieties. Since the early seventies, we have seen several critical editions of neoclassical plays unedited since the eighteenth or early nineteenth century, by authors such as Cadalso, García de la Huerta, García Malo, López de Ayala, Nicolás Moratín, and Trigueros, and a surge of critical interest in them, although some of the authors that are becoming the object of increased attention, such as Cienfuegos, Gálvez de Cabrera, and Montiano, are still waiting to have all or most of their plays made available in modern scholarly editions. Scholars who have been particularly active in the study of neoclassical theater include Russell Sebold, Guillermo Carnero and Emilio Palacios Fernández. Among the most thorough scholarly work dealing wholly or largely with the poetics of neoclassicism, we must mention recent books by José Checa Beltrán, *Razones del buen gusto (Poética española del neoclasicismo)* [*Reasons of Good Taste. Neoclassical Spanish Poetics*] (1998), María José Rodríguez Sánchez de León, *La crítica dramática en España (1789–1833)* [*Spanish Scholarship on Drama, 1789–1833*] (2000), and Helmut C. Jacobs, *Belleza y buen gusto. Las teorías de las artes en la literatura española del siglo XVIII* [*Beauty and Good Taste. Discourses on Art in Eighteenth-century Spanish Literature*] (2001; original German version 1996).

Despite this increased critical attention, Jesús Pérez Magallón can claim, as he does, that his book is "the first monograph published in Spanish concerned exclusively with neoclassical theater" (7). That does not mean, however, that he attempts to present a sweeping panorama on the subject, with a complete repertoire of authors and titles, details on performances and critical reactions to them, analyses of theoretical polemics and foreign influences, considerations of institutional and political contexts, or a periodization attempting to account for the changing theoretical and practical issues surrounding the neoclassical movement along its century-long development.

In fact, the book deals with none of the above. Its aim is very straightforward: "to present and reflect on the central concerns articulated by the neoclassicists in their dramatic production" (7). The author attempts to do so mainly by analyzing the characters and plots of some forty plays, chosen according to the vague criterion of "representativeness," a term on which the author does not elaborate. This is problematic not only because of the specific choices (for example, Bretón de los Herreros, one the most prolific and popular authors of neoclassical comedy, is not represented), but also because it skirts the question of what, exactly, constitutes a neoclassical play. Why include genres such as the comic *sainetes* [one-act farce] (generally disliked by eighteenth-century neoclassicists) or Jovellanos's sentimental drama *El delincuente honrado* [*The Honest Criminal*] but not, for example, plays that are at least formally neoclassical such as Martínez de la Rosa's *La conspiración de Venecia* [*The Venice Conspiracy*] or Larra's *Macías*? It is not that there are no grounds to exclude these plays from consideration; in fact, most literary histories include them under the rubric of Romanticism. But if the criteria applied are not exclusively formal, then they need to be explained. If such plays are excluded because the issues they address do not match with the reformist concerns of the neoclassical tragedies here studied, then we need to understand that we are not dealing with Spanish neoclassical theater as a whole, but only with its Enlightenment phase.

Be that as it may, Pérez Magallón's book, within its chosen restriction to what is articulated in the texts themselves, is a well-organized and intelligent exposition of the major political and social themes in reformist neoclassical tragedy and comedy. The book has two main parts. The first (Chapter 1) deals with Spanish neoclassical theory of drama, and the second (Chapters 2–4, comprising the bulk of the study) deals with the thematic and ideological analysis of the plays. The book ends with a brief overview of critical studies on neoclassical theater, an annotated bibliography, and a name index.

One of the virtues of the first chapter on neoclassical dramatic theory is that it pays particular attention to the little-explored period from the late seventeenth century to the beginnings of the neoclassical movement proper, which the author situates in the 1730s. Pérez Magallón has emerged as one of the leading experts on this transitional "time of the *novatores* [innovative intellectuals]," with his critical edition—in tandem with Russell Sebold—of the Count of Fernán Núñez's *El hombre práctico* [*The Practical Man*] (1686) and his extensive panoramic study of the period, *Construyendo la modernidad. La cultura española en el tiempo de los novatores (1675–1725)* [*Constructing Modernity. Spanish Culture done at the time of the innovative intellectuals, 1675–1725*], which appeared shortly after the book under review. Following his exposition of Fernán Núñez's views on theater (from discourse

XXVII of *El hombre práctico*) [*The Practical Man*], Pérez Magallón deals at some length with Bances Candamo's Aristotelian classicism, arguing that his views on theater are a step in the direction of the Enlightenment because his appeal to Aristotle and Horace stems not from an uncritical subservience to *auctoritas* [authority] but from the awareness that the classical authors' poetics are themselves the product of reason applied to accumulated experience.

Pérez Magallón argues that what separates eighteenth-century neoclassicism from its Golden Age predecessors is that it builds a bridge between theory and practice as it aligns itself with enlightened social reformism and assimilates the philosophical rehabilitation of observation and experience. The "rules of art" should not be understood as the product of a dogmatic attitude but as the rational articulation of accumulated practical experience. After expanding on this insight, the first chapter provides a well-organized account of neoclassical dramatic theory, relying heavily on Ignacio de Luzán's 1737 *Poética* [*Poetics*] and Pedro Estala's writings on comedy and tragedy, and less heavily on Mayans, Montiano, Nicolás and Leandro Moratín, Díez González, Sánchez Barbero, Masdeu, and a few others. The key concepts of good taste, dramatic *illusio* [illusion], imitation—of ideal nature and of literary models—verisimilitude, the unities, and dramatic economy are explained in their mutual relations and as means toward the ultimate goal of combining pleasure with instruction and "creating a space of rational communication between public and playwright" where the former will find "a mirror in which it can identify itself" (48). Missing is a consideration of a concept that seems to me central to neoclassical dramatic theory, that of *decoro* or propriety. A final section of the chapter deals mainly with the ideal characteristics and aims of the classical dramatic genres, tragedy and comedy, but also with the place of minor comical genres such as the *sainete* [one-act farce], and with the tensions and transformations in the hierarchical edifice of neoclassical poetics created by the rise of "mixed" genres such as sentimental comedy and urban tragedy. Overall, the chapter provides a useful synthesis of neoclassical dramatic theory, although diachronic considerations are largely avoided.

Chapter 2 on tragedy begins by examining the difficulties in reconciling the Aristotelian view of tragedy with the reform-oriented practice of neoclassicist authors, whose tragedies are "a field of reflection focusing on (political) power and the new socially acceptable forms of heroism" (73), premised on an unquestioned but not servile acceptance of monarchy. When the conflict stems ultimately from villainy rather than fate, tragedy becomes something like "discussion drama" (I borrow the term from Donald Shaw), a showcase of reasonable statesmanship confronting passions. The bulk of the chapter examines the major themes in neoclassical tragedy, on the basis of analyses, often quite detailed, of some twenty plays. The themes include: models of the good monarch and of the tyrant; issues of legitimacy and mixed blood; the protagonism of chieftain Pelayo, elevated to mythical restorer of the fatherland and "expressing metaphorically the process of (re)construction of the country" (100); the relation between the king and his subjects, and the choices faced by the latter when the king becomes a tyrant; the new model of the nobleman, characterized above all by virtue and patriotism; and the figure of the royal counselor as moral guide, flatterer or manipulator. The first section of chapter 4 returns to tragedy to explore the construction of female characters, where the prevalence of misogynistic commonplaces (women as fragile, fickle, and untrustworthy, prone to manipulation and adultery) and the desired model of the bourgeois family result in an image of the ideal woman constructed around the values of fidelity, honor, honesty, obedience, and resignation.

Neoclassical comedy, the topic of chapter 3, attempts to change through laughter, or later also through sensibility and tears, patterns of behavior in the middle sectors of society that are perceived to be unacceptable or at odds with reformist goals. As in the previous chapter, the analysis of some twenty plays (including a couple of *sainetes*) [one-act farce] provides an overview of major themes: love, interest, and marriage; social mobility; hypocrisy and the obsession with appearances; truthfulness and trust; religiosity, or rather its absence from the plays; paternal authority, the upbringing of children, and filial obedience. (Obedience, says Pérez Magallón, is in neoclassical comedy the overarching code that takes the place of Baroque honor.) Section 2 of chapter 4 revisits misogynistic attitudes and the construction of the ideal woman, this time in comedy, as it explores the obsession with fashion and its ambivalent status for the reformists, as a spur for the economy and as a cause of overconsumption resulting in moral corruption. Section 3 examines the construction of the ideal male citizen, the *hombre de bien* [Honest Man], in contrast with undesirable social types such as the *petimetre* [fop]. The former is characterized by moral integrity, patriotism, usefulness, compassion, and the interiorization of honor, understood as inner contentment stemming from virtuous behavior, rather than as socially sanctioned. The *petimetre*, by contrast, is the fop, the vain, feminized man who seeks social recognition through the display of surface appearances of cultural refinement.

The final pages of the book offer a brief overview of critical studies on neoclassical theater, an annotated select bibliography, and an index of names. The bibliography of primary works includes only the plays, but not the major theoretical works dealt with in the first chapter. An index of play titles would have been useful as well. The book has a number of printing errors and a few slips: Martínez de la Rosa's tragedy *La viuda de Padilla* [*Padilla's Widow*] is twice ascribed to Quintana (83, 298); Iriarte's comedy *La señorita malcriada* [*The Bad-Mannered Young Lady*] is retitled (178) *La señorita mimada* [*The Spoiled Lady*] (an interference from his other comedy, *El señorito mimado*) [*The Spoiled Young Gentleman*]; the year of publication of John A. Cook's book is 1959 and not 1957 (295). There is also a factual error in the final overview of critical studies: The author laments that there is no modern edition of a critical text as essential as Clavijo's *El Pensador* [*The Thinker*]. There is: *Antología de "El Pensador"* [*Anthology of "The Thinker"*], edited by Sebastián de la Nuez Caballero, Islas Canarias, 1989. It includes the essays on the *autos sacramentales* [eucharistic play] that Pérez Magallón refers to in the first chapter.

Despite these few faults, Pérez Magallón's monograph accomplishes what it sets out to accomplish. It is a perceptive and well-written mapping of the major themes of reformist Spanish neoclassical theater. It draws attention to some plays heretofore ignored by scholars, and relates them thematically to the better-known ones. It highlights both the commonalities and the variations in the ways these plays engage specific reformist concerns. It will be a fertile resource for students of eighteenth-century theater in general, and particularly for scholars approaching eighteenth-century texts—not only plays—within a thematic orientation centered on social and political issues.—José A. Valero

Pérez Magallon, Jesús. "Hacia un nuevo discurso poético en el tiempo de los novatores." *Bulletin Hispanique*, 103 (2001), 449–79.

Pérez Priego, Miguel Ángel. "La Biblia y el teatro religioso medieval y renacentista." Pp. 111–33 of *Judíos en la literatura española*. Edited by Iacob M. Hassán and Ricardo Izquierdo Benito. Cuenca: Universidad de Castilla–La Mancha, 2001.

Pont, Jaume. "Huérfanos y expósitos en la obra en prosa de Antonio Ros de Olano." Pp. 231–53 of *Historia social y literatura. Familia y clases populares en España (siglos XVIII–XIX)*. Edited by Roberto Fernández and Jacques Soubeyroux. Lérida: Milenio, 2001.

Pont, Virginie. "Afterword". Pp. 382–89 of *Las Casas face à l'esclavage des Noirs: vision critique du "Onzième Remède" (1516)/Las Casas frente a la esclavitud de los negros: visión crítica del "Undécimo Remedio" (1516)*. Edited by Victorien Lavou Zoungbo. Perpignan: Université de Perpignan, 2001.

Profeti, Maria Grazia. "El espacio del teatro y el espacio del texto: Metastasio en España en la primera mitad del siglo XVIII." Pp. 263–91 of *La ópera en España e Hispanoamérica. Actas del Congreso Internacional, "La ópera en España y en Hispanoamérica. Una creación propia."* Madrid,

29.XI/3.XII de 1999. Edited by Emilio Casares Rodicio and Álvaro Torrente. Madrid: ICCMU, 2001.

Rabaté, Colette. "La familia popular en la trilogía de Wenceslao Ayguals de Izco." Pp. 209–29 of *Historia social y literatura. Familia y clases populares en España (siglos XVIII–XIX)*. Edited by Roberto Fernández and Jacques Soubeyroux. Lérida: Milenio, 2001.

Ribao Pereira, Montserrat. "Del humor y los humores en el *Jardín de Venus*. Las otras fábulas de Samaniego." *Dieciocho*, 24 (2001), 203–16.

Ríos Carratalá, Juan Antonio. "La Biblioteca Virtual Miguel de Cervantes. Obras del Siglo XVIII." *Dieciocho*, 24 (2001), 297–326.

Risco, Antonio. "Mantener una casa en Madrid. Modelos familiares y economía doméstica hacia 1766" Pp. 37–56 of *Historia social y literatura. Familia y clases populares en España (siglos XVIII–XIX)*. Edited by Roberto Fernández and Jacques Soubeyroux. Lérida: Milenio, 2001.

Rodicio, Emilio Casares, and Álvaro Torrente (eds.). *La ópera en España e Hispanoamérica. Actas del Congreso Internacional, "La ópera en España y en Hispanoamérica. Una creación propia."* Madrid, *29.XI/3.XII de 1999*. Madrid: ICCMU, 2001.

Rodríguez Puértolas, Julio. "La poesía de la Baja Edad Media." Pp. 87–109 of *Judíos en la literatura española*. Edited by Iacob M. Hassán and Ricardo Izquierdo Benito. Cuenca: Universidad de Castilla–La Mancha, 2001.

Rueda, Ana. *Cartas sin lacrar: la novela epistolar y la España ilustrada, 1789–1840*. Madrid: Iberoamericana, 2001. Pp. 524; bibliography; index.

Saint–Lu, André. "Bartolomé de Las Casas et la *Traité des Nègres*." Pp. 15–22 of *Las Casas face à l'esclavage des Noirs: vision critique du "Onzième Remède" (1516)/Las Casas frente a la esclavitud de los negros: visión crítica del "Undécimo Remedio" (1516)*. Edited by Victorien Lavou Zoungbo. Perpignan: Université de Perpignan, 2001.

Sala Valldaura, Josep María. "Los afectos sociales y domésticos en el teatro de Fernández de Moratín: el beso de doña Francisca y Rita." Pp. 113–29 of *Historia social y literatura. Familia y clases populares en España (siglos XVIII–XIX)*. Edited by Roberto Fernández and Jacques Soubeyroux. Lérida: Milenio, 2001.

Samaniego, Félix María de. *Obras completas*. Edited by Emilio Palacios Fernández. Madrid: Fundación José Antonio de Castro, 2001. Pp. 663; illustrations; index.

Samper, Edgar. "La representación de la familia obrera en el teatro social de fines del siglo XIX: *El pan del pobre* de Félix González Llana y José Francos Rodríguez (1894), *Juan José* de Joaquín Dicenta (1895) y *Teresa* de "Clarín" (1895)." Pp. 286–97 of *Historia social y literatura. Familia y clases populares en España (siglos XVIII–XIX)*. Edited by Roberto Fernández and Jacques Soubeyroux. Lérida: Milenio, 2001.

Santa, Àngels, and Antoine Court. "Familia y clases populares en las traducciones de *Geneviève* de Lamartine durante el siglo XIX." Pp. 256–66 of *Historia social y literatura. Familia y clases populares en España (siglos XVIII–XIX)*. Edited by Roberto Fernández and Jacques Soubeyroux. Lérida: Milenio, 2001.

Schraibman, José. "La visión ecuménica de Galdós." Pp. 353–73 of *Judíos en la literatura española*. Edited by Iacob M. Hassán and Ricardo Izquierdo Benito. Cuenca: Universidad de Castilla–La Mancha, 2001.

Sebold, Russell P. *La perduración de la modalidad clásica. Poesía y prosa españolas de los siglos XVII a XIX*. Salamanca: Universidad de Salamanca, 2001. Pp. 270; index.

Sebold, Russell P. "La 'restauración' de la poesía, alma del movimiento neoclásico." *Salina*, 15 (2001), 123–31.

Sommer-Mathis, Andrea. "La ópera y la fiesta cortesana: los intercambios entre Madrid y la corte imperial de Viena."pp. 293–316 of *La ópera en España e Hispanoamérica. Actas del Congreso Internacional, "La ópera en España y en Hispanoamérica. Una creación propia." Madrid, 29.XI/3.XII de 1999*. Edited by Emilio Casares Rodicio and Álvaro Torrente. Madrid: ICCMU, 2001.

Soubeyroux, Jacques. "Marginalidad y familia popular en la novela y la prensa de finales del siglo XVIII: evolución ideológica de un sistema de representación literaria." Pp. 141–56 of *Historia social y literatura. Familia y clases populares en España (siglos XVIII–XIX)*. Edited by Roberto Fernández and Jacques Soubeyroux. Lérida: Milenio, 2001.

Stein, Louise K. "De la contera del mundo: las navegaciones de la ópera entre dos mundos y varias culturas." Pp. 79–94 of *La ópera en España e Hispanoamérica. Actas del Congreso Internacional, "La ópera en España y en Hispanoamérica. Una creación propia." Madrid, 29.XI/3.XII de 1999*. Edited by Emilio Casares Rodicio and Álvaro Torrente. Madrid: ICCMU, 2001.

Stiffoni, Gian Giacomo. "La ópera en tiempos de Carlos III (1759–1788)." Pp. 317–41 of *La ópera en España e Hispanoamérica. Actas del Congreso Internacional, "La ópera en España y en*

Hispanoamérica. Una creación propia." Madrid, 29.XI/3.XII de 1999. Edited by Emilio Casares Rodicio and Álvaro Torrente. Madrid: ICCMU, 2001.

Tardieu, Jean-Pierre. "De l' 'undécimo remedio' de Las Casas (1516) au projet de traite des Noirs de 1518." Pp. 41–58 of *Las Casas face à l'esclavage des Noirs: vision critique du "Onzième Remède" (1516)/Las Casas frente a la esclavitud de los negros: visión crítica del "Undécimo Remedio" (1516)*. Edited by Victorien Lavou Zoungbo. Perpignan: Université de Perpignan, 2001.

Torres Nebrera, Gregorio (ed.). *"Celestina": recepción y herencia de un mito literario*. Cáceres: Universidad de Extremadura, 2001. Pp. 207; index.

Fernando de Rojas's *La Celestina* (1499), arguably Spain's second most important literary work, has exerted considerable influence on the letters and the arts of all periods. *Celestina: recepción y herencia de un mito literario* [*Celestina: Reception and Endurance of a Literary Myth*], a collection of essays edited by Gregorio Torres Nebrera, deals precisely with the reception and the legacy of this modern classic from the sixteenth century up to the present. It touches upon a variety of issues including echoes, intertextual references, imitations, theatrical and cinematic adaptations, and fictional reworkings.

The book is divided into six chapters. In Chapter 1 (17–49) Emilio Blanco traces *La Celestina*'s extraordinary success in the sixteenth century, as evident in the number of editions, translations and critical reviews that it produced. This surge in popularity recedes in the 1600s, as other types of fiction gradually begin to gain more notoriety. Ignacio Arellano's contribution in chapter two (51–72) stresses the relatively small presence of Rojas' masterwork in the *comedia nueva* [*New Comedy*], due to the incompatibility between the role of the tragicomic in *La Celestina* vis-à-vis the poetics that informs seventeenth-century Spanish theatre. Joaquín Álvarez Barrientos is responsible for chapter three (73–96), where he chronicles the most relevant commentaries on *La Celestina* during the eighteenth and the nineteenth centuries.

Chapters four to six shift the emphasis away from the reception of the work. In Chapter 4 (97–124) Felipe B. Pedraza Jiménez offers a detailed account of the adaptations of *La Celestina* for the stage elapsing a period of almost four hundred years. Manuel Ángel Vázquez Medel does the same with the cinematic versions in Chapter 5 (125–41), while providing the reasons why films based on Rojas's work have been for the most part failures. Finally, the editor, Torres Nebrera, devotes Chapter 6 (143–207) to a series of artistic experiments aimed at re-creating the spirit of the *Tragicomedia*, either by keeping faith with the original or by departing from it.

The contributors to this volume are to be commended for providing an incredibly rich and well-documented source of information about *La Celestina*'s presence in Western culture. The specialist in search of data will hence find in it an extremely useful departure point for his or her own pursuits. On the other hand, a scholar less engaged in the medieval or the early modern periods will probably feel somewhat overwhelmed by the erudite tone of some of the chapters. While aware of the challenges of striking a balance between historical and critical approaches to literature, I wished that this book had paid slightly more attention to the latter. In this respect, I find Vázquez Medel's theoretical considerations on what a cinematic adaptation of a literary work ought to be particularly refreshing. Unfortunately, other articles remain a mere catalogue of names and years and do not care much to stimulate the reader's intellectual curiosity.

The subtitle of the volume rightly asserts that *La Celestina* is a literary myth. Having said that, perhaps the biggest shortcoming of the volume has to do with its inability to define *why* it is indeed one. In other words, what is it that makes the *Tragicomedia* [*Tragicomedy*] one of the most subversive and universal pieces of literature ever written? Is it the originality of its design, as María Rosa Lida de Malkiel proposed in her 1962 seminal study? Is it its generic indeterminacy, half way between the humanistic comedy and the modern novel? Is it the characterization of the protagonist, Celestina, the archetypal representation of the procuress as a charming, cunning, selfish, and materialistic old woman imbued with magical powers? Or is it rather the nihilistic portrayal of a society absolutely devoid of ethical and religious values, a reflection of the *converso* [*converted Jew*] Rojas's pessimistic views on what in 1948 Américo Castro was to call the historical reality of Spain? A preliminary chapter responding to these and other similar questions from a variety of critical perspectives would have proved immensely valuable.

A discrepancy between Celestina and *La Celestina* also arises in the content of this book. While the title seems to refer to the fictional character (Celestina), the articles deal for the most part with the legacy of the entire work (*La Celestina*.) The confusion is all the more striking in light of the fact that it is the old procuress that has universally come to incarnate, along with Don Quijote [Don Quixote], Don Juan and Carmen, an essential representation of the Spanish psyche. In failing to adequately distinguish between the protagonist and the text itself, the editor of this volume misses once again an excellent opportunity to answer the question of what constitutes a literary myth.—Toni Dorca.

Torres Nebrera, Gregorio. "Preliminar." Pp. 9–16 of *"Celestina": recepción y herencia de un mito literario*. Edited by Gregorio Torres Nebrera. Cáceres: Universidad de Extremadura, 2001.

Torres Nebrera, Gregorio. "La reescritura y la reinvención del mito." Pp. 143–207 of *"Celestina": recepción y herencia de un mito literario*. Edited by Gregorio Torres Nebrera. Cáceres: Universidad de Extremadura, 2001.

Vázquez Medel, Manuel Ángel. "*La Celestina*, de la literatura al cine." Pp. 125–41 of *"Celestina": recepción y herencia de un mito literario*. Edited by Gregorio Torres Nebrera. Cáceres: Universidad de Extremadura, 2001.

Vilalta, María José. "Desmontando la tradición: la desmitificación de la familia campesina tradicional en los *Drames Rurals* de Víctor Català." Pp. 299–319 of *Historia social y literatura. Familia y clases populares en España (siglos XVIII–XIX)*. Edited by Roberto Fernández and Jacques Soubeyroux. Lérida: Milenio, 2001.

Voltaire, Francois-Marie Arouet de. *Epistolario inglés; Cándido*. Translated by Leandro Fernández de Moratín. Barcelona: LIBSA, 2001. Pp. 283.

Williams, Jerry M. "A New Text in the Case of Ana de Castro: Lima's Inquisition on Trial." *Dieciocho,* 24 (2001), 7–32.

Zamora, Andrés. "Guerrillas ideológicas y estéticas en la *Raquel* (breviario español de cómo marginar al enemigo)." *Dieciocho,* 24 (2001), 261–78.

Zoungbo, Victorien Lavou (ed.). *Las Casas face à l'esclavage des Noirs: vision critique du "Onzième Remède" (1516)/Las Casas frente a la esclavitud de los negros: visión crítica del "Undécimo Remedio" (1516)*. Perpignan: Université de Perpignon, 2001. Pp. 389.

Foreign Languages and Literatures

French Literature and Language

Albes, Claudia. "Der Autobiograph als Botaniker: Zur poetologischen Funktion von Linnés Systema Naturae in Rousseaus 'Les reveries du promeneur solitaire." Pp. 213–38 of *Erschriebene Natur: Internationale Perspektiven auf Texte des 18. Jahrhunderts*. Edited by Michael Scheffel. Bern: Peter Lang, 2001.

Aldridge, A. Owen. "John Adams Confronts Turgot." *Studies in Eighteenth-Century Culture*, 30 (2001), 91–104.

Alimento, Antonella. "Il 'secolo dell'Unigenitus'? Politica e religione in Francia nel secolo dei Lumi." *Rivista di Storia e Letteratura Religiosa*, 37 (2001), 323–46.

Altman, Janet Gurkin. "Strategic Timing: Women's Questions, Domestic Servitude, and the Dating Game in Montesquieu." *Eighteenth-Century Fiction*, 13 (2001), 325–48.

Andres, Bernard. "A l'orient du septentrion, ou zelim dans la gazette littéraire de Montreal (1778–1779)." *Tangence*, 65 (2001), 60–71.

Andres, Bernard. "D'une mère partie a la patrie canadienne: Archéologie du patriote au XVIIIe siècle." *Voix et Images: Littérature Quèbècoise*, 26 (2001), 474–97.

Andrews, Richard. "From Beaumarchais to Da Ponte: A New View of the Sexual Politics of 'Figaro.'" *Music and Letters*, 82 (2001), 214–33.

Ansart, Guillaume. "Jansenist Themes and Influences in Prévost's Cleveland." Pp. 47–55 of *Voltaire, Religion and Ideology, Women's Studies, History of the Book, Passion in the Eighteenth Century*. Edited by Anthony Strugnell. Oxford: Voltaire Foundation, 2001.

Ansart, Guillaume. "Rousseau, Bataille, et le principe de l'utilité classique." *French Studies: A Quarterly Review*, 55 (2001), 25–35.

Aravamudan, Srinivas. "Progress through Violence or Progress from Violence? Interpreting the Ambivalences of the Histoire des Deux Indes." Pp. 259–80 of *Progrès et violence au XVIIIe siècle*. Edited by Valerie Cossy and Deidre Dawson. Paris: Honoré Champion, 2001.

Arbetti, Flavia. "Les attitudes di Lady Hamilton." *Quaderni di Lingue e Letterature*, 26 (2001), 5–19.

Arbo, Alessandro. "Diderot et l'hieroglyphe musical." *Recherches sur Diderot et sur l' Encyclopédie*, 30 (2001), 65–80.

Aron, Paul, Sophie Basch, Manuel Couvreur, and others (eds.) *Vérité et littérature au XVIIIe siècle*. Mélanges rassemblés en l'honneur de Raymond Trousson. Introduction by Valerie van Crugten Andre. (Colloques Congres et Conferences sur le Dix-Huitième Siècle 2.) Paris: Honoré Champion, 2001. Pp. 346.

Astbury, Katherine. "National Identity and Politicisation in Fiction up to the Revolution: The Example of the Moral Tale." *Literature and History*, 10 (2001), 6–17.

Balcou, Jean (ed.). *Bretagne et lumières: Mélanges offerts à Monsieur le Professeur Jean Balcou*. (Université de Bretagne occidentale et C.N.R.S., Centre d'études des correspondances et journaux intimes des XIXe et XXe siècles.) Brest: Université de Bretagne occidentale, Centre d'études des correspondances et journaux intimes des XIXe et XXe siècles, 2001. Pp. 407.

Bandry, Anne. "A Bibliography of Sterne in French." *Shandean: An Annual Devoted to Laurence Sterne and His Works*, 12 (2001), 91–113.

Bauer Funke, Cerstin. "Aline et Léonore ou les effets de la violence: Violence et progrès dans Aline et Valcour ou le Roman philosophique du marquis de Sade." Pp. 167–86 of *Progrès et violence au XVIIIe siècle*. Edited by Valerie Cossy and Deidre Dawson. Paris: Honoré Champion, 2001.

Bell, David A. "Canon Wars in Eighteenth-Century France: The Monarchy, the Revolution and the 'Grands hommes de la patrie.'" *Modern Language Notes*, 116 (2001), 705–38.

Belleguic, Thierry. "Les bijoux indiscrets ou la tentation du savoir." Pp. 83–108 of *Théories et debats esthétiques au Dix-Huitième siècle: Elements d'une enquete/Debates on Aesthetics in the Eighteenth Century: Questions of Theory and Practice*. Edited by Elisabeth Décultot and Mark Ledbury. Paris: Honoré Champion, 2001.

Benac, Karine. "Marivaux disciple de Pascal? Les 'Deux Ordres' du divertissement dans L'Indigent Philosophe." *Litteratures*, 45 (2001), 151–67.

Bender, John. "Enlightenment Fiction and the Scientific Hypothesis." Pp. 236–60 of *Eighteenth-Century Genre and Culture: Serious Reflections on Occasional Forms: Essays in Honor of J. Paul Hunter*. Edited by Dennis Todd and Cynthia Wall. Newark: University of Delaware Press, 2001.

Bérenguier, Nadine. "D'un mémoire judiciaire a une Cause célèbre: Le Parcours d'une femme adultere." *Dalhousie French Studies*, 56 (2001), 133–43.

Bernier, Marc André. "La question du despotisme oriental en France sous le regne du sultan Zeokinizul." *Tangence*, 65 (2001), 52–59.

Bernier, Marc André. *Libertinage et figures du savoir: Rhétorique et roman libertin dans la France des Lumières, 1734–1751*. Québec: Presses de l'Université Laval, 2001. Pp. 273; bibliography.

Biondi, Carminella. "Il 'variolico veleno' alla corte di Parma nella corrispondenza Du Tillot-D'Argental." Pp. 69-89 of *Un viaggio infinito...: Salute, malattia e morte*. Edited by Carmelina Imbroscio. Bologna: CLUEB, 2001.

Birn, Raymund F. *Forging Rousseau: Print, Commerce and Cultural Manipulation in the Late Enlightenment*. (Studies on Voltaire and the Eighteenth Century 8.) Oxford: Voltaire Foundation, 2001. Pp. ix + 281; illustrations.

Boccazzi, Barbara Mazza. "'La luna d'agosto': Appunti e spunti di trattatistica architettonica da Lodoli à Laugier." *Quaderni Veneti*, 33 (2001), 109–25.

Boixareu, Mercedes. "Le Theme de la Juive de Tolede dans les précédents espagnols de Cazotte." Pp. 25–41 of *Vérité et littérature au XVIIIe siècle*. Edited by Paul Aron and others. Paris: Honoré Champion, 2001.

Bokobza Kahan, Michele. "Une Conscience cartelee: Dulaurens." *Revue d' Histoire Littéraire de la France*, 101 (2001), 1367–82.

Bonnet, Jean Claude. "Le culte des grands hommes en France au XVIIIe siècle ou la defaite de la monarchie." *Modern Language Notes*, 116 (2001), 689–704.

Bottiglia, William F. "A Garden of Hope." Pp. 81–87 of *Readings on Candide*. (Greenhaven Press Literary Companion to World Literature.) Edited by Thomas Walsh. San Diego: Greenhaven, 2001.

Boulerie, Florence. "La Vérité palpable de Diderot contre les généralisations théoriques d'Helvétius." Pp. 69–78 of *Théories et débats esthétiques au dix huitième siècle: Elements d'une enquete/Debates on Aesthetics in the Eighteenth Century: Questions of Theory and Practice*. Edited by Elisabeth Décultot and Mark Ledbury. Paris: Honoré Champion, 2001.

Bourgeois, Muriel, Olivier Guerrier, Laurence Vanoflen (eds.). *Littérature et morale 16e-18e siècle de l'humaniste au philosophe.* (Collection U.; Lettres.) Paris: Armand Colin, 2001. Pp. 192.

Brady, Patrick. "From Chaos to Control: The Subversive Structure of Desire." *Australian Journal of French Studies,* 38 (2001), 69–78.

Brady, Valentini Papadopoulou. "'Manon Lescaut, c'est lui': A Study of Point of View in Prévost's *Manon Lescaut.*" *Intertexts,* 5 (2001), 156–67.

Braun, Theodore E. D. "Chaos, Contingency, and Candide." *1650–1850: Ideas, Aesthetics, and Inquiries in the Early Modern Era,* 6 (2001), 199–209.

Brillant Annequin, Anick. "Oedipe de Voltaire: Tragédie dramatique ou drame tragique?" *Recherches et Travaux,* 59 (2001), 15–41.

Brocherioux, Chrystele. "Vauvenargues nationaliste." *Studi Francesi,* 45 (2001), 533–41.

Brown, Gregory S. "The Self-Fashionings of Olympe De Gouges, 1784–1789." *Eighteenth-Century Studies,* 34 (2001), 383–401.

Brunel, Pierre. "Pasiphae et le taureau blanc: Voltaire, Chenier, François Noel." Pp. 43–56 of *Vérité et littérature au XVIIIe siècle.* Edited by Paul Aron and others. Paris: Honoré Champion, 2001.

Bruyn, Adrienne, Pieter Muysken, and Maaike Verrips. "Double–Object Constructions in the Creole Languages: Development and Acquisition." Pp. 329–73 of *Language Creation and Language Change: Creolization, Diachrony, and Development.* Edited by Michel DeGraff. Cambridge: MIT Press, 2001.

Buffat, Marc. "Pour un spectateur distant." *Eighteenth-Century Life,* 25 (2001), 68–79.

Byrne, Patrick. "Second Thoughts on the Dénouement of *Les Liaisons Dangereuses.*" *Modern Language Review,* 96 (2001), 964–72.

Candaux, Jean Daniel. "Un Hommage a Jean-Jacques Rousseau dans la mouvance du Prince de Ligne." Pp. 57–65 of *Vérité et littérature au XVIIIe siècle.* Edited by Paul Aron and others. Paris: Honoré Champion, 2001.

Cardy, Michael. "Place and Space in Two Eighteenth-Century French Texts." Pp. 49–59 of *Frontières flottantes: Lieu et espace dans les cultures francophones du Canada/Shifting Boundaries: Place and Space in the Francophone Cultures of Canada*. Edited by Jaap Lintvelt. Amsterdam: Rodopi, 2001.

Carlin, Claire (ed.). *Le mariage sous l'Ancien Régime*. (Dalhousie French Studies 56.) Halifax: Dalhousie University, 2001. Pp. 166; illustrations.

Chammas, Jacqueline. "L'Inceste: 'Crime' ou 'Droit de la nature'? La Loi de l'interdit dans l'Icosameron de Casanova." Pp. 33–47 of *Lumen*. (Selected Proceedings from the Canadian Society for Eighteenth-Century Studies/Travaux Choisis de la societé Canadienne d'Étude du Dix-Huitième Siècle 20.) Edited by William Kinsley. Kelowna: Academic, for the Canadian Society for Eighteenth-Century Studies, 2001.

Charbonneau, Frédéric. "Regime et sensibilité: Manger, pleurer et boire dans les Mémoires de Marmontel." *French Forum*, 26 (2001), 21–37.

Charles, Shelly. "Fortune des Illustres: La Traduction anglaise des Illustres Françaises." *Eighteenth-Century Fiction*, 14 (2001), 95–109.

Chartier, Pierre. "Le Pouvoir des fables ou la verité selon Jacques." *Recherches sur Diderot et sur l' Encyclopédie*, 30 (2001), 47–64.

Chauderlot, Fabienne Sophie. "'Becoming-Image': Deleuzian Echoes in Jacques Rivette's La Religieuse." *Eighteenth-Century Life*, 25 (2001), 88–100.

Cherpak, Clifton. "Using Low Comedy to Mock Philosophic Pretensions." Pp. 105–11 of *Readings on Candide*. (Greenhaven Press Literary Companion to World Literature.) Edited by Thomas Walsh. San Diego: Greenhaven, 2001.

Cirakman, Asli. "From Tyranny to Despotism: The Enlightenment's Unenlightened Image of the Turks." *International Journal of Middle East Studies*, 33 (2001), 49–68.

Clack, Beverley. "Sade: Forgiveness and Truth in a Desacralised Universe." *Literature and Theology: An International Journal of Theory, Criticism and Culture*, 15 (2001), 262–75.

Cladis, Mark S. "The End of the Private Life: Rousseau, Redemption, and Tragedy." *Soundings: An Interdisciplinary Journal*, 84 (2001), 51–77.

Cook, Malcolm. "La Fiction courte en France, 1790–1800." *Eighteenth-Century Fiction*, 13 (2001), 197–211.

Cornand, Suzanne. "La Lettre d'indignation ou l'éloquence dans la correspondance de Madame de Graffigny." *Revue d' Histoire Litteraire de la France*, 101 (2001), 37–50.

Cornille, Jean-Louis. *La lettre française: De Crébillon fils à Rousseau, Laclos, Sade*. (Accent 26.) Leuven: Peeters, 2001. Pp. 131.

Cornille, Jean-Louis. "The Go-Between." *Pretexts: Literary and Cultural Studies*, 10 (2001), 163–77.

Cortey, Mathilde. *L'invention de la courtisane au XVIIIe siècle dans les romans-mémoires des "filles du monde" de Madame Meheust à Sade (1732–1797)*. Paris: Éditions Arguments, 2001. Pp. ii + 307; illustration, bibliography.

Cossy, Valerie. "An English Touch: Laurence Sterne, Jane Austen, et le roman sentimental en Suisse Romande." *Annales Benjamin Constant*, 25 (2001), 131–60.

Cossy, Valerie. "'Pour qui écrire desormais?': Esthétique et révolution dans les oeuvres d'Isabelle de Charriere et Germaine de Stael." Pp. 233–55 of *Progrès et violence au XVIIIe siècle*. Edited by Valerie Cossy and Deidre Dawson. Paris: Honoré Champion, 2001.

Cossy, Valerie, and Deidre Dawson (eds.). *Progres et violence au XVIIIe siècle*. Introduction by Valerie Cossy; Preface by Michel Delon and Jochen Schlobach. (International Eighteenth-Century Studies/Etudes Internationales sur le Dix-Huitième Siècle: Series Published for the International Society of Eighteenth-Century Studies 3.) Paris: Honoré Champion, 2001. Pp. 458.

Coudreuse, Anne. *Le refus du pathos au XVIIIe siècle*. (Babeliana 3.) Paris: Honoré Champion, 2001. Pp. 270.

Coulet, Henri. "Destin du conte moral." *Eighteenth-Century Fiction*, 13 (2001), 247–58.

Coulet, Henri. "Rousseau, Diderot, les amants et la courtisane." Pp. 67–75 of *Vérité et littérature au XVIIIe siècle*. Edited by Paul Aron and others. Paris: Honoré Champion, 2001.

Coward, David. "Restif de la Bretonne and Time." *Australian Journal of French Studies*, 38 (2001), 129–40.

Foreign Languages and Literatures

Cronk, Nicholas. *Études sur les Journaux de Marivaux.* (Bibliothèque portative de la Fondation Voltaire.) Oxford: Voltaire Foundation, 2001. Pp. 172.

Crugten André, Valerie Van. "Syncrétisme et dérision parodique dans Pauliska ou la perversité moderne de Reveroni Saint-Cyr." *Revue d' Histoire Littéraire de la France*, 101 (2001), 1551–71.

Cryle, P. M.. *The Telling of the Act: Sexuality as Narrative in Eighteenth- and Nineteenth-Century France.* Newark: University of Delaware Press, 2001. Pp. 433; bibliography, index.

Curran, Andrew. *Sublime Disorder: Physical Monstrosity in Diderot's Universe.* (Studies on Voltaire and the Eighteenth Century 1.) Oxford: Voltaire Foundation, 2001. Pp. xi +171.

Dalnekoff, Donna Isaacs. "Eldorado as an 'Impossible Dream.'" Pp. 64–71 of *Readings on Candide.* (Greenhaven Press Literary Companion to World Literature.) Edited by Thomas Walsh. San Diego: Greenhaven, 2001.

Darlow, Mark. "'Apprendre aux hommes à mourir': The Theatrical Adaptations of Paul et Virginie." *European Studies: A Journal of European Culture, History, and Politics*, 17 (2001), 129–42.

Davison, Rosena. "Happy Marriage: Myth or Reality in Eighteenth-Century France? The Case of Madame d'Épinay and Her Family." *Dalhousie French Studies,* 56 (2001), 116–24.

Dawson, Deidre. "A quel prix le jardin de Candide? Progrès et Violence dans l'oeuvre de Voltaire." Pp. 187–204 of *Progrès et violence au XVIIIe siècle.* Edited by Valerie Cossy and Deidre Dawson. Paris: Honoré Champion, 2001.

Dawson, Robert L. "Marmontel Made in Britain." *Australian Journal of French Studies*, 38 (2001), 107–23.

De Ligne, Prince Charles-Joseph: *Fragments ee l'histoire de ma vie, II.* Edited with an introduction by Jeroom Vercruysse. (Age des Lumieres 13.) Paris: Honoré Champion, 2001. Pp. 624.

Décultot, Elisabeth, and Mark Ledbury (eds.). *Théories et débats esthétiques au dix huitième siècle: Elements d' une enquête/Débates on Aesthetics in the Eighteenth Century: Questions of Theory and Practice.* Introduction by Elisabeth Décultot and Mark Ledbury; Preface by Jochen Schlobach and Jean Mondot. (International Eighteenth-Century Studies/Études Internationales sur le Dix-Huitième Siècle: Series Published for the International Society of Eighteenth Century Studies 4.) Paris: Honoré Champion, 2001. Pp. 340.

Degott, Pierre. "De Racine a Händel: Les Tribulations d'Esther." *Bulletin de la Societe d' Etudes Anglo Americaines des XVIIe et XVIIIe Siècles*, 52 (2001), 35–50.

DeJean, Joan. "Was the Eighteenth Century Long Only in England?" *Eighteenth-Century Fiction*, 13 (2001), 155–62.

Deloffre, Frédéric. "L'Écrivain éditeur posthume dans la littérature clandestine." *Travaux de Littérature*, 14 (2001), 279–98.

Deloffre, Frédéric. "Une 'Oeuvre fondatrice': Les Illustres Françaises." *Eighteenth-Century Fiction*, 13 (2001), 213–34.

Delon, Michel. "François Pages, romancier presse." Pp. 91–99 of *Vérité et littérature au XVIIIe siècle*. Edited by Paul Aron and others. Paris: Honoré Champion, 2001.

Delon, Michel. "L'Etrangete de Chardin et la gene de Diderot." *Romanistische Zeitschrift für Literaturgeschichte/Cahiers d' Histoire des Littératures Romanes*, 25 (2001), 295–308.

Delon, Michel. "Variations du roman-liste: Du temps individuel au temps historique." *Eighteenth Century Fiction*, 13 (2001), 259–77.

Derson, Didier. "La Théâtralite du discours romanesque sadien." *Revue d' Histoire du Théâtre*, 4 (2001), 353–68.

Derson, Didier. "Narration et didascalies dans l'oeuvre romanesque du Marquis de Sade." *Revue d' Histoire du Théâtre*, 4 (2001), 369–77.

Desné, Roland. "Autour de la lettre de Diderot à Landois." Pp. 101–18 of *Vérité et littérature au XVIIIe siècle*. Edited by Paul Aron and others. Paris: Honoré Champion, 2001.

Didier, Beatrice. *Diderot dramaturge du vivant*. (Écriture.) Paris: Presses Université de France, 2001. Pp. 213.

Dionne, Ugo. "Admirable et cavalier: Le XVIIIe Siècle de Philippe Sollers." Pp. 19–31 of *Lumen*. (Selected Proceedings from the Canadian Society for Eighteenth-Century Studies /Travaux Choisis de la societé Canadienne d'Étude du Dix-Huitième Siècle 20.) Edited by William Kinsley. Kelowna: Academic, for the Canadian Society for Eighteenth-Century Studies, 2001.

Foreign Languages and Literatures

Dokou, Christina. "Derrida's Travels: Swift at Large in the Academy." *Eighteenth-Century: Theory and Interpretation*, 42 (2001), 113–41.

Dorati, Marco. "Jan Potocki interprete di Erodoto." *Acme: Annali della Facolta di Lettere e Filosofia dell' Universita degli Studi di Milano*, 54 (2001), 3–34.

Droixhe, Daniel. "Les Ameriques du jeune Turgot." Pp. 119–36 of *Vérité et littérature au XVIIIe siècle*. Edited by Paul Aron and others. Paris: Honoré Champion, 2001.

Dutton, Dianne. "De la rhétorique a la narration: Les Exempla dans l'Entretien d'un père avec ses enfants de Denis Diderot." Pp. 13–26 of *The Documentary Impulse in French Literature*. Edited by Buford Norman. Amsterdam: Rodopi, 2001.

Dziedzic, Andrzej. "Liberté, proprieté et sexualité dans le Supplement au voyage de Bougainville." *Chimères: A Journal of French Literature*, 25 (2001), 45–55.

Ecker, Eva. "Die deutschen Übersetzungen und Bearbeitungen von Marivaux' Liebeslustspielen im 18. Jahrhundert." *Maske und Kothurn: Internationale Beiträge zur Theaterwissenschaft*, 46 (2001), 167–93.

Ehrard, Jean. "'Mangeront-ils?': Note sur Les repas de quelques heros de romans du XVIIIe siècle." Pp. 137–43 of *Vérité et littérature au XVIIIe siècle*. Edited by Paul Aron and others. Paris: Honoré Champion, 2001.

Eigeldinger, Frederic S. "Avatars du manuscrit des Rêveries: De Girardin a Dupeyrou." Pp. 145–61 of *Vérité et littérature au XVIIIe siècle*. Edited by Paul Aron and others. Paris: Honoré Champion, 2001.

Elmarsafy, Ziad. "Submission, Seduction, and State Propaganda in Favart's Soliman II, ou les trois sultanes." *French Forum*, 26 (2001), 13–26.

Enckell, Pierre. "Le Comte de Caylus, ses amis et Les etrennes de la Saint-Jean, 1738–1751." *Revue d' Histoire Litteraire de la France*, 101 (2001), 123–34.

Eon de Beaumont, Charles Geneviève Louis Auguste André Timothée d': *The Maiden of Tonnerre: The Vicissitudes of the Chevalier and the Chevaliere d'Eon*. Edited and translated by Roland A. Champagne, Nina Ekstein, and Gary Kates. Baltimore: Johns Hopkins University Press, 2001. Pp. xxiv + 207.

Erlat, Jale. "XVIII. Yuzyilda Bir Frankofon: Isabelle de Charrière." *Edebiyat Fakultesi Dergisi/Journal of the Faculty of Letters*, 18 (2001), 1–13.

Fabiano, Andrea. "Metastasio, Voltaire, Diderot, Marmontel e l'opera francese." *Problemi di Critica Goldiana*, 8 (2001), 203–21.

Fauskewåg, Svein Eirik. *Sade ou La tentation totalitaire: Étude sur l'anthropologie littéraire dans La nouvelle Justine et L'histoire de Juliette.* (Les Dix-Huitièmes Siècles 49.) Paris: Honoré Champion, 2001. Pp. 196.

Ferris, David S. "Before the Museum: Diderot and the Salon." *Rivista di Estetica*, 41 (2001), 78–85, 173–80.

Fido, Franco. "Carlo Gozzi e Diderot dopo 'Le Bourru bienfaisant': Palinodie di antigoldonisti." *Rivista di Letterature Moderne e Comparate*, 54 (2001), 427–36.

Fink, Beatrice. "Saint-John de Crevecoeur's Tale of a Tuber." *Eighteenth-Century Life*, 25 (2001), 225–34.

Fiszer, Stanislaw. *L' image de la Pologne dans l'oeuvre de Voltaire.* (Studies on Voltaire and the Eighteenth Century 5.) Oxford: Voltaire Foundation, 2001. Pp. xv + 188; illustrations.

Florack, Ruth (ed.). *Tiefsinnige Deutsche, frivole Franzosen: Nationale Stereotype in deutscher und französischer Literatur.* Stuttgart: Metzler, 2001. Pp. xii + 931; illustrations.

Forget, Danielle. "Figures, politesse et organisation textuelle." *Journal of Pragmatics: An Interdisciplinary Journal of Language Studies*, 33 (2001), 1157–72.

Foucart, Claude. "Rom und das klassische Ideal." Pp. 685–713 of *Die Wende von der Aufklärung zur Romantik 1760–1820: Epoche im Überblick.* Edited by Horst-Albert Glaser. Amsterdam: Benjamins, 2001.

Gallouët, Catherine. *Marivaux, journaux et fictions.* Orléans: Paradigme, 2001. (Références 19.) Pp. 166.

Gargett, Graham. "Plagiarism, Translation and the Problem of Identity: Oliver Goldsmith and Voltaire." *Eighteenth-Century Ireland/Iris an da Chultur*, 16 (2001), 83–103.

Gevrey, Françoise. "La Redéfinition des genres dans l'Encyclopédie." *Kairos*, 18 (2001), 91–101.

Gierl, Martin. "Kompilation und die Produktion von Wissen im 18. Jahrhundert." Pp. 63–94 of *Die Praktiken der Gelehrsamkeit in der frühen Neuzeit*. Edited by Helmut Zedelmaier. Tübingen: Max Niemeyer Verlag, 2001.

Glaser, Horst-Albert. "Annex: Giacomo Casanova." Pp. 161–70 of *Die Wende von der Aufklärung zur Romantik 1760–1820: Epoche im Überblick*. Edited by Horst-Albert Glaser. Amsterdam: Benjamins, 2001.

Glaser, Horst-Albert. "Annex: Marquis de Sade." Pp. 305–11 of *Die Wende von der Aufklärung zur Romantik 1760–1820: Epoche im Überblick*. Edited by Horst-Albert Glaser. Amsterdam: Benjamins, 2001.

Glaser, Horst-Albert. "Weltumsegler und ihre Reiseberichte." Pp. 15–22 of *Die Wende von der Aufklärung zur Romantik 1760–1820: Epoche im Überblick*. Edited by Horst-Albert Glaser. Amsterdam: Benjamins, 2001.

Goetz, Charlotte. *Marat en famille: La Saga des Mara(t), II: Suisse, Grande-Bretagne, Hollande, France, Russie: La Correspondance de Jean Mara avec Frederic-Samuel Ostervald et la Société typographique de Neuchatel (1769–1782)*. (Chantiers: Marat 7.) Brussels: Pole Nord, 2001. Pp. 325.

Goldstein, Marc Allan (ed.). *Social and Political Thought of the French Revolution 1788–1797: An Anthology of Original Texts*. Abridged edition. Translated by Marc Allan Goldstein. New York: Peter Lang, 2001.

Goldzink, Jean, Marie Helene Cotoni, and Genevieve Artigas Menant. "Des Difficultés sur la religion aux Illustres Françaises: Ecarts et interpretations." *Revue d' Histoire Litteraire de la France*, 101 (2001), 313–26.

Goodden, Angelica. *Diderot and the Body*. (Legenda: Research Monographs in French Studies.) Oxford: European Humanities Research Centre, 2001. Pp. x + 209.

Gordon, Felicia. "'This Accursed Child': The Early Years of Marie Madeleine Jodin (1741–90), Actress, Philosophe and Feminist." *Women's History Review*, 10 (2001), 229–48.

Gordon, Felicia, and P. N. Furbank. *Marie Madeleine Jodin 1741–1790: Actress, Philosophe and Feminist*. (Women and Gender in the Early Modern World.) Aldershot: Ashgate Publishing Company, 2001. Pp. xii + 224.

Gray, Patricia, and Wallace Kirsop. "L'Art du prospectus: L'Écrivain éditeur et son public." *Travaux de Littérature*, 14 (2001), 361–74.

Grenon, Anne France. "La Formulation de la loi morale dans Le Spectateur français de Marivaux." *Revue d' Histoire Litteraire de la France*, 101 (2001), 1163–80.

Grosperrin, Jean Philippe. "Le 'Tour' des mouvements dans les Journaux de Marivaux." *Litteratures*, 45 (2001), 105–31.

Gsteiger, Manfred. "Vom 'edlen Wilden' zum 'homme naturel'." Pp. 649–61 of *Die Wende von der Aufklärung zur Romantik 1760–1820: Epoche im Überblick*. Edited by Horst-Albert Glaser. Amsterdam: Benjamins, 2001.

Guarnieri, Elisabetta. "Louis Guillaume Coutonnier e il suo 'Metodo per imparar facilmente il francese' (Milano: 1734, 1739, 1747)." *Acme: Annali della Facolta di Lettere e Filosofia dell' Universita degli Studi di Milano*, 54 (2001), 245–63.

Hakim, Zeina. "Le langage en Révolution." *Versants: Revue Suisse des Litteratures Romanes/Rivista Svizzera di Letterature Romanze/Schweizerische Zeitschrift für Romanische Literaturen*, 39 (2001), 45–64.

Hammer, Stephanie Barbe. "Romanticism and Reaction: Hampton's Transformation of *Les Liaisons Dangereuses*." Pp. 117–31 of *Modern Dramatists: A Casebook of Major British, Irish, and American Playwrights*. Edited by Kimball King. New York: Routledge, 2001.

Hammersley, Rachel. "Camille Desmoulins's Le Vieux Cordelier: A Link between English and French Republicanism." *History of European Ideas*, 27 (2001), 115–32.

Hassler, Gerda. "La Discussion sur l'universalité de la langue francaise et la comparaison des langues: Une Rupture épistémologique." Pp. 15–39 of *Changements politiques et statut des langues: Histoire et épistémologie 1780–1945*. Edited by Marie-Christine-Kok Escalle. Amsterdam: Rodopi, 2001.

Havens, George R. "Using Irony as a Form of Satire." Pp. 98–104 of *Readings on Candide*. (Greenhaven Press Literary Companion to World Literature.) Edited by Thomas Walsh. San Diego: Greenhaven, 2001.

Henry, Patrick. "Mythical and Symbolic Gardens." Pp. 88–96 of *Readings on Candide*. (Greenhaven Press Literary Companion to World Literature.) Edited by Thomas Walsh. San Diego: Greenhaven, 2001.

Hoang, Lethuy. *Les Mille et Une Nuits: A travers l'infini des espaces et des temps: Le Conteur Galland, le conte et son public.* (Currents in Comparative Romance Languages and Literatures 90.) New York: Peter Lang, 2001. Pp. x + 201.

Hodson, Christopher. "'In Praise of the Third Estate': Religious and Social Imagery in the Early French Revolution." *Eighteenth-Century Studies,* 34 (2001), 337–62.

Howells, Robin. "The Peruvienne and Pathos." *French Studies,* 55 (2001), 453–66.

Huchette, Jocelyn. "Y a-t-il un 'caractère national' des auteurs? La Problematique du gout dans la critique voltairienne des littératures étrangères." Pp. 155–67 of *Une histoire de la "fonction auteur" est elle possible?* Actes du colloque organisé par le Centre de recherche LiDiSa (Littérature et Discours du Savoir). Edited by Nicole Jacques Lefevre. Saint-Etienne: Université de Saint-Etienne, 2001.

Hunter, Andy. "The Peregrinations of Auld Robin Gray and Eugenie Grandet." *Etudes Ecossaises,* 7 (2001), 183–93.

Ida, Hisashi. "Sens moral et sociabilité naturelle: L'Influence de la philosophie morale écossaise sur Diderot." *Études de Langue et Littérature Françaises,* 78 (2001), 69–83.

Imbroscio, Carmelina. "Mesmer a Parigi: Entusiasmi di massa e satira popolare intorno al magnetismo animale." Pp. 119–36 of *Un viaggio infinito...: Salute, malattia e morte.* Edited by Carmelina Imbroscio. Bologna: CLUEB, 2001.

Imbroscio, Carmelina (ed.). *Un viaggio infinito...: Salute, malattia e morte. Percorsi di lettura tra Belgio, Francia e Italia in ricordo di Paola Vecchi.* (Heuresis: Strumenti 20.) Bologna: CLUEB, 2001. 190 pp.

Jacobs, Helmut C. "'Je suis excellent pantomime': Musik und Pantomime in Denis Diderots Le Neveu de Rameau." *Romanistische Zeitschrift für Literaturgeschichte/Cahiers d' Histoire des Littératures Romanes,* 25 (2001), 309–37.

Johnson, Daniel C. "La Polémique musicale dans Julie ou la Nouvelle Héloise de Jean-Jacques Rousseau." Pp. 557–65 of *Jean Jacques Rousseau, politique et nation.* Edited by Robert Thiery. Paris: Honoré Champion, 2001.

Johnson, James H. "Versailles, Meet Les Halles: Masks, Carnival, and the French Revolution." *Representations,* 73 (2001), 89–116.

Johnston, Guillemette. "Constitutive Elements of the Discourse of Natural Instruction in Rousseau's Emile: Situations and Implications." *Romanic Review*, 92 (2001), 245–58.

Joly, Raymond. "De la ponctuation, à propos de Marivaux." Pp. 123–35 of *Lumen*. (Selected Proceedings from the Canadian Society for Eighteenth-Century Studies/Travaux Choisis de la société Canadienne d'Étude du Dix-Huitième Siècle 20.) Edited by William Kinsley. Kelowna: Academic, for the Canadian Society for Eighteenth-Century Studies, 2001.

Jones, Jennifer M. "Personals and Politics: Courting la citoyenne in Le courier de l'hymen." *Yale French Studies*, 101 (2001), 171–81.

Kavanagh, Thomas M. "Coupling the Novel: Reading Bodies in La Morlière's Angola." *Eighteenth-Century Fiction*, 13 (2001), 389–413.

Kehrès, Jean-Marc. *Sade et la rhétorique de l'exemplarité*. (Dix-Huitièmes Siècles 64.) Paris: Honoré Champion, 2001. Pp. 184.

Kempton, Adrian. "Diderot's Clarissa and Laclos' Cecilia: Virtuous English Heroines as Models for an Emerging Aesthetic of the Novel in France." *Franco British Studies: Journal of the British Institute in Paris*, 31 (2001), 37–61.

Kinsley, William, Benoit Melançon, and Anne Richardot (eds.). *Lumen*. (Selected Proceedings from the Canadian Society for Eighteenth-Century Studies/Travaux Choisis de la société Canadienne d'Étude du Dix-Huitième Siècle 20.) Kelowna: Academic, for the Canadian Society for Eighteenth-Century Studies, 2001. Pp. vi + 160.

Kirsop, Wallace. "Canonical Novels for Gentlemen's Libraries." *Australian Journal of French Studies*, 38 (2001), 166–76.

Kopanev, Nikolai Alexandrovitch. "Marc Michel Rey, libraire-éditeur de J.-J. Rousseau et de Catherine II.." Pp. 697–706 of *Jean Jacques Rousseau, politique et nation*. Edited by Robert Thiery. Paris: Honoré Champion, 2001.

Kovacs, Katalin. "La Naissance d'un genre littéraire: La Critique d'art au XVIIIe siècle." Pp. 211–32 of *Théories et débats esthétiques au dix huitième siècle: Éléments d'une enquête/Debates on Aesthetics in the Eighteenth Century: Questions of Theory and Practice*. Edited by Elisabeth Décultot and Mark Ledbury. Paris: Honoré Champion, 2001.

Kozul, Mladen. "L'Eloquence sadienne: De la propagande philosophique a la rhetorique de la fiction." Pp. 109–22 of *Theories et debats esthetiques au dix huitième siècle: Elements d'une enquete*

/Debates on Aesthetics in the Eighteenth Century: Questions of Theory and Practice. Edited by Elisabeth Décultot and Mark Ledbury. Paris: Honoré Champion, 2001.

Kusch, Manfred. "The Symbols of the River and the Garden." Pp. 57–63 of *Readings on Candide*. (Greenhaven Press Literary Companion to World Literature.) Edited by Thomas Walsh. San Diego: Greenhaven, 2001.

Labrosse, Claude. "Nouveauté et la Nouvelle Héloise." *Eighteenth-Century Fiction*, 13 (2001), 235–46.

Lafon, Henri. "Le Roman au miroir du dramatique." *Eighteenth-Century Fiction*, 13 (2001), 437–59.

Lagerqvist, Hans. "Jean-Jacques Rousseau et le langage humain: Conformisme, subjectivité et modernité dans l'Essai sur l'origine des langues." *Zeitschrift für Romanische Philologie*, 117 (2001), 402–29.

Langille, E. M., and G. P. Brooks. "How English Translators Have Dealt with Candide's Homosexual Allusions." *Literary Research/Recherche Littéraire: A Journal of the International Comparative Literature Association/Une Revue de l' Association Internationale de Littérature Comparée*, 18 (2001), 367–87.

Lanser, Susan. "'Au sein de vos pareilles': Sapphic Separatism in Late Eighteenth-Century France." *Journal of Homosexuality*, 41 (2001), 105–16.

Le Ru, Véronique. "D'Alembert et les gens de lettres." *Kairos*, 18 (2001), 171–82.

Leca Tsiomis, Marie. "L'Etoile de Diderot: Tours et detours de l'auteur." Pp. 141–53 of *Histoire de la "fonction auteur" est elle possible?* Edited by Nicole Jacques-Lefevre. Saint-Etienne: Université de Saint-Etienne, 2001.

Lecerf, Guy. "Modeliser la couleur: Art de la mémoire, travail d'aveugle?" *Kairos*, 18 (2001), 143–70.

Lee, Young Mock. "Diderot et la lutte parlementaire au temps de l'Encyclopédie, II." *Recherches sur Diderot et sur l' Encyclopédie*, 30 (2001), 93–126.

Leger, Benoit. "Traduire ou omitter les psaumes: La Version de Desfontaines (1717)." *TTR: Traduction, Terminologie, Redaction: Etudes sur le Texte et Ses Transformations*, 14 (2001), 65–94.

Lerner, Lawrence Scott. "Beyond Gregoire: A Third Discourse on Jews and the French." *Modern Judaism*, 21 (2001), 199–215.

Letzter, Jacqueline, and Robert Adelson. *Women Writing Opera: Creativity and Controversy in the Age of the French Revolution*. (Studies on the History of Society and Culture 43.) Berkeley: University of California Press, 2001. Pp. xvii + 341.

Levasseur, Susan J. "'All Monstrous, All Prodigious Things': Anna Barbauld's 'The Rights of Woman' and Mary Wollstonecraft's Revolution in Female Manners." *Nineteenth-Century Feminisms*, 5 (2001), 10–36.

Lévêque, Laure. *Le roman de l'histoire: 1780-1850*. (Collection Critiques littéraires.) Paris: L'Harmattan, 2001. Pp. 402; bibliography.

Liandrat Guigues, Suzanne. "L'Echiquier rivettien." *Eighteenth-Century Life*, 25 (2001), 80–87.

Liesegang, Kerstin. "'Les Livres les plus utiles sont ceux dont les lecteurs font eux-mêmes la moitié': Parcours educatif et travail du lecteur dans deux contes 'mineurs' en prose de Voltaire: L'Homme aux quarante écus et La Princesse de Babylone." Pp. 111–32 of *Literarischer Kanon und Fremdsprachenunterricht*. Edited by Georg Fehrmann. Bonn: Romanistischer Verlag, 2001.

Lu, Jin. "En vers ou en prose? Les Débats sur la tragédie a l'age des Lumières." Pp. 139–53 of *Théories et débats esthétiques au dix huitième siècle: Élements d'une enquête/Debates on Aesthetics in the Eighteenth Century: Questions of Theory and Practice*. Edited by Elisabeth Décultot and Mark Ledbury. Paris: Honoré Champion, 2001.

Luccichenti, Furio. "Casanova e gli ebrei." *Intermediaire des Casanovistes*, 18 (2001), 23–33.

Manning, Rita C. "Rousseau's Other Woman: Collette in Le Devin du village." *Hypatia: A Journal of Feminist Philosophy*, 16 (2001), 27–42.

Marchal, Roger. "Des Satyres parmi les nymphes: Contes moraux et nouvelles Idylles de Diderot et Salomon Gessner." *Travaux de Littérature*, 14 (2001), 309–19.

Marchal, Roger (ed.). *Vie des salons et activités littéraires: de Marguerite de Valois à Mme. de Staël; actes du colloque international de Nancy [1999]*. (Collection Publications du Centre d'Étude des Milieux Littéraires 2.) Nancy: Presses Université de Nancy, 2001. Pp. 343; illustrations.

Marlan, Dawn. "The Seducer as Friend: The Disappearance of Sex as a Sign of Conquest in *Les Liaisons Dangereuses*." *PMLA,* 116 (2001), 314–28.

Martin, Christophe. "'Microlectures': Sujets mineurs et finesse de perception dans les Journaux de Marivaux." *Litteratures*, 45 (2001), 133–49.

Mason, Haydn. "Using Characters to Disprove Optimism." Pp. 39–46 of *Readings on Candide.* (Greenhaven Press Literary Companion to World Literature.) Edited by Thomas Walsh. San Diego: Greenhaven, 2001.

Mason, Haydn. "Voltaire et George Keate." Pp. 181–91 of *Vérité et littérature au XVIIIe siècle.* Edited by Paul Aron and others. Paris: Honoré Champion, 2001.

Mattauch, Hans. "Le Mirliton enchanteur: Historique d'un mot a la mode en 1723." *Révue d' Histoire Littéraire de la France*, 101 (2001), 1255–67.

May, Georges. "La Rehabilitation du roman français: Souvenirs et conjectures." *Eighteenth-Century Fiction*, 13 (2001), 147–54.

May, Gita. "The Status of Eighteenth-Century Studies." *French Review*, 75 (2001), 318–25.

McMahon, Darrin M. "Narratives of Dystopia in the French Revolution: Enlightenment, Counter-Enlightenment, and the Isle des Philosophes of the Abbé Balthazard." *Yale French Studies,* 101 (2001), 103–18.

Menil, Alain. "Reflexions sur une 'erreur seduisante': La Religieuse de Rivette." *Eighteenth-Century Life*, 25 (2001), 101–15.

Merrick, Jeffrey. "'Brutal Passion' and 'Depraved Taste': The Case of Jacques-François Pascal." *Journal of Homosexuality*, 41 (2001), 85–103.

Meylan, Claire. "Quand les critiques repondent a Casanova." Pp. 201–08 of *Fiction d'-auteur? Le Discours biographique sur l'auteur de l'Antiquité a nos jours.* Edited by Sandrine Dubel. Paris: Honoré Champion, 2001.

Miller, Nancy K. "Cover Stories: Enlightenment Libertinage, Postmodern Recyclage." *Eighteenth-Century Fiction*, 13 (2001), 477–99.

Miller, Paul Allen. "Disciplining the Lesbian: Diderot's *La Religieuse*." *Intertexts*, 5 (2001), 168–81.

Millner, Jacqueline. "André Chenier's Astonishing Revolutionary Language in the Iambs." *Dalhousie French Studies,* 57 (2001), 10–24.

Mondot, Jean. "Goethe und die Französischen Lumières oder Voltaire und kein Ende." *Goethe-Jahrbuch,* 118 (2001), 75–90.

Montoya, Alicia. "Caesar the Father in Marie-Anne Barbier's *La Mort de Cesar* (1709)." Pp. 319–38 of *Recreating Ancient History: Episodes from the Greek and Roman Past in the Arts and Literature of the Early Modern Period.* Edited by Karl Enenkel. Leiden: Brill, 2001.

Moscovici, Claudia. "An Ethics of Cultural Exchange: Diderot's Supplement Au Voyage De Bougainville." *CLIO: A Journal of Literature, History, and the Philosophy of History,* 30 (2001), 289–307.

Moser Verrey, Monique. "Le Langage du corps romanesque des Illustres Françaises (1713) a La Sorcière de Verberie (1798)." *Eighteenth-Century Fiction,* 13 (2001), 349–88.

Mostefai, Ourida. "La violence pamphletaire et ses stratégies en France a l'epoque des Lumieres." Pp. 281–95 of *Progrès et violence au XXIIIe siècle.* Edited by Valerie Cossy and Deidre Dawson. Paris: Honoré Champion, 2001.

Motsch, Andreas. *Lafitau et l'émergence du discours éthnographique.* (Imago Mundi 2.) Sillery: Septentrion, 2001. Pp. 295; illustrations.

Mourao, Manuela. "The Compromise of Enlightened Rationalism in Diderot's *La Religieuse.*" *Romance Quarterly,* 48 (2001), 223–38.

Moureau, Francois. "Bois Bresil, Amazones et reveries coloniales: Paradoxes bresiliens des Lumières françaises." Pp. 209–22 of *Vérité et littérature au XVIIIe siècle.* Edited by Paul Aron and others. Paris: Honoré Champion, 2001.

Moureau, Francois. "L'Infidelité de Lucinde ou 'Amour outrage': Un Roman inédit du debut du XVIIIe Siècle." *Australian Journal of French Studies,* 38 (2001), 79–93.

Mulsow, Martin. "Gegen die Fälschung der Vergangenheit: Philologie bei Mathurin Veyssière La Croze." Pp. 333–47 of *Philologie und Erkenntnis: Beiträge zu Begriff und Problem Frühneuzeitlicher Philologie.* Edited by Ralph Hafner. Tübingen: Max Niemeyer Verlag, 2001.

Naginski, Erika. "The Object of Contempt." *Yale French Studies,* 101 (2001), 32–53.

Nakagawa, Hisayasu. "La Logique de l'inacheve d'Emile et Sophie." Pp. 223–33 of *Vérité et littérature au XVIIIe siècle*. Edited by Paul Aron and others. Paris: Honoré Champion, 2001.

Nell, Sharon Diane. "The Last Laugh: Carnivalizing the Feminine in Piron's 'La Puce.'" Pp. 165–90 of *Carnivalizing Difference: Bakhtin and the Other*. Edited by Peter I. Barta. London: Routledge, 2001.

Niccoli, Elena. "L'apocalisse nella storia: Poesia, profezia e rivoluzione." *Strumenti Critici: Rivista Quadrimestrale di Cultura e Critica Letteraria*, 16 (2001), 189–223.

Niklaus, Robert. "La Constitution avancée par Condorcet en 1787 dans ses Lettres d'un bourgeois de New-Haven a un citoyen de Virginie sur l'inutilité de partager le pouvoir legislatif entre plusieurs corps." Pp. 235–46 of *Vérité et littérature au XVIIIe siècle*. Edited by Paul Aron and others. Paris: Honoré Champion, 2001.

O Gallchoir, Cliona. "Gender, Nation and Revolution: Maria Edgeworth and Stephanie-Felicite De Genlis." Pp. 200–16 of *Women, Writing and the Public Sphere, 1700–1830*. Edited by Elizabeth Eger. Cambridge: Cambridge University Press, 2001.

O'Neal, John C. "Nature's Culture in Du Bos's *Reflexions critiques sur la poésie et sur la peinture*." Pp. 15–27 of *Art and Culture in the Eighteenth Century: New Dimensions and Multiple Perspectives*. Edited by Elise Goodman. Newark: University of Delaware Press, 2001.

Pacini, Giulia. "'Celle dont la voix publique vous a nommé le père': Olympe de Gouges's memoire de Madame de Valmont (1788)." *Women in French Studies,* 9 (2001), 207–19.

Pearson, Roger. "Searching for Optimism in a Cruel World." Pp. 33–38 of *Readings on Candide*. (Greenhaven Press Literary Companion to World Literature.) Edited by Thomas Walsh. San Diego: Greenhaven, 2001.

Pekacz, Jolanta T. "Gendered Discourse as a Political Option in Pre-Revolutionary France." Pp. 331–46 of *Progrès et violence au XVIIIe siècle*. Edited by Valerie Cossy and Deidre Dawson. Paris: Honoré Champion, 2001.

Phillips, John. *Sade: The Libertine Novels*. London, England: Pluto, 2001. Pp. x + 204.

Pister, Danielle. *L'image du prêtre dans la littérature classique: XVIIe–XVIIIe siècles*. Actes du colloque organisé par le Centre "Michel Baude—Littérature et spiritualité" de l'Université de Metz, 20-21 novembre 1998. (Recherches en littérature et spiritualité 1.) Bern: Peter Lang, 2001. Pp. x + 278; illustrations.

Plagnol Dieval, Marie Emmanuelle. "Editer le théâtre de société: Le Cas de Carmontelle." *Travaux de Littérature*, 14 (2001), 321–34.

Pott, Sandra. "Critica Perennis: Zur Gattungsspezifik gelehrter Kommunikation im Umfeld der Bibliotheque Germanique (1720–1741)." Pp. 249–73 of *Die Praktiken der Gelehrsamkeit in der Frühen Neuzeit*. Edited by Helmut Zedelmaier. Tübingen: Max Niemeyer Verlag, 2001.

Pratt, Alan R. "Voltaire's Black Humor." Pp. 112–20 of *Readings on Candide*. (Greenhaven Press Literary Companion to World Literature.) Edited by Thomas Walsh. San Diego: Greenhaven, 2001.

Pucci, Suzanne Rodin. *Sites of the Spectator: Emerging Literary and Cultural Practice in Eighteenth-Century France*. (Studies on Voltaire and the Eighteenth Century 9.) Oxford: Voltaire Foundation, 2001. Pp. ix + 202.

Quéro, Dominique. "Note bibliographique sur le comte de Caylus et le 'Théâtre du Chateau de Morville'." *Revue d' Histoire Littéraire de la France*, 101 (2001), 135–45.

Quintili, Paolo (ed.). *La pensée critique de Diderot: Matérialisme, science et poésie à l'âge de l'Encyclopédie 1742–1782*. (Les Dix-Huitièmes Siècles 62.) Paris: Honoré Champion, 2001. Pp. 566.

Reed, Gail S. "Playing on His Readers' Desires." Pp. 121–27 of *Readings on Candide*. (Greenhaven Press Literary Companion to World Literature.) Edited by Thomas Walsh. San Diego: Greenhaven, 2001.

Regan, Shaun. "Translating Rabelais: Sterne, Motteux, and the Culture of Politeness." *Translation and Literature*, 10 (2001), 174–99.

Renwick, John. *Jean-François Marmontel (1723–1799): dix études*. (Les Dix-Huitièmes Siècles 51.) Paris: Honoré Champion, 2001. Pp. 376.

Revelli, Giorgetta (ed.). *Da Ulisse a Ulisse (il viaggio come mito letterario). Atti del convegno internationale, Imperia, 5–6 Ottobre 2000*. Pisa: Istituti Editoriali e Poligrafici Internazionali, 2001. Pp. 314.

Rivière, Marc Serge. "Women's Responses to Voltaire's Writings in the Eighteenth Century: 'a Silencing of the Feminine.'" *New Zealand Journal of French Studies*, 22 (2001), 5–27.

Roberts, Ian F. "Maupertuis: Doppelgänger of Doctor Moreau." *Science Fiction Studies*, 28 (2001), 261–74.

Saggiorato, Laura. "Le Journal de Lausanne: La Sensibilité au quotidien, 1786–1798." *Annales Benjamin Constant*, 25 (2001), 51–130.

Saint Amand, Pierre. "Lumieres et vengeance." Pp. 363–77 of *Progrès et violence au XVIIIe siècle*. Edited by Valerie Cossy and Deidre Dawson. Paris: Honoré Champion, 2001.

Sarrazin, Veronique. "L'Auteur éditeur de ses oeuvres a la fin du XVIIIe siècle: Aspects légaux et économiques." *Travaux de Littérature*, 14 (2001), 335–60.

Sato, Junji. "L'Origine et les sensations: Jean-Jacques Rousseau et les problèmes de l'"autobiographie."" *Études de Langue et Littérature Francaises*, 78 (2001), 55–68.

Sauvage, Emmanuelle. "La Tentation du théâtre dans le roman: Analyse de quelques tableaux chez Sade et Richardson." Pp. 147–60 of *Lumen*. (Selected Proceedings from the Canadian Society for Eighteenth-Century Studies/Travaux Choisis de la societe Canadienne d'Etude du Dix-Huitième Siècle 20.) Edited by William Kinsley. Kelowna: Academic, for Canadian Society for Eighteenth-Century Studies, 2001.

Scherr, Arthur. "Women's Equality in *Candide*." Pp. 129–40 of *Readings on Candide*. (Greenhaven Press Literary Companion to World Literature.) Edited by Thomas Walsh. San Diego: Greenhaven, 2001.

Schoenaers, Christian. "Deux 'diaristes' goréens: Stanislas de Boufflers et Joseph Boly." *Revue Generale*, 136 (2001), 67–77.

Schroder, Volker. "Entre l'oraison funèbre et l'éloge historique: L'Hommage aux morts a l'Académie francaise." *Modern Language Notes*, 116 (2001), 666–88.

Scott, Clive. "Landscapes of the Line: Verse-Features and the Perception of Nature in Romantic and Pre-Romantic Poetry." Pp. 189–212 of *Erschriebene Natur: Internationale Perspektiven auf Texte des 18. Jahrhundets*. Edited by Michael Scheffel. Bern: Peter Lang, 2001.

Seferian, Catherine. "Des frères jumeaux aux faux frères de Jacob, la réception du Paysan parvenu de Marivaux: L'Exploration methodique d'un reseau complexe." *Oeuvres et Critiques: Revue Internationale d' Etude de la Reception Critique d' Etude des Oeuvres Littéraires de Langue Francaise*, 26 (2001), 152–62.

Seite Salaun, Armelle. "De Loaisel de Treogate a Chateaubriand;." Pp. 83–98 of *Enfance et voyages de Chateaubriand: Armorique, Amerique*. Edited by Jean Balcou. Paris: Honoré Champion, 2001.

Sermain, Jean Paul. "Désir d'écriture et amour de soi dans les journaux de Marivaux." *Litteratures*, 45 (2001), 95–104.

Sgard, Jean. "Le Mot 'roman.'" *Eighteenth Century Fiction*, 13 (2001), 183–95.

Showalter, English. "Mme De Graffigny, Reader of Fiction." *Eighteenth-Century Fiction*, 13 (2001), 461–76.

Showalter, English. "Transformations du genre romanesque au XVIIIe Siècle." *Eighteenth-Century Fiction*, 13 (2001), 139–499.

Singerman, Alan J. "Film Forum: Suzanne Simonin: *La Réligieuse de Diderot* (1966) by Jacques Rivette." *Eighteenth-Century Life*, 25 (2001), 64–117.

Sola, Anne de. "Traduction et trafic d'influences: The Illustrious French Lovers de Penelope Aubin et Les Illustres Françaises de Robert Challe." *French Studies*, 55 (2001), 327–38.

Sozzi, Lionello. "Jean-Jacques Rousseau a Turin." Pp. 247–63 of *Vérité et littérature au XVIIIe siècle*. Edited by Paul Aron and others. Paris: Honoré Champion, 2001.

Spaas, Lieve. "Paul et Virginie: The Shipwreck of an Idyll." *Eighteenth-Century Fiction*, 13 (2001), 315–24.

Spacks, Patricia Meyer. "Ambiguous Practices." Pp. 150–64 of *Eighteenth Century Genre and Culture: Serious Reflections on Occasional Forms: Essays in Honor of J. Paul Hunter*. Edited by Dennis Todd and Cynthia Wall. Newark: University of Delaware Press, 2001.

Spedding, Patrick. "Shameless Scribbler or Votary of Virtue? Eliza Haywood, Writing (and) Pornography in 1742." Pp. 237–51 of *Women Writing, 1550–1750*. Edited by Jo Wallwork. Bundoora: Meridian, 2001.

Sprenger, Scott. "Off with His Head: Robespierre and the Terror of the Ideal Document." Pp. 27–38 of *The Documentary Impulse in French Literature*. Edited by Buford Norman. Amsterdam: Rodopi, 2001.

Steigerwald, Jorn, Olivier Mannoni, and Françoise Mancip Renaudie. "Arcadie historique: Paul et Virginie de Bernardin de Saint-Pierre, entre classicisme et préromantisme." *Revue Germanique Internationale*, 16 (2001), 69–86, 188–90.

Stewart, Joan Hinde. "Reading Lives 'a la manière des romans de Crebillon.'" *Eighteenth-Century Fiction*, 13 (2001), 415–35.

Strugnell, Anthony. "Fable et vérité: Strategies narrative et discursive dans les ecrits de Diderot sur le colonialisme." *Recherches sur Diderot et sur l' Encyclopedie* 30 (2001), 35–46.

Strugnell, Anthony (ed.). *Voltaire, Religion and Ideology, Women's Studies, History of the Book, Passion in the Eighteenth Century.* (Studies on Voltaire and the Eighteenth Century 12.) Oxford: Voltaire Foundation, 2001. Pp. 476.

Sumi, Yoichi. "'Atmosphère' et 'atmosphère': Essai sur la Cyclopaedia et le premier Prospectus de l'Encyclopédie." Pp. 271–84 of *Vérité et littérature au XVIIIe siècle.* Edited by Paul Aron and others. Paris: Honoré Champion, 2001.

Tarin, René. Diderot et la Révolution française: Controverses et polémique autour d'un philosophe. (Dix-Huitièmes Siècles 55.) Paris: Honoré Champion, 2001. Pp. 179; illustrations; facsimiles; bibliography.

Terdiman, Richard. "Political Fictions: Revolutionary Deconstructions in Diderot." *Yale French Studies,* 101 (2001), 153–70.

Terrasse, Jean. "La Contamination des genres chez Diderot: Contes, nouvelles, entretetiens ou dialogues philosophiques?" *Eighteenth-Century Fiction*, 13 (2001), 279–300.

Thiery, Robert (ed.). *Jean-Jacques Rousseau, Politique et Nation*. Paris: Honoré Champion, 2001. Pp. xxiv + 1,163; plates; illustrations.

Thomas, Downing A. "Pastoral against Tragedy in Hippolyte et Aricie." Pp. 409–19 of *Racine et/ou le classicisme.* Edited by Ronald W. Tobin. (Biblio 17.) Tübingen: Narr, 2001.

Thomas, Ruth P. "Theatre as Metaphor in Mme De Charriere's *Caliste.*" *Women in French Studies,* 9 (2001), 152–64.

Tippner, Anja. "'Wissende Unschuld': Selbstinszenierung und Repräsentation in den Memoiren Katharinas II." *Deutsche Vierteljahrsschrift für Literaturwissenschaft und Geistesgeschichte*, 75 (2001), 422–45.

Tobin, Ronald W. (ed.). *Racine et, ou le classicisme: Actes du colloque conjointement organisé par la North American Society for Seventeenth Century French Literature et la Société Racine, University of California, Santa Barbara [1999].* (Biblio 17.) Tübingen: Narr, 2001. Pp. 505.

Toledano Buendia, Carmen. "Robinson Crusoe naufraga en tierras espanolas." *Babel: Revue Internationale de la Traduction/International Journal of Translation*, 47 (2001), 35–48.

Topazio, Virgil W. "Voltaire's Attack on Optimism Has a Humanitarian Goal." Pp. 47–55 of *Readings on Candide*. (Greenhaven Press Literary Companion to World Literature.) Edited by Thomas Walsh. San Diego: Greenhaven, 2001.

Trousson, Raymond. "Le Dolbreuse de Loaisel de Treogate: Du roman libertin au 'roman utile.'" *Eighteenth-Century Fiction*, 13 (2001), 301–13.

Trousson, Raymond. *Visages de Voltaire: XVIIIe–XIXe siècles*. (Dix-Huitièmes Siècles 63.) Paris: Honoré Champion, 2001. Pp. 460; bibliography; index.

Tunstall, Kate E. "Diderot's *Promena de Vernet*, or the Salon as Landscape Garden." *French Studies*, 55 (2001), 339–49.

Vallois, Marie Claire, and John Galvin. "Gendering the Revolution: Language, Politics, and the Birth of a Nation (1789–1795)." *South Atlantic Quarterly*, 100 (2001), 423–45.

Van Strien Chardonneau, Madeleine. "Le Statut du francais, langue seconde selon Isabelle de Charriere: Langue de culture, langue utilitaire?" Pp. 41–52 of *Changements politiques et statut des langues: Histoire et épistémologie 1780–1945*. Edited by Marie-Christine-Kok Escalle. Amsterdam: Rodopi, 2001.

Vecchi, Paola. "Immagini della malattia, della morte e dell'aldila nell'opera di Louis-Sebastien Mercier." Pp. 11–19 of *Un viaggio infinito...: Salute, malattia e morte*. Edited by Carmelina Imbroscio. Bologna: CLUEB, 2001.

Versini, Laurent. "Diderot éditeur de soi-meme et des autres." *Travaux de Littérature*, 14 (2001), 299–307.

Versini, Laurent. "Diderot et la verite." Pp. 285–96 of *Vérité et littérature au XVIIIe siècle*. Edited by Paul Aron and others. Paris: Honoré Champion, 2001.

Volpilhac Auger, Catherine. "Du bon usage des corrections: L'Édition posthume de L'Ésprit des lois et les manuscrits de La Brede." *Revue d' Histoire Littéraire de la France*, 101 (2001), 1181–91.

Waeber, Jacqueline. "'Cette horrible innovation': The First Version of the Recitative Parts of Rousseau's 'Le Devin du village.'" *Music and Letters*, 82 (2001), 177–213.

Wagner, Jacques (ed.). *La voix dans la culture et la littérature françaises (1713–1875). Actes du Colloque du Centre de recherches révolutionnaires et romantiques, Université Blaise-Pascal (1997).* (Révolutions et romantismes 2.) Clermont-Ferrand: Presses universitaires Blaise Pascal, 2001. Pp. 416; bibliography.

Walker, Lesley H. "Sweet and Consoling Virtue: The Memoirs of Madame Roland." *Eighteenth-Century Studies*, 34 (2001), 403–19.

Walsh, Thomas, ed. *Readings on Candide.* (Greenhaven Press Literary Companion to World Literature.) San Diego: Greenhaven, 2001. 172 pp.

Weber, Caroline, Howard G. Lay (eds.). *Fragments of Revolution.* (Yale French Studies 101.) New Haven: Yale University Press, 2001. Pp. 230; illustrations.

Weber, Caroline. "Freedom's Missed Moment." *Yale French Studies,* 101 (2001), 9–31.

Whatley, Janet. "Dissoluble Marriage, Paradise Lost: Suzanne Necker's Reflexions sur le divorce." *Dalhousie French Studies,* 56 (2001), 144–53.

Wolfgang, Aurora. "Les Salonnières: Reclaiming the Literary Field." *Intertexts*, 5 (2001), 114–28.

Wolper, Roy S. "Candide the 'Dunce-King': Exploring Evil through a Band of Fools." Pp. 141–50 of *Readings on Candide.* (Greenhaven Press Literary Companion to World Literature.) Edited by Thomas Walsh. San Diego: Greenhaven, 2001.

Yim, Denise. "Madame de Genlis's *Adèle et Théodore*: Its Influence on an English Family's Education." *Australian Journal of French Studies*, 38 (2001), 141–57.

Zecchi, Lina. "La scia pulviscolare di una metafora illuminista." Pp. 55–73 of *Il velo dissolto: Visione e occultamento nella cultura francese e francofona.* Edited by Franca Zanelli Quarantini. Bologna: CLUEB, 2001.

German and Slavic Literatures and Languages

Aleknaviciene, Ona. "Henricho Lyzijaus Laiskas Augustui Hermannui Francke'i." *Archivum Lithuanicum*, 3 (2001), 187–206.

Allan, Sean. *The Stories of Heinrich von Kleist: Fictions of Security*. Rochester: Camden House, 2001. Pp. 243.

Allerkamp, Andrea. "An/Ruf: Quelle, Nahme, Stimme: Zu Friedrich Hölderlins 'Hyperion.'" *Weimarer Beiträge*, 47(2001), 559–575.

Allert, Beate. "Hidden Aspects of Goethe's Writings on Color, Seeing, and Motion and Their Significance for a Feminist Visual Theory." Pp. 144–91 of *Bodies of Resistance: New Phenomenologies of Politics, Agency, and Culture*. Edited by Laura Doyle. Evanston: Northwestern University Press, 2001.

Amelin, Maksim. "Schastliveishii Poet Vremen Ekateriny: Apologiia Vasiliia Petrova." *Voprosy Literatury*, 6 (2001), 243–50.

Ammerlahn, Hellmut. "Der Strukturparallelismus von Wilhelms kreativer, bildender und tätiger Vergangenheitsbewältigung in Goethes Meister-Romanen." *Goethe Yearbook*, 10 (2001), 154–90.

Anderegg, Johannes. *Schreibe mir oft! Zum Medium Brief zwischen 1750 und 1830*. Göttingen: Vandenhoeck und Ruprecht, 2001. Pp. 144.

Anderegg, Johannes. "'...Wenn ich Dir es nicht mittheilen könnte': Zu Goethes Briefen an Charlotte von Stein auf der Reise nach Rom." *Goethe Yearbook*, 10 (2001), 84–98.

Andreeva, Nadezhda. *Nemskata literatura v Bulgariia prez Vuzrazhdaneto. [Deutsche Literatur in Bulgarien zu der nationalen Wiedergeburt]*. [Bulgaria]: Kralitsa Mab, 2001. Pp. 533.

Antoine, Annette. *Literarische Unternehmungen der Spätaufklärung*. Volume I: *Der Verleger Friedrich Nicolai, die 'Straußfedern' und ihre Autoren*. Volume II: *Die Korrespondenz von Johann Gottwerth Müller (1743-1828) und Friedrich Nicolai (1733-1811): Edition und Kommentar*. (Epistemata: Reihe Literaturwissenschaft 365.) Würzburg: Königshausen und Neumann, 2001. Pp. 259; 172.

Aoki, Atsuko. "Die Struktur der doppelten Wiederholung in Schillers 'Fiesco'." *LiLi: Zeitschrift für Literaturwissenschaft und Linguistik*, 31 (2001), 132–39.

Arbetti, Flavia. "Le Attitudes di Lady Hamilton." *Quaderni di Lingue e Letterature*, 26 (2001), 5–19.

Foreign Languages and Literatures

Arburg, Hans Georg von. "Essais de physiognomonie: La Mise en scene critique d'une science precaire dans les ecrits de Georg Christoph Lichtenberg." Pp. 253–80 of *Theories et debats esthetiques au dix huitième siècle: Elements d' une enquete/Debates on Aesthetics in the Eighteenth Century: Questions of Theory and Practice*. Edited by Elisabeth Décultot and Mark Ledbury. Paris: Honoré Champion, 2001.

Arons, Wendy. "From Miss Sara Sampson to Miss Julie: Naturalist Configurations of the Fallen Woman." *Text and Presentation: The Journal of the Comparative Drama Conference*, 22 (2001), 147–57.

Aspalter, Christian M. "Über die Unpässlichkeit des Gelächters: Joseph Felix (von) Kurz-Bernardons 'Prinzessin Pumphia.'" *Modern Austrian Literature*, 34 (2001), 1–20.

Auerochs, Bernd. "Die Unsterblichkeit der Dichtung: Ein Problem der 'Heiligen Poesie' des 18. Jahrhunderts." Pp. 69–87 of *Begründungen und Funktionen des Kanons: Beiträge aus der Literatur und Kunstwissenschaft, Philosophie und Theologie*. Edited by Gerhard R. Kaiser. Heidelberg: Carl Winter Universitätsverlag, 2001.

Avetisian, V. A. "'Gete I Karleil': K Voprosu O Formirovanii Getevskoi Kontseptsii Mirovoi Literatury." *Izvestiia Akademii Nauk, Seriia Literatury i Iazyka*, 60 (2001), 27–37.

Bahr, Ehrhard. "Goethe and the Concept of Bildung in Jewish Emancipation." Pp. 16–28 of *Goethe in German Jewish Culture*. Edited by Klaus L. Berghahn. Rochester: Camden House, 2001.

Bahr, Ehrhard, and Walter K. Stewart. "North American Goethe Dissertations: 1989–99 Supplement." *Goethe Yearbook*, 10 (2001), 263–75.

Baldwin, Claire. "Authority and Interpretation in G. C. Lichtenberg's Commentaries on William Hogarth." Pp. 261–78 of *The Construction of Textual Authority in German Literature of the Medieval and Early Modern Periods*. Edited by James F. Poag. Chapel Hill: University of North Carolina Press, 2001.

Bancaud-Maënen, Florence. "Lichtenberg: l'ironie ou le sourire de l'esprit." Pp. 116–29 of *Lectures d'une oeuvre. Les aphorismes de Lichtenberg*. Edited by Jean Mondot. Paris: Éditions du temps, 2001.

Barbera, Sandro. "Stella e la maga Armida: la funzione del mito e il suo declino in 'Stella.'" *Cultura tedesca,* 17 (2001), 23–47.

Barkemeyer, Karen. "Listening to the Voice of/as the Other: Friedrich Hölderlin and the Deconstruction of the 'German nation.'" *Germanic Review*, 76 (2001), 234–53.

Barkhoff, Jurgen. "Tanz der Körper–Tanz der Sprache: Körper und Text in Friedrich Schillers Gedicht 'Der Tanz.'" *Jahrbuch der Deutschen Schillergesellschaft: Internationales Organ für Neuere Deutsche Literatur*, 45 (2001), 147–63.

Barry, David. "Faustian Pursuits: The Political-Cultural Dimension of Goethe's Weltliteratur and the Tragedy of Translation." *German Quarterly*, 74 (2001), 164–85.

Barton, Karin. "Goethe über alles: Recent books on parallel lives." *Eighteenth-Century Studies*, 34 (2001), 630–37.

Bartsch, Michael. "Was enthält Fausts Phiole?" *Goethe-Jahrbuch*, 118 (2001), 346–50.

Bauer, Joachim, and Gerhard Müller. "Lehr- und Wanderjahre: Goethes Weg durch die Geheimgesellschaften." *Goethe-Jahrbuch*, 118 (2001), 31–45.

Baum, Richard. "Der Genius Italiens: Goethes dritte Reise in den Süden als Wendepunkt im Schaffensprozeß." Pp. 1–55 of *Goethe und Italien*. Edited by Willi Hirdt and Birgit Tappert. Bonn: Bouvier, 2001.

Baumbach, Gerda. "Kreuzerkomödie: '[...] um einen Kreuzer kann man von redenden Marionetten nicht viel fordern.'" *Maske und Kothurn: Internationale Beiträge zur Theaterwissenschaft*, 44 (2001 [1998]), 101–31.

Beetz, Manfred. "Vom 'selbsttätigen Widerstand' des Schönen. Schillers Dramaturgie des Publikums in 'Wallenstein.'" Pp. 205–30 of *"Das Schöne soll sein." Aisthesis in der europäischen Literatur.* Edited by Peter Heßelmann and Michael Huesmann. Göttingen: Aisthesis, 2001.

Beetz, Manfred. "Von der galanten Poesie zur Rokokolyrik. Zur Umorientierung erotischer und anthropologischer Konzepte in der ersten Hälfte des 18. Jahrhunderts." Pp. 33–61 of *Literatur und Kultur des Rokoko*. Edited by Matthias Luserke, Reiner Marx, and Reiner Wild. Göttingen: Vandenhoeck & Ruprecht, 2001.

Behrens, Rudolf. "Schrift und Stimme: Illusionen der Gegenwart und ihre Zerstörung im französischen Briefroman des 18. Jahrhunderts." Pp. 189–206 of *Sinne und Verstand: Ästhetische Modellierungen der Wahrnehmung um 1800*. Edited by Caroline Welsh, Christina Dongowski, and Susanna Lulé. Würzburg: Königshausen & Neumann, 2001.

Behrens, Rudolf. "Um 1700: Galanterie als Konfiguration von Préciosité, Libertinage und Pornographie (am Beispiel der Lettres portugaises)." Pp. 275–305 of *Der galante Diskurs: Kommunikationsideal und Epochenschwelle*. Edited by Thomas Borgstedt and Andreas Solbach. Dresden: Thelem, 2001.

Bemofsky, Susan. "Hölderlin as Translator: The Perils of Interpretation." *Germanic Review*, 76 (2001), 215–33.

Bennett, Benjamin. *Goethe as Woman: The Undoing of Literature*. (Kritik: German Literary Theory and Cultural Studies.) Detroit: Wayne State University Press, 2001. Pp. 320.

Benrath, Gustav Adolf. "Die Freundschaft zwischen Goethe und Jung-Stilling." Pp. 157–70 of *Goethe und der Pietismus*. Edited by Hans-Georg Kemper. Tübingen: Max Niemeyer Verlag, 2001.

Bergengruen, Maximilian. "L'Esthetique de l'illusion: Sur le rapport entre le gout, la morale et la signification dans la 'Critique de la faculte de juger.'" *Revue Germanique Internationale*, 16 (2001), 147–63, 95–96.

Berghahn, Klaus L. "Ein klassischer Chiasmus: Goethe und die Juden, die Juden und Goethe." *Goethe Yearbook*, 10 (2001), 203–21.

Berghahn, Klaus L., and Jost Hermand (eds.). *Goethe in German-Jewish Culture*. (Studies in German Literature Linguistics and Culture.) Rochester: Camden House, 2001. Pp. xiii + 190.

Berghahn, Klaus L., and Sara B. Young. "Patterns of Childhood: Goethe and the Jews." Pp. 3–15 of *Goethe in German Jewish Culture*. Edited by Klaus L. Berghahn. Rochester: Camden House, 2001.

Berkovskii, Naum Iakovlevich. *Romantizm v Germanii*. Sankt Peterburg: Azbuka-klassika, 2001.

Berkowitz, Joel, and Jeremy Dauber. "Translating Yiddish Dramas of the Jewish Enlightenment." *Metamorphoses: Journal of the Five College Seminar on Literary Translation*, 9 (2001), 90–112.

Bersier, Gabrielle. "Goethe's Geology in Flux: Vulcanism and Neptunism in the Translation of Richard Payne Knight's 'Expedition into Sicily' and the 'Italian Journey.'" Pp. 35–45 of *Goethe, Chaos, and Complexity*. Edited by Herbert Rowland. Amsterdam: Rodopi, 2001.

Bilstein, Johannes. "Engel oder: Nachbarn in unseren Augen." *Neue Sammlung: Vierteljahres-Zeitschrift für Erziehung und Gesellschaft*, 41 (2001), 637–49.

Birus, Hendrik. "Goethes Italienische Reise als Einspruch gegen die Romantik." Pp. 116–34 of *Europäische Begegnungen—Die Faszination des Südens. Acta Ising 2000*. Edited by Stefan Krimm and Ursula Triller. München: Bayerischer Schulbuchverlag 2001.

Bishop, Paul (ed.). *A Companion to Goethe's 'Faust': Parts I and II*. (Studies in German Literature Linguistics and Culture.) Rochester: Camden House, 2001. Pp. 319; bibliography.

Blamberger, Günter, Sabine Doering, and Klaus Müller-Salget (eds.). *Kleist-Jahrbuch 2001*. Stuttgart: Metzler 2001. Pp. Viii + 336.

Blinn, Hansjürgen. "Shakespeare im Rokoko: 'Natur und Grazie' in Wielands Shakespeare-Übersetzung." Pp. 147–66 of *Literatur und Kultur des Rokoko*. Edited by Matthias Luserke, Reiner Marx, and Reiner Wild. Göttingen: Vandenhoeck & Ruprecht, 2001.

Blödom, Andreas. "Vom Deutschen zum Dänen: Der Literat Christian Levin Sander in Kopenhagen um 1800." Pp. 77–94 of *Dänisch-deutsche Doppelgänger: Transnationale und bikulturelle Literatur zwischen Barock und Moderne*. Edited by Heinrich Detering, Anne-Bitt Gerecke, and Johan de Mylius. Göttingen: Wallstein, 2001.

Bluhm, Lothar, and Achim Hölter (eds.). *"Daß gepfleget werde der feste Buchstab." Festschrift für Heinz Rölleke zum 65. Geburtstag*. Trier: Wissenschaftlicher Verlag, 2001. Pp. xi+ 559.

Bluhm, Lothar. "'Du kommst mir vor wie Saul, der Sohn Kis' ... Wilhelm Meisters Lehrjahre zwischen 'Heilung' und 'Zerstörung'." Pp. 122–40 of *"daß gepfleget werde der feste Buchstab." Festschrift für Heinz Rölleke zum 65. Geburtstag*. Edited by Lothar Bluhm and Achim Hölter. Trier: Wissenschaftlicher Verlag, 2001.

Bluhm, Lothar. "Goethes 'incalculable Productionen.' Zur Kontextualität von Wilhelm Meisters Lehrjahren und den Unterhaltungen deutscher Ausgewanderten." Pp. 35–50 of *Der europäische Roman zwischen Aufklärung und Postmoderne. Festschrift zum 65. Geburtstag von Jürgen C. Jacobs*. Edited by Friedhelm Marx and Andreas Meier. Weimar: VDG, 2001.

Boa, Elizabeth. "Die Geschichte der O oder die (Ohn-) Macht der Frauen: 'Die Wahlverwandtschaften' im Kontext des Geschlechterdiskurses um 1800." *Goethe-Jahrbuch*, 118 (2001), 217–33.

Boening, Thomas. *Alterität und Identität in literarischen Texten von Rousseau und Goethe bis Celan und Handke.* Freiburg: Rombach, 2001. Pp. 368.

Böhm, Arnd. "Epic and the History of Faust." *Modern Language Studies*, 31 (2001), 79–97.

Böhm, Arnd. "Margarete's Innocence and the Guilt of Faust." *Deutsche Vierteljahrsschrift für Literaturwissenschaft und Geistesgeschichte*, 75 (2001), 216–50.

Böhm, Arnd. "Typology and History in the 'Rattenlied' (Faust I)." *Goethe Yearbook*, 10 (2001), 65–83.

Bollacher, Martin. "Aufklärungspositionen des jungen Goethe." *Goethe-Jahrbuch*, 118 (2001), 158–70.

Bollacher, Martin. "Goethes Konzeption der Weltliteratur." Pp. 169–85 of *Ironische Propheten: Sprachbewußtsein und Humanität in der Literatur von Herder bis Heine.* Edited by Markus Heilmann and Birgit Wägenbaur. Tübingen: Narr, 2001.

Bonacchi, Silvia. "Ewald Christian von Kleist und J. M. R. Lenz im Kontext der Rokokolyrik." Pp. 177–95 of *Literatur und Kultur des Rokoko.* Edited by Matthias Luserke, Reiner Marx, and Reiner Wild. Göttingen: Vandenhoeck & Ruprecht, 2001.

Bonifazio, Massimo. "'Rappresentazioni compiutamente simboliche': La 'mise en abyme' nell'opera di Novalis." *Strumenti Critici: Rivista Quadrimestrale di Cultura e Critica Letteraria*, 16 (2001), 441–55.

Böning, Holger. "Pressewesen und Aufklärung—Intelligenzblätter und Volksaufklärer;" Pp. 69–119 of *Pressewesen der Aufklärung: Periodische Schriften im Alten Reich.* Edited by Sabine Doering-Manteuffel, Josef Mancal, and Wolfgang Wüst. (Colloquia Augustana 15.) Berlin: Akademie-Verlag, 2001.

Borchert, Angela. "Goethe's Eulogy for Duchess Anna Amalia: Re-Membering Classicism." *Modern Language Studies*, 31 (2001), 59–77.

Borges, Jorge Luis. "La literatura alemana en la epoca de Bach." *Letras Libres*, 3 (2001), 25–28.

Borgestedt, Thomas, and Andreas Solbach (eds.). *Der galante Diskurs: Kommunikationsideal und Epochenschwelle.* (Arbeiten zur Neueren deutschen Literatur 6.) Dresden: Thelem, 2001. Pp. 368; illustrations.

The period around 1700 brought forth a considerable production of German "gallant" novels and poems. Musicologists have come to terms with an eighteenth-century "gallant" style in music. Christian Thomasius and his followers propagated the fashion of "gallant" conduct. The concept of a "gallant period" has, however, remained questionable even among specialists of the German literature where it originated—most of all since the production to be analyzed under the term is no longer read. The period itself seems to have been one of transition, if not one out of touch with all the European developments around 1700. Most experts of German literature prefer to focus on the two neighboring periods: The baroque, so the general notion, suffered a trivialization after the 1680s, while the enlightenment, beginning with philosophical debates at the very same time did not reach the literary genres before the 1730s.

Andreas Solbach's and Thomas Borgsted's volume of eighteen contributions on the gallant period—an English version of the title could be *The Gallant Discourse: Ideal of Communication and Threshold Between the Epochs*—is in this situation a courageous attempt to revitalize research necessary to cover nearly half a century. The gallant fashion came from France—to some extent as an answer to the discourse of the "*préciosité*" (articles by Helga Meise, Emanuel Peter, and Jörn Steigerwald). It arrived in Germany forty years later as a competitive behavior to be adopted by every man planning his career, claims the article by Andreas Solbach. Even Poland was affected by the ideal, though without developing a comparable vernacular literature, claim Miroslawa Czarnecka and Jolanta Szafarz.

The gallant movement disrupted traditions of the German Baroque. It promoted a lighter and more licentious poetry, as Thomas Borgstedt, Ferdinand van Ingen, Knut Kiesant, and Peter Rusterholz explicate in their articles. Dirk Niefanger concludes in his analysis that it was on the other hand the very fashion which ultimately provoked the advocates of the Enlightenment to call for an improved national literature. The musicologist remains somewhat outside of this discussion as the periodization he deals with is different.

The articles selected give a fragmented view, in line with established notions: The gallant fashion was adopted by Germany's young generation at a time when the Enlightenment—to be imported from England—was already waiting. Most contributors imply that the gallant period served—at least with the necessary turbulence if not with the disaster—out of which the new period could emerge. The volume does, however, not deal with "gallant" novels written after the 1690s. A few early eighteenth-century poems find interpretations—mainly under the question of how Baroque aesthetics were treated after 1700. The problematic production remains effectively outside the picture and so does the rest of Europe. The gallant "conduite" flourished in Germany around 1700 not as an antiquated mode of conduct but as the very style needed to communicate with the Western neighbors. None of the articles mention the wars which had moved the German Empire into the center of Europe after the events of 1688/89. The volume does not explain how "baroque" music could sell in Venice, Vienna, and Dresden as much as in London at the time, how Bohemian musicians could survive in London, or a painter such as Kneller from Lübeck, or a theater manager such as the Swiss Count Heidegger, or a composer such as Handel, or a King such as George I. German intellectuals toured through Europe without noting the epochal divergence, and Dutch newspapers and international books published in the Netherlands in French editions were read all over Europe at the very same time. We seem to need a concept of a European period, and the fashion of French "gallant" behavior could be an integral part of this concept, yet the present volume hardly goes into this direction. Rather, it discusses the late seventeenth- and early eighteenth-century as something particularly German in order to strengthen a view of Germany's belated development which was misleading when first formulated by Gottsched and his followers in the middle of the eighteenth century.

The bigger problem remains of how the present discourse of German scholarship will fit into the framework of modern international research. Dirk Niefanger's contribution offers an effective way out of the dilemma: we might reconsider the concept of the gallant period and differentiate between a concept fashionable around 1700 and a concept established by Gottsched and his followers after 1730 in an attempt to stigmatize the preceding period. With a group of colleagues Niefanger has already announced a new volume of research on the period for October 2004. The title *Kulturelle Orientierung um 1700: Traditionen, Programme, konzeptionelle Vielfalt* to be published with Max Niemeyer Verlag promises the more open perspective on the period.—Olaf Simons

Bosse, Heinrich. "Klopstocks 'Kriegslied' (1749): Militärische Poesiepolitik im 18. Jahrhundert." *Jahrbuch des Freien Deutschen Hochstifts*, (2001), 41–99.

Brandes, Peter. "Goethes Na(H)Me." *Weimarer Beiträge: Zeitschrift für Literaturwissenschaft, Ästhetik und Kulturwissenschaften*, 47 (2001), 540–58.

Braun, Werner. "Plundersweiler und die musikalischen Jahrmärkte." Pp. 115–33 of *Goethe: Ungewohnte Ansichten*. Edited by Karl Richter. St. Ingbert: Röhrig, 2001.

Braungart, Wolfgang. "'Und was du hast, ist/Athem zu holen.' Hölderlins hymnisches Fragment 'Der Adler'." *Hölderlin-Jahrbuch*, 32 (2000–2001), 246–62.

Breuer, Ingo: "Schauplätze jämmerlicher Mordgeschichte: Tradition der Novelle und Theatralität der Historia bei Heinrich von Kleist." *Kleist-Jahrbuch*, (2001), 196-225.

Brinkmann, Reinhold. "Kennst Du Das Buch? Oder: Die Vertreibung der Musiknoten aus 'Wilhelm Meisters Lehrjahren.'" *Goethe-Jahrbuch*, 118 (2001), 289–303.

Brown, Hilary. "Sarah Scott, Sophie Von La Roche, and the Female Utopian Tradition." *Journal of English and Germanic Philology*, 100 (2001), 469–81.

Brown, Jane K. "Der Drang zum Gesang: On Goethe's Dramatic Form." *Goethe Yearbook*, 10 (2001), 115–24.

Brown, Jane K. "When Is Conservative Modern? Or, Why Bother with Goethe?" *Modern Language Studies*, 31 (2001), 35–43.

Buchheit, Vinzenz. "Sendungsbewusstsein beim frühen Herder." *Euphorion: Zeitschrift für Literaturgeschichte*, 95 (2001), 1–15.

Busch, Werner. "Die Rolle der englischen Kunst für Goethes Kunstbegriff." *Goethe-Jahrbuch*, 118 (2001), 187–201.

Butler, Michael. "Goethe and Switzerland." *Publications of the English Goethe Society*, 70 (2001), 16–28.

Calhoon, Kenneth S. "The Gothic Imaginary: Goethe in Strasbourg." *Deutsche Vierteljahrsschrift für Literaturwissenschaft und Geistesgeschichte*, 75 (2001), 5–14.

Cho, Woo-Ho. "Kultur-Topographie und Kulturkonzepte in Wielands Romanen." *Deutschlandforschung*, 10 (2001), 163–86.

Choi, Yeun-Soo. *Frauenbild und Familienstruktur in Lessings Dramen*. Femwald: Litblockin, 2001. Pp. 220.

Cloot, Julia. *Geheime Texte: Jean Paul und die Musik*. Berlin: De Gruyter, 2001. Pp. ix + 346.

Cooper, Barry. "Beethoven's 'Abendlied' and the 'Wiener Zeitschrift'." *Music and Letters*, 82 (2001), 234–50.

Crisman, William. "Which Galatea? Complicating While Clarifying Wackenroder's Key Passage." *Germanic Notes and Reviews*, 32 (2001), 148–53.

Crotti, Ilaria, Piermario Vescovo, and Ricciarda Ricorda. *Il mondo vivo: Aspetti del romanzo, del teatro e del giornalismo nel Settecento italiano*. (Ricerche/Facoltà di lettere e filosofia dell'Università di Venezia 17.) Pavova: Il Poligrafo, 2001. Pp. 235.

Cullhed, Anna. "Nio greker, en herdinna och Goethe: om lyrikens kanon 1746-1806. [Nine Greeks, a shepherdess, and Goethe]." *TFL: Tidskrift för litteraturvetenskap*, 3 (2001), 3–15.

Curran, Jane V. "Goethe and Schubert: Songs and Settings." *Germanic Notes and Reviews*, 32 (2001), 159–63.

Czarnecka, Miroslawa. "Elzbieta Druzbacka (1698/9–1765)—die sarmatische Sappho." Pp. 41–52 of *Der galante Diskurs: Kommunikationsideal und Epochenschwelle*. Edited by Thomas Borgstedt and Andreas Solbach. Dresden: Thelem, 2001.

Czubaty, Jaroslaw. "Progress and Violence in Political Reality: The Case of Political Imagination of the Elite of the Russian Empire at the Turn of the Eighteenth Century." Pp. 53–70 of *Progres et violence au XVIIIe siècle*. Edited by Valerie Cossy and Deidre Dawson. Paris: Honoré Champion, 2001.

Daiber, Jürgen. *Experimentalphysik des Geistes: Novalis und das romantische Experiment*. Göttingen: Vandenhoeck & Ruprecht, 2001. Pp. 336.

Dambacher, Eva. "Schiller-Bibliographie: 2000 und Nachträge." *Jahrbuch der Deutschen Schillergesellschaft: Internationales Organ für Neuere Deutsche Literatur*, 45 (2001), 433–88.

Dangel Pelloquin, Elsbeth. "'You Kiss by Th' Book': Plädoyer für eine literarische Osculologie." *Jahrbuch der Deutschen Schillergesellschaft: Internationales Organ für Neuere Deutsche Literatur*, 45 (2001), 359–79.

Daniel, Thilo. "Johann Michael von Loens Auseinandersetzung mit Nikolaus Ludwig von Zinzendorf und der Brüdergemeine." Pp. 25–43 of *Goethe und der Pietismus*. Edited by Hans-Georg Kemper. Tübingen: Max Niemeyer Verlag, 2001.

Danilevskii, R. Iu. "Russkaia Literaturnaia Mysl' I Nasledie G. E. Lessinga." *Russkaia Literatura: Istoriko Literaturnyi Zhurnal*, 4 (2001), 90–108.

Davies, Mererid Puw. *The Tale of Bluebeard in German Literature: From the Eighteenth Century to the Present*. (Oxford Modern Languages and Literature Monographs.) Oxford: Clarendon Press, 2001. Pp. xiii + 279.

Davies, Steffan. "Goethe, Theatre and Politics: Götz von Berlichingen from 1771 to 1804." *Publications of the English Goethe Society*, 70 (2001), 29–45.

Dawson, Ruth P. *The Contested Quill: Literature by Women in Germany, 1770–1800*. Newark: University of Delaware Press, 2001. Pp. 415.

De Michelis, Cesare G. "Il Viaggio Sentimentale: Appunti E Motivi; Atti Del Convegno Internazionale, Imperia, 5–6 Ottobre 2000." Pp. 91–97 of *Da Ulisse a Ulisse (Il Viaggio Come Mito Letterario)*. Edited by Giorgetta Revelli. Pisa: Istituti Editoriali e Poligrafici Internazionali, 2001.

Destro, Alberto, and Charles Hindley. "The Guilty Hero, Or: The Tragic Salvation of Faust." Pp. 56–75 of *A Companion to Goethe's Faust: Parts I and II*. Edited by Paul Bishop. Rochester: Camden House, 2001.

Di Benedetto, Arnaldo. "Interesse di Goethe per Alfieri." Pp. 69–75 of *Goethe und Italien*. Edited by Willi Hirdt and Birgit Tappert. Bonn: Bouvier, 2001.

Dickinson, Sara. "The Russian Tour of Europe before Fonvizin: Travel Writing as Literary Endeavor in Eighteenth-Century Russia." *Slavic and East European Journal*, 45 (2001), 1–29.

Diederichsen, Uwe. "Goethes Wahlverwandtschaften–Auch ein juristischer Roman?" *Goethe-Jahrbuch*, 118 (2001), 142–57.

Dohm, Burkhard. "Radikalpietistin und 'Schöne Seele': Susanna Katharina von Klettenberg." Pp. 111–33 of *Goethe und der Pietismus*. Edited by Hans-Georg Kemper. Tübingen: Max Niemeyer Verlag, 2001.

Doyle, Laura (ed.). *Bodies of Resistance: New Phenomenologies of Politics, Agency, and Culture*. Evanston: Northwestern University Press, 2001. Pp. xxxiv + 305.

Drochmalnik, Daniel. "Mendelsohns Begriff 'Zeremonialgesetz' und der europäische Antizeremonialismus: Eine begriffliche Untersuchung." Pp. 128–60 of *Recht und Sprache in der Deutschen Aufklärung*. Edited by Ulrich Kronauer. Tübingen: Max Niemeyer Verlag, 2001.

Drotvinas, Vincentas. "Friedricho Wilhelmo Haacko laiskas Gotthilfui Augustui Franckei." *Acta Linguistica Lithuanica/Lietuviu Kalbotyros Klausimai*, 45 (2001), 179–86.

Durrani, Osman. "The Character and Qualities of Mephistopheles." Pp. 76–94 of *A Companion to Goethe's Faust: Parts I and II*. Edited by Paul Bishop. Rochester: Camden House, 2001.

Dye, Ellis. "Figurations of the Feminine in Goethe's Faust." Pp. 95–121 of *A Companion to Goethe's Faust: Parts I and II*. Edited by Paul Bishop. Rochester: Camden House, 2001.

Ecker, Eva. "Die deutschen Übersetzungen und Bearbeitungen von Marivaux' Liebeslustspielen im 18. Jahrhundert." *Maske und Kothurn: Internationale Beiträge zur Theaterwissenschaft*, 46 (2001), 167–93.

Egger, Irmgard. *Diätetik und Askese: Zur Dialektik der Aufklärung in Goethes Romanen*. München: Fink, 2001. Pp. 284.

Egger, Irmgard. "Eikones: Zur Inszenierung der Bilder in Goethes Romanen." *Goethe-Jahrbuch*, 118 (2001), 260–73.

Egger, Irmgard. "'Verbinden mehr als trennen': Goethe und die plastische Anatomie." *Germanisch-Romanische Monatsschrift*, 51 (2001), 45–53.

Ehrich-Haefeli, Verena. "Die Syntax des Begehrens: Zum Sprachwandel am Beginn der bürgerlichen Moderne: Sophie La Roche: Geschichte des Fräuleins von Sternheim, Goethe: Die Leiden des jungen Werther." Pp. 139–69 of *Sprachkontakt Sprachvergleich Sprachvariation; Festschrift für Gottfried Kolde zum 65. Geburtstag*. Edited by Kirsten Adamzik. Tübingen: Max Niemeyer Verlag, 2001.

Eibl, Karl, and Bernd Scheffer (eds.). *Goethes Kritiker.* Paderborn: Mentis, 2001. Pp. 208.

Endres, Johannes. "Inzest und Tabu als Modelle literarischer Epochenerfahrung." *Deutsche Vierteljahrsschrift für Literaturwissenschaft und Geistesgeschichte*, 75 (2001), 446–62.

Erlin, Matt. "Urban Experience, Aesthetic Experience, and Enlightenment in G. E. Lessing's *Minna von Barnhelm*." *Monatshefte für Deutschsprachige Literatur und Kultur*, 93 (2001), 20–35.

Esaka, Tetsuya. "Zur Entstehungsgeschichte von Schillers Dom Karlos." *Jahrbuch der Deutschen Schillergesellschaft: Internationales Organ für Neuere Deutsche Literatur*, 45 (2001), 131–46.

Esleben, Jorg. "Georg Forster's Dialectic of Imperialist Desire." *Seminar: A Journal of Germanic Studies*, 37 (2001), 305–22.

Esterhammer, Angela. "Locationary Acts: Blake's Jerusalem and Hölderlin's Patmos." Pp. 178–90 of *Placing and Displacing Romanticism*. Edited by Peter J. Kitson. Aldershot: Ashgate, 2001.

Fechner, Jörg Ulrich. "Ein wiedergefundener Brief von Lenz aus Weimar 1776 an Friedrich Leopold Graf Stolberg." Pp. 23–36 of *Jakob Michael Reinhold Lenz: Vom Sturm und Drang zur Moderne*. Edited by Andreas Meier. Heidelberg: Carl Winter Universitätsverlag, 2001.

Fiedler, Sabine. "'Bela Dam,' Cu Al Vi Placus, Se Akompanon Mi Kuragus? Zur Übersetzung von Goethes Faust ins Esperanto." *Interlinguistische Informationen*, Supplement 6 (2001), 128–45.

Fink, Karl J. "Goethe's Intensified Border." Pp. 93–104 of *Goethe, Chaos, and Complexity*. Edited by Herbert Rowland. Amsterdam: Rodopi, 2001.

Fischer, Bernd. "Fremdbestimmung und Identitätspolitik in 'Die Hermannsschlacht'." Pp. 165–78 of *Kleists Erzählungen und Dramen: Neue Studien*. Edited by Paul Michael Lützeler and David Pan. Würzburg: Königshausen & Neumann, 2001.

Fischer-Lichte, Erika. "Mißlingende Inkorporation?: Zur rituellen Struktur des 'Prinz Friedrich von Homburg.'" Pp. 151–64 of *Kleists Erzählungen und Dramen: Neue Studien*. Edited by Paul Michael Lützeler and David Pan. Würzburg: Königshausen & Neumann, 2001.

Foi, Maria Carolina. "Schillers Wilhelm Tell: Menschenrechte, Menschenwürde und die Würde der Frauen." *Jahrbuch der Deutschen Schillergesellschaft: Internationales Organ für Neuere Deutsche Literatur*, 45 (2001), 193–223.

Foley, Stephen Merriam. "Remembering Goethe: Essays for the 250th Anniversary." *Modern Language Studies*, 31 (2001), 5–164.

Forster, Eckart. "Goethe and the 'Auge des Geistes.'" *Deutsche Vierteljahrsschrift für Literaturwissenschaft und Geistesgeschichte*, 75 (2001), 87–101.

Freschi, Marino. "Il Cagliostro di Goethe." *Cultura tedesca*, 17 (2001), 73–88.

Fricke, Harald. "Literaturtheorie und gelbe Zettel: Zur Neuedition von Goethes Spruchprosa." Pp. 55–70 of *Goethe-Philologie im Jubiläumsjahr: Bilanz und Perspektiven*. Edited by Jochen Golz. Tübingen: Max Niemeyer Verlag, 2001.

Friedrich, Hans-Edwin. "'Ewig lieben,' zugleich aber 'menschlich lieben'?: Zur Reflexion der empfindsamen Liebeskonzeption von Gellert und Klopstock bis Goethe und Jacobi." *Aufklärung*, 13 (2001), 148–89.

Friedrich, Hans Edwin. "Nützliche oder grausame Natur? Naturkonstruktion in der spätaufklärerischen Robinsonade (Campe, Wezel)." Pp. 289–308 of *Erschriebene Natur: Internationale Perspektiven auf Texte des 18. Jahrhunderts*. Edited by Michael Scheffel. Bern: Peter Lang, 2001.

Friedrich, Heinz. "Vom Nutzen und Nachteil der Aufklärung für das Leben." *Goethe-Jahrbuch*, 118 (2001), 22–30.

Fuhrmann, Helmut. *Zur poetischen und philosophischen Anthropologie Schillers: Vier Versuche*. Würzburg: Königshausen und Neumann, 2001. Pp. 196.

Garber, Jörn. "Begriff, Hypothese, Faktum: Christoph Martin Wielands kulturalistische Kritik am Natur- und Staatsrecht." Pp. 205–29 of *Recht und Sprache in der deutschen Aufklärung*. Edited by Ulrich Kronauer. Tübingen: Max Niemeyer Verlag, 2001.

Gardt, Andreas. "Das rationalistische Konzept der Fachsprache: Gottfried Wilhelm Leibniz." Pp. 37–52 of *Recht und Sprache in der deutschen Aufklärung*. Edited by Ulrich Kronauer. Tübingen: Max Niemeyer Verlag, 2001.

Gaskill, Howard. "'Aus der dritten Hand': Herder and His Annotators." *German Life and Letters*, 54 (2001), 210–18.

Gaskill, Howard. "Tieck's Juvenilia: Ossianic Attributions." *Modern Language Review*, 96 (2001), 747–61.

Gephart, Werner. "Goethe als 'Gesellschaftsforscher'? Eine soziologische Lektüre der 'Italienischen Reise.'" Pp. 105–124 of *Goethe und Italien*. Edited by Willi Hirdt and Birgit Tappert. Bonn: Bouvier, 2001.

Gerhard, Anselm. "Goethes 'Herrliche Dichtungen' und Schuberts 'Grosse Freiheit': Ein Spannungsverhältnis—Einmal anders betrachtet." *Goethe-Jahrbuch*, 118 (2001), 304–14.

Gibbons, James. "J. M. R. Lenz's Der Landprediger: An Adaptation of the Vicar of Wakefield 'Tradition'?" *Colloquia Germanica: Internationale Zeitschrift für Germanistik*, 34 (2001), 213–36.

Gibbons, James. "Laying the Moral Foundations: Writer, Religion and Late Eighteenth-century Society—The Case of J. M. R. Lenz." *German Life and Letters* 54 (2001), 137–54.

Gibbons, James. "Politics and the Playwright: J. M. R. Lenz and *Die Soldaten*." *Modern Language Review*, 96 (2001), 732–46.

Glaser, Horst-Albert, and György M. Vajda (eds.). *Die Wende von der Aufklärung zur Romantik 1760–1820: Epoche im Überblick*. (Comparative History of Literatures in European Languages/Histoire Comparee des Litteratures de Langues Europeennes 14.) Amsterdam: Benjamins, 2001. Pp. 760.

Goethe, Johann Wolfgang, and Johann Gottlob von Quandt. *Von den herrlichsten Kunstwerken umgeben ... : Der Briefwechsel zwischen Johann Wolfgang von Goethe und Johann Gottlob von Quandt*. Edited by Walter Schmitz. Dresden: Thelem, 2001. Pp. lxxi + 369; illustrations.

Golz, Jochen, ed. *Goethe-Philologie im Jubiläumsjahr: Bilanz und Perspektiven; Kolloquium der Stiftung Weimarer Klassik und der Arbeitsgemeinschaft für Germanistische Edition, 26. Bis 27. August 1999*. (Beihefte zu Editio 16.) Tübingen: Max Niemeyer Verlag, 2001. Pp. vi + 194; illustration.

Goodman, Katherine R. "Of Gifts, Gallantries, and Horace: Luise Kulmus (Gottsched) in Her Early Letters." *Women in German Yearbook: Feminist Studies in German Literature and Culture*, 17 (2001), 77–102.

Görisch, Reinhard. *Jahresschriften der Claudiusgesellschaft*. Hamburg: Otto Heinevetter, 2001. Pp. 65; bibliography.

Götze, Karl Heinz. "Macht—Vernunft—Liebe: Zu Lichtenbergs Liebessemantik." Pp. 95–115 of *Lectures d'une oeuvre. Les aphorismes de Lichtenberg*. Edited by Jean Mondot. Paris: Éditions du temps, 2001.

Götze, Martin. *Ironie und absolute Darstellung: Philosophie und Poetik in der Frühromantik*. Paderborn: Schöningh, 2001. Pp. 409.

Grage, Joachim, and Michael Scheffel. "Anfänge deutscher und skandinavischer Naturpoesie oder Die Ausdifferenzierung europäischer Nationalliteraturen im Zeichen des Irdischen Vergnügens in Gott." Pp. 25–71 of *Erschriebene Natur: Internationale Perspektiven auf Texte des 18. Jahrhunderts*. Edited by Michael Scheffel. Frankfurt: Peter Lang, 2001.

Grair, Charles A. "Seducing Helena: The Court Fantasy of Faust II, Act III." *Goethe Yearbook*, 10 (2001), 99–114.

Gratzke, Michael. "'Wer kann mit Blut und Feu'r die Worte färben?' Natur, Gewalt und die Erfindung von Männlichkeit bei Ewald von Kleist." *Beiträge zur Kleist-Forschung* (2001), 163-211.

Greiner, Bernhard. "'Die große Lücke in unserer dermaligen Literatur auszufüllen': Die unausführbare Tragödie 'Robert Guiskard'." Pp. 135–49 of *Kleists Erzählungen und Dramen: Neue Studien*. Edited by Paul Michael Lützeler and David Pan. Würzburg: Königshausen & Neumann, 2001

Grimm, Sieglinde. "Fichtes Gedanke der Wechselwirkung in Hölderlins Empedokles-Tragödie." *Poetica*, 33 (2001), 191-214.

Grosche, Stefan. *"Zarten Seelen ist gar viel gegönnt": Naturwissenschaft und Kunst im Briefwechsel zwischen C. G. Carus und Goethe*. Göttingen: Wallstein, 2001. Pp. 308; illustration.

Gsteiger, Manfred. "Vom 'edlen Wilden' zum 'homme naturel.'" Pp. 649–61 of *Die Wende von der Aufklärung zur Romantik 1760–1820: Epoche im Überblick*. Edited by Horst-Albert Glaser. Amsterdam: Benjamins, 2001.

Gutjahr, Ortrud, and Harro Segeberg (eds.). *Klassik und Anti-Klassik: Goethe und seine Epoche*. Würzburg: Königshausen & Neumann, 2001. Pp. 310.

Gutjahr, Ortrud. "Charlotte von Steins 'Dido'— eine Anti-Iphigenie?" Pp. 219–46 of *Klassik und Anti-Klassik: Goethe und seine Epoche*. Edited by Ortrud Gutjahr and Harro Segeberg. Würzburg: Königshausen & Neumann, 2001.

Guthke, Karl S. *Goethes Weimar und "Die große Öffnung in die weite Welt."* Wiesbaden: Harrassowitz, 2001. Pp. 202; illustrations.

Foreign Languages and Literatures

Gulke, Peter. "Verschwiegene Humanität: Mozarts Entführung und Goethes Iphigenie." *Goethe-Jahrbuch*, 118 (2001), 171–75.

Haase, Fee Alexandra. "Vom Brief zum Buch: Zur Gattung Brief in Christoph Martin Wielands Rezeption antiker Schriften im Zusammenhang mit der Literatur der Neuzeit." *Studia Theodisca*, 8 (2001), 117–33.

Habrich, Christa. "Alchemie und Chemie in der pietistischen Tradition." Pp. 45–77 of *Goethe und der Pietismus*. Edited by Hans-Georg Kemper. Tübingen: Max Niemeyer Verlag, 2001.

Hafner, Ralph. "Das Erkenntnisproblem in der Philologie um 1700: Zum Verhältnis von Polymathie und Aporetik bei Jacob Friedrich Reimmann, Christian Thomasius und Johann Albert Fabricius." Pp. 95–128 of *Philologie und Erkenntnis: Beiträge zu Begriff und Problem Frühneuzeitlicher Philologie*. Edited by Ralph Hafner. Tübingen: Max Niemeyer Verlag, 2001.

Hafner, Ralph. "Philologische Festkultur in Hamburg im ersten Drittel des 18. Jahrhunderts: Fabricius, Brockes, Telemann." Pp. 349–78 of *Philologie und Erkenntnis: Beiträge zu Begriff und Problem frühneuzeitlicher Philologie*. Edited by Ralph Hafner. Tübingen: Max Niemeyer Verlag, 2001.

Hahn, Barbara. "Augen. Blicke. Augenblicke: Metaphern des Sehens zwischen Charlotte von Stein und Goethe." *Deutsche Vierteljahrsschrift für Literaturwissenschaft und Geistesgeschichte*, 75 (2001), 60–70.

Hahn, Barbara, and Heidi Swanson. "Demarcations and Projections: Goethe in the Berlin Salons." Pp. 31–43 of *Goethe in German Jewish Culture*. Edited by Klaus L. Berghahn. Rochester: Camden House, 2001.

Hahn, Karl-Heinz: *"Dann ist Vergangenheit beständig ...": Goethe-Studien*. (Schriften der Goethe-Gesellschaft 68.) Weimar: Böhlau, 2001. Pp. 215; illustrations.

Hamilton, John T. "Thunder from a Clear Sky: On Lessing's Redemption of Horace." *Modern Language Quarterly*, 62 (2001), 203–18.

Hamlin, Cyrus. "Goethe's Faust and the Philosophers." Pp. 221–42 of *A Companion to Goethe's Faust: Parts I and II*. Edited by Paul Bishop. Rochester: Camden House, 2001.

Hammer, Stephanie. *Schiller's Wound: The Theater of Trauma from Crisis to Commodity*. (Kritik: German Literary Theory and Cultural Studies.) Detroit: Wayne State University Press, 2001. Pp. 192; bibliography, index.

Häntzschel, Günter. "'Überschriften' und 'Kapitel': Die 'Welt' der Venetianischen Epigramme Goethes." *Lichtenberg-Jahrbuch*, 12 (2000 [2001]), 127–44.

Hart, Gail K. "Doing Time in Schiller's Eighteenth Century: C. F. D. Schubart as Political Prisoner, or the Man in the Hole." *Pacific Coast Philology*, 36 (2001), 1–9.

Hass-Zumkehr, Ulrike. "Spiegelungen der Rechtssprache in der Lexikographie." Pp. 53–71 of *Recht und Sprache in der deutschen Aufklärung*. Edited by Ulrich Kronauer. Tübingen: Max Niemeyer Verlag, 2001.

Haug, Christine. "'Schlimme Bücher, so im Verborgenen herumgehn, thun mehr schaden, als die im öffentlichen Laden ligen...': Literarische Konspiration und Geheimliteratur in Deutschland zur Zeit der Aufklärung." *Leipziger Jahrbuch zur Buchgeschichte*, 11 (2001), 11–63.

Heilmann, Markus, and Birgit Wägenbaur (eds.). *Ironische Propheten: Sprachbewusstsein und Humanität in der Literatur von Herder bis Heine; Studien für Jürgen Brummack zum 65. Geburtstag.* Tübingen: Narr, 2001. Pp. 295; illustrations.

Hein, Karsten. *Ottilie von Goethe (1796-1872): Biographie und literarische Beziehungen der Schwiegertochter Goethes.* (Europäische Hochschulschriften.) Frankfurt: Peter Lang, 2001. Pp. 698.

Heinz, Jutta. "'Ein Park, der blosse einfache Natur ist': Zu einigen Parallelen von Gartenkunst und Romantheorie im 18. Jahrhundert." Pp. 253–70 of *Der imaginierte Garten*. Edited by Günter Oesterle and Harald Tausch. Göttingen: Wallstein, 2001.

Heinz, Jutta. "Wezel und die Frauen: Prototypen feministischer Argumentationsstrukturen im späten 18. Jahrhundert." *Wezel-Jahrbuch*, 4 (2001), 120-41.

Henke, Silke. "Das Goethe-Inventar als archivisches Findhilfsmittel und Quelle der Goethe-Philologie: Ergebnisse und Nutzungsmöglichkeiten." Pp. 87–98 of *Goethe-Philologie im Jubiläumsjahr: Bilanz und Perspektiven*. Edited by Jochen Golz. Tübingen: Max Niemeyer Verlag, 2001.

Hentschel, Uwe. "'Besuche in Briefen': Die epistolare Praxis der Anakreontiker und Gellerts Briefreform." *Orbis litterarum*, 56 (2001), 378–95.

Hentschel, Uwe. "'Briefe sind Spiegel der Seelen': Epistolare Kultur des 18. Jahrhunderts zwischen Privatheit und Öffentlichkeit." *Lessing-Yearbook*, 33 (2001), 183–200.

Herboth, Franziska. *Satiren des Sturm und Drang: Innenansichten des literarischen Feldes zwischen 1770 und 1780.* Hannover: Wehrhahn, 2001. Pp. 312.

Herrmann, Britta. "La vie comme roman: transformations mediales du fictif entre classicisme et romantisme." *Revue Germanique Internationale*, (2001), 47–68.

High, Jeffrey L. (ed.). *Die Goethezeit: Werke, Wirkung, Wechselbeziehungen; Eine Festschrift für Wilfried Malsch.* Göttingen: Schwerin, 2001. Pp. vii + 451.

Hildebrand, Olaf. "Im 'Irrgarten' der Paradoxien: Goethe, Diderot und Le Neveu du Rameau." *Goethe-Jahrbuch*, 118 (2001), 91–107.

Hilger, Stephanie. "The Feminine Performance of Class in Chr. F. Gellert's Leben der Schwedischen Gräfin von G." *Seminar: A Journal of Germanic Studies*, 37 (2001), 283–304.

Hilger, Stephanie. "The 'Weibliche Geschlechte' in the Mirror of the Early German Enlightenment: Class and Gender in Johann Christoph Gottsched's *Die vernünftigen Tadlerinnen*." *Lessing Yearbook/Jahrbuch*, 33 (2001), 127–49.

Hirdt, Willi (ed.). *Goethe und Italien.* (Studium universale 22.) Bonn: Bouvier, 2001. Pp. viii + 353; illustrations.

Hodkinson, James. "Genius Beyond Gender: Novalis, Women and the Art of Shapeshifting." *Modern Language Review*, 96 (2001), 103–15.

Hoff, Karin. "Grenzenlose Erinnerungen: Friederike Bruns kosmopolitischer Selbstentwurf." Pp. 95–107 of *Dänisch-deutsche Doppelgänger: Transnationale und bikulturelle Literatur zwischen Barock und Moderne.* Edited by Heinrich Detering, Anne-Bitt Gerecke, and Johan de Mylius. Göttingen: Wallstein, 2001.

Hoffmann, Daniel. "'Der Löwe brüllt, wer sollte sich nicht fürchten?' Zur utopischen Restauration der alten Stammburg in Goethes 'Novelle.'" *Zeitschrift für Deutsche Philologie*, 120 (2001), 527–39.

Hofmann, Michael. "Literatur und kulturelle Differenz: Problemkonstellationen in Geschichte und Gegenwart." *Weimarer Beiträge: Zeitschrift für Literaturwissenschaft, Ästhetik und Kulturwissenschaften*, 47 (2001), 387–402.

Hollmer, Heide, and Albert Meier. "'Die Erde ist nicht überall einerlei!': Landschaftsbeschreibungen in Karl Philipp Moritz's Reiseberichten aus England und

Italien." Pp. 263–88 of *Erschriebene Natur: Internationale Perspektiven auf Texte des 18. Jahrhunderts*. Edited by Michael Scheffel. Bern: Peter Lang, 2001.

Hollmer, Heide, and Albert Meier (eds.) *Dramenlexikon des 18. Jahrhunderts*. München: Beck 2001. Pp. 350.

Hollmer's and Meier's collection of short descriptions of eighteenth-century dramas is based on the correct assumption that the eighteenth-century dramatic landscape in Germany is still "terra incognita," since literary history so far has concerned itself only with a tiny percentage of the plays that were read and performed during that century. It is an assumption that would likely be endorsed by readers who, for example, have ever wondered why the bourgeois tragedy (a total canon of three plays) is considered an important genre in eighteenth-century drama, or by those who are familiar with the extraordinary depth and variety of forgotten dramatic traditions (such as women's drama). The stated goal of Hollmer's and Meier's collection is to include now-famous as well as obscure texts, to the extent that they were "characteristic" for the eighteenth-century theatrical landscape ("characteristic," in the editors' rather vague definition, indicating either the popularity of the work or its "representativeness" as an example for a popular genre). The one to two page-descriptions of each play, organized alphabetically by author, generally attempt some historical contextualization and offer a short plot summary followed by a one-paragraph interpretation and (at most) one or two secondary sources.

Hollmer and Meier are quite right in stating that research on eighteenth-century drama has been selective and inadequate; whether their lexicon contributes to amending that situation is another question. Much of the book, for one thing, is dedicated to authors and plays that are part of the standard eighteenth-century canon (such as Johann Christoph Gottsched, Lessing, Schiller, Goethe, and Lenz). 21 of the volume's 350 pages are dedicated to Goethe alone; by comparison, only about 16 pages total are spent on the 7 women authors appearing in the volume. To me, it seems worth asking the question why about one quarter of the book is spent on relatively famous writers: while there is an argument to be made for comprehensibility, the blurbs on plays by Goethe and Co. essentially duplicate those that can be found in standard lexica from Kosch to Kindler. In the cases of well-known, well-researched writers, the one or two secondary sources listed at the end of each summary can hardly begin to do justice to the immense quantity and diversity of research already done. That applies even to the still underresearched women writers, where more often than not—in the cases of Sophie Albrecht, Marianne Ehrmann, Luise Adelgunde Gottsched, and Charlotte von Stein, for example—the most recent research has been ignored. In terms of women's dramatic activity, the volume does not keep its promise of treating obscure as well as famous plays: only those women authors who have been most extensively researched to date have been included (Sophie Albrecht, Marianne Ehrmann, Luise Adelgunde Gottsched, Catherine the Great, Karoline Neuber, Charlotte von Stein, and Caroline von Wolzogen), while many others (Sophie Eleonore Titzenhofer, Eleonore Thon, Christiane Karoline Schlegel, Victoria von Rupp, Amalie von Imhoff, to name just a few) have been ignored.

Given the obvious fact that comprehensiveness is impossible, it would have made more sense to train the volume's focus on the true "terra incognita" of eighteenth-century drama: the obscure plays by unknown or underresearched writers, male or female, some of whom appear here and many others of whom had to cede their place to the canonical Greats who have already been much better and more extensively researched than this volume can represent. Treating obscure authors, male or female, would mandate inclusion of comprehensive bibliographical data of recent research, rather than merely listing one or two (usually already outdated) secondary sources, or, in some cases, no secondary literature at all (and that includes cases where such literature does exist). As it is, it is difficult to see how Hollmer's and Meier's book can serve as the basis for further research: the plot summaries pique the readers' interest, only to abandon them at the research stage. Scholars on canonical "great" dramatists from Gottsched to Goethe clearly no longer need this volume; scholars on more obscure playwrights like the few women mentioned here will, in many cases, find it lagging behind existing research. While its contribution to drama research is thus questionable, the volume does convey a glimpse of what must have been a fascinating and varied eighteenth-century dramatic landscape, a landscape later compressed to include only the standard plays by a few elite authors that now make up our "literary history."—Susanne Kord

Holm, Christiane. "Die verliebte Psyche und ihr galanter Bräutigam: Das Roman-Projekt von Susanna Elisabeth und Johann Ludwig Prasch." Pp. 53–86 of *Der galante Diskurs: Kommunikationsideal und Epochenschwelle*. Edited by Thomas Borgstedt and Andreas Solbach. Dresden: Thelem, 2001.

Hörner, Wolfgang (ed.). *Jean Paul und das Bier: "Bier, Bier, Bier, wie es auch komme"*. Hannover: Wehrhahn, 2001. Pp. 73.

Huerkamp, Josef, and Georg Meyer-Thurow (eds.). *"Die Einsamkeit, die Natur und meine Feder, dies ist mein einziger Genuß": Christian August Fischer (1771–1829): Schriftsteller und Universitätsprofessor*. (Bielefelder Schriften zu Linguistik und Literaturwissenschaft 15.) Bielefeld: Aisthesis, 2001. Pp. 486.

Hughes, Lindsey. "From Caftans into Corsets: The Sartorial Transformation of Women During the Reign of Peter the Great." Pp. 17–32 of *Gender and Sexuality in Russian Civilisation*. Edited by Peter I. Barta. London: Routledge, 2001.

Hummel, Adrian. "Bürger Voß: Leben, Werk und Wirkungsgeschichte eines schwierigen Autors." Pp. 137–67 of *Johann Heinrich Voß: Idylle, Polemik und Wohllaut*. (Göttinger Bibliotheksschriften 18.) Edited by Elamer Mittler and Inka Tappenbeck. Göttingen: Niedersächsische Staats- und Universitätsbibliothek, 2001.

Hurlebusch, Klaus. *Klopstock, Hamann und Herder als Wegbereiter autorzentrischen Schreibens: Ein philologischer Beitrag zur Charakterisierung der literarischen Moderne*. (Studien und Texte zur Sozialgeschichte der Literatur 86.) Tübingen: Max Niemeyer Verlag, 2001. Pp. v + 117.

llgner, Richard. *Die Ketzermythologie in Goethes "Faust."* Herbolzheitn: Cetitaurus, 2001. Pp. 194.

Ikeuchi, Osamu. *Gete-san konbanwa*. Tokyo: Shueisha, 2001. Pp. 254.

Iltcheva, Radoslava. "Pierre le Grand et son image litteraire: Entre le progres et la violence." Pp. 205–32 of *Progres et violence au XVIIIe siècle*. Edited by Valerie Cossy and Deidre Dawson. Paris: Honoré Champion, 2001.

Jaeger, Stephan. "Poèmes classiques-romantiques: le sujet lyrique entre deux eaux." *Revue Germanique Internationale,* (2001), 9–26.

Jahn, Bernhard. "Das Hörbarwerden des unerhörten Ereignisses: Sinne, Künste und Medien in Goethes Novelle." *Euphorion: Zeitschrift für Literaturgeschichte,* 95 (2001), 17–37.

Jakob, Hans-Joachim. *Die Folianten bilden Gelehrte, die Broschüren aber Menschen: Studien zur Flugschriftenliteratur in Wien 1781 bis 1791.* Frankfurt: Peter Lang, 2001. Pp. 282.

Johnson, Laurie. "Psychic, Corporeal, and Temporal Displacements in 'Die Familie Schroffenstein'." Pp. 121–33 of *Kleists Erzählungen und Dramen: Neue Studien.* Edited by Paul Michael Lützeler and David Pan. Würzburg: Königshausen & Neumann, 2001.

Jolle, Jonas. "Goethe's Translation of Pindar's Fifth Olympian Ode." *Goethe Yearbook,* 10 (2001), 50–64.

Jones, Michael T. "Schiller Trouble: The Tottering Legacy of German Aesthetic Humanism." *Goethe Yearbook,* 10 (2001), 222–45.

Jones, W. Gareth. "Russian Literature in the Eighteenth Century." Pp. 25–35 of *The Routledge Companion to Russian Literature.* Edited by Neil Cornwell. London: Routledge, 2001.

Joost, Ulrich. "'Schmierbuchmethode bestens zu empfehlen': Lichtenbergs 'Sudelbücher'-Aphorismen." Pp. 24–35 of *Lectures d'une oeuvre. Les aphorismes de Lichtenberg.* Edited by Jean Mondot. Paris: Éditions du temps, 2001.

Joost, Ulrich, Alexander Neumann, and Wolfgang Promies (eds.). *Lichtenberg-Jahrbuch 2000.* Saarbrücken: Saarbrücker Druckerei und Verlag, 2001. Pp. 250; bibliography, illustration.

Kany, Roland. "Tiefblickende Augen, wunderliche Phantasien: Ein Hamann-Fund und seine Bedeutung." *Jahrbuch der Deutschen Schillergesellschaft: Internationales Organ für Neuere Deutsche Literatur,* 45 (2001), 11–24.

Kausch, Karl-Heinz. *Das Kulturproblem bei Wieland.* Würzburg: Königshausen und Neumann 2001. Pp. 355.

Kemper, Hans Georg. "'Göttergleich': Zur Genese der Genie-Religion aus pietistischem und hermetischem 'Geist'." Pp. 171–208 of *Goethe und der Pietismus.* Edited by Hans-Georg Kemper. Tübingen: Max Niemeyer Verlag, 2001.

Kemper, Hans Georg, and Hans Schneider (eds.). *Goethe und der Pietismus.* (Hallesche Forschungen 6.) Tübingen: Max Niemeyer Verlag, 2001. Pp. viii + 278.

Kenkel, Karen J. "Monstrous Women, Sublime Pleasure, and the Perils of Reception in Lessing's Aesthetics." *PMLA,* 116 (2001), 545–61.

Kerry, Paul E. *Enlightenment Thought in the Writings of Goethe: A Contribution to the History of Ideas.* (Studies in German Literature Linguistics and Culture.) Rochester: Camden House, 2001. Pp. 184; bibliography, index.

Kiefer, Sascha. "'Gesellige Bildung': Ein Ideal des Rokoko und seine Fortschreibung in Goethes 'Unterhaltungen deutscher Ausgewanderten' (1795)." Pp. 235–49 of *Literatur und Kultur des Rokoko.* Edited by Matthias Luserke, Reiner Marx, and Reiner Wild. Göttingen: Vandenhoeck & Ruprecht, 2001.

Kiefer, Sebastian. "Wortmusik und mystische Erfahrung: Anmerkungen zu Goethes Gedicht 'Selige Sehnsucht'." *Weimarer Beiträge: Zeitschrift für Literaturwissenschaft, Ästhetik und Kulturwissenschaften,* 47 (2001), 403–17.

Kiesant, Knut. "Galante Dichtung am Berliner Hof: Zur galanten Dichtung Johann von Bessers (1654–1729)." Pp. 111–26 of *Der galante Diskurs: Kommunikationsideal und Epochenschwelle.* Edited by Thomas Borgstedt and Andreas Solbach. Dresden: Thelem, 2001.

Kim, Gyu Chang. *Vermittlungs- und Übersetzungsgeschichte Goethes in Korea.* (Tübinger Studien zur deutschen Literatur 17.) Frankfurt: Peter Lang, 2001. Pp. 207.

Kimball, Roger. "Schiller's 'Aesthetic Education.'" *New Criterion,* 19 (2001), 12–19.

Kimura, Naoji. *Jenseits von Weimar: Goethes Weg zum Fernen Osten.* (Euro Sinica. 8.) Berlin: Peter Lang, 2001. Pp. 207.

Kister, Stefan. *Text als Grab: Sepulkrales Gedenken in der deutschen Literatur um 1800.* Bielefeld: Aisthesis, 2001. Pp. 250; illustrations.

Kleine, Sabine. "Mimesis und Imagination." Pp. 443–59 of *Die Wende von der Aufklärung zur Romantik 1760–1820: Epoche im Überblick.* Edited by Horst-Albert Glaser. Amsterdam: Benjamins, 2001.

Kleinschmidt, Erich. "Brüchige Diskurse: Orientierungsprobleme in Friedrich Schillers 'Die Verschwörung des Fiesko zu Genua'." *Jahrbuch des Freien Deutschen Hochstifts,* (2001), 100–121.

Kohlschein, Franz. "Brauchtum in der Satire der Aufklärung: Zur 'Bildergalerie katholischer Missbräuche' von Joseph Richter." *Österreichische Zeitschrift für Volkskunde,* 55 (2001), 425–43.

Kohn, Brigitte. *"Denn wer die Weiber haßt, wie kann der leben?": Die Weiblichkeitskonzeption in Goethes 'Wilhelm Meisters Lehrjahren' im Kontext von Sprach und Ausdruckstheorie des ausgehenden 18. Jahrhunderts.* Würzburg: Königshausen und Neumann, 2001. Pp. 461.

Koltes, Manfred. "Die Regestausgabe der Briefe an Goethe: Geschichte—Aufgaben— Stand." Pp. 99–111 of *Goethe-Philologie im Jubiläumsjahr: Bilanz und Perspektiven.* Edited by Jochen Golz. Tübingen: Max Niemeyer Verlag, 2001.

König, Peter. "Idiomate patrio dicitur: Die Stellung deutscher Rechtsausdrucke in Christian Wolffs Jus Naturae." Pp. 113–27 of *Recht und Sprache in der deutschen Aufklärung.* Edited by Ulrich Kronauer. Tübingen: Max Niemeyer Verlag, 2001.

Kordela, A. Kiarina. "It Looks Down Upon Us (Allegorical Fields and Repetitive Errors)." *Modern Language Studies,* 31 (2001), 99–129.

Koselleck, Reinhart. "Begriffliche Innovationen der Aufklärungssprache: Festvortrag Donnerstag, 29.01.1998." Pp. 4–26 of *Recht und Sprache in der deutschen Aufklärung.* Edited by Ulrich Kronauer. Tübingen: Max Niemeyer Verlag, 2001.

Kosenina, Alexander. "Friedrich Nicolai's Satires on Philosophy." *Monatshefte für Deutschsprachige Literatur und Kultur,* 93 (2001), 290–99.

Kosenina, Alexander. "Will er 'auf ein Theater warten, welches da kommen soll'?: Kleists Ideen zur Schauspielkunst." *Kleist-Jahrbuch,* (2001), 38-54.

Krause, Frank. "Stoische Ungeduld. Johann Christoph Gottsched: Der Sterbende Cato (1732)." *German Life and Letters,* 54 (2001), 191–209.

Kremer, Detlef. *Romantik.* Stuttgart: Metzler, 2001. Pp. viii + 339.

Kreutzer, Hans Joachim. "'Amphitryon': Mythos und Drama." Pp. 179–90 of *Kleists Erzählungen und Dramen: Neue Studien.* Edited by Paul Michael Lützeler and David Pan. Würzburg: Königshausen & Neumann, 2001.

Krippendorff, Ekkehart. *Jefferson und Goethe.* (EVA-Duographien 12.) Hamburg: Europäische Verlagsanstalt, 2001. Pp. 212; illustrations.

Kronauer, Ulrich. "Die Darstellung kultureller Differenz in Verordnungen und anderen die 'Zigeuner' betreffenden Texten des 18. Jahrhunderts." Pp. 95–108 of *Die Macht der Differenzen: Beiträge zur Hermeneutik der Kultur*. Edited by Reinhard Düssel, Geert Edel, and Ulrich Schödlbauer. Heidelberg: Synchron, 2001.

Kronauer, Ulrich, and Jörn Garber (eds.). *Recht und Sprache in der deutschen Aufklärung*. (Hallesche Beiträge zur europäischen Aufklärung 14.) Tübingen: Max Niemeyer Verlag, 2001. Pp. 233; illustration.

Krüger-Fürhoff, Irmela Marei. *Der versehrte Körper: Revisionen des klassizistischen Schönheitsideals*. Göttingen: Wallstein, 2001. Pp. 236.

Kugler, Stefani, and Dagmar Heinze. "Von der Unmöglichkeit, den Anderen zu lieben: Caroline von Wolzogens 'Die Zigeuner' und Caroline Auguste Fischers 'William der Neger.'" Pp. 135–54 of *Das Subjekt und die Anderen: Interkulturalität und Geschlechterdifferenz vom 18. Jahrhundert bis zur Gegenwart*. Edited by Herbert Uerlings, Karl Hölz, and Viktoria Schmidt-Linsenhoff. (Studienreihe Romania 16.) Berlin: Erich Schmidt, 2001.

Kunzel, Christine. "Knabe trifft Röslein auf der Heide: Goethes 'Heidenröslein' im Kontext einer Poetik sexueller Gewalt." *Ariadne: Forum für Frauen und Geschlechtergeschichte*, 39 (2001), 56–61.

Kurscheidt, Georg. "Überlegungen zur Kommentierung von Briefen; mit Beispielen aus Goethes Briefen." Pp. 147–65 of *Goethe-Philologie im Jubiläumsjahr: Bilanz und Perspektiven*. Edited by Jochen Golz. Tübingen: Max Niemeyer Verlag, 2001.

Kurth Voigt. Liselotte E. "Zimmermanns Ueber die Einsamkeit (1784/85): Zur Rezeption des Werkes." *Modern Language Notes*, 116 (2001), 579–95.

Lamport, F. J. "'Eine wahrhaft Ossianische oder Kosegartensche Wirkung ...': Patriotic Landscapes of the Goethezeit." *Publications of the English Goethe Society*, 70 (2001), 56–73.

Lange, Horst. "Wolves, Sheep, and the Shepherd: Legality, Legitimacy, and Hobbesian Political Theory in Goethe's Götz von Berlichingen." *Goethe Yearbook*, 10 (2001), 1–30.

Langner, Beatrix K.. *Hölderlin und Diotima: Eine Biographie*. Frankfurt: Insel, 2001. Pp. 226.

Lappo Danilevskii, K. Iu. "Lessing I Vinkel'man V 'Zhurnale Iziashchnykh Iskusstv' V. I. Grigorovicha." *Russkaia Literatura: Istoriko Literaturnyi Zhurnal*, 2 (2001), 105–16.

Laudin, Gérard. "L'homme de lettres, le savant et le philosophe: Lichtenberg au temps des vaches maigres de la littérature." Pp. 74–94 of *Lectures d'une oeuvre: Les aphorismes de Lichtenberg*. Edited by Jean Mondot. Paris: Éditions du temps, 2001.

Lawitschka, Valerie (ed.). *Hölderlin: Philosophie und Dichtung;* Turm-Vorträge 1992-98. Tübingen: Edition Isele, 2001. Pp. 320.

Leask, Nigel. "Salons, Alps and Cordilleras: Helen Maria Williams, Alexander von Humboldt, and the Discourse of Romantic Travel." Pp. 217–35 of *Women, Writing and the Public Sphere, 1700 1830*. Edited by Elizabeth Eger. Cambridge: Cambridge University Press, 2001.

Lebedeva, O. B., and A. S. Ianushkevich. "Neizvestnye Perevody V. A. Zhukovskogo Iz Gete." *Russkaia Literatura: Istoriko Literaturnyi Zhurnal*, 2 (2001), 76–82.

Leger, Sylvie. *Thérèse Huber, femme écrivain*. Villeneuve d'Ascq: Presses universitaires du Septentrion, 2001. Pp. 404.

Leistner, Bernd. "Mutationen eines Schiller-Zitats." *Goethe-Jahrbuch,* 118 (2001), 351–52.

Lennartz, Rita. "'Angesicht zu Angesicht.' Lebende Bilder und tote Buchstaben in Goethes 'Die Wahlwandtschaften'." Pp. 145–183 of *Bildersturm und Bilderflut: Zur schwierigen Anschaulichkeit der Moderne*. Edited by Helmut J. Schneider. Bielefeld: Aisthesis 2001.

Lennartz, Rita. "Attitüde und Gewand—Vom Umschreiben der Kunst: Goethes 'Sendschreiben' von 1812 über 'Der Tänzerin Grab'." Pp. 135–80 of *Goethe und Italien*. Edited by Willi Hirdt and Birgit Tappert. Bonn: Bouvier, 2001.

Lennartz, Rita. "Feuer und Flamme. Figuratives Spiel in Brentanos 'Ponce de Leon'." Pp. 187–201 of *Theorie der Komödie—Poetik der Komödie*. (Aisthesis Studienbuch 2.) Edited by Ralf Simon. Bielefeld: Aisthesis, 2001.

Lindemann-Stark, Anke. *Leben und Lebensläufe des Theodor Gottlieb von Hippel*. St. Ingbert: Röhrig, 2001. Pp. 384.

Linder, Jutta. *"Falsche Tendenzen": Der Staatsdiener Goethe und der Dichter*. Catanzaro: Rubbettino, 2001. Pp. 204.

Lohmeier, Anke Marie. "'Arte aut Marte': Über Ewald von Kleist, Dichter und Soldat." Pp. 121–33 of *Literatur und Kultur des Rokoko*. Edited by Matthias Luserke, Reiner Marx, and Reiner Wild. Göttingen: Vandenhoeck & Ruprecht, 2001.

Luke, David. "Translating Faust: A Personal Statement." Pp. 271–82 of *A Companion to Goethe's Faust: Parts I and II*. Edited by Paul Bishop. Rochester: Camden House, 2001.

Lu, Yixu. "Die Theatralität des Göttlichen: Über Kleists Amphityron." *Kleist-Jahrbuch,* (2001), 148–59.

Lulé, Susanna, and Olivier Mannoni. "L'Opera comme modele esthetique chez Goethe et E. T. A. Hoffmann." *Revue Germanique Internationale,* 16 (2001), 123–39, 92–93.

Luserke-Jaqui, Matthias (ed.). *Goethe nach 1999: Positionen und Perspektiven*. Göttingen: Vandenhoeck & Ruprecht, 2001. Pp. 175; illustration.

Luserke-Jaqui, Matthias (ed.). *Goethe und Lenz: Die Geschichte einer Entzweiung; eine Dokumentation*. (Insel-Taschenbuch 2750.) Frankfurt am Main: Insel, 2001. Pp. 199.

Luserke, Matthias, Reiner Marx, and Reiner Wild (eds.). *Literatur und Kultur des Rokoko*. Göttingen: Wallstein, 2001. Pp. 328; illustrations.

Lützeler, Paul Michael. "Verführung und Missionierung: Zu den Exempeln in 'Die Verlobung in St. Domingo'." Pp. 35–48 of *Kleists Erzählungen und Dramen: Neue Studien*. Edited by Paul Michael Lützeler and David Pan. Würzburg: Königshausen & Neumann, 2001.

Lützeler, Paul Michael, and David Pan (eds.). *Kleists Erzählungen und Dramen: Neue Studien*. Würzburg: Königshausen & Neumann, 2001. Pp. 263.

Maaser, Michael. "Goethe und kein Ende? Das Goethe-Jubiläum 1999 und sein Ertrag." *Historische Zeitschrift,* 273 (2001), 95–266.

MacDonald, Robert David. "*Faust*: The Play in Production." Pp. 283–89 of *A Companion to Goethe's Faust: Parts I and II*. Edited by Paul Bishop. Rochester: Camden House, 2001.

Maier, Hans-Joachim. *Zwischen Bestimmung und Autonomie: Erziehung, Bildung und Liebe im Frauenroman des 18. Jahrhunderts. Eine Literatursoziologische Studie von Christian F. Gellerts Leben der schwedischen Gräfin von G*** und Sophie von La Roches Geschichte des Fräuleins von Sternheim*. (Germanistische Texte und Studien 65.) Hildesheim: Olms-Weidmann, 2001. Pp. 406.

Manger, Klaus. "Goethe und die deutschen Aufklärer." *Goethe-Jahrbuch,* 118 (2001), 46–57.

Manzoni, Beccaria Giulia. *Col core sulla penna: Lettere 1791–1841*. Edited by Grazia Maria Griffini. (Quaderni Manzoni 2.) Milano: Centro Nazionale Studi Ma, 2001. Pp. xliv + 366; illustrations.

Marchal, Roger. "Des satyres parmi les nymphes: contes moraux et nouvelles idylles de Diderot et Salomon Gessner." *Travaux de littérature*, 14 (2001), 300–19.

Marrades, Julián, and Manuel E. Vázquez (eds.). *Hölderlin: Poesía y pensamiento*. (Pre-Textos 1.) Valencia: Coleción filo-sofías, 2001. Pp. 198.

Martindale, Charles. "The Aesthetic Turn: Latin Poetry and the Judgement of Taste." *Arion: A Journal of Humanities and the Classics*, 9 (2001), 63–89.

Martinson, Steven D. "Organizing Chaos: 'Organisation' in Herder and Goethe's Werther and Faust." Pp. 135–46 of *Goethe, Chaos, and Complexity*. Edited by Herbert Rowland. Amsterdam: Rodopi, 2001.

Martus, Steffen. "Man setzet sich eben derselben Gefahr aus, welcher man andre aussetzet': Autoritative Performanz in der Literarischen Kommunikation am Beispiel von Bayle, Bodmer und Schiller." *Zeitschrift für Deutsche Philologie*, 120 (2001), 481–501.

Marx, Reiner. "Anakreontik als lyrische Initiation: Zu Lessings 'Kleinigkeiten' und Goethes 'Annette'." Pp. 135–45 of *Literatur und Kultur des Rokoko*. Edited by Matthias Luserke, Reiner Marx, and Reiner Wild. Göttingen: Vandenhoeck & Ruprecht, 2001.

Mazza, Ethel Matala de. "Recht für bare Münze: Institution und Gesetzeskraft in Kleists 'Zerbrochnem Krug'." *Kleist-Jahrbuch*, (2001), 160–77.

McCarthy, John A. "The 'Pregnant Point': Goethe on Complexity, Interdisciplinarity, and Emergence." Pp. 17–31 of *Goethe, Chaos, and Complexity*. Edited by Herbert Rowland. Amsterdam: Rodopi, 2001.

Meer, Jan Ij van der. "The Literary System of the Stanislaw Age in Poland: Its Participants." *Russian, Croatian and Serbian, Czech and Slovak, Polish Literature*, 49 (2001), 449–88.

Meier, Andreas (ed.). *Jakob Michael Reinhold Lenz: Vom Sturm und Drang zur Moderne*. (Beihefte zum Euphorion: Zeitschrift für Literaturgeschichte 41.) Heidelberg: Carl Winter Universitätsverlag, 2001.

Meinhold, Günter. *'Zauberflöte' und 'Zauberflöten' Rezeption : Studien zu Emanuel Schikaneders Libretto 'Die Zauberflöte' und seiner literarischen Rezeption*. Frankfurt: Peter Lang, 2001. Pp. 313.

Mellemgaard, Signe. "Natur og unatur: Oplysning og opdragelse i. C. G. Salzmanns roman Carl von Carlsberg." *Folk og Kultur*, (2001), 89–104.

Memmolo, Pasquale. "Goethes Lachen in Italien: Et in Arcadia ego!" Pp. 181–202 of *Goethe und Italien*. Edited by Willi Hirdt and Birgit Tappert. Bonn: Bouvier, 2001.

Mengel, S. "Russkie Perevody Khall'skikh Pietistov: Simeon Todorskii, 1729–1735 Gg." *Vestnik Moskovskogo Universiteta, Seriia 9, Filologiia* 3 (2001), 89–103.

Menze, Ernest A. "Benjamin Franklin Seen with German Eyes: Selective Co-Optations by German Authors." *Yearbook of German American Studies*, 36 (2001), 29–46.

Mergenthaler, Volker. "'So theil' ich alles, was ich sehe…in fünf gevierte Fächer ein': Zum wahrnehmungsgeschichtlichen Ort von Barthold Heinrich Brockes' Thürmchen zu Ritzebüttel." Pp. 121–44 of *Erschriebene Natur: Internationale Perspektiven auf Texte des 18. Jahrhunderts*. Edited by Michael Scheffel. Bern: Peter Lang, 2001.

Meyer, Urs. *Politische Rhetorik: Theorie, Analyse und Geschichte der Redekunst am Beispiel des Spätaufkärers Johann Gottfried Seume*. Paderbom: Mentis, 2001. Pp. 292.

Michel, Christoph. "Goethe, die Kinder und die Magie des Wortes: Überlegungen zu dem Gedicht 'Alter Feuersegen'." Pp. 333–44 of *Goethe: Ungewohnte Ansichten*. Edited by Karl Richter. St. Ingbert: Röhrig, 2001.

Michel, Paul. "Das Buch der Natur bei Johann Jacob Scheuchzer (1672–1733)." Pp. 169–93 of *Vox Sermo Res: Beiträge zur Sprachreflexion, Literatur und Sprachgeschichte vom Mittelalter bis zur Neuzeit*. Edited by Wolfgang Haubrichs. Stuttgart: Hirzel, 2001.

Miller, Norbert. "'Du hast mir deines Angesichts Züge bewährt…': 'Der zerbrochne Krug' und die Probe auf den Augenblick." Pp. 215–39 of *Kleists Erzählungen und Dramen: Neue Studien*. Edited by Paul Michael Lützeler and David Pan. Würzburg: Königshausen & Neumann, 2001.

Minter, Catherine J. "Literary *Empfindsamkeit* and Nervous Sensibility in Eighteenth-Century Germany." *Modern Language Review*, 96 (2001), 1016–28.

Mittler, Elmer, and Inka Tappenbeck (eds.). *Johann Heinrich Voß: Idylle, Polemik und Wohllaut.* (Göttinger Bibliotheksschriften 18.) Göttingen: Niedersächsische Staats- und Universitätsbibliothek, 2001. Pp. 298; illustrations.

Mix, York Gothart. "Das Ende des Rokoko und die Formierung eines autonomen Lyrikmarktes in Deutschland (J.G. Herder, J.W.L. Gleim, G.A. Bürger)." Pp. 211–22 of *Literatur und Kultur des Rokoko.* Göttingen: Vandenhoeck & Ruprecht, 2001.

Mix, York Gothart. "Nationale Selbst- und Fremdbilder in der Mode- und Alamodekritik des 'Hinkenden Boten' und anderer populärer Kalender des 18. Jahrhunderts." *Internationales Archiv für Sozialgeschichte der Deutschen Literatur,* 26 (2001), 56–71.

Mondot, Jean. "Goethe und die französischen lumieres oder Voltaire und kein Ende." *Goethe-Jahrbuch,* 118 (2001), 75–90.

Moog Grünewald, Maria. "Der Sänger im Schild—oder: Über den Grund ekphrastischen Schreibens." Pp. 1–19 of *Behext von Bildern? Ursachen, Funktionen und Perspektiven der textuellen Faszination durch Bilder.* Edited by Heinz J. Drugh. Heidelberg: Carl Winter Universitätsverlag, 2001.

Moretti, Vito. *Le forme dell'identità: Dall'Arcadia al decadentismo.* (Nuova universale Studium, 100.) Roma: Studium, 2001. Pp. 219.

Muenzer, Clark S. "Wandering among Obelisks: Goethe and the Idea of the Monument." *Modern Language Studies,* 31 (2001), 5–34.

Mülder-Bach, Inka. "Kommunizierende Monaden: Herders literarisches Universum." Pp. 41–52 of *Sinne und Verstand: Ästhetische Modellierungen der Wahrnehmung um 1800.* Edited by Caroline Welsh, Christina Dongowski, and Susanna Lulé. Würzburg: Königshausen & Neumann, 2001.

Müller, Ernst Ludwig. *Christoph Heinrich Hölty: Leben und Werk.* Egelsbach: Fouqué, 2001. Pp. 272.

Müller, Peter. "Lenz und Goethe, Jena und Weimar." *Weimarer Beiträge: Zeitschrift für Literaturwissenschaft, Ästhetik und Kulturwissenschaften,* 47 (2001), 292–99.

Münster, Reinhold. *Friedrich von Hagedorn: Personalbibliographie; mit einem Forschungsbericht und einer Biographie des Dichters.* Würzburg: Königshausen und Neumann, 2001. Pp. 126; bibliography.

Naeve Bucher, Ursula. *Schönes Fräulein darf ich's wagen, Ihnen Arm und Geleite anzutragen? Zu Annäherung, Werbung, Versuchung und Verführung in der Schwedischen und deutschen Literatur des 18. Jahrhunderts.* (Acta Universitatis Stockholmiensis: Stockholmer Germanistische Forschungen 58.) Stockholm: Almqvist & Wiksell, 2001.

Nägele, Rainer. "The Pure Gaze." *Deutsche Vierteljahrsschrift für Literaturwissenschaft und Geistesgeschichte*, 75 (2001), 27–38.

Nell, Sharon Diane. "The Last Laugh: Carnivalizing the Feminine in Piron's 'La Puce'." Pp. 165–90 of *Carnivalizing Difference: Bakhtin and the Other.* Edited by Peter I. Barta. London: Routledge, 2001.

Nemoianu, Virgil. "From Goethe to Guizot: The Conservative Contexts of 'Wilhelm Meisters Wanderjahre.'" *Modern Language Studies*, 31 (2001), 45–58.

Neuhaus, Stefan. "'Dass die Zärtlichkeit noch barbarischer zwingt als Tyrannenwut!': Zur Problematisierung von Familienstrukturen in Schillers Dramen." *Jahrbuch für Internationale Germanistik*, 33 (2001), 98–111.

Niefanger, Dirk. "Die Chance einer ungefestigten Nationalliteratur: Traditionsverhalten im galanten Diskurs." Pp. 147–64 of *Der galante Diskurs: Kommunikationsideal und Epochenschwelle.* Edited by Thomas Borgstedt and Andreas Solbach. Dresden: Thelem, 2001.

Niefanger, Dirk. "Narrative Verwandlungen: Ein intermediales Verfahren in Bildbeschreibungen Wilhelm Heinses, Heinrich von Kleists und Johann Wolfgang von Goethes." *Jahrbuch der Deutschen Schillergesellschaft: Internationales Organ für Neuere Deutsche Literatur*, 45 (2001), 224–49.

Niekerk, Carl. "Men in Pain: Disease and Displacement in 'Der Findling.'" Pp. 107–19 of *Kleists Erzählungen und Dramen: Neue Studien.* Edited by Paul Michael Lützeler and David Pan. Würzburg: Königshausen & Neumann, 2001.

Niggl, Günter. "Goethes Pietismus-Bild in Dichtung und Wahrheit." Pp. 257–68 of *Goethe und der Pietismus.* Edited by Hans-Georg Kemper. Tübingen: Max Niemeyer Verlag, 2001.

Niggl, Günter. *Studien zur Literatur der Goethezeit.* (Schriften zur Literaturwissenschaft 17.) Berlin: Duncker & Humblot, 2001. Pp. 324.

Nikolova, Irena. *Complementary Modes of Representation in Keats, Novalis and Shelley.* (Studies in Nineteenth Century British Literature 18.) New York: Peter Lang, 2001.

Objartel, Georg. "Semantische Individualisierung: Ansätze zu Goethe." Pp. 305–17 of *Sprache im Leben der Zeit: Beiträge zur Theorie, Analyse und Kritik der deutschen Sprache in Vergangenheit und Gegenwart; Helmut Henne zum 65. Geburtstag*. Edited by Armin Burkhardt. Tübingen: Max Niemeyer Verlag, 2001.

Objartel, Georg. "Sprachreflexivität bei Goethe: Sogenannt: Mit vergleichenden Ausblicken;" Pp. 97–104 of *Die deutsche Sprache der Gegenwart; Festschrift für Dieter Cherubim zum 60. Geburtstag*. Edited by Stefan J. Schierholz. Frankfurt: Peter Lang, 2001.

Oehlenschläger, Eckart. "Goethes Schrift 'Das Römische Carneval': Ein Versuch über die Formalisierbarkeit des Tumults." Pp. 221–39 of *Goethe und Italien*. Edited by Willi Hirdt and Birgit Tappert. Bonn: Bouvier, 2001.

Oergel, Maike. "'Wie es wirklich wurde': The Modern Need for Historical Fiction, or the Inevitability of the Historical Novel." Pp. 435–49 of *Travellers in Time and Space: The German Historical Novel/Reisende durch Zeit und Raum: Der deutschsprachige historische Roman*. Edited by Osman Durrani. Amsterdam: Rodopi, 2001.

Oesterle, Günter. "Figurations esthétiques dans le classicisme et le romantisme: 'l'instant fécond' et l'arabesque." *Revue Germanique Internationale*, (2001), 141–6.

Ohm, Reinhard. *"Unsere jungen Dichter": Wielands literaturästhetische Publizistik im Teutschen Merkur zur Zeit des Sturm und Drang und der Frühklassik (1773–1789)*. (Schriftenreihe Literaturwissenschaft 52.) Trier: Wissenschaftlicher Verlag, 2001. Pp. 198.

Ohrgaard, Per. "Anmerkungen zum Reden und Schweigen in Wilhelm Meisters Lehrjahren." *Goethe-Jahrbuch*, 118 (2001), 176–86.

Ohrgaard, Per. "Die Nachfolge Schillers? Über Oehlenschlägers 'Correggio' und Goethe." *Das achtzehnte Jahrhundert*, 25 (2001), 231–47.

Ondrejovic, Slavomir. "Slovencina V Diele Mithridates Johanna Christopha Adelunga a Johanna Severina Vatera." *Slovenska Rec: Casopis pre Vyskum Slovenskeho Jazyka*, 66 (2001), 321–36.

Ott, Michael. *Das ungeschriebene Gesetz: Ehre und Geschlechterdifferenz in der deutschen Literatur um 1800*. (Rombach Wissenschaften. Reihe Litterae 81.) Freiburg: Rombach, 2001. Pp. 368.

Pan, David. "The Aesthetic Foundations of Morality in 'Das Erdbeben in Chili.'" Pp. 49–59 of *Kleists Erzählungen und Dramen: Neue Studien*. Edited by Paul Michael Lützeler and David Pan. Würzburg: Königshausen & Neumann, 2001.

Patzer, Georg. *Gotthold Ephraim Lessing: "Nathan der Weise."* Stuttgart: Klett, 2001. Pp. 64.

Peitsch, Helmut. *Georg Forster: A History of His Critical Reception.* (German Life and Civilization 34.) New York: Peter Lang, 2001. Pp. 352.

Peters, Kirsten. *Der Kindsmord als schöne Kunst betrachtet: Eine motivgeschichtliche Untersuchung der Literatur des 18. Jahrhunderts.* (Epistemata. Reihe Literaturwissenschaft 350.) Würzburg: Königshausen & Neumann, 2001. Pp. 243.

Phelan, Anthony. "The Classical and the Medieval in *Faust* II." Pp. 144–68 of *A Companion to Goethe's Faust: Parts I and II.* Edited by Paul Bishop. Rochester: Camden House, 2001.

Pikulik, Lothar. *Signatur einer Zeitenwende: Studien zur Literatur der frühen Moderne von Lessing bis Eichendorff.* Göttingen: Vandenhoeck & Ruprecht, 2001. Pp. 222; illustrations.

Ponzi, Mauro. "Goethes Bild von Rom: Fiktion und Wahrheit." Pp. 275–291 of *Goethe und Italien.* Edited by Willi Hirdt and Birgit Tappert. Bonn: Bouvier, 2001.

Powers, Elizabeth. "From Genre to Gender: On Goethe's 'Der Wandrer'." *Goethe Yearbook,* 10 (2001), 31–49.

Promies, Wolfgang. "Lichtenberg—ein 'Chamfort allemand'?" Pp. 14–23 of *Lectures d'une oeuvre. Les aphorismes de Lichtenberg.* Edited by Jean Mondot. Paris: Éditions du temps, 2001.

Pulvirenti, Grazia. "Nel giardino di Belriguardo: Il mito dell'artista romantico nel Torquato Tasso di Goethe." *Confronto Letterario: Quaderni del Dipartimento di Lingue e Letterature Straniere Moderne dell' Universita di Paviae del Dipartimento di Linguistica e Letterature Comparate dell' Universita di Bergamo,* 18 (2001), 87–108.

Pulvirenti, Grazia. "'L'illusione consapevole': 'Proserpina' e l'opera d'arte totale." *Cultura tedesca,* 17 (2001), 97–115.

Raihala, Lorelle. "Who Has Control of the Marquise's Life?" Pp. 93–106 of *Kleists Erzählungen und Dramen: Neue Studien.* Edited by Paul Michael Lützeler and David Pan. Würzburg: Königshausen & Neumann, 2001.

Rajabzadah, Hashim. "Iraniyan va Zhapani-ha az nigah-i Kampfir." *Name ye Anjoman: Quarterly Journal of Society for the Appreciation of Cultural Works and Dignitaries,* 1 (2001), 103–46 (right), 5–6 (left).

Reed, Terence James. *Humanpraxis Literatur: Essays um Goethe*. (Kulturwissenschaftliche Reihe/ Collegium Europaeum Jenense 3.) Jena: VDG, 2001. Pp. 87.

Regener, Ursula. "Gedanken über Rosen: Galantes bei Johann Christian Günther." Pp. 181–198 of *Der galante Diskurs: Kommunikationsideal und Epochenschwelle*. Edited by Thomas Borgstedt and Andreas Solbach. Dresden: Thelem, 2001.

Rehfeld, Hans Jürgen. "'Sonne, du grosses Gestirn' (F. Nietzsche), Goethes Schlesische Reise. Mit einem Seitenblick auf Heinrich von Kleists Reise ins Riesengebirge." *Beiträge zur Kleist-Forschung*, (2001), 213-41.

Reitemeier, Frauke. *Deutsch-englische Literaturbeziehungen: Der historische Roman Sir Walter Scotts und seine deutschen Vorläufer*. (Beiträge zur englischen und amerikanischen Literatur 18.) Paderborn: Schöningh 2001. Pp. 290; tables, bibliography, index.

In the prologue to his translation of Goethe's *Goetz*, Sir Walter Scott commended the historical novel *Hermann von Unna* by the German woman author Benedikte Naubert (published anonymously in 1789, English translation in 1794), as an "excellent romance." Reitermeier's study, her revised Göttingen dissertation (1999), sets out to specify and describe the influence of German historical novels, mostly of the last quarter of the eighteenth century, on Scott's writings. This approach is exactly the study's weakness: it defines novels with historical topics before Scott as precursors to Scott's model and evaluates them almost exclusively against Scott's production. This approach in turn gives little original information about the novels in question, their authors, and their interest in and use of historical topics in literature. As to be expected, Reitemeier comes to the conclusion that, indeed, Scott is likely to have been more influenced by Naubert's novels than by contemporary English novels, as he applied a technique similiar to Naubert's of writing on two levels, with a fictional character acting against a historical background (251). However, what Scott valued highly in Naubert's novels might not have been their treatment of history, but the romances and the importance of gothic effects and supernatural elements (246).

The study sets out to quantify the influence of Naubert's novels on Scott as claimed by Kurt Schreinert in 1941. (Reitemeier does not, however, problematize nationalistic interests around 1940 in claiming German origins for the historical novel as genre.) Besides novels by the prolific woman author Naubert (well-known in scholarship on German women authors) Reitemeier unearths (mostly from the collection of the library at Corvey) three forgotten male authors (Ignaz Aurelius Feßler, August Gottlieb Meißner, Veit Weber, pseudonym for Leonhard Wächter) who produced a plethora of fairly popular novels in German with historical topics published between 1781 and 1807. Reitemeier treats the German writers as a group who attempted historical novels before Scott. It is symptomatic that none of the authors' names appear in the headlines, nor is cohesive information on the writers and their works easily to be found in the book. Consequently, the book is not indexed under Naubert or eighteenth-century German literature or women writers and tends to be overlooked in eighteenth-century scholarship.

In her chapter on English historical novels before Scott, Reitemeier examines thiry-five novels, quite a few of which were published anonymously. They were published between 1779 (Bicknell, *Prince Arthur*) and 1812 (West, *Loyalists*). The criterion for inclusion appears to have been what was accessible to the author, mostly at the National Library of Scotland. Unlike the four authors on the German book market, there were no British writers who stood out as particularly productive in this genre. This is clearly a neglected area of research in the shadow of Scott that deserves more attention.

Reitemeier examines both German and English novels not by authors or in groups with stylistic similarities, but she divides them into two groups, the first having historical main characters (defined as they are known to have lived under that name), the second fictional ones. Within Naubert's works and also within the English novels, she finds an additional subgroup of novels whose main characters she terms pseudo-historical ("pseudohistorisch") which she defines as (fictional) sons or daughters of historical characters. This reviewer proposes that the term pseudo-historical might be more useful for main characters that have historical names, but where the novel completely changes and reinterprets the few known facts of their lives, such as in the case of Naubert's novel on Barbara Blomberg, mother of emperor Charles V's illegitimate son. Reitemeier's interesting observation that both Naubert and the English writers produced a high number of novels with female main characters set in the distant past results in interesting, albeit disparate observations which lead not to a conclusion, but to a series of asterisks (literally) in her statistics tables. Taken further, her observations might lead to conclusions about the role of historical novels of the long eighteenth century in writing women's history, parallel to and contradictory to historiography being established as a male domain in Germany at the end of the eighteenth century. On the other hand, much of Naubert's mixed genre production, such as her *Velleda, ein Zauberroman* [*Velleda, a Novel of Magic*] might be compared to early nineteenth-century British "imaginative historiography" (Lynne Hamer) which combined historical contents of legends and sagas with narrative techniques of novels. Such works lack a clear and historically sound foundation for the line of events which Reitemeier considers essential for Scott, a model which he therefore did not adopt.

Additional chapters of the book describe the availability of translations and other aspects of receptions of German literature in early nineteenth-century Britain as well as Scott's reception of German texts in particular. They provide valuable insights, especially on the image of German Romantics and cultural transfer, but they are not well integrated. This book tries to do too much in the overarching frame without giving sufficient room for the foundation. On the one hand its ambitious goal is to reevaluate early historical narratives and trace the origins of the historical novel before Scott including cross-cultural connections. Reitemeier falls short and offers vague conclusions because her groundwork, the inventory of lesser-known and forgotten texts and their readership has turned up more material than scholars have been aware of. These historical narratives deserve to be studied further and on their own, not just as possible precursors to Scott.—Waltraud Maierhofer

Renner, Ursula. "Eros, Melancholie und Medien: Goethes 'Amor als Landschaftsmahler.'" *Jahrbuch des Freien Deutschen Hochstifts*, (2001), 1–29.

Rennie, Nicholas. "Between Pascal and Mallarmé: Faust's Speculative Moment." Pp. 117–33 of *Goethe, Chaos, and Complexity*. Edited by Herbert Rowland. Amsterdam: Rodopi, 2001.

Rennie, Nicholas. "'Schilderungssucht' and 'Historische Krankheit': Lessing, Nietzsche, and the Body Historical." *German Quarterly*, 74 (2001), 186–96.

Richter, Elke. "Zur historisch-kritischen Gesamtausgabe von Goethes Briefen" Pp. 123–45 of *Goethe-Philologie im Jubiläumsjahr: Bilanz und Perspektiven*. Edited by Jochen Golz. Tübingen: Max Niemeyer Verlag, 2001.

Richter, Karl. "Rokoko-Reminiszenzen in Goethes 'West-östlichem Divan.'" Pp. 277–88 of *Literatur und Kultur des Rokoko*. Edited by Matthias Luserke, Reiner Marx, and Reiner Wild. Göttingen: Vandenhoeck & Ruprecht, 2001.

Richter, Karl, and Gerhard Sauder (eds.) *Goethe: Ungewohnte Ansichten*. (Annales Universitatis Saraviensis 17.) St. Ingbert: Röhrig, 2001. Pp. 386; illustrations.

Richter, Karl, and Herbert Wender. "Vorüberlegungen zu einer historisch-kritischen Ausgabe von Goethes Gedichten." Pp. 43–54 of *Goethe-Philologie im Jubiläumsjahr: Bilanz und Perspektiven*. Edited by Jochen Golz. Tübingen: Max Niemeyer Verlag, 2001.

Riege, Helmut. "Zur Edition von Klopstocks Briefwechsel in der Hamburger Klopstock-Ausgabe." Pp. 63–64 of *"Ich an Dich": Edition, Rezeption und Kommentierung von Briefen; Alfred Doppler zum 80. Geburtstag gewidmet*. Edited by Werner M. Bauer. Innsbruck: Institut für Deutsche Sprache, Literatur und Literaturkritik, 2001.

Roberts, Marilyn. "The Memoirs of Wilhelmina of Bayreuth: A Story of Her Own." *Eighteenth-Century Women: Studies in Their Lives, Work, and Culture*, 1 (2001), 129–64.

Robertson, Ritchie. "Literary Techniques and Aesthetic Texture in Faust." Pp. 1–27 of *A Companion to Goethe's Faust: Parts I and II*. Edited by Paul Bishop. Rochester: Camden House, 2001.

Rommel, Gabriele (ed.). *Novalis: Das Werk und seine Editoren*. [Exhibition catalogue]. Wiederstedt, 2001. Pp. 271; illustrations.

Rowland, Herbert, ed. *Goethe, Chaos, and Complexity*. (Internationale Forschungen zur Allgmeinen und vergleichenden Literaturwissenschaft 55.) Amsterdam: Rodopi, 2001. Pp. xix + 201; illustrations.

Sasse, Günter. "Der Gesang als Medium der Sozialdisziplinierung in Goethes Roman Wilhelm Meisters Wanderjahre." *Goethe-Jahrbuch*, 118 (2001), 274–88.

Sasse, Günter. "'Die Zeit des Schönen ist vorüber': Wilhelm Meisters Weg zum Beruf des Wundarztes in Goethes Roman Wilhelm Meisters Wanderjahre Oder Die Entsagenden." *Internationales Archiv für Sozialgeschichte der Deutschen Literatur*, 26 (2001), 72–97.

Sauder, Gerhard. "Aufklärerische Bibelkritik und Bibelrezeption in Goethes Werk." *Goethe-Jahrbuch*, 118 (2001), 108–25.

Sauder, Gerhard. "Der Dämmerung Schleier und Goethes 'Zueignung'" Pp. 279–310 of *Goethe: Ungewohnte Ansichten*. Edited by Karl Richter. St. Ingbert: Röhrig, 2001.

Sauder, Gerhard. "Tiecks 'Vernachlässigter Lenz'." Pp. 37–46 of *Jakob Michael Reinhold Lenz: Vom Sturm und Drang zur Moderne*. Edited by Andreas Meier. Heidelberg: Carl Winter Universitätsverlag, 2001.

Sautermeister, Gert. "Brennpunkte der Aphoristik Lichtenbergs." Pp. 172–203 of *Lectures d'une oeuvre: Les aphorismes de Lichtenberg*. Edited by Jean Mondot. Paris: Éditions du temps, 2001.

Scheffel, Michael. "Das Buch der Natur und die Schrift des Dichters: Barthold Heinrich Brockes und die Folgen." Pp. 26–39 of *Erschriebene Natur: Internationale Perspektiven auf Texte des 18. Jahrhunderts*. Edited by Michael Scheffel. Bern: Peter Lang, 2001.

Scheffel, Michael (ed.). *Erschriebene Natur: Internationale Perspektiven auf Texte des 18. Jahrhunderts*. (Jahrbuch für Internationale Germanistik A 66.) Bern: Peter Lang, 2001.

Schellenberg, Renata. "The Genesis of Goethe's Last Novel: Wilhelm Meisters Wanderjahre (1821)." *New German Review: A Journal of Germanic Studies*, 17 (2001), 47–63.

Schindler, Stephan K. "Die blutende Brust der Amazone: Bedrohliche weibliche Sexualität in Kleists 'Penthesilea..'" Pp. 191–202 of *Kleists Erzählungen und Dramen: Neue Studien*. Edited by Paul Michael Lützeler and David Pan. Würzburg: Königshausen & Neumann, 2001.

Schindler, Stephan K. *Eingebildete Körper: Phantasierte Sexualität in der Goethezeit*. Tübingen: Stauffenburg, 2001. Pp. 258.

Schlichtmann, Silke. *Geschlechterdifferenz in der Literaturrezeption um 1800? Zu zeitgenössischen Goethe-Lektüren*. (Untersuchungen zur deutschen Literaturgeschichte 107.) Tübingen: Max Niemeyer Verlag, 2001. Pp. viii + 303.

Schlipphacke, Heidi M. "Eros and Community: C. F. Gellert's Das Leben der schwedischen Gräfin von G***." *Germanic Review*, 76 (2001), 70–89.

Schlosser, Rainer. "Die Gazzetta di Weimar als Quelle italienischer Erstbelege." *Romanische Forschungen*, 113 (2001), 171–89.

Schmidt, Benjamin Marius. *Denker ohne Gott und Vater: Schiller, Schlegel und der Entwurf von Modernität in den 1790ern*. Stuttgart: Metzler, 2001. Pp. xi + 326.

Schmidt, Michael. "Die 'Liebhaberin der Vernunft' und ihr 'Rechthaber': Zum Verfahren der Lächerlichkeitsprobe in Lessings Komödie 'Minna von Barnhelm oder das Soldatenglück'." *Nordlit: Arbeidstidsskrift i litteratur*, 9 (2001), 29–44.

Schmiesing, Ann. "Lessing's Reading of Racinian Tragedy." *Seminar: A Journal of Germanic Studies*, 37 (2001), 113–28.

Schneider, Erich. "Geschichte Schreiber des Luxus, nicht seine Priester": Das 'Journal des Luxus und der Moden' (1786–1827)." *Rückert-Studien*, 13 (2000/01) 89–109.

Schneider, Helmut J. "Goethes Schauspiel 'Torquato Tasso' und Tassos Hirtenspiel 'Aminta': Eine Skizze zum Fortleben der pastoralen Tradition." Pp. 313–27 of *Goethe und Italien*. Edited by Willi Hirdt and Birgit Tappert. Bonn: Bouvier, 2001.

Schneider, Helmut J. "Das Licht der Welt: Geburt und Bild in Goethes Faustdichtung." *Deutsche Vierteljahrsschrift für Literaturwissenschaft und Geistesgeschichte*, 75 (2001), 102–22.

Schneider, Manfred. "Die Welt im Ausnahmezustand: Kleists Kriegstheater." *Kleist-Jahrbuch*, (2001), 104–19.

Schneiders, Werner. "Aufklärung als memento mori?" *Das achtzehnte Jahrhundert*, 25 (2001), 83–96.

Schossler, Franziska, and Paul Bishop. "Progress and Restorative Utopia in Faust II and Wilhelm Meister Wanderjahre." Pp. 169–93 of *A Companion to Goethe's Faust: Parts I and II*. Edited by Paul Bishop. Rochester: Camden House, 2001.

Schrader, Hans Jürgen. "Salomonis Schlüssel für die 'halbe Höllenbrut': Radikalpietistisch tingierte 'Geist–Kunst' im Faustschen 'Studierzimmer.'" Pp. 231–56 of *Goethe und der Pietismus*. Edited by Hans-Georg Kemper. Tübingen: Max Niemeyer Verlag, 2001.

Schubert, Gerd (ed.). *Jahrbuch der Johann-Gottfried-Schnabel-Gesellschaft 2000-2001. Schnabeliana. Beiträge und Dokumente zu Johann Gottfried Schnabels Leben und Werk und zur Literatur und Geschichte des frühen 18. Jahrhunderts*. St. Ingbert: Röhrig, 2001. Pp. 177; illustrations, facsimiles.

Schulz, Friedrich. *Briefe*. Edited by Gerhard Kosellek. Bielefeld: Aisthesis, 2001. Pp. 266.

Schulz, Georg M. *Jacob Michael Reinhold Lenz*. (Reclams UB 17629.) Stuttgart: Reclam, 2001. Pp. 300; illustrations.

Schutjer, Karin Lynn. *Narrating Community after Kant: Schiller, Goethe, and Hölderlin*. Detroit: Wayne State University Press, 2001. Pp. 272.

Schwartz, Peter J. "Eduard's Egotism: Historical Notes on Goethe's Elective Affinities." *Germanic Review*, 76 (2001), 41–68.

Schwieder, Gabriele. *Goethes "West östlicher Divan": Eine poetologische Lektüre*. Köln: Böhlau, 2001. Pp. viii + 242.

Scimonello, Giovanni. "Benjamin, Adorno e Hölderlin: interpretazione dell'ode 'Dichtermut'/'Blödigkeit.'" *Cultura tedesca,* 18 (2001), 111–28.

Seifert, Siegfried. "Goethe-Bibliographie 2000." *Goethe-Jahrbuch*, 118 (2001), 523–71.

Seume, Johann Gottfried. *Spaziergang nach Syrakus im Jahre 1802*. Edited with an Introduction by Jörg Drews. Frankfurt: Insel, 2001. Pp. 455; illustrations.

Shaw, Gisela. "Theodor Gottlieb von Hippel (1741–1796) als Wegbereiter der Frauenbewegung in Deutschland: 'Lachender Philosoph' oder 'Prophet'?" *German Life and Letters*, 54 (2001), 273–90.

Siepe, Franz. "Wieland und der prodikeische Herkules: Zu einem Detail in Kraus Gemälde Wieland im Kreis seiner Familie und zu Wielands lyrischem Drama Die Wahl des Herkules." *Jahrbuch der Deutschen Schillergesellschaft: Internationales Organ für Neuere Deutsche Literatur*, 45 (2001), 73–96.

Simonis, Annette. "Die 'neue Mythologie' der Aufklärung: Karl Philipp Moritz' Mythenpoetik im diskursgeschichtlichen Kontext." *Jahrbuch der Deutschen Schillergesellschaft: Internationales Organ für Neuere Deutsche Literatur*, 45 (2001), 97–130.

Simons, Olaf. *Marteaus Europa oder Der Roman, bevor er Literatur wurde: eine Untersuchung des deutschen und englischen Buchangebots der Jahre 1710 bis 1720*. Amsterdam: Rodopi 2001. Pp. 765.

Sinopoli, Franca. "La Representation de la douleur: Contradictions du classicisme chez Lessing et chez Schiller." Pp. 281–88 of *Theories et debats esthetiques au dix huitième siècle: Elements d' une enquete/Debates on Aesthetics in the Eighteenth Century: Questions of Theory and Practice*. Edited by Elisabeth Décultot and Mark Ledbury. Paris: Honoré Champion, 2001.

Smith, Peter D. "'Was die Welt im Innersten zusammenhält': Scientific Themes in Goethe's Faust." Pp. 194–220 of *A Companion to Goethe's Faust: Parts I and II*. Edited by Paul Bishop. Rochester: Camden House, 2001.

Soboth, Christian. "Willkommen und Abschied: Der junge Goethe und der Pietismus." Pp. 209–30 of *Goethe und der Pietismus*. Edited by Hans-Georg Kemper. Tübingen: Max Niemeyer Verlag, 2001.

Solbach, Andreas. "Der galante Geschmack." Pp. 225–76 of *Der galante Diskurs: Kommunikationsideal und Epochenschwelle*. Edited by Thomas Borgstedt and Andreas Solbach. Dresden: Thelem, 2001.

Sørensen, Bengt Algot. "Friederike Brun in den 'Bonstettiana.'" *Das achtzehnte Jahrhundert*, 25 (2001), 279–82.

Spicker, Friedemann. "'Für den Verstand kann man nicht zu lakonisch sein, aber wohl für die Phantasie': Jean Paul als Aphoristiker—nach und neben Lichtenberg." *Lichtenberg-Jahrbuch*, 12 (2000 [2001]), 82–96.

Stellmacher, Wolfgang. *Goethes "Puppenspiel": Vom Sinn und Gewinn der zyklischen Komposition*. Frankfurt: Peter Lang, 2001. Pp. 198.

Stepanov, V. P. "Izmenenie Chastotnosti Upotrebitel'nykh Imen Na Protiazhenii Xviii Veka." *Russkaia Literatura: Istoriko Literaturnyi Zhurnal*, 2 (2001), 71–75.

Stephens, Anthony. "Stimmengewebe: Antithetik und Verschiebung in 'Die heilige Cäcilie oder die Gewalt der Musik.'" Pp. 77–91 of *Kleists Erzählungen und Dramen: Neue Studien*. Edited by Paul Michael Lützeler and David Pan. Würzburg: Königshausen & Neumann, 2001.

Stephenson, R. H. "The Diachronic Solidity of Goethe's Faust." Pp. 243–70 of *A Companion to Goethe's Faust: Parts I and II*. Edited by Paul Bishop. Rochester: Camden House, 2001.

Stewart, Tom. "Melancholia, Masturbation, and Lesesucht in *Anton Reiser*." *Focus on German Studies: A Journal on and Beyond German Language and Literature*, 8 (2001), 97–108.

Stievermann, Jan. "'Man Doing' and 'Man Listening': A Comparison of Ralph Waldo Emerson's Nature and Novalis' Die Lehrlinge zu Sais." *Literaturwissenschaftliches Jahrbuch im Auftrage der Görres-Gesellschaft*, 42 (2001), 125–44.

Strack, Friedrich. "Von Goethe und Schiller verkannt und gegängelt?: Hölderlins Auseinandersetzung mit der Weimarer Klassik." *Jahrbuch des Freien Deutschen Hochstifts*, (2001), 122–50.

Streitberger, Fritz. *Der Freiheit eine Gasse: Die Lebensgeschichte des Christian Friedrich Daniel Schubart.* Bietigheim: Salzer, 2001. Pp. 135.

Sullivan, John. "The Epistolary Style of Simeon Denisov." *Slavonica*, 7 (2001), 42–61.

Swales, Martin. "The Character and Characterization of Faust." Pp. 28–55 of *A Companion to Goethe's Faust: Parts I and II*. Edited by Paul Bishop. Rochester: Camden House, 2001.

Tantillo, Astrida Orle. *Goethe's Elective Affinities and the Critics.* (Studies in German Literature Linguistics and Culture.) Rochester: Camden House, 2001. Pp. 270; bibliography.

Tateo, Francesco (ed.). *Le svolte nella letteratura italiana.* 5 volumes. Bari: Edizioni B.A. Graphis, 2001.

Tellini, Gino. "Ancora su Goethe e Manzoni." Pp. 341–53 of *Goethe und Italien*. Edited by Willi Hirdt and Birgit Tappert. Bonn: Bouvier, 2001.

Thums, Barbara, and Olivier Mannoni. "Paradigmes classiques et romantiques d'une esthethique de la distance chez Karl Philipp Moritz et Wilhelm Heinrich Wackenroder." *Revue Germanique Internationale*, 16 (2001), 101–22, 191–92.

Tippner, Anja. "'Wissende Unschuld': Selbstinszenierung und Repräsentation in den Memoiren Katharinas II." *Deutsche Vierteljahrsschrift für Literaturwissenschaft und Geistesgeschichte*, 75 (2001), 422–45.

Vaget, Hans Rudolf. "The 'Augenmensch' and the Failure of Vision: Goethe and the Trauma of Dilettantism." *Deutsche Vierteljahrsschrift für Literaturwissenschaft und Geistesgeschichte*, 75 (2001), 15–26.

Vaget, Hans Rudolf. "'Massig boshaft': Faust Gefährte. Goethes Mephistopheles im Lichte der Aufklärung." *Goethe-Jahrbuch*, 118 (2001), 234–46.

Vaget, Hans Rudolf. "Neue Wege zu Goethes Faust?" *Colloquia Germanica: Internationale Zeitschrift für Germanistik*, 34 (2001), 57–64.

Vaget, Hans Rudolf. "Wer vieles bringt, wird manchem etwas bringen: Zur Situtation der Faust-Philologie im Jubilaumsjahr 1999." Pp. 29–42 of *Goethe-Philologie im Jubiläumsjahr: Bilanz und Perspektiven*. Edited by Jochen Golz. Tübingen: Max Niemeyer Verlag, 2001.

Van der Laan, James M. "Faust and Textual Chaos." Pp. 105–15 of *Goethe, Chaos, and Complexity*. Edited by Herbert Rowland. Amsterdam: Rodopi, 2001.

Van Ingen, Ferdinand: "Epochenschwelle und Gattungskonvention in der Galanten Dichtung: Liebesklage und Abschied." Pp. 87–110 of *Der galante Diskurs: Kommunikationsideal und Epochenschwelle*. Edited by Thomas Borgstedt and Andreas Solbach. Dresden: Thelem, 2001.

Vincent, Deirdre. "Text as Image and Self-Image: The Contextualization of Goethe's Dichtung und Wahrheit (1810–1813)." *Goethe Yearbook*, 10 (2001), 125–53.

Vollhardt, Friedrich. *Selbstliebe und Geselligkeit: Untersuchungen zum Verhältnis von naturrechtlichem Denken und moraldidaktischer Literatur im 17. und 18. Jahrhundert*. (Communicatio 26.) Tübingen: Max Niemeyer Verlag, 2001. Pp. vii + 393.

Vollmann, Ralf. "Der Beitrag über Tibetisch in Adelungs 'Mithridates' 1806." *Asiatische Studien/Etudes Asiatiques: Zeitschrift der Schweizerischen Asiengesellschaft/Revue de la Societe Suisse Asie*, 55 (2001), 493–528.

Vulpius, Christian August. *Glossarium für das 18. Jahrhundert*. Edited by Alexander Kosenina. (Fundstücke 1.) Hannover: Wehrhahn, 2001. Pp. 112.

A discussion of Christian Vulpius usually begins with the date 12 July 1788, when the author's sister, Christiane Vulpius, requested Goethe to find some suitable work for her brother. Since scholarship has long been more fascinated by Christiane Vulpius (E. Klessmann, S. Damm), often the discussion ends there as well. Christian Vulpius, best known for his wildly successful *Rinaldo Rinaldini, der Räuberhauptmann* [*Rinaldo rinaldini, the Robber-chief*] (1799), is also the author of seventy-seven prose works, forty-three plays, and twenty-four collections of poetry or songs, including the publication of the *Glossarium* [*Glossary*] when he was only twenty-six year old. Vulpius also edited four journals, contributed numerous reviews, and penned over nine-hundred letters before he died in 1827. Trained as a lawyer, the young and often impoverished Vulpius worked in the Göschen publishing house, in the Weimar Court Theater, and as a private secretary, before finally settling in as the librarian at the Ducal Library in Weimar. A few brave souls (A. Meier, E. Larkin, R. Simanowski—not Somanowski as given in the notes) have sought to establish Vulpius' credentials as an insightful critic of his times and disseminator of the values of the Enlightenment. This slim volume of 110 pages will further that aim considerably.

Following the tradition of satirical dictionaries (Rabener, Lichtenberg, Cranz, and others), which Prof. Košenina skillfully points out in the afterword, the *Glossarium* of 1788 contains nearly 600 aperçus on the most diverse issues of his age. They range from one-word responses "MÄRTIRERBUCH, ein Ehestandsjournal" ["book of martyrs, a matrimony journal"] to elaborations of a page or so on "DICHTER, KUSS, WELT" ["poet, kiss, world"]. In his witty, insightful and occasionally mocking descriptions, Vulpius reveals the breadth of his reading as he cites Platon, Sebastian Brand, Opitz, Shakespeare, Wieland (often), Herder, Richardson, Rousseau, Goethe, Schiller, and many others including himself.

Arranged alphabetically, the conceptual starting point may be the role of the satirist: "SATIRIKER, ein Mann, welcher seines Lebens nicht sicher ist, weil er die Wahrheit zur Schau trägt." ["Satirist: a man whose life is not safe because he exhibits truth."] With piercing exactness he lampoons humanity, even if not without sympathy:

"MENSCH, ist, mit dem alten Dichter Opitz, zu reden: des Glükes Ball, die Phantasey der Zeit." [A human being is, in the words of the old poet Opitz: fortune's ball, time's fantasy."] But even as humanity is the object of another's will, it is also most capable of inflicting harm: "RAUBTHIER, bedeutet der Mensch." ["Beast of prey, meaning, human being."] In short, the portrayed world is not a friendly, inhabitable place: "WELT, ist ein Ort, wo, wie Göthens Werther sagt, nicht leicht einer den andern versteht." ["World, that is a place, as Goethe's Werther says, where hardly anyone understands anyone else."] Neither philosophy, a frozen weather vane that points only in one direction, nor the university ("UNIVERSITÄT, der schönste ort, an der Quelle Durst zu leiden." ["University, the most beautiful place to suffer thirst at the spring."]) provides a corrective. Indeed, thoughtful reflection seems out of fashion: "NACHDENKEN, eine menschliche Eigenschaft, welche bald ganz und gar aus der Mode kommen wird." ["Reflecting, a human characteristic which will soon become totally unfashionable."] Not without some bitterness, then death becomes a friend: "TOD, der beste Freund der Menschen." ["Death, men's best friend."] But given the genre, such speculations are to be taken with a grain of salt.

Not surprisingly, Vulpius takes aim at the literary institutions and the convoluted financial arrangements they bring: "DICHTER, eine Menschengattung, welche sich des Hungers nicht erwehren kann, und doch von Göttermalen, Nektar und Ambrosia spricht." [Poets, a group of humans which cannot fend of hunger, and yet speaks of feasts of the gods, of nectar and ambrosia."] Poets and writers are taken advantage of: "NACHDRUCKER, sind privilegierte Diebe. . ." ["Reprinters are privileged thieves."] And the reviewers too are moved only by resentment: "REZENSENT, gewöhnlich, ein Mann, der es nicht leiden kann, daß jemand etwas Gutes geschrieben hat, welcher nicht sein oder seiner Sekte Freund ist." [Reviewer, ordinarily a man who cannot tolerate it that someone who is not his or his group's friend has written something good."] Only the translator, the ÜBERSETZER, which Vulpius himself was, seems to find favorable commentary.

With some virulence Vulpius satirizes the vicious and hypocritical religious scene of his day, largely from the perspective of German Lutheranism: "JESUITISMUS [soll] wie die Pest im Finstern schleichen." ["Jesuitism, prowling like pestilence in the dark."] "PFAFFEN, auch Priester, welche in der Welt das gröste Unglük anrichteten." ["Parsons, or priests, who do the utmost misfortune in the world."] He does not spare the ÄBTISSIN [abbess], the KARDINAL [cardinal], and the NONNE [nun]. Nor are the arrogant ILLUMINATEN [illuminati] found to differ from the Jesuits.

Vulpius further satirizes the social classes, e.g., the BAUER [peasant] as pack mule of the state and the ADEL [nobility] as uselessly privileged. Interestingly, no BÜRGER [bourgeois], the class to which Vulpius aspired, is mentioned. Vulpius, who came to value conservative political views, similarly makes fun of the ideal of his fellow patriots: "VATERLAND, eine Frazze, welche nur schwachköpfichte Menschen amusirt." ["Fatherland, a grimace which amuses only feeble-minded humans."]

Even less significant matters are objects of Vulpius's satire. The doctor is vilified for his greed; attention to modishness and sentimentality are critiqued. Relations between men and women find ample parody in the text. While UNMÄSIGKEIT [immodesty] and UNBESTÄNDIGKEIT [fickleness] are female virtues (although Vulpius in many other texts presents a surprisingly positive portrayal of women), marriage is mocked: "EHE, eine wechselseitige Verbindung zwischen einem männlichen und einem weiblichen Geschöpf sich lebenslang Weh und Leid zu klagen." ["Marriage, a mutual relation between a male and a female creature in order to wail and commiserate all their life long."]

Much is playful and much is serious in this satiric text. But if one is familiar with other aspects of Vulpius' writing and life, one realizes that he sides fully with the ethical aims of the limited *Selbstdenken* of the conservative Enlightenment and the aesthetic stance of the Weimar Classicists, Goethe and Schiller, whom he defended against Kotzebue. The entries indicate Vulpius' strong affirmation of eudaemonistic (not hedonistic, not enthusiastic) principles as well as the need for moral rectitude grounded in reason and nature.

We are indebted to the editor, Košenina, for this entertaining and informative volume, for he again reminds us that we remain interested in the eighteenth century because, in its problematical social, political and religious institutions, it resembles our own.—Edward T. Larkin

Wagner, Irmgard. "Goethe's Bohemian Traces Or: Marienbad Mirrorings." *Modern Language Studies*, 31 (2001), 151–62.

Wahl, Volker. "Goethes Amtliche Schriften als Editionsaufgabe des Thüringischen Hauptstaatsarchivs Weimar." Pp. 175–94 of *Goethe-Philologie im Jubiläumsjahr: Bilanz und Perspektiven*. Edited by Jochen Golz. Tübingen: Max Niemeyer Verlag, 2001.

Warminksi, Andrzej. "Returns of the Sublime: Positing and Performative in Kant, Fichte, and Schiller." *Modern Language Notes*, 116 (2001), 964–78.

Weder, Christine. "Moral Interest and Religious Truth: On the Relationship between Morality and Religion in Novalis." *German Life and Letters*, 54 (2001), 291–309.

Weigel, Sigrid. "Der 'Findling' als 'gefährliches Supplement'." *Kleist-Jahrbuch,* (2001), 120–34.

Weigelt, Horst. "Johann Kaspar Lavater und Goethe: Zwischen Nähe und Distanz." Pp. 135–56 of *Goethe und der Pietismus*. Edited by Hans-Georg Kemper. Tübingen: Max Niemeyer Verlag, 2001.

Weimar, Klaus. "Der Blick und die Gewalt der Stimme: Zu Die Natürliche Tochter." *Deutsche Vierteljahrsschrift für Literaturwissenschaft und Geistesgeschichte*, 75 (2001), 39–59.

Weiss, Hermann F. "Unbekannte Zeugnisse zu Friedrich von Hardenberg und seinem Umkreis." *Literaturwissenschaftliches Jahrbuch im Auftrage der Görres-Gesellschaft*, 42 (2001), 83–123.

Weissberg, Liliane. "Life as a Goddess: Henriette Herz Writes Her Autobiography." *Braun Lectures in the History of the Jews in Prussia*, 6 (2001), 5–40.

Weissengruber, Erik. "'Can One Not Be Serious, Even When Laughing?': British Translations of G. E. Lessing's Minna von Barnhelm, 1786–1805." *Metamorphoses: Journal of the Five College Seminar on Literary Translation*, 9 (2001), 51–74.

Weizsäcker, Richard von. "Can Goethe Guide Us through the Process of European Union?" Pp. 25–39 of *A New Germany in a New Europe*. Edited by Todd Herzog. New York: Routledge, 2001.

Welsh, Caroline, Christina Dongowski, and Susanna Lulé (eds.). *Sinne und Verstand: Ästhetische Modellierungen der Wahrnehmung um 1800*. Würzburg: Königshausen & Neumann, 2001. Pp. 244.

Wicke, Andrea. "Politisches und galantes Verhaltensideal im frühen 18. Jahrhundert: Überschneidungen und Differenzen." Pp. 313–30 of *Der galante Diskurs: Kommunikationsideal und Epochenschwelle*. Edited by Thomas Borgstedt and Andreas Solbach. Dresden: Thelem, 2001.

Wieckenberg, Ernst-Peter. "Johann Heinrich Voß, 'Tausend und eine Nacht' und einige vergessene Gedichte." *Lichtenberg-Jahrbuch*, 12 (2000 [2001]), 97–126.

Wieczorrek, Michael. "Stil und Status: Juristisches Schreiben im 18. Jahrhundert." Pp. 99–112 of *Recht und Sprache in der deutschen Aufklärung*. Edited by Ulrich Kronauer. Tübingen: Max Niemeyer Verlag, 2001.

Wiethölter, Waltraud (ed.). *Der junge Goethe: Genese und Konstruktion einer Autorschaft*. Tübingen: Francke, 2001. Pp. 184.

Wiethölter, Waltraud. "'Ursprünglicher Gedanken Refrain-Wiederholung': Zum Phänomen frühromantischer Zyklik." *Deutsche Vierteljahrsschrift für Literaturwissenschaft und Geistesgeschichte*, 75 (2001), 587–656.

Williams, John R. "The Problem of the Mothers." Pp. 122–43 of *A Companion to Goethe's Faust: Parts I and II*. Edited by Paul Bishop. Rochester: Camden House, 2001.

Wilson, W. Daniel. "'Humanitätssalbader': Goethe's Distaste for Jewish Emancipation, and Jewish Responses." Pp. 146–64 of *Goethe in German Jewish Culture*. Edited by Klaus L. Berghahn. Rochester: Camden House, 2001.

Winter, Susanne. "Tra ragione e passione: Turandot di Carlo Gozzi e di Friedrich Schiller." *Problemi di Critica Goldiana*, 8 (2001), 223–51.

Wintermeyer, Rolf. "Selbsterfahrung und Sprachdenken bei Lichtenberg." Pp. 130–71 of *Lectures d'une oeuvre: Les aphorismes de Lichtenberg*. Edited by Jean Mondot. Paris: Éditions du temps, 2001.

Woesler, Winfried. "Brauchen wir eine neue Ausgabe von Lessings Briefwechsel?" Pp. 75–94 of *'Ich an Dich': Edition, Rezeption und Kommentierung von Briefen*. Edited by Werner M. Bauer. Innsbruck: Institut fur Deutsche Sprache, Literatur und Literaturkritik, 2001.

Wolf, Norbert Christian. *Streitbare Ästhetik: Goethes kunst- und literaturtheoretische Schriften 1771–1789*. Tübingen: Max Niemeyer Verlag 2001. Pp. ix + 566.

Worley, Sharon. "Ethical Aesthetics and the Immutable Model in Friedrich Schiller's on the Aesthetic Education of Man and Dorothea Schlegel's Florentin." *New German Review: A Journal of Germanic Studies*, 17 (2001), 107–38.

Zehm, Edith. "Überlieferung und Textherstellung: Textprobleme im zweiten Band der Edition von Goethes Tagebüchern." Pp. 113–22 of *Goethe-Philologie im Jubiläumsjahr: Bilanz und Perspektiven*. Edited by Jochen Golz. Tübingen: Max Niemeyer Verlag, 2001.

Zelle, Carsten. "Die Geburt der Natur aus dem Geiste der Rhetorik: Zur Schematisierung von Natur und Genie bei Dennis und Goethe." Pp. 145–67 of *Erschriebene Natur: Internationale Perspektiven auf Texte des 18. Jahrhunderts*. Edited by Michael Scheffel. Bern: Peter Lang, 2001.

Zelle, Carsten. "Von der Ästhetik des Geschmacks zur Ästhetik des Schönen." Pp. 371–97 of *Die Wende von der Aufklärung zur Romantik 1760–1820: Epoche im Überblick*. Edited by Horst-Albert Glaser. Amsterdam: Benjamins, 2001.

Ziolkowski, Theodore. "Das Treffen in Buchenwald oder der vergegenwärtigte Goethe." *Modern Language Studies*, 31 (2001), 131–50.

Zymner, Rüdiger. "Lenz und Shakespeare." Pp. 11–21 of *Jakob Michael Reinhold Lenz: Vom Sturm und Drang zur Moderne*. Edited by Andreas Meier. Heidelberg: Carl Winter Universitätsverlag, 2001.

Italian Literature and Language

Ajello, Epifanio. *Carlo Goldoni: L'Esattezza e lo sguardo*. (Civiltà letteraria italiana 20). Salerno: Edisud, 2001. Pp. 356; illustration.

Bersier, Gabrielle. "Goethe's Geology in Flux: Vulcanism and Neptunism in the Translation of Richard Payne Knight's Expedition into Sicily and the Italian Journey." Pp. 35–45 of *Goethe, Chaos, and Complexity*. Edited by Herbert Rowland. Amsterdam: Rodopi, 2001.

Bertipaglia, Giuliana. "Ossian and Cesarotti: Poems and Translations." *Studies in Scottish Literature*, 32 (2001), 132–39.

Blanc, Olivier, and Jeffrey Merrick. "The 'Italian Taste' in the Time of Louis XVI, 1774–92." *Journal of Homosexuality*, 41 (2001), 69–84.

Bordin, Michele. "Retorica della negazione e morale della rinuncia: Altre postille alla 'Sinderesi' di Giacinta (Goldoni, Avventure della villeggiatura, III, 4)." *Problemi di Critica Goldiana*, 8 (2001), 93–131.

Brook, Clodagh. "Giuseppe Ungaretti: Translator of William Blake." *Forum Italicum*, 35 (2001), 368–82.

Caesar, Ann Hallamore. "History or Pre-History? Recent Revisions in the Eighteenth-Century Novel in Italy." *Journal of Romance Studies*, 1 (2001), 133–41.

Calimani, Anna Vera Sullam. "Ippolito Pindemonte e la lingua Inglese." *Quaderni Veneti*, 34 (2001), 179–98.

Capano, Daniel A. "El binarismo simetrico como operador del humor en 'Il servitore di due padroni" de Carlo Goldoni." *Letras*, 44 (2001), 69–76.

Chammas, Jacqueline. "L'inceste: 'Crime' ou 'droit de la nature'? La loi de l'interdit dans l'icosameron de Casanova;." Pp. 33–47 of *Lumen*. Edited by William Kinsley. (Lumen: Proceedings of the Canadian Society for Eighteenth-Century Studies/Actes de la societe Canadienne d'etude du dix huitième siècle 20.) Kelowna: Academic, for Canadian Society for Eighteenth-Century Studies, 2001.

Chaplin, Sue. "Romance and Sedition in the 1790s: Radcliffe's the Italian and the Terrorist Text." *Romanticism: The Journal of Romantic Culture and Criticism*, 7 (2001), 177–90.

Cicali, Gianni. "Strategie drammaturgiche di un contemporaneo di Goldoni: Pietro Trinchera (1702–1755)." *Problemi di Critica Goldiana*, 8 (2001), 133–201.

Clerici, Luca (ed.). *Il viaggiatore meravigliato. Italiani in Italia [1714–1996]*. (EST 189.) Milano: Il Saggiatore, 2001. Pp. xxx + 372.

Costa Zalessow, Natalia. "Fragments from an Autobiography: Petronilla Paolini Massimi's Struggle for Self-Assertion." *Italian Quarterly*, 38 (2001), 27–35.

Costa Zalessow, Natalia. "Teresa Carniani Malvezzi and Vincenzo Monti." *Rivista di Studi Italiani*, 19 (2001), 48–64.

Crotti, Ilaria, Gilberto Pizzamiglio, and Piermario Vescovo, eds. *Putte, zanni, rusteghi: Scena e testo nella Commedia Goldoniana*. (Pleiadi 53.) Ravenna: Longo, 2001.

Danesi, Marcel. "Metafora e senso: Un'interpretazione Vichiana delle ricerche recenti sulla metafora." *Forum Italicum*, 35 (2001), 23–47.

Di Brazza, Fabiana. "Pindemonte, Vittorelli, Antonio di Brazza: Nuove Testimonianze." *Quaderni Veneti*, 33 (2001), 127–35.

Fido, Franco. "Carlo Gozzi e Diderot dopo 'Le Bourru Bienfaisant': Palinodie di Antigoldonisti." *Rivista di Letterature Moderne e Comparate*, 54 (2001), 427–36.

Foucart, Claude. "Rom und das klassische Ideal." Pp. 685–713 of *Die Wende von der Aufklärung zur Romantik 1760–1820: Epoche im Überblick*. Edited by Horst-Albert Glaser. Amsterdam: Benjamins, 2001.

Gaborik, Patricia. "Layers of Othering: Missing Politics in Translation of Carlo Gozzi's Turandot." *Metamorphoses: Journal of the Five College Seminar on Literary Translation*, 9 (2001), 75–89.

Giannetti, Valeria. "Il Sermone sulla mitologia di Vincenzo Monti." *Lettere Italiane*, 53 (2001), 509–24.

Glaser, Horst Albert. "Annex: Giacomo Casanova." Pp. 161–70 of *Die Wende von der Aufklärung zur Romantik 1760–1820: Epoche im Überblick*. Edited by Horst-Albert Glaser. Amsterdam: Benjamins, 2001.

Guerci, Luciano. "Appunti sulla letteratura controrivoluzionaria in Italia (1789–1799)." *Pensiero Politico: Rivista di Storia delle Idee Politiche e Sociali*, 34 (2001), 255–67.

Longman, Stanley V. "Theatrical Warfare in Eighteenth-Century Venice." *Text and Presentation: The Journal of the Comparative Drama Conference*, 22 (2001), 113–25.

Lukoschik, Rita Unfer. "Die 'Gelehrte Frau Elisabetta Caminer Turra, Zu Vicenza': Eine Kulturvermittlerin des 18. Jahrhunderts." Pp. 32–52, 457 of *Märkte, Medien, Vermittler: Zur interkulturellen Vernetzung von Literatur und Film*. Edited by Manfred Engelbert. Göttingen: Wallstein, 2001.

Marchi, Gian Paolo. "Mascheroniana." *Quaderni di Lingue e Letterature*, 26 (2001), 125–31.

Marienberg, Sabine. "L'agire semiotico in Vico e Hamann." *Bollettino del Centro di Studi Vichiani*, 31–32 (2001), 87–93.

Meylan, Claire. "Quand les critiques repondent a Casanova." Pp. 201–08 of *Fiction d' auteur? Le discours biographique sur l' auteur de l' antiquite a nos jours*. Edited by Sandrine Dubel. Paris: Honoré Champion, 2001.

Momo, Arnaldo. "Considerazioni intorno a qualche 'Lieto Fine' Goldoniano fra testo e scena." *Problemi di Critica Goldiana*, 8 (2001), 7–91.

Morgana, Silvia. "Volta e la lingua della comunicazione scientifica." *Acme: Annali della Facolta di Lettere e Filosofia dell' Universita degli Studi di Milano*, 54 (2001), 205–26.

Naddeo, Barbara Ann. "Urban Arcadia: Representations of the 'Dialect' of Naples in Linguistic Theory and Comic Theater, 1696–1780." *Eighteenth Century Studies*, 35 (2001), 41–65.

Padoan, Giorgio. "Correzioni d'autore al sior Todero Brontolon." Pp. 175–99 of *Putte, zanni, rusteghi: Scena e testo nella commedia Goldoniana*. Edited by Ilaria Crotti. Ravenna: Longo, 2001.

Padoan, Giorgio. "Dalla filologia testuale all'analisi drammaturgica: Il sior Todero Brontolon." Pp. 201–322 of *Putte, zanni, rusteghi: Scena e testo nella commedia Goldoniana*. Edited by Ilaria Crotti. Ravenna: Longo, 2001.

Padoan, Giorgio. "Gli arlecchini di Carlo Goldoni." Pp. 81–110 of *Putte, zanni, rusteghi: Scena e testo nella commedia Goldoniana*. Edited by Ilaria Crotti. Ravenna: Longo, 2001.

Padoan, Giorgio. "Goldoni, Marmontel, Zanetti: La dedica de la casa nova." Pp. 323–37 of *Putte, zanni, rusteghi: Scena e testo nella commedia Goldoniana*. Edited by Ilaria Crotti. Ravenna: Longo, 2001.

Padoan, Giorgio. "I 'Rusteghi,' Todero e i presunti limiti ideologici della Borghesia Veneziana." Pp. 151–73 of *Putte, zanni, rusteghi: Scena e testo nella commedia Goldoniana*. Edited by Ilaria Crotti. Ravenna: Longo, 2001.

Padoan, Giorgio. "L'erede di Molière." Pp. 111–50 of *Putte, zanni, rusteghi: Scena e testo nella commedia Goldoniana*. Edited by Ilaria Crotti. Ravenna: Longo, 2001.

Padoan, Giorgio. "L'esordio di Goldoni: La conquista della moralita." Pp. 11–44 of *Putte, zanni, rusteghi: Scena e testo nella commedia Goldoniana*. Edited by Ilaria Crotti. Ravenna: Longo, 2001.

Padoan, Giorgio. "L'impegno civile di Carlo Goldoni." Pp. 45–80 of *Putte, zanni, rusteghi: Scena e testo nella commedia Goldoniana*. Edited by Ilaria Crotti. Ravenna: Longo, 2001.

Perocco, Daria. "Non foscolo, ma." *Quaderni Veneti*, 34 (2001), 199–218.

Pizzamiglio, Gilberto. "Due rimandi ariosteschi nel raggiratore di Goldoni?" *Quaderni Veneti*, 34 (2001), 145–54.

Pozzi, Francesco. "Il barnabita Carlo Schiera e un nuovo manoscritto settecentesco delle odi pariniane." *Aevum: Rassegna di Scienze Storiche, Linguistiche, e Filologiche*, 75 (2001), 759–80.

Puppa, Paolo. "Goldoni, per voci sole e qualche regia." *Quaderni Veneti*, 34 (2001), 155–63.

Riva, Massimo. "Per Speculum Melancholiae: The Awakening of Reason Engenders Monsters." Pp. 279–96 of *Monsters in the Italian Literary Imagination*. Edited by Keala Jewell. Detroit: Wayne State University Press, 2001.

Roy, Jeanne Helene. "Fashioning Identities: Casanova's Encounter with La Charpillon." *Intermediaire des Casanovistes*, 18 (2001), 1–9.

Rusi, Michela. "Abusi 'Gaddiani' nella Venezia del Settecento (Antonio Bianchi)." *Quaderni Veneti*, 34 (2001), 129–44.

Schlosser, Rainer. "Die Gazzetta Di Weimar als Quelle italienischer Erstbelege." *Romanische Forschungen*, 113 (2001), 171–89.

Sidorsky, David. "The Historical Novel as the Denial of History: From 'Nestor' Via the 'Vico Road' to the Commodius Vicus of Recirculation." *New Literary History: A Journal of Theory and Interpretation*, 32 (2001), 301–26.

Toaff, Ariel. "Giovanni Antonio Costanzi, ultimo censore di librai ebraici a Roma (1745–1756 Ca.)." *Rassegna Mensile di Israel*, 67 (2001), vi–vii, 203–14 (left).

Toubiana, Guy. "Kasanova karnavalut i sotsialnoto probraziavane." Pp. 273–81 of *Da mislim drugoto obrazi, stereotipi, krizi: XVIII–XX Vek/To Think the Other: Images, Stereotypes, Crisis: 18th–20th Centuries*. Edited by Nikolai Aretov. Sofia: Kralitsa Mab, 2001.

Vescovo, Piermario. "Goldoni Teorico." *Quaderni Veneti*, 34 (2001), 165–77.

Winter, Susanne. "La polemique deguisee en conte de fees dramatise: L'amore delle tre melarance et l'augellino belverde de Carlo Gozzi." Pp. 155–83 of *Theories et debats esthetiques au dix huitième siècle: Elements d' une enquete/Debates on Aesthetics in the Eighteenth Century: Questions of Theory and Practice*. Edited by Elisabeth Décultot and Mark Ledbury. Paris: Honoré Champion, 2001.

Winter, Susanne. "Tra ragione e passione: Turandot di Carlo Gozzi e di Friedrich Schiller." *Problemi di Critica Goldiana,* 8 (2001), 223–51.

Zamboni, Lidia. "Francesco Bianchini a Londra nel 1713." *Quaderni di Lingue e Letterature*, 26 (2001), 71–86.

VI: British Literatures

Abbott, Rob. *Jane Austen: A Beginner's Guide*. London: Hodder & Stoughton, 2001. Pp. x + 84; bibliography; illustrations.

Aebischer, Pascale. "'Steal[ing] out O' Th' Old Plays' in John Lacy's *Sauny the Scott: Or, the Taming of the Shrew*." *Restoration and 18th Century Theatre Research*, 16 (2001), 24–41.

Ahrens, Rüdiger. "The Cultural Context of the Dennis-Pope Controversy." Pp. 175-88 of *Renaissance Humanism—Modern Humanism(s): Festschrift for Claus Uhlig*. (Anglistische Forschungen, 301.) Edited by Walter Göbel and Bianca Ross. Heidelberg: C. Winter, 2001.

Alexander, Andrew. "'That Young Politician': Mr. B. and the Question of Authenticity in *Pamela*." Pp. 23–31 of *Proceedings of the Eighth Annual Northern Plains Conference on Earlier British Literature*. Edited by Robert J. De Smith. Sioux Center: Dordt College, 2001.

Alexander, Joy. "Anything Goes? Reading *Mansfield Park*." *Use of English,* 52 (2001), 239–51.

Alkon, Paul. "Deja Vu All Over Again: Three More Books on Samuel Johnson." *Review*, 23 (2001), 175–86.

Allen, David. "Greeks, Indians, and the Scottish Presbyterian: Dissident Arguments for Vegetarianism in Enlightenment Scotland." Pp. 265–97 of *1650–1850: Ideas, Aesthetics, and Inquiries in the Early Modern Era*. Volume 6. Edited by Kevin L. Cope. New York: AMS Press, 2001.

Andreadis, Harriette. *Sappho in Early Modern England: Female Same-Sex Literary Erotics, 1550–1714*. (The Chicago Series on Sexuality, History, and Society.) Chicago: University of Chicago Press, 2001. Pp. xiii + 254; bibliography; illustrations.

Archer, John Michael. *Old Worlds: Egypt, Southwest Asia, India, and Russia in Early Modern English Writing*. Stanford: Stanford University Press, 2001. Pp. ix + 241; bibliography.

Ardila, J. A. G. "La Influencia de la Narrativa del Siglo de Oro en la Novela Britanica del XVIII." *Revista de Literatura,* 63 (2001), 401–23.

Ardila, John G. "Cervantes y la Quixotic Fiction: El Hibridismo Generico." *Cervantes: Bulletin of the Cervantes Society of America,* 21 (2001), 43–65.

Armbruster, Karla, and Kathleen R. Wallace (eds.). *Beyond Nature Writings: Expanding the Boundaries of Ecocriticism*. Charlottesville: University Press of Virginia, 2001. Pp. x + 372.

Aron, Paul, Sophie Basch, Manuel Couvreur, Jacques Marx, Eric Van der Schueren, Valerie Van Crugten-André, and Roland Mortier. *Vérité et Littérature Au XVIIIe Siècle*. Paris: Honoré Champion, 2001. Pp. 346.

Asbach, Olaf, and Dieter Huning. "L'état de Nature et la Fondation du Droit: L'abbé de Saint-Pierre Comme Intermédiaire Entre Hobbes et Rousseau." Pp. 153–67 of *Jean-Jacques Rousseau, Politique et Nation*. Edited by Robert Thiery. Paris: Honoré Champion, 2001.

Asfour, Lana. "Sterne's First Female Reader in France: Julie de Lespinasse." *Shandean: An Annual Devoted to Laurence Sterne and His Works,* 12 (2001), 31–36.

Astington, John H. "Two Seventeenth-Century Actors: New Facts." *Theatre Notebook: A Journal of the History and Technique of the British Theatre,* 55 (2001), 2–5.

Austen, Jane. *Sense and Sensibility: Complete Text with Introduction, Historical Contexts, Critical Essays*. (New Riverside Editions.) Edited by Beth Lau. Boston: Houghton Mifflin, 2001. Pp. 386; bibliography.

Austin, Michael. "Aphra Behn, Mary Pix, and the Sexual Politics of Primogeniture." *Restoration and 18th Century Theatre Research,* 16 (2001), 13–23.

Avetisian, V. A. "Gete I Karleil': K Voprosu O Formirovanii Getevskoi Kontseptsii Mirovoi Literatury." *Izvestiia Akademii Nauk, Seriia Literatury i Iazyka,* 60 (2001), 27–37.

VI: British Literatures

Bachman, Maria K. "The Confessions of Pamela: 'a Strange Medley of Inconsistence.'" *Literature and Psychology*, 47 (2001), 12–33.

Backscheider, Paula R. "Fashioning Novels, Novelizing Fashions." Pp. 190–217 of *Eighteenth-Century Genre and Culture: Serious Reflections on Occasional Forms: Essays in Honor of J. Paul Hunter*. Edited by Dennis Todd and Cynthia Wall. Newark: University of Delaware Press, 2001.

Baer, Joel H. "Penelope Aubin and the Pirates of Madagascar: Biographical Notes and Documents." *Eighteenth-Century Women*, 1 (2001), 49–62.

Bailey, Anne Hall. "Charlotte Lennox's *The Female Quixote*: The Reconciliation of Enlightenment Philosophies." *Tennessee Philological Bulletin*, 38 (2001), 9–18.

Bainbridge, Beryl. *According to Queeney*. New York: Carroll & Graf Publishers, 2001. Pp. v + 216.

Beryl Brainbridge's *According to Queeney* is a polished, finely wrought, acrid portrait of the Streatham coterie, and one likely to produce intense ambivalence among eighteenth-century scholars. It is perhaps best described as a bleak modernist reworking of Piozzi's *Anecdotes*. Tonally, the novel is detached, austere, icy. The figures at Bolt Court—Mrs. Williams, Mrs. Desmoulins, Levet, Poll—have a pervasive odd ugliness about them, as if they were being performed by the inmates of Charenton. The Streatham Park scenes are Chekhov in Hell. What we observe is a circle of self-involved idle rich dining, drinking, gossiping, watching Sophy Streatfield make tears—all in seemingly inconsequential fashion—while constructing lives that will either result in, or be spoiled by, the next disastrous blow of fate.

The modus operandi of the novel is an obsessive intertextuality. When Bainbridge writes, "Mrs. Williams hated everybody. Levet despised Mrs. Desmoulins and did not love Mrs. Williams; Poll cared for no one and was a stupid slut besides," a Johnsonian recognizes lines from his letters—"Williams hates every body. Levet hates Desmoulins and does not love Williams. Desmoulins hates them both. Poll loves none of them"—and his description of Poll as "a stupid slut" in Fanny Burney's diary. Later in the novel, Johnson describes his father teaching him "in a gentle voice" how to swim and we recall the *blanda voce* of his Latin poem on the topic. The borrowings are so frequent, dense, and wide-ranging, they give the novel the feel of a fantastically ambitious collage. Bainbridge's characterizations range from the gratuitously strange to the deeply intuitive. Mrs. Desmoulins, for example, figures as the one woman who loves Johnson as a man—an unrequited passion by turns pathetic and bizarre. Hester Thrale, her most convincing character, appears not as an innately generous woman, but as an egoist heroically struggling to practice generosity—while her chilly, remote daughter Queeney alone perceives the narcissism behind the nurturance. This is Bainbridge at her best, and could well alter the way one thinks of the author of the *Anecdotes*.

The portrait of Johnson himself is dramatic, to be sure, but will satisfy no one who knows him well. What Bainbridge gives us most powerfully is his physical presence: the overwhelming fact of this rough, scarred, stormy, unpredictable giant. She also deftly captures his sensitivity, his neediness, and his surprising gift for befriending children. On the other hand, she makes a clearly conscious decision not even to attempt to register Johnson's intellect. Lacking the spoken *Ramblers* of Boswell's *Life*, we find it hard to believe this man did, or even could, write the published ones. Nor does she capture the *heroic* quality of Johnson's sanity. Bainbridge presents with unsettling effectiveness the "vile melancholy" (blended here of sensuality and guilt) that tormented him; but Johnson didn't *suffer* his pathology, he *fought* it—and his greatest writings are dispatches from the front. If Boswell's Johnson stands in the arena fighting back the beasts that assail him, Bainbridge's lies down and lets himself be devoured. Readers who know the Streatham coterie will find her book engaging, provocative, and elegant, but they will still feel the weakness in the portrait at its core.—Lance Wilcox

Baines, Paul. *The Complete Critical Guide to Alexander Pope.* New York: Routledge, 2001. Pp. xiv + 219; bibliography.

Bander, Elaine. "Gossip as Pleasure, Pursuit, Power, and Plot Device in Jane Austen's Novels." *Persuasions: Journal of the Jane Austen Society of North America*, 23 (2001), 118–29.

Bandry, Anne. "De la Contradiction dans Quelques Romans Anglais du XVIIIe Siècle." *Bulletin de la Société d'Études Anglo-Américaines des XVIIe et XVIIIe Siècles*, 53 (2001), 175–87.

Bandry, Anne. "Gulliver et la Machine a Compter: Une Etude De Specifictes." *Bulletin de la Société d'Études Anglo-Américaines des XVIIe et XVIIIe Siècles,* 53 (2001), 145–57.

Bannerji, Himani, Shahrzad Mojab, and Judith Whitehead (eds.). *Of Property and Propriety: The Role of Gender and Class in Imperialism and Nationalism.* Toronto: University of Toronto Press, 2001. Pp. xii + 244; bibliography.

Barber, Tabitha. "Mary Beale (1633–1699)." Pp. 105–17 of *Englische Frauen der Frühen Neuzeit: Dichterinnen, Malerinnen, Mäzeninnen.* Edited by Gesa Stedman. Darmstadt: Wissenschaftliche Buchgesellschaft, 2001.

Barchas, Janine. "Before Print Culture: Mary, Lady Chudleigh, and the Assimilation of the Book." Pp. 15–35 of *Eighteenth-Century Genre and Culture: Serious Reflections on Occasional Forms: Essays in Honor of J. Paul Hunter.* Edited by Dennis Todd and Cynthia Wall. Newark: University of Delaware Press, 2001.

Barnard, Alan J. "Anthropology, Race, and Englishness: Changing Notions of Complexion and Character." *Eighteenth-Century Life,* 25 (2001), 94–102.

Barnes, Diana. "The Restoration of Royalist Form in Margaret Cavendish's Sociable Letters." Pp. 201–14 of *Women Writing, 1550–1750.* Edited by Jo Wallwork and Paul Salzman. Bundoora: Meridian Bundoora, 2001.

Barron, Stephanie. *Jane and the Prisoner of Wool House, Jane Austen Mystery.* New York: Bantam Books, 2001. Pp. ix + 291.

VI: British Literatures

Barth, Marilyn. "Exploring the Book Arts through One Fine Copy of *The Castle of Otranto*." *Eighteenth-Century Novel*, 1 (2001), 287–310.

Basker, James G. "Intimations of Abolitionism in 1759: Johnson, Hawkesworth, and Oroonoko." *Age of Johnson*, 12 (2001), 47–66.

Basker, James G. "Multicultural Perspectives: Johnson, Race, and Gender." Pp. 64–79 of *Johnson Re-Visioned: Looking Before and After*. (Bucknell Studies in Eighteenth-Century Literature and Culture.) Edited by Philip Smallwood. Lewisburg: Bucknell University Press, 2001.

Battestin, Martin C. "Dr. Johnson and the Case of Harry Fielding." Pp. 96–113 of *Eighteenth-Century Genre and Culture: Serious Reflections on Occasional Forms: Essays in Honor of J. Paul Hunter*. Edited by Dennis Todd and Cynthia Wall. Newark: University of Delaware Press, 2001.

Beach, Adam R. "The Creation of a Classical Language in the Eighteenth Century: Standardizing English, Cultural Imperialism, and the Future of the Literary Canon." *Texas Studies in Literature and Language,* 43 (2001), 117–41.

Beckford, William. *Vathek with the Episodes of Vathek*. Edited by Kenneth W. Graham. Peterborough, Ontario: Broadview Press, 2001. Pp. 397.

The problematic textual history of *Vathek* and its *Episodes* is a never-ending chronicle of misinformation and mistranslation. During Beckford's lifetime, he projected a single unified narrative consisting of four interconnected stories, the main frame story, *Vathek*, integrated with "The History of the Princes and Friends Alasi and Firouz," "The History of Prince Bakiarokh," and "The History of Princess Zulkaïs and the Prince Kalilah," a grand design that he was never to achieve. None of the *Episodes* saw publication until the twentieth century when two of the three were published in *The English Review* for 1909 and in French text editions by Guy Chapman (Constable, 1929), J. B. Brunius (Edition Stock, 1948), Ernest Giddey (Editions Rencontre, 1962), and Maurice Lévy (Flammarion, 1981). The first English version of *Vathek* had been the translation by the Reverend Samuel Henley published in 1786, a rendering that had both Beckford's approval and collaboration, but not his permission to publish. The third English version of *Vathek* was published in 1816 and offered a text prepared by Beckford himself with corrections, emendations, and notes based on earlier flawed versions. As Graham notes is his 1975 article, "Vathek in English and French" (*Studies in Bibliography: Papers of the Bibliographical Society of the University of Virginia*, vol. 28: 153–66), "The versions of *Vathek* in English and French do differ and the differences are significant...Neither Beckford nor Henley felt constrained to make the English version a faithful representation of the French." The annotations to *Vathek* in the Broadview edition reaffirm the fact that there can never be an absolutely definitive edition of Beckford's odd novel in either English or French, although Beckford seems to have come to prefer the English over the French in his later lifetime.

Graham's new edition of *Vathek with the Episodes of Vathek* both takes into consideration the authority of the English version and fulfills Beckford's dream of a thematically unified single work conjoining *Vathek* with its *Episodes*. The primary aim of the Broadview edition is the reinstatement of Beckford "at his most creative and least inhibited," a goal that is admirably accomplished in no small degree by the installation of the newly located version of the suppressed first *Episode* translated by Graham "to counteract the malign influence of the only published version of the first *Episode*" done by Sir Frank T. Marzials in 1912. By unearthing among the Beckford papers in the Bodleian Library the manuscript of the suppressed version of the first *Episode* (Bodleian Library, Ms. Beckford d.13) and translating it, Graham has provided Beckford scholars and general readers with a graphic link to the "uninhibited" Beckford, since the homosexual love theme of this new version of the first *Episode* (referred to as "the *Firouz* version") contrasts sharply with the homosexual-become-heterosexual love theme of the Marzials translation. In the suppressed version, Beckford makes no concessions to the rigid sexual standards of the culture and no apologies, implicit or explicit, for the homosexual charges of the Powderham Castle scandal that had driven him from England. For comparative purposes, the Marzials translation (titled "The History of Prince Alasi and the Princess Firouzkah") is included as "Appendix A."

The superiority of Graham's edition to its twentieth-century predecessors is immediate and obvious. While *Vathek* has been printed and edited numerous times in the twentieth century, no edition in English properly connects and harmonizes *Vathek* with its *Episodes* in accordance with Beckford's original intentions. Editions in English using the Marzials translations of *The Episodes of Vathek* have been compiled by Lin Carter (Ballantine, 1971), Robert J. Gemmett (Associated University Presses, 1975), and Malcolm Jack (Dedalus, 1994). The Lin Carter edition prints *Vathek* **and** the *Episodes* in contrast to the Broadview edition that prints Vathek **with** the *Episodes*. All prior editions of the *Episodes* must now be regarded as fallacious in light of Graham's discovery of the authentic first *Episode* among the overlooked Beckford papers. An inspection of secondary bibliographies of Beckford criticism shows a paucity of critical writing about the *Episodes*, a vacuum in Beckford studies that this edition does much to redress. By restoring the true first *Episode*, this edition offers the reader the total *Vathek* as Beckford envisioned it together with such unique features a four maps of the Middle East to guide the reader through *Vathek*'s infernal geography of various heavens and hells on earth. Cogent footnotes reveal Beckford's compendious knowledge of Islamic literature, history, and culture, while preserving the tone of Beckford's and Henley's original notes in their extensive use of Barthélémy d'Herbelot's *Bibliothèque Orientale* (1697). The other appendixes are equally valuable to the researcher. Appendix B contains commentaries on Beckford's Orientalism, the choice of texts, and the analytic and textual issues generated by the bilingual nature of the main tale and its satellite tales in French and English. By beginning the volume with a chronology of Beckford's life and ending it with a carefully selected bibliography of "Works Cited/Recommended Reading" the Broadview edition nicely bookends the curious life of "the Caliph of Fonthill" with due recognition of such scholars as André Parreaux and Robert J. Gemmett who have contributed so much to the advancement of Beckford studies. Regretably, some of Graham's own work on Beckford such as his essay "Beckford's 'Vathek': A Study in Ironic Dissonance" (*Criticism*, XIV [1972]: 243–52) is not among the "Recommended Reading" and certainly should be.

The organization of the edition compels the user to approach and appreciate *Vathek* in the rebellious context of the *Episodes,* particularly the importance of first *Episode* with its "pattern of sexual extremism," thus forestalling any future study of *Vathek* as an isolated work. Vathek's "sensuality and curiosity," "rebellion and atrocity," "ambition and incest," (all Graham's chapter subtitles) are reflected in the unruly characters and hedonistic motifs of the *Episodes*. Since the question of *Vathek*'s Gothicism still seems a worthwhile topic for debate, some discussion of *Vathek*'s mixture of genres and the formal relationship of *Vathek*'s amalgam of dissonant styles to the *Episodes* deserves mention in the Introduction as does the pursuit of the persistent question of *Vathek*'s Gothicism. The nature of *Vathek*'s Gothicism as well as other intriguing questions of genre, however, remain unaddressed as do the affinities of the grotesque comedy of both *Vathek* and its *Episodes* with later forms of dark or negative Romanticism. Lastly, might there exist other "lost" versions of the *Episodes* among the Beckford Papers in the Bodleian or elsewhere? Or has an evolving text finally reached a fixed state?

The Edition is dedicated to the members of The Beckford Round Table whose scholarship is acknowledged throughout the volume. Inevitably, it will face comparisons with what must now be called the "limited" editions of *Vathek* done by Peter Fairclough and Mario Praz (Penguin Books, 1968, as one of three Gothic novels), E. F. Bleiler (Dover Publications, 1966, as one of three Gothic novels), Roger Lonsdale (Oxford University Press, 1970;

VI: British Literatures

reissued as an Oxford World Classics paperback 1998), and Malcolm Jack (Pickering aned Chatto, 1993), probably the four most widely used classroom texts. Given its special emphasis on the totality of *Vathek* with its *Episodes*, the Broadview Edition should supersede all of these and should rapidly establish itself as the preferred text for our time in its superlative illumination of one of the most bizarre classics of eighteenth-century literature.—Frederick S. Frank, Allegheny College

Beer, John. "Why Were Buncle's Eyes Closed? The 2001 Toast." *Charles Lamb Bulletin*, 115 (2001), 70–71.

Bell, Maureen, Shirley Chew, Simon Eliot, Lynette Hunter, and James L. W. West, III (eds.). *Re-Constructing the Book: Literary Texts in Transmission*. Aldershot: Ashgate Publishing Company, 2001. Pp. xi + 231.

Bell, Robert H. "Sterne's Anatomy of Folly." *Literary Imagination*, 3 (2001), 21–41.

Bender, John. "Enlightenment Fiction and the Scientific Hypothesis." Pp. 236–60 of *Eighteenth-Century Genre and Culture: Serious Reflections on Occasional Forms: Essays in Honor of J. Paul Hunter*. Edited by Dennis Todd and Cynthia Wall. Newark: University of Delaware Press, 2001.

Benedict, Barbara. "Publishing and Reading Poetry." Pp. 63–82 of *The Cambridge Companion to Eighteenth-Century Poetry*. Edited by John Sitter. Cambridge: Cambridge University Press, 2001.

Berg, Temma F. "Engendering the Gothic: Clara Reeve Redecorates the Castle of Otranto." *Reader: Essays in Reader-Oriented Theory, Criticism, and Pedagogy*, 44 (2001), 53–78.

Berger, Dieter A. "Aristokratische Geschlechter-Räume in der englischen Restaurationskomödie." Pp. 37–50 of *Geschlechter-Räume: Konstruktionen von "Gender" in Geschichte, Literatur und Alltag*. Edited by Margarete Hubrath. Köln, Weimar and Wien: Böhlau, 2001.

Berglund, Lisa. "Allegory in the *Rambler*." *Papers on Language and Literature*, 37 (2001), 147–78.

Bernstein, Jeremy. "The Man Who Was Junius." *Gettysburg Review*, 14 (2001), 249–84.

Berry, Amanda. "Edmund Burke, Public Eye." Pp. 43–63 of *Romantic Generations: Essays in Honor of Robert F. Gleckner*. Edited by Ghislaine McDayter, Guinn Batten, Barry Milligan, and Peter Manning. Lewisburg: Bucknell University Press, 2001.

Bertipaglia, Giuliana. "Ossian and Cesarotti: Poems and Translations." *Studies in Scottish Literature,* 32 (2001), 132–39.

Bertuol, Roberto. "The Square Circle of Margaret Cavendish: The 17th-Century Conceptualization of Mind by Means of Mathematics." *Language and Literature,* 10 (2001), 21–39.

Bessière, Jean (ed.). *Commencements Du Roman.* Paris: Honoré Champion, 2001. Pp. 216.

Bhattacharya, Nandini. "Family Jewels: George Colman's *Inkle and Yarico* and Connoisseurship." *Eighteenth-Century Studies,* 34 (2001), 207–26.

Bhattacharya, Nandini. "James Cobb, Colonial Cacophony, and the Enlightenment." *SEL,* 41 (2001), 583–603.

Black, Jeremy. *Eighteenth-Century Britain, 1688–1783.* (Palgrave History of Britain.) New York: Palgrave, 2001. Pp. viii + 312.

Blackwell, Bonnie. "*Tristram Shandy* and the Theater of the Mechanical Mother." *ELH,* 68 (2001), 81–133.

Blakemore, Steven and Fred Hembree. "Edmund Burke, Marie Antoinette, and the Procédure Criminelle." *Historian,* 63 (2001), 505–20.

Blasker, James G. "Smollett's Racial Consciousness in *Roderick Random*." Pp. 77–90 of *1650–1850: Ideas, Aesthetics, and Inquiries in the Early Modern Era.* Volume 6. Edited by Kevin L. Cope. New York: AMS Press, 2001.

Blewett, David (ed.). *Passion and Virtue: Essays on the Novels of Samuel Richardson.* Toronto: University of Toronto Press, 2001. Pp. xv + 344; bibliography; plates; illustrations.

Bode, Christoph, and Fritz-Wilhelm Neumann (eds.). *Re-Mapping Romanticism: Gender–Text–Context.* Essen: Blaue Eule, 2001. Pp. 209.

Bogel, Fredric V. *The Difference Satire Makes: Rhetoric and Reading from Jonson to Byron.* New York: Cornell University Press, 2001. Pp. ix. + 262; bibliography.

As Frederick V. Bogel points out in this challenging reconfiguration of the theory of Augustan satire, criticism of the past fifty years has been guided by assumptions that satire is a "full-fledged artistic mode" not merely "a symptom of ill humor or personal spite," that the satiric voice is that of a "particular and highly conventionalized persona," and that the satirist takes note of "an object that exists anterior to the satiric attack" (2). Bogel argues that while formalist criticism of satire "has insisted on its clarity, its stability, and its ultimate if not apparent lack of ambiguity," satire is actually "a double structure," one component of which closely resembles the traditional formalist and historicist accounts of the genre, the second component of which "works precisely against the first and, with it, produces much of the difficulty, profundity, and interest of the satiric mode"(4). The satirist has always been regarded as "a holy scourge expelling dangerous figures from society"(29). Indeed the satirist's insistence that satiric violence is inevitably inspired by the magnitude of the evils with which it contends has made it easier for critics to defend satiric attacks on moral grounds"(12), inducing the reader to "align our reading selves with the satirist, and therefore to set ourselves against the object of satire"(13). As Bogel insists, however, it is just as likely that "we attack figures, distance ourselves from them, because we sense their threatening proximity to us as because they are already so different from us."

In short, satire "is a rhetorical means to the production of difference in the face of a potentially compromising similarity, not the articulation of differences already securely in place"(42). This discovery has significant consequences for Augustan mock-form. As Bogel argues, traditional accounts of mock form tend to preserve "faith in clear distinctions: between mock-epic, and epic, small and great, and so on"(22). But "such distinctions are far from clear and secure. These works seem to have sprung not simply from veneration for the ancient and elevated or from scorn for the modern and low but from a wild fascination with the possibility of writing as though such distinctions were inoperative or unreal"(22). Such works "suggest that we take the "mock"—in formulas like 'mock–heroic'—to signify not mockery, but surrogacy, substitute or counterfeit status"(22). Indeed, all forms of parody and mimicry involve some measure of engagement or reenactment; all forms of imitation involve "an act of identification, even when that identification is then enlisted in an effort of repudiation"(25). Chapters devoted to *Volpone*, *Jonathan Wild*, Swift's poems, Byron's *Beppo*, and *The Beggar's Opera*, work out the implications of these assertions. Bogel's final chapter investigates the connection between Augustan satiric rhetoric and the ambiguous response to the "very idea of categorical distinctness"(215). In the final analysis, however, it is the careful, often original, analysis of satiric "difference," that marks Bogel's most significant contribution to the theory of Augustan satire.—Roger D. Lund

Bony, Alain. "Du Discours du Jardin au Silence du Sublime: Le Proche et le Lointain dans L'esthétique Paysagere d'Addison." *Bulletin de la Société d'Études Anglo-Américaines des XVIIe et XVIIIe Siècles*, 52 (2001), 91–115.

Borovaia, Olga V. "Translation and Westernization: *Gulliver's Travels* in Ladino." *Jewish Social Studies*, 7 (2001), 149–68.

Boswell, James. *The Correspondence and Other Papers of James Boswell Relating to the Making of the Life of Johnson*. Edited by Marshall Waingrow. Edinburgh: Edinburgh University Press, 2001. Pp. lxxxvi + 524; bibliography.

Botting, Fred (ed.). *The Gothic*. Cambridge: Brewer, 2001. Pp. 184; illustrations.

Boucé, Paul-Gabriel. "Gulliver Phallophorus and the Maids of Honour in Brobdingnag." *Bulletin de la Société d'Études Anglo-Américaines des XVIIe et XVIIIe Siècles*, 53 (2001), 81–98.

Boucé, Paul-Gabriel. "Death in Gulliver's Travels: The Struldbruggs Revisited." *Q/W/E/R/T/Y: Arts, Litteratures & Civilisations du Monde Anglophone*, 11 (2001), 37–46.

Boulukos, George E. "Daniel Defoe's Colonel Jack, Grateful Slaves, and Racial Difference." *ELH,* 68 (2001), 615–31.

Boulukos, George. "The Grateful Slave: A History of Slave Plantation Reform in the British Novel." *Eighteenth-Century Novel,* 1 (2001), 161–79.

Bour, Isabelle. "Corps, Paysage, Nation ou Comment le Roman Britannique Est Devenu Moderne (Radcliffe, Owenson, Scott)." Pp. 159–72 of *Modernité et Romantisme.* Edited by Isabelle Bour, Eric Dayre, and Patrick Nee. Paris: Honoré Champion, 2001.

Bour, Isabelle. "Du Meta-Romanesque Chez Defoe." Pp. 65–75 of *Commencements Du Roman.* Edited by Jean Bessière,. Paris: Honoré Champion, 2001.

Bour, Isabelle, Eric Dayre, and Patrick Nee (eds.). *Modernite et Romantisme.* Paris: Honoré Champion, 2001. Pp. 395.

Boyd, Diane E. "'Professing Drudge': Charlotte Smith's Negotiation of a Mother-Writer Author Function." *South Atlantic Review,* 66 (2001), 145–66.

Bradshaw, Penny. "Dystopian Futures: Time-Travel and Millenarian Visions in the Poetry of Anna Barbauld and Charlotte Smith." *Romanticism on the Net: An Electronic Journal Devoted to Romantic Studies,* 21 (2001).

Brahami, Frederic. "Hume: Le Scepticisme et la Nature Humaine." *Magazine Litteraire,* 394 (2001), 48–50.

Breckmann, Patricia C. "Clothes of Pamela's Own: Shopping at B—— Hall." *Eighteenth-Century Life,* 25 (2001), 201–13.

Breuer, Horst. "Szenisches Erzahlen bei Jane Austen." *Zeitschrift fur Anglistik und Amerikanistik,* 49 (2001), 361–74.

Breunig, Hans Werner. "Jane Austen: Romantic? British Empiricist?" Pp. 163–81 of *Re-Mapping Romanticism: Gender–Text–Context.* Edited by Christoph Bode and Fritz-Wilhelm Neumann. Essen: Blaue Eule, 2001.

Brewer, Lisa K. "Encroaching Upon the Male Prerogative: Margaret Cavendish and the Construction of a Female Author." *Kentucky Philological Review,* 15 (2001), 15–21.

Brewton, Vince. "'He to Defend: I to Punish': Silence and the Duel in *Sense and Sensibility.*" *Persuasions: Journal of the Jane Austen Society of North America,* 23 (2001), 78–89.

Bridges, Elizabeth. *"The Most Essential Parts of Good Government": The Exclusion Crisis Plays of Aphra Behn.* n.p., 2001. Pp. iv + 235.

Brockhaus, Cathrin. "Aphra Behn (1640–1689)." Pp. 119–36 of *Englische Frauen der Frühen Neuzeit: Dichterinnen, Malerinnen, Mäzeninnen.* Edited by Gesa Stedman. Darmstadt: Wissenschaftliche Buchgesellschaft, 2001.

Broich, Ulrich. "Huren, Hehler, Straßenräuber: Zur literarischen Repräsentation des Verbrechens im England des frühen 18. Jahrhunderts." Pp. 13–41 of *Kriminalität und Verbrechen in der Gesellschaft.* (Wissenschaft und Philosophie, 41.) Edited by Venanz Schubert. St. Ottilien: EOS, 2001.

Brosch, Renate. "Spectacular Emotions: Edmund Burke's Redefinition of Visible Identity." Pp. 22–37 of *Engendering Images of Man in the Long Eighteenth Century.* Edited by Walter Göbel, Saskia Schabio and Martin Windisch. Trier: WVT Wissenschaftlicher Verlag Trier, 2001.

Brown, Hilary. "Sarah Scott, Sophie Von La Roche, and the Female Utopian Tradition." *Journal of English and Germanic Philology,* 100 (2001), 469–81.

Brown, John Russell. *The Oxford Illustrated History of Theatre.* New York: Oxford University Press, 2001. Pp. viii + 582; bibliography; illustrations; maps.

Brown, Laura. *Fables of Modernity: Literature and Culture in the English Eighteenth Century.* Ithaca: Cornell University Press, 2001. Pp. xii + 273; bibliography; illustrations.

Laura Brown's cultural fables are constructed from recurrent, concrete images, whose connotations are teased out of particular more or less familiar seventeenth- and eighteenth-century poems and prose texts until they take on symbolic force. Some of these images have been discussed before—Lady Credit, for instance, or pets in Srinivas Aravamudan's incisive and disturbing *Tropicopolitans* (1999). But here they are linked associatively to create an image of modernity as a dynamic and fluid, unstable and leveling capitalist system of exchange.

Chapter I explores images of London's open sewer system in Swift's "Description of a City Shower," Gay's "Trivia," Rochester's "Ramble in St James' Park," Pope's "Dunciad," and Robert Gould's "Love given o're," where the sewer's mingling of waste of all kinds from all parts of the city is associated with the promiscuity of the whore (or vice versa), to represent the leveling of all qualities and ranks characteristic of the urban, metropolitan experience. The rain-produced torrents in Swift's poem link the sewer to the torrents and oceans examined in Chapter II. Here Johnson's "Vanity of Human Wishes," Young's "Ocean," and particular poems by Denham, Dryden, Tickell, and Pope are used to identify a "collective story" about these images as nationalist representations of England's global expansion, and of the hopes and fears, *pax britannica* and belligerency, produced by English "mercantile capitalism." Lady Credit, who is tracked in Chapter III through Defoe, *The Spectator,* medical discourses on hysterick women, and the sentimental heroine, is associated with the ocean inasmuch as both were used to represent "the mystery of trade" as well as the potent volatility and dangerous infirmities of feeling and of finance. In Chapter IV, Dulness in Pope's "Dunciad" is Lady Credit's daughter, and her feminized equivalent in the burgeoning book trade. As the locus of several intersecting cultural fables, the analysis of Pope's poem in this chapter draws together all the images heretofore discussed. The last two chapters focus more particularly on cultural fables associated with race. In Chapter V, the image of the native prince is shown to progressively lose its strangeness and cultural alterity as it is sentimentalized and pursued through reports of visits to London by American and West Indian kings, Behn's novella *Oronooko* and Southerne's stage adaptation, Shebbeare's play *Lydia, The Ballad of the Indian King*, and Defoe's *Captain Singleton*, Mackenzie's *Julia de Roubigne*, and Anna Maria Mackenzie's *Slavery*—just as in Chapter VI, exploration of Pope's mixed catalogue of "Men, monkies, Lap-Dogs, Parrots" in "The Rape of the Lock" in some sense returns us to the confusion of men, animals and things in the initial city sewer.

This summary does not do justice the imaginative tissue of admirable readings in this book. These enrich our understanding of many poems and prose passages that are standard fare in the classroom and make this a very useful book. They also constitute model readings in the sense that they return close reading to cultural studies and convincingly demonstrate the heuristic value of detailed historical and cultural information for the minute interpretation of texts. In linking literature and history in this way, Laura Brown makes a timely move away from the sweeping theoretical apriorism that has, unfortunately, discredited cultural studies in many quarters.

The weaknesses of *Fable of Modernity* derive from its sometimes unjustified generalizations and from its efforts to align itself with a particular post-Marxist view of modernity. The "encounter with difference" disappears in generalizations, for instance, when images of the whore's genital sink in two misogynist poems become "*the* female body" or when a handful of poems become "the poetry of the period." There is a circularity in the claim that "the feminization of the forces of history is a striking characteristic of the cultural expression of the period" when the introduction points out that Brown has actively sought out images involving gender to redress the traditional masculinism of modernity studies. While the "newly conceived conjunctions of race or gender and modernity" constructed in this book have all the seductive appeal and poetic truth of fables, the generalizations are not firmly anchored either in the eighteenth century or in modernity. Take for instance the recurrent fable about the leveling of hierarchies. Part of the point of Swift's "Description of a City Shower" and indeed of Rochester's "St. James' Park" is surely that the sewer, the shower and the park are *remarkable* for joining and jumbling together categories of people who would normally be kept apart in a city where different ranks occupied different geographical districts and where hierarchy was reinscribed in spatial terms. Are modernity's cities less ghettoized by income, race and class? Has the structure of capitalism's businesses and corporations really been less hierarchical? We may wish to ask why we continue to project cultural fables such as those so brilliantly expounded in this book onto our past, present and future.—Eve Tavor Bannet

Brown, Leslie Ellen. "An Essay Suggesting an Important Application of the Highland Music: Moral Sentiment and the Oeconomic Ode." Pp. 317–32 of *1650–1850: Ideas, Aesthetics, and Inquiries in the Early Modern Era*. Volume 6. Edited by Kevin L. Cope. New York: AMS Press, 2001.

Brown, Murray L. "George Washington in the Popular British Press, 1775–1784." Pp. 107–19 of *George Washington in and as Culture*. Edited by Kevin L. Cope, William S. Pederson, and Frank Williams. New York: AMS Press, 2001.

Brownstein, Rachel. "Personal Experience Paper." Pp. 220–31 of *Personal Effects: The Social Character of Scholarly Writing*. Edited by Deborah H. Holdstein and David Bleich. Logan: Utah State University Press, 2001.

VI: British Literatures

Brownstein, Rachel M. "Out of the Drawing Room, Onto the Lawn." Pp. 13–21 of *Jane Austen in Hollywood*. Edited by Linda Troost and Sayre N. Greenfield. Lexington: University Press of Kentucky, 2001.

Bruni, Francesco (ed.). *"Le Donne, I Cavalier, L'arme, Gli Amori": Poema E Romanzo: La Narrativa Lunga in Italia*. Venice: MarsilioVenice, Italy, 2001. Pp. viii + 446.

Brunstrom, Conrad. "'Be Male and Female Still: An ABC of Hyperbolic Masculinity in the Eighteenth Century." Pp. 29–48 of *Presenting Gender: Changing Sex in Early-Modern Culture*. (Bucknell Studies in Eighteenth-Century Literature and Culture.) Edited by Chris Mounsey. Lewisburg: Bucknell University Press, 2001.

Brunstrom, Conrad. "'Not Worth Going to See': The Place of Ireland in Samuel Johnson's Imagination." *Eighteenth-Century Ireland/Iris an da Chultur*, 16 (2001), 73–82.

Bruyn, Frans de. "Anti-Semitism, Millenarianism, and Radical Dissent in Edmund Burke's Reflections on the Revolution in France." *Eighteenth-Century Studies*, 34 (2001), 577–600.

Bryant, Arthur. *Pepys. The Man in the Making, 1633–1669*. Preface by Reba N. Soffer. London: House of Stratus, 2001.

Bryant, Arthur. *Pepys. Saviour of the Navy, 1683–1689*. Preface by Reba N. Soffer. London: House of Stratus, 2001.

Bryant, Arthur. *Pepys. The Years of Peril, 1669–1689*. Preface by Reba N. Soffer. London: House of Stratus, 2001.

Budd, Adam. "Moral Correction: The Refusal of Revision in Henry Fielding's *Amelia*." *Lumen*, 20 (2001), 1–17.

Buickerood, James G. "Clarification of Some Matters Pertinent to the Question of the Authorship of Two Dissertations Concerning Sense, and the Imagination, with an Essay on Consciousness (1728)." *Notes and Queries*, 48 (2001), 406–09.

Burdan, Judith. "*Mansfield Park* and the Question of Irony." *Persuasions: Journal of the Jane Austen Society of North America*, 23 (2001), 197–204.

Burgess, Miranda J. "Bearing Witness: Law, Labor, and the Gender of Privacy in the 1720s." *Modern Philology*, 98 (2001), 393–422.

Burke, Tim. "'Humanity Is Now the Pop'lar Cry': Laboring-Class Writers and the Liverpool Slave Trade, 1787–1789." *Eighteenth Century: Theory and Interpretation,* 42 (2001), 245–63.

Burney, Fanny. *Journals and Letters.* Edited by Peter Sabor and Lars E. Troide.. New York: Penguin, 2001. Pp. xxx + 589; bibliography.

Burns, William E. "'By Him the Women Will Be Delivered from That Bondage, Which Some Has Found Intolerable': M. Marsin, English Millenarian Feminist." *Eighteenth-Century Women,* 1 (2001), 19–38.

Burroughs, Catherine. "British Women Playwrights and the Staging of Female Sexual Initiation: Sophia Lee's *The Chapter of Accidents* (1780)." *Romanticism on the Net: An Electronic Journal Devoted to Romantic Studies,* 23 (2001).

Burton, Vicki Tolar. "John Wesley and the Liberty to Speak: The Rhetorical and Literacy Practices of Early Methodism." *College Composition and Communication,* 53 (2001), 65–91.

Bywaters, David. "Historicism Gone Awry: Recent Work on John Dryden." Pp. 245–55 of *John Dryden: A Tercentenary Miscellany.* Edited by Susan Green and Steven N. Zwicker. San Marino: Huntington Library, 2001.

Campe, Ruediger. "Was Heiäyt: Eine Statistik Lesen? Beobachtungen Zu Daniel Defoe's *A Journal of the Plague Year.*" *MLN,* 116 (2001), 521–35.

Canfield, J. Douglas, and Maja-Lisa Von Sneidern (eds.). *The Broadview Anthology of Restoration & Early Eighteenth-Century English Drama,* Broadview Anthologies of English Literature. Orchard Park: Broadview, 2001. Pp. xxi + 1977; illustrations; map.

Carboni, Pierre. "Aux Confins de l'ailleurs et du Moi: Extension Géographique et Définition, *The Seasons* de James Thomson." *Bulletin de la Société d'Études Anglo-Américaines des XVIIe et XVIIIe Siècles,* 52 (2001), 145–54.

Carboni, Pierre. "The Castle of Indolence De James Thomson. L'etrange *Songe De La Raison.*" *Études Ecossaises,* 7 (2001), 29–40.

Carnell, Rachel K. "Clarissa's Treasonable Correspondence: Gender, Epistolary Politics, and the Public Sphere." Pp. 114–34 of *Passion and Virtue: Essays on the Novels of Samuel Richardson.* Edited by David Blewett. Toronto: University of Toronto Press, 2001.

Carnell, Rachel K. "The Very Scandal of her Tea Table: Eliza Haywood's Response to the Whig Public Sphere." Pp. 255–73 of *Presenting Gender: Changing Sex in Early-Modern Culture*. (Bucknell Studies in Eighteenth-Century Literature and Culture.) Edited by Chris Mounsey. Lewisburg: Bucknell University Press, 2001.

Caron, Richard, Joscelyn Godwin, Wouter J. Hanegraaff, and Jean-Louis Vieillard-Baron (eds.). *Esotérisme, Gnoses & Imaginaire Symbolique: Melanges Offerts a Antoine Faivre*. Louvain: Peeters, 2001. Pp. xii + 948; illustrations.

Carruthers, Gerard. "A Manuscript Fragment of an Unsigned and Undated Draft Letter by David Hume on the Ossian Controversy in the Mitchell Library, Glasgow (Oli, P.26)." *Notes and Queries*, 48 (2001), 419.

Casal, Elvira. "Laughing at Mr. Darcy: Wit and Sexuality in *Pride and Prejudice*." *Persuasions: The Jane Austen Journal On-Line*, 22 (2001).

Cash, Arthur H. "Sterne, Hall, Libertinism, and a Sentimental Journey." *Age of Johnson*, 12 (2001), 291–327.

Casler, Jeanine. "The Primacy of the 'Rougher' Version: Neo-Conservative Editorial Practices and Clara Reeve's *Old English Baron*." *Papers on Language and Literature*, 37 (2001), 404–37.

Cavaliero, Roderick. *The Last of the Crusaders: The Knights of St. John and Malta in the Eighteenth Century*. Valletta: Progress Press, 2001. Pp. x + 298; bibliography; illustrations; maps.

Caywood, Cynthia, and Bonnie A. Hain. "Breaking the Confining Silence: Unstable Valences and Language in Aphra Behn's *The Rover*." *Restoration and 18th-Century Theatre Research*, 16 (2001), 24–39.

Centlivre, Susanna. "The Busybody." Pp. 75–144 of *Eighteenth-Century Women Dramatists*. Edited by Melinda C. Finberg. Oxford: Oxford University Press, 2001.

Chaber, Lois A. "'Sufficient to the Day': Anxiety in *Sir Charles Grandison*." Pp. 268–94 of *Passion and Virtue: Essays on the Novels of Samuel Richardson*. Edited by David Blewett. Toronto: University of Toronto Press, 2001.

Chapin, Chester. "Samuel Johnson and Joseph Addison's Anti-Jacobite Writings." *Notes and Queries*, 48 (2001), 38–40.

Chapin, Chester. "Samuel Johnson: Latitudinarian or High Churchman?" *Cithara: Essays in the Judaeo-Christian Tradition,* 41 (2001), 35–43.

Chaplin, Sue. "Romance and Sedition in the 1790s: Radcliffe's *The Italian* and the Terrorist Text." *Romanticism,* 7 (2001), 177–90.

Charles, Sebastien. "L'immaterialisme en Terre Ennemie: La Pensée Berkeleyenne dans le Materialisme des Lumières." *Lumen,* 20 (2001), 46–69.

Chezaud, Patrick. "Lumieres Irrationnelles d'Ecosse et la Fin du Baroque." *Études Écossaises,* 7 (2001), 97–110.

Chiba, Yasuki. "'Chichi' Naki Ato Ni Kaku to Iukoto: Suuifuto Oke Monogatari No Kontekusuto." *Eigo Seinen/Rising Generation,* 147 (2001), 179–83.

Choi, Inhwan. "The Scot in Empire: A Study of Smollett's *Roderick Random* and *Humphry Clinker.*" *British and American Fiction to 1900,* 8 (2001), 229–54.

Choi, Julie. "Engendering the Modern Individual: Empire, Class and Nation in *Evelina.*" *Feminist Studies in English Literature,* 8 (2001), 1–31.

Christmas, William J. "Eighteenth-Century Laboring-Class Poets." *Eighteenth Century: Theory and Interpretation,* 42 (2001), 187–278.

Christmas, William J. "An Emendation to Mary Collier's *The Woman's Labour.*" *Notes and Queries,* 48 (2001), 35–38.

Chung, Ewha. "Samuel Richardson's *Sir Charles Grandison* as the 'Middle-Class Aristocrat': Redefining the Eighteenth-Century English Hero and Nation." *Journal of English Language and Literature/Yongo Yongmunhak,* 47 (2001), 1173–89.

Chung, Rebecca. "A Woman Triumphs: From *Travels of an English Lady in Europe, Asia, and Africa* (1763) by Lady Mary Wortley Montagu." Pp. 110–24 of *Travel Knowledge: European "Discoveries" in the Early Modern Period.* Edited by Ivo Kamps and G. Singh. New York: Palgrave, 2001.

Claésson, Dick. "Introduction to 'Beckford's Letter from Geneva to Lord Thurlow, 22 May 1778.'" *The Beckford Journal,* 7 (2001), 18–20.

Clark, Lorna. "The Diarist as Novelist: Narrative Strategies in the Journals and Letters of Frances Burney." *English Studies in Canada,* 27 (2001), 283–302.

Clark, Lorna. "The Family in the Novels of Sarah Harriet Burney." *Lumen*, 20 (2001), 71–81.

Clark, J. C. D., and Howard Erskine-Hill. *Samuel Johnson in Historical Context*. New York: Palgrave, 2001. Pp. xii + 318; bibliography; illustrations.

Clarke, Stephen. "No More Green Cloth Boardings: The Fastidious Book Collecting of William Beckford." *The Beckford Journal*, 7 (2001), 39–44.

Clery, E. J. "Horace Walpole's the Mysterious Mother and the Impossibility of Female Desire." Pp. 23–46 of *The Gothic*. Edited by Fred Botting. Cambridge: Brewer, 2001.

Clingham, Greg. "Knightly Chetwood's *A Short Account of Some Passages of the Life and Death of Wentworth Late Earle of Roscommon*." *Restoration: Studies in English Literary Culture, 1660–1700*, 25 (2001), 117–38.

Clingham, Greg. "Resisting Johnson." Pp. 19–36 of *Johnson Re-Visioned: Looking Before and After*. (Bucknell Studies in Eighteenth-Century Literature and Culture.) Edited by Philip Smallwood. Lewisburg: Bucknell University Press, 2001.

Coetzee, J. M. "Daniel Defoe, *Robinson Crusoe*." Pp. 17–22 of *Stranger Shores: Literary Essays, 1986–1999*. Edited by J. M. Coetzee. New York: Viking, 2001.

Coetzee, J. M. "Samuel Richardson, *Clarissa*." Pp. 23–33 of *Stranger Shores: Literary Essays, 1986–1999*. Edited by J. M. Coetzee. New York: Viking, 2001.

Coetzee, J. M. *Stranger Shores: Literary Essays, 1986–1999*. New York: Viking, 2001. Pp. viii + 295; bibliography.

Coetzee, J. M. "What Is a Classic?" Pp. 1–16 of *Stranger Shores: Literary Essays, 1986–1999*. Edited by J. M. Coetzee. New York: Viking, 2001.

Cohen, Michèle. "The Grand Tour: Language, National Identity and Masculinity." *Changing English*, 8 (2001), 129–41.

Cohen, Paula Marantz. "The Talking Life: Boswell and Johnson." *Boulevard*, 17 (2001), 115–26.

Cohen, Ralph. "The Return to the Ode." Pp. 203–24 of *The Cambridge Companion to Eighteenth-Century Poetry*. Edited by John Sitter. Cambridge: Cambridge University Press, 2001.

Collins, Amanda. "Jane Austen, Film, and the Pitfalls of Postmodern Nostalgia." Pp. 79–89 of *Jane Austen in Hollywood*. Edited by Linda Troost and Sayre N. Greenfield. Lexington: University Press of Kentucky, 2001.

Collins, Irene. *Jane Austen and the Clergy*. London: Hambledon and London, 2001. Pp. 256; illustrations.

Conlin, Jonathan G. W. "High Art and Low Politics: A New Perspective on John Wilkes." *Huntington Library Quarterly*, 64 (2001), 357–81.

Conway, Alison. *Private Interests: Women, Portraiture, and the Visual Culture of the English Novel, 1709–1791*. Toronto: University of Toronto Press, 2001. Pp. xii + 293; bibliography; plates.

In *Private Interests*, Alison Conway focuses on the cultural exchange between eighteenth-century portrait painting and the novel, which opens up an imaginative space for conceptions of women's subjectivity and agency that previous discussions on visuality have neglected. Conway writes to expand the paradigm set out by Michel Foucault in *Discipline and Punish* and carried on by John Bender and Nancy Armstrong, arguing for a more nuanced exploration of the disciplining gaze, particularly in relation to women and the domestic sphere: "In its representation of the portrait, I argue, the novel entertains the idea of private interests as both decorous and illicit," which creates a dialectic that "highlights women's capacity to claim agency as spectacles and spectators, as subjects figured as both embodied and critical within the visual moment created by the novel's representation of the portrait" (4). The portrait signals a disruptive force because it encourages and resists spectatorship, generating an interpretive crisis in the viewer and complicating the power of the gaze.

Conway sets up her argument by outlining the divided response to novels and portraits, which reflected the conflict between private and public interests. Novels generated anxiety through the solitary activity of reading and the sometimes perverse association of reader and text and portraits through the narcissistic self-display of the subject and the voyeuristic consumption of the image. Blurring the clear distinction between positive and negative responses to each, Conway argues, is the active attempt on the part of writers and painters to tap into the power of eroticized and pedagogical aspects of visual and verbal images.

Focusing on Delarivier Manley's *The New Atalantis*, Conway explains that Manley uses portraiture to explore the power of visual pleasure, although she separates politics and pleasure in her erotic tableaux of seduced, abandoned, and ruined women. The two modes of portraitures that Manley exploits are the male, state portraits and the Restoration courtesan portraits. Juxtaposing the private scandals of Whig politicians and the public eroticism of famous prostitutes, Manley resists women's passive objectification and sexual victimization.

In her discussion of Samuel Richardson's *Clarissa*, Conway begins with the portrait of Clarissa dressed in the Vandyke style. Clarissa's portrait serves as both the object and subject of Clarissa's virtue. Richardson's novel offers two modes of spectatorship. The first is an idealized mode that encourages readers to admire and sympathize with Clarissa. The second is Lovelace's epistemology of the visual, in which he defines and controls Clarissa's meaning. By the end of the narrative, however, Clarissa escapes and thwarts Lovelace's visual control. Her elaborate death preparations are simultaneously public and private, enabling her to reestablish her public identity and personal agency.

Conway addresses two novels influenced by Richardson's version of female virtue and visibility: Eliza Haywood's *The History of Miss Betsy Thoughtless* and Henry Fielding's *Amelia*. Haywood and Fielding, as they rewrite the tragic ending of *Clarissa*, address the vexed issue of female embodiment in two distinct ways. Haywood explores women's roles as spectacles and spectator; Fielding focuses on women's visibility and idealization. The miniature portrait links Conway's discussion of the two narratives. As a sentimental object and a commodity, the miniature traverses the boundaries between private and public. In both novels, this intimate object reflects the heroines' success in securing visual power: "Both Betsy and Amelia gain an idealized form of domestic tranquillity as a result of the visual dynamics they set in motion" (149).

In Lawrence Sterne's novels, particularly *Tristram Shandy* and *A Sentimental Journey*, Conway sees a progression from open interpretive spaces to a more narrowly focused gaze. Indeed, *Tristram Shandy*'s circulation of visual power, in the form of exchanged glances and bawdy stares, is replaced in *Journey* by an authorial libertine gaze that wrests interpretive power away from female characters and from readers. As Conway demonstrates, the use of portraits in each novel reflects the two vastly different visual agendas.

Private Interests ends with an examination of Angelica Kauffman's self-portraits, Mary Wollstonecraft's *Mary, a Fiction* (1788), and Elizabeth Inchbald's *A Simple Story* (1791). Conway first describes Kauffman's successful negotiation of private and public spheres through her allegorical self-portraits. Conway then takes up two novelists who offer thinly-disguised autobiographies of their own. Wollstonecraft's antipathy toward both the novel form and the portrait throughout *Mary* reflects her inability to imagine embodied female agency. Inchbald, on the other hand, aligns herself with Kauffman's celebration of women's spectatorship and creates an optimistic version of the feminine.

Conway's book richly exemplifies the productive, interdisciplinary trends in English studies. Weighted heavily to the close readings of novels, *Private Interests* still incorporates detailed analysis of portraits and art theory. This study, therefore, seems to offer less to the art historian than to the literary critic. Yet it does indeed offer a great deal to eighteenth-century scholars. Carefully supported and ultimately persuasive, *Private Interests* provides a nuanced approach to visuality and the culture of the novel.—Mercy Cannon

Conway, Alison. "The Protestant Cause and a Protestant Whore: Aphra Behn's *Love Letters*." *Eighteenth-Century Life*, 25 (2001), 1–19.

Coote, Stephen. *Samuel Pepys: A Life*. New York: Palgrave, 2001. Pp. xiii + 386; plates.

Cope, Kevin L. (ed.). *1650–1850: Ideas, Aesthetics, and Inquiries in the Early Modern Era*. Volume 6. New York: AMS Press, 2001. Pp. xvi + 405; illustrations.

Cope, Kevin L. "Imageless Supermen and Women in Interregnum Interstices: Davenant's Apparitional Drama and the Restoration of Commonwealth 'Entertainments.'" Pp. 3–21 of *Engendering Images of Man in the Long Eighteenth Century*. Edited by Walter Goebel, Saskia Schabio, and Martin Windisch. Trier: Wissenschaftlicher Verlag Trier, 2001.

Cope, Kevin L., William S. Pederson, and Frank Williams (eds.). *George Washington in and as Culture*. New York: AMS Press, 2001. Pp. xix + 324; illustrations.

Cossy, Valérie. "L'écriture de la Paternité ou L'enfance des Pères: Prevost-Dassier, Sir Walter Finch ... et Victor Frankenstein." *Lettre de Zuylen et du Portet: Bulletin Genootschap Belle de Zuylen/Isabelle de Charriere*, 26 (2001), 6–12.

Cossy, Valerie. "An English Touch: Laurence Sterne, Jane Austen, et Le Roman Sentimental En Suisse Romande." *Annales Benjamin Constant*, 25 (2001), 131–60.

Cossy, Valerie, Deidre Dawson, Michel Delon, and Jochen Schlobach (eds.). *Progrès et Violence au XVIIIe Siècle*. Paris: Honoré Champion, 2001. Pp. 458.

Cottegnies, Line. "L'esclave, Le Prince Et Le Libertin: Espace Colonial et Figures de L'aTranger Dans *Oroonoko* d'Aphra Behn." *Bulletin de la Société d'Études Anglo-Américaines des XVIIe et XVIIIe Siècles*, 52 (2001), 75–89.

Cotterill, Anne. "'Rebekah's Heir': Dryden's Late Mystery of Genealogy." Pp. 201–26 of *John Dryden: A Tercentenary Miscellany*. Edited by Susan Green and Steven N. Zwicker. San Marino: Huntington Library, 2001.

Cowley, Hannah. "The Belle's Stratagem." Pp. 211–80 of *Eighteenth-Century Women Dramatists*. Edited by Melinda C. Finberg. Oxford: Oxford University Press, 2001.

Craciun, Adriana, Kari E. Lokke, and Madelyn Gutwirth (eds.). *Rebellious Hearts: British Women Writers and the French Revolution*. Albany: State University of New York Press, 2001. Pp. xii + 395; illustrations.

Craig, Sheryl Bonar. "The Value of a Good Income: Money in *Emma*." *Persuasions: The Jane Austen Journal On-Line*, 22 (2001).

Creeber, Glen, Toby Miller, and John Tulloch (eds.). *The Television Genre Book*. London: British Film Institute, 2001. Pp. xi + 163; illustrations.

Cronk, Nicholas. "Lord Hervey and Voltaire's Letters Concerning the English Nation." *Notes and Queries*, 48 (2001), 409–11.

Cross, Ashley J. "From Lyrical Ballads to Lyrical Tales: Mary Robinson's Reputation and the Problem of Literary Debt." *Studies in Romanticism*, 40 (2001), 571–605.

Curley, Thomas M. "Johnson and the Irish: A Postcolonial Survey of the Irish Literary Renaissance in Imperial Great Britain." *Age of Johnson*, 12 (2001), 167–97.

Curran, Stuart. "Dynamics of Female Friendship in the Later Eighteenth Century." *Nineteenth-Century Contexts*, 23 (2001), 221–39.

D'Souza, Florence. "Robert Orme (1728–1801), Pionnier De L'historiographie De L'inde." *Bulletin de la Société d'Études Anglo-Américaines des XVIIe et XVIIIe Siècles*, 52 (2001): 231–45.

VI: British Literatures

Dachez, Hélène. "Le Proche et le Lointain Dans *Clarissa* (1747–1748) de Samuel Richardson: Entre Sens et Contre-Sens." *Bulletin de la Société d'Études Anglo-Américaines des XVIIe et XVIIIe Siècles,* 52 (2001), 173–87.

Dalporto, Jeannie. "Landscape, Labor, and the Ideology of Improvement in Mary Leapor's 'Crumble-Hall.'" *Eighteenth Century: Theory and Interpretation,* 42 (2001), 228–44.

Daly, Patrick J., Jr. "Monarchy, the Disbanding Crisis, and Samuel Garth's Dispensary." *Restoration: Studies in English Literary Culture, 1660–1700,* 25 (2001), 35–52.

Dames, Nicholas. "Austen's Nostalgics." *Representations,* 73 (2001), 117–43.

Danchin, Pierre. *The Prologues and Epilogues of the Eighteenth Century: The Fourth Part, 1761–1776.* Paris: Messene, 2001.

Daniel, Clay. "Milton and the Restoration: Some Reassessments." *Connotations: A Journal for Critical Debate,* 11 (2001), 201–21.

Davies, Kate. "A Moral Purchase: Femininity, Commerce, and Abolition, 1788–1792." Pp. 133–59 of *Women, Writing and the Public Sphere, 1700–1830.* Edited by Elizabeth Eger, Charlotte Grant, Cliona O Gallchoir, and Penny Warburton. Cambridge: Cambridge University Press, 2001.

Davis, Lydia. *Samuel Johnson Is Indignant: Stories.* New York: McSweeney's Books, 2001. Pp. 201.

Davis, Paul. "'But Slaves We Are': Dryden and Virgil, Translation and the 'Gyant Race.'" *Translation & Literature,* 10 (2001), 110–27.

Davis, Paul. "Dryden at His Tercentenary." *Translation & Literature,* 10 (2001), 128–35.

Davison-Pegon, Claire. "Le Moine (de Lewis) D'antonin Artaud: Le Souffle du Double." *Bulletin de la Société d'Études Anglo-Américaines des XVIIe et XVIIIe Siècles,* 52 (2001), 189–204.

Day, W. G. "Orthographical Sterne." *Shandean: An Annual Devoted to Laurence Sterne and His Works,* 12 (2001), 117–19.

Daybell, James. (ed.) *Early Modern Women's Letter Writing, 1450–1700.* New York: Palgrave, 2001. Pp. xiv + 213; bibliography.

De Gooyer, Alan. "Sensibility and Solitude in Cowley's Familiar Essay." *Restoration: Studies in English Literary Culture, 1660–1700,* 25 (2001), 1–18.

De Michelis, Cesare G. "Il Viaggio Sentimentale: Appunti E Motivi." Pp. 91–97 of *Da Ulisse a Ulisse.* (Il Viaggio Come Mito Letterario.) Edited by Giorgetta Revelli. Pisa: Istituti Editoriali e Poligrafici Internazionali, 2001.

De Montluzin, Emily Lorraine. "Topographical, Antiquarian, Astronomical, and Meteorological Contributions by George Smith of Wigton in the *Gentleman's Magazine,* 1735–59." *ANQ,* 14 (2001), 5–12.

Dearden, James S. "The Chace: Hunting for Somervile." *Book Collector,* 50 (2001), 346–64.

Debus, Allen G. "The Scribleriad: Alchemy in an Eighteenth-Century Mock-Heroic Poem." *Cauda Pavonis: Studies in Hermeticism,* 20 (2001), 19–24.

Defoe, Daniel. *Writings on Travel, Discovery, and History.* 8 volumes. Edited by W. R. Owens, Philip Nicholas Furbank, John McVeagh, A. Wear, N. H. Keeble, and David Hayton. London: Pickering & Chatto, 2001.

Defoe, Daniel. *The Consolidator.* Edited by Michael Seidel, Maximillian E. Novak, and Joyce D. Kennedy. New York: AMS Press, 2001. Pp. lvii + 288; illustrations.

The Consolidator was first published in 1705, shortly after "The True Born Englishman" made Defoe a literary celebrity (1701) and "The Shortest Way with Dissenters" landed him in the pillory (1702). Elements from both of these previous satires find their way into *The Consolidator,* as do elements from Jonathan Swift's 1704 work, *The Tale of the Tub.* Like Swift's *Tale, The Consolidator* is largely a thinly veiled narration of the history and current state of England's three major religious factions (Catholics, Anglicans, and Dissenters). Like Swift's work, *The Consolidator* intersperses this narration with long, seemingly purposeless digressions. Defoe's digressions, however, do not carry the same logical force that Swift's do; rather than acting as satiric vehicles themselves, the digressive paragraphs in *The Consolidator* simply dilute the focus of the satire and decrease the effectiveness of the argument.

The major plot device of *The Consolidator* is a journey to the moon. The narrator first visits China, whose considerable achievements in learning and scientific progress, he discovers, has been acquired through frequent visits to the Lunar World, to which they alone have access. The "Consolidator" of the title is a kind of spaceship that conveys the Chinese, and eventually the narrator, to the Moon. It is also, though, an allegory for the English House of Commons, whose 513 members correspond exactly to the members of that body. Once on the Moon, the narrator is able to look at the Earth through special lenses that give the lunar perspective on our world and to interact with the inhabitants, whose religious politics bear a striking resemblance to those of England in the early eighteenth century. Through this device, Defoe simply narrates, with a standard Dissenting spin, the recent religious history of England, using the "Solunarian Church" in the role of the Church of England, "Crolians" to represent Dissenters, and the all-negating "Abrogratzians" as stand-ins for of Roman Catholics.

There is plenty of fault to be found in this deservedly obscure work of Daniel Defoe. The satire is rarely clever. Other than making up a few new names, Defoe does nothing to give the Lunar world its own identity, and even the

VI: British Literatures

marginally interesting narrative is too long and too digressive to hold much interest for contemporary readers. No fault, however, can be found in the edition. The editorial apparatus is superb. The work is introduced with an excellent essay by the editors, and more than a hundred pages of elaborate end notes track down every allusion and historical reference in the 156 pages of text.

In the past, *The Consolidator* has always held some interest for students of Defoe, admirers of Swift, and those interested in early forms of what we now call "science fiction." The Stoke-Newington edition of this venerable work provides a standard scholarly edition for anyone who may have reason to refer to it in the future.—Michael Austin

DeForest, Mary, and Eric Johnson. "The Density of Latinate Words in the Speeches of Jane Austen's Characters." *Literary and Linguistic Computing*, 16 (2001), 389–401.

Dereli, Cynthia. "In Search of a Poet: The Life and Work of Elizabeth Hands." *Women's Writing*, 8 (2001), 169–82.

Descargues, Madeleine. "Tristram Shandy and the Appositeness of War." *Shandean: An Annual Devoted to Laurence Sterne and His Works*, 12 (2001), 63–77.

Deschamps, Yannick. "Le Debat Sur L'union Anglo-Ecossaise. La Derniere Phase (1706–1707)." *Études Ecossaises,* 7 (2001), 195–207.

De Smith, Robert J. (ed.). *Proceedings of the Eighth Annual Northern Plains Conference on Earlier British Literature.* Sioux Center: Dordt College, 2001. Pp. 98; illustrations.

Desné, Roland. "Autour de la Lettre de Diderot a Landois." Pp. 101–18 of *Vérité et Littérature Au XVIIIe Siècle*. Edited by Paul Aron, Sophie Basch, Manuel Couvreur, Jacques Marx, Eric Van der Schueren, Valerie Van Crugten-André, and Roland Mortier. Paris: Honoré Champion, 2001.

Diana, M. Casey. "Emma Thompson's *Sense and Sensibility* as Gateway to Austen's Novel." Pp. 140–47 of *Jane Austen in Hollywood*. Edited by Linda Troost and Sayre N. Greenfield. Lexington: University Press of Kentucky, 2001.

Diaz Bild, Aida. "Charlotte Smith y el Arte de Escribir." Pp. 197–209 of *Polifonas Textuales: Ensayos in Honorem Maria del Carmen Fernandez Leal*. Edited by Manuel Brito and Juan Ignacio Oliva. La Laguna: Revista Canaria de Estudios Ingleses (RCEI), 2001.

Dickson, Rebecca. "Misrepresenting Jane Austen's Ladies: Revising Texts (and History) to Sell Films." Pp. 44–57 of *Jane Austen in Hollywood*. Edited by Linda Troost and Sayre N. Greenfield. Lexington: University Press of Kentucky, 2001.

Dokou, Christina. "Derrida's Travels: Swift at Large in the Academy." *Eighteenth Century: Theory and Interpretation,* 42 (2001), 113–41.

Dolan, Brian. *Ladies of the Grand Tour: British Women in Pursuit of Enlightenment and Adventure in Eighteenth-Century Europe*. New York: HarperCollins, 2001. Pp. xi + 337; bibliography; illustrations; plates.

Dole, Carol M. "Austen, Class, and the American Market." Pp. 58–78 of *Jane Austen in Hollywood*. Edited by Linda Troost and Sayre N. Greenfield. Lexington: University Press of Kentucky, 2001.

Donnelly, Jerome. "Dryden and the Exoteric Tradition: *Absalom and Achitophel* and the Ages of Man." Pp. 219–29 of *Dryden and the World of Neoclassicism*. Edited by Wolfgang Görtschacher and Holger Klein. Tubingen: Stauffenburg, 2001.

Donoghue, Frank. "Avoiding the 'Cooler Tribunal of the Study': Richard Brinsley Sheridan's Writer's Block and Late Eighteenth-Century Print Culture." *ELH*, 68 (2001), 831–56.

Doody, Margaret Anne. "The Gnostic Clarissa." Pp. 210–45 of *Passion and Virtue: Essays on the Novels of Samuel Richardson*. Edited by David Blewett. Toronto: University of Toronto Press, 2001.

Doody, Margaret Anne. "'A Good Memory Is Unpardonable': Self, Love, and the Irrational Irritation of Memory." *Eighteenth-Century Fiction*, 14 (2001), 67–94.

Doring, Jurgen. "Die Bedeutung des Hogarth Act Von 1735 für die Englische Graphik und ihr Verhaltnis zur Tagesliteratur." Pp. 38–50 of *Sister Arts: Englische Literatur Im Grenzland Der Kunstgebiete*. Edited by Joachim Möller. Marburg: Jonas, 2001.

Dougal, Theresa A. "Teaching Conduct or Telling a New Tale? Priscilla Wakefield and the Juvenile Travellers." *Eighteenth-Century Women*, 1 (2001), 299-319.

Drescher, Horst W. "Un 'man of feeling' à Paris. Le journal intime d'Henry Mackenzie, célèbre romancier écossais du XVIIIème siècle." *Bulletin de l'Association Franco-Ecossaise* 34 (2001), 3–6.

Dryden, John. *John Dryden: Selected Poems*. Edited by Steven N. Zwicker and David A. Bywaters. London: Penguin Books, 2001. Pp. xxiv + 582; illustrations.

Dryden, Robert G. "John Gay's *Polly*: Unmasking Pirates and Fortune Hunters in the West Indies." *Eighteenth-Century Studies* 34, (2001), 539–57.

Dryden, John. *John Dryden: Selected Poems*. Edited by Steven N. Zwicker and David A. Bywaters. London: Penguin Books, 2001. Pp. xxiv + 582; illustrations.

Duane, Anna Mae. "Confusions of Guilt and Complications of Evil: Hysteria and the High Price of Love at *Mansfield Park*." *Studies in the Novel*, 33 (2001), 402–15.

Duff, Virginia M. "'[F]Allen by Mistaken Rules': Anne Finch's 'the Bird and the Arras' and the Subtle Indictment of Domestic Confinement and Marriage Law." *Eighteenth-Century Women*, (2001), 39–48.

Duff, Virginia. "'I Should Not Care to Mix My Breed': Gender, Race, Class, and Genre in Mary Davys's *The Accomplished Rake, or Modern Fine Gentleman*." *Eighteenth-Century Novel*, 1 (2001), 311–25.

Dugaw, Dianne. *Deep Play: John Gay and the Invention of Modernity*. Newark: University of Delaware Press, 2001. Pp. 322; bibliography; illustrations.

Dussinger, John A. "'Ciceronian Eloquence': The Politics of Virtue in Richardson's *Pamela*." Pp. 27–51 of *Passion and Virtue: Essays on the Novels of Samuel Richardson*. Edited by David Blewett. Toronto: University of Toronto Press, 2001.

Dykstal, Timothy. "The Habits of Highly Effective People: Pedagogy and the Problem of *Amelia*." Pp. 114–35 of *Eighteenth-Century Genre and Culture: Serious Reflections on Occasional Forms: Essays in Honor of J. Paul Hunter*. Edited by Dennis Todd and Cynthia Wall. Newark: University of Delaware Press, 2001.

Earl, John. "Harold Scott, the Comus Court, and the Choice Spirits' Assembly." *Theatre Notebook: A Journal of the History and Technique of the British Theatre*, 55 (2001), 130–45.

Dryden, John. *John Dryden: Selected Poems*. Edited by Steven N. Zwicker and David A. Bywaters. London: Penguin Books, 2001. Pp. xxiv + 582; illustrations.

Edgecombe, Rodney Stenning. "Gray's 'Elegy' and Thomas Brown's 'Pastoral on the Death of Queen Mary.'" *Notes and Queries*, 48 (2001), 413.

Edgecombe, Rodney Stenning. "Gray's 'Elegy Written in a Country Churchyard..'" *Explicator*, 59 (2001), 76–78.

Eger, Elizabeth. "Representing Culture: 'The Nine Living Muses of Great Britain' (1779)." Pp. 104–132 of *Women, Writing and the Public Sphere, 1700–1830*. Edited by Elizabeth Eger, Charlotte Grant, Cliona O Gallchoir, and Penny Warburton. Cambridge: Cambridge University Press, 2001.

Eger, Elizabeth, Charlotte Grant, Cliona O Gallchoir, and Penny Warburton (eds.). *Women, Writing and the Public Sphere, 1700–1830*. Cambridge: Cambridge University Press, 2001. Pp. xii + 320; bibliography; illustrations.

This collection of articles presents women's contribution and relation to the public sphere in a hitherto almost uninvestigated light. Until now, whenever literary critics have focused on women writers of the eighteenth century, they have done this by portraying them as creating a sphere of their own. The present volume, by contrast, seeks to stress women writers' contribution to the broader picture of cultural transformation that took place in the eighteenth century. Throughout, the contributors to this volume have taken it as their guiding principle to analyze contemporary sources, a practice that makes this volume a remarkably rich treasure-trove for all readers who, though academically minded, do not have easy access to original eighteenth-century material.

In Socratic manner, the editors regard it as their first duty to define the two terms public and private. They emphasize that in all the articles the discussion of the private and public spheres has to be seen against the background of the transition from a pre-industrialized, aristocratic society to an industrialized, commercialized society. In this discussion, it is important for a twenty-first-century reader to understand what the public sphere really meant for women, who at that time were severely restricted in their legal and political rights. The first section, "Women in the Public Eye," looks at women who either operated in the public sphere or were transported into the public sphere as a result of gossip. As do several other contributors, Markman Ellis sharply criticizes Jürgen Habermas's account of the eighteenth century, *The Structural Transformation of the Public Sphere*. Habermas, according to Ellis, gave an inaccurate account of coffee houses in that he described them as open to all, thereby disregarding the fact that they were in reality exclusive meeting places for educated male citizens, and that women, for example, were admitted only as members of the serving staff. Caroline Gonda discusses what could be regarded as eighteenth-century gossip magazines, which brought various types of women, such as murderesses, fallen women, and those who married far above their own social status, into the public gaze.

Section two, "Consuming Arts," looks at women's representation in, and contribution to, the fine arts. Charlotte Grant examines the close connection between morality and the visual arts in the eighteenth century, as, for example, in the work of William Hogarth, and also in the choice of exhibition venues, such as the Vauxhall Gardens or the Foundling Hospital. Still within the context of morality, Elizabeth Eger shows how it was not until the second half of the eighteenth century, when discussions as to the public purpose and utility of art took place, that women were believed to have a civilizing force on society and that they should therefore take part in the social and cultural progress. Section three, "Learned Ladies: From Bluestockings to Cosmopolitan Intellectuals," begins with general observations on Bluestocking feminism and emphasizes the important contribution it made through its social, ideological, and political focus to the creation of private and public spheres. In what follows, three major figures of Bluestocking feminism are discussed, Catharine Macaulay, Maria Edgeworth, and Helen Maria Williams. In "Catharine Macaulay: History, Republicanism and the Public Sphere," Susan Wiseman seems almost to reproach Catharine Macaulay for having presented a "masculinized history" of seventeenth-century England. Macaulay's approach to history-writing, Wiseman complains, was still rooted in a discourse of national male virtue. Wiseman's criticism here seems rather severe if one takes into account the fact that at the time Macaulay wrote about, that is 1603–89, women were not allowed to take an active part in politics. It thus seems only natural that the majority of the protagonists in Macaulay's *History* are male. Cliona Ó Gallchoir makes it clear in her article that, although feminism was only in its early stages at the end of the eighteenth century, it was as yet very modest indeed in its demands. Maria Edgeworth, for example, although she strongly advocated a woman's right to publish, regarded a woman's taking part in the public sphere as unseemly and female leadership as having a corrupting effect on women.

Similarly, in the final section of the volume, "The Female Subject," two articles on Mary Wollstonecraft portray her as only moderate in her ideas of women's freedom. Wollstonecraft, it is argued, reproached women for their self-love and tried to make patriotic citizens out of them; this, however, meant for her that women should remain within the domestic sphere which she saw really as a public sphere in that a well-organized family would have a formative

VI: British Literatures

influence on well-organized society. To what extent a woman could participate in the public sphere is analyzed by Penny Warburton in "Theorising Public Opinion: Elizabeth Hamilton's Model of Self, Sympathy and Society." Elizabeth Hamilton, Warburton argues, is an example of the fact that women could, through the publication of political writings, make a major contribution to the public sphere even though they were allowed neither to vote nor to stand for Parliament.

This volume is a well-researched study on women and their relation to the public sphere in the eighteenth century. It examines the various ways in which women were portrayed, or portrayed themselves, and provides many interesting insights into hitherto less researched fields. One of its many strengths is clearly the host of contemporary sources that are adduced to paint a vivid picture of the time under discussion. And finally, one should not omit to mention the extensive notes that accompany each individual chapter and which are further evidence of the hard work that has been put into this book by all the contributors.—Melanie Maria Just

Eisenberg, Dan. "A Letter to Dr. Percy." *Cervantes: Bulletin of the Cervantes Society of America,* 21 (2001), 95–140.

Elfenbein, Andrew. "Lesbian Aestheticism on the Eighteenth-Century Stage." *Eighteenth-Century Life,* 25 (2001), 1–16.

Ellington, H. Elisabeth. "'A Correct Taste in Landscape': Pemberley as Fetish and Commodity." Pp. 90–110 of *Jane Austen in Hollywood.* Edited by Linda Troost and Sayre N. Greenfield. Lexington: University Press of Kentucky, 2001.

Ellison, Julie. "News, Blues, and Cowper's Busy World." *Modern Language Quarterly,* 62 (2001), 219–37.

Ellwood, Gracia Fay. "How Not to Father: Mr. Bennet and Mary." *Persuasions: The Jane Austen Journal On-Line,* 22 (2001).

Emsley, Sarah. "The Last Pages of *Emma*: Austen's Epithalamium." *Persuasions: Journal of the Jane Austen Society of North America,* 23 (2001), 188–96.

Erickson, Robert A. "'Written in the Heart': Clarissa and Scripture." Pp. 170–209 of *Passion and Virtue: Essays on the Novels of Samuel Richardson.* Edited by David Blewett. Toronto: University of Toronto Press, 2001.

Escott, Angela. "The School of Eloquence and 'Roasted Square Caps': Oratory and Pedantry as Fair Theatrical Game?" *Women's Writing,* 8 (2001), 59–79.

Ezell, Margaret. "'Household Affaires Are the Opium of the Soul': Damaris Masham and the Necessity of Women's Poetry." Pp. 49–65 of *Write or Be Written: Early Modern Women Poets and*

Cultural Constraints. Edited by Barbara Smith and Ursula Appelt. Aldershot: Ashgate Publishing Company, 2001.

Fabian, Bernhard, and Marie-Luise Spieckermann. "Pope in Eighteenth-Century Germany: A Bibliographical Essay (II)." *Swift Studies* 16 (2001), 5–30.

Fairer, David. "Creating a National Poetry: The Tradition of Spenser and Milton." Pp. 177–202 of *The Cambridge Companion to Eighteenth-Century Poetry*. Edited by John Sitter. Cambridge: Cambridge University Press, 2001.

Fanning, Christopher. "The Voices of the Dependent Poet: The Case of Mary Barber." *Women's Writing*, 8 (2001), 81–97.

Farnsworth, Rodney. "Mothers, Children, and the Other: Emotions About Children in Stäel's *Corinne* and Austen's *Sense and Sensibility*." *Prism(s): Essays in Romanticism*, 9 (2001), 123–38.

Fauske, Christopher. *Jonathan Swift and the Church of Ireland, 1710–1724: An Accidental Patriot*. Dublin: Irish Academic Press, 2001. Pp. 294.

Feldmann, Doris. "The Detection of the *homo politicus*: Textual/Sexual Politics in William Godwin's *Caleb Williams*." Pp. 68–80 of *Engendering Images of Man in the Long Eighteenth Century*. Edited by Walter Göbel, Saskia Schabio and Martin Windisch. Trier: WVT Wissenschaftlicher Verlag Trier, 2001.

Fendler, Susanne. "From Knight to Gentleman: The Changing Image of Man in the Early English Novel." Pp. 266–77 of *Engendering Images of Man in the Long Eighteenth Century*. Edited by Walter Göbel, Saskia Schabio, and Martin Windisch. Trier: WVT Wissenschaftlicher Verlag Trier, 2001.

Ferriss, Suzanne. "Emma Becomes Clueless." Pp. 122–29 of *Jane Austen in Hollywood*. Edited by Linda Troost and Sayre N. Greenfield. Lexington: University Press of Kentucky, 2001.

Fielitz, Sonja. "John Dryden as Critic and Translator of Ovid: The *Metamorphoses*, or, Neo-Classical Standards Put to the Test." Pp. 155–67 of *Dryden and the World of Neoclassicism*. Edited by Wolfgang Görtschacher and Holger Klein. (SECL—Studies in English and Comparative Literature, 17.) Tübingen: Stauffenburg, 2001.

Finberg, Melinda C. (ed.). *Eighteenth-Century Women Dramatists*. Oxford: Oxford University Press, 2001. Pp. lxi + 380; bibliography; chronology.

Fitzgerald, Lauren. "(In)Alienable Rights: Property, Feminism, and the Female Body from Ann Radcliffe to the Alien Films." *Romanticism on the Net: An Electronic Journal Devoted to Romantic Studies,* 21 (2001).

Fleck, Andrew. "Guyomar and Guyon: Dryden's Debt to Spenser in *The Indian Emperour.*" *Notes and Queries,* 48 (2001), 26–28.

Fletcher, Loraine. *Charlotte Smith: A Critical Biography.* New York: Palgrave, 2001. Pp. xi + 401; illustrations.

In her book *Reflections on Biography,* Paula R. Backscheider writes, "It is the job of the biographer to interpret, but the more invisible the interpretation and even the judgment are the better the book reads—and the more subversive it is" (3). The 2001 paperback edition of Fletcher's 1998 book achieves, for the most part, an objectivity about Smith that makes this biography on the cusp of the subversive Backscheider writes about. The process of biography writing itself must be akin to submersing oneself into the very consciousness of an absent subject and, therefore, must be considered a triumph of the will more often than a labor of love. In many literary biographies, readers wonder, "Whose will triumphed? Author or biographer?" Not in the case of this biography.

While Fletcher's admiration for Smith is not invisible, it is tempered with an appreciation of what twentieth-century audiences yearn for in their reading; of one of Smith's sonnets Fletcher writes: "For a modern taste, an immediate improvement can be made merely by taking out the exclamation marks, so averse we are to the surprised and declamatory; unfortunately, her tendency in revising was to add the screamers" (51). Fletcher's work considers the literature not only from a critical light but also from the process, including the intricacies of book production, information about how Smith wrote, publishing details, edition additions and emendations (as well as illustrations and engravings), the list of subscribers, and the approximate profit for Smith. Without insulting Smith's ability to budget or economize (as other critics have done), Fletcher brings to life the difficult time Smith had in balancing her acquired tastes with the circumstances she was reduced to as a result of leaving a profligate husband with their nine living children in tow.

In the first and second chapters, "Exile" and "Writing to Live" respectively, Fletcher inserts Smith into the cultural and literary milieu of the eighteenth century, carefully explaining how Smith might have first learned of slavery, its connections to the East India Trade, Smith's concept of spirituality, and her love of the botanical that, although not uncommon in the eighteenth-century, exceeded the affinity her contemporaries had for wide open spaces and the flora that abound there. "Exile" begins (aptly) with Smith's marriage to Benjamin Smith, then flashes back to her previous life, attachments, and education. The biography analyzes Smith's publications in chronological order, beginning with *Elegaic Sonnets and other Essays,* the translations *Manon Lescaut, or, the Fatal Attachment,* and *The Romance of Real Life.* The first two chapters also include analyses of *Emmeline* and *Ethelinde.* Most of Fletcher's reading of Smith's novels revolves around the idea that the castle stands in as a complete emblem of British law and government; the more dilapidated the castle, the more scathing Smith's comment on the institutions by which she was oppressed. Fletcher writes, "The Gothic house and its antitypes provide implicit political comment and controlling structures for her sprawling plots. But the ironist who is liberal or radical starts with a considerable disadvantage" (122). Since this biography's publication, however, several critical articles have built upon and/or razed this vein of criticism.

Chapter three, "Girondism," delineates the political overtones of Smith's middle novels. Informed by Burke's *Reflections on the Revolution in France,* which was published in November, 1790, *Celestina, Desmond* (drawn from the materials of her brief visit to Paris in 1791), and *The Banished Man* were among the most sporadically received of Smith's oeuvre. Freedom is at issue in each; Fletcher asserts that "Religion and the state buttress each other, threatening or crushing individual liberty" (135). Fletcher's treatment of *The Old Manor House* inadvertently suggests one reason for this novel's emergence as Smith's most commercially successful (at least in the late twentieth century): "Charlotte's guarded and hesitant style is most pronounced in *The Old Manor House*, which is poised between the revolutionism of *Desmond* and the conservative stance of *The Banished Man*" (168). This novel is also the least autobiographical: "Unlike the earlier novels the *Old Manor House* makes no appeal to public sympathy in the form of author-representative characters....More interesting to the biographer are the nocturnal meetings of Orlando and Monimia in Volume One and all they represent of sex in rebellion against society. Given Charlotte's way of harnessing her life to power her writing, one might be forgiven for wondering about this" (189). Here, the biographer appears again, playfully wondering if Smith's own nocturnal meetings informed those of Monimia and Orlando. Given Fletcher's later reporting that Sophia Lee's *Life of a Lover* "agreeably shocked," although Smith thought it "quite risqué," suggests otherwise (327).

Chapter 4, "An Interest in Green Leaves," examines *The Wanderings of Warwick* (1794) and her six children's books including *Rural Walks* (1795), *Rambles Farther* (1796), and *A History of England* (1806). The children's books, like her poetry, were especially imbued with the language and ideology of Sensibility, according to Fletcher. The biographer writes, "Charlotte thought an education which encouraged outdoor pursuits made a healthy antidote to the taste of luxuries and sexual precocity of girls growing up in towns. A program of social awareness and contact with poverty, however paternalistic and condescending it may seem now, must have had some effect on several generations of villagers who had no access to other help" (229). This may be seen as one of the weaknesses of the paperback edition of the biography; Sensibility has been recently reworked and reloaded with cultural significance that this biography does not take into account. Smith's children's books stress, according to Fletcher, the crucial blend of the cultivation of Sensibility with the memorization of poetry and classic literature. The ghost of the canon is once again present in the biography, as Fletcher notes that "The lines Charlotte introduces from her favorite eighteenth-century writers are often ones chosen by David Nichol Smith for his *Oxford Book of Eighteenth Century Verse* in 1926" (232).

In her discussion of *Montalbert*, Fletcher shows how Smith "radicalizes" Burney, revising her "claustrophobic" conclusions for the novel's heroine Rosalie (242). Fletcher consistently alludes to without naming what Sarah W. R. Smith in *Fetter'd or Free* has called "the sister plot": the interweaving of two stories that mirror or inform one another in which one sister is rewarded and the other punished for obeying or stepping outside patriarchal boundaries. This chapter's jumbled feel of overlapping editions, publications, removals from lodging to lodging escalates, lending the reader of the biography a disoriented feeling that perhaps reflects Smith's own sense of being the captain of an unmoored family for many years. The irony is that, while establishing herself as a writer, she was most often not established in any one locale for very long. Smith's situation created in her a honed sense of compassion, the primary emotion that impelled her to pen *The Narrative of the Loss of the Catharine* for the benefit of one of the single mother survivors of that tragedy, which remains Smith's sole foray into journalism. Chapter 5, "The Goddess of Botany," is dedicated to showing how Smith's politics have been revamped; whereas society could offer some small hope for a character like Emmeline, *The Young Philosopher's* Laura finds protection in "nature alone" (269).

An entire chapter devoted to another woman writer who has eclipsed Smith's presence in the literary canon seems odd in a biography dedicated to arguing Smith's lasting importance in the development of English letters. Nonetheless, that's what we have in Chapter 6, "Jane Austen," whose writings Fletcher links to Smith's. This chapter's use of secondary sources proves Fletcher's most exhaustive in the biography; but while Austen borrowed often the materials of Smith's narratives, Austen was "hostile to some of the ideas she found" in Smith's work (304). By Austen's time, Smith's reputation as Jacobin, although that name described only one section of her voluminous work, had taken hold. Fletcher maintains that the house metaphor Austen popularizes is owed to Smith: "Other novelists of the nineteenth and twentieth centuries seized on Smith's house metaphor, though usually through Austen and without knowing where it originated..." the biographer shows her objectivity by demurring that "comparison(s) will usually end in Austen's favor" (317).

Chapter 7, "Beachy Head," is devoted to the poems of the same name but includes the lament that Smith's "talent was distorted and wasted in Trust correspondence" in the last five years of her life (320). The chapter gives many depressing details, including this assessment of her sad decision to sell her library of over one-thousand volumes to allay debts. For the treasury of volumes she had been collecting since she was twenty, Smith: "got only about £150 for them, and missed them acutely; it must have felt like the end of her career" (323). Despite the despair such a moment might occasion for a writer, Fletcher chooses to accentuate the positive; Smith had "an ability to cut off from the hostile present, or at least to distance herself in word-play or stories," thus showing how integral a writing life must have been for a woman who often wrote letters riddled with misery. Fletcher elucidates the meaning of the title of Smith's final book of poems, explaining that "beachy" means the "end of a journey" as well as "death": a fitting title for a work published three months after Smith died. In this last, best work of poetry, Smith sets a new direction for herself. Fletcher writes, "Unlike the Romantics, she was learning how to register the cruelty and wastefulness as well as the beauty of Nature. Her voice was developing in distinctive ways" (336).

Readers of Charlotte Smith's oeuvre have all of the versions and revisions of the eighteenth-century novel, the inspiring development of a poet, and even an ill-fated drama at their disposal. More compelling than Fletcher's connections between Smith's life and her plot lines is the biographer's suggestion that Smith is among the most prolific, if not exemplary, professional woman writers of her time.—Diane Boyd

Fludernik, Monika. "Noble Savages and Calibans: Dryden and Colonial Discourse." Pp. 273–88 of *Dryden and the World of Neoclassicism*. Edited by Wolfgang Görtschacher and Holger Klein. Tubingen: Stauffenburg, 2001.

Fludernik, Monika. "Sympathetic Affect and Artful Deception: Rhetorical Ambivalence in William Godwin's *Caleb Williams*." Pp. 81–96 of *Engendering Images of Man in the Long Eighteenth Century*. Edited by Walter Göbel, Saskia Schabio and Martin Windisch. Trier: WVT Wissenschaftlicher Verlag Trier, 2001.

Fortunati, Vita, Rita Monticelli, and Maurizio Ascari (eds.). *Travel Writing and the Female Imaginary*. Bologna: Pàtron, 2001. Pp. 140; illustrations.

Foster, Gavin. "Ignoring the Tempest: Pepys, Dryden, and the Politics of Spectating in 1667." Pp. 5–22 of *John Dryden: A Tercentenary Miscellany*. Edited by Susan Green and Steven N. Zwicker. San Marino: Huntington Library, 2001.

Franklin, Michael (ed.). *The European Discovery of India: Key Indological Sources of Romanticism*. 6 volumes. London: Ganesha, 2001. Pp. 2600.

Michael Franklin is making a heroic effort to save the seminal texts of early Orientalism from oblivion (or resurrect them, if they are already there)—last year's nine-volume *Representing India: Indian Culture and Imperial Control in Eighteenth-Century British Orientalist Discourse* (London: Routledge) is now followed by the equally impressive six-volume *European Discovery of India*. The texts in this new set illustrate the negotiations between politics and scholarship in the study of Indian culture and religion in the late eighteenth and early nineteenth centuries. This period witnessed two complementary developments:

1) the shift from treating Indian natives as equals or at least collaborators to disrespecting any contribution from indigenous people in politics and scholarship; and

2) the shift from using scholarship for well-intentioned, if not always entirely successful, projects of colonial administration to pursuing scholarship for its own sake or for literary purposes.

From a twenty-first-century, post-Said point of view, these are depressing developments. However, they are still highly important because of how they illuminate how events and theories have to coincide to lead to such heinous political scenarios as the nineteenth-century British occupation of India.

The facsimile texts in the six volumes of the scarily expensive *European Discovery of India* fall into four categories. The largest comprises the translations of Sanskrit works of philosophy and literature by English scholars: Charles Wilkins' versions of the *Bhāgvăt-Gggtâ* (1784) and *Heetôpadçs* (1787), Sir William Jones' renderings of *Gítagóvinda* (1789) and of Kâlidâsa's *Sacontalá* (1789), and Horace Hayman Wilson's translations of Kâlidâsa's *Mégha Dúta* (1814) and of the *Vishńu Puráńa* (1840). Second, there are works of scholarship like Jones's essay "On the Mystical Poetry of the Persians and Hindus," Friedrich Schlegel's "On the Indian Language, Literature, and Philosophy," and Henry Thomas Colebrooke's collected *Essays on the Religion and Philosophy of the Hindus*. The two other categories are represented with one work each: travel literature with William Hodges' *Travels in India, During the Years 1780, 1781, 1782, & 1783* (with excellent reproductions of the engravings) and miscellaneous writing with Francis Gladwin's Calcutta periodical *Asiatic Miscellany* (inexplicably in a 1787 London abridgement).

Not all works are strictly from the eighteenth century (even in the long version), but they all come from the time before the dark of nineteenth-century Macaulay-style Orientalism settled on India. Each work comes with a well-informed and highly informative introduction to the writer and context. Some introductions delve into interpretations of the text—those for *Gítagóvinda* and the *Mégha Dúta* are particularly good—while others stick to brief summaries preparing the reader for the following work. The travel narrative with its visual and verbal depictions of India and the Calcutta periodical with its mix of literature—in translation or by British writers in India—history, travel, and politics are especially interesting, and it is good to have them available in an accessible form.

While the texts in *The European Discovery* are appropriately chosen, immaculately reproduced, and expertly set up, some details remain unclear. For instance, the variety of the material—though it shows beyond doubt how much of a *European* phenomenon early Orientalism was—raises the question whether Franklin might not have stuck to one genre, for instance translations of Sanskrit material or early travel narratives, which are particularly difficult to get a hold of. The works are nicely presented, but the selection of editions to reproduce, as in the case of the *Asiatic Miscellany*, is nowhere explained. The introductions could have gone easier on biography and offered more interpretation—it is a shame that there is still no book on eighteenth-century representations of India from Franklin, clearly the most informed and insightful critic writing about this era and area of the world. Finally, the steep price of the volumes raises troubling question. As library budgets become smaller and smaller, one would hope that publishers could find a way to make this material available at a more affordable price. Until then, the libraries than can afford to put *The European Discovery of India* on their shelves should count themselves lucky.—Norbert Schürer

Frohock, Richard. "Violence and Awe: The Foundations of Government in Aphra Behn's New World Settings." Pp. 41–58 of *Women at Sea: Travel Writing and the Margins of Caribbean Discourse*. Edited by Lizabeth Paravisini-Gebert and Ivette Romero-Cesareo. New York: Palgrave, 2001.

Fruchtman, Jack, Jr. "The Politics of Sensibility: Helen Maria Williams's *Julia* and the Terror in France." *Eighteenth-Century Women*, 1 (2001), 185–202.

Fuentes, Yvonne. "Two Endings to a Same Deception: The Stories of Federica and Caelia." *Hispanofila*. 131 (2001), 21–30.

Fujii, Tetsu. "Bamingamu Daigaku Eibungaku-Ka Jonson Senta No Gaiyo." *Eigo Seinen/Rising Generation*, 146 (2001), 797.

Fujii, Tetsu. "A Note on a Variant Copy of Hawkins's *The Life of Samuel Johnson*, Ll.D." *Notes and Queies,* 48 (2001), 429–30.

Fujii, Tetsu. "Why Chalmers?: A Note on a Life of Hawkins." *Notes and Queries*, 48 (2001), 433–34.

Fulford, Tim. "'Nature' Poetry." Pp. 109–32 of *The Cambridge Companion to Eighteenth-Century Poetry.* Edited by John Sitter. Cambridge: Cambridge University Press, 2001.

Fuller, Graham. "Cautionary Tale." Pp. 77–81 of *Film/Literature/Heritage: A Sight and Sound Reader.* Edited by Ginette Vincendeau. London: British Film Institute, 2001.

Fullerton, Susannah, and Anne Harbers (eds.). *Jane Austen: Antipodean Views.* Neutral Bay: Wellington Lane Press, 2001. Pp. 168; illustrations.

Fulton, David. "A Holiday from High Tone: Politics and Genre in Andrew Davies' Adaptation of Daniel Defoe's *Moll Flanders*." *EnterText: An Interactive Interdisciplinary E-Journal for Cultural and Historical Studies and Creative Work*, 1 (2001), 132–56.

Furbank, P. N., and W. R. Owens "Defoe and King William: A Sceptical Enquiry." *Review of English Studies,* 52 (2001), 227–32.

Furbank, P. N., and W. R. Owens. "Defoe's 'South-Sea' and 'North-Sea' Schemes: A Footnote to a *New Voyage Round the World*." *Eighteenth-Century Fiction,* 13 (2001), 501–08.

Gabbard, Christopher D. "'The She-Tyrant Reigns': Mary Ii and the Tullia Poems." *Restoration: Studies in English Literary Culture, 1660–1700*, 25 (2001), 103–16.

Gadeken, Sara. "'A Method of Being Perfectly Happy': Technologies of Self in the Eighteenth-Century Female Community." *Eighteenth-Century Novel,* 1 (2001), 217–35.

Gailor, Genoveffa Giambona. "Pioneering English Women Writers: Hannah More and Mary Wollstonecraft." *Zenith: A Literary Magazine,* 7 (2001), 28–31.

Gardiner, Anne Barbeau. "Dryden, Bower, Castlemaine, and the Imagery of Revolution, 1682–1687." *Eighteenth-Century Life,* 25 (2001), 135–46.

Gardner, Kevin J. "George Farquhar's the Recruiting Officer: Warfare, Conscription, and the Disarming of Anxiety." *Eighteenth-Century Life*, 25 (2001), 43–61.

Gargett, Graham. "Oliver Goldsmith and Voltaire's *Lettres Philosophiques*." *Modern Language Review*, 96 (2001), 952–63.

Gargett, Graham. "Plagiarism, Translation and the Problem of Identity: Oliver Goldsmith and Voltaire." *Eighteenth-Century Ireland/Iris an da Chultur*, 16 (2001), 83–103.

Gaskill, Howard. "'Aus Der Dritten Hand': Herder and His Annotators." *German Life and Letters*, 54 (2001), 210–18.

Gaskill, Howard. "Tieck's Juvenilia: Ossianic Attributions." *Modern Language Review*, 96 (2001), 747–61.

Gautier, Gary. "Slavery and the Fashioning of Race in *Oroonoko*, *Robinson Crusoe*, and Equiano's *Life*." *Eighteenth Century: Theory and Interpretation*, 42 (2001), 161–79.

Gelber, Michael Werth. "John Dryden and *The Battle of the Books*." Pp. 139–56 of *John Dryden: A Tercentenary Miscellany*. Edited by Susan Green and Steven N. Zwicker. San Marino: Huntington Library, 2001.

Geller, Jaclyn. "The Unnarrated Life: Samuel Johnson, Female Friendship, and the Rise of the Novel Revisited." Pp. 80–98 of *Johnson Re-Visioned: Looking Before and After*. (Bucknell Studies in Eighteenth-Century Literature and Culture.) Edited by Philip Smallwood. Lewisburg: Bucknell University Press, 2001.

Geng, Li-Peng. "The Loiterer and Jane Austen's Literary Identity." *Eighteenth-Century Fiction*, 13 (2001), 579–92.

Gerrrard, Christine. "Political Passions." Pp. 37–62 of *The Cambridge Companion to Eighteenth-Century Poetry*. Edited by John Sitter. Cambridge: Cambridge University Press, 2001.

Gerard, W. B. "Sterne in Wedgwood: 'Poor Maria' and the 'Bourbonnais Shepherd.'" *Shandean: An Annual Devoted to Laurence Sterne and His Works*, 12 (2001), 78–88.

Gibbons, James. "J. M. R. Lenz's Der Landprediger: An Adaptation of *The Vicar of Wakefield* 'Tradition'?" *Colloquia Germanica: Internationale Zeitschrift für Germanistik*, 34 (2001), 213–36.

Gibbons, Luke. "'Subtilized into Savages': Edmund Burke, Progress, and Primitivism." *South Atlantic Quarterly*, 100 (2001), 83–109.

Gilbert, Deidre. "Joanna Baillie, Passionate Anatomist: Basil and Its Masquerade." *Restoration and 18th Century Theatre Research*, 16 (2001), 42–54.

Gillespie, Stuart. "John Dryden, Classicist and Translator." *Translation & Literature,* 10 (2001), 1–2.

Gillespie, Stuart. *John Dryden, Classicist and Translator*. Edinburgh: Edinburgh University Press, 2001. Pp. ix + 151; bibliography; illustrations.

Gindele, Karen C. "The Flavor of a Peach." *Review,* 23 (2001), 245–56.

Giovannelli, Laura. *Falsi D'autore: Percy, Macpherson, Chatterton*. Pisa: ETS, 2001. Pp. 280; bibliography.

Giovanopoulos, Anna-Christina. "The Bloody Register: Representations of Violence in 17th- and 18th-Century England." Pp. 67–79 of *The Aesthetics and Pragmatics of Violence*. Edited by Michael Hensen and Annette Pankratz. Passau: Stutz, 2001.

Giroud, Vincent. *Theater & Anti-Theater in the 18th Century: A Tercentennial Exhibition*. New Haven: Beinecke Rare Book & Manuscript Library Yale University, 2001. Pp. 36; illustrations.

Gladfelder, Hal. *Criminality and Narrative in Eighteenth-Century England: Beyond the Law*. Baltimore: Johns Hopkins University Press, 2001. Pp. xiii + 281; bibliography.

Members of the emerging middle class in eighteenth-century England were obsessed with crime stories about pirates, highwaymen, and otherwise wayward characters tending toward deviant social and/or sexual behavior. Rogue narratives, criminal ballads, pamphlets, and trial reports proliferated in the early part of the century, giving way to crime fiction, one of the most important genres in the rise of the novel period. Pioneers of the crime novel, such as Daniel Defoe and later Henry Fielding, invented the criminal as a marketable commodity but also as an instructive guide, one who could lead readers down the path to hell, repent, and then help readers find their ways back to the gates of heaven.

Scholars of eighteenth-century British literature have paid much attention to the crime genre, citing its importance to the origination and rise of the novel. Hal Gladfelder pays homage to critics who have investigated the crime genre and criminal biographies, such as Lincoln Faller, John Richetti, Michael McKeon, John Bender, and D. A. Miller. Gladfelder notes that much of the scholarly interest in the eighteenth-century crime genre to date has tended to coincide with the seminal work of Michel Foucault; the emphasis has been on surveillance. Gladfelder's book, however, departs from this tradition. He argues that his own study "diverges most fundamentally . . . in shifting the focus of discussion from the institutions of law (the prison, the police) and the law's strategies of surveillance and control to the experience of the outlaw: the social forces and forms of identity that violate the boundaries of legality" (8). Gladfelder concentrates on the relationship between reader, author, and criminal personality. That is, the reader experiences a significant sense of identification with the criminal mind, personality, and behavior. In Gladfelder's estimation, Defoe compels the reader to "confront his or her own likeness in the text" (14). The resulting reader identification with the criminal personality establishes firstly what the author calls the "universal inheritance of sin," a sense that the difference between the law-abiding citizen and the criminal is slight indeed. Secondly, the reader in Gladfelder's argument is able to identify with the criminal mind, so much so that he or she begins to share the guilt that the character possesses. The analysis proposes that the audience and author experience both "panic" and "guilt" as they simultaneously desire the deviant activity. Gladfelder states that "crime narratives, and the novels that derive from them tend to legitimate, to project as desirable, the very disruptive potentialities they set out to contain" (8). In this sense, Gladfelder's argument runs counter to understanding the criminal biography as a morally instructive text. Here, crime is an occasion to protest and resist authority and even, as the author puts it, to "advocate resistance to the institutions of justice and their prefabricated narratives of crime and retribution, and this resistance to the authorized narratives of criminality runs, as a countercurrent, through all the forms of crime literature" (9). In other words, authors such as Defoe create criminals with whom readers will be able to identify and sympathize; readers might find parts of themselves in these deviant personalities and acts of depravity.

In order to demonstrate the strands of connection, identification, and collusion between audience, author, and criminal, Gladfelder focuses in Part I on the various early eighteenth-century crime genres: criminal biography, the picaresque, trial reports, and gallows speeches. In Part II, the author considers Defoe's *Colonel Jack*, *Moll Flanders*, and *Roxana*. Next, he turns to Henry Fielding's writings (both fictive and his trial writing when serving as a magistrate). In the epilogue, Gladfelder concentrates predominantly on William Godwin's *Caleb Williams* in order to show "ways in which the criminal narrative had over the course of the eighteenth century become a necessary vehicle for articulating cultural anxieties and longings" (16).

In sum, Gladfelder's scholarship is smart, thorough, and provocative. Eighteenth-Century scholars will find *Criminality and Narrative in Eighteenth-Century England: Beyond the Law* a unique and valuable contribution to the studies of crime literature and the eighteenth-century novel. Additionally, the study advances our understanding of the identity, experience, and disposition of the eighteenth-century reader. Individuality is achieved through deviance (or empathy for deviance) as a form of protest.—Robert Dryden

Glasenapp, Jorn. "Das Bild stets vor Augen oder William Gilpin Und Der Pittoreske Landschaftskult Des Ausgehenden 18. Jahrhunderts." Pp. 169–88 of *Erschriebene Natur: Internationale Perspektiven Auf Texte Des 18. Jahrhunderts*. Edited by Michael Scheffel and Dietmar Gotsch. Bern: Peter Lang, 2001.

Glaser, Horst Albert. "Weltumsegler und Ihre Reiseberichte." Pp. 15–22 of *Die Wende Von Der Aufklarung Zur Romantik 1760–1820: Epoche im Uberblick*. Edited by Horst Albert Glaser, Gyorgy M. Vajda, and Francois Crouzet. Amsterdam: Benjamins, 2001.

Göbel, Walter. "Samuel Johnson and Laurence Sterne. Versions of 18th-Century Humanism." Pp. 217–27 of *Renaissance Humanism – Modern Humanism(s): Festschrift for Claus Uhlig*. (Anglistische Forschungen, 301.) Edited by Walter Göbel and Bianca Ross. Heidelberg: Winter, 2001.

Göbel, Walter. "Sarah and Henry Fielding's Definitions of the 'Man of Feeling.'" Pp. 176–91 of *Engendering Images of Man in the Long Eighteenth Century*. Edited by Walter Göbel, Saskia Schabio and Martin Windisch. Trier: WVT Wissenschaftlicher Verlag Trier, 2001.

Göbel, Walter, Saskia Schabio, and Martin Windisch. (eds.). *Engendering Images of Man in the Long Eighteenth Century*. Trier: WVT Wissenschaftlicher Verlag, 2001. Pp. xiii + 295.

VI: British Literatures

Gobin, Charles E. "Dangerous Persuasions: Correspondence as Presence in Clarissa." Pp. 91–111 of *1650–1850: Ideas, Aesthetics, and Inquiries in the Early Modern Era*. Volume 6. Edited by Kevin L. Cope. New York: AMS Press, 2001.

Gohrbandt, Detlev. "Judging the Virtues of Gendered Speech in Eighteenth-Century Fables." Pp. 133–48 of *Engendering Images of Man in the Long Eighteenth Century*. Edited by Walter Göbel, Saskia Schabio and Martin Windisch. Trier: WVT Wissenschaftlicher Verlag Trier, 2001.

Goldgar, Bertrand A. "Imitation and Plagiarism: The Lauder Affair and Its Critical Aftermath." *Studies in the Literary Imagination*, 34 (2001), 1–16.

Goldstein, Philip (ed.). *Communities of Cultural Value: Reception Study, Political Differences, and Literary History*. Edited by Philip Goldstein. Lanham: Lexington Books, 2001. Pp. vii + 241.

Goldstein, Philip. "Feminism and Poststructuralist Criticism: The Reception of *Pride and Prejudice*." In *Communities of Cultural Value: Reception Study, Political Differences, and Literary History*. Edited by Philip Goldstein. Lanham: Lexington Books, 2001.

Goldsworthy, Cephas. *The Satyr: An Account of the Life and Work, Death and Salvation, of John Wilmot, Second Earl of Rochester*. London: Weidenfeld & Nicolson, 2001. Pp. vii + 295; bibliography.

Gonda, Caroline. "Misses, Murderesses, and Magdalens: Women in the Public Eye." Pp. 53–71 of *Women, Writing and the Public Sphere, 1700–1830*. Edited by Elizabeth Eger, Charlotte Grant, Cliona O Gallchoir, and Penny Warburton. Cambridge: Cambridge University Press, 2001.

Goodridge, John. "John Clare and Eighteenth-Century Poetry: Pomfret, Cunningham, Bloomfield." *Eighteenth Century: Theory and Interpretation*, 42 (2001), 264–78.

Gorak, Jan (ed.). *Canon Vs. Culture: Reflections on the Current Debate*. Edited by Jan Gorak. New York: Garland, 2001. Pp. xv + 227.

Gorak, Jan. "Reflections on the Eighteenth-Century Canon: Disciplinary Change in the Humanities." Pp. 191–212 of *Canon Vs. Culture: Reflections on the Current Debate*. Edited by Jan Gorak. New York: Garland, 2001.

Goring, Paul. "Anglicanism, Enthusiasm and Quixotism: Preaching and Politeness in Mid-Eighteenth Century Literature." *Literature & Theology*, 15 (2001), 326–41.

Görlach, Manfred. *Eighteenth-Century English*. Heidelberg: Winter, 2001.

Görtschacher, Wolfgang, and Holger Klein (eds.). *Dryden and the World of Neoclassicism*. Tübingen: Stauffenburg, 2001. Pp. xiii + 295; bibliography.

Görtschacher, Wolfgang. "Of Virtuous Inclinations and Moral Goodness: John Dryden's *Troilus and Cressida: Or, Truth Found too Late*." Pp. 115–25 of *Dryden and the World of Neoclassicism*. Edited by Wolfgang Görtschacher and Holger Klein. (SECL—Studies in English and Comparative Literature, 17.) Tübingen: Stauffenburg, 2001.

Gottlieb, Evan. "The Astonished Eye: The British Sublime and Thomson's 'Winter.'" *Eighteenth Century: Theory and Interpretation*, 42 (2001), 43–57.

Gould, Timothy. "Engendering Aesthetics: Sublimity, Sublimation, and Misogyny in Burke and Kant." Pp. 40–60 of *Maps and Mirrors: Topologies of Art and Politics*. Edited by Steve Martinot. Evanston: Northwestern University Press, 2001.

Gqola, Pumla Dineo. "'Where There Is No Novelty, There Can Be No Curiosity': Reading Imoinda's Body in Aphra Behn's *Oroonoko or, the Royal Slave*." *English in Africa*, 28 (2001), 105–17.

Grabes, Herbert (ed.). *Writing the Early Modern English Nation: The Transformation of National Identity in Sixteenth- and Seventeenth-Century England*. Amsterdam: Rodopi, 2001. Pp. xv + 199.

Graham, Kenneth W. "An Introduction to the Broadview Edition of *Vathek* with *The Episodes of Vathek*." *The Beckford Journal*, 7 (2001), 11–17.

Grant, Charlotte. "The Choice of Hercules: The Polite Arts and 'Female Excellence' in Eighteenth-Century London." Pp. 75–103 of *Women, Writing and the Public Sphere, 1700–1830*. Edited by Elizabeth Eger, Charlotte Grant, Cliona O Gallchoir, and Penny Warburton. Cambridge: Cambridge University Press, 2001.

Gray, Alasdair. *A Short Survey of Classic Scottish Writing*. Edinburgh: Canongate Press, 2001. Pp. xiv + 159; bibliography.

Green, Susan, and Steven N. Zwicker (eds.). *John Dryden: A Tercentenary Miscellany*. San Marino: Huntington Library, 2001. Pp. vii + 255; bibliography; illustrations.

Greene, Richard. "Mary Leapor: The Problem of Personal Identity." *Eighteenth Century: Theory and Interpretation*, 42 (2001), 218–27.

VI: British Literatures

Greene, Richard. "Sir Beelzebub's Syllabub; or, Edith Sitwell's Eighteenth Century." *Lumen*, 20 (2001), 101–09.

Gregg, Stephen H. "A 'Truly Christian Hero': Religion, Effeminacy, and Nation in the Writings of the Societies for Reformation of Manners." *Eighteenth-Century Life*, 25 (2001), 17–28.

Gregori, Flavio. "John Gay's Fables: A Childish Work?" Pp. 47–56 of *Hearts of Lightness: The Magic of Children's Literature*. Edited by Laura Tosi. Venice: Cafoscarina, 2001.

Griffin, Michael. "Delicate Allegories, Deceitful Mazes: Goldsmith's Landscapes." *Eighteenth-Century Ireland/Iris an da Chultur*, 16 (2001), 104–17.

Griffin, Robert J. "*Roxana*: The 1740 Version." *Center & Clark Newsletter*, 38 (2001), 5–6.

Griffin, Robert J. "The Age of 'the Age of' Is Over: Johnson and New Versions of the Late Eighteenth Century." *Modern Language Quarterly*, 62 (2001), 377–91.

Griffith, Elizabeth. "The Times." Pp. 145–210 of *Eighteenth-Century Women Dramatists*. Edited by Melinda C. Finberg. Oxford: Oxford University Press, 2001.

Griswold, Mac. "Planting the English Landscape Garden: There Were Flowers." *Raritan*, 20 (2001), 80–106.

Gross, Gloria Sybil. "In a Fast Coach with a Pretty Woman: Jane Austen and Samuel Johnson." *Age of Johnson*, 12 (2001), 199–253.

Grossman, Joyce. "Social Protest and the Mid-Century Novel: Mary Collyer's *The History of Betty Barnes*." *Eighteenth-Century Women*, 1 (2001), 165–84.

Grossman, Kathryn M., Michael E. Lane, Benedicte Monicat, and Willa Z. Silverman (eds.). *Confrontations: Politics and Aesthetics in Nineteenth-Century France*. Amsterdam: Rodopi, 2001. Pp. 311; music.

Grundy, Isobel. *Lady Mary Wortley Montagu*. Oxford: Oxford University Press, 2001. Pp. 704; bibliography; plates; illustrations; table; maps.

Guest, Kristen (ed.). *Eating their Words: Cannibalism and the Boundaries of Cultural Identity*. New York: State University of New York Press, 2001. Pp. 219; bibliography.

In general literary parlance, the term "cannibalism" is used to point out the absolute divide or alterity existing between civilization and savagery. Each of the essays in Kristen Guest's collection, however, challenges the ways cannibalism is used to support such alterity. As the title suggests, the volume is limited to "textual" cannibalism, while the subtitle describes the focus of each essay: as Guest puts it, "the discourse of cannibalism persistently gives voices to the diverse marginal groups it is supposed to silence and questions the dominant ideologies it is evoked to support" (3). In other words, cannibalism effectively functions as an ambivalent term that, while yoked to savagery, can also be used to describe the so-called civilization that uses the term.

In one of the more poignant essays from the volume, "Robinson Crusoe Inc(orporates): Domestic Economy, Incest, and the Trope of Cannibalism," Minaz Jooma explores the relationship between cannibalism and domestic economy. According to Jooma, "domestic relations in *Robinson Crusoe* are repeatedly concerned with the violation of bodily and psychic boundaries" (62), especially between the prodigal Crusoe and his relationships with his father as well as the captain of the Turkish rover. Jooma suggests that Crusoe is a slave whose body is available for "sexual consumption" by the Turkish captain (66). Jooma describes how after his shipwreck, Crusoe is "rebirthed" on shore and then "cannibalizes" his new "mother," the ship itself. While she does touch on the more "literal" cannibalism in the novel, Jooma is primarily concerned with cannibalism as a metaphor. Crusoe's symbolic cannibalism "of several maternal bodies that yield food and supplies ultimately gives him the means to gain ascendancy over the would-be cannibal victims, the cannibals themselves and all other potential marauders" (73). For Jooma, Crusoe learns from his father and from the Turkish captain how to "incorporate" the savages he encounters into a "domestic economy—an economy in which those held captive by a monopoly on consumables are quietly compelled to do as the colonizer, Crusoe, desires" (73). The import is that Crusoe is a cannibal as much as the savages are, and he learns his cannibalism partly from English domestic economy.

Further essays in the volume explore Spenser's description of the "Savage Nation" in Book 6 of *The Fairie Queene* as descriptions of New World natives. According to Robert Viking O'Brien, these descriptions suggest European unease with its own consumptions through colonization. In another essay, Mark Buchan describes how Achilles desires to eat Hector's dead body, but then decides to remain within the bounds of civilization, while the Cyclops has no civilization and thus breaks no societal code when he eats Odysseus's men. Julia Wright explicates Maturin's *Melmoth the Wanderer* as a novel about the consumption of land through inheritance and the change in the national economy as it moves from aristocracy to capitalism. Kristen Guest explores depictions of cannibalism in Victorian "lower-class" melodrama as a form of "reverse consumption," representing the upper class consumption of the lower class. In one of the more fun essays in the collection, Santiago Colas describes how Latin and South American revolutionaries appropriated cannibalism as an ambivalent trope that could be used to represent revolution. The next essays study New Zealand author Ian Wedde's novel *Symmes Hole* and Margaret Atwood's *Wilderness Tips* while the last essay provides a critique of the way cannibalism is often used in contemporary literary criticism, demonstrating the way "ocular proof" was used to show that literal cannibalism existed. According to Geoffrey Sanborn, the proof that cannibalism existed was often suspect, and modern critics should read representations of cannibalism as contextually performative.

The nine essays collected in the volume appropriately complicate the term "cannibalism" and demonstrate how its usage is often ambivalent. While it is generally used to solidify the self/other divide, it may often work against the divide to show the similarities between civilization and savagery. The collection may prove useful for critics working within any period, especially for those who desire to read a collection that combines critical complexity with close-reading strategies.—Chad Wilson

Gunn, Daniel P. "Is *Clarissa* Bourgeois Art?" Pp. 135–51 of *Passion and Virtue: Essays on the Novels of Samuel Richardson*. Edited by David Blewett. Toronto: University of Toronto Press, 2001.

VI: British Literatures

Haddad, Emily A. "Body and Belonging(s): Property in *The Captivity of Mungo Park*." Pp. 124–44 of *Colonial and Postcolonial Incarceration*. Edited by Graeme Harper. New York: Continuum, 2001.

Haggerty, George E. "Walpoliana." *Eighteenth-Century Studies*, 34 (2001), 227–49.

Haggerty, George E. "Sir Charles Grandison and the 'Language of Nature.'" Pp. 317–31 of *Passion and Virtue: Essays on the Novels of Samuel Richardson*. Edited by David Blewett. Toronto: University of Toronto Press, 2001.

Hale, John K. "Arrows (and Arrowroot) in Jane Austen's *Emma*." *Persuasions: Journal of the Jane Austen Society of North America*, 23 (2001), 219–21.

Hale, John K. "Austen's *Emma*." *Explicator*, 59 (2001), 122–24.

Hall, Dennis. "On Idleness: Dr. Johnson on Millennial Malaise." *Kentucky Philological Review*, 15 (2001), 28–32.

Hamilton, Patricia L. "Bathsua Makin's Essay and Daniel Defoe's 'An Academy for Women'." *Seventeenth-Century News*, 59, (2001), 146–53.

Hammond, Brean. "The City in Eighteenth-Century Poetry." Pp. 83–108 of *The Cambridge Companion to Eighteenth-Century Poetry*. Edited by John Sitter. Cambridge: Cambridge University Press, 2001.

Hanley, Brian. *Samuel Johnson as Book Reviewer: A Duty to Examine the Labors of the Learned*. Newark: University of Delaware Press, 2001. Pp. 293; bibliography.

Harbinson, Michael. "Keats and Dryden—Source or Analogue?" *Notes and Queries*, 48 (2001), 138–40.

Hardin, Michael. "Colonizing the Characters of Daniel Defoe: J. M. Coetzee's *Foe*." *Notes on Contemporary Literature*, 31 (2001), 9–10.

Harman, Claire. *Fanny Burney: A Biography*. Alfred A. Knopf, 2001. Pp. xxvi + 417; bibliography; illustrations.

Any biographer of Frances Burney must confront an overwhelming amount of primary evidence that survives from the tribe of writers known as the Burney family. Furthermore, one must be familiar with the considerable body of scholarship that has been published about Burney and her works. And with more than five biographies of Burney appearing in the past half century, a biographer must establish the need for another. In her preface, Clare Harman distinguishes hers from her predecessors' by the evaluation and the weight that she will give the surviving evidence. With regard to the *Memoirs of Doctor Burney*, Harman suggests that her most formidable predecessor, Joyce Hemlow, has given it more authority than it deserves. Harman proceeds to write an engaging account of Burney's life yet one that differs little in the primary details and events from Hemlow's. As her narrative unfolds, Harman highlights the discrepancies that she finds in the evidence that she has examined and attempts to interpret these inconsistencies. However, her interpretations are not always convincing, and in at least one instance, she shows that she has not kept up with current Burney scholarship. In order to evaluate Harmon's biography, it may be useful to consider some of the points where hers differs from Hemlow's.

Harman's book offers ancillary material not included in Hemlow's. Whereas Hemlow's biography includes six plates and nine illustrations, Harman's comes replete with two sections of glossy plates containing a total of thirty-six illustrations of people and scenes related to Burney's life. Most of the illustrations included in Hemlow's work have been reproduced in Harman's. The inclusion of the additional ones is welcome, however, noticeably absent in Harmon's book is any reproduction of Burney's handwriting. Given the wealth of manuscripts that Burney left to posterity, an illustration of at least one is desirable. Harman provides two interesting appendices of material not included by Hemlow. Both highlight Burney's intellectual capacity. The first, she titles "Fanny Burney Undergoes a Memory Test." It offers two transcripts for comparison of Lord Thurlow's opening speech at the trial of Warren Hastings in 1788, at which Burney was present; one is Burney's account which she recalled later for her father and recorded in her Diary; the other is that of a shorthand writer making a transcription for the official record. From the comparison, one can see Burney's memory, at least in this instance, was remarkably accurate. The second appendix reprints J. N. Waddell's *Notes and Queries* article of 1980, "Additions to the O.E.D. from the Writings of Fanny Burney." If one has not seen this article, it testifies to Burney's inventiveness with neologisms.

Within the main text of her biography, Harmon occasionally differs with Hemlow. For example, Harman appears to disagree with respect to the identification of Burney's maternal grandfather, thus presenting the reader with two men, one of whom who may have been Burney's ancestor. Yet the evidence that she provides is inconclusive and points to the possibility that the two men are indeed one and the same person. In another instance, Hemlow offers a retelling of Burney's account of an incident that took place in 1817. Burney had gone for a walk with her dog along the coast at Ilfracombe and found herself trapped by the rising tide on a rocky protuberance. In Burney's dramatic account, the incident is life-threatening. Harman retells the same event yet questions Burney's veracity. She cites a short letter of 1912 in which the same incident is described by the son of a friend of Burney's son, Alex. In this letter, the threat to Burney is minimized and even the presence of the dog is denied. Harman proceeds to offer an interpretation as to why Burney would exaggerate and alter the details in her account. In her evaluation, she gives more weight to evidence four times removed and nearly one hundred years after the event than to Burney's firsthand account written six years after the fact. Unfortunately, Harman misses an opportunity where the evidence does warrant a departure from Hemlow, when she cites the publication date of *Cecilia* as June 12, 1782. The correct publication date for *Cecilia*, July 12, 1782, has been established since 1980 when Alvaro Ribeiro published his article "The Publication Date of Fanny Burney's *Cecilia*" in *Notes and Queries*. In summary, although Harman's biography places Burney's life in the hands of a popular reading audience in an attractive and readable format—which is always a welcome occasion—a more careful treatment of the subject is desired.—Catherine M. Rodriguez

Harper, Graeme (ed.). *Colonial and Postcolonial Incarceration*. New York: Continuum, 2001. Pp. x + 264; illustrations.

Harrington, Dana. "Gender, Commerce, and the Transformation of Virtue in Eighteenth-Century Britain." *Rhetoric Society Quarterly*, 31 (2001), 33–52.

VI: British Literatures

Harris, Jocelyn. "Protean Lovelace." Pp. 92–113 of *Passion and Virtue: Essays on the Novels of Samuel Richardson*. Edited by David Blewett. Toronto: University of Toronto Press, 2001.

Harris, Martin. "The 'Witchcraft' of Media Manipulation: *Pamela* and *The Blair Witch Project*." *Journal of Popular Culture,* 34 (2001), 75–107.

Harth, Phillip. "The Text of Dryden's Poetry." Pp. 227–44 of *John Dryden: A Tercentenary Miscellany*. Edited by Susan Green and Steven N. Zwicker. San Marino: Huntington Library, 2001.

Hashinuma, Katsumi. "The Economic Theme in *Gulliver's Travels*." *Hitotsubashi Journal of Arts and Sciences*, 42 (2001), 41–58.

Haskell, Dennis. *Samuel Johnson in Marrickville*. Todmorden: Arc, 2001. Pp. 81.

Hawes, Clement. "Johnson's Cosmopolitan Nationalism." Pp. 37–63 of *Johnson Re-Visioned: Looking Before and After*. (Bucknell Studies in Eighteenth-Century Literature and Culture.) Edited by Philip Smallwood,. Lewisburg: Bucknell University Press, 2001.

Haynes, Kenneth. "Dryden: Classical or Neoclassical?" *Translation & Literature,* 10 (2001), 67–77.

Haywood, Eliza. *The Selected Works of Eliza Haywood*. 3 volumes. Edited by Alexander Pettit, Patrick Spedding, Margo Collins, Jerry Beasley, Christine Blouch, and Kathryn King. London: Pickering & Chatto, 2001. Pp. 1,368.

Helbig, Jörg (ed.). *Erzählen und Erzähltheorie Im 20. Jahrhundert*. Heidelberg: Carl Winter Universitatsverlag, 2001. Pp. 412; portraits.

Helo, Ari. "The Historicity of Morality: Necessity and Necessary Agents in the Ethics of Lord Kames." *History of European Ideas,* 27 (2001), 239–55.

Hensen, Michael, and Annette Pankratz (eds.). *The Aesthetics and Pragmatics of Violence*. Passau: Stutz, 2001. Pp. 272; illustrations.

Herman, Ruth. "Enigmatic Gender in Delarivier Manley's *New Atalantis*." Pp. 202–24 of *Presenting Gender: Changing Sex in Early-Modern Culture*. (Bucknell Studies in Eighteenth-Century Literature and Culture.) Edited by Chris Mounsey. Lewisburg: Bucknell University Press, 2001.

Herman, Ruth. "A New Attribution to Delavivier Manley?" *Notes and Queries,* 48 (2001), 401–03.

Herzog, Gunter. "Picturesque Sisters: Das 'Bild' als Intermediales Medium in Literatur, Malerei und Gartenkunst des 18. Jahrhunderts." Pp. 76–92 of *Sister Arts: Englische Literatur Im Grenzland der Kunstgebiete*. Edited by Joachim Möller. Marburg: Jonas, 2001.

Hewson, Lance. "Style and Translation." *Anglophonia: French Journal of English Studies*, 9 (2001), 193–204.

Heyl, Christopher. "The Metamorphosis of the Mask in Seventeenth- and Eighteenth-Century London." Pp. 114–34 of *Masquerade and Identities: Essays on Gender, Sexuality, and Marginality*. Edited by Efrat Tseëlon. New York: Routledge, 2001.

Hill, Lisa. "Eighteenth-Century Anticipations of the Sociology of Conflict: The Case of Adam Ferguson." *Journal of the History of Ideas*, 62 (2001), 281–99.

Hill, Ruth. "Modern Science as Emergent Culture: Luzán's 'Juicio De Paris Renovado: Fabula Epica.'" *Hispanofila*, 132 (2001), 53–68.

Hoagwood, Terence Allan. "Elizabeth Inchbald, Joanna Baillie, and Revolutionary Representation in the 'Romantic' Period." Pp. 293–316 of *Rebellious Hearts: British Women Writers and the French Revolution*. Edited by Adriana Craciun, Kari E. Lokke, and Madelyn Gutwirth. Albany: State University of New York Press, 2001.

Hogg, James. "Dryden versus Shadwell: A Study in Literary Polemics." Pp. 41–74 of *Dryden and the World of Neoclassicism*. Edited by Wolfgang Görtschacher and Holger Klein. (SECL—Studies in English and Comparative Literature, 17.) Tübingen: Stauffenburg, 2001.

Hogle, Jerrold E. "The Gothic at Our Turn of the Century: Our Culture of Simulations and the Return of the Body." Pp. 153–79 of *The Gothic*. Edited by Fred Botting. Cambridge: Brewer, 2001.

Holdstein, Deborah H., and David Bleich (eds.). *Personal Effects: The Social Character of Scholarly Writing*. Logan: Utah State University Press, 2001. Pp. 385.

Holland, Peter, and Michael Patterson. "Eighteenth-Century Theater." Pp. 255–98 of *The Oxford Illustrated History of Theatre*. Edited by John Russell Brown. New York: Oxford University Press, 2001.

Holmes, Martin. "A Song Attributed to Dryden: A Postscript." *Library: The Transactions of the Bibliographical Society*, 2 (2001), 65–68.

VI: British Literatures

Holmesland, Oddvar. "Aphra Behn's *Oroonoko*: Cultural Dialectics and the Novel." *ELH*, 68 (2001), 57–79.

Honold, Alexander. "Das Glück des Schiffbrüchigen: Robinson, Ein Held Der Westlichen Welt." *Weimarer Beitrage: Zeitschrift für Literaturwissenschaft, Ästhetik und Kulturwissenschaften*, 47 (2001), 165–86.

Hopes, Jeffrey. "*Vanité des Vanités: An Apology for the Life of Colley Cibber* et L'autobiographie du Texte." *Bulletin de la Société d'Études Anglo-Américaines des XVIIe et XVIIIe Siècles*, 52 (2001), 129–43.

Hopkins, Lisa. "Mr. Darcy's Body: Privileging the Female Gaze." Pp. 111–21 of *Jane Austen in Hollywood*. Edited by Linda Troost and Sayre N. Greenfield. Lexington: University Press of Kentucky, 2001.

Horne, William C. "Samuel Johnson Discovers the Arctic: A Reading of a 'Greenland Tale' as Arctic Literature." Pp. 75–90 of *Beyond Nature Writings: Expanding the Boundaries of Ecocriticism*. Edited by Karla Armbruster and Kathleen R. Wallace. Charlottesville: University Press of Virginia, 2001.

How, James. "Clarissa's Cyberspace: The Development of Epistolary Space in Richardson's *Clarissa*." *Eighteenth-Century Novel*, 1 (2001), 37–69.

Hudson, Nicholas. "'Britons Never Will Be Slaves': National Myth, Conservatism, and the Beginnings of British Antislavery." *Eighteenth-Century Studies*, 34 (2001), 559–76.

Hughes, Derek. *The Theatre of Aphra Behn*. New York: Palgrave, 2001. Pp. vii + 230; bibliography.

Hughes's study of Aphra Behn's theatrical work is a welcome addition to Behn scholarship from Janet Todd, Jacqueline Pearson, Jane Spencer, and others. As his opening prologue makes clear, Hughes's intention is to offer a detailed, contextualized reading of Behn's dramatic *oeuvre*, and he provides a welcome space to consider Behn's often neglected works such as *The Younger Brother*, *The Town Fopp*, and *The Emperor of the Moon*. Most satisfyingly, he attempts to give a sense of the theatrical context in which Behn's work operated and was staged. This careful attention to the theatrical and the useful appendix listing the key players referred to offer the reader a refreshing view of Behn's contribution to the canon.

Hughes begins by briefly situating Behn within the proto-feminist conduct discourses and the misogynist satire of the Restoration period. The study of the full range of Behn's dramatic *oeuvre* allows Hughes to assess the extent of Behn's shifting position between these poles since he looks not only at her "feminist" comedy, but also her tragicomedies. The treatment of women, of power, and of the monarchy are themes that he traces through the plays, and he argues for a flexible reading of Behn's politics and proto-feminism in the light of the contemporary political moment and of theatrical pragmatics.

Hughes links Behn to her writing contemporaries, studying her rivalry notably with Dryden and Shadwell and her collaboration with theater companies and actors. The real strength of the book lies in the detailed studies of each play, which frequently reflect upon the use of staging, theater spaces and scenery and the actors recruited for each role. From these theatrical pragmatics Hughes draws insights into the thematic force and significance of each play, such as his particularly fruitful examination of the stage crown as a prop and symbol in *The Roundheads*. Theatre scholars may wish that Hughes had had space to take further this revealing performance analysis, but this study offers a highly readable and thoughtful contribution to the burgeoning industry of Behn scholarship.—Jane Milling

Hughes, Derek (ed.). *Eighteenth-Century Women Playwrights*. London: Pickering & Chatto, 2001. 6 volumes; bibliography.

Huhn, Peter. "The Precarious Autopoiesis of Modern Selves: Daniel Defoe's *Moll Flanders* and Virginia Woolf's *The Waves*." *European Journal of English Studies*, 5 (2001), 335–48.

Hunt, Lynn, and Margaret Jacob. "The Affective Revolution in 1790s Britain." *Eighteenth-Century Studies*, 34 (2001), 491–521.

Hunter, Andy. "The Peregrinations of Auld Robin Gray and Eugenie Grandet." *Études Ecossaises*, 7 (2001), 183–93.

Hunter, J. Paul. "Couplets and Conversation." Pp. 11–36 of *The Cambridge Companion to Eighteenth-Century Poetry*. Edited by John Sitter. Cambridge: Cambridge University Press, 2001.

Hurst, Jane. *Jane Austen and Alton*. Alton: J. Hurst, 2001. Pp. 36; bibliography; illustrations; maps.

Huse, Ann A. "Cleopatra, Queen of the Seine: The Politics of Eroticism in Dryden's *All for Love*." Pp. 23–46 of *John Dryden: A Tercentenary Miscellany*. Edited by Susan Green and Steven N. Zwicker. San Marino: Huntington Library, 2001.

Hutner, Heidi. *Colonial Women: Race and Culture in Stuart Drama*. New York: Oxford University Press, 2001. Pp. ix + 141; bibliography.

Ikegame, Naoko. "Uiriamu Bureiku No Geijutsu Kyoiku Shiso Ni Kansuru Ichi Kosatsu: Reinoruzu No Geijutsu Ni Kansuru Koenshu E No Kakikomi O Chushin Ni." *Ochanomizu Joshi Daigaku Jimbun Kagaku Kiyo*, 54 (2001), 177–86.

Ingram, Allan. "The Vision at Slains: Boswell's Supernatural Encounters." *Études Ecossaises*, 7 (2001), 7–20.

VI: British Literatures

Innocenti, Loretta. "L'antiromanzo Sterniano Tra Umorismo E Sensibilitāi." Pp. 157–73 of *"Le Donne, I Cavalier, L'arme, Gli Amori": Poema E Romanzo: La Narrativa Lunga in Italia*. Edited by Francesco Bruni. Venice: MarsilioVenice, Italy, 2001.

Insalaco, Danielle. "Thinking of Italy, Making History: Johnson and Historiography." Pp. 99–113 of *Johnson Re-Visioned: Looking Before and After*. (Bucknell Studies in Eighteenth-Century Literature and Culture.) Edited by Philip Smallwood. Lewisburg: Bucknell University Press, 2001.

Irlam, Shaun. "'Wish You Were Here': Exporting England in James Grainger's *The Sugar-Cane*." *ELH*, 68 (2001), 377–96.

Ishii, Shigemitsu. "Tokugawa Shogun's Tristram Shandy." *Shandean: An Annual Devoted to Laurence Sterne and His Works*, 12 (2001), 22–29.

Iwanisziw, Susan B. "The Shameful Allure of Sycorax and Wowski: Dramatic Precursors of Sartje, the Hottentot Venus." *Restoration and 18th-Century Theatre Research*, 16 (2001), 3–23.

Jack, Malcolm. "The Professor of Paederasty." *The Beckford Journal*, 7 (2001), 45–46.

Jacobus, Mary. "Intimate Connections: Scandalous Memoirs and Epistolary Indiscretion." Pp. 274–89 of *Women, Writing and the Public Sphere, 1700–1830*. Edited by Elizabeth Eger, Charlotte Grant, Cliona O Gallchoir, and Penny Warburton. Cambridge: Cambridge University Press, 2001.

Jamoussi, Zouheir. *La Liberté dans L'oeuvre de Defoe: Entre la Réalité et la Fiction*. Tunis: Centre de Publication Universitaire, 2001. Pp. 104.

Jerinic, Maria. "Challenging Englishness: Frances Burney's *The Wanderer*." Pp. 63–84 of *Rebellious Hearts: British Women Writers and the French Revolution*. Edited by Adriana Craciun, Kari E. Lokke, and Madelyn Gutwirth. Albany: State University of New York Press, 2001.

Johnson, Claudia L. "The Divine Miss Jane: Jane Austen, Janeites, and the Discipline of Novel Studies." Pp. 118–32 of *Reception Study: From Literary Theory to Cultural Studies*. Edited by James L.Machor and Philip Goldstein. New York: Routledge, 2001.

Johnston, Freya. "Diminutive Observations in Johnson's *Journey to the Western Islands of Scotland*." *Age of Johnson*, 12 (2001), 1–16.

Jones, Charles. "John Wild of Littleleek, an Early Eighteenth-Century Spelling Reformer, and the Evolution of a New Alphabet." *English Language and Linguistics*, 5 (2001), 17–40.

Jones, Wendy. "The Dialectic of Love in *Sir Charles Grandison*." Pp. 295–316 of *Passion and Virtue: Essays on the Novels of Samuel Richardson*. Edited by David Blewett. Toronto: University of Toronto Press, 2001.

Jooma, Minaz. "Robinson Crusoe Inc(Orporates): Domestic Economy, Incest, and the Trope of Cannibalism." Pp. 57–78 of *Eating Their Words: Cannibalism and the Boundaries of Cultural Identity*. Edited by Kristen Guest and Maggie Kilgour. New York: State University of New York Press, 2001.

Jordan, Sarah. "From Grotesque Bodies to Useful Hands: Idleness, Industry, and the Laboring Class." *Eighteenth-Century Life*, 25 (2001), 62–79.

Jung, Sandro. "William Shenstone and James Thomson: A New Poem." *Notes and Queries*, 48 (2001), 411–13.

Kairoff, Claudia Thomas. "Eighteenth-Century Women Poets and Readers." Pp. 157–76 of *The Cambridge Companion to Eighteenth-Century Poetry*. Edited by John Sitter. Cambridge: Cambridge University Press, 2001.

Kamps, Ivo, and G. Singh (eds.). *Travel Knowledge: European "Discoveries" in the Early Modern Period*. New York: Palgrave, 2001. Pp. Vii + 274; illustrations.

Kaplan, Deborah. "Mass Marketing Jane Austen: Men, Women, and Courtship in Two Film Adaptations." Pp.177–87 of *Jane Austen in Hollywood*. Edited by Linda Troost and Sayre N. Greenfield. Lexington: University Press of Kentucky, 2001.

Karian, Stephen. "Reading the Material Text of Swift's Verses on the Death." *SEL*, 41 (2001), 515–44.

Kayman, Martin A. "The 'New Sort of Specialty' and the 'New Province of Writing': Bank Notes, Fiction and the Law in *Tom Jones*." *ELH*, 68 (2001), 633–53.

Keane, Angela. "The Anxiety of (Feminine) Influence: Hannah More and the Counterrevolution." Pp. 109–34 of *Rebellious Hearts: British Women Writers and the French Revolution*. Edited by Adriana Craciun, Kari E. Lokke, and Madelyn Gutwirth. Albany: State University of New York Press, 2001.

VI: British Literatures

Keegan, Bridget. "Cobbling Verse: Shoemaker Poets of the Long Eighteenth Century." *Eighteenth Century: Theory and Interpretation,* 42 (2001), 195–217.

Keegan, Bridget. "Georgic Transformations and Stephen Duck's *The Thresher's Labour.*" *SEL,* 41 (2001), 545–62.

Keevak, Michael. "George Psalmanazar: Impostor, Traveler." Pp. 91–101 of *Crossings: Travel, Art, Literature, Politics.* Edited by Rudolphus Teeuwen. Taipei: Bookman, 2001.

Keipert, Helmut. *Pope, Popovskij Und Die Popen: Zur Entstehungsgeschichte Der Russischen Übersetzung Des "Essay on Man" Von 1757, Abhandlungen Der Akademie Der Wissenschaften in Göttingen, Philologisch-Historische Klasse.* Göttingen: Vandenhoeck & Ruprecht, 2001. Pp. 94.

Keith, Jennifer. "'Pre-Romanticism' and the Ends of Eighteenth-Century Poetry." Pp. 271–90 of *The Cambridge Companion to Eighteenth-Century Poetry.* Edited by John Sitter. Cambridge: Cambridge University Press, 2001.

Kelley, Anne. "'In Search of Truths Sublime': Reason and the Body in the Writings of Catherine Trotter." *Women's Writing,* 8 (2001), 235–50.

Kelly, Gary. "Bluestocking Feminism." Pp. 163–80 of *Women, Writing and the Public Sphere, 1700–1830.* Edited by Elizabeth Eger, Charlotte Grant, Cliona O Gallchoir, and Penny Warburton. Cambridge: Cambridge University Press, 2001.

Kempton, Adrian. "Diderot's Clarissa and Laclos' Cecilia: Virtuous English Heroines as Models for an Emerging Aesthetic of the Novel in France." *Franco-British Studies,* 31 (2001), 37–61.

Kennedy, Deborah. "The Ruined Abbey in the Eighteenth Century." *Philological Quarterly,* 80 (2001), 501–23.

Kennedy, Deborah. "Benevolent Historian: Helen Maria Williams and Her British Readers." Pp. 317–336 of *Rebellious Hearts: British Women Writers and the French Revolution.* Edited by Adriana Craciun, Kari E.Lokke, and Madelyn Gutwirth. Albany: State University of New York Press, 2001.

Keohane, Catherine. "'Too Neat for a Beggar': Charity and Debt in Burney's *Cecilia.*" *Studies in the Novel,* 33 (2001), 379–401.

Kerr, Douglas. "Timothy Mo's Man Sundae, and Other Overseas Workers." *Journal of Commonwealth Literature,* 36 (2001), 15–27.

Kerr, Heather. "Trembling Hyphen/Shaking Hinge: Margaret Cavendish and Queer Literary Subjectivity." Pp. 215–36 of *Women Writing, 1550–1750*. Edited by Jo Wallwork and Paul Salzman. Bundoora: Meridian, 2001.

Kewes, Paulina. "'[A] Play, Which I Presume to Call Original': Appropriation, Creative Genius, and Eighteenth-Century Playwriting." *Studies in the Literary Imagination,* 34 (2001), 17–47.

Kewes, Paulina. "'The State Is out of Tune': Nicholas Rowe's *Jane Shore* and the Succession Crisis of 1713–14." *Huntington Library Quarterly,* 64 (2001), 283–308.

Keymer, Tom, and Peter Sabor (eds.). *The Pamela Controversy: Criticisms and Adaptations of Samuel Richardson's Pamela, 1740–1750*. 6 volumes. London: Pickering & Chatto, 2001. Illustrations; facsimiles.

Kiberd, Declan. *Irish Classics.* Cambridge: Harvard University Press, 2001. Pp. xvi + 704; bibliography.

King, Amy M. "Linnaeus's Blooms: Botany and the Novel of Courtship." *Eighteenth-Century Novel,* 1 (2001), 127–60.

King, Kathryn R. "The Novel before Novels (with a Glance at Mary Hearne's *Fables of Desertion*)." Pp. 36–57 of *Eighteenth-Century Genre and Culture: Serious Reflections on Occasional Forms: Essays in Honor of J. Paul Hunter*. Edited by Dennis Todd and Cynthia Wall. Newark: University of Delaware Press, 2001.

King, Thomas A. "The Fop, the Canting Queen and the Deferral of Gender." Pp. 94–135 of *Presenting Gender: Changing Sex in Early-Modern Culture.* (Bucknell Studies in Eighteenth-Century Literature and Culture.) Edited by Chris Mounsey. Lewisburg: Bucknell University Press, 2001.

Kleine, Sabine. "Ästhetik des Hässlichen." Pp. 411–31 of *Die Wende von der Aufklärung zur Romantik 1760–1820: Epoche im Überblick*. Edited by Horst Albert Glaser, Gyorgy M. Vajda, and Francois Crouzet. Amsterdam: Benjamins, 2001.

Kliman, Bernice. "Cum Notis Variorum: Thomas Davies, Eighteenth-Century Commentator on Shakespeare: Marginalia and Published Notes." *Shakespeare Newsletter,* 51 (2001), 83.

Knights, Elspeth. "'The Library, of Course, Afforded Everything': Jane Austen's Representation of Women Readers." *English: The Journal of the English Association,* 50 (2001), 19–38.

VI: British Literatures

Knox-Shaw, Peter. "Defoe and the Politics of Representing the African Interior." *Modern Language Review,* 96 (2001), 938.

Kosmetatou, Elizabeth. "What's in a Name? Jane Austen's *Persuasion* and the Puzzle of Poor Richard." *Persuasions: Journal of the Jane Austen Society of North America,* 23 (2001), 215–18.

Kostova, Ludmilla. "Constructing Oriental Interiors: Two Eighteenth-Century Women Travellers and Their Easts." Pp. 17–33 of *Travel Writing and the Female Imaginary*. Edited by Vita Fortunati, Rita Monticelli, and Maurizio Ascari. Bologna: Patron, 2001.

Kraft, Elizabeth. "Ethics, Politics, and Heterosexual Desire in Aphra Behn's *The Rover*." *Essays in Theatre/Études Théâtrales,* 19 (2001), 111–25.

Kreis–Schinck, Annette. *Women, Writing, and the Theater in the Early Modern Period: The Plays of Aphra Behn and Susanne Centlivre*. Madison: Fairleigh Dickinson University Press, 2001. Pp. 273; bibliography.

Kroll, Richard. "The Double Logic of Don Sebastian." Pp. 47–69 of *John Dryden: A Tercentenary Miscellany*. Edited by Susan Green and Steven N. Zwicker. San Marino: Huntington Library, 2001.

Krysmanski, Bernd. "William Hogarths Kritik an der Balance des Peintres: Roger De Piles, Jonathan Richardson, Mark Akenside und Joseph Spence im Fadenkreuz der Englischen Satire." Pp. 51–75 of *Sister Arts: Englische Literatur im Grenzland der Kunstgebiete*. Edited by Joachim Möller. Marburg: Jonas, 2001.

Kubeck, Elizabeth. "The Key to Stowe: Toward a Patriot Whig Reading of Eliza Haywood's *Eovaai*." Pp. 225–54 of *Presenting Gender: Changing Sex in Early-Modern Culture*. (Bucknell Studies in Eighteenth-Century Literature and Culture.) Edited by Chris Mounsey. Lewisburg: Bucknell University Press, 2001.

La Rochefoucauld, François duc de, and Aphra Behn. *Seneca Unmasqued: A Bilingual Edition of Aphra Behn's Translation of La Rochefoucauld's Maximes*. Edited by Irwin Primer. New York: AMS Press, 2001. Pp. lvi + 198; bibliography; illustrations.

Labbe, Jacqueline M. "Metaphoricity and the Romance of Property in the Old Manor House." *Novel,* 34 (2001), 216–31.

Laffrado, Laura. "Constructing the Subaltern: White Creole Culture and Raced Captivity in Eighteenth-Century Dutch Suriname." *Studies in Eighteenth-Century Culture*, 30 (2001), 31–48.

Laidlow, Jonathan. "A Compendium of Shandys: Methods of Organizing Knowledge in Sterne's *Tristram Shandy*." *Eighteenth-Century Novel*, 1 (2001), 181–200.

Lamb, Jonathan. "Modern Metamorphoses and Disgraceful Tales." *Critical Inquiry*, 28 (2001), 133–66.

Lamb, Jonathan. "Recent Studies in the Restoration and Eighteenth Century." *SEL*, 41 (2001), 623–75.

Lams, Victor J. *Clarissa's Narrators*. New York: Peter Lang, 2001. Pp. x + 172; bibliography.

Landry, Donna. "Horsy and Persistently Queer: Imperialism, Feminism and Bestiality." *Textual Practice*, 15 (2001), 467–85.

Lange, Horst. "Wolves, Sheep, and the Shepherd: Legality, Legitimacy, and Hobbesian Political Theory in Goethe's Gotz Von Berlichingen." *Goethe Yearbook: Publications of the Goethe Society of North America*, 10 (2001), 1–30.

Laurence, Anne. "'Begging Pardon for All Mistakes or Errors in This Writeing I Being a Woman & Doing Itt Myselfe': Family Narratives in Some Early Eighteenth-Century Letters." Pp. 194–206 of *Early Modern Women's Letter Writing, 1450–1700*. Edited by James Daybell. Houndmills: Palgrave, 2001.

Le Faye, Deirdre. *Jane Austen's World*. London: Frances Lincoln, 2001. Pp. 208; illustrations; maps.

Le Faye, Deirdre. "Lord Brabourne's Edition of Jane Austen's Letters." *Review of English Studies*, 52 (2001), 91–102.

Leask, Nigel. "Salons, Alps and Cordilleras: Helen Maria Williams, Alexander von Humboldt, and the Discourse of Romantic Travel." Pp. 217–35 of *Women, Writing and the Public Sphere, 1700–1830*. Edited by Elizabeth Eger, Charlotte Grant, Cliona O Gallchoir, and Penny Warburton. Cambridge: Cambridge University Press, 2001.

Leduc, Guyonne. "Langues Inventées et Langue Anglaise dans *Gulliver's Travels* de Swift et dans 'The Voyages of Mr. Job Vinegar' de Fielding." *Bulletin de la Société d'Études Anglo-Américaines des XVIIe et XVIIIe Siècles*, 53 (2001), 99–143.

Lee, Inkyu. "A Reading of Samuel Johnson's *Rasselas*." *British and American Fiction to 1900*, 8 (2001), 91–115.

Lee, Yoon Sun. "Giants in the North: Douglas, the Scottish Enlightenment, and Scott's Redgauntlet." *Studies in Romanticism*, 40 (2001), 109–21.

Lennon, Thomas M. "Berkeley on the Act-Object Distinction." *Dialogue: Canadian Philosophical Review/Revue Canadienne de Philosophie*, 40 (2001), 651–67.

Lessenich, Rolf. "Tory versus Whig: John Dryden's Mythical Concept of Kingship." Pp. 243–56 of *Dryden and the World of Neoclassicism*. Edited by Wolfgang Görtschacher and Holger Klein. (SECL—Studies in English and Comparative Literature, 17.) Tübingen: Stauffenburg, 2001.

Levine, Joseph M. "Jonathan Swift and the Idea of History." Pp. 79–94 of *Eighteenth-Century Genre and Culture: Serious Reflections on Occasional Forms: Essays in Honor of J. Paul Hunter*. Edited by Dennis Todd and Cynthia Wall. Newark: University of Delaware Press, 2001.

Levy, Maurice. *Boswell, Un Libertin Melancolique: Sa Vie, Ses Voyages, Ses Amours et Ses Opinions*. Grenoble: ELLUG, 2001 Pp. 414.

Lewis, Jayne. "The Type of a Kind: Or, the Lives of Dryden." *Eighteenth-Century Life*, 25 (2001), 3–18.

Linden, Stanton J. "Margaret Cavendish and Robert Hooke: Optics and Scientific Fantasy in the Blazing World." Pp. 611–23 of *Esoterisme, Gnoses & Imaginaire Symbolique: Melanges Offerts a Antoine Faivre*. Edited by Richard Caron, Joscelyn Godwin, Wouter J. Hanegraaff, and Jean-Louis Vieillard-Baron. Louvain: Peeters, 2001.

Linney, Verna. "A Passion for Art, a Passion for Botany: Mary Delany and Her Floral 'Mosaiks.'" *Eighteenth-Century Women*, 1 (2001), 203–35.

Lockwood, Thomas. "Subscription-Hunters and Their Prey." *Studies in the Literary Imagination*, 34 (2001), 121–35.

Lokke, Kari E. "'The Mild Dominion of the Moon': Charlotte Smith and the Politics of Transcendence." Pp. 85–106 of *Rebellious Hearts: British Women Writers and the French Revolution*. Edited by Adriana Craciun, Kari E. Lokke, and Madelyn Gutwirth. Albany: State University of New York Press, 2001.

Lonsdale, Roger. "Thomas Gray, David Hume and John Home's Douglas." Pp. 57–70 of *Re-Constructing the Book: Literary Texts in Transmission*. Edited by Maureen Bell, Shirley Chew, Simon Eliot, Lynette Hunter, and James L. W. West, III . Aldershot: Ashgate Publishing Company, 2001.

Looser, Devoney. "Feminist Implications of the Silver Screen." Pp. 159–76 of *Jane Austen in Hollywood*. Edited by Linda Troost and Sayre N. Greenfield. Lexington: University Press of Kentucky, 2001.

Lorraine de Montluzin, Emily. "Beyond Gibbon: John Whitaker's Other Contributions to the English Review." *Notes and Queries*, 48 (2001), 430–33.

Love, Harold. "Roger L'estrange's Criticism of Dryden's Elocution." *Notes and Queries,* 48 (2001), 398–400.

Lurbe, Pierre. "*Le Beggar's Opera* (1728), Ou la Danse Macabre de John Gay." *Bulletin de la Société d'Études Anglo-Américaines des XVIIe et XVIIIe Siècles*, 52 (2001), 117–27.

Lutz, Alfred. "Representing Scotland in *Roderick Random* and *Humphry Clinker*: Smollett's Development as a Novelist." *Studies in the Novel*, 33 (2001), 1–17.

Lynn, Steven, Adam Rounce, George Justice, and Laura J. Rosenthal (eds.). "The Eighteenth Century." *Year's Work in English Studies*, 79 (2001), 381–442.

Mabry, Rochelle. "Fighting Fire with Fire: Reclaiming Phallocentric Conventions in Feminine Costume Dramas." *West Virginia University Philological Papers*, 48 (2001), 107–14.

Macey, J. David, Jr. "Amiable Deception and Flaming Fancy: Samuel Jackson Pratt and the Literature(s) of Benevolence." *Philological Review,* 27 (2001), 25–35.

Macfarlane, Alan. "David Hume and the Political Economy of Agrarian Civilization." *History of European Ideas*, 27 (2001), 79–91.

Machor, James L., and Philip Goldstein (eds.). *Reception Study: From Literary Theory to Cultural Studies*. New York: Routledge, 2001. Pp. xvii + 393.

Mack, Ruth. "The Historicity of Johnson's Lexicographer." *Representations*, 76 (2001), 61–87.

MacKenzie, Niall. "'A Great Affinity in Many Things': Further Evidence for the Jacobite Gloss on 'Swedish Charles.'" *Age of Johnson*, 12 (2001), 255–72.

VI: British Literatures

MacKenzie, Niall. "A Mid-Eighteenth-Century Precedent for Burns's Rising Sun?" *Notes and Queries*, 48 (2001): 414–19.

MacKenzie, Niall. "'Dougal Maccullony, I Am Glad to See Thee!': Gaelic Etymology, Jacobite Culture, and 'Exodus Politics.'" *Scottish Studies Review*, 2 (2001), 29–60.

MacWilliams, David C. "'Hurrying into the Shrubbery': The Sublime, Transcendence, and the Garden Scene in *Emma*." *Persuasions: Journal of the Jane Austen Society of North America*, 23 (2001), 133–38.

Mahoney, John L. "The True Story: Poetic Law and License in Johnson's Criticism." Pp. 185–98 of *1650–1850: Ideas, Aesthetics, and Inquiries in the Early Modern Era*. Volume 6. Edited by Kevin L. Cope. New York: AMS Press, 2001.

Mahoney, John L. "Contemporary Attitudes toward Biography and the Case of Walter Jackson Bate's Samuel Johnson." Pp. 333–47 of *1650–1850: Ideas, Aesthetics, and Inquiries in the Early Modern Era*. Volume 6. Edited by Kevin L. Cope. New York: AMS Press, 2001.

Manning, Gillian. *Libertine Plays of the Restoration*, Everyman Library. London: J. M. Dent, 2001. Pp. lxiii + 787; bibliography.

Markman, Ellis. "Coffee-Women, the Spectator and the Public Sphere in the Early Eighteenth Century." Pp. 27–51 of *Women, Writing and the Public Sphere, 1700–1830*. Edited by Elizabeth Eger, Charlotte Grant, Cliona O Gallchoir, and Penny Warburton. Cambridge: Cambridge University Press, 2001.

Martinez, Marc. "'Offensive Matter': La Mise en Scene du Corps Grotesque dans Gulliver's Travels." *Q/W/E/R/T/Y: Arts, Litteratures & Civilisations du Monde Anglophone*, 11 (2001), 47–58.

Martinot, Steve (ed.). *Maps and Mirrors: Topologies of Art and Politics*. Evanston: Northwestern University Press, 2001. Pp. xxxix + 342.

Maruca, Lisa. "Political Propriety and Feminine Property: Women in the Eighteenth-Century Text Trades." *Studies in the Literary Imagination*, 34 (2001), 79–99.

Mason, Tom, and Adam Rounce. "'Looking Before and After'?: Reflections on the Early Reception of Johnson's Critical Judgments." Pp. 134–66 of *Johnson Re-Visioned: Looking Before and After*. (Bucknell Studies in Eighteenth-Century Literature and Culture.) Edited by Philip Smallwood. Lewisburg: Bucknell University Press, 2001.

Mason, Tom. "'Et Versus Digitos Habet': Dryden, Montaigne, Lucretius, Virgil, and Boccaccio in Praise of Venus." *Translation & Literature*, 10 (2001), 89–109.

Mason, Tom. "John Dryden: The Living and the Dead." *Translation & Literature,* 10 (2001), 136–45.

Matyaszewski, Pawel. "Le Progres Viole ou Le Mal De La Revolution Selon Edmund Burke." Pp. 349–61 of *Progres et Violence au XVIIIe Siècle*. Edited by Valerie Cossy, Deidre Dawson, Michel Delon, and Jochen Schlobach. Paris: Honoré Champion, 2001.

May, James E. "Winchester College Ms 58: Fair Copies of Two Paraphrases by the Revd. Dr. William Broome." *Notes and Queries*, 48 (2001), 29–31.

Mazella, David. "'Justly to Fall Unpitied and Abhorr'd': Sensibility, Punishment, and Morality in Lillo's *The London Merchant*." *ELH*, 68 (2001), 795–830.

Mazzone, Stefania. "Il Costituzionalismo Inglese: L'ermeneutica Della Prassi in David Hume." *Pensiero Politico: Rivista di Storia delle Idee Politiche e Sociali*, 34 (2001), 353–89.

McCarthy, William. "Review Essay: The Piozzi Letters." *Age of Johnson:*, 12 (2001), 399–420.

McCarthy, William. "Why Anna Letitia Barbauld Refused to Head a Women's College: New Facts, New Story." *Nineteenth-Century Contexts*, 23 (2001), 349–79.

McCarthy, William, and Elizabeth Kraft (eds.). *Anna Letitia Barbauld: Selected Poetry and Prose*. Orchard Park: Broadview, 2001. Pp. 519; bibliography.

McDayter, Ghislaine, Guinn Batten, Barry Milligan, and Peter Manning (eds.). *Romantic Generations: Essays in Honor of Robert F. Gleckner*. Lewisburg: Bucknell University Press, 2001. Pp. 301.

McDonald, Irene B. "The Chawton Years (1809–1817)—'Only' Novels." *Persuasions: The Jane Austen Journal On-Line,* 22 (2001).

McInelly, Brett C. "Exile or Opportunity? The Plight of the Transported Felon in Daniel Defoe's *Moll Flanders* and *Colonel Jack*." *Genre (California),* 22 (2001), 210–17.

McIntosh-Varjabedian, Fiona. "La Cathedrale Chez Hume dans l'histoire d'angleterre: Un Non-Lieu?" Pp. 39–48 of *La Cathédrale*. Edited by Joelle Prungnaud, Alain Montandon, and Jean-Marc Moura. Villeneuve d'Ascq, France: Université Charles de Gaulle, 2001.

VI: British Literatures

McKean, Thomas A. "The Fieldwork Legacy of James Macpherson." *Journal of American Folklore*, 114 (2001), 447–63.

McKenzie, D. F. "Congreve and the Integrity of the Text." Pp. 34–41 of *Re-Constructing the Book: Literary Texts in Transmission*. Edited by Maureen Bell, Shirley Chew, Simon Eliot, Lynette Hunter, and James L. W. West, III. Aldershot: Ashgate Publishing Company, 2001.

McLaverty, J. *Pope, Print, and Meaning*. New York: Oxford University Press, 2001. Pp. vi + 257; bibliography; illustrations.

McLoughlin, Timothy O. "Conquest, Liberty and Empire: Anomalies and Contradictions in Eighteenth-Century Writing." *Bulletin de la Société d'Études Anglo-Américaines des XVIIe et XVIIIe Siècles*, 53 (2001), 189–200.

McMaster, Juliet. "Reading Body Language: A Game of Skill." *Persuasions: Journal of the Jane Austen Society of North America*, 23 (2001), 90–104.

McMaster, Juliet. "*Sir Charles Grandison*: Richardson on Body and Character." Pp. 246–67 of *Passion and Virtue: Essays on the Novels of Samuel Richardson*. Edited by David Blewett. Toronto: University of Toronto Press, 2001.

McMinn, Joseph. "Swift and Theatre." *Eighteenth-Century Ireland/Iris an da Chultur*, 16 (2001), 35–46.

McRae, Andrew. "Female Mobility and National Space in Restoration England: The Travel Journals of Celia Fiennes." Pp. 105–13 of *Women Writing, 1550–1750*. Edited by Jo Wallwork and Paul Salzman. Bundoora: Meridian, 2001.

Medoff, Jeslyn. "'Very Like a Fiction': Some Early Biographies of Aphra Behn." Pp. 247–69 of *Write or Be Written: Early Modern Women Poets and Cultural Constraints*. Edited by Barbara Smith and Ursula Appelt. Aldershot: Ashgate Publishing Company, 2001.

Meeker, Kevin. "Is Hume's Epistemology Internalist or Externalist?" *Dialogue: Canadian Philosophical Review/Revue Canadienne de Philosophie*, 40 (2001), 125–46.

Meier, Jurg. "Romantic Love as a Narrative Emotion in Jane Austen's *Emma*." *Prism(s): Essays in Romanticism*, 9 (2001), 65–86.

Menneteau, Patrick. "Aspects de L'irrationnel dans La Philosophie de David Hume." *Études Ecossaises*, 7 (2001), 111–24.

Menzies, Ruth. "'That Infernal Habit of Lying': La Tradition du Voyage Imaginaire et le Discours Prefaciel des *Gulliver's Travels*." *Q/W/E/R/T/Y: Arts, Litteratures & Civilisations du Monde Anglophone*, 11 (2001), 59–70.

Messenger, Ann. *Pastoral Tradition and the Female Talent: Studies in Augustan Poetry*. New York: AMS Press, 2001. Pp. ix + 248; bibliography.

In the middle of a chapter on Sarah Dixon, Messenger pauses for the briefest of moments to share with the reader a piece of personal information: "That creative activity can reduce depression is psychologically valid. It worked for Jane Barker, at least some of the time. It works for me" (143). Though apparently in keeping with the general aim of the book—to draw connections between female authors' lives and the pastoral poems they wrote—this moment stands out, not as a bit of strategic scholarly confessionalism, but as a brave intimation shared in the spirit of kinship with her subjects as well as audience. While some of her current readers will have, I did not know Messenger and have only recently become aware of her work. Much of it was published posthumously, after several years of battling with cancer. "It works for me." So matter-of-fact and, I presume, powerfully understated. If I was initially discomforted by this sentence, it is only because I have long since taken for granted that such generosity is extremely rare in academic writing. Messenger's gesture reminded me of other possibilities. In the final chapter of the book she offers an imaginative biography of Anne Killigrew's emotional life. Messenger is the kind of reader and writer she would push us into becoming. A loss indeed to be lamented.

Yet the move has its limits, as Messenger herself concedes: "judged by the standards of respectable scholarship, my story is fiction. Better to leave Killigrew out of this kind of study until someone manages the miracle of finding more information about her life" (196). It may be psychologically valid that creativity can reduce depression, but after leaving behind Messenger's own testimonial, how are readers supposed to assess the statement's truth? The central thesis of this book is that women used pastoral to "say something directly or indirectly about their lives...about the world they as women lived in, including their marginal position as artists, about the things that happened to them, their feelings, their relationships, their thoughts" (11). But the age-old question nags: where precisely are the intersections between life and art? Messenger deals with this issue on a case by case basis—sometimes more or less dubiously—but it would have been better had she dealt more generally with the theoretical issues involved for more than just one paragraph of her first chapter. It is the one major flaw of the book but one not easily passed over.

The title foreshadows this problem. Happily, far from defining *the* "pastoral tradition" in a limited way, the book devotes four chapters to describing multiple generic traditions: the retirement pastoral, the pastoral elegy, the Christian pastoral, and the mock- or anti-pastoral (Messenger terms it "upside-down pastoral"). Likewise, the book's five chapters on individual female writers—Behn, Finch, Chudleigh, Dixon, and Leapor—trace rather divergent poetic practices notwithstanding their shared pastoral heading. (The book's strength lies in its illuminating close-readings of individual poems; students should mine it for its gems.) And yet, because the book's focus is on "female" talent, in each chapter a "male" paradigm of the pastoral tradition is typically established for contrastive purposes. In male retirement poetry, for example, the poet chooses a life of solitude mixed with the delightful pleasures of food, drink, books, and most of all, sex. Of course, the form is founded not only on the idea of retiring from something (usually urban business or politics or war), but on the poet's ability to *choose* to retire from it. Of such choices and pleasures, women had little part. And so by and large, the female retirement pastoral expresses wishes mainly for safety, love, and female friendship.

This sounds plausible—and to be fair Messenger is less schematic than a synopsis must be, often mentioning exceptions and noting tonal variations in poems by several authors as well as in the oeuvre of one author. Nevertheless a leap typically occurs, as when it is stated that in retirement pastoral, men write more from Horace and women, even when veiling themselves in literary convention, from their lives and feelings. Or when, in the chapter on upside-down pastoral, women poets are said to eschew the form because they were more concerned with "adapting art into modes of expressing the truths of their own lives, their own realities. The kind of poetry that, however artfully and however tacitly, debunked the art of the genre in which they had deep roots, held few attractions for them." Or when, after supposing that to a considerable extent women and men mourn similarly, nevertheless it is maintained that "it is true that women's elegies are more frequently expressive of personal feeling...when the dead are admired poets, whether male or female, whether personal friends or distant models, women elegists make them the real subjects of their poems, not a taking-off place for disquisitions on the profession of poetry" (113).

With individual writers, Messenger resorts to the same move. On Sarah Dixon: "Is she telling her own story in the Sylvia-to-Strephon poems? I can't be sure. But given women poets' tendency to write from the heart, to use the conventions of pastoral to mask autobiography, I think this may be Miss Dixon's own experience" (153). But this is the question precisely to be answered: when and where does one deem a literary allusion merely conventional, and where does one make room for emotional expression? Johnson's criticisms of (Milton's) pastoral and (Hammond's) love elegy are not mentioned, but they can at this late date certainly be challenged. Almost always, Messenger chooses to read the male poets as "detached," "professional," "crafted," "artistic," and their female counterparts as "emotional." Where the first chapter discovers the history of gendered literary typing (as in, women accepted and were permitted to write pastoral because it was a "female form"), the other chapters seem to bury that knowledge and exhume all the old stereotypes.

The book's title invokes Eliot's famous essay, "Tradition and the Individual Talent," in which he said (Modernist) talent is at once shaped by and shapes the literary canon, managing simultaneously to be both traditional and individual. It is probable that Messenger would like to tackle the implicit masculinity of Eliot's account, to demonstrate that women too belong to and influence tradition. This is the argument of an older generation, and it is thanks to scholars such as Messenger that students of the eighteenth century today no longer need to be persuaded that women writers are worth reading. What is less clear, however, is that their place in the tradition is determined by their willingness to emote more than men. Because she is so adept at tracking details (she demonstrates a remarkable ability to recall and organize a vast catalogue of poetry), at hearing minor differences in poetic voices that to others merely blend into one unintelligible chorus, I wish she had maintained more categorical openness. Does the distinction of male and female change when considering working-class poets (Messenger discusses Leapor's desire to speak for working women but does not refer to any men)? when considering poets with homoerotic desires? Do male and female pastoral sound different when the subject is the enslaved? the imprisoned? What happens to female pastoral once sentimentalism enables men to shed tears? once sentimentalism turns emotional outburst itself into conventional behavior?—Michael Rotenberg-Schwartz

Miles, Robert. "Abjection, Nationalism and the Gothic." Pp. 47–70 of *The Gothic*. Edited by Fred Botting. Cambridge: Brewer, 2001.

Miller, Eric. "Aphra Behn's Tigers." *Dalhousie Review*, 81 (2001), 47–65.

Miller, Judith Davis. "The Politics of Truth and Deception: Charlotte Smith and the French Revolution." Pp. 337–63 of *Rebellious Hearts: British Women Writers and the French Revolution*. Edited by Adriana Craciun, Kari E. Lokke, and Madelyn Gutwirth. Albany: State University of New York Press, 2001.

Miller, Stephen. *Three Deaths and Enlightenment Thought: Hume, Johnson, Marat*. Lewisburg: Bucknell University Press, 2001. Pp. 219; bibliography; illustrations.

The title of Miller's book is likely to raise questions in the minds of curious readers. How are deaths, and the idea of death, connected to the main current of Enlightenment thinking? (One does not think of Voltaire, d'Alembert, d'Holbach, Diderot, and Rousseau as figures whose ideas of life were driven by the idea of death.) How are Hume, Johnson, and Marat going to be connected, either in terms of their relation to the Enlightenment or in terms of death? (Marat, especially, seems the odd man of this trio.) The title sets a test that needs to be met by intensive thesis-making, but it is a test that the book itself does not pass. If one begins by asking how Miller is going to frame a coherent book on the basis of such disparate material, one concludes that he has not done so. Miller begins with a chapter on eighteenth-century interest in the deathbed and in death as a public, signifying act. He goes on to chapters on Hume, Johnson, and Marat, and concludes with a chapter on the Enlightenment itself.

The basic procedure in the chapters on his three major figures is to move outward from their deaths. He begins by briefly recounting the death scene and reactions to it. The deaths are then seen as manifestations of a each figure's "deathbed project," metaphorically in the chapter on Marat, where the section entitled "Marat's Deathbed Project" rapidly goes on to state that "Marat did not have a deathbed project." (Marat's deathbed project, therefore, becomes his paranoid concern for the suppression of enemies of the revolution, such as the traitors whose names he thought Charlotte Corday, his assassin, would reveal to him. Hume's project was to show the futility of fearing death and, hence, the needlessness of religion; Johnson's, in contrast, was to promote traditional religion.) The "deathbed project" then leads to an exposition of what Miller sees as the Enlightenment position articulated in the various works of the decedents, and the discussion focuses primarily on the issues of religion and politics. This survey is expanded to include their the views of friends and associates: Smith and Gibbon, in the case of Hume; Burke and Reynolds in the case of Johnson; David, Priestley, Price, and Paine in the case of Marat. Each chapter concludes with an assertion that the "deathbed project" has failed-Hume's because religious enthusiasm was not a major problem in the late eighteenth century, Johnson's because "the connection between religion and politics was less clear than Johnson allowed," and Marat's because "most citizens of France had come to the conclusion that radical patriotism had been an unhealthy phenomenon." The chapters are woven together by frequent comparisons between the views of the various figures.

In part, the connections, especially the view of Johnson as an Enlightenment figure, are based on skewed terms. Johnson, for example, gets to be a member of Enlightenment not because of his interest in science, his empiricism, his common sense, and his insistence that people face the reality of experience, however uncomfortable (elements of Johnson's thought that Miller does not discuss), but because he is opposed to superstition and fanaticism. He also shared Enlightenment thought on lesser matters—his defense of progress and his view that luxury was more helpful to society than not, views that might well have been shared by nineteenth-century industrialists not usually considered Enlightenment thinkers. Miller has granted Johnson a place in the Enlightenment for the wrong reasons. If one asserts, perhaps more accurately, that a characteristic of the Enlightenment is its opposition to religious authority, Johnson's place seems inappropriate. Hume and Johnson were both, although for different reasons, political conservatives, and for Miller such conservatism, or at least acquiescence in the authority of the state for the good of society, is another Enlightenment hallmark. Even Priestley and Price drew short of open revolution. Paine turned out to be irrelevant, and Marat, of course, was dead. Locke, Montesquieu, Kant, Franklin, Jefferson, and Godwin are, in three cases, not mentioned at all or, in the others, mentioned only in passing and not in a political context. The broader political issues that they and other liberal Enlightenment thinkers addressed are not discussed.

That figures associated with the Enlightenment disagreed with each other on many subjects has long been recognized, and the various opinions recorded here do not change the picture. Miller's project is to undermine or deny the secular, liberal, socialist Enlightenment and to replace it with a conservative Enlightenment that sees religion as useful if not true and government as authoritative if not right. But his terms are too vague and his canvas too narrow to be very convincing, although I must confess a disinclination to be convinced in any case. In the end, the Enlightenment itself grows dim. Miller concludes that "all the writers discussed in this study were interested in the question of progress." But the formulation "interested in the question of progress" is hardly a precise and useful way of identifying membership in the family of Enlightenment thinkers. Miller's book is pleasantly written, and its summaries of various positions are accurate and interesting. But its approach is undefined, and the notion of seeing the Enlightenment through the deaths of Hume, Johnson, and Marat seems unrewarding.—Charles A. Knight

Millington, Jon. "Dramatisations of *Vathek*: Genlis and After." *The Beckford Journal*, 7 (2001), 34–38.

Milne, Anne. "Gender, Class, and the Beehive: Mary Collier's 'The Woman's Labour' (1739) as Nature Poem." *Isle: Interdisciplinary Studies in Literature and Environment*, 8 (2001), 109–29.

Minma, Shinobu. "Self–Deception and Superiority Complex: Derangement of Hierarchy in Jane Austen's *Emma*." *Eighteenth-Century Fiction*, 14 (2001), 49–65.

Miyazaki, Toshizo. "Tanjun Na Hanashi (5): Kaiwa." *Eigo Seinen/Rising Generation*, 147 (2001), 275.

Moglen, Helene. *The Trauma of Gender: A Feminist Theory of the English Novel*. Berkeley: University of California Press, 2001. Pp. x + 216.

Helene Moglen sets up two tasks for herself. The first is to challenge the notion that the rise of the middle class is the primary factor in creating the rise of the novel. The second is that the prevailing device is realism. For her first premise, she posits that "the novel came into being as a response to the sex-gender system that emerged in England in the late seventeenth and early eighteenth centuries" (1). For her second point, she established a binary, similar to McKeon's in his *Origins of the English Novel 1600–1740* and in line with Todorov's theory of the fantastic, that breaks the novel's development down into two separate traditions: the fantastic and the realistic. The two ideas are interrelated by their expression of rising individualism. Realism, the social form, naturalizes the inequities of gender, while the fantastic deals with interiority of characters, thereby realizing the character as predominantly as object. Moglen uses the remaining chapters to outline her thesis by examining several traditional novels from the period: *Robinson Crusoe*, *Clarissa*, *Tristram Shandy*, and *The Castle of Otranto*. Her chapter on Defoe focuses on his ideology of the individual, one based on the business model associated with the rise of a capitalistic society. His fictions represent not only the "ideology of possessive individualism" (19), but also showed the clashes between the existing sex-gender based systems. His works are written primarily in the mode of realism, despite what Moglen refers to as Defoe's own "powerful fantasy of social, economic, and psychological autonomy" (17). Chapter 2 argues that *Clarissa* "is a product of an emergent pornographic imagination, which Richardson, in both senses, represented" (59). Moglen states that the novel is divided into three separate narrative moments. Realism dominates the first, covering the events of the conflict in Clarissa's family. The second section, the long mid-section, is fantastic. And the third section, post-rape, is sublime. The sex-gender roles are demonstrated by Clarissa dominating the first and last sections and Lovelace the middle. "(W)holes and Noses: The Indeterminacies of *Tristram Shandy*," Chapter 3, discusses how this novel is at the crossroads of the two modes, realism and fantasy. Tristram Shandy's subject is male subjectivity. His fantasy is that of wholeness, and the realism is the fragmentation inherent in trying to shape a reality. The final realization is, of course, that everyone's life is farcical in nature. Her chapter on Horace Walpole and *The Castle of Otranto* looks at a novel that, as its mode, is fantasy. This self, differing from that of *Tristram Shandy*, is one that is constructed by its relation to others, rather than from within the self. Walpole's anti-hero is a monstrous parody of the hero, a combination of capitalism and the sex-gender system, that previous novels have developed previously. Gothic texts also "portray the horrifying emptiness of a secularized world. Representing irrational impulses, they do not claim access to a higher integrative truth but attest to meanings that elude language and analysis" (111).

In her conclusion, Moglen realizes that her analysis has been arranged around a bimodal configuration of individual, as well as novelistic, development and accepts that this is, perhaps, inevitable. In an age prior to Freud, "The novel emerged to manage the effects of the trauma of gender. Its bimodal narratives stunningly revealed the misfortunes that men and women have suffered, but these same narratives also concealed them from consciousness" (146). The point of fiction, however, is to reside beside theory in order to fulfill the need for complex and ambiguous representation that enables identification.— Kit Kincade

Möller, Joachim (ed.). *Sister Arts: Englische Literatur im Grenzland der Kunstgebiete*. Marburg: Jonas, 2001. Pp. 183; illustrations.

Montag, Warren. "Gulliver's Solitude: The Paradoxes of Swift's Anti-Individualism." *Eighteenth Century: Theory and Interpretation,* 42 (2001), 3–19.

Montoya, Pablo. "Un Robinson Cercano." *Revista Universidad de Antioquia*, 264 (2001), 24–30.

Mooney, James E. *Eighteenth-Century Catalogues of the Yale College Library*. New Haven: Yale University Beinecke Library, 2001. Pp. xxi + 151; illustrations.

Moore, Lucy. *Amphibious Thing: The Life of Lord Hervey*. London: Penguin, 2001. Pp. 384; bibliography; illustrations.

Moran, Leslie J. "Law and the Gothic Imagination." Pp. 87–109 of *The Gothic*. Edited by Fred Botting. Cambridge: Brewer, 2001.

Morgan, Peter. "The Omnipotence of Simulacra: Charles II and the Divine Right of Signs." *Concentric: Literary and Cultural Studies,* 27 (2001), 67–86.

Morillo, John D. *Uneasy Feelings: Literature, the Passions, and Class from Neoclassicism to Romanticism*. New York: AMS Press, 2001. Pp. viii + 313; bibliography.

Morris, David B. "A Poetry of Absence." Pp. 225–48 of *The Cambridge Companion to Eighteenth-Century Poetry*. Edited by John Sitter. Cambridge: Cambridge University Press, 2001.

Morris, Ivor. "Jane Austen and Her Men." *Persuasions: The Jane Austen Journal On-Line*, 4 (2001).

Moskal, Jeanne. "Napoleon, Nationalism, and the Politics of Religion in Mariana Starke's Letters from Italy." Pp. 161–190 of *Rebellious Hearts: British Women Writers and the French Revolution*. Edited by Adriana Craciun, Kari E. Lokke, and Madelyn Gutwirth. Albany: State University of New York Press, 2001.

Moss, Joyce, and Lorraine Valestuk (eds.). *British and Irish Literature and Its Times: Celtic Migrations to the Reform Bill (Beginnings–1830s)*. (World Literature and Its Times 3.) Detroit: Gale, 2001. Pp. xli + 549; bibliography; illustrations.

Mounsey, Chris (ed.). Presenting Gender: Changing Sex in Early-Modern Culture. (Bucknell Studies in Eighteenth-Century Literature and Culture.) Lewisburg: Bucknell University Press, 2001. Pp. 301; bibliography; illustrations.

Mounsey, Chris. "'To the Women of Both Sexes': Christopher Smart, Mrs. Mary Midnight, the Voice of the Dissident Woman Writer." Pp. 274–93 of *Presenting Gender: Changing Sex in Early-Modern Culture*. (Bucknell Studies in Eighteenth-Century Literature and Culture.) Edited by Chris Mounsey. Lewisburg: Bucknell University Press, 2001.

Murphy, Michael. "Allan Ramsay's Contribution to Theatre in Edinburgh, 1719–1739." *Scottish Studies Review*, 2 (2001), 9–28.

Murray, John Condon. *Gulliver's Travels: A Witness Exploration of Humanity in Search of the Answer to the Question "Who Am I?"* Lincoln: iUniverse.com Inc., 2001. Pp. xi + 99; bibliography.

Murray, John Condon. (ed.). *Redefining the 'Self': Selected Essays on Swift, Poe, Pinter, and Joyce*. San Jose: Author's Choice Press, 2001. Pp. xi + 77; bibliography.

Nachumi, Nora. "Seeing Double: Theatrical Spectatorship in *Mansfield Park*." *Philological Quarterly*, 80 (2001), 233–52.

Nachumi, Nora. "'As if!': Translating Austen's Ironic Narrator to Film." Pp. 130–39 of *Jane Austen in Hollywood*. Edited by Linda Troost and Sayre N. Greenfield. Lexington: University Press of Kentucky, 2001.

Naguschewski, Dirk, and Sabine Schrader (eds.). *Sehen, Lesen, Begehren: Homosexualität in Franzosischer Literatur und Kultur*. Berlin: Tranvia Frey, 2001. Pp. 280.

Nagy, Joseph Falaky. "Observations on the Ossianesque in Medieval Irish Literature and Modern Irish Folklore." *Journal of American Folklore*, 114 (2001), 436–46.

Nakahara, Akio. "J. D. Furiman Samyueru Jonson Shoshi O Yomu." *Eigo Seinen/Rising Generation*, 147 (2001), 482–84.

Narain, Mona. "Body and Politics in Aphra Behn's *Love Letters between a Nobleman and His Sister*." Pp. 151–62 of *Women Writing, 1550–1750*. Edited by Jo Wallwork and Paul Salzman. Bundoora: Meridian, 2001.

Nardin, Jane. "Hannah More and the Problem of Poverty." *Texas Studies in Literature and Language*, 43 (2001), 267–84.

Nardin, Jane. "Hannah More and the Rhetoric of Educational Reform." *Women's History Review*, 10 (2001), 211–27.

Nassaar, Christopher S. "The Farquhar and Arbuthnot Connections in Oscar Wilde's *A Woman of No Importance*." *Notes and Queries,* 48 (2001), 158–62.

Nate, Richard. "'Plain and Vulgarly Express'd': Margaret Cavendish and the Discourse of the New Science." *Rhetorica,* 19 (2001), 403–17.

Nell, Sharon Diane. "Woman in the Eighteenth Century." *Intertexts,* 5 (2001). Special issue.

Nelson, Robin. "Jane Austen Adaptations." P. 40 of *The Television Genre Book*. Edited by Glen Creeber, Toby Miller, and John Tulloch. London: British Film Institute, 2001.

New, Melvyn. "Reading Sterne through Proust and Levinas." *Age of Johnson*, 12 (2001), 329–60.

Newcastle, Margaret Cavendish, Duchess of. *Observations Upon Experimental Philosophy*. Edited by Eileen O'Neill. Cambridge University Press, 2001. Pp. xlvii + 287; bibliography.

Nichol, Donald W. "The New Foundling Hospital for Wit: From Hanbury Williams to John Wilkes." *Studies in the Literary Imagination*, 34 (2001), 101–19.

Nicklas, Pascal. "The Refinement of Violence: Concepts of Civilization and *The Man of Feeling.*" Pp. 297–330 of *Progres et Violence Au XVIIIe Siècle*. Edited by Valerie Cossy, Deidre Dawson, Michel Delon, and Jochen Schlobach. Paris: Honoré Champion, 2001.

Niederhoff, Burkhard. "Erotik und Empfindsamkeit in a Sentimental Journey." *Anglia: Zeitschrift fur Englische Philologie,* 119 (2001), 20–38.

Nigro, Jeffrey A. "Estimating Lace and Muslin: Dress and Fashion in Jane Austen and Her World." *Persuasions: Journal of the Jane Austen Society of North America,* 23 (2001), 50–62.

Nixon, Cheryl L. "Maternal Guardianship by 'Nature' and 'Nurture': Eighteenth-Century Chancery Court Records and *Clarissa*." *Intertexts,* 5 (2001), 128–55.

Nixon, Cheryl L. "Balancing the Courtship Hero: Masculine Emotional Displays in Film Adaptations of Austen's Novels." Pp. 22–43 of *Jane Austen in Hollywood*. Edited by Linda Troost and Sayre N. Greenfield. Lexington: University Press of Kentucky, 2001.

Noble, Yvonne. "Charles Coffey and John Mottley: An Odd Couple in Grub Street." *Restoration and 18th Century Theatre Research,* 16 (2001), 1–12.

Noble, Yvonne. "Light Writing from a Dark Winter: The Scriblerian *Annus Mirabilis*." *Eighteenth-Century Life,* 25 (2001), 19–31.

Noble, Yvonne. "Virgilian Bees in Dryden." Pp. 169–79 of *Dryden and the World of Neoclassicism.* Edited by Wolfgang Görtschacher and Holger Klein. Tubingen: Stauffenburg, 2001.

Noggle, James. *The Skeptical Sublime: Aesthetic Ideology in Pope and the Tory Satirists.* New York: Oxford University Press, 2001. Pp. ix + 269; bibliography.

Nolan, Jerry. "*Liber Veritatis* or Why has the Child been so Abused?" *The Beckford Journal,* 7 (2001), 2–10.

Northrop, Douglas A. "The Role of the Narrator in Aphra Behn's *Oroonoko*." Pp. 15–22 of *Proceedings of the Eighth Annual Northern Plains Conference on Earlier British Literature.* Edited by Robert J. De Smith. Sioux Center: Dordt College, 2001.

Norton, David Fate. "From John Locke to Dugald Stewart." *Journal of the History of Ideas,* 62 (2001), 359–65.

Novak, Maximillian E. *Daniel Defoe: Master of Fictions: His Life and Ideas.* New York: Oxford University Press, 2001. Pp. xi + 756; bibliography; illustrations.

On the acknowledgment page of his monumental biography of Daniel Defoe, Maximillian E. Novak recounts that the early stages of the project included significant collaboration with Paula R. Backscheider, who went on to publish her own biography of Defoe, *Daniel Defoe: His Life* (Johns Hopkins University Press, 1989). It is fitting that the two most significant biographies of Defoe in print share this common genealogy: the two books stand side by side as nearly perfect complements of the other's approach. Backscheider's is the more traditional biography, emphasizing the important dates of Defoe's life, the people he knew, the causes he fought for, and the historical contexts in which he wrote. As the best biographers do, Backscheider brings all of this background information expertly to bear on Defoe's work as a writer.

Novak's biography, on the other hand, starts with Defoe's writings and uses them to extract elements of Defoe's life that have always remained impervious to more traditional biographical methods. *Daniel Defoe: Master of Fictions* is both biography and literary criticism. This is especially true in the later chapters that deal with the works for which Defoe is best remembered: *Robinson Crusoe, Moll Flanders, Journal of the Plague Year,* and *Roxanna.* These chapters survey the reception of Defoe's major works over the past 270 years, cite generously from modern scholarship, and offer fresh interpretations of the works that they analyze. In earlier chapters, Novak relies heavily on his knowledge of some four hundred or so published books by Defoe to reconstruct the author's early life and to make connections across works that produce fresh insights into his career.

Novak never becomes so wrapped up in literary interpretation that he forgets his job as a biographer. His analyses of both major and minor works always throw new light on his subject and set up inferences about Defoe's life that are both plausible and enlightening. Unlike so many other writers who employ literary criticism as a method of biography, Novak is very clear about the inferential nature of his project. His prose includes a fair amount of meta-discourse designed to tell the reader what can be said with certainty about Defoe, what can be reasonably inferred, what can be considered probable, and what can only be guessed at. The result is a compelling, intellectually honest, and genuinely enlightening biography of one of the most often-described, but little-understood writers in English history. The biography always keeps the picture of Defoe, the writer, in the foreground, and Defoe's writings eclipse all other source material as the best way to reconstruct that picture.

If *Daniel Defoe: Master of Fictions* has a weakness, it is simply this: that Novak has read and considered Defoe's words more carefully than Defoe himself ever did and, on occasion, assumes a certain amount of consistency between works—and even within a single work—that may very well have been beyond the intentions of the author. But this is the flip side of the work's most considerable strength: that its author, in his forty-year career as a scholar of Defoe and of eighteenth-century literature in general, has read so much of, and thought so carefully about, Defoe's corpus that he can draw with authority conclusions that have been beyond the expertise of anyone else who has ever written on the subject. The end result is a work of acute and insightful scholarship that serves as a capstone to the life's work of a major scholar and as a biography that will stand, with Backscheider's earlier work, as a starting point for Defoe scholarship in the coming generations.—Michael Austin

O'Brien, John. "Busy Bodies: The Plots of Susanna Centlivre." Pp. 165–89 of *Eighteenth-Century Genre and Culture: Serious Reflections on Occasional Forms: Essays in Honor of J. Paul Hunter*. Edited by Dennis Todd and Cynthia Wall. Newark: University of Delaware Press, 2001.

O Gallchoir, Cliona. "Gender, Nation and Revolution: Maria Edgeworth and Stehanie-Felicite de Genlis." Pp. 200–16 of *Women, Writing and the Public Sphere, 1700–1830*. Edited by Elizabeth Eger, Charlotte Grant, Cliona O Gallchoir, and Penny Warburton. Cambridge: Cambridge University Press, 2001.

O'Loughlin, Katrina. "'Having Lived Much in the World': Inhabitation, Embodiment and English Women Travellers' Representations of Russia in the Eighteenth Century." *Women's Writing*, 8 (2001), 419–39.

Olsen, Thomas Grant. "Reading and Righting *Moll Flanders*." *SEL*, 41 (2001), 467–81.

Orr, Bridget. *Empire on the English Stage: 1660–1714*. Cambridge: Cambridge University Press, 2001. Pp. 360; bibliography.

This study claims to be the first large-scale attempt by a literary historian to analyze the deeper implications of the representations of colonial issues in Restoration drama. Until now, emphasis has almost exclusively been laid on Dryden and his manner of dealing with matters of empire; Bridget Orr, without by any means neglecting Dryden, looks at a large number of plays that have Empire as their topic but which have never been part of a literary canon and have over the course of the centuries been almost forgotten. Orr does in her book what is demanded by post-colonial critics; that is, she rereads the literature of the past in order to detect references to colonialism, but she does not adopt the often obfuscating jargon of post-colonialism. Rather, she re-reads these plays with a strong emphasis on the historical and sociological background against which they were written and thus seeks to show the important contribution they made to the shaping of European perspectives on non-European societies.

In the first chapter, which might have been more appropriately called "Introduction," Orr explains the incidence of colonial issues in Restoration plays with the fact that it was the time of incipient colonial expansion and settlement and that before the English had built their Empire on which the sun never set, they were preoccupied with fear of Dutch and French rivals for overseas possessions, a fear that was frequently reflected in the plays. In general terms, Orr stresses that the surface presentation of exotic settings often implies a political subtext that deals with internal English affairs, that is, the foreign is used to cast light on the familiar. In the subsequent chapters, Orr applies this general observation to individual plays.

In chapter two, Orr discusses how heroic drama was an especially appropriate vehicle for the presentation of matters of colonialism in that a focus on patriotism helped to encourage feelings of national supremacy over other colonial powers. She identifies two types of plays in this category, one set within the areas of European expansion, the other within Eastern empires. The Eastern empires are usually portrayed as cruelly barbarian and thus justify being taken over by civilized European, particularly English, forces. In chapters three and four, Orr picks out two of these Eastern empires, the Ottoman and the Moghul, in order to illustrate her thesis. In a close analysis of plays dealing with the Turkish Empire, she shows how this defined through contrast the virtues of a free Protestant country such as England. The large number of "Turkish plays" in around the year 1680 Orr explains in terms of the immediate threat the Turkish forces posed to Europe by the siege of Vienna, and similarly, the frequent references to Eastern empires such as the Persian and Moghul empires, are explained by the establishment of new trading arrangements in the area.

The same practice of self-definition by the use of contrast with foreign countries is employed in the "Spanish plays," as Orr successfully demonstrates. Here, the cruelty of the Spanish towards the natives of central and south America is used to emphasize the glorious, humane achievements of free Protestant England as against absolutist, Catholic Spain. Orr's analysis of "Spanish plays" is focused almost exclusively on Dryden, something she laments in other writers as she had stressed in chapter one, whereas only a brief section is devoted to writers such as Davenant and Mary Pix.

In Chapter 6, Orr focuses on writers who have been almost completely forgotten by literary critics, namely male writers of utopian plays, such as John Weston, Edward Howard, Charles Hopkins, and Peter Motteux. Also in this context, Orr explains the proliferation of these plays with the socio-historical background of the time: the increasingly widespread debates as to how to organize and govern the newly-acquired territories led writers to invest their own fantasies with utopian qualities. During the reign of Queen Anne, these utopian fantasies often presented Amazons ruling the natives.

Towards the end of her book, Orr focuses on what the plays reveal about the meaning colonial expansion had for England. She detects evidence of the extent to which masculine social status and character were shaped by this expansion and how new types appear in society and on stage, types that are associated with the colonies, such as merchants, planters, and sea-captains. But Orr also sees in these plays a revelation of the contempt that seems to have been prevalent at the time for those who actually went out to the colonies, as a protracted period in the colonies threatened their idea of national identity, whereas those who remained in England and still managed to make a profit out of colonial territories enjoyed high social esteem.

Orr's account of empire on the English stage is eminently readable, refreshingly free from needless critical jargon, and straightforward in its way of dealing with the subject matter. Orr's practice of rereading these plays against their historical and sociological background is commendable and could serve as an example for other literary historians who set out to deal with a similar topic.—Melanie Maria Just

Orr, Bridget. "Poetic Plate-Fleets and Universal Monarchy: The Heroic Plays and Empire in the Restoration." Pp. 71–97 of *John Dryden: A Tercentenary Miscellany*. Edited by Susan Green and Steven N. Zwicker. San Marino: Huntington Library, 2001.

Ortiz de Zarate Fernandez, Amalia, and Rodrigo Browne Sartori. "El Sindrome de Insularidad y Aislamiento en *Robinson Crusoe*: Analisis Comparativo Intercultural." *Especulo: Revista de Estudios Literarios*, 17 (2001).

Pajares Infante, Eterio. "La Primera Traduccion Espanola de *Tom Jones*: Analisis Critico." *Dieciocho: Hispanic Enlightenment*, 24 (2001), 245–60.

Palmer, Sally. "'I Prefer Walking': Jane Austen and 'the Pleasantest Part of the Day.'" *Persuasions: Journal of the Jane Austen Society of North America*, 23 (2001), 154–65.

Paradise, Nathaniel. "From Poet to Novelist: Women Writers and the Literary Marketplace." *Eighteenth-Century Women*, 1 (2001), 237–62.

Paravisini-Gebert, Lizabeth. "Cross-Dressing on the Margins of Empire: Women Pirates and the Narrative of the Caribbean." Pp. 59–98 of *Women at Sea: Travel Writing and the Margins of Caribbean Discourse*. Edited by Lizabeth Paravisini-Gebert and Ivette Romero-Cesareo. New York: Palgrave, 2001.

Paravisini-Gebert, Lizabeth, and Ivette Romero-Cesareo (eds.). *Women at Sea: Travel Writing and the Margins of Caribbean Discourse*. New York: Palgrave, 2001. Pp. 320; bibliography.

Park, Hyungji. "'Entirely without Words' in *Emma*: The Narrative Conspiracy against Jane Fairfax." *British and American Fiction to 1900*, 8 (2001), 177–200.

Park, Julia. "Following Footpaths in *Emma*: Actual and Metaphorical." *Persuasions: Journal of the Jane Austen Society of North America*, 23 (2001), 139–47.

Park, Jusik. "'The Estate of Hostility': Hobbesian Philosophy in Rochester's 'A Satyr against Reason and Mankind.'" *Journal of English Language and Literature/Yongo Yongmunhak*, 47 (2001), 997–1015.

Parker, Jan. "Teaching Troubling Texts: Virgil, Dryden, and Exemplary Translation." *Translation & Literature*, 10 (2001), 33–50.

Parker, Keiko. "'What Part of Bath Do You Think They Will Settle In?': Jane Austen's Use of Bath in *Persuasion*." *Persuasions: Journal of the Jane Austen Society of North America*, 23 (2001), 166–76.

Parrinder, Patrick. "Highway Robbery and Property Circulation in Eighteenth-Century English Narratives." *Eighteenth-Century Fiction*, 13 (2001), 509–28.

VI: British Literatures

Patterson, Diana. "Foliation Jokes in Tristram Shandy." Pp. 163–83 of *1650–1850: Ideas, Aesthetics, and Inquiries in the Early Modern Era*. Volume 6. Edited by Kevin L. Cope. New York: AMS Press, 2001.

Payne, Darin. "Effacing Difference in the Royal Society: The Homogenizing Nature of Disciplinary Dialogue." *Rhetoric Review*, 20 (2001), 94–112.

Pearson, Hesketh. *Johnson and Boswell*. Second edition. London: House of Stratus, 2001.

Pellicer, Juan Christian. "Dryden, Chesterfield, and Johnson's 'Celebrated Letter': A Case of Compound Allusion." *Notes and Queries*, 48 (2001), 413–14.

Pender, Patricia. "Competing Conceptions: Rhetorics of Representation in Aphra Behn's Oroonoko." *Women's Writing*, 8 (2001), 457–71.

Pepys, Samuel. *The Diary of Samuel Pepys*. London: Kuperard, 2001. Pp. 336.

Pepys, Samuel. *The Diary of Samuel Pepys*. Edited by Richard Le Gallienne. New York: Modern Library, 2001. Pp. xxxv + 310.

Pepys, Samuel. *The Diary of Samuel Pepys: A New and Complete Transcription*. Edited by Robert Latham and William Matthews 2001. Pp. 368; bibliography.

Perkins, Pam. "Planting Seeds of Virtue: Sentimental Fiction and the Moral Education of Women." *Cardiff Corvey: Reading the Romantic Text*, 6 (2001).

Perman, David. *Scott of Amwell: Dr. Johnson's Quaker Critic*. Ware: Rockingham Press, 2001. Pp. 368; bibliography; illustrations; maps.

Pettit, Alexander. "The Adventures of Peter Wilkins: Desire, Difference, and the Fallacy of Comic Convention." *Eighteenth Century: Theory and Interpretation*, 42 (2001), 91–112.

Pettit, Alexander. "Rex v. Curll: Pornography and Punishment in Court and on the Page." *Studies in the Literary Imagination*, 34 (2001), 63–78.

Picard, Liza. *Dr. Johnson's London: Coffee-Houses and Climbing Boys, Medicine, Toothpaste and Gin, Poverty and Press-Gangs, Freakshows and Female Education*. New York: St. Martin's Press, 2001. Pp. xxi + 362; bibliography; plates, illustrations.

Picard draws heavily on *Gentleman's Magazine* materials for short entries within sections on the place, the poor, the middling, and the rich. Rev. (favorably; with another book) by Peter Earle in *TLS* (January 5, 2001), 26.

Picard, Liza. *Dr Johnson's London: Life in London 1740–1770*. London: Phoenix, 2001. Pp. 384; bibliography; illustrations; facsimiles; maps.

Pierce, John B. "Pamela's Textual Authority." Pp. 8–26 of *Passion and Virtue: Essays on the Novels of Samuel Richardson*. Edited by David Blewett. Toronto: University of Toronto Press, 2001.

Pitcher, E. W. "Who Wrote the Essay 'on Sensibility'—William Jackson or Edmund." *ANQ*, 14 (2001), 15–16.

Pix, Mary. "The Innocent Mistress." Pp. 1–74 of *Eighteenth-Century Women Dramatists*. Edited by Melinda C. Finberg. Oxford: Oxford University Press, 2001.

Plumsky, Roger. "Dryden's *Absalom and Achitophel*." *Explicator*, 60 (2001), 12–15.

Poliakov, O. Iu. "'Korol' Lir' V Periodicheskikh Izdaniiakh Anglii XVIII V.: K Probleme Transformatsii Metoda Deskriptivnoi Kritiki." *Vestnik Moskovskogo Universiteta. Seriia, 9* (2001), 63–76.

Poole, Ralph J. "Michel Tourniers Anal/yse von Daniel Defoe's *Robinson Crusoe*." Pp. 121–60 of *Sehen, Lesen, Begehren: Homosexualität in Französischer Literatur und Kultur*. Edited by Dirk Naguschewski and Sabine Schrader. Berlin: Tranvia Frey, 2001.

Porter, James. "'Bring Me the Head of James Macpherson' the Execution of Ossian and the Wellspring of Folkloristic Discourse." *Journal of American Folklore*, 114 (2001), 396–435.

Porter, James (ed.). "James Macpherson and the Ossian Epic Debate." *Journal of American Folklore*, (2001), 396–514. Special issue.

Potkay, Adam. "Hume's 'Supplement to Gulliver': The Medieval Volumes of the History of England." *Eighteenth-Century Life*, 25 (2001), 32–46.

Potkay, Adam (ed.). "Essays in Honor of Robert P. Maccubbin: The Interdisciplinary Approach." *Eighteenth Century Life*, 25, (2001). Pp. 1–270.

Potter, Tiffany. "'A God-Like Sublimity of Passion': Eliza Haywood's Libertine Consistency." *Eighteenth-Century Novel,* 1 (2001), 95–126.

Potter, Tiffany. "'Decorous Disruption': The Cultural Voice of Mary Davys." *Eighteenth-Century Women,* 1 (2001), 63–93.

Pratt, Kathryn. "Charlotte Smith's Melancholia on the Page and Stage." *SEL*, 41 (2001), 563–81.

Prescott, Sarah. "Provincial Networks, Dissenting Connections, and Noble Friends: Elizabeth Singer Rowe and Female Authorship in Early Eighteenth-Century England." *Eighteenth-Century Life*, 25 (2001), 29–42.

Prescott, Sarah and David E. Shuttleton. "Mary Chandler, Elizabeth Rowe, and 'Ralph's Miscellany': Coincidental Biographical and Bibliographical Findings." *Notes and Queries,* 48 (2001), 31–34.

Price, Bronwen. "A Rhetoric of Innocence: The Poetry of Katherine Philips, 'The Matchless Orinda.'" Pp. 223–46 of *Write or Be Written: Early Modern Women Poets and Cultural Constraints*. Edited by Barbara Smith and Ursula Appelt. Aldershot: Ashgate Publishing Company, 2001.

Price, Steven R. "The Autography Manuscript in Print: Samuel Richardson's Type Font Manipulation in *Clarissa*." Pp. 117–35 of *Illuminating Letters: Typography and Literary Interpretation*. Edited by Paul C. Gutjahr and Margaret L. Benton. Amherst: University of Massachusetts Press, 2001.

Priestley, Sharon L. "'Happy to Worship in a Romish Church': Boswell and Roman Catholicism." *Studies in Scottish Literature,* 32 (2001), 150–63.

Pruitt, John. "Some Current Publications." *Restoration: Studies in English Literary Culture, 1660–1700,* 25 (2001), 139–69.

Prungnaud, Joelle, Alain Montandon, and Jean-Marc Moura (eds.). *La Cathédrale*. Villeneuve d'Ascq: Université Charles de Gaulle, 2001. Pp. 304; plates; illustrations.

Punter, David, and Elizabeth Bronfen. "Gothic: Violence, Trauma, and the Ethical." Pp. 7–21 of *The Gothic*. Edited by Fred Botting. Cambridge: Brewer, 2001.

Raber, Karen. *Dramatic Difference: Gender, Class, and Genre in the Early Modern Closet Drama*. Newark: University of Delaware Press, 2001. Pp. 338; bibliography.

Radford, Andrew. "Samuel Pepys and the 'Riding.'" *Notes and Queries,* 48 (2001), 28–29.

Raphael, Linda Schermer. *Narrative Skepticism: Moral Agency and Representations of Consciousness in Fiction*. Madison: Fairleigh Dickinson University Press, 2001. Pp. 238.

Rawson, Claude. "Thoughts on Adventurers: Fielding to Byron." Pp. 136–49 of *Eighteenth-Century Genre and Culture: Serious Reflections on Occasional Forms: Essays in Honor of J. Paul Hunter*. Edited by Dennis Todd and Cynthia Wall. Newark: University of Delaware Press, 2001.

Rawson, Claude. "Gulliver and Others: Reflections on Swift's 'I' Narrators." *Q/W/E/R/T/Y: Arts, Litteratures & Civilisations du Monde Anglophone*, 11 (2001), 71–80.

Rawson, Claude Julien. *God, Gulliver, and Genocide : Barbarism and the European Imagination, 1492–1945*. Oxford: New York, 2001. Pp. xvi + 401; bibliography; illustrations.

Ray, Joan Klingel. "Austen's *Sense and Sensibility*." *Explicator*, 60 (2001), 15–19.

Real, Hermann J. "Allegorical Adventure and Adventurous Allegory: Gulliver's 'Several Ridiculous and Troublesome Accidents' in Brobdingnag." *Q/W/E/R/T/Y: Arts, Litteratures & Civilisations du Monde Anglophone*, 11 (2001), 81–87.

Real, Hermann J. "Corinna's Dream, Again." *Notes and Queries*, 48 (2001): 34–35.

Real, Hermann J. "Gulliver and the Moons of Mars, Once More." *East-Central Intelligencer*, 15 (2001), 7–8.

Real, Hermann J. *Securing Swift: Selected Essays*. Dublin: Maunsel & Co., 2001. Pp. xiv + 353; illustrations.

Real, Hermann J. (ed.). *Swift Studies. The Annual of the Ehrenpreis Center for Swift Studies*. Volume 16. Munich: Fink, 2001. Pp.136.

This year's issue comprises, like most of its predecessors, a valuable collection of articles on Swift and related writers and matters. In the first article, Bernhard Fabian and Marie-Luise Spieckermann continue their account of the reception of Pope in eighteenth-century Germany, which they had begun in the previous issue of *Swift Studies*. It is again an outstanding example of thorough scholarship and makes interested readers look forward with great enthusiasm to the many volumes still to come. Once Fabian and Spieckermann's ambitious project on the reception of all British writers in Germany in the years 1680 to 1810 is completed, the reader will have access to an invaluable work on transcultural exchange in the eighteenth century.

Three of the essays contained in this year's issue deal with questions of interpretation. In "Swift's *Tale*, the Renaissance Anatomy, and Humanist Invective," W. Scott Blanchard examines to what extent *A Tale of a Tub* is embedded in the world of Renaissance anatomy, one of the many angles from which one can approach the *Tale*, but one which has so far not received the critical attention it deserves. In "Dismembered Body," Charles Greg Kelley contests the view held by many some time ago that Swift was a heartless misanthrope. He found evidence to the contrary in a host of sources from popular culture, which he analyses in this article. Susann P. Reilly, in "'A Soil So Unhappily Ccultivated': Balnibarbi and Swift's Georgic Vision of Ireland," gives further evidence as to how topical *Gulliver's Travels* really was. By identifying what goes on in Balnibarbi with actual events and people in Ireland at the time Swift wrote the satire, Reilly convincingly compares Ireland to Balnibarbi. An article of documentary character is presented by Stephen Karian in "Swift's Epitaph for Stella?". Karian here provides a Latin inscription believed to have been written by Swift shortly after Stella's death; this inscription has only recently been discovered as being written on a copy of *Verses on the Death of Dr. Swift*, a copy which is now in the possession of Baylor University.

This year's issue closes with a real highlight of Swiftiana. In "Seeking an Enduring Image: Rupert Barber, Jonathan Swift, and the Profile Portrait," the art historian Arthur S. Marks has brought together fifteen illustrations of portraits of Swift, illustrations that are most beautifully reproduced here. Marks examines these portraits and points out differences and similarities between them, and how the fact that Swift himself showed little enthusiasm for having his likeness painted could have affected the various portraits. As always, the volume ends with the editor's extensive bibliography of recent work on Jonathan Swift.—Melanie Maria Just

Real, Hermann J. "That 'Flower of Swift's Cynicism,' The Lady's Dressing Room, Again." *East-Central Intelligencer*, 15 (2001), 8–13.

Regan, Shaun. "Translating Rabelais: Sterne, Motteux, and the Culture of Politeness." *Translation & Literature*, 10 (2001), 174–99.

Ribble, Frederick G. "Fielding and William Young." *Studies in Philology*, 98 (2001), 457–501.

Ribble, Frederick G. "Fielding's Rapprochement with Walpole in Late 1741." *Philological Quarterly*, 80 (2001), 71–81.

Richardson, John. "Alexander Pope's *Windsor Forest*: Its Context and Attitudes toward Slavery." *Eighteenth-Century Studies*, 35 (2001), 1–17.

Richardson, John. "Christian and/or Ciceronian: Swift and Gulliver's Fourth Voyage." *Cambridge Quarterly*, 30 (2001), 37–49.

Richardson, John. "Pope's *Windsor-Forest*." *Explicator*, 59 (2001), 118–20.

Richardson, John. "Swift, 'A Modest Proposal' and Slavery." *Essays in Criticism*, 51 (2001), 404–23.

Richetti, John. "Secular Crusoe: The Reluctant Pilgrim Re-Visited." Pp. 58–78 of *Eighteenth-Century Genre and Culture: Serious Reflections on Occasional Forms: Essays in Honor of J. Paul Hunter*. Edited by Dennis Todd and Cynthia Wall. Newark: University of Delaware Press, 2001.

Rigamonti, Antonella, and Laura Favero Carraro. "Women at Stake: The Self-Assertive Potential of Gambling in Susanna Centlivre's *The Basset Table*." *Restoration and 18th Century Theatre Research*, 16 (2001), 53–62.

Rivero, Albert J. "The Place of Sally Godfrey in Richardson's *Pamela*." Pp. 52–72 of *Passion and Virtue: Essays on the Novels of Samuel Richardson*. Edited by David Blewett. Toronto: University of Toronto Press, 2001.

Rizzo, Betty. "'Downing Everybody': Johnson and the Grevilles." *Age of Johnson*, 12 (2001), 17–46.

Roberts, Marilyn. "The Memoirs of Wilhelmina of Bayreuth: A Story of Her Own." *Eighteenth-Century Women*, 1 (2001), 129–64.

Robinson, David Michael. "The Abominable Madame De Murat." *Journal of Homosexuality*, 41 (2001), 53–67.

Robinson, David Michael. "The Metamorphosis of Sex(uality): Ovid's 'Iphis and Ianthe' in the Seventeenth and Eighteenth Centuries." In *Presenting Gender: Changing Sex in Early-Modern Culture*. Edited by Chris Mounsey. (Bucknell Studies in Eighteenth-Century Literature and Culture.) Lewisburg: Bucknell University Press, 2001.

Rodriguez, Ileana. "Apprenticeship as Citizenship and Governability." Pp. 341–66 of *The Latin American Subaltern Studies Reader*. Edited by Ileana Rodriguez. Durham: Duke University Press, 2001.

Rodriguez, Ileana (ed.). *The Latin American Subaltern Studies Reader*. Durham: Duke University Press, 2001. Pp. xii + 459.

Rollyson, Carl. "Samuel Johnson: Dean of Contemporary Biographers." *Biography: An Interdisciplinary Quarterly*, 24 (2001), 442–47.

Roper, Alan. "Innuendo in the Restoration." *Journal of English and Germanic Philology*, 100 (2001), 22–39.

Roper, Alan. "Who's Who in *Absalom and Achitophel*?" Pp. 99–138 of *John Dryden: A Tercentenary Miscellany*. Edited by Susan Green and Steven N. Zwicker. San Marino: Huntington Library, 2001.

Rosenbaum, Susan. "'A Thing Unknown, without a Name': Anna Laetitia Barbauld and the Illegible Signature." *Studies in Romanticism*, 40 (2001), 369–99.

Rosengarten, Richard. *Henry Fielding and the Narration of Providence: Divine Design and the Incursions of Evil*. Basingstoke: Palgrave, 2001. Pp. 192.

Ross, Ian Campbell. "Sterne, Swift, Orrery, and the 'Rabelaisian Fragment.'" *Notes and Queries,* 48 (2001), 422–25.

Ross, Margaret Clunies. *The Old Norse Poetic Translations of Thomas Percy.* Turnhout: Brepols, 2001. Pp. xii + 290.

Rosslyn, Felicity. "Dryden: Poet or Translator?" *Translation & Literature,* 10 (2001), 21–32.

Rousseau, George S. "Ingenious Pain: Fiction, History, Biography, and the Miraculous Eighteenth Century." *Eighteenth-Century Life*, 25 (2001), 47–62.

Rousseau, George S. "Towards a Geriatric Enlightenment." Pp. 3–43 of *1650–1850: Ideas, Aesthetics, and Inquiries in the Early Modern Era.* Volume 6. Edited by Kevin L. Cope. New York: AMS Press, 2001.

Roy, G. Ross. "A Burnsian Odd Couple." *Studies in Scottish Literature,* 32 (2001), 216–17.

Roy, G. Ross. "An Early Indian Mystic and Robert Burns." *Studies in Scottish Literature*, 32 (2001), 218–20.

Roy, G. Ross. "A Prototype for Robert Burns's Kilmarnock Edition?" *Studies in Scottish Literature,* 32 (2001), 213–16.

Rumbold, Valerie. "Cut the Caterwauling: Women Writers (Not) in Pope's *Dunciads.*" *Review of English Studies*, 52 (2001), 524–39.

Runge, Laura L. "Beauty and Gallantry: A Model of Polite Conversation Revisited." *Eighteenth-Century Life,* 25 (2001), 43–63.

Russell, Anne. "'Public' and 'Private' in Aphra Behn's Miscellanies: Women Writers, Print, and Manuscript." Pp. 29–48 of *Write or Be Written: Early Modern Women Poets and Cultural Constraints.* Edited by Barbara Smith and Ursula Appelt. Aldershot: Ashgate Publishing Company, 2001.

Russell, Gillian. "'Keeping Place': Servants, Theater and Sociability in Mid–Eighteenth-Century Britain." *Eighteenth Century: Theory and Interpretation*, 42 (2001), 21–42.

Ruwe, Donelle. "Guarding the British Bible from Rousseau: Sarah Trimmer, William Godwin, and the Pedagogical Periodical." *Children's Literature: Annual of The Modern Language Association Division on Children's Literature and The Children's Literature Association*, 29 (2001), 1–17.

Ryan, Vanessa L. "The Physiological Sublime: Burke's Critique of Reason." *Journal of the History of Ideas*, 62 (2001), 265–79.

Rylance, Rick, and Judy Simons (eds.). *Literature in Context*. New York: Palgrave, 2001. Pp. 274; bibliography.

Rytting, Jenny Rebecca. "Jane Austen Meets Carl Jung: Pride, Prejudice, and Personality Theory." *Persuasions: The Jane Austen Journal On-Line*, 22 (2001).

Salber, Cecilia. "Bridget Jones and Mark Darcy: Art Imitating Art...Imitating Art." *Persuasions: The Jane Austen Journal On-Line*, 22 (2001).

Salzman, Paul (ed.). *An Anthology of Seventeenth-Century Fiction*. New York: Oxford University Press, 2001. Pp. xxxiii + 562.

Sambrook, James. "'A Just Balance between Patronage and the Press': The Case of James Thomson." *Studies in the Literary Imagination*, 34 (2001), 137–53.

Samet, Elizabeth D. "A Prosecutor and a Gentleman: Edmund Burke's Idiom of Impeachment." *ELH*, 68 (2001), 397–418.

Samuelian, Kristin Flieger. "'Piracy is our only option': Postfeminist Intervention in *Sense and Sensibility*." Pp. 148–58 of *Jane Austen in Hollywood*. Edited by Linda Troost and Sayre N. Greenfield. Lexington: University Press of Kentucky, 2001.

Sanborn, Geoffrey. "The Missed Encounter: Cannibalism and the Literary Critic." Pp. 187–204 of *Eating Their Words: Cannibalism and the Boundaries of Cultural Identity*. Edited by Kristen Guest and Maggie Kilgour. New York: State University of New York Press, 2001.

Sanders, Arthrell D. "The Student: Matters of Publication." *CLA Journal*, 45 (2001), 69–86.

Sandhu, Sukhdev. "Sterne and the 'Coal-Black Jolly African.'" *Shandean: An Annual Devoted to Laurence Sterne and His Works*, 12 (2001), 9–21.

Sandiford, Keith. "Vertices and Horizons with Sugar: A Tropology of Colonial Power." *Eighteenth Century: Theory and Interpretation*, 42 (2001), 142–60.

Sandock, Mollie. "'I Burn with Contempt for My Foes': Jane Austen's Music Collections and Women's Lives in Regency England." *Persuasions: Journal of the Jane Austen Society of North America*, 23 (2001), 105–17.

Sauvage, Emmanuelle. "La Tentation Du Théâtre dans le Roman: Analyse De Quelques Tableaux Chez Sade et Richardson." *Lumen*, 20 (2001), 147–60..

Sanchez Hernandez, Elena. "'An Undigested Heap of Thoughts': La Conversion del Libertino." Pp. 243–50 of *Polifonias Textuales: Ensayos in Honorem Maria del Carmen Fernandez Leal*. Edited by Manuel Brito and Juan Ignacio Oliva. La Laguna: Revista Canaria de Estudios Ingleses (RCEI), 2001.

Scheffel, Michael, and Dietmar Gotsch (eds.). *Erschriebene Natur: Internationale Perspektiven Auf Texte Des 18. Jahrhunderts*. Bern: Peter Lang, 2001. Pp. 333; illustrations.

Scheick, William J. "An Inward Power and Authority: John Davenport's Seditious Piety." *Religion and Literature*, 33 (2001), 1–21.

Schellenberg, Betty A. "Enclosing the Immovable: Structuring Social Authority in *Pamela* 2." Pp. 73–91 of *Passion and Virtue: Essays on the Novels of Samuel Richardson*. Edited by David Blewett. Toronto: University of Toronto Press, 2001.

Schellenberg, Betty A. "Frances Sheridan Reads John Home: Placing Sidney Bidulph in the Republic of Letters." *Eighteenth-Century Fiction*, 13 (2001), 561–77.

Scherwatzky, Steven D. "'Complicated Virtue': The Politics of Samuel Johnson's *Life of Savage*." *Eighteenth-Century Life*, 25 (2001), 80–93.

Scheuermann, Mona. "Hannah More and the English Poor." *Eighteenth-Century Life*, 25 (2001), 237–51.

Schmidgen, Wolfram. "Robinson Crusoe, Enumeration, and the Mercantile Fetish." *Eighteenth-Century Studies*, 35 (2001), 19–39.

Schürer, Norbert. "A New Novel by Charlotte Lennox." *Notes and Queries*, 48 (2001). 419–22.

Schweitzer, Corie. "Public Good and Private Mischief: Daniel Defoe's Journal of Three Nations in a *Journal of the Plague Year*." *Eighteenth-Century Novel*, 1 (2001), 253–69.

Scott, Clive. "Landscapes of the Line: Verse-Features and the Perception of Nature in Romantic and Pre-Romantic Poetry." Pp. 189–212 of *Erschriebene Natur: Internationale Perspektiven Auf Texte Des 18. Jahrhunderts*. Edited by Michael Scheffel and Dietmar Gotsch. Bern: Peter Lang, 2001.

Segal, Lore. "The Uses of Story: Jane Austen on Our Unwillingness to Be Parted from Our Money." *Antioch Review,* 59 (2001), 252–58.

Selwyn, David. "Games and Play in Jane Austen's Literary Structures." *Persuasions: Journal of the Jane Austen Society of North America,* 23 (2001), 15–28.

Seo, Yeong-yoon. "The Change of Political Power in Restoration England: Congreve's *The Way of the World.*" *Journal of English Language and Literature/Yongo Yongmunhak,* 47 (2001), 487–503.

Seybert, Gislinde. "Schreibende Frauen." Pp. 141–52 of *Die Wende Von Der Aufklarung Zur Romantik 1760–1820: Epoche Im Uberblick.* Edited by Horst Albert Glaser, Gyorgy M. Vajda, and Francois Crouzet. Amsterdam: Benjamins, 2001.

Shaffer, Julie. "Cross-dressing the Nature of Gender in Mary Robinson's *Walsingham.*" Pp. 136–70 of *Presenting Gender: Changing Sex in Early-Modern Culture.* (Bucknell Studies in Eighteenth-Century Literature and Culture.) Edited by Chris Mounsey. Lewisburg: Bucknell University Press, 2001.

Sharma, Anjana. "A Different Voice: Mary Hays's the Memoirs of Emma Courtney." *Women's Writing,* 8 (2001), 139–67.

Sheehan, Richard Johnson, and Denise Tillery. "Margaret Cavendish, Natural Philosopher: Negotiating between Metaphors of the Old and New Sciences." *Eighteenth-Century Women,* 1 (2001), 1–18.

Sherbo, Arthur. "W. R. in Robert Burns's Commonplacebook 1783–1785." *Notes and Queries,* 48 (2001), 117–18.

Sherman, Sandra. "The Law, Confinement, and Disruptive Excess in Hays's *The Victim of Prejudice.*" Pp. 131–61 of *1650–1850: Ideas, Aesthetics, and Inquiries in the Early Modern Era.* Volume 6. Edited by Kevin L. Cope. New York: AMS Press, 2001.

Shields, Carol. *Jane Austen.* New York: Viking, 2001. Pp. 185.

Shifflett, Andrew. "'Subdu'd by You': States of Friendship and Friends of the State in Katherine Phillips's Poetry." Pp. 177–95 of *Write or Be Written: Early Modern Women Poets and Cultural Constraints.* Edited by Barbara Smith and Ursula Appelt. Aldershot: Ashgate Publishing Company, 2001.

VI: British Literatures

Silver, Sean R. "Some Current Publications." *Restoration: Studies in English Literary Culture, 1660–1700,* 25 (2001), 53–82.

Sim, Stuart. "Sterne-Chaos-Complexity." *Eighteenth-Century Novel,* 1 (2001), 201–15.

Simms, Norman. "Childish Anxieties in the Adventures of Lemuel Gulliver." *Q/W/E/R/T/Y: Arts, Litteratures & Civilisations du Monde Anglophone,* 11 (2001), 89–96.

Simons, Judy. "Jane Austen: *Persuasion.*" Pp. 91–104 of *Literature in Context.* Edited by Rick Rylance and Judy Simons. Houndmills: Palgrave, 2001.

Siskin, Clifford. "Novels and Systems." *Novel: A Forum on Fiction,* 34 (2001), 202–15.

Sisman, Adam. *Boswell's Presumptuous Task: The Making of the Life of Dr. Johnson.* New York: Farrar, Straus, and Giroux, 2001. Pp. xxii + 351; bibliography; illustrations.

Sitter, John E. "Introduction: The Future of Eighteenth-Century Poetry." Pp. 1–10 of *The Cambridge Companion to Eighteenth-Century Poetry.* Edited by John Sitter. Cambridge: Cambridge University Press, 2001.

Sitter, John E. "Questions in Poetics: Why and How Poetry Matters." Pp. 133–56 of *The Cambridge Companion to Eighteenth-Century Poetry.* Edited by John Sitter. Cambridge: Cambridge University Press, 2001.

Sitter, John E. (ed.). *The Cambridge Companion to Eighteenth-Century Poetry.* Cambridge: Cambridge University Press, 2001. Pp. 318.

I'll state from the outset that I have been and continue to be a great fan and beneficiary of the Cambridge Companion series (as a student as well as a teacher) and that John Sitter's contribution to it is one for which we can all be grateful. But I have often thought the series awkwardly titled. One supposes it evokes a casualness signifying an eschewal of "completeness" as an illusory goal and an acceptance of (contemporary) topicality as inevitable and satisfactory. Gone are "the Ages of" a few male authors, and present are essays that approach the book's subject in socio-political, economic, aesthetic, formal, and thematic ways. The breadth of information contained herein is vast (although, one might wish for a greater presence of Johnson, a bit of information on continental poetry, and some linkage to trends in other arts); moreover, despite the need for economy, its depth is surprising. In almost every essay, the best moments occur when, finished with opening summary, the authors provide examples and detailed readings of lesser known texts. As the etymology of "companion" would suggest, the collection is a store of nourishing material.

Sitter's claim for this book is that it will offer perspectives that explain but also empathize with its subject. In this, the book is quite successful. But who is its ideal reader? Under the series title, Cambridge's catalogue states that its intention is to provide "students and other readers with stimulating introductions to particular authors, genres, and periods in the history of literature and drama." I can imagine giving J. Paul Hunter's essay on couplets to a group of undergraduate students, but other essays, I suspect, would prove too detailed, too difficult, or both. Because the contributors are committed to recovering forgotten writers and ignored aspects of the period, it's even possible that the essays would be useful only in a carefully crafted graduate class or to advanced graduate students. On the other hand, the introductory parts of many of these essays rehearse matters that will already be quite familiar to scholars.

On familiarity: it is a shame that no essay here covers the critical tradition of eighteenth-century poetry. Only two handfuls of sources either cited in footnotes or listed in the "Further Reading" sections appended to each chapter date back to the first half of the twentieth century. The references overwhelmingly refer to work done since the seventies. I do not recall a nod to Saintsbury or even Martin Price or Donald Davie's older scholarship. And more recent major texts like Marshall Brown's *Preromanticism*, Margaret Anne Doody's *The Daring Muse*, or Patricia Meyer Spacks's (Spacks is one of the contributors) *The Poetry of Vision* are barely grappled with. One risk involved with this lack is that students will receive the recital of recent critical perspectives uncritically as fact. A second, more meaningful, risk is that it may end conversation precisely where one might begin. For example, Hunter's excellent essay fails to mention Earl Wasserman's influential *The Subtler Language*, though both argue that the period's attraction to the couplet has something to do with its larger cultural habits and preoccupations. A discussion of Wasserman's reading, including its strengths and weaknesses, might help students grasp what is at stake for Hunter, and for themselves, in claiming that the couplet is or is not a "closed" form. Likewise, it may be true, as Tim Fulford says, that patriotism and nationalism are encoded into eighteenth-century landscapes, but a student inclined to investigate more aesthetic approaches to landscape would not know where to turn for information.

That said, a good companion is one who offers stimulating conversation. This is one of Sitter's stated goals, to have us all engage as "active readers" of eighteenth-century poetry who can perceive its playfulness as well as its seriousness. While the essays overlap in ways that will certainly provoke readers to respond, however, they are not literally in dialogue with each other (as, for example, some of the essays in *The Cambridge Companion to Blake* are). This is unfortunate, as many opportunities for deeper analysis are lost. For example, the first three essays, by Hunter, Christine Gerrard and Barbara Benedict, provide different contexts in which to place poetry: the social sphere, the political sphere, and the literary marketplace. Where Hunter's essay reminds readers of the function poetry played in the social fabric, Benedict's shows the extent to which poetry was itself shaped by market forces. On one hand, then, the poetic expansiveness typical of eighteenth-century poetry is said already to be written into the couplet form; on the other, it is said to be driven by the explosion of presses and the commodification of genres. How would either scholar address this dichotomy?

Gerrard's essay explains some of the political controversies of the century and contends that poetry has less and less to say about these over time. With the exception of Churchill's satiric salvos, after the 1740s, Gerrard suggests, political/satiric verse is replaced either by the elegiac or the imaginative. One wonders if perhaps politics might be differently construed so as to include a wider range of poetic responses to it. Is elegy necessarily apolitical? Here Gerrard might have taken note of a brilliant remark in Spacks's essay, that sensibility could also encompass frustration and even anger. Such anger often appears in abolitionist poetry of the latter century.

Another missed opportunity for interesting dialogue resides in the tension between Claudia Thomas Kairoff's essay on women poets and David Fairer's on the influence of Spenser and Milton. Kairoff writes that whereas men's poems reflect the influence of a classical education, women's show the influence of English "classics," such as Milton, Dryden, Swift, and Pope. Fairrer, on the other hand, discusses the way poets learned to absorb, rather than merely mimic Spenser and Milton as well as to shed themselves of Popeian style. Milton is the great influence here, and his blank verse is said to unleash "dynamic" and "organic" forces in eighteenth-century poetry. What he means by these terms is less than clear, but Doody's *Daring Muse* and Blanford Parker's *The Triumph of the Augustans* might have been mentioned to help identify other sources of, if not "organicism," at least the "literal" or mundane. For example, why Dryden's translation of *The Georgics* (Fairrer does not mention them) would not likewise have an influence on the expansiveness of eighteenth-century poetry is never addressed. But more to the point, here readers will want to return to Hunter, whose couplets are supposed to be equally expansive, and to Benedict, whose market forces might not require Milton for capaciousness. How might students reconcile Kairoff's and Fairrer's quite different narratives of literary influence?

This could go on forever, as each essay seems a close cousin to the others. It is impossible in limited space to account for each of the rich essays in this collection—and they are all rich—but a simple summary of them will suggest manifold interrelationships. Brean Hammond's essay charts the city as it appears in eighteenth-century poetry and does so first by defining its extremities as the "polite" and "revolutionary." Where the first comments, from a distanced position and in an urbane voice, on the moral condition of city life, the latter exposes and condemns, in a more immediate and angry tone, the power and privilege on which the city is founded. Tim Fulford's essay reviews the by-now-standard ideological view of rural landscape but does well to notice the tendency for this to reveal itself as aggression in poets such as Thomson and Grainger. David Morris reveals that much of the century's poetry is driven by a desire itself signaled by "absences" most often evoked by the specter of ruins, dreams, or death. Spacks's aforementioned essay on the poetics of sensibility helpfully differentiates eighteenth-century anguish from a Romantic acceptance of alienation. Where Romantic heroes are superior because separate, the poet of sensibility feels diminished, and often indignant, because her feelings, as well as reason, do not square with a social world. Jennifer Keith's entry shares much with Spacks's, arguing that latter-century poetry is marked by a refusal to find consolation in transcendence but rather accepts a painful emptying-out of the self. Keith's essay amounts to a sophisticated apology for late eighteenth-century poetry, one that thankfully refuses "post-Augustan" and "preromantic" labels and seeks to understand the poetry on its own terms.

The two most outstanding essays of the collection are Ralph Cohen's and Sitter's own contribution. Sitter's essay is on poetic treatises of the period and argues that earlier attitudes about poetry prove more flexible than Romantic notions, which, though more lofty, were also more narrowing and restrictive. The commonplace attitude maintains that eighteenth-century poetry is rule-bound and prescriptive, but Sitter demonstrates that it is practical and pluralist. Whereas Dennis's religious vision of poetry serves as a precedent for Coleridge's utopian vision, the main strand of thought in the period derives from Addison's interest in expressions that marry direct perception and imagination. For much of the century, then, mimesis enables passionate expression—a notion lost once genius and passion become the purpose, and not merely an aspect, of poetry.

Cohen has made a career out of brilliant essays, and he continues to illuminate here, arguing that the mid-century proliferation of odes does not signal a move towards greater expressivity but to academic, scholarly work. The Wartons' "turn" to the greater ode was indeed activated by a rejection of moralizing, but the move was toward concepts of "invention" and "imagination" that were defined by classical education and literary knowledge. It is the lesser ode that embraces the emotional—and while the Wartons eschew what they consider a mere vulgar form, novelists like Richardson and, later, sentimental sonneteers like Charlotte Smith, in turn reject elitist allegories of states of mind for more direct treatment of effusion. In a remarkable moment, Cohen suggests that Pamela's "turn to personal feeling does for her class what the ode writers do when they return poetry to originary claims about poetry and the poet—except that they are addressing an audience from a different class" (213–14). Again, one can here imagine that the book's entire chorus of scholars would hit many interesting notes in responding to this one. But it is up to the reader to play with the dissonances and create new harmonies.

Sitter's introduction to the collection discusses the tendency for eighteenth-century poets to think about, and speak to, the future. This is perhaps a projection of an understandable editorial anxiety. He need not worry. As it teaches students to read actively and sympathetically the poetry of our period, the collection will create and remain relevant to the future it desires.—Michael Rotenberg-Schwartz

Skinner, John. *An Introduction to Eighteenth-Century Fiction: Raising the Novel*. New York: Palgrave, 2001. Pp. xi + 317; bibliography.

Smallwood, Philip. "Dryden's Criticism as Transfusion." *Translation & Literature*, 10 (2001), 78–88.

Smallwood, Philip. "Ironies of the Critical Past: Historicizing Johnson's Criticism." Pp. 114–33 of *Johnson Re-Visioned: Looking Before and After.* (Bucknell Studies in Eighteenth-Century Literature and Culture.) Edited by Philip Smallwood. Lewisburg: Bucknell University Press, 2001.

Smallwood, Philip (ed.). *Johnson Re-Visioned: Looking Before and After.* (The Bucknell Studies in Eighteenth-Century Literature and Culture.) Lewisburg: Bucknell University Press, 2001. Pp. 179; bibliography.

Smith, Barbara, and Ursula Appelt (eds.). *Write or Be Written : Early Modern Women Poets and Cultural Constraints.* Aldershot: Ashgate, 2001. Pp. xxiii + 281; bibliography.

Smith, Charlotte. *The Collected Letters of Charlotte Smith.* Edited by Judith Phillips Stanton. Bloomington: Indiana University Press, 2001. Pp. 768.

Smith, Johanna M. "Constructing the Nation: Eighteenth Century Geographies for Children." *Mosaic: A Journal for the Interdisciplinary Study of Literature,* 34 (2001), 133–48.

Sneidern, Maja-Lisa Von. "'Monk' Lewis's Journals and the Discipline of Discourse." *Nineteenth-Century Contexts*, 23 (2001), 59–88.

Sola, Anne de. "Traduction et Trafic D'influences: *The Illustrious French Lovers* de Penelope Aubin et les Illustres Francaises de Robert Challe." *French Studies*, 55 (2001), 327–38.

Souter, Kay Torney. "Jane Austen and the Reconsigned Child: The True Identity of Fanny Price." *Persuasions: Journal of the Jane Austen Society of North America,* 23 (2001), 205–14.

Southam, B. C. *Jane Austen's Literary Manuscripts: A Study of the Novelist's Development through the Surviving Papers.* New York: Athlone Press, 2001. Pp. xv + 159; bibliography; illustrations.

Sowerby, Robin. "Augustan Dryden." *Translation & Literature,* 10 (2001), 51–66.

Spacks, Patricia Meyer. "Ambiguous Practices." Pp. 150–64 of *Eighteenth-Century Genre and Culture: Serious Reflections on Occasional Forms: Essays in Honor of J. Paul Hunter.* Edited by Dennis Todd and Cynthia Wall. Newark: University of Delaware Press, 2001.

Spacks, Patricia Meyer. "The Poetry of Sensibility." Pp. 249–70 of *The Cambridge Companion to Eighteenth-Century Poetry.* Edited by John Sitter. Cambridge: Cambridge University Press, 2001.

Spedding, Patrick. "Shameless Scribbler or Votary of Virtue? Eliza Haywood, Writing (and) Pornography in 1742." Pp. 237–51 of *Women Writing, 1550–1750*. Edited by Jo Wallwork and Paul Salzman. Bundoora: Meridian, 2001.

Spence, Jon. *A Century of Wills: From Jane Austen's Family, 1705–1806*. Paddington: Jane Austen Society of Australia, 2001. Pp. vi + 120; bibliography; plates; facsimiles; genealogical table.

Spencer, Susan, Margo Collins, Albert J. Rivero, and George Justice (eds.). *The Eighteenth-Century Novel*. 2 volumes. New York: AMS Press, 2001.

This inaugural edition of essays regarding Restoration and eighteenth-century prose, edited by Susan Spencer, offers a nice variety of topics and approaches. The essays included provide a mixture of new conversations and continued discussions. The collection, with fourteen essays and three book reviews, is useful for the serious scholar researching these particular texts and topics but also will provide an interesting read for the lover of eighteenth-century studies.

In "Spies, Pirates, and White Slaves: Encounters with the Algerines in Three Early American Novels," Jennifer Margulis looks at three American novels that deal primarily with America and the Barbary Coast. In contrast to previous criticism of these texts, Margulis contends that these texts offer a sympathetic view of the North African and a subtle critique of America.

In "Clarissa's Cyberspace: The Development of Epistolary Space in Richardson's *Clarissa*," James How argues for Clarissa's ability to develop an "epistolary space," much like the twenty-first-century notion of cyberspace. How particularly argues with the poststructuralist reading, which fails to account for the fact that after Clarissa's language begins to break down and as she is moving towards her death, that she appears a more powerful speaker and writer (37).

In "Clarissa Harlowe, Pleasant Rawlins, and Eighteenth-Century Discourses of Law," Beth Swan places the events of *Clarissa* in context with an actual trial in 1702 in which Haagen Swendsen is indicted "for abducting and forcibly marrying an heiress, Pleasant Rawlins," in order to gain her money (71).

In "'A God-like Sublimity of Passion': Eliza Haywood's Libertine Consistency," Tiffany Potter explores how "the cultural discourse of libertinism," although typically associated with the masculine, is deeply threaded throughout Eliza Haywood's work. She further argues that Haywood herself "was considered a libertine in her own time by many of her readers" (96).

In "Linnaeus's Blooms: Botany and the Novel of Courtship," Amy M. King looks closely at the works of botanist Carl Linnaeus and finds a connection between his sexualized language applied to botany and the burgeoning use of those same botanical terms by eighteenth-century authors to describe sexuality in their works.

In "The Grateful Slave: A History of Slave Plantation Reform in the British Novel, 1750–1780," George Boulukos insists that the compromise put forward by many eighteenth-century texts, which have been understood as anti-slavery, should instead be read as attempts to reform the institution rather than abolish it.

In "A Compendium of Shandys: Methods of Organizing Knowledge in Sterne's *Tristram Shandy*," Jonathan Laidlow disagrees with the reading of *Tristram Shandy* "as a precursor of twentieth-century Modernism and Postmodernism" and claims it is "better viewed in the light of an eighteenth-century modernism" (181).

In "Sterne, Chaos, Complexity," Stuart Sim sees an "intersection of metaphysics, physics, and literary practice" in Sterne's *Tristram Shandy*. He looks particularly at Hume as well as chaos and complexity theory, and he considers "the relationship between narrative, consciousness, and a world governed by the operations of chaos and complexity" (201).

In "'A Method of Being Perfectly Happy': Technologies of the Self in the Eighteenth-Century Female Community," Sara Gadeken looks at Sarah Scott's *Millennium Hall* (1762), Sarah Fielding's *David Simple* (1744), Mrs. Bilson's *History of the Countess of Dellwyn* (1759), and Mary Hamilton's *Munster Village* (1778) and argues that each text resists "the Lockean theory of property and social contract." Instead, she writes that they focus on constructing a model community that demonstrates the necessary virtues of successfully functioning in a community when one is an individual "produced by and embedded in her community" and when one's "capacities develop within a context of nonconsensual relations, namely a society and a family, which she does not choose" (217).

In "Questing for Family in *Joseph Andrews* and *David Simple*," Lori Walk contests earlier criticism of Sarah Fielding's *David Simple* and Henry Fielding's *Joseph Andrews* and alleges, "Family is at the center of the development of both Joseph and David as they move, seek, observe, and confront the worlds around them" (237).

In "Public Good and Private Mischief: Daniel Defoe's Journal of Three Nations in *A Journal of the Plague Year*," Corie Schweitzer challenges the "critical consensus" that Defoe writes *A Journal of the Plague Year* as a sympathetic piece to the poor classes. She considers "both Defoe's class ideologies as they reflect the immediate political and economic history surrounding the writing of the Journal and the way he uses the genre of this fictional novel (originally marketed as a true autobiographical journal) to make his case for the middle class" (254).

In "Class, Gender, and Domesticity in Maria Edgeworth's *Belinda*," Nicholas Mason discusses class, gender, and domesticity in Maria Edgeworth's *Belinda*. After providing a brief overview of recent criticism dealing with *Belinda* and domesticity, Mason goes on to argue that his article will demonstrate that domesticity in *Belinda* is "more than a system for proper female behavior." He insists that "the domesticity Edgeworth advocates is a summons for all members of polite society, whether female or male, to live up to their gender- and class-based responsibilities" (272).

In "Exploring the Book Arts through One Fine Copy of *The Castle of Otranto*," Marilyn L. Barth looks closely at the print history of Horace Walpole's *The Castle of Otranto*. Her account includes a detailed description of the Smithsonian's edition's special features and a brief biography of Walpole.

In "'I should not care to mix my breed': Gender, Race, Class, and Genre in Mary Davys' *The Accomplished Rake, or Modern Fine Gentlemen*," Virginia Duff discusses miscegenation on many levels: the text, the author, the genre, and the period.

The book reviews included in the collection are Julia Stern's *The Plight of Feeling: Sympathy and Dissent in the Early American Novel*—reviewed by Gareth Evans, Timothy Mowl's *William Beckford: Composing for Mozart*—reviewed by Dick Claesson, and Mary Seidman Trouille's *Sexual Politics in the Age of Enlightenment: Women Writers Read Rousseau*—reviewed by Mary McAlpin.—Amy E. Harris Tan

Stapleton, M. L. "Ovid the Rakehell: The Case of Wycherley." *Restoration: Studies in English Literary Culture, 1660–1700,* 25 (2001), 85–102.

Steggle, Matthew. "Macflecknoe and Cynthia's Revels." *Notes and Queries,* 48 (2001), 397–98.

Stevenson, David. "A Note on the Scotsman Who Inspired *Fanny Hill*." *Scottish Studies Review,* 2 (2001), 39–45.

Stevenson, Kay Gilliland. *Milton to Pope, 1650–1720.* New York: Palgrave, 2001. Pp. x + 292; bibliography; illustrations.

Stewart, Philip. "The Rise of I." *Eighteenth-Century Fiction,* 13 (2001), 163–81.

Stewart, Joan Hinde. "Reading Lives a la Maniere des Romans de Crebillon.'" *Eighteenth-Century Fiction,* 13 (2001), 415–35.

VI: British Literatures

Stillman, Peter G. "'With a Moral View Design'd': *Gulliver's Travels* as a Utopian Text." *Q/W/E/R/T/Y: Arts, Litteratures & Civilisations du Monde Anglophone*, 11 (2001), 97–107.

Stillman, Robert E. "The State (out) of Language: Dryden's *Annus Mirabilis* as a Restoration Paradigm for Scientific Revolution." *Soundings*, 84 (2001), 201–27.

Stovel, Bruce. "Jane Austen and the Pleasure-Principle." *Persuasions: Journal of the Jane Austen Society of North America*, 23 (2001), 63–77.

Stovel, Nora Foster. "'Every Savage Can Dance': Choreographing Courtship." *Persuasions: Journal of the Jane Austen Society of North America*, 23 (2001), 29–49.

Straub, Kristina. "Feminine Sexuality, Class Identity, and Narrative Form in the Newgate Calendars." Pp. 218–35 of *Eighteenth-Century Genre and Culture: Serious Reflections on Occasional Forms: Essays in Honor of J. Paul Hunter*. Edited by Dennis Todd and Cynthia Wall. Newark: University of Delaware Press, 2001.

Struever, Nancy S. "Hobbes and Vico on Law: A Rhetorical Gloss." *New Vico Studies*, 19 (2001), 63–85.

Sumi, Yoichi. "'Atmosphere' et 'Atmosphere': Essai sur la Cyclopaedia et le Premier Prospectus de L'encyclopedie." Pp. 271–84 of *Vérité et Littérature au XVIIIe Siècle*. Edited by Paul Aron, Sophie Basch, Manuel Couvreur, Jacques Marx, Eric Van der Schueren, Valerie Van Crugten–André, and Roland Mortier. Paris: Honoré Champion, 2001.

Swan, Beth. "Clarissa Harlowe, Pleasant Rawlins, and Eighteenth-Century Discourses of Law." *Eighteenth-Century Novel*, 1 (2001), 71–93.

Swan, Beth. "Raped by the System: An Account of *Clarissa* in the Light of Eighteenth-Century Law." Pp. 113–29 of *1650–1850: Ideas, Aesthetics, and Inquiries in the Early Modern Era*. Volume 6. Edited by Kevin L. Cope. New York: AMS Press, 2001.

Swift, Jonathan. *Gulliver's Travels, and, a Modest Proposal*. Edited by Richard Gravil. London: Longman, 2001. Pp. 120; bibliography.

Swift, Jonathan. *Gulliver's Travels*. Edited by Robert DeMaria New York: Penguin, 2001. Pp. xxx + 305; bibliography; illustrations; maps.

Swift, Jonathan. *Los Viajes De Gulliver*. Madrid: Estudio Didáctico, 2001. Pp. 185.

Swift, Jonathan. *Les Voyages De Gulliver*. Edited by Anne Bouin and Antoine Ronzon Toulouse: Milan, 2001. Illustrations.

Syrotinski, Michael, and Ian Maclachlan (eds.). *Sensual Reading: New Approaches to Reading and Its Relation to the Senses*. Lewisburg: Bucknell University Press, 2001. Pp. 350.

Tadie, Alexis. "From the Ear to the Eye: Perceptions of Language in the Fictions of Laurence Sterne." Pp. 106–23 of *Sensual Reading: New Approaches to Reading and Its Relation to the Senses*. Edited by Michael Syrotinski and Ian Maclachlan. Lewisburg: Bucknell University Press, 2001.

Tagge, Anne. "Steeped in Jane Austen on a Sri Lankan Mountaintop." *Chronicle of Higher Education*, 48 (2001), B5.

Taylor, E. Derek. "Mary Astell's Ironic Assault on John Locke's Theory of Thinking Matter." *Journal of the History of Ideas*, 62 (2001), 505–22.

Teeuwen, Rudolphus (ed.). *Crossings: Travel, Art, Literature, Politics*. Taipei: Bookman, 2001. Pp. xi + 300; illustrations.

Thomas, Richard F. *Virgil and the Augustan Reception*. Cambridge: Cambridge University Press, 2001. Pp. xx + 324; bibliography.

Thompson, Helen. "How *The Wanderer* Works: Reading Burney and Bourdieu." *ELH*, 68 (2001), 965–89.

Thompson, James. "Teaching Notes." *Radical Teacher: A Socialist, Feminist, and Anti-Racist Journal on the Theory and Practice of Teaching*, 61 (2001), 43–44.

Thompson, Peggy. "Abuse and Atonement: The Passion of Clarissa Harlowe." Pp. 152–69 of *Passion and Virtue: Essays on the Novels of Samuel Richardson*. Edited by David Blewett. Toronto: University of Toronto Press, 2001.

Thomson, Peter. "English Renaissance and Restoration Theatre." Pp. 173–219 of *The Oxford Illustrated History of Theatre*. Edited by John Russell Brown. New York: Oxford University Press, 2001.

Thorn, Jennifer. "'Althea Must Be Open'd': Eliza Haywood, Individualism, and Reproductivity." *Eighteenth-Century Women*, 1 (2001), 95–127.

VI: British Literatures

Thorne, Christian. "Thumbing Our Nose at the Public Sphere: Satire, the Market, and the Invention of Literature." *PMLA*, 116 (2001), 531–44.

Tilby, Michael J. "Opposition and Its Literary Expression in the Late Restoration: A 'Self-Conscious Model'." Pp. 88–104 of *Confrontations: Politics and Aesthetics in Nineteenth-Century France*. Edited by Kathryn M. Grossman, Michael E. Lane, Benedicte Monicat, and Willa Z. Silverman. Amsterdam: Rodopi, 2001.

Todd, Dennis, and Cynthia Wall (eds.). *Eighteenth-Century Genre and Culture: Serious Reflections on Occasional Forms: Essays in Honor of J. Paul Hunter*. Newark: University of Delaware Press, 2001. Pp. 316; bibliography.

Toker, Leona. "Conspicuous Leisure and Invidious Sexuality in Jane Austen's *Mansfield Park*." *Connotations: A Journal for Critical Debate*, 11 (2001), 222–40.

Toledano Buendia, Carmen. "Apuntes sobre la Traduccion de la Novela Inglesa del Siglo XVIII en Espana." Pp. 23–30 of *Polifonias Textuales: Ensayos in Honorem Maria Del Carmen Fernandez Leal*. Edited by Manuel Brito and Juan Ignacio Oliva. La Laguna: Revista Canaria de Estudios Ingleses (RCEI), 2001.

Toledano Buendia, Carmen. "*Robinson Crusoe* Naufraga en Tierras Españolas." *Babel: Revue Internationale de la Traduction/International Journal of Translation*, 47 (2001), 35–48.

Tomaselli, Sylvana. "The Most Public Sphere of All: The Family." Pp. 239–56 of *Women, Writing and the Public Sphere, 1700–1830*. Edited by Elizabeth Eger, Charlotte Grant, Cliona O Gallchoir, and Penny Warburton. Cambridge: Cambridge University Press, 2001.

Tomlinson, Charles. "Why Dryden's Translations Matter." *Translation & Literature*, 10 (2001), 3–20.

Tomlinson, Sophie. "Harking Back to Henrietta: The Sources of Female Greatness in Katherine Philips's *Pompey*." Pp. 179–90 of *Women Writing, 1550–1750*. Edited by Jo Wallwork and Paul Salzman. Bundoora: Meridian, 2001.

Tóibín, Colm (ed.). *The Penguin Book of Irish Fiction*. New York: Penguin Books, 2001. Pp. xxxiv + 1,085; bibliography.

Tosi, Laura (ed.). *Hearts of Lightness: The Magic of Children's Literature*. Venice: Cafoscarina, 2001. Pp. 197.

Trevor, William (ed.). *The Oxford Book of Irish Short Stories*. Oxford: New York, 2001. Pp. xvi + 563.

Troost, Linda, and Sayre N. Greenfield . "The Mouse That Roared: Patricia Rozema's *Mansfield Park*." Pp. 188–204 of *Jane Austen in Hollywood*. Edited by Linda Troost and Sayre N. Greenfield. Lexington: University Press of Kentucky, 2001.

Troost, Linda, and Sayre Greenfield. "Watching Ourselves Watching." Pp. 1–12 of *Jane Austen in Hollywood*. Edited by Linda Troost and Sayre N. Greenfield. Lexington: University Press of Kentucky, 2001.

Troost, Linda, and Sayre N. Greenfield. (eds). *Jane Austen in Hollywood*. Lexington: University Press of Kentucky, 2001. Pp. 221; bibliography; illustrations.

Few scholarly works excite sufficient demand to require a second edition within three years of the first publication, but this collection of essays on Austen and Hollywood has attracted an audience far beyond academe. The volume analyzes the recent spate of film adaptations of Austen's novels, not simply in terms of the quality or "faithfulness" of the productions but for what they reveal about their fans. While each contributor exhibits a solid grounding in Austen scholarship, the collection is at least as concerned with contemporary culture as with Austen's milieu, and although the essays are serious and scholarly, they are calculated to be intelligible to the thoughtful layperson. As the editors point out, adaptations of the novels "have more to tell us about our own moment in time than about Austen's writing. In watching them, we watch ourselves." The included essays address the familiar themes of property, gender, and class, but turn the magnifying class upon late twentieth-century viewers and critics. The self-congratulatory attitude of those who pride themselves on their viewing discernment comes under the microscope, as do shifting concepts of masculinity and romance. American reception of British productions, the differences between British and American directors, and the construction of American nostalgia for a country-house culture are other pertinent topics. Several essays—notably by Devoney Looser, Lisa Hopkins, and Kristen Fleiger Samuelian—grapple with filmmakers' ambiguous, possibly feminist, interpretations of the novels: the authors do not always agree about the degree to which such interpretations succeed. This second edition includes one new essay on Patricia Rozema's *Mansfield Park*.—Leslie Richardson

Tseëlon, Efrat (ed.). *Masquerade and Identities: Essays on Gender, Sexuality, and Marginality*. New York: Routledge, 2001. Pp. xx + 180; illustrations.

Tyler, Natalie. *The Friendly Jane Austen: A Well-Mannered Introduction to a Lady of Sense & Sensibility*. New York: Penguin Books, 2001. Pp. xix + 299; bibliography; illustrations.

Uhm, Yong-Hee. "Locke, Vico, Wordsworth." *Nineteenth-Century Literature in English*, 4 (2001), 147–70.

Uhrig, Reinhard. *Changing Ideas, Changing Texts: First-Person Novels in the Early Modern Period, Francion, Courasche and Moll Flanders*. New York: P. Lang, 2001. Pp. 286; bibliography; illustrations.

VI: British Literatures

Varney, Andrew. "Philips's 'Deluded Peasant' and Addison's 'Enchanted Hero.'" *Notes and Queries*, 48 (2001), 403–05.

Vasconcelos, Sandra Guardini T. *Literature and Cinema: Images of Feminity in Pride and Prejudice*, (Working Papers in British Studies 5.) São Paulo: Humanitas/FFLCH-USP, 2001. Pp. 31.

Velcic, Vlatka. "Postmodern and Postcolonial Portrayals of Colonial History: Contemporary Novels About the Eighteenth Century." *Tennessee Philological Bulletin*, 38 (2001), 41–48.

Viano, Francesca Lidia. "Barbarism and Religion: Il Gibbon Di Pocock." *Pensiero Politico: Rivista di Storia delle Idee Politiche e Sociali*, 34 (2001), 119–25.

Vincendeau, Ginette (ed.). *Film/Literature/Heritage: A Sight and Sound Reader*. London: British Film Institute, 2001. Pp. xxxi + 300; illustrations.

Voogd, Peter de. "Uncle Toby in 3d." *Shandean: An Annual Devoted to Laurence Sterne and His Works*, 12 (2001), 122–24.

Wahrman, Dror. "The English Problem of Identity in the American Revolution." *American Historical Review*, 106 (2001), 1236–62.

Waldron, Mary. *Jane Austen and the Fiction of Her Time*. Cambridge: Cambridge University Press, 2001. Pp. ix + 194; bibliography.

Walpole, Horace. *The Castle of Otranto*. Edited by Michael Gamer. London: Penguin, 2001. Pp. xiii + 159.

Walk, Lori. "Questing for Family in *Joseph Andrews* and *David Simple*." *Eighteenth-Century Novel*, 1 (2001), 237–52.

Walker, William. "Addison's Mastery of Locke." Pp. 45–78 of *1650–1850: Ideas, Aesthetics, and Inquiries in the Early Modern Era*. Volume 6. Edited by Kevin L. Cope. New York: AMS Press, 2001.

Wallace, Elizabeth Kowaleski. "Theatricality and Cosmopolitanism in Hannah Cowley's *The Belle's Stratagem*." *Comparative Drama*, 35 (2001), 415–33.

Wallace, Miriam. "Mary Hays's 'Female Philosopher': Constructing Revolutionary Subjects." Pp. 233–60 of *Rebellious Hearts: British Women Writers and the French Revolution*. Edited by Adriana Craciun, Kari E. Lokke, and Madelyn Gutwirth. Albany: State University of New York, 2001.

Wallwork, Jo. "Old Worlds and New: Margaret Cavendish's Response to Robert Hooke's Micrographia." Pp. 191–200 of *Women Writing, 1550–1750*. Edited by Jo Wallwork and Paul Salzman. Bundoora: Meridian, 2001.

Wallwork, Jo, and Paul Salzman (eds.). *Women Writing, 1550–1750*. Bundoora: Meridian, 2001. Pp. 256.

Walsh, Sean. "'Our Lineal Descents and Clans': Dryden's Fables Ancient and Modern and Cultural Politics in the 1690s." Pp. 175–200 of *John Dryden: A Tercentenary Miscellany*. Edited by Susan Green and Steven N. Zwicker. San Marino: Huntington Library, 2001.

Warburton, Penny. "Theorising Public Opinion: Elizabeth Hamilton's Model of Self, Sympathy and Society." Pp. 257–73 of *Women, Writing and the Public Sphere, 1700–1830*. Edited by Elizabeth Eger, Charlotte, Grant, Cliona O Gallchoir, and Penny Warburton. Cambridge: Cambridge University Press, 2001.

Warner, Christopher J. "The Question of Misogynistic Polemic in Elkanah Settle's the Female Prelate (1680 and 1689)." *Restoration: Studies in English Literary Culture, 1660–1700*, 25 (2001), 19–34.

Watanabe, Koji. "1727nen No Jonasan Suwifuto (1): Saigo No Kikoku." *Eigo Seinen/Rising Generation*, 147 (2001), 408–10.

Watanabe, Koji. "1727nen No Jonason Suwifuto (2): Mohitotsu No Sanbun." *Eigo Seinen/Rising Generation*, 147 (2001), 486–88.

Watanabe, Koji. "1727nen No Jonasan Suwifuto (3): Suwifuto No Raillery." *Eigo Seinen/Rising Generation*, 147 (2001), 551–53.

Waters, John. "Topographical Poetry and the Politics of Culture in Ireland, 1772–1820." Pp. 221–44 of *Romantic Generations: Essays in Honor of Robert F. Gleckner*. Edited by Ghislaine McDayter, Guinn Batten, Barry Milligan, and Peter Manning. Lewisburg: Bucknell University Press, 2001.

Weinbrot, Howard D. "Johnson and the Jacobite Truffles." *Age of Johnson*, 12 (2001), 273–290.

Weinman, Jaime J. "Dryden and Purcell's King Arthur: A Production History." *Restoration and 18th Century Theatre Research*, 16 (2001), 40–52.

Wenner, Barbara Britton. "From 'Four White Cows Disposed at Equal Distances' to the 'Fine, Shady Bower': Importance of Place in the *Juvenilia*." *Persuasions: Journal of the Jane Austen Society of North America*, 23 (2001), 148–53.

West, Russell. "All Sujet and No Fabula? *Tristram Shandy* and Russian Formalism." Pp. 283–302 of *Erzählen und Erzähltheorie Im 20. Jahrhundert*. Edited by Jorg Helbig. Heidelberg: Carl Winter Universitatsverlag, 2001.

West, Russell. "To the Unknown Reader: Constructing Absent Readership in the Eighteenth-Century Novel: Fielding, Sterne and Richardson." *Arbeiten aus Anglistik und Amerikanistik*, 26 (2001), 105–23.

Westfall, Marilyn. "A Sermon by the 'Queen of Whores.'" *SEL*, 41 (2001), 483–97.

Whyman, Susan. "Gentle Companions: Single Women and their Letters in Late Stuart England." Pp. 177–93 of *Early Modern Women's Letter Writing, 1450–1700*. Edited by James Daybell. New York: Palgrave, 2001.

Wieselhuber, Franz. "Models of National Identity in Restoration Pamphlets." Pp. 131–48 of *Writing the Early Modern English Nation: The Transformation of National Identity in Sixteenth- and Seventeenth-Century England*. Edited by Herbert Grabes. Amsterdam: Rodopi, 2001.

Wiesenfarth, Joseph. "Jane Austen's Family of Fiction: From Henry and Eliza to Darcy and Eliza." *Persuasions: The Jane Austen Journal On-Line*, 22 (2001).

Williams, Carolyn. "Inhumanly Brought Back to Life and Misery: Mary Wollstonecraft, *Frankenstein*, and the Royal Humane Society." *Women's Writing*, 8 (2001), 213-34.

Williams, Carolyn D. "Women Behaving Well: Early Modern Images of Female Courage." Pp. 49–75 of *Presenting Gender: Changing Sex in Early-Modern Culture*. (Bucknell Studies in Eighteenth-Century Literature and Culture.) Edited by Chris Mounsey. Lewisburg: Bucknell University Press, 2001.

Williamson, Karin. "Voice, Gender, and Augustan Verse Epistle." Pp. 76–93 of *Presenting Gender: Changing Sex in Early-Modern Culture*. (Bucknell Studies in Eighteenth-Century Literature and Culture.) Edited by Chris Mounsey. Lewisburg: Bucknell University Press, 2001.

Wilner, Arlene Fish. "'Thou Hast Made a Rake a Preacher': Beauty and the Beast in Richardson's *Pamela*." *Eighteenth-Century Fiction*, 13 (2001), 529–60.

Wilputte, Earla A. "Eliza Haywood's Frederick, Duke of Brunswick-Lunenburgh." *SEL*, 41 (2001), 499–514.

Wilson, Fiona. "The Diary of Thomas Campbell: An Irishman in England." *Wasafiri: Journal of Caribbean, African, Asian and Associated Literatures and Film*, 34 (2001), 24–28.

Wilson, Margaret. *Jane Austen's Family and Tonbridge*. Chawton: Jane Austen Society, 2001. Pp. 60; bibliography; illustrations; maps.

Wilton-Ely, John. "'Gingerbread and Sippets of Embroidery': Horace Walpole and Robert Adam." *Eighteenth-Century Life*, 25 (2001), 147–69.

Wiltshire, John. "Mrs. Bennet's Least Favorite Daughter." *Persuasions: Journal of the Jane Austen Society of North America*, 23 (2001), 179–87.

Wiltshire, John. *Recreating Jane Austen* Cambridge University Press, 2001. Pp. 192; bibliography.

In some ways, John Wiltshire's *Recreating Jane Austen* extends the work of his *Jane Austen and the Body* (1992), which focused on desire *in* the works of Austen. In this book, he focuses on desire *for* the works of Austen. Wiltshire explains that *Recreating Jane Austen* focuses upon "the general topic of artistic recreation and remaking, and the role Jane Austen plays in the contemporary cultural imagination" (ix), emphasizing the concept of creativity inherent in adaptation. In stressing the creative nature of recreations, Wiltshire centers the third chapter on the idea that Austen herself adapted Shakespeare. But Wiltshire's point is not that Austen somehow copied Shakespeare's plots or characters; instead, he suggests that Austen intellectually "processed" Shakespeare's works in a sophisticated manner that bears a similarity to the ways in which some filmmakers have "processed" Austen. In fact, Wiltshire proposes that scriptwriters and filmmakers "be understood as readers" (5) and that, "[r]ather than thinking of these works as piracies or abductions of the original text, I argue that they are best read as recreations" (6). This, then, is the reason for reintroducing creativity into critical discourse, and Wiltshire uses the work of psychoanalyst Donald Winnicott to underpin his own discussions of creativity. By examining not only recreations of Austen but also Austen's recreations and the creations of her characters, Wiltshire illuminates the inventiveness of influence from many points of view in a thorough discussion of the truly creative nature of adaptation.

Yet Wiltshire occasionally raises some interesting issues that tantalize more than they inform the reader, such as when he asserts that the adaptation or remaking "of earlier works into other media is an important feature of the current landscape" (2) without explaining how or why—and without directly explaining how current reworkings of Austen function differently from past appropriations. For example, he asserts that the topic of his book "is not so much the imitations or recreations of Jane Austen, as the process of imitation or recreation itself" (7) without delineating the reasons why Austen should serve as the book's focus. Similarly, Wiltshire acknowledges that Austen had to learn to adapt the "inwardness" of Shakespearean soliloquies into a technique more suited to the novel, doing so through the method of free, indirect speech. He further declares that film adaptations will need to find a way to express "inwardness" commensurate with the abilities and limitations of that media. But in what ways does this make unique the current landscape of adaptation?

However, these unexplored issues only point to the richness of Austen studies. Wiltshire's book affirms that "of all the writers in the canon, Jane Austen is the one around whom [...] a] fantasy of access, [...] a] dream of possession, weaves its most powerful spell" (17). The continuing challenge to Austen scholars is to pursue the kinds of important issues that Wiltshire raises in an effort to establish the reasons for the spell under which Austen places writers and re-creators.—Kathryn Strong

Wind, Astrid. "Irish Legislative Independence and the Politics of Staging American Indians in the 1790s." *Symbiosis: A Journal of Anglo-American Literary Relations,* 5 (2001), 1–16.

Winn, James A. "Past and Present in Dryden's Fables." Pp. 157–74 of *John Dryden: A Tercentenary Miscellany.* Edited by Susan Green and Steven N. Zwicker. San Marino: Huntington Library, 2001.

Wiseman, Susan. "Catherine Macaulay: History, Republicanism and the Public Sphere." Pp. 181–99 of *Women, Writing and the Public Sphere, 1700–1830.* Edited by Elizabeth Eger, Charlotte Grant, Cliona O Gallchoir, and Penny Warburton. Cambridge: Cambridge University Press, 2001.

Wood, Nigel. "Jonathan Swift: *Gulliver's Travels.*" Pp. 63–77 of *Literature in Context.* Edited by Rick Rylance and Judy Simons. Houndmills: Palgrave, 2001.

Woolf, Virginia. "Jane Austen at Sixty." *Brick,* 68 (2001), 152–54.

Wright, Glenn. "Geoffrey the Unbarbarous: Chaucerian 'Genius' and Eighteenth-Century Antimedievalism." *English Studies,* 82 (2001), 193–202.

Wu, Eleanor B. Morris. "A Variety of Narrative Voices in Henry Fielding's *Jonathan Wild.*" *Fu Jen Studies: Literature & Linguistics,* 34 (2001), 75–98.

Yamanouchi, Hisaaki. "The Fair Commands the Song: William Cowper and Women." *Wordsworth Circle,* 32 (2001), 101–06.

Yang, Wonkyung. "'My Mother's Marriage Settlement': The Representation of Marriage Contract in *Tristram Shandy.*" *Journal of English Language and Literature/Yongo Yongmunhak*, 47 (2001), 3–17.

Yoder, R. Paul. "Blake's Pope." Pp. 23–42 of *Romantic Generations: Essays in Honor of Robert F. Gleckner.* Edited by Ghislaine McDayter, Barry Milligan, Peter Manning, and Guinn Batten. Lewisburg: Bucknell University Press, 2001.

Youngberg, Quentin. "The Sensitive Swift: Coming to Terms with the Dean's Beneficent Satire." Pp. 33–38 of *Proceedings of the Eighth Annual Northern Plains Conference on Earlier British Literature.* Edited by Robert J. De Smith. Sioux Center: Dordt College, 2001.

Zelle, Carsten. "Die Geburt der Natur aus dem Geiste der Rhetorik: Zur Schematisierung von Natur und Genie bei Dennis und Goethe." Pp. 145–67 of *Erschriebene Natur: Internationale Perspektiven Auf Texte Des 18. Jahrhunderts*. Edited by Michael Scheffel and Dietmar Gotsch. Bern: Peter Lang, 2001.

Zimpfer, Nathalie. "Tradition et Contradiction: *A Tale of a Tub* de Swift." *Bulletin de la Société d'Études Anglo-Américaines des XVIIe et XVIIIe Siècles,* 53 (2001), 161–73.

Zionkowski, Linda. *Men's Work: Gender, Class, and the Professionalization of Poetry, 1660–1784*. New York: Palgrave, 2001. Pp. viii + 279; bibliography.

Zunshine, Lisa. "Eighteenth-Century Print Culture and the 'Truth' of Fictional Narrative." *Philosophy and Literature,* 25 (2001), 215–32.

VII: New World Literatures and Languages

American Literature and Language

Adams, Stephen. *The Best and Worst Country in the World: Perspectives on Early Virginia Landscape.* Charlottesville: University Press of Virginia, 2001. Pp. xii + 305; illustrations; maps.

Andrews, William L. "Benjamin Banneker's Revision of Thomas Jefferson: Conscience Versus Science in the Early American Antislavery Debate." Pp. 218–41 of *Genius in Bondage: Literature of the Early Black Atlantic.* Edited by Vincent Carretta and Philip Gould. Lexington: University Press of Kentucky, 2001.

Arch, Stephen Carl. *After Franklin: The Emergence of Autobiography in Post-Revolutionary America, 1770–1830.* Hanover: University Press of New England, 2001. Pp. xiv + 241.

Arner, Robert D. "The Sources and Significance of Joseph Dumbleton's 'The Paper Mill': Augustan American Poetics and the Culture of Print in Colonial Williamsburg." Pp. 199–224 of *Finding Colonial Americas: Essays Honoring J. A. Leo Lemay.* Edited by Carla Mulford and David S. Shields. Newark: University of Delaware Press, 2001.

Bacon, Jacqueline. "Rhetoric and Identity in Absalom Jones and Richard Allen's *Narrative of the Proceedings of the Black People, During the Late Awful Calamity in Philadelphia.*" *Pennsylvania Magazine of History and Biography*, 125 (2001), 61–90.

Bauer, Ralph. "Millennium's Darker Side: The Missionary Utopias of Franciscan New Spain and Puritan New England." Pp. 33–49 of *Finding Colonial Americas: Essays Honoring J. A. Leo*

Lemay. Edited by Carla Mulford and David S. Shields. Newark: University of Delaware Press, 2001.

Bross, Kristina. "Dying Saints, Vanishing Savages: 'Dying Indian Speeches' in Colonial New England Literature." *Early American Literature*, 36 (2001), 325–52.

Byrd, William, II. *The Commonplace Book of William Byrd II of Westover*. Edited by Kevin Berland, Jan Kirsten Gilliam, and Kenneth A. Lockridge. Chapel Hill: Published for the Omohundro Institute of Early American History and Culture, Williamsburg, Virginia, by the University of North Carolina Press, 2001. Pp. xv + 319.

Cahill, Edward. "An Adventurous and Lawless Fancy: Charles Brockden Brown's Aesthetic State." *Early American Literature*, 36 (2001), 31–70.

Carretta, Vincent. "'Property of Author': Olaudah Equiano's Place in the History of the Book." Pp. 130–50 of *Genius in Bondage: Literature of the Early Black Atlantic*. Edited by Vincent Carretta and Philip Gould. Lexington: University Press of Kentucky, 2001.

Carretta, Vincent, and Philip Gould (eds.). *Genius in Bondage: Literature of the Early Black Atlantic*. Lexington: University Press of Kentucky, 2001. Pp. 272; illustrations; map.

Castillo, Susan, and Ivy Schweitzer (eds.). *The Literatures of Colonial America: An Anthology*. Malden: Blackwell Publishers, 2001. Pp. xxii + 602; illustrations; maps.

Carson, David J. "Edward Taylor and Puritan Entrepreneurship." *Studies in Puritan American Spirituality*, 7 (2001), 111–41.

Cope, Kevin L. "How General George Outlived His Own Funeral Orations." Pp. 65–98 of *George Washington in and as Culture*. Edited by Kevin L. Cope, William S. Pederson, and Frank Williams. New York: AMS Press, 2001.

Cowell, Pattie. "'Much depends upon my knowing': The Education of Polly Hewson." Pp. 316–30 of *Finding Colonial Americas: Essays Honoring J. A. Leo Lemay*. Edited by Carla Mulford and David S. Shields. Newark: University of Delaware Press, 2001.

Crain, Caleb. *American Sympathy: Men, Friendship and Literature in the New Nation*. New Haven: Yale University Press, 2001. Pp. x + 310; illustrations.

Caleb Crain's *American Sympathy: Men, Friendship, and Literature in the New Nation* contributes substantially to the growing body of scholarship on masculinity in American culture of the eighteenth and nineteenth centuries. In an idiosyncratic work that melds literary criticism with ample amounts of history and biography, Crain argues that the diaries of John Fishbourne Mifflin and James Gibson, the letters and novels of Charles Brockden Brown, the journals and essays of Ralph Waldo Emerson, and Herman Melville's *Billy Budd* are linked as literary works by their efforts to "represent a man's feelings for another man" (9). Crain names this feeling of friendship "sympathy," and his aim is first to show that this sympathy, a concept alien to twenty-first-century readers, was crucial to the nation and to the nation's literature at its birth and second to show the way sympathy itself and the representations of it changed as the nation changed.

At the start, *American Sympathy* makes its case for the cultural importance of sympathy by retelling the story of John André, the British officer who was hanged in America for conspiring with Benedict Arnold. The decision to hang Andre was made by George Washington over the objection of many, notably among them Alexander Hamilton, who came to know and love Andre while he was imprisoned in America. Even for Washington, the decision to execute Andre was a political necessity but not a desirable one. (Arnold was the true villain and thus the preferred choice for execution, but he had escaped to England.) Before and after his capture, Andre displayed honor, accepting his fate with grace. According to Crain, while Andre sided with the enemy he "stood for...an ideal to which America as a nation aspired—the disinterested fraternity of men" (2). This ideal of fraternity, of sympathy, mattered so much because America was to be a nation in which the more traditional bonds that connected people would be severed in the name of liberty. How the role of sympathy changed both in men's lives and in literature is Crain's topic as his study moves forward.

This conceptual framework, while perhaps overly broad, nonetheless gives Crain considerable space for imaginative rereadings of canonical American texts and the lives of their authors. In his study of Charles Brockden Brown, for example, Crain examines the novelist's early letters to and from male friends as a means to reconsidering his novels. "Brown," Crain writes, "seems to have learned how to turn sympathy into literature by using a circle of intimate male friends as guineau pigs for his experiments" (14). Similarly, Crain begins his fascinatingly detailed study of Emerson by contrasting Emerson's largely passionless second marriage ("I marry impersonally" Emerson wrote in his journal in 1840 [qtd. in Crain 179]) with more emotional relationships Emerson formed with male friends. Focusing on Emerson's biography, his writings in his journal, and his essays, Crain argues that Emerson essentially transferred the feeling of sympathy (with distinct sexual overtones)—through a process Crain names "hierotomy"—away from his male friends and into his writing: "the essay 'Friendship' has cut itself off from the desire that generated it, its author's wish to reach another man" (234). Crain boldly links this separation to the emergence of the American literary marketplace, in which, he argues, "the work had to be cut off from the author so that any purchaser of the text could find meaning and pleasure there" (234).

The final chapter is an inventive rereading on Melville's *Billy Budd* as a late-nineteenth-century enactment of the tragic consequences of the severance of sympathy from its object; Crain asserts that it is a "strong negative example of the configuration of literature and sentiment" that is his subject (269). In reading Captain Vere's decision to execute Billy Budd as a consequence of what happens when sympathy is separated from its object, Crain challenges both traditional readings that valorize Vere and more recent readings that find latent homosexual desire to be the novel's driving force. Crain argues that the story of Billy's execution constitutes an angry reprisal of the story of John Andre. Ending the study this way provides a symmetry that befits a work so elegantly argued.—Evan Brier

Craven, Wayne. "Washington Allston and *Ut Pictura Poesis*: The Romantic Artist as Poet and Cultivated Intellectual." Pp. 261–73 of *Finding Colonial Americas: Essays Honoring J. A. Leo Lemay*. Edited by Carla Mulford and David S. Shields. Newark: University of Delaware Press, 2001.

Daly, Robert. "Lexias and Agency in Anne Bradstreet." *Studies in Puritan American Spirituality*, 7 (2001), 1–22.

Desrochers, Robert, Jr. "'Surprizing Deliverance'? Slavery and Freedom, Language, and Identity in the *Narrative* of Briton Hammon, 'a Negro Man.'" Pp. 190–98 of *Genius in Bondage: Literature of the Early Black Atlantic*. Edited by Vincent Carretta and Philip Gould. Lexington: University Press of Kentucky, 2001.

Edwards, Jonathan. *Sermons and Discourses*. Edited by M. X. Lesser. (The Works of Jonathan Edwards 19.) New Haven: Yale University Press, 2001. Pp. xiv + 849.

Egan, Jim. "'To Bring *Mary-land* into *England*: English Identities in Colonial American Writing." Pp. 125–36 of *Finding Colonial Americas: Essays Honoring J. A. Leo Lemay*. Edited by Carla Mulford and David S. Shields. Newark: University of Delaware Press, 2001.

Ellis, Markman. "Ignatius Sancho's *Letters*: Sentimental Libertinism and the Politics of Form." Pp. 199–217 of *Genius in Bondage: Literature of the Early Black Atlantic*. Edited by Vincent Carretta and Philip Gould. Lexington: University Press of Kentucky, 2001.

Elrod, Eileen Razzari. "Moses and the Egyptian: Religious Authority in Olaudah Equiano's *Interesting Narrative*." *African American Review*, 35 (2001), 409–25.

Equiano, Olaudah. *The Interesting Narrative of the Life of Olaudah Equiano*. Edited by Angelo Costanzo. Peterborough: Broadview Press, 2001. Pp. 330.

Fink, Beatrice. "Saint-John de Crèvecoeur's Tale of a Tuber." *Eighteenth-Century Life*, 25 (2001), 225–34.

Finseth, Ian. "'A Melancholy Tale': Rhetoric, Fiction, and Passion in *The Coquette*." *Studies in the Novel*, 33 (2001), 125–59.

Flesch, William. "The Conjuror's Trick, or How to Rhyme." *Literary Imagination*, 3 (2001), 184–204.

Frank, Armin Paul. "Ebenezer Cook's *The Sot-Weed Factor*: An Intercultural Reading." Pp. 64–78 of *Finding Colonial Americas: Essays Honoring J. A. Leo Lemay*. Edited by Carla Mulford and David S. Shields. Newark: University of Delaware Press, 2001.

Frankel, Matthew Cordova. "'Nature's Nation' Revisited: Citizenship and the Sublime in Thomas Jefferson's *Notes on the State of Virginia*." *American Literature*, 73 (2001), 695–726.

Gautier, Gary. "Slavery and the Fashioning of Race in *Oroonoko*, *Robinson Crusoe*, and Equiano's *Life*." *Eighteenth Century: Theory and Interpretation*, 42 (2001), 161–79.

Gildersleeve, D. Britton. "'I Had a Religious Mother': Maternal Ancestry, Female Spaces, and Spiritual Synthesis in Elizabeth Ashbridge's *Account*." *Early American Literature*, 36 (2001), 371–94.

Giles, Paul. *Transatlantic Insurrections: British Culture and the Formation of American Literature, 1730–1860*. Philadelphia: University of Pennsylvania Press, 2001. Pp. 262.

Paul Giles's *Transatlantic Insurrections: British Culture and the Formation of American Literature, 1730-1860* makes a compelling case for reconsidering the relationship between British and early American literature from a comparative perspective. Giles's rejection of the Cold War-influenced, exceptionalist notion of a distinctly "American" literature that held sway in the academy for decades is by now commonplace. However, Giles also finds fault with more recent formulations of early American literature as essentially postcolonial, a product of a relationship that was imperial both politically and culturally. Thus the creative call for a comparative study of British and early American literature: "I am concerned," he writes in his introduction, "with American literature not as subordinate to an imperial British literature, but rather as something that develops parallel to it" (2). As a result, Giles's reading of the relationship between British and American culture revolves less around "questions of ethnocentric consciousness and conflict" and more on "the more discomfiting figures of mirroring and twinning, where mutual identities are not so much independently asserted but sacrilegiously travestied" (2).

The meaning of this formulation is slow to reveal itself, but that does not make Giles's early chapters any less insightful. The first two chapters focus on the generally neglected influence of Alexander Pope on obscure early American poets Mather Byles and John Trumbull. Typically, Giles notes, the influence of Pope on early American literature is suppressed in order to make the case of Milton's impact on the revolutionary American imagination. But Pope's popularity in America was considerable, and so too was his influence. Using Pope to draw attention to what is distinctive in Byles and Trumbull and then using Byles and Trumbull as a means to rereading Pope as a maker of "devilishly two-faced" art (69), Giles shows the value of what he calls his "transatlantic framework" (69) before moving on to more canonical American subjects and their English counterparts.

Chapters Three and Four focus on two "exemplars of American identity," as Giles puts it (70), Benjamin Franklin's *Autobiography* and Thomas Jefferson's *Notes on the State of Virginia*. Franklin's text is read in unlikely relation to the novels of Samuel Richardson. As in previous chapters, Giles's insights along the way—fresh readings of both Franklin and Richardson that focus on both as writers of wholly paradoxical guides to virtue—are sometimes more convincing and more concrete than his summation about the relationship between them, which is obscure: "the textual productions of both Franklin and Richardson institutionalize transgressive styles of duality as they circulate according to Enlightenment principles of transnational comparison and formal exchange" (91).

Subsequent chapters continue in this vein and flesh out some of Giles's theoretical formulations. Starting with the rarely noted fact that Jane Austen wrote her most celebrated novels while England was at war with America, Giles finds connections between Austen's family romances and the ultimate breakdown of the dysfunctional family that America and England once constituted. Similarly, he finds that the works of Washington Irving can be read in a different light "if they are understood as reflecting the suppressed trauma of internecine conflict in the first generation after the American Revolution" (142). Irving, Giles argues, is perhaps the best example of what the transnational approach can do for American writers, because he best exemplifies "an American author whose status is diminished by any forced affiliation with agendas of literary nationalism" (142). Giles next aims, in a chapter that draws on Kristeva's theoretical model of perversion, to revise our notion of Hawthorne and Trollope as "embodiments of native literary traditions" (165), before concluding with a perhaps too-brief consideration of

Equiano and Poe. As the chapters progress, Giles's goals become clearer: to draw particular attention to burlesque elements in American literature, often written in imitation of British writers, that have been suppressed from more conventional formulations of distinctively American literature. His larger case, that the emergence of these two national literary traditions are shaped in profound ways by the relationship between the two nations, is convincingly made.

Giles's argument is sometimes obscure but it is always imaginative and often compelling. His grasp of recent scholarship, moreover, is outstanding; generous allusions to the work of others makes *Transatlantic Insurrections* exceptionally useful for scholars of early American and seventeenth- and eighteenth-century British literatures.—Evan Brier

Gillespie, Joanna Bowen. *The Life and Times of Martha Laurens Ramsay, 1759–1811*. Columbia: University of South Carolina Press, 2001. Pp. xxviii + 315; illustrations; maps.

Gould, Philip. "'Remarkable Liberty': Language and Identity in Eighteenth-Century Black Autobiography." Pp. 116–29 of *Genius in Bondage: Literature of the Early Black Atlantic*. Edited by Vincent Carretta and Philip Gould. Lexington: University Press of Kentucky, 2001.

Gura, Philip F. "Writing the Literary History of Eighteenth-Century America: A Prospect." Pp. 164–85 of *The World Turned Upside Down: The State of Eighteenth-Century American Studies at the Beginning of the Twenty-First Century*. Edited by Michael V. Kennedy and William G. Shade. Bethlehem: Lehigh University Press, 2001.

Guruswamy, Rosemany Fithian. "'Thou Hast the Holy Word': Jupiter Hammon's 'Regards' to Phillis Wheatley." Pp. 190–98 of *Genius in Bondage: Literature of the Early Black Atlantic*. Edited by Vincent Carretta and Philip Gould. Lexington: University Press of Kentucky, 2001.

Hucko, Christine. "Female Writers, Women's Networks, and the Preservation of Culture: The Schwenkfelder Women of Eighteenth-Century Pennsylvania." *Pennsylvania History*, 68 (2001), 101–30.

Imbarrato, Susan Clair. "Genteel Confusion: Reading Class Structure in Dr. Alexander Hamilton's *Itinerarium*." Pp. 153–69 of *Finding Colonial Americas: Essays Honoring J. A. Leo Lemay*. Edited by Carla Mulford and David S. Shields. Newark: University of Delaware Press, 2001.

Kamrath, Mark L. "Charles Brockden Brown and the 'Art of he Historian': An Essay Concerning (Post) modern Historical Understanding." *Journal of the Early Republic*, 21 (2001), 231–60.

VII: New World Literatures and Languages

Kazanjian, David. "Charles brockden Brown's Biloquial Nation: National Culture and White Settler Colonialism in *Memoirs of Carwin the Biloquist*." *American Literature*, 73 (2001), 459–96.

Kennedy, Jennifer T. "Dath Effects: Revisiting the Conceit of Franklin's *Memoir*." *Early American Literature*, 36 (2001), 201–34.

Kennedy, Michael V., and William G. Shade (eds). *The World Turned Upside Down: The State of Eighteenth-Century American Studies at the Beginning of the Twenty-First Century*. Bethlehem: Lehigh University Press, 2001. Pp. 336.

Kullman, Colby H. "Benjamin Franklin's Humor and the America Revolution: An Explosion of Popular Satirical Techniques." Pp. 269–77 of *George Washington in and as Culture*. Edited by Kevin L. Cope, William S. Pederson, and Frank Williams. New York: AMS Press, 2001.

Kutchen, Larry. "The 'Vulgar Thread of the Canvas': Revolution and the Picturesque in Ann Eliza Bleeker, Crèvecoeur, and Charles Brockden Brown." *Early American Literature*, 36 (2001), 395–425.

Larkin, Edward. "Seeing Through Language: Narrative, Portraiture, and Character in Peter Oliver's *The Origin & Progress of the American Revolution*." *Early American Literature*, 36 (2001), 427–54.

Lemay, J. A. Leo. "An Attribution of *Reflections on Courtship and Marriage* (1746), to Benjamin Franklin." *Papers of the Bibliographic Society of America*, 95 (2001), 59–96.

Lindman, Janet Moore, and Michelle Lise Tarter (eds.). *A Centre of Wonders: The Body in Early America*. Ithaca: Cornell University Press, 2001. Pp. vii + 283; illustrations.

Little, Ann M. "'Shoot that rogue for he hath an Englishman's coat on!': Cultural Cross-Dressing on the New England Frontier, 1620–1760." *New England Quarterly*, 74 (2001), 238–73.

Longacre, Mark Garrett. "Timothy Dwight's Rhetorical Ideology of Taste in Federalist Connecticut." *Rhetorica*, 19 (2001), 93–124.

Mattek, Michael C. "A Curious Little book: Francis Glass's *Washingtonii Vita*." Pp. 179–96 of *George Washington in and as Culture*. Edited by Kevin L. Cope, William S. Pederson, and Frank Williams. New York: AMS Press, 2001.

McCarthy, Keely. "Conversion, Identity, and the Indian Missionary." *Early American Literature*, 36 (2001), 353–69.

McClatchy, J. D. (ed.). *Bright Pages: Yale Writers 1701–2001*. New Haven: Yale University Press, 2001. Pp. 540.

Messmer, Marietta. "Negotiations of Cultural Identity and Poetic Agency in Anne Bradstreet's Seventeenth-Century London and Boston Editions." *Studies in Puritan American Spirituality*, 7 (2001), 51–79.

Micklus, Robert. "The Reception of Dr. Alexander Hamilton's *History of the Tuesday Club*, Ten Years After." Pp. 170–82 of *Finding Colonial Americas: Essays Honoring J. A. Leo Lemay*. Edited by Carla Mulford and David S. Shields. Newark: University of Delaware Press, 2001.

Minor, Dennis. "Shaved Monkeys, Sleepy Students, and Dangerous Kegs: Revolutionary War Humor and Satire." Pp. 99–106 of *George Washington in and as Culture*. Edited by Kevin L. Cope, William S. Pederson, and Frank Williams. New York: AMS Press, 2001.

Mulford, Carla, and David S. Shields (eds.). *Finding Colonial Americas: Essays Honoring J. A. Leo Lemay*. Newark: University of Delaware Press, 2001. Pp. 481; illustrations.

Murray, Laura J. "Joining Signs with Words: Missionaries, Metaphors, and the Massachusett Language." *New England Quarterly*, 74 (2001), 62–93.

Myles, Anne G. "From Monster to Martyr: Re-Presenting Mary Dyer." *Early American Literature*, 36 (2001), 1–30.

Oberg, Barbara. "Benjamin Franklin's 'Observations on the Means of Extinguishing a Fire': An Addition to the Franklin Canon." Pp. 331–42 of *Finding Colonial Americas: Essays Honoring J. A. Leo Lemay*. Edited by Carla Mulford and David S. Shields. Newark: University of Delaware Press, 2001.

Olson, Alison Gilbert. "Pennsylvania Satire Before the Stamp Act." *Pennsylvania History*, 68 (2001), 507–32.

Pasley, Jeffrey L. *"The Tyranny of Printers": Newspaper Politics of the Early Republic*. Charlottesville: University Press of Virginia, 2001. Pp. xviii + 517.

Perkins, Pam. "Writing Republican Femininity: the Letters of Eliza Southgate Brown." *Symbiosis*, 5 (2001), 121–37.

VII: New World Literatures and Languages

Potkay, Adam. "History, Oratory, and God in Equiano's *Interesting Narrative*." *Eighteenth-Century Studies*, 34 (2001), 600–14.

Rinehart, Lucy. "'Manly Exercises': Post-Revolutionary Performances of Authority in the Theatrical Career of William Dunlap." *Early American Literature*, 36 (2001), 263–93.

Round, Philip H. "Anne Bradstreet's *Several Poems* and the Rise of Christian Belletrism in Eighteenth-Century New England." *Studies in Puritan American Spirituality*, 7 (2001), 23–50.

Royot, Daniel. "Long Live *la Différence*: Humor and Sex in Franklin's Writings." Pp. 170–82 of *Finding Colonial Americas: Essays Honoring J. A. Leo Lemay*. Edited by Carla Mulford and David S. Shields. Newark: University of Delaware Press, 2001.

Sayre, Gordon M. "Communion in Captivity: Torture, Martyrdom, and Gender in New France and New England." Pp. 50–63 of *Finding Colonial Americas: Essays Honoring J. A. Leo Lemay*. Edited by Carla Mulford and David S. Shields. Newark: University of Delaware Press, 2001.

Scheick, William J. "'The Captive Exile Hasteth': Increase Mather, Meditation, and Authority." *Early American Literature*, 36 (2001), 183–200.

Scheick, William J. "Renaissance Art and Puritan Heraldry: Edward Taylor's 'Meditation 1.15.'" *Studies in Puritan American Spirituality*, 7 (2001), 81–109.

Shields, John C. *The American Aeneas: Classical Origins of the American Self*. Knoxville: University of Tennessee Press, 2001. Pp. 480; illustrations.

The Outdoor Life Network advertised the 2004 Tour de France with a series of commercials referring to "The Cyclism." In them, a *sçop* appears and harkens viewers to listen to the dynamics of an historical event about to unfold before them, to prepare for a tale of the named mighty contenders who battle for victory, to behold the Cyclism. Though the rhetoric is without rhyme and unsung, the hero is well sung. The commercial campaign suggests to sports fans that the Tour de France has become a modern-day epic of national significance, international participation, with Lance Armstrong as the warrior-king hero. The main question that the upcoming broadcasts will answer is whether American Lance Armstrong can win his sixth Tour de France in a row, an historical record. This momentous event becomes more than a bicycle road race where international contenders and multinational teams cycle across France; it becomes "The Cyclism." Such sort of mythmaking emerges again and again in cultures that, as Regina Schwartz argues in *The Curse of Cain: The Violent Legacy of Monotheism* (1997), remember a pattern from the past, then forget the past pattern as the present cultural moment transmogrifies the old elements into something new. In *The American Aeneas: Classical Origins of the American Self*, John C. Shields chooses to label this process "a pattern of acceptance and denial" (xxvii, 205), claiming that "most Americans are adept at accepting and then denying" (117). According to Shields, Americans follow this pattern with both the classical and Biblical myths, represented by Aeneas and Adam, but especially in their relationship to locating "the idea of 'Americanness'" in classical sources, in which case there exists "an entrenched refusal to entertain the possibility" of such roots (xxvii). He argues that even though the *Aeneid*, along with other classical texts, deeply informs our culture, we Americans sublimate the myth of Aneas to the myth of Adam. For well-educated Americans who know even of the influences of thinkers like Hume, Montesquieu, Locke on founders of what became the United States government, the rhetoric "entrenched refusal" seems rather strong. Chapter 5 in fact challenges this rhetoric by effectively if not innovatively discussing the influence of such Enlightenment authors on American discourse. Even the OLN 2004 summer commercials for the Tour de France suggest Americans still have some familiarity with classical stories; however, it is possible that, in line with Shields' arguments, more Americans might have noted the literary resonances in the ads if a Biblical story had been chosen for representation.

The American Aeneas traces the use of the Aeneas myth in American literary and cultural production from long before the United States existed up through the American Renaissance and, to some extent, contemporary American culture, noting Americans' complex and shifting responses to classical influences. According to Shields, the Aeneas myth became subsumed by the myth of Adam in 1784 when the "formative, voiced gesturing toward the new nation's defining document [the U.S. Constitution] wrought a self-conscious transformation of the People into Americans" (276). He argues that "the price paid for denying the classical origins of the American self has been high" (277), but notes that in cultural transfers, whether that of Aeneas or Adam, "change will lead to improvement. It matters not that failure may (and does) occur; the dynamism of renewal holds out an ineluctable promise of success" (xl). And he invites us to transform the way we approach American studies by recovering, with him, more of the vibrant myth of Aeneas as it manifests itself in American texts. In a sense, Shields proposes an epic task, for he wants us to expand anew the literary canon to include neglected material sources and to revisit well-read texts with this new lens largely determining the scope of our gaze. He starts the story, standing in as a figure who wages war, sometimes achieving success, sometimes facing failure, sometimes exhibiting insight, sometimes showing hubris, but making heroic strides to expand discussions of American literature and culture and our patterns of cultural redefinition by illuminating the "tension" between the Biblical and the classical modes of discourse (xxiv).

Largely in chronological order, Shields offers textual evidence to chart the shifting use of classicism in American culture according to the following configuration: "From around 1500 to the 1620s, both of these discourses traveled alongside one another, with the classical slightly privileged over the Adamic, probably as a result of the Renaissance enthusiasm for reclamation of classical knowledge" (71). This differs slightly from his introductory comments that during this period "both myths run alongside each other, making fecund connections but *neither* privileged" (emphasis added; xxxix). *The American Aeneas* moves through three more periods that Shields defines in this way:

[F]rom 1620 to about 1720, the Adamic myth is slightly valorized by the Puritan adventure. From the 1720s through the time of the construction of the United States Constitution, the Vergilian or classical mode (in the form of secular Enlightenment and Deism) dominates, and Adam effectively becomes Aeneas. Finally, from about 1790 until the present, the Adamic myth is promoted to such a degree that Aeneas yields, leaving Adam in a position of dominance. (xxxix)

Using this time line to give *The American Aeneas* its structure, Shields both demonstrates and opens for further exploration the extent to which classical ideas and literary techniques shape America's identity-formation, past and present.

Through his textual analyses of narratives, meditations, epics, pastorals, elegies, literary independence poems, religious discourses, and political writings, Shields tracks how the earliest explorers to the American Renaissance authors, while all "invest[ing] their work with an American ambiance," rely upon classical sources in an attempt to create an American identity that avoids British or European sources for literary form and that valorizes pietas for God, family, and country, particularly in promoting the epic enterprises of American Exceptionalism and Manifest Destiny that bolstered the cultural imperatives to create in the New World, like Aeneas before them, a

VII: New World Literatures and Languages 471

new government that supplants the way of life of the native occupants and, in fact, comes to dominate the world (x, xxvii–xxxv, 37, 65, 84, 156–58, 182, 209). Shields waffles but ultimately admits early Americans claimed to create rather than created writing distinct from the British (xl, 94, 266), a ready response for our knowledge that Milton in *Paradise Lost* (along with other British authors) combines the myths of Aeneas and Adam. In discussing the American elegy, he points out and then provides evidence that, although Milton's works proved popular in the American colonies, none of the colonial poems featured in *American Aeneas* "derives its form from Milton's pastoral elegy [*Lycidas*]" (132); moreover, he notes that "by the 1720s in England, the pastoral elegy was an essentially dead genre, not to be revived until Shelley's *Adonais*" published in 1821 (154). In fact, even earlier, much like Plato's response to the dangers of poetry, John Calvin, Richard Baxter, and Thomas Hooker warned Puritans against inspiration from the Muses. America's almanac poets and writers like Jane Turrell, Anne Bradstreet, John Saffin, and Benjamin Tompson show their independence when they ignore such warnings (40, 78). To further illuminate the persistent drive for independence displayed by American authors, Shields references other scholarship that demonstrates how "during the eighteenth century, Great Britain harbored a growing hostility toward classical thought and culture, particularly Vergil[, that]…merged with a general rejection of neoclassicism in preference for the evolving romantic mode" (267). In contrast, between 1720 and 1790 the pastoral elegy proved popular in America (155), comprising the "genre of literary independence poems" that emerged not from studying British works but more directly from the ancient eclogues and pastoral elegies that the American authors studied in their Latin grammar school training or private tutoring (88, 99, 155). The propensity to compare expansion into the New World with "Aeneas's perilous sea voyage to discover the land to the west" prevailed in writings by the English, Italians, Portuguese, French, and Spaniards long before the Puritan jeremiad (xxvi). Addressing how this European tendency to accommodate pagan authors to Christian thought persisted throughout the Middle Ages and Renaissance, Shields notes some of the twelfth- through seventeenth-century Christian humanists who, thinking Virgil "purloined" his material from the Bible, rendered the *Aeneid* as a story about "the process of maturation" and "the acquisition of wisdom" (xxx–xxxi). In the end, Americans accept and refigure the classical and European-explorer narratives, adding the Adamic myth to translate Aeneas' gods into Judeo-Christianity's monotheistic deity.

In recovering what he deems "aggressive declarations of American literary self-sufficiency" that emerged well before Ralph Waldo Emerson's 1837 Phi Beta Kappa address, *The American Scholar* (85), Shields calls for a reevaluation of the stature of Early American writings, a challenge we will face if we wish to consider ourselves learned or to insure a learned posterity. In sum, contrary to "the universal approach among students of American culture," from Shields' analyses we should now recognize "Early Americans were committed to cultural independence long before 1776" (155). Do Americanists universally doubt early colonists' commitment to cultural independence being that an independent nation did emerge? Or, have Americanists rather distinguished the emergence of American writings from American literature? While Shields's own analyses of American forgetfulness and transformation of their mythos will compel other scholars to heed his call, readers must adjust their palates, shore up their patience for pompousness, for Shields heavily seasons *The American Aeneas* with statements about our mistaken "universal approach" and our "cultural blindness" (xxi, xxii, xxv, xxviii, xlv). Even though his own evidence as well as his own plea to the scholarly community suggests that through time cultural literacy changes, a now well-understood occurrence when stories move across space and in time and then get retold and revised and reshaped along the way, Shields calls us blind: "A powerful attitudinal imperative sustains the hegemony of the Adamic myth, making it the only mode of discourse accepted with the field of American Studies. Thus those who would study American culture move into the field already predisposed to a cultural blindness which militates against recognition of the Aeneas myth. This narrowness of vision contributes mightily, I think, to a regrettable pattern which many (but not enough) identify in the United States today—that learning itself is being valued less highly" (xlv). Shields asks us to believe we are universally not only ignorant of the source materials and approach he presents but so blind that we never considered such approaches ourselves. Perhaps if he were as sensitive to the rights of the blind as he suggests he is to the rights of women, African-Americans, and Native-Americans, he would rephrase this. I likewise find Shields's assessment of Americanists and students of American culure fascinating in light of current home-schooling students, all pre-teen, who recently visited my home and discussed their current studies with me and how they, on their own, noticed in early American culture the classical resonances, having previously studied the Roman culture. It seems no real revelation to an educated high school student, much less an Americanist, that "Roman ideals of political and moral action shaped the lives and characters of the authors of the United States Constitution" (xxvi); basic civics, American government, American history, even American literature courses would cover this. American folk heroes like Davy Crockett and Paul Bunyan also hearken to the Aeneas myth. Shields' argument, in a sense, suggests that only the "intellectual elite" among our nation's settlers, founders, and citizens have ever known the myth of Aeneas (xxxv). This works to a certain degree, but Shields then takes it rather far when he begins to attack what we might call today's or yesterday's "intellectual elite" for scholarship that fails to underscore the influence of Aeneas in America.

At times *The American Aeneas* effectively uses previous scholarship, like in its integration of material from Nathan O. Hatch's *The Democratization of American Christianity* (1989); more often, the text simply oversimplifies and reduces current readings, starting with those of Sacvan Bercovitch (xxi), whose work Shields elsewhere also upholds as laudatory, and continuing with the work of Hyatt H. Waggoner, and Boris Ford (349-50), among others. Similarly, though Shields uses Robert D. Richardson's *Myth and Literature in the American Renaissance* (1978) to support some of his arguments (291, 384), he also states that Richardson's conclusions about Nathaniel Hawthorne's relationship to classical literature are "incredible," that is, incredibly wrong, he implies (297). Shields notes that he like his predecessors disregarded the importance of classicism in American culture, "hardly guessing then that I had been programmed by the hegemonic Adamic myth to arrive at just such a determination" (xxii). Addressing his own previous skepticism about the importance of the Aeneas or classical influence in American culture, particularly when Shields presents dated but nonetheless useful models in such unflattering terms (x), does not go far in helping establish a sense of common ground with Americanists and in fact might dissuade them from reviewing the evidence itself. With deprecating remarks that attribute a kind of intellectual downfall in our culture to Americanists' past ignorance, Shields might create resistance in readers he hopes to inform, engage in conversation, and intellectually challenge. These sorts of digressions, somewhat distracting from his important arguments that do contribute to the field, might leave readers guessing if Shields writes for atonement or sympathy as much as for presenting us with a new pattern for approaching American writings. In a sense, he does in his Preface what he argues we find in the "Preface" to Phillis Wheatley's *Poems on Various Subjects*: "While it may have been the fashion of the day to register such a disclaimer, this published statement contradicts real circumstance and signals the construction of a mask, one most likely designed to increase the sales of her volume" (119). In following a convention used in sixteenth-, seventeenth-, and eighteenth-century works by women, Shields further establishes his perceived sense of marginalization and his consequent need for subversion. The rubric works for Shields, but not without eliciting the reader's reservations.

While it's certainly myopic to refute cultural influences upon one's thinking and important to acknowledge that a single perspective at a single point in time rarely proves all-encompassing, it is another thing to seemingly desire to replace what one finds as one hegemonic system with another that might one day be seen by scholars as hegemonic or, at least, lacking—in this case, in fully defining the American self. Shields considers "inevitable" his "critique of the hegemony of the Adamic mode of discourse" (also referred to as "monolithic hegemony" [xxvii], "obstructed" scholarly efforts due to "the hegemony of the Adamic myth" [62]) but does not want us to construe that "as a negative assessment of the work of other students of American letters and culture"; he asks, "How could I censure the work of others when I myself have exemplified the dominance of the American Adam?" (xxiv). In a way, he protests too much. Shields at times goes beyond challenging or furthering others' arguments; his tone becomes flippant and boastful; his self-deprecation transforms into self-righteous attack, making some arguments more likely to bring insult and close-mindedness than to open up the conversation. A somewhat pompous tone emerges when, on one hand, Shields argues that the Adamic myth holds validity and, on other hand, argues that it is hegemonic. If a reader responds to Shields' tone toward past American Studies rather than to his many interesting source materials and analyses that expand the field, such a reader might deem Shields' behavior as posturing. With greater success and authority, Shields presents his recovery project as epic in tone, asserting that *The American Aeneas* presents "startling evidence" of what "had contributed mightily" to America's self-identification process, using works that "demonstrate an originality and independence whose temper predicts the struggle for political and economic independence" (x). He succeeds in identifying examples of the prevalent Aeneas mythos in early American culture.

Shields begins the reevaluation process when he devotes chapters two and three to novel readings of Edward Taylor's private poetry and public sermons and of Cotton Mather's *Magnalia Christi Americana*. Shields demonstrates that, in *Magnalia Christi Americana*, Sir William Phips becomes "an American Aeneas figure" who is "a military and political figure and sometimes and adventurer" (67): "Mather constructs the prototype of America's self-made entrepreneurial man who also moves within his community as a thoroughly political being" (68), thereby he "celebrates the first full-blown American capitalist" who will "gain" and "seize" as an outgrowth of "loyalty to a homeland in this world" and suggests that "the New Testament's denial of worldly goods was unsound, perhaps even in error. That is to say, acquisition and wealth not only became celebrated but stood as concrete evidence of moral worth" (70, 75). Though Mather repeatedly denounces the myth of Aeneas for its erroneous heathenism, he saturates the *Magnalia* with classicism, particularly with the "syncretization of Phoebus and Jesus" and with borrowings from Vergil's *Aeneid*, including the structure for his work (58, 63).

Taylor's denial of classicism emerges differently. In public sermons he alludes to Midas's avarice and Alexander's worldly ambition (43, 50); the classics, then, may demonstrate what we ought not to be or do. In his private poetry, however, he approaches classicism as an intellectual humanist using conceits "within the Renaissance tradition of employing classical allusions, as well as within the orthodox Christian practice of typology" (44). Shields, for this one author expanding "classical" to include the Egyptian—not just Greco-Roman—mythos, presents an interesting analysis of the classical allusions in Taylor's poetry and sermons. However, these Egyptian references seem akin to epics' digressions because Shields elsewhere does not explore such references. That Shields stops exploring such allusions may in part relate to recent criticism like Jeffrey Steele's *The Representation of the Self in the American Renaissance* (1987) and *Transfiguring America: Myth, Ideology, and Mourning in Margaret Fuller's Writing* (2001) or Janet Gabler-Hover's *Dreaming Black/Writing White: The Hagar Myth in American Cultural History* (2000). While *The American Aeneas* looks at Nathaniel Hawthorne's "My Kinsman Major Molineaux" and at Herman Melville's *Billy Budd* for classical influences, it excludes mention of Margaret Fuller, trained by her father to be fluent in Greek and Latin, prevalent user of ancient mythologies in works like *Woman in the Nineteenth Century* and in her entire Conversation series. Nor does it mention Henry David Thoreau's interest in Troy or any of the Transcendentalists' explorations of classical myths from the middle east; their positions on slavery, native Americans, or Mexicans; or—despite the bibliographic entry of Larry J. Reynolds' *European Revolutions and the American Literary Renaissance* (1988)—their transference of America's republican democratic ideals onto the Italian Revolution of 1848. Granted, many of these ideas have elsewhere found a forum. If Americanists, however, wish to expand upon Shields' efforts and those already present in the field, such topics might be explored anew or more fully using outgrowths from Shields' lines of inquiry into the influences of classicism on the American culture and the literature it produces.

Accordingly, Shields calls Americanists to engage in more extensive treatments of other source material by noting that his treatment of the satire and pamphlet are but "brief observations" and that his approach might be employed to help reevaluate Latin American literature as well as North American literature (156, 338). Another wide-open area for application is twentieth- and twenty-first century texts, for which Shields offers no explications. Paul Woodruff's *Reverence: Renewing a Forgotten Virtue* (2002) and Loren Eiseley's *The Unexpected Universe* (1972), for example, would benefit from readings that applied the myth of Aeneas to the American construction of self. Instead of analyzing contemporary documents, he attests that as an Americanist interested in Early American literature, he perceives himself as having a marginalized status due to our longstanding failure to recognize that "America was invented first in terms of the Aeneas myth," that our country's founders constructed a shift to the Adamic myth that went undetected, and that this in turn marginalizes early American literature (337). Shields clearly shifts from literary analysis to polemics when reacting to the current American culture; in fact, he shifts far from theories of Foucault, Said, and Derrida that he uses elsewhere toward a kind of essentialism and universalism:

> While we all need to learn tolerance, we also must discourage intolerance.... [A]wareness of the Adam and Aeneas dialectic can facilitate constructive human interaction....Let us first locate our true origins, our true selves; then we can the better muster the stamina and maturity to move toward "knowing about others."...Again what is needed is a critical patriotism, one tempered by compassion, when dealing with other nations of our shrinking globe....Lifting the siege of America's classical origins will expedite construction of a fully traversable path through these ostensibly chaotic whirlwinds and will lend new dignity to the American self or selves. (354, 355, 357, 362)

In a sense Shields in *The American Aeneas* dons the hat of historian, literary critic, and popular psychologist.

Of the literary and historical arguments Shields does make in *The American Aeneas*, the most underdeveloped and disingenuous are the politically correct mentions: "Since historically each strand of the Adam and Aeneas dialectic is patriarchal and racist (but need not remain so), that dialectic embraces both racial and feminist issues" (xliv). He goes on to argue that we Americanists still maintain a "hegemonic attitude" toward "marginalized minorities in American culture" (251), but he does not tell us in what culture minorities avoid marginalization or receive greater respect. And his supporting evidence is sparse, appears sporadically, and at times seems interesting but tangential to the discussion and analysis at hand. For example, in analyzing the pastoral in America, Shields notes how historian Beverley critiques "whites' interference in Native American affairs" and states that "*The History* represents one of the earliest attempts to defend Native Americans" (104). These observations are not unwelcome and do suggest new approaches to early American discourse, but they are a jarring change of topic really deserving their own series of articles or collection of essays. So, though Shields desires for *The American Aeneas* to help "eradicate...racism" toward Native Americans and African Americans as well as the hegemonic policies toward minorities like these and women (xii, 34), he only sprinkles his study with any textual analyses to support this. Perhaps to Shields, who announces his own Native American "biological origins" (xi, 353), his most important minority explorations in light of the Aeneas myth involve settlers' treatments of the indigenous people in north America (xxxi, 33, 37). More often than he finds defenses of Native Americans in early American writings, he finds that the strands of the Adamic and Aeneas myths converge "at the expense of Native American occupants" (37). For example, Shields suggests how "[o]ne line from the *Aeneid* could have carried considerable weight in justifying the early settlers' seizure of land from Native Americans, this purpose not so moral" (xxxi); for, "[u]pon arrival in this new land, Aeneas encounters a people who have to be supplanted before he can take possession of the new land" (xxxiii). This is perhaps his weakest argument about the classical origins of the American self. That patterns of liberation lead to patterns of oppression and that patterns of oppression lead to patterns of liberation seems more to be an evident recurrence in history than to echo a single epic or classical discourse. Nonetheless, Shields suggests that the Aeneas myth's relationship with cultural minorities would be an area for future scholars to explore more fully.

Similarly, Shields nods to "woman's part in bringing about the establishment of the American cultural self" (290); yet, besides the discussion of Phillis Wheatley's work, he fails to expand much upon those contributions or others by African Americans or other works that address slavery. He does make an interesting but somewhat tenuous argument that Crèvecoeur indicts American industriousness because of the institution of slavery (114–16). Moreover, when extensively discussing the American pastoral, Shield's best discussion of the subversive pastoral appears with his analysis of Phillis Wheatley's subversive use of "smiles" and her "carving out her own property, the property of her imagination," using Sylvanus who "symbolized release from any and all 'iron bands'"; eventually Shields goes so far as to compare Wheatley with Baraka and Malcolm X and to suggest her images for the pastoral emerge from her African memories (122, 125, 129). Given my own research on North Carolina slave George Moses Horton whose poetic works use many similar strategies, I am inclined to respect the idea that Wheatley's poetry proves more subversive than we sometime acknowledge. In Chapter 6, Shields argues that Wheatley's complete works, in total a sort of epic poem in his eyes, respond to "her oppressors" and the "freedom struggle" (225, 246, 250), for we see a "pattern of donning a mask and uttering harmless, acceptable generalities" to advance "the cause of freedom" (123, 128). While Shields may present an unusual and unusually creative argument about

Wheatley's oeuvre, he successfully reopens for exploration early African American letters both in terms of classical resonances and subversive tactics.

Including the analyses of Wheatley, *The American Aeneas* devotes more than fifty percent of its length to the eighteenth-century. Shields traces the great reverence for classics that stimulated the American drive for independence between 1720 and 1789 (205): "These writers, unlike those writing before the 1720s, feel no compunction about expressing themselves in a purely aesthetic manner" (81); they publicly use Horace much like Edward Taylor does in his private poetry: "with no apology or attempt to Christianize their sources... feeling no necessity for explanation" (81). *The American Aeneas* presents a very nice analysis of *Pietas et Gratulatio* (*Devotion and Gratitude*), a 1761 collection by Harvard College faculty and graduates planned by Francis Bernard, royal governor of New Jersey and Massachusetts who uses the noun *Columbia* "to identify the Atlantic colonies. The use of this noun confirms that the American colonies by this time were thinking of themselves as a unit, a collective body with a common purpose, albeit a loose one"; *Columbia* is referred to as a "Country." So despite Loyalist leanings, Bernard helped further the American identity (91) when he "asserts a radical discontinuity between the literary cultures of Great Britain and America" (94). He also helps build the American self by promoting "civic pietas" (94) and thus is "art in the service of politics" (95). Shields devotes chapter five to exploring how this amalgamation led to the likely manifestation of "George Washington's dynamic enactment of the Vergilian Moment," which solidified "a cohesive American self" that reflected the biblical and classical mythos and did not "duplicate the past but...improve[d] upon it" (163, 204). Hence, the *American Aeneas* can expand upon our understanding of early American writings as well as early American performances and presentations.

Prior to the strong chapter on the rhetoric surrounding George Washington, Shields illustrates how the Aeneas myth manifests itself in cultural artifacts beyond writings. He offers us a dazzling analysis of Eunice Bourne's embroidery panel *The Fishing Lady*. His rhetorical analysis of the piece leads him to infer that its scene demonstrates "a classless society, an unpretentious home life, and a secular atmosphere of tolerance" that is "pastoral yet domestic" (82). "In short," Shields concludes, "this panel represents a self-sufficient, already independent American, enjoying a latter-day version of the classical world's mythical golden age, as described, for example, in Vergil's fourth eclogue" (83). Revealing the prevalence of this image in early America and among America's early leaders, Shields explains how First Lady Martha Custic Washington worked at embroidering such a panel just before she died (83). Shields limits his analyses of the rhetoric in cultural artifacts to a textile, broadside, and painting (*The Apotheosis of George Washington*, 164, *Groupe of Aeneas*, 188). While scholarship by art and architectural historians, among others, notes the classical rhetoric in American architecture, sculpture, and painting, Shields offers scholars in American Studies a model for creating connections among cultural productions leading to more illuminative cultural readings.

Throughout most of the eighteenth century, then, Puritan Americans easily accommodated pietas to the Adamic discourse, which "effectively blurred the difference between the classical and the biblical modes" (160). However, the discourse changes between 1763 and 1800 as America begins to think of itself as a nation (xxxviii). Shields explains that while "such religious movements as the Great Awakening arose to counter the advancing Aeneas myth", they "were not so successful until after 1800" when a new nation existed (112). The religious push for the dominance of the myth of Adam, however, could not succeed until the advent of universal education in the United States of America.

In several presentations that will engage scholars interested in early American education, Shields shows us the calculated merger of Aeneas and Adam that persists today as a Christianized Aeneas. This radically departed from the efforts by Philip Freneau and Henry Brackenridge, who, Shields argues, "democratize the notion of epic heroism so that it embraces the ordinary American" (98). In part, the effort "launched by Noah Webster almost immediately after the signing, in 1783, of the Treaty of Paris ending the American Revolution" followed "Virgil's narrative of how Latin derived from the language of the peoples of Latium and how Aeneas's descendants would keep their identification as Latins directly parallels a campaign," which emphasized "retaining a self-earned, independent identity and name" (xxxii, xxiv). Shields amply expands upon this idea in Chapter 5, showing how Noah Webster and Benjamin Rush next led a crusade (later supporters include Benjamin Franklin, Samuel

Goodrich, Anthony Benezet, and William Livingston, who adopted John Locke's theories of a working class and upper class educational distinction) to remove classical studies from the curricula of public schools (111, 194–209, 260–68). The opponents to this pedagogical shift include Samuel Knox, Timothy Dwight, Edgar Allan Poe, and John Quincy Adams (286–89). While Shields' extensive treatments of Edward Taylor and Cotton Mather do show that Calvinistic authors publicly favor the Adam myth (71), he also concludes that "the first indication of this promotion [of the myth of Adam over that of Aeneas] originated not (as one may expect) in the discourse of Calvinistic Protestantism, but in that of education" (259). Indeed, "It was largely the perception of the politicians and educational reformers that, if American cultural cohesiveness was to be accomplished, *all* had to appeal to the Adamic mythos of this 'middling sort'" [or, "the People" (210), the term Shields later adopts from Declaration of Independence] (31, 98), who were much more informed as a whole in Biblical stories than in classical ones. These cultural shapers thus upheld the intelligentsia's earlier use of the way of Aeneas as "the American Way" by consciously extending the Adamic myth to include it quietly or masked (276–77, 162). While Shields acknowledges that, at its best, "ancient Rome permitted all races and most religions to persist" (xliii–xliv), he also states that the Adamic myth is more democratic than the Aeneas myth because Americans, past and present, more readily identify it. Thus, because few attended the all-male college preparatory grammar schools and literacy was declining from the almost universal status it once held for both sexes, early American leaders rendered the Aeneas myth elitist and undemocratic.

In chapters eight and nine, Shields suggests that Nathaniel Hawthorne's "My Kinsman, Major Molineaux" and Herman Melville's *Billy Budd, Sailor (An Inside Narrative)* assert plainly the presence of the Aeneas myth. Chapter 8, "The Persistence of the American Aeneas in Hawthorne," offers an at-times brilliant reading of Hawthorne's short story. The analysis of *Billy Budd,* while sometimes interesting (322, 324, 329), on the whole proves itself underdeveloped and uneven (294, 307, 312). Shields uses a string of tentative words like "probably" and "perhaps" and "could have" and "speculation" and "tenuous connection" (312–13). As mentioned earlier, Shields leaves scholars of nineteenth-century, twentieth-century, and contemporary American literature and all of Latin American literature ample room for exploration into the reverberations of the Aeneas myth.

No doubt a greater exploration of the convergent use of these myths in our literary history might yield new interpretations of cultural, economic, and religious practices. Had *The American Aeneas* maintained that "the literature written by Early Americans, particularly, reflects more complex attitudes than students of Early American studies have recognized" (xxiii), Shields would have appeared less deprecating and more inviting. It's not the use of 'student' as distinct from 'scholar' that I like here; one might even note the redundancy of 'students' and 'studies'; what I appreciate, though, is the invitation that those of us interested in American studies begin to recognize a new level of complexity to early American texts, a level in part less pursued currently because Americans' studies of Latin and the classics prove significantly less commonplace than they once did. Shields' presentation of "the dialectic of Adam and Aeneas" directs us to see again American eclecticism and inclusivity (xxiv), where the culture assimilates parts of once-competing modes; this process even supports Shields's own arguments, for it is not so unlike how ancient Roman culture—so lauded by early Americans—emerged after the Romans conquered Greece.

Just as his primary sources do, Shields's endnotes and bibliography prove impressive in scope. The index will not help readers find uses of literary theory that inform *The American Aeneas* or many scholarly texts that Shields's arguments refute or laud; however, it will help interested scholars locate Shields's arguments on fifteenth-century author Peter Martyr; sixteenth-century author Richard Eden; seventeenth-century authors Cotton Mather, George Sandys, Daniel Russell, Anne Bradstreet. Benjamin Tompson, John Saffin, Edward Taylor, Daniel Russell, Urian Oakes, and John Norton II; eighteenth-century figure George Washington and authors Phyllis Wheatley, Jane Turrell, East Apthorp, John Adams, Aquila Rose, Joseph Breintnall, John Perkins, Richard Lewis, George Webb, Jacob Taylor, Francis Bernard, John Trumbull, William Livingston, Thomas Cradock, J. Hector St. John de Crèvecoeur, Thomas Godfrey, Joseph Seccombe, Jeremy Belknap, Joseph Green, Elias Bockett, and Jonathan Mitchell Sewall; and nineteenth-century authors Joel Barlow, Ralph Waldo Emerson, Nathaniel Hawthorne, Herman Melville, Henry David Thoreau, and William Holmes McGuffey. Although uneven and inconsistent at times, if readers get past the Preface and maintain patience, *The American Aeneas* makes important contributions that can inform how we teach and that do offer new avenues for scholarly exploration.—Deshae E. Lott

Shufflelton, Frank. "A Continental Poetics: Scientific Publishing and Scientific Society in Eighteenth-Century America." Pp. 277–91 of *Finding Colonial Americas: Essays Honoring J. A. Leo Lemay*. Edited by Carla Mulford and David S. Shields. Newark: University of Delaware Press, 2001.

Shuffelton, Frank. "On Her Own Footing: Phillis Wheatley on Freedom." Pp. 175–89 of *Genius in Bondage: Literature of the Early Black Atlantic*. Edited by Vincent Carretta and Philip Gould. Lexington: University Press of Kentucky, 2001.

Sievers, Julie. "Awakening the Inner Light: Elizabeth Ashbridge and the Transformation of Quaker Community." *Early American Literature*, 36:2 (2001), 235–62.

Sivils, Matthew Wynn. "Native American Sovereignty and Old Deb in Charles Brockden Brown's *Edgar Huntly*. *American Transcendental Quarterly*, 15 (2001), 293–304.

Stabile, Susan M. "A 'Doctrine of Signatures': The Epistolary Physics of Ester Burr's Journal." Pp. 109–26 of *A Centre of Wonders: The Body in Early America*. Edited by Janet Moore Lindman and Michele Lise Tarter. Ithaca: Cornell University Press, 2001.

Stabile, Susan M. "Under the Wisteria: the Topography of Sarah Wister's Commonplace Book." Pp. 227–48 of *Finding Colonial Americas: Essays Honoring J. A. Leo Lemay*. Edited by Carla Mulford and David S. Shields. Newark: University of Delaware Press, 2001.

Tamer, Annette C. "Richard Lewis's Poetics of Anti-mercantilism." Pp. 137–52 of *Finding Colonial Americas: Essays Honoring J. A. Leo Lemay*. Edited by Carla Mulford and David S. Shields. Newark: University of Delaware Press, 2001.

Tarter, Michele Lise. "Quaking in the Light: The Politics of Quaker Women's Corporeal Prophecy in the Seventeenth-Century Transatlantic World." Pp. 145–62 of *A Centre of Wonders: The Body in Early America*. Edited by Janet Moore Lindman and Michele Lise Tarter. Ithaca: Cornell University Press, 2001.

Tennenhouse, Leonard. "Caribbean Degeracy and the Problem of Masculinity in Charles Brockden Brown's *Ormond*." Pp. 104–21 of *Finding Colonial Americas: Essays Honoring J. A. Leo Lemay*. Edited by Carla Mulford and David S. Shields. Newark: University of Delaware Press, 2001.

Toulouse, Teresa A. "Hannah Duston's Bodies: Domestic and Colonial Male Identity in Cotton Mather's *Decennium Luctuosum*." Pp. 193–209 of *A Centre of Wonders: The Body in Early America*. Edited by Janet Moore Lindman and Michele Lise Tarter. Ithaca: Cornell University Press, 2001.

Vaughan, William. "Orality, Divinity, Sublimity: Jonathan Edwards and the Ethics of Incorporation." *College Literature*, 28 (2001), 127–43.

Weyler, Karen A. "Race, Redemption, and Captivity in *A Narrative of the Lord's Wonderful Dealings with John Marrant, a Black* and *Narrative of the Uncommon Sufferings and Surprising Deliverance of Briton Hammon, a Negro Man*." Pp. 39–53 of *Genius in Bondage: Literature of the Early Black Atlantic*. Edited by Vincent Carretta and Philip Gould. Lexington: University Press of Kentucky, 2001.

Winkfield, Unca Eliza. *The Female American, or, The Adventures of Unca Eliza Winkfield*. Edited by Michelle Burnham. Peterborough: Broadview Press, 2001. Pp. 196; illustrations.

Winship, Michael. "Were There Any Puritans in New England?" *New England Quarterly*, 74 (2001), 118–38.

Ziff, Larzer. *Return Passages: Great American Travel Writing, 1780–1910*. New Haven: Yale University Press, 2001. Pp. 320; illustrated.

Australia, New Zealand, and Adjacent Literatures and Cultures (1999 Imprints)

Adams, Mark, and Nicholas Thomas. *Cook's Sites: Revisiting History*. Dunedin: University of Otago Press with Centre for Cross-Cultural Research, Australian National University, 1999. Pp. 196; illustrations; maps; bibliographical references.

In 1773 William Hodges produced paintings of the antipodean environment and of the Maori people. The authors have revisited the sites of contact between Cook's crews in Dusky Sound and Queen Charlotte Sound. The photographs and text examine the traces of the past.

Agnew, Vanessa. "Dissecting the Cannibal: Comparing the Function of the Autopsy Principle in the Diaries and Narratives of Captain Cook's Second Voyage." Pp. 50–60 of *Marginal Voices, Marginal Forms: Diaries in European Literature and History*. Edited by Rachel Langford and Russell West. Amsterdam: Rodopi, 1999.

VII: New World Literatures and Languages

Anderson, Grahame, and Wendy Pool. "The King Who Lived at the Point: Isaac Gilsemans's Contribution to the Records of Abel Tasman's Visit to Tongatapu in 1643." *Turnbull Library Record*, 32 (1999), 13–29; illustrations; map.

The authors argue that Abel Tasman was visited by the local Tu'i Kanokupolu Mataele Tu'apiko and not the Tu'i Tonga as is commonly assumed. They use two detailed views drawn by Gilsemans during the visit of the *Heemskerck* and *Zeehaen* to analyze types of canoes used, the compound of the king, clothing, the protocol of the Tongans and the explorers, and the position of the ships. The article includes a diagram of the intermarriages between the Tongatapu kings in the 16th to 18th centuries.

Aughton, Peter. *Endeavour: The Story of Captain Cook's First Great Epic Voyage*. Moreton-in-Marsh: Windrush Press, 1999. Pp. 216; maps; bibliographical references; index.

Bader, Hans-Dieter, and Peter McCurdy, with the assistance of Jefferson Chapple (eds.). *Proceedings of the Waka Moana Symposium 1996: Voyages from the Past to the Future*. [Auckland]: New Zealand National Maritime Museum with Te Papa National Services, 1999. Pp. xiii + 325; illustrations; maps; bibliographical references.

This volume deals with maritime anthropology and offers contributions on traditional Oceanic canoe building, sailing and navigating in the Pacific Islands, including New Zealand.

Barber, Ian G. "Early Contact Ethnography and Understanding: An Evaluation of the Cook Expeditionary Accounts of the Grass Cove Conflict." Pp. 156–79 of *Voyages and Beaches: Pacific Encounters, 1769–1840*. Edited by Alex Calder, Jonathan Lamb, and Bridget Orr. Honolulu: University of Hawaii Press, 1999.

Barnhart, William Clifford. *A Protestant Empire: Evangelicals and the Foreign Missionary Revival in Britain, 1790–1820* (1998). Pp. 251. Dissertation Abstracts International, Section A: The Humanities and Social Sciences 60/02 (August 1999), 516. Abstract number: DA9920396.

This article examines evangelical contributions to imperial sentiment in late Hanoverian England. Evangelicals have become synonymous with the British anti-slavery movement in the late eighteenth century, thus overshadowing the degree to which they actively supported Britain's imperial interests. And when the connection between evangelical foreign missions and the promotion of the British Empire has provoked scholarly attention, it has usually been within the context of the New Imperialism of the late nineteenth century. However, as this study demonstrates, the modern era in British Protestant missions was inaugurated by the evangelical revival of the late eighteenth century and given shape during a period of rapid imperial growth and over two decades of war against revolutionary France. Based mainly on published materials such as sermons, pamphlets, poems and periodicals, this study illustrates how issues of war and empire were central to the conceptualization and marketing of the foreign missionary movement by evangelicals in the late eighteenth century. It is an investigation of one way in which empire was promoted at home in the form of missionary societies, rather than the unfolding of imperial policies in the colonies.

Bell, Leonard. "Augustus Earle's *The Meeting of the Artist and the Wounded Chief Hongi, Bay of Islands, New Zealand, 1827*, and his Depictions of other New Zealand Encounters: Contexts and Connections." Pp. 241–64 of *Voyages and Beaches: Pacific Encounters, 1769–1840*. Edited by Alex Calder, Jonathan Lamb, and Bridget Orr. Honolulu: University of Hawaii Press, 1999.

Bernard, Michel. *La colonisation pénitentiaire en Australie, 1788–1868*. Paris: L'Harmattan, 1999. Pp. 271; maps; bibliographical references; index.

Blain, Michael. *Clergy in the Diocese of Auckland, 1814–1868: A Directory of Anglican Clergy Who Served in the Northern Part of New Zealand, Including the Provinces of Taranaki and Auckland, and in the Southern Pacific, Between 1814 and 1868*. Compiled by Michael Blain with the Anglican Church in Aotearoa, New Zealand, and Polynesia. [Auckland]: Diocese of Auckland, 1999. Pp. 124; bibliographical references; index.

Calder, Alex, Jonathan Lamb, and Bridget Orr (eds.). *Voyages and Beaches: Pacific Encounters, 1769–1840*. Honolulu: University of Hawaii Press, 1999. Pp. viii + 344; illustrations; maps; bibliographical references; index.

Casella, Eleanor Conlin. *Dangerous Girls and Gentle Ladies: Archaeology and Nineteenth Century Australian Female Convicts* (1999). Pp. 305. Dissertation Abstracts International, Section A: The Humanities and Social Sciences 60/06 (December 1999), 2103. Abstract number 9931200.

Casella examines female convicts, transported to the Australian penal colony of Van Diemen's Land (renamed Tasmania in 1855) between 1803 and 1854. Approximately 12,000 of these exiled convicts were women. Incarcerated within a networked system of female prisons, inmates were subjected to punishment and reformation through moral classification, bodily mortification, surveillance, hard labor, and physical confinement. Far from passively accepting these disciplinary mechanisms, the female convicts of Van Diemen's Land actively manipulated their material world to minimize their institutionalized disadvantage. This dissertation interweaves documentary, architectural, geographic and archaeological sources of data to illuminate the strategic construction of gender identity and daily negotiation of power relations that shaped these female prisons. It draws on feminist and French critical theory and focuses on the Ross Female Factory, the last remaining prison site to retain archaeological deposits related to the nineteenth-century female convicts.

Chancellor, Edward. *Devil Take the Hindmost: A History of Financial Speculation*. New York: Farrar, Straus, Giroux, 1999. Pp. xiv + 386; bibliographical references; index.

This volume includes a chapter on "'This Bubble World': The Origins of Financial Speculation," on "Stockjobbing in 'Change Alley: The Projecting Age of the 1690s" and on "The Never-to-be-forgot or Forgiven South-Sea Scheme."

VII: New World Literatures and Languages

Christian, Glynn. *Fragile Paradise*. Revised edition. Sydney: Doubleday, 1999. Pp. xv + 447; illustrations; bibliography; index.

Biography of Fletcher Christian (1764–93) who was involved in the mutiny on the *Bounty* [1789] and spent the rest of his life on Pitcairn Island.

Clark, Steve H. (ed.). *Travel Writing and Empire: Postcolonial Theory in Transit*. London: Zed, 1999. Pp. 264.

Coldrey, Barry M. *Good British Stock: Child and Youth Migration to Australia*. (Research Guide, National Archives of Australia 11.) Canberra: National Archives of Australia, 1999. Pp. 220; illustrations; facsimiles; bibliographical references.

Coleman, Deirdre. "Claire Clairmont and Mary Shelley: Identification and Rivalry within the 'Tribe of the Otaheite Philosophers.'" *Women's Writing*, 6 (1999), 309–28.

This essay focuses on Mary Wollstonecraft Shelley's (1797–1851) novel Frankenstein ([1818]), the author's relationship to Clara Mary Jane Clairmont (1798–1879) and the influence of Jean-Jacques Rousseau's (1712–78) *Julie, ou la Nouvelle Héloïse* (1761).

Coleman, Deirdre (ed.). *Maiden Voyages and Infant Colonies: Two Women's Travel Narratives of the 1790s*. London: Leicester University Press, 1999. Pp. xviii + 247; illustrations; bibliographical references; index.

This book comprises Anna Maria Falconbridge's *Narrative of Two Voyages to the River Sierra Leone During the Years 1791–1793* and Mary Ann Parker's *A Voyage Round the World, in the Gorgon Man of War*. Both travel reports include material on the eighteenth-century slave trade.

Cook, Andrew. "Alexander Dalrymple and the Hydrographic Office." Pp. 53–68 of *Pacific Empires: Essays in Honour of Glyndwr Williams*. Edited by Alan Frost and Jane Samson. Carlton South: Melbourne University Press, 1999.

Cook, James. *Endeavour: Captain Cook's Journal, 1768–71*. [Canberra]: National Library of Australia with the National Maritime Museum, 1999. 1 CD-ROM + 1 insert (pp. 16; illustrations).

This CD-ROM includes a digital facsimile of James Cook's *Endeavour* journal, with J. C. Beaglehole's complete, indexed transcript; supplementary text on the people, places and discoveries from Cook's voyage. It also provides video footage and a virtual tour of the *Endeavour* replica and biographies of the crew.

Cook, James. *The Journals of Captain Cook. Prepared from the Original Manuscript by J. C. Beaglehole for the Hakluyt Society, 1955–67.* Selected and edited by Philip Edwards. London: Penguin, 1999. xiv + 646; maps; bibliographical references; index.

A new one-volume abridged edition based on the 4-volume Hakluyt Society edition.

Cook, James. *The Journals of Captain James Cook on His Voyages of Discovery.* Edited from the Original Manuscripts: Four Volumes and a Portfolio. Volume. I: *The Voyage of the Endeavor, 1768–1771*; Volume II: *The Voyage of the Resolution and Adventure, 1772–1775*; Volume III: *The Voyage of the Resolution and Discovery,* 1776–1780 (part 1); *The Life of Captain James Cook* (part 2); Volume IV: *Charts & Views Drawn by Cook and his Officers.* Edited by J. C. Beaglehole. Rochester: Boydell Press, in association with Horden House, Sydney, 1999. Pp. cclxxxiv + 696; pp. clxx + 1028; pp. ccxxiv + 720/viii + 928; pp. viii + 68; illustrations; maps; bibliographical references.

Cook, James. *The Voyages of Captain Cook.* Edited by John Barrow. Hertfordshire: Wordsworth Editions, 1999. Pp. xvii + 470.

Cook, Judith. *To Brave Every Danger. Das trotzige Leben der Mary Bryant: Die unglaubliche Geschichte einer Räuberin im 18. Jahrhundert.* Translated by Anne Büchel. Reinbek bei Hamburg: Rowohlt, 1999. Pp. 292; map; bibliographical references.

Biography of female convict Mary Bryant [b. 1765] and her life in Botany Bay.

Coote, Jeremy. "Computerizing the Forster ("Cook"), Arawe, and Founding Collections at the Pitt Rivers Museum." *Pacific Arts*, 19/20 (1999), 48–80.

Coote describes the extent of the cataloguing of the Pacific collections at the museum and the Pacific photographic collection and Pacific exhibitions mounted from the typological displays. He focuses on the museum's Pacific collections: the Forster ("Cook") collection, the Founding collection, and the collection arising from the Arawe Project. He provides examples of how catalogue records for Pacific items, such as Maori tools and a store-house door, are entered and annotated on the museum data base, and discusses the role of computerization in making the museum collections accessible to the international research community.

Craik, George L[illie] [1798–1866]. *The New Zealanders.* Facsimile edition. Christchurch: Kiwi Publishers, 1999. Pp. iv + 424; illustrations; bibliographical references.

Written around the experiences of John Rutherford [b. 1796?], "the white chief" who, after his shipwreck on the East Coast of the North Island, was adopted by a Maori tribe, tattooed, and given wives and rank.

VII: New World Literatures and Languages

Croft, Julian. "A Sense of Industrial Place—The Literature of Newcastle, New South Wales, 1797–1997." *Antipodes: A North American Journal of Australian Literature*, 13 (1999), 15–20.

The essay examines poetry and fiction, focusing on the role of landscape and the impact of industrialism.

Crosby, R[on]. D. *The Musket Wars: A History of Inter-Iwi Conflict 1806–45.* Birkenhead: Reed Books, 1999. Pp. 392; illustrations; maps; bibliographical references; index.

Crozet, Julien Marie. *Crozet's Voyage to Tasmania, New Zealand, the Ladrone Islands, and the Philippines in the Years 1771–1772.* Translated by Henry Ling Roth. Christchurch: Kiwi Publishing, 1999. Pp. xxiii + 148.

Daunton, Martin, and Rick Halpern (eds.). *Empire and Others: British Encounters with Indigenous Peoples, 1600–1850.* Philadelphia: University of Pennsylvania Press, 1999. Pp. xii + 400; bibliographical references; index.

Dening, Greg. "The Hegemony of Laughter: Purea's Theatre." Pp. 127–46 of *Pacific Empires: Essays in Honour of Glyndwr Williams.* Edited by Alan Frost and Jane Samson. Carlton South: Melbourne University Press, 1999.

Dixson, Miriam. *The Imaginary Australian: Anglo-Celts and Identity, 1788 to the Present.* Sydney: University of New South Wales Press, 1999. Pp. viii + 216.

Dixson, Miriam. *The Real Matilda: Woman and Identity in Australia, 1788 to the Present.* Fourth updated edition. Sydney: University of New South Wales Press, 1999. Pp. 318; bibliographical references; index.

Dixon's volume discusses the history of women and women's rights in Australia.

Douglas, Bronwen. "Art as Ethno-Historical Text: Science, Representation and Indigenous Presence in Eighteenth and Nineteenth Century Oceanic Voyage Literature." Pp. 65–99 of *Double Vision: Art Histories and Colonial Histories in the Pacific.* Edited by Nicholas Thomas and Diane Losche, assisted by Jennifer Newell. Cambridge: Cambridge University Press, 1999.

Douglas-Hamilton, Jill, and Anne Savage. *Napoleon, the Empress, & the Artist: The Story of Napoleon, Josephine's Garden at Malmaison, Redouté & the Australian Plants.* Preface by Bernard Chevallier; foreword by Bernard Smith. East Roseville: Kangaroo Press, 1999. Pp. xi + 244; illustrations; bibliographical references; index.

This volume focuses on Pierre Joseph Redouté (1759–1840), whose botanical illustrations were held in high esteem by Napoleon I, Emperor of the French (1769–1821) and his wife Josephine (1763–1814).

During, Simon. "Pacific Colonialism and the Formation of Literary Culture." Pp. 285–303 of *Voyages and Beaches: Pacific Encounters, 1769–1840*. Edited by Alex Calder, Jonathan Lamb, and Bridget Orr. Honolulu: University of Hawaii Press, 1999.

Edmond, Rod. "Missionaries of Tahiti, 1797–1840." Pp. 226–40 of *Voyages and Beaches: Pacific Encounters, 1769–1840*. Edited by Alex Calder, Jonathan Lamb, and Bridget Orr. Honolulu: University of Hawaii Press, 1999.

Egan, Jack (ed.). *Buried Alive: Sydney 1788–92: Eyewitness Accounts of the Making of a Nation*. Sydney: Allen & Unwin, 1999. Pp. 384.

Estensen, Miriam. *Discovery: The Quest for the Great South Land*. New York: St. Martin's Press, 1999. Pp. x + 286; illustrations, maps; bibliographical references; index.

Filihia, Meredith. "Rituals of Sacrifice in Early Post-European Contact with Tonga and Tahiti." *Journal of Pacific History*, 34 (1999), 5–22.

This volume provides a comparative study of the ritual of human sacrifice in the highly stratified societies of Tonga and Tahiti in the period immediately following the commencement of European contact. It looks at the form of the ritual, the occasions on which it was performed, and argues that although sacrifice was usually performed in order for the chiefly elite to gain some benefit, both chiefs and commoners made use of the ritual for political ends. It also briefly discusses human sacrifice in Hawaii, in order to demonstrate the validity of the conclusions drawn in the paper within the wider context of Polynesia.

Fisher, Robin. "Vancouver's Vision of Native Peoples: The Northwest Coast and Hawaii." Pp. 147–63 of *Pacific Empires: Essays in Honour of Glyndwr Williams*. Edited by Alan Frost and Jane Samson. Carlton South: Melbourne University Press, 1999.

Flannery, Timothy (ed.). *The Explorers: Epic First Hand Accounts of Exploration in Australia*. Introduction by Tim Flannery. London: Phoenix, 1999. Pp. 385; bibliographical references.

Flynn, Dennis O., Lionel Frost, and A. J. H. Latham (eds.). *Pacific Centuries: Pacific and Pacific Rim History Since the Sixteenth Century*. (Routledge Explorations in Economic History 12.) London: Routledge, 1999. Pp. x + 261; illustrations; bibliographical references; index.

VII: New World Literatures and Languages 485

This collection is comprised of case studies on the Spanish colonial interest in the Philippines, in the silk trade, the ecology and history of the Pacific islands, the maritime trade and agro-ecology of South China, rice as an economic factor, various gold rushes, the wheat trade, Asian-American exchanges.

Forbes, David W., and Samuel A. Cooke (eds.). *Hawaiian National Bibliography 1780–1900, I: 1780–1830.* Foreword by Samuel A. Cooke. Honolulu: University of Hawaii Press with Hordern House, 1999. Pp. xxi + 527.

This volume deals with American literature and its connections to Hawaii, 1700–1999.

Frappell, Ruth (ed. and comp.). *Anglicans in the Antipodes: An Indexed Calendar of the Papers and Correspondence of the Archbishops of Canterbury, 1788–1961, Relating to Australia, New Zealand, and the Pacific.* (Bibliographies and Indexes in Religious Studies 50.) Foreword by Keith Rayner. Westport: Greenwood Press, 1999. xvi + 440; maps; bibliographical references; indexes.

Frappell has collected the correspondence and papers of the Archbishops of Canterbury: John Moore; William Howley; Charles Thomas Longley; Archibald Campbell Tait; Edward White Benson; Frederick Temple; Randall Thomas Davidson; Cosmo Gordon Lang; William Temple; Geoffrey Francis Fisher. In Appendix A, she gives a list of Archbishops of Canterbury, Bishops of London, Archbishops and Bishops in Australia, Archbishops and Bishops in New Zealand and the Pacific; in appendix B she lists Lambeth Degrees in Australia, New Zealand, and Melanesia.

Frost, Alan. "The Spanish Yoke: British Schemes to Revolutionise Spanish America, 1739–1807." Pp. 33–52 of *Pacific Empires: Essays in Honour of Glyndwr Williams.* Edited by Alan Frost and Jane Samson. Carlton South: Melbourne University Press, 1999.

Frost, Alan. *Voyage of the Endeavour: Captain Cook and the Discovery of the Pacific.* St. Leonards: Allen & Unwin, 1999. Pp. xxxvii + 196; illustrations; maps; bibliography; index.

Frost, Alan, and Jane Samson (eds.). *Pacific Empires: Essays in Honour of Glyndwr Williams.* Carlton South: Melbourne University Press, 1999. Pp. xii + 334; illustrations; maps; bibliographical references; index.

Frost, Warwick. "Alfred Crosby's Ecological Imperialism Reconsidered: A Case Study of European Settlement and Environmental Change on the Pacific Rim." 171–87 of *Pacific Centuries: Pacific and Pacific Rim History Since the Sixteenth Century.* Edited by Dennis O. Flynn, Lionel Frost, and A. J. H. Latham. London: Routledge, 1999.

Frugé, August, and Neal Harlow. *A Voyage to California, the Sandwich Islands, and Around the World in the Years 1826–1829.* Translated by August Frugé and Neal Harlow; introduction by August Frugé. Berkeley: University of California Press, 1999. Pp. xxx + 254.

The book focuses on Auguste Bernard Duhaut-Cilly [1790–1849] and his work *Voyage autour du monde, principalement à la Californie et aux îles Sandwich, pendant les années 1826, 1827, 1828, et 1829* [1834–35]. There is special interest in treatment of California and Hawaii.

Geiringer, Claudia. "Ko Te Heke Ra O Maruiwi: Theories About the First Wave of Settlement." Pp. 15–30 of *When the Waves Rolled in Upon Us: Essays in Nineteenth-Century Maori History by History Honours Students, University of Otago 1973–93*. Edited by Michael Reilly and Jane Thomson; foreword by Erik Olssen. Dunedin: University of Otago Press, 1999.

George, Alexander S. *William Dampier in New Holland: Australia's First Natural Historian*. Hawthorn: Bloomings Books, 1999. Pp. xx + 171; illustrations; bibliography; index.

Gudgeon, Thomas Wayth [d. 1890]. *The History and Doings of the Maoris, From the Year 1820 to the Signing of the Treaty of Waitangi in 1840*. Facsimile edition. Christchurch: Kiwi Publishers, 1999. Pp. 94; bibliographical references.

Hart, Elliot. "The Chatham Islands: A Brief History." *New Zealand Memories*, 21 (1999), 385, 438–41.

Hart outlines the history of the islands from European discovery in 1791 by Lieutenant William Broughton up to 1970.

Henderson, James. *Sent Forth a Dove: Discovery of the Duyfken*. Nedlands: University of Western Australia Press, 1999. Pp. xiv + 218; illustrations; bibliographical references; index.

This is a volume on the ship (and replica) *Duyfken*, which was involved in the Dutch discovery and seventeenth-century exploration of Australia.

Hewson, Helen. *Australia: 300 Years of Botanical Illustration*. Foreword by HRH The Prince of Wales. Collingwood: CSIRO Publishing, 1999. Pp. 228; bibliographical references; index.

Hohepa, Pat. "My Musket, My Missionary, And My Mana." Pp. 180–201 of *Voyages and Beaches: Pacific Encounters, 1769–1840*. Edited by Alex Calder, Jonathan Lamb, and Bridget Orr. Honolulu: University of Hawaii Press, 1999.

Home, Edward. *A First Fleet Letter to a Gentleman in Edinburgh*. (First Fleet Books 5.) Canberra: Mulini Press, 1999. Pp. 26; illustrations.

This was first published in 1789 as "Some Account of New Holland and the Discovery of a Chain of Islands in the Pacific Ocean; in a Letter from Edward Home, Carpenter, to a Gentleman in Edinburgh."

VII: New World Literatures and Languages

Houlahan, Mark. "The Canon on the Beach: H. T. Kemp Translating *Robinson Crusoe* and *The Pilgrim's Progress*." Pp. 304–16 of *Voyages and Beaches: Pacific Encounters, 1769–1840*. Edited by Alex Calder, Jonathan Lamb, and Bridget Orr. Honolulu: University of Hawaii Press, 1999.

Hunt, Susan. *Terre Napoléon: Australia Through French Eyes, 1800–1804*. [Sydney]: Historic Houses Trust of New South Wales in association with Hordern House, 1999. Pp. 148; illustrations; maps; bibliographical references.

This is a catalogue of an exhibition held at the Museum of Sydney, February 27–May 30, 1999, in collaboration with the Collection Charles-Alexandre Lesueur of Muséum d'histoire naturelle. It focuses on French artists/natural history illustrators Charles Alexandre Lesueur (1778–1846) and Nicolas-Martin Petit (1777–1804), and on their work for French explorer Nicolas Baudin (1754–1803).

Jenkin, Robert. "Strangers in Mohua: Abel Tasman's Exploration of New Zealand: An Investigation of the First Recorded Contact between Maori and Pakeha, December 18th and 19th, 1642." Takaka: Golden Bay Museum, 1999. Pp. 60; illustrations; maps; plans.

King, Robert J. "Francisco Muñoz y San Clemente and His 'Reflections on the English Settlements of New Holland.'" *British Library Journal*, 25 (1999), 55–76.

King's essay focuses on Spanish author Francisco Muñoz y San Clemente's "Reflexiones sobre los establecimientos Ingleses de la Nueva-Holanda" and his treatment of British colonialism in the South Seas (manuscript study; British Library; edition of MS Additional 19264; English language translation).

Lamb, Jonathan. "Re-Imagining Juan Fernandez: Probability, Possibility and Pretence in the South Seas." Pp. 19–43 of *Double Vision: Art Histories and Colonial Histories in the Pacific*. Edited by Nicholas Thomas and Diane Losche, assisted by Jennifer Newell. Cambridge: Cambridge University Press, 1999.

Langford, Rachael, and Russell West (eds.). *Marginal Voices, Marginal Forms: Diaries in European Literature and History*. Amsterdam: Rodopi, 1999. Pp. 211.

Liebersohn, Harry. "Images of Monarchy: Kamehameha I and the Art of Louis Choris." Pp. 44–64 of *Double Vision: Art Histories and Colonial Histories in the Pacific*. Edited by Nicholas Thomas and Diane Losche, assisted by Jennifer Newell. Cambridge: Cambridge University Press, 1999.

Lines, William J. *Taming the Great South Land: A History of the Conquest of Nature in Australia*. New edition with a new afterword by the author. Athens: University of Georgia Press, 1999. Pp. xx + 347; illustrations; maps; bibliography; index.

Lummis, Trevor. *Life and Death in Eden: Pitcairn Island and the Bounty Mutineers.* London: Victor Gollancz, 1999. Revised edition. Pp. 255; illustrations; map; bibliographical references; index.

Mabberley, David. *Ferdinand Bauer: The Nature of Discovery.* London: Merrell Holberton, 1999. Pp. 128; illustrations.

This is a study on Australian wildlife painting by Ferdinand Bauer [1760–1826], published in cooperation with the Natural History Museum, London.

Mackay, David. "Exploring the Pacific, Exploring James Cook." Pp. 251–69 of *Pacific Empires: Essays in Honour of Glyndwr Williams.* Edited by Alan Frost and Jane Samson. Carlton South: Melbourne University Press, 1999.

Mackay, David. "Myth, Science, and Experience in the British Construction of the Pacific." Pp. 100–13 of *Voyages and Beaches: Pacific Encounters, 1769–1840.* Edited by Alex Calder, Jonathan Lamb, and Bridget Orr. Honolulu: University of Hawaii Press, 1999.

Martin, Angus. "Le Rêve océanien en France et le récit océanien à la veille de la Révolution: *Le Chant tahïtien* (1786) de Jean-Antoine Joseph de Bry." Pp. 235–47 of *Variété: Perspectives in French Literature, Society and Culture.* Edited by Marie Ramsland. Frankfurt: Peter Lang, 1999.

Martin's essay examines Jean-Antoine Joseph Debry [1760–1834] and his prose work *Chant tahïtien*; his treatment of exoticism and relationship to Oceania.

Mawer, Granville Allen. *Ahab's Trade: The Saga of South Seas Whaling.* St. Leonards: Allen & Unwin, 1999. Pp. xiv + 393; illustrations; map; bibliography; index.

McHugh, P. G. "A Tribal Encounter: The Presence and Properties of Common-Law Language in the Discourse of Colonization in the Early Modern Period." Pp. 114–31 of *Voyages and Beaches: Pacific Encounters, 1769–1840.* Edited by Alex Calder, Jonathan Lamb, and Bridget Orr. Honolulu: University of Hawaii Press, 1999.

McHugh, P. G. "Australasian Narratives of Constitutional Foundation." Pp. 98–114 of *Quicksands: Foundational Histories in Australia and Aotearoa New Zealand.* Edited by Klaus Neumann, Nicholas Thomas, and Hilary Erickson. Sydney: University of New South Wales Press, 1999.

McKinney, Sam. *Bligh! The Whole Story of the Mutiny Aboard H.M.S. Bounty.* Victoria: Horsdal & Schubart, 1999. Pp. x + 190; bibliographical references; index.

VII: New World Literatures and Languages 489

McLean, Ian. "Under Saturn: Melancholy and the Colonial Imagination." Pp. 131–62 of *Double Vision: Art Histories and Colonial Histories in the Pacific*. Edited by Nicholas Thomas and Diane Losche, assisted by Jennifer Newell. Cambridge: Cambridge University Press, 1999.

McNeill, John R. "Islands in the Rim: Ecology and History in and Around the Pacific, 1521–1996." Pp. 70–84 of *Pacific Centuries: Pacific and Pacific Rim History Since the Sixteenth Century*. Edited by Dennis O. Flynn, Lionel Frost, and A. J. H. Latham. London: Routledge, 1999.

Moloughney, Brian, and Jim Ng (eds.). *Chinese in Australasia and the Pacific: Old and New Migrations and Cultural Change: Conference for the Study of Overseas Chinese, Hutton Lecture Theatre, 20–21 November 1998: New Zealand Conference of ASCADAPI, Association for the Study of Chinese and Their Descendants in Australasia and the Pacific Islands*. [Dunedin]: University of Otago, [1999]. Pp. 252; illustrations; maps; bibliographical references.

Morris, Graham P. *Son of Caledon: The Story of Scottish Colour-Sergeant William Wilson [1777–1836] of the Royal Engineers, British Army (1797–1820) and Later Superintendent of Convicts at Port Macquarie, NSW, and His Wife Maria De Jesus De Costa-Reis, of Portugal & Their Family in Australia from 1823–1998*. Kilsyth: Graham P. Morris, 1999. Pp. 334; illustrations; bibliographical references.

Motohashi, Ted. "The Discourse of Cannibalism in Early Modern Travel Writing." Pp. 83–99 of *Travel Writing and Empire: Postcolonial Theory in Transit*. Edited and with an introduction by Steve Clark. London: Zed, 1999.

Neumann, Klaus, Nicholas Thomas, and Hilary Erickson (eds.). *Quicksands: Foundational Histories in Australia and Aotearoa New Zealand*. Sydney: University of New South Wales Press, 1999. Pp. xxii + 281.

Newton, Douglas (ed.). *Arts of the South Seas: Island Southeast Asia, Melanesia, Polynesia, Micronesia: The Collections of the Musée Barbier-Mueller. Arts des mers du Sud. English*. Translation from the French by David Radzinowicz Howell. München: Prestel, 1999. Pp. 368; illustrations; maps.

Nicholson, John. *Fishing for Islands: Traditional Boats and Seafarers of the Pacific*. St. Leonards: Allen & Unwin, 1999. Pp. 40; illustrations.

Nicholson provides a history of boats and boating in Oceania; emigration and immigration; discovery and exploration.

Nicol, John [1755–1825]. *The Life and Adventures of John Nicol, Mariner* [1776–1801]. Edited and with an introduction by Tim Flannery. First American edition New York: Atlantic Monthly Press, 1999. Pp. 198; maps; bibliographical references; index.

In his many voyages the Scottish-born sailor John Nicol twice circumnavigated the globe, visiting every inhabited continent while witnessing and participating in many of the greatest events of exploration and adventure in the eighteenth century. His autobiography contains material on his visit to the Sandwich Islands (Hawaii) where he was entertained by the king's court mere days after the murder of Captain James Cook, and on his relationship with Sarah Whitlam, a convict bound for the Botany Bay prison colony, with whom he fostered a son on his way to Australia.

Nordyke, Eleanor C., in collaboration with James A. Mattison, Jr. (eds.). *Pacific Images: Views from Captain Cook's Third Voyage: Engravings and Descriptions from A Voyage to the Pacific Ocean, volumes I, II, and III, and the Atlas by Captain James Cook and Captain James King, published as the Official Edition of the Lords Commissioners of the Admiralty, in London, 1784.* [Honolulu]: Hawaiian Historical Society, 1999. Pp. xxvi + 174; illustrations; maps; bibliographical references; index.

Oldfield, Audrey. *The Great Republic of the Southern Seas: Republicans in Nineteenth-Century Australia*. Sydney: Hale & Iremonger, 1999. Pp. 280; illustrations; bibliography; index.

The British settlement in Australia began amid the great republican movements of the late eighteenth century, and from its earliest days republican ideals affected political thinking in the colony. In this study, Audrey Oldfield investigates the subject from a biographical angle, concentrating on the people involved in the republican debate throughout the century: from the Scottish martyr Thomas Muir, convicted of sedition in 1793, to Henry Lawson, writing "The Song of the Republic" in 1887. She explores such questions as: Did transportation to siphon off agitators and urban poor save Britain from revolution and republicanism? Was there ever any likelihood that Australia might have chosen republican constitutions in the 1850s? Was there a deliberate attempt by Britain and Australian monarchists to subvert republicanism in the federation period?

Parkin, Ray. *H. M. Bark* Endeavour: *Her Place in Australian History; with an Account of Her Construction, Crew and Equipment and a Narrative of Her Voyage on the East Coast of New Holland in the Year 1770.* Carlton South: Melbourne University Press, 1999. Pp. xi + 467; illustrations; bibliographical references; index.

Pieske, Burghard. *Bounty Bay: 5000 nasse Meilen im Pazifik: Auf den Spuren von Captain Bligh.* Bielefeld: Delius Klasing, 1999. Pp. 304; illustrations; maps.

Pocock. J. G. A. "Nature and History, Self and Other: European Perceptions of World History in the Age of Encounter." Pp. 25–43 of *Voyages and Beaches: Pacific Encounters, 1769–1840.* Edited by Alex Calder, Jonathan Lamb, and Bridget Orr. Honolulu: University of Hawaii Press, 1999.

VII: New World Literatures and Languages

Porter, Andrew. "The Career of William Ellis: British Missions, the Pacific, and the American Connection." Pp. 193–214 of *Pacific Empires: Essays in Honour of Glyndwr Williams*. Edited by Alan Frost and Jane Samson. Carlton South: Melbourne University Press, 1999.

Porter, Andrew. "North American Experience and British Missionary Encounters in Africa and the Pacific, c. 1800–1850. Pp. 345–63 of *Empire and Others: British Encounters with Indigenous Peoples, 1600–1850*. Edited by Martin Daunton and Rick Halpern. Philadelphia: University of Pennsylvania Press, 1999.

Porter, Andrew (ed.). *The Oxford History of the British Empire*. Volume 3: *The Nineteenth Century*. Oxford: Oxford University Press, 1999. Pp. xxii + 774.

Ramsland, Marie (ed.). *Variété: Perspectives in French Literature, Society and Culture*. Frankfurt: Peter Lang, 1999. Pp. 349; illustrations.

Reilly, Michael, and Jane Thomson (eds.). *When the Waves Rolled in Upon Us: Essays in Nineteenth-Century Maori History by History Honours Students, University of Otago 1973–93*. Dunedin: University of Otago Press, 1999. Pp. 2223; illustrations; maps.

Retter, Catharine, and Shirley Sinclair. *Letters to Ann: The Love Story of Matthew Flinders and Ann Chappelle*. Pymble: Angus & Robertson, 1999. Pp. ix + 150; illustrations; bibliographical references.

This volume documents the correspondence between Matthew Flinders (1774–1814), involved in the history of European discovery and exploration of Australia, and Ann Chappelle (1772–1852).

Riddle, Shane. "'Spanish Tahiti': Mapping the Eastern Pacific in the 18th Century." *New Zealand Map Society Journal*, 12 (1999), 26–34.

Riddle discusses voyages from Peru to Tahiti and other Spanish activities in the region in the 1770s and considers the maps drawn during this period as an attempt to construct a "Spanish Tahiti."

Rosenthal, Michael. "The Penitentiary as Paradise." Pp. 103–30 of *Double Vision: Art Histories and Colonial Histories in the Pacific*. Edited by Nicholas Thomas and Diane Losche, assisted by Jennifer Newell. Cambridge: Cambridge University Press, 1999.

Smith, S[tephenson]. Percy [1840–1922]. *Maori Wars of the Nineteenth Century: The Struggle of the Northern Against the Southern Maori Tribes Prior to the Colonisation of New Zealand in 1840*. Christchurch: Kiwi Publishers, 1999. Pp. 490; illustrations; tables.

This is a facsimile of the second and enlarged edition: Christchurch: Whitcombe & Tombs, 1910. The first edition was published as *Wars of the Northern Against the Southern Tribes of New Zealand in the Nineteenth Century*.

State Library of New South Wales (ed.). *Mutiny on the Bounty: The Story of Captain William Bligh, Seaman, Navigator, Surveyor and of the Bounty Mutineers*. New South Wales: Rolf Harris; Poole: Chris Lloyd, 1999. Pp. 112; illustrations; bibliographical references; index.

Tasker, John. *Chain of Evidence: Who Were the First Humans to Visit New Zealand?* Hastings: Kanuka Press, 1999. Pp. 201; illustrations; maps; bibliographical references.

Tasker includes a chapter on the European "discovery" and exploration up to 1840.

Taillemite, Etienne. *Marins français à la découverte du monde: de Jacques Cartier à Dumont d'Urville*. [Paris]: Fayard, 1999. Pp. 725; maps; bibliographical references; index.

Tcherkezoff, Serge. "Who said the 17th–18th Centuries Papalagi/'Europeans' Were 'Skybursters'? A Eurocentric Projection onto Polynesia." *Journal of the Polynesian Society*, 108 (1999), 417–25.

Tcherkezoff cites references to the use of "Papalangi" and dialectal variations used in different parts of Polynesia, from first contact with Europeans until the present. He analyzes these accounts for clues as to the etymology of the term, considers Polynesian cosmology in an attempt to determine whether early Europeans were seen as beings of the sky, and looks at other hypotheses.

Thomas, Nicholas. "Liberty and License: The Forsters' Accounts of New Zealand Sociality." Pp. 132–55 of *Voyages and Beaches: Pacific Encounters, 1769–1840*. Edited by Alex Calder, Jonathan Lamb, and Bridget Orr. Honolulu: University of Hawaii Press, 1999.

Thomas, Nicholas. *Possessions: Indigenous Art, Colonial Culture*. London: Thames and Hudson, 1999. Pp. 304; illustrations; bibliographical references; index.

This volume examines New Zealand and Australian folk art, primitive influences on modern art, and colonial culture.

Thomas, Nicholas, Diane Losche, and Jennifer Newell (eds.). *Double Vision: Art Histories and Colonial Histories in the Pacific*. Cambridge: Cambridge University Press, 1999. Pp. xii + 289; illustrations; bibliographical references; index.

Turnbull, Paul. "Enlightenment Anthropology and the Ancestral Remains of Australian Aboriginal People." Pp. 202–25 of *Voyages and Beaches: Pacific Encounters, 1769–1840*.

VII: New World Literatures and Languages 493

Edited by Alex Calder, Jonathan Lamb, and Bridget Orr. Honolulu: University of Hawaii Press, 1999.

Turner, Stephen. "A History Lesson: Captain Cook Finds Himself in the State of Nature." Pp. 89–99 of *Voyages and Beaches: Pacific Encounters, 1769–1840*. Edited by Alex Calder, Jonathan Lamb, and Bridget Orr. Honolulu: University of Hawaii Press, 1999.

Van Zanden, Henry. *1606 Discovery of Australia*. Perth: Rio Bay Enterprises, 1999. Pp. viii + 142; illustrations; maps; bibliographical references; index.

Waterhouse, Richard. "'The Vision Splendid': Conceptualising the Bush, 1813–1913." *Journal of Popular Culture*, 33 (1999), 23–34.

Williams, Glyndwr. "'To Make Discoveries of Countries Hitherto Unknown': The Admiralty and Pacific Exploration in the Eighteenth Century." Pp. 13–31 of *Pacific Empires: Essays in Honour of Glyndwr Williams*. Edited by Alan Frost and Jane Samson. Carlton South: Melbourne University Press, 1999.

Winks, Robin W. (ed.). *The Oxford History of the British Empire*. Volume 5: *Historiography*. Oxford University Press, 1999. Pp. xxiv + 731.

This is a study of the history and historiography of the British Commonwealth and British colonies.

Wolfe, Patrick. *Settler Colonialism and the Transformation of Anthropology: The Politics and Poetics of an Ethnographic Event*. (Writing Past Colonialism Series.) London: Cassell, 1999. Pp. ix + 246; illustrations; bibliography.

Wolfe writes on the history of anthropology in Australia and its entanglement with racism, imperialism, and frontier and pioneer life.

Wood, Houston. *Displacing Natives: The Rhetorical Production of Hawai'i*. Lanham: Rowman & Littlefield Publishers, 1999. Pp. xii + 223; illustrations; bibliography; index.

This volume contains chapters on the "Violent Rhetoric of Names" and on "Captain James Cook, Rhetorician."

Australia, New Zealand, and Adjacent Literatures and Cultures (2000 Imprints)

Anderson, Hugh. *Farewell to Judges & Juries: The Broadside Ballad & Convict Transportation to Australia, 1788–1868*. Hotham Hill: Red Rooster, 2000. xxxiv + 611; illustrations; some musical scores; bibliographical references.

Armitage, David. *The Ideological Origins of the British Empire*. Cambridge: Cambridge University Press, 2000. Pp. xi + 239; bibliographical references; index.

Balme, Christopher B. "Sexual Spectacles: Theatricality and the Performance of Sex in Early Encounters in the Pacific." *The Drama Review: A Journal of Performance Studies*, 44 (2000), 67–85.

Balme examines English and European literature between 1700–99; the role of cross-cultural contact; the treatment of female sexuality; ritual behavior as performance in Tahitian culture.

Banks, Sir Joseph [1743–1820]. *The Letters of Sir Joseph Banks: A Selection, 1768–1820*. Edited by Neil Chambers. Foreword by David Mabberley; introduction by Harold Carter. London: Imperial College Press, 2000. Pp. xliii + 420; illustrations.

Barker, Anthony. *What Happened When: A Chronology of Australia from 1788*. New updated and revised edition. St. Leonards: Allen & Unwin, 2000. Pp. xi + 505; index.

Bartlett, Thomas. "The 1798 Rebellion in Perspective." Pp. 13–23 of *Ireland and Australia, 1798–1998: Studies in Culture, Identity, and Migration*. Edited by Philip Bull, Frances Devlin-Glass, and Helen Doyle. Sydney: Crossing Press, 2000.

Bassett, Judith, Keith Sinclair, and Marcia Stenson. *The Story of New Zealand*. Auckland: Reed, 2000. Pp. 223; illustrations; facsimiles; maps.

Bonyhady, Tim. *The Colonial Earth*. Carlton: Miegunyah Press, 2000. Pp. xi + 432; illustrations.

When the First Fleet sailed for New South Wales in 1787, the British government ordered Governor Phillip to preserve the cattle, sheep and hogs he brought with him, but not the environment he found. Yet Phillip and his officers were quick to try to protect Australia's land. This book challenges the equation of colonization with destruction.

Booker, John, and Russell Craig. *John Croaker: Convict Embezzler*. Carlton South: Melbourne University Press, 2000. Pp. x + 206; illustrations; maps; bibliographical references; index.

This biography of John Croaker (1788–1824) also includes the history of prisoner employment in New South Wales, and the history of the Australian brewing industry.

Borofsky, Robert. "Cook, Lono, Obeyesekere, and Sahlins." Pp. 421–42 of *Remembrance of Pacific Pasts: An Invitation to Remake History*. Edited by Robert Borofsky. Honolulu: University of Hawaii Press, 2000.

Borofsky, Robert (ed.). *Remembrance of Pacific Pasts: An Invitation to Remake History*. Honolulu: University of Hawaii Press, 2000. Pp. xvi + 557; illustrations; bibliographical references; index.

Bowman, Stanley Mackenzie. *The History of a Bowman Family in Australia: The First 200 Years, 1798–1998*. Dubbo: Development and Advisory Publications Australia, 2000. Pp. 168. Illustrations; maps.

Brome, Richard [d. 1652?]. *The Antipodes*. Edited by David Scott Kastan and Richard Proudfoot. London: Nick Hern, 2000. Pp. xii + 153.

This is a new edition of a Jacobean city comedy first printed in London in 1640. Written in an age of travel and exploration, the play reflects contemporary ideas about the southern hemisphere and employs them in a humorous play-within-the-play with the aim of recalling the main character Peregrine (an obsessive reader of travel books) to his marital duties.

Brown, Anthony J. *Ill-Starred Captains: Flinders and Baudin*. With a foreword by Tim Flannery. Hindmarsh: Crawford House Publishing, 2000. Pp. xix + 512; illustrations; maps; bibliographical references; index.

Brown's volume documents the journeys of discovery to Australia under Matthew Flinders (1774–1814) and Nicolas Baudin (1754–1803).

Brunt, Peter William. *The Sublime and the "Civilized" Subject: History, Painting, and Cook's Second Voyage* (2000). Pp. 260. Dissertation Abstracts International, Section A: The Humanities and Social Sciences 61/01 (July 2000), 3. Abstract Number DA9953644.

Brunt examines a number of images by William Hodges from Cook's second voyage in relation to the eighteenth century discourse on the sublime. While the encounter with the sublime inaugurates and empowers the "civilized" subject, author argues that it is also characterized by another movement: a sublime upon a sublime, which interrupts this teleological end, diverting it to more ambiguous goals and displacing the subject's sense of empowerment by an apprehension of power's instability. The author proposes, furthermore, that the scene of the sublime has geographical and cultural, as well as historical, settings: it "happens" in the encounter with others on "beaches" in faraway places. Introduction outlines this double movement of the sublime. Chapter 1 looks at Hodges' "landing" paintings, suggesting that they allegorize the "turn" in the aesthetic ideology of Reynolds's

Discourses in which the aspiration to a certain kind of sublime—the classical ideal of universality in painting—is interrupted and, in effect, derailed by the intuition of another which exactly overshadows the first. Chapter 2 analyzes two paintings by Hodges based on an encounter with a Maori family in Dusky Bay New Zealand in conjunction with the film *Once Were Warriors*. Both narratives, despite their disparities, are about the transformation from "savagery" to "civility" (figured in the ideal of the domestic bourgeois family) as enabled through the agency of sublime encounters. Chapter 3 examines Hodges's painting of the ruined monuments of Easter Island and its pendant of Tahiti in relation to Poussin's painting, *Et in Arcadia Ego*, each of which is pervaded by an elegiac mood constitutive of "civilized" subjectivity as, again, the displaced effect of a sublime encounter. In all these chapters, author shows these transformations to be more equivocal than they at first appear. Indeed, the sublime, author argues, *is* this equivocation. To reveal it as such, as the author aims to do here, is less to undermine the "civilized" subject as to restore it to the multiple cultural and historical indeterminacies at its origin.

Bruyn, Frans de. "Reading Het groote tafereel der dwaasheid: An Emblem Book of the Folly of Speculation in the Bubble Year 1720." *Eighteenth-Century Life*, 24 (2000), 1–42.

This is an essay on Netherlandic literature from the eighteenth century, especially satire and its treatment of the South Sea Bubble in relation with economic and cultural change.

Bull, Philip, Frances Devlin-Glass, and Helen Doyle (eds.). *Ireland and Australia, 1798–1998: Studies in Culture, Identity, and Migration*. Sydney: Crossing Press, 2000. Pp. xiii + 367; bibliographical references.

These papers from the tenth Irish-Australian Conference held in Melbourne in September and October 1998, focus on the history of emigration and immigration. They represent Australia's principal scholarly commemoration of the Irish Rebellion of 1798 and its outcomes for both countries.

Bullard, Allice. *Exile to Paradise: Savagery and Civilization in Paris and the South Pacific, 1790–1900*. Stanford: Stanford University Press, 2000. Pp. 380; illustrations; bibliography; index.

This volume is a history of French penal colonies, especially the deportation of French rebels related to the Paris Commune to New Caledonia.

Caplan, Jane (ed.). *Written on the Body: The Tattoo in European and American History*. Princeton: Princeton University Press, 2000. Pp. xxiii + 318; illustrations.

Carey, Hilary M.. "'Attempts and Attempts': Responses to Failure in Pre- and Early Victorian Missions to the Australian Aborigines." Pp. 45–61 of *Mapping the Landscape: Essays in Australian and New Zealand Christianity: Festschrift in Honour of Professor Ian Breward*. (American University Studies, Series IX, History, 193.) Edited by Susan Emilsen and William W. Emilsen. New York: Peter Lang, 2000.

Carroll-Burke, Patrick. *Colonial Discipline: The Making of the Irish Convict System*. Dublin: Four Courts, 2000. Pp. 256; bibliographical references; index.

VII: New World Literatures and Languages

Burke gives a history of prisons and a general history of Ireland during the 18th and 19th century.

Carlsson, Susanne Chauvel. *Pitcairn: Island at the Edge of Time*. Rockhampton: Central Queensland University Press, 2000. Pp. 238; illustrations; bibliography; index.

Carlsson presents a book on social customs and the history of Pitcairn Island, final destination of the mutineers from the *Bounty* (1798).

Davison, Graeme. "Colonial Origins of the Australian Home." Pp. 6–25 of *A History of European Housing in Australia*. Edited with an introduction by Patrick Troy. Cambridge: Cambridge University Press, 2000.

Denoon, Donald, and Philippa Mein-Smith, with Marivic Wyndham. *A History of Australia, New Zealand, and the Pacific*. Oxford: Blackwell, 2000. Pp. xiv + 523; illustrations; bibliography; index.

A history of Australia, New Zealand, and the Pacific from the earliest settlements to the present. Usually viewed in isolation, these societies are covered here in a single account, in which the authors show how the peoples of the region constructed their own identities and influenced those of their neighbors. By broadening the focus to the regional level, this volume develops analyses of economic, social and political history which transcend national boundaries. The result is a work which both describes the aspirations of European settlers and reveals how the dispossessed and marginalized indigenous peoples negotiated their own lives as best they could. The authors demonstrate that both these stories are the strands of a single history.

Dingle, Tony. "Necessity the Mother of Invention, Or, Do-It-Yourself." Pp. 57–76 of *A History of European Housing in Australia*. Edited with an introduction by Patrick Troy. Cambridge: Cambridge University Press, 2000.

Dose, Gerd, and Bettina Keil (eds.). *Writing in Australia: Perceptions of Australian Literature in Its Historical and Cultural Context. A Series of Lectures Given at Hamburg University on the Occasion of the 1st Festival of Australian Literature in Hamburg 1995*. Münster: Lit Verlag, [2000]. Pp. vi + 227.

Druett, Joan. *Rough Medicine: Surgeons at Sea in the Age of Sail*. New York: Routledge, 2000. Pp. x + 270; illustrations; bibliographical references; index.

This volume includes an examination of naval medical practice in the South Pacific Ocean, especially in relation with whaling.

Emilsen, Susan, and William W. Emilsen (eds.). *Mapping the Landscape: Essays in Australian and New Zealand Christianity: Festschrift in Honour of Professor Ian Breward*. (American University Studies, Series IX, History 193.) New York: Peter Lang, 2000. Pp. viii + 356; portrait.

Emmett, Ross B. (eds.) *Great Bubbles*. 3 volumes. Volume 1: *Tulip Mania* (edited with John Law); Volume 2: *The Mississippi Scheme and Bubble. The English Financial Revolution and Exchange Alley*; Volume 3: *South Sea Bubble*. Brookfield: Pickering & Chatto, 2000. Pp. xxxi + 271; vi + 252; vi + 426; illustrations; bibliographical references; index.

These volumes focus on the history of the South Sea Company, reactions to the South Sea Bubble (1720), the Mississippi Scheme and the seventeenth-century Tulip mania, the history of the Compagnie des Indes, and the history of finance and speculation during the eighteenth century.

Esleben, Jörg. *Enlightenment Canvas: Cultures of Travel, Ethnographic Aesthetics, and Imperialist Discourse in Georg Foster's Writings* (1999). Pp. 284. Dissertation Abstracts International, Section A: The Humanities and Social Sciences 60/10 (April 2000), 3651. Abstract number DA9947612.

Esleben examines the ambivalent relationships of conjunctions of travel literature, ethnography, anthropology, and aesthetics to European imperialism in the writings of Georg Forster (1754–94). In late-eighteenth-century Europe, particularly Germany, Forster's account of James Cook's second circumnavigation from 1772 to 1775, *A Voyage around the World* (1777), his subsequent essays and reviews, his translations of travel literature and of the Indian drama *Sakuntal* by Kalidasa, and his second travel account, *Ansichten vom Niederrhein* (1791), made him an eminent practitioner and theoretician of travel writing as well as contributor to ethnography, philosophical anthropology, and aesthetic theory. Based on a conception of discourse as formation of knowledge and power, this study argues that the combinations of ethnographic, anthropological, and aesthetic discourses in Forster's writings engaging with non-European cultures participate ambivalently in European imperialism: these writings contribute to the formulation of European cultural authority and of an imperialist "civilizing mission," but they also put this authority into question by revealing the contradictory, ambivalent, antagonistic moments involved in formulating cultural difference and authority. Study contains a detailed examination of the relationships between ethnographic representations of the bodies, arts, and social structures of Pacific islanders, aesthetic discourse, and imperialist power in "A Voyage around the World."

Flannery, Tim (ed.). *Two Classic Tales of Australian Exploration; 1788 by Watkin Trench; Life and Adventures by John Nicol*. Introduction by Tim Flannery. Melbourne: Text Publishing, 2000. Pp. viii + 280 + 198; maps; illustrations; bibliographical references; index.

This edition was first published as two separate volumes: One tale is by Watkin Trench (1758 or 1759–1833); one tale is by John Nicol (1755–1825). The books deal with the First Fleet, seafaring life, and the history of settlement in Botany Bay.

Flinders, Matthew (1774–1814). *Voyage to Terra Australis: Matthew Flinders' Great Adventures in the Circumnavigation of Australia*. Edited and introduced by Tim Flannery. Melbourne: Text Publishing, 2000. Pp. xxiv + 268; illustrations; map.

VII: New World Literatures and Languages

Fordyce, Linda, and Kirsten MacLehn. *The Bay: A History of Community at Titahi Bay*. Titahi Bay, New Zealand: Titahi Bay Residents & Ratepayers Progressive Association, 2000. Pp. 200; illustrations; maps; bibliographical references; index.

This book records the development of a community at Titahi Bay, from before the time of Maori settlement through to beach resort plans and state housing projects; it includes chapters on early Maori settlement 1300–1820 and on the arrival of the first Europeans 1820–40.

Forster, Georg. *A Voyage Round the World*. Edited by Nicholas Thomas and Oliver Berghof, assisted by Jennifer Newell. Honolulu: University of Hawaii Press, 2000. 2 volumes. Pp. xlvii + 475; xv + 477; 860; illustrations; maps; bibliographical references; index.

Forster, Johann Reinhold. *The Language of the Noble Savage*. Compiled by Karl H. Rensch. Canberra: Archipelago Press, 2000. Pp. vii + 349; illustrations; bibliographical references.

Forster studies the linguistic fieldwork of Reinhold Forster (1729–98) and George Forster in Polynesia on James Cook's (1728–79) second voyage to the Pacific (1772–1775).

Frame, T[homas], and Kevin R. Baker. *Mutiny! Naval Insurrections in Australia and New Zealand*. St. Leonards: Allen & Unwin, 2000. Pp. xi + 283; illustrations; bibliographical references; index.

Fuchs, Anne. "How to Be a Pilgrim and a Cartographer at the Same Time: Some Deliberations on Intercultural Understanding." Pp. 191–207 of *The Notion of Intercultural Understanding in the Context of German as a Foreign Language*. Edited by Theo Harden, Arnd Witte, and Jeanne Riou; introduction by Theo Harden and Arnd Witte. Oxford: Peter Lang, 2000.

This essay examines Georg Forster and his prose narrative *Reise um die Welt* (1778–80); his treatment of the other, compared to ethnography.

Garber, Jörn (ed.). *Wahrnehmung—Konstruktion—Text: Bilder des Wirklichen im Werk Georg Forsters*. (Hallesche Beiträge zur Europäischen Aufklärung 12.) Tübingen: Niemeyer, 2000. Pp. vi + 233.

Garber, Peter M. *Famous First Bubbles: The Fundamentals of Early Manias*. Cambridge: MIT Press, 2000. Pp. xi + 163; illustrations; map; bibliographical references; index.

Garber's study of speculation history includes chapters on the history of the Compagnie des Indes, the seventeenth century Tulip mania, and the South Sea Bubble in Great Britain in 1720.

Gilbert, Steve (ed.), with the collaboration of Cheralea Gilbert. *Tattoo History: A Source Book: An Anthology of Historical Records of Tattooing Throughout the World*. New York: Juno Books, 2000. Pp. 216; illustrations; map; bibliographical references.

This history of tattooing includes some material on the European voyages of discovery, Joseph Banks, the Islands in the Pacific, Samoa, the Marquesas, and New Zealand.

Grant, John (b. 1776). *This Beauteous, Wicked Place: The Letters and Journals of John Grant, Gentleman Convict*. Edited by Yvonne Cramer. Canberra: National Library of Australia, 2000. Pp. 224; illustrations.

Guest, Harriet. "Curiously Marked: Tattooing and Gender Difference in Eighteenth-Century British Perceptions of the South Pacific." Pp. 83–101 of *Written on the Body: The Tattoo in European and American History*. Edited by Jane Caplan. Princeton: Princeton University Press, 2000.

Hall, Barbara. *A Desperate Set of Villains: The Convicts of the* Marquis Cornwallis, *Ireland to Botany Bay 1796*. Coogee: B. Hall, 2000. Pp. 288; illustrations; map; bibliographical references; index.

Hall-Jones, John. *Milford Sound: An Illustrated History of the Sound, the Track and the Road*. Invercargill: Craig, 2000. Pp. 147.

This book includes material on the period of discovery and exploration and on the history of the design and construction of roads.

Harrison, Jennifer. "'I Beg Your Leave to Accquaint You': Irish-Australian Improvements to Convict Transportation." Pp. 90–101 of *Ireland and Australia, 1798–1998: Studies in Culture, Identity, and Migration*. Edited by Philip Bull, Frances Devlin-Glass, and Helen Doyle. Sydney: Crossing Press, 2000.

Hemming, Christine A. *The Art of the French Voyages to New Zealand 1769–1846*. Auckland: Heritage Press, 2000. Pp. 91; illustrations; bibliography.

Hemming gives pictorial representations of New Zealand and the social life and customs of its Maori inhabitants, by members of the early French voyages of discovery and exploration.

Hiney, Tom. *On the Missionary Trail: A Journey Through Polynesia, Asia, and Africa with the London Missionary Society*. First American edition. New York: Atlantic Monthly Press, 2000. Pp. ix + 367; illustrations; maps; bibliographical references; index.

VII: New World Literatures and Languages 501

Hiney includes material on the journeys of Daniel Tyerman (1773–1828) and George Bennet (b. 1776) to Oceania and on the history of the London Missionary Society.

Holden, Robert. *Orphans of History: The Forgotten Children of the First Fleet*. Melbourne: Text Publishing, 2000. Pp. 219; illustrations; bibliographical references.

Hölz, Karl, Viktoria Schmidt-Linsenhoff, and Herbert Uerlings (eds.). *Beschreiben und Erfinden: Figuren des Fremden vom 18. bis zum 20. Jahrhundert.* (Trierer Studien zur Literatur 34.) Introduction by Karl Hölz. Frankfurt: Peter Lang, 2000. Pp. 240.

Hooker, Brian. "Identifying Cook's Discoveries in Hauraki Gulf—1769." *New Zealand Map Society Journal*, 12 (2000), 93–95.

This is an examination of the chart of the Hauraki Gulf produced by James Cook in 1769 and attempts to identify the features marked and named, particularly those near the approaches to the Waitemata Harbour.

Hoving, Ab, and Cor Emke. *The Ships of Abel Tasman*. Introduction by Peter Sigmond. Hilversum: Verloren, 2000. Pp. 144; illustrations; maps; folded leaves of plates; bibliographical references; 1 computer optical disc. (Title on CD-ROM: *De schepen van Abel Tasman = The Ships of Abel Tasman*. Translation of *De schepen van Abel Tasman*.)

This CD-ROM describes shipbuilding in the Netherlands during the seventeenth century and the discoveries and explorations of Abel Janszoon Tasman (1603?–59).

Johnston, Anna. "On the Importance of Bonnets: The London Missionary Society and Politics of Dress in Nineteenth-Century Polynesia." *New Literatures Review*, 36 (2000), 114–27.

Johnston Includes late eighteenth and early nineteenth century material.

Joy, Samuel. *The Logbook of the* Mary Mitchell *Friday 22nd April–Tuesday 27th of September 1836: Being the Journal of the American Whaling Vessel* Mary Mitchell *commanded by Captain Samuel Joy While at Cloudy Bay During the New Zealand Bay Whaling Season of 1836*. Edited and annotated [that is, written] by Kit Stevens. Porirua: Ambergris, 2000. Pp. 110; illustrations; bibliographical references.

Julen, Hans. *A History of Tasmania's West Coast: From Abel Tasman to Zeehan Railway Station*. Launceston: H. Julen, 2000. Pp. 66; illustrations; plans.

King, Michael. *Moriori: A People Rediscovered*. Revised edition. Auckland: Viking, 2000. Pp. 227; illustrations; maps; bibliographical references; index.

King's is an early history of New Zealand people(s) and their connection with Chatham Islands.

Kitson, Peter J. "'The Eucharist of Hell': Or, Eating People is Right. Romantic Representations of Cannibals." *Romanticism-on-the-Net: An Electronic Journal Devoted to Romantic Studies*, 17 (2000), no pagination.

Knightley, Phillip. *Australia: A Biography of a Nation*. London: Jonathan Cape, 2000. Pp. vii + 373; bibliographical references; index.

Kronauer, Ulrich. "Georg Forsters Einleitung zu *Cook der Entdecker*: Forsters Auseinandersetzung mit Rousseau über Fortschritt und Naturzustand." Pp. 31–42 of *Wahrnehmung—Konstruktion— Text: Bilder des Wirklichen im Werk Georg Forsters*. Edited by Jörn Garber. Tübingen: Niemeyer, 2000.

Kronauer focuses on Forster's (1754–1794) treatment of progress, compared to nature sources in Jean-Jacques Rousseau (1712–1778).

Lamb, Jonathan, Vanessa Smith, and Nicholas Thomas (eds.). *Exploration & Exchange: A South Seas Anthology, 1680–1900*. Chicago: University of Chicago Press, 2000. Pp. xxv + 359; illustrations; maps; bibliographical references; index.

This anthology contains a number of short but well commented excerpts from eighteenth-century explorations of the South Pacific: for example, by William Dampier on the discovery of New Holland; by Samuel Wallis on the discovery of Tahiti; by James Cook, Joseph Banks and John Hawkesworth on the voyage of the *Endeavour*; by Richard Simson and George Anson respectively on the exploration of Juan Fernandez; by William Wilson on missionary voyages to Tahiti; by Edward Roberts on the Marquesa Islands; by Johann Reinhold Forster on cannibalism; by William Wales on the Transit of Venus observed from the Dusky Sound in New Zealand; by James Morrison on the Mutiny on the *Bounty*.

Langdon, Robert. "An Alternative Explanation for Alleged Wreckage of the Caravel *San Lesmes* Found at Amanu." *Journal of Pacific History* 35 (2000), 309–312.

Langdon argues that the wreckage found on Amanu Atoll in the Tuamotu Archipelago by archaeologists of the Groupe de recherche en archeologie navale (GRAN) in 2000 is not from the 16th century Spanish caravel *San Lesmes* but from the early nineteenth century British trading vessel, the *Hercules*.

Langdon, Robert. "'Dusky Damsels': Pitcairn Island's Neglected Matriarchs of the Bounty Saga." *Journal of Pacific History*, 35 (2000), 29–47.

Langdon reexamines the 1920s and 1930s studies of American physical anthropologist Harry L. Shapiro on the inheritance of anthropometric and qualitative traits among descendants of the *Bounty* mutineers and their

Polynesian wives on Norfolk and Pitcairn Islands. He argues that many Tahitians of the *Bounty*'s time were descended from European seamen of the lost caravel *San Lesmes*, who had settled in the Society Islands in 1526.

Leask, Nigel. "Irish Republicans and Gothic Eleutherarchs: Pacific Utopias in the Writings of Theobald Wolfe Tone and Charles Brockden Brown." *Huntington Library Quarterly: Studies in English and American History and Literature*, 63 (2000), 347–67.

Leask examines Irish author Wolfe Tone (1763–1798) and his poem "Sandwich Islands Memorandum," its treatment of utopia, and its relationship to America and the French Revolution. He compares him to Charles Brockden Brown (1771–1810), especially his *Memoirs of Carwin the Biloquist* (1815) and *Wieland* (1798).

Ledyard, John. "From *A Journal of Captain Cook's Last Voyage*." Pp. 37–48 of *American Sea Writing: A Literary Anthology*. Edited by Peter Neill; foreword by Nathaniel Philbrick. New York: Library of America, 2000.

Lewis, Miles. "Making Do." Pp. 41–56 of *A History of European Housing in Australia*. Edited with an introduction by Patrick Troy. Cambridge: Cambridge University Press, 2000.

Maack, Annegret. "'It's All Contrary'—Utopian Projections in the Antipodes." *Antipodes: A North American Journal of Australian Literature*, 14 (2000), 123–28.

Marsden, Susan. "The Introduction of Order." Pp. 26–40 of *A History of European Housing in Australia*. Edited with an introduction by Patrick Troy. Cambridge: Cambridge University Press, 2000.

Matthews, Tony. *Shipwrecks and Seafarers' Scandals: True Tales from Colonial Queensland and the South Pacific*. Warwick: CQU Press, 2000. Pp. 250; illustrations; bibliographical references; index.

Maxwell-Stewart, Hamish, and Ian Duffield. "Skin Deep Devotions: Religious Tattoos and Convict Transportation to Australia." Pp. 118–35 of *Written on the Body: The Tattoo in European and American History*. Edited by Jane Caplan. Princeton: Princeton University Press, 2000.

McIntyre, Perry, and Adele Cathro. *Thomas Dunn: Convict and Chief Constable and His Descendants*. Spit Junction: PR Ireland, 2000. Pp. 230; illustrations; maps; bibliographical references; index.

This is a biography of New South Wales Prisoner Thomas Dunn (d. 1832) from Ireland and his family.

Mitchell, Glenn. "An Industry Time Forgot." Pp. 77–85 of *A History of European Housing in Australia*. Edited with an introduction by Patrick Troy. Cambridge: Cambridge University Press, 2000.

Molony, John N[eylon]. *The Native-Born: The First White Australians*. Carlton South: Melbourne University Press, 2000. Pp. xi + 252; illustrations; maps; bibliographical references; index.

Australian history, social life and customs, 1788–1851, are the focus of this volume.

Moore, Andrew. "The United Irishmen and South-West Sydney: A Reconsideration of the Waldersee Thesis." Pp. 34–47 of *Ireland and Australia, 1798–1998: Studies in Culture, Identity, and Migration*. Edited by Philip Bull, Frances Devlin-Glass, and Helen Doyle. Sydney: Crossing Press, 2000.

National Library of Australia. *The World Upside Down: Australia 1788–1830*. Canberra: National Library of Australia, 2000. Pp. v + 58; 6 leaves of plates; illustrations, facsimiles; bibliographical references. http://www.nla.gov.au/exhibitions/upsidedown.

These are essays to accompany the exhibition "The World Upside Down: Australia 1788–1833," at the National Library of Australia (March 4–June 25, 2000). They include European eyewitness accounts of indigenous peoples, first impressions by female visitors, British reactions to the landscape of New South Wales, and memories of childhood experience in the Australian colonies.

Neill, Peter (ed.). *American Sea Writing: A Literary Anthology*. Foreword by Nathaniel Philbrick. New York: Library of America, 2000. Pp. xxi + 671; bibliographical references.

O'Farrell, Patrick James. *The Irish in Australia: 1788 to the Present*. Revised edition. Notre Dame: University of Notre Dame Press, 2000. Pp. 363; illustrations; bibliographical references; index.

Since the First Fleet of 1788, the Irish have been coming to Australia. They were the beginning of a central, colorful and profoundly influential element in Australia's evolution into a nation different and separate from Britain. Commencing with Irish convicts, feared and despised, followed by free Irish immigrants and settlers into the often hostile texture of colonial life, they came to see themselves as patriotic Australians, integrating into all levels and facets of national life and character, many occupying the highest positions in the land in government, law and commerce. This edition features a revised final chapter, which deals with the changing relationship between Australians, new Irish and Irish Australians.

O'Neill, Pamela, and Jonathan M. Wooding (eds.). *Literature and Politics in the Celtic World: Papers from the Third Australian Conference of Celtic Studies, University of Sydney, July 1998*. (Sydney Series in Celtic Studies 4.) Sydney: Foundation for Celtic Studies, University of Sydney, 2000. Pp. vii + 384.

VII: New World Literatures and Languages

Phillips, Caroline. *Waihou Journeys: The Archaeology of 400 Years of Maori Settlement*. Auckland: Auckland University Press, 2000. Pp. xiv + 194.

Phillips, Roderick. *A Short History of Wine*. London: Allen Lane, 2000. Pp. xxi + 369; maps; bibliographical references; index.

This volume is comprised of chapters on "Wine in New Worlds: The Americas, Africa and Australia, 1500–1800" and on "Wine, Enlightenment and Revolution: Europe in the Eighteenth Century."

Porter, David. "from *Journal of a Cruise Made to the Pacific Ocean*." Pp. 52–57 of *American Sea Writing: A Literary Anthology*. Edited by Peter Neill; foreword by Nathaniel Philbrick. New York: Library of America, 2000.

Protos, Alec. *The Road to Botany Bay: The Story of Frenchmans Road Reandwick Through the Journals of Laperouse and the First Fleet Writers*. Compiled with an introduction by Alec Protos. Revised edition. Sydney: Randwick & District Historical Society, 2000. Pp. 32; illustrations; maps.

These historical sources are related to the First Fleet (1787–88), Jean-Francois de Galaup, Comte de La Perouse (1741–88), and the settlement of New South Wales.

Rice, Anthony. *Voyages of Discovery*. German. *Der verzauberte Blick: Das Naturbild berühmter Expeditionen aus drei Jahrhunderten*. Translated by Fried Schmitz. München: Verlag Frederking & Thaler, 2000. Pp. 335; illustrations; bibliographical references; index.

In his volume Rice offers travel reports by James Cook, Joseph Banks and Sydney Parkinson on their journey onboard the *Endeavour*; by James Cook, Johann and Georg Forster on their search for "Terra Australis"; by Matthew Flinders and Ferdinand Bauer on their voyage onboard the *Investigator*.

Robson, John. *Captain Cook's World: Maps of the Life and Voyages of James Cook, R. N.* Auckland: Random House New Zealand, 2000. Pp. 212; [chiefly collection of] maps; bibliographical references.

Schaffeld, Norbert. "The Making of a Myth: Irish Convicts, Diggers and Bushrangers in Australian Literature." Pp. 65–94 of *Writing in Australia: Perceptions of Australian Literature in Its Historical and Cultural Context. A Series of Lectures Given at Hamburg University on the Occasion of the 1st Festival of Australian Literature in Hamburg 1995*. Edited by Gerd Dose and Bettina Keil. Münster: Lit Verlag, [2000].

Seixo, Maria Alziro (ed.). *Travel Writing and Cultural Memory/Ecriture du voyage et mémoire culturelle*. Foreword by Maria Alziro Seixo. (Proceedings of the XVth Congress of the International

Comparative Literature Association '"iterature as Cultural Memory," Leiden, August 16–22, 1997, volume 9.) Amsterdam: Rodopi, 2000. Pp. 293.

Sellick, Douglas R. G. (comp.). *First Impressions, Albany: Travellers' Tales 1791–1901*. Reprint. Perth: Western Australian Museum, 2000. Pp. xiii + 234; illustrations.

Sinclair, Keith. *A History of New Zealand*. Revised edition with additional material by Raewyn Dalziel. Auckland: Penguin, 2000. Pp. 396; bibliographical references; index.

Scott, Bill. "Traditional Ballad Verse in Australia." *Folklore*, 111 (2000), 309–13.

Smith, Bernard. "Constructing 'Pacific' Peoples." Pp. 152–68 of *Remembrance of Pacific Pasts: An Invitation to Remake History*. Edited by Robert Borofsky. Honolulu: University of Hawaii Press, 2000.

This essay deals with James Cook's perception of indigenous peoples.

Stratmann, Silke. *Myths of Speculation: The South Sea Bubble and 18th-Century English Literature*. (Münchner Studien zur neueren englischen Literatur= Munich Studies in English Literature 10.) München: Fink, 2000. Pp. 218; illustrations; bibliographical references.

Based on the author's thesis, this book was previously published in part under the title *South Sea's at Best a Mighty Bubble*.

Taylor, Brian. "Ossian and the Antipodes: The Macpherson Controversy and Some Australian Connections With It." [Page numbers unavailable] *Literature and Politics in the Celtic World: Papers from the Third Australian Conference of Celtic Studies, University of Sydney, July 1998*. (Sydney Series in Celtic Studies 4.) Edited by Pamela O'Neill and Jonathan M. Wooding. Sydney: Foundation for Celtic Studies, University of Sydney, 2000.

Thomson, Arthur S[aunders]. *The Story of New Zealand: Past and Present, Savage and Civilized*. Facsimile edition. Christchurch: Kiwi Publishers, 2000. Pp. ix + 331; vii + 368; illustrations; maps; bibliographical references; index.

Thompson includes material on New Zealand prior to 1840.

Tolron, Francine. *La Nouvelle-Zélande: du duel au duo? Essai d'histoire culturelle*. Toulouse: Presses Universitaires du Mirail, 2000. Pp. 338; illustrations; map; bibliography.

Tolron covers pre-colonial history of New Zealand/Oceania.

VII: New World Literatures and Languages

Toohey, John. *Captain Bligh's Portable Nightmare.* New York: Harper Collins Publishers, [2000]. Pp. vii + 211; illustrations; maps; bibliographical references.

This biographical work emphasizes Bligh's (1754–1817) great mapmaking skills, used to particular effect while he was exploring with Captain Cook; discovers his guilt over Cook's death at Kealakekua Bay; examines the failure of the Bounty expedition (1789) and the myths that surround it, the trails and retributions that followed Bligh's return to England, his successes as a navigator and as a vice-admiral fighting next to Nelson at the Battle of Copenhagen. Toohey dismisses the black legend of the cruel and foulmouthed Captain William Bligh.

Troy, Patrick (ed.). *A History of European Housing in Australia.* Introduction by Patrick Troy. Cambridge: Cambridge University Press, 2000. Pp. xiv + 325.

This is a history of Australian material culture, 1700–1999.

Uerlings, Herbert. "Geschlecht und Fortschritt: Zu Georg Forsters Reise um die Welt und dem Diskurs der 'Universalgeschichten des weiblichen Geschlechts.'" Pp. 13–44 of *Beschreiben und Erfinden: Figuren des Fremden vom 18. bis zum 20. Jahrhundert.* (Trierer Studien zur Literatur 34.) Edited by Karl Hölz, Viktoria Schmidt-Linsenhoff, and Herbert Uerlings; introduction by Karl Hölz. Frankfurt: Peter Lang, 2000.

Vaggioli, Dom Felice (1845–1921). *History of New Zealand and Its Inhabitants.* Translated by John Crockett. (Originally published 1896 in Parma.) Dunedin: University of Otago Press, 2000. Pp. xxiii + 340; illustrations.

Veit, Walter F. "Voyages of Dicovery and the Critique of European Civilization." Pp. 57–82 of *Travel Writing and Cultural Memory/Ecriture du voyage et mémoire culturelle.* (Proceedings of the XVth Congress of the International Comparative Literature Association "Literature as Cultural Memory," Leiden, August 16–22, 1997, volume 9.) Edited with foreword by Maria Alziro Seixo Amsterdam: Rodopi, 2000. Pp. 293.

Voigt, Johannes. "The Origin of Australian National Consciousness." Pp. 19–36 of *Writing in Australia: Perceptions of Australian Literature in Its Historical and Cultural Context. A Series of Lectures Given at Hamburg University on the Occasion of the 1st Festival of Australian Literature in Hamburg 1995.* Edited by Gerd Dose and Bettina Keil. Münster: Lit Verlag, [2000].

Waterhouse, Henry. *The First Map of Port Jackson (as Chartered by Midshipman Waterhouse & Lt. Bradley 1788); Bennelong's Spearhead, from the Spear Broken from Govr. Phillip's Shoulder by Lt. Waterhouse at Manly 1790; Henry Waterhouse's First Fleet Manuscript 1788–1791; Capt. Waterhouse RN's Letter to Viscount Sydney Reporting His Purchase and Importation of the Colony's First Merion Sheep and Thoroughbred Horses. Sydney Cove 1797: All in Facsimile Form.* (Australian Desiderata.) Sydney: R. & L. Waterhouse, 2000. 14 leaves of plates; illustrations; map.

This is a limited edition of twenty copies. It deals with the correspondence of Henry Waterhouse (d. 1812); early cartography in Australia (Port Jackson and Broken Bay) involving Arthur Phillip (1738–1814), Bennelong (1764?–1813), and the ship *Sirius*.

Waterhouse, Richard. "Australian Legends: Representations of the Bush, 1813–1913." *Australian Historical Studies*, 31 (2000), 201–21.

Webb, Vivienne. *Les sauvages de la Mer Pacifique: Manufactured by Joseph Dufour et Cie 1804 after a Design by Jean Gabriel Charvet*. Sydney: Art Gallery of New South Wales; Canberra: National Gallery of Australia, [2000]. (Australian Collection Focus 7.) Pp. 48; illustrations; bibliographical references.

This is a volume on landscape in art, early European views of Polynesians, and the history of French wallpapers.

Australia, New Zealand, and Adjacent Literatures and Cultures (2001 Imprints)

Aimer, Don. "Pacific Dreaming." *New Zealand Geographic*, 51 (2001), 62–78.

Aimer provides the backgrounds for the fascination of eighteenth century Europeans with Polynesia and its inhabitants. He focuses on the voyages of explorers such as James Cook, noting the contributions to science made by their observations of plants, animals, and the way of life of the peoples encountered. He refers to the popularity of books published on the Pacific, and to observations of the transit of Venus and suggests that, despite moments of disillusion, the idea of the noble savage lived on into the twentieth century, under the patronage of anthropologist Margaret Mead.

Alexander, Alison, with Prue Torney-Parlicki. *A Wealth of Women: Australian Women's Lives from 1788 to the Present*. Potts Point: Duffy & Snellgrove, 2001. Pp. ix + 300; illustrations; bibliographical references; index.

Anderson, Grahame. *The Merchant of the Zeehaen: Isaac Gilsemans and the Voyages of Abel Tasman*. Wellington: Te Papa Press, 2001. Pp. x + 162; illustrations; maps; bibliographical references; index.

Arnold, Ken. *Australia, Somewhere in Time: A Brief History of the Navigators, the Explorers, and the Colonies Leading Up to and Including Federation*. Bendigo: Crown Castleton Publishers, 2001. Pp. 335; illustrations; maps; bibliographical references; index.

Attwood, Bain, and Fiona Magowan (eds.). *Telling Stories: Indigenous History and Memory in Australia and New Zealand*. Wellington: Bridget Williams Books; Crows Nest: Allen & Unwin, 2001. Pp. xvii + 269; illustrations.

VII: New World Literatures and Languages

Badger, Geoffrey Malcolm. *Explorers of Australia.* East Roseville: Kangaroo Press, 2001. Pp. viii + 312; illustrations; maps; bibliographical references; index.

Barrington, George (1755–1804). *George Barrington's Voyage to Botany Bay: Retelling a Convict's Travel Narrative of the 1790s.* Edited by Suzanne Rickard. London: Leicester University Press, 2001. Pp. xxiv + 181; illustrations; map; bibliographical references and index.

This fully annotated edition identifies the work's original textual sources and illuminates its complex publishing history. It also focuses on contemporary debates concerning penal settlement, punishment, racial encounters and the manipulation of knowledge. George Barrington's surprising credentials as author allowed an exotic interpretation of events and inflamed European curiosity about the colony's settlement. Shrewd publishers exploited the famous name and presented a seamless and colorful assemblage cut from official journals, revealing the extent of close contact with aboriginal peoples, the treatment of convicts and discovery of unusual plants and animals. Bearing all the hallmarks of authenticity, Barrington's account gained a singular place in popular contemporary travel and exploration literature, providing the foundation for a long series of embellished and illustrated histories. Botany Bay's reputation for cruel deprivation often overshadowed tales of opportunity presented to the talented. Barrington's revival as a reformed convict helped transform his own image, while the narrative's insights into the rigors of transportation, the struggle for survival and daily life in the penal colony initiated a lively convict travel literature. Barrington's work has become known as *Voyage to Botany Bay*. The version of Barrington's *Voyage* used in this work is entitled: *An Impartial and Circumstantial Narrative of the Present State of Botany Bay, in New South Wales... by George Barrington, now Superintendent of the Convicts at Paramata,* published circa 1793 by S. & J. Bailey, London.

Belich, James. *Making Peoples: A History of the New Zealanders: From Polynesian Settlement to the End of the Nineteenth Century.* Auckland: Penguin, 2001. Pp. 497; maps; bibliography; index.

This volume covers New Zealand history to 1840.

Bender, Barbara, and Margot Winer (eds.). *Contested Landscapes: Movement, Exile and Place.* Oxford: Berg, 2001. Pp. xvi + 372; plates; illustrations; maps.

Bergin, Tom. *Sunken Sagas: Whalers of the Coral Sea: The Forgotten Pioneers of Queensland, 1793–1852.* Queensland: Bergin Publications, 2001. Pp. iv + 186; illustrations; maps; bibliographical references.

Binney, Judith (ed.). *The Shaping of History: Essays from the New Zealand Journal of History.* Wellington: Bridget Williams Books, 2001. Pp. xvi + 422; illustrations; bibliography.

Bird Rose, Deborah. "The Saga of Captain Cook: Remembrance and Morality." Pp. 76–95 of *Telling Stories: Indigenous History and Memory in Australia and New Zealand.* Edited by Bain Attwood and Fiona Magowan. Wellington: Bridget Williams Books/Crows Nest: Allen & Unwin, 2001.

Bligh, John H. *Vice Admiral William Bligh FRS: A Biography*. Rochester: John Bligh, 2001. Pp. 341; illustrations; bibliographical references; index.

Bligh, William (1754–1817), and Edward Christian (1758–1823). *The Bounty Mutiny*. (Penguin Classics.) With an introduction by R. D. Madison. New York: Penguin Books, 2001. Pp. xxv + 254; illustrations; bibliographical references.

Blosseville, Jules-Alphonse-René Poret, Baron de (1802–1833). "Blosseville's *Projet d'une colonie pénale à la Nouvelle Zélande*: Text and Translation." Translated with an introduction by Martin Purdy. *New Zealand Journal of French Studies*, 22 (2001), 5–41.

Cobeldick, Trevor. "The First New Zealand." *History Now*, 7 (2001), 6–10.

Cobeldick investigates the earliest use of the name "New Zealand" for a Dutch discovery in the eastern seas. Backgrounds the voyage of the yacht *Duifken* (Duyfken) in 1605–1606, under the auspices of the Vereenigde Oostindische Compagnie (VOC) United East Indies Company, and discusses the use of the name "New Zealand" for a piece of the New Guinea coast on a map produced by one of the complement of the ship. Traces the later names for this first "New Zealand."

Conlin Casella, Eleanor. "Landscapes of Punishment and Resistance: A Female Convict Settlement in Tasmania, Australia." Pp. 103–20 of *Contested Landscapes: Movement, Exile and Place*. Edited by Barbara Bender and Margot Winer. Oxford: Berg, 2001.

Cosgrove, Peter (ed.). *Australia: The Complete Story*. Foreword and introduction by Peter Cosgrove. Noble Park: Five Mile Press, 2001. Pp. 912; illustrations; maps; 1 CD-ROM; indexes.

Crawford, Patricia, and Philippa Maddern (eds.). *Women as Australian Citizens: Underlying Histories*. Carlton South: Melbourne University Press, 2001. Pp. xii + 284; illustrations.

Creed, Barbara, and Jeanette Hoorn (eds.). *Body Trade: Captivity, Cannibalism, and Colonialism in the Pacific*. Introduction by Barabara Creed and Jeanette Hoorn; foreword by Peter Hulme. Annandale: Pluto Press, 2001. Pp. xxii + 296; illustrations; bibliography; index.

Captivity, cannibalism, the circus, trading in bodies, prostitution, the Stolen Generation: this book examines the historical and cultural significance of the way in which the human body has been held captive, traded and placed on display throughout the western world.

Crocombe, R. G. *The South Pacific*. Rewritten, updated, and expanded edition. Suva: Institute of Pacific Studies, University of the South Pacific, 2001. Pp. 790; illustrations; maps; bibliographical references; index.

VII: New World Literatures and Languages

Crocombe includes information relevant for the study of eighteenth-century literature and culture.

Cuthbertson, Bern. *In the Wake of Bass and Flinders: 200 Years On: The Story of the Re-Enactment Voyages 200 Years on in the Whaleboat* Elizabeth *and the Replica Sloop* Norfolk *to Celebrate the Bicentenary of the Voyages of George Bass and Matthew Flinders*. Sandy Bay: Bern and Jan Cuthbertson, 2001. Pp. xi + 321; illustrations; maps; bibliographical references.

This is a volume on Matthew Flinders's (1774–1814) and George Bass's (1771–1803) journeys to Australia.

Davison, Graeme, John Hirst, and Stuart Macintyre. (eds.). *The Oxford Companion to Australian History*. Revised edition. South Melbourne: Oxford University Press, 2001. Pp. xx + 722; maps; index.

Day, David. *Claiming a Continent: A New History of Australia*. Pymble: Harper Collins, 2001. Pp. 352; bibliographical references; index.

Dugard, Martin. *Farther Than Any Man: The Rise and Fall of Captain James Cook*. Crow's Nest: Allen & Unwin, 2001. Pp. xiv + 287; maps; index.

Ellingson, Terry Jay. *The Myth of the Noble Savage*. Berkeley: University of California Press, 2001. Pp. xxii + 445; illustrations; bibliography; index.

Entrecasteaux, Antoine Raymond Joseph de Bruni, chevalier d' (1737–93). *Voyage de Dentrecasteaux, envoyé à la recherche de La Pérouse*. English. *Voyage to Australia & the Pacific, 1791–1793*. Edited and translated by Edward Duyker and Maryse Duyker. Carlton South: Melbourne University Press, 2001. Pp. xliii + 392; illustrations; maps; bibliographical references; index.

Esleben, Jörg. "Georg Forster's Dialectic of Imperialist Desire." *Seminar: A Journal of Germanic Studies*, 37 (2001), 305–22.

Espák, Gabriella Tóthné. "Perceptions of the Land and the Aborigine in Australia." *British and American Studies/Revista de Studii Britanice si Americane*, 7 (2001), 47–61.

This essay covers European treatment of landscape and Australian aborigines during the long eighteenth century.

Farrell, Rita. "Women and Citizenship in Colonial Australia." Pp. 115–40 of *Women as Australian Citizens: Underlying Histories*. Edited by Patricia Crawford and Philippa Maddern. Carlton South: Melbourne University Press, 2001.

Fitzsymonds, Eustace (ed.). *Connoisseurs in Paintings: George Frankland and the Aborigines of Van Diemen's Land*. Adelaide: James Dally, 2001. Pp. 32; illustrations; bibliographical references.

This volume deals with the art of Aboriginal Tasmanian George Frankland (1800–38) and the History of Tasmania, 1803–1900.

Flynn, Dennis O., Arturo Giráldez, and James Sobredo (eds.). *European Entry in the Pacific: Spain and the Acapulco-Manila Galleons*. Brookfield: Ashgate Publishing Company, 2001. (The Pacific World 4.) Pp. xliii + 392; illustrations.

Freycinet, Louis Claude Desaulses de (1779–1842). *Reflections on New South Wales 1788–1839*. [that is, *Voyage autour du monde*. English. Selections.] Potts Point: Hordern House, 2001. Pp. xxi + 670; illustrations; maps; bibliographical references; index.

Now translated into English for the first time from the original publication of Freycinet's *Voyage autour du monde* (Paris, 1824–44) by Thomas Brendan Cullity, Jean and Bernice Pasquier, and Katharine Pratt Freycinet's examination of the history and progress of the colony of New South Wales during the first fifty-two years, based on his visit to Port Jackson as commander of the *Uranie* in 1819, his earlier visit with the *Baudin* voyage in 1802, his interviews and subsequent correspondence with the colonists themselves, and his close analysis of the published literature to 1839. This edition is limited to three-hundred copies.

Frost, Lucy, and Hamish Maxwell-Stewart. *Chain Letters: Narrating Convict Lives*. Carlton South: Melbourne University Press, 2001. Pp. xiv + 248; illustrations; bibliographical references.

Fulford, Tim, and Peter J. Kitson (eds.), advisory editor Tim Youngs. *Travels, Explorations and Empires: Writings from the Era of Imperial Expansion, 1770–1835*. 2 sets of 4 volumes. Volumes 1–4: *Travel Writings on North America, the Far East, North and South Poles and the Middle East*. Volumes 5–8: *Travel Writings on Africa, India, The Caribbean, South Seas and Australasia*. London: Pickering & Chatto, 2001. Pp. xlii + 405; xxiii + 389; xxii + 401; xxviii + 368; xxxvi + 441; xvi + 336; xxi + 412 ; xxvii + 445; illustrations; bibliographies; indexes.

These volumes are anthologies with facsimile editions of eighteenth-century and early nineteenth-century travel documents.

Fullerton, Susannah, and Anne Harbers (eds.). *Jane Austen: Antipodean Views*. Neutral Bay: Wellington Lane Press, 2001. Pp. 168; illustrations; index.

Furbank, P. N., and W. R. Owens. "Defoe's 'South-Sea' and 'North-Sea' Schemes: A Footnote to A New Voyage Round the World." *Eighteenth-Century Fiction*, 13 (2001), 501–08.

VII: New World Literatures and Languages

Garvey, Robert. *To Build a Ship: The VOC Replica Ship, Duyfken.* Crawley: University of Western Australia under Tuart House, 2001. Pp. 104; illustrations.

This volume is about the ship (and replica) *Duyfken* which was involved in the Dutch discovery and seventeenth-century exploration of Australia; its design and construction; pictorial works.

Gascoigne, John. *Joseph Banks and His Abiding Legacy.* London: Menzies Centre for Australian Studies, 2001. (London Papers in Australian Studies 2.) Pp. 12; bibliographical references.

Gosden, Chris, and Chantal Knowles. *Collecting Colonialism: Material Culture and Colonial Change.* Oxford: Berg, 2001. Pp. xxi + 234; illustrations; bibliography; index.

Gosden examines the history of material culture in Papua New Guinea, and of foreign influences on civilizations in Oceania, especially the British impact on its colonies in the Pacific.

Griffin, Gwen. *Female Skeletons in the Cupboard: Stories of Convict Women at Port Macquarie.* Port Macquarie: Port Macquarie Historical Society, 2001. Pp. [not available]; illustrations; bibliographical references; index.

Griffin provides a history of women prisoners in the penal colony of New South Wales, Port Macquarie.

Guest, Kristen (ed.). *Eating Their Words: Cannibalism and the Boundaries of Cultural Identity.* Foreword by Maggie Kilgour; introduction by Kristen Guest. New York: State University of New York Press, 2001. Pp. ix + 219.

Harcourt, Rex. *Southern Invasion—Northern Conquest: Story of the Founding of Melbourne.* Blackburn South: Golden Point Press, 2001. Pp. x + 247; illustrations; maps; bibliography; index.

Hoyle, Arthur. *The Life of John Hunter: Navigator, Governor, Admiral. (1738– 1821).* (First Fleet Books 6.) Canberra: Mulini Press, 2001. Pp. 189; illustrations; maps; bibliographical references; index.

This is a biography of the early Australian Governor of New South Wales, John Hunter (1738–1821) and the First Fleet (1787–88).

Ingram, Edward. The *British Empire as a World Power.* London: Frank Cass, 2001. Pp. xiv + 282; bibliographical references; index.

Irvine, Nancy. *Mary Reibey, Molly Incognita: A Biography of Mary Reibey (1777 to 1855) and Her World*. Second edition. Sydney: Library of Australian History, 2001. Pp. xviii + 161; illustrations; maps; bibliographical references.

Johnson, Richard. *The Search for the Inland Sea: John Oxley, Explorer, 1783–1828*. Carlton South: Melbourne University Press, 2001. Pp. xii + 305; illustrations; maps; bibliographical references; index.

This is a biography of John Oxley, with a focus on his explorations in the Australian Lachlan River Region and the Macquarie River Region, New South Wales.

Kirch, Patrick Vinton, and Roger Curtis Green. *Hawaiki, Ancestral Polynesia: An Essay in Historical Anthropology*. Cambridge: Cambridge University Press, 2001. Pp. xvii + 375; illustrations; maps; bibliography; indexes.

Kitson, Peter J. (ed.). *Placing and Displacing Romanticism*. Introduction by Peter J. Kitson. Aldershot: Ashgate Publishing Company, 2001. Pp. xv + 232.

Kitson, Peter J. "Romantic Displacements: Representing Cannibalism." Pp. 204–25 of *Placing and Displacing Romanticism*. Edited and with an introduction by Peter J. Kitson. Aldershot: Ashgate Publishing Company, 2001.

Kitson, Peter J. (ed.). *Travels, Explorations and Empires: Writings from the Era of Imperial Expansion, 1770–1835*. Volume 8: *South Seas and Australasia*. London: Pickering & Chatto, 2001. Pp. xxvii + 445; illustrations; bibliography, index.

Kitson has compiled an anthology with facsimile editions of eighteenth-century and early nineteenth-century travel documents, including excerpts from texts by John Hawkesworth, James Cook, Johann Reinhold Forster, Georg Forster, David Samwell, George Keate, William Bligh, George Hamilton, Mary Ann Parker, David Collins, Robert Southey, George Vason, Matthew Flinders, and John Martin.

Lamb, Jonathan. *Preserving the Self in the South Seas, 1680–1840*. Chicago: University of Chicago Press, 2001. Pp. xii + 345; illustrations; bibliography; index.

Lamb's collection includes chapters on "The Romancing of the Civil Self," "Political Theories of the Self," " The Romance of Navigation," "Science and Collecting," "Scurvy," "The Polynesian Person and the Spread of Leprosy," " From Juan Fernandez to New Zealand," "Void Contracts and Subtle Islands," "Patriots in Paradise," "Starlings and Parrots; Keate and Sympathy," and "The Settlement of New Zealand."

VII: New World Literatures and Languages 515

Mageo, Jeannette Marie (ed.). *Cultural Memory: Reconfiguring History and Identity in the Postcolonial Pacific.* Honolulu: University of Hawaii Press, 2001. Pp. vi + 222; bibliographical references; index.

Mageo examines social aspects of memory, group identity, and intergroup ethnic relations with a focus on case studies from the smaller Pacific islands, not on Australia or New Zealand. But also offers more general reflections on the impact of the "encounter" between Oceania and western colonial forces and their culture of memory.

Maroto Camino, Mercedes. "Maps, Traffic, and Representation: The Iberian Pacific in the Sixteenth Century." Pp. 31–54 of *Crossings: Travel, Art, Literature, Politics.* Edited with introduction by Rudolphus Teeuwen. Taipei: Bookman, 2001.

Maroto examines Spanish literature 1600–99; the focus of interest on Pedro Fernández de Quirós (d. 1615) and his travel narrative *Relación de un memorial que ha presentado a su Magestad* (1610); his treatment of exploration in Oceania; his relationship to cartographers; representation of colonialism; compared to Antonio Pigafetta,(1480/91?– 1534?), especially his *Relazione del primo viaggio intorno al mondo*.

Marquardt, Karl Heinz. *Captain Cook's Endeavour.* Revised edition. London: Conway Maritime Press, 2001. Pp. 136; illustrations; fold-out plan; bibliographical references.

Mayer, Matthew. "Criminal History Transported: An Enquiry into the Literary Origins of Australian Convict Narratives." *Australian Studies*, 16 (2001), 45–62.

McCarthy, Kathleen D. (ed.). *Women, Philanthropy, and Civil Society.* Bloomington: Indiana University Press, 2001. Pp. v + 314.

McDonald, Ean. *Finders Keepers, Or, Terra to Let, Or, Who Put Australia on the Map?* Revised edition. Gooseberry Hill: Ean McDonald, 2001. 50 leaves; illustrations; maps.

Nautical astronomy, navigation, discovery, and exploration of Australia to 1788 are subjects explored in this volume.

McLean, Gavin. *Captain's Log: New Zealand's Maritime History.* Auckland: Hodder Moa Beckett, 2001. Pp. 224.

McNeill, J. R. (ed.). *Environmental History in the Pacific World.* (The Pacific World 2.) Brookfield: Ashgate Publishing Company, 2001. Pp. xxix + 385.

Meaney, Neville. "Britishness and Australian Identity. The Problem of Nationalism in Australian History and Historiography." *Australian Historical Studies*, 32 (2001), 76–90.

Monin, Paul. *This Is My Place: Hauraki Contested, 1769–1875.* Wellington: Bridget Williams Books, 2001. Pp. 284; illustrations; bibliographical references; index.

Moran, Kevin James. *Rottnest. Volume One: Ghosts of Wadjemup: A History of the Discovery, the Settlement, Aboriginal Penal Colony, Boy's Reformatory, the Development of Rottnest as a Holiday Isle.* Perth: Vision Syndicate, 2001. Pp. 219; illustrations; map; bibliographical references.

Morgenroth, Matthias. *Nachrichten aus dem Land der Gegenfüssler: Untersuchungen zur deutschen Australienliteratur.* Tübingen: Stauffenburg, 2001. Pp. 333; illustrations; bibliographical references.

Musée national des arts d'Afrique et d'Océanie. *Kannibals et vahinés: imagerie des mers du Sud* [exposition], Paris, Musée national des arts d'Afrique et d'Océanie, 23 octobre 2001–18 février 2002. Commissaire Roger Boulay. Paris: Réunion des musée nationaux, 2001. Pp. 183; illustrations; bibliographical references.

This is a catalogue of an exhibition on the history of Oceania, including aspects such as indigenous peoples in popular culture, Pacific Islanders and their first contact with Europeans, cultural assimilation, travel descriptions, and south seas inhabitants perceived as curiosities and wonders.

National Library of Australia. *Cook & Omai: The Cult of the South Seas.* A collection of essays and catalogue of the exhibition "Cook & Omai: The Cult of the South Seas," held at the National Library of Australia in association with the Humanities Research Centre, the Australian National University Catalogue. Curated for the National Library of Australia by Michelle Hetherington in association with Iain McCalman and Alexander Cook of the Humanities Research Centre, The Australian National University. Canberra: National Library of Australia, 2001. Pp. v + 66; illustrations.

This volume comprises Michelle Hetherington's "The Cult of the South Seas," Iain McCalman's "Spectacles of Knowledge: OMAI as Ethnographic Travelogue," Christa Knellwolf's "Comedy in the OMAI Pantomime," Caroline Turner's "Images of Mai," Harriet Guest's "Omai's Things," Alexander Cook's "The Art of Ventriloquism: European Imagination and the Pacific," Paul Turnbull's "Mai, the Other Beyond the Exotic Stranger," and Greg Dening's "O Mai! This is Mai: A Masque of a Sort."

National Library of Australia. *Cook & Omai: The Cult of the South Seas.* (Pandora Electronic Collection.) Canberra: National Library of Australia, 2001. http://www.nla.gov.au/exhibitions/omai

In 1774, the first Polynesian to visit London traveled to England with the crew of Captain Cook's second Pacific voyage and became an overnight sensation. Seen as a living example of the "Noble Savage," Omai (b. 1753?) as he was known, was discussed by scientists and philosophers, celebrated in all the best circles and written about in everything from poetry to pornography. He proved a lightning rod for European anxieties regarding imperialism, civilization, and the true nature of mankind. The artistic and literary legacy of Omai's encounter with Europe provides a fascinating insight into European culture in a moment of transition, when old certainties were collapsing and new ones were yet to form. *Cook & Omai: The Cult of the South Seas* has been developed by the National Library of Australia in association with the Humanities Research Centre of the Australian National University. The online version of the exhibition includes interpretive text and images from the Library's Rex Nan Kivell Collection.

Pocock, J. G. A. "Tangata Whenua and Enlightenment Anthropology." Pp. 38–61 of *The Shaping of History: Essays from the New Zealand Journal of History*. Edited by Judith Binney. Wellington: Bridget Williams Books, 2001.

Prickett, Stephen. "Schleiermacher Among the Aborigines." Pp. 321–28 of *Colonies, Missions, Cultures in the English Speaking World: General and Comparative Studies*. Edited with an introduction by Gerhard Stilz.. Tübingen: Stauffenburg, 2001.

Examines the influence of David Collins (1756–1810), "Account of the English Colony in New South Wales" (1798) on Friedrich Ernst Schleiermacher (1768–1834), "Über die Religion: Reden an die Gebildeten unter ihren Verachtern" (1799).

Reece, Bob. *The Origins of Irish Convict Transportation to New South Wales*. Houndmills: Palgrave, 2001. Pp. xx + 373; illustrations; maps; bibliography; index.

This study explores the pre-history of Irish convict transportation to New South Wales which began with the *Queen* in April 1791. It traces earlier attempts to revive the trans-Atlantic convict trade and the frustrated efforts by Irish authorities to join in the Botany Bay scheme after 1786. The nine Irish shipments to North America and the West Indies are described in detail for the first time, including the dramatic outcomes in Nova Scotia, Newfoundland, and the Leeward Islands, which eventually forced the Home Office to find space for Irish convicts on the Third Fleet. These events are related against the background of Dublin's burgeoning crime rate in the 1780s, the critical insecurity of its prison system and the troubled political relationship between Ireland and Britain.

Rees, Sian. *The Floating Brothel: The Extraordinary True Story of an Eighteenth-Century Ship and its Cargo of Female Convicts*. London: Headline, 2001. Pp. 248; illustrations; maps, bibliographical references; index.

"Not much attempt had been made to enforce discipline among the women, many of them London prostitutes, who had turned the ship into a floating brothel at her various ports of call." Such is the general view of the voyage of the *Lady Julian* from England to the new colony of New South Wales, transporting more than two-hundred convict women, mainly taken from London's fever-ridden, overcrowded Newgate Gaol. The reality was both more complex and more interesting, dramatically different from the well-known stories of hellish journeys to Australia. The women aboard the *Lady Julian* arrived in Australia healthier and happier than they had ever been before. According to custom, each sailor was entitled to take a woman, an arrangement that brought privileges to the women as well as relief for the men. John Nicol, steward and ship's cooper for the voyage, fell deeply in love with nineteen-year-old Sarah Whitelam, convicted of theft worth more than fifty-one shillings. Their child was one of several born during the voyage. What happened to them after arriving at Port Jackson is one of the many fascinating stories in this lively and refreshing book. Sian Rees casts a new light on an important and under-documented corner of Australia's history.

Roe, Michael. *The State of Tasmania: Identity at Federation Time*. Hobart: Tasmanian Historical Research Association, 2001. Pp. 268; maps; bibliographical references; index.

Roe includes early nineteenth-century material.

Russell, Lynette. *Savage Imaginings: Historical and Contemporary Constructions of Australian Aboriginalities*. Melbourne: Australian Scholarly Publishing, 2001. Pp. xiii + 134; illustrations; bibliography; index.

Russell explores the dominant discussions in Australian Aboriginal history. Its central tenet is that European textual representations of Aboriginal Australians have characteristically involved images and imaginings of primitivism, great antiquity and sameness. The author argues that Aboriginal-focused museum displays, textual studies and photo-essays have reduced Aboriginal culture to a moment frozen in pre-contact time.

Sanborn, Geoffrey. "The Missed Encounter: Cannibalism and the Literary Critic." Pp. 187–204 of *Eating Their Words: Cannibalism and the Boundaries of Cultural Identity*. Edited by Kristen Guest. New York: State University of New York Press, 2001.

Schmidt, Benjamin. *Innocence Abroad: The Dutch Imagination and the New World, 1570–1670*. Cambridge: Cambridge University Press, 2001. Pp. xxix + 450; illustrations; bibliography.

Smith, Bernhard, Terry Smith, and Christoph Heathcote. *Australian Painting 1788–2000*. Fourth and extended edition, with additional chapters by Terry Smith and Christoph Heathcote. Melbourne: Oxford University Press, 2001. Pp. xi + 630.

Smith, Keith Vincent. *Bennelong: The Coming in of the* Eora, *Syndney Cove, 1788–1792*. East Roseville: Kangaroo Press: Viacom, 2001. Pp. x + 182; illustrations; maps; bibliographical references; index.

This book deals with an early encounter between the Aboriginal Australian Bennelong (around 1764–1813) and explorer Arthur Phillip (1738–1814).

So'o, Asofou. "Pacific Missions with Special Reference to Samoa." Pp. 221–34 of *Colonies, Missions, Cultures in the English Speaking World: General and Comparative Studies*. Edited by Gerhard Stilz. Introduction by Gerhard Stilz. Tübingen: Stauffenburg, 2001.

VII: New World Literatures and Languages 519

Sprod, Dan. *The Usurper: Jorgen Jorgenson and His Turbulent Life in Iceland and Van Diemen's Land, 1780–1841.* Sandy Bay, Tasmania: Blubber Head Press, 2001. Pp. xiii + 718; illustrations; maps; bibliographical references; index.

This is a biography of Jørgen Jürgensen (b. 1780)

Staniforth, Mark, and Michael Hyde (eds.). *Maritime Archaeology in Australia: A Reader.* Blackwood: Southern Archaeology, 2001. Pp. x + 337; illustrations; maps; bibliographical references.

This volume comprises forty-five research papers some of which examine the material culture related to early European settlement of Australia; for example, Mark Staniforth on "Dependant Colonies: The Importation of Material Culture into the Australian Colonies: 1788–1850"; M. Nash on "The *Sydney Cove* Historic Shipwreck: 1797"; J. Campbell on "Eighteenth Century Clubs from HMS *Pandora*: A Preliminary Analysis"; L. Pigott on "The Surgeon's Equipment from the Wreck of the HMS *Pandora*"; J. Pasveer, A. Buck and M. van Huystee on "Victims of the *Batavia* [that is, a Dutch East Indiaman wrecked off Western Australia in 1629) Mutiny: Physical, Anthropological and Forensic Studies of the Beacon Island Skeletons."

Stilz, Gerhard (ed.). *Colonies, Missions, Cultures in the English Speaking World: General and Comparative Studies.* Introduction by Gerhard Stilz. Tübingen: Stauffenburg, 2001. Pp. 486.

Swain, Shurlee. "Women and Philanthropy in Colonial and Post-Colonial Australia." Pp. 428–43 of *Women, Philanthropy, and Civil Society.* Edited by Kathleen D. McCarthy. Bloomington: Indiana University Press, 2001.

Teeuwen, Rudolphus (ed.). *Crossings: Travel, Art, Literature, Politics.* Introduction by Rudolphus Teeuwen. Taipei: Bookman, 2001. Pp. xi + 300; maps.

Tuckey, J[ames]. H[ingston] (1776–1816). An *Account of a Voyage to Establish a Colony at Port Philip in Bass's Strait, On the South Coast of New South Wales, in His Majesty's Ship Calcutta, in the Years 1802–3–4. By J. H. Tuckey Esq., First Lieutenant of the Calcutta.* (Sullivan Bay Historical Series 1.) Edited by Richard E. Cotter. Red Hill, Victoria in Australia: Lavender Hill Multimedia for Friends of the Collins Settlement, Sorrento, 2001. Pp. v + 114; illustrations.

Villiers, Alan. *Captain Cook, the Seamen's Seaman: A Study of the Great Discoverer.* Illustrated by Adrian Small. London: Penguin, 2001. Pp. 255; illustrations; bibliographical references; index.

Williams, Christiane Kuechler. *The Discovery of an Erotic Paradise: An Investigation into the European Reception of the South Pacific Islands in the 18th Century* (2001). Pp. 346. Dissertation

Abstracts International, Section A: The Humanities and Social Sciences 62/04 (October 2001), 1426. Abstract number DA3012094

Williams examines various literary responses to the discovery of the South Pacific islands and possible motivations for a sudden, short-lived frenzy that swept across Europe with images of paradisiacal, erotic-exotic islands in the second half of the eighteenth century. Chapter 1 summarizes the history of Pacific discoveries from Magellan to Cook. Chapter 2 discusses common relations between Europe and its Other and shows several functions that the "foreign" South Pacific served in the late eighteenth century. Chapter 3 includes an overview of the genre of travel literature and reflects on the publishing success of South Seas travelogues. In Chapter 4 the argument is made that the South Pacific occupied a special position within the eighteenth-century consciousness, because it, unlike Africa, Asia, and the Americas, the islands offered the prototype of the Noble Savage as well as an ideal stage for European colonial and sexual desires. For the sciences they offered challenging new data including an entire new race for anthropology. Chapter 5 carries out a close analysis of nine South Pacific travelogues from England, France, and Germany written between 1765 and 1785 and analyzes idealizing motifs such as the image of paradise/utopia, the Noble Savage, and a merging of antiquity and native cultures. In addition, this thesis establishes an underlying notion of feminization and sexualization of the South Seas in literature and art, based on the parallel of woman and land in the act of conquest. The fascination of the enlightened male middle class with the islands can be attributed to their sexual dissatisfaction with the de-sexualized European woman, which in the eighteenth century was restricted to a maternal role. The chapter concludes by examining the extent to which travelogues belonged to developing pornographic genres. Chapter 6 analyzes three major negative aspects of the South Seas: cannibalism, "abnormal" sexuality, and syphilis. Chapter 7 offers a short description of the German (un)colonial situation. An examination of nine German literary productions about the South Pacific, written between 1770 and 1810, shows that German authors projected their longing for the colonial and sexual adventures onto the South Pacific.

Wright, Julia M. "Devouring the Disinherited: Familial Cannibalism in [Charles Robert] Maturin's *Melmoth the Wanderer* (1802)." Pp. 79–105 of *Eating Their Words: Cannibalism and the Boundaries of Cultural Identity*. Edited by Kristen Guest. New York: State University of New York Press, 2001.

Wright, Robert Edward. *The Life and Times of Pierce Collits, Convict, Pioneer & Innkeeper*. Sydney: R. Wright, 2001. Pp. i + 37; illustrations.

This is a biography of prisoner Pierce Collits (1769–1848) in New South Wales.

Special Section: Late Entries and Reviews

Printing and Bibliographical Studies

Adams, David. *Bibliographie des oeuvres de Denis Diderot, 1739–1900*. Vols. 1–2. Ferney-Voltaire: Centre International d'étude du XVIIIe siècle, 2000. Pp. 464; 480; illustrations. See *ECCB*, 26 (2000), I:4.

Rev. by Jo-Ann McEachern in *British Journal of Eighteenth-Century Studies*, 25 (2002), 267–68.

Albertan, Christian, and Anne-Marie Chouillet. "Autographes et documents." *Recherches sur Diderot et sur l'Encyclopédie*, 28 (2000), 167–87.

Atteberry, John, and John Russell. *Ratio Studiorum: Jesuit Education, 1540–1773*. Chestnut Hill: John J. Burns Library, Boston College, 1999. Pp. 64; illustrations.

Avery, Gillian. "Intimations of Mortality: The Puritan and Evangelical Message to Children." Pp. 87–110 (with illustrations) in *Representations of Childhood Death*. Edited by Gillian Avery and Kimberley Reynolds. London: Macmillan, 2000.

Baines, Paul. *The House of Forgery in Eighteenth-Century Britain*. Aldershot: Ashgate Publishing Company, 1999. Pp. 204; notes; illustrations; index.

Barbier, Frédéric (ed.). *Les trois révolutions du livre*. Actes du colloque internationale de Lyon/Villeurbanne. [Special issue of] *Revue française d'histoire du livre*, nos. 106–09 (2000). Pp. 324.

Containing papers from a 1998 colloque at Lyon/Villeurbanne. Includes Barbier's "D'une mutation l'autre: Les temps longs de l'histoire du livre" (7–18); Dominique Varry's "Le compagnon et l'atelier artisanal: L'exemple de Lyon" (93–118); Dominique Bougé-Grandon's "Enseigner les livres: Le témoignage de François de Los Rios" (119–32); Sabine Juratic's "Entre tradition et innovation: Les ateliers typographiques parisiens au XVIIIe siècle" (133–54); Pierre Rétat's "Les gazettes européennes de langue française: La réception" (155–68); Eva Ring's "La Typographie Royale de Buda" (169–208); Carla Hesse's "Communication et révolution politique: L'exemple de la France" (209–18); Louis André's "Une révolution de papier: Le papier et la 'seconde révolution du livre'" (219–30); Alain Nave's "De la stéréotypie" (231–46); and James Mosley's "Antiquité et industrie: Un nouveau langage typographique" (247–60).

Bayerische Staatsbibliothek and Universitätsbibliothek München. *Münchner Altbestandskatalog: Bayerische Staatsbibliothek 1501–1840, Universitätsbibliothek München 1501–1850 = Munich Catalogue of Early Printed Books: Bavarian State Library 1501–1840, Munich University Library 1501–1850.* Munich: Saur, 2000. CD-ROM disc and loose-leaf handbook with search instructions in English and German and installation instructions in German.

Bell, Maureen, Shirley Chew, Simon Eliot, Lynette Hunter, and James L. W. West III (eds.). *Reconstructing the Book: Literary Texts in Transmission.* Aldershot: Ashgate, 2001. Pp. 231.

Includes C. Y. Ferdinand's "The Economics of the Eighteenth-Century Provincial Book Trade: The Case of Ward and Chandler" (42–56). Rev. by Julian Warner in *Library Quarterly*, 72 (2002), 398–99.

Blom, Frans, Joseph Blom, Frans Korsten, and Geoffrey Scott (comps.). *English Catholic Books 1701–1800: A Bibliography.* Brookfield: Ashgate, 1996. Pp. xl + 356; indices of printers and publishers and of titles. See *ECCB*, 22–24 (1996–1998), 29.

Rev. by John Farrell in *Journal of Ecclesiastical History*, 48 (1997), 587; (favorably; with another book) by Juliet McLaren in *Scriblerian*, 33 (2001), 222–23.

Bödeker, Hans Erich, and Ernst Hinrichs (eds.). *Alphabetisierung und Literalisierung in Deutschland in der Frühen Neuzeit.* (Wolfenbütteler Studien zur Aufklärung, 26.) Tübingen: Max Niemeyer, 1999. Pp. vi + 366; charts, graphs, illustrations; maps; tables.

The sixteen essays include the editors' introduction, Andrea Hofmeister's "Ländliche Alphabetisierung in Südniedersachsen: 'Großtraum' Göttingen und nordwestliches Harzvorland" (11–32); Norbert Winnige's "Alphabetisierung in Althessen: Zum Stand der Signierfähigkeit in Hessen-Kassel um 1800" (33–67); Reiner Prass's "Preußich-gewerblicher Vorsprung und katholischländliche Rückständigkeit? Zur Alphabetisierungs in Minden-Ravensberg und Corvey-Paderborn" (69–93); Jens Riederer's "Prämie der Aufklärung: Zum Alphabetisierungsvorsprung im Fürstentum Halberstadt gegenüber der Magdeburger Börde um 1800" (95–118); Susan Klehn's "Alphabetisierung in der Stadt Braunschweig um 1800: Die Magnigemeinde als Stichprobe" (141–62); Bettina Busch-Geertsema's "'Elender als auf dem elendesten Dorfe'? Elementarbildung und Alphabetisierung in Bremen am Beginn des 19. Jahrhunderts" (181–200); Anne-Kristin Kupke's "Elementarschulunterricht in Kursachsen um 1670" (225–52); Gisela Teistler's "Fibeln als Dokumente für die Entwicklung der Alphabetisierung: Ihre Entstehung und Verbreitung bis 1850" (255–81; illustrations); Reinhart Siegert's "Zur Alphabetisierung in den

Special Section: Late Entries and Reviews

deutschen Regionen am Ende des Jahrunderts: Methodische Überlegungen und inhaltliche Bausteine aus Quellenmaterial der Volksaufklärung" (283–307); and Alfred Messerli's "Literale Normen und Alphabetisierung im 18. und 19. Jahrhundert in der Schweiz" (309–26).

Boisvert, Marcel. *L'Éducation de la jeune fille de province dans Balzac*. Montreal: Guérin, 2000. Pp. v + 242.

Bookbinding 2000. Proceedings: A Collection of Papers from the June 2000 Conference Celebrating the Installation and Opening of the Bernard C. Middleton Collection of Books on the History and Practice of Bookbinding. Rochester: Melbert B. Cary, Jr., Graphics Arts Collection, Wallace Library, Rochester Institute of Technology, 2000. Pp. 103; illustrations (chiefly colored).

The six essays include Middleton's own "Facsimile Printing for Antiquarian Books," treating techniques for replacement of damaged leaves; Marianne Tidcombe's "Women Bookbinders in Britain before the First World War"; and Peter Waters's "The Preservation of Library Material in a Digital Age" (surveying such topics as causes of deterioration and preservation methods). Rev. by Jeffrey Barr in *SHARP News*, 12, no. 2 (Spring 2003), 7–8.

Boyle, John, Fifth Earl of Cork and Orrery. *Remarks on the Life and Writings of Dr. Jonathan Swift*. Edited by João Fróes. Newark: University of Delaware Press, 2000. Pp. 461; appendices with "Orrery Manuscript Notes in his Annotated Copies of Remarks on Swift" [327–433]; bibliographical descriptions; frontispiece; index.

Rev. by James E. May in *East-Central Intelligencer*, 15 (2001), 38–40; by John V. Price in *Notes and Queries*, n.s. 49 (2002), 144; by Claude Rawson in *Review of English Studies*, n.s. 52, 455–57; (favorably) by Ian Campbell Ross in *Eighteenth-Century Ireland*, 15 (2000), 199–201.

Carter, Sebastian. "Printing and the Mind of Man." *Matrix*, 20 (2000), 172–80.

Retrospective look at famous book exhibition in London, 1963.

Castillo Gómez, Antonio (ed.). *Escribir y leer en el siglo de Cervantes*. Barcelona: Gedisa, 1999. Pp. 362.

Twelve conference papers with some discussions reaching into the mid 1600s.

Chouillet, Anne Marie, and Laurent Loty. "Carnet bibliographique." *Recherches dur Diderot et sur Encyclopédie*, 28 (2000), 189–91.

Clayton, Tim. "George Clarke Print Collection Now Online." *Print Quarterly*, 17 (2000), 392.

On 8,000 prints George Clarke bequeathed to Worcester College. See http://prints.worc.ox.ac.uk.

Clifford, Timothy. *Designs of Desire: Architectural and Ornament Prints and Drawings 1500–1850.* Edinburgh: National Galleries of Scotland, 1999. Pp. 328; fully illustrated.

Catalogue of an exhibition in Glasgow and Edinburgh from Nov. 1999 to June 2000.

Colclough, Stephen. *Reading Experience, 1700–1840: An Annotated Register of Sources for the History of Reading in the British Isles.* (History of the Book on Demand, 6.) Reading: Simon Eliot, 2000. Pp. xi + 118.

Colclough, Stephen. Recovering the Reader: Commonplace Books and Diaries as Sources of Reading Experience." *Publishing History,* 44 (1998), 5–37.

Comminey, Shawn. "The Society for the Propagation of the Gospel in Foreign Parts and Black Education in South Carolina, 1702–1764." *Journal of Negro History,* 84 (1999), 360–69.

Copsey, Tony. *Suffolk Writers from the Beginning until 1800: A Catalogue of Suffolk Authors with Some Account of Their Lives and a List of Their Writings.* Ipswich: Book Company (distributed Ipswich: Claude Cox Rare Books), 2000. Pp. 558.

Rev. (favorably) by Peter Isaac in *Quadrat,* no. 12 (January 2001), 33–34.

Craske, Matthew. *William Hogarth.* (British Artists.) London: Tate Publishing, 2000. Pp. 80; bibliography; illustrations (some in color); index.

Rev. in rev. essay "New Hogarth Studies" by Timothy Erwin in *Eighteenth-Century Studies,* 36 (2003), 304–08, noting appreciatively that Craske's introduction to Hogarth, "published for the Tate Gallery, . . . links the social milieu of the painter to the journalism of the period."

Desachy, Matthieu. *Livres et bibliothèques en Rouergue (XIVe–XVIIIe siècle).* Rodez: Revue du Rouergue, 2000. Pp. 183; illustrations.

Debenedetti, Elisa (ed.). *700 Disegnatore: Incisioni, progetti, caricature.* (Studi sul Settecento romano 13.) Rome: Bonsignori, 1997. Pp. 301; illustrations (some in color); index.

Includes Simona Ciofetta's "Alcune edizioni di architettura di Gian Giacomo e Domenico De Rossi: Fasi preparatorie e finalità dell'opera" (65–82; 13 illustrations); Antonella Pampalone's "I'volti' della storia nelle caricature della collezione di Pier Leone Ghezzi (parte II)" (83–140; bibliography; 156 illustrations); Giulia Fusconi and Alida Moltedo's "Pier Leone Ghezzi, un incisore ignoto e l'edizione delle *Camere Sepolcrali*" (141–60; illustrations); Bruno Contardi's "Piranesi in Campidoglio" (161–83; illustrations); Elisa Debenedetti's "Giuseppe Barberi, un diario visivo idealmente dedicato alla famiglia Altieri" (183–227; 40 illustrations); Segio Pace's "Disegni per un'accademia domestica: Note sull'opera architettonica di Giuseppe Barberi (Roma 1746–1809)" (229–64; 40 illustrations); Susanna Pasquali's "Echi di una committenza illustre: Un disegno anonimo dell'Accademia di

S. Luca attribuito alla cerchia di Mario Asprucci" (265–77; 10 illustrations); Maria Rosaria Nappi's "Una committente inglese per l'editoria romana: La duchessa di Devonshire e l'Eneide di Virgilio" (279–96; 14 illustrations).

Dekker, Rudolf. *Childhood Memory and Autobiography in Holland: From the Golden Age to Romanticism*. London: Macmillan, 2000. Pp. 174; illustrations.

Rev. (favorably) by Ulla Bergstrand in *Children's Books History Society Newsletter*, 68 (2000), 21–26.

Desachy, Matthieu. *Livres et bibliothèques en Rouergue (XIVe–XVIIIe siècle)*. Rodez: Revue du Rouergue, 2000. Pp. 183; illustrations.

Eidelberg, Martin. "'Ce joli morceau': *Le Royaume de l'amour* de Watteau." *Revue de l'Art*, 123 (1999), 39–46.

Enniss, Stephen. "The Role of the Artifact in a Facsimile Age." *RBM: A Journal of Rare Books, Manuscripts, and Cultural History*, 1 (2000), 46–47.

Feyel, Gilles. *L'Announce et la nouvelle: La presse d'information en France sous l'Ancien Régime (1630–1789)*. Oxford: Voltaire Foundation, 2000. Pp. vii + 1387; bibliography; illustrations; indices. See *ECCB*, 26 (2000), 47.

Rev. by Pierre Rétat in *British Journal for Eighteenth-Century Studies*, 25 (2002), 285.

Findlay, James A. *ABC Books and Related Materials: Selections from the Nyr Indictor Collection of the Alphabet: An Exhibition Catalogue*. Ft. Lauderdale: F. L. Bienes Center for the Literary Arts, 2000. Pp. 64; illustrations.

Rev. (favorably) by Pat Garrett in *Children's Books History Society Newsletter*, 69 (April 2001), 24.

Francisco Goya, Capricci, Disastri della Guerra, Follie: Opere grafiche della Fondazione Antonio Mazzotta. Introduction by Tulliola Spara gni. Milan, 2000. Pp. 120; checklist; 182 illustrations.

Briefly noted in *Print Quarterly*, 17 (2000), 392–93.

Frasca, R. "'To rescue the Germans out of Sauer's hands': Benjamin Franklin's German-language Printing Partnerships." *Pennsylvania Magazine of History and Biography*, 121:4 (1997), 329–50.

García Ejarque, Luis. *Historia de la lectura pública en España*. (Biblioteconomía y administración cultural 35.) Gijón: Trea, 2000. Pp. xvi + 533; index.

Garside, Peter, and E. R. Showerling. *The English Novel 1770–1829: A Bibliographical Survey of Prose Fiction Published in the British Isles.* Volume 2: 1800–1829. New York: Oxford University Press, 2000. Pp. 500.

Gauss, Ulrike (ed.). *Giovanni Battista Piranesi—Die poetische Wahrheit. Die Radierungen.* With commentary by Ulrike Gauss, Corinna Höper, Stefan Heinlein, Jeannette Stoschek. Stuttgart: Hatje, 1999. Pp. 512; 380 illustrations.

Goodman, Roy E. "A Selected Guide to Printed Materials Relating tothe Iconography and Artifacts of Benjamin Franklin." Pp. 170–82 of *Finding Colonial Americas: Essays Honoring J. A. Leo Lemay.* Edited by Carla Mulford. Newark: University of Delaware Press, 2001.

Green, James N. "Thinking about Benjamin Franklin's Library." Pp. 343–56 of *Finding Colonial Americas: Essays Honoring J. A. Leo Lemay.* Edited by Carla Mulford. Newark: University of Delaware Press, 2001.

Greene, John C. *Theatre in Belfast, 1736–1800.* Bethlehem: Lehigh University Press, 2000. Pp. 311; bibliography; index.

Principally a calendar of plays. Rev. (favorably) by William J. Burling in *East-Central Intelligencer*, 15, no. 1 (January 2001), 34; by Robert Mahony in *Eighteenth-Century Ireland / Iris an dá chultúr*, 16 (2001), 142–43; by David Thomas in *Review of English Studies*, n.s. 53 (2002), 151–52.

Groom, Nick. *The Making of Percy's "Reliques."* New York: Oxford University Press, 1999. Pp. xiii + 290.

Hacker, Rupert (ed.). *Beiträge zur Geschichte der Bayerischen Staatsbibliothek.* (Schriftenreihe der Bayerischen Staatsbibliothek, 1.) Munich: Saur, 2000. Pp. 410; index.

Rev. by Franz Obermeier in *Wolfenbütteler Notizen zur Buchgeschichte*, 26 (2001), 145–48.

Hendrix, Lee, and Thea Vignau-Wilberg. *An Abecedarium: Illuminated Alphabets from the Court of the Emperor Rudolf II.* Los Angeles: J. Paul Getty Museum, 1997. Pp. 64; colored illustrations.

Illustrations from pages of the manuscript *Mira calligraphiae monumenta*, published in 1992 by the Getty Museum and Thames & Hudson. On German lettering, copybooks, and illuminated manuscripts to 1800, focused on work of Joris Hoefnagel (d. 1601).

Henkel, A. K. "Leibniz Bibliography 1998." *Studia Leibnitiana*, 30:2 (1998), 229–54.

Special Section: Late Entries and Reviews

Hill, Sarah H., and Sue Evans Vrooman. *Native Lands: Indians and Georgia*. Atlanta: Atlanta History Center, 1999. Pp. 49; colored illustrations; catalog for an exhibition.

Hinterding, Erik, Ger Luijten, Martin Royalton-Kisch, and Ernst van de Wetering. *Rembrandt, the Printmaker*. Chicago: Fitzroy-Dearborn, 2000. Pp. 384; illustrations (some in color).

Published on the occasion of an exhibition in 2000–01 at the Rijksmuseum, Amsterdam, and in 2001 at the British Museum; catalog translated from Dutch. With "Rembrandt the Printmaker: The Shaping of an Oeuvre" by Luijten; "Watermark Research as a Tool for the Study of Rembrandt's Etchings" by Hinterding; "Remarks on Rembrandt's Oil-Sketches for Etchings" by Ernst van de Wetering; "The Role of Drawings in Rembrandt's Printmaking" by Royalton-Kisch; and the catalog.

Houghton Library. *Stage, Ballroom, and Parlour: Selections from the Ruth N. and John M. Ward Collection of Music for Dance and Theatre in the Harvard Theatre Collection: An Exhibition*. Cambridge: Harvard College Library, 2000. Pp. 47; exhibition catalogue; illustrations.

Huisstede, P. van, and P. J. Brandhorst (comps.). *Dutch Printers' Devices, 15th–17th Century: A Catalogue with CD-ROM*. 3 vols. Nieuwkoop: HES; de Graaf, 1999. Pp. viii + 1639; illustrations.

Rev. by Jochen Becker in *Quaerendo*, 32 (2002), 304–15; by Ursula Rautenberg and Oliver Duntze in *Buchhandelsgeschichte* (2001), B34–37.

Jahrbuch der Auktionspreise für Bücher, Handschriften und Autographen (JAP). Vol. 50: for 1999. Stuttgart: Hauswedell, 2000. Pp. 838 + CD-ROM.

Kaimowitz, Jeffrey H. *Bentley's World: The Greek and Latin Classics & Their Influence in 18th-Century Britain*. Hartford: Watkinson Library, Trinity College, 1997. Pp. 27; illustrations.

Kaimowitz, Jeffrey H. *Birds in Print: A Survey of Major Illustrating Processes, 1500–1998*. Hartford: Watkinson Library, Trinity College, 1999. Pp. 12; catalogue for exhibition [February–June, 1999]; illustrations.

Kaiser, Gerhard R., and Siegried Seifert (eds.). *Friedrich Justin Bertuch (1747–1822), Verleger, Schriftsteller und Unternehmer in klassischen Weimar*. Tübingen: Niemeyer, 2000. Pp. viii + 719; 55 illustrations; index. See *ECCB*, 26 (2000), 80.

Rev. (favorably) by John L. Flood in *Library*, 7th ser., 2 (2001), 89–90.

Keane, Angela. *Women Writers and the English Nation in the 1790s: Romantic Belongings*. Cambridge: Cambridge University Press, 2000. Pp. 200; bibliography; index.

Angela Keane demonstrates that Ann Radcliffe, Helen Maria Williams, Charlotte Smith, Mary Wollstonecraft, and Hannah More, presented identities and published types of content which enabled them to participate in shaping the commercial, progressive, individually redeeming and aesthetic Romantic ideals which we find in the better-known writing of their male contemporaries. She reveals these writers had to struggle with or evade evolving domestic norms whose effect prevented women from identifying as productive members of imagined communities except through their relationship to a family network. Her argument is that nationalism, patriarchal marital and capitalist arrangements, and the 1790s perception of print culture as inescapably politicized and radical turned women who wanted literally or imaginatively to leave a feminized restrictive home into ostracized exiles or isolated wanderers. Unless they were mothers or performed a maternal function, they were made to feel they belonged nowhere, to no one or had no one attached to them because no one was dependent on their care. This, even when they lived among family and friends, functioned as successful *salonnières*, or conducted commercial business. Following a qualified variant of Habermas's theories, Keane shows that in the 1790s and afterward, the public sphere is "newly masculinized" (8) and, especially for women, writing and publishing become potentially strongly suspect activities.

In five chapters Keane explores how her five women writers coped with impinging norms that would characterize their ways of life and vocation as an alien aberration. She begins by examining neglected aspects of Ann Radcliffe's novels and her nearly forgotten travel book, *A Journey Made in the Summer of 1794*. In all these Radcliffe develops a Rousseauistic critique of injustices which typified the *ancien régime* in the minds of her readers, and imagines benign human communities rooted in shared memories of local pasts and cultural learning, and in progressive enlightened interaction between people through commerce. Radcliffe writes effective anti-war propaganda through retelling the recent past (e.g., the seiges of Mentz and Manheim), and she condemns repressive Catholic dogma, ways of life, and non-modern epistemology. Radcliffe is only partly actuated by her Protestant, Whiggish, and liberal background. The insight that makes her recognize the importance of imaginary terrors, a loss of autonomy, and physiological deprivation is the same which creates her haunted picturesque landscapes and Wordsworthian therapeutic pilgrimages. Keane builds on Terry Castle's essay, "The Spectralization of the Other in *The Mysteries of Udolpho* (in *The New Eighteenth Century*, edited by Felicity Nussbaum and Laura Brown [New York: Methuen, 1987] 231–53, 307–10), to suggest that for Radcliffe "home" becomes a spectral place where shared benevolence, physical comfort and individual fulfillment is made freely available to reader and writer through the consciousness which imagines it.

Since unlike what has happened to Radcliffe's work, the intended and actual social and political uses of Helen Maria Williams's imaginative and travel writings have not been neglected, Keane moves on to study Williams's work to see how it contributes to our understanding of Romantic poetics as well as the contemporary failure of an ideal of cosmopolitanism to take hold and of progressive political ideals to lead to effective legislative action in England. Keane shows how Williams and Charlotte Smith demonstrated a rare courage when they persisted in arguing that the failure, perversions, and fearful violence that the French revolution led to did not invalidate Enlightenment egalitarian and humane ideals; while Hannah More exploited virulent anti-French propaganda to campaign for an emerging counter-revolutionary evangelical value system and restrained bourgeois behavior, Williams and Smith praised French culture for initiating reformist ideals and promotion of salon life and aristocratic manners and taste. Like Mary Wollstonecraft in her *An Historical and Moral View of the Origin and Progress of the French Revolution* (1794), Williams and Smith were occasionally willing sympathetically to dramatize women's heterosexual desires finding fulfillment outside the prevailing marital codes. In her close reading of Williams's eight-volume *Letters Written in France* (covering a span from 1790 to 1816), Keane characterizes these Letters as a "narrative of desire." Williams writes from the vantage point of a "regained paradise" looking back on devastation and loss (71). Family romances and emotional appeals alternate with stories of imprisonment, catalogues of executions, and "an overwhelming sensation of exile" where Williams is "reduced to the status of a motherless Gothic heroine, in flight from phantoms and despots" (70), mourning for the French people, for a lost dream of an international community, for a time when men and women were encouraged to place shared subjective idealisms in the public sphere.

As Keane says, in her analysis of Charlotte Smith's 1792 epistolary novel, *Desmond* "was the only work of British fiction to comment directly on the events of the French revolution as they unfolded" (81), and, like Williams's *Letters*, participated in the debate over the French revolution between Burke and Paine. Keane concentrates on those of Smith's novels which explore "the condition of exile" (91), dramatize and explicitly comment on the economic, social and political realities of English society, argue for Enlightenment ideals, and suggest why the French revolution degenerated into terror and civil war. In Keane's effort to introduce the reader to Smith's powerful novels which are not well known, she sometimes loses sight of larger issues and provides a series of too sketchy perfunctory plot summaries, description, and analysis. She has, however, chosen well. While *The Banished Man* (1794) falls off badly in its fourth volume, and (until recently) has been discussed only disparagingly, the book's early phases include a depiction of cycles of violence, famine, corrupt anarchy, and anguish in the French countryside; like Radcliffe in her *Journey*, Smith presents real sieges on the European continent; her hero, D'Alonville, is a homeless French aristocrat, an *emigré*, who becomes involved with a historical Polish patriot. Keane shows that *The Banished Man* does not, as has been suggested, "capitulate to counter-revolutionary sentiment," but, in the teeth of a depiction of ruthless familial and class feuds, "reasserts the cosmopolitan fantasy that underpinned early revolutionary philosophy" (94). The trope of exile and the brutalities of mercenary wars dominate Keane's analysis of Smith's historical novel, *The Old Manor House* (1793) as Keane focuses on the hero's time fighting on the American continent in the late 1770s. Keane does ample justice to Smith's last long novel, *The Young Philosopher* (1798) by a careful examination of Smith's imaginative exploration of sexual politics, of the repression, powerlessness and homelessness of women, and of isolated flight and imprisonment, much of it brought about by emotional blackmail and corrupt manipulation of law and familial and sexual mores.

Keane is at times too defensive. She defends Smith's dismissal of Desmond's French mistress who has had a child by him on the grounds that Smith is not unconsciously yielding to, but exposing how "nationalistic sentiment" can lead to erasing individuals (88). Keane never brings up the "hollow" hypocrisies underlying the heroine's rectitude (examined by Diana Bowstead in "Charlotte Smith's *Desmond*: The Epistolary Novel as Ideological Argument," *Fetter'd or Free: British Women Novelists, 1670–1815*, edited by Mary Anne Schofield and Cecilia Macheski [Athens: Ohio University Press, 1986], 237–63). Keane seems unaware that Smith's displacements testify far more to her desire for satisfying heterosexual love and adult male companionship in an imagined community (very like those with which Radcliffe closes her novels) than they do to any regret she is exiled from typical English milieus. A longing for fulfilling adult heterosexual love, bitterness, and intense grief over individual injustices she and her children have suffered fuel Smith's work. Smith produces morally confused work as the norms of respectability coerce her into obscuring the anger and frustrations that induce her to write.

On the other hand, Keane's defense of Mary Wollstonecraft's *A Vindication of the Rights of Woman* (1792) against those who have argued the book presents "a puritan sexual ethic with such passionate conviction that self-denial seems a libidinized activity" is persuasive (Cora Kaplan, "Wild Nights," *Sea Changes: Culture and Feminism* [Thetford: Thetford Press, 1986], 35–36). Keane argues that Wollstonecraft "tried and failed to resist" the exploitation of women's bodies by men, contemporary political, social, and economic arrangements and ranked hierarchies. Wollstonecraft sought to enable women to live as fully socialized a life as men, and to have access to a life of the mind equivalent to their particular talents. Like Charlotte Smith, Mary Wollstonecraft experienced the reality that, contrary to what was professed by moralists in print, laws and customs were not set up to support women who were mothers. In her *Letters Written During a Short Residence in Sweden, Denmark and Norway* (1796) and private letters to Gilbert Imlay, Wollstonecraft exposes the amorality and hardening of individuals which some of the actual practices of commerce inculcate. She was driven to publish by passionate indignation over socially-accepted practices which led to high infant mortality and abandoned children; to women whose bodies were exhausted and were without either an absolute legal right to economic support or ability to achieve economic security on their own. Wollstonecraft argues the power women gain over men through their sexuality is debasing and ephemeral. Keane concedes that Wollstonecraft did write about adult sexuality pessimistically and from a proscriptive standpoint, but Wollstonecraft's warnings, disdain for co-opted women, and depressive stance are not meant to deprive women of pleasure; rather she seeks to protect them because she was convinced that her experience of powerlessness against violence and of sexuality and motherhood as abject and alienated was common.

Keane concludes by modifying recent attempts to re-position Hannah More as a "revolutionary reformer" and to present her as someone who conferred power on women (e.g., Anne K. Mellor, *Mothers of the Nation: Women's Political Writing in England, 1780–1830* [Bloomington: Indiana University Press, 2000] 13–38). Keane focuses on how More's "canny manipulation of the press, social connection and economic patronage" (134) was aimed at offering readers "a programme of emotional and mental discipline" (145) intended to repress political activities on behalf of legislative reforms. More wanted to prevent the ordinary person from gaining access to publish in the press. She urged women to educate themselves with the limited aim of being "of practical use" to their families and to those whom the marketplace and contemporary hierarchies had severely disadvantaged. She argued they must conform to middle class norms, and be especially "scrupulous" in their sexual relationships, to be allowed to exercise this power ("The Practical Use of Female Knowledge," *The Female Spectator: English Women Writers before 1800*, edited by Mary Mahl and Helene Koon [Bloomington: Indiana University Press, 1977], 287–96). Ironically, More found herself "vilified" (152) and was silenced when she took an active role in establishing schools, women's clubs and explicitly promoted an "evangelical religion of the heart." She was attacked by conservative members of the Established church as a female attempting to wrest inappropriate authority; it was insinuated her "enthusiasms" disguised an "uncontrollable sexuality" (152, 157). Unfortunately, Keane omits More's popular novel, *Coelebs in Search of a Wife* (1808): in this novel a genuinely genial tone and satirically comic scenes whose targets are complicated, and which have some of the ambiguity of life, replace the grating condescension and transparently simplified politics of More's *Cheap Repository Tracts* (1795–97) and the flattery of More's letters to patrons and friends which mar them and have created an antipathy for More among some modern scholars. Analysis and quotation from *Coelebs* reveals why this novel found a receptive audience and remained in print for decades.

Nonetheless, the real strength of Keane's book derives from her decision not to concentrate on novels; she situates those novels she covers amid the varied contentious print culture of the 1790s and deals at length with her subjects' intelligent and perceptive non-fiction. She reveals the strategies and deformations of women's texts that arise when women attempt to publish in a marketplace dominated by norms inimical to presenting real women's lives and to giving power to women "to take their place in whatever discourse is essential to action and the right to have one's part matter" (Carolyn Heilbrun, *Writing a Woman's Life* [New York: Ballantine Books, 1988], 18). The one demur I would register is the absence of any questioning of the assumption that individuals function best when they feel they belong to some imagined large community, preferably one rooted in memories going back to childhood. Keane is particularly troubled by "the level of institutional 'misrecognition' of women's place in civil society and the contradictory status of mothers in the discourse of nationhood" (162) that continues in our own time. "Internationalism" as an ideal may today seem a poignant "fantasy" (14–15, 55, 76), but in a book professedly "Utopian in purpose" (161), it's troubling to see the power of nationalism, capitalism and present state and familial institutions presented as apparently immutable.—Ellen Moody

Kerhervé, Alain. "La bibliothèque virtuelle d'une grande dame du XVIIIe siècle: Les livres dans la correspondance de Mary Delany (1700–1788)." *Bulletin de la société d'études anglo-américaines des XVIIe et XVIIIe siècles*, 50 (2000), 137–66.

Knapen, Luc (ed.). *La Bibliothèque de l'Abbaye de Saint-Hubert en Ardenne au dix-septième siècle*. 2 vols. Leuven: Bibliotheek van de Faculteit der Godgeleerdheid, 1999. Bibliography; index.

Vol. 1 is on the intellectual and religious life of the Benedictine community; Vol. 2 is a bibliography focused on a 1665 conscriptus. Rev. by Augustine J. Curley in *Libraries and Culture*, 37 (2002), 279–80.

Special Section: Late Entries and Reviews

Kümmerling-Meibauer, Bettina. *Klassiker der Kinder- und Jugendliteratur: Ein internationales Lexicon.* 2 vols. Stuttgart and Weimar: S. B. Metzler, 1999. Pp. 1236; illustrations.

With 534 articles on classics of children's literature from over sixty-five countries. Rev. by Brian Alderson in *Children's Books Historical Society Newsletter*, no. 70 (July 2001), 34–36.

Lathem, Edward Connery (comp.), and Marcus A. McCorison. *English Verse and Literary Prose Published in America before 1776: A Bibliography.* Worcester: American Antiquarian Society, 2000. CD-ROM + booklet (pp. 25 + [6]).

The CD-ROM contains Lathem's bibliography and notes (Ph.D. thesis from Oxford University, 1961). The printed guidebook, or introduction, by McCorison discusses Lathem and his bibliography and exemplifies the use of the CD-ROM.

Lee, Jennifer B., and Miriam Mandelbaum. *Seeing Is Believing: 700 Years of Scientific and Medical Illustration.* New York: New York Public Library, 1999. Pp. 76; catalogue for an exhibition (October 1999–February 2000); illustrations (some in color).

Lethbridge, Stefanie. "Anthological Reading Habits in the Eighteenth Century: The Case of Thomson's *Seasons*." Pp. 89–103 in *Anthologies of British Poetry: Critical Perspectives from Literary and Cultural Studies*. Edited by Barbara Korte, Stefanie Lethbridge, and Ralf Schneider. Amsterdam: Rodopi, 2000.

Lorenzo, Luciano García (ed.). *Autoras y actrices en la historia del teatro español.* Murcia: Universidad y Festival de Almagro, 2000. Pp. 349.

Magill, Frank N. (ed.). *Dictionary of World Biography: The Seventeenth and Eighteenth Centuries.* Volume 4. Chicago: Fitzroy Dearborn Publishers, 1999. Pp. xvii + 1515; illustrations.

May, James E. "Who Will Edit the ESTC? (and have you checked OCLC lately?)." *Analytical and Enumerative Bibliography*, n.s. 12 (2001), 288–304.

Mayfield, E., and R. Fordyce. "Dissertations of Note." *Children's Literature*, 28 (2000), 275–88.

McCorkle, Barbara B. *The Early Maps of New England: An Exhibition from the Collection of The Kenneth Spencer Research Library, University of Kansas, Lawrence, Kansas, October 2000–January 2001.* Lawrence: University of Kansas, [2000]. Pp. 16.

Moore, Fabienne. "Homer Revisited: Anne Le Fevre Dacier's Preface to her Prose Translation of the *Iliad* in Early Eighteenth-Century France." *Studies in the Literary Imagination*, 33 (2000), 87–107.

Moral, Rafael del (comp.). *Enciclopedia de la novela española*. Barcelona: Planeta, 1999. Pp. 712; bibliography; chronology.

Alphabetical list of Spanish fiction from the Renaissance on. Rev. in *College and Research Libraries*, 62 (2001), 159–60.

North, Roger. *Notes of Me: The Autobiography of Roger North*. Edited by Peter Millard. Toronto: University of Toronto Press, 2000. Pp. 354.

O'Malley, Tom, and Clive Soley. *Regulating the Press*. London, and Sterling: Pluto Press, 2000. Pp. 244; index.

Theoretical and critical study with late twentieth-century focus. Rev. by Aled Jones in *Media History*, 7 (2001), 190–91.

Peacey, J. T. "Marchamont Nedham and the Lawrans Letters." *Bodleian Library Record*, 17, no. 1 (April 2000), 24–35.

Argues that Nedham, editing the weekly newspaper *Mercurius Pragmaticus* in late 1748, was the author of a group of intelligence letters (in the Hyde Collection) from London to royalist exile Sir Edward Nicholas in France.

Peña, Margarita (ed.). *La palabra amordazada: Literatura censurada por la Inquisición*. Mexico City: Facultad de Filosofía y Letras, Universidad Nacional Autónoma de Mexico, 2000. Pp. 129.

Covers dances, songs, popular, religious, and satirical literature censored in sixteenth through nineteenth centuries; with censured texts in the Archivo General de la Nación.

Perrot, Jean. *Jeux et enjeux du livre d'enfance et de jeunesse*. Paris: Editions du Cercle de la Librairie, 1999. Pp. 414; 8 color plates.

Rev. (favorably) by Gillian Adams in *Libraries and Culture*, 38 (2003), 84–85.

Piereth, Wolfgang. *Bayerns Pressepolitik und die Neuordnung Deutschlands nach den Befreiungskriegen*. Munich: C. H. Beck, 1999. Pp. 1 + 330; illustrations; index.

Special Section: Late Entries and Reviews

Raven, James (ed.). *Free Print and Non-Commercial Publishing since 1700*. Aldershot.: Ashgate, 2000. Pp. xiv + 258; graphs; illustrations; index; index; tables. See *ECCB*, 26 (2000), I:123–24.

Rev. Alexandra Franklin in *SHARP News*, 10, no. 3 (Summer 2001), 6–7; by T. H. Howard-Hill in *Papers of the Bibliographical Society of America*, 95 (2001), 139–40.

On the one hand, this volume offers lots of interesting information on the subject of free print, which includes posted broadsides, religious literature given away for free, vanity publications, commemorative volumes, and propaganda material. On the other hand, *Free Print* demonstrates the central problem of the new discipline known as "history of the book" or "book history"—its difficulty in finding or constructing connections between historical research on material objects and literary interpretation of cultural artifacts.

Apart from James Raven's introductory essay, seven of the ten other contributions deal with the long eighteenth century. The most successful article is David Money's investigation of commemorative verse produced by the Oxford and Cambridge university presses between 1564 and 1763. At one point, Money subtly dissects the power relations between the tutor Anthony Alsop and his pupil and patron James Cecil, 5th Earl of Salisbury as demonstrated in the placement of their poetry in one book—but at the same time he also shows how the poetical rhetoric of one Sir John Williams enacts the competition between Oxford and London for cultural capital.

Other articles, however, stop short of analyzing the texts they wonderfully contextualize. Marcus Wood, for instance, thoroughly investigates the publications of the abolitionist movement in England and identifies the Society for Effecting the Abolition of the Slave Trade's 1788 seal as well as their 1789 print "The Description of a Slave Ship" as the most important records in that movement. But then, even though there are reproductions of those documents, he hardly says anything *about* them. Similarly, Leslie Howsam argues that the Religious Tract Society (later British and Foreign Bible Society) had a particular agenda in *not* giving Bibles away as gifts—namely to increase their commodity value—but never closely reads the actual texts of the Bibles that the RTS sold.

Furthermore, some essays to *Free Print* offer mostly historical information on the Americas, but little analysis. James Raven's article on mission literature in colonial America, for instance, is another one of his many well-researched and well-documented contributions to book history (with lots of informative numbers and tables). However, after mentioning *Proposals for Encouraging Learning and Religion in the Foreign Plantations* (1695) by Thomas Bray, apparently the most popular publication of this instigator of the Society for the Propagation of Christian Knowledge, Raven unfortunately does not analyze its text. Florence Jumonville gives a similarly comprehensive survey of broadsides in the streets of New Orleans between 1764 and 1900 with tantalizing reproductions, but does not look at the rhetorical or stylistic make-up of the texts in any detail.

Two other essays look beyond the realm of the English language. Anindita Ghosh investigates the attempts of missionaries to spread Christianity in Bengal at the beginning of the nineteenth century and shows how they failed because they brought print into an oral culture, because they employed the formal language of literal translations of the Bible, because they insisted on prose in a poetry-oriented culture, and because the Bible demanded silent reading in a culture that was used to public recitations. Reminiscent of old-school bibliography, Anna Giulia Cavagna follows the transmission of knowledge in the Enlightenment across national boundaries by tracing the provenance of books written by, and given away to, friends, colleagues, libraries, and societies by the Italian civil servant and astronomer Giovanni Giacomo Marinoni. Her thesis that Marinoni was trying to unify amateurs and experts could have been strengthened in the texts of the books, but those are never presented.

As James Raven explains in his introduction, book history is about "exploring historical conditions in the printing house, publishing and reviewing communities, distributive agencies, and readerships and reading performance [by way of] printing sites, print-shop practice, composition, print runs, paper-making, typographical innovation, the reconstruction of local writing communities and local reception, to methods for identifying texts, authors and reviews, the recording and interpretation of marginalia, marks of ownership and provenance" (8). In this project, free print plays a particular role because it forces the scholar to rethink the role of the readers (who are no longer also purchasers of the text) and of national boundaries (since free print made borders particularly permeable). However, the scholarship in this particular volume mostly stays in the realm of historical research, and does not quite fulfill the promise of the history of the book to cross the disciplines of historical and literary studies and illuminate both of them.—Norbert Schürer

Schenck, David H. J. *Directory of the Lithographic Printers of Scotland, 1820–1870: Their Locations, Periods, and a Guide to Artistic Lithographic Printers.* (Occasional Publications of the Edinburgh Bibliographical Society.) Edinburgh: Edinburgh Bibliographical Society; New Castle: Oak Knoll, 2000. Pp. 124; facsimiles.

Scott, Patrick. *John Milton & Seventeenth-Century Culture from the Collections of the Thomas Cooper Library.* Columbia: Thomas Cooper Library, University of South Carolina, 2000. Pp. 36; bibliography; exhibition catalogue; illustrations.

Sharpe, Kevin. "Representations and Negotiations: Texts, Images, and Authority in Early Modern England." *Historical Journal*, 42:3 (1999), 853–81.

Sheridan, Thomas E. (ed.). *Empire of Sand: The Seri Indians and the Struggle for Spanish Sonora, 1645–1803.* Tucson: University of Arizona Press, 1999. Pp. 600.

Soler i Fabregat, Ramon. *El libro de arte en España durante la edad moderna.* (Biblioteconomía y administración cultural, 43.) Gijón: Trea, 2000. Pp. 213.

Stark, W. "Kant's Last Manuscript in the Berlin *Staatsbibliothek*." *Kant-Studien*, 90:4 (1999), 510–11.

Stole, Ingeborg. *Totentanz und Obrigkeit: Illustrierte Erbauungsliteratur von Conrad Meyer im Kontext reformierter Bilderfeindlichkeit im Zürich des 17. Jahrhunderts.* (Europäische Hochschulschriften, ser. 28, vol. 343.) Frankfurt am Main: Peter Lang, 1999. Pp. viii + 418.

Revised doctoral thesis (1995) on relation of word and image within Zurich artist Conrad Meyer's *Sterbensspiegel* (1650).

Stoomberg, Harriet J. *High Heads: Spotprenten over haarmode in de achttiende eeuw: Uitgegeven door Matthew en Mary Darly / High Heads: Hair Fashions Depicted in Eighteenth-Century Satirical Prints: Published by Matthew and Mary Darly.* (Rijksmuseum Twenthe, 11.) Amsterdam: Rijksmuseum, 1999. Pp. 63; exhibition catalogue in English and Dutch; illustrations (some in color).

Special Section: Late Entries and Reviews

The Darlys produced many prints from 1758–1778. Rev. by David Alexander in *Print Quarterly*, 17 (2000), 173–75.

Strugnell, Anthony (ed.). *From Letter to Publication: Studies on Correspondence and the History of the Book. With the Besterman Lecture 2000*. (SVEC, 2001: 10.) Oxford: Voltaire Foundation, 2001. Pp. v + 295.

Includes Robert Darnton's "J.-P. Brissot et la Société typographique de Neuchâtel (1779–1787)" and Daniel Droixhe's "Signatures clandestines et autres essais sur les contrefaçons de Liège et de Maastricht au XVIII siècle."

Tilley, Joy. *A Catalogue of the Donations Made to Norwich City Library, 1608–1656*. Cambridge: Libri Pertinentes, 2000. Pp. ix + 120; bibliography; 9 illustrations; author/title index.

Rev. (favorably) by J. F. Fuggles in *Book Collector*, 50 (2001), 582–83; (favorably) by David Stoker in *SHARP News*, 11, no. 1 (Winter 2001/02), 14.

Tombarel-Fauconnier, Annick. *Index des écrits sur la musique et de quelques écrits scientifiques de Jean-Jacques Rousseau*. Genève: Slatkine, 1999. Pp. ii + 446.

Trimmer, Sarah. *The Guardian of Education: A Periodical Work*. With a new Introduction by Matthew Grenby. 5 volumes. Bristol: Thoemmes Press, 2000.

Facsimile edition (London: J. Hatchard, 1802–1806). Rev. by Andrea Immel in *Children's Books History Society Newsletter*, 77 (2003), 32–33.

Vorlesungsverzeichnisse der Universität Königsberg (1720–1804). (Forschungen und Materialien zur Universitätgeschichte, I: 1–2.) Edited, with an introduction and index, by Michael Oberhausen and Riccardo Pozzo. 2 vols. Stuttgart: Frommann-Holzboog, 1999.

Concerns university prospectuses. Rev. by Ulrich Johannes Schneider in *Das achtzehnte Jahrhundert*, 25 (2001), 294–96.

Watanabe-O'Kelly, Helen, and Anne Simon (comps.). *Festivals and Ceremonies: A Bibliography of Works Relating to Court, Civic and Religious Festivals in Europe 1500–1800*. London: Mansell, 2000. Pp. xx + 533; indices. See *ECCB*, 26 (2000), I:154.

Rev. (favorably) by John L. Flood in *Library*, 7th series, 2 (2001), 89.

Wheeler, Susan. *Five Hundred Years of Medicine in Art: An Illustrated Catalogue of Prints and Drawings in the Clements C. Fry Collection Held at the Harvey Cushing / John Hay Whitney Medical Library,*

Yale University. Aldershot.: Ashgate, 1999. Pp. xxvii + 363; bibliography; 1700 illustrations; indices.

Windle, John, and Karma Pippin. *Mary Wollstonecraft Godwin, 1759–1797: A Bibliography of First and Early Editions, with Briefer Notes on Later Editions and Translations.* 2nd Edition. New Castle: Oak Knoll Press, 2000. Pp. xvi + 71; illustrations.

Winearls, Joan. *Art on the Wing: British, American and Canadian Illustrated Bird Books from the Eighteenth to the Twentieth Century.* Toronto: Thomas Fischer Rare Book Library, 1999. Pp. 80; illustrations.

Wolf, Christoph, and others [Harvard students in Music 215r]. *Johann Sebastian Bach (1685–1750): "The Man from whom all true musical wisdom proceeded": A 250th Anniversary Exhibition.* Cambridge: Houghton Library and Eda Kuhn Music Library, Harvard University, 2000. Pp. 51; exhibition catalogue; facsimiles.

Zipes, Jack (ed.). *When Dreams Came True: Classical Fairy Tales and Their Tradition.* New York: Routledge, 1999. Pp. x + 238; illustrations; index.

Historical, Social, and Economic Studies:
Europe, Africa, Asia, Central and South America

Adamson, John (ed.). *The Princely Courts of Europe: Ritual, Politics and Culture Under the Ancien Regime 1500–1750.* London: Seven Dials, 1999. Pp. 352; illustrations.

Alimento, A. "Un gioco di cacchi? Aspetti e problemi di storia politica della Francia pre-rivoluzionaria." *Revista Storica*, 110:2 (1998), 529–72.

Allan, D. "'In-the-bosome-of-a-shaddowie-grove': Sir George Mackenzie and the Consolations of Retirement." *History of European Ideas*, 25:5 (1999), 251–73.

Allison, R. J. "The Origins of African-American Culture." *Journal of Interdisciplinary History*, 30:3 (1999), 475–81.

Alvis, J. "Milton and the Declaration of Independence." *Interpretation: A Journal of Political Philosophy*, 25:3 (1998), 367–405.

Special Section: Late Entries and Reviews

Aravamudan, Srinivas. *Tropicopolitans: Colonialism and Agency, 1688–1804*. Durham: Duke University Press, 2000. Pp. x + 424; illustrations.

Arrom, Silvia Marina. *Containing the Poor: The Mexico City Poor House, 1774–1871*. Durham: Duke University Press, 20000. Pp. 408.

Assereto, G. "Il mal di pietra: L'insurrezione genovese del 1746 e la controversia su Balilla." *Studi Setteceteschi*, 18 (1998), 335–66.

Aten, D., M. N. J. Lucassen, and V. J. M. L. Wijnekus. *De Atlas van de Engels–Russische invasie in 1799*. Zaltbommel: Europese Bibliotheek, 1999. Pp. 44; illustrations; portraits.

Atteberry, John, and John Russell. *Ratio Studiorum: Jesuit Education, 1540–1773*. Chestnut Hill: John J. Burns Library, Boston College, 1999. Pp. 64; illustrations.

Aulinas, L. R. "Riformismo contro rivoluzione? Verso la fine di un falso dilemma nella storiografia spagnola sul XVIII secolo." *Studi Storci*, 36:1 (1995), 103–26.

Aumètre, J., and others (eds.). *Rousseau, Anticipateur-Retardtaire*. Québec: Pressses de l'Université Laval, 2000. Pp. 344.

Bach, Reinhard. *Rousseau, économie politique*. Montmorency: Musée Jean-Jacques Rousseau, 1999. Pp. 367; illustrations.

Backouche, Isabelle. *La Trace du fleuve: La Seine et Paris (1750–1850)*. Paris: Éditions de l'École des hautes études en sciences sociales, 2000. Pp. 430.

Baker, M. "Lord Nelson and John Bowsher." *Mariner's Mirror*, 86 (2000), 310–12.

Bannister, J. "Convict Transportation and the Colonial State in Newfoundland, 1789." *Acadiensis*, 2 (1998), 95–123.

Baranger, Denis. *Le Parlementarisme des origines: Essai sue les conditions de formation d'un exécutif responsable en Angleterre, des années 1740 au début de l'âge victorien*. Paris: Presses universitaires de France, 1999. Pp. 416.

Barbero, A. "Una nobilitàprovinciale sotto l'Antico Regime: Il *Nobiliare du Duché d'Aoste* di J. B. De Tillier." *Revista Storica Italiana*, 109:1 (1997), 5–48.

Barbiche, Bernard. *Les Institutions de la monarchie française à l'époque moderne, XVIe–XVIIIe siècle.* Paris: Presses universitaires de France, 1999. Pp. 448.

Barendse, R. J. "Trade and State in the Arabian Seas: A Survey from the Fifteenth to the Eighteenth Century." *Journal of World History*, 11 (2000), 173–225.

Baridon, Michel. "The Cultural Historian and the Garden." *Lumen*, 19 (2000), 23–37.

Baridon, Michel. "Les deux grandes tournants du S iècle des lumières." *Dix-huitième siècle*, 31 (1999), 15–31.

Barker, T. M. "A Debacle of the Peninsular War: The British-Led Amphibious Assault Against Fort Fuengirola, 14–15 October 1810." *Journal of Military History*, 64:1 (2000), 9–52.

Barrett, Thomas M. *At the Edge of Empire: The Terek Cossacks and the North Caucasus Frontier, 1700–1860.* Boulder: Westview Press, 1999. Pp. xv + 243; illustrations.

Baten, Joerg. *Ernaehrung und wirtschaftliche Entwicklung in Bayern (1730–1880).* (Beitraege zur Wirtschafts- und Sozialgeschichte 82.) Stuttgart: Steiner, 1999. Pp. 217.

Beaur, Gérard (ed.). *La terre et les hommes: France et Grande-Bretagne, XVIe–XVIIIe siècles.* Paris: Hachette, 1998. Pp. 256.

Beaurepaire, Pierre-Yves. "À la recontre de l'Auter et du Frère: Voyageurs et francs-maçons dans la France des Lumières." Pp. 62–70 of *Le Voyage en France 1750–1914*. Edited by Jean-Denys Devauges and Didier Masseau. Compiègne: Société des amis du Musée national de la voiture et du tourisme, Château de Compiègne, 2000.

Beaurepaire, Pierre-Yves. "*Les Véritables Auteurs de la Révolution de France de 1789* démasqués: Discours de persécution et crimes d'indifférenciation chez F. N. Sourdat de Troyes." *Dix-huitième siècle*, 32 (2000), 403–21.

Bechtel, Guy. *Les Quatre Femmes de Dieu: La putain, la sorcière, la sainte et Bécassine.* Paris: Plon, 2000. Pp. 328.

Beckles, Hilary. *Centering Woman: Gender Discourses in Caribbean Slave Society.* Kingston: M. Wiener, 1999. Pp. xxv + 211.

Bedell, J. "Archaeology and Probate Inventories in the Study of Eighteenth-Century Life." *Journal of Interdisciplinary History*, 31 (2000), 223–45.

Special Section: Late Entries and Reviews

Ben-Amos, I. K. "Gifts and Favors: Informal Support in Early Modern England." *Journal of Modern History*, 72:2 (2000), 295–338.

Benton, L. "The Legal Regime of the South Atlantic World, 1400–1750: Jurisdictional Complexity as Institutional Order." *Journal of World History*, 11 (2000), 27–56.

Bernier, Olivier. *The World in 1800*. New York: Wiley, 2000. Pp. xi + 452; maps; illustrations; portraits.

Bernstein, Jeremy. *Dawning of the Raj: The Life and Times of Warren Hastings*. Chicago: Ivan E. Dee, 2000. Pp. xi + 319; illustrations; map.

Bertière, Simone. *La Reine et la favorite: Les reines de France au temps des Bourbons, tome 3*. Paris: Fallois, 2000. Pp. 592.

Biagianti, I. "Dalla 'Paix perpetuelle' alla neutralità generale: L'opera di Saint-Pierre in Italia nel XVIII secolo." *Revista Storica Italiana*, 110:1 (1998), 222–50.

Bisha, R. "Reconstructing the Voice of a Noblewoman of the Time of Peter the Great: Daria Mikhailovna Menshikova, an Exercise in (Pseudo) Autobiographical Writing." *Rethinking History*, 2 (1998), 51–63.

Black, Jeremy. "Britain as a Military Power, 1688–1915." *Journal of Military History*, 64:1 (2000), 159–78.

Black, Jeremy. "Britain 1800." *History Today*, 50:11 (2000), 29–35.

Bluche, François. *Louis XV*. Paris: Perrin, 2000. Pp. 308.

Blussé, Leonard, and Femme S. Gaastra (eds.). *On the Eighteenth Century as a Category of Asian History: Van Leur in Retrospect*. Aldershot: Ashgate, 1998. Pp. 322.

Bodineau, Pierre, and Michel Verpeaux. *Histoire constitutionnelle de la France*. Paris: Presses universitaires de France, 2000. Pp. 127.

Boes, M. R. "Jews in the Criminal-Justice System of Early Modern Germany." *Journal of Interdisciplinary History*, 30 (19999), 407–35.

Bois, Pierre-André, Raymond Heitz, and Roland Krebs (eds.). *Voix conservatrices et réactionnaires dans les périodiques allemands de la Révolution française à la Restauration.* (Convergences 13.) New York: Peter Lang, 1999. Pp. xxvi + 431.

Boissonade, Euloge, and Christiane Laroque. *Rouget de Lisle.* Paris: France–Empire, 1999. Pp. 327; illustrations.

Boisvert, Marcel. *L'Éducation de la jeune fille de province dans Balzac.* Montreal: Guérin, 2000. Pp. v + 242.

With a lengthy discussion of the education of girls in the early nineteenth century.

Bonifas, Gilbert (ed.). *Conservatismes anglo-américains, XVIIIe et XIXe siècles.* Nice: Centre de recherche sur les écritres de lange anglaise de l'université de Nice-Sophia-Antipolis, 1999. Pp. 215.

Bourguet-Rouveyre, Josiane. "Bonaparte vû par les memorialistes français: une image à facettes." *Annales historiques de la révolution française,* 318 (1999), 601–14.

Bray, Francesca. *Technology and Gender: Fabrics of Power in Late Imperial China.* Berkeley: University of California Press, 1997. Pp. xvi + 419; illustrations; table; maps; glossary.

Bredin, Miles. *The Pale Abyssinian: A Life of James Bruce, African Explorer.* London: HarperCollins, 2000. Pp. xiv + 290; illustrations; maps; portraits; [16 pp.] of plates.

Bret, Patrice. *L'Egypte au temps de l'expédition de Bonaparte, 1798–1801.* Paris: Hachette littératures, 1998. Pp. 340; illustrations; maps.

Bret, Patrice. *L'Expedition d'Egypte, une entreprise des Lumières 1798–1801: Actes du colloque international.* Paris: Hachette littératures, 1998. Pp. xviii + 436; illustrations.

Brianta, Donata. "Education and Training in the Mining Industry, 1750–1860: European Models and the Italian Case." *Annals of Science,* 57:3 (2000), 267–300.

Brod, M. "Politics and Prophecy in Seventeenth-Century England: The Case of Elizabeth Poole." *Albion,* 31:3 (1999), 395–412.

Brown, D. "Reassessing the Influence of the Aristocratic Improver: The Example of the Fifth Duke of Bedford (1765–1802)." *Agricultural History Review,* 47:2 (1999), 182–95.

Special Section: Late Entries and Reviews

Brown, H. G. "Domestic State Violence: Repression from the Croquants to the Comune." *Historical Journal*, 42:3 (1999), 597–622.

Buchan, John. *The Massacre of Glencoe*. Staplehurst: Spellmont, 1999. Pp. 176.

Bullock, S. C. "A Mumper Among the Gentle: Tom Bell, Colonial Confidence Man." *William and Mary Quarterly*, 55:2 (1998), 231–58.

Bumsted, J. M. "The Land Question of Prince Edward Island and the Quitrent Controversy of 1802–1806." *Acadiensis*, 29:2 (2000), 102–19.

Burke, Edmund. *On Empire, Liberty, and Reform: Speeches and Letters*. Edited by David Bromwich. New Haven: Yale University Press, 2000. Pp. 536.

Burnard, T. "Slave naming Patterns: Onomastics and the Taxonomy of Race in Eighteenth-Century Jamaica." *Journal of Interdisciplinary History*, 31:3 (2000), 325–46.

Bushman, R. L. "Markets and Composite Farms in Early America." *William and Mary Quarterly*, 55:3 (1998), 351–74.

Caine, Barbara. *Gendering European History 1780–1920*. New York: Continuum, 1999. Pp. 224.

Cambry, Jacques. *Voyage dans le Finistère ou État de ce Département en 1794 et 1795*. Quimper: Société archéologique du Finistère, 1999. Pp. lxiv + 504; illustrations.

Carré, Jacques. "Le Jardin urbain au XVIIIe siècle." *Bulletin de la société d'études anglo-américaines des XVIIe et XVIIIe siécles*, 51 (2000), 185–200.

Carter, Philip. *Men and the Emergence of Polite Society, Britain 1660–1800*. London: Longman, 2000. Pp. 224; illustrations.

Cartuyvels, Yves. *D'où le Code pénal? Une approche généalogique des primers codes pénaux absolutistes au XVIIe siècle*. Montréal: Presses de l'Université de Montréal, 1996. Pp. xv + 404.

Casler, Jeanine. "Aging and Opportunity: Growing Older in Clara Reeve's *School for Widows*." *Journal of Aging and Identity*, 4 (1999), 111–26.

Cavaillé, Jean-Pierre. "De la construction des appearances au culte de la transparence: Simulation et dissimulation entre le XVIe et le XVIIIe siècle." *Littératures classiques*, 34 (1998), 73–102.

Cavendish, R. "The French Surrender Malta, September 5th, 1800." *History Today*, 50:9 (2000), 54–55.

Ceretti, M. "Alessandro Verri: Lettere sulla Rivoluzione francese (1791–1800)." *Rivista Storica*, 3:109 (1997), 803–52.

Cervantes, Xavier. *L'Angleterre au XVIII siècle*. Rennes: Presses universitaires de Rennes, 1998. Pp. 171.

Chase, H. V. "Philip Thomas (1747–1815): Physician, Patriot, Politician." *Maryland Medical Journal*, 48:5 (1999), 207–13.

Chastenet de Puységur, Armand-Marie-Jacques. *Un somnambule dédordonné? Journal du traitement magnétique dujeune Hébert*. Edited by Jean-Pierre Peter. Le Plessis-Robinson: Institut synthélabo pour le progrès de la connaissance, 1999. Pp. 306.

Chater, K. "'Where There's a Will': Black Britons in the Eighteenth Century." *History Today*, 50:4 (2000), 26–27.

Chatterjee, I. "A Slave's Quest for Selfhood in Eighteenth-Century Hindustan." *Indian Economic and Social History Review*, 37 (2000), 53–86.

Chevet, Jean-Michel. *La terre et les paysas en France et en Grande-Bretagne du début du XVIIe à la fin du XVIIIe siècle*. 2 volumes. Paris: Messene, 1998.

Chézaud, Patrick. "Culture de la Nature au XVIIIe siècle ou Le Sens dans le jardin." *Bulletin de la société d'études anglo-américaines des XVIIe et XVIIIe siècles*, 51 (2000), 129–40.

Christofferson, M. S. "An Antitotalitarian History of the French Revolution: François Furet's *Penser la Revolution française* in the Intellectual Politics of the Late 1970s." *French Historical Studies*, 22:4 (1999), 557–611.

Churchman, Nancy. "Public Debt Policy and Public Extravagance: The Ricardo–Malothus debate." *History of Political Economy*, 31:4 (2000), 653–74.

Special Section: Late Entries and Reviews

Clark, A. "Gender and Politics in the Long Eighteenth Century." *History Workshop*, 48 (1999), 252–57.

Clark, J. C. D. *English Society 1660–1832: Religion, Ideology and Politics During the Ancien Regime*. Cambridge: Cambridge University Press, 2000. Pp. xii + 580.

Clark, Peter. *British Clubs and Societies, 1580–1800: The Origins of an Associational World*. New York: Oxford University Press, 2000. Pp. 516.

Coetzee, Carli. "The Double-Sided Signature: The South African Career of Johannes Van der Kemp (1747–1811)." *Pretexts: Literary and Cultural Studies*, 9 (2000), 207–14.

Cohen, S. S. "William Hodgson: An English Merchant and Unsung Friend to American Revolutionary Captives." *Pennsylvania Magazine of History and Biography*, 123:1–2 (1999), 57–85.

Colander, David. "The Death of Neoclassical Economics." *Journal of the History of Economic Thought*, 22:2 (2000), 127–44.

Coleman, J. "The History of Political Thought in a Modern University: The First Henry Tudoe Memorial Lecture (Delivered March 1999, University of Durham)." *History of Political Thought*, 21:1 (2000), 152–71.

Comminey, Shawn. "The Society for the Propagation of the Gospel in Foreign Parts and Black Education in South Carolina, 1702–1764." *Journal of Negro History*, 84 (1999), 360–69.

Conrad, Lawrence I., Michael Neve, Vivian Nutton, Roy Porter, and Andrew Wear. *Histoire de la lutte contre la maladie: La tradition médicale occidentale, de la Antiquité à la fin du Siècle des lumières*. Translated by Sophie Mayeux, Simone Rozenberg, and Paul Rozenberg. Le Plessis-Robinson: Institut synthélabo pour le progrès de la connaissance, 1999. Pp. xi + 524.; illustrations.

Conway, Stephen. *The British Isles and the War of American Independence*. New York: Oxford University Press, 2000. Pp. 408.

Cookson, J. E. "The Napoleonic Wars, Military Scotland and Tory Highlandism in the Early Nineteenth Century." *Scottish Historical Review*, 78 (1999), 60–75.

Cornette, Joël. *La Monarchie entre Renaissance et Révolution: 1515–1792*. Paris: Seuil, 2000. Pp. 503.

Cosgrove, Denis. "Global Illumination and Enlightenment in the Geographies of Vincenzo Coronelli and Athanasius Kircher." Pp. 33–66 of *Geography and Enlightenment*. Edited by David N. Livingstone and Charles W. Withers. Chicago: University of Chicago Press, 1999.

Crane, Elaine Forman. "Political Dialogue and the Spring of Abagail's Discontent." *William and Mary Quarterly*, 56:4 (1999), 745–74.

Crawford, C. "Patients' Rights and the Law of Contract in Eighteenth-Century England." *Social History of Medicine*, 13 (2000), 381–410.

Crépin, Annie. "Le 18 Brumaire, un étape importante dans la constitution d'une armée nouvelle." *Annales historiques de la révolution française*, 318 (1999), 663–76.

Crosland, Margaret. *Madame de Pompadour: Sex, Culture and Power*. Stroud: Sutton, 2000. Pp. 224; plates; illustrations.

Curtis, L. P. "The Four Erins: Feminine Images of Ireland, 1780–1900." *Eire–Ireland*, 33 (1998), 70–102.

Czouz-Tornare, Alain-Jacques. "La reception du 18 Brumaire en Helvétie." *Annales historiques de la révolution française*, 318 (1999), 727–46.

Da Passano, M. "Della democrazia direttoriale all'oligarchia senatoria: Le vicende costituzionali della Repubblica Ligure (1797–1805)." *Studi Settecenteschi*, 17 (1997), 287–334.

Darby, M. "Bligh's Disciple: Matthew Flinders's Journal of *HMS Providence* (1791–3)." *Mariner's Mirror*, 86 (2000), 401–11.

Davids, Karel. "Patents and Patentees in the Dutch Republic Between c1580 and 1720." *History and Technology*, 16:3 (2000), 263–84.

Davis, J. A. "The Neapolitan Revolution of 1799–1999: Between History and Myth." *Journal of Modern Italisn Studies*, 4 (1999), 350–79.

De Bruyn, Frans. "Reading *Het groote tafereel der dwaasheid*: An Emblem Book of the Folly of Speculation in the Bubble Year 1720." *Eighteenth Century Life*, 24:2 (2000), 1–42.

Dejongh, G. "New Estimates of Land Productivity in Belgium, 1750–1850." *Agricultural History Review*, 47:1 (1999), 7–28.

Special Section: Late Entries and Reviews

Derby, M. "Lieutenants' Passing Certificates: William Bligh and Peter Heywood." *Mariner's Mirror*, 86 (2000), 197–99.

Desan, Suzanne. "Reconstituting the Social After the Terror: Family, Property and the Law in Popular Politics." *Past & Present*, 164 (1999), 81–121.

Desan, Suzanne. "What's After Political Culture? Recent French Revolutionary Historiography." *French Historical Studies*, 23:1 (2000), 163–96.

Devine, T. M. *The Scottish Nation, 1700–2000.* London: Penguin Press, 2000. Pp. 720.

De Vries, Marleen. "Dichten is zilver, zwijgne is goud; vrowen in letterkundige genootschappen, 1772–1800." *De Achttiende Eeuw*, 31:2 (1999), 187–213.

Dickinson, H. T. (ed.). *Britain and the American Revolution.* London: Longman, 1998. Pp. xii + 284; maps.

Di Rienzo, E. "Giustizia e lotta politica in Francia nei manoscritti de Marc-Antoine Jullien de Paris (1794–96)." *Studi Storici*, 39:3 (1998), 645–74.

Di Rienzo, E. "'Leri in Francia, oggi in Italia': Neogiacobinismo e questione italiana nei manoscritti di Marc-Antoine Jullien de Paris (1796–1801)." *Studi Storici*, 37:1 (1996), 593–628.

Di Rienzo, E. "Nascita di una nazione: La missione in Vandea e in Bretagna di Marc-Antoine Jullien de Paris." *Revista Storica Italiana*, 110:2 (1998), 411–62.

Dixon, C. "Cutting Out the *Caroline*." *Mariner's Mirror*, 86 (2000), 50–59.

Dobuzinskis, Laurent. "Serge Kolm on Social Justice and the Social Contract: A Contextual Analysis and a Critique." *European Legacy*, 5:5 (2000), 687–702.

Doerflinger, Johannes. "Anselm Desing, 1699–1772, und seine Globen." *Der Glousfreund*, 47–48 (1999), 229–42.

Dojnov, S. "Bulgarian Emigrants in Russia (in the Second Half of the 18th Century)." *Bulgarian History Review*, 1–2 (1999), 48–71.

Dolan, Brian. *Exploring European Frontiers: British Travellers in the Age of Enlightenment.* London: Macmillan, 2000. Pp. 232.

Douglas. Hugh. *Jacobite Spy Wars: Moles, Rogues, and Treachery.* Stroud: Sutton, 2000. Pp. 269.

Dubois, L. "'The Price of Liberty': Victor Hugues and the Administration of of Freedom in Guadeloupe, 1794–1798." *William and Mary Quarterly*, 56:2 (1999), 363–92.

Dubois, L. "La Republique Metissée: Citizenship, Colonialism, and the Borders of French History." *Cultural Studies*, 14:1 (2000), 15–34.

Dubois, Laurent. *Les Esclaves de la République: L'Histoire oubliée de la première émancipation, 1789–1794.* (Liberté de l'esprit.) Paris: Calmann-Lévy, 1999. Pp. 240.

Dunlop, Ian. *Louis XIV.* London: Chatto and Windus, 1999. Pp. xii + 487.

Dunn, P. M. "Dr. William Buchan and His Domestic Medicine." *Archives of Diseases of Childhood and Fetal and Neonatal Education*, 43:6 (2000), 71–73.

Dupuy, Pascal. "Le 18 Brumaire en Grande-Bretagne: le témoignage de la presse et de la caricature." *Annales historiques de la révolution française*, 318 (1999), 773–87.

Durey, M. "The British Secret Service and the Escape of Sir Sidney Smith from Paris in 1798." *History*, 84:275 (1999), 437–57.

Dziembowski, Edmond. *Un nouveau patriotisme français. 1750–1770: La France face à la puissance anglaise à l'époque de la guerre de Sept Ans.* Oxford: Voltaire Foundation, 1998. Pp. vii + 566; illustrations.

Edney, Matthew H. "Reconsidering Enlightenment Geography and Map Making: reconnaisance Mapmaking Archive." Pp. 165–98 of *Geography and Enlightenment.* Edited by David N. Livingstone and Charles W. Withers. Chicago: University of Chicago Press, 1999.

Edwards, L. "Horatio Nelson and Lady Hamilton's Twins." *Mariner's Mirror*, 86 (2000), 313–15.

Ellis, J. "Georgian Town Gardens." *History Today*, 50 (2000), 38–45.

Eltis, David. *The Rise of African Slavery in the Americas.* Cambrisge: Cambridge University Press, 2000. Pp. xvii + 353; maps.

Evangelisti, S. "Wives, Widows, and Brides of Christ: Marriage and the Convent in the Historiography of Early Modern Italy." *Historical Journal*, 43:1 (2000), 233–47.

Special Section: Late Entries and Reviews

Fairweather, Maria. *The Pilgrim Princess: A life of Princess Zinaida Volkonsky.* New York: Carroll & Graf, 1999. Pp. xv + 316; illustrations; plates.

Farr, D. "John Blackwell and Daniel Cox: Further Notes on Their Activities in Restoration England and British North America." *Pennsylvania Magazine of History and Biography*, 123:3 (1999), 227–33.

Faure, Michel. "John Millar ou la culture politique d'un homme des Lumières." Pp. 209–27 of *Ecosse des Lumières: lw XVIIIe siècle autrement.* Edited by Pierre Morère. Grenoble: Université Stendhal, 1997.

Ferrone, V. "L'illuminismo italiano e la revoluzione napoletana del '99." *Studi Storici*, 40:4 (1999), 993–1084.

Finkelman, Paul (ed.). *Slavery and the Law.* Madison: Madison House, 1997. Pp. 465.

Fisher, Judith W. "Creating Another Identity: Aging Actresses in the Eighteenth Century." *Journal of Aging and Identity*, 4 (1999), 57–77.

Fisher, M. H. "Representing 'His' Women: Mirza Abu Talib Khan's 1801 *Vindication of the Liberties of Asiatic Women.*" *Indian Economic and Social History Review*, 37 (2000), 216–37.

Flannery, Tim (ed.). *The Life and Adventures of John Nicol, Mariner.* Edinburgh: Canongate, 2000. Pp. 198.

Fletcher, A. "Manhood, the Male Body, Courtship and the Household in Early Modern England." *History*, 84:275 (1999), 419–36.

Foley, Michael. *The Politics of the British Constiturion.* (Political Analyses Series.) Manchester: Manchester University Press,, 1999. Pp. viii + 296.

Fox, Robert, and Agusti Nieto-Galan (eds.). *Natural Dyestuffs and Industrial Culture in Europe, 1750–1880.* Canton: Science History Publications, 1999. Pp. xxix + 354; illustrations; maps.

Franks, J. "The Taking of Geeriah Fort and Town, 1756: Amphibious Operations in Indian Waters." *Mariner's Mirror*, 86 (2000), 468–71.

Fox, Robert, and Anthony Turner (eds). *Luxury Trades and Consumerism in Ancien Régime Paris: Studies in the History of the Skiled Workforce.* Aldershot: Ashgate, 1998. Pp. 336.

French, H. R. "Social Status, Localism and the 'Middle Sort of People' in England, 1620–1750." *Past and Present*, 166 (2000), 66–99.

Frey, Manuel. *Macht und Moral des Schenkens: Staat und Bürgerliche Mäzene vom Späten 18. Jahrhundert bis zur Gegenwart.* (Buergerlichkeit, Wertewandel, Maezenatentum 4.) Berlin: Fannei & Walz Verlag, 1999. Pp. 306.

Friedeberg, R. V. "From Collective Representation to the Right to Individual Defence: James Steuart's *Ius Populi Vindicatum* and the Use of Johannes Althusius's *Politica* in Restoration Scotland." *History of European Ideas*, 24:1 (1998), 19–42.

Frost, O. W. "Getting the Record Straight: Georg Steller's Plant Collecting on Kayak Island, Alaska, 1741." *Pacific Northwest Quarterly*, 90:3 (1999), 115–22.

Fudge, E. "Monstrous Acts: Bestiality in Early Modern England." *History Today*, 50 (2000), 20–25.

Gainot, Bernard. "Enquête sur le 'suicide' de Victor Bach." *Annales historiques de la révolution française*, 318 (1999), 615–38.

Gainot, Bernard. "Un projet avorté d'intégration républicaine: L'institution nationale des colonies (1797–1802)." *Dix-huitième siècle*, 32 (2000), 371–401.

García Ejarque, Luis. *Historia de la lectura pública en España*. (Biblioteconomía y administración cultural, 35.) Gijón, Spain: Trea, 2000. Pp. xvi + 533; index.

Garnot, Benoît. *Crime et justice aux XVIIe et XVIIIe siècles*. Paris: Imago, 2000. Pp. 208.

Garnot, Benoit. *Justice et société en France aux XVIe, XVIIe, et XVIIIe siècles*. Paris: Ophrys, 2000. Pp. 249.

Garrigus, J. D. "White Jacobins/Black Jacobins: Bringing the Haitian and French Revolutions Together in the Classroom." *French Historical Studies*, 23:2 (2000), 259–75.

Gascoigne, John. *Science, Politics and Universities in Europe, 1600–1800*. Aldershot: Ashgate, 1998. Pp. 304.

Geiter, M. K. "William Penn and Jacobitism: A Smoking Gun? The Attempted Restoration of James II to the English Throne." *Historical Research*, 73:180 92000), 213–18.

Special Section: Late Entries and Reviews

Gibson, J. R. "Sitka Versus Kodiak: Countering the Tingit Threat and Situating the Colonial Capital in Russian America." *Pacific History Review*, 67:1 (1998), 67–98.

Gilleir, Anke. "De individualiteit van de vrouwelijkheid of geslacht van het universele: Johanna Schopenhauer (1766–1838) en de Weimarer Klassik." *De Achttiende Eeuw*, 31:2 (1999), 129–42.

Gilli, Marita. "Une vision allemande du 18 Brumaire. *Les résultats de ma mission à Paris dans le mois de Brumaire an VIII*, de Jospeh von Gorres." *Annales historiques de la révolution française*, 318 (1999), 747–54.

Girollet, Anne. *Victor Schoelcher, républicain: approche juridique et politique de l'œuvre d'un fondateur de la République*. Paris: Éditions Karthala, 2000. Pp. 409.

Goldsmith, Netta Murray. *The Worst of Crimes: Homosexuality and the Law in Eighteenth-Century London*. Aldershot: Ashgate, 1998. Pp. 232.

Gordon, F. "*Vues Legislatives Pour les Femmes* (1790): A Reformist–Feminist Vision—'And we too are citizens.'" *History of Political Thought*, 20:4 (1999), 649–73.

Gragg, L. "The Pious and the Profane: The Religious Life of Early Barbados Planters." *Historian*, 62:2 (2000), 264–83.

Granderoute, Robert. "Comment perfectionner l'éducation ou les propositions de Dominique-François Rivard." *Dix-huitième siècle*, 31 (1999), 451–60.

Gretchanaïa, Elena. "Deux lettres de la princesse de Tarente à la comtesse Golovina." *Dix-huitième siècle*, 31 (1999), 331–43.

Greer, Alan. *Habitants, marchands et seigneurs: La société rurale du bas Richelieu, 1740–1840*. Quebec: Septentrion, 2000. Pp. 358.

Griffin, J. P. "Famous Names in Toxicology: Inoculators and Vaccinators of the 18th Century, III." *Adverse Drug Reactions and Toxicology Review.*, 19:1 (2000), 17–33.

Grimm, Jürgen. "Quand s'arrête le siècle de Louis XIV?" *Littratures classiquesé*, 34 (1998), 237–48.

Guerci, L. "Incredulità e rigenerazione nella Lombardia del triennio repubblicano." *Revista Storica Italiana*, 109:1 (1997), 49–120.

Guilhaumou, Jacques. *L'Avènement des porte-parole de la République (1789–1792). Essai de synthèse sur les langages de la Révolution française*. Villeneuve-d'Ascq: Presses universitaires du Septentrion, 1998. Pp. 306.

Guillery, Peter. "The Further Adventures of Mary Lacy: 'Seaman,' Shipwright, Builder." *History Workshop Journal* 49 (2000), 212–19.

Gutierrez de Pineda, Virginia. *Miscegenación y Cultura en la Columbia Colonial, 1750–1810*. 2 volumes. Santafe de Bogota: Ediciones Uniandes, 1999.

Gvosdev, Nikolas K. *Imperial Policies and Perspectives Toward Georgia, 1760–1819*. New York: St. Martin's Press, 2000. Pp. 216.

Haggerty, George E. *Men in Love: Masculinity and Sexuality in the Eighteenth Century*. New York: Columbia University Press, 2000. Pp. 214.

Haines, R., and R. Shlomowitz. "Explaining the Mortality Decline in the Eighteenth-Century Slave Trade." *Economic History Review*, 53:2 (2000), 262–83.

Hamilton, Jill. *Marengo: The Myth of Napoleon's Horse*. London: Fourth Estate, 2000. Pp. 246; illustrations.

Hanlon, Gregory. *Early Modern Italy, 1550–1800: Three Seasons in European History*. New York: St. Martin's Press, 2000. Pp. 400.

Hardman, John, and Munro Price (eds.). *Louis XVI and the comte de Vergennes: Correspondence 1774–1787*. Oxford: Voltaire Foundation, 1998. Pp. xvii + 403; portraits.

Harpham, Edward J. "Economics and History: Books II and III of the *Wealth of Nations*." *History of Political Thought*, 20:3 (1999), 438–55.

Harpham, Edward J. "The Problem of Liberty in the Thought of Adam Smith." *Journal of the History of Economic thought*, 22:2 (2000), 217 ff.

Harris, John. *Industrial Espionage and Technology Transfer: Britain and France in the 18th Century*. Aldershot: Ashgate, 1998. Pp. 680.

Hartley, S. "John Hunter: The Scientific Surgeon—'don't think, try; be patient, be accurate...'" *Journal of Investigative Surgery*, 12:6 (1999), 305–06.

Special Section: Late Entries and Reviews

Hatcher, J. "Labour, Leisure and Economic Thought Before the Nineteenth Century." *Past and Present*, 160 (1998), 64–115.

Haydon, Colin, and William Doyle (eds.). *Robespierre*. Cambridge: Cambridge University Press, 2000. Pp. 268.

Hedenborg, Susanna. "The World Is Full of Sorrow: Infant Mortality in Stockholm, 1754–1850." *Scandanavian Economic History Review*, 48:1 (2000), 64–80.

Hemmings, Ray. *Liberty or Death: The Struggle for Democracy in Britain, 1780–1830*. New York: New York University Press, 2000. Pp. 192.

Hibbert, Christopher. *George III: A Personal History*. New York: Basic Books, 1998. Pp. xv + 464; illustrations.

Hill, Sarah H., and Sue Evans Vrooman. *Native Lands: Indians and Georgia*. Atlanta: Atlanta History Center, 1999. Pp. 49; colored illustrations; catalogue for an exhibition.

Hollman, Guy. "The Economics of Conservatism or the Case for Mercantilism Reassessed." Pp. 117–31 of *Conservatismes anglo-américains, XVIIIe et XIXe siècles*. Edited by Gilbert Bonifas. Nice: Centre de recherche sur les écritres de lange anglaise de l'université de Nice-Sophia-Antipolis, 1999.

Honeyman, Katrina. *Women, Gender and Industrialisation in England 1700–1870*. New York: St. Martin's Press, 2000. Pp. 224.

Hook, Michael, and Walter Ross. *The "Forty-Five": The Last Jacobite Rebellion*. Edinburgh: National Library of Scotland, 1999. Pp. ix + 144; illustrations; maps.

Hopkin, David M. "Sons and Lovers: Popular Images of the Conscript, 1798–1870." *Modern and Contemporary France*, 9 (2000), 19–36.

Hoppit, Julian. *England After the Glorious Revolution, 1689–1727*. New York: Oxford University Press, 2000. Pp. 600.

Houston, Rab. *Madness and Society in Eighteenth-Century Scotland*. New York: Oxford University Press, 2000. Pp. 482.

Hughes, Lindsey. *Russia in the Age of Peter the Great*. New Haven: Yale University Press, 1998. Pp. xxx + 602; illustrations; map.

Huysseune, Michel. "Virtuous Citizens and Noble Savages of the New World: The Contamination, Juxtaposition and (Mis)Representation of Cultural Models in Enlightenment France." Pp. 47–62 of *Images of America: Through the European Looking-Glass*. Edited by William Chew III. Bruxelles: Vubpress, 1997.

Iaeys, G. "Virtuous Commerce and Free Theology: Political Economy and the Dissenting Academies 1750–1800." *History of Political Thought*, 20:1 (1999), 141–72.

Ingram, Allan. "Political Hypochondria: The Case of James Boswell." Pp. 1–17 of *Conservatismes anglo-américains, XVIIIe et XIXe siècles*. Edited by Gilbert Bonifas. Nice: Centre de recherche sur les écritres de lange anglaise de l'université de Nice-Sophia-Antipolis, 1999.

Ingram, Allan. "Sanity, Madness and the People Next Door: Neighbours and Normalcy in Eighteenth-Century England." *Le spectateur européen*, 1 (2000), 75–90.

Jacob, Margaret C. *The Enlightenment: Brief History with Documents*. London: Palgrave, 2000. Pp. 240.

Jaffe, James A. *Striking a Bargain: Work and Industrial Relations in England, 1780–1850*. Manchester: Manchester University Press, 2000. Pp. 256.

Jaume, Lucien (ed.). *Coppet, creuset de l'esprit libéral: Les ideées politiques et constitutionnelles du groupe de Madame de Staël*. Paris: Presses universitaires d'Aix-Marseille, 2000. Pp. 242.

Jennings, Jeremy. "Intellectuals and Political Culture." *European Legacy*, 5 (2000), 781–94.

Jeremy, David J. *Artisans, Entrepreneurs and Machines: Essays in Early Anglo-American Textile Industries, 1770–1840s*. Aldershot: Ashgate, 1998. Pp. 364.

Joffrin, Laurent. *Les Batailes de Napoléon*. Paris: Seuil, 2000. Pp. 244; illustrations.

Johnson, Whittington B. *Race Relations in the Bahamas, 1784–1834: The Nonviolent Transformation from a Slave to a Free Society*. Fayetteville: University of Arkansas Press, 1999. Pp. 208.

Jomini, Antoine Henri, baron de. *Guerres de la Révolution (1792–1797)*. Paris: Hachette, Littératures, 1998. Pp. 439.

Jones, Greta, and Elizabeth Malcolm (eds.). *Medicine, Disease, and the State in Ireland, 1650–1940*. Cork: Cork University Press, 1999. Pp. x + 278; illustrations.

Special Section: Late Entries and Reviews

Jourdan, Annie. "L'image de Paris dans l'œuvre de Jean-Jacques Rousseau: Du rêve à la mémoire." Pp. 37–57 of *Paris: de l'image à la mémoire: Representations artistiques, littéraires, sociopolitiques*. Amsterdam: Rodopi, 1997.

Jourdan, Annie. "La republique Batave et le 18 Brumaire. La grande illusion." *Annales historiques de la révolution française*, 318 (1999), 755–72.

Karoly, L. "The 1739–1740 Plague Epidemic in County Tolna." *Orvosi Hetilop*, 140:34 (1999), 1895–97.

Kelly, James. *Henry Flood: Patriots and Politics in Eighteenth-Century Ireland*. Dublin: Four Courts Press, 1998. Pp. 486.

Kevorkian, Tanya. "The Rise of the Poor, Weak, and Wicked: Poor Care, Punishment, Religion, and Patriarchy in Leipzig, 1700–1730." *Journal of Social History*, 34:1 (2000), 163–81.

Kidd, C. "The Rehabilitation of Scottish Jacobitism." *Scottish Historical Review*, 77 (1998), 58–76.

Kiddy, Elizabeth W. "Ethnic and Racial Identity in the Brotherhoods of the Rosary of Minas Gerais, 1700–1830." *The Americas*, 56:2 (1999), 221–52.

King, P. "The Rise of Juvenile Delinquency in England 1780–1840: Changing Patterns of Perception and Prosecution." *Past & Present*, 160 (1998), 116–66.

King, Steven. *Poverty and Welfare in England, 1700–1850*. Manchester: Manchester University Press, 2000. Pp. 256.

Knight, Franklin W. "The Haitian Revolution." *American Historical Review*, 105:1 (2000), 103–15.

Knighton, C. S. "Some Pepysian Addenda at Magdalene College, Cambridge." *Mariner's Mirror*, 86 (2000), 148–56.

Kross, Jessica. "Mansions, Men, Women, and the Creation of Multiple Publics in Eightenth-Century British North America." *Journal of Social History*, 33:2 (2000), 385–408.

Kubik, T. R. W. "How Far the Swor? Militia Tactics and Politics in the *Commonwealth of Oceania*." *History of Thought*, 19:2 (1998), 186–212.

Kuiters, W. G. J. "Law and Empire: The Armenians Contra Verelst, 1769–77." *Journal of Imperial and Commonwealth History*, 28:2 (2000), 1–22.

Kujula, A. "The Breakdown of Society: Finland in the Great Northern War, 1700–1714." *Scandinavian Journal of History*, 25 (2000), 69–86.

Lake, P., and M. Questier. "Puritans, Papists, and the 'Public Sphere' in Early Modern England: the Edmund Campion Affair in Context." *Journal of Modern History*, 72:3 (2000), 587–627.

Landford, Paul. *Englishness Identified: Maners and Character, 1650–1850*. New York: Oxford University Press, 2000. Pp. 350.

Landry, N. "Process of Inventory Goods Among the Sea Folk of Ile-Royale in the 18th Century." *Acadiensis*, 28:2 (1999), 71–92.

Langford, Paul. *Englishness Identified: Manners and Character 1650–1850*. New York: Oxford University Press, 2000. Pp. xii + 389.

Larrère, Catherine. *Actualité de Montesquieu*. Paris: Presses de Sciences, 1999. Pp. 130.

Lauwaert, Françoise. *Le Meutre en Famille: Parricide et Infanticide en Chine, XVIIIe–XIXe Siècle*. Paris: Odile Jacob, 1999. Pp. 366.

Lavery, Brian (ed.). *Shipboard Life and Organisation, 1731–1815*. (Navy Records Society Publications 138.) Aldershot: Ashgate, 1998. Pp. 682.

Law, R., and P. E. Lovejoy. "Borgu in the Atlantic Slave Trade." *African Economic History*, 27 (1999), 69–92.

Le Clercq, Chrestien. *Nouvelle relation de la Gaspésie*. Montréal: Presses de l'Université de Montréal, 1999. Edited by Réal Ouellet. Pp. 796.

Leduc, Guyonne. *L'Éducation des Anglaises au XVIIIe siècle: La Conception de Henry Fielding*. Paris: L'Harmattan, 1999. Pp. 415.

Leduc, Guyonne. *Vie, formes, et lumières: Homage à Paul Denizot*. [Villeneuve-d'Ascq]: Société d'études anglo-américaines, 1999. Pp. 304; portrait.

Lee, D., and T. Fulford. "Virtual Empires." *Cultural Critique*, 44 (2000), 3–28.

Special Section: Late Entries and Reviews

Le Fevre. "The Duke of Grafton's Fighting Instructions of 1687." *Mariner's Mirror*, 85 (1999), 456–58.

Le Goff, T. J. A. *France 1661–1789: Anatomy of the Ancien Régime*. New York: Oxford University Press, 2000. Pp. 288.

Lemaire, Jean-François. *Les Blessés dans les armées napoléoniennes*. Paris: Lettrage distribution, 1999. Pp. 336.

Leneman, Leah. *The Scottish Experience of Divorce and Separation, 1684–1830*. Edinburgh: Edinburgh University Press, 1998. Pp. vi + 354.

Lentz, Thierry. *Le Grand Consulat*. Paris: Fayard, 1999. Pp. 627.

Leuwers, Hervé. "République et relations entre les peuples. Quelques éléments de l'idéal républicain autour de Brumaire an VIII." *Annales historiques de la révolution française*, 318 (1999), 677–94.

Leveque, Pierre. "La marine française au 18 Brumaire." *Annales historiques de la révolution française*, 318 (1999), 639–64.

Linn, Patricia Y. C. E. "Citizenship, Military Families, and the Creation of a New Definition of 'Deserving Poor' in Britain, 1793–1815." *Social Politics, Gneder, State and Society*, 7:1 (2000), 5–46.

Little, P. "The First Unionists? Irish Protestant Attitudes to Union with English, 1653–9." *Irish Historical Studies*, 32 (2000), 44–58.

Livesey, J. "Agrarian Ideology and Commercial Republicanism in the French Revolution." *Past & Present*, 157, (1997), 94–121.

Livingstone, David N., and Charles W. Withers (eds.). *Geography and Enlightenment*. Chicago: university of Chicago Press, 1999. Pp. viii + 456; illustrations; maps.

Lockerby, E. "The Deportation of the Acadians from Ile St.-Jean, 1758." *Acadiensis*, 27:2 (1998), 45–94.

López, Emilio la Parra. "Les changements politiques en Espagne après Brumaire." *Annales historiques de la révolution française*, 318 (1999), 695–712.

Luebke, D. M. "Frederick the Great and the Celebrated Case of the Millers Arnold (1770–1779): A Reappraisal." *Central European History*, 32:4 (1999), 379–408.

Luoma-Aho, Mika. "Carl Schmitt and the Transformation of the Political Subject." *European Legacy*, 5:5 (2000), 703–16.

Lupo, Massimo. "Reorganization of the Public Education System in the Kingdom of Naples During the French Period." *Journal of Modern Italian Studies*, 4 (1999), 329–49.

Luzzatto, S. "Il bacio di Grégoire: La 'rigenerazione' degli ebrei nella Francia del 1789." *Studi Settecenteschi*, 17 (1997), 265–86.

Macinnes, A. "Britain, 1700: The State of the Islands at a Crucial Moment in British State Formation." *History Today*, 50:10 (2000), 39–45.

Macleod, Emma Vincent. *A War of Ideas: British Attitudes to the Wars Against Revolutionary France, 1792–1802.* Aldershot: Ashgate, 1998. Pp. 256.

Maffre, Claude. "La difficile intégration des noirs à la fin du XVIIIe siècle." Pp. 221–33 of *Formen der Aufklärung und ihrer Rezeption: Expressions des Lumières et de leur réception Festschrift zum 70. Geburtstag von Ulrich Ricken*. Tübingen: Stauffenberg Verlag, 1999.

Marchand, Patrick. "Turgot et les messageries: Vers un nouvel ordre du transport public." Pp. 17–25 of *Le Voyage en France 1750–1914*. Edited by Jean-Denys Devauges and Didier Masseau. Compiègne: Société des amis du Musée national de la voiture et du tourisme, Château de Compiègne, 2000.

Marshall, Alan. *The Age of Faction: Court Politics, 1660–1702.* Manchester: Manchester University Press, 1999. Pp. 256.

Marshall, John. "Some Intellectual Consequences of the English Revolution." *European Legacy*, 5:4 (2000), 515–30.

Marshall, Peter J. "The Making of an Imperial Icon: The Case of Warren Hastings." *Journal of Imperial and Commonwealth History*, 27 (1999), 1–16.

Matthews, M. D. "Mercantile Shipbuilding Activity in South-West Wales, 1740–1829." *Welsh History Review*, 19:3 (1999), 400–24.

Special Section: Late Entries and Reviews

Maza, Sarah C. *Vies privées, affaires publiques: Les causes célèbres de la France prérévolutionnaire.* Paris: Fayard, 1997. Pp. 384.

McBride, I. R. "'When Ulster Joined Ireland': Anti-popery, Presbyterian Radicalism and Irish Republicanism in the 1790s." *Past & Present*, 157 (1997), 63–93.

McCallum, Paul. "Historical Pattern as Political Rhetoric: Tory Uses of the Restoration Trope in Power and Opposition." *Studies in Eighteenth-Century Culture*, 29 (2000), 201–39.

McClain, M. "The Duke of Beaufort's Tory Progress Through Wales, 1684." *Welsh History Review*, 18:4 (1997), 592–620.

McLoughlin, Thomas O. *Contesting Ireland: Irish Voices Against England in the Eighteenth Century.* Dublin: Four Courts Press, 1999. Pp. 248.

McMahon, D. M. "The Counter-Enlightenment and the Low-Life of Literature in Pre-revolutionary France." *Past & Present*, 159 (1998), 77–112.

Meadows, R. Darrell. "Engineering Exile: Social Networks and the French Atlantic Community, 1789–1809." *French Historical Studies*, 23:1 (2000), 67–102.

Medlin, Dorothy. "The Composition and Publication History of André Morellet's *Mémoires sur le dix-huitième siècle et sur la Révolution*". *Diderot Studies*, 28 (2000), 123–40.

Menedelson, Sara, and Patricia Crawford. *Women in Early Modern England 1550–1720.* New York: Clarendon Press, 1998. Pp. xvi + 480; illustrations.

Mercer, Matthew. "Dissenting Academies and the Education of the Laity, 1750–1850." *History of Education*, 30 (2000), 35–58.

Mercier-Faivre, Anne-Marie (ed.). *Un supplément à l'Encyclopédie, le monde primitif d'Antoine Court de Gébelin, suivi d'une édition du génie allégorique et symbolique de l'Antiquité, extrait du Monde primitif (1773).* Paris: H. Champion, 1999. Pp. 506; illustrations.

Merlotti, A. "A proposito di una recente riedizione della *Vita* di Pietro Giannone." *Revista Storica Italiana*, 111:1 (1999), 543–81.

Millward, James A. *Beyond the Pas: Economy, Ethnicity, and Empire in Quing Central Asia, 1759–1864.* Stanford: Stanford University Press, 1998. Pp. xxii + 353.

Minerbi, M. "Condorcet di fronte alla caduta della monarchia." *Studi Settecenteschi*, 18 (1998), 179–214.

Minuti, R. "La 'tirannia delle leggi.' Note sul Giappone di Montesquieu." *Studi Settecenteschi*, 17 (1997), 83–110.

Mirabeau, Victor Riqueti, Marquis de. *Les Bières flottantes de négriers: Un discours non prononcé sur l'abolition de la traite des Noirs (novembre 1789–mars 1790)*. Text established and annotated by Marcel Dorigny. Saint-Étienne: Publications de l'Université de Saint-Étienne, 2000. Pp. 158.

Monaque, R. "Latouche-Treville: The Admiral Who Defied Nelson." *Mariner's Mirror*, 86 (2000), 272–84.

Montefiore, Simon Sebag. *Prince of Princes: The Life of Potemkin*. London: Weidenfeld & Nicolson, 2000. Pp. xiv + 634; ilustrations; plates; portraits.

Montesquieu, Charles Louis de Secondat, Baron de. *Réflexions sur la monarchie universelle en Europe*. (Les classiques de la pensée politique 17.) Geneva: Droz, 2000. Pp. 126.

Moore, Lucy. *Amphibious Thing: The Life of Lord Hervey*. New Yrok: Viking Press, 2000. Pp. 376.

Mowl, Tim, and Brian Earnshaw. *An Insular Rococo: Architecture, Politics, and Society in Ireland and England, 1710–1770*. London: Reaktion Books, 1999. Pp. ix + 358; illustrations; maps; portraits.

Murphey, R. "Westernisation in the Eighteenth-Century Ottoman Empire: How Far, How Fast?" *Byzantine and Modern Greek Studies*, 23 (1999), 116–39.

Muskett, P. "Andrew Reid: An Eighteenth-Century Supercargo." *Mariner's Mirror*, 85 (1999), 405–10.

Myers, A. D. "Ethnic Distinctions and Wealth Among Colonial Jamaican Merchants, 1685–1716." *Social Science History,*, 22:1 (1998), 47–81.

Neill, Anna. "Buccaneer Ethnography: Nature, Culture, and Nation in the Journals of William Dampier." *Eighteenth-Century Studies*, 33:2 (1999–2000), 165–80.

Special Section: Late Entries and Reviews

Nicholson, M. "The Continental Journeys of Andrew Duncan Junior: A Physician's Education and the International Culture of Eighteenth-Century Medicine." *Clio Medica*, 56 (2000), 89–119.

Nicolai, Giorgio Maria. *Il Grande Orso bianco: Viaggiatori italiani in Russia*. Rome: Bulzoni, 1999. Pp. 577.

Norholdt, Gerard Schulte. "Are All Men Created to Be Universal? Dutch Cultural and Scientific Societies in the Decades Around 1800." *De Achttiende Eeuw*, 31:2 (1999), 163–72.

Oestmann, Guenther. "Der Mondglobus Tobias Mayers, 1723–1762." *Der Globusfreund*, 47–48 (1999), 221–28.

O'Regan, Philip. *Archbishop William King of Dublin (1650–1729) and the Constitution in Church and State*. Dublin: Four Courts Press, 2000. Pp. 355.

Osborne, Thomas. *Aspects of Enlightenment: Social Theory and the Ethics of truth*. Lanham: Rowman & Littlefield, 1998. Pp. xv + 216.

Pairault, François. *Gaspard Monge: Le fondateur de Polytechnique*. Paris: Tallandier, 2000. Pp. 524.

Park, Mungo. *Travels in the Interior*. Edited by Kate Ferguson Masters. Durham: Duke University Press, 2000. Pp. 407; illustrations; maps.

Parthasarathi, P. "Rethinking Wages and Competitiveness in the Eighteenth Century: Britain and South India." *Past & Present*, 158 (1998), 79–109.

Pasquino, G. "The Election of the Tenth President of the Italian Republic." *Journal of Modern Italian Studies*, 4 (1999), 405–15.

Payen, Philippe. *Les arrêts de règlement du Parlement de Paris au XVIIIe siècle: dimension et doctrine*. Paris: Presses universitaires de France, 1997. Pp. 526.

Picard, Liza. *Dr. Johnson's London: Coffee Houses and Climbing Boys, Medicine, Toothpaste and Gin, Poverty and Press-gangs, Freakshows and Female Education*. London: Weidenfeld & Nicholson, 2000; New York: St. Martin's, 2001. Pp. xxi + 362; illustrations (some in color); maps.

Picard draws heavily on *Gentleman's Magazine* materials for short entries within sections on the place, the poor, the middling, and the rich. Rev. (favorably; with another book) by Peter Earle in *TLS* (5 January 2001), 26.

Platt, K. M. F. "History and Despotism, or Hayden White vs. Ivan the Terrible and Peter the Great." *Rethinking History*, 3:3 (1999), 247–69.

Pocock, J. G. A. "Enlightenment and Counter-Enlightenment, Revolution and Counter-Revolution: A Eurosceptical Enquiry." *History of Political Thought*, 20:1 (1999), 125–39.

Poole, R. "Making Up for Lost Time." *History Today*, 49:12 (1999), 4046.

Price, Richard. *British Society, 1670–1880: Dynamism, Containment, and Change*. Cambridge: Cambridge University Press, 2000. Pp. 349.

Quinn, J. "Theobald Wolfe Tone and the Historians." *Irish Historical Studies*, 32 (2000), 113–28.

Ragussis, M. "Jews and Other 'Outlandish Englishmen': Ethnic Performance and the Invention of British Identity Under the Georges." *Critical Inquiry*, 26 (2000), 773–97.

Ramel, Stig. *Gustaf Mauritz Armfely: Fondateur de la Finlande*. Paris: esprit ouvert, 1999. Pp. 384.

Rao, Anna Maria. "Les exiles italiens et Brumaire." *Annales historiques de la révolution française*, 318 (1999), 713–26.

Rao, Anna Maria. "La rivoluzione francese e la scoperta della politica." *Studi Storici*, 36:1 (1996), 163–214.

Rapport, Michael. *Nationality and Citizenship in Revolutionary France: The Treatment of Foreigners 1789–1799*. New York: Oxford University Press, 2000. Pp. x + 2000.

Raughter, R. "A Discreet Benevolence: Female Philanthrophy and the Catholic Resuegence in Eighteenth-Century Ireland." *Women's History Review*, 6:4 (1997), 465–84.

Reynaud, Denis, and Chantal Thomas, (eds.). *La Suite àl'ordinaire prochain: La représentation du monde dans les gazettes (XVIIIe siècle)*. Lyon: Presses universitaires de Lyon, 1999. Pp. 293.

Ricard, Alain (ed.). *Voyages de découverte en Afrique: Anthologie 1790–1890*. Paris: Robert Laffont, 2000. Pp. 1,100.

Richards, Eric. *The Highland Clearances: People, Landlords, and Rural Turmoil*. Edinburgh: Birlinn, 2000. Pp. xii + 379; illustrations; maps; plates.

Special Section: Late Entries and Reviews

Richards, Eric. *Patrick Sellar and the Highland Clearances: Homicide, Eviction, and the Price of Progress.* Edinburgh: Polygon, 2000. Pp. xi + 440; illustrations; maps.

Robb, P. "Credit, Work, and Race in 1790s Calcutta: Early Colonialism Through a Contemporary European View." *Indian Economic and Social History Review*, 37 (2000), 1–25.

Rodriguez, Catherine M. "A Story of Her Own: Hester Lynch Piozzi's *Autobiography*." *Journal of Aging and Identity*, 4 (1999), 127–38.

Rosanvallon, Pierre. *La Démocratie inachevée: Histoire de la souveraineté du peuple en France.* (Bilbiothèque des histoires.) Paris: Gallimard, 2000. Pp. 472.

Rosner, Lisa, and John Theibault. *A Short History of Europe, 1600–1815: Contests for a Reasonable World.* Armonk: M. E. Sharpe, 2000. Pp. xi + 450; illustrations.

Rosove, Michael H. *Let Heroes Speak: Antarctic Explorers, 1772–1922.* Washington, D. C.: U. S. Naval Institute Press, 2000. Pp. 320.

Rothenberg, Gunther E. *Les Guerres Napoléoniennes 1796–1815.* (Atlas des guerres.) Paris: Autrement, 2000. Pp. 224; illustrations.

Rotondò, A. "Stampa periodica olandese e opinione pubblica europea nel Settecento: La 'Bibliotèque raisonnée' 1728–1753." *Revista Storica Italiana*, 110:1 (1998), 166–221.

Rouet, D. "The Giving of First Names in Port Royal During the 17th and 18th Centuries: Evolution and Methods of Attribution." *Acadiensis*, 27:2 (1998), 26–44.

Rowell, E. "Bermuda, the Royal Navy, and the Austen Family." *Mariner's Mirror*, 86 (2000), 457–59.

Rudolph, J. "Rape and Resistance: Women and Consent in Seventeenth-Century English Legal and Political Thought." *Journal of British Studies*, 39 (2000), 157–84.

Russell, Gillian. "'Faro's Daughters': Female Gamesters, Politics, and the Discourse of Finance in 1790s Britain." *Eighteenth-Century Studies*, 33:4 (2000), 481–504.

Safier, Neil. "Mapping Myths: The Cartographic Boundaries Between Science and Speculation on La Condamine's 'Amazon,' 1743–44." *The Portolan*, 46 (1999–2000), 8–27.

Sâgean, Mathieu. *Relation des aventures de Mathieu Sâgean, Canadien*. Edited by Pierre Berthiaume. Montréal: Presses de l'Université de Montréal, 1999. Pp. 227.

Salmon, J. H. M. "Liberty by Degrees: Raynal and Diderot on the British Constitution." *History of Political Thought*, 20:1 (1999), 87–106.

Sander, S. "Learning Before Enlightenment? On the Popular MedicineManuscripts of the Physician and Best Selling Author Christoph von Hellwig (1663–1721)." *Medizinhistorisches Journal*, 34:3–4 (1999), 245–308.

Schneider, Zoe A. "Women Before the Bench: Female Litigants in Early Modern Normandy." *French Historical Studies*, 23:1 (2000), 1–32.

Scheuermann, Mona. "Ferocious Countenance: The Upper Classes Look at the Poor." *Age of Johnson*, 11 (2000), 53–79.

Scott, D. "The Barweis Affair: Political Allegiance and the Scots During the British Civil Wars." *Englsih Historical Review*, 463 (2000), 843–63.

Scott, Jonathan. *England's Troubles: Seventeenth-Century English Political Instability in European Context*. Cambridge: Cambridge University Press, 2000. Pp. 536.

Seth, Catriona. "Chateaubriand comparatiste: La recherche du bonheur perdu dans l'*Essai sur les Révolutions*." *Bulletin de la Société Chateaubriand*, 40 (1998), 30–38.

Sharpe, P. "The Female Labour Market in English Agriculture During the Industrial Revolution: Expansion or Contraction?" *Agricultural History Review*, 47:2 (1999), 161–81.

Shaw, John Stuart. *The Political History of Eighteenth-Century Scotland*. (British History in Perspective Series.) New York: St. Martin's Press, 1999. Pp. vii + 151.

Shaw, L. M. E. *The Anglo-Portuguese Alliance and the English Merchants in Portugal, 1654–1810*. Aldershot: Ashgate, 1998. Pp. 256.

Shepard, A. "Social Control, Authority and Deviance in Early Modern England." *History Workshop*, 48 (1999), 240–47.

Smythe, W. R. "Benjamin Rush's Death." *Journal of the American College of Surgeons*, 190:4 (2000), 471–82.

Special Section: Late Entries and Reviews

Solovjova, K., and A. Vovnyanko. "The Rise and Decline of the Lebedev–Lastochkin Company: Russian Colonization in South Central Alaska, 1787–1798." *Pacific Northwest Quarterly*, 90:4 (1999), 191–205.

Sonnenberg-Stern, Karina. *Emancipation nad Poverty: the Ashkenazi Jews of Amsterdam, 1796–1850*. New York: St. Martin's Press, 2000. Pp. 200.

Sparrow, Elizabeth. *Secret Service: British Agents in France, 1792–1815*. Woodbridge: Boydell Press, 1999. Pp. xvi + 459; illustrations.

Stammers, M. "The Hand Maiden and Victim of Agriculture: The Port of Wells-Next-the-Sea, Norfolk, in the Eighteenth and Nineteenth Centuries." *Mariner's Mirror*, 86 (2000), 60–65.

Stevens, D. "Orphans and Musicians in Venice: A Unique System of Social Support in 18th-Century Venice That Brought Great Economic, Social and Cultural Benefits." *History Today*, 50 (2000), 22–27.

Stevenson, David, and Marie-Cécle Révauger. "Ecosse et franc-maçonnerie." Pp. 229–42 of *Ecosse des Lumières: le XVIIIe siècle autrement*. Edited by Pierre Morère. Grenoble: Université Stendhal, 1997.

Stewart, A. "The Last Chief: Dougal Stewart of Appin (died 1764)." *Scottish Historical Review*, 76 (1997), 203–21.

Stobart, Jon, and Alastair Owens (eds.). *Urban Fortunes: Property and Inheritance in the Town, 1700–1900*. Aldershot: Ashgate, 2000. Pp. 240.

Storrs, Christopher. *War, Diplomacy, and the Rise of Savoy, 1690–1720*. New York: Cambridge University Press, 1999. Pp. xiv + 345; illustrations.

Sturkenboom, Dorothee. "Historicizing the Gender of Emotions: Changing Perceptions in Dutch Enlightnment Thought." *Journal of Social History*, 34:1 (2000), 55–75.

Stuurman, Siep. "The Creation of Concepts in Political Theory; The Invention of Modern Equality." *Intellectual News*, 6–7 (2000), 41–51.

Sussman, Charlotte. *Consuming Anxieties: Consumer Protest, Gender, and British Slavery, 1713–1833*. Stanford: Stanford University Press, 2000. Pp. 293.

Sweet, R. "Freemen and Independence in English Borough Politics c. 1770–1830." *Past & Present*, 161 (1998), 84–115.

Syrett, D. "The Raising of American Troops for Service in the West Indies During the War of Austrian Succession, 1740–1." *Historical Research*, 73:180 (2000), 20–32.

Tackett, T. "Conspiracy Obsession in a Time of Revolution: French Elites and the Origins of the Terror, 1789–1792." *American Historical Review*, 105:3 (2000), 691–713.

Teltscher, Kate. "'Maidenly and Well Nigh Effeminate': Constructions of Hindu Masculinity and Religion in Seventeenth-Century English Texts." *Postcolonial Studies: Culture, Politics, Economy*, 3:2 (2000), 159–70.

Thévenot, Marie-Hélène. "Flora McDonald (1722–1790), la Jeanne d'Arc écossaise: myth et réalité." *Etudes écossaises*, 3 (1996), 89–101.

Thiesse, Anne-Marie. *La Création des identités nationales: europe XVIIIe–XXe siècle*. Paris: Seuil, 1999. Pp. 320.

Todd, M. "Profane Pastimes and the Reformed Community: The Persistence of Popular Festivities in Early Modern Scotland." *Journal of British Studies*, 39 (2000), 123–56.

Tournebize, Cassïlde. "Recueil de lettres relatives à Anthony Murray fils, de Dollerie et de Grange, Dunfermline, tué à Culloden en 1746." *Études écossaises*, 4 (1997), 239–67.

Trampus, A. "Riforme, Giuseppinismo et Lumi nella monarchia asburgica: Nuovi studi sulla figura del cancelliere Kaunits." *Revista Storica Italiana*, 110:3 (1998), 985–1004.

Trudel, Marcel. *Le Régime militaire et la disparition de la Nouvelle-France, 1759–1764*. Montreal: Fides, 1999. Pp. 570.

Tucker, P. "The Early History of the Court of Chancery: A Comparative Study." *English Historical Review*, 115:463 (2000), 791–811.

Tulard, Jean. *Murat*. Paris: Fayard, 2000. Pp. 473.

Vainio-Korhonen, Kirsi. "Handicrafts as Professions and Sources of Income in Late Eighteenth and Early Nineteenth Century Turku (Abo): A Gender Viewpoint to Economic History." *Scandanavian Economic History Review*, 48:1 (2000), 40–63.

Special Section: Late Entries and Reviews

Van den Berg, Richard. "Differential rent in the 1760s: Two Neglected French Contributions." *European Journal of the History of Economic Thought*, 7:2 (2000), 181 ff.

Varry, Dominique. "De la Bastille à Bellecour: Une 'canaille littéraire' Taupin Dorval." Pp. 571–82 of *Le Livre et l'historien: Études offertes en l'honneur du professeur Henri-Jean Martin*. Edited by Frédéric Barbier and others. Genève: Droz, 1997.

Velasquez, E. A. "The Scottish Enlightenment in Thought and Practice." *Interpretation: A Journal of Political Philosophy*, 27:3 (2000), 279–304.

Villani, P. "Agenti e diplomatici francesci in Italia durante la Rivoluzione: Eymar e la sua mission a Genova (1793)." *Studi Storici*, 36:4 (1996), 957–76.

Von Bonstetten, Karl Viktor. *Neue Schriften 1798–1802. Historisch-kritische Ausgabe in swei Teilbänden auf Grund gedruckter und handschriftlicher Textvorlagen*. Edited by Doris Walser-Wilhelm and Peter Walser-Wilhelm. Frankfurt am Main: Peter Lang, 2000. Pp. xxxv + 480; illustrations.

Wagner, Jacques (ed.). *Journalisme et religion*. (Eighteenth-Century French Intellectual History 6.) New York: Peter Lang, 2000. Pp. xviii + 413.

Wagner, Peter. "Penser la science en termes de différences sexuelles: *Une expérience sur un oiseau dans une pompe à air* de Joseph Wright of Derby." *Dix-huitième siècle*, 31 (1999), 283–301.

Wahrmann, Dror. "Percy's Prologue: From Gender Play to Gender Panic in Eighteenth-Century England." *Past & Present*, 159 (1998), 113–60.

Walker, B. L. "The Early Modern Japanese State and Ainu Vaccinations: Redefining the Body Politic 1799–1868." *Past & Present*, 163 (1999), 121–60.

Walker, J. "Gambling and Venetian Noblemen c. 1500–1700." *Past & Present*, 162 (1999), 28–69.

Walsham, Alexandra. *Providence in Early Modern England*. New York: Oxford University Press, 1999. Pp. xviii + 387; illustrations.

Wareham, T. "The Duration of Frigate Command During the Revolutionary and Napoleonic Wars." *Mariner's Mirror*, 86 (2000), 412–23.

Watanabe-O'Kelly, Helen, and Anne Simon (comps.). *Festivals and Ceremonies: A Bibliography of Works Relating to Court, Civic and Religious Festivals in Europe 1500–1800*. London: Mansell, 2000. Pp. xx + 533; indices. See *ECCB*, 26 (2000), I:154.

Rev. (favorably) by John L. Flood in *Library*, 7th ser., 2 (2001), 89.

Webb, Vivienne, and others. *Les Sauvages de la Mer Pacifique: Manufactured by Joseph Dufour et Cie 1804–1805 after a Design by Jean-Gabriel Charvet*. Seattle: University of Washington Press, 2000. Pp. 48.

Webb, Timothy. "Coleridge and Robert Emmet: Reading the Text of the Irish Revolution." *Irish Studies Review*, 8 (2000), 303–24.

Webster, T. "The Word of God and the Ethics of the Religious Past in Northern Ireland." *Rethinking History*, 2:3 (1998), 387–96.

Weil, Rachel. *Political Passions: Gender, the Family and Political Argument in England, 1680–1714*. Manchester: Manchester University Press, 2000. Pp. 300.

Whatley, Christopher A. *A Scottish Society, 1707–1830*. Manchester: Manchester University Press, 2000. Pp. 336.

Whatmore, R. "The Political Economy of Jean-Baptiste Say's Republicanism." *History of Political Thought*, 20:3 (1998), 439–56.

Whyman, Susan E. *Sociability and Power in Late Stuart England: The Cultural Worlds of the Verneys, 1660–1720*. New York: Oxford University Press, 2000. Pp. xiv + 287.

Whyte, Ian. *Migration and Society in Britain, 1550–1830*. New York: St. Martin's Press, 2000. Pp. 176.

Willette, T. "1799–1899: Heroic Memory in the Centennial of the Repubblica Napoletana." *Journal of Modern Italian Studies*, 4 (1999), 369–79.

Williams, H. G. "'Learning suitable to the situation of the poorest classes': The National Society and Wales, 1811–1839." *Welsh History Review*, 19:3 (1999), 425–52.

Wirtschafter, Elise Kimerling. *Social Identity in Imperial Russia*. DeKalb: Northern Illinois University Press, 1997. Pp. xi + 260; illustrations; maps.

Special Section: Late Entries and Reviews

Wokler, R. "The Manuscript Authority of Political Thoughts." *History of Political Thought*, 20:1 (1999), 107–23.

Woloch, Isser. *Napoleon and His Collaborators: The Making of a Dictatorship*. New York: W. W. Norton, 2000. Pp. 281.

Wood, Marcus. *Blind Memory: Visual Representations of Slavery in England and America, 1780–1865*. New York: Routledge, 1999. Pp. xxi + 341; illustrations.

Yeo, Eileen Janes. "The Creation of 'Motherhood' and Women's Responses in Britain and France, 1750–1914." *Women's History Review*, 8:2 (1999), 201–18.

Zook, Melinda S. *Radical Whigs and Conspiratorial Politics in Late Stuart England*. University Park: Penn State University Press, 1999. Pp. xxi + 234.

Historical, Social, and Economic Studies: North America

Allen, Ethan. *The Narrative of the Captivity of Col. Ethan Allen*. Edited by Stephen Carl Arch. Acton: Copley Publishing Group, 2000. Pp. xxvii + 73; map.

Allen, W. B., and Kevin A. Cloonan. *The Federalist Papers: A Commentary*. New York: Peter Lang, 2000. Pp. ix + 429.

Appleby, Joyce. *Inheriting the Revolution: The First Generation of Americans*. Cambridge: Belknap Press, 2000. Pp. viii + 322; illustrations.

Arbour, Keith. "One Last Word: Benjamin Franklin and the Duplessis Portrait of 1778." *Pennsylvania Magazine of History and Biography*, 118 (1994), 183–208.

Ardanaz, Margarita, and others (eds.). *Estudios de la mujer en el ámbito de los países de habla inglesa, I*. Madrid: Universidad Complutense de Madrid, 1994. Pp. viii + 448.

Baker, Emerson W., and John G. Reid. *The New England Knight: Sir William Phips, 1651–1695*. Toronto: University of Toronto Press, 1998. Pp. xxiv + 359; illustrations; maps.

Ball, Terrance. "'The Earth Belongs to the Living': Thomas Jefferson' and the Problem of Intergenerational Relations." *Environmental Politics*, 9 (2000), 61–77.

Bank, Rosemarie K. "Archiving Culture: Performance and American Museums in the Earlier Nineteenth Century." Pp. 37–51 of *Performing America: Cultural Nationalism in American Theater*. Edited by Jeffery D. Mason and J. Ellen Gainor. Ann Arbor: University of Michigan Press, 1999.

Barger, J. "Washington's Mount Vernon." *American History*, 34 (1999), 46–47.

Barkan, Elliott Robert (ed.). *A Nation of Peoples: A Sourcebook on America's Multicultural Heritage*. Westport: Greenwood Press, 1999. Pp. xv + 583; illustrated.

Baseler, Marilyn C. *"Asylum for Mankind": America 1607–1800*. Ithaca: Cornell University Press, 1998. Pp. xi + 353.

Bassard, Katherine Clay. *Spiritual Interrogations: Culture, Gender, and Community in Early African American Women's Writing*. Princeton: Princeton University Press, 1999. Pp. 183.

Beaudry, Catherine A. "The Library of Isaac Norris II: The Formation of an Educated Reader in the Philadelphia of the Early Enlightenment." *East-Central Intelligencer*, 8 (1994), 6–13.

Ben-Amos, Dan, and Liliane Weissberg (eds.). *Cultural Memory and the Construction of Identity*. Detroit: Wayne State University Press, 1999. Pp. 333.

Bénot, Yves. "La Révolution française entre les Indiens et le modèle américain." *Dix-huitième siècle*, 32 (2000), 351–69.

Berg, Susan. "'Make Me a Good End': A Roll Through the Ancient Sport of Lawn Bowling." *Colonial Williamsburg*, 21 (1999), 26–29.

Blake, David Haven, Jr. "'Posterity Must Judge': Private and Public Discourse in the Adams–Jefferson Letters." *Arizona Quarterly*, 50 (1994), 1–30.

Bodenhorn, H. "A Troublesome Caste: Height and Nutrition of Antebellum Virginia's Rural Free Blacks." *Journal of Economic History*, 59 (1999), 972–96.

Bogue, Margaret Beattie. *Fishing the Great Lakes: An Environmental History, 1783–1933*. Madison: University of Wisconsin Press, 2000. Pp. xix + 444; illustrations.; maps.

Bollacher, Martin (ed.). *Johann Gottfried Herder: Geschichte und Kultur*. Würzburg: Königshausen & Neumann, 1994. Pp. xii + 414.

Special Section: Late Entries and Reviews

Bouton, Terry. "A Road Closed: Rural Insurgency in Post-Independence Pennsylvania." *Journal of American History*, 87 (2000), 855–77.

Breen, Louise A. "Praying with the Enemy: Daniel Gookin, King Philip's War, and the Dangers of Intercultural Mediatorship." Pp. 101–22 of *Empire and Others: British Encounters with Indigenous Peoples, 1600–1850*. Edited by Martin Daunton and Rick Halpern. Philadelphia: University of Pennsylvania Press, 1999.

Breen, T. H. "Subjecthood and Citizenship: The Context of James Otis's Radical Critique of John Locke." *New England Quarterly*, 71 (1998), 378–403.

Breig, James. "Thomas Jeferson Orders an Orrey: Worlds of Patience and a Model of the Solar System." *Colonial Willliamsburg* (2000), 34–38.

Brown, David. "Jeffersonian Ideology and the Second Party System." *The Historian*, 62 (1999), 17–30.

Brown, Kathleen. "Native Americans and Early Modern Concepts of Race." Pp. 79–100 of *Empire and Others: British Encounters with Indigenous Peoples, 1600–1850*. Edited by Martin Daunton and Rick Halpern. Philadelphia: University of Pennsylvania Press, 1999.

Buckley, Thomas E. "Reflections on a Wall." *William and Mary Quarterly*, 56 (1999), 795–800.

Burgett, Bruce. *Sentimental Bodies: Sex, Gender, and Citizenship in the Early Republic*. Princeton: Princeton University Press, 1998. Pp. 213.

Burstein, Andrew. "Jefferson's Rationalizations." *William and Mary Quarterly*, 57 (2000), 183–97.

Burstein, Andrew. "Mr. Jefferson and His Constant Companions." *Virginia Quarterly Review*, 74 (1998), 142–45.

Burstein, Andrew. "The Problem of Jefferson Biography." *Virginia Quarterly Review*, 70 (1994), 403–20.

Burstein, Andrew. *Sentimental Democracy: The Evolution of America's Romentic Self-Image*. New York: Hill & Wang, 1999. Pp. xxi + 406.

Bush, H. K. "The Declaration of Independence as Spectacle." *Cultural Studies*, 14 (2000), 361–64.

Butler, Jon. *Becoming America: The Revolution Before 1776.* Cambridge: Harvard University Press, 2000. Pp. 320.

Butler, L. S. "Blackbeard's Revenge." *American History,* 35 (2000), 18–24.

Campbell, James. *Recovering Benjamin Franklin: An Exploration of a Life of Science and Service.* Chicago: Open Court, 1999. Pp. x + 302.

Canny, Nicholas. "Writing American History; or, Reconfiguring the History of Colonial British America." *Journal of American History,* 86 (1999), 1093–1115.

Carter, Edward C., II (ed.). *Surveying the Record: North American Scientific Exploration to 1930.* Philadelphia: Memoirs of the American Philosophical Society, 1999. Pp. xv + 344; illustrations.

Caron, Nathalie. *Thomas Paine contre l'imposture des prêtres.* Paris: L'Harmattan, 1998. Pp. 543.

Cawley, A. S. "A Pasionate Affair: The Master–Servant Relationship in Seventeenth-Century Maryland." *The Historian,* 61 (1999), 751–63.

Chard, Chloe. "Lassitude and Revival in the Warm South: Relaxing and Exciting Travel, 1750–1830." *Clio Medica,* 56 (2000), 179–205.

Chase, H. V. "Philip Thomas (1747–1815): Physician, Patriot, Politician." *Maryland Medical Journal,* 48 (1999), 207–13.

Chu, J. M. "An Independent Means: The American Revolution and the Rise of a National Economy." *Journal of Interdisciplinary History,* 31 (2000), 63–71.

Cizauskas, Albert. "Jefferson and Kosciusko: Two Views of Equality." *Baltic States Quarterly of Arts & Sciences,* 40 (1994), 45–50.

Cleary, Patricia. *Elizabeth Murray: A Woman's Pursuit of Independence In Eighteenth-Century America.* Amherst: University of Massachusetts Press, 2000. Pp. xii + 279; illustrations; portraits.

Cleary, Patricia. "Making Men and Women in the 1770s: Culture, Class, and Commerce in the Anglo-American World." Pp. 98–116 of *A Shared Experience: Men, Women, and the History of Gender.* Edited by Laura McCall and Donald Yacovone. New York: New York University Press, 1998.

Special Section: Late Entries and Reviews

Cline, Edward. "'Thus in the beginning of the world was America.'" *Colonial Willliamsburg* (1999), 29–35.

Collinson, S. "President or King?" *History Today*, 50 (2000), 9–15.

Conger, Danielle E. "Making Mothers: Medical Discourse and the Birth of the Middle-class Mother, 1750–1850." *Transactions and Studies of the College of Physicians of Philadelphia*, 21 (1999), 43–48.

Conlin, M. F. "The American Mission of Citizen Pierre-Auguste Adet: Revolutionary Chemistry and Diplomacy in the Early Republic." *Pennsylvania Magazine of History and Biography*, 124 (2000), 489–520.

Cornell, Saul. *The Other Founders: Anti-Federalism and the Dissenting Tradition in America, 1788–1828*. Chapel Hill: Published for the Omohundro Institute of Early American History and Culture, Williamsburg, Virginia, by the University of North Carolina Press, 1999. Pp. xvi + 327; maps.

Countryman, Edward. *Americans: A Collision of Histories*. New York: Hill and Wang, 1996. Pp. xxiii +294; maps.

Crane, Elaine Forman. "Political Dialogue and the Spring of Abigail's Discontent." *William and Mary Quarterly*, 56 (1999), 745–74.

Crèvecoeur, Hector St. Jean de. *Letters from an American Farmer*. Edited by Susan Manning. New York: Oxford University Press, 1997. Pp. xlvi + 235.

Crews, Ed. "Firearms and the Founders." *Colonial Williamsburg* (2000), 54–58.

Crocker, Matthew H. *The Magic of the Many: Josiah Quincy and the Rise of Mass Politics in Boston, 1800–1830*. Amherst: University of Massachusetts Press, 1999. Pp. xiv + 222; maps.

Crothers, A. G. "Public Culture and Economic Liberalism in Post-Revolutionary Northern Virginia, 1780–1820." *Canadian Review of American Studies*, 29 (1999), 61–90.

Dawson, Matthew Q. *Partisanship and the Birth of America's Second Party, 1796–1800: Stop the Wheels of Government*. Westport: Greenwood Press, 2000. Pp. xiv + 245.

Dickinson, H. T. *Britain and the American revolution*. London: Longman, 1998. Pp. xii + 284; maps.

Ditz, Toby L. "Shipwrecked, or Masculinity Imperiled: Mercantile Representations of Failure and the Gendered Self in Eighteenth-Century Philadelphia." *Journal of American History*, 81 (1994), 51–80.

Dreisbach, Daniel L. "Thomas Jefferson and the Danbury Baptists Revisited." *William and Mary Quarterly*, 56 (1999), 805–16.

Dunnavent, R. B. "Broadsides and Brown Water: The U.S. Navy in Riverine Warfare During the War of 1812." *American Neptune*, 59 (1999), 199–210.

Ellis, Joseph J. "Intimate Enemies: When John Adams Was Elected President and Thomas Jefferson Vice President, Each Came to See the Other as a Traitor. Out of Their Enmity Grew Our Modern Political System." *American Heritage*, 51 (2000), 80–88.

Ellis, Joseph J. "Jefferson: Post-DNA." *William and Mary Quarterly*, 57 (1999), 125–38.

Ellison, Julie. *Cato's Tears and the Making of Anglo-American Emotion*. Chicago: University of Chicago Press, 1999. Pp. xi + 299; illustrations.

Elmer, Jonathan. "The Archive, the Native American, and Jefferson's Convulsions." *Diacritics: A Review of Contemporary Criticism*, 28 (1998), 5–24.

Eltis, D., and S. L. Engerman. "The Importance of Slavery and the Slave Trade to Industrializing Britain." *Journal of Economic History*, 60 (2000), 123–44.

Emmett, Ross B. (ed.). *Great Bubbles: Reactions to the South Sea Bubble, the Mississippi Scheme and the Tulip Mania Affair*. 3 volumes. London: Pickering & Chatto, 2000. Pp. 1,050; illustrations.

Faery, Rebecca Blevins. *Cartographies of Desire: Captivity, Race and Sex in the Shaping of an American Nation*. Norman: University of Oklahoma Press, 1999. Pp. x + 275; illustrations.

Felsenstein, Frank (ed.). *English Trader, Indian Maid: Representing Gender, Race, and Slavery in the New World: An Inkle and Yarico Reader*. Baltimore: Johns Hopkins University Press, 1999. Pp. xiii + 317; illustrations.

Fenn, Elizabeth A. "Biological Warfare in Eighteenth-Century North America: Beyond Jeffery Amherst." *Journal of American History*, 86 (2000), 1552–81.

Special Section: Late Entries and Reviews

Ferguson, Robert A. "Becoming American: High Treason and Low Invective in the Republic of Laws." Pp. 103–33 of *The Rhetoric of Law*. Edited by Austin Sarat and Thomas R. Kearns. Ann Arbor: University of Michigan Press, 1994.

Ferling, J. "Thomas Jefferson Scrapbooks Revealed." *American History*, 34 (2000), 8.

Ferling, J., and L. E. Braverman. "John Adams's Health Reconsidered." *William and Mary Quarterly*, 55 (1998), 83–104.

Fleming, Thomas. *Duel: Alexander Hamilton, Aaron Burr, and the Future of America.* New York: Basic Books, 2000. Pp. 420.

Fleming, Thomas. "George Washington, Spymaster." *American Heritage*, 51 (2000), 45–51.

Flores, Daniel. "A Very Different Story: Exploring the Southwest from Monticello with the Freeman and Custis Expedition of 1806." *Montana: A Magazine of Western History*, 50 (2000), 2–17.

Foster, Thomas A. "Deficient Husbands: Manhood, Sexual Incapacity, and Male Marital Sexuality in Seventeenth-Century New England." *William and Mary Quarterly*, 56 (1999), 723–44.

Fouché, Nicole. *Franklin et Jefferson, aux sources de l'amitié franco-américaine, 1776–1808.* (Biographies américaines.) Paris: Michel Houdiard, 2000. Pp. 102.

Foucrier, Annick, and Philippe Jacquin. *Meriwether Lewis et William Clarke: la traversée d'un continent, 1803–1808.* (Biographies américaines.) Paris: Michel Houdiard, 2000. Pp. 102.

Franklin, Benjamin. *The Papers of Benjamin Franklin.* Volume XXXV: May 1 through October 31, 1781. Edited by Barbara B. Oberg, Ellen R. Cohn, Jonathan R. Dull, Karen Duval, Leslie J. Lindenauer, Kate M. Ohno, and Claude A. Lopez. New Haven: Yale University Press, 1999. Pp. 832.

Friedenberg, Z. B. "Musculoskeletal surgery in Eighteenth Century America." *Clinical Orthopaedics*, 374 (2000), 10–16.

Gable, Eric, and Richard Handler. "Public History, Private Memory: Notes from the Ethnography of Colonial Williamsburg, Virginia, USA." *Ethnos*, 65 (2000), 237–52.

Gambles, A. "Free Trade and State Formation: the Political Economy of Fisheries Policy in Britain and the United Kingdom Circa 1780–1850." *Journal of British Studies*, 39 (2000), 288–316.

Gaustad, Edwin S. "Thomas Jefferson, Danbury Baptists, and 'Eternal Hostility.'" *William and Mary Quarterly*, 56 (1999), 801–04.

Gelles, Edith B. *"First Thoughts": Life and Letters of Abigail Adams*. New York: Twayne, 1998. Pp. xvi + 204.

Gentile, G. P. "General Arnold and the Historians." *Journal of Military History*, 64 (2000), 179–80.

Gibson, A. "Ancients, Moderns and Americans: The Republicanism–Liberalism Debate Revisited." *History of Political Thought*, 21 (2000), 261–307.

Gill, Harold B., Jr. "Christmas in Colonial Virginia." *Colonial Williamsburg*, 21 (1999), 10–13.

Gill, Harold B., Jr. "First Session in the New Capitol." *Colonial Williamsburg*, 21 (1998), 21–23.

Gillespie, Joanna Bowen. "Fileopietism as Citizenship, 1810: Letters from Martha Laurens Ramsay to David Ramsay, Jr." *Early American Literature*, 29 (1994), 141–65.

Goldsmith, L. "'To profit by his skill and to traffic on his crime': Prison Labor in Early 19th-century Massachusetts." *Labor History*, 40 (1999), 439–57.

Gomez, M. A. "African Identity and Slavery in the Americas." *Radical History Review*, 75 (1999), 111–20.

Gordon-Read, Annette. "Engaging Jefferson: Blacks and the Founding Father." *William and Mary Quarterly*, 57 (2000), 171–82.

Gould, Philip. "Representative Men: Jeremy Belknap's American Biography and the Political Culture of the Early Republic." *A/B: Auto/Biographical Studies*, 9 (1994), 83–97.

Grasso, Christopher. *A Speaking Aristocracy: Transforming Public Discourse in Eighteenth-Century Connecticut*. Chapel Hill: Published for the Omohundro Institute of Early American History and Culture, Williamsburg, Virginia, by the University of North Carolina Press, 1999. Pp. viii + 511; illustrations.

Special Section: Late Entries and Reviews

Greene, Jack P. "The American Revolution." *American History Review*, 105 (2000), 93–102.

Greene, Nathanael. *The Papers of General Nathanael Greene*. Volume XI: 7 April–30 September 1782. Edited by Dennis M. Conrad, Roger N. Parks, Elizabeth C. Stevens, and Nathaniel N. Shipton. Chapel Hill: University of North Carolina Press, 2000. Pp. 855.

Greer, Allan. "Colonial Saints: Gender, Race, and Hagiography in New France." *William and Mary Quarterly*, 57 (2000), 332–48.

Grubb, F. "The Transatlantic Market for British Convict Labor." *Journal of Economic History*, 60 (2000), 94–122.

Gutzman, K. R. Constantine. "The Virginia and Kentucky Resolutions Reconsidered: 'An Appeal to the Real Laws of Our Country.'" *Journal of Southern History*, 66 (2000), 473–96.

Haffis, C. M. "Washington's Gamble, L'Enfant's Dream: Politics, Design, and the Founding of the National Capital." *William and Mary Quarterly*, 56 (1999), 745–74.

Hall, Timothy D. *Contested Boundaries: Itinerancy and the Reshaping of the Colonial American Religious World*. Durham: Duke University Press, 1994. Pp. x + 196.

Hamilton, P. "Revolutionary Principles and Family Loyalties: Slavery's Transformation in the St. George Tucker Household of Early National Virginia." *William and Mary Quarterly*, 55 (1998), 531–56.

Harvey, Lisa St. Clair. "Mr. Jefferson's Wolf: Slavery and Suburban Robot." *Journal of American Culture*, 17 (1994), 79–89.

Heath, Barbara J. *Hidden Lives: The Archaeology of Slave Life at Thomas Jefferson's Poplar Forest*. Charlottesville: University Press of Virginia, 1999. Pp. vii + 81; illustrations.

Henigman, Laura. *Coming into Communion: Pastoral Dialogues in Colonial New England*. Albany: State University of New York Press, 1999. Pp. xi + 234.

Higginbotham, D. "The Federalized Militia Debate: A Neglected Aspect of Second Amendment Scholarship." *William and Mary Quarterly*, 55 (1998), 39–58.

Horsman, Reginald. *The New Republic: The United States of America, 1789–1815*. (The Longman History of America.) London: Longman, 2000. Pp. ix + 275.

Huebner, Timothy S. *The Southern Judicial Tradition: State Judges and Sectional Distinctiveness, 1790–1890.* Athens: University of Georgia Press, 1999. Pp. xiii + 263.

Hume, Ivor N. "'Weird Sisters, Hand in Hand...': Witchcraft and Evil Spirits." *Colonial Williamsburg,* 21 (1998), 14–19.

Hutson, James H. "Thomas Jefferson's Letter to the Danbury Baptists: A Controversy Rejoined." *William and Mary Quarterly,* 56 (1999), 775–90.

Ignatiev, Noel. "The Revolution as an African-American Exuberance." *Eighteenth-Century Studies,* 27 (1994), 605–13.

Isenberg, Andrew C. *The Destruction of the Bison: An Environmental History, 1750–1920.* New York: Cambridge University Press, 2000. Pp. 198.

Johnson, Whittington B. *Race Relations in the Bahamas, 1784–1834: The Nonviolent Transformation from a Slave to a Free Society.* Fayetteville: University of Arkansas Press, 1999. Pp. 208.

Jones, George Fenwick. "Portrait of an Irish Entrepreneur in Colonial Agusta: John Rae, 1708–1772." *Georgia Historical Quarterly,* 83 (1999), 427–47.

Kale, Wilford. "Educating a Colony: the First Trustees of the College of William and Mary in Virginia." *Colonial Williamsburg,* 22 (2000), 25–28.

Kasakoff, A. B., and J. W. Adams. "The Effects of Migration, Place, and Occupation on Adult Mortality in the American North, 1740–1880." *Historical Methods,* 33 (2000), 115–30.

Kaufmann, Eric. "American Exceptionalism Reconsidered: Anglo-Saxon Ethnogenesis in the 'Universal' Nation, 1776–1850." *Journal of American Studies,* 33 (1999), 437–58.

Keane, John. *Tom Paine: A Political Life.* Boston: Little, Brown, 1995. Pp. xxii + 64; illustrations; map.

Kemp, Anthony. "The Negation of the Past and the Creation of American Radicalism." *Early American Literature,* 30 (1995), 182–87.

Kennedy, Roger G. *Burr, Hamilton, and Jefferson: A Study in Character.* New York: Oxford University Press, 2000. Pp. xix + 476; illustrations; maps.

Special Section: Late Entries and Reviews

Key, J. P. "Indians and Ecological Conflict in Territorial Arkansas." *Arkansas Historical Quarterly*, 59 (2000), 129–46.

Kierner, Cynthia A. *Beyond the Household: Women's Place in the Early South, 1700–1835.* Ithaca: Cornell University Press, 1998. Pp. xi + 295; illustrated.

Kizilos, P. "Revolutionary Sharpshooter." *Zamerican History*, 35 (2000), 16.

Kortenhauf, K. D. "Republican Ideology and Wartime Reality: Thomas Mifflin's Struggle as the First Quartermaster General of the Continental Army, 1775–1778." *Pennsylvania Magazine of History and Biography*, 122 (1998), 179–210.

Kriz, Kay Dian. "Curiosities, Commodities, and Transplanted Bodies in Hans Sloane's 'Natural History of Jamaica.'" *William and Mary Quarterly*, 57 (2000), 35–78.

Kashatus, W. C. "Revolution with Pen & Ink." *American History*, 34 (2000), 52–58.

Kramnick, Isaac, and R. Laurence Moore. "The Baptists, the Bureau, and the Case of the Missing Lines." *William and Mary Quarterly*, 56 (1999), 817–22.

Kupperman, Karen Ordahl. *America in European Consciousness, 1493–1750.* Chapel Hill: Published for the Institute of Early American History and Culture, Williamsburg, Virginia, by the University of North Carolina Press, 1995. Pp. xii + 428; illustrations.

Landsman, Ned C. *From Colonials to Provincials: American Thought and Culture, 1680–1760.* New York: Twayne, 1997. Pp. xv + 223; illustrations; maps.

Larson, Chiles T. A. "Albemarle Pippins." *Colonial Williamsburg*, 21 (1998), 28–32.

Larson, Rebecca. *Daughters of Light: Quaker Women Preaching and Prophesying in the Colonies and Abroad, 1700–1775.* New York: Knopf, 1999. Pp. x + 399; illustrations.

Laurens, Henry. *The Papers of Henry Laurens.* Volume XV: December 1778–August 31, 1782. Edited by David R. Chesnutt and C. James Taylor. Columbia: University of South Carolina Press, 1999. Pp. 768.

Lawson, Russell M. *The American Plutarch: Jeremy Belknap and the Historian's Dialogue with the Past.* Westport: Praeger, 1998. Pp. viii + 173; illustrations.

Leiner, Frederick C. *Millions for Defense: The Subscription Warships of 1798.* Annapolis: Naval Institute Press, 1999. Pp. viii + 262.

Leonard, Thomas C. "Recovering 'Wretched Stuff' and the Franklins' Synergy." *New England Quarterly*, 72 (1999), 444–55.

Lepore, Jill. *In the Name of War: King Philip's War and the Origins of American Identity.* New York: A. A. Knopf, 1998. Pp. xxviii + 337; illustrations; maps.

Lewis, James A. *Neptune's Militia: The Frigate* South Carolina *During the American Revolution.* Kent: Kent State University Press, 1999. Pp. 288; illustrations; maps.

Lewis, Jan. "Introduction to Forum: Thomas Jefferson and Sally Hemmings Redux." *William and Mary Quarterly*, 57 (2000), 121–24.

Linder, Marc, and Lawrence S. Zacharias. *Of Cabbages and King County: Agriculture and the Formation of Modern Brooklyn.* Iowa City: University of Iowa Press, 2000. Pp. x + 478; illustrations; map.

Lockley, Timothy J. "Trading Encounters Between Non-Elite Whites and African-Americans in Savannah, 1790–1860." *Journal of Southern History*, 66 (2000), 25–48.

Longsworth, Polly. "Jefferson's 'alleged child': Could He have Been Michael Brown, Murdered with George Wythe?" *Colonial Williamsburg*, 21 (1999), 10–19.

Looney, J. Jefferson. *Nurseries of Letters and Republicanism: A Brief History of the American Whig-Cliosophic Society and Its Predecessors, 1765–1941.* Princeton: Trustees of the Whig-Cliosophic Society, 1996. Pp. xii + 72; [4] pp. of plates; illustrations.

Lopez, Claude-Anne. *My Life with Benjamin Franklin.* New Haven: Yale University Press, 2000. Pp. 288.

Louis, Jeanne Henriette. "La sainte expérience de la Pennsylvanie (1682–1756) gage de la royauté spirituelle et de la France-Amérique." Pp. 541–51 of *La France-Amérique (XVIe–XVIIIe siècle). Actes du XXXVe colloque intenational d'etudes humanistes.* (Travaux du Centre d'etudes supérieures de la Renaissance de Tours. La savoir de Mantice 5.) Edited by Frank Lestringant. Paris: Honoré Champion, 1998.

Special Section: Late Entries and Reviews

Lynch, James V. "The Limits of Revolutionary Radicalism: Tom Paine and Slavery." *Pennsylvania Magazine of History and Biography*, 123 (1999), 177–99.

Manning, Susan. "Industry and Idleness in Colonial Virginia: A New Approach to William Byrd II." *Journal of American Studies*, 28 (1994),169–90.

Mass, John. "To Disturb the Assembly: Tarleton's Charlottesville Raid and the British Invasion of Virginia, 1781." *Virginia Cavalcade*, 49 (2000), 148–57.

Matar, Nabil. *Turks, Moors, and Englishmen in the Age of Discovery*. New York: Columbia University Press, 1999. Pp. xi + 268; illustrations; maps.

Maxey, D. W. "Samuel Hopkins, the Holder of the First U. S. Patent: A Study of Failure." *Pennsylvania Magazine of History and Biography*, 122 (1998), 3–37.

McCall, Laura, and Donald Yacovone (eds.). *A Shared Experience: Men Women, and the History of Gender*. New York: New York University Press, 1998. Pp. xvi + 387; illustrations.

McCartney, Martha W. "Jean-Nicolas Desandrouins and His Overlooked Map of 18th Century Williamsburg: A Closer Look at a Seemingly Familiar of the City in 1781 Turns Up Heretofore Unnoticed Detaila." *Colonial Williamsburg*, 21 (1999–2000), 45–48.

McCartney, Martha W. "Richman, Poorman, Beggarman, Thief: Down but Not Out in Colonial Virginia." *Colonial Williamsburg*, 22 (2000), 18–23.

McCraw, Thomas K. "The Strategic Vision of Alexander Hamilton." *The American Scholar*, 63 (1994), 31–57.

McDonald, Forrest. *States' Rights and the Union: Imperium in Imperio, 1776–1876*. Lawrence: University Press of Kansas, 2000. Pp. 282.

McDonald, Robert M. S. "Thomas Jefferson's Changing Reputation as Author of the 'Declaration of Independence': The First Fifty Years." *Journal of the Early Republic*, 19 (1999), 169–95.

McDowell, G. L. "The Language of Law and the Foundations of American Constitutionalism." *William and Mary Quarterly*, 55 (1998), 375–98.

Messer, "'A Species of treason and not the least dangerous kind': The Treason Trials of Abraham Carlisle and John Roberts." *Pennsylvania Magazine of History and Biography*, 123 (1999), 303–32.

Miller, Cynthia. "William Small and the Making of Thomas Jefferson's Mind." *Colonial Williamsburg*, 22 (2000), 30–33.

Miller, Marla R. "'My Part Alone': The World of Rebecca Dickinson, 1787–1802." *New England Quarterly*, 71 (1998), 341–77.

Middleton, S. "The Transformation of Eighteenth-Century America." *Historical Journal*, 42 (1999), 1147–53.

Mikalachki, Jodi. "'What Is an American': The European Heritage of Hector St. John de Crèvecœur." Pp. 567–81 of *La France-Amérique (XVIe–XVIIIe siècle). Actes du XXXVe colloque intenational d'etudes humanistes.* (Travaux du Centre d'etudes supérieures de la Renaissance de Tours. La savoir de Mantice 5.) Edited by Frank Lestringant. Paris: Honoré Champion, 1998.

Miller, Nathan. *Broadsides: The Age of Fighting Sail, 1775–1815.* New York: John Wiley, 2000. Pp. 400; illustrations; maps; portraits.

Mires, C. "In the Shadow of Independence Hall: Vernacular Activities and the Meanings of Historic Places." *Public History*, 21 (1999), 49–64.

Mizelle, Brett. "'Man Cannot Behold It Without Contemplating Himself': Monkeys, Apes, and Human Identity in the Early Republic." *Pennsylvania History*, 66 (1999), 144–73.

Montgomery, Dennis. "'If ponies rode men and grass ate the cows': Just What Tune Was in the Air When the World Turned Upside Down?" *Colonial Williamsburg*, 21 (1999), 33–39.

Morgan, D. T. "Benjamin Franklin: Champion of Generic Religion." *The Historian*, 62 (2000), 722–29.

Morgan, Jennifer L. "'Some Could Suckle Over Their Shoulder': Male Travelers, Female Bodies, and the Gendering of Racial Ideology, 1500–1770." *William and Mary Quarterly*, 3rd series 54 (1997), 167–92.

Morris, John D. *Sword of the Border: Major General Jacob Jennings Brown, 1775–1828.* Kent: Kent State University Press, 1999. Pp. 368; illustrations; maps.

Special Section: Late Entries and Reviews

Moss, Kay K. *Southern Folk Medicine, 1750–1820*. Columbia: University of South Carolina Press, 1999. Pp. 259.

Mulford, Carla. "Figuring Benjamin Franklin in American Cultural Memory." *New England Quarterly*, 72 (1999), 415–43.

Mulford, Carla. "*Huehuetlatolli*, Early American Studies, and the Problem of History." *Early American Literature*, 30 (1995), 146–61.

Myers, J. P. "Mapping Pennsylvania's Western Frontier in 1756." *Pennsylvania Magazine of History and Biography*, 123 (1999), 3–29.

Myers, J. P. "The New Way to the Forks of the Ohio: Reflections on John Pott's Map of 1758." *Pennsylvania Magazine of History and Biography*, 122 (1998), 385–410.

Neiman, Fraser D. "Coincidence or Causal Connection: the Relationship Between Thomas Jefferson's Visits to Monticello and Sally Hemmings's Conceptions." *William and Mary Quarterly*, 57 (2000), 198–210.

Nelson, Dana D. *National Manhood: Capitalist Citizenship and the Imagined Fraternity of White Men*. Durham: Duke University Press, 1998. Pp. xiv + 344.

Nelson, Larry L. *A Man of Distinction Among Them: Alexander McKee and British–Indian Affairs Along the Ohio Country Frontier, 1754–1799*. Kent: Kent State University Press, 1999. Pp. 280; illustrations; maps.

Newman, S. P. "Reading the Bodies of Early American Seafarers." *William and Mary Quarterly*, 55 (1998), 59–82.

Nicholls, Michael L. "Strangers Settling Among Us: The Sources and Challenge of Urban Free Black Population of Early Virginia." *Virginia Magazine of History and Biography*, 108 (2000), 155–79.

Norling, Lisa. *Captain Ahab Had a Wife: New England Women and Whalefishery 1720–1870*. Chapel Hill: University of North Carolina Press, 2000. Pp. 372.

O'Brien, Karen. "David Ramsay and the Delayed Americanization of American History." *Early American Literature*, 29 (1994), 1–18.

Olson, A. "The Pamphlet War Over the Paxton Boys." *Pennsylvania Magazine of History and Biography*, 123 (1999), 31–55.

O'Neil, Robert M. "The 'Wall of Separation' and Thomas Jefferson's Views on Religious Liberty." *William and Mary Quarterly*, 56 (1999), 791–94.

Onuf, Peter S. "Every Generation Is an 'Independent Nation': Colonization, Miscegenation, and the Fate of Jefferson's Children." *William and Mary Quarterly*, 57 (2000), 153–70.

O'Shaughnessey, Andrew Jackson. *An Empire Divided: The American Revolution and the British Caribbean*. Philadelphia: University of Pennsylvania Press, 2000. Pp. 392.

Ostrander, Gilman M. *Republic of Letters: The American Intellectual Community, 1776–1865*. Madison: Madison House, 1999. Pp. xvi + 379.

Paredes Manzanero, Matilde. "British Florida Women Through the Eyes of Male Travelers (1763–1783)." Pp. 441–48 of *Estudios de la mujer en el ámbito de los países de habla inglesa, I*. Edited by Margarita Ardanaz and others. Madrid: Universidad Complutense de Madrid, 1994.

Park, Edwards. "Our Flag Was Still There." *Smithsonian*, 31 (2000), 22–26.

Park, Edwards. "To Bathe or Not to Bathe: Coming Clean in Colonial America." *Colonial Williamsburg*, 22 (2000), 12–16.

Pasley, Jeffrey L. "The Two National Gazettes: Newspapers and the Embodiment of American Political Parties." *Early American Literature*, 35 (2000), 51–86.

Perkins, Elizabeth A. *Border Life: Experience and Memory in the Revolutionary Ohio Valley*. Chapel Hill: University of North Carolina Press, 1998. Pp. xiv + 253; illustrations; maps.

Perry, Dennis R. "'Novelties and Stile Which All Out-Do': William Hubbard's Historiography Reconsidered." *Early American Literature*, 20 (1994), 166–82.

"Racial Consciousness and Nation-Building in the Early Republic." [Special issue.] *Journal of the Early Republic*, 19 (1999).

Ranlet, Philip. "In the Hands of the British: The Treatment of American POWs During the War of Independence." *The Historian*, 62 (2000), 731–58.

Special Section: Late Entries and Reviews

Reid-Maroney, Nina. *Philadelphia's Enlightenment, 1740–1800: Kingdom of Christ, Empire of Reason*. Westport: Greenwood Press, 2000. Pp. 216.

Richards, Leonard L. *The Slave Power: The Free North and Southern Domination, 1780–1860*. Baton Rouge: Louisiana State University Press, 2000. Pp. 208.

Rickard, S. "Conversations with Malthus." *History Today*, 49 (1999), 47–53.

Robarge, David. *A Chief Justice's Progress: John Marshall from Revolutionary Virginia to the Supreme Court*. (Contributions in American History 185.) Westport: Greenwood Press, 2000. Pp. xxv + 364; illustrations.

Roberts, Rita. "Patriotism and Political Criticism: The Evolution of Political Consciousness in the Mind of a Black Revolutionary Soldier." *Eighteenth-Century Studies*, 27 (1994), 569–88.

Rogow, Arnold A. *A Fatal Friendship: Alexander Hamilton and Aaron Burr*. New York: Hill and Wang, 1998. Pp. 351.

Rohrs, Richard C. "Sectionalism, Political Parties, and the Attempt to Relocate the National Capital in 1814." *The Historian*, 62 (2000), 535–55.

Rombes, Nicholas. "Cheating with Sound: Imagining Civic Culture in Federalist Culture." *Arizona Quarterly*, 54 (1998), 1–24.

Saeger, James Schofield. *The Chaco Mission Frontier: The Guaycuruan Experience*. Tuscon: University of Arizona Press. 2000. Pp. xviii + 266.

James Saeger's brief but detailed case study of the acculturation experience of the Guaycuruan peoples of the Gran Chaco in the post-contact period is a book with a purpose: to revise what the author feels to be the overgeneralizing tendencies of David Sweet's earlier – and radical – indictment of the Catholic mission system. Sweet, some readers may recall, saw that system as fundamentally responsible for everything from demographic disaster to psychological alienation. That this may have been true for some peoples in some areas Saeger does not deny. But to all, everywhere? To sustain the argument, Saeger contends, one would have to demonstrate one of two things: either that a very high degree of homogeneity existed within of the experiences of native peoples, so that what was said of one group would apply to all, or that homogeneity did not matter. Sweet's own evidential base, Saeger notes, draws almost exclusively upon data drawn from the record of sedentary peoples already familiar with settled agriculture. What happens when one tests his work with a group like the Guaycuruans, predominantly hunter/gatherers whose experience with Catholic missions came long after the contact period?

In general, Saeger finds that with a people whose contact and interaction with Europeans preceded its entry into mission life—a life that, when it came, involved only part of the population group and was, at the individual level, often quite sporadic even then—Sweet's thesis either does not hold or needs serious modification. It does not hold, for example, in the case of demographic catastrophe: it may be that for many aboriginal groups the mission system's concentration of populations, together with successful missionary efforts to restrict diet, intensified the impact of Old World diseases; for the Guaycuruans, however, the radical die-off (Saeger is—rather uncritically—in the camp of the "high counters" in the ongoing debate on population decline) took place during a much earlier period. By the time the mission experience began in the 1740s, Saeger argues, diseases had reached an endemic stage among these people, who were—and would continue to be—seen as remarkably healthy. In other areas, such as in the more complex matter of an alienating alteration of subsistence patterns and work roles, Sweet's claims may hold, but only in a modified, more subdued way. Saeger grants that a dramatic alteration in lifestyle certainly was experienced by many males, transformed as they were from hunter-warriors into something akin to Sweet's "unwaged rural proletarians," but for women, captives, and servants, whose lifestyles within the pre-mission Guaycuruan situation was already akin to that, there was little change. And even for men, Saeger contends, the change may not have run very deep, for whatever the actual lifestyle, self-perception was still built largely on a hunter-warrior-combat model. Through these examples and many others, Saeger demonstrates convincingly that while there was indeed a long and significant transition from "aboriginal" to "indigenous", the mission experience —in this case, at any rate—was by no means the catalytic element.

A word on method: having no written Guaycuruan record from which to draw, yet committed not only to getting, but concentrating upon, the perspective of the Guaycuruans, Saeger adopts the technique of "reading through" the written record to hear the native voices "which call faintly to us through Spanish documents," setting to one side whatever assertions, opinions, and judgments the writers of the documents might have expressed and gauging instead what the *actions* delineated in these accounts might indicate about *attitudes*. We will find no "Guaycuruan" point of view, Saeger grants, if ever there was one, but we can find viewpoints – viewpoints that can be gleaned from behavior. Yet even in the hands of a scholar as sophisticated as Saeger, the method, admirable though its goal may be, sometimes leaves the reader unsure of the results. An example: about an incident described early in the book, Saeger writes: "In 1638 Tobas and Mocobis [subgroups of the Abipones—Saeger's constant emphasis is upon the intense localism that drove power distribution] asked Father Gaspar Osorio for a mission, but they must have reconsidered, because they took the priest's head in 1639." One finds there an action, certainly, but can one divine from it an attitude? A moment of violence in a time-specific situation? A surfacing of an antagonistic stance toward the prospect of control deeply programmed into the culture? Something else? "Reading through" does not help here. Still, overall one gains confidence from Saeger's generally measured, cautious employment of the technique. One feels rather less confident, however, about the validity of Saeger's tendency to draw from studies very far afield. There has been much excellent work produced in recent years on the acculturation experience in North American situations, a literature with which Saeger is obviously comfortable. However, should a scholar who has taken Sweet to task for assuming too much cross-cultural similarity really place such confidence in resemblances between the Guaycuruan experience and that of the Carolina Catawbas studied by James Merrell, or the Canadian tribes of Christopher Miller and George Hammill?

Still, Saeger is generally careful to see such comparisons as suggestive, not shaping. In all, the work is most illuminating on the complex acculturation process in the Gran Chaco, and, in the process, forcefully corrective of Sweet's work.—David Sloan

Saillant, John. "The Black Body Erotic and the Republican Body Politic 1790–1820." Pp. 89–111 of *Sentimental Men: Masculinity and the Politics of Culture*. Edited by Mary Chapman and Glenn Hendler. Berkeley: University of California Press, 1999.

Sarat, Austin, and Thomas R. Kearns (eds.). *The Rhetoric of Law*. Ann Arbor: University of Michigan Press, 1994. Pp. 341.

Special Section: Late Entries and Reviews

Sargent, Sarah E. "Elizabeth and Thomas Roper, Proprietors: Tavern Keeping in Colonial Virginia." *Virginia Cavalcade*, 48 (1999), 4–13.

Sarson, S. "Distribution of Wealth in Prince George's County, Maryland, 1800–1820." *Journal of Economic History*, 60 (2000), 847–55.

Sassaman, R. "In Search of the Penobscot Expedition." *American History*, 35 (2000), 8 ff.

Schmidt, Klaus H., and Fritz Fleischmann (eds.). *Early America Re-Explored: New Readings in Colonial, Early National, and Antebellum Culture*. New York: Peter Lang, 2000. Pp. ix + 599; illustrations.

Schwarzchild, Edward. "From the Physiognotrace to the Kinematoscope: Visual Technology and the Preservation of the Peale Family." *Yale Journal of Criticism*, 12 (1999), 57–71.

Seelye, John. *Memory's Nation: the Place of Plymouth Rock*. Chapel Hill: University of North Carolina Press, 1998. Pp. xv + 699.

Self, Robert L. "The Collaboration of Thomas Jefferson and John Hemings: Furniture Attributed to the Monticello Joinery." *Winterthur Portfolio: A Journal of American Material Culture*, 33 (1998), 231–48.

Selig, Robert A. "François Joseph Paul Comte de Grasse, the Battle of the Virginia Capes, and the American Victory at Yorktown." *Colonial Williamsburg*, 21 (1999), 26–32.

Selig, Robert A. "A French Volunteer who Lived to Rue America's Revolution: Denis Jean Florimond du Langlois, Marquis du Bouchet." *Colonial Williamsburg*, 21 (1999), 16–25.

Selig, Robert A. "From Newport to Yorktown: Following the Road to Victory." *Colonial Williamsburg*, 22 (2000), 66–71.

Selig, Robert A. "The Iconography of Triumph and Surrender: Yorktown, Virginia, 19 October 1781, Two o'Clock in the Afternoon." *Colonial Williamsburg*, 22 (2000), 72–77.

Selig, Robert A. "Who Were the Huguenots?" *Colonial Williamsburg*, 21 (1999), 67–71.

Sheldon, Garrett Ward. *The Political Philosophy of James Madison*. Baltimore: Johns Hopkins University Press, 2000. Pp. 152.

Sheridan, Thomas E. (ed.). *Empire of Sand: The Seri Indians and the Struggle for Spanish Sonora, 1645–1803*. Tucson: University of Arizona Press, 1999. Pp. 600.

Shields, David S. "Anglo-American Clubs: Their Wit, Their Heterodoxy, Their Sedition." *William and Mary Quarterly*, 51 (1994), 293–304.

Short, John Renne. "A New Mode of Thinking: Creating a National Geography in the Early Republic." Pp. 19–50 of *Surveying the Record: North American Scientific Exploration to 1930*. Edited by Edward C. Carter II. Philadelphia: Memoirs of the American Philosophical Society, 1999.

Shuffleton, Frank. "Binding Ties: The Public and Domestic Spheres in Jefferson's Letters to His Family." Pp. 28–47 of *Thomas Jefferson and the Education of a Citizen*. Edited by James Gilreath. Washington, D. C.: Library of Congress, 1999.

Slonim, S. "The Founders' Fears of Foreign Influence." *Mid-America Historical Review*, 81 (1999), 126–46.

Smith, D. S. "Population and Political Ethics: Thomas Jefferson's Demography of Generations." *William and Mary Quarterly*, 56 (1999), 591–612.

Smith, M. M. "Culture, Commerce, and Calendar Reform in Colonial America." *William and Mary Quarterly*, 55 (1998), 557–84.

Springman, K. T. "Thomas Paine's Response to Lord North's Speech on the British Peace Proposals." *Pennsylvania Magazine of History and Biography*, 121 (1997, 351–70.

St. George, Robert Blair. "Placing Race at Jefferson's Monticello." Pp. 231–63 of *Cultural Memory and the Construction of Identity*. Edited by Dan Ben-Amos and Liliane Weissberg. Detroit: Wayne State University Press, 1999.

Staloff, Darren. *The Making of an American Thinking Class: Intellectuals and Intelligentsia in Puritan Massachusetts*. New York: Oxford University Press, 1998. Pp. xv + 276.

Stanton, Lucia. "The Other End of the Telescope: Jefferson Through the Eyes of His Slaves." *William and Mary Quarterly*, 57 (2000), 139–52.

Summers, J. H. "What Happened to Sex Scandals? Politics and Peccadilloes, Jefferson to Kennedy." *Journal of American History*, 87 (2000), 825–54.

Special Section: Late Entries and Reviews

Sweet, James H. "The Iberian Roots of American Racist Thought." *William and Mary Quarterly*, 54 (1997), 143–66.

Takagi, Midori. *"Rearing Wolves to Our Own Destruction": Slavery in Richmond, Virginia, 1782–1865.* Charlottesville: University Press of Virginia, 1999. Pp. xi + 187.

Taylor, S. "Yellow Fever: Politics and Class Relations in Philadelphia, 1793–1805." *Transactions and Studies of the College of Physicians of Philadelphia*, 21 (1999), 5–58.

Theobald, Mary Miley. "Splendor and Mystery." *Colonial Williamsburg*, 21 (1998), 24–27.

Theobald, Mary Miley. "Virginia's Early Jews: Just Passing Through." *Colonial Williamsburg*, 22 (2000), 39–43.

Tise, Larry E. *The American Counterrevolution: A Retreat from Liberty, 1783–1800.* Mechanicsburg: Stackpole Books, 1999. Pp. 672.

Tise, Larry E. *Benjamin Franklin and Women.* University Park: Pennsylvania State University Press, 2000. Pp. 224; illustrations.

Trees, Andy. "Private Correspondence for the Public Good: Thomas Jefferson to Elbridge Gerry, 26 January 1799." *Virginia Magazine of History and Biography*, 108 (2000), 217–54.

Ulrich, Laurel Thatcher. "Wheels, Looms, and the Gender Division of Labor in Eighteenth-Century New England." *William and Mary Quarterly*, 55 (1998), 3–38.

Van Beusekom, M., and F. Ngolet. "Teaching Radical History: Africans and the Roots of Early American Culture." *Radical History Review*, 75 (1999), 109–10.

Vickers, D., and V. Walsh. "Young Men and the Sea: The Sociology of Seafaring in Eighteenth-Century Salem, Massachusetts." *Socal History*, 24 (1999), 17–38.

Vincent, Stephen A. *Southern Seed, Northern Soil: African-American Farm Communities in the Midwest, 1765–1900.* Bloomington: Indiana University Press, 1999. Pp. xi + 187.

Walling, Karl-Friedrich. *Republican Empire: Alexander Hamilton on War and Free Government.* Lawrence: University Press of Kansas, 2000. Pp. xii + 356.

Walsh, Lorena S. "Slavery at Carter's Grove in the Early Eighteenth Century." *Virginia Cavalcade*, 47 (1998), 110–25.

Washington, George. *The Papers of George Washington, Presidential Series.* Volume IX: September 1791–February 1792. Edited by Mark A. Mastromarino and Jack D. Warren Jr. Charlottesville: University Press of Virginia, 2000. Pp. 672.

Washington, George. *The Papers of George Washington, Revolutionary War Series.* Volume X: June–August 1777. Edited by Frank E. Grizzard, Jr. Charlottesville: University Press of Virginia, 2000. Pp. 750.

Washington, George. *The Papers of George Washington, Revolutionary War Series.* Volume XI: August–October 1777. Edited by Philander D. Chase and Edward G. Lengel. Charlottesville: University Press of Virginia, 2000. Pp. 730.

Weil, François. *Histoire de New York.* Paris: Fayard, 2000. Pp. 378.

Werlen, Hans-Jakob. "'Philadelphia kann überall liegen': Herder, Benjamin Franklin und das Ethos des homo œconomicus." Pp. 303–17 of *Johann Gottfried Herder: Geschicthe und Kultur.* Edited by Martin Bollacher. Würzburg: Königshausen & Neumann, 1994.

Wilmerding, John. *Compass and Clock: Defining Moments in American Culture: 1800, 1850, 1900.* New York: Harry N. Abrams, 1999. Pp. 256; illustrations.

Wilson, Lisa. "A Marriage 'Well-Ordered': Love Power, and Partnership in Colonial New England." Pp. 70–97 of *A Shared Experience: Men, Women, and the History of Gender.* Edited by Laura McCall and Donald Yacovone. New York: New York University Press, 1998.

Wokeck, Marianne S. *Trade in Strangers: the Beginnings of Mass Migration to North America.* University Park: Pennsylvania State University Press, 1999. Pp. xxx + 319; maps.

Wood, Roger. "'The History Is Concisely This': Thomas Paine's Account of the Peasants' Revolt." *Studies in Medievalism*, 6 (1994), 5–20.

Wright, D. R. "The Atlantic Slave Trade and New England Slavery: How We Remember, How We Forget." *Journal of American Ethnic History*, 20 (2000), 78–81.

Wright, E. "Benjamin Franklin: An American in Lodon." *History Today*, 50 (2000), 18–25.

Wright, R. E. "Artisans, Banks, and the Election of 1800." *Pennsylvania Magazine of History and Biography*, 122 (1998), 211–39.

York, N. L. "The First Continental Congress and the Problem of American Rights." *Pennsylvania Magazine of History and Biography*, 122 (1998), 353–83.

Young, Jeffrey Robert. *Domesticating Slavery: The Master Class in Georgia and South Carolina, 1670–1837*. Chapel Hill: University of North Carolina Press, 1999. Pp. xii + 336.

Young, Joanne. "The Prescient Minister of Jamestown." *Colonial Williamsburg*, 21 (1998), 33–37.

Philosophy, Science, and Religion

Aichele, A. "The Foundation of Hermeneutics as a Work of Art: The Relation Between Metaphysical and Aesthetical Truth in Alexander Gottlieb Baumgarten." *Studia Leibnitiana*, 31 (1999), 82–90.

Allen, Richard C. *David Hartley on Human Nature*. Albany: State University of New York Press, 1999. Pp. 469.

Anstey, Peter R. "*De anima* and Descartes: Making Up Aristotle's Mind." *History of Philosophy Quarterly*, 17 (2000), 237–60.

Avery, Gillian. "Intimations of Mortality: The Puritan and Evangelical Message to Children." Pp. 87–110 (with illustrations) in *Representations of Childhood Death*. Edited by Gillian Avery and Kimberley Reynolds. London: Macmillan, 2000. Pp. xvi + 246; bibliography; index.

Bailey, Hilary Rhodes. "*Jacques le fataliste*, Chaos, and the Free Will Debate." Pp. 51–63 of *Disrupted Patterns: On Chaos and Order in the Enlightenment*. Edited by Theodore E. D. Braun and John A. McCarthy. Amsterdam: Rodopi, 2000.

Baird, John D. "Note on the Date of Publication of the English Translation of Lavoisier's *Traité Elementaire de Chymie*." *Ambix*, 46:3 (1999), 171.

Baird, John D. "Note on the Date of Publication of the English Translation of Lavoisier's *Traité Elementaire de Chymie*." *Ambix*, 47:2 (2000), 47.

Baldwin, M. "Assaying Robert Boyle." *Isis*, 90 (1999), 772–74.

Barbone, S., and L. Rice. "Spinoza and Necessary Existence." *Philosophia*, 27:1–2 (1999), 87–97.

Bassler, O. B. "Leibniz on the Indefinite as Infinite." *Review of Metaphysics*, 51:4 (1998), 849–74.

Bassler, O. B. "The Leibnizian Continuum in 1671." *Studia Leibnitiana*, 30 (1998), 1–23.

Bassler, O. B. "Towards Paris: The Growth of Leibniz's Paris Mathematics or the Pre-Paris Mathematics." *Studia Leibnitiana*, 30 (1998), 160–80.

Bates, David. "The Mystery of Truth: Louis Claude de Saint-Martin's Enlightened Mysticism." *Journal of the History of Ideas*, 61 (2000), 635–55.

Bates, Don. "*Machina Ex Deo*: William Harvey and the Meaning of Instrument." *Journal of the History of Ideas*, 61 (2000), 577–93.

Baxter, Donald L. M. "Hume's Labyrinth Concerning the Idea of Personal Identity." *Hume Studies*, 24 (1998), 203–33.

Bayle, Pierre. *Various Thoughts on the Occasion of a Comet*. Edited by Robert C. Bartlett. Albany: State University of New York Press, 2000. Pp. xv + 267.

Bedini, Silvio A. *Patrons, Artisans, and Instruments of Science, 1600–1750*. Ashgate: Aldershot, 1999.

Benitez, Miguel, Antony McKenna, Gianni Paganini, and Jean Salem (eds.). *Materia actuosa: Antiquité, age classique, Lumières: Mélanges en l'honneur d' Olivier Bloch*. Paris: Honore Champion, 2000. Pp. 747.

Benz, August. *Die Moralphilosophie von Thomas Reid zwischen Tradition und Innovation*. (St. Galler Studien zur Politikwissenschaft 23.) Bern: Haupt, 2000. Pp. ix + 276.

Bérenguier, Nadine. "The Politics of Happy Matrimony: Cerfvol's *La Gamologie ou l'Education des Filles Destinés au Mariage*." *Studies in Eighteenth-Century Culture*, 29 (2000), 173 ff.

Special Section: Late Entries and Reviews

Beretta, M. "At the Source of Western Science: The Organization of Experimentalism at the Accademis-del-Cimento (1657–1667)." *Notes and Records of the Royal Society of London*, 54 (2000), 215–22.

Bermudez, José. "The Originality of Cartesian Skepticism: Did It Have Ancient or Medieval Antecedents?" *History of Philosophy Quarterly*, 17 (2000), 333–60.

Bernschneider-Reif, S. "Laboratories, Distilleries, Balm Makers: The Oil Activity in Thuringen Forest from the 17th to the 19th Century." *Pharmazie in Unserer Zeit*, 29 (2000), 213–19.

Bever, E. "Witchcraft Fears and Psychosocial Factors in Disease." *Journal of Interdisciplinary History*, 30 (2000), 573–90.

Bietenholz, Peter G. *Daniel Zwicker, 1612–1678: Peace, Tolerance, and God the One and Only.* Florence: Olschki, 1999. Pp. 330.

Bitbol-Hespéridès, Annie. "Descartes, Reader of Harvey: The Discovery of the Circulation of Blood in Context." *Graduate Faculty Philosophy Journal*, 22 (2000), 15–40.

Black, Joseph. *The Correspondence of Joseph Black.* Edited by Jean Jones and Robert Anderson. Aldershot: Ashgate, 2000. Pp. 1,200.

Blay, Michel. *Reasoning with the Infinite: From the Closed World to the Mathematical Universe.* Translated by M. B. DeBevoise. Chicago: University of Chicago Press, 1998. Pp. x + 216; illustrations.

Blondy, Alain. "La naissance de la science préhistorique." Pp. 165–75 of *Visualisation*. Edited by Roland Mortier. Berlin: Berlin Verlag Arno Spitz, 1999.

Blouet, Olwyn M. "Bryan Edwards, FRS, 1743–1800." *Notes and Records of the Royal Society*, 54:2 (2000), 215–22.

Bobro, Marc E. "Thinking Machines and Moral Agency in Leibniz's *Nouveau Essais*." *Studia Leibnitiznz*, 30:2 (1998), 178–93.

Boewe, Charles. "John Bradbury (1768–1823), Kentucky's Forgotten Naturalist." *Filson Club History Quarterly*, 74:3 (2000), 221–49.

Booth, C. C. "Choosing a Dermatological Hero for the Millennium: Robert Willan (1757–1812)." *Clinical and Experimental Dermatology*, 25:1 (2000), 85–86.

Bordes, Philippe. "David's Portrait of the Comte de Turenne at Williamstown." *Burlington Magazine*, 142:1166 (2000), 276–80.

Borsay, Anne. "An Example of Political Arithmetic: The Evaluation of Spa Therapy at the Georgian Bath Infirmary, 1742–1830." *Medical History*, 44:2 (2000), 149–72.

Botul, Jean-Baptiste. *La Vie sexuelle d'Emmanuel Kant."* Paris: Mille et une nuits, 1999. Pp. 93.

Braffort, Paul. *Science et littérature: Les deux cultures, dialogues et controverses pour l'an 2000.* Paris: Diderot, 1998 Pp. 307; illustrations.

Braun, Theodore E. D., and John A. McCarthy (eds.). *Disrupted Patterns: On Chaos and Order in the Enlightenment.* Amsterdam: Rodopi, 2000. Pp. xiii + 219; illustrations.

Breathnach, C. S. "Joseph Black (1728–1799): An Early Adept in Quantification and Interpretation." *Journal of Medical Biography*, 8:3 (2000), 149–55.

Bredekamp, Horst. *Thomas Hobbes Visuelle Strategien. Des Leviathan: Das Urbild Des Modernen Staates.* Berlin: Akademie Verlag, 2000. Pp. 264.

Brenni, P. "La funzione degli strumenti scientifici nella didattica fra Settecento e Ottocento." *Studi Settecenteschi*, 18 (1998), 421–30.

Bret, Patrice. *Lavoisier et l'Encyclopé die méthodique: Le manuscritdes régisseurs des Poudres et salpêtres pour le Dictionnaire de l'artillerie (1787).* Firenze: L. S. Olschki, 1997. Pp. 202; illustrations.

Bret, Patrice, Christiane Demeulenaere-Douyère, and Liliane Hilaire-Pérez. *Des matériaux pour l'histoire: Archives et collections scientifiques et techniques du XVIIIe siècle à nous jours.* Paris: ENS Editions, 2000. Pp. 99.

Brianta, Donata. "Education and Training in the Mining Industry, 1750–1860: European Models and the Italian Case." *Annals of Science*, 57:3 (2000), 267–300.

Brooke, J. H. "'Wise-men-nowadays-think-otherwise': John Ray, Natural Theology and the Meanings of Anthropocentrism." *Notes and Records of the Royal Sociaty of London*, 54 (2000), 199–213.

Brown, G. I. *Scientist, Soldier Statesman, Spy: Count Rumford, the Extraordinary Life of a Scientific Genius.* Gloucestershire: Sutton, 1999. Pp. x + 182; illustrations; portraits; [8] pp. of plates; facsimiles.

Special Section: Late Entries and Reviews

Brown, Gillian. *The Consent of the Governed: The Lockean Legacy in Early American Culture.* Cambridge: Harvard University Press, 2001. Pp. 237.

Brown, Michael. "Francis Hutchinson and the Molesworth Connection." *Eighteenth-Century Ireland–Iris an dá chultúr*, 14 (1999), 62–76.

Buffon, Georges Louis LeClerc de. *Natural History, General & Particular.* 9 volumes. Bristol: Thoemmes, 2000.

Burchell, D. "The Disciplined Citizen: Thomas Hobbes, Neostoicism and the Critique of Classical Citizenship." *Australian Journal of Politics and History*, 45:4 (1999), 506–25.

Burnard, T. "'The countrie continues sicklie': White Mortality in Jamaica, 1655–1780." *Social History of Medicine*, 12 (1999), 45–72.

Burr, Sandra J. "Inspiring Lunatics: Biographical Portraits of the Lunar Society's Erasmus Darwin, Thomas Day, and Joseph Priestly." *Eighteenth Century Life*, 24:2 (2000), 111–27.

Capet, Antoine. "La correspondence conservatrice du whig Burke." Pp. 19–34 of *Conservatismes anglo-américains, XVIIIe et XIXe siècles*. Edited by Gilbert Bonifas. Nice: Centre de recherche sur les écritres de lange anglaise de l'université de Nice-Sophia-Antipolis, 1999.

Carrell, Jennifer Lee. "Newton's Vice: Some Say Alchemy Inspired Our Greatest Scientist." *Smithsonian*, 31 (2000), 130–44.

Carrithers, D. W. "Montesquieu's Philosophy of Punishment." *History of Political Thought*, 19:2 (1998), 213–40.

Carroll, J. W. "Humean Justified Belief." *Philosophical Quarterly*, 48:192 (1998), 373–78.

Chapman, H. C. "Divine Remembrance: Hölderlin, Nancy, and the Finitude of Thought." *Philosophy Today*, 43:3 (1999), 250–65.

Chen, S. "Locke's Political Arguments for Toleration." *History of Political Thought*, 19:2 (1998), 167–85.

Cherni, Amor. "Brute Matter and Organic Matter in Buffon." *Graduate Faculty Philosophy Journal*, 22 (2000), 87–105.

Chézaud, Patrick. "James Burnett, Lord Monboddo et le débat autour de l'origine du langage dans l'Ecosse du XVIIIe siècle." Pp. 285–318 of *Ecosse des Lumières: le XVIIIe sièvle autrement*. Edited by Pierre Morère. Grenoble: Université Stendhal, 1997.

Chézaud, Patrick. "Thomas Reid et le sens commun." Pp. 243–76 of *Ecosse des Lumières: le XVIIIe sièvle autrement*. Edited by Pierre Morère. Grenoble: Université Stendhal, 1997.

Choudhury, Mita. "Despotic Habits: The Critique of Power and Its Abuses in an Eighteenth-Century Convent." *French Historical Studies*, 23:1 (2000), 33–66.

Christen, A. G., and J. A. Christen. "Martin Van Butchell (1735–1814): The Eccentric, 'Kook' Dentist of Old London." *Journal of the History of Dentistry*, 43:3 (1999), 99–104.

Chu, Pingyi. "Trust, Instruments, and Cross-Cultural Scientific Exchanges: Chinese Debate Over the Shape of the Earth, 1600–1800." *Science in Context*, 12:3 (1999), 385–412.

Ciardi, M. "Medicina, tecnologia civile e militare, filosofia naturale: L'insegnamento della fisica nel Regno del Sardegna." *Studi Settecenteschi*, 18 (1998), 217–48.

Clark, S. "Hume's Definition of Miracles Revised." *American Philosophical Quarterly*, 36:1 (1999), 49–57.

Claydon, Tony, and Ian McBride (eds). *Protestantism and National Identity: Britain and Ireland c. 1650–c. 1850*. New York: Cambridge University Press, 1998. Pp. xi + 317; illustrations.

Cohen, Huguette. "Diderot's Cosmic Games: Revisiting a Dilemma." Pp. 9–20 of *Disrupted Patterns: On Chaos and Order in the Enlightenment*. Edited by Theodore E. D. Braun and John A. McCarthy. Amsterdam: Rodopi, 2000.

Colerus, Johannes, Jean M. Lucas, and Dominique de Saint-Glain. *Vies de Spinoza*. Paris: Allia, 1999. Pp. 132.

Contardi, S. "Visibiltà e autoapprendimento: Aspetti della didattica fisica nella Toscana di Pietro Leopoldo." *Studi Settecenteschi*, 18 (1998), 343–66.

Cook, M. "The Ontological Status of Malebranchean Ideas." *Journal of the History of Philosophy*, 36:4 (1998), 525–44.

Cope, Kevin L. "John Locke Didn't Have It All Locked Up, or, Locke on the Emergence, Development, and Branching of Knowledge, Education, Politics, Religion, and Hairdress-

Special Section: Late Entries and Reviews

ing." Pp. 91–105 of *Disrupted Patterns: On Chaos and Order in the Enlightenment.* Edited by Theodore E. D. Braun and John A. McCarthy. Amsterdam: Rodopi, 2000.

Copeland, David A. *Benjamin Keach and the Development of Baptist Traditions in Seventeenth-Century England.* (Studies in Religion and Society 48.) Lewiston: E. Mellen, 2000. Pp. 220.

Costa, Michael. "Hume on the Very Idea of a Relation." *Hume Studies*, 34:1 (1998), 71–94.

Cowen, David L. *Pharmacopoeias and Related Literature in Britain and America, 1618–1847.* Aldershot: Ashgate Publishing Company, 2000. Pp. 320.

Cox, James A. "Nonconformist Joseph Priestley." *Colonial Williamsburg*, 21 (1998), 54–62.

Craik, A. D. D. "James Ivory, F. R. S., Mathematician: 'The most unlucky perosn that ever existed.'" *Notes and Records of the Royal Society of London*, 54 (2000), 223–47.

Crawford, C. "Patients' Rights and the Law of Contract in Eighteenth-Century England." *Social History of Medicine*, 13 (2000), 381–409.

Cronk, Nicholas (ed.). *Études sur le Fils naturel et les Entretiens sur le Fils naturel de Diderot.* Oxford: Voltaire Foundation, 2000. Pp. ix + 324.

Cunningham, A. "Kantian Ethics and Intimate Attachments." *American Philosophical Quarterly*, 36:4 (1999), 279–94.

Cusset, Catherine. *No Tomorrow: The Ethics of Pleasure in the French Enlightenment.* Charlottesville: University Press of Virginia, 1999. Pp. xiv + 208.

D'Alessandro, Giuseppe. *L'Illuminismo Dimenticato: Johann Gottfried Eichhorn (1752–1827) e il suo tempo.* Naples: Liguori Editore, 2000. Pp. 389.

Dalton, S. "Subjectivity and Orientation in Levinas and Kant." *Continental Philosophy Review*, 32:4 (1999), 433–49.

Darwall, S. "Sympathetic Liberalsim: Recent Work on Adam Smith." *Philosophy and Public Affairs*, 28:2 (1999), 139–64.

Davie, William. "Hume's General Point of View." *Hume Studies*, 24 (1998), 275–94 *Hume Studies*, 24 (1998), 203–33.

Davis, P. "Thomas Hobbes's Translations of Homer: Epic and Anticlericalism in Late Seventeenth-Century England." *Seventeenth Century*, 12 (1997), 231–55.

Décultot, Élisabeth. "Winckelmann naturaliste: L'histoire naturelle et la naissance de l'histoire de l'art." *Dix-huitième siècle*, 31 (1999), 179–94.

De Franceschi, Sylvio Hermann. "L'autorité pontificate face au legs de l'antiromanisme catholique et régaliste des Lumières." *Archivium Historiae Pontificiae*, 38 (2000), 119–63.

Delacampagne, Christian. *Le Philosophe et le tyran*. (Perspectives critiques.) Paris: Presses universitaires de France, 2000. Pp. 248.

Démoris, René. "Chardin et la lettre: Le rouge et le blanc." *Revue de l'A.I.R.E.*, 24 (2000), 15–21.

Denby, David J. "Sensuslisme, esthétique sentimentale et démocratie." *Dix-huitième siècle*, 31 (1999), 123–39.

Desile, Patrick. "Illuminations et feux d'artifice." *Revue d'esthetique*, 28 (1997), 53 *Bulletin de la société d'études anglo-américaines des XVIIe et XVIIIe siècles*, 50 (2000), 167–89.

Despoix, Philippe. "Measurement of the World and European Representation in the 18th Century: The British Program to Measure Longitudes at Sea." *Revur d'histoire des sciences*, 53:2 (2000), 205–33

Dingwall, H. M. "'To be insert in the mercury': Medical Practitioners and the Press in Eighteenth-Century Edinburgh." *Social History of Medicine*, 13 (2000), 23–44.

Downing, L. "The Status of Mechanism in Locke's *Essay*." *Philosophical Review*, 107:3 (1998), 381–414.

Drayton, Richard. *Nature's Government: Science, Imperial Britain, and the "Improvement" of the World*. New Haven: Yale University Press, 2000. Pp. xi + 416; illustrations.

Dreisbach, Daniel L. "George Mason's Pursuit of Religious Liberty in Revolutionary Virginia." *Virginia Magazine of History & Biography*, 108 (2000), 5–44.

Duchesneau, François. "Diderot et la physiologie de la sensibilité." *Dix-huitième siècle*, 31 (1999), 195–216.

Special Section: Late Entries and Reviews

Duchesneau, François, Guy Lafrance, and Claude Piché (eds.). *Kant actuel: Essais en hommage à Pierre Laberge*. Montréal: Bellarmin, 2000. Pp. 303; portrait.

Duddy, Thomas. "Toland, Berkeley, and the Irrational Hypothesis." *Eighteenth-Century Ireland–Iris an dá chultúr*, 14 (1999), 49–61.

Duffield, Holley Gene. *Historical Dictionary of the Shakers*. (Historical Dictionaries of Religions, Philosophies, and Movements.) Lanham: Scarecrow Press, 2000. Pp.xxvi + 219.

Duflo, Colas. *La finalité dans la nature: De Descartes à Kant*. Paris: Presses universitaires de France, 1996. Pp. 128.

Dumouchel, Daniel. "Le sublime et les limites du sensible: Perception scientifique et subjectivité esthétique chez Addison et Kant." *Dix-huitième siècle*, 31 (1999), 61–75.

Dupre, L. "Kant's Theory of History and Progress." *Review of Metaphysics*, 51:4 (1998), 813–28.

Eadie, M. J. "Robert Whytt and the Pupils." *Journal of Clinical Neurosciences*, 7:4 (2000), 295–97.

Edwards, Jonathan. *The Works of Jonathan Edwards*. Volume XVII: The "Miscellanies," 501–832. Edited by Ava Chamberlain. New Haven: Yale University Press, 2000. Pp. 602.

Engstrand, I. H. W. "Of Fish and Men: Spanish Marine Science During the Late Eighteenth Century." *Pacific History Review*, 69 (2000), 3–30.

Eveleth, D. "'The Romanian privilege' in French Medicine and Anti-Semitism." *Social History of Medicine*, 11 (1998), 213–32.

Faaborg, R. W. "Berkeley and the Argument from Microscopes." *Pacific Philosophical Quarterly*, 80:4 (1999), 301–23.

Farinella. C. I 'luoghi' della fisica a Genova fra Settecento e Ottocento." *Studi Setteceteschi*, 18 (1998), 249–78.

Fenn, Elizabeth A. "Biological Warfare in Eighteenth-Century North America: Beyond Jeffrey Amherst." *Journal of American History*, 86 (2000), 1552–80.

Ferguson, S. "Are Locke's Abstract Ideas Fictions?" *Review of Metaphysics*, 53:1 (1999), 127–40.

Ferraresi, A. "La fisica sperimentale tra università e ginnasi nella Lombardia austriaca." *Studi Setteceteschi*, 18 (1998), 279–320.

Ferret, Olivier. "Les paradoxes d'un anti-philosophe: *L'Éloge historique de monseigneur le du de Bourgogne*, par J.-J. Lefranc de Pompignan." *Dix-huitième siècle*, 31 (1999), 429–49.

Fields, Polly Stevens. "Samson Occom and/in the Missionary Position: Consideration of a Native American Preacher in 1770s Colonial America." *Wordaworth Circle*, 32 (2001), 14–20.

Fine, Gail. "Descartes and Ancient Skepticism: Reheated Cabbage?" *Philosophical Review*, 109 (2000), 195–234.

Fisher, M., and E. Watkins. "Kant on the Material Ground of Possibility: From the 'Only Possible Argument' to *The Critique of Pure Reason*." *Review of Metaphysics*, 52:2 (1998), 369–95.

Flikschuh, K. "Freedom and Constraint in Kant's *Metaphysical Elements of Justice*." *History of Political Thought*, 20:2 (1999), 250–71.

Foisneau, Luc. *Hobbes et la toute-puissance de Dieu*. (Fondements de la politique.) Paris: Presses Universitaires de France, 2000. Pp. 421.

Frankel, S. "Politics Rhetoric: The Intended Audience of Spinoza's *Tractus Theologico-Politicus*." *Review of Metaphysics*, 52:4 (1999), 897–924.

Freiberg, M. "Going Gregorian, 1582–1752: A Summary View." *Catholic Historical Review*, 86:1 (2000), 1–19.

Freydberg, Bernard. *Provocative Form in Plato, Kant, Nietzsche (and Others)*. New York: Peter Lang, 2000. Pp. xii + 211.

Friday, J. "Hume's Sceptical Standard of Taste." *Journal of the History of Philosophy*, 36:4 (1998), 545–66.

Fuchs, Michel. "L'axe masculin/féminin chez Edmund Burke: De l'esthétique à la politique." *Dix-huitième siècle*, 31 (1999), 461–77.

Gabhart, M. "Spinoza on Self-Preservation and Self-Destruction." *Journal of the History of Philosophy*, 37:4 (1999), 613–28.

Special Section: Late Entries and Reviews

Gacto, M. "The Bicentennial of a Forgotten Giant: Lazzaro Spallanzani (1729–1799)." *International Microbiology*, 2:4 (1999), 273–74.

Gargett, Graham. "Voltaire's *Lettres philosophiques* in Eighteenth-Century Ireland." *Eighteenth-Century Ireland–Iris an dá chultúr*, 14 (1999), 77–98.

Garms, Jörg. "Materialen zur Kunsttätigkeit der gegenreformatorischen Orden in Österreich and in anderen Ländern der Habsburgermonarchie bis 1800: VII. Das Archiv des Piaristenorderns (Fortsetzung)." *Römische Historische Mitteilungen,* 42 (2000), 351–81.

Geshwind, M. "Dr. Chamberlen's Anodyne Teething Necklaces." *Journal of the History of Dentistry*, 43:3 (1999), 115–18.

Giudice, F. "Giovanni Rizzetti, l'ottica newtoniana e la legge di rirazione." *Studi Setteceteschi*, 18 (1998), 45–64.

Goldstein, Joel A. "A Matter of Great Magnitude: The Conflice Over Arithmetization in 16th-, 17th-, and 18th-Century Editions of Euclid's *Elements* Books I Through VI (1561–1795)." *Historia Mathematica*, 27:1 (2000), 36–53.

Gosetti, J. A. "The Poetic Politics of Dwelling: Hölderlin, Kant, and Heidegger." *International Studies in Philosophy*, 30:1 (1998), 57–71.

Gosetti, J. A. "Revolutions in the Subject of Language: Hölderlin to Kristeva." *International Studies in Philosophy*, 31:1 (1999), 61–76.

Goulemot, Jean M. "Histoire littéraire et histoire des idées du XVIIIe siè cle à l'épreuve de la Révolution." *Modern Language Notes*, 114 (1999), 629–46.

Gregorio, Tullio. *Genèse de la raison classique de Charron à Descartes*. Paris: PUF-épiméthée, 2000. Pp. xi + 63.

Griswold, Charles L., Jr. *Adam Smith and the Virtues of Enlightenment*. Cambridge: Cambridge University Press, 2000. Pp. 426.

Gross, A. G., J. E. Harmon, and M. S. Reidy. "Argument and 17th-Century Science: A Rhetorical Analysis with Sociological Implications." *Social Studies of Science*, 30 (2000), 371–96.

Grove, Allen W. "Sexual Chaos: The Gothic 'Formula' and the Politics of Complexity." Pp. 107–18 of *Disrupted Patterns: On Chaos and Order in the Enlightenment*. Edited by Theodore E. D. Braun and John A. McCarthy. Amsterdam: Rodopi, 2000.

Habermas, Jurgen. "From Kant to Hegel and Back Again: The Move Toward Detranscendentalization." *European Journal of Philosophy*, 7:2 (1999), 129–57.

Haines, R., and R. Schlomowitz. "Explaining the Modern Mortality Decline: What Can We Learn from Sea Voyages?" *Social History of Medicine*, 11 (1998), 15–48.

Hallberg, Peter. "The Nature of Collective Individuals: J. G. Herder's Concept of Community." *History of European Ideas*, 26 (1999), 291–304.

Hanna, Robert. "How Do We Know Necessary Truths? Kant's Answer." *European Journal of Philosophy*, 6:2 (1998), 115–45.

Harley, D. "Rhetoric and the Social Construction of Sickness and Healing." *Social History of Medicine*, 12 (1999), 407–35.

Haskell, Y. "New Wings on Old Vessels? Scientific Didactic Poetry Between Antiquity and Modernity." *Studies in the History and Philosophy of Science*, 31A (2000), 173–88.

Haslam, Thomas J. "Benjamin Franklin, David Hume, Autobiography, and the Jealousy of Empire." Pp. 292–306 of *Finding Colonial Americas: Essays Honoring J. A. Leo Lemay*. Edited by Carla Mulford. Newark: University of Delaware Press, 2001.

Hayles, N. Katherine. "Enlightened Chaos." Pp. 1–5 of *Disrupted Patterns: On Chaos and Order in the Enlightenment*. Edited by Theodore E. D. Braun and John A. McCarthy. Amsterdam: Rodopi, 2000.

Herbert, G. B. "Fichte's Deduction of Rights from Self-Consciousness." *Interpretation: A Journal of Political Philosophy*, 25:2 (1998), 201–22.

Herrick, James A. *The Radical Rhetoric of the English Deists: The Discourse of Skepticism, 1680–1750*. Columbia: University of South Carolina Press, 1997. Pp. ix + 249.

Hilbert, M. "Herschel's Investigation of the Nature of Radiant Heat: The Limitations of Experiment." *Annals of Science*, 56:4 (1999), 357–78.

Special Section: Late Entries and Reviews

Hlobil, Tomás. "Two Concepts of Language and Poetry: Edmund Burke and Moses Mendelssohn." *British Journal for the History of Philosophy*, 8:3 (2000), 447–58.

Hobbes, Thomas. *Léviathan*. (Folio Essais.) Translated by Gérard Mairet. Paris: Gallimard, 2000. Pp. 1,027.

Horstmann, F. "A Building-Block in Kepler Reception: Thomas Hobbes's *Physica coelestis*." *Studia Leibnitana*, 30:2 (1998), 135–60.

Hugues, Sylvie. "Esthétique et épistémologie: Science, Religion, Sensation." *Dix-huitième siècle*, 31 (1999), 141–58.

Hund, J. "Is the *Critique of Pure Reason* Asociological?" *South African Journal of Philosophy*, 17:1 (1998), 8–21.

Hund, J. "Postscript: The Possibility of a Kantian Sociology." *Philosophy of the Social Sciences*, 30:1 (2000), 113–29.

Hunt, A. "The Lord's Supper in Early Modern England." *Past & Present*, 161 (1998), 39–83.

Hunwick, Andrew. "Le rôle de textes clandestins dans la philosophie du baron d'Holbach (1723–1789)." *Essays in French Literature*, 37 (2000), 62–87.

Ibrahim, Annie. "Une philosophie d'aveugle: La matière fait de l'esprit." *Recherches dur Diderot et sur Encyclopédie*, 28 (2000), 97–106.

Iliffe, Robert. "An Interregnum Parody of Music, Magic, and Natural Language: Seth Ward's *Vindiciæ Academiorum*." *Intellectual News*, 8 (2000), 69–70.

Imlay, R. A. "Contingency, Reason and Necessary Goodness in Leibniz." *Studia Leibnitiana*, 30:2 (1998), , 194–203.

Imlay, R. A. "Leibniz's Cosmological Argument and the Alleged Reflexivity of Sufficient Reason." *Studia Leibnitiana*, 31:1 (1999), 73–81.

Irons, Charles F. "The Spiritual Fruits of Revolution: Disestablishment and the Rise of the Virginia Baptists." *Virginia Magazine of History & Biography*, 108 (2000), 159–86.

Iturrate, José. "Confradía de sacerdotes en los Valles de Arraya y La Minoria en honor de la Purísima Concepción de la Virgen María." *Scriptorium Victoriense*, 47 (2000), 167–214.

Jackson, M. W. "Labor, Skills, and Practices in the Scientific Enterprise: Recent Works in the Cultural History of Science." *Journal of Modern History*, 71 (1999), 902–13.

Jacovides, Michael. "Cambridge Changes of Color." *Pacific Philosophical Quarterly*, 81:2 (2000), 142–63.

Jami, Catherine. "'European Science in China' or 'Western Learning'? Representations of Cross-Cultural Transmissions, 1600–1800." *Science in Context*, 12:3 (1999), 413–34.

Janiak, A. "Space, Atoms and Mathematical Divisibility in Newton." *Studies in the History and Philosophy of Science*, 31A (2000), 203–30.

Jankovic, Vladimir. "The Place of Nature and the Nature of Place: The Chorographic Challenge to the History of British Provincial Science." *History of Science*, 38 (2000), 251–70.

Jespers, F. "*Dieu veut bien souffrir des anthropologies*: Leibniz's Use of Images of God." *Studia Leibnitiana*, 30 (1998), 103–15.

Jesseph, Douglas M. *Squaring the Circle: The War Between Hobbes and Wallis*. Chicago: University of Chicago Press, 1999. Pp. xiv + 419; illustrations.

Johns, A. "Identity, Practice, and Trust in Early Modern Natural Philosophy." *Historical Journal*, 42:4 (1999), 1125–45.

Johnson, Laurie. "The Aesthetic Authority of Disorder in Friedrich Schlegel's Philosophy." Pp. 119–34 of *Disrupted Patterns: On Chaos and Order in the Enlightenment*. Edited by Theodore E. D. Braun and John A. McCarthy. Amsterdam: Rodopi, 2000.

Jollet, Étienne. "Les rapports entre les sciences et les beaux-arts dans les écrits de C.-H. Watelet: Pour une représentation de l'ordre de la nature." *Dix-huitième siècle*, 31 (1999), 217–31.

Joly, Bernard. "Les leçons de morale de Descartes à la princesse Élisabeth." Pp. 65–77 of *Lettre et réflexion morale: La lettre, miroir de l'âme*. Edited by Geneviève Haroche-Bouzinac. Paris: Klincksieck, 1999.

Jones, Colin. "Pulling Teeth in Eighteenth-Century Paris." *Past and Present*, 166 (2000), 100–45.

Special Section: Late Entries and Reviews

Jones, W. E. "Can We Infer Naturalism from Scepticism? Hume's *Treatise of Human Nature*." *Philosophical Quarterly*, 50:201 (2000), 433–51.

Jullien, François. *Fonder la morale: Dialogue de Mencius avec un philosophe des Lumières*. Paris: Grasset, 1995. Pp. 219.

Kagawa, Chiaki. "The Mind-Body Debate: Studies in Descartes' Philosophy in Japan." *Intellectual News*, 6–7 (2000), 70–81.

Kassler, Michael, and Philip Olleson. *Samuel Wesley, 1766–1837: A Source Book*. Aldershot: Ashgate, 2000. Pp. 350.

Kavanagh, Thomas M. "Crébillon's Chaotics of Desire." Pp. 135–46 of *Disrupted Patterns: On Chaos and Order in the Enlightenment*. Edited by Theodore E. D. Braun and John A. McCarthy. Amsterdam: Rodopi, 2000.

Kay, Carol. "Valuing Practices in Hume." *New Literary History*, 30 (1999), 757–67.

Keller, Eve. "Embryonic Individuals: The Rhetoric of Seventeenth-Century Embryology and the Construction of Early-Modern Identity." *Eighteenth-Century Studies*, 33 (2000), 321–48.

Kemal, S. "Aesthetic License: Foucault's Modernism and Kant's Post-Modernism." *International Journal of Philosophical Studies*, 7 (1999), 281–303.

Kemp, Catherine. "Two Meanings of the Term 'Idea': Acts and Contents in Hume's *Treatise*." *Journal of the History of Ideas*, 61 (2000), 675–90.

Kerslake, Lawrence. "Les *Observations sur l'éloquence* de l'abbé de Saint-Pierre." *Dix-huitième siècle*, 31 (1999), 305–28.

Kim, Mi Guyng. "Chemical Analysis and the Domains of Reality: Wilhelm Homberg's *Essais de Chémie, 1702–1709*." *Studies in History and Philosophy of Science*, 31A:1 (2000), 37–70.

Kinghorn, Kenneth Cain. "Richard Boardman: American Methodism's First Superintendent." *Asbury Theological Journal*, 55 (2000), 17–35.

Kirscher, Roger. "Les néologues autour de Friedrich Nicolai et de sa revue *Allgemeine Deutsche Bibliothek* (1765–1792). Une volonté de réforme théologique 'éclairée.'" *Dix-huitième siècle*, 32 (200), 445–56.

Kleingeld, P. "Kant on the Unity of Theoretical and Practical Reason." *Review of Metaphysics*, 52:2 (1998), 311–39.

Knee, Philip, and Gérald Allard (eds.). *Rousseau juge de Jean-Jacques: Études de les Dialogues.* (Pensée libre 7.) Ottawa: Association nord-américaine des études Jean-Jacques Rousseau, 1998. Pp. 238.

Koistinen, O. "On the Consistency of Spinoza's Modal Theory." *Southern Journal of Philosophy*, 36:1 (1998), 61–80.

Koistinen, O., and A. Repo. "Compossinility and Being in the Same World in Leibniz's Metaphysics." *Studia Leibnitiana*, 31 (199), 196–214.

Kollerstrom, N. "The Path of Halley's Comet, and Newton's Late Apprehension of the Law of Gravity." *Annals of Science*, 56:4 (1999), 331–56.

Koriako, D. "Undemonstrable Sentences, Made-Up Conceptions: Kant on the Use of Mathematical Arguments in Philosophy." *Studia Leibnitiana*, 30 (1998), 24–48.

Kossler, M. "The Transcendental Appearance in the Paralogisms of Pure reason According to the First Edition of *Kritik der reinen Vernunft*." *Kant-Studien*, 90:1 (1999), 385–409.

Kramnick, Jonathan Brodie. "Locke's Desire." *Yale Journal of Criticism*, 12 (1999), 189–208.

Kremer, M. "Liberty and Revolution in Burke's *Letter to the Sheriffs of Bristol*." *Interpretation: A Journal of Political Philosophy*, 26:1 (1998), 77–97.

Kuflik, Arthur. "Hume on Justice to Animals, Indians, and Women." *Hume Studies*, 34:1 (1998), 53–70.

Kuhn, Hans Wolfgang, and Halgard Kuhn. "Untersuchungen zur Säkularisation der Abtei St. Maximin hart vor Trier. Die Überlieferung von Archiv, Bibliothek and Zimelien." *Jahrbuch fur westdeutsche Landesgeschichte*, 26 (2000), 99–197.

Kusukawa, S. "The *Historia Piscium* (1686)." *Notes and Records of the Royal Society of London*, 54 (2000), 179–97.

Laberge, Pierre, Guy Lafrance, and Denis Dumas. *L'Année 1795: Kant, essai sur la paix*. Paris: J. Vrin, 1997. Pp. 405.

Special Section: Late Entries and Reviews

Lafon, Sylvie. "Si loin, si proche: Les Highlands, les Lowlands et le 'complexe d'eloignement' de l'Ecosse des Lumières." *Le spectateur européen*, 1 (2000), 59–74.

La Mettrie, Julian Offray de. *Discours sur le bonheur*. Paris: L'arche, 2000. Pp. 128.

Langford, S., and M. Ramachandran. "Rigidity, Occasional Identity and Leibniz Law." *Philosophical Quarterly*, 50:201 (2000), 518–26.

Langsam, H. "Kant's Compatibilism and His two Conceptions of Truth." *Pacific Philosophical Quarterly*, 81:2 (2000), 164–88.

Lannoy, Cyprien. "La sensibilité épistémologique de Diderot: Expression mat rialiste d'un désir d'eternité." *Recherches sur Diderot et sur l'Encyclopdie*, 27 (199), 59–88.

Lantin, R. "On Kant's Argument in the Second Analogy." *Philosophia*, 27:3–4 (1999), 483–95.

Larson, Rebecca. *Daughters of Light: Quaker Women Preaching and Prophesying in the Colonies and Abroad, 1700–1775*. New York: Knopf, 1999. Pp. x + 399; illustrations.

Lassman, Peter. "Enlightenment, Cultural Crisis, and Politics: The Role of Intellectuals from Kant to Habermas." *European Legacy*, 5 (2000), 815–28.

Lavoisier, Antoine Laurent. *Œuvres de Lavoisier: Correspondance. Volume VI: 1789–1791*. Edited by Henry Kagan and Patrice Bret. Paris: Académie de sciences, 1997. Pp. xviii + 491; illustrations.

La Volpa, Anthony J. "Fichte's Road to Kant." Pp. 200–29 of *Representations of the Self from the Renaissance to Romanticism*. Edited by Patrick Coleman, Jayne Lewis, and Jill Kowalik. Cambridge: Cambridge University Press, 2000.

Lawlor, Clark, and Akihito Suzuki. "The Disease of the Self: Representing Consumption, 1700–1830." *Bulletin of the History of Medicine*, 74:3 (2000), 458–94.

Lawrence, Christopher, and Stephen Shapin (eds.). *Science Incarnate: Historical Embodiments of Natural Knowledge*. Chicago: University of Chicago Press, 1998. Pp. vii + 342; illustrations.

Lee, Hyun Sang, and Allen C. Guelzo (eds.). *Edwards in Our Time: Jonathan Edwards and the Shaping of American Religion*. Grand Rapids: William B. Eerdmans, 1999. Pp. xiv + 214.

Le Jallé, Éléonore. *Hume et la régulation morale.* Paris: Presses universitaires de France, 1999. Pp. 136.

Lequan, Maï. *La Chimie selon Kant.* Paris: Presses universitaires de France, 2000. Pp. 136.

Levenduski, Cristine. *Peculiar Power: A Quaker Woman Preacher in Eighteenth-Century America.* Washington, D.C.: Smithsonian Institution Press, 1996. Pp. x + 171; illustrations.

Levinger, M. "Kant and the Origins of Prussian Constitutionalism." *History of Political Thought,* 19 (1998), 241–63.

Levy, Lia. *L'Automate spirituel: La naissance de la subjectivité modern d'après l'Ethique de Spinoza.* Assen: Van Gorcum, 2000. Pp. xii + 365.

Lieberman, D. "Jeremy Bentham: Biography and Intellectual Biography." *History of Political Thought,* 20:1 (1999), 187–204.

Lilla, M. "Kant's Theological–Political Revolution." *Review of Metaphysics,* 52:2 (1998), 397–434.

Lindman, Janet Moore, and Michele Lise Tarter (eds.). *A Centra of Wonders: The Body in Early America.* Ithaca: Cornell University Press, 2001. Pp. vii + 283; illustrations.

Lister, A. "Scepticism and Pluralism in Thomas Hobbes's Political Thought." *History of Political Thought,* 19:1 (1998), 35–50.

Lodge, P. "Leibniz's Heterogeneity Argument Against the Cartesian Conception of Body." *Studia Leibnitiana,* 30 (1998), 83–102.

Long, C. P. "Two Powers, One Ability: The Understanding and Imagination in Kant's Critical Philosophy." *Southern Journal of Philosophy,* 36:2 (1998), 233–53.

Look, Brandon. "From the Metaphysical Union of Mind and Body to the Real Union of Monads: Leibniz on *supposita* and *vincula-substantiala*." *Southern Journal of Philosophy,* 36:4 (1998), 505–29.

Special Section: Late Entries and Reviews

Loptson, Peter. "Hume Multiperspectival Pluralism and Authorial Voice." *Hume Studies*, 24 (1998), 313–34.

Los, Willeke. "Locke en Nederland: De receptie van zijn ideeën over individualiteit in opvoeding en onderwijs bij P. A. Verwer (1796–1757) en K. Van der Palm (1730–1789)." *De Achttiende Eeuw*, 31:2 (1999), 173–86.

Madden, Edward H. "Ethan Allen, His Philosophical Side." *Transactions of the Charles S. Peirce Society*, 35 (1999), 270–83.

Maggioni, F., C. Occhipinti, and G. Zanchin. "Headaches in *Domestic Medicine* by William Buchan." *Italian Journal of Neurological Sciences*, 12:2 (1998), 109–15.

Malcolm, N. "The Publications of John Pell, F. R. S. (1611–1685): Some New Light and Some Old Confusions." *Notes and Records of the Royal Society of London*, 54 (2000), 275–92.

Malcolm, N. "The Title Page of *Leviathan*, Seen in a Curious Perspective." *Seventeenth Century*, 13 (1998), 124–55.

Malebranche, Nicolas de. *Dialogues on Metaphysics and on Religion*. Edited by Nicholas Jolley and David Scott. Cambridge: Cambridge University Press, 1997. Pp. 287.

Malm, Mats. "On the Technique of the Sublime." *Comparative Literature*, 52 (2000), 1–10.

Malpas, J. "Constituting the Mind: Kant, Davidson and the Unity of Consciousness." *International Journal of Philosophical Studies*, 7:3 (1999), 1–30.

Maltese, G. "On the Relativity of Motion in Leonhard Euler's Science." *History of the Exact Sciences*, 54:4 (2000), 319–48.

Mander, W. J. "Edward Caird's Neo-Kantian Idealism." *Modern Schoolman*, 76:1 (1998), 33–42.

Marciano, Alain, and Maud Pelissier. "The Influence of Scottish Enlightenment on Darwin's Theory of Cultural Evolution." *Journal of the History of Economic Thought*, 22:2 (2000), 239 ff.

Marcucci, S. "'Moral Friendship' in Kant." *Kant-Studien*, 90:4 (1999), 434–41.

Martin, Frank. "Two Angels by Bernardo Cametti in Madrid." *Burlington Magazine*, 142:1163 (2000), 104–07.

Mays, S. "Age-dependent Cortical Bone Loss in Women from 18th Century and Early 19th Century London." *American Journal of Physical Anthropology*, 112:3 (2000), 349–61.

Mazlish, Bruce. "Ernst Cassirer's Enlightenment: An Exchange with Robert Wokler." *Studies in Eighteenth-Century Culture*, 29 (2000), 349–59.

McAllister, J. W. "Universal Regularities and Initial Conditions in Newtonian Physics." *Synthese*, 120:3 (1999), 325–43.

McCarthy, John A. "Beyond a Philosophy of Alternatives: Chaos, Cosmology, and the Eighteenth Century." Pp. 21–36 of *Disrupted Patterns: On Chaos and Order in the Enlightenment*. Edited by Theodore E. D. Braun and John A. McCarthy. Amsterdam: Rodopi, 2000.

McCorkle, Barbara B. *The Early Maps of New England: An Exhibition from the Collection of The Kenneth Spencer Research Library, University of Kansas, Lawrence, Kansas, October 2000–January 2001*. Lawrence: University of Kansas, [2000]. Pp. 16.

McMahon, S. "John Ray (1627–1705) and the Act of Uniformity 1662." *Notes and Records of the Royal Society of London*, 54 (2000), 153–78.

Meeker, Kevin. "Hume: Radical Sceptic or Naturalized Epistemologist?" *Hume Studies*, 34:1 (1998), 31–52.

Meistad, Tore. *Martin Luther and John Wesley on the Sermon on the Mount*. Lanham: Scarecrow Press, 1999. Pp. 352.

Menendez Torrellas, G. "Mathematics and Harmony: A Possible Influence of Pythagorean Sources on the Music Theory of Leibniz." *Studia Leibnitiana*, 31:1 (1999), 34–54.

Menneteau, Patrick. "La position du sens commun de James Oswald comme réponse à John Locke, à David Hume et à la religion naturelle." Pp. 277–83 of *Ecosse des Lumières: le XVIIIe sièvle autrement*. Edited by Pierre Morère. Grenoble: Université Stendhal, 1997.

Menninghaus, Winfried. "Le mouvement du rire chez Kant." *Dix-huitième siècle*, 32 (2000), 265–77.

Special Section: Late Entries and Reviews

Mertens, J. "From Tubal Cain to Faraday: William Whewell as a Philosopher of Technology." *History of Science*, 38 (2000), 321–42.

Michael, M. A. "Locke's *Second Treatise* and the Literature of Government." *Interpretation: A Journal of Political Philosophy*, 25:3 (1998), 407–27.

Michaelis, L. "The Deadly Goddess: Friedrich Hölderlin on Politics and Fate." *History of Political Thought*, 20:2 (1999), 225–49.

Miele, Michele, O.P. "Le missioni populari nel Sud e le iniziative del gruppo fondato da L. Fiorillo, O.P. (+1737)." *Archivum Fratrum Praedicatorum*, 70 (2000), 365–443.

Milburn, John R. *Adams of Fleet Street, Instrument Makers to King George III*. Aldershot: Ashgate, 2000. Pp. xix + 420; illustrations..

Miller, David Philip. "'Puffing Jamie': The Commercial and Ideological Importance of Being a 'philosopher' in the Case of the Reputation of James Watt (1736–1819)." *History of Science*, 38:1 (2000), 1–24.

Miller, Jacqueline C. "The Body Politic and the Body Somatic: Benjamin Rush's Fear of Social Disorder and His Treatment of Yellow Fever." Pp. 61–74 of *A Centre of Wonders: The Body in Early America*. Edited by Janet Moore Lindman and Michele Lise Tarter. Ithaca: Cornell University Press, 2001.

Miller, Peter N. *Peiresc's Europe: Learning and Virtue in the Seventeenth Century*. London: Routledge, 2000. Pp. 270.

Mirabeau, Marquis de, and François Quesnay. *Traité de la monarchie*. (Cahiers d'économie politique.) Paris: l'Harmattan, 2000. Pp. 192.

Moggach, D. "Reciprocity, Elicitation, Recognition: the Thematics of Intersubjectivity in the Early Fichte." *Dialogue: Canadian Philosophical Review*, 38:2 (1999), 271–96.

Mongenot, Christine. "J'ai un talent pour la morale: Mme de Maintenon et la tentation de la direction spirituelle dans sa correspondance avec les Dames de Saint-Louis à Saint-Cyr." Pp. 133–147 of *Lettre et réflexion morale: La lettre, miroir de l'âme*. Edited by Geneviève Haroche-Bouzinac. Paris: Klincksieck, 1999.

Mongin, P., and N. Sigot. "Halevy's Bentham Is Bentham." *Philosophy*, 74:288 (1999), 271–81.

Morgan, David T. "Benjamin Franklin: Champion of Generic Religion." *The Historian*, 62 (2000), 723–30.

Mori, Gianluca. *Bayle philosophe*. Paris: Honoré Champion, 1999. Pp. 416.

Morrissey, M. "Interdisciplinarity and the Study of Early Modern Sermons." *Historical Journal*, 42:4 (1999), 1111–23.

Mortier, Roland. "L'actualité des Lumières à la fin du XXE siècle." *Revue des sciences morales et philosophiques*, 3 (1998), 45–56.

Mortier, Roland (ed.). *Visualisation*. Berlin: Berlin Verlag Arno Spitz, 1999. Pp. xxi + 290; illustrations.

Moyal, G. "A Brief Note on Clarity and Distinctness in Descartes's *First Meditation*." *Studia Leibnitiana*, 31 (1999), 91–98.

Mullin, Amy. "Descartes and the Community of Inquirers." *History of Philosophy Quarterly*, 17 (2000), 1–28.

Murdoch, Dugald. "The Cartesian Circle." *Philosophical Review*, 108 (1999), 221–44.

Murphy, Mark C. "Desire and Ethics in Hobbes's *Leviathan*: A Response to Professor Deigh." *Journal of the History of Philosophy*, 38:2 (2000), 259–68.

Nachtomy, O. "The Individual's Place in the Logical Space: Leibniz on Possible Individuals and Their Relations." *Studia Leibnitiana*, 30:2 (1998), 161–77.

Nagel, Jennifer. "The Empiricist Conception of Experience." *Philosophy*, 75 (2000), 345–76.

Nastasi, P. "Domenico Scinà e la fisica Palermitana fra Settecento e Ottocento." *Studi Setteceteschi*, 18 (1998), 377–406.

Neill, Alex. "'An Unaccountable Pleasure': Hume on Tragedy and the Passions." *Hume Studies*, 24 (1998), 335–54.

Nelles, Paul. "Saint-Beuve Between the Renaissance and Enlightenment. *Journal of the History of Ideas*. 61:3 (2000), 473–92.

Special Section: Late Entries and Reviews

Nelson, E. Carles. "Patrick Browne (ca. 1720–1790),, Irish Physician, Historian, and Caribbean Botanist: A Brief Biography with an Account of His Lost Medical Dissertations." *Huntia*, 11:1 (2000), 5–16.

Neugebauer, P., J. P. Thomas, and O. Michel. "The 'Case' of Joseph Haydn: A Rhinological Patient During the Eighteenth Century." *Laryngoscope*, 110:7 (2000), 1078–81.

Nicoletta, Julie. "The Gendering of Order and Disorder: Mother Ann Lee and Shaker Architecture." *New England Quarterly*, 74 (2001), 303–16.

Nichols, R. "Space, Individuation and the Identity of Indiscernibles: Leibniz's Triumph Over Strawson." *Studia Leibnitiana*, 31 (1999), 181–95.

Noonan, Harold W. "Animalism versus Lockeanism: A Current Controversy." *Philosophical Quarterly*, 48:192 (1998), 302–18.

Ohry, A. "Some Medical Aspects of Daniel Defoe and Robinson Crusoe." *Harefuah*, 135:1–2 (1998), 77–79.

Oldroyd, D. "Non-written Sources in the Study of the History of Geology: Pros and Cons, in the light of the Views of Collingwood and Foucault." *Annals of Science*, 56:4 (1999), 395–415.

O'Neal, John C. "Esthétique et épistémologie sensualiste." *Dix-huitième siècle*, 31 (1999), 77–91.

Osler, Margaret J. "Rethinking the Scientific Revolution: New Historiographical Directions." *Intellectual News*, 8 (2000), 21–30.

Oswald, John. *The Cry of Nature or an Appeal to Mercy and to Justice on Behalf of the Persecuted Animals.* (Mellen Animal Rights Library 8.) Edited with an introduction by Jason Hribal. Lewiston: E. Mellen, 2000. Pp. 82.

Oswald, P. H., and E. Charles Nelson. "Jamaican Plant Genera Named by Patrick Browne (ca. 1720–1790): A Checklist with an Attempt at an Etymology." *Huntia*, 11:1 (2000), 17–30.

Overhoff, Jürgen. *Hobbes's Theory of the Will: Ideological Reasons and Historical Circumstances.* Lanham: Rowman & Littlefield, 2000. Pp. x + 266.

Owen, David. *Hume's Reason*. New York: Oxford University Press, 2000. Pp. 234.

Paden, R. "Monomania and the War of All Against All." *Philosophia*, 27:1–2 (1999), 69–86.

Pantin, I. "New Philosophy and Old Prejudices: Aspects of the Reception of Copernicanism in a Divided Europe." *Studies in the History and Philosophy of Science*, 30A (1999), 237–62.

Parchment, S. "The Mind's Eternity in Spinoza's *Ethics*." *Journal of the History of Philosophy*, 38 (2000), 349–82.

Parmentier, Marc. "Le problème de Molyneux de Locke à Diderot." *Recherches dur Diderot et sur Encyclopédie*, 28 (2000), 13–23.

Parrett, H. "Kant on Music and the Hierarchy of the Arts." *Journal of Aesthetics and Art Criticism*, 56:3 (1998), 251–64.

Pedersen, K. M. "Water-filled Telescopes and the Pre-history of Fresnel's Ether Dragging." *Archives for the History of the Exact sciences*, 54:6 (2000), 499–564.

Pepe, L. "Matematica e fisica nei collegi del Settecento." *Studi Setteceteschi*, 18 (1998), 407–20.

Perullo, N. "Topics, Criticism, Grammatology: The Thought of Vico Seen Through the Works of Derrida." *Aut Aut*, 293–94 (1999), 183–220.

Peterfreund, Stuart. "Imagination at a Distance: Bacon's Epistemological Double-Bind, Natural Theology, and the Way of Scientific Explanation in the Seventeenth and Eighteenth Centuries." *The Eighteenth Century: Theory and Interpretation*, 41 (2000), 110–40.

Pfau, Thomas. "The Voice of Critique: Aesthetic Cognition after Kant." *Modern Language Quarterly*, 60:3 (1999), 321–52.

Pipes, Richard. *Property and Freedom*. New York: Vintage Books, 1999. Pp. xvi + 328.

Piccioto, Joanna. "Optical Instruments and the Eighteenth-Century Observer." *Studies in Eightenth-Century Cuklture*, 29 (2000), 123–53.

Piller, C. "Doing What Is Best." *Philosophical Quarterly*, 50:199 (2000), 208–26.

Pipes, Richard. *Property and Freedom*. New York:: Vintage Books, 1999. Pp. xvi + 328.

Pitassi, Maria-Cristina. "Firman Abauzit (1679–1767), ou de l'hétérodoxie discrète." *Bulletin de la société de l'histoire du protestantisme français,* 146 (2000), 717–28.

Special Section: Late Entries and Reviews

Pitt, A. "The Religion of the Moderns: Freedom and Authenticity in Constant's *De la religion*." *History of Political Thought*, 21:1 (2000), 67–87.

Plomp, R. "A Longitude Timekeeper by Isaac Thuret with the Balance Spring Invented by Christiaan Huygens." *Annals of Science*, 56:4 (1999), 379–94.

Portolano, M. "John Quincy Adams's Rhetorical Crusade for Astronomy." *Isis*, 91 (2000), 480–503.

Pozzo, R. "Kant Within the Tradition of Modern Logic: The Role of the 'Introduction: Idea of a Transcendental Logic." *Review of Metaphysics*, 52:2 (1998), 295–310.

Principato, Aurelio. "L'éloquence révolutionnaire: Idéologie et légende." Pp. 1019–37 of *Histoire de la rhétorique dans l'Europe moderne, 1450–1950*. Edited by Marc Fumaroli. Paris: Presses universitaires de France, 1999.

Prunier, Clotilde. "L'éducation et le Livre: Controverses religieuses Écosse au XVIIIe." *Bulletin de la société d'études anglo-américaines des XVIIe et XVIIIe siècles*, 50 (2000), 67–79.

Pruss, A. R. "Leibniz's Approach to Individuation and Strawson's Criticism." *Studia Leibnitiana*, 30 (1998), 116–23.

Putterman, E. "The Role of Public Opinion in Rousseau's Conception of Property." *History of Political Thought*, 20:3 (1999), 417–37.

Pyle, Cynthia M. "Text as Body/Body as Text: Humanists' Approach to the World Around Them and the Rise of Science." *Intellectual News*, 8 (2000), 7–14.

Quehen, H. D. "Politics and Scholarship in the Ignatian Controversy." *Seventeenth Century*, 13 (1998), 69–84.

Quintili, Paolo. "Diderot, l'esthétique et la naturalisme: L'autre science de l'interprétation de la nature." *Dix-huitième siècle*, 31 (1999), 269–82.

Randles, W. G. L. *The Unmaking of the Medieval Christian Cosmos, 1500–1760: From Solid Heavens to Boundless Æther*. Aldershot: Ashgate, 1999. Pp. 290.

Ratcliff, M. J. "Wonders, Logic, and Microscopy in the Eighteenth Century: A History of the Rotifer." *Science in Context*, 13:1 (2000), 93–120.

Raylor, T. "Thomas Hobbes and the Mathematical Demonstration of the Sword." *Seventeenth Century*, 15 (2000), 175–98.

Reeves, E. "Old Wives' Tales and the New World Syatem: Gilbert, Galileo, and Kepler." *Configurations*, 7:3 (1999), 301–54.

Reid, Thomas. *Thomas Reid: Essays on the Intellectual Powers of Man: A Critical Edition*. Edited by Derek R. Brooks. University Park: Pennylvania State University Press, 2000. Pp. 340.

Reiss, Timothy J. "Revising Descartes: On Subject and Community." Pp. 16–38 of *Representations of the Self from the Renaissance to Romanticism*. Edited by Patrick Coleman, Jayne Lewis, and Jill Kowalik. Cambridge: Cambridge University Press, 2000.

Riley, J. C. "Why Sickness and Death Rates Do Not Move Parallel to One Another Over Time." *Social History of Medicine*, 12 (1999), 101–24.

Robel, Gilles. "David Hume, John Bull et Siater peg." Pp. 151–85 of *Ecosse des Lumières: le XVIIIe siècle autrement*. Edited by Pierre Morère. Grenoble: Université Stendhal, 1997.

Robson, D. W. "Anticipating the Brethren: The Reverend Charles Nisbet Critiques the French Revolution." *Pensylvania Magazine of History and Biography*, 121:4 (1997), 303–28.

Rogozinski, Jacob. *Le Don de la loi: Kant et l'éthique*. Paris: Presses universitaires de France, 1999. Pp. 352.

Rosen, F. "Crime, Punishment, and Liberty." *History of Political Thought*, 20:1 (1999), 173–85.

Rosen, F. "James Burns and Jeremy Bentham." *History of Political Thought*, 20:1 (1999), 3–6.

Rothman, P. "By 'the light of his own mind': The Story of James Ferguson, Astronomer." *Notes and Records of the Royal Society of London*, 54 (2000), 33–45.

Rousseau, Jean-Jacques. *Spiritualité de Jean-Jacques Rousseau*. Montmorency: Museé Jean-Jacques Rousseau, 1998. Pp. 365; illustrations.

Roxburgh, Kenneth. "Thomas Gilllespie and Philip Doddridge." *Journal of the United Reformed Church History Society*, 6 (1999), 262–72.

Roy, Jean. *Le Souffle de l'espérance: Le poliotique entre le rêve et la raison*. Montréal: Bellarmin, 2000. Pp. 612.

Rudwick, Martin. "George Cuvier's Paper Museum of Fossil Bones." *Archives of Natural History*, 27 (2000), 51–68.

Ruffner, J. A. "Newton Propositions or Comets: Steps in Transition, 1681–84." *Archive for the History of the Exact Sciences*, 54:4 (2000), 259–77.

Ruin, H. "Leibniz and Heidegger on Sufficient Reason." *Studia Leibnitiana*, 30 (1998), 49–67.

Saccone, G. M. "The Ambitious Relation Between Hobbes' Rhetorical Appeal to English History and His Deductive Method in *A Dialogue*." *History of European Ideas*, 24:1 (1998), 1–17.

Saillant, John. "Traveling in Old and New Worlds with John Jea, the African Preacher, 1773–1816." *Journal of American Studies*, 33:3 (1999), 473–90.

Salter, J. "Sympathy with the Poor: Theories of Punishment in Hugo Grotius and Adam Smith." *History of Political Thought*, 20:2 (1999), 205–24.

Sammons, Christa, and Cyrus Hamlin. *Goethe the Scientist*. New Haven: Beinecke Rare Book and Manuscript Library, 1999. Pp. 63; exhibition catalogue; illustrations (some in color)

Sanchez, J. R. B., and A. G. Belmer. "Medical Applications of Chemistry in Early Nineteenth-Century France." *Ambix*, 47:1 (2000), 1–28.

Santesso, Aaron. "Aesthetic Chaos in the Age of Reason." Pp. 37–48 of *Disrupted Patterns: On Chaos and Order in the Enlightenment*. Edited by Theodore E. D. Braun and John A. McCarthy. Amsterdam: Rodopi, 2000.

Scarani, P. "Johann Wofgang Goethe (1749–1832): Creator of the Term and Concept of Morphology." *Pathologica*, 92:1 (2000), 45–49.

Schaer, Roland, and Lyman Tower Sargent (eds.). *L'Utopie: La quête de la société idéale en Occident*. Paris: Bibliothèque nationale de France, 2000. Pp. 368; illustrations.

Schelling, Friedrich Wilhelm Joseph von. *Philosophie de l'art*. Translated by Caroline Sulzer and Alain Pernet. Grenoble: Éditions Jérôme Millon, 1999. Pp. 397.

Scherer, I. "The Problem of the *a priori* in Sensibility: Revisiting Kant's and Hegel's Theories of the Senses." *Review of Metaphysics*, 52:2 (1998), 341–67.

Schettino, E. "L'insegnamento della fisica sperimentale a Napoli seconda metà del Settecento." *Studi Setteceteschi*, 18 (1998), 367–76.

Schmeisser, Martin. "'Lusus serius,' or Why Alchemy Went into Disrepute." *Intellectual News*, 8 (2000), 66–69.

Schneider, M. "Thought and Action of the Monads: Leibniz's Foundation of Subjectivity." *Studia Leibnitiana*, 30 (1998), 68–82.

Scott, David. "Occasionalism and Occasional Causation in Descartes' Philosophy." *Journal of the History of Philosophy*, 38 (2000), 503–28.

Secada, Jorge. *Cartesian Metaphysics: The Scholastic Origins of Modern Philosophy*. Cambridge: Cambridge University Press, 2000. Pp. xii + 333.

Seeman, Erik. "Lay Conversion Narratives: Investigating Ministerial Intervention." *New England Quarterly*, 71 (1998), 629–34.

Segal, Gideon. "Beyond Subjectivity: Spinoza's Cognitivism of the Emotions." *British Journal for the History of Philosophy*, 8:1 (2000), 1–20.

Serjeantson, Richard. "Playing Philosophically: Isaac Newton and John Bate's *Mysteries of Art and Nature*." *Intellectual News*, 8 (2000), 70–72.

Shapin, S. "Descartes the Doctor: Rationalism and Its Therapies." *British Journal for the History of Science*, 33:116 (2000), 131–54.

Sherratt, Y. "Adorno and Horkheimer's Concept of 'Enlightenment.'" *British Journal for the History of Philosophy*, 8:3 (2000), 521–44.

Simonis, Linda. "Science et esthétique chez les francs-maçons: l'exemple des illuminés de Bavière." *Dix-huitième siècle*, 32 (2000), 457–71.

Slomp, G. "From Genus to Species: The Unravelling of Hobbesian Glory." *History of Political Thought*, 19:4 (1998), 552–69.

Smit, H. "The Role of Reflection in Kant's *Critique of Pure Reason*." *Pacific Philosophical Quarterly*, 80:2 (1999), 203–23.

Special Section: Late Entries and Reviews

Smith, J. E. "On the Fate of Composite Substances after 1704." *Studia Leibnitiana*, 30:2 (19998), 204–10.

Smyth, Jim (ed.). *Revolution, Counter-Revolution and Union: Ireland in the 1790s*. New York: Cambridge University Press, 2000. Pp. 257.

Snobelen, S. D. "Isaac Newton, Heretic: The Strategies of a Nicodemite." *British Journal for the History of Science*, 32:115 (2000), 381–419.

Snyder, L. J. "Renovating the *Novum Organum*: Bacon, Whewell and Induction." *Studies in the History and Philosophy of Science*, 30A (1999), 531–57.

Sommereux, Ann. "La bienveillance et le grand tout." Pp. 187–207 of *Ecosse des Lumières: le XVIIIe sièvle autrement*. Edited by Pierre Morère. Grenoble: Université Stendhal, 1997.

Sorell, Tom. "Descartes, the Divine Will, and the Ideal of Psychological Stability." *History of Philosophy Quarterly*, 17 (2000), 361–82.

Spallanzani, Mariafranca. "Dal 'Dictionnaire des songes' di Descartes all'*Encyclopédie* di Diderot e D'Alembert." Edited by Daniela Gallingani and Marianna Tagliani. *I sogni della conoscenza: Les rêves du savoir. Actes du séminaire de l"Université de Bologna*. Firenze: Central editoriale toscano, 1998.

Spinoza, Benedictus de. *Traité de l'amendement de l'intellect*. Translated by Bernard Pautrat. Paris: Allia, 1999. Pp. 192.

Spinoza, Benedictus de. *Traité théologico-politique*. (Épiméthée.) Translated by Jacqueline Lagrée and Pierre-François Moureau. Paris: Presses universitaires de France, 1999. Pp. 862.

Stafford, J. M. "Hume on Luxury: A Response to John Dennis." *History of Political Thought*, 20 (1999), 646–48.

Stedall, J. A. "Catching Proteus: The Collaborations of John Wallis and William Brouncker, Part 1: Squaring the Circle." *Notes and Records of the Royal Society of London*, 54 (2000), 317–31.

Stenger, Gerhardt. "Vertu et vérité dans *le Fils naturel*." Pp. 65–78 of *Études sur le Fils naturel et les Entretiens sur le Fils naturel de Diderot*. Edited by Nicholas Cronk. Oxford: Voltaire Foundation, 2000.

Stern, R. "Going Beyond the Kantian Philosophy: On McDowell's Hegelian Critique of Kant." *European Journal of Philosophy*, 7:2 (1999), 247–69.

Stevenson, Gordon Park. "Humean Self-Consciouness Explained." *Hume Studies*, 34:1 (1998), 95–129.

Stock, Barbara. "Spinoza and the Immortality of the Mind." *History of Philosophy Quarterly*, 17 (2000), 381–404.

Stolberg, Michael. "Self-Pollution, Moral Reform, and the Venereal Trade: Notes on the Sources and Historical Context of *Onania* (1716)." *Journal of the History of Sexuality*, 9:1–2 (2000), 37–61.

Stone, J. C. "Robert Gordon and the Making of the First Atlas of Scotland." *Northern Scotland*, 18 (1998), 15–29.

Strauss, D. F. M. "Kant and Modern Physics: The Synthetic *a priori* and the Distinction Between Modal Function and Entity." *South African Journal of Philosophy*, 19:1 (2000), 26–40.

Szczekalla, M. "'Leviathan' and 'Behemoth': Nature and History in the Works of Hobbes." *Sæculum*, 49 (1998), 280–95.

Tait, L. Gordon. *The Piety of John Witherspoon: Pew, Pulpit, and Public Forum*. Louisville: Geneva Press, 2001. Pp. xxiii + 256; illustrations.

Tallerud, B. "*Febris upsaliensis* at the End of the 18th Century: A Mysterious Epidemic nearly Stopped the Scientific Career of Linne." *Lakartidningen*, 96:51–52 (1999), 5806–08.

Tarlton, Charles D. "Rehabilitating Hobbes: Obligation, Anti-Fascism and the Myth of a 'Taylor Thesis.'" *History of Political Thought*, 10:3 (1998), 407–38.

Taylor, Jacqueline. "Justice and the Foundations of Social Morality in Hume's *Treatise*." *Hume Studies*, 34:1 (1998), 5–30.

Teute, Fredrika. "The Loves of the Plants; or, The Cross-Fertilization of Science and Desire at the End of the Eighteenth Century." *Huntington Library Quarterly*, 63 (2000), 319–45.

Thompson, C. B. "Young John Adams and the New Philosophic Rationalism." *William and Mary Quarterly*, 55:2 (1998), 259–80.

Special Section: Late Entries and Reviews

Tolbert, J. T. "Fabri de Peiresc's Quest for a method to Calculate Terrestrial Longitude." *Historian*, 61:4 (1999), 801–19.

Trebiliani, Maria Luisa. "Crisi di Rapporti Stato-Chiesa nella Reppublica di Lucca (1713)." *Rivista di Storia della Chiesa in Italia*, 54 (2000), 71–89.

Tuchman, Phyllis. "The Quiet Mastery of Jean-Siméon Chardin." *Smithsonian*, 31:3 (2000), 80–88.

Tweedale, G. "Sources in the History of Occupational Health: The Turner and Newall Archive." *Social History of Medicine*, 13 (2000), 515–33.

Vaccari, Ezio. "Mining and Knowledge of the Earth in Eighteenth-Century Italy." *Annals of Science*, 57:2 (2000), 163–80.

Van Bunge, Wiep. "A New Research Project: Cartesianism, Spinozism, and Empiricism, 1650–1750." *Intellectual News*, 6–7 (2000), 100–06.

Van Bunge, Wiep. "Spinoza in English, 1700–1900." *Intellectual News*, 6–7 (2000), 65–70.

Van der Laan, J. M. "Essayistic Orders of Chaos." Pp. 191–201 of *Disrupted Patterns: On Chaos and Order in the Enlightenment*. Edited by Theodore E. D. Braun and John A. McCarthy. Amsterdam: Rodopi, 2000.

Varani, G. "The Beginnings of Leibniz's Theory of Rheoric: Jakob Thomasius's Teachings on Rhetoric and Melanchthon's Grammatical Legacy." *Studia Leibnitiana*, 31:1 (1999), 6–33.

Vaughan, M. "Slavery, Smallpox, and Revolution: 1792 in Ile de France." *Social History of Medicine*, 13 (2000), 411–28.

Vermeule, Blakey. *The Party of Humanity Writing Moral Psychology in Eighteenth-Century Britain*. Baltimore: Johns Hopkins University Press, 2000. Pp. 280.

Vieira, Antonio. *Le Saut en clair-obscur. Sermons baroques*. Genève: Ad Solem, 2000. Pp. 204.

Vignolles, H. "Distance of the Stars in the 18th Century: John Michell's Magnitude Scale." *Archives for the History of the Exact Sciences*, 55:1 (2000), 77–101.

Villis, Carl. "Bernardo Bellotto's Seven Large Views of Rome, c. 1743." *Burlington Magazine*, 142:1163 (2000), 76–81.

Wade, N. J. "Jean Théophile Desaguilers (1683–1744) and Eighteenth Century Vision Research." *British Journal of Psychology*, 91:2 (2000), 275–85.

Wait, E. "A Phenomenological Reply to Berkeley's 'Water Experiment.'" *South African Journal of Philosophy*, 17:2 (1998), 104–11.

Walis, Ruth. "Cross-currents in Astronomy and Navigation: Thomas Hornsby, FRS (1733–1810)." *Annals of Science*, 57:3 (2000), 219–40.

Watkins, E. "The Argumentative Structure of Kant's *Metaphysical Foundations of Natural Science*." *Journal of the History of Philosophy*, 36:4 (1998), 567–93.

Watts, Ruth. *Gender, Power and the Unitarians in England, 1760–1860*. (Women and Men in History.) New York: Longman, 1998. Pp. xii + 236.

Waxman, Wayne. "The Point of Hume's Skepticism with Regard to Reason." *Hume Studies*, 24 (1998), 235–73.

Webster, C. "La reinvenzione di Robert Boyle." *Revista Storica Italiana*, 109:1 (1997), 298–307.

Weekley, Carolyn J. "Edward Hicks: Quaker Minister and Artist." *Colonial Williamsburg*, 21 (1998), 68–74.

White, J. S. "The 1653 English Edition of *De motu cordis*, Shown to be Harvey's Vernacular Original and Revealing Crucial Aspects of His Pre-Circulation Theory and Its Connection to the Discovery of the Circulation of the Blood." *History and Philosophy of the Life Sciences*, 21 (1999), 65–91.

Williams, G. "Kant and the Question of Meaning." *Philosophical Forum*, 30:2 (1999), 115–31.

Williams, G. "Nietzsche's Response to Kant's Morality." *Philosophical Forum*, 30:3 (1999), 201–16.

Wilson, C. "Savagery and the Supersensible: Kant's Universalism in Historical Context." *History of European Ideas*, 24:4–5 (1998), 315–30.

Wokler, Robert. "The Enlightenment Project as Betrayed by Modernity." *History of European Ideas*, 24:45 (1998), 301–13.

Special Section: Late Entries and Reviews

Wokler, Robert. "Ernst Cassirer's Enlightenment: An Exchange with Bruce Mazlish." *Studies in Eighteenth-Century Culture*, 29 (2000), 335–48.

Wolloch, Nathaniel. "Christian Huygen's Attitude Toward Animals." *Journal of the History of Ideas*, 61:3 (2000), 415–32.

Worrall, J. "The Scope, Limits, and Distinctiveness of the Method of 'Deduction from the Phenomena': Some Lessons from Newton's 'Demonstrations' in Optics." *British Journal for the Philosophy of Science*, 51:1 (2000), 45–80.

Wouldenberg, R. V. "Thomas Reid on Memory." *Journal of the History of Philosophy*, 37:1 (1999), 117–33.

Wrigley, R. "Pathological Topographies and Cultural Itineraries: Mapping 'Mal'aria in 18th- and 19th-Century Rome." *Clio Medica*, 56 (2000), 207–28.

Wulf, S. J. "Ambivalent Romanticism: Art and Aesthetic Insight in Philosophy and Politics." *History of European Ideas*, 25 (1999), 275–89.

Yolton, John W. *Realism and Appearances: An Essay in Ontology*. Cambridge: Cambridge University Press, 2000. Pp. xiii + 157.

Young, J. "Poets and Rivers: Heidegger on Holderlin's *Der Ister*." *Dialogue–Canadian Philosophical Review*, 38:2 (1999), 391–416.

Yovel, Yirmiyahu (ed.). *Desire and Affect: Spinoza as Psychologist*. New York: Little Room Press, 1999. Pp. xvii + 294; illustrations.

Yovel, Yirmiyahu. "Kant's Practical Reason as Will: Interest, Recognition, Judgment, and Choice." *Review of Metaphysics*, 52:2 (1998), 267–94.

Zagorin, P. "Hobbes Without Grotius." *History of Political Thought*, 21:1 (2000), 16–40.

Zucker, Ross. "Unequal Property and Its Premises in Liberal Theory." *History of Philosophy Quarterly*, 17 (2000), 29–55.

Fine Arts: Painting, Prints, Drawing, Sculpture, Architecture

"American and Canadian Dissertations [in the Visual Arts], 1998." *Art Bulletin*, 81 (1999), 327–37.

Amic, Sylvain, and Sylvie Patry. "Les recueils de costumes àl'usage des peintres (XVIIIe–XIXe siècles): Un genre éditorial au service de la peinture d'histoire?" *Histoire de l'art*, 46 (2000), 39–66.

Asleson, Robyn, Shelley M. Bennett, Mark Leonard, and Shearer West (eds.). *A Passion for Performance: Sarah Siddons and Her Portraitists*. Los Angeles: J. Paul Getty Museum, 1999. Pp. xvii + 142; illustrations.

Bailey, Gauvin Alexander. *Art on the Jesuit Missions in Asia and Latin America, 1542–1773*. Toronto: University of Toronto Press, 2000. Pp. xii + 310; illustrations; plates.

Ballon, Hilary. *Louis Le Vau: Mazarin's College, Colbert's Revenge*. Princeton: Princeton University Press, 1999. Pp. ix + 248; bibliography; index; 109 black and white plates.

Barker, Elizabeth E. "New Light on 'The Orrey': Joseph Wright and the Representation of Astronomy in 18th- Century Britain." *British Art Journal*, 1 (2000), 29–37.

Baskins, Cristelle L. "On Seventeenth-Century Dutch Art." *The European Legacy*, 5:5 (2000), 729–32.

Baudino, Isabelle. "La presse et le développement du marché de l'art à Londres dans la première moitié du XVIIIe siècle." *Bulletin de la société d'études anglo-américaines des XVIIe et XVIIIe siècles*, 50 (2000), 233–45.

Belhaouari, Luis. "Jean Démosthène Dugourc: Graveur de *Sacrifice à Vénus*, d'après un tableau de Caspar Netscher anciennement dans les collections du Palais Royale." *Nouvelles de l'estampe*, 170 (2000), 27–34.

Black, Bernard. "Canova's Lost Model for Hercules and Lichas Preserved in Bronze: The Definitive French Casts, the Copies and the Confusions." *Apollo*, 152, n.s. 463 (2000), 13–21.

Bodard, Diane H. "Domenico Maria Muratori's Last Painting." *Burlington Magazine*, 142:1163 (2000), 108–11.

Special Section: Late Entries and Reviews

Bok, Marten Jan. "The Painter and His World: The Socioeconomic Approach to Seventeenth-Century Dutch Art." Pp. 224–46 of *The Golden Age of Dutch Painting in Historical Perspective*. Edited by Frans Grijzenhout and Henk van Veen. English edition translated by Andrew McCormick. Cambridge: Cambridge University Press, 1999.

Boomgaard, Jerorn. "Sources and Styles From the Art of Reality to the Reality of Art." Pp. 166–83 of *The Golden Age of Dutch Painting in Historical Perspective*. Edited by Frans Grijzenhout and Henk van Veen. English edition translated by Andrew McCormick. Cambridge: Cambridge University Press, 1999.

Bouchard, Nathalie Lemoine. "L.-N. Van Blarenberghe et le 'Traité sur la Cavalerie' de Drummond de Melfort." *Histoire del'art*, 45 (1999), 57–69.

Carasso, Dedalo. "A New Image: German and French Thought on Dutch Art, 1775–1860." Pp. 108–29 of *The Golden Age of Dutch Painting in Historical Perspective*. Edited by Frans Grijzenhout and Henk van Veen. English edition translated by Andrew McCormick. Cambridge: Cambridge University Press, 1999.

Cervantes, Xavier. "'The Famous Painter of Views Canaletti of Venice': Canaletto entre l'Italie et l'Angleterre." *Le spectateur européen*, 2 (2000), 111–34.

Châtel, Laurent. "'Getting the Picture' of the Picturesque: Some Thoughts on the Greatest British Aesthetic Muddle of the Eighteenth and Nineteenth Centuries." *Bulletin de la société d'études anglo-américaines des XVIIe et XVIIIe siècles*, 50 (2000), 229–50.

Chézaud, Patrick. "Jean Siméon Chardin et la peinture des idées britanniques." *Bulltin de la société d'études anglo-américaines des XVIIe et XVIIIe siècles*, 51 (2000), 251–72.

Christiansen, Keith. "Tiepolo, Theater, and the Notion of Theatricality." *Art Bulletin*, 81:4 (1999), 665–92.

Clifford, Jane. "Miss Berry and Canova: A Singular Relationship." *Apollo*, 152, n.s. 463 (2000), 3–12.

Collins, Jeffrey. "Obelisk Design by Giovanni Stern." *Burlington Magazine*, 142:1163 (2000), 90–100.

Coutu, Joan. "'A very good and seigneurial design': The Duke of Richmond's Academy in Whitehall." *British Art Journal*, 1 (2000), 47–54.

Craske, Matthew. *William Hogarth*. (British Artists.) London: Tate Publishing; Princeton: Princeton University Press, 2000. Pp. 80; bibliography; illustrations (some in color); index.

Rev. in rev. essay "New Hogarth Studies" by Timothy Erwin in *Eighteenth-Century Studies*, 36 (2003), 304–08, noting appreciatively that Craske's introduction to Hogarth, "published for the Tate Gallery, . . . links the social milieu of the painter to the journalism of the period."

Cross, David A. *A Striking Likeness: The Life of George Romney*. Aldershot: Ashgate, 2000. Pp. xiv + 258; plates; illustrations.

Dassas, Frédéric. *L'Illusion baroque: L'architecture de 1600 à 1750*. Paris: Gallimard, 1999. Pp. 160.

Dawson, Deirdre. "La peinture des sentiments moraux: Gavin Hamilton et Jacques-Louis David." Pp. 319–42 of *Ecosse des Lumières: le XVIIIe siècle autrement*. Edited by Pierre Morère. Grenoble: Université Stendhal, 1997.

Debenedetti, Elisa (ed.). *700 Disegnatore: Incisioni, progetti, caricature*. (Studi sul Settecento romano, 13.) Rome: Bonsignori, 1997. Pp. 301; illustrations (some in color); index.

Includes Simona Ciofetta's "Alcune edizioni di architettura di Gian Giacomo e Domenico De Rossi: Fasi preparatorie e finalità dell'opera" (65–82; 13 illustrations); Antonella Pampalone's "I'volti' della storia nelle caricature della collezione di Pier Leone Ghezzi (parte II)" (83–140; bibliography; 156 illustrations); Giulia Fusconi and Alida Moltedo's "Pier Leone Ghezzi, un incisore ignoto e l'edizione delle *Camere Sepolcrali*" (141–60; illustrations); Bruno Contardi's "Piranesi in Campidoglio" (161–83; illustrations); Elisa Debenedetti's "Giuseppe Barberi, un diario visivo idealment dedicato alla famiglia Altieri" (183–227; 40 illustrations); Segio Pace's "Disegni per un'accademia domestica: Note sull'opera architettonica di Giuseppe Barberi (Roma 1746–1809)" (229–264; 40 illustrations); Susanna Pasquali's "Echi di una committenza illustre: Un disegno anonimo dell'Accademia di S. Luca attribuito alla cerchia di Mario Asprucci" (265–277; 10 illustrations); Maria Rosaria Nappi's "Una committente inglese per l'editoria romana: La duchessa di Devonshire e l'Eneide di Virgilio" (279–96; 14 illustrations).

Deconinck-Brossard, Françoise. "Recréation picturale d'une réécration musicale: Le Tableau de la famille Sharp par Zoffany." *Bulletin de la société d'études anglo-américaines des XVIIe et XVIIIe siècles*, 51 (2000), 273–80.

De Jongh, E. "The Iconological Approach to Seventeenth-Century Dutch Painting." Pp. 200–23 of *The Golden Age of Dutch Painting in Historical Perspective*. Edited by Frans Grijzenhout and Henk van Veen. English edition translated by Andrew McCormick. Cambridge: Cambridge University Press, 1999.

Special Section: Late Entries and Reviews

De Jongh, E. "Seventeenth-Century Dutch Art Seen through a Political Prism." Pp. 141–62 of *The Golden Age of Dutch Painting in Historical Perspective*. Edited by Frans Grijzenhout and Henk van Veen. English edition translated by Andrew McCormick. Cambridge: Cambridge University Press, 1999.

Démoris, René. "Peinture et science au Siècle des lumières: L'invention d'un clivage." *Dix-huitième siècle*, 31 (1999), 45–60.

De Vries, Lyckle. "'The Felicitous Age of Painting': Eighteenth-Century Views of Dutch Art in the Golden Age." Pp. 29–44 of *The Golden Age of Dutch Painting in Historical Perspective*. Edited by Frans Grijzenhout and Henk van Veen. English edition translated by Andrew McCormick. Cambridge: Cambridge University Press, 1999.

D'Oench, Ellen G. *"Copper into Gold": Prints by John Raphael Smith, 1751–1812*. New Haven: Yale University Press, for the Paul Mellon Center for Studies in British Art, 1999. Pp. xiv + 300; illustrations.

Eidelberg, Martin. "'Ce joli morceau': *Le Royaume de l'amour* de Watteau." *Revue de l'Art*, 123 (1999), 39–46.

Eidelberg, Martin. "'Landskips...dark and gloomy': Reintroducing Henry Ferguson." *Apollo*, 152, n.s. 463 (2000), 27–36.

Eusman, Elmer. "Ploos van Amstel's Mark" *Print Quality*, 17 (2000), 248–61.

Francisco Goya, Capricci, Disastri della Guerra, Follie: Opere grafiche della Fondazione Antonio Mazzotta. Introduction by Tulliola Spargani. Milan, 2000. Pp. 120; checklist; 182 illustrations.

Briefly noted in *Print Quarterly*, 17 (2000), 392–93.

Gauss, Ulrike (ed.). *Giovanni Battista Piranesi—Die poetische Wahrheit. Die Radierungen*. With commentary by Ulrike Gauss, Corinna Höper, Stefan Heinlein, Jeannette Stoschek. Stuttgart: Hatje, 1999. Pp. 512; 380 illustrations.

Gibson-Wood, Carol. *Jonathan Richardson: Art Theorist of the Enlightenment."* New Haven: Yale University Press, for the Paul Mellon Center for Studies in British Art, 2000. Pp. vii + 264; illustrations.

Glendenning, Nigel, Enriqueta Harris, and Francis Russell. "Lord Grantham and the Taste for Velàzquez: 'The Electric Eel of the Day.'" *Burlington Magazine*, 141:1159 (1999), 598–605.

Greuze, Jean-Baptiste. *The Laundress*. Edited by Colin B. Bailey. Los Angeles: J. Paul Getty Museum, 2000. Pp. 92; illustrations.

Griffiths, Antony. "Goethe, Boerner, and the Artists of Their Time." *Print Quarterly*, 17 (2000), 51–52.

Griffiths, Antony. "'The Print in Stuart Britain' Revisited." *Print Quarterly*, 17 (2000), 115–22.

Grijzenhout, Frans. "Between Reason and Sensitivity: Foreign Views of Dutch Painting, 1660–1800." Pp. 11–28 of *The Golden Age of Dutch Painting in Historical Perspective*. Edited by Frans Grijzenhout and Henk van Veen. English edition translated by Andrew McCormick. Cambridge: Cambridge University Press, 1999.

Grijzenhout, Frans, and Henk van Veen (eds.). *The Golden Age of Dutch Painting in Historical Perspective*. English edition translated by Andrew McCormick. Cambridge: Cambridge University Press, 1999. Pp. xiii + 333; bibliography; end notes; index; list of contributors; 73 black and white plates.

The editors of *The Golden Age of Dutch Painting in Historical Perspective* have assembled a collection of essays reflecting the respective aesthetic standards and concerns of three centuries of critiques of seventeenth-century Dutch art. As the editors explain, "The present collection of essays offers neither another survey of seventeenth-century Dutch art nor a new interpretation, but rather a description of the various visions of it that have come and gone" (4). The anthology, accordingly, presents a wide variety of viewpoints, which, in turn, serve as critiques of the art critics and historians, themselves.

The foci of the essays are the paintings produced between circa 1580–1680, within the geographic boundaries of the Dutch Republic (5). The essays are divided chronologically, reflecting different periods—and perspectives—in Dutch art scholarship. The essays in the first section, *Art Lovers*, addresses views of Dutch art by critics in the outside world who analyzed the artists in terms of their positions in society. Frans Grijzenhout's contribution is particularly relevant: "Between Reason and Sensitivity: Foreign Views of Dutch Painting, 1660–1800 (11–28). The several essays in the second section, *Ideologues*, are concerned with the political and ideological focus of Dutch art criticism between the late eighteenth- and early twentieth centuries, as seen both within the Netherlands (by Dutch critics) and from the perspectives of German and French writers. In this regard, N. C. F. Van Sas ("Dutch Nationality in the Shadow of the Golden Age: National Culture and the Nation's Past, 1780–1914,"49–68) and Dedalo Carasso ("A New Image: German and French Thought on Dutch Art, 1775–1860," 108–29) address the political and specifically nationalistic concerns of the large group of art critics writing from this perspective. The third section, *Art Historians*, focuses on what the editors describe as the "art-historical scholarship"(5) which originated in the nineteenth-century and has continued to shape Dutch art criticism through the end of the twentieth-century. E. H. Kossmann's "Seventeenth-Century Dutch Art in the Eyes of Historians" (184–99) is representative.

The writing styles vary considerably. Some are quite engaging, presenting different perspectives and analyses, such as E. De Jongh's "The Iconological Approach to Seventeenth-century Dutch Painting" (200–23), and Jerorn Boomgaard's "Sources and Style: From the Art of Reality to the Reality of Art" (166–83). Others, such as de Vries' essay on eighteenth-century views of Dutch art ("'The Felicitous Age of Painting': Eighteenth-Century Views of Dutch Art in the Golden Age," 29–43) appear to be simply collections of factual material. De Vries concludes "We have found no evidence of a coherent, comprehensive view of the art of the Golden Age. Not until the nineteenth century would an attempt be made to capture the essence of the period with a single term, such as 'realist' or 'bourgeois'" (43).

The essays are generally well documented, and with some notable exceptions, substantial information is incorporated within the texts of the essays, rather than buried in footnotes. There are layers of critics and historians presented in these essays, however, many of which are poorly or incompletely documented, and the student or researcher will often be hard-pressed to identify the sources of many of the quotations and references. In the essay "Seventeenth-Century Dutch Art Seen through a Political Prism," for example, E. de Jongh quotes Adama van Scheltema's essay of 1922 on the artist and society, "Kunstenaar en samenleving" (154), which was previously published as a series of articles in the *Socialistische Gids,* the scholarly monthly of the Sociaal-Democratische Arbeiderspartij (Social-Democratic Workers party, or SDAP), but neither the 1922 essay nor its original publications is referenced in the bibliography. Scheltema's essay, as quoted by De Jongh, references, in turn, the nineteenth-century historian Robert Fruin, "...who ascribed the sudden florescence and proleferation of painting [during the Dutch Golden Age] to purely material factors: for lack of other investment opportunities, a great deal of capital went into art" (154). Regrettably, neither van Scheltema's nor Fruin's essays are documented with bibliographical references. There are similar problems in Boomgaard's essay ("Sources and Style: From th Art of Reality to the Reality of Art," 166–83), in which he addresses German art historian Alois Riegl's notion that "art developed according to '*Kunstwollen*'...which he translates as the manner in which "...at a given point, people wished to see natural things represented" (177). This notion may be interpreted as describing the way art is analysed at a given time, with particular reference to the subject matter of Golden Age Dutch Paintings. The reader will look in vain, however, for a reference to the source of Riegl's critical remarks (Alois Riegl,. "Naturwerk und Kunstwerk I,"*Gesammelte Aufsätze.* (Augsburg, 1901; 51–64).

The essays in this collection trace the changes in perspective in discussions and studies of Dutch Golden Age paintings, which was critiqued first by amateurs concerned with establishing the "Dutchness" of these paintings, then by historians, and most recently, by art historians. The use of archives has expanded significantly in the more recent studies, with a concomitant increase in the amount and quality of information available. Now with far more data available, the approach used by art historians has become more comprehensive, and focuses more on analysis, offering different interpretations rather than striving to reach specific conclusions, such as establishing the "Dutchness" of Dutch Art. In a way, this collection of essays follows the modern *Kunstwollen*, showing in its comprehensiveness, the changing perspectives during since the seventeenth century when the paintings of the Golden Age were created.

The most significant limitation in the editors' attempts to present a comprehensive survey is evident in the final essay, Eric J. Sluijter's "New Approaches in Art History and the Changing Image of Seventeenth-Century Dutch Art Between 1960 and 1990" (247–76). While acknowledging that "modern art-historical research on seventeenth-century Dutch art is a highly international affair,...and the foreign contribution to this field is—in contrast to other aspects of the Netherlands' history and culture—considerably greater than that of the Dutch themselves" (274), Sluijter, nevertheless, restricts his discussion of these "new approaches" to those of Dutch scholars, exclusively. This rather contradictory perspective, however, serves rather to reinforce earlier historians' efforts to identify and fix the "Dutchness" of Golden Age paintings, and stands as a final statement in this survey of the changing perspectives in the four centuries since the paintings themselves were created.

This collection of essays may not be as useful to the study of Dutch Art, specifically, as to the study of art history and art criticism, generally. Lay art enthusiasts with a general knowledge of Dutch art will find much of interest in the essays, but the collection will be most appreciated by readers familiar with Dutch history, in particular, the period from 1600–1900, and the Netherlands' role as a major trading capital—Jeff Warwick

Grosskurth, Brian. "Shifting Monuments: Falconet's *Peter the Great* Between Diderot and Eisenstein." *Oxford Art Journal*, 23 (2000), 49–78.

Guicharnaud, Hélène. "Louis de Boullogne au réfectoire des Petits Pères." *Gazette des Beaux Arts*, 136 (2000), 49–56.

Guilding, Ruth. "The 2nd Earl of Egremont's Sculpture Gallery at Petworth: A Plan by Charles Townley." *Apollo*, 151:n.s. 458 (2000), 27–29.

Haar. James. "Some Sixteenth-Century 'Thematic' Madrigal Anthologies." Pp. 65–80 of *Music in the Theater, Church, and Villa: Essays in Honor of Robert Lamar Weaver and Norma Wright Weaver*. Edited by Susan Parisi. (Detroit Monographs in Musicology/Studies in Music 28.) Warren: Harmonie Park Press, 2000.

Hansell, Kathleen Kuzmick. "Mozart's Milanese Theatrical Works." Pp. 195–212 of *Music in the Theater, Church, and Villa: Essays in Honor of Robert Lamar Weaver and Norma Wright Weaver*. Edited by Susan Parisi. (Detroit Monographs in Musicology/Studies in Music 28.) Warren: Harmonie Park Press, 2000.

Harriss, Ernest II. "Johann Mattheson: The Enlightenment, *L'Eclaircissement*, or *Die Aufklärung*." Pp. 187–94 of *Music in the Theater, Church, and Villa: Essays in Honor of Robert Lamar Weaver and Norma Wright Weaver*. Edited by Susan Parisi. (Detroit Monographs in Musicology/Studies in Music 28.) Warren: Harmonie Park, 2000.

Harskamp, Jaap. "Renaissance and Renovation: The Influence of Lenoir's *Musée des monumens français*, 1795–1816." *Gazette des Beaux Arts*, 136:1580 (2000), 103–08.

Heinichen, Johann David. *Neu erfundene und gründliche Anweisung zu volkommener Erlernung des General-Basses. Reprint der Ausgabe Hamburg 1711*. Herausgegeben von Wolfgang Horn. (Documenta Musicologica Erste Reihe: Druckschriften-Faksimiles.) (Association Internationale des Bibliothèques Musicales; Archives et Centres de Documentation Musicaux; Internationale Gesellschaft für Musikwissenschaft.) Kassel: Bärenreiter, 2000. Pp. 27 + 284; editorial notes; facsimile edition.

Hinterding, Erik, Ger Luijten, Martin Royalton-Kisch, and Ernst van de Wetering. *Rembrandt, the Printmaker*. Chicago: Fitzroy-Dearborn, 2000. Pp. 384; illustrations (some in color).

Published on the occasion of an exhibition in 2000–2001 at the Rijksmuseum, Amsterdam, and in 2001 at the British Museum; catalogue translated from Dutch. With "Rembrandt the Printmaker: The Shaping of an Oeuvre" by Luijten; "Watermark Research as a Tool for the Study of Rembrandt's Etchings" by Hinterding; "Remarks on Rembrandt's Oil-Sketches for Etchings" by Ernst van de Wetering; "The Role of Drawings in Rembrandt's Printmaking" by Royalton-Kisch; and the catalogue.

Special Section: Late Entries and Reviews

Hornsby, Clare. "Carlo Labruzzi: An Album of Thirteen Aquatints Dedictaed to Sir Richard Colt Hoare." *Apollo*, 151:n.s. 457 (2000), 3–8.

Jollet, Étienne. "Between Allegory and Topography: The Project for a Statue to Louis XVI in Brest (1785–1786) and the Question of the Pedestal in Public Statuary in Eighteenth-Century France." *Oxford Art Journal*, 23 (2000), 49–78.

Jollet, Étienne. "Le rire chez Fragonard." *Dix-huitième siècle*, 32 (2000), 165–80.

Jones, Sue, and Katheryn Calley Galitz. "Jacques-Louis David's Portrait of Comtesse Vilain XIII." *Burlington Magazine*, 142:1166 (2000), 301–03.

Julien, Pascal. "Pierre Legros, sculpteur romain." *Gazette des Beaux-Arts*, 135:1574 (2000), 189–214.

Kloek, J. J. "To the Land of Rembrandt: The Formation of a Literary Image of Seventeenth-Century Art in the Nineteenth Century." Pp. 91–107 of *The Golden Age of Dutch Painting in Historical Perspective*. Edited by Frans Grijzenhout and Henk van Veen. English edition translated by Andrew McCormick. Cambridge: Cambridge University Press, 1999.

Klonk, Charlotte. *Science and the Perception of Nature: British Landscape Art in the Late Eighteenth and Early Nineteenth Centuries*. New Haven: Yale University Press, 1996. Pp. 208.

Koolhaas, Eveline, and Sandra De Vries. "Back to a Glorious Past: Seventeenth-Century Art as a Model for the Nineteenth Century." Pp. 141–62 of *The Golden Age of Dutch Painting in Historical Perspective*. Edited by Frans Grijzenhout and Henk van Veen. English edition translated by Andrew McCormick. Cambridge: Cambridge University Press, 1999.

Kossmann, E. H. "Seventeenth-Century Dutch Art in the Eyes of Historians." Pp. 184–99 of *The Golden Age of Dutch Painting in Historical Perspective*. Edited by Frans Grijzenhout and Henk van Veen. English edition translated by Andrew McCormick. Cambridge: Cambridge University Press, 1999.

Krill, Rosemary Troy. *Early American Decorative Arts, 1620–1860: A Handbook for Interpreters*. Lanham: AltaMira, for the American Association for State and Local History, 2000. Pp. 430.

Laing, Alistair. "Sir Rowland and Lady Winn: A Conversation piece in the Library at Nostell Priory." *Apollo*, 151 (2000), 14–18.

Lavezzi, Élisabeth. "Peinture et savoirs scientifiques. Le cas des *Observations sur la peinture* (1753) de Jacques Gautier d'Argoty." *Dix-huitième siècle*, 31 (1999), 233–47.

Ledbury, Mark. "Unpublished Letters to Jacques-Louis David from His Pupils in Italy." *Burlington Magazine*, 142:1166 (2000), 296–300.

Ledbury, Mark. "'Vous avés achevé mes tableux': Michel-Jean Sedaine and Jacques-Louis David." *British Journal for Eighteenth-Century Studies*, 23 (2000), 59–84.

Libourel, Jean-Louis. "Les voiture de côté, ou l'art d'admirer la nature." Pp. 34–40 of *Le Voyage en France 1750–1914*. Edited by Devauges Jean-Denys and Didier Masseau. Compiègne: Société des amis du Musée national de la voiture et du tourisme, Château de Compiègne, 2000.

Lovell, Margaretta M. "Copley and the Case of the Blue dress." *Yale Journal of Criticism*, 11 (1998), 53–67.

Marsden, Jonathan. "Napoleon's Bust of 'Malbrouk.'" *Burlington Magazine*, 142:1166 (2000), 303–06.

Martin, Ann Smart, and J. Ritchie Garrison (eds.). *American Material Culture: The Shape of the Field*. Winterthur: Henry Francis du Pont Winterthur Museum, 1997. Pp. 428; illustrations.

McClellan, Andrew. "The Life and Death of a Royal Monument: Bouchardon's *Louis XV*." *Oxford Art Journal*, 23 (2000), 1–28.

McVerry, John. "William Blathwayt at Dyrham." *Apollo*, 151:n.s. 458 (2000), 36–42.

Meijers, Debora J. "Two Princely German Collections and the Image of Seventeenth-Century Dutch Art." Pp. 130–40 of *The Golden Age of Dutch Painting in Historical Perspective*. Edited by Frans Grijzenhout and Henk van Veen. English edition translated by Andrew McCormick. Cambridge: Cambridge University Press, 1999.

Miles, E. G. "'Memorials of great & good men who were my friends': Portraits in the Life of Oliver Wolcott, Jr." *Proceedings of the American Antiquarian Society*, 107:1 (1997), 105–59.

Miller, Lillian B., Sydney Hart, and David C. Ward (eds.). *The Selected Papers of Charles Wilson Peale and His Family*. Volume 5: *The Autobiography of Charles Wilson Peale*. New Haven: Yale University Press, 2000. Pp. 560.

Special Section: Late Entries and Reviews

Nemerov, Alexander. "The Ashes of Germanicus and the Skin of Painting: Sublimation and Money in Benjamin West's *Agrippina.*" *Yale Journal of Criticism*, 11 (1998), 11–27.

Ogée, Frédéric. "Chardin's Time: Reflections on the Tercentenary Exhibition and Twenty Years of Chardin Scholarship." *Eighteenth-Century Studies*, 33 (2000), 431–50.

Ogée, Frédéric. "Je-sais-quoi: la représentation des formes du vivant dans l'œuvre de William Hogarth." *Dix-huitième siècle*, 31 (1999), 249–68.

Paul, Carole. *Making a Prince's Museum: Drawings for the Late-Eighteenth-Century Redecoration of the Villa Borghese*. Los Angeles: Getty Research Institute, 2000. Pp. viii + 173; illustrations.

Pelletier, Monique. "Les guides routiers au XVIIIe siècle: Tradition et innovations (l'exemple de l'itinéraire Paris Compiègne." Pp. 7–16 of *Le Voyage en France 1750–1914*. Edited by Devauges Jean-Denys and Didier Masseau. Compiègne: Société des amis du Musée national de la voiture et du tourisme, Château de Compiègne, 2000.

Pressly, William L. "The Reappearance of a Portrait by James Bary: 'D. Solly' and 'thought's exchange.'" *British Art Journal*, 1 (2000), 62–66.

Pupil, François. "La Miniature dans la Peinture." *Gazette des Beaux Arts*, 136 (2000), 124–40.

Ramos, Julie. "Laboratoire d'une nouvelle forme d'art: L'édition des 'Minnelieder' (1803) illustrée par Phillip Otto Runge." *Histoire de l'art* (1999), 71–84.

Ridgway, Christopher, and Robert Williams (eds.). *Sir John Vanbrugh and Landscape Architecture in Baroque England, 1690–1730*. Stroud: Suttton, in association with the National Trust, 1999. Pp. xiv + 242; illustrations; maps; portraits.

Rosenberg, Pierre, and Marie-Anne Dupuy (eds.). *Dominique-Vivant Denon: L'œil de Napoléon*. Paris: Réunion des Musées nationaux, 1999. Pp. 540; illustrations.

Catalogue of an exhibition at the Louvre.

Screech, Timon. *Sex and the Floating World: Erotic Images in Japan, 1700–1820*. Honolulu: University of Hawaii Press, 1999. Pp. 319; illustrations.

Shanes, Eric. "Turner at the British Institution in 1806: A Canvas United in a World Divided." *Apollo*, 150:452 (1999), 30–36.

Sluijter, Eric J. "New Approaches in Art History and the Changing Image of Seventeenth-Century Dutch Art between 1960 and 1990." Pp. 247–76 of *The Golden Age of Dutch Painting in Historical Perspective*. Edited by Frans Grijzenhout and Henk van Veen. English edition translated by Andrew McCormick. Cambridge: Cambridge University Press, 1999.

Smiles, Sam. *Eye Witness: Artists and Visual Documentation in Britain, 1770–1830*. Aldershot: Ashgate, 2000. Pp. x + 216; illustrations.

Smiles, Sam. *J. M. W. Turner*. Princeton: Princeton University Press, 2000. Pp. 80; illustrations.

Sørensen, Bent. "Some Sources for Piranesi's Early Architectural Fantasies." *Burlington Magazine*, 142:1163 (2000), 82–89.

Stevenson, C. "Hogarth's Mad King and His Audiences." *History Workshop*, 49 (2000), 25–43.

Sweetman, John. *The Artist and the Bridge, 1700–1900*. Aldershot: Ashgate, 2000. Pp. xii + 208; illustrations.

Van Sas, N. C. F. "Dutch Nationality in the Shadow of the Golden Age: National Culture and the Nation's Past, 1780–1914." Pp. 49–68 of *The Golden Age of Dutch Painting in Historical Perspective*. Edited by Frans Grijzenhout and Henk van Veen. English edition translated by Andrew McCormick. Cambridge: Cambridge University Press, 1999.

Verplanck, Anne. "The Social Meaning of Portrait Miniatures in Philadelphia, 1760–1820." Pp. 195–223 of *American Material Culture: The Shape of the Field*. Edited by Ann Smart Martin and J. Ritchie Garrison. Winterthur: Henry Francis du Pont Winterthur Museum, 1997.

Wendors, Richard. "After Sir Joshua." Pp. 260–70 of *Representations of the Self from the Renaissance to Romanticism*. Edited by Partick Coleman, Jayne Lewis, and Jill Kowalik. Cambridge: Cambridge University Press, (2000).

Wind, Barry. *A Foul and Pestilential Congregation": Images of "Freaks" in Baroque Art*. Aldershot: Ashgate, 2000. Pp. 240.

Wine, Humphrey. "Quelques aspects de l'interaction entre la science, la technique et les beaux-arts." *Dix-huitième siècle*, 31 (1999), 107–22.

Wintermute, Alan, and Colin B. Bailey. *Watteau and His Circle: French Drawing from 1700–1750*. New York: Merrill Holberton Publishers, 2000. Pp. 268; illustrations.

Youngquist, P. "In the Face of Beauty: Camper, Bell, Reynolds, Blake." *Word and Image*, 16:4 (2000), 319–34.

Fine Arts: Theater

Betzwieser, Thomas. "Musical Setting and Scenic Movement: Chorus and *chœur dansé* in Eighteenth-Century Parisian Opéra." *Cambridge Opera Journal*, 12 (2000/Online publications: 20 March, 2001), 1–28.

Dobson, M. "A Dog at All Things: The Transformation of the Onstage Canine, 1550–1850." *Performance Research*, 5:2 (2000), 116–24.

Frantz, Pierre. "Rire et théâtre carnavalesque pendant la Révolution." *Dix-huitième siècle*, 32 (2000), 291–306.

Glen, Robert. "'Adieu the Delights of the Stage': An Anti-Methodist Song of 1746." *Notes and Queries*, n.s. 46 (1999), 350–56.

Gustafson, Sandra M. *Eloquence in Power: Oratory and Performance in Early America*. Chapel Hill: University of North Carolina Press, 2000. Pp. 287; illustrations.

Hillmer, Rüdiger. *Die napoleonische Theaterpolitik: Geschäftstheater in Paris 1799–1815*. Köln: Böhlau Verlag, 1999. Pp. xiii + 536; maps.

Houchin, John H. "The Struggle for Virtue: Professional Theatre in 18th Century Philadelphia." *Theatre History Studies*, 19 (1999), 167–88.

Hume, Robert D. "Jeremy Collier and the Future of the London Theater in 1698." *Studies in Philology*, 96:4 (1999), 480–511.

Johnson, Odai. "Thomas Jefferson and the Colonial American Stage." *Virginia Magazine of History and Biography*, 108 (200), 139–54.

Kaplan, Deborah. "Learning 'to speak the English language': *The Way of the World* on the Twentieth-Century American Stage." *Theatre Journal*, 49 (1997), 301–21.

Mannucci, Erica J. *Il Patriota e il vaudeville. Teatro, publico e porter nella Parigi della Rivoluzione*. Naples: Vivarium, 1998. Pp. 540.

Mason, Jeffrey D., and J. Ellen Gainor (eds.). *Performing America: Cultural Nationalism in American Theater.* Ann Arbor: University of Michigan Press, 1999. Pp. vi + 250; illustrations.

McPherson, Heather. "Masculinity, Femininity, and the Tragic Sublime: Reinventing Lady Macbeth." *Studies in Eighteenth-Century Culture,* 29 (2000), 299–333.

Nicassio, Susan Vidiver. *Tosca's Rome: The Play and the Opera in Historical Perspective, with a New Appendix..* Chicago: University of Chicago Press, 1999. Pp. xix + 343. Appendices; bibliography; chapter notes; index; musical examples; 49 black-and-white plates.

This book has its inspiration in the author's passionate devotion to Puccini's opera *Tosca*. The opera, in turn, was inspired by the 1887 play by the French dramatist Victorien Sardou entitled *La Tosca* (distinguished from the opera here, as in the book, by the definite article). Sardou's play is based on a fictionalisation of his interpretation of events in Rome in the years 1798–1800 and *Tosca's Rome* thus completes the circle by placing the opera in the context of the political, social, and cultural background of its period.

As implied by its title, *Tosca's Rome* has two interrelated themes. The first of these is the opera itself, the second, the historical setting of Rome at the end of the eighteenth century. Chapter 1, of the two introductory chapters, is devoted to the story of the opera's creation, from its roots in Sardou's inspiration, followed by Puccini's obsession with the story after first viewing *La Tosca* in Milan in 1889, to its opening in Rome, in 1900. The chapter includes extensive detail on the political and religious situation in Italy during the writing of the opera, and the influence of these contemporary circumstances on the composer. In contrast, Chapter 2, *Rome without a Pope,* paints a detailed picture of life in Rome during the last years of the eighteenth century. There follow three chapters devoted to "The Painter's Rome," "The Singer's Rome," and "The Policeman's Rome," reflecting the backgrounds of the three principal protagonists of the opera—Cavaradossi, Tosca, and Scarpia, respectively. A major part of the book (one-hundred pages) consists in four chapters dealing with the three acts of the opera, and the "Entr'acte" after Act One. There are three Appendices relating to the writing of the opera: Appendix I compares in detail the actions of opera and play, the latter covering a longer period of time, while Appendix II discusses briefly the making of the libretto. Appendix III, new to the paperback edition, is entitled "1896 Working Papers for *Tosca*." It provides an account of documents, found recently at Colleretto, which throw new light on the creation of the opera, including a description of Puccini's discarded material.

In his distillation of *La Tosca* for the operatic stage, Puccini and his collaborators condensed the action to a sixteen-hour period between midday on 17 June and 4:00 a.m. on June 18, 1800. The date is fixed by reference to the battle of Marengo, reports of which reached Rome at that time (first the premature announcement of an Austrian alliance victory, followed by news of Napoleon' late rally). While there is no suggestion that the plot is other than fiction, there is no doubt that it is a plausible invention written with a high degree of realism. The frontispiece provides a map of the northwest quarter of Rome showing the relevant landmarks: the Church of Sant'Andrea della Valle, the Farnese Palace, the Argentina Theatre where Tosca was engaged, and the dominating Castel Sant'Angelo. Only the location of Cavaradossi's villa is a fiction. Inscribed on the map are the routes through the streets followed by the major participants during the course of the action. Nicassio points out, however, these are not without dramatic inconsistencies and logistical impossibilities.

The details and the characters ring true—the insecure prison system, the romantic painter dabbling in radical politics, involved in a liaison with a rising star of the opera, who lives for her art and for love, and the lascivious and sadistic police chief who exploits the relationship to his own ends. In separate chapters, Nicassio suggests the contemporary backgrounds of each of these characters and identifies from a mass of anecdotal and substantiated stories possible real-life models for the roles in Sardou's play. Cavaradossi, for example, could be a former student of David, whose pupils dominated the Prix-de-Rome at the time. Tosca could be one of many young opera singers

Special Section: Late Entries and Reviews

to emerge from convent education in Verona and elsewhere, gradually replacing *castrati* in the female roles (Nicassio also provides a detailed account of the history of opera in Rome during the eighteenth century).

The last four chapters, devoted to the opera itself, provide a comprehensive and extremely detailed analysis of the music, the libretto, the motivations of the characters and their actions on- and off-stage. Nicassio, here, displays her musical as well as her historical knowledge. Her analysis and discussion illustrates how little flexibility can be exercised by directors of this opera if full justice is to be done to Puccini's invention!

Nicassio has based her book on a mass of meticulously researched and clearly presented evidence. The bibliography lists primary sources in Rome, London, Milan, and New York, as well as fifteen pages of secondary sources. It is to be regretted, however, that the bibliography is not divided into two sections, on "Tosca" and on "Rome," respectively, thus clearly separating fiction from fact— Peter Schofield

O'Brien, John. "Harlequin Britain: Eighteenth-Century Pantomime and the Cultural Location of Entertainment(s)." *Theatre Journal*, 50 (1998), 489–510.

Plagnol-Diéval, Marie-Emmanuelle. "Le théâtre de Carmontelle: jeux de miroir et jeu de société." *Revue d'histoire du théâtre*, 2 (1997), 163–78.

Richards, Jeffrey H. "Brogue Irish Take the American Stage, 1767–1808." *New Hibernia Review*, 3:3 (1999), 47–64.

Scherl, Adolf. *Berufstheater in Prag 1680–1739*. Wien: Verlag der Oesterreichischen Akademie der Wissenschaften, 1999. Pp. 245.

Strand, Ginger. "The Theater and the Republic: Defining Party on Boston's Rival Stages." Pp. 19–36 of *Performing America: Cultural Nationalism in American Theater*. Edited by Jeffrey D. Mason and J. Ellen Gainor. Ann Arbor: University of Michigan Press, 1999.

White, Barbara. "Music Drama on the Concert Stage: Voice, Character and Performance in Judith Weir's *The Consolations of Scholarship*." *Cambridge Opera Journal*, 12 (2000/Online publications: 20 March, 2001), 55–79.

Fine Arts: Music

Angelis, Marcello de. The Magical Moment in Mozart's *Zauberflöte*, and a Note on the Production of the Opera at the Teatro di Santa Maria in Florence in 1818." Pp. 259–62 of *Music in the Theater, Church, and Villa: Essays in Honor of Robert Lamar Weaver and Norma Wright Weaver*. Edited by Susan Parisi. (Detroit Monographs in Musicology/Studies in Music 28.) Warren: Harmonie Park Press, 2000.

Bartlet, M. Elizabeth C. *Étienne-Nicolas Méhul and Opera: Source and Archival Studies of Lyric Theatre During the French Revolution, Consulate and Empire*. 2 volumes. Heilbronn: Musik-Edition Galland, 1999. Pp. xxviii + 912; illustrations.

Bashford, Christins, and Leanne Langley (eds.). *Music and British Culture, 1785–1914: Essays in Honour of Cyril Ehrlich*. New York: Oxford University Press, 2000. Pp. 488; illustrations; music examples.

Belfy, Jeanne Marie. "Henry Wolking's Ballet Forever Yesterday." Pp. 291–306 of *"Music in the Theater, Church, and Villa: Essays in Honor of Robert Lamar Weaver and Norma Wright Weaver*. Edited by Susan Parisi. (Detroit Monographs in Musicology/Studies in Music 28.) Warren: Harmonie Park Press, 2000.

Bower, Calvin M. "Alleluia, Cofitemini Domino, Qoniam Bonus—An *Allewluia, Versus, Sequentia*, and *Five Prosae* recorded in Aquitanian Sources." Pp. 3–30 of *Music in the Theater, Church, and Villa: Essays in Honor of Robert Lamar Weaver and Norma Wright Weaver*. Edited by Susan Parisi. (Detroit Monographs in Musicology/Studies in Music 28.) Warren: Harmonie Park Press, 2000.

Brunner, Lance W. "The Tao of Singing: On the Schola Hungarica's Interpretation of the Nonantolan Sequences." Pp. 33–50 of *Music in the Theater, Church, and Villa: Essays in Honor of Robert Lamar Weaver and Norma Wright Weaver*. Edited by Susan Parisi. (Detroit Monographs in Musicology/Studies in Music 28.) Warren: Harmonie Park Press, 2000.

Burden, Michael (ed.). *Henry Purcell's Operas: The Complete Texts*. New York: Oxford University Press, 2000. Pp. 544; illustrations.

Cantagrel, Gilles. *Passion Bach: L'album d'une vie*. Paris: Textuel, 2000. Pp. 214; illustrations.

Carroll, Paul. *Baroque Woodwind Instruments: A Guide to Their History, Repertoire and Basic Technique*. Aldershot: Ashgate, 1999. Pp. 194.

Cash, Alice Hudnall. "Wanda Landowska and the Revival of the Harpsichord." Pp. 277–84 of *Music in the Theater, Church, and Villa: Essays in Honor of Robert Lamar Weaver and Norma Wright Weaver*. Edited by Susan Parisi. (Detroit Monographs in Musicology/Studies in Music 28.) Warren: Harmonie Park Press, 2000.

Chusid, Martin (ed.). *A Companion to Schubert's 'Schwanengesang.' History, Poets, Analysis, Performance*. New Haven: Yale University Press, 2000. Pp. ix + 230; bibliography; chapter notes; index; musical examples; tables.

Special Section: Late Entries and Reviews

Chusid, Martin (ed.). *Franz Schubert, 'Schwanengesang.' Facsimiles of the Autograph Score and Sketches, and Reprint of the First Edition.* New Haven: Yale University Press, 2000. Pp. xxiv + 149; editorial notes; end notes; musical examples.

This is the first time that the complete autograph score of Schubert's *Schwanengesang* appears in facsimile (Walter Dürr's 1978 facsimile is missing "Die Taubenpost"), and the significance of the event is underscored by the concurrent issue of a companion volume of essays written by various scholars. Included in the handsome facsimile volume are the few surviving sketches for the work and the 1829 first edition issued by Tobias Haslinger. Textually, the first edition differs little from the autograph score, which had served as the *Stichvorlage* (the copy of the music on which the first edition was directly based). It is however a beautiful piece of engraving, and its inclusion in the facsimile volume allows us an unusual opportunity to enjoy something of the quality of Haslinger's work, which was highly regarded by his Viennese contemporaries. (This estimation may be better appreciated by comparing the *Schwanengesang* first edition with some of the less-beautiful first editions (such as those of Beethoven's String Quartet in F minor, Op. 95 and the "Archduke" Trio, Op. 97) previously issued by S. A. Steiner, whose firm Haslinger took over completely in 1826.)

The photography for the facsimiles is sharp and the reproduction is in monochrome halftone. For ease of reference, the editor has thoughtfully supplied measure numbers corresponding to the music at the bottom of each page of the autograph score. That the facsimiles of the sketches and the autograph score do not appear in shades of color that mimic the original sources as closely as modern technology can allow is a real pity, for the different layers of writing and the many subtleties of a composer's hand often represent aspects of the compositional process that a monochrome reproduction simply cannot capture. For this reason, Chusid's commentary on the sketches, and on the alterations and corrections that Schubert made in the autograph score, are particularly helpful, even though it cannot take the place of a firsthand examination by anyone engaged in an in-depth study of the manuscripts.

The essays in the companion volume discuss *Schwanengesang*'s early reception (Walburga Litschauer, 5–13); the poets of the work, namely Rellstab, Heine, and Seidl (Martin Chusid, 14–52); and issues of performance and analysis (Chusid, Walter Dürr, Steven Lubin, and Edward Cone). Among these, Cone's "Repetition and Correspondence in *Schwanengesang*" (53–89) is particularly important. Arguing against the traditional categorization of songs into either strophic, through-composed, or modified strophic because it leaves out other songs that do not conform to these three categories, Cone offers in its place a bipartite classification comprising Type A and Type B. Type A includes all the three song categories in the traditional categorization by virtue of the fact that their design "explicitly depends on correspondence between words and music" (54). Type B refers to "songs whose music exhibits a design, such as a conventional "generic" form, that is explicable in absolute musical terms" (54). These are songs that are "more abstractly designed" (55) and Cone gives, as generic examples, the *da capo aria* and a song crafted in sonata form. The value of Cone's classification becomes evident in the way he uses it as a firm basis for his analysis and criticism of Schubert's music and text-setting in *Schwanengesang*. Brilliant and perceptive, the discussion ends with an examination of "Die Taubenpost," the only setting of a poem in the work that is not by Rellstab or Heine. Cone believes that Schubert meant this song, based on a text by Seidl, to be an essential "addendum to the two conjoined cycles" (85). This claim contradicts two previous and very different notions about *Schwanengesang*: (a) that the songs, although published posthumously under a fitting single title, do not form a cycle; and (b) that the Rellstab songs do indeed form a cycle, while the Heine songs may be viewed as cyclic if they are rearranged in an order reflecting the original poetic source.

Cone's claim that *Schwanengesang* features two conjoined song cycles with their component songs laid out in Schubert's original order is shared by Chusid, who makes a strong and convincing argument for it in "The Sequence of the Heine Songs and Cyclicism in *Schwanengesang* (159–73)." To be sure, Schubert has written out the seven Rellstab songs and six Heine songs as two separate groups in the autograph ("Die Taubenpost" comes at the end after the Heine songs), and it seems to me that the way in which he sometimes begins, within the same group, one song after another in the same page already indicates that he either meant the songs of each group to relate to each other in the sequence that he has specified, or that the sequence is totally arbitrary. In either case, the notion that the Heine songs should be rearranged to form a viable cycle, which some scholars have put forth, cannot hold.

Of the remaining essays in the volume, I should mention in particular Chusid's helpful "Texts and Commentary" (90–151) and Steven Lubin's "The Three Styles of *Schwanengesang*" (191–204). The former is a comprehensive discussion of the songs taken one at a time (and repeating some of the commentary already offered in the facsimile volume), while the latter is an insightful probe into the different voices of late Schubert. A discography by Richard Lesueur (205–10) listing recordings of the work dating back to as early as 1934 forms the last chapter of this useful volume—Seow-Chin Ong

Chusid, Martin. "The Poets of *Schwanengesang*: Rellstab, Heine, and Seidl." Pp. 14–52 of *A Companion to Schubert's 'Schwanengesang.' History, Poets, Analysis, Performance*. Edited by Martin Chusid. New Haven: Yale University Press, 2000.

Chusid, Martin. "The Sequence of the Heine songs and Cyclicism in *Schwanengesang*. Pp. 159–73 of *A Companion to Schubert's 'Schwanengesang'. History, Poets, Analysis, Performance*. Edited by Martin Chusid. New Haven: Yale University Press, 2000.

Chusid, Martin. "Texts and Commentary." Pp. 90–158 of *A Companion to Schubert's "Schwanengesang." History, Poets, Analysis, Performance*. Edited by Martin Chusid. New Haven: Yale University Press, 2000.

Cohen, Alabert. "Musicians, Amateurs, and Collectors: Early French Auction Catalogues as Musical Sources." *Music & Letters*, 81:1 (2000), 1–12.

Cone, Edward T. "Repetition and Correspondence in *Schwanengesang*. Pp. 53–89 of *A Companion to Schubert's 'Schwanengesang.' History, Poets, Analysis, Performance*. Edited by Martin Chusid. New Haven: Yale University Press, 2000.

Crosby, Brian. "Stephen and Other Paxtons: An Investigation into the Identities and Careers of a Family of Eighteenth-Century Musicians." *Music & Letters*, 81:1 (2000), 13–40.

Degott, Pierre. "Le livret d'oratorio au XVIIIe siècle: Quelle sorte de livre?" *Bulletin de la société d'études anglo-américaines des XVIIe et XVIIIe siiècles*, 50 (2000), 81–98.

Deshoulières, Christophe. *L'Opéra baroque et la scène moderne*. Paris: Fayard, 2000. Pp. 984.

Donaldson, William. *The Highland Pipe and Scottish Society, 1750–1950: Transmission, Change and the Concept of Tradition*. East Linton: Tuckwell, 2000. Pp. x + 518.

Special Section: Late Entries and Reviews

Dorival, Jérôme. *La Cantate française au XVIIIe siècle.* Paris: Presses universitaires de France, 1999. Pp. 127; music.

Dubois, Pierre. "Les impressions successives: Jardins, musiques et temporalité dans *The Elements of Criticism* de Henry Home, Lord Kames." *Bulletin de la société d'études anglo-américaines des XVIIe et XVIIIe siècles*, 51 (2000), 215–28.

Etzion, J. "Spanish Music as Perceived in Western Music Historiography: A Case of the Black Legend." *International Review of the Aesthetics and Sociology of Music*, 29:2 (1998), 93–120.

Fanelli, J. G. "The Manfredini Family of Musicians of Pistoia, 1684–1803." *Studi Musicali*, 26:1 (1997), 187 ff.

Fink, M. "The Ball Scenes in Operas." *International Review of the Aesthetics and Sociology of Music*, 28:2 (1998), 169–88.

Fruchtman, Caroline S. "The Influence of Architect and Playwright Sir John Vanbrugh and His Musical Taste on the London Stage, 1696–1711." Pp. 145–58 of *Music in the Theater, Church, and Villa: Essays in Honor of Robert Lamar Weaver and Norma Wright Weaver.* Edited by Susan Parisi. (Detroit Monographs in Musicology/Studies in Music 28.) Warren: Harmonie Park Press, 2000.

Gianturco, Carolyn. "The 'Staging' of Genres Other Than Opera in Baroque Italy." Pp. 113–30 of *Music in the Theater, Church, and Villa: Essays in Honor of Robert Lamar Weaver and Norma Wright Weaver.* Edited by Susan Parisi. (Detroit Monographs in Musicology/Studies in Music 28.) Warren: Harmonie Park Press, 2000.

Gibson, John G. *Traditional Gaelic Bagpiping, 1745–1945.* Montreal: McGill–Queen's University Press, 2000. Pp. 424.

Glixon, Jonathan E., and Beth L. Glixon. "Oil and Opera Don't Mix: The Biography of Sant'Aponal, a Seventeenth-Century Venetian Opera Theater." Pp. 131–44 of *Music in the Theater, Church, and Villa: Essays in Honor of Robert Lamar Weaver and Norma Wright Weaver.* Edited by Susan Parisi. (Detroit Monographs in Musicology/Studies in Music 28.) Warren: Harmonie Park Press, 2000.

Green, Jonathan D. *A Conductor's Guide to the Choral-Orchestral Works of J. S. Bach.* Lanham: Scarecrow Press, 2000. Pp. ix + 622.

Heinichen, Johann David. *Neu erfundene und gründliche Anweisung zu volkommener Erlernung des General-Basses. Reprint der Ausgabe Hamburg 1711.* Herausgegeben von Wolfgang Horn. (Documenta Musicologica Erste Reihe: Druckschriften-Faksimiles.) (Association Internationale des Bibliothèques Musicales; Archives et Centres de Documentation Musicaux; Internationale Gesellschaft für Musikwissenschaft.) Kassel: Bärenreiter, 2000. Pp. 27 + 284; editorial notes; facsimile edition.

See also Johann Mattheson, *Der volkommene Capellmeister (Hamburg, 1739). Studienausgabe im Neusatz des Textes und der Noten.*

The two books under consideration here are the product of an excellent initiative by Bärenreiter Verlag to make widely available some of the most important primary texts of the eighteenth century. Johann David Heinichen's (1683–1729) *Anweisung* is the earlier chronologically, dating from 1711, and it is a treatise on the art of thorough bass, a staple practice of both composers and performers of the time. This is Heinichen's first foray into a subject that occupied him throughout his life and culminated in his magisterial compendium *Der General-Bass in der Composition* published in Dresden in 1728. Prefaced by an excellent introduction by Wolfgang Horn, this facsimile edition of the 1711 treatise makes the work available for the first time in modern print. This is especially welcome as the treatise is not only important in itself, but also lends itself as a sounding board for comparisons with the 1728 treatment which, as a complete rewriting and enlargement, represents Heinichen's mature thoughts on the subject. What intervened between the two editions and influenced his ideas was Heinichen's sojourn in Venice, 1711–16, where he went to compose operas and absorb the Italian operatic style. Heinichen's work on thorough bass influenced all other contemporary German theorists of the time, including Mattheson who repeatedly drew attention to his name in his theoretical works. The reason for Heinichen's long influence is that he viewed thorough bass not only as the art of accompaniment, but also as the embodiment of musical composition itself, and with this view, his treatises carried significant original thought and insight.

Mattheson was a seasoned treatise writer with more than a dozen major volumes and a number of smaller works published during his life. He viewed musical composition as part of the larger context of his period's intellectuality, and his *Der volkommene Capellmeister* is perhaps the single most important German treatise of the first half of the eighteenth century. It deserves this title not only because of the sheer volume and comprehensiveness of its coverage, but also because of the depth and insight of Mattheson's views. In short, this is the work of maturity of an excellent musical mind of the Enlightenment. This new release in the 'Bärenreiter Studienausgaben' series provides a faithful transcription of the text and musical examples in modern script. The emphasis here is on transcription, retaining all language and punctuation irregularities and aiming to provide a study-text with as few editorial interventions as possible, while at the same time bypassing the difficulties associated with reading German facsimili of the period. The treatise itself hardly need any introduction at all. Although written from a German perspective, the image of musical thought it captures carries large elements of pan-European validity. Furthermore, some particularly important topics for modern historians are those new areas that Mattheson ventured into, as for example the relationship between rhetoric and musical composition, a theory of melody writing, and the expression of the Affections. All these were emerging concepts in eighteenth-century musical aesthetics, and Mattheson's treatment of these subjects is of paramount importance. One wishes that the publication of similar titles by Bärenreiter continues.—Vassilis Vavoulis

Heyink, R. "Niccolo Jommelli, Maestro di Cappella of Santa Maria dell'Anima in Rome, the German National Church." *Studi Musicali*, 26:2 (1997), 417–43.

Special Section: Late Entries and Reviews

Hunter, Mary. *The Culture of Opera Buffa in Mozart's Vienna: A Poetics of Entertainment*. Princeton: Princeton University Press, 1999. Pp. xiii + 331; appendices; bibliography; index; musical examples.

The title of this ambitious and impressive book encapsulates a tension that is all but inescapable when discussing *opera buffa* in Vienna in the later eighteenth century. On one side, Mozart so dominates our perceptions that all musical events at that time seem peripheral to him, and even the city itself should be thought of as his. Yet, on the other side, an examination of his cultural context can be leveling to the extent that Mozart vanishes into the crowd of his contemporaries and Vienna, then, seems to have belonged either to nobody, or just as much to the likes of Salieri, Sarti, and Vincente Martin y Soler. Mary Hunter embraces rather than fights this tension, allowing it to give her study a twin-agenda. Explicitly, her book is not about Mozart (24), rather, she investigates the conventions and habits of the 130 or so *opere buffe* produced in Vienna between 1770 and 1790, focusing particularly on issues of gender and class. Hunter, however, realises that most readers will come to the subject through Mozart, and one of the things she wants to explain is how Mozart's comic masterpieces fit into the world of this repertory (24). The book, accordingly, is divided into three parts, the first two concerned with the repertory as a whole, and the third with a contextual case-study of *Così fan tutte*.

Hunter first considers how *opere buffe* functioned as entertainment, framing this within the wider context of late-eighteenth-century Viennese society (Chapters 1–3). Her concern is to show how the repertory's pleasure-giving qualities were not simply ends in themselves, but were also reflections of social class structures. The amusing reversals and transgressions of prevailing class-hierarchies, for example, are constrained within an overall structure that ultimately serves to reinforce the existing social status quo. The portrayal of female characters is also interestingly dealt with, in the light of the bourgeois reconfiguring of gender roles at that time.

Part Two (Chapters 4–7) addresses the social implications of the closed structural units, aria and ensemble, in *opera buffa*. Arias, the cornerstone for communicating character, are classified into five types: *buffa, serva/contadina*, noble, rage, and sentimental. Most of the types are illustrated with an example quoted in complete score. Ensembles are divided into two types—those which occur in mid-act, and those which begin or end an act. Discussion focuses particularly on the assertion of individual versus collective identity. Form is analysed, yet formalism is avoided. If the dissection leaves the reader to piece together the operas as wholes, that is a challenge to relish, given Hunter's stimulus.

The final section of the book (Chapters 8–9) places *Così fan tutte* within the context revealed in the rest of the text. First, *Così* is put in conversation with interlocutors both literary (Ovid, Boccaccio, Ariosto) and musical—Salieri's *La grotta di Trofonio*, which is shown to be a kind of anti-model. Audience recognition of this intertextuality is considered to be part of the pleasure-giving power of opera buffa. Hunter then turns to *Così's* relationship with conventions. *Così* is a particularly apt choice here, for, as Hunter argues, this opera is not simply conventional, but profoundly about the *meaning* of convention (24). Generic types are shown to appear in unexpected circumstances, and social themes are illustrated in Despina's relationship to her superiors. Hunter closes with a reassessment of the long-debated "mismatch" between da Ponte's playful lyrics and Mozart's exquisite music. While most previous critics have sought to divorce the transcendent Mozart from the trivial da Ponte, Hunter re-joins them, locating the music's raw sensual beauty within the overall dramaturgical fabric.

In laying out the "poetics of entertainment"—the book's subtitle—Hunter both provides new thoughts on familiar works and an invaluable guide to the rest of the *buffa* repertory in Viennese opera repertory. Her concept of "conversation," which amounts to exploring the network of relationships between composers, librettists, audiences, works, and conventions, allows her to shuttle between one type of material and another, as well as between the particular and the general, with a deftness that proves illuminating on both sides. In providing a methodological approach that can easily be transferred, this book will be valuable to everyone with an interest in opera and its meanings—D. J. Burn

Kassler, Michael, and Philip Olleson. *Samuel Wesley (1766–1837): A Source Book*. Aldershot: Ashgate, 2000. Pp. xxiii + 765; portrait.

Kennesen, Claude. *Musical Prodigies: Perilous Journeys, Remarkable Lives*. Portland: Amadeus Press, 1999. Pp. 351; bibliography, illustrations.

On Christmas Eve, 1781, an event took place at the court of Joseph II in Vienna which was to prove the genesis of the piano competition and, in a different sense, the origin of this highly entertaining book by Claude Kennesen. On that occasion, the greatest prodigy the world has ever known, Wolfgang Amadeus Mozart, displayed his talents in the presence of the Emperor in apposition to those of the celebrated Italian pianist and composer, Muzio Clementi. While not a competition per se, it was so regarded by the assembled guests and by Emperor Joseph, who declared Mozart the winner by sending him a prize of fifty ducats. From this interesting event sprang two branches of musical history, the instrumental competition with all its implications for individual careers, and the amazing and inexplicable phenomenon of the musical prodigy. Although musical competitions are far removed, today, from the demonstrations of skill and musical "tricks" that characterized Mozart's performances for the royal courts of Europe, these exhibitions and Mozart's astounding virtuosity still serve as the silent, unverbalized paradigms, the "bench-marks" for the recitals and competitions of contemporary artists.

The very existence of the musical prodigy is as mesmerizing as it is difficult to comprehend. Kennesen has done an outstanding job of combining a plethora of anecdotal material sufficient to satisfy the most avid of readers who cannot get enough of the lives of famous people with a thoughtful consideration of just what the phenomenon of the highly gifted musical child consists of. Most of this discussion is contained in the illuminating *Reader's Guide*, which appears as the second of two introductory chapters and a postlude by the singer Bejun Mehta. The author then proceeds to give synopses of the childhoods of famous musicians, as well as the notable events of their later lives, beginning with Mozart, Paganini, and Clara Schumann, and continuing with Pablo Casals, Jascha Heifetz, Emanuel Feuermann, Gregor Piatigorsky, and Artur Rubenstein.

After touching on the younger prodigies Glenn Gould, Martha Argerich, Daniel Barenboim, and Van Cliburn, the subject of competitions is taken up with a consideration of the relationship between winning competitions in the twentieth century and the procurement of artist management (Leopold Mozart's *ad hoc* role for much of his son's career), followed by a detailed description of the First Tchaikovsky Competition in Moscow in 1958 and the First International Henryk Wieniawski Violin Competition in 1935. The latter occasions look into the lives and careers of such extraordinary violinists as David Oistrakh, Henri Temianka, Ida Haendel, and Ginette Neveu, whose career was tragically cut short at the age of thirty-one. Also included are the eminent artists Isaac Stern, Janos Starker, Yehudi Menuhin, Mstislav Rostropovich, Ruggiero Ricci, Zara Nelsova, Jacqueline du Pré, Yo-Yo Ma, and a selection of outstanding representatives of other instruments such as the guitarist Andrés Segovia, the bassist Gary Karr, the violist William Primrose, and the percussionist Evelyn Glennie. The lives and careers of some singers and conductors and one composer, Samuel Barber, together with three very touching portraits of the gypsy violinist Kató Havas and two of Kennesen's own cello students, Eric Wilson and the remarkable Shauna Rolston, complete the book.

Throughout, one is struck by both the luminous quality inherent in these unusually gifted lives and by the tastefulness of Kennesen's awe and understanding of them. A personal acquaintance with a number of the artists mentioned did not deter this reviewer from eagerly devouring page after page of fascinating detail. This is a book both to enjoy as a breathtaking page turner and as a serious presentation of that elusive ideal, the *Wunderkind*—Roy Bogas

Kirkendale, Warren. "Ciceronians Versus Aristotelians on the *ricercar* as Exordium, from Bembo to Bach." *Studi Musicali*, 26:1 (1997), 3–54.

Special Section: Late Entries and Reviews

Kirkendale, Warren. "On te Rhetorical Interpretation of the *ricercar* and J. S. Bach's *Musical Offering*." *Studi Musicali*, 26:2 (1997), 331–76.

Lawson, Colin. *The Early Clarinet: A Practical Guide.* (Cambridge Handbooks to the Historical Performance of Music.) Cambridge: Cambridge University Press, 2000. Pp. xiii + 128; illustrations.

LeSueur, Richard. "A *Schwanengesang* Discography." Pp. 205–10 of *A Companion to Schubert's 'Schwanengesang'. History, Poets, Analysis, Performance.* Edited by Martin Chusid. New Haven: Yale University Press, 2000.

Lester, Joel. *Bach's Works for Solo Violin: Style, Structure, Performance.* New York: Oxford University Press, 2000. Pp. 175.

Link, Dorothea. "A Newly Discovered Accompanied Recitative to Mozart's 'Vado, ma dove', KV583." *Cambridge Opera Journal*, 12 (2000/Online publication: March 20, 2001), 29–50.

Litschauer, Walburga. "The Origin and Early Reception of *Schwanengesang*. Pp. 5–13 of *A Companion to Schubert's "Schwanengesang." History, Poets, Analysis, Performance.* Edited by Martin Chusid. New Haven: Yale University Press, 2000.

Lubin, Steven. "The Three Styles of *Schwanengesang*: A Pianist's Perspective." Pp. 191–204 of *A Companion to Schubert's 'Schwanengesang'. History, Poets, Analysis, Performance.* Edited by Martin Chusid. New Haven: Yale University Press, 2000.

McGeary, Thomas. "Heidegger, Handel, Opera, and F-ting." *Handel Institute Newsletter*, 11:1 (2000), [4–6].

Morelli, A. "Dissemination of Italian Oratorios During the 17th Century." *Studi Musicali*, 26:1 (1997), 105–86.

Murray, Sterling E. *The Music of Antonio Rosetti (Anton Rösler) ca. 1750–1792: A Thematic Catalog.* Edited by J. Bunker and Marilyn S. Clark. (Detroit Studies in Music Bibliography 76.) Warren: Harmonie Park Press, 1996. Pp. lvii + [865]; appendices; bibliography; diagrams; facsimiles; indices; musical examples; black and white plates; table of concordances.

Since the eighteenth century, thematic catalogues, in one form or another, have been a very common tool of composers and music scholars alike, for documenting compositions. Thematic catalogues compiled by composers, themselves, are similar to a musical autobiography since they usually list in chronological order each composition, including the first theme of the piece as well as other important information, such as instrumentation and text source(s). In the nineteenth century, music scholars aggressively created thematic catalogues for major composers and by the late twentieth century it was difficult to find any well-known composer who did not have a thematic catalogue listing his or her compositions. Murray's thematic catalogue of Rosetti's music is a welcome addition to this long tradition.

Antonio Rosetti (also known as Anton Rösler or Rössler) was a double bass player and composer from Bohemia. Because of the various surnames he used during his life, it has been difficult for historians to recreate his activities and identify his compositions, since his surnames were common to a number of musicians at this time. His early musical training was acquired as part of his Jesuit schooling, and in 1773 (at approximately age twenty-three) he entered the service of Kraft Ernst, Prince von Oettingen-Wallerstein (near Augsburg), serving as both a livery servant and double bass player in the *Hofkapelle*. His musical abilities were evidently appreciated, and by the following year, he was promoted to court musician, and in 1785 became *Kapellmeister*. Rosetti produced various compositions during the 1770s and 1780s, most notably a Requiem Mass for the death of the Prince's young wife (1776), several pieces of church music, an oratorio, and a large body of music for the Wallerstein court: symphonies, wind partitas, solo keyboard works, and concertos. Because of his poor financial situation, Rosetti left Wallerstein in 1789 for a position as music director for Friedrich Franz I (1756–1837), Duke of Mecklenburg-Schwerin at Ludwigslust. In his three brief years of service at the Duke's court, he wrote a number of large-scale compositions and received commissions from several distinguished patrons including the Elector of Trier and the King of Prussia.

Rosetti was a prolific and diverse composer despite his short life, and his extant works include more than two-hundred pieces of music in almost every instrumental and vocal genre. These are preserved in more than four-hundred fifty musical sources—both manuscripts and prints—which are contained in some two-hundred seventy-five archives, libraries and private collections scattered throughout twenty-three countries. Murray's thematic catalogue of Rosetti's music is well-organized with a clearly laid out format and style, and attests to his extensive sleuthing in identifying and authenticating Rosetti's compositions. Murray presents a short biography of Rosetti's life and a discussion of the previous thematic catalogue by Oskar Kaul (originally published in 1912 and reprinted in 1968). Comprehensive information is provided for each entry (if known and if applicable) including details of instrumentation and vocal scoring, musical and poetic incipits, concordances, and, where known, details pertaining to the work's composition, and a schedule of modern editions, recordings, print and manuscript sources. His discussion of Rosetti's music includes, perforce, an account of the "other" Rosetti's and Rösler's whose compositions have become entangled with those composed by the Wallerstein Rosetti (xxi–v). Questionable or uncertain attributions and known spurious attributions are clearly identified.

What is slightly more unusual in this thematic catalogue is the breadth of documentation provided in Part 2, for copyists and watermarks, in particular. Murray not only lists the various copyists by name or number (642), but also provides full-page facsimiles of the various handwriting (642–83; 698–732). Despite the catalogue's comprehensiveness and Murray's careful attention to detail, some of his practices are questionable, among these, his idiosyncratic system of abbreviations (for example, "kyb" for keyboard instrument, and both "cl" and "trp" for "trumpet copies of the original scores (s)" and "[*clarino(I)*]"). Somewhat more disturbing, however, besides the lack of copies of Rosetti's works, are several notation errors in the incipits themselves. These may represent merely inaccurate proofreading, but raise doubts as to the possibility of yet more errors in the catalogue.

Overall, Murray's thematic catalogue of Rosetti's compositions is an important musical publication to help promote the compositions of this composer. Few of his works have been published in recent years and even fewer have been recorded. With this catalog and the promise of a forthcoming book on Rosetti's life and stylistic study of his music by Sterling Murray, this oversight will surely change—Patricia Debly

Music in the Theater, Church, and Villa: Essays in Honor of Robert Lamar Weaver and Norma Wright Weaver. Edited by Susan Parisi with the collaboration of Ernest Harriss II and Calvin M.

Bower. (Detroit Monographs in Musicology/Studies in Music 28.) Warren: Harmonie Park Press, 2000. Pp. xx + 327; musical examples; tables; black and white illustrations; index.

Music in the Theater, Church, and Villa is a *festschrift* honoring Robert Lamar Weaver and Norma Wright Weaver on the occasion of their seventy-fifth birthdays. Robert and Norma Weaver's years of work in Italian archives have contributed greatly to our understanding of Italian music and culture of the seventeenth and eighteenth centuries, particularly in Florence. and the essays by friends, colleagues and former students pay tribute to their research and findings. The essays are organized in approximate chronological order according to subject—five articles concerning music before 1600, eleven on music from 1600 to 1800, and four on music since 1800. The most substantive contributions to the Weaver *Festschrift* are two articles dealing with correspondence emanating from Florence. The first, "The Unknown Letters of Marco da Gagliano" by Edmond Strainchamps (89–112), adds twenty-seven letters to the 29 published in 1889 by Emil Vogel. Gagliano was a Florentine composer, cleric, and *maestro di cappella* at Santa Maria del Fiore and the Medici court. In addition to his normal duties, he composed music for court entertainments in Mantua. The correspondence between Gagliano and Duke Ferdinando Gonzaga of Mantua provides a rich description of musical life in Florence, Mantua, and Rome from the late sixteenth century through the first half of the seventeenth. In addition to his commentary on the curious relationship between Gagliano and Gonzaga, Strainchamps provides useful indices to Gagliano's letters, facsimiles and texts of the new letters. William Holmes' article on the correspondence of impresario Marchese Luca Casimiro degli Albizzi ("The Correspondence of the Impresario Luca Casimiro degli Albizzi: An Index;" 159–86) is another significant contribution to research in the details and "business arrangements" of Florentine opera production.

Further important contributions to the Weaver festschrift include Susan Parisi's article "*La finte pazzie* of Ferdinando Rutini: A Rediscovered Florentine Opera Buffa of the Late Eighteenth Century" (233–58), Marita McClymond's discussion of Alfieri's contribution to the change in operatic aesthetics at the end of the eighteenth century ("Alfieri and the Revitalization of Opera Seria"; 227–32). John A. Rice traces a parallel shift in Viennese operatic conventions in "Violence, Pathos, and Comedy in Salieri's *La finte scema*" (213–26). His description of external circumstances contributing to the failure of Salieri's 1775 *opera buffa* concludes with Giovanni de Gamerra's preface to the libretto and texts of annotations Salieri added to the autograph score years after the opera's unsuccessful premiere.

Several articles address performance practices, such as Jonathan and Beth Glixon's article on the colorful history of the Venetian theatre Sant'Aponal ("Oil and Opera Don't Mix: the Biography of Sant'Aponal, a Seventeenth-Century Venetian Opera Theater"; 131–44) and Carolyn Gianturco's discussion of staged oratorios by Handel and Alessandro Scarlatti, and various celebratory cantatas ("The 'Staging' of Genres Other Than Opera in Baroque Italy," 113–30).

Also of interest are essays by Carolyn Fruchtman's on "The Influence of Architect and Playwright Sir John Vanbrugh and His Musical Taste on the London Stage, 1696–1711" (145–58), describing Vanbrugh's role in redirecting the artistic tastes of London theatergoer, and Ernest Harriss II, who addresses the musical and aesthetic influence of Johann Mattheson ("Johannn Mattheson: The Enlightenment, *L'Éclaircissement,* or *Die Aufklärung,*" 187–94). In Harriss's view, Mattheson was a pragmatist and empiricist steeped in English philosophical thought, rather than a rationalist indebted to French neoclassical ideals, as is commonly held. Two remaining contributions relevant to eighteenth-century studies concern Mozart and Italy. Regrettably, Marcello de Angelis' very brief article on Mozart's *Zauberflöte* is garbled and poorly organized ("The Magical Moment in Mozart's Zauberflöte, and a Note on the Production of the Opera at the Teatro di S. Maria in Florence in 1818," 259–62). Kathleen Kuzmick Hansell's "Mozart's Milanese Theatrical Works" (195–212), on the other hand, provides an illuminating discussion of three dramatic works commissioned by the Regio Ducal Teatro in Milan—*Mitridate, re di Ponto* (1770), *Ascanio in Alba* (1771), and *Lucio Silla* (1772)—and their contributions in preparing the young composer for his later operatic successes. Especially useful is her detailed discussion of how works for Italian theaters were commissioned, prepared, and performed, and the details of this process in Mozart's Milanese commissions. Also included are very useful tables providing details of scenes in the three Milanese works and the disposition of orchestras in Turin, Milan, Rome, and Naples from 1737 to 1845. Hansell concludes with further information on performance practice at the Milanese opera, the manner in which young Mozart deployed the forces available to him, and his reception in Italy to the present time.

The *Festschrift* honoring the Weavers' scholarship is a worthy tribute to their many years of meticulous scholarship. The various articles by their students and colleagues contribute new insights to a growing body of documentary and historical material—Jean M. Widaman

Owens, S. "Regimental and Courtly Oboe Bands in Early Eighteenth-Century Wurttemburg." *Journal of Band Research*, 34:2 (1999), 1–18.

Panetta, V. J. "Organ Motets by Giovanni Gabriele." *Studi Musicali*, 26:1 (1997), 55–72.

Parisi, S. "Bologna Q.27.IV–V: A New Manuscript Source of Italian Monody and Canzonette." *Studi Musicali*. 26:1 (1997), 73–104.

Parisi, Susan. "*Le finte pazzie* of Ferdinado Rutini: A Rediscovered Florentine Opera Buffa of the Late Eighteenth Century." Pp. 233–58 of *Music in the Theater, Church, and Villa: Essays in Honor of Robert Lamar Weaver and Norma Wright Weaver*. Edited by Susan Parisi with the collaboration of Ernest Harriss II and Calvin M. Bower. (Detroit Monographs in Musicology/Studies in Music 28.) Warren: Harmonie Park Press, 2000.

Parrott, Andrew. *The Essential Bach Choir*. Rochester: Boydell Press, 2000. Pp. xi + 223; illustrations.

Pont, Abraham. "Not Vagaries but Varieties: Handel's 'Inconsistencies' Authenticated." *Handel Institute Newsletter*, 11:1 (2000), [1–4].

Pruett, Lilan P. "An Organ Building Project of the Sixteenth Century: The Large Organ of St. Vitus Cathedral in Prague." Pp. 81–88 of *Music in the Theater, Church, and Villa: Essays in Honor of Robert Lamar Weaver and Norma Wright Weaver*. Edited by Susan Parisi with the collaboration of Ernest Harriss II and Calvin M. Bower. (Detroit Monographs in Musicology/Studies in Music 28.) Warren: Harmonie Park Press, 2000.

Rice, John A. "Violence, Pathos, and Comedy in Salieri's *La finta scema*." Pp. 213–26 of *Music in the Theater, Church, and Villa: Essays in Honor of Robert Lamar Weaver and Norma Wright Weaver*. Edited by Susan Parisi with the collaboration of Ernest Harriss II and Calvin M. Bower. (Detroit Monographs in Musicology/Studies in Music 28.) Warren: Harmonie Park Press, 2000.

Special Section: Late Entries and Reviews

Sadie, Julie Anne (ed.). *Companion to Baroque Music.* Foreword by Christopher Hogwood. London: J. M. Dent & Sons, 1990; Berkeley: University of California Press, 1998 (paperback). Pp. xviii + 549; bibliography; chronology; index; musical examples; facsimiles; maps; black and white plates.

"By acquiring this book, you have gained the materials for exploring anew the Baroque era of music" (xv), In this introduction to the *Companion to Baroque Music*, the words "exploring anew" imply an audience of well-informed readers able to actively engage with its contents. Compiler/editor Julie Anne Sadie maintains, however, that the book "is designed to be accessible to enthusiasts while at the same time being a useful tool for specialists" (xv). The *Companion*'s exhaustive store of information may be enticing to the musicological sleuth, but it may prove daunting to the average music lover. Where other musical "Companions" present information in dictionary format or as essays grouped by topic, the *Companion to Baroque Music* uses a combination of formats—dictionary, essay, and chronology—in conjunction with one another. The first section, "Places and Persons," occupies nearly two-thirds of the book and is central to its chief purpose—allowing the reader to view musicians in their geographical/temporal context. Composers, singers, instrumentalists, and instrument makers are listed alphabetically according to the city of their principal employ, with cross references to other places where they worked. Cities in turn, are organized by country or region—Italy, France, Northern Europe, Central Europe, the British Isles, the Low Countries, and the Iberian peninsula and its New World colonies—each preceded by an illuminating essay.

Parts II and III contain brief essays on Baroque performing forces and performance practice issues. Part IV, a chronology, "reflects the geographic ordering of the 'Places and People' section and presents both significant details of the lives of musicians and events relating to institutions and music. Consequently, the relative import of the events, however selectively chosen for inclusion, may not always be self-evident" (xvi). Sadie explains that "the somewhat unorthodox format of the *Companion* is intended to help the reader re-examine assumptions and confront fallacies" (xvi). Regrettably, the format is rather cumbersome, and, as a consequence, the assumptions and fallacies that Sadie and the authors of the essays hope will be reexamined may go unnoticed by most readers.

The "Select Bibliography of Recent Books in English" corresponds to the first three sections of the *Companion*, with separate subdivisions for each country or region and the essays of Parts II and III. The bibliography has been updated through 1997 in the 1998 paperback edition, and is adequate for the general reader but would prove more useful to the specialist if it included works in other languages. The bibliography is adequate for general readers, but would prove more useful to the specialist if it included works in other languages. The index is the key to examining the complex web of relationships among persons, places, and institutions cited in the text, but, unaccountably, it fails to list musical compositions, instruments, or terms that might be helpful to the non-specialist. As is often the case, this work has demonstrated once again that it is difficult to balance the needs of the professional musician and the general music lover in a single volume. The *Companion to Baroque Music* is a rich source of information, but the readers' "rewards" may be obtained only with considerable effort—Jean M. Widaman

Sadie, Stanley. *Mozart and His Operas.* New York: St. Martin's Press, 2000. Pp. xiv + 238; illustrations; plates.

Sawyer, John E. "Irony and Borrowing in Handel's *Agrippina*." *Music & Letters*, 80:4 (1999), 531–59.

Smither, Howard E. "Historicism in Nineteenth-Century German Oratorio." Pp. 263–76 of *Music in the Theater, Church, and Villa: Essays in Honor of Robert Lamar Weaver and Norma Wright Weaver.* Edited by Susan Parisi with the collaboration of Ernest Harriss II and Calvin M.

Bower. (Detroit Monographs in Musicology/Studies in Music 28.) Warren: Harmonie Park Press, 2000.

Spaethling, Robert (ed.). *Mozart's Letters, Mozart's Life*. New York: Norton, 2000. Pp. xiii + 409; illustrations.

Stinson, Russell. *The Orgelbüchlein*. New York: Oxford University Press, 2000. Pp. 208.

Strainchamps, Edmond. "The Unknown Letters of Marco da Gagliano." Pp. 89–112 of *Music in the Theater, Church, and Villa: Essays in Honor of Robert Lamar Weaver and Norma Wright Weaver*. Edited by Susan Parisi with the collaboration of Ernest Harriss II and Calvin M. Bower. (Detroit Monographs in Musicology/Studies in Music 28.) Warren: Harmonie Park Press, 2000.

Supicic, I. "From renaissance to Baroque Times: Some Considerations of Social History." *International Review of the Aesthetics and Sociology of Music*, 28:2 (1997), 133–42.

Talbot, Michael. *Venetian Music in the Age of Vivaldi*. Aldershot: Ashgate, 2000. Pp. 384.

Tocchini, G. "Neapolitan Libretti, Tuscan-Roman Libretti: Origins of the Goldonian *commedia per musica*." *Studi Musicali*, 26:2 (1997), 377–415.

Trojan, J. "*Burlesca per il carnevale* (1732): An *opera bouffe* from the Musical Collection of the Cistercian Monastery in Osek, West Bohemia, with an Accompanying Libretto in Latin and Czech." *Hudebni Veda*, 35:4 (1998), 319–41.

Türk, Daniel Gottlob. *Daniel Gottlob Türk on the Role of the Organist in Worship (1787)*. Edited and translated by Margot Ann Greenlimb Woolard. Lanham: Scarecrow Press, 2000. Pp. xxv + 171; illustrations.

Volek, T. "Czech Chateau Music Ensembles of the 18th Century in the European Context." *Hudebni Veda*, 34 (1997), 404–10.

Wolf, Christoph, and others [Harvard students in Music 215r]. *Johann Sebastian Bach (1685–1750): "The Man from whom all true musical wisdom proceeded": A 250th Anniversary Exhibition*. Cambridge: Houghton Library and Eda Kuhn Music Library, Harvard University, 2000. Pp. 51; exhibition catalogue; facsimiles.

Zeiss, Laurel E. "Mozart or Not? The Musical Evidence." *Cambridge Opera Journal*, 12 (March 2000/Online publications: March 20, 2001), 51–54.

Special Section: Late Entries and Reviews

Foreign Literatures and Languages: Iberian

Castillo Gómez, Antonio (ed.). *Escribir y leer en el siglo de Cervantes*. Barcelona: Gedisa, 1999. Pp. 362.

Twelve conference papers with some discussions reaching into the mid-1600s.

Foreign Literatures and Languages: French

Abbatista, G. "La prima volta dell'Abate Raynal: *L'Histoire du Stadhoudérate* il repubblicanesimo olandese." *Studi Settecenteschi*, 17 (1997), 111–51.

Abrantès, Mme d'. *Une soirée chez Mme Geoffrin*. (Le cabinet des lettrés.) Paris: Gallimard, 2000. Pp. 170.

Albertan-Coppola, Sylviane. "Les voyages portugais dans l'*Histoire générale des voyages* de l'abbé Prévost." *Dix-huitième siècle*, 31 (1999), 491–506.

Aldridge, A. Owen. "John Adams Meets the Abbé Mably." *Dalhousie French Studies*, 52 (2000), 88–99.

Andrès, Bernard. "Le fantasme du champ littéraire dans la *Gazette de Montréal* (1778–1779)." *Études françaises*, 36:3 (2000), 9–26.

Andries, Lise. "État des recherches: Présentation." *Dix-huitième siècle*, 32 (2000), 7–18.

Ansart, Guillaume, "Aspects of Rationality in Diderot's *Supplément au voyage de Bougainville*." *Diderot Studies*, 28 (2000), 11–19.

Artigas-Menant, Geneviève. "La plume et les Lumières: le manuscrit outil de progrès." *Lumen*, 19 (2000), 1–21.

Audidière, Sophie. "La *Lettre sur les aveugles* et l'éducation des sens." *Recherches dur Diderot et sur Encyclopédie*, 28 (2000), 67–82.

Bayard, Pierre. *Comment améliorer les œuvres ratées?* Paris: Minuit, 2000. Pp. 176.

Becq, Annie. "Le XVIIe siècle au miroir du XVIIIe." *Littératures classiques*, 34 (1998), 251–66.

Belleguic, Thierry. "L'oeil et le tourbillon: Épistémologie et poétique du *pathos* dans 'La promenade Vernet.'" *Dix-huitième siècle*, 32 (2000), 485–502.

Bénot, Yves. "Correspondance: À propos d'une citation de Diderot par Jean Guéhenno." *Dix-huitième siècle*, 32 (2000), 742–43.

Bernardin de Saint-Pierre, Jacques Henri. *Paul and Virginie*. Fort Augustus: Ghislaine, 1997. Pp. 88; illustrations; map.

Bernardin de Saint-Pierre, Jacques Henri. *Paul et Virginie*. Edited by Elyette Roussel. (Lectures Clé en français facile.) [Paris]: Clé international, 1998. Pp. 63; illustrations.

Bernier, Marc André. "La *Lettre sur les sourds et muets* (1751) de Denis Diderot: Une rhétorique du *pnctum temporis*." *Lumen*, 18 (1999), 1–11.

Berthiaume, Pierre, and Danielle Forget. "Entre la polémique et le littéraire: Le baron de Lahontan." *Canadian Journal of Rhetorical Studies/L Revue canadienne d'études rhétoriques*, 9 (1998), 73–96.

Bertrand, Dominique. "La cacophonie des rires dans *la Pucelle* de Voltaire." *Dix-huitième siècle*, 32 (2000), 129–44.

Bertrand, Gilles. "Masque et séduction dans la Venise de Casanova." *Dix-huitième siècle*, 31 (1999), 407–28.

Bièvre, Marquis de. *Métaphysique du calembour et autres jeux sur les mots d'esprit*. Paris: Payot, 2000. Pp. 158.

Black, Moishe. "Lucretius Tells Diderot: Here's the Plan." *Diderot Studies*, 28 (2000), 39–58.

Bokobza Kahan, Michèle. *Libertinage et folie dans le roman du 18e siècle*. Louvain: Peeters, 2000. Pp. 291.

Bonnel, Roland. "La géographie morale de la campagne dans les *Contes moraux* de Marmontel." *Dalhousie French Studies*, 52 (2000), 64–82.

Bostoen, Karel. "La langue que j'ai oubliée: Belle de Zuylen et le néerlandais." *Rapports-Het Franse Boek*, 70 (2000), 110–16.

Special Section: Late Entries and Reviews

Bouabane, Stéphanie. "Entre *brevitas* et digressions narratives: le dilemme du romancier dans la première moitié du XVIIIe siècle." *Lumen*, 18 (1999), 13–25.

Boulerie, Florence. "La littérature pour apprendre le réel? Ambiguïtés du statut de la littérature chez deux pédagogues des Lumières, Rousseau et La Chalotais." *Littératures classiques*, 37 (1999), 201–11.

Bourdin, Jean-Claude. "Le matérialisme dans la *Lettre* sur lea aveugles." *Recherches dur Diderot et sur Encyclopédie*, 28 (2000), 83–96.

Braun, Theodore E. D. "Montesquieu, *Lettres persanes*, and Chaos. Pp. 79–90 of *Disrupted Patterns: On Chaos and Order in the Enlightenment*. Edited by Theodore E. D. Braun and John A. McCarthy. Amsterdam: Rodopi, 2000.

Brady, Patrick. "Chaos, Complexity, Catastrophe and Control in Marivaux's *La Vie de Marianne*. Pp. 65–78 of *Disrupted Patterns: On Chaos and Order in the Enlightenment*. Edited by Theodore E. D. Braun and John A. McCarthy. Amsterdam: Rodopi, 2000.

Brot, Muriel. "La corres pondance de Raynal." *Recherches dur Diderot et sur Encyclopédie*, 28 (2000), 135–49.

Brown, Gregory S. "Scripting the Patriotic Playwright in Enlightenment Era France: Louis-Sebastien Mercier's Self-Fashionings Between 'Court' and 'Public.'" *Historical Reflections*, 26:1 (2000), 31–57.

Brown, H. G. "An Unmasked Man in a *milieu de memoire*: the Abbé Slier as Sans-Peur the Brigand Priest." *Historical Reflections*, 26:1 (2000), 1–30.

Buchs, Arnaud. "Diderot: écrire la peinture. Poétique de la *Lettre sur les sourds et les muets*." *Poétique*, 121 (2000), 115–24.

Buffat, Marc. "Les *Lettres à Sophie Volland*: morale et correspondance amoureuse." Pp. 79–87 of *Lettre et réflexion morale: La lettre, miroir de l'âme*. Edited by Geneviève Haroche-Bouzinac. Paris: Klincksieck, 1999.

Burt, E. S. "Regard for the Other: Embarrassment in the *Quatrième promenade*." *L'Ésprit créateur*, 39:4 (1999), 54–67.

Byrne, P. W. "Opportunistic Argument in *Manon Lescaut*." *Esays in French Literature*, 35–36 (1998–99), 22–49.

Cammagre, Geneviève. "Diderot, de la *Correspondance aux Salons*: Énonciation épistolaire et critique d'art." *Dix-huitième siècle*, 32 (2000), 473–84.

Candaux, Jean-Daniel. "Le voyage minéralogique dans la France des Lumières." Pp. 29–33 of *Le Voyage en France 1750–1914*. Edited by Devauges Jean-Denys and Didier Masseau. Compiègne: Société des amis du Musée national de la voiture et du tourisme, Château de Compiègne, 2000.

Cavallin, Jean-Christophe. *Chateaubriand et "l'homme aux songes": L'initiation à la poésie dans les "Mémoires d'outre-tombe."* (Écrivains.) Paris: Preses universitaires de France, 2000. Pp. 244.

Cave, Christophe. "Le rire des anti-philosophes." *Dix-huitième siècle*, 32 (2000), 227–39.

Cecchi, Annie. *Mishima Yukio: Esthétique classique, univers tragique d'Apollon et Dionysos à Sade et Bataille.* Paris: Honoré Champion, 1999. Pp. 278.

Cellard, Jacques. *Un génie dévergondé: Nicolas-Edme Rétif, dit "de Bretonne."* Paris: Plon, 2000. Pp. 595; illustrations.

Chamayou, Anne. "Diderot polygraphe dans les *Lettres à Sophie Volland*." Pp. 163–70 of *Éloge de l'adrese: Actes du colloque de l'Université d'Artois. 02–03 avril 1998.* Edited by Anne Chamayou. Arras: Artois Presses Université, 2000.

Charney, Ann. *Le Jardin de Rousseau.* Montréal: Flammarion Québec, 1999. Pp. 252.

Charrak, André. "Géométrie et métaphysique dans la *Lettre sur les aveugles* de Diderot." *Recherches dur Diderot et sur Encyclopédie*, 28 (2000), 43–53.

Charrier, Marianne. "'Grand sujet de disserter si on pouvait le faire sans ennuyer les autres et s'attrister soi même': La réflexion morale dans les lettres de Mme Riccoboni à D. Garrick et à R. Liston." Pp. 89–105 of *Lettre et réflexion morale: La lettre, miroir de l'âme.* Edited by Geneviève Haroche-Bouzinac. Paris: Klincksieck, 1999.

Charrier-Vozel, Marianne. "Les billets de Beaumarchais le libertin." *Revue de l'A.I.R.E.*, 25–26 (2000), 65–76.

Charrière, Isabelle de. *Sir Walter Finch et son fils William.* Edited by Valérie Cossy. (Collection XVIIIe siècle.) Paris: Desjonquères, 2000. Pp.152.

Chartier, Pierre. "Présentation." *Recherches dur Diderot et sur Encyclopédie*, 28 (2000), 5.

Special Section: Late Entries and Reviews

Chastang, Marie-Laure. "Voltairiana." *Essays in French Literature*, 35–36 (1998–99), 50–68.

Chastel-Rousseau, Charlotte. "Promenades d'Anglais sur la place Louis XV ou les aperçus critiques d'un mode d'embellissement 'a la française.'" *Dix-huitième siècle*, 32 (2000), 521–35.

Châtelet, Gabrielle Émilie Le Tonnelier de Breteuil du. *Lettres d'amour au marquis de Saint-Lambert*. Paris: Paris-Méditerranée, 1997. Pp. 275.

Chouillet, Anne-Marie, and Laurent Loty. "Carnet bibliographiques." *Recherches sur Diderot et sur l'Encyclopédie*, 29 (2000), 211–13.

Cook, Malcolm. "Laclos: Two Unpublished Letters." *British Journal for Eighteenth-Century Studies*, 23 (2000), 37–42.

Cook, Malcolm, and Marie-Emmanuelle Plagnol-Diéval (eds.). *Anecdotes, faits-divers, contes, nouvelles, 1700–1820: Actes du colloque d'Exeter de 1998*. (French Studies of the Eighteenth and Nineteenth Centuries 5.) Berne: Peter Lang, 2000. Pp. 302.

Corbin, Alain. "Des origines de la perception du paysage." Pp. 59–61 of *Le Voyage en France 1750–1914*. Edited by Devauges Jean-Denys and Didier Masseau. Compiègne: Société des amis du Musée national de la voiture et du tourisme, Château de Compiègne, 2000.

Crampe-Casnabet, Michèle. "Qu'appelle-t-on sentir?" *Recherches dur Diderot et sur Encyclopédie*, 28 (2000), 55–66.

Crébillon, Prosper Jolyot de. *Rhadamisthe et Zénobie*. Montpellier: Espaces 3, 1999. Pp. 86.

Crépu, Michel. *La Confusion des lettres* Paris: Grasset, 1999. Pp. 250.

Cronk, Nicholas (ed.). *Études sur le Traité sur le tolérance de Voltaire*. Oxford: Voltaire Foundation, 2000. Pp. vi + 324.

Cryle, Peter. "État présent de la critique sadienne." *Dix-huitième siècle*, 31 (1999), 507–24.

Curran, Andrew. "Diderot's Revisionism: Enlightenment and Blindness in the *Lettres sur les aveugles*." *Diderot Studies*, 28 (2000), 75–94.

Darlow, Mark. *Maîtres et valets dans dans la comédie française du XVIIIe siècle*. (Connaissance d'une thème.) Paris: Bréal, 2000. Pp. 125.

Davies, Simon. "Un lettre inédite de Jean-Jacques Rousseau (1769)." *Dix-huitième siècle*, 31 (1999), 329–30.

Delon, Michel. "Des rats dans les catacombes de l'esprit." Pp. 331–41 of *Le Mythe en littérature: Essais offerts à Pierre Brunel*. Edited by Yves Chevrel and Camille Durnoulié. Paris: Universitaires de France, 2000. Pp. 403.

Delon, Michel. "Souvenirs balzaciens de 'Faublas.'" *L'Année balzacienne* (1999), 17–27.

Denon, Vivant, and others (eds.). *Lettres à Isabella Tetochi, 1788–1816*. Paris: Paris-Méditerrainée, 1998. Pp. 272.

Deprun, Jean. "De Baudelaire à Gilbert...et retour: Note sur un hémistiche voyageur." *Bulletin baudelairien* (1997), 48–49.

Diaz, Brigitte. "Morales de la lettre. La correspondence de jeunesse de madame Roland (1767–1780." Pp. 151–61 of *Lettre et réflexion morale: La lettre, miroir de l'âme*. Edited by Geneviève Haroche-Bouzinac. Paris: Klincksieck, 1999.

Diderot, Denis. *Lettera sui ciechi per quelli che ci vedono*. Firenze: La Nuova Italia, 1999. Pp. 138.

Dionne, Ugo. "Diviser pour régner: Découpage et chapitration romanesque." *Poétique*, 118 (1999), 131–55.

Duflo, Colas. "La fin du finalisme: Les deux natures: Holmes et Sanderson." *Recherches dur Diderot et sur Encyclopédie*, 28 (2000), 107–31.

Edmiston, William G. "Plots, Patterns, and Challenges to Gender Ideology in Gomez and Sade." *The French Review*, 73:3 (2000), 463–74.

Fink, Beatrice. "The Divine Brought Down to Earth: Three Recent Sade Biographies." *Eighteenth-Century Life*, 24:2 (2000), 106–10.

Fumaroli, Marc. "Le premier redécouvreur de Guez de Balzac: Joseph Joubert." *Littératures classiques*, 33 (1998), 21–26.

Gomez-Géraud, Marie-Christine, and Philippe Antoine (eds.). *Roman et récit de voyage: Écriture de fiction, écriture du voyage*. Actes du colloque "Roman et récit de voyage," décembre 1999, à l'Université de Picardie–Jules Verne. Paris: Presses de l'Université Paris–Sorbonne, 2000. Pp. 256.

Special Section: Late Entries and Reviews

Goulemot, Jean M. "Guez de Balzac, l'épistolier au siècle ds Lumières." *Littératures classiques*, 33 (1998), 149–58.

Groult, Martine. *D'Alembert et la mécanique de la vérité dans l'Encyclopédie* Paris: Honore Champion, 1999. Pp. 505; illustrations.

Haroche-Bouzinac, Geneviève (ed.). *Lettre et réflexion morale: La lettre, miroir de l'âme*. Paris: Klincksieck, 1999. Pp. 195.

Haroche-Bouzinac, Geneviève. "Madame de Graffigny et les épistoliers français du XVIIIe siècle." *Revue de l'A. I. R. E.*, 23 (1999), 59–61.

Harrison, David. "The Wisdom of Candide: En Reconnaissance de Jean Perkins." *ADFL Bulletin*, 31:3 (2000), 30–32.

Hawcroft, Michael. *Rhetoric: Readings in French Literature*. New York: Oxford University Press, 2000. Pp. 268.

Herman, Jan, and Christian Angelet. *Recueil de préfaces de romans du XVIIIe siècle*. Volume 1: *1700–1750*; Volume 2: *1751–1899*. Saint-Étienne: Presses universitaires de Saint-Étienne, 1999.

Huchette, Jocelyn. "La 'gaieté française' ou la question du caractère national dans la dé finition du rire, de *l'Esprit des lois à De la littrature*." *Dix-huitièeme siécle*, 32 (2000), 97–109.

Imbruglia, G. "Lo storico e l'opinione pubblica Raynal dalle 'Nouvelle littéraires' all'*Histoire des deux Indies*." *Studi Settecenteschi*. 17 (1997), 153–85.

Iotti, Gianni. "L'ignorance d'Usbek: Considérations sur les *Lettres persanes*." *Dix-huitième siècle*, 31 (1999), 479–90.

Laclos, Pierre Choderlos de. *Harreman arriskutsuak*. Edited by Jon Muñoz Otaegi. Bizkaia: Ibaizabal, 1997. Pp. 533.

Laclos, Pierre Choderlos de. *Les Liaisons dangereuses*. First New York Public Library Collectors Edition. Edited by Ernest Christopher Dowson. New York: Doubleday, 1998. Pp. xxvi + 467; illustrations.

Laclos, Pierre Choderlos de. *Les Liaisons dangereuses*. Edited by Caroline Jacot Grapa. Paris: Gallimard, 1997. Pp. 218.

Laclos. Pierre Choderlos de. *Les Liaisons dangereuses*. Edited and translated by Douglas Parmée. (Oxford World's Classics.) New York: Oxford University Press, 1998. Pp. xl + 402.

Laclos. Pierre Choderlos de. *Niebezpieczne zwiazki*. Edited by Tadeusz Zelenski. Warsaw: Prószynski s S-ka, 1999. Pp. 388.

Laclos. Pierre Choderlos de. *Niebezpieczne zwiazki*. Edited by Tadeusz Zelenski. Warsaw: CIL Polska, 2000. Pp. 382.

Laclos. Pierre Choderlos de. *Opasnye sviazi*. Moscow: Terra, 1997. Pp. 348.

Laclos, Pierre Choderlos de. *P.-A. Choderlos de Laclos:* Les liaisons dangereuses. Edited by Michel Delon. Paris: Presses universitaires de France, 1999. Pp. 138.

Lafargue, Catherine. "Exemples de violence dans La Paysanne pervertie." *Études rétiviennes*, 31 (1999), 181–90.

Lafon, Henri. *Espaces romanesques du XVIIIe siècle, 1670–1820: de Madame de Villedieu à Nodier.*. Paris: PUF, 1997. Pp. 216.

L'Aminot, Tanguy. *Émile et l'éducation*. Montmorency: Musée Jean-Jacques Rousseau, 1997. Pp. 340; illustrations.

Lamy, Bernard. *La Rhétorique ou l'art de parler*. Edited by Benoit Timmermans. Paris: Presses universitaires de France, 1999. Pp. 600.

Lapierre, Solange. *La contribution de Pierre Abel de Boyer à la lexicographie (anglais et Français) du XVIIIe siècle*. Montréal: Université de Montréal, 1999. Pp. 118.

Lasowski, Patrick Wald (ed.). *Romanciers libertins du XVIIIe siècle*. Volume 1. (Bibliothèque de la Pléiade 472.) Paris: Galliard, 2000. Pp. cviii + 1,341, illustrations.

Leigh, John. *The Search for Enlightenment: An Introduction to Eighteenth-Century French Writing*. Lanham: Roman & Littlefield Publishers, 1999. Pp. 176; illustrations.

Le Ru, Véronique. "La *Lettre sur les aveugles* et le bâton de la raison." *Recherches dur Diderot et sur Encyclopédie*, 28 (2000), 25–41.

Special Section: Late Entries and Reviews

Magri–Mourgues, Véronique. "*Corinne* et le voyage." Pp. 11–25 of *Lectures de* Corinne *ou l'Italie de Germaine de Staël*. Edited by Jean-Marie Seillan. Nice: Université de Nice-Sophia Antipolis, 2000.

Maher, R. "'Le veritable champ du sublime'? The Ode in France in the Seventeenth Century." *Seventeenth Century*, 15:2 (2000), 244–65.

Maistre, Xavier de. *Viagem ao redor do meu quarto*. (Classicos Mercado Aberto.) Porto Alegre: Mercado Aberto, 1998. Pp. 173.

Maistre, Xavier de. *Voyage autou de ma chambrer*. (La petite collection 277.) Paris: Éditions Mille et une nuits, 2000. Pp. 85.

Mall, Laurence. "D'Homère à Fénelon à Rousseau: Les problèmes du modèle das le livre V d'*Émile*." *Studi Francesi*, 127 (1999), 30–43.

Mall, Laurence. "Une autobiolecture: L'*Essai sur les règnes de claude et de Néron* de Diderot." *Diderot Studies*, 28 (2000), 111–22.

Mason, Haydn. "Voltaire and Sir Everard Fawkener." *British Journal for Eighteenth-Century Studies*, 23 (2000), 1–11.

Masseau, Didier. "La marquise de La Ferté-Imbault, reine antiphilosophe des Lanturelus." Pp. 35–50 of *Les Dérèglements de l'rat: Formes et procédures de l'illégitimité culturelle en France (1715–1924)*. Edited by Pierre Popovic and Érik Vigneault. Montréal: Presses de l'Université de Montréal, 2000.

Maxient, Jocelyn. *Le XVIIIe siècle de Milan Kundera, ou Diderot investi par le roman contemporain*. Paris: Presses universitaires de France, 1998. Pp. 314.

Melançon, Benoît. "Letters, Diary, and Autobiography in Eighteenth-Century France." Pp. 151–70 of *Representations of the Self from the Renaissance to Romanticism*. Edited by Patrick Coleman, Jayne Lewis, and Jill Kowalik. Cambridge: Cambridge University Press, 2000.

Meslier, Jean. *Mémoire: Extraits*. Edited by Armand Farrachi. Paris: Exils, 2000. Pp. 134.

Moore, Fabienne. "Homer Revisited: Anne Le Fevre Dacier's Preface to her Prose Translation of the *Iliad* in Early Eighteenth-Century France." *Studies in the Literary Imagination*, 33, no. 2 (2000), 87–107.

Mortier, Roland. "Julie de Lespinasse, femme savante et âme sensible." Pp. 235–45 of *La sensibilité dans la littérature française au XVIIIe siècle*. (Biblioteca della ricerca. Cultura straniera 86.) Edited by Franco Piva. Paris: Didier érudition, 1998.

Moser-Verrey, Monique. "Les dîners des *Lettres neuchâteloises* au gré cœurs sensibles." *Rapports-Het Franse Boek*, 70 (2000), 79–85.

Moureau, François. "Dans les coulisses de 'Samson: Voltaire et le nouvelliste." Pp. 321–29 of *Voltaire en Europe: Hommage à Christiane Mervaud*. Edited y Michel Delon and Catriona Seth. Oxford: Voltaire Foundation, 2000.

Moscovici, Claudia. "Beyond the Particular and the Universal: D'Alembert's 'Discours préliminaire' to the *Encyclopédie*." *Eighteenth-Century Studies*, 33 (2000), 103–18.

Nablow, Ralph A. "Voltaire, Molière, and *La Guerre civile de Genève*." *Romance Notes*, 40:1 (1999), 49–58.

Pasini, M. "Jean-Jacques Dortous de Mairan e Madame du Châtelet: Frammenti di una querelle." *Studi Settecenteschi*, 17 (1997), 63–82.

Pedersen, Christian Bank. "Les traits de Diderot: La critique d'art en tableau." *Poétique*, 120 (1999), 427–57.

Pelckmans, Paul. "Les surenchères du concernment: Belle et ses frères." *Rapports-Het Franse Boek*, 70 (2000), 101–09.

Piroux, Lorraine. "Staged Truth and Travel Epistemology in the *Lettre à d'Alembert sur les spectacles*." *Studies in Eighteenth-Century Culture*, 29 (2000), 155–72.

Richard, Odile. "Les jardins de Diderot dans les *Lettres à Sophie Volland*. *Revue de l'A. I. R. E.*, 23 (1999), 21–33.

Rivara, Annie, and Antony McKenna (eds.). *Le Roman des années trente: la génération de Prévost et de Marivaux*. Saint-Etienne: Publications de l'Université de Saint-Etienne, 1998. Pp. 167.

Sade, Marquis de. *Français, encore un effort si vous voulez être républicains!* Paris: Max Milo, 2000. Pp. 185; illustrations.

Sade, Marquis de. *Letters from Prison*. Edited by Richard Seaver. New York: Arcade Publishers, 1998. Pp. 401; illustrations.

Special Section: Late Entries and Reviews

Saint-Simon, Louis de Rouvroy, duc de. *Memoirs*. 3 volumes. Edited and translated by Lucy Norton. London: Prion, 2000. Pp. 525; 525; 522.

Salazar, Philippe-Joseph. "'The author writes like a Briton': la réception de Balzac en Angleterre." *Littératures classiques*, 33 (1998), 247–62.

Samson, Guillemette. "Une 'Belle' anglaise: Isabelle de Zuylen/Mme de Charrière." *Rapports-Het Franse Boek*, 70:2 (2000), 72–78.

Seillan, Jean-Marie (ed.). *Lectures de* Corinne *ou l'Italie de Germaine de Staël*. Nice: Université de Nice-Sophia Antipolis, 2000. Pp. 92.

Seth, Catrionia. "À sa voix tout sur la terre se change en poésie: les improvisations dans *Corinne*." Pp. 131–54 of *"Un deuil éclatant du bonheur": Corinne ou l'Italie/Madame de Staël*. Edited by Jean-Pierre Perchellet. Orléans: Paradigme, 1999.

Seth, Catrionia. "L'éloge des infidèles dans les œuvres de jeunesse de Parny." *Cahiers Roucher-André Chénier*, 17 (1998), 63–70.

Seth, Catriona. "Louvet et la poésie." Pp. 233–54 of *Entre libertinage et Révolution, Jean-Baptiste Louvet*. Strasbourg: Presses universitaires de Strasbourg, 1999.

Seth, Catriona. "La part des anges: signes et présages dans *Corinne ou l'Italie*" Pp. 181–204 of *"Une mélodie intellectuelle": Corinne ou l'Italie de Germaine de Staël*. Edited by Christine Planté, C. Pouzoulet, and Alain Vaillant. Montpellier: Université Paul Valéry, 2000.

Seth, Catriona. "Traduction, transposition ou œuvre de fiction pure, la nouvelle exotique à la fin du XVIIIe siècle." Pp. 193–206 of *La Nouvelle de langue française aux frontières des autres denres, du Moyen Âge à nos jours*. Louvain: Quorum, 1998.

Seth, Catriona. "Une âme exilée sur la terre. Corinne: un mythe moderne de la transgression." Pp. 99–129 of *Mme de Staël*. Edited by Michel Delon and F. Mélonio. Paris: Presses d'Université Paris-Sorbonne, 2000.

Seth, Catriona. "Verlaine et la poèsie profane du XVIIIe siècle." Pp. 179–91 of *Verlaine: 1896–1996*. Edited by M. Bercot. Paris: Klincksieck, 1998.

Seth, Catrionia. "Voltaire pragmatique: l'argent dans le *Traité sur la tolérance*." Pp. 191–204 of *Études sur le Traité sur la tolérance de Voltaire*. Edited by Nicolas Cronk. Oxford: Voltaire Foundation, 1999.

Sheridan, Geraldine. "Warring Translations: Prévost's *Doyen de Killerine* in the Irish Press." *Eighteenth Century Ireland–Iris an dá cultúr*, 14 (1999), 99–116.

Siess, Jürgen. "Images et rapport de places dans le discours epistolaire de Madame du Deffand et Madame Riccoboni." *L'Esprit Créateur*, 60 (2000), 38–49.

Sol, Antoinette. "'Se répandre en paroles.' Notions of Identity in Mme de Bénouville's Pensées errantes." *Intertexts*, 4 (2000), 129–43.

Stewart, Philip. "Le roman à clefs à l'époque des Lumières." Pp. 183–95 of *Les Dérèglements de l'rat: Formes et procédures de l'illégitimité culturelle en France (1715–1924)*. Edited by Pierre Popovic and Érik Vigneault. Montréal: Presses de l'Université de Montréal, 2000.

Strien-Chardonneau, Madeleine van. "Lettres (1793–1805) d'Isabelle de Charrière à son neveu, Willem-René van Tuyll van Serookskerken: Une éducation aristocratique et post-révolutionnaire." *Rapports-Het Franse Boek*, 70 (2000), 86–93.

Stroev, Alexandre. "Des dessins inédits du marquis de Sade." *Dix-huitièma siècle*, 32 (2000), 323–42.

Sylvos, Françoise. "La lettre en chiffre(s): Du quantifiable et du secret." *Revue de l'A.I.R.E.*, 25–26 (2000), 33–42.

Vanpée, Janie. "Performing Justice: The Trials of Olympe de Gouges." *Theatre Journal*, 51 (1999), 47–65.

Vega, Judith. " Sade's libertijnse republick. Over pornografische parabels en esthetische politiek." *Jaarboek voor Vrouwengeschiedenis*, 20 (2000), 109–33.

Wagner, Jacques (ed.). *Lesage, écrivain (1695–1735)*. Amsterdam: Rodopi, 1997. Pp. xviii + 366; illustrations.

Went-Daoust, Yvette, and Léo van Maris. "État de la question. La correspondance de Belle deZuylen (Isabelle de Charrière)." *Revue de l'A.I.R.E.*, 25–26 (2000), 4–16.

Wood, Dennis. "Isabelle de Charrière moraliste." *Rapports-Het Franse Boek*, 70 (2000), 94–100.

Young-Mock, Lee. "Diderot et la lutte parlementaire au temps de l'*Encyclopédie*." *Recherches sur Diderot et sur l'Encyclopédie*, 29 (2000), 45–69.

Special Section: Late Entries and Reviews

Foreign Literatures and Languages: Germanic and Slavic

Bunzel, Wolfgang, Konrad Feilchenfeldt, and Walter Schmitz (eds.). *"Schnittpunkt Romantik": Text- und Quellenstudien zur Literatur des Jahrhunderts. Festschrift für Sibylle von Steinsdorff.* Tübungen: Max Niemeyer Verlag, 1997. Pp. viiii + 354; portrait.

Dekker, Rudolf. *Childhood Memory and Autobiography in Holland: From the Golden Age to Romanticism.* London: Macmillan, 2000. Pp. 174; illustrations.

Rev. (favorably) by Ulla Bergstrand in *Children's Books History Society Newsletter*, no. 68 (November 2000), 21–26.

Goodman, Katherine R. *Amazons and Apprentices: Women and German Parnassus in the Early Enlightenment.* Woodbridge: Camden House, 2000. Pp. 316.

Hansen, Angela. *"Der Hofmeister" von J. M. R. Lenz: Ein Versuch einer Neuinterpretation.* Bern: Peter Lang, 2000. Pp. 312.

Lacoue-Labarthe, P. "The Theater of Hölderlin." *Aut Aut*, 293–94 (2000), 153–66.

Nerius, Dieter. *Beiträge zur deutschen Orthographie.* Edited by Petra Ewald and Bernd Skibitzki. (Sprache-System und Tätigkeit 34.) Frankfurt am Main: P. Lang, 2000. Pp. 420.

Novalis (Friedrich von Hardenberg). *Le Brouillon général.* Paris: Allia, 2000. Pp. 350.

Novalis (Friedrich von Hardenberg). *Schriften. Sechster Bend 1.–2. Teilband. Der dichterische Jungendnachlass (1788–1791) und Stammbucheintagungen (1791–1792).* Edited by Hans-Joachim Mähl. Stuttgart: Kohlhammer, 2000. Pp. 675; 590.

Otto, Véronique. "Grimm correcteur de Catherine II: Sur un 'Fonds Grimm' inconnu." *Dix-huitième siècle*, 31 (1999), 395–406.

Rose, Sven-Erik. "The Funny Business of the Swedish East India Company: Gender and Imperial Joke-Work in Jacob Wallenberg's Travel Writing." *Eighteenth-Century Studies*, 33:2 (1999–2000), 217–32.

Rosenfield, Kathrin H. "Getting Inside Sophocles' Mind Through Hölderlin's *Antigone*." *New Literary History*, 30 (1999), 107–27.

Zeidlerin, Susanna Elisabeth. *Jungferlicher Zeitvertreiber: Das ist allerhand Deusche Gedichte Bey Häusslicher Arbeit und stiller Einsamkeit verfertiget und zusammen getragen von Susannen Elisabeth Zeidlerin. Neudruck der Ausgabe von 1686.* Edited by Cornelia Niekus Moore. Frankfurt am Main: P. Lang, 2000. Pp. xlvi + 139; illustrations.

Foreign Literatures and Languages: Multiple Language Traditions

Zipes, Jack (ed.). *When Dreams Came True: Classical Fairy Tales and Their Tradition.* New York: Routledge, 1999. Pp. x + 238; illustrations; index.

British Literatures

Archer, Jean Barbara, and Gordon Leslie Herries Davies. "Inspiration from Nature and Some Plays Written by John O'Keeffe (1747–1823)." *Archives of Natural History*, 27 (2000), 123–35.

Austen, Jane. *Œuvres romanesques complètes, I.* (Bibliothèque de la Pléaide.) Paris: Gallimard, 2000. Pp. 1,160.

Bandry, Anne. "*The Visitor*, the Inspectress, Selima, Obadiah et Tristram, ou comment s'anime le *Public Ledger* en 1760–1761." *Bulletin de la société d'études anglo-américaines des XVIIe et XVIIIe siècles*, 50 (2000), 283–98.

Basker, James G. "'The Next Insurrection': Johnson, Race, and Rebellion." *Age of Johnson*, 11 (2000), 37–51.

Beal, Joan C. *English Pronunciation in the Eighteenth Century: Thomas Spence's* Grand Repository of the English Language. New York: Oxford University Press, 1999. Pp. 256.

Beveridge, A. "Teetering on the verge of complete sanity': Boswell's Life of Boswell." *Journal of the Royal Society of Medicine*, 93:8 (2000), 434–37.

Biberman, Matthew. "Milton, Marriage, and a Woman's Right to Divorce." *Studies in English Literature 1500–1900*, 39 (1999), 131–53.

Bony, Alain. "Affairs de famille: Déja vu et reconnaissance dans *Joseph Andrews*." *Études Anglaises*, 53:4 (2000), 413–27.

Bony, Alain. "*Lascivia Philomema*: Beauté, *wit* et sexe dans l'esthétique addisonienne." *Bulletin de la société d'études anglo-américaines des XVIIe et XVIIIe siècles*, 50 (2000), 261–82.

Boulard, Claire. *Presse et socialisation féminine en Angleterre de 1690 à 1750: Conversations à l'heure du thé*. Paris: L'Harmattan, 2000. Pp. 537; illustrated.

Boyle, John, Fifth Earl of Cork and Orrery. *Remarks on the Life and Writings of Dr. Jonathan Swift*. Edited by João Fróes. Newark: University of Delaware Press; Cranbury: Associated University Presses, 2000. Pp. 461; appendices with "Orrery Manuscript Notes in his Annotated Copies of Remarks on Swift" [327–433]; bibliographical descriptions; frontispiece; index.

Rev. by James E. May in *East-Central Intelligencer*, 15, no. 1 (January 2001), 38–40; by John V. Price in *Notes and Queries*, n.s. 49 (2002), 144; by Claude Rawson in *Review of English Studies*, n.s. 52 (2001), 455–57; (favorably) by Ian Campbell Ross in *Eighteenth-Century Ireland*, 15 (2000), 199–201.

Bundock, Michael. "Johnson's 'Vile Melancholy' and *The Life of Savage*." *Age of Johnson*, 11 (2000), 177–85.

Carboni, Pierre. "Les penseurs écossais des belles lettres." Pp. 22–56 of *Ecosse des Lumières: le XVIIIe siècle autrement*. Edited by Pierre Morère. Grenoble: Université Stendhal, 1997.

Carney, Sean. "The Passion of Joanna Baillie: Playwright as Martyr." *Theatre Journal*, 52 (2000), 227–52.

Charke, Charlotte. *Narrative of the Life of Mrs. Charlotte Charke*. Edited by Robert Rehder. London: Pickering & Chatto, 2000. Pp. 171.

Charles, Shelly. "De la traduction au pastiche: *L'Histoire du chevalier Grandisson*." *Eighteenth-Century Fiction*, 13:1 (2000), 129–40.

Chaudhuri, Rosinka. "'Young India: A Bengal Eclogue': Or Meat-Eating, Race, and Reform in a Colonial Poem." *Interventions: International Journal of Postcolonial Studies*, 2 (2000), 424–41.

Chézaud, Patrick. "Robert Fergusson, poète du Sens Commun." *Études écossaises*, 4 (1997), 31–42.

Cowper, William. *The Centenary Letters*. Edited by Simon Malpas. Manchester: Fyfield, 2000. Pp. xxi + 162.

Daly, P. J. "John Gay's *The Fan* and the Paper War of 1713." *Clio*, 29:3 (2000), 249–69.

Davenport, Hester. *Faithful Handmaid: Fanny Burney at the Court of King George III*. Stroud: Sutton, 2000. Pp. xvi + 240; plates; illustrations; portraits.

Davis, Leith. *Acts of Union: Scotland and the Literary Negotiation of the British Nation, 1707–1830*. Stanford: Stanford University Press, 1998. Pp. viii + 219.

Descargues, Madeleine. "*Le Spectator* à la recherche d'équilibres précaires." *Bulletin de la société d'études anglo-américaines des XVIIe et XVIIIe siècles*, 50 (2000), 247–59.

Deutsch, Helen. "Symptomatic Correspondences: the Author's Case in Eighteenth-Century Britain." *Cultural Critique*, 42 (1999), 35–80.

Devereux, Janice. "Hannah More's Notebook." *Notes and Queries*, 244 (1999), 447–48.

Donoghue, Frank. "Avoiding the 'cooler tribunal of the study': Richard Brinsley Sheridan's Writer's Block and Late Eighteenth-Century Print Culture." *ELH*, 68 (2001), 831–56.

Downie, J. A. "Johnson's Politics." *Age of Johnson*, 11 (2000), 81–104.

Dresher, Horst W. "Henry Mackenzie: Lumières et sentiment." Pp. 87–103 of *Ecosse des Lumières: le XVIII siècle autrement*. Edited by Pierre Morère. Grenoble: Université Stendhal, 1997.

Duval, Gilles. "John Dunton (libraire et auteur, 1659–1733) ou la versatilité." *Bulletin de la société d'études anglo-américaines des XVIIe et XVIIIe siècles*, 50 (2000), 209–18.

Eberle-Sinatra, Michael (ed.). *Mary Shelley's Fictions: From Frankenstein to Falkner*. New York: Macmillan, 2000. Pp. xxvi + 250.

Edwards, Karen L. *Milton and the Natural World: Science and Poetry in* Paradise Lost. Cambridge: Cambridge University Press, 1999. Pp. xii + 265.

Eger, Elizabeth, Charlotte Grant, Clíona O Gallchoire, and Penny Warburton (eds.). *Women, Writing and the Public Sphere, 1700–1830*. Cambridge: Cambridge University Press, 2001. Pp. xi + 320.

Includes Eger's "Representing Culture: 'The Nine Living Muses of Great Britain' (1779)" (104–32); and Ellis Markman's "Coffee-Women, *The Spectator* and the Public Sphere in the Early Eighteenth Century" (27–52).

Special Section: Late Entries and Reviews

Ennis, Daniel J. "The Making of the Poet Laureate, 1730." *Age of Johnson*, 11 (2000), 217–35.

Fields, Polly S. "Charlotte Charke and the Liminality of Bi-Gendering: A Study of the Canonical Works." Pp. 221–39 of *A Pilgrimage for Love: New Essays in Early Modern Literature*. Edited by Sigrid King. Tempe: Arizona Center for Medieval and Renaissance Studies, 2000.

Fields, Polly S. "George Lillo and the Victims of Economic Theory." *Studies in the Literary Imagination*, 32:2 (1999), 77–88.

Folkenflik, Robert. "The New Model Eighteenth-Century Novel." *Eighteenth-Century Fiction*, 12:2–3 (2000), 459–78.

Furbank, Philip N., and W. R. Owens. "Defoe, the De la Faye Letters and *Mercurius Politicus*." *British Journal for Eighteenth-Century Studies*, 23 (2000), 13–20.

Galibert, Thierry. "*Le Moine* de Matthew G. Lewis veçu par Antonin Artaud." *Revue d'histoire littéraire de la France*, 99:5 (1999), 1079–86.

Gardiner, Ellen. *Regulating Readers: Gender and Literary Criticism in the Eighteenth-Century Novel*. Newark: University of Delaware Press, 2000. Pp. 198.

Goldgar, Bertrand A. "Imitation and Plagiarism: The Lauder Affair and Its Critical Aftermath." *Studies in the Literary Imagination*, 34 (Spring 2001), 1–16.

Graham, Kenneth W. *Vathek with the Episodes of Vathek*: The Role of the Suppressed 'Story of Alasi and Firouz.'" *East-Central Intelligencer*, n.s. 14:3 (2000), 10–12.

Groom, Nick (ed.). *Thomas Chatterton and Romantic Culture*. New York: St. Martin's Press, 1999. Pp. 256.

Gunn, Daniel P. "The Lexicographer's Task: Language, Reason, and Idealism in Johnson's *Dictionary* Preface." *Age of Johnson*, 11 (2000), 105–24.

Harman, Claire. *Fanny Burney: A Biography*. New York: HarperCollins, 2000. Pp. 430.

Hawes, Clement (ed.). *Christopher Smart and the Enlightenment*. New York: St. Martin's Press, 2000. Pp. 308.

Hopes, Jeffrey. "Scottish Unionism and the Beginnings of Defoe Criticism." *Études écossaises*, 4 (1997), 159–65.

Hoveler, Diane Long. "Reading the Wound: Wollstonecraft's *Wrongs of Woman, or Maria* and Trauma Theory." *Studies in the Novel*, 31:4 (1999), 387–408.

Hsia, Adrian. *The Vision of China in the English Literature of the Seventeenth and Eighteenth Centuries.* Hong Kong: Chinese University Press, 1998. Pp. xi + 404.

Hunter, J. Paul. "Serious Reflections on Daniel Defoe (with an Excursus on the Farther Adventures of Ian Watt and Two Notes on the Present State of Literary Studies)." *Eighteenth-Century Fiction*, 12:2–3 (2000), 227–37.

Jordan, Sarah. "Samuel Johnson and Idleness." *Age of Johnson*, 11 (2000), 145–76.

King, A. "Englishmen, Scots and Marchers: National and Local Identities in Thomas Gray's 'Scalacronica.'" *Northern History*, 36 (2000), 217–31.

Komisaruk, Adam. "'So Guided by a Silken Cord': *Frankenstein*'s Family Values." *Studies in Romanticism*, 38:2 (1999), 409–42.

Korshin, Paul J. "Samuel Johnson's Life Experience with Poverty." *Age of Johnson*, 11 (2000), 3–20.

Lamb, J. "'The Rime of the Ancient Mariner,' a Ballad of the Scurvy." *Clio Medica*, 56 (2000), 157–77.

Lewis, Jayne, and Maximillian E. Novak. "Dryden 2000." *The Center & Clark Newsletter*, 36 (2000), 3–5.

Loussouarn, Sophie. "La littérature enfantine en Angleterre au XVIIIe siècle." *Bulletin de la société d'études anglo-américaines des XVIIe et XVIIIe siècles*, 50 (2000), 99–114.

Lynch, Diedre. "Personal Effects and Sentimental Fictions." *Eighteenth-Century Fiction*, 12:2–3 (2000), 345–68.

Mack, Robert L. *Thomas Gray*. New Haven: Yale University Press, 2000. Pp. 736; illustrations.

Mackenzie, Henry. *Literature and Literati: The literary Correspondence of Henry Mackenzie Volume 1: Letters 1766–1827; Volume 2: Notebooks, 1763–1824.* Edited by Horst W. Drescher. Frankfurt-am-Main: Peter Lang, 1999. Pp. 392.

Special Section: Late Entries and Reviews

McKeon, Michael. "Watt's *Rise of the Novel* within the Tradition of the Rise of the Novel." *Eighteenth-Century Fiction*, 12:2–3 (2000), 253–76.

Morère, Pierre. "Addison et Steele: Éthique, esthétique et sentiment dans *The Spectator*." *Bulletin de la société d'études anglo-américaines des XVIIe et XVIIIe siècles*, 50 (2000), 301–24.

Morère, Pierre. "James Beattie (1735–1803): Imitation et sources vives." *Etudes écossaises*, 4 (1997), 43–54.

Murray, Nicholas. *World Enough and Time: the Life of Andrew Marvell*. New York: St. Martin's Press, 1999. Pp. 294; illustrations.

Neregal, V. "Language and Power in Pre-Colonial Western India: Textual Hierarchies, Literate Audiences and Colonial Philology." *Indian Economic and Social History Review*, 37 (2000), 259–94.

Novak, Maximillian E. "Gendered Cultural Criticism and the Rise of the Novel: The Case of Defoe." *Eighteenth-Century Fiction*, 12:2–3 (2000), 239–52.

O'Quinn, Daniel. "Scissors and Needles: Inchbald's *Wives as They Were, Maids as They Are* and the Governance of Sexual Exchange." *Theatre Journal*, 51 (1999), 105–25.

Park, Youngwon. *Milton and Isaiah: A Journey Through the Drama of Salvation in* Paradise Lost. New York: Peter Lang, 2000. Pp. xii + 143.

Phillips, M. "William Blake in Lambeth." *History Today*, 50:11 (2000), 18–25.

Phillips, Philip Edward. *John Milton's Epic Invocations: Converting the Muse* New York: Peter Lang, 2000. Pp. xii + 159.

Preston, Thomas R. "Moral Spin Doctoring, Delusion, and Chance: Wakefield's Vicar Writes an Enlightenment Parable." *Age of Johnson*, 11 (2000), 237–81.

Puel, Marc. "La Ville et le luxe dans *Humphry Clinker*." *Cercles: Revue pluridisciplinaire du monde anglophone*, 1:1 (2000). Electronic article. http://www.cercles.com/vol1_ni/puel.pdf.

Richetti, John. "Ideas and Voices: The New Novel in Eighteenth-Century England." *Eighteenth-Century Fiction*, 12:2–3 (2000), 327–44.

Robinson, Roger. "Nature's Kindly Plan: A New Look at James Beattie and His Poetry." *Eighteenth-Century Scotland*, 12 (1998), 7–11.

Seymour, Miranda. *Mary Shelley*. London: John Murray, 2000. Pp. xvi + 655; plates; illustrations.

Sher, Richard B. "Boswell on Robertson and the Moderates: New Evidence." *Age of Johnson*, 11 (2000), 205–15.

Sorensen, Janet. "Smollett and the Scottish Language of British Cultural Identity." *Eighteenth-Century Scotland*, 13 (1999), 8–12.

Stevenson, Kay Gilliland. *Milton to Pope, 1650–1720*. Basingstoke: Macmillan, 2000. Pp. 320; illustrations.

Stock, R. D. "Samuel Johnson and the Snares of Poverty." *Age of Johnson*, 11 (2000), 21–36.

Swift, Jonathan. *The Correspondence of Jonathan Swift, D. D., in Four Volumes*. Volume 1: *Letters 1690–1714*. Edited by David Wooley. Bern: Peter Lang, 2000. Pp. 650.

Tankard, Paul. "A Clergyman's Reading: Books Recommended by Samuel Johnson." *Age of Johnson*, 11 (2000), 125–43.

Tennenhouse, Leonard. "The Americanization of Clarissa." *Yale Journal of Criticism*, 11 (1998), 177–96.

Terry, Richard (ed.). *James Thomson: Essays for the Tercentenary*. Liverpool: Liverpool University Press, 2000. Pp. 279; illustrations.

Tomalin, Claire. *Jane Austen, passions discrètes*. Paris: Autrement, 2000. Pp. 410.

Topia, André. "*Eveline*: la porosité des frontières." *Études Anglaises*, 53:4 (2000), 413–27.

Trimmer, Sarah. *The Guardian of Education: A Periodical Work*. With a new Introduction by Matthew Grenby. 5 volumes. Bristol: Thoemmes Press; Tokyo: Editions Synapse, 2000.

Facsimile edition (London: J. Hatchard, 1802–1806). Rev. by Andrea Immel in *Children's Books History Society Newsletter*, no. 77 (November 2003), 32–33.

Special Section: Late Entries and Reviews

Urstad, Tone Sundt. *Sir Robert Walpole's Poets: The Use of Literature as Government Propaganda, 1721*–1742. Newark: University of Delaware Press, 1999. Pp. 297.

Velissariou, Aspasia. "*A Trip to Scarborough*; or, How 'to undergo a bungling Reformation.'" *Bulletin de la société d'études anglo-américaines des XVIIe et XVIIIe siècles*, 50 (2000), 325–37.

Wall, Cynthia. *The Literary and Cultural Spaces of Restoration London*. Cambridge: Cambridge University Press, 1998. Pp. xviii + 277; illustrations.

Whittaker, Jason. *William Blake and the Myths of Britain*. New York: St. Martin's Press, 1999. Pp. 215.

Woodberry, Bonnie. "The Mad Body as the Text of Culture in the Writings of Mary Lamb." *Studies in English Literature 1500–1900*, 39 (1999), 659–74.

Yoshinaka, T. "'Perhaps' in Marvell's 'Bermudas.'" *Seventeenth Century*, 13 (1998), 22–35.

New World Literatures and Languages

Arnold, Laura. "'Now...Didn't Our People Laugh?: Female Misbehavior and Algonquin Culture in Mary Rowlandson's Captivity and Restoration." *American Indian Culture and Research*, 21:4 (1997), 1–28.

Babb, Valerie Melissa. *Whiteness Visible: The Meaning of Whiteness in American Literature and Culture*. New York: New York University Press, 1998. Pp. xi + 227; illustrations; maps.

Baepler, Paul (ed.). *White Slaves, African Masters: An Anthology of American Barbary Captivity Narratives*. Chicago: University of Chicago Press, 1999. Pp. xiii + 310; illustrations.

Bak, John. "Tossing 'the book' Out with the Bath Water: Republican Sentiment in *The Contrast* (1787) by Royall Tyler." *Bulletin de la société d'études anglo-américaines des XVIIe et XVIIIe siècles*, 50 (2000), 167–89.

Barton, Paul. "Narrative Intrusion in *Charlotte Temple*: A Closet Feminist's Strategy in an American Novel." *Women & Language*, 23 (2000), 26–33.

Bassard, Katherine Clay. *Spiritual Interrogations: Culture, Gender, and Community in Early African-American Women's Writing*. Princeton: Princeton University Press, 1999. Pp. 183.

Benchérif, Osman. *The Image of Algeria in Anglo-American Writings, 1785–1962*. Lanham: University Press of America, 1997. Pp. xix + 269.

Benito, Jesús, and Ana Manzanas. "The (De)Construction of the Other in *The Interesting Narrative of the Life of Olaudah Equiano*." Pp. 47–56 of *Black Imagination and the Middle Passage*. Edited by Maria Diedrich, Henry Louis Gates, and Carl Pederson. New York: Oxford University Press, 1999.

Bly, Antonio T. "Wheatley's 'To the University of Cambridge, in New England....'" *Explicator*, 55 (1997), 205–08.

Boswell, Parley Ann. "Mary White Rowlandson Remembers Captivity: A Mother's Anguish, a Woman's Voice." Pp. 109–18 of *Woman's Life-Writing: Finding Voice/Building Community*. Edited by Linda S. Coleman. Bowling Green: Bowling Green State University Popular Press, 1997.

Bray, Alan. "The Curious Case of Michael Wigglesworth." Pp. 205–15 of *A Queer World: The Center for Lesbian and Gay Studies Reader*. Edited by Martin B. Duberman. New York: New York University Press, 1997.

Brown, Charles Brockden. *Ormond, or, The Secret Witness*. Edited with an introduction by Mary Chapman. Orchard Park: Broadview Press, 1999. Pp. 301.

Brown, Gillian. "Fables and the Forming of Americans." *Modern Fiction Studies*, 43 (1997), 115–43.

Brown, Gillian. ""The Quixotic Fallacy." *Novel*, 32 (1999), 250–74.

Burgett, Bruce. "Masochism and Male Sentimentalism: Charles Brockden Brown's Clara Howard." Pp. 205–25 of *Sentimental Men: Masculinity and the Politics of Culture*. Edited by Mary Chapman and Glenn Hendler. Berkeley: University of California Press, 1999.

Bushman, Richard. "A Poet, a Planter, and a Nation of Farmers." *Journal of the Early Republic*, 19 (1999), 1–14.

Carretta, Vincent. "Olaudah Equiano or Gustavus Vassa? New Light on an Eighteenth-Century Question of Identity." *Slavery and Abolition*, 20 (1999), 96–105.

Coleman, Linda S. (ed.). *Woman's Life-Writing: Finding Voice/Building Community*. Bowling Green: Bowling Green State University Popular Press, 1997. Pp. 281.

Special Section: Late Entries and Reviews

Coupe, Lynda Wolfe. *Images of the Hunter in American Life and Literature*. New York: Peter Lang, 2000. Pp. 224.

Craig, Raymond. *A Concordance to the Complete Works of Anne Bradstreet*. 2 volumes. Lewiston: Edward Mellen Press, 2000. Pp. 648.

Dempsey, Jack. "Reading the Revels: The Riddle of May Day in *New English Canaan*." *Early American Literature*, 34 (1999), 283–312.

Diedrich, Maria, Henry Louis Gates, and Carl Pederson (eds.). *Black Imagination and the Middle Passage*. New York: Oxford University Press, 1999. Pp. xvi + 320.

Downes, Paul. "Constitutional Secrets: 'Memoirs of Carwin' and the Politics of Concealment." *Criticism*, 39 (1997), 89–117.

Drexler, Michael. "Managing the Public: Strategic Publication in Franklin and Whitman." *Modern Language Studies*, 28:2 (1998), 55–67.

Duberman, Martin B. (ed.). *A Queer World: The Center for Lesbian and Gay Studies Reader*. New York: New York University Press, 1997. Pp. xii + 705.

Fetterly, Judith. "'My Sister! My Sister!': The Rhetoric of Catherine Sedgwick's Hope Leslie." *American Literature*, 70 (1998), 491–516.

Franklin, Benjamin. *Franklin on Franklin*. Edited by Paul M. Zall. Lexington: University Press of Kentucky, Pp. 2000. Pp. 315.

Gardner, Jared. *Master Plots: Race and the Founding of an American Literature, 1787–1845*. Baltimore: Johns Hopkins University Press, 1998. Pp. xvii + 238; illustrations.

Glaude, Eddie S., Jr. *Exodus! Religion, Race, and Nation in Early Nineteenth-Century Black America*. Chicago: University of Chicago Press, 2000. Pp. x + 216.

Goddu, Teresa A. *Gothic America: Narrative, History, and Nation*. New York: Columbia University Press, 1997. Pp. x + 227.

Gray, Edward G., and Norman Fiering (eds.). *The Language Encounter in the Americas, 1492–1800: A Collection of Essays*. New York: Berghahan Books, 2000. Pp. x + 342; illustrations.

Greene, Roland. *Unrequited Conquests: Love and Empire in the Colonial Americas.* Chicago: University of Chicago Press, 1999. Pp. xii + 289; illustrations.

Hebel, Odo J. "'A Stranger in a Strange Land': *Some Account of the Fore Part of the Life of Elizabeth Ashbridge* (1774) and the (Inter)cultural Inscription of American Autobiographical Writing." Pp. 183–200 of *Early America Re-Explored: New Readings in Colonial, Early National, and Antebellum Culture.* Edited by Klaus H. Schmidt and Fritz Fleischmann. New York: Peter Lang, 2000.

Irmscher. Christoph. *The Poetics of Natural History: From John Bartram to William James.* New Brusnwick: Rutgers University Press, 1999. Pp. xvii + 357; illustrations.

Joy, Neill R. "Politics and Culture: The Dr. Franklin–Dr. Johnson Connection, with an Analogue." *Prospects,* 23 (1998), 59–105.

Kelleter, Frank. "Puritan Missionaries and the Colonization of the New World: A Reading of John Eliot's *Indian Dialogues* (1671)." Pp. 71–106 of *Early America Re-Explored: New Readings in Colonial, Early National, and Antebellum Culture.* Edited by Klaus H. Schmidt and Fritz Fleischmann. New York: Peter Lang, 2000.

Kendrick, Robert. "Other Questions: Phillis Wheatley and the Ethics of Interpretation." *Cultural Critique,* 38 (1997–98), 39–64.

Leask, Nigel. "Irish Republicans and Gothic Eleutherarchs: Pacific Utopias in the Writings of Theobals Wolfe Tone and Charles Brockden Brown." *Huntington Library Quarterly,* 63 (2000), 347–67.

Lee, Robert A., and W. M. Verhoeven (eds.). *Making America/Making American Literature: Franklin to Cooper.* Amsterdam: Rodopi, 1996. Pp. 360.

Leonard, Thomas C. "Recovering 'Wretched Stuff' and the Franklins' Synergy." *New England Quarterly* 72 (1999), 444–55.

Luciano, Dana. "'Perverse Nature': *Edgar Huntly* and the Novel's Reproductive Disorders." *American Literature,* 70 (1998), 1–27.

Mulford, Carla. "Franklin, Modernity, and Themes of Dissent in the Early Modern Era." *Modern Language Studies,* 28:2 (1998), 13–27.

Special Section: Late Entries and Reviews

Murphy, Graham J., and Edward William Pitcher (eds.). *The Irish in Popular Literature in the Early American Republic: Paddy Whacking*. (Studies in British and American Magazines 3.) Lewiston: Edward Mellen Press, 1999. Pp. 428.

Murphy, Joseph. "The Loafer and the Loaf-Buyer: Whitman, Franklin, and Urban Space." *Modern Language Studies*, 28:2 (1998), 41–54.

Noah, Mordecai. *The Selected Writings of Mordecai Noah*. Edited by Michael Schuldiner and Daniel J. Kleinfeld. Westport: Greenwood Press, 1999. Pp. viii + 171; illustrations.

Peyer, Bernd. *The Tutor'd Mind: Indian Missionary-Writers in Antebellum America*. Amherst: University of Massachusetts Press, 1997. Pp. x + 420; illustrations.

Pitcher, E. W. ""Inventing Humorous Indians in Early American Literature." *ANQ: A Quarterly Journal of Short Articles, Notes, and Reviews*, 12 (1999), 41–49.

Rice, Grantland. "Cognitive Patterns and Aesthetic Deformations in Post-Revolutionary American Writing: A Preliminary Inquiry." Pp. 13–23 of *Reciprocal Influences: Literary Production, Distribution, and Consumption in America*. Edited by Steven Fink and Susan S. Williams. Columbus: Ohio State University Press, 1999.

Richards, Jeffrey H. "Revolution, Domestic Life, and the End of 'common mercy' in Crevecoeur's *Landscapes*." *William and Mary Quarterly*, 55:2 (1998), 281–96.

Richardson, Gary. "Nationalizing the American Stage: The Drama of Royall Tyler and William Dunlap as Post-Colonial Phenomena." Pp. 221–48 of *Making America/Making American Literature: Franklin to Cooper*. Edited by Robert A. Lee and W. M. Verhoeven. Amsterdam: Rodopi, 1996.

Roberson, Susan L. (ed.). *Women, America, and Movement: Narratives of Relocation*. Columbia: University of Missouri Press, 1998. Pp. viii + 291; illustrations.

Roberts-Miller, Patricia. *Voices in the Wilderness: Public Discourse and the Paradox of Puritan Rhetoric*. Tuscaloosa: University of Alabama Press, 1999. Pp. xiii + 209.

Ryals, Kay Ferguson. "America, Romance, and the Fate of the Wandering Woman: The Case of Charlotte Temple." Pp. 81–105 of *Women, America, and Movement: Narratives of Relocation*. Edited by Susan L. Roberson. Columbia: University of Missouri Press, 1998.

Sabino, Robin, and Jennifer Hall. "The Path Not Taken: Cultural Identity in *The Interesting Narrative of the Life of Olaudah Equiano*." *MELUS*, 24 (1999), 5–19.

Salisbury, Neal. "Contextualizing Mary Rowlandson: Native Americans, Lancaster and the Politics of Captivity." Pp. 107–50 of *Early America Re-Explored: New Readings in Colonial, Early National, and Antebellum Culture*. Edited by Klaus H. Schmidt and Fritz Fleischmann. New York: Peter Lang, 2000.

Sayre, Gordon M. "Abridging Between Two Worlds: John Tanner as American Indian Autobiographer." *American Literary History*, 11 (1999), 480–99.

Sayre, Gordon M. (ed.). *American Captivity Narratives: Selected Narratives with Introduction*. Boston: Houghton Mifflin, 2000. Pp. x + 453; illustrations.

Schmidt, Klaus H. "A Scotsman in British America; or Up Against Provincialism: The Construction of Individual and Collective Identities in Dr. Alexander Hamilton's *Itinerarium*." Pp. 151–81 of *Early America Re-Explored: New Readings in Colonial, Early National, and Antebellum Culture*. Edited by Klaus H. Schmidt and Fritz Fleischmann. New York: Peter Lang, 2000.

Schmidt, Klaus, and Fritz Fleischmann (eds.). *Early America Re-Explored: New Readings in Colonial, Early National, and Antebellum Culture*. New York: Peter Lang, 2000. Pp. ix + 599.

Shuffleton, Frank. "Tower, Desire, and American Cultural Studies." *Early American Literature*, 34 (1999), 94–102.

Stadler, Gustavus. "Magawisca's Body of Knowledge: Nation Building in *Hope Leslie*." *Yale Journal of Criticism*, 12 (1999), 41–56.

Thompson, Gary Richard, and Eric Carl Link. *Neutral Ground: New Traditionalism and the American Romance Controversy*. Baton Rouge: Louisiana State University Press, 1999. Pp. xvi + 267.

Toulouse, Teresa A. "'American Puritanism' and Mary White Rowlandson's *Narrative*." Pp. 137–58 of *Challenging Boundaries: Gender and Periodization*. Edited by Joyce W. Warren and Margaret Dickie. Athens: University of Georgia Press, 2000.

Twagilimana, Aimable. *Race and Gender in the Making of an African American Literary Tradition*. New York: Garland Publishers, 1997. Pp. xxiii + 177.

Special Section: Late Entries and Reviews

Vickers, Anita. "Social Corruption and the Subversion of the American Success Story in *Arthur Mervyn*." *Prospects*, 23 (1998), 129–46.

Warren, Joyce W., and Margaret Dickie (eds.). *Challenging Boundaries: Gender and Periodization*. Athens: University of Georgia Press, 2000. Pp. xxiv + 296.

Wesley, Marilyn C. *Secret Journeys: The Trope of Women's Travel in American Literature*. Albany: State University of New York Press, 1999. Pp. xviii + 167.

Winiarski, D. L. "'Pale blewish lights' and a Dead Man's Groan: Tales of the Supernatural from Eighteenth-Century Plymouth, Massachusetts." *William and Mary Quarterly*, 55:4 (1998), 497–530.

Zafar, Rafia. *We Wear the Mask: African Americans Write American Literature, 1760–1870*. New York: Columbia University Press, 1997. Pp. xi + 249.

Addendum (Fine Arts)

Ziskin, Rochelle. *The Place Vendôme: Architectural and Social Mobility in Eighteenth-Century Paris*. Cambridge: Cambridge University Press, 1999.

Index

Aarsleff, Hans   121
Abarca Vásquez, Carlos A.   19
Abauzit, Firman   612
Abbatini, Antonio Maria   246
Abbatista, Guido   19, 99, 649
Abbott, Rob   367
Abdullah, Thabit A. J.   19
Abel, Frederick L.   235
Abing, Kevin   99
Abkoude, Johannes van   61, 164
Abrantès, Mme. d'   649
Abu-Tarbush, José   99
Acanfora, Elisa   217
Acemoglu, Daron   99
Aceves Pastrana, Patricia   99, 100, 106, 107, 112, 114, 117, 122, 130, 132, 133, 134, 136, 154, 162, 180, 181, 188, 190, 197, 204, 207
Adam, Robert   246, 458
Adamoli, Pierre   86
Adams, Abigail (also: Abagail)   571, 574
Adams, Beverly   99
Adams, Christine   35
Adams, David   521
Adams, J. W.   576
Adams, John   66, 291, 476, 568, 572, 573, 618, 649
Adams, John Quincy   476, 613
Adams, Mark   478
Adams, Stephen   461
Adamson, Christopher   99
Adamson, John   536

Adamzik, Kirsten   326
Addison, Joseph   375, 381, 447, 455, 572, 597, 663, 667
Adelman, Howard Tzvi   100
Adelson, Robert   245, 251, 306
Adelung, Johann Christoph   346, 356
Adet, Pierre-Auguste   571
Adkins, Cecil   231
Adler, Hans   19
Adler, Kraig   105
Adorno, Theodor W.   247, 353, 616
Aebischer, Pascale   367
Afanasii of Kholmogory (Archbishop)   171–72
Aftalion, Fred   100
Ageeva, Olga Genievna   19
Agesci, Bernard d'   227
Agnesi, Maria Gaetana   169
Agnew, Robin A. L.   100
Agnew, Vanessa   478
Àguilar Piñal, Francisco   265
Aguilonius, Franciscus   115
Aguirrezabala, Marcela   19
Agujari, Lucrezia   264
Ahishali, Recep   19
Åhlström, Olof   231
Ahrens, Rüdiger   367
Aichele, A.   589
Aimer, Don   508
Ajello, Epifanio   360
Akenside, Mark   417
Akyeampong, Emmanuel   100

Al-Amin B., Shaykh 197
Al-Jabarti, Abd al-Rahman 35
Alatorre, Antonio 19, 100
Albert, Heinrich 248
Albertan, Christian 521
Albertan-Coppola, Sylviane 649
Alberti, Carmelo 259
Albes, Claudia 291
Albrecht, Sophie 334
Albright, Ann Cooper 229
Albright, Carol Bonomo 100
Alchon, Suzanne Austin 20
Aldini, Nicolò Nicoli 100
Aldrich, Putnam 230
Aldridge, A. Owen 291, 649
Alejos-Grau, Carmen José 100
Aleknaviciene, Ona 315
Alexander I 131
Alexander VII 125
Alexander, Alison 508
Alexander, Andrew 367
Alexander, Joy 367
Alexandre, Josette 100
Alfieri, Vittorio 325, 645
Alfonso, S. 179
Alfonso-Goldfarb, Ana Maria 100
Algarotti, Francesco 145
Algor, Catherine 20
Alimento, A. 536
Alimento, Antonella 291
Alkon, Paul 367
Allan, D. 536
Allan, David 20
Allan, Sean 316
Allard, Gérald 604
Allen, David 367
Allen, Ethan 567, 607
Allen, Lee N. 101
Allen, Richard 104, 461
Allen, Richard C. 589
Allen, W. B. 567
Allerkamp, Andrea 316
Allert, Beate 316

Allihn, Ingeborg 231
Allison, Henry E. 101
Allison, R. J. 536
Allston, Washington 463
Almeida, Jaime de 101
Alonso, Francisco 267–68
Alpert, Michael 101
Alphonsus X 278
Alsop, Anthony 533
Althusius, Johannes 548
Altman, Janet Gurkin 291
Alvarez, J. 217
Álvarez Barrientos, Joaquín 265, 278, 289
Alvis, J. 536
Alzate y Ramírez, José Antonio de 99, 100, 106, 107, 112, 114, 117, 122, 130, 132, 133, 134, 136, 154, 162, 180, 181, 188, 190, 197, 204, 207
Amalric, Jean-Pierre 20
Amalvi, Christian 101
Amar y Borbón, Josefa 69
Amelang, James 101
Amelin, Maksim 316
Ameriks, Karl 156
Amerman, Richard H. 101
Amherst, Jeffery, General 572, 597
Amic, Sylvain 622
Ammerlahn, Hellmut 316
Amory, Hugh 7
Amstel, Ploos van 625
Ancarani, Maria Elisabetta 101
Ancillon, Louis Frédéric 101, 118
Anderegg, Johannes 316
Anderson, Benedict 13
Anderson, Frank G., Jr. 101
Anderson, Fred 20
Anderson, Grahame 479, 508
Anderson, Hugh 494
Anderson, Robert 591
Anderson, Stephanie 101
Anderson, Timothy G. 101
Anderson-Gold, Sharon 102

Index

Andioc, René 275–76, 283
Andor, Eszter 102, 117, 129, 130, 131, 151, 160, 174, 175, 179, 186, 191, 203, 204, 207
André, John 463
André, Louis 522
Andreadis, Harriette 368
Andreev, Andrei IUr'evich 20
Andreev, Stefan 50, 143
Andreeva, Nadezhda 316
Andrés, Bernard 291, 649
Andrés Turrión, Maria Luisa de 102
Andrew, Donna T. 20
Andrew, Patricia R. 223
Andrews, Jonathan 20, 83, 102
Andrews, Richard 231, 291
Andrews, William L. 461
Andries, Lise 649
Andronov, Ilja 20
Angelet, Christian 655
Angelis, Marcello de 635, 645
Angulo Egea, María 265
Animan Akassi, Clément 265
Anna Amalia of Prussia 321
Anne, Queen 15, 433
Anning, Mary 139
Anquetil-Duperron, Abraham Hyacinthe 94
Ansart, Guillaume 102, 291, 649
Anson, George 502
Anstey, Peter R. 589
Antognazza, Maria Rosa 102
Antoine, Annette 316
Anzur, Tea 20, 102
Aoki, Atsuko 316
Appelt, Ursula 393–94, 423, 437, 441, 444, 448
Appleby, John H. 102
Appleby, Joyce 567
Apthorp, East 476
Aravamudan, Srinivas 291, 377, 537
Arbell, Mordechai 102
Arbetti, Flavia 291, 316

Arbo, Alessandro 231, 292
Arbour, Keith 103, 567
Arburg, Hans Georg von 317
Arbuthnot, Dr. John 189, 430
Arc, Joan of (Jeanne d' Arc) 564
Arce, Daniel Mendoza de 231
Arch, Stephen Carl 461, 567
Archer, Jean Barbara 662
Archer, John Michael 368
Ardanaz, Margarita 567, 582
Ardila, John G. 368
Arellano, Ignacio 266, 289
Aretov, Nikolai 364
Argerich, Martha 642
Argoty, Jacques Gautier d' 630
Arias Martínez, Manuel 103
Ariosto, Ludovico 641
Aristotle 125, 150, 285
Armbruster, Karla 368, 411
Armfely, Gustaf Mauritz 560
Armillas Vicente, Jose A. 103
Armitage, David 494
Armstrong, Lance 469
Armstrong, Nancy 384
Arner, Robert D. 461
Arnheim, Arthur 20, 103
Arnold, Benedict 463
Arnold, Denis 262
Arnold, Elsie 262
Arnold, General 574
Arnold, Ken 508
Arnold, Laura 669
Arnstein, Walter L. 95
Arntz, Katherine 21
Aron, Paul 292, 293, 294, 296, 298, 299, 307, 309, 312, 313, 314, 368, 389, 451
Arons, Wendy 317
Aronnica, Ferdinando 103
Arras, Sainte-Marie-Madeleine d' 125
Arrenberg, Reinier 61, 164
Arrom, Silvia Marina 537
Arru, Angiolina 21

Artaud, Antonin 387, 665
Artigas-Menant, Geneviève 21, 301, 649
Arzano, Simone 103
Asad, M. N. M. Kamil 103
Asbach, Olaf 21, 368
Asbury, Francis (Methodist bishop) 195
Ascari, Maurizio 397, 417
Asch, Ronald G. 21
Asfour, Lana 368
Ashbee, Andrew 231
Ashbridge, Elizabeth 465, 477, 672
Asleson, Robyn 217, 622
Aspalter, Christian M. 317
Aspromourgos, Tony 103
Asprucci, Mario 525, 624
Assereto, G. 537
Astbury, Katherine 292
Astell, Mary 202, 452
Astington, John H. 368
Astruc, Jean 78
Aten, D. 537
Athanassoglou-Kallmeyer, Nina 218
Atkinson, John 7
Atteberry, John 521, 537
Attems, Carlo Michele d' 123
Atwood, Margaret 406
Attwood, Bain 508, 509
Aub, Max 279
Aubin, Anne-Marie 21
Aubin, Penelope 312, 369, 448
Audidière, Sophie 649
Audisio, Gabriel 21
Auerochs, Bernd 317
Aughton, Peter 479
August the Strong (August I, Elector of Saxonia, later also August II of Poland) 82
Aulinas, L. R. 537
Aumètre, J. 537
Austen, Jane 8, 15, 296, 367, 368, 370, 376, 379, 381, 384, 385, 386, 387, 389, 390, 391, 393, 394, 396, 399, 400, 403, 405, 407, 411, 412, 413, 414, 416, 417, 418, 420, 421, 422, 423, 427, 428, 429, 430, 434, 438, 442, 444, 448, 449, 451, 452, 453, 454, 455, 457, 458–59, 465, 512, 561, 662
Austern, Linda Phyllis 103
Austin, Michael 368, 388–89, 431–32
Avellán, Don Salvador 273
Avery, Gillian 521, 589
Avetisian, V. A. 317, 368
Avogadro, Amedeo 119
Axtell, James 21
Ayguals de Izco, Wenceslao 272
Aymes, Jean-René 266, 272
Azevedo, Cecilia 103
Azyr, Vicq d' 181
Baader, Maria Benjamin 103
Baartman, Sartje 413
Baarsen, Reinier J. 218
Babb, Valerie Melissa 669
Babell, William 247
Bach, Carl Philipp Emanuel 250–51
Bach, Jeffrey 103
Bach, Johann Christian 250–51
Bach, Johann Sebastian 230–31, 232–33, 234, 238, 241, 242, 250–51, 252, 255, 321, 536, 636, 639, 643, 648
Bach, Reinhard 537
Bach, Victor 548
Bach, Wilhelm Friedemann 250–51
Bachmann, Maria K. 369
Backouche, Isabelle 537
Backscheider, Paula R. 369, 395, 431
Backus, Isaac 185
Bacon, Francis 120, 612, 617
Bacon, Jacqueline 104, 461
Bader, Hans-Dieter 479
Badger, Geoffrey Malcolm 509
Badía Cabrera, Miguel A. 104
Baecque, Antoine de 21
Baepler, Paul 669
Baer, Joel H. 369

Baggerman, Arianne 21
Bahar, Saba 104
Bahr, Ehrhard 3, 104, 317
Bailey, Anne Hall 369
Bailey, Colin B. 227, 626, 632
Bailey, Gauvin Alexander 622
Bailey, Hilary Rhodes 589
Baillie, Joanna 401, 410, 663
Bainbridge, Beryl 369–70
Baines, Paul 370
Baird, John D. 589
Baitugan, Boris 104
Bak, John 669
Baker, Edward 266
Baker, Emerson W. 104, 567
Baker, Keith Michael 104
Baker, Kevin R. 499
Baker, M. 537
Baker, N. K. 244
Baker, Theodore 249
Bakewell, Sarah 21
Bakhtin, Mikhail 309, 345
Bakken, Dawn E. 104
Balano, Randy Carol 21
Balcou, Jean 292, 311
Baldwin, Claire 317
Baldwin, M. 589
Ball, Terrance 567
Balle, Robert 133
Ballon, Hilary 622
Balme, Christopher B. 494
Balthazard, Abbé 307
Balzac, Guez de 654, 655
Balzac, Honoré de 523, 540, 654, 659
Bancaud-Maënen, Florence 317
Bander, Elaine 370
Banderier, Gilles 104
Bandry, Anne 3, 292, 370, 662
Bank, Rosemarie K. 568
Bankert, Norbert R. 104
Banks, Sir Joseph 36, 124, 494, 500, 502, 505, 513
Banneker, Benjamin 461

Bannerji, Himani 370
Bannet, Eve Tavor 377–78
Bannister, J. 537
Bar-Shany, Michael 231
Baraka, Amiri 474
Baranger, Denis 537
Barbauld, Anna Laetitia 306, 376, 422, 440
Barber, Ian G. 479
Barber, Mary 394
Barber, Rupert 439
Barber, Samuel 642
Barber, Tabitha 370
Barbera, Sandro 317
Barberi, Giuseppe 524, 624
Barbero, A. 537
Barbiche, Bernard 22, 538
Barbier, Frédéric 521–22, 565
Barbier, Marie-Anne 308
Barbolani di Montauto, Novella 218
Barbone, S. 590
Barchas, Janine 3–4, 370
Barclay, Robert (Captain) 77
Bardet, Jean-Pierre 22
Bareau, Juliet Wilson 218
Barenboim, Daniel 642
Barendse, R. J. 538
Barfield, Rodney D. 104
Barger, J. 568
Bari, Abdul 104
Baridon, Michel 538
Barkan, Elliott Robert 568
Barkemeyer, Karen 318
Barker, Anthony 494
Barker, Elizabeth E. 622
Barker, Hannah 22
Barker, Jane 424
Barker, Michael 105
Barker, Nicolas 22
Barker, T. M. 538
Barkhoff, Jurgen 318
Barlow, Joel 476
Barnard, Alan J. 22, 370

Barnard, T. C. 22
Barnard, Timothy P. 22
Barnes, Diana 370
Barnett, S. J. 22, 105
Barnhart, William Clifford 479–80
Barnuevo, Peralta 17
Baroja, Pío 279
Barquist, David L. 105
Barr, William 105
Barras, Vincent 186
Barrett, Thomas M. 538
Barrington, Daines 190
Barrington, George 509
Barron, Stephanie 370
Barrow, John 482
Barry, David 318
Barry, Robert J. 6
Barta, Peter I. 309, 335, 345
Barth, J. Robert 105
Barth, Marilyn 4, 371, 450
Barth-Scalmani, Gunda 22
Bartlet, M. Elizabeth C. 636
Bartlett, Robert C. 590
Bartlett, Thomas 105, 494
Barton, Karin 318
Barton, Paul 669
Bartram, John 672
Bartsch, Michael 318
Bary, James 631
Basch, Sophie 292, 368, 389, 451
Baseler, Marilyn C. 568
Bashford, Christins 636
Basker, James G. 4, 371, 662
Baskins, Cristelle L. 622
Bass, George 511
Bassard, Katherine Clay 568, 669
Basset, Francis 227
Bassett, Judith 494
Bassler, O. B. 590
Basso, Matthew 22
Bastien, Pascal 22
Bataille, Georges 210, 652
Bataille, Robert R. 291

Bate, John 616
Bate, Walter Jackson 421
Baten, Jörg 22, 538
Bates, A. W. 105
Bates, David 590
Bates, Don 590
Bates, Elisha 99
Batoni, Pompeo 227
Battestin, Martin C. 371
Batten, Guinn 373, 422, 456, 459
Battenberg, J. Friedrich 23, 105
Baude, Michel 309
Baudelaire, Charles 654
Baudin, Nicolas 495
Baudino, Isabelle 622
Bauer, Aaron M. 105
Bauer, Ferdinand 488, 505
Bauer, Joachim 23, 318
Bauer, Ralph 461–62
Bauer, Werner M. 350, 359
Bauer Funke, Cerstin 292
Baum, Richard 318
Baumann, Anette 23
Baumann, Ursula 23
Baumbach, Gerda 318
Baumgarten, Alexander Gottlieb 150, 589
Baverel-Croissant, Marie-Françoise 105
Baxter, Donald L. M. 106, 590
Baxter, Richard 108, 471
Bayard, Pierre 649
Bayle, Pierre 12, 14, 203, 342, 590, 610
Bayly, C. A. 23
Bayly, Susan 23
Beach, Adam R. 371
Beachy, Robert 23
Beaglehole, J. C. 481, 482
Beahrs, Virginia 231
Beal, Joan C. 662
Beale, Mary 370
Bealer, Bonnie K. 209
Beasley, Jerry 409
Beattie, J. M. 23

Index

Beattie, James 667, 668
Beatty, John D. 5, 23
Beauclerk, Lady Di 53
Beaud-Ladoire, Paule 23
Beaudry, Catherine A. 568
Beaufort, Duke of 557
Beaumarchais, Pierre Augustin Caron de 231, 291, 652
Beaur, Gérard 538
Beaurepaire, Pierre-Yves 538
Beavan, Iain 7, 106
Beauvalet-Boutouyre, Scarlett 23
Bechtel, Guy 538
Beckage, Donna 231
Becker, Peter 23
Beckford, William 226, 371–73, 382, 383, 404, 427, 431, 450, 665
Beckles, Hilary 538
Becq, Annie 649
Bedell, J. 538
Bedford, Fifth Duke of 260, 540
Bedini, Silvio A. 590
Beer, John 373
Beethoven, Ludwig van 231, 234, 236, 238, 241, 243, 244, 245, 247, 248, 249, 250, 251, 258, 260, 262, 263, 324, 637
Beetz, Manfred 318
Begheyn, Paul 106
Behn, Aphra 368, 371, 377, 378, 381, 385, 386, 398, 400, 404, 411, 411–12, 417, 423, 424, 425, 429, 431, 435, 441, 465
Behrendt, Stephen D. 24
Behrens, Rudolf 318, 319
Beicken, Suzanne J. 241
Bek, Michael 106
Belanger, Terry 14
Belaubre, Christophe 106
Belfy, Jeanne Marie 636
Belhaouari, Luis 622
Belich, James 509
Belknap, Jeremy 476, 574, 578

Bell, Sir Charles 633
Bell, David A. 24, 292
Bell, Leonard 480
Bell, Martin 106
Bell, Maureen 5, 6, 373, 420, 423, 522
Bell, Robert H. 373
Bell, Tom 541
Bella, Stefano della 223
Belleguic, Thierry 292, 650
Bellesi, Sandro 218
Belloste, Augustin 163
Bellotto, Bernardo 219, 619
Belmer, A. G. 615
Bély, Lucien 24
Bemofsky, Susan 319
Ben-Amos, Dan 568, 586
Ben-Amos, I. K. 539
Ben-Chaim, Michael 106
Ben-Naeh, Yaron 24, 106
Ben-Ur, Aviva 106
Benac, Karine 292
Benavente, Countess-Duchess of 267, 268
Bénavidès, Christine 39
Benchérif, Osman 670
Bender, Barbara 509, 510
Bender, John 292, 373, 384, 401
Benedict, Barbara M. 24, 106, 373, 446
Beneš, Mirka 218
Benezet, Anthony 476
Benhamou, Reed 24
Benítez, Leonel Rodríguez 106
Benítez, Miguel 590
Benito, Jesús 670
Benito Aguado, María Teresa 24
Benjamin, Walter 353
Bennelong 508, 518
Bennet, George 501
Bennett, Benjamin 319
Bennett, James 109
Bennett, Shelley M. 217, 622
Bénouville, Madame de 660
Bénot, Yves 568, 650

Benrath, Gustav Adolf 319
Bentham, Jeremy 122, 205, 606, 609, 614
Bentley, G. E., Jr. 218
Bentley, Richard 527
Benton, L. 539
Benton, Margaret L. 437
Benz, August 590
Benzoni, Gino 24
Berceo, Gonzalo de 278
Bercot, M. 659
Bercovitch, Sacvan 472
Berengo, Marino 101, 186
Bérenguier, Nadine 293, 590
Beretta, M. 591
Beretta, Marco 106, 107
Berg, Peter 5
Berg, Susan 568
Berg, Temma F. 373
Berg, Wesley 238
Bergengruen, Maximilian 319
Berger, Dieter A. 373
Bergerac, Cyrano de 190
Berggren, Ulf 231
Berghahn, Cord-Friedrich 24, 107
Berghahn, Klaus L. 104, 107, 144, 148, 149, 192, 212, 317, 319, 331, 359
Berghof, Oliver 499
Bergin, Tom 509
Berglund, Lisa 373
Bergmann, Walter 257–58
Bergquist, Lars 107
Berke, Dietrich 232
Berkel, Klaas van 218, 222
Berkeley, George 101, 118, 124, 419, 597, 620
Berkemer, Georg 24, 50, 54, 64
Berkovskii, Naum Iakovlevich 319
Berkowitz, Joel 319
Berland, Kevin 462
Bermúdez, Isabel Cristina 30, 107
Bermudez, José 591
Bernal, Luz Fernanda Azuela 107

Bernand, Carmen 107
Bernard, Francis 475, 476
Bernard, Michel 480
Bernardi, Walter 25, 107
Bernardin de Saint Pierre, Jacques Henri 297, 312, 650
Bernardini, Paolo 25, 102, 107, 109, 111, 128, 134, 137, 153, 159, 168, 175, 177, 182, 188, 190, 211
Bernasconi, Robert 25
Bernat, Chrystel 108, 110, 118, 124, 179, 213
Bernier, Marc André 24, 293, 650
Bernier, Olivier 539
Bernschneider-Reif, S. 591
Bernstein, Jeremy 373, 539
Berry, Amanda 373
Berry, Helen 25
Bersier, Gabrielle 319, 360
Berteau, Pierre C. 25, 107
Berthiaume, Pierre 108, 650
Bertière, Simone 539
Bertini, Giuseppe 219
Bertipaglia, Giuliana 360, 374
Bertomeu Sánchez, José Ramón 25, 136
Bertrand, Dominique 650
Bertrand, Gilles 650
Bertuch, Friedrich Justin 527
Bertuol, Roberto 374
Besser, Johann von 337
Bessière, Jean 374, 376
Betzwieser, Thomas 633
Bever, E. 591
Beveridge, A. 662
Beverley, Robert 474
Bhattacharya, Nandini 374
Biagianti, I. 539
Bianchi, Antonio 364
Bianchi, Diana 25, 108
Bianchini, Francesco 365
Biancolelli, Domenico 259
Biba, Otto 232
Biberman, Matthew 662

Bicalho, Maria Fernanda Baptista 25
Bicknell, Alexander 348
Bideaux, Michel 258
Bidima, Jean-Godefroy 266
Bidulph, Sidney 443
Bieganska, Anne 25
Biermann, Veronica 219
Bietenholz, Peter G. 591
Bièvre, Marquis de 650
Bigelow, Ann Clymer 108
Biheron, Marie Marguerite 28, 110
Bilby, Kenneth M. 51, 145
Bilson, Mrs. 449
Bilstein, Johannes 320
Binder, Harald 108
Binkley, Thomas 254–55
Binney, Judith 509, 517
Biondi, Carminella 293
Birchmore-Timney, Carol 94
Birkett, Stephen 232
Birn, Raymond F. 26, 293
Birnstiel, Eckart 108, 110, 118, 124, 179, 213
Birus, Hendrik 320
Bisha, R. 539
Bishop, Paul 320, 325, 326, 331, 341, 350, 352, 353, 354, 355, 359
Bissell, R. Ward 220
Bitbol-Hespéridès, Annie 591
Bittoun-Debruyne, Nathalie 266
Black, Bernard 622
Black, Frank Gees 5
Black, Jeremy 26, 108, 374, 539
Black, Joseph 591, 592
Black, J. William 108
Black, Kathryn Smith 205
Black, Moishe 650
Blackburn, Anne M. 26, 108
Blackwell, Bonnie 9, 108, 374
Blackwell, John 547
Blackwell, Marilyn S. 108
Blain, Michael 480
Blake, David Haven, Jr. 568

Blake, William 7, 198, 218, 227, 238, 327, 361, 446, 459, 633, 669
Blakemore, Steven 374
Blakiston, Francis 204
Blamberger, Günter 320
Blanc, Olivier 360
Blanchard, W. Scott 438
Blanco, Emilio 266, 289
Blanquie, Christophe 26
Blasco Ibáñez, Vicente 279
Blasio, Silvia 219
Blasker, James G. 374
Blathwayt at Dyrham, William 630
Blay, Michel 26, 109, 591
Bleeker, Ann Eliza 467
Bleich, David 378, 410
Bleiler, E. F. 372
Blewett, David 374, 380, 381, 391, 393, 406, 407, 409, 414, 423, 436, 440, 443, 452
Blewitt, Paul 109
Bligh, John H. 510
Bligh, William 90, 488, 490, 491, 507, 510, 514, 544, 545
Blin, Françoise 185
Blinn, Hansjürgen 320
Blödom, Andreas 320
Blom, Frans 522
Blom, Joseph 522
Blomberg, Barbara 349
Blondy, Alain 591
Bloomfield, Robert 403
Blosseville, Jules-Alphonse-René Poret, Baron de 510
Blouch, Christine 409
Blouet, Olwyn M. 591
Bluche, François 539
Bluhm, Andreas 109
Bluhm, Lothar 320
Blussé, Leonard 539
Bly, Antonio T. 670
Boa, Elizabeth 320
Boardman, Richard 603

Boarini, Serge 109
Bobrick, Benson 109
Bobro, Marc E. 591
Boccaccio, Giovanni 641
Boccazzi, Barbara Mazza 293
Boch, Julie 109
Bockett, Elias 476
Bockholdt, Rudolf 232
Bodard, Diane H. 622
Bode, Christoph 374, 376
Bödeker, Hans Erich 26, 522–23
Bodenhorn, H. 568
Bodineau, Pierre 539
Bodmer, Johann Jacob 342
Bodoni, Giambattista 4
Boening, Thomas 321
Boer, Dick E. H. de 26
Boerhaave, Herman 159
Boerner, Carl Gustav 626
Boes, M. R. 539
Boewe, Charles 591
Bogas, Roy 240–41, 642
Bogel, Fredric V. 374–75
Bogen, David S. 109
Bogucka, Maria 26, 27
Bogue, David 109
Bogue, Margaret Beattie 568
Böhm, Arnd 321
Böhm, Günter 109
Böhme, Katrin 109
Bois, Pierre-André 540
Boisson, Didier 27, 110
Boissonade, Euloge 540
Boisvert, Marcel 523, 540
Boixareu, Mercedes 293
Bok, Marten Jan 623
Bokobza Kahan, Michèle 293, 650
Boles, John B. 110, 115
Bollacher, Martin 321, 568, 588
Bolton, Herbert Eugene 27
Boly, Joseph 311
Bolzano, Bernard 125
Bombi, Andrea 266

Bonacchi, Silvia 321
Boncompain, Jacques 27
Bondeson, Jan 27
Bongiovanni, Carmela 232
Bonifas, Gilbert 540, 551, 552, 593
Bonifazio, Massimo 321
Böning, Holger 321
Bonincontro, Eleonora 110
Bonnel, Roland 650
Bonnet, Charles 84, 195
Bonnet, Jean-Claude 293
Bonney, Richard 27, 110, 124, 146, 156
Bònoli, Fabrizio 110
Bontemps, Alex 27
Bony, Alain 375, 662, 663
Bonyhady, Tim 494
Boogert, Maurits H. van den 27
Booker, John 494–95
Boomgaard, Jerorn 623, 626, 627
Booth, C. C. 591
Booth, Ken 34, 72, 85
Borchert, Angela 321
Bordes, Philippe 592
Bordin, Michele 361
Bordo, Michael D. 27
Borelli, Giovanni Alfonso 121
Borgen, Peder 110
Borges, Jorge Luis 321
Borgestedt, Thomas 321–22
Borghese, Giovanni Battista 228
Borghetti, Maria-Novella 79
Borgstedt, Thomas 319, 324, 335, 337, 345, 348, 354, 356, 359
Born, Karl Erich 52
Borofsky, Robert 495, 506
Borovaia, Olga V. 375
Borsay, Anne 592
Bosbach, Franz 110, 124, 146, 156
Bosco, Madonna del 101
Bosse, David 27
Bosse, Heinrich 323
Bost, Hubert 110
Bostoen, Karel 650

Index

Boswell, James   16, 369, 370, 375, 383, 412, 419, 437, 445, 552, 662, 668
Boswell, Parley Ann   670
Bots, Hans   110
Botteri, Lauro   219
Bottiglia, William F.   293
Botting, Fred   375, 383, 410, 425, 428
Botul, Jean-Baptiste   592
Bouabane, Stéphanie   651
Boucé, Paul-Gabriel   375
Bouchard, Nathalie Lemoine   623
Bouchardon, Jacques-Philippe   630
Boucher, David   27
Boudreau, George W.   28, 43, 44, 54, 83, 84, 88
Boufflers, Stanislas-Jean, Chevalier de   311
Bougainville, Louis-Antoine, Comte de   299, 308, 649
Bougé-Grandon, Dominique   522
Bouguer, Pierre   131
Bouilly, Jean-Nicolas   262
Bouin, Anne   452
Boulard, Claire   663
Boulay, Roger   516
Boulerie, Florence   293, 651
Boulinier, Georges   28, 110
Boullogne, Louis de   628
Boulukos, George E.   376, 449
Bour, Isabelle   376
Bourbón, Don Carlos Maria Isidro de   173
Bourdieu, Pierre   452
Bourdin, Jean-Claude   651
Bourgeois, Muriel   294
Bourguet-Rouveyre, Josiane   540
Bourguinat, Nicolas   28
Bourne, Eunice   475
Bouton, Terry   569
Bouveresse, Jacques   111
Bower, Calvin M.   636, 644–46, 647–48
Bower, George   399
Bowman, Carl F.   160

Bowman, Stanley Mackenzie   495
Bowron, Edgar Peters   219
Bowsher, John   537
Bowstead, Diana   529
Boxall, Maria   232
Boyajian, James C.   111
Boyce, D. George   28
Boyd, Diane   376, 395–97
Boyd, Malcolm   232–33
Boyer, Paul S.   149
Boyer, Pierre Abel de   656
Boyle, John, Fifth Earl of Cork and Orrery   523, 663
Boyle, Nicholas   111
Boyle, Robert   152, 158, 174, 183, 195, 589, 620
Boyleau, Simon   238
Brabourne, Lord   418
Braccesi, Alessandro   110
Bracci, Pietro   225
Bracken, David   111
Brackenridge, Henry   475
Bradbury, John   591
Braddick, M. J.   28
Braden, Jutta   28
Bradfield, Katherine   197
Brading, D. A.   111
Bradley, James E.   28, 111, 170, 176, 204, 206, 209
Brashaw, Penny   376
Bradstreet, Anne   124, 171, 188, 464, 468, 469, 471, 476, 671
Brady, Patrick   294, 651
Brady, Valentini Papadopoulou   294
Braffort, Paul   592
Braganza, Catherine of   163
Brahami, Frédéric   376
Brainerd, David   182
Brake, Wayne te   111
Brakensiek, Stefan   28
Brana-Shute, Rosemary   49
Brand, Sebastian   356
Brandes, Peter   323

Branfoot, Crispin 111
Brandhorst, P. J. 527
Branson, Susan 28, 111
Braun, Mark 111
Braun, Theodore E. D. 294, 589, 592, 594, 595, 600, 602, 603, 608, 615, 619, 651
Braun, Werner 323
Braungart, Wolfgang 323
Braunschweig, Karl 233
Braverman, L. E. 573
Bray, Alan 670
Bray, Francesca 540
Bray, Thomas 533
Brazdil, Rudolf 206
Breashears, Caroline 4
Breathnach, C. S. 592
Breazeale, Daniel 112
Brech, Alison 28, 112
Breckmann, Patricia C. 376
Bredekamp, Horst 592
Bredin, Miles 540
Breen, Louise A. 112, 569
Breen, T. H. 28, 569
Breig, James 569
Breintnall, Joseph 476
Bremer, Manuel E. 112
Brenni, P. 592
Brentano, Clemens 340
Bresc-Bautier, Geneviève 112
Breslaw, Elaine G. 112
Bressler, Ann Lee 29, 112
Bret, Patrice 112, 540, 592, 605
Brett, Phillip 239
Breuer, Dieter 29
Breuer, Horst 376
Breuer, Ingo 323
Breunig, Hans Werner 376
Brewer, John 3
Brewer, Lisa K. 376
Brewer, William D. 112
Brewton, Vince 377
Brianta, Donata 540, 592

Bric, Maurice J. 29
Bridges, Elizabeth 377
Brier, Evan 463, 465–66
Briesemeister, Dietrich 89
Briley, Ron 29
Brillant Annequin, Anick 294
Brinkmann, Reinhold 323
Brissot, J.-P. 16, 37, 535
Brito, Émilio 443
Brito, Manuel 389, 453
Broadie, Alexander 112
Brocherioux, Chrystele 294
Brockes, Barthold Heinrich 331, 343, 351
Brockhaus, Cathrin 377
Brockmann, Thomas 110, 124, 146, 156
Brod, M. 540
Brodeur, Patrice 112
Brodeur, Raymond 117
Broers, Michael 113
Broich, Ulrich 377
Brome, Richard 495
Bromley, J. S. 29
Bromwich, David 541
Bronfen, Elizabeth 437
Brontolon, Todero 363
Brook, Clodagh 361
Brooke, Frances 263, 264
Brooke, J. H. 592
Brooks, Derek R. 614
Brooks, Francis 113
Brooks, G. P. 305
Brooks, Richard S. 113
Broome, William 422
Brosch, Renate 377
Brosche, Peter 113
Bross, Kristina 462
Brot, Muriel 651
Broughton, William 486
Brouncker, William 617
Brouzeng, Paul 100, 103, 110, 113, 116, 117, 119, 120–21, 123, 125,

126, 128, 131, 134, 143, 167, 171, 180–81, 199, 202
Brown, Alan K. 35
Brown, Anthony J. 495
Brown, Callum G. 113
Brown, Charles Brockden 462, 463, 466, 467, 477, 503, 670, 671, 672, 675
Brown, D. 540
Brown, David 569
Brown, Eliza Southgate 468
Brown, G. I. 592
Brown, Gillian 29, 593, 670
Brown, Gregory S. 294, 651
Brown, H. G. 541, 651
Brown, Hilary 323, 377
Brown, Iain Gordon 223
Brown, Jacob Jennings 580
Brown, Jane K. 323
Brown, John Russell 377, 410, 452
Brown, Kathleen 569
Brown, Kendall W. 29
Brown, Kenneth 113
Brown, Laura 29, 377–78, 528
Brown, Leslie Ellen 378
Brown, Marshall 446
Brown, Michael 578, 593
Brown, Murray L. 378
Brown, Robert 173
Brown, Roger L. 113
Brown, Stewart J. 113
Brown, Thomas 391
Brown, Tracy L. 114
Browne, Patrick 71, 175, 611
Brownstein, Rachel M. 378, 379
Brozek, Josef 208
Bruce, James 540
Bruck, Michael von 161
Bruckmann, Patricia C. 29
Brügge, Joachim 233
Brumwell, Stephen 29
Brun, Friederike 333, 354
Brunel, Pierre 294

Bruni, Francesco 379, 413
Brunius, J. B. 371
Brunner, Lance W. 636
Brunstrom, Conrad 379
Brunt, Peter William 495–96
Bruyn, Adrienne 294
Bruyn, Frans de 379, 496
Bry, Jean-Antoine Joseph de (also: Debry) 488
Bryant, Arthur 379
Bryant, Mary 482
Bucer, Martin 108
Buchan, John 541
Buchan, Mark 406
Buchan, William 546, 607
Büchel, Anne 482
Buchheit, Vinzenz 323
Buchs, Arnaud 651
Buchwald, Jed Z. 114
Buck, A. 519
Buckingham, James Silk 78
Buckle, Stephen 114
Buckley, Thomas E. 569
Buczynski, Alexander 29
Budd, Adam 379
Budd, Graham E. 114
Bueno, Antonio González 114
Bueno, Eva Paulino 266
Buffat, Marc 294, 651
Buffon, Georges Louis LeClerc, Comte de 165, 593
Buickerood, James G. 379
Bulatov, Vladimir E. 29
Bull, John 614
Bull, Philip 494, 496, 500, 504
Bullard, Allice 496
Bullen, J. B. 219
Buller, Arthur 123
Bullock, S. C. 541
Bumsted, J. M. 541
Bundock, Michael 663
Bungener, Patrick 114
Bunker, J. 643–44

Bunyan, John 182, 487
Bunyan, Paul 472
Bunzel, Wolfgang 661
Buonarroti, Michaelangelo 220
Burchell, D. 593
Burdan, Judith 379
Burden, Michael 636
Burgess, Miranda J. 379
Burgett, Bruce 569, 670
Burgio, Alberto 114
Burguière, André 30
Burhans, Bruce J. 30
Burigny, Jean Lévesque de 124
Burke, Edmund 80, 189, 211, 373, 374, 377, 379, 395, 400, 404, 422, 426, 442, 529, 541, 593, 598, 601, 604
Burke, Tim 30, 380
Burkhardt, Armin 346
Burn, D. J. 250–51, 641
Burnard, T. 541, 593
Burnard, Trevor 30
Burnett, James 594
Burney, Charles (Dr.) 264, 408
Burney, Fanny (Frances) [d'Arblay] 369, 380, 382, 396, 407–08, 413, 415, 452, 664, 665
Burney, Sarah Harriet 383
Burnham, Michelle 478
Burnim, Kalman A. 264
Burns, James 614
Burns, Robert 421, 441, 444
Burr, Aaron 573, 576, 583
Burr, Ester 477
Burr, Sandra J. 593
Burns, William E. 114, 380
Burroughs, Catherine 380
Burroughs, George 177
Burstein, Andrew 569
Burt, E. S. 651
Burton, John D. 114
Burton, Vicki Tolar 380
Busch, Werner 323
Busch-Geertsema, Bettina 522

Bush, H. K. 569
Bushman, R. L. 541
Bushman, Richard 670
Butler, Joseph 155, 176
Butler, Jon 114, 570
Butler, L. S. 570
Butler, Michael 323
Butterfield, Kevin 114
Butterwick, Richard 30
Buttner, Manfred 115
Buyssens, Danielle 115
Byles, Mather 465
Byrd, Ronald 30
Byrd II (of Westover), William 462, 479
Byrne, P. W. 651
Byrne, Patrick 294
Byron, George Gordon, Lord 374–75, 438
Byrt, John 233
Bywaters, David 380, 390, 391
Caballero Espericueta, Mariano 30
Caballero Fernández-Rufete, Carmelo 266–67
Cadalso, José de 265, 267–68, 277, 284
Cadé, Michel 268–69
Caesar, Ann Hallamore 361
Caffentzis, C. George 115
Caffort, Michel 115, 219
Cahill, David 115
Cahill, Edward 462
Cain, Robert J. 5
Cain, Tubal 609
Caine, Barbara 541
Caird, Edward 607
Calaça, Carlos Eduardo 30, 167
Calaresu, Melissa 30
Calder, Alex 479, 480, 484, 486, 487, 488, 490, 492–93
Calderón de la Barca, Pedro 266–67
Caldwell, Michael 3–4
Calhoon, Kenneth S. 323
Calhoon, Robert M. 115
Calimani, Anna Vera Sullam 361

Index

Calvin, John 34, 176, 471
Cambry, Jacques 541
Cameron, David Kerr 30
Cametti, Bernardo 608
Cammagre, Geneviève 652
Campbell, Colin D. 115
Campbell, George 88
Campbell, J. 519
Campbell, James 569
Campbell, Sabrina 115
Campbell, Thomas 458
Campe, Ruediger 380
Campenhausen, Christoph von 115
Camper, Petrus 633
Campion, Edmund 554
Camplani, Clara 269
Campos, José Antonio 269
Canales, Jimena 115
Canaletto (Giovanni Antonio Canal) 623
Candamo, Bances 285
Candaux, Jean-Daniel 115, 294, 652
Canfield, J. Douglas 380
Cañizares, José de 269, 278
Cañizares-Esguerra, Jorge 30
Canning, Joseph 31
Cannon, Mercy 384–385
Canny, Nicholas 570
Canova, Antonio 622, 623
Cansinos-Asséns, Rafael 279
Cantagrel, Gilles 636
Cantor, Geoffrey 116
Canuel, Mark 116
Capano, Daniel A. 361
Capdevila, Néstor 269
Capet, Antoine 593
Caplan, Jane 496, 500, 503
Caplin, William E. 233
Capone, Stefania 107
Carasso, Dedalo 623, 626
Caravaggio, Michelangelo Merisi da 220, 225, 227, 228
Carboni, Pierre 380, 663
Cardano, Girolamo 198

Cardy, Michael 295
Carew, Derek 234
Carey, Hilary M. 496
Carlebach, Elisheva 116
Carlin, Claire 295
Carlisle, Abraham 580
Carlos III, King 45, 268, 278, 288–89
Carlos IV, King 186, 267
Carlos V, King 280
Carlson, Andrew 116
Carlson, David J. 116
Carlsson, Susanne Chauvel 497
Carman, Judith E. 234
Carmichael, Gershom 141
Carmontelle, Louis de 310, 635
Carneiro, Henrique Soares 116, 269
Carnell, Rachel K. 380, 381
Carnero, Guillermo 284
Carney, Sean 663
Carofano, Pierluigi 219
Caron, Nathalie 570
Caron, Richard 381, 419
Carozzi, Albert V. 116
Carpenter, Richard 164
Carr, Dawson W. 225
Carraro, Laura Favero 439
Carré, Jacques 541
Carrell, Jennifer Lee 593
Carreras, Juan José 269
Carretta, Vincent 62, 72, 94, 461, 462, 464, 465, 466, 477, 478, 670
Carrithers, D. W. 593
Carroll (of Carollton), Charles 256–57
Carroll, J. W. 593
Carroll, Noël 219
Carroll, Paul 636
Carroll-Burke, Patrick 116, 496–97
Carruthers, Gerard 381
Carson, David J. 462
Carswell, John 31
Carter, Brian 116
Carter, Edward C., II 570, 586
Carter, Elizabeth 13

Carter, Harold 494
Carter, Lin 372
Carter, Philip 31, 541
Carter, Sebastian 523
Cartier, Jacques 492
Carton, Fernand 31
Cartuyvels, Yves 541
Carus, Carl Gustav 330
Carvajal, Tomás de 281
Casal, Elvira 381
Casals, Pablo 642
Casanova, Jean-Claude 31
Casanova de Seingalt, Giacomo Girolamo 295, 301, 306, 307, 361, 362, 363, 364, 650
Casanovas, Juam 116
Casanueva, Fernando 31
Casares Rodicio, Emilio 266–67, 269, 270, 276, 277, 279, 280, 281, 287, 288–89
Casas, Bartolomé de las (also: Las Casas) 269, 273, 277, 279–80, 282, 286, 287, 289, 290
Casella, Eleanor Conlin 480, 510
Cash, Alice Hudnall 636
Cash, Arthur H. 381
Cashin, Edward J. 116
Casler, Jeanine 381, 541
Casler, Lawrence 234
Cassese, Michele 117
Cassini, Alain de 125
Cassini, Anna 117
Cassini, Daniel de 125
Cassini, Giovanni Domenico (also Jean-Dominique) 100, 103, 110, 113, 116, 119, 120–21, 123, 125, 126, 128, 131, 134, 143, 167, 171, 199, 202
Cassini, Jacques 180–81
Cassini, Patrice de 125
Cassirer, Ernst 608, 620
Castillo, Benito del 117
Castillo Gómez, Antonio 523, 649

Castillo, Susan 462
Castle, Terry 528
Castlemaine, Roger, Earl of 399
Castleman, Bruce A. 31
Castlenau, Henriette de (Madame de Murat) 440, 564
Castro, Américo 289
Castro, Ana de 290
Castro, Taurino Burón 117
Català, Víctor 290
Catherine II 'the Great,' Empress 32, 37, 81, 90, 246, 304, 313, 334, 355, 661
Cathro, Adele 503
Caulier, Brigitte 117
Cavagna, Anna Giulia 533
Cavaillé, Jean-Pierre 542
Cavaliero, Roderick 31, 381
Cavallin, Jean-Christophe 652
Cavallo, Sandra 117
Cave, Christophe 652
Cavendish, Margaret, Duchess of Newcastle 175, 370, 374, 376, 416, 419, 430, 444, 456
Cavendish, R. 542
Cawley, A. S. 570
Caylus, Comte de 299, 310
Caywood, Cynthia 381
Cazotte, Jacques 293
Cebrian, Reyes Bertolin 113
Cecchi, Annie 652
Cecil, James, Fifth Earl of Salisbury 533
Cedeño, Aristófanes 269
Celan, Paul 321
Celeda, Jaroslav 248
Cellard, Jacques 652
Centlivre, Susanna 381, 417, 432, 439
Ceretti, M. 542
Cerezo, Guindo 270
Cerfvol, Sieur de 590
Cerman, Markus 21, 31, 93
Cerruti, Solbiati 234
Cerruti, Silvio 234

Index

Certeau, Michel de   135
Cervantes, Miguel de   287, 290, 369, 393, 523, 649
Cervantes, Xavier   542, 623
Cesarani, David   117
Cesareo, Francesco C.   117
Cesarotti, Melchiorre   360, 374
Chaber, Lois A.   381
Chabot, Jean-Luc   31
Chàline, Olivier   117
Challe, Robert   312, 448
Chalmers, Alexander   12, 14
Chalmers, George   399
Chalmers, Mary E.   118
Chamayou, Anne   652
Chamayou, Fabienne   118
Chamberlain, Ava   597
Chamberlen, Dr.   599
Chambers, Ephraim   17
Chambers, Neil   494
Chamfort, Sébastien Roche Nicolas   347
Chammas, Jacqueline   295, 361
Champagne, Roland A.   299
Champion, Françoise   107
Champion, J. A. I.   118
Champion, Neil   118
Chan, Hok-lam   118
Chancellor, Edward   480
Chandler, Mary   437
Chang, Hasok   118
Chantin, Jean-Pierre   31, 118
Chapin, Chester   381, 382
Chaplin, Sue   361, 382
Chapman, Guy   371
Chapman, H. C.   593
Chapman, Mary   584, 670
Chappelle, Ann   491
Chapple, Jefferson   479
Charack, André   234
Charbonneau, Frédéric   295
Chard, Chloe   570
Chardin, Jean-Siméon   619, 623
Chardin, Teilhard de   298, 596

Charke, Charlotte Cibber   663, 665
Charles I, King   220
Charles II, King   428
Charles V, Emperor   349
Charles, S. J.   118
Charles, Sébastien   382
Charles, Shelly   295, 663
Charlton, David   258
Charney, Ann   652
Charpillon, Marie   364
Charrak, André   652
Charrier, Marianne   652
Charrier-Vozel, Marianne   652
Charrière, Isabelle Agneta de (Belle van Zuylen)   296, 300, 313, 314, 385, 650, 652, 658, 659, 660
Charron, Pierre   599
Charteris, Richard   234
Chartier, Pierre   295, 652
Charvet, Jean Gabriel   508
Chase, Gilbert   235
Chase, H. V.   542, 570
Chase, Philander D.   588
Chastang, Marie-Laure   653
Chastel-Rousseau, Charlotte   653
Chastenet de Puységur, Arman-Marie-Jacques   542
Chateaubriand, François René   311, 562, 652
Châtel, Laurent   623
Chatel de Brancion, Laurence   32
Châtelet, Gabrielle Émilie le Tonnelier de Breteuil du (Madame de Châtelet)   653, 658
Chater, K.   542
Chatterjee, I.   542
Chatterton, Thomas   401, 665
Chaucer, Geoffrey   459
Chauderlot, Fabienne Sophie   295
Chaudhuri, Rosinka   663
Chavis, John   179
Checa Beltrán, José   284
Cheetham, Mark A.   118, 219

Chen, S. 593
Chénier, André 294, 308
Cherkasov, Petr Petrovich 32
Cherni, Amor 593
Cherpak, Clifton 295
Chesnutt, David R. 577
Chesterfield, Philip Dormer Stanhope, Earl of 435
Chetwood, Knightly 383
Cheuse, Alan 118
Chézaud, Patrick 382, 542, 594, 663
Chevallier, Bernard 483–84
Chevet, Jean-Michel 542
Chevrel, Yves 654
Chew, Shirley 6, 373, 420, 423, 522
Chew, William, III 552
Chézaud, Patrick 623
Chiappe, Jean-François 32
Chiba, Yasuki 382
Chigi, Fabio 186
Chinchilla Pawling, Perla 118
Chinnici, Ileana 119
Chisick, Harvey 32
Chiu, Peng-sheng 32
Cho, Woo-Ho 324
Chohan, Sandeep 119
Choi, Inhwan 382
Choi, Julie 382
Choi, Yeun-Soo 324
Choquette, Leslie 32
Choris, Louis 487
Choudhury, Mita 594
Chouillet, Anne Marie 521, 523, 653
Christen, A. G. 594
Christen, J. A. 594
Christian, Charles W. 119
Christian, Edward 510
Christian, Fletcher 481
Christian, Glynn 481
Christiane, Fürstin von der Osten-Sacken 58
Christiansen, Keith 219–21, 623
Christiansen, Palle Ove 32
Christie, Nancy 119, 152
Christina, Queen 219
Christmas, William J. 382
Christofferson, M. S. 542
Chu, J. M. 570
Chu, Pingyi 594
Chudleigh, Lady Mary 3–4, 370, 424
Chung, David 119
Chung, Ewha 382
Chung, Rebecca 382
Churchill, Charles 446
Churchman, Nancy 542
Chusid, Martin 636, 637–38, 643
Chuvin, Pierre 68
Ciampolini, M. 221
Ciappara, Frans 32, 119
Ciardi, M. 594
Ciardi, Marco 119
Cibber, Colley 411
Cicali, Gianni 361
Cicchini, Marco 32
Cicero, Marcus Tullius 391
Cicovacki, Predrag 119
Cid, Jesús-Antonio 270
Cienfuegos, Beatriz (Crossdresser) 281, 284
Cigoli, Ludovico (Cardi da) 221
Ciobanu, Veniamin 32
Ciofetta, Simona 524, 624
Cirakman, Asli 32, 295
Cislo, Waldemar 119
Cizauskas, Albert 570
Clack, Beverley 295
Cladis, Mark S. 295
Claésson, Dick 382, 450
Clairmont, Claire 381
Clairmont, Clara Mary Jane 481
Clare, John 403
Clarin, Leopoldo Alas 288
Clark, A. 543
Clark, Anthony 33
Clark, David H. 32, 119
Clark, Gregory 33

Clark, J. C. D. 383, 543
Clark, Lorna 382, 383
Clark, Marilyn S. 643–44
Clark, Peter 543
Clark, S. 594
Clark, Stephen P. H. 32, 119
Clark, Steve H. 481, 489
Clark, Stuart 119
Clark, Suzannah 103, 120, 234
Clark, William 23
Clark, William (Lewis and Clark) 61, 174, 180, 199, 210, 573
Clarke, George 523
Clarke, Stephen 383
Clavijo y Fajardo, José 286
Claydon, Tony 594
Clayton, Lawrence 120
Clayton, Tim 523
Cleary, Patricia 570
Cleaveland, Timothy 120
Cleland, John 450
Clementi, Muzio 642
Clemit, Pamela 139
Clerici, Luca 361
Clery, E. J. 383
Cliburn, Van 642
Clifford, Jane 623
Clifford, Timothy 524
Cline, Edward 571
Clingham, Greg 383
Cloonan, Kevin A. 567
Cloot, Julia 324
Clune, John James 120
Cobb, David A. 59
Cobb, James 374
Cobbett, William 89
Cobeldick, Trevor 510
Cock, Randolph 120
Coetzee, Carli 543
Coetzee, J. M. 383, 407
Coffey, Charles 431
Coffman, Elesha 120
Cohen, Alabert 638

Cohen, Daid E. 120
Cohen, Huguette 594
Cohen, I. Bernhard 114
Cohen, Michèle 383
Cohen, Paula Marantz 383
Cohen, Ralph 383, 447
Cohen, S. S. 543
Cohn, Ellen R. 573
Cohon, Rachel 120
Coigny, Aimée 54
Colander, David 543
Colas, Santiago 406
Colbert de Croissy, Charles-Joachim 622
Colclough, Stephen 524
Coldrey, Barry M. 481
Cole, Michael 221
Colebrook, Henry Thomas 398
Coleman, Deirdre 481
Coleman, Dorothy 120
Coleman, J. 543
Coleman, Linda S. 670
Coleman, Patrick 605, 614, 632, 657
Coleman, Terry 33
Coleridge, Samuel Taylor 116, 145, 206, 447, 666
Colerus, Johannes 594
Coley, Noel G. 120
Colin, Jacques 120–21
Collani, Claudia von 33
Collette, Sophie 33, 121
Colley, Linda 13, 141
Collier, Jeremy 633
Collier, Mary 382, 427
Collingwood, Robin George 611
Collins, Amanda 384
Collins, David 514, 517
Collins, Dennis 234
Collins, Irene 384
Collins, Jeffrey 623
Collins, Margo 409, 449–50
Collinson, S. 571
Collits, Pierce 520
Collyer, Mary 405

Colman, George, (the Younger) 413, 572
Colomba, Giovanni 264
Columbus, Christopher 108
Come, Arnold B. 121
Comminey, Shawn 524, 543
Comte, Auguste 169
Conacher, I. D. 121
Condamine, Charles Maria de la 80, 189, 561
Condette-Marcant, Anne-Sophie 33
Condillac, Etienne Bonnot de 121
Condorcet, Marie-Jean Antoine Nicolas Caritat, Marquis de 309, 558
Cone, Edward T. 637, 638
Conermann, Stephan 33
Conforti, Maria 121
Conger, Danielle E. 571
Congreve, William 423, 444
Conlin, Jonathan G. W. 384
Conlin Casella, Eleanor 480, 510
Conlin, M. F. 571
Connolly, Sean J. 33
Connolly, William R. 121
Conrad, Dennis M. 575
Conrad, Lawrence I. 543
Conrad, Margaret 33
Constant, Benjamin 311, 613
Constantine, David 33
Contardi, Bruno 524, 624
Contardi, S. 594
Conway, Alison 384–85, 385
Conway, Stephen 33, 543
Cook, Alan 121
Cook, Alexander 516
Cook, Andrew 481
Cook, Della Collins 174
Cook, Ebenezer 464
Cook, G. C. 121
Cook, James (Captain) 478, 479, 481, 482, 485, 488, 490, 493, 495–96, 498, 499, 501, 502, 503, 505, 506, 507, 508, 509, 511, 514, 515, 516–17, 519, 520
Cook, John A. 283, 286
Cook, Judith 482
Cook, M. 594
Cook, Malcolm 296, 653
Cook, Noble David 20, 31, 33
Cook (of Needham), Robert 189
Cooke, Samuel A. 485
Cookson, J. E. 543
Cooper, Barry 234, 324
Cooper, James Fenimore 672, 673
Cooper, Kenneth 254
Coote, Jeremy 482
Coote, Stephen 385
Cope, Kevin L. 5, 29, 30, 63, 66, 68, 71, 75, 77, 85, 87, 228, 367, 374, 378, 385, 403, 421, 435, 441, 444, 451, 455, 462, 467, 468, 594–95
Copeland, David A. 595
Copernicus, Nicolas 612
Copley, John Singleton 630
Copsey, Tony 524
Coquard, Claude 34
Corbin, Alain 653
Corcoran, Patrick 168
Corday, Charlotte 426
Cordonnier, Alexis 34
Coré, Filhos de 266
Corkery, Daniel 93
Cornand, Suzanne 296
Corneille, Pierre 42, 104
Cornelis, Bart 218
Cornell, Saul 571
Cornette, Joël 543
Cornille, Jean-Louis 296
Cornwallis, Charles, First Marquess Cornwallis 129
Cornwell, Neil 336
Corona Páez, Sergio Antonio 34
Coronelli, Vincenzo 544
Corot, Jean Baptiste Camille 229
Corp, E. 234
Corral, Marco Arturo Moreno 122

Cortés, Rocío 270
Cortés-Conde, Roberto 27
Cortey, Mathilde 296
Cosandey, Fanny 34
Cosgrove, Denis 544
Cosgrove, Peter 510
Cosimo II de Medici 220
Cosimo III 229
Cosme, Alba Dolores Morales 122
Cossy, Valérie 34, 291, 292, 296, 297, 308, 309, 311, 324, 335, 385, 386, 422, 430, 652
Costa, Michael 595
Costa Zalessow, Natalia 361
Costanzi, Giovanni Antonio 364
Costanzo, Angelo 464
Costilla, Nora Reyes 122
Cotoni, Marie-Hélène 301
Cottegnies, Line 386
Cotter, Richard E. 519
Cotterill, Anne 386
Cotticelli, Francesco 258–60
Cotton, John 122
Cottret, Bernard 34
Coudreuse, Anne 296
Coulet, Henri 296
Coull, James R. 34
Countryman, Edward 571
Coupe, Lynda Wolfe 671
Courier, Paul-Louis 60
Courreges, Hélène de 122
Court, Antoine 288
Court de Gébelin, Antoine 557
Coutonnier, Louis Guillaume 302
Coutu, Joan 623
Couty, Mathieu 34
Couvreur, Manuel 292, 368, 389, 451
Cowan, Brian 34
Cowans, Jon 34
Coward, David 296
Cowart, G. 221
Cowell, Pattie 462
Cowen, David L. 53, 137–38, 148, 179, 212, 595
Cowley, Abraham 388
Cowley, Hannah 386, 455
Cowper, William 6, 129, 182, 393, 459, 663
Cox, Daniel 547
Cox, James A. 595
Cox, Michael 34, 72, 85
Craciun, Adriana 386, 410, 413, 414, 415, 419, 425, 428, 455
Cradock, Thomas 476
Craig, Raymond 671
Craig, Russell 494–95
Craig, Sheryl Bonar 386
Craik, A. D. D. 595
Craik, George L[illie]. 482
Crain, Caleb 462–63
Cramer, John B. 242
Cramer, Wilhelm 246
Cramer, Yvonne 500
Crampe-Casnabet, Michèle 653
Crane, Elaine Forman 544, 571
Cranz, August Friedrich 356
Craske, Matthew 524, 624
Craven, Wayne 463
Crawford, Alan Pell 34
Crawford, C. 544, 595
Crawford, Michael J. 40
Crawford, Patricia 510, 511, 557
Crawford, Richard 234–36
Crawford, William H. 35
Crébillon, Claude Prosper Jolyot de (Crébillon fils) 313, 450, 603, 653
Crecelius, Daniel 35
Creeber, Glen 386, 430
Creed, Barbara 510
Creed, Brad 122
Crépin, Annie 544
Crépu, Michel 653
Crespí, Juan 35
Crespo Solana, Ana 35
Cresswell, M. J. 122
Cresti, Federico 122

Crèvecoeur, Hector Saint-John de 300, 464, 467, 474, 476, 571, 580, 673
Crews, Ed. 571
Crick, Olly 263
Crimmins, James E. 122
Crisman, William 324
Croaker, John 494–95
Croce, Benedetto 259
Crocker, Matthew H. 571
Crocker, Robert 113, 122, 133, 153, 161, 174, 182, 187, 190, 195
Crockett, Davy 472
Crockett, John 507
Crocombe, R. G. 510–11
Croft, Julian 483
Croll, Gerhard 236
Crome, A. F. W. 176
Cronk, Nicholas 297, 386, 595, 617, 653, 659
Crosby, Alfred 485
Crosby, Brian 638
Crosby, R[on]. 483
Crosland, Margaret 544
Cross, Ashley J. 386
Cross, David A. 624
Crothers, A. G. 571
Crotti, Ilaria 324, 361, 363, 364
Crouch, Margaret A. 123
Crouzet, François 402, 416, 444
Crowne, John 247
Crowston, Clare Haru 35–36
Croxson, Bronwyn 36
Crozet, Julien Marie 483
Crugten-André, Valerie van 292, 297, 368, 389, 451
Crummey, Robert O. 36
Cruse, Bernard W. 123
Crusius, Gabriele 48
Cruz, Béatriz Nates 123
Cruz, Enrique Normando 36
Cruz, Ramón de la 279, 281
Cryle, P. M. 297
Cryle, Peter 653

Csetri, Elek 123
Cudworth, Ralph 153
Cullen, Fintan 123
Cullen, Louis M. 123
Cullhed, Anna 324
Cullity, Thomas Brendan 512
Culpepper, Charles 152
Cumberland, Richard 144
Cunja, Vesna 123
Cunningham, A. 595
Cunningham, Andrew 123
Cunningham, John 403
Curley, Thomas M. 386
Curll, Edmund 12, 435
Curran, Andrew 297, 653
Curran, Jane V. 324
Curran, Stuart 36, 386
Curtin, Nancy J. 123
Curtin, Philip 36
Curtis, Bruce 123
Curtis, L. P. 544
Curtis, Peter 573
Cusset, Catherine 595
Cuthbertson, Bern 511
Cuvier, George 615
Cuvier, Georges 169
Cysat, Renward 53
Czarnecka, Miroslawa 322, 324
Czouz-Tornare, Alain Jacques 544
Czubaty, Jaroslav 324
D'Afflitto, Chiara 221
D'Alembert Le Rond, Jean 17, 305, 425, 617, 655, 658
D'Alessandro, Giuseppe 595
D'Antuono, Nancy 259
D'arcy, Frank 37
D'Costa, Anthony 124
D'Elfer, Charles 236
D'Oench, Ellen G. 625
D'Souza, Florence 386
Da Passano, M. 544
Da Ponte, Lorenzo (Emanuele Conegliano) 231, 235, 291, 641

Index

Dabas, Bal Kishan 36
Dachez, Hélène 387
Dacier, Anne Le Fevre 532, 657
Dadelsen, Georg von 232
Daiber, Jürgen 324
Daliès, Nandou 123
Dalporto, Jeannie 36, 387
Dalrymple, Alexander 481
Dalnekoff, Donna Isaacs 297
Dalton, S. 595
Daly, P. J. 664
Daly, Patrick J., Jr. 387
Daly, Robert 124, 464
Dalziel, Raewyn 506
Dambacher, Eva 324
Dames, Nicholas 387
Damm, S. 356
Dampier, William 486, 502, 558
Danchin, Pierre 387
Danckwardt, Marianne 236
Danesi, Marcel 362
Danforth, Susan 36, 124
Dangel Pelloquin, Elsbeth 325
Daniel, Clay 387
Daniel, Stephen H. 124
Daniel, Thilo 325
Danilevskii, R. Iu 325
Danson, Edwin 36
Dante, Alighieri 248
Darby, M. 544
Darcel, Jean-Louis 36
Darlow, Mark 297, 653
Darly, Mary 534–35
Darly, Matthew 534–35
Darnton, Robert 16, 37, 40, 66, 535
Darrigol, Olivier 124
Darwall, S. 595
Darwin, Charles 607
Darwin, Erasmus 593
Dashkova, E. R. 37
Dassas, Frédéric 624
Daston, Lorraine 37
Dauber, Jeremy 319

Dauberval, Jean Bercher 261
Daunou, Pierre Claude François 68
Daunton, Martin 483, 491, 569
Davenant, William 385, 433
Davenport, Hester 664
Davenport, John 443
David, François 124
David, Jacques-Louis 426, 592, 624, 629, 630, 634
Davids, Karel 37, 544
Davidson, Donald 607
Davidson, Jenny 37, 124
Davie, Donald 446
Davie, William 595
Davies, Andrew 399
Davies, Benjamin 236
Davies, Gordon Leslie Herries 662
Davies, John 201
Davies, Kate 387
Davies, Mererid Puw 325
Davies, Simon 654
Davies, Steffan 325
Davies, Thomas 416
Davis, J. A. 544
Davis, Leith 664
Davis, Lydia 387
Davis, Martin L. 124
Davis, Michael T. 5
Davis, P. 596
Davis, Paul 387
Davis, Richard 164
Davis, Robert C. 124
Davis, Whitney 221
Davison, Doris M. 124
Davison, Graeme 497, 511
Davison, Rosena 297
Davison-Pegon, Claire 387
Davys, Mary 391, 437, 450
Dawson, Deidre 34, 291, 292, 296, 297, 308, 309, 311, 324, 335, 386, 422, 430, 624
Dawson, Matthew Q. 571
Dawson, Robert L. 297

Dawson, Ruth P. 37, 325
Day, David 511
Day, John 104
Day, Thomas 104, 168, 593
Day, W. G. 387
Daybell, James 387, 418, 457
Dayre, Eric 376
De Bruyn, Frans 544
De Franceschi, Sylvio Hermann 596
De Gooyer, Alan 388
De Jesus de Costa-Reis, Maria 489
De Jong, Willem R. 125
De Jongh, E. 624, 625, 626, 627
De Ligne, Prince Charles-Joseph 297
De Michelis, Cesare G. 325, 388
De Montluzin, Emily Lorraine 388
De Pierris, Graciela 125
De Piles, Roger 417
De Rossi, Domenico 524, 624
De Smith, Robert J. 367, 389, 431, 459
De Sousa, Mathias 109
De Tillier, J. B. 537
De Vries, Lyckle 625, 626
De Vries, Marleen 545
De Vries, Sandra 629
Dean, Michael Emmans 125
Dean, Winton 260, 262
Deans-Smith, Susan 125
Dear, Peter Robert 37
Dearden, James S. 388
Débarbat, Suzanne 100, 103, 110, 113, 116, 117, 119, 120–21, 123, 125, 126, 128, 131, 134, 143, 167, 171, 180–81, 199, 202
Debenedetti, Elisa 524–25, 624
DeBevoise, M. B. 591
Debly, Patricia 643–44
Debus, Allen G. 388
Deconinck-Brossard, Françoise 624
Décultot, Elisabeth 292, 293, 297, 304–05, 306, 317, 353, 365, 596
Dedieu, Jean-Pierre 60
Deffand, Madame du 660

Defoe, Daniel 5, 8, 314, 375, 376, 377, 378, 380, 383, 388–89, 399, 400, 401, 402, 405, 406, 407, 411, 412, 413, 414, 417, 422, 427, 428, 432, 434, 436, 439, 443, 450, 453, 454, 465, 487, 512, 611, 665, 666, 667
DeForest, Mary 389
Degardin, Alain 92, 207
Degott, Pierre 298, 638
DeGraff, Michel 294
DeJean, Joan 298
Dejongh, G. 544
Dekker, Rudolf 21, 525, 661
Delacampagne, Christian 596
Delacroix, Eugène 218, 224
Delâge, Denys 37
Delambre, Jean Baptiste Joseph 184
Delany, Mary 419, 530
Delbecke, Maarten 125
Deleuze, Gilles 295
Delille, Gérard 37, 125
Delisle, Joseph Nicolas 102
Dellaborra, Maria Teresa 236
Delmaire, Danielle 37
Deloffre, Frédéric 298
Delon, Michel 296, 298, 386, 422, 430, 654, 656, 658, 659
Delporte, Christiophe 125
DeMaria, Robert 451
Demel, Bernhard 38
Demelas, Marie-Danielle 126
Demerson, Paula de 38
Demeulenaere-Douyère, Christiane 126, 592
Demkin, A. V. 38
Démoris, René 596, 625
Demoulins, Camille 302
Dempsey, Jack 671
Denby, David J. 596
Denham, John 377
Dening, Greg 483, 516
Denis, Gilles 38, 126
Denisov, Simeon 355

Dennis, John   69, 367, 447, 460, 617
Denon, Dominique-Vivant   631, 654
Denoon, Donald   497
Denzel, Markus A.   82
Deol, Jeevan   38
Deppermann, Arnulf   126
Deprun, Jean   654
Derby, M.   545
Dereli, Cynthia   389
Derex, Jean-Michel   38
DeRogatis, Amy   126
Derrida, Jacques   299, 389, 473, 612
Derson, Didier   298
Desachy, Matthieu   524, 525
Desaix, Général (Louis Charles Antoine des Aix)   101
Desaguilers, Jean Théophile   620
Desan, Suzanne   545
Descargues, Madeleine   389, 664
Descartes, René   109, 113, 126, 165, 591, 597, 599, 602, 603, 606, 610, 614, 616, 617, 619
Deschamps, Yannick   389
DesChene, Dennis   126
Deschênes, Gaston   38
Desfontaines, Pierre François Guyot, Abbé de   305
Desforges, Jane   126
Deshoulière, Christophe   638
Desile, Patrick   596
Desing, Anselm   545
Delisle, Nicolas   102
Desmond, Jane C.   229
Desmoulins, Camille   302
Desné, Roland   298, 389
Desplat, Christian   38
Despoix, Philippe   596
Desrochers, Robert, Jr.   464
Destro, Alberto   325
Detering, Heinrich   320, 333
DeTurk, Sabrina   221
Deutsch, Helen   664
Devauges, Jean-Denys   538, 556, 652, 653
Devereux, Janice   664
Devine, T. M.   545
Devine, Thomas Martin   38
Devlin-Glass, Frances   494, 496, 500, 504
Di Benedetto, Amaldo   325
Di Brazza, Antonio   362
Di Brazza, Fabiana   362
Di Rienzo, E.   545
Diana, M. Casey   389
Diamante, J. B.   270
Diaz, Brigitte   654
Diaz, Ramón Lourido   126
Diaz Bild, Aida   389
Diáz Esteban, Fernando   270, 278
Díaz-Mas, Paloma   270, 278
Diaz-Trechuelo, Lourdes   126
Dibble, Abigail (Graves)   104
Dibble, Ernest F.   126
Dickerman, Edmund H.   208
Dickie, Margaret   674, 675
Dickinson, H. T.   545, 571
Dickinson, Rebecca   580
Dickinson, Sara   325
Dickson, Rebecca   389
Dideriksen, Gabriella   260–62
Diderot, Denis   17, 55, 63, 89, 153, 292, 293, 295, 296, 297, 299, 300, 301, 303, 304, 305, 306, 307, 308, 310, 312, 313, 314, 333, 342, 362, 389, 415, 426, 521, 523, 562, 589, 594, 595, 596, 605, 612, 613, 617, 627, 649, 650, 651, 652, 653, 654, 656, 657, 658, 660
Didier, Béatrice   298
Diederichsen, Uwe   325
Diedrich, Maria   670, 671
Dietl, Ralph   126
Díez, Fernando   38
Díez González, Rosa Maria   285
Diggins, John Patrick   126
Dils, Ann   229

Dilworth, John 241
Dine, Sarah Blank 127
Dingle, Tony 497
Dingwall, H. M. 596
Dionne, Ugo 298, 654
DiStefano, Roberto 127
Ditchfield, G. M. 47, 138
Ditt, Karl 38
Ditz, Toby L. 572
Dixon, C. 545
Dixon, Jeremiah 36
Dixon, Sarah 424, 425
Dixon, Simon 58
Dixson, Miriam 483
Djerassi, Carl 127
Dobson, M. 633
Dobuzinskis, Laurent 545
Dodd, William 240
Doddridge, Philip 614
Doerflinger, Johannes 545
Doering-Manteuffel, Sabine 39, 320, 321
Dohm, Burkhard 326
Dojnov, S. 545
Dokou, Christina 299, 389
Dolan, Brian 39, 390, 545
Dolan, Frances E. 127
Dolci, Carlo 221
Dole, Carol M. 390
Domergue, Lucienne 20, 39
Dominicis, Giulia de 127
Dompnier, Bernard 39
Donaldson, William 638
Donat, James G. 127
Dongowski, Christina 318, 344, 358
Donnelly, Jerome 390
Donoghue, Frank 5, 390, 664
Doody, Margaret Anne 8, 390, 446
Dopfel, Costanza Gislon 258–60
Dorati, Marco 299
Dorca, Toni 289–90
Dorigny, Marcel 558
Doring, Jurgen 390

Dorival, Jérôme 639
Dorleijn, G. J. 5
Dormois, Jean-Pierre 39
Dorosz, Janina 27
Dörrer, Fridolin 127
Dortous de Mairan, Jean-Jacques 658
Dorval, Taupin 565
Dose, Gerd 497, 505, 507
Doss, Chriss H. 127
Dougal, Theresa A. 390
Douglas, Bronwen 483
Douglas, Hugh 546
Douglas, Sir James 419
Douglas-Hamilton, Jill 483–84
Dougherty, Keith L. 39
Downes, Paul 671
Downie, J. A. 664
Downing, L. 596
Dowson, Ernest Christopher 655
Doyle, Anthony 39
Doyle, Helen 494, 496, 500, 504
Doyle, Laura 316, 326
Doyle, Peter 127
Doyle, William 39, 551
Dracobly, Alex 75–76
Draper, Anthony J. 39
Drayton, Richard 596
Dreisbach, Daniel L. 127, 572, 596
Drescher, Horst W. 390, 666
Drescher, Seymour 128
Dresher, Horst W. 664
Drews, Jörg 353
Dresser, Madge 39
Drexler, Michael 671
Driancourt-Girod, Janine 39, 128
Drinker, Elizabeth 111, 127, 148
Driscoll, Elizabeth Monahan 140
Drochmalnik, Daniel 326
Droïxhe, Daniel 16, 37, 40, 66, 299, 535
Drotvinas, Vincentas 326
Drowne, Solomon, Jr. 128
Droz, Jacques 68

Index 703

Druett, Joan 497
Drugh, Heinz J. 344
Drury, Marjule Anne 40, 128
Druzbacka, Elzbieta 324
Dryden, John 377, 380, 386, 387, 390, 390, 391, 394, 395, 397, 399, 400, 401, 404, 407, 409, 410, 412, 417, 419, 420, 422, 431, 432, 433, 434, 436, 440, 441, 446, 447, 448, 450, 451, 453, 456, 459, 666
Dryden, Robert G. 390, 401–02
Du Bos, Jean Baptiste, Abbé 309
Du Bois Marcus, Nancy 128
Du Châtelet, Madame 138, 155, 180, 182, 208, 213, 215
Du Halde, J. B. 128
Du Toit, Alexander 129
Duane, Anna Mae 391
Dubel, Sandrine 307, 363
Duberman, Martin B. 670, 671
Dubin, Lois 40, 128
Dubois, Laurent 546
Dubois, Paul-André 128
Dubois, Pierre 639
Dubovitski, A. B. 128
Dubuis, Michel 270
Ducerceau, Jacques Androuet 227
Duchesne, Ricardo 40
Duchesneau, François 596, 597
Duck, Stephen 415
Duclos, Charles Pinot 108
Duddy, Thomas 597
Dudley, William S. 40
Duff, Virginia M. 391, 450
Duffield, Holley Gene 597
Duffield, Ian 503
Duffy, Michael 40
Duflo, Colas 597, 654
Dufour, Hortense 40
Dufour et Cie, Joseph 508, 566
Dugard, Martin 511
Dugaw, Dianne 391
Dugourc, Jean-Démosthène 622

Duhart, Frédéric 40
Duhaut-Cilly, Auguste Bernard 486
Dulaurens, Henri Joseph 293
Dull, Jonathan R. 573
Dumaitre, Paule 128
Dumas, Denis 604
Dumbleton, Joseph 461
Dumont, Simone 128
Dumont d'Urville, Jules Sébastien César 492
Dumouchel, Daniel 597
Dumouchel, Paul 129
Duncan, Andrew, Jr. 559
Dunlap, William 469, 673
Dunlop, Ian 546
Dunn, P. M. 546
Dunn, Walter S., Jr. 40–41
Dunn, Thomas 503
Dunnavent, R. B. 572
Dunne, Tim 34, 72, 85
Dunton, John 664
Dupas, Didier Mathias 41, 129
Depeyron, Pierre Alexandre 299
Duplessis, Joseph Siffred 567
Dupre, L. 597
Dupuy, Marie-Anne 631
Dupuy, Pascal 546
Duran, Yves 41
Durand-Coquard, Claudine 34
Durante, Sergio 236
Durey, M. 546
Durey, Michael 129
During, Simon 484
Durnbaugh, Donald F. 129
Durnoulié, Camille 654
Dürr, Alfred 232
Dürr, Walter 637
Durrani, Osman 326, 346
Dury, Andrew 29
Düssel, Reinhard 339
Dussinger, John A. 5, 41, 391
Duteil, Jean-Pierre 41
Dutton, Dianne 299

Duval, Gilles 664
Duval, Karen 573
Duyker, Edward 511
Duyker, Maryse 511
Dwight, Timothy 467, 476
Dye, Ellis 326
Dyer, Mary 175, 468
Dykstal, Timothy 41, 391
Dziedzic, Andrzej 299
Dziembowski, Edmond 546
Eadie, M. J. 597
Earl, John 391
Earle, Augustus 480
Earle, Rebecca 42
Earnshaw, Brian 558
Eberle-Sinatra, Michael 664
Eby, Jack 236
Eccleshall, Robert 28
Eck, Otto van 21
Ecker, Eva 299, 326
Eddy, Donald D. 6
Eddy, M. D. 42, 129
Eddy, Thomas 99
Edel, Geert 339
Eden, Richard 476
Eden, William 39
Edgcumbe, John 224
Edgecombe, Rodney Stenning 236, 391
Edgeworth, Maria 309, 392, 432, 450
Edmiston, John M. 108
Edmiston, William G. 654
Edmond, Rod 484
Edney, Matthew H. 546
Edwards, Bryan 591
Edwards, James 4
Edwards, Jonathan 129, 149, 173, 197, 207, 212, 464, 478, 597, 605
Edwards, Karen L. 664
Edwards, L. 546
Edwards, Philip 482
Egan, Jack 484
Egan, Jim 464
Eger, Elizabeth 6, 9, 42, 309, 340, 387, 391, 392–93, 403, 404, 413, 415, 418, 421, 432, 453, 456, 459, 664
Egger, Irmgard 326
Egremont, Second Earl of 628
Egremont (Lord) 226
Ehmer, Josef 21, 31, 93
Ehrard, Jean 299
Ehrenpreis, Stefan 129
Ehrich-Haefeli, Verena 326
Ehrmann, Marianne 334
Eibl, Karl 327
Eichendorff, Joseph von 347
Eichhorn, Johann Gottfried 595
Eicholz, Hans L. 129
Eidelberg, Martin 525, 625
Eigeldinger, Frederic S. 299
Eiseley, Loren 473
Eisenbach, Ulrich 42
Eisenberg, Dan 393
Eisenstein, Sergei 627
Ekstein, Nina 299
Elazar, Daniel J. 42, 129
Elbel, Martin 130
Elfenbein, Andrew 393
Eliot, John 672
Eliot, Simon 6, 373, 420, 423, 522
Eliot, Thomas Stearns 425
Élisabeth, Princess (of France) 602
Elizabeth I, Queen 193
Ella, George M. 129
Ellingson, Terry Jay 511
Ellington, H. Elisabeth 393
Elliot, Andrew 51
Elliott, Mark C. 42
Ellis, J. 546
Ellis, Joseph J. 572
Ellis, Markman 6, 9, 392, 421, 464
Ellis, William 491
Ellison, Julie 6, 393, 572
Ellison, Paul M. 236
Ellwood, Gracia Fay 393
Elm, Veit 42
Elmarsafy, Ziad M. 42, 299

Index

Elmer, Jonathan 572
Elrod, Eileen Razzari 130, 464
Eltis, D. 572
Eltis, David 546
Elwell, Frank W. 130
Emch-Deriaz, Antoinette 130
Emerson, Ralph Waldo 354, 463, 471, 476
Emilsen, Susan 496, 497
Emilsen, William W. 496, 497
Emke, Cor 501
Emmett, Ross B. 498, 572
Emsley, Sarah 393
Enckell, Pierre 299
Endelman, Todd M. 42
Endres, Johannes 327
Enenkel, Karl 308
Engelbert, Manfred 362
Engels, Jens Ivo 42
Engelstein, Laura 130
Engerman, S. L. 572
Engerman, Stanley L. 42, 159
England, John (Bishop) 157
Engstrand, Iris H. W. 42, 130, 597
Ennis, Daniel J. 665
Enniss, Stephen 525
Entenmann, Robert 43
Entrecasteaux, Antoine Raymond Joseph de Bruni, Chevalier d' 511
Éon, Monsieur d' 57
Éon de Beaumont, Charles Geneviève Louis Auguste André Thimotée d' 299
Épinay, Louise Florence Petronille Tardieu d'Esclavelles, Marquise d' 297
Equiano, Olaudah (Gustavus Vassa the African) 72, 130, 400, 464, 465, 466, 670, 674
Erickson, Hilary 488, 489
Erickson, Robert A. 393
Erlat, Jale 300
Erlin, Matt 327
Erskine, Ebenezer 130
Erskine-Hill, Howard 383
Esaka, Tetsuya 327
Escalle, Marie-Christine-Kok 302, 314
Escamilla González, Iván 130
Escott, Angela 393
Eshet, Dan 130
Esleben, Jörg 327, 511
Espák, Gabriella Tóthné 511
Espido Freire, Mila 270
Espinosa, José Manuel 162
Espronceda, José de 272
Esquilache, Marqués de (Leopoldo de Gregorio) 278
Esquivel Triana, Ricardo 43
Estala, Pedro 285
Estensen, Miriam 484
Esterhammer, Angela 327
Esterházy, Almerie 248
Etter, Brian 236
Etzion, J. 639
Euclid 599
Euler, Leonhard 607
Eusman, Elmer 625
Eustace, Nicole 43, 130
Evangelisti, S. 546
Evans, Caleb 147
Evans, Chris 43
Evans, Gareth 450
Evans, James 164
Eveleth, D. 597
Evelyn, John 215
Everaert, Guido 93
Everist, Mark 260
Ewald, Petra 661
Ewell, Terry B. 236
Externbrink, Sven 21
Ezell, Margaret 393–94
Faaborg, R. W. 597
Fabian, Bernhard 394, 438
Fabiano, Andrea 300
Fabila, René Avilés 130
Fabricius, Johann Albert 331
Fabris, Dinko 270

Faery, Rebeca Blevins 572
Fagan, Patrick 43, 131
Faggionato, Raffaella 131
Faidit, Jean-Michel 131
Fairclough, Peter 372
Fairer, David 394, 446
Fairfax, Jane 434
Fairweather, Maria 547
Falconbridge, Anna Maria 481
Falconet, Étienne Maurice 627
Falino, Jeannine 43
Faller, Lincoln B. 401
Fallon, Peter K. 43
Fanelli, J. G. 639
Fanning, Christopher 394
Faraday, Michael 133, 609
Farinella, C. 597
Farley, James J. 43–44
Farnsworth, Rodney 394
Faroqhi, Suraiya 131
Farquhar, George 399, 430
Farquharson, Henry 102
Farr, D. 547
Farr, David 131
Farrachi, Armand 657
Farrell, Rita 511
Fatio, Olivier 131
Fauchois, Yann 131
Fauque, Danielle 131
Faure, Michel 547
Faus Prieto, Alfredo 43
Fauske, Christopher 394
Fauskewåg, Svein Eirik 300
Fauve-Chamoux, Antoinette 44
Favart, Charles Simon 299
Fawkener, Sir Everard 657
Fay, Mary Ann 44
Fea, John 44, 131
Fechner, Jörg Ulrich 327
Federhofer, Marie-Theres 44
Feest, Christian F. 131
Fehrenbacher, Don E. 44
Fehrmann, Georg 306

Feijoo, Benito 266
Feilchenfeldt, Konrad 661
Feldmann, Doris 394
Feliú de San Pedro, Benito de 270
Fell, Charles 127
Felsenstein, Frank 572
Fendler, Susanne 394
Fénelon (François de Salignac de La Mothe-Fénelon) 657
Feng, Hongqian 132
Feng, Lisheng 132
Fengzuo, Xue 198
Fenn, Elizabeth A. 44, 132, 572, 597
Fenning, Hugh 132
Feo, Roberto de 221
Ferdinand, C[hristine]. Y. 6, 522
Ferdinando Gonzaga of Mantua, Duke 645
Ferguson, Adam 148, 410
Ferguson, Henry 625
Ferguson, James 614
Ferguson, Niall 132
Ferguson, Robert A. 573
Ferguson, S. 597
Ferguson, Sally 132
Fergusson, Robert 663
Ferling, J. 573
Ferm, Robert L. 132
Fernán Núñez, Count of 284
Fernández, Pura 270
Fernández, Roberto 266, 270, 271–73, 276, 277, 279, 282, 283, 286, 287, 288, 290
Fernández Albaladejo, Pablo 44
Fernández Álvarez, Manuel 273
Fernández de Moratín, Leandro 267, 271, 285, 287, 290
Fernández de Moratín, Nicolás 268, 285
Fernández de Santa Cruz, Manuel 214
Fernández Fernández, Olga 273
Fernández García, José 89
Fernández Retamar, Roberto 273
Fernando VII, King 186

Index

Ferraresi, A. 598
Ferraro, Giovanni 44, 132
Ferraz, Marcia H. M. 132
Ferret, Olivier 598
Ferris, David S. 300
Ferriss, Suzanne 394
Ferrone, V. 547
Ferrone, Vincenzo 44
Ferrús Antón, Beatriz 281–82
Feßler, Ignaz Aurelius 348
Fester, Nicolás 79
Fetterly, Judith 671
Feuermann, Emanuel 642
Feuillée, Louis 134
Feyel, Gilles 525
Fichte, Johann Gottlieb 112, 330, 358, 600, 605, 609
Fido, Franco 300, 362
Fiedler, Sabine 327
Field, Clive D. 132
Fielding, Harry 371
Fielding, Henry 8, 9, 283, 375, 379, 384, 391, 401, 402, 414, 418, 434, 438, 439, 440, 450, 455, 457, 459, 554, 662
Fielding, Sarah 402, 449, 450
Fields, Polly Stevens 44, 598, 665
Fielitz, Sonja 394
Fiennes, Celia 423
Fiering, Norman 25, 102, 107, 109, 111, 128, 134, 137, 153, 159, 168, 175, 177, 182, 188, 190, 211, 671
Figeac, Michel 44
Filatova, Elena 161
Filihia, Meredith 484
Filomarino, Ascanio (Cardinal) 225
Finberg, Melinda C. 381, 386, 394, 405, 436
Finch, Anne [Kingsmill], Countess of Winchilsea 391, 424
Finch, Sir Walter 385, 652
Finch, William 652
Findlay, James A. 525

Fine, Gail 598
Fink, Beatrice 300, 464, 654
Fink, Karl J. 327
Fink, Steven 673
Fink, M. 639
Finkelman, Paul 547
Finseth, Ian 464
Finzsch, Norbert 126, 132, 133, 187
Fiorillo, L. 609
Fischer, Bernd 327
Fischer, Caroline Auguste 339
Fischer, Christian August 335
Fischer-Lichte, Erika 327
Fisher, Howard J. 133
Fisher, Judith W. 547
Fisher, M. 598
Fisher, M. H. 547
Fisher, N. R. R. 133
Fisher, Robin 484
Fisk, Charles 236–37
Fiszer, Stanislaw 300
Fitch, Donald 238
Fitzgerald, Lauren 395
Fitzgerald, Patrick 45
Fitzherbert, Maria 70
Fitzsymonds, Eustace 512
Flach, Werner 133
Flamsteed, John 32, 119
Flannery, Tim 490, 495, 498, 547
Flaxman, John 226
Fleck, Andrew 395
Fleeman, J. D. 6
Fleischmann, Fritz 585, 672, 674
Fleming, Thomas 573
Fleming, William 94
Flesch, William 464
Flesler, Daniela 273
Fletcher (of Madeley), John 200
Fletcher, A. 547
Fletcher, Loraine 395–97
Fleuriot, Jacques 133
Flikschuh, K. 598
Flinders, Matthew 491, 495, 498, 505,

511, 514, 544
Flood, Henry 553
Florack, Ruth 300
Florenskij, Pavel 146
Flores, Daniel 573
Flores, Ramón Sánchez 133
Florido, Francisco 167
Flothius, Marius 238
Flotzinger, Rudolf 238
Fludernik, Monika 397
Flynn, Dennis O. 484–85, 489, 512
Flynn, James T. 133
Fogarty, Gerald P. 133
Fogel, Robert W. 133
Fogg, G. E. 133
Fogleman, Aaron 133
Foi, Maria Carolina 327
Foisneau, Luc 598
Foley, Michael 547
Foley, Stephen Merriam 328
Folkenflik, Robert 665
Fonvizin, Denis Ivanovich 325
Forbes, David W. 485
Forbes, Sir John 100
Force, James E. 133
Ford, Boris 472
Ford, Brian J. 45, 133
Fordyce, George 120
Fordyce, Linda 499
Fordyce, R. 531
Foreman, Amanda 45
Forero Romero, Juan Carlos 45
Forget, Danielle 300, 650
Forkel, Johann Nikolaus 232, 253
Fornasari, Liletta 221
Forster, Antonia 6, 14
Forster, Eckart 134, 328
Forster, Georg 327, 347, 482, 492, 499, 502, 505, 507, 511, 514
Forster, Johann Reinhold 482, 499, 502, 505, 514
Forster, Marc R. 45, 134
Fort, Bernadette 221

Fortescue, John 45
Fortunati, Vita 397, 417
Fortune, Nigel 262
Foster, Gavin 397
Foster, George M. 148
Foster, Hannah Webster 464
Foster, Thomas A. 573
Foucart, Claude 300, 362
Foucault, Michel 199, 384, 401, 473, 603, 611
Fouché, Nicole 573
Foucrier, Annick 573
Fouilleron, Joel 134
Fouquet, Nicolas 105
Fox, Robert 547
Fraanje, Maarten 58
Fragonard, Jean-Honoré 629
Frame, T[homas]. 499
Francesconi, Daniele 45
Francis, Richard 134
Franchke, August Hermann 315
Francke, Gotthilf August 326
Franco, Adolfo Olea 134
Franco-Rubio, Gloria A. 45
Franits, Wayne E. 218, 221–23, 224, 225, 226, 228, 229
Frank, Allen J. 134
Frank, André Gunder 40
Frank, Armin Paul 464
Frank, Frederick S. 371–73
Frank, Michael 134
Frankel, Matthew Cordova 464
Frankel, Rachel 134
Frankel, S. 598
Frankenstein, Victor 385
Frankland, George 512
Franklin, Benjamin 6, 51, 52, 67, 163, 171, 343, 426, 461, 465, 467, 468, 469, 475, 525, 526, 567, 570, 573, 578, 580, 581, 587, 588, 600, 610, 671, 672, 673
Franklin, Michael 397–98
Franks, J. 547

Index

Frantz, John B. 134
Frantz, Pierre 633
Franzinetti, G. 101
Frappell, Ruth 485
Frasca, R. 525
Frasca-Spada, Marina 45, 134
Frasi, Giulia 242
Frati, Paola 137
Frederick, Duke of Brunswick-Lunenburgh 458
Frederick the Great (Friedrich II von Preussen [Prussia]), King 229, 556
Frederick William II (Friedrich Wilhelm II), King 255
Freeman, Joanne B. 45
Freeman, Thomas 573
Freemanova, Michaela 238
Freiberg, M. 598
Freiberg, Stanley 231
Freitas, R. 238
French, H. R. 548
Freneau, Philip 475
Freschi, Marino 328
Fresnel, Augustin 612
Freud, Sigmund 149, 427
Frey, Manuel 45, 135, 548
Freycinet, Katharine Pratt 512
Freycinet, Louis Claude Desaulses de 512
Freydberg, Bernard 598
Frézier, Amédée 171
Fricke, Harald 328
Friday, J. 598
Friedeberg, R. V. 548
Friedenberg, Z. B. 573
Friedländer, David 124
Friedman, Jean E. 135
Friedrich Franz I, Duke of Mecklenburg-Schwerin at Ludwigslust 644
Friedrich Wilhelm I, King 81
Friedrich, Hans-Edwin 328
Friedrich, Heinz 328
Friesen, Ilse E. 135

Frisch, Walter 238
Frischer, Bernard D. 223
Fritzsche, Peter 45
Fróes, João 523, 663
Froeschlé, Michel 134, 135
Froeschlé-Chopard, Marie-Hélène 135
Frohock, Richard 398
Froide, Amy M. 46
Frolich, Martha 238
Frost, Alan 481, 483, 484, 485, 488, 491, 493
Frost, Lionel 484–85, 489
Frost, Lucy 512
Frost, O. W. 548
Frost, Warwick 485
Fruchtman, Caroline S. 639, 645
Fruchtman, Jack, Jr. 398
Frugé, August 485–86
Fruin, Robert 627
Frye, Northrop 431
Fu, Banghong 135
Fuchs, Anne 499
Fuchs, Michel 598
Fudge, E. 548
Fuentes, Yvonne 273–75, 398
Fuhrmann, Helmut 328
Fuhrmann, Martin 46
Fujii, Tetsu 398, 399
Fukala, Radek 135
Fulford, T. 554
Fulford, Tim 399, 446, 447, 512
Fuller, Graham 399
Fuller, Margaret 473
Fullerton, Susannah 399, 512
Fulton, David 399
Fulton, Henry L. 141–42
Fumaroli, Marc 46, 613, 654
Funaro, Liana Elda 135
Furbank, P[hilip]. N[icholas]. 5, 260, 301, 388, 399, 512, 665
Furdell, Elizabeth Lane 135
Furet, François 542
Furiman, J. D. 429

Furner, Mark 135
Fusconi, Giulia 524, 624
Fuseli, Henry 226
Füssel, Marian 135
Fyke, Karen 68
Gaastra, Femme S. 539
Gabaldón, Rodrigo 273–75
Gabbard, Christopher D. 399
Gabhart, M. 598
Gable, Eric 573
Gabler-Hover, Janet 473
Gaborik, Patricia 362
Gabrieli, Giovanni 646
Gabrielli, Caterina 264
Gacto, M. 599
Gadeken, Sara 399, 449
Gaeddert, William K. 234
Gagliano, Marco da 645, 648
Gahan, Daniel 135
Gailor, Genoveffa Giambona 399
Gailus, Manfred 46, 135
Gainor, J. Ellen 568, 634, 635
Gainot, Bernard 46, 548
Gainot, Benoît 548
Gainsborough, Thomas 223
Galaup, Jean-François de, Comte de La Pérouse (also: Lapérouse) 505
Galdós, Benito Perez 288
Galibert, Thierry 665
Galilei, Galileo 614
Galitz, Katheryn Calley 629
Gallaher, Matthew C. 247
Galley, Chris 136
Gallingani, Daniela 617
Gallouët, Catherine 300
Galvani, Luigi 25, 107
Gálvez, María Rosa 275–76
Gálvez de Cabrera, María Rosa 284
Galvin, John 314
Gambelli, Delia 259
Gambles, A. 574
Gamer, Michael 455
Gamerra, Giovanni de 645

Gamlieli, Nissim Benjamin 71
Gandt, François de 46, 125, 132, 136, 138, 145, 146, 155, 163, 165, 180, 182, 193, 206, 208
Gantet, Claire 46
Garampi, Francesco 206
Garampi, Giuseppe (Cardinal) 206
Garber, Jörn 328, 339, 499, 502
Garber, Peter M. 499
Garceau, Dee 22
García, Alberto Saladino 136
García de la Huerta, Vicente 278, 284
García Fraile, Dámaso 276
Garciá Belmar, Antonio 25, 46, 136
García de Leon, Porfirio 136
García Ejarque, Luis 525, 548
García Malo, Ignacio 284
García-Melero, José Enrique 136
Gardiner, Anne Barbeau 399
Gardiner, Ellen 665
Gardiner, J. S. J. 172
Gardner, Jared 671
Gardner, Kevin J. 399
Gardt, Andreas 328
Gargett, Graham 300, 599
Garms, Jörg 136, 599
Garrard, Mary 219
Garrick, David 239, 263–64, 652
Garrigus, J. D. 548
Garrigus, John D. 137
Garrioch, David 46, 137
Garrison, J. Ritchie 630, 632
Garside, Peter 526
Garth, Samuel 387
Gartner, Lloyd P. 137
Garvey, Robert 513
Gascoigne, John 513, 548
Gaskill, Howard 328, 400
Gaspar, David Barry 46
Gassendi, Pierre 172
Gassman, Florian Leopold 264
Gassmann, Gunther 137
Gates, Henry Louis 670, 671

Index

Gaufrido, Giacomo 219
Gauss, Ulrike 526, 625
Gaustad, Edwin S. 137, 574
Gautier, Gary 400, 465
Gaveaux, Pierre 262
Gaviano, Marie-Pierre 90
Gavira Márquez, Maria Concepción 46
Gay, John 375, 377, 390, 391, 405, 420, 664
Gazzaniga, Valentina 137
Geaves, Ron A. 119
Geggus, David Patrick 47
Geiger, Ludwig 144
Geiringer, Claudia 486
Geiringer, Karl 230
Geiter, M. K. 548
Gelber, Michael Werth 400
Geller, Jaclyn 400
Gellert, Christian Fürchtegott 241, 328, 332, 333, 341, 351
Gelles, Edith B. 574
Gembero Ustárroz, María 277
Geminiani, Francesco 240
Gemmett, Robert J. 372
Genet-Rouffiac, Nathalie 137
Geng, Li-Peng 400
Genlis, Stéphanie-Félicité du Crest de Saint Aubin de 309, 315, 432
Gentile, G. P. 574
Gentileschi, Artemisia 219–21
Gentileschi, Orazio 219–21, 225
Geoffrin, Madame 649
Geoghegan, Vincent 28
George, Alexander S. 486
George, Enoch 124
George I, King 322
George III, King 551, 609, 664
George IV, King 70
Georgelin, Yvon 103
Georgopoulou, Maria 223
Gephart, Werner 329
Geraci, Robert P. 137, 156, 157, 158, 159, 171–72, 173

Geraghty, Antony 223
Gerard, W. B. 400
Gerber, Ernst 252
Gere, Cathy 137
Gerecke, Anne-Bitt 320, 333
Gerhard, Anselm 329
Gerrard, Christine 400, 446
Gertz, Steven 119
Gerzina, Gretchen Holbrook 47
Geshwind, M. 599
Gessner, Salomon 306, 342
Getz, Christine 238
Gevitz, Norman 137–38
Gevrey, Françoise 300
Ghezzi, Pier Leone 524, 624
Ghosh, Anindita 533
Giacomo, Gian 524, 624
Giannetti, Valeria 362
Giannone, Pietro 185, 557
Gianturco, Carolyn 639, 645
Gibb, John 164
Gibbon, Edward 211, 420, 426, 455
Gibbons, J. M. 47, 138, 400
Gibbons, James 329
Gibbons, Luke 138, 400
Gibson, A. 574
Gibson, J. R. 549
Gibson, James 463
Gibson, John G. 639
Gibson, William 47, 138
Gibson-Wood, Carol 625
Giddey, Ernest 371
Gierl, Martin 301
Gies, David Thatcher 275–76
Giessauf, Johannes 33, 47
Giglberger, Veronika 238
Gil Novales, Alberto 47, 138
Gilard, Céline 271, 276
Gilbert, Cheralea 500
Gilbert, Deidre 401
Gilbert, Steve 500
Gilbert, William 614, 654
Gildersleeve, D. Britton 465

Giles, Paul 465–66
Gill, Harold B., Jr. 574
Gill, Miriam 223
Gilleir, Anke 549
Gillespie, Joanna Bowen 466, 574
Gillespie, Stuart 401
Gillespie, Thomas 614
Gilli, Marita 549
Gilliam, Jan Kirsten 462
Gilpin, William 402
Gilreath, James 586
Gilseman, Isaac 479, 508
Gindele, Karen C. 401
Giné Janer, Marta 276
Ginio, Eyal 47, 138
Giovannelli, Laura 401
Giovanopoulos, Anna-Christina 401
Giráldez, Arturo 512
Girardin, René, Le Marquis de 299
Gireau-Geneaux, Annie 138
Girodet (-Trioson), Anne-Louis 228
Girollet, Anne 549
Giroud, Vincent 401
Giroust, François 236
Giudice, F. 599
Giuseppe II 117
Giusti, A. M. 223
Giusti Maccari, Patrizia 223
Gladfelder, Hal 47, 401–02
Gladwin, Francis 398
Glasenapp, Jorn 402
Glaser, Horst-Albert 300, 301, 302, 329, 330, 337, 360, 362, 402, 416, 444
Glass, Francis 467
Glass, Marguerite 222, 229
Glaude, Eddie S., Jr. 671
Gleba, Gudrun 26
Glen, Marilyn 138
Glen, Robert 633
Glendinning, Nigel 267, 268, 625
Glennie, Evelyn 642
Glixon, Beth L. 639, 645

Glixon, Jonathan E. 639, 645
Glover, William 138
Gluck, Christoph Willibald, Ritter von 236, 246
Goalen, Martin 223
Göbel, Walter 47, 367, 377, 385, 394, 397, 402, 403
Gobin, Charles E. 403
Godard, Jean-Luc 249
Goddu, Teresa A. 671
Godfrey, Peter B. 47, 138
Godfrey, Thomas 476
Godsey, William D., Jr. 138
Godwin, Joscelyn 381, 419
Godwin, William 15, 48, 112, 139, 394, 397, 402, 426, 441
Goethe, Johann Wolfgang von 3, 104, 107, 134, 144, 145, 148, 149, 150, 151, 157, 192, 200, 203, 207, 212, 243, 308, 316, 317, 318, 319, 320, 321, 323, 324, 325, 326, 327, 328, 329, 330, 331, 332, 333, 334, 335, 336, 337, 338, 339, 340, 341, 342, 343, 344, 345, 346, 347, 348, 349, 350, 351, 352, 353, 354, 355, 356, 357, 358, 359, 360, 418, 460, 615, 626
Goethe, Ottilie von 332
Goetz, Charlotte 301
Gogoleva, Alla Anatol'evna 47
Gohrbandt, Detlev 403
Golay, Eric 47
Golden, Janet 139
Goldgar, Bertrand A. 6, 403, 665
Goldoni, Carlo 360, 361, 362, 363, 364, 648
Goldsmith, L. 574
Goldsmith, Netta Murray 549
Goldsmith, Oliver 15, 300, 329, 400, 405, 667
Goldstein, Joel A. 599
Goldstein, Jonathan 139
Goldstein, Marc Allan 48, 139, 301

Goldstein, Philip 403, 413, 420
Goldsworthy, Cephas 403
Goldzink, Jean 301
Golinski, Jan 139
Gollar, C. Walker 155
Golovina, Comtesse 549
Golz, Jochen 328, 329, 332, 338, 339, 349, 350, 355, 358, 360
Gomez, M. A. 574
Gomez, Madeleine de 654
Gómez Camargo, Miguel 266–67
Gomez-Géraud, Marie-Christine 654
Gómez-Moreno, Ángel 276–77
Gonda, Caroline 392, 403
González de Garay, María Teresa 277
González de Zárate, Francisco 277
González Marín, Luis Antonio 277
González y González, Enrique 48
Goodden, Angelica 301
Goodfriend, Joyce D. 128
Goodhue, Thomas W. 139
Goodlad, Graham 139
Goodman, Elise 222, 223, 309
Goodman, Katherine R. 329, 661
Goodman, Roy E. 6, 526
Goodrich, Samuel 475–76
Goodridge, John 403
Goodwin, Charles H. 139
Gookin, Daniel 569
Gorak, Jan 403
Gordon, F. 549
Gordon, Felicia 48, 260, 301
Gordon, Robert 618
Gordon-Read, Annette 574
Goring, Paul 403
Görisch, Reinhard 329
Görlach, Manfred 403
Gorner, Paul 139
Gorres, Joseph von 549
Görtschacher, Wolfgang 390, 394, 397, 404, 410, 419, 431
Gosden, Chris 513
Göse, Frank 48

Gosetti, J. A. 599
Gotsch, Dietmar 402, 443, 460
Gottlieb, Evan 404
Gottsch, Silke 48
Gottsched, Johann Christoph 322, 333, 334, 338
Gottsched, Louise Adelgunde Victorie (see also: Luise Kulmus) 329, 334
Götze, Karl Heinz 329
Götze, Martin 330
Gouges, Olympe de 294, 309, 660
Gould, Glenn 642
Gould, Philip 62, 72, 94, 461, 462, 464, 466, 477, 478, 574
Gould, Robert 377
Gould, Timothy 404
Gouldbourne, Ruth 139
Goulemot, Jean M. 599, 655
Goya [y Lucientes], Francisco José de 218, 525, 625
Goyhenetche, Manex 48
Gozzi, Carlo 362, 365
Gozzi, Gasparo 300
Gqola, Pumla Dineo 404
Grabes, Herbert 404, 457
Graf, E. C. 277
Graffigny, Françoise D'Issembourg D'Happoncourt de 296, 312, 655
Grafton, Duke of 555
Grage, Joachim 330
Gragg, L. 549
Graham, Gargett 400
Graham, Kenneth W. 48, 139, 371–73, 404, 665
Graham, Tommy 139
Graille, Patrick 48
Grainger, James 153, 413, 447
Grair, Charles A. 330
Gramain-Kibleur, Pascale 48, 140
Gramberg, Gerhard Anton 48
Gramlich-Oka, Bettina 140
Granados, Enrique 279
Granderoute, Robert 549

Grandet, Eugenie 303, 412
Grange, Cyril 48
Grant, Charlotte 6, 387, 391, 392–93, 392, 403, 404, 413, 415, 418, 421, 432, 453, 456, 459, 664
Grant, John 500
Grantham, Lord 625
Grapa, Caroline Jacot 655
Grasse, François Joseph Paul, Comte de 585
Grasso, Christopher 574
Grateau, Philippe 49
Gratian 203
Gratton, D. J. 140
Gratzke, Michael 330
Graun, Johann Gottlieb 250
Grave, Floyd K. 238
Gravelot, Hubert François 9
Graves, Rolande 49
Gravil, Richard 451
Gray, Alasdair 404
Gray, Edward G. 671
Gray, Patricia 301
Gray, Robin 303, 412
Gray, Stephen 32, 119
Gray, Thomas 7, 13, 391, 420, 666
Graziani, Carlo 255–56
Greaves, Richard L. 140
Green, James N. 526
Green, John C. 526
Green, Jonathan D. 639
Green, Joseph 476
Green, Roger Curtis 514
Green, Susan 380, 386, 397, 400, 404, 409, 412, 417, 433, 440, 456, 459
Greenagel, Frank L. 140
Greenberg, Robert 140
Greene, Jack P. 49, 575
Greene, Nathanael 575
Greene, Richard 49, 404, 405
Greene, Roland 672
Greenfield, Sayre N. 379, 384, 389, 390, 393, 394, 411, 414, 420, 429, 430, 442, 454
Greenshields, Malcolm R. 51, 147
Greer, Alan 549
Greer, Allan 575
Gregg, Stephen H. 49, 140, 405
Gregoire, Lucien 306
Gregori, Flavio 405
Gregori, Mina 217, 218, 219, 221, 223, 225, 226, 227, 229
Gregorio, Tullio 599
Gregory, James 180–81
Greiner, Bernhard 330
Grellet, Stephen 99
Grenberg, Jeanine M. 140
Grenby, Matthew 535, 668
Grenon, Anne France 302
Grenon, Michel 140
Gretchanaïa, Elena 549
Greuze, Jean-Baptiste 227, 626
Greve, James R. 140
Greyerz, Kaspar von 140
Grier, Michelle 143
Griffin, Gwen 513
Griffin, J. P. 549
Griffin, Mark C. 140
Griffin, Michael 405
Griffin, Patrick 49, 141–42
Griffin, Robert J. 405
Griffini, Grazia Maria 342
Griffith, Elizabeth 405
Griffith, Paddy 49
Griffiths, Antony 626
Griffiths, Steve 142
Grijzenhout, Frans 623, 624, 625, 626–27, 629, 630, 632
Grimm, Friedrich Melchior, Freiherr von 661
Grimm, Jürgen 549
Grimm, Sieglinde 330
Grimmelshausen, Hans Jakob Christoph von 454
Grinberg, Keila 49
Griscom, John 99

Grise, Philippe 49, 143
Griswold, Charles L., Jr. 599
Griswold, Mac 143, 405
Grizzard, Frank E., Jr. 588
Groemer, Gerald 143
Gronim, Sara Stidstone 143
Gronke, Horst 49
Groom, Nick 526, 665
Grosche, Stefan 330
Grosperrin, Jean Philippe 302
Gross, A. G. 599
Gross, Gloria Sybil 405
Gross, Robert A. 49
Gross, Suzanne 238
Grossi, Filipo 143
Grosskopf, Jan Schenk 143
Grosskurth, Brian 627
Grossman, Carol 7
Grossman, Joyce 405
Grossman, Kathryn M. 405, 453
Grotius, Hugo 91, 161, 615
Groult, Martine 655
Grout, Donald J. 238, 246
Grove, Allen W. 600
Groves, Eric W. 143
Grozdanova, Elena 50, 143
Grubb, F. 575
Grumet, Robert S. 143
Grundy, Isobel 405
Gsteiger, Manfred 302, 330
Guangdi, Li 176
Guarino, Francesco 220
Guarnieri, Elisabetta 302
Gudermann, Rita 38
Gudgeon, Thomas Wayth 486
Guéhenno, Jean 650
Guelzo, Allen C. 605
Guenther, Karen 143
Guerci, L. 549
Guerci, Luciano 362
Guereña, Jean-Louis 277
Guerrier, Olivier 294
Guest, Harriet 500, 516

Guest, Ivor Forbes 230
Guest, Kristen 405–06, 414, 442, 513, 518, 520
Guicharnaud, Hélène 628
Guicharnaud-Tollis, Michèle 277
Guijarro Mora, Víctor 50, 143
Guilding, Ruth 628
Guilhaumou, Jacques 550
Guillery, Peter 550
Guizot, François Pierre Guillaume 345
Gulke, Peter 331
Gundolf, Friedrich 144
Gunn, Daniel P. 406, 665
Gunnarsdóttir, Ellen 144
Gunst, Peter 144
Günther, Johann Christian 348
Gunther-Canada, Wendy 144
Gupta, Ashin Das 50
Gura, Philip F. 466
Guruswamy, Rosemary Fithian 466
Gustafson, Sandra M. 633
Guthke, Karl S. 330
Gutiérrez Bueno, Pedro, 25, 46, 136
Gutiérrez de Pineda, Virginia 550
Gutiérrez de Vegas, Fernando 270
Gutiérrez Escudero, Antonio 50
Gutjahr, Ortrud 330
Gutjahr, Paul C. 437
Gutwirth, Madelyn 386, 410, 413, 414, 415, 419, 425, 428, 455
Gutzman, K. R. Constantine 575
Gvosdev, Nikolas K. 550
Haack, Friedrich Wilhelm 326
Haakonssen, Knud 144
Haar, James 628
Haase, Fee Alexandra 331
Haberlein, Mark 82, 192
Habermas, Jürgen 392, 528, 600, 605
Habrich, Christa 331
Hacker, Rupert 526
Haddad, Emily A. 407
Haechler, Jean 50
Haeffli, Anton 239

Haendel, Ida 642
Haffis, C. M. 575
Hafner, Ralph 308, 331
Hafstein, Valdimar 144
Hafter, Daryl 50
Hagedorn, Friedrich von 344
Haggerty, George E. 407, 550
Hagihara, Mamoru 144
Hague, Hope 144
Hahn, Barbara 144, 331
Hahn, Karl-Heinz 331
Hain, Bonnie A. 381
Haines, Catharine M. C. 144
Haines, R. 550, 600
Hakim, Zeina 302
Hale, John K. 407
Hales, Sir Edward 201
Halévy, Elie 609
Hall, A. Rupert 50, 144
Hall, Barbara 500
Hall, Dennis 407
Hall, Douglas Gordon Hawkins 50
Hall, Jennifer 674
Hall, Leslie 50
Hall, Nigel 50
Hall, Richard 50
Hall, Roland 144
Hall, Timothy D. 575
Hall-Jones, John 500
Hallberg, Peter 600
Hallengren, Anders 107
Halleux, Robert 145
Halley, Edmond 121, 604
Halliday, E. M. 50
Halloran, Brian M. 50, 145
Halpern, Rick 483, 491, 569
Hamada, Masami 145
Hamann, Johann Georg 335, 336, 362
Hamburger, Michael 262
Hamer, Lynne 349
Hamid, Ahmud Fauzi Abdul 145
Hamilton, Alexander 112, 463, 466, 468, 573, 576, 579, 583, 587, 674

Hamilton, Elizabeth 393, 456
Hamilton, Emma 291, 316, 546
Hamilton, Frances 145
Hamilton, Gavin 624
Hamilton, George 514
Hamilton, Hugh Douglas 629
Hamilton, Jill 550
Hamilton, John T. 331
Hamilton, Mary 449
Hamilton, P. 575
Hamilton, Patricia L. 407
Hamilton, Sir William 33
Hamlin, Cyrus 331, 615
Hamm, E. P. 145
Hammer, Stephanie Barbe 145, 302, 331
Hammersley, Rachel 302
Hammill, George 584
Hammon, Briton 464, 478
Hammon, Jupiter 466
Hammond, Brean 407, 447
Hammond, Christopher 145
Hammond, John 425
Hamon, Etienne 224
Hamou, Philippe 145
Hampton, Christopher 302
Handel, George Frederick (Georg Friedrich Händel) 233, 234, 235, 239–40, 241–42, 243, 245, 246, 247, 250, 298, 322, 643, 645, 646, 647
Handke, Peter 321
Handler, Jerome S. 51, 145
Handler, Richard 573
Hands, Elizabeth 389
Hanegraaff, Wouter J. 381, 419
Haney, David P. 145
Haney, Frank 146
Hanley, Brian 7, 407
Hanlon, Gregory 550
Hanna, Robert 146, 600
Hansel, Joelle 146
Hansell, Kathleen Kuzmick 628, 645
Hansen, Angela 661
Hanshaw, Mark E. 146

Index 717

Hanson, James A. 146
Häntzschel, Günter 332
Hara, Junichiro 146
Harber, W. H. 146
Harbers, Anne 399, 512
Harbinson, Michael 407
Harbison, P. 224
Harcourt, Rex 513
Hardach, Gerd 42
Harden, Theo 499
Hardenberg, Friedrich von 358
Hardin, Michael 407
Harding, Vanessa 51
Hardman, John 550
Hardy, Jean-Pierre 51
Harer, Ingeborg 254–55
Hareven, Tamara K. 21, 31, 93
Harford, Emmanuel 158
Harley, D. 600
Harley, J. B. 51
Harlow, Neal 485–86
Harman, Claire 407–08, 665
Harmon, J. E. 599
Haroche-Bouzinac, Geneviève 146, 602, 609, 651, 652, 654, 655
Harper, Graeme 407, 408
Harpham, Edward J. 550
Harrington, Dana 408
Harris, Ann Sutherland 219
Harris, Cath 146
Harris, Dianne 218
Harris, Ellen T. 239–40, 242
Harris, Enriqueta 625
Harris, Ian 146
Harris, Jocelyn 409
Harris, John 17, 550
Harris, Martin 409
Harrison, David 655
Harrison, Jennifer 500
Harrison, Paul 51
Harriss, Ernest, II 628, 644–46, 647–48
Harskamp, Jaap 628

Hart, Edward H. 51
Hart, Elliot 486
Hart, Gail K. 332
Hart, Sydney 630
Harth, Phillip 409
Hartley, David 589
Hartley, S. 550
Hartweg, Frédéric 146
Harvey, Brian W. 240–41
Harvey, Bruce A. 147
Harvey, Karen 51
Harvey, Lisa St. Clair 575
Harvey, Ross 241
Harvey, William 137, 590, 591, 620
Hashinuma, Katsumi 409
Haskell, Dennis 409
Haskell, Y. 600
Haslam, Thomas J. 51, 600
Haslinger, Tobias 637
Hass-Zumkehr, Ulrike 332
Hassán, Iacob M. 265, 270, 276–77, 277–79, 280, 281, 283, 286, 287, 288
Hassler, Gerda 302
Hastings, Adrian 146
Hastings, Warren 408, 539, 556
Hatch, Nathan O. 472
Hatcher, J. 551
Hatvany, Matthew G. 147
Haubrichs, Wolfgang 343
Haug, Christine 332
Hautebert, Joel 51
Havas, Kató 642
Havens, George R. 302
Hawcroft, Michael 655
Hawes, Clement 409, 665
Hawgood, Barbara J. 51, 147
Hawkes, David 147
Hawkesworth, John 371, 502, 514
Hawkins, Sir John 399
Hawney, Theophilus 234
Hawthorne, Nathaniel 465, 472, 473, 476

Hayden, J. Michael 51, 147
Hayden, Roger 147
Haydn, Franz Joseph 232, 235, 238, 239, 248, 249, 250, 251, 255, 611
Haydon, Colin 551
Hayes, Derek 51, 147
Hayes, John 223
Hayles, N. Katherine 600
Hayman, Francis 9
Haynes, Kenneth 409
Hays, Mary 444, 455
Hayton, David 52, 388
Haywood, Eliza 9, 312, 381, 384, 409, 417, 436, 449, 452, 458
Hearne, John 147
Hearne, Mary 416
Heath, Barbara 575
Heathcote, Christoph 518
Hebel, Odo J. 672
Heck, Anne Godrich 258
Heck, Thomas F. 258, 259
Hedenborg, Susanna 551
Hedenstrom, Mathias von 201
Hedin, Thomas F. 224
Hedquist, Valerie 222, 224
Heesen, Anke te 52
Hegel, Georg Wilhelm Friedrich 600, 615, 618
Heidegger, Count 322
Heidegger, Martin 599, 614, 621, 643
Heifetz, Jascha 642
Heilbron, John L. 52, 147
Heilbrun, Carolyn 530
Heilmann, Markus 321, 332
Hein, Karsten 332
Heine, Darlene Clark 46, 52, 86
Heine, Heinrich 148, 321, 637
Heinichen, Johann David 628, 640
Heinlein, Stefan 526, 625
Heinse, Wilhelm 345
Heinz, Jutta 332
Heinze, Dagmar 339
Heisters, Lorenz 188

Heitz, Raymond 540
Heitzenrater, Richard P. 147
Hejja, Julianna Erika 52
Helbig, Jörg 409, 457
Hellmann, Birgitt 23
Hellmuth, Thomas 52
Hellwig, Christoph von 562
Helmstadter, Axel 52, 147
Helo, Ari 409
Helvétius, Bonheur d' 293
Hembree, Fred 374
Hemings, John 585
Hemlow, Joyce 408
Hemming, Christine A. 500
Hemmings, Ray 551
Hemmings, Sally 578, 581
Henderson, James 486
Hendler, Glenn 584, 670
Henley, Samuel 371, 372
Hendrix, Lee 526
Henigman, Laura 575
Henke, Silke 332
Henkel, A. K. 526
Henning, Hansjoachim 52
Henningsen, Peter 52
Henriksen, Jan-Olav 147
Henrikson, Alan K. 147
Henry, Patrick 302
Hensen, Michael 401, 409
Hentsch, Thierry 52, 147
Hentschel, Uwe 332
Hepokoski, James 241
Herbelot, Barthélémy d' 372
Herbert, Francis 29
Herbert, G. B. 600
Herbert, Z. 223
Herboth, Franziska 333
Herder, Johann Gottfried 321, 323, 328, 335, 342, 344, 356, 400, 568, 588, 600
Herger, Csabane 52, 148
Herman, Bernard L. 52
Herman, Jan 655

Herman, Ruth 409
Hermand, Jost 104, 107, 144, 148, 149, 192, 212, 319
Hernández, Bartolome 103
Hernández-Sáenz, Luz María 148
Hernández-Sánchez, Eulalia 270
Herndon, Ruth Wallis 53
Heron-Allen, Edward 240
Herren, Madeleine 148
Herreros, Bretón de los 284
Herrick, James A. 600
Herrmann, Britta 333
Herschel, William 600
Hertel, Christiane 222, 224
Hervey, Lord 428, 558
Herz, Henriette 358
Herzfeld, Erika 53
Herzog, Gunter 410
Herzog, Todd 358
Hesse, Carla 522
Heßelmann, Peter 318
Hetherington, Michelle 516
Hewson, Helen 486
Hewson, Lance 410
Hewson, Polly 462
Heyer, Georgette 561
Heyink, R. 640
Heyl, Christopher 410
Heywood, Peter 545
Hibbert, Christopher 53, 551
Hicks, Carola 53
Hicks, Edward 620
Hiebl, Ewald 52
Higby, Gregory J. 53, 95, 137–38, 148, 179, 212
Higginbotham, D. 575
Higgins, Antony 279
High, Jeffrey L. 333
Highfill, Philip H., Jr. 264
Hight, Marc A. 148
Hilaire-Pérez, Liliane 592
Hilbert, M. 600
Hildebrand, David 256–57

Hildebrand, Ginger 256–57
Hildebrand, Olaf 333
Hilger, Stephanie 333
Hikino, Kyosuke 148
Hill, Arthur E. 241
Hill, Harvey 148
Hill, Jacqueline 53
Hill, Lisa 148, 410
Hill, Ruth 279, 410
Hill, Sarah H. 527, 551
Hill, W. E. 240
Hille, Martin 53
Hiller, Johann Adam 241
Hillmer, Rüdiger 633
Hilson, Ian 12
Hilton, Mary 148
Himrod, David K. 113
Hindley, Charles 325
Hiney, Tom 500–01
Hinrichs, Ernst 522–23
Hinterding, Erik 527, 628
Hippel, Theodor Gottlieb von 340, 353
Hirdt, Willi 318, 325, 329, 333, 340, 343, 347, 352, 355
Hirsch, Alison Duncan 148
Hirst, John 511
Hitchcock, Edward 149
Hitchcock, H. Wiley 236
Hitchcock, Tim 53
Hitzel, Frédéric 53
Hlobil, Tomás 601
Hoagwood, Terence Allan 410
Hoang, Lethuy 303
Hoare, Henry 264
Hoare, Sir Richard Colt 629
Hobbes, Thomas 129, 160, 206, 214, 368, 418, 434, 451, 592, 593, 596, 598, 601, 602, 606, 610, 611, 614, 615, 616, 618, 621
Hochedlinger, Michael 53
Hochreiter, Martina 241
Hodges, William 398, 478, 495, 496
Hodgins, Bruce 170

Hodgson, Barbara 149
Hodgson, William 543
Hodkinson, James 333
Hodson, Christopher 149, 303
Hoeber, Francis W. 149
Hoecherl-Alden, Gisela 149
Hoetzl, Ernest 254–55
Hoff, Karin 333
Hoffman, Abigail Kursheedt 164
Hoffmann, Daniel 333
Hoffmann, E. T. A. 341
Hoffmann, Roald 127
Hofmann, Michael 333
Hofmeister, Andrea 522
Hofstetter, Michael 53
Hogan, John 53
Hogarth, William 69, 221, 317, 390, 392, 417, 524, 624, 631, 632
Hogg, James 410
Hogle, Jerrold E. 410
Hogwood, Christopher 647
Hohepa, Pat 486
Holbach, Paul Henri Thiry, Baron d' 426, 601
Holbach, Rudolf 26
Holden, Robert 501
Hölderlin, Friedrich 316, 317, 319, 323, 327, 330, 339, 340, 342, 352, 353, 354, 593, 599, 609, 621, 661
Holdstein, Deborah H. 378, 410
Holenstein, André 54
Holland, Peter 410
Hollinshead, Janet E. 149
Hollman, Guy 551
Hollmer, Heide 333–34, 334–35
Holm, Christiane 335
Holman, Peter 241
Holmes, Martin 410
Holmes, Paula Elizabeth 149
Holmes, Reverend 654
Holmes, Richard 54
Holmes, Stephen R. 149
Holmes, William 645

Holmesland, Oddvar 411
Hölter, Achim 320
Hölty, Christoph Heinrich 344
Holub, Robert C. 149
Hölz, Karl 339, 501, 507
Holzem, Andreas 149
Holzhey, Helmut 149–50
Homberg, Wilhelm 603
Home, Edward 486
Home, Henry, Lord Kames 409, 639
Home, John 420, 443
Homer 406, 532, 596, 657
Honer, John 224
Honeyman, Katrina 551
Hongi (chieftain of Maori tribe) 480
Hongmou, Chen 80
Honold, Alexander 411
Hood, Paxton 150
Hook, Michael 551
Hooke, Robert 419, 456
Hooker, Brian 501
Hookham, Thomas 471
Hoorn, Jeanette 510
Höper, Corinna 526, 625
Hopes, Jeffrey 411, 665
Hopkin, David M. 551
Hopkins, Charles 432
Hopkins, Lisa 411
Hopkins, Samuel 154, 579
Hopper, Isaac 99
Hoppit, Julian 551
Horace (Quintus Horatius Flaccus) 223, 285, 329, 331, 424, 475
Horkheimer, Max 616
Horn, Wolfgang 628, 640
Horne, William C. 411
Hörner, Wolfgang 335
Hornsby, Clare 629
Hornsby, Thomas 620
Horsman, Reginald 575
Horstmann, F. 601
Horstmann, Monika 54
Horton, George Moses 474

Hoskovec, Jiri 208
Hotchkiss, Gregory K. 151
Houchin, John H. 633
Houlahan, Mark 487
Houlbrook, Matt 151
Houston, Alan 150
Houston, R. A. 54, 151
Houston, Rab 551
Houston, Robert 54, 151
Houzawa, Naohide 151
Hov, Live 151
Hoveler, Diane Long 666
Hoving, Ab 501
How, James 411, 449
Howard, Edward 433
Howells, Robin 303
Howsam, Leslie 533
Hoxsie, Russell 151
Hoyle, Arthur 513
Hoyos, Camilo 154
Hoz, Juan de la 278
Hribal, Jason 611
Hsia, Adrian 666
Hsia, Ke-chin 151
Hsia, R. Po-chia 151
Hsu, Ginger Cheng-chi 224
Hubb'ard, William 582
Huber, Brad R. 148, 152, 204
Huber, Thérèse 340
Hubert, Olivier 152
Hubrath, Margarete 373
Huchette, Jocelyn 303, 655
Hucho, Christine 152
Hudon, Christine 152, 465
Hudson, Nicholas 411
Huebner, Timothy S. 576
Huerkamp, Josef 335
Huertas, Monique de 54
Huesmann, Michael 318
Hughes, Christopher G. 224
Hughes, Derek 7, 411–12
Hughes, Lindsey 335, 551
Hughes, Peter 152

Hugues, Sylvie 601
Hugues, Victor 546
Huhn, Peter 412
Huisstede, P. van 527
Hull, Gillian 152
Hullinger, David 152
Hulme, Hank 152
Hulme, Peter 510
Humboldt, Alexander von 340, 418
Hume, David 45, 51, 101, 104, 106, 115, 118, 120, 121, 125, 133, 154, 161, 165, 166, 168, 172, 173, 183, 186, 191, 200, 376, 381, 420, 422, 423, 425–26, 436, 470, 590, 593, 594, 595, 598, 600, 603, 604, 606, 607, 608, 610, 611, 614, 617, 618, 620
Hume, Ivor N. 576
Hume, Robert D. 260–62, 263, 633
Hummel, Adrian 335
Humphreys, Joshua 43–44
Humuta, Don Marcos 173
Hund, J. 601
Hung, Ho-fung 54
Huning, Dieter 368
Hunt, A. 601
Hunt, John Dixon 223
Hunt, Lynn 412
Hunt, Susan 487
Hunter, Andy 303, 412
Hunter, Brooke 54
Hunter, David 234, 241
Hunter, Ian 150, 152
Hunter, J. Paul 3, 292, 312, 369, 370, 371, 373, 391, 412, 416, 419, 432, 438, 439, 445, 446, 448, 451, 453, 666
Hunter, James 54
Hunter, John 513, 550
Hunter, Lynette 6, 373, 420, 423, 522
Hunter, Mary 641
Hunter, Michael 152
Hunwick, Andrew 601

Hurlebusch, Klaus 335
Hurley, David Ross 241–42
Huron, David 242
Hurpin, Gérard 54, 153
Hurst, Jane 412
Huse, Ann A. 412
Husserl, Edmund 139
Hutcheson, Francis (Bishop) 141
Hutchinson, Dale L. 162
Hutchinson, Francis 593
Hutson, James H. 576
Hutner, Heidi 412
Hutton, Gordon 153
Hutton, Sarah 153
Huxley, Andrew 178
Huygens, Christiaan 180–81, 621
Huysseune, Michel 552
Huystee, M. van 519
Hyde, Edward, First Earl of Clarendon 13
Hyde, Michael 519
Iaeys, G. 552
Iakolev, Sergei Evgen'evich 54
Ianne, Antonia 242
Ianushkevich, A. S. 340
Ibánez, María Ignacia 268
Ibrahim, Annie 601
Ickringill, Steve 45
Ida, Hisashi 303
Ignatiev, Noel 576
Ikegame, Naoko 412
Ikeuchi, Osamu 335
Ilgner, Richard 335
Iliffe, Robert 601
Illari, Bernardo 279
Iltcheva, Radoslava 335
Imbarrato, Susan Clair 466
Imbroscio, Carmelina 293, 303, 314
Imbruglia, Girolamo 55, 153, 655
Imlay, Gilbert 529
Imlay, R. A. 601
Inchbald, Elizabeth 385, 410, 667
Inclán, Valle 279

Ingamells, John 224
Ingen, Ferdinand van 322
Ingham, Cynthia Jo 153
Ingram, Allan 412, 552
Ingram, Edward 513
Ingres, Jean Auguste Dominique 228
Innocenti, Loretta 413
Insalaco, Danielle 413
Ionov, Igor' Nikolaevich 55
Iotti, Gianni 655
Iriarte, Tomás de 286
Irlam, Shaun 153, 413
Irmscher, Christoph 672
Irons, Charles F. 601
Irr, Caren 55
Irvine, Nancy 514
Irving, Washington 465
Isaac, Peter 7
Isakhov, Salavat Midkhatovich 104
Isenberg, Andrew C. 576
Ishii, Shigemitsu 413
Isla, José Francisco de 280
Islaev, Faizulkhak Gabdulkhakovich 55
Islamoglu, Huri 55
Islamov, Tofik Muslimovich 153
Israel, Jonathan Irvine 153
Iturrate, José 601
Ivan the Terrible 560
Ivory, James 595
Iwanisziw, Susan B. 413
Izquierdo Benito, Ricardo 265, 270, 276–77, 277–79, 280, 281, 283, 286, 287, 288
Jabour, Anya 153
Jack, Malcolm 373, 413
Jackson, Charles Thomas 180
Jackson, Dianah Leigh 55, 153
Jackson, Edmund 436
Jackson, Kent P. 153
Jackson, M. W. 602
Jackson, Robert H. 154
Jackson, William 436
Jacob, Margaret C. 7, 55, 154, 412, 552

Index

Jacobi, Friedrich Heinrich 328
Jacobs, Diane 154
Jacobs, Helmut C. 279, 303
Jacobsen, Anja Skaar 154
Jacobsen, Douglas 154
Jacobus, Mary 413
Jacovides, Michael 602
Jacques-Lefevre, Nicole 303, 305
Jacquet de la Guerre, Elizabeth-Claude 220, 246
Jacquette, Dale 154
Jacquin, Frédéric 55
Jacquin, Philippe 573
Jaeger, Stephan 335
Jaffe, Catherine 279
Jaffe, James A. 55, 552
Jägers, Regine 55
Jahn, Bernhard 336
Jai Singh II, Maharaja 207
Jakob, Hans-Joachim 336
James II, King 548
James, Donald W., Jr. 175
James, William 175, 672
Jami, Catherine 602
Jamoussi, Zouheir 413
Jander, Owen 242
Janiak, A. 602
Janitzek, Martina 242
Jankovic, Vladimir 602
Jansen, Cornelius 31, 102, 118, 209, 291
Jansen, Guido 218
Jappe, Anselm 93
Jaramillo, Ana María Hermillo 154
Jardine, Lisa 154
Jarnoux, Philippe 55
Jauhiainen, Peter D. 154
Jaume, Lucien 552
Jea, John 615
Jean Paul (Johann Paul Friedrich Richter) 324, 335, 354
Jean-Denys, Devauges 630, 631
Jeffares, N. 224

Jefferson, Thomas 50, 85, 95, 96, 127, 129, 338, 426, 461, 464, 465, 567, 568, 569, 570, 572, 573, 574, 575, 576, 578, 579, 580, 581, 582, 585, 586, 587, 633
Jenkin, Robert 487
Jenkins, Cliff 214
Jenkins, Jennifer R. 242
Jenks, Timothy
Jenne, Natalie 230–31
Jennings, Jeremy 552
Jensen, Geoffrey 49, 55
Jeremy, David J. 552
Jerinic, Maria 413
Jespers, F. 602
Jesseph, Douglas M. 602
Jesus, Marie-Joseph de l'Enfant 164
Jewell, Keala 364
Jezierski, Andrzej 56
Jiraskova, Alena 56
Joaquín Dicenta, Juan José de 288
Jobst, Kerstin S. 56
Jodin, Marie Madeleine 48, 260, 301
Jodziewicz, Thomas W. 154
Joffrin, Laurent 552
Jogėla, Vytautas 155
Johns, A. 602
Johnson, Christian 121
Johnson, Claudia L. 413
Johnson, Daniel C. 303
Johnson, Eric 389
Johnson, James H. 303
Johnson, Laurie 336, 602
Johnson, Lee 224
Johnson, Maria Poggi 155
Johnson, Odai 633
Johnson, Richard 514
Johnson, Samuel 6, 7, 13, 16, 74, 79, 165, 172, 196, 367, 369, 370, 371, 377, 379, 381, 382, 383, 387, 399, 400, 402, 405, 407, 409, 411, 413, 419, 420, 421, 425–26, 435–36, 440, 443, 445, 448, 456, 559, 662,

663, 664, 665, 666, 668, 672
Johnson, Sherry 56
Johnson, Simon 99
Johnson, Whittington B. 552, 576
Johnston, Andrew John Bayly 56
Johnston, Anna 501
Johnston, Freya 413
Johnston, Guillemette 304
Johnston, René 56
Johnstone, H. Diack 243
Jolle, Jonas 336
Jollet, Étienne 602, 629
Jolley, Nicholas 607
Joly, Bernard 155, 602
Joly, Raymond 304
Jomini, Antoine Henri, Baron de 552
Jommelli, Niccolo 640
Jones, Absalom 104, 461
Jones, Alun R. 224
Jones, Charles 414
Jones, Colin 602
Jones, Dorothy 56
Jones, George Fenwick 155, 576
Jones, Greta 552
Jones, Jean 591
Jones, Jennifer M. 304
Jones, Joseph 279
Jones, Marshall B. 155
Jones, Michael T. 336
Jones, Philip Henry 7
Jones, Simon 243
Jones, Sue 629
Jones, W. E. 603
Jones, W. Gareth 336
Jones, Wendy 414
Jones, William 77, 184
Jones, Sir William (orientalist) 398
Jonson, Ben 374–75, 450
Jooma, Minaz 406, 414
Joost, Ulrich 336
Jordan, David P. 155
Jordan, Sarah 414, 666
Joseph II, Emperor of Austria 642

Josephine (wife of Napoleon Bonaparte) 483–84
Jost, Peter 243
Joubert, Joseph 654
Jourda, Pierre 258
Jourdan, Annie 21, 74, 553
Jové, Antoni 272, 279
Jovellanos y Ramírez, Gaspar Melchor de 273, 281, 284
Joy, Neill R. 672
Joy, Samuel 501
Joyce, James 429
Juengel, Scott 155
Juet, Hubert 56
Julen, Hans 501
Julia, Dominique 39
Juliani, Richard N. 155
Julien, Pascal 155, 629
Jullien, François 603
Jumonville, Florence 533
Jung, Carl 442
Jung, Hans Rudolf 155
Jung, Sandro 414
Jung-Stilling, Johann Heinrich 319
Junius 373
Juratic, Sabine 522
Jurdjevic, Mark 56
Jürgensen, Jørgen (also: Jorgen Jorgenson) 519
Jurgenson, William 232
Jurt, Joseph 56
Just, Melanie Marie 392–93, 432–33, 438–39
Justice, George 420, 449–50
Jutong, Wu 164
Jutte, Robert 155
Kaboré, Boniface 155
Kadane, Matthew 156
Kagan, Henry 605
Kagan, Susan 243
Kagawa, Chiaki 603
Kahn, Jean 156
Kaimowitz, Jeffrey H. 527

Index

Kairoff, Claudia Thomas 414, 446
Kaiser, Gerhard R. 317, 527
Kaldenbach, Kees 224–25
Kale, Wilford 576
Kalidasa 498
Kalik, Judith 156
Kalista, Zdenek 156
Kallen, Stuart A. 156
Kalm, Máximo José 279
Kamehameha I 487
Kampmann, Christoph 156
Kamrath, Mark L. 466
Kamps, Ivo 382, 414
Kan, Sergei 156
Kankei, Jidan 151
Kant, Immanuel 25, 91, 101, 102, 105, 112, 114, 118, 119, 126, 133, 140, 143, 146, 150, 156, 158, 159, 161, 162, 163, 165, 168, 188, 194, 202, 203, 204, 206, 207, 208, 209, 211, 213, 215, 219, 231, 352, 358, 404, 426, 534, 592, 595, 597, 598, 599, 600, 601, 603, 604, 605, 606, 607, 608, 612, 613, 614, 615, 616, 618, 620, 621
Kanter, Douglas 156
Kany, Roland 336
Kapitzke, Robert L. 56, 156
Kaplan, Cora 529
Kaplan, Deborah 414, 633
Kaplan, Steven L. 56
Kapón, Uriel Macías 278, 279
Karajan, Herbert von 262
Kardasis, Vassilis 57
Karhausen, L. R. 156
Karian, Stephen E. 94, 185, 414, 439
Karl Friedrich von Baden, Markgraf 67
Karoly, L. 553
Karp, Serguei 57
Karr, Gary 642
Kasakoff, A. B. 576
Kashatus, W. C. 577
Kassler, Jamie C. 243

Kassler, Michael 157, 243, 603, 642
Kates, Gary 57, 299
Katz, Melissa R. 225
Kauffman, Angelica 385
Kaufman, Matthew H. 57
Kaufmann, Eric 576
Kaul, Oskar 644
Kausch, Karl-Heinz 336
Kavanagh, Thomas M. 304, 603
Kay, Carol 603
Kayman, Martin A. 414
Kazanjian, David 467
Keach, Benjamin 595
Keane, Angela 414, 527–30
Keane, John 576
Kearns, Daniel F. 157
Kearns, Gerry 157
Kearns, Thomas R. 573, 584
Keate, George 307, 514
Keats, John 345, 407
Keble, John 155
Keeble, N. H. 388
Keefe, Simon P. 243–44
Keegan, Bridget 415
Keevak, Michael 57, 415
Kefeli, Agnès 157
Kehrès, Jean-Marc 304
Keil, Bettina 497, 505, 507
Keipert, Helmut 415
Keith, Jennifer 415, 447
Keller, Eve 603
Kelleter, Frank 672
Kelley, Anne 415
Kelley, Charles Greg 438
Kelley, Donald R. 57, 157
Kelly, Gary 415
Kelly, James 553
Kelly, Joseph 157
Kemal, S. 603
Kemp, Anthony 576
Kemp, Catherine 603
Kemp, H. T. 487
Kemper, Hans-Georg 319, 325, 326,

331, 336, 345, 352, 354, 358
Kempton, Adrian   304, 415
Kences, James   104
Kendall, Gavin   57
Kendrick, Robert   672
Kenkel, Karen J.   337
Kennedy, Adrienne   231
Kennedy, Deborah   415
Kennedy, Hugh   35, 57
Kennedy, Jennifer T.   467
Kennedy, Joyce D.   388–89
Kennedy, Máire   8, 57
Kennedy, Michael V.   57, 466, 467
Kennedy, Roger G.   576, 577
Kennesen, Claude   642
Kenney, Alice P.   157
Kenri, Bakuhan   151
Kenshur, O.   157
Keohane, Catherine   415
Kepler, Johannes   601, 614
Kerhervé, Alain   530
Kerman, Joseph   244, 260
Kerov, Valeri Vsevolodovich   157
Kerr, Douglas   415
Kerr, Heather   416
Kerry, Paul E.   157, 337
Kersh, Rogan   57
Kerslake, Lawrence   603
Kertzer, David I.   157
Kessel, Martina   57
Kevorkian, Tanya   553
Kewes, Paulina   8, 416
Key, J. P.   577
Keymer, Thomas   8–9
Keymer, Tom   416
Keynes, Milo   157
Khaleeli, Zhaleh   157
Khan, Mirza Abu Talib   547
Khandekar, Narayan   225
Khanna, Vinod C.   58
Khodarkovsky, Michael   137, 156, 157, 158, 159, 171–72, 173
Khoury, Dina Rizk   58, 158

Khristoforova, N. V.   58
Kiberd, Declan   416
Kidd, C.   553
Kidd, Colin C.   158
Kiddy, Elizabeth W.   553
Kiefer, Sascha   337
Kiefer, Sebastian   337
Kierkegaard, Søren   147, 244
Kierner, Cynthia A.   577
Kiesant, Knut   322, 337
Kieven, Elisabeth   225
Kilgour, Maggie   414, 442, 513
Killigrew, Anne   424
Kim, Gyu Chang   337
Kim, Jin-Ah   244
Kim, Mi Gyung   158, 603
Kimball, Roger   337
Kimbel, Edith   254–55
Kimbel, Michael   254–55
Kimura, Naoji   337
Kincade, Kit   427–28
King, A.   666
King, Amy M.   416, 449
King, James   490
King, Kathryn R.   409, 416
King, Kimball   302
King, Michael   501–02
King, Moll   25
King, P.   553
King, Robert J.   487
King, Sigrid   665
King, Steven   553
King, Stewart R.   58
King, Thomas A.   416
King of Dublin, William (Archbishop)   559
Kingdon-Ward, Martha   257–58
Kinghorn, Kenneth Cain   603
Kinnaman, Ted   158
Kinsley, William   295, 298, 304, 311, 361
Kiple, Kenneth F.   158
Kirch, Patrick Vinton   514

Index

Kircher, Athanasius 544
Kirillov, V. V. 158
Kirk, Brian 158
Kirk, James 113, 158, 169
Kirkendale, Warren 642, 643
Kirkham, Linda M. 58
Kirkland, Trevor 158
Kirnberger, Johann Philipp 230
Kirsop, Wallace 301, 304
Kirscher, Roger 603
Kister, Stefan 337
Kitson, Peter J. 327, 502, 512, 514
Kivy, Peter 245
Kizilos, P. 577
Klassen, Sherri 58
Klehn, Susan 522
Klein, Herbert S. 159
Klein, Holger 390, 394, 397, 404, 410, 419, 431
Klein, Joachim 58
Kleine, Sabine 337, 416
Kleinfeld, Daniel J. 673
Kleingeld, P. 604
Kleingeld, Pauline 159
Kleinschmidt, Erich 337
Kleist, Ewald Christian von 321, 330, 340
Kleist, Heinrich von 316, 323, 327, 330, 336, 338, 341, 342, 345, 346, 347, 348, 351, 352, 354
Klessmann, E. 356
Klettenberg, Susanna Katharina von 326
Klieber, Rupert 159
Klier, John 159, 161
Kliman, Bernice 416
Kloek, J. J. 629
Kloek, Wouter Theodore 218
Klonk, Charlotte 629
Klooster, Wim 159
Klopstock, Friedrich Gottlieb 323, 328, 335, 350
Knapen, Luc 530
Knapp, Éva 159, 205

Knee, Philip 604
Knell, S. J. 159
Kneller, Sir Godfrey 322
Knellwolf, Christa 516
Knight, Charles A. 425–26
Knight, Franklin W. 58, 553
Knight, Richard Payne 319, 360
Knight, William 106
Knightley, Phillip 502
Knighton, C. S. 553
Knights, Elspeth 416
Knoblauch, Hubert 159
Knoeff, Rina 159
Knowles, Chantal 513
Knox, Samuel 476
Knox-Shaw, Peter 417
Koch, Heinrich Christoph 243, 245, 252
Kochan, James 58
Koehn, Barbara 58
Kohlschein, Franz 338
Kohn, Brigitte 338
Koistinen, O. 604
Kok, Jan Piet Filedt 218
Kolchinsky, Eduard I. 159
Kollerstrom, N. 604
Kolm, Serge 545
Kolneder, Walter 254
Koltes, Manfred 338
Komisaruk, Adam 666
Komlos, John 159
Kondakov, Jurij Evgen'evich 159
König, Peter 338
Kontler, László 160
Koolhaas, Eveline 629
Koon, Helene 530
Koos, Greg 160
Kopanev, Nikolai Alexandrovitch 304
Kord, Susanne 334–35
Kordela, A. Kiarina 338
Koriako, D. 604
Korman, Gerd 160
Korshin, Paul J. 666

Korsten, Frans   522
Korte, Barbara   531
Kortenhauf, K. D.   577
Kosch, Wilhelm   334
Kosciusko, Thaddeus   570
Kosegarten, Gotthard Ludwig   339
Kosellek, Gerhard   352
Kosellek, Reinhart   338
Kosenina, Alexander   338, 356–57
Koslofsky, Craig   160
Kosmetatou, Elizabeth   417
Kossigan, Patrice   279–80
Kossler, M.   604
Kossmann, E. H.   626, 629
Kost, A.   200
Kostova, Ludmilla   417
Kotel'nikov, Esaul E. N.   159
Kottman, Karl A.   160
Kotzebue, August von   357
Kovacs, Katalin   304
Kow, Simon   160
Kowalik, Jill   605, 614, 632, 657
Kowalská, Eva   160
Kowalski, Waldemar   160
Kozul, Mladen   304–05
Kraft Ernst, Prinz von Oettingen-Wallerstein   644
Kraft, Elizabeth   417, 422
Kramer, Lawrence   243
Kramnick, Isaac   577
Kramnick, Jonathan Brody   604
Kraus, Georg Melchior   353
Kraus, Gerlinde   58
Krause, Frank   338
Krawehl, Otto-Ernst   82
Kraybill, Donald B.   160
Krebs, Roland   540
Kreczmar, Agnieszka   169
Kreis-Schinck, Annette   417
Kremer, Detlef   338
Kremer, M.   604
Kresin, Oleksii   58
Kretzschmar, Louise   160

Kreutzer, Hans Joachim   338
Krieger, Alex   59, 66
Krill, Rosemary Troy   629
Krimm, Stefan   320
Krippendorff, Ekkehart   338
Krishna, V. V.   59
Kristeva, Julia   465, 599
Kriz, Kay Dian   577
Kroll, Richard   417
Kronauer, Ulrich   326, 328, 332, 338, 339, 359, 502
Kronick, David A.   59, 160
Kross, Jessica   553
Krüger-Furhoff, Irmela Marei   339
Krysmanski, Bernd   417
Kubeck, Elizabeth   417
Kubik, T. R. W.   553
Kuehn, Manfred   161
Kuehn, Thomas   22, 83
Kuflik, Arthur   604
Kugle, Scott Alan   161
Kugler, Stefani   339
Kuhn, Halgard   604
Kuhn, Hans Wolfgang   604
Kuhn, Laura   249
Kuiters, W. G. J.   554
Kujula, A.   554
Kuklick, Bruce   161
Kulenkampff, Jens   161
Kullman, Colby H.   467
Kulmus, Luise (see also: Gottsched)   329
Kümmerling-Meibauer, Bettina   531
Kundera, Milan   657
Kunzel, Christine   339
Kupke, Anne-Kristin   522
Kupperman, Karen Ordahl   577
Kuppers-Braun, Ute   161
Kurscheidt, Georg   339
Kurth-Voigt, Liselotte E.   339
Kurz-Bernardons, Joseph Felix (von)   317
Kusch, Manfred   305
Kushkumbaev, Aibolat Kairsliamovich   59

Index

Kushner, Tony 161
Kusukawa, S. 604
Kutchen, Larry 467
Kutty, Bilal Ahmad 161
Kuzniaeva, Sofia 161
Kyba, Daniel A. 161
Kylmäkoski, Merja 59
L'Affilard, Michel 230
L'Aminot, Tanguy 656
L'estrange, Roger 420
La Brède, Baron de (see: Montesquieu)
La Chalotais, Louis-René de Caradeuc de 651
La Charpillon, Marie 364
La Ferté-Imbault, Marquise 657
La Mettrie, Julian Offray de 605
La Morlière, Charles de 304
La Nöe, Jérôme de 120–21
La Roche, Sophie von 323, 326, 341, 377
La Rochefoucauld, François, Duc de 417
La Volpa, Anthony J. 605
Labbe, Jacqueline M. 417
Laberge, Pierre 604
Laborde, Jean-Benjamin de 34
Labouvie, Eva 59
Labrosse, Claude 305
Laclos, Pierre Choderlos de 304, 415, 655
Lacoue-Labarthe, P. 661
Lacour, Eva 59
Lacy, John 367
Lacy, Mary 550
Lafargue, Catherine 656
Laffey, Paul 161
Laffrado, Laura 59, 418
Lafiteau, Joseph François 131, 308
Lafon, Henri 305, 656
Lafon, Sylvie 605
Lafont, Jean Marie 59
Lafrance, Guy 597, 604
Lagerqvist, Hans 305
Lagrée, Jacqueline 161, 617

Lahontan, Louis Armand de Lom d'Arce 80, 650
Lai, Whalen 161
Laidlow, Jonathan 418, 449
Laing, Alistair 629
Laiskas, Henricho Lyzijaus 315
Lake, P. 554
Lamb, Charles 373
Lamb, J. 666
Lamb, Jonathan 418, 479, 480, 484, 486, 487, 488, 490, 492–93, 502, 514
Lamb, Mary 669
Lambert, John 131
Lambert, Patricia M. 140
Lamartine, Geneviève de 288
Lamont, Stewart 59
Lamport, F. J. 339
Lamprecht, Oliver 59
Lams, Victor J. 418
Lamy, Bernard 656
Landau, Philippe-Èfraïm 161
Landes, Joan B. 59
Landford, Paul 554
Landois, Paul 298, 389
Landowska, Wanda 636
Landry, Donna 418
Landry, N. 554
Landsman, Ned C. 60, 577
Lane, Michael E. 405, 453
Langdon, Robert 502–03
Lange, Horst 339, 418
Langford, Paul 554
Langford, Rachel 478, 487
Langford, S. 605
Langhans, Edward A. 264
Langille, E. M. 305
Langley, Leanne 636
Langlois, Denis Jean Florimond du (Marquis du Bouchet) 585
Langner, Beatrix K. 339
Langsam, H. 605
Lannoy, Cyprien 605

Lanser, Susan 305
Lantin, R. 605
Laperriere, Guy 162
Lapierre, Solange 656
Laponce, J. A. 60
Lappo Danilevskii, K. Iu 339
Lara, María de la Paz Ramos 162
Larguier, Gilbert 60
Larkin, E. 356
Larkin, Edward T. 356–57, 467
Laroque, Christiane 540
Larra, Mariano José de 272, 284
Larrère, Catherine 554
Larrimore, Mark 162
Larsen, Clark Spencer 140, 162, 208, 213
Larsen, Jens Peter 242
Larson, Chiles T. A. 577
Larson, Duane H. 137
Larson, Edward J. 162
Larson, Rebecca 577, 605
Larsson, Jonas 60
LaRue, Jan 245
Lasowski, Patrick Wald 656
Lässig, Simone 162
Lassman, Peter 605
Lassus, Orlando 252
Latham, A. J. H. 484–85, 489
Latham, John 162
Latham, Robert 435
Lathem, Edward Connery 531
Laudin, Gérard 340
Laugier, Marc-Antoine 293
Laurence, Anne 418
Laurence, Janet 60
Laurens, Henry 577
Laursen, C. 118
Lautman, Jean-Pierre 60
Lauwaert, Françoise 554
Laux-Huetz de Lemps, Claire 60
Lavater, Johann Kaspar 358
Lavery, Brian 554
Lavezzi, Elisabeth 630

Lavoisier, Antoine Laurent de 106, 107, 592, 605
Lavroff, Dmitri Georges 60
Lavrov, Aleksandr 162
Law, John 498
Law, R. 554
Lawitschka, Valerie 340
Lawlor, Clark 605
Lawrence, Christopher 605
Lawson, Colin 643
Lawson, Henry 490
Lawson, Russell M. 578
Laxton, Paul 51
Lay, Howard G. 315
Lazarus, Rachel Mordecai 135
Lazo, Yolanda 162
Le Brun-Gouanvic, Claire 263
Le Cat, Claude Nicolas 49, 54, 143, 153, 163, 193
Le Clercq, Chrestien 554
Le Faye, Deirdre 418
Le Fevre, Peter 555
Le Flem, Jean-Paul 60
Le Gallienne, Richard 435
Le Goff, T. J. A. 555
Le Jallé, Éléonore 606
Le Ru, Véronique 305, 656
Le Rue, Véronique 163
Le Textier, Antoine 264
Le Vau, Louis 622
Leapor, Mary 36, 49, 387, 404, 424, 425
Leask, Nigel 340, 418, 503, 672
Lebedeva, O. B. 340
Leca Tsiomis, Marie 305
Lecerf, Guy 305
Leclerc, Guy 227, 245
Lecourt, Dominique 163
Ledbetter, David 245
Ledbury, Mark 292, 293, 297, 304–05, 306, 317, 353, 365, 630
Lederer, Josef-Horst 245
Leduc, Christophe 60, 163

Index

Leduc, Guyonne 418, 554
Ledyard, John 503
Lee, Ann 134, 176, 611
Lee, D. 554
Lee, Haiyan 60
Lee, Hyun Sang 605
Lee, Inkyu 419
Lee, Jennifer B. 531
Lee, Robert A. 672, 673
Lee, Sophia 380, 396
Lee, Wayne E. 60
Lee, Yoon Sun 419
Lee, Young Mock 305
Leech, Peter 163, 245
Leeuwenhoek, Antony van 223
Lefebvre, Bernard 163
Lefèvre, Wolfgang 163
Lefrand de Pompignan, J.-J de 598
Legay, Marie-Laure 61
Leger, Benoit 305
Leger, Sylvie 340
Legros, Pierre 629
Leibniz, Gottfried Wilhelm von 102, 111, 116, 138, 149, 150, 163, 165, 180, 212, 328, 526, 591, 601, 602, 604, 605, 606, 608, 610, 611, 613, 614, 616, 619
Leigh, Edward, Lord 183
Leigh, John 656
Leiner, Frederick C. 578
Leistner, Bernd 340
Leitz, Robert C., III 5
Lequan, Maï 606
Leland, John 122
Lemaire, Jean-François 555
Lemay, J. A. Leo 467
Lemercier, Jean-Pierre 163
LeMinor, Jean-Marie 163
Lena, Alberto 163
Leneman, Leah 555
Lengel, Edward G. 588
Lenman, Bruce 61
Lennartz, Rita 340
Lennon, Thomas M. 419
Lennox, Charlotte 369, 443
Lenoir, Alexandre 628
Lenoir, Frederic 107
Lentz, Thierry 555
Lenz, Jacob Michael Reinhold 47, 138, 321, 327, 329, 334, 341, 342, 344, 351, 352, 360, 400, 661
Lenzi Iacomelli, Carlotta 225
León, Leonardo 61
León, Sánchez de 284
Leonard, Mark 225, 622
Leonard, Thomas C. 578, 672
Leopoldo, Pietro 594
Lepore, Jill 578
Lerner, Lawrence Scott 163, 306
Lesage, Alano René (also: Alain René) 280, 660
Leshchilovskaia, Inna Ivanovna 163
Leslie, Charles Powell 39
Lespinasse, Julie de (Mademoiselle) 368, 658
Lessenich, Rolf 419
Lesser, M. X. 464
Lessing, Gotthold Ephraim 147, 317, 324, 325, 327, 331, 334, 337, 339, 342, 347, 349, 351, 352, 353, 358, 359
Lester, Joel 643
Lestringant, Frank 578, 580
Leseueur, Charles Alexandre 487
LeSueur, Richard 638, 643
Leszczynska, Cecylia 56
Lethbridge, Stefanie 531
Letzter, Jacqueline 245, 306
Lèu, Yimin 128
Leunig, Timothy 184
Leuwers, Hervé 555
Levasseur, Susan J. 306
Lévêque, Laure 306
Leveque, Pierre 555
Levenduski, Christine M. 606
Lever, Maurice 61

Levinas, Choderlos de 430, 495
Levine, Joseph M. 419
Levinger, M. 606
Levine, Neil Ann Stuckey 163
Levis, R. Barry 164
Levy, Janet M. 245
Levy, Lia 606
Lévy, Maurice 371, 419
Lewis, Alison 164
Lewis, Brian 61
Lewis, C. L. E. 159
Lewis, James A. 578
Lewis, Jan 578
Lewis, Jayne 419, 605, 614, 632, 657, 666
Lewis, Marilyn 164
Lewis, Matthew G. "Monk" 448, 665
Lewis, Meriwether (Lewis and Clark) 61, 174, 180, 199, 210, 573
Lewis, Miles 503
Lewis, Richard 476, 477
Leza, José Máximo 280
Li, Hsiao-t'i 61
Li, Liukun 164
Liandrat Guigues, Suzanne 306
Libin, Laurence 246
Libo, Kenneth 164
Libourel, Jean-Louis 630
Lichtenberg, Georg Christoph 317, 329, 336, 340, 347, 351, 354, 356
Lida de Malkiel, María Rosa 289
Lieberman, D. 606
Liebersohn, Harry 487
Lieburg, Fred van 61, 164
Liedtke, Rainer 164
Liedtke, Walter 222, 225
Liesegang, Kerstin 306
Light, Dale B. 155
Lilla, M. 606
Lillo, George 422, 665
Lim, Seung-Hwi 164
Lincoln, Margarette 61
Lind, William S. 61

Lindemann-Stark, Anke 340
Linden, Stanton J. 419
Lindenauer, Leslie J. 573
Linder, Jutta 340
Linder, Marc 578
Lindgren, Lowell E. 260–62
Lindman, Janet Moore 164, 172, 467, 477, 478, 606, 609
Lindmark, Daniel 164
Lines, William J. 487
Link, Dorothea 643
Link, Eric Carl 674
Linn, Patricia Y. C. E. 555
Linn[a]eus, Carolus (Linné, Carl von) 291, 416, 449, 618
Linney, Verna 419
Linton, Marisa 61
Lintvelt, Jaap 295
Lippincott, Louise 109
Lipsius, Justus 196
Lisle, Viscount 164
Lisovskii, Iraklu (Bishop) 133
Lister, A. 606
Lister, W. 246
Liston, R. 652
Litschauer, Walburga 643
Little, Ann M. 164, 467
Little, Meredith 230–31
Little, P. 555
Little, Patrick 164
Littleton, Charles 152
Liu, Peng 165
Liu, Zhenggang 165
Livesey, James 61, 555
Livingston, William 476
Livingstone, David N. 544, 546, 555
Lobachev, S. V. 165
Locke, John 29, 69, 82, 114, 123, 132, 144, 146, 148, 168, 171, 172, 173, 177, 190, 192, 193, 195, 197, 199, 202, 214, 426, 431, 450, 452, 454, 455, 470, 476, 569, 593, 594–95, 596, 597, 604, 607, 608, 609, 611,

Index

612
Lockerby, E. 555
Lockley, Timothy James 62, 578
Lockridge, Kenneth A. 462
Lockwood, Thomas 9, 419
Locqueneux, Robert 165
Lodge, P. 606
Lodge, Paul 165
Lodoli, Carlo 293
Loen, Johann Michael von 325
Loesch, Perk 62
Loft, Anne 58
Lohmeier, Anke Marie 340
Loiselle, Kenneth 17–18
Loker, Zvi 165
Lokke, Kari E. 386, 410, 413, 414, 415, 419, 425, 428, 455
Lombardi, Daniela 62
Lomnicki, Nikola Škrlec 74
Long, C. P. 606
Longacre, Mark Garrett 467
Longman, Stanley V. 363
Longstaffe-Gowan, Todd 165, 225
Longsworth, Polly 578
Lonsdale, Roger 372, 420
Look, Brandon 606
Looney, J. Jefferson 578
Looser, Devoney 420, 454
Lope de Vega (Carpio), Félix 278
Lopez, Claude A. 573, 578
López, Emilio la Parra 555
López Cano, Rubén 280
López de Ayala, Pilar 284
López Martínez, María Isabel 270
Loptson, Peter 165, 607
Lorenzo, Luciano García 531
Lorieux, Denis 62
Lorizzo, Loredana 225
Lorraine de Montluzin, Emily 420
Los, Willeke 607
Losche, Diane 483, 487, 489, 491, 492
Löscher, Valentine Ernst 181
Losh, Sara 219

Losonsky, Michael 165
Lott, Deshae E. 469–77
Loty, Laurent 523, 653
Loughran, Trish 165
Louis XIV, King 56, 137, 170, 546, 549
Louis XV, King 61, 236, 539, 630, 653
Louis XVI, King 32, 360, 629
Louis, Jeanne Henriette 578
Louis-Courvoisier, Micheline 62, 165
Loussouarn, Sophie 666
Louvet, Jean-Baptiste 659
Lovattini, Giovanni 264
Love, Harold 420
Lovejoy, P. E. 554
Lovejoy, Paul E. 62
Loveland, Jeff 62, 165
Lovell, Margaretta M. 630
Lovell, W. George 20, 31, 33
Lowe, Thomas 242
Lowengard, Sarah 62, 165
Lowerre, Kathryn 246, 263–64
Lowerson, John 62
Lowrey, John 225
Lowth, Robert 16
Loyola, Ignatius 613
Loz, Hypolite Radegonde 55
Lu, Jin 306
Lu, Yixu 341
Lubbock, Tom 218
Lubin, Steven 637, 638, 643
Luca Casimiro degli Albizzi, Marchese 645
Lucas, Jean M. 594
Lucassen, M. N. J. 537
Lucena Salmoral, Manuel 280
Luccichenti, Furio 306
Luciano, Dana 672
Ludwig, Bernd 166
Ludwig, Ernst 252
Ludwig, Frieder 166
Ludwin, Dawn M. 166
Luebke, D. M. 556
Lühning, Helga 246

Luijten, Ger   527, 628
Luisi-Weichsel, Yvonne   254–55
Luke, David   341
Lukoschik, Rita Unfer   362
Lulé, Susanna   318, 341, 344, 358
Lully, Jean-Baptiste   254
Lummis, Trevor   488
Lund, Roger D.   374–75
Luo, Bingliang   62
Luoma-Aho, Mika   556
Lupo, Massimo   556
Luque Alcaide, Elisa   62, 166
Lurbe, Pierre   420
Luria, Sarah   62
Luserke, Matthias   318, 320, 321, 337, 340, 341, 342, 349
Luserke-Jaqui, Matthias   341
Lushpai, Vladimir Borisovich   63, 166
Luther, Martin   34, 128, 131, 160, 608
Lütteken, Laurenz   246
Lutz, Alfred   420
Lützeler, Paul Michael   327, 330, 336, 338, 341, 343, 345, 346, 347, 351, 354
Luzán, Ignacio de   273, 277, 279, 410
Luzzato, S.   556
Lynch, Deidre   666
Lynch, James V.   579
Lynch, John   63
Lynch, William T.   166
Lynn, John A.   63
Lynn, Michael R.   63
Lynn, Steven   420
Lyons, Clare A.   166
Lyons, Jack C.   166
Lyotard, Jean-François   206
Lyttelton, George, Lord   15
Ma, Yo-Yo   642
Maack, Annegret   503
Maas, David E.   63, 341
Maaser, Michael   341
Mabberley, David   488, 494
Mably, Abbé   649

Mabry, Rochelle   420
Macaulay, Catherine   392, 459
Macaulay, John Allen   63, 166
Macauley, Melissa   63
Macauly, Thomas Babington   398
MacClintock, Carol   254
Maccullony, Dougal   421
MacDonald, Stuart   166
MacDonald, Robert David   341
Macey, J. David, Jr.   420
Macfarlane, Alan   420
MacGregor, Arthur   63, 166
Machado Phillips, Rebecca   106
Macheski, Cecilia   529
Machor, James L.   413, 420
Machosky, Brenda   144
Macinnes, A.   556
Macintyre, Stuart   511
Maciulyte, Kristina   63, 166
Mack, Robert L.   666
Mack, Ruth   420
Mackay, David   488
Mackenzie, Alexander   51
Mackenzie, Anna Maria   378
Mackenzie, Sir George   536
Mackenzie, Henry   378, 390, 430, 664, 666
MacKenzie, Niall   420, 421
MacLachlan, Ian   452
Maclean, Kama   166
MacLehn, Kirsten   499
MacLeod, Emma Vincent   556
Macpherson, James   328, 339, 360, 374, 381, 400, 401, 423, 436, 506
MacWilliams, David C.   421
Madden, Edward H.   607
Maddern, Philippa   510, 511
Maddox, Randy L.   166
Madison, Dolley   96
Madison, James   585
Madison, R. D.   510
Maeder, Ernesto J. A.   63
Maffeis, Rodolfo   225

Index

Maffre, Claude 556
Magellan, Fernando 520
Mageo, Jeannette Marie 515
Maggioni, F. 607
Magill, Frank N. 531
Magowan, Fiona 508, 509
Magnin, Charles 167
Magri-Mourgues, Véronique 657
Maguire, Leonard J. 180
Mahan, Alfred Thayer 63
Maher, R. 657
Mähl, Hans-Joachim 661
Mahl, Mary 530
Mahler, Gustave 262
Mahling, Christoph-Hellmut 246
Mahlke, Regina 167
Mahoney, John L. 421
Maier, Hans-Joachim 341
Maierhofer, Waltraud 348–49
Maimon, Salomon 112, 167, 202
Mainer, José-Carlos 278, 280
Maintenon, Madame de 609
Maio, Marcos Chor 167
Mairet, Gérard 601
Maistre, Joseph de 160
Maistre, Xavier de 657
Maitte, Corine 64
Makin, Bathsua 407
Makuzu, Tadano 140
Malatian, Teresa 65
Malcolm, Elizabeth 552
Malcolm, N. 607
Malcolm X 474
Malebranche, Nicolas de 181, 607
Malettke, Klaus 21
Malik, Iftikhar H. 64, 167
Malik, Zahiruddin 64
Mall, Laurence 657
Mallarmé, Stéphane 349
Mallet, David 15
Malm, Mats 607
Malone, Edmund 13
Malpas, J. 607

Malpas, Simon 663
Maltese, G. 607
Malvezzi, Teresa Carniani 361
Manby, George 105
Mancal, Josef 39, 246, 321
Mandelbaum, Miriam 531
Mandelbrote, Scott 9, 12, 14
Mandell, Charlotte 21
Mander, W. J. 607
Manfredi, Tommaso 167
Manger, Klaus 341
Manley, Delarivier (Mary) 384, 409
Mann, Alastair J. 64
Mann, Bruce H. 90
Mann, Judith W. 219–21
Mann, Kristin Dutcher 167
Mann, Michael 64
Manning, Gillian 421
Manning, Peter 373, 422, 456, 459
Manning, Rita C. 306
Manning, Susan 571, 579
Mannoni, Olivier 312, 341, 355
Mansel, Philip 64
Mansfield, William 231
Mantilla, R. Luis Carlos 167
Mannucci, Erica J. 633
Manuel-Gismondi, Vincent 167
Manzanas, Ana 670
Manzoni, Beccaria Giulia 342, 355
Mapp, Paul 64, 167
Marat, Jean Paul 172, 301, 425–26
Marcacci, Marco 167
Marcet, Jane 104
Marchal, Roger 306, 342
Marchand, Patrick 556
Marchena Fernández, Juan 64
Marchi, Gian Paolo 362
Marciano, Alain 607
Marcil, Yasmine 16, 167
Marco, Guy 246
Marcos Marín, Francisco 281
Marcucci, S. 607
Marczali, Henrik 144

Margulis, Jennifer 449
Maria (Spanish Infanta) 220
María Luisa (Queen) 267
Maria-Theresa, Empress 191
Marichal, Carlos 64
Marie Antoinette, Queen 40, 374
Marienberg, Sabine 362
Marín, Miguel Ángel 281
Mariña, Jacqueline 168
Marino, Daniela 64
Marinoni, Giovanni Giacomo 533
Maris, Léo van 660
Marivaux, Pierre Carlet Chamblain de 292, 294, 297, 299, 300, 302, 304, 307, 311, 312, 326, 651, 658
Mark, W. Oldenburg 137
Marker, Gary 64
Marks, Arthur S. 439
Markworth, Tino 149–50
Marlan, Dawn 307
Marmontel, Jean François 295, 297, 300, 310, 650
Maroto Camino, Mercedes 515
Marpurg, Friedrich Wilhelm 230
Marquardt, Karl Heinz 515
Marrades, Julián 342
Marrant, John 478
Marsden, Jonathan 630
Marsden, Susan 503
Marsden, William E. 168
Marshall, Alan 556
Marshall, John 168, 556
Marshall, Peter J. 64, 65, 556
Marshall, Patricia Phillips 168
Marshall, Robert 242
Marsin, M. 380
Marteau, Pierre 353
Martí, Marc 65, 281–82
Martin, Angus 488
Martin, Ann Smart 630, 632
Martin, Christophe 307
Martin, Frank 608
Martin, Jean-Clément 65

Martin, Joel W. 168
Martin, John 514
Martin, Olivier 65
Martin, Philippe 168
Martin, Xavier 65, 168
Martìn y Soler, Vincente 641
Martindale, Charles 342
Martinez, Marc 421
Martínez de la Rosa, Francisco 284, 286
Martinot, Steve 404, 421
Martinson, Steven D. 342
Martschukat, Jürgen 65
Martus, Steffen 342
Martyr, Peter 476
Maruca, Lisa 9–10, 421
Marvell, Andrew 667, 669
Marx, Friedhelm 320
Marx, Hans Joachim 247
Marx, Jacques 368, 389, 451
Marx, Reiner 318, 320, 321, 337, 340, 341, 342, 349
Marx, William 168
Mary II, Queen 391, 399
Marzagalli, Silvia 168
Marzials, Sir Frank T. 372
Mascarenhas, Vijay 168
Masdeu, Edgar 285
Masham, Damaris Cudworth 393–94
Maslen, K. I. D. 10
Mason, Charles 36
Mason, George 596
Mason, Haydn 307, 657
Mason, J. C. S. 168
Mason, Jeffrey D. 568, 634, 635
Mason, Lowell 235
Mason, Nicholas 450
Mason, Tom 421, 422
Mass, John 579
Masseau, Didier 538, 556, 630, 631, 652, 653, 657
Masters, Bruce 168
Masters, Kate Ferguson 559
Mastrogregori, Massimo 65

Index

Mastromarino, Mark A. 588
Masui, Shitsuyo 169
Matar, Nabil 169, 579
Mather, Cotton 469, 473, 476, 478
Mati, Francesco 219
Matsuura, Shigeru 169
Mattauch, Hans 307
Mattek, Michael C. 467
Matteis, Nicola 243
Matteson, Johann 252, 628, 640, 645
Matthews, Christopher N. 65
Matthews, M. D. 556
Matthews, Tony 503
Matthews, William 435
Matthieu, Jacques 65
Mattison, James A., Jr. 490
Maturin, Charles Robert 406, 520
Matusikova, Lenka 169
Matyaszewski, Pawel 422
Mauch, Christof 65
Mauerer, Esteban 65
Maupertius, Pierre Louis Moreau de 310
Maur, Eduard 66
Maurer, Trude 169
Mawer, Granville Allen 488
Maxey, D. W. 579
Maxient, Jocelyn 657
Maxwell-Stuart, Hamish 503, 512
Maxwell-Stuart, P. G. 169
May, Georges 307
May, Gita 307
May, James E. 10, 422, 531
Mayans, Gregorio 285
Mayer, Matthew 515
Mayers, Tobias 559
Mayeux, Sophie 543
Mayfield, E. 531
Mayhew, Robert J. 66, 169
Mays, S. 608
Mayson, Walter 240
Maza, Sarah C. 557
Mazarin, Armand Charles de la Porte (Cardinal) 622
Mazarin, Mancini 23
Mazek, Dorota 66, 169
Mazella, David 422
Mazlish, Bruce 608, 620
Mazuecos, Eugenia 117
Mazza, Ethel Matala de 342
Mazzinghi, Joseph 261
Mazzone, Stefania 422
Mazzotti, Massimo 169
McAllister, J. W. 608
McAlpin, Mary 450
McBride, I. R. 557
McBride, Ian 594
McCaffrey, John F. 169
McCall, Laura 22, 570, 579, 588
McCallum, Paul 557
McCalman, Iain 516
McCarthy, John A. 342, 589, 592, 594, 595, 600, 602, 603, 608, 615, 619, 651
McCarthy, Kathleen D. 515, 519
McCarthy, Keely 169, 468
McCarthy, William 422
McCartney, Martha W. 579
McClain, M. 557
McClatchy, J. D. 468
McCleave, Sarah 230–31
McClellan, Andrew 630
McClellan, Chris 169
McClelland, Ivy 283
McClymond, Marita 645
McConnell, Anita 28, 112
McCorkle, Barbara B. 66, 531, 608
McCorison, Marcus A. 531
McCormick, Andrew 623, 624, 625, 626–27, 629, 630, 632
McCoy, Rebecca 169
McCraw, Thomas K. 579
McCullough, David 66
McCurdy, Peter 479
McDannell, Coleen 170
McDayter, Ghislaine 373, 422, 456, 459
McDermott, Rachel Fell 170

McDonald, Archie P. 66
McDonald, Ean 515
McDonald, Flora 564
McDonald, Forrest 579
McDonald, Irene B. 422
McDonald, Robert M. S. 579
McDowell, G. L. 579
McDowell, John 618
Mcevansoneya, Philip 226
McEvoy, John 170
McEwan, Bonnie G. 170
McFarland, Cynthia 170, 210
McGaw, Judith A. 66
McGeary, Thomas 643
McGillivray, Duncan 161
McGowen, Randall 20
McGrayne, Sharon Bertsch 170
McGuffey, William Holmes 476
McHugh, P. G. 488
McHugh, Timothy J. 170
McInelly, Brett C. 422
McIntosh-Varjabedian, Fiona 422
McIntyre, Perry 503
McKay, Barry 7
McKean, Thomas A. 423
McKee, Alexander 581
McKenna, Antony 590, 658
McKenzie, D. F. 423
McKeon, Michael 401, 427, 667
McKinney, Sam 488
McKinstry, E. Richard 10
McLaren, Martha 66
McLaverty, J. 10, 423
McLean, Gavin 515
McLean, Ian 489
McLeod, Jacqueline 46, 52, 86
McLeod, Kenneth 239–40, 241–42
McLoughlin, Timothy O. 423
McLoughlin, Thomas O. 557
McMahon, Darrin M. 66, 170, 307, 557
McMahon, S. 608
McMaster, Juliet 423
McMillan, Samuel 130

McMinn, Joseph 423
McMullin, B. J. 247
McNab, David 170
McNamee, Robert V. 37, 40, 66
McNeil, David 66
McNeill, John R. 489, 515
McOuat, Gordon 170
McPherson, Heather 634
McRae, Andrew 423
McVeagh, John 388
McVerry, John 630
Mead, Margaret 508
Meadows, R. Darrell 557
Meaney, Neville 515
Médeuil, Joseph Crassous de 96
Media, Baja Edad 287
Medlin, Dorothy 557
Medoff, Jeslyn 423
Mee, Bob 67
Meeker, Kevin 423, 608
Meer, Jan Ij van der 342
Meheust, Madame 296
Mehta, Bejun 642
Méhul, Étienne Nicolas 636
Meier, Albert 333–34, 334–35, 356
Meier, Andreas 320, 327, 342, 351, 360
Meier, Jurg 423
Meijers, Debora J. 630
Mein-Smith, Philippa 497
Meinhold, Günter 343
Meise, Helga 322
Meißner, August Gottlieb 348
Meistad, Tore 608
Melamed, Daniel 233
Melançon, Benoît 304, 657
Meléndez, Mariselle 282
Meléndez Valdés, Juan 268, 281
Melfort, Drummond de 623
Mellemgaard, Signe 342
Mellor, Anne Kostelanetz 530
Mélonio, Françoise 659
Melton, James Van Horn 67, 170, 171
Melville, Herman 463, 473, 476, 488,

Index

581
Memmolo, Pasquale 343
Menchi, Silvana Seidel 22, 83
Mencius 603
Mendelssohn, Moses 24, 107, 326, 601
Mendes da Costa, Emanuel 116
Menedelson, Sara 557
Meneguello, Cristina 74
Menegus Bornemann, Margarita 67
Menendez Torrellas, G. 608
Mengel, S. 343
Menil, Alain 307
Menneteau, Patrick 423, 608
Menninghaus, Winfried 608
Menshikova, Daria Mikhailovna 539
Menuhin, Yehudi 642
Menze, Ernest A. 67, 171, 343
Menzies, Archibald 143, 152
Menzies, Ruth 424
Meoni, L. 226
Mercer, Christia 171
Mercer, Frank 264
Mercer, Matthew 171, 557
Mercier, Gilbert 67
Mercier, Louis Sébastien 32, 314, 651
Mercier, Philip 9
Mercier-Faivre, Anne Marie 557
Merck, Johann Heinrich 44
Meredith, William 247
Mergenthaler, Volker 343
Merlotti, A. 557
Merrell, James 584
Merrick, Jeffrey 67, 307, 360
Merritt, J. F. 53, 67, 84
Mertens, J. 609
Meslay, Olivier 226
Meslier, Jean 657
Messenger, Ann 424–25
Messer 580
Messerli, Alfred 523
Messmer, Marietta 171, 468
Metastasio, Pietro (pseud. for P. Antonio Domenico Bonaventura Trapassi)
273, 279, 286–87, 300
Métayer, Christine 67
Metternich, Clemens, Prince of 132
Metzger, Hans-Dieter 171
Metzler, Guido 67
Meyen, Franz Julius Ferdinand 105
Meyer, Annette 171
Meyer, Conrad 534
Meyer, Jeffrey F. 171
Meyer, Thomas 49
Meyer, Urs 343
Meyer-Thurow, Georg 335
Meyers, Robert 171
Meylan, Claire 307, 363
Meynell, Guy 171
Miampica, Wilfrid 282
Michael, M. A. 609
Michaelis, L. 609
Michaels, Leon 171
Michéa, Hubert 171
Michel, Christoph 343
Michel, O. 611
Michel, Paul 343
Michelangelo (Michelagniolo Buonarroti) 220
Michell, John 619
Michels, Georg 171–72
Michon, Jacques 67
Micklus, Robert 468
Middleton, S. 580
Midnight, Mary 429
Miele, Michele 609
Mifflin, John Fishbourne 463
Mifflin, Thomas 577
Mignot, Arthur T. 172
Mikalachki, Jodi 580
Milburn, John R. 609
Miles, E. G. 630
Miles, M. 67
Miles, Robert 425
Miles, Thomas 87
Milford, T. A. 172
Milhous, Judith 260–62, 263

Millar, Andrew 7, 15
Millar, John 547
Millard, Peter 532
Miller, Christopher 584
Miller, Cynthia 580
Miller, D. A. 401
Miller, David W. 172
Miller, David Philip 609
Miller, Eric 425
Miller, Jacqueline C. 172, 609
Miller, James 67
Miller, Jonathan 172, 262
Miller, Judith Davis 425
Miller, Judy 204
Miller, Lillian B. 630
Miller, Malcolm 247
Miller, Marla R. 580
Miller, Michael 177
Miller, Nancy K. 307
Miller, Nathan 580
Miller, Norbert 343
Miller, Paul Allen 307
Miller, Peter N. 172, 609
Miller, Stephen 172, 425–26
Miller, Tim R. 68
Miller, Toby 386, 430
Milligan, Berry 373, 422, 456, 459
Milling, Jane 411–12
Millington, Jon 226, 427
Millner, Jacqueline 308
Mills, Elizabeth Shown 172
Mills, Randy J. 172
Millward, James A. 557
Milne, Anne 427
Milton, J. R. 172, 173
Milton, John 147, 387, 394, 425, 446, 450, 465, 471, 534, 536, 662, 664, 667, 668
Minart, Gérard 678
Minerbi, Alessandra 71
Minerbi, M. 558
Mines, Mattison 68
Minevich, Pauline M. 260

Minkema, Kenneth P. 173
Minken, Anne 68, 173
Minma, Shinobu 427
Miño Grijalva, Manuel 68
Minor, Dennis 468
Minor, Heather Hyde 226
Minter, Catherine J. 343
Minuti, R. 558
Mirabeau, Victor Riqueti, Marquis de 558, 609
Mirafuentes Galván, José Luis 173
Mires, C. 580
Mitchell, Glenn 504
Mitchell, Robert W. 247
Mitchell, Trent A. 190
Mittler, Elmar 335, 344
Mix, York Gothart 344
Miyazaki, Toshizo 427
Mizelle, Brett 580
Mo, Timothy 415
Moggach, D. 609
Moglen, Helene 427–28
Mohrmann, Ruth-Elisabeth 68
Moitte, Jean-Guillaume 125
Molesworth, Robert 593
Molière (Jean Baptiste Poquelin) 279, 363, 658
Molina del Villar, América 68
Molineaux, Major 473, 476
Moller, Horst 68
Möller, Joachim 390, 410, 417, 428
Möller, Lenelotte 68
Mollier, Jean-Yves 67
Molony, John N[eylon]. 504
Moloughney, Brian 489
Moltedo, Alida 524, 624
Molyneux, William 612
Momo, Arnaldo 363
Monaque, R. 558
Monboddo, James Burnet, Lord 594
Moncada Maya, José Omar 107
Mondot, Jean 297, 308, 317, 329, 336, 340, 344, 347, 351, 359

Money, David 533
Monge, Gaspard 559
Mongeig Goguel, Catherine 226
Mongenot, Christine 609
Mongin, P. 609
Monicat, Benedicte 405, 453
Monin, Paul 516
Monro, Alexander 20
Monro, John 83, 102
Montandon, Alain 422, 437
Montag, Warren 428
Montagu, Elizabeth 13
Montagu, Lady Mary Wortley 44, 68, 382, 405
Montaigne, Michel Eyquem de 422
Montefiore, Simon Sebag 558
Montegón, Pedro 273, 282
Monteiro, Nuno Gonçalo F. 68
Montesquieu (Charles Louis de Secondat, Baron de la Brède) 94, 267, 291, 314, 426, 470, 554, 558, 593, 651
Montgomery, Dennis 580
Monti, Vincenzo 361
Montiano (y Luyando), Augustín de 284, 285
Monticelli, Rita 397, 417
Montlinot, Charles-Antoine-Joseph Leclerc de 69
Montoya, Alicia 308
Montoya, Pablo 428
Moody, Barry 33
Moody, Ellen 527–30
Moody, Margaret Josephine 69
Moog Grünewald, Maria 344
Mooney, James E. 11, 428
Moore, A. F. 247
Moore, Andrew 504
Moore, Brian L. 58, 69
Moore, Cornelia Niekus 662
Moore, D. T. 173
Moore, Fabienne 532, 657
Moore, Lucy 69, 428, 558
Moore, R. Laurence 577

Moral, Rafael del 532
Moral Roncal, Antonio Manuel 173
Moran, Kevin James 516
Moran, Leslie J. 428
Moran Orti, Manuel 173
Morant Deusa, Isabel 69
Moratín, Nicolás 284
More, Hannah 70, 399, 414, 429, 430, 443, 528, 530, 664
More, Henry 122
Morellet, André 92, 557
Morelli, A. 643
Moreno, Deborah 173
Moreno, Gómez 278
Morère, Pierre 547, 594, 608, 614, 617, 624, 663, 664, 667
Moretti, Vito 344
Morgan, David T. 580, 610
Morgan, Jennifer 580
Morgan, Kenneth 30, 69, 173
Morgan, Peter 428
Morgana, Silvia 363
Morgenroth, Matthias 516
Morgues, Mathieu de 164
Mori, Gianluca 610
Morillo, John D. 69, 428
Morineau, Michel 69
Morissey, M. 610
Moritz, Karl Philipp 333–34, 353, 354, 355
Morris, David B. 428, 447
Morris, Graham P. 489
Morris, Ivor 428
Morris, John D. 580
Morris, Richard K. 223
Morrison, James 502
Morriss, Roger 40
Morrissey, M. 610
Mortier, Roland 69, 358, 389, 451, 591, 610, 658
Moscoso, Javier 69, 173
Moscovici, Claudia 308, 658
Moser Verrey, Monique 308, 658

Moskal, Jeanne 428
Mosley, James 522
Moss, Joyce 428
Moss, Kay K. 581
Mossner, Ernest Campbell 173
Mostashari, Firouzeh 173
Mostefai, Ourida 308
Motohashi, Ted 489
Motsch, Andreas 308
Mott, Luiz 173, 174
Motteux, Pierre 310, 433, 439
Mottley, John 431
Moulin, Anne Marie 678
Moulton, Gary E. 61
Mounsey, Chris 69, 379, 381, 409, 416, 417, 429, 440, 444
Moura, Jean-Marc 422, 437
Mourao, Manuela 308
Moureau, François 308, 658
Moureau, Pierre-François 617
Mowl, Tim 558
Mowl, Timothy 450
Moyal, G. 610
Mozart, Leopold 642
Mozart, Wolfgang Amadeus 156, 232, 235, 236, 238, 241, 243, 243–44, 245, 246, 247, 248, 249, 250, 260, 331, 628, 635, 641, 642, 645, 646, 647, 648
Muchembled, Richard 174
Muchembled, Robert 69
Muenzer, Clark S. 344
Muffat, Georg 254–55
Muhly, Frank 174
Mülder-Bach, Inka 344
Mulford, Carla 6, 51, 52, 96, 461–62, 463, 464, 466, 468, 469, 477, 526, 581, 600, 672
Müller, Ernst Ludwig 344
Müller, Gerhard 23, 318
Müller, Johann Gottwerth 316
Muller, Michael 70, 174
Muller, Michael G. 70

Müller, Peter 344
Müller-Bahlke, Thomas J. 174
Müller-Salget 320
Mulligan, Lotte 174
Mullin, Amy 610
Mulsow, Martin 308
Mungello, D. E. 174
Muñoz, Antonio 283
Muñoz y San Clemente, Francisco 487
Munson, Cheryl Ann 174
Munson, James 70
Münster, Reinhold 344
Muir, Thomas 490
Murat, Madame (see also: Castlenau, Henriette) 440, 564
Muratori, Lodovico Antonio 622
Murdoch, Dugald 610
Murillo, Bartolomé Estéban 226, 229
Murphey, R. 558
Murphy, Gary 53
Murphy, Graham J. 673
Murphy, John A. 70
Murphy, Joseph 673
Murphy, Larry 174
Murphy, Mark C. 610
Murphy, Michael 429
Murphy, Thomas 70, 174
Murray, Anthony, Jr. 564
Murray, Dian H. 70
Murray, Elizabeth 570
Murray, John Condon 429
Murray, Laura J. 174, 468
Murray, Nicholas 667
Murray, Sterling E. 643–44
Mursell, Gordon 175
Musa, Sulaiman 70, 175
Muskett, P. 558
Musschenbroek, Petrus van 50, 143
Mussmann, Olaf 70
Muto, Giovanni 175
Muysken, Pieter 294
Myers, A. D. 558
Myers, Herbert W. 247

Index

Myers, J. P. 581
Myers, Marya C. 175
Myers, Myer 105
Myles, Anne G. 175, 468
Mylius, Johan de 320, 333
Myrone, Martin 226
Nablow, Ralph A. 658
Nachtomy, O. 610
Nachumi, Nora 429
Naddeo, Barbara Ann 363
Nadell, Pamela S. 106, 175, 196
Naeve Bucher, Ursula 345
Nagel, Jennifer 610
Nägele, Rainer 345
Naginski, Erika 308
Naguschewski, Dirk 70, 82–83, 429, 436
Nagy, Josef Falaky 429
Nahon, Gérard 175
Naidu, B. Narasingaraja 175
Nakagawa, Hisayasu 309
Nakahara, Akio 429
Nancy, Jean-Luc 593
Napoleon I, Emperor (Napoléon Bonaparte) 37, 65, 113, 168, 227, 483–84, 487, 540, 552, 555, 561, 565, 567, 630, 631, 633, 634
Nappi, Maria Rosaria 525, 624
Naragon, Steve 156
Narain, Mona 429
Nardin, Jane 70, 429, 430
Nash, M. 519
Nassaar, Christopher S. 430
Nastasi, P. 610
Nate, Richard 175, 430
Naubert, Benedikte 348
Nave, Alain 522
Naveda Chávez-Hita, Adriana 70
Naylor, James 146
Necker, Suzanne 315
Nedham, Marchamont 532
Nee, Patrick 376
Neher-Bernheim, Renée 70

Neidleman, Jason Andrew 71
Neill, Alex 610
Neill, Anna 558
Neill, Peter 503, 504, 505
Neiman, Fraser D. 581
Neisser, Barbara 49
Nell, Sharon Diane 309, 345, 430
Nelles, Paul 610
Nelson, Dana D. 581
Nelson, E. Charles 71, 175, 611
Nelson, Horatio Viscount (Admiral) 33, 63, 95, 507, 537, 546, 558
Nelson, John K. 71, 175
Nelson, Larry L. 581
Nelson, Robin 430
Nelsova, Zara 642
Nemerov, Alexander 631
Nemoianu, Virgil 345
Nepomuceno, Giovanni 167
Neregal, V. 667
Nerius, Dieter 661
Neuber, Caroline 334
Neuendorff, Otto 175
Neufeld, Hermann 175
Neugebauer, P. 611
Neugebauer, Wolfgang 71
Neuhaus, Stefan 345
Neumann, Alexander 336
Neumann, Fritz-Wilhelm 374, 376
Neumann, Klaus 488, 489
Neve, Michael 543
Neveu, Ginette 642
Nevitt, H. Rodney 222, 226
New, Melvyn 430
Newberry, Paul A. 176
Newell, Jennifer 483, 487, 489, 491, 492, 499
Newman, John Henry (Cardinal) 155
Newman, S. P. 581
Newport, Kenneth G. C. 210
Newson, Linda 176
Newton, Douglas 489
Newton, John 182

Newton, Sir Isaac 32, 46, 50, 106, 114, 119, 125, 132, 133, 136, 138, 144, 145, 146, 155, 157, 163, 182, 183, 184, 193, 196, 208, 215, 593, 602, 604, 615, 616, 617, 621
Ng, Jim 489
Ng, On-Cho 176
Ngolet, F. 587
Ni, Peimin 176
Nicassio, Susan Vidiver 634–35
Niccoli, Elena 309
Nichol, Donald W. 430
Nicholls, Michael L. 581
Nichols, David A. 71
Nichols, Joel A. 176
Nichols, R. 611
Nicholson, John 489
Nicholson, M. 559
Nicklas, Pascal 430
Nicodemus 617
Nicol, John 490, 498, 517, 547
Nicolai, Friedrich 48, 316, 338, 603
Nicolai, Giorgio Maria 559
Nicolas, Gilbert 71
Nicoletta, Julie 176, 611
Niderst, Alain 124
Niederhoff, Burkhard 430
Niefanger, Dirk 322, 345
Niekerk, Carl 345
Nieto-Galan, Agustí 71, 547
Nietzsche, Friedrich 147, 348, 349, 598, 620
Niewójt, Monika 71
Niggl, Günter 345
Nigro, Jeffrey A. 430
Nikitin, Nikolai Ivanovich 176
Niklaus, Robert 309
Nikolova, Irena 345
Nikolow, Sybilla 176
Nikon, Patriarch 165
Nini, Yehuda 71
Nisbet, Charles 614
Nitsch, Friedrich August 215

Nixon, Cheryl L. 430
Noah, Mordecai 673
Noble, Yvonne 431
Nochlin, Linda 219
Nodier, Charles 656
Noel, Charles C. 176
Noel, François 294
Noel, Jan 176
Noggle, James 431
Nolan, Jerry 431
Noll, Mark A. 177
Nollet, Jean-Antoine 106
Noonan, Harold W. 611
Nora, Pierre 71
Nordyke, Eleanor C. 490
Norholdt, Gerard Schulte 559
Norling, Lisa 581
Norman, Buford 299, 312
Norman, Larry F. 262
Norr, Lynette 162
Norrington, Roger 262
Norris, Isaac, II 568
Norris, Jim 177
North, Lord 586
North, Roger 532
Northrup, Douglas A. 431
Norton, David Fate 177, 431
Norton, John, II 476
Norton, Lucy 659
Norton, Mary Beth 177
Novak, Maximillian E. 388–89, 431–32, 666, 667
Novakov, Anna 219–21
Novalis (Friedrich von Hardenberg) 209, 213, 321, 324, 345, 350, 354, 661
Novinsky, Anita 71, 177
Novopashina, Lidiia Iur'evna 72
Nuchelmans, J. C. F. 177
Nuez Caballero, Sebastián de la 286
Nuland, Sherwin B. 177
Núñez Sánchez, Jorge 72
Nuovo, Victor 177
Nussbaum, Felicity 72, 528

Nuttall, Geoffrey F. 177
Nutton, Vivian 543
O Crummey, Robert 90
O Gallchoire, Clíona 6, 309, 387, 391, 392–93, 403, 404, 413, 415, 418, 421, 432, 453, 456, 459, 664
Oakes, Urian 476
O'Brien, John 432, 635
O'Brien, Karen 11, 13, 14, 581
O'Brien, Robert Viking 406
Oberhausen, Michael 535
Oberg, Barbara 468, 573
Obeyesekere, Gananath 495
Objartel, Georg 346
Occhipinti, C. 607
Occom, Samson 44, 598
O'Connor, Thomas 72
O'Dea, Michael 72
Oden, Tom 177
Oehlenschläger, Eckart 346
Oehler, K. Eberhard 177
Oergel, Maike 346
Oesterle, Günter 332, 346
Oestmann, Guenther 559
O'Fahey, R. S. 177
O'Farrell, Patrick James 504
Ogata, Amy F. 226
Ogborn, Miles 72
Ogée, Frédéric 631
Ogoula, Landry 282
Ogundiran, Akinwumi O. 72
O'Hara, Matthew 178
OhAnnrachain, Eoghan 178
OhAnnrachain, Tadg 178
Ohm, Reinhard 346
Ohno, Kate M. 573
Ohrgaard, Per 346
Ohry, A. 611
Oistrakh, David 642
O'Keefe, John 662
Okudaira, Ryuji 178
O'Loughlin, Katrina 72, 432
Olden-Jørgensen, Sebastian 178

Oldfield, Audrey 490
Oldroyd, D. 611
Oleskiewicz, Mary 247
Olin, Margaret 178
Oliphant, John 72
Oliva, Juan Ignacio 389, 443, 453
Oliveira, Rosiska Darcy de 178
Oliver, Peter 467
Olleson, Philip 157, 178, 243, 603, 642
Olmi, Giuseppe 178
Olsen, Thomas Grant 432
Olson, A. 582
Olson, Alison Gilbert 178, 468
Olssen, Erik 486
O'Malley, Tom 532
Omai 516–17
O'Neal, John C. 309, 611
O'Neil, Robert M. 582
O'Neill, Eileen 430
O'Neill, Pamela 504, 506
Ondo, Danielle Ada 282
Ondrejovic, Slavomir 346
Ong, Seow-Chin 236–37, 637–38
Onuf, Peter S. 582
Ophälders, Markus 247
Opitz, Martin 356, 357
Opsomer, Carmélia 178
Opwis, Felicitas 178
O'Quinn, Daniel 667
Orchard, Stephen 179
O'Regan, Philip 559
O'Reilly, Robert Bray 260–61
Orlandi, Giuseppi 179
Orlin, Lena Cowen 179
Orme, Robert 386
Ormsby-Lennon, Hugh 179
Orr, Bridget 432–33, 479, 480, 484, 486, 487, 488, 490, 492–93
Orrery, John Boyle, Earl of 441
Orser, Charles E., Jr. 65, 72
Orsi, Robert A. 225
Orsted, Hans Christian 154
Ortiz de Zarate Fernandez, Amalia 434

O'Shaughnessey, Andrew Jackson 582
Osborne, Thomas 559
Osiander, Andreas 72
Osler, Margaret J. 611
Osorio, Father Gaspar 584
Ossian (see also: James Macpherson) 328, 339, 360, 374, 381, 400, 436, 506
Ostgergard, Derek E. 226
Ostervald, Frédéric Samuel 301
Ostrander, Gilman Marston 582
Ostrow, S. F. 227
Oswald, James 608
Oswald, John 611, 611
Oswald, P. H. 611
Othow, Helen Chavis 179
Otis, James 569
Ott, Michael 346
Otto, Véronique 661
Overhoff, Jürgen 611
Ovid (Publius Ovidius Naso) 394, 440, 450, 641
Owczarski, Adam 179
Owen, David 611
Owen, John 142
Owens, Alastair 563
Owens, S. 646
Owens, Samantha 247
Owens, W. R. 5, 388, 399, 512, 665
Owenson, Miss Sydney 376
Pabst-Béziat, Annette 179
Pace, Segio 524, 624
Pacini, Giulia 309
Pacini, Monica 72
Pacini, Piero 226
Pack, Spencer J. 73
Paden, R. 612
Padoan, Giorgio 363, 364
Paer, Ferdinando 232
Paganini, Nicoló 218, 642
Paganini, Gianni 590
Pages, François 298
Paine, Thomas 12, 426, 529, 570, 586, 588
Paine, Tom 576, 579
Pairault, François 559
Paisiello, Giovanni 261
Paiva, Eduardo França 73
Paiva, José Pedro 179
Pajares Infante, Eterio 283, 434
Palacios Fernández, Emilio 284, 287
Palisca, Claude V. 238
Pallaga, Franco 219
Palmer, Sally 434
Palti, Elias José 73
Palumbo, Onofrio 220
Pampalone, Antonella 524, 624
Pamphili (Cardinal) 239
Pan, David 327, 330, 336, 338, 341, 343, 345, 346, 347, 351, 354
Panetta, V. J. 646
Pankratz, Annette 401, 409
Panova, Snezhka 73
Pantin, I. 612
Paradis, Olivier 179
Paradise, Nathaniel 11, 434
Parascandola, John 179
Paravisini-Gebert, Lizabeth 398, 434
Parchment, S. 612
Pardoe, Elizabeth Lewis 179
Pare, Ambroise 128
Paredes Manzanero, Matilde 582
Paris, Marc-Antoinne Jullien de 545
Parisi, Susan 628, 635, 636, 639, 644–46, 647–48
Park, Edwards 582
Park, Hyungji 434
Park, John Sungmin 180
Park, Julia 434
Park, Jusik 434
Park, Katherine 37
Park, Maria Hester 251
Park, Mungo 407, 559
Park, Thomas 251
Park, Youngwon 667
Parker, Blanford 446

Index

Parker, Jan 434
Parker, Keiko 434
Parker, Mara E. 255–56
Parker, Mary Ann 481, 514
Parkin, Ray 490
Parkinson, Sydney 505
Parks, Roger N. 575
Parmée, Douglas 656
Parmentier, Marc 180, 612
Parnham, David 180
Parreaux, André 372
Parrett, H. 612
Parrinder, Patrick 434
Parrott, Andrew 646
Parthasarathi, Prasannan 73, 559
Pascal, Blaise 166, 189, 292, 349
Pascal, Jacques-François 307
Pasini, M. 658
Pasley, Jeffrey L. 73, 468, 582
Pasquali, Susanna 524, 624
Pasquier, Bernice 512
Pasquier, Jean 512
Pasquino, G. 559
Passeron, Irène 180
Passola i Tejedor, Antoni 283
Pasternack, Lawrence 180
Pasveer, J. 519
Patkas, Ronald D. 180
Paton, Bruce C. 180
Paton, Diana 73
Patry, Sylvie 622
Patte, Jean-Yves 77
Patterson, Diana 435
Patterson, Michael 410
Patterson, Richard 180
Patzer, Georg 347
Paul, Carole 631
Paul, Michael C. 180
Pautrat, Bernard 617
Paxman, David 73, 180
Paxton, Stephen 638
Payen, Philippe 559
Payne, Darin 435

Payne, E. A. 180
Peacey, J. T. 532
Peale, Charles Wilson 630
Pearson, Hesketh 435
Pearson, Jacqueline 411
Pearson, Roger 309
Pedersen, Christian Bank 658
Pedersen, Kurt Møller 180–81, 612
Pederson, Carl 670, 671
Pederson, William S. 29, 30, 63, 66, 68, 71, 75, 77, 85, 87, 228, 378, 385, 462, 467, 468
Pedraza Jiménez, Felipe B. 278, 283, 289
Pedrosa, José Manuel 283
Peel, Sir Robert 156
Peiresc, Fabri de 609, 619
Peitsch, Helmut 347
Pekacz, Jolanta T. 309
Pelayo, Menéndez 265
Pelckmans, Paul 658
Pelissier, Maud 607
Pell, John 607
Pelletier, Monique 181, 631
Pellicari, Medardo 227
Pellicer, Juan Christian 435
Pellisier, Robert 283
Peña, Margarita 532
Pencak, William A. 28, 43, 44, 54, 83, 84, 88
Pender, Patricia 435
Penn, William 548
Pennant, Thomas 162
Pennell, C. R. 29, 70, 73, 74, 86
Penskoi, Vitali Viktorovich 73
Penslar, Derek J. 181
Pepe, L. 612
Pepys, Samuel 379, 385, 397, 435, 437, 553
Peral Vega, Emilio 279
Percy, Dr. 393
Percy, Thomas 401, 441, 526, 565
Pérez Galdós, Benito 272

Pérez González, Maria Luisa 73
Pérez Magallón, Jesús 283–86
Pérez Priego, Miguel Ángel 286
Pérez Puente, Leticia 48, 181
Pérez Romero, Emilio 73
Pérez Samper, María de los Ángeles 73
Pergolesi, Giovanni Battista 250
Periquet y Zuaznábar, Fernando 279
Perkins, Elizabeth A. 582
Perkins, John 476
Perkins, Pam 435, 468
Perman, David 435
Pernet, Alain 615
Perocco, Daria 364
Peron, François 101
Pérotin-Dumon, Anne 74
Perrin, Liese M. 181
Perrot, Jean 532
Perry, Dennis R. 582
Perry (of Dublin), Thomas 240
Peruga, Mónica Bolufer 69
Perullo, N. 612
Peset, José Luis 181
Pesic, Peter 247
Pessin, Andrew 181
Peter I 'the Great,' Emperor 335, 539, 551, 560, 627
Peter II 163
Peter, Emanuel 322
Peter, Jean-Pierre 542
Peterfreund, Stuart 612
Peters, Kirsten 347
Peterson, Mark A. 181
Petit, Nicolas-Martin 487
Petrarch (Francesco Petrarca) 168
Pettit, Alexander 12, 409, 435
Petzoldt, Klaus 181
Peumery, Jean-Jacques 181
Peyer, Bernd 673
Pfau, Thomas 612
Pfeil, Tom 74
Phelan, Anthony 347
Philbrick, Nathaniel 503, 504, 505

Philip, 'King' (Metacomet, Chief of the Wampanoag) 183, 569, 578
Philip IV, King 220
Philipp, Thomas 74
Philips, Katherine 437, 453
Phillip, Arthur (Governor of Australia) 494, 507–08, 518
Phillips, Carla Rahn 74
Phillips, Caroline 505
Phillips, John 309
Phillips, Katherine 444
Phillips, M. 667
Phillips, Michael 227
Phillips, Philip Edward 667
Phillips, Roderick 505
Philo (of Alexandria) 196
Phips, Sir William 473, 567
Piatigorsky, Gregor 642
Picard, Georges 74
Picard, Liza 74, 435–36, 559
Picciotto, Joanna 612
Piché, Claude 597
Pickstone, John V. 181
Pierce, John Benjamin 436
Piereth, Wolfgang 532
Pieske, Burghard 490
Pietsch, Theodore W. 181
Pigafetta, Antonio 515
Pigott, L. 519
Pigott, Louis J. 162
Pijning, Ernst 74, 182
Pike, L. 247
Pikulik, Lothar 347
Piller, C. 612
Pincus, Steven 150
Pindar (-os) 336
Pindemonte, Ippolito 362
Pingué, Danièle 74
Pinilla Monroy, German 182
Pinter, Harold 429
Pinto, John 225
Piper, John 182
Pipes, Richard 612

Index

Pippin, Karma 536
Pippins, Albemarle 577
Piranesi, Giovanni Battista (Giambattista) 226, 228, 524, 526, 624, 625, 632
Piron, Alexis 308, 345
Piroux, Lorraine 658
Pister, Danielle 309
Pitassi, Maria-Cristina 612
Pitcher, Edward William 436, 673, 673
Pitt, A. 613
Pius VI, Pope 127
Pius VII, Pope 113
Piva, Franco 658
Piva, Paolo 182
Pix, Mary 368, 433, 436
Pizzamiglio, Gilberto 361, 364
Plagnol Diéval, Marie-Emmanuelle 310, 635, 653
Plank, Geoffrey 74
Planté, Christine 659
Platania, Marco 79
Plath, Wolfgang 232
Platner, Ernst 112
Plato 128, 356, 598
Platt, K. M. F. 560
Playford, Henry 241
Pleve, Igor R. 74
Plomp, R. 613
Plumier, Charles 181
Plummer, Marguerite R. 75
Plumsky, Roger 436
Poag, James F. 317
Pocock, J. G. A. 490, 517, 560
Pocock, John 211, 455
Poe, Edgar Allan 429, 466, 476
Pohl, Karl Heinrich 162
Pointon, Marcia R. 227
Poirier, Roger 75
Poke, Christopher 227
Polet, Jean 75
Poliakov, O. Iu 436
Polisensky, Josef 182
Pomeau, René 182

Pomfret, John 403
Pommyer, l'Abbé 224
Pompadour, Jeanne Antoinette Poisson, Marquise de 544
Ponchartrain, Jérôme de 56
Poniatowski, Stanislaw August 71
Pont, Abraham 646
Pont, Jaume 272, 286
Pont, Virginie 286
Ponzi, Mauro 347
Pool, Wendy 479
Poole, Kenneth 75
Poole, R. 560
Poole, Ralph J. 436
Pooley, Julian 12
Poovey, Mary 154
Pope, Alexander 10–11, 367, 370, 377, 378, 394, 415, 423, 431, 438, 439, 441, 446, 450, 459, 465, 668
Popkin, Jeremy D. 75
Popkin, Richard H. 118, 182
Popovic, Pierre 657, 660
Popovskij, Nikolaj 415
Porret, Michel 182
Porter, Andrew 491
Porter, David 505
Porter, James 436
Porter, Roy 75–76, 182, 183, 543
Portolano, M. 613
Portowitz, Adena 247
Potemkin, Grigori Alexandrowitsch 558
Potkay, Adam 183, 436, 469
Potocki, Jan 299
Pott, John 581
Pott, Sandra 76, 310
Potter, Elizabeth 183
Potter, Tiffany 436, 437, 449
Pourciau, Bruce 183
Poussin, Nicolas 224, 225, 496
Poutrin, Isabelle 34
Pouzoulet, C. 659
Powers, Elizabeth 347
Pozzi, Francesco 364

Pozzo, R. 613
Pozzo, Riccardo 535
Prasch, Johann Ludwig 335
Prasch, Susanna Elisabeth 335
Prasmantaite, Aldona 183
Prass, Reiner 522
Pratt, Alan R. 310
Pratt, Kathryn 437
Pratt, Samuel Jackson 420
Praud, Jocelyne 76
Praz, Mario 372
Pré, Jacqueline du 642
Preda, Alex 76
Prescott, Sarah 437
Presotto, Marco 269
Pressly, William L. 631
Preston, Thomas R. 12, 667
Prévost, (d'Exile), Antoine-François, Abbé 102, 291, 294, 395, 649, 651, 658, 660
Prévost, Guillaume-Jean (called: Prévost-Dossier) 385
Price, Bronwen 437
Price, Charles Gower 247
Price, Curtis 260, 263
Price, Martin 446
Price, Munro 550
Price, Richard 426, 560
Price, Stephen R. 437
Prickett, Stephen 517
Priestley, Joseph 426, 593, 595
Priestley, Sharon L. 437
Primer, Irwin 417
Primrose, William 642
Principato, Aurelio 613
Profeti, Maria Grazia 286–87
Promies, Wolfgang 336, 347
Protos, Alec 505
Proust, Marcel 430
Provizer, Norman 75
Pruett, Lilan P. 646
Prüfer, Thomas 76
Pruitt, John 437

Prungnaud, Joëlle 422, 437
Prunier, Clotilde 613
Pruss, A. R. 613
Pryor (of Gateside), William 241
Psalmanazar, George 57, 415
Ptolemy (Claudius Ptolemaeus) 198
Pucci, Suzanne Rodin 76, 262, 310
Puccini, Giacomo 634
Puel, Marc 667
Pufendorf, Samuel, Freiherr von 149
Pugsley, Nathaniel K. 138
Pulkert, Oldrich 248
Pulsipher, Jenny Hale 183
Pulvirenti, Grazia 347
Punter, David 437
Pupil, François 631
Puppa, Paolo 364
Purcell, Henry 241, 247, 456, 636
Purcell, Mark 183
Purdy, Martin 510
Purea 483
Purkinje, Jan Evangelista 208
Pursell, Carroll 66, 76
Putterman, E. 613
Pyle, Cynthia M. 613
Pythéas le Massaliote 103
Qi, Han 76
Qingping, Deng 215
Quadros, Eduardo Gusmao de 77, 183
Quandt, Johann Gottlob von 329
Quantin, Jean-Louis 183
Quarantini, Franca Zanelli 315
Quehen, H. D. 613
Queneau, Jacqueline 77
Quéro, Dominique 310
Quesnay, François 609
Questier, M. 554
Quinault, Roland 77
Quincy, Josiah 571
Quinn, Frederick 184
Quinn, J. 560
Quintanilla, Luis de 172
Quintili, Paolo 310, 613

Index

Quirós, Pedro Fernández de 515
Raab, Arnim 248
Raab, Michael 248
Rabaté, Colette 272, 287
Rabe, Robert 77
Rabelais, François 310, 439, 441
Rabener, Gottlieb Wilhelm 356
Raber, Karen L. 437
Rabuzzi, Daniel A. 77
Racine, Jean 298, 313
Rack, Henry D. 184
Radcliffe, Ann 361, 376, 382, 395, 528, 529
Radford, Andrew 437
Radford, Peter 77
Radzinowicz Howell, David 489
Rae, John 576
Ragan, Bryant T., Jr. 67
Ragan, Edward D. 77
Ragussis, M. 560
Rahikainen, Marjatta 77
Raihala, Lorelle 347
Raina, Dhruv 184
Raj, Kapil 77, 184
Rajabzadah, Hashim 347
Ramachandran, M. 605
Ramati, Ayval 184
Rameau, Jean François 303, 333
Rameau, Jean-Philippe 120
Ramel, Stig 560
Ramm, Friederike 252–53
Ramón, José 46
Ramos, Julie 631
Ramsay, Allan 223, 429
Ramsay, David 581
Ramsay, David, Jr. 574
Ramsay, Martha Laurens 466, 574
Ramsland, Marie 488, 491
Randles, W. G. L. 613
Ranlet, Philip 582
Rao, Anna Maria 560
Raphael, Linda Schermer 438
Rapley, Elizabeth 155

Rapport, Michael 560
Ras, Norberto 77
Rashid, Samory 184
Ratcliff, Marc J. 184, 613
Ratner, Leonard G. 248
Raudzens, George 108, 113, 115, 170, 176, 184, 199
Raughter, R. 560
Raven, James 12, 14, 533–34
Ravid, Benjamin C. I. 124
Rawson, Claude Julien 184, 438
Ray, Aniruddha 77
Ray, Joan Klingel 438
Ray, John 592, 608
Ray, Mark Douglas 184
Rayet, Georges 119
Raylor, T. 614
Raynal, Abbé 562, 649, 651, 655
Rayner, Keith 485
Razzell, Peter 184
Real, Hermann J. 438–39
Reardon, Colleen 185
Rebel, Hermann 77
Recker, Jo Ann M. 185
Recuenco Pérez, Julian 185
Reddy, William M. 78
Redouté, Pierre Joseph 484
Rée, Peta 78
Reece, Bob 517
Reed, Gail S. 310
Reed, Terence James 348
Reedy, Gerald 185
Rees, Keith van 5
Rees, Sian 78, 517–18
Reeve, Clara 373, 381, 541
Reeves, E. 614
Regan, Shaun 310, 439
Regener, Ursula 348
Reger, Max 238
Rehder, Robert 663
Rehding, Alexander 103, 120, 234
Rehfeld, Hans Jürgen 348
Rehm, Wolfgang 248

Reibey, Mary 514
Reicha, Antoine 243
Reichler, Claude 185
Reid, Andrew 558
Reid, David 55, 154
Reid, John G. 567
Reid, Thomas 139, 176, 213, 590, 594, 614, 621
Reid-Maroney, Nina 78, 185, 583
Reidy, M. S. 599
Reijen, Paul van 248
Reill, Peter Hanns 104
Reilly, Michael 486, 491
Reilly, Robin 78
Reilly, Susan P. 439
Reimmann, Jacob Friedrich 331
Reinhold, Carl Leonhard 215
Reis, Elizabeth 185
Reiss, Timothy J. 614
Reitemeier, Frauke 348–49
Rellstab, Ludwig 634
Rembrandt (Rembrandt Harmensz. van Rijn) 527, 628
Renard, Jacques 48
Renaudie, Françoise Mancip 312
Renner, Ursula 349
Rennie, Nicholas 349
Rensch, Karl H. 499
Renwick, John 310
Renwick, William 248
Repo, A. 604
Resch, Rita M. 234
Réstif de la Bretonne (et la ville), Nicolas Edme (also: Rétif) 296, 652, 656
Rétat, Pierre 522
Retter, Catharine 491
Révauger, Marie-Cécile 563
Revelli, Giorgetta 310, 325, 388
Rey, Marc Michel 304
Reynard, Pierre Claude 78
Reynaud, Denis 560
Reynolds, Kimberley 521, 589
Reynolds, Sir Joshua 224, 426, 495, 632, 633
Reynolds, Larry J. 473
Reynolds, Simon 109
Rheinberger, Rudolf 185
Ribao Pereira, Montserrat 287
Ribble, Frederick G. 439
Ribeiro, Alvaro 408
Ricard, Alain 560
Ricci, Ruggiero 642
Riccoboni, Marie-Jeanne (de Heurles Laboras de Mezières) 652, 655
Rice, Anthony 505
Rice, Grantland S. 673
Rice, John A. 645, 646
Rice, L. 590
Richard, Jacques 78
Richard, Odile 658
Richardot, Anne 304
Richards, Annette 248
Richards, Eric 560, 561
Richards, Jeffrey H. 635, 673
Richards, Leonard L. 583
Richards, Peter Judson 185
Richardson, David 62
Richardson, Gary A. 673
Richardson, John 88, 201, 439
Richardson, Jonathan 417, 625
Richardson, Leslie 454
Richardson, Robert D. 472
Richardson, Samuel 8–9, 10, 29, 108, 311, 356, 367, 369, 374, 376, 380, 381, 382, 383, 384, 386, 391, 393, 403, 406, 407, 409, 411, 414, 415, 416, 418, 423, 427, 430, 436, 437, 440, 443, 447, 449, 451, 452, 457, 465, 668
Richetti, John 401, 439, 667
Richmond, Duke of 623
Richter, Elke 349
Richter, Joseph 338
Richter, Karl 343, 349, 350
Richters, Fredrik 231
Richters, Hendrik 231

Index 753

Rickard, Suzanne 509, 583
Ricorda, Ricciarda 324
Ricuperati, Giuseppe 78, 185, 186
Riddle, Shane 491
Ridgway, Christopher 631
Rieder, Philip 186
Riederer, Jens 522
Riege, Helmut 350
Riegl, Alois 627
Riethmüller, Jürgen 78
Rigal, Laura 78, 186
Rigamonti, Antonella 439
Rigaudière, Albert 33
Rijk, Michel Nuss de 227
Riley, J. C. 61
Rinehart, Lucy 469
Ring, Eva 522
Ringrose, David R. 272
Ríos Carratalá, Juan Antonio 287
Riou, Jeanne 499
Risco, Antonio 39, 272, 287
Rispoli, Gennaro 194
Ritzmann, Iris 186
Riva, Massimo 364
Rivara, Annie 658
Rivard, François 549
Rivero, Albert J. 440, 449–50
Rivers, Isabel 6, 9, 11, 12–14, 16, 18, 78, 186
Rivette, Jacques 295, 307, 312
Rivière, Marc Serge 310
Rizo Castellón, José 78
Rizzetti, Giovanni 599
Rizzo, Betty 440
Robarge, David 583
Robb, P. 561
Robel, Gilles 614
Robbins, Louise E. 79
Roberson, Susan L. 673
Roberts, Edward 502
Roberts, Ian F. 310
Roberts, John 580
Roberts, Marilyn 350, 440

Roberts, Rita 583
Roberts-Miller, Patricia 673
Robertson, John Kent 186
Robertson, Ritchie 350
Robertson, William 129, 668
Robespierre, Maximilien de 68, 551
Robev, Nikola 86
Robinson, David Michael 440
Robinson, James A. 99
Robinson, Mary 386, 444
Robinson, Paul 251, 260, 262, 263
Robinson, Roger 668
Robson, D. W. 614
Robson, John 505
Rocchietti, Joseph 100
Roche, Daniel 79, 186
Rochester, John Wilmot, Second Earl of 377, 378, 403, 434
Rockmore, Tom 112
Rodén, Marie-Louise 186
Rodriguez, Catherine M. 407–08, 561
Rodriguez, Ileana 440
Rodríguez, María José 284
Rodriquez, José 278
Rodríguez López-Brea, Carlos M. 186
Rodríguez Puértolas, Julio 278, 287
Roe, Michael 518
Roeber, A. Gregg 186–87
Roffidal-Motte, Emilie 187
Rogal, Samuel J. 187
Rogers, G. A. J. 187
Rogers, Pat 12
Roggero, Marina 79
Roglieri, Maria Ann 248
Rogoff, Leonard 187
Rogow, Arnold A. 583
Rogozinski, Jacob 614
Rohr, Deborah Adams 248
Rohrbasser, Jean-Marc 79
Rohrer, S. Scott 187
Rohrs, Richard C. 583
Rojas, Fernando de 289
Rojas Navarro, Alfredo 273–75

Roland, Madame (Manon Philipon) 93, 314, 654
Rollyson, Carl 79, 440
Rolston, Shauna 642
Roman, Alain 79
Rombes, Nicholas 583
Romeiro, Adriana 79
Romero-Cesareo, Ivette 398, 434
Romero Jaramillo, Dolcey 79
Rommel, Gabriele 350
Rommelt, Stefan W. 79
Romney, George 624
Ronzon, Antoine 452
Roper, Alan 440
Roper, Elizabeth 585
Roper, Thomas 585
Ros de Olano, Antonio 272, 286
Rosa, Mario 79, 187
Rosa, Pacecco de 220
Rosand, Ellen 248
Rosanvallon, Pierre 561
Rose, Aquila 476
Rose, Deborah Bird 509
Rose, Emily C. 187
Rose, Hugh James 206
Rose, Stephen 248
Rose, Sven Erik 661
Rosen, F. 614
Rosenbaum, Susan 440
Rosenberg, Pierre 227, 631
Rosenfeld, Sophia 79
Rosenfield, Kathrin H. 661
Rosengarten, Richard 440
Rosenthal, Angela 221
Rosenthal, Laura J. 420
Rosenthal, Michael 491
Rosetti, Antonio (Anton Rösler or Rössler) 643–44
Rosner, Lisa 561
Rosove, Michael H. 561
Ross, Bianca 367, 402
Ross, D. Reid 187
Ross, Ian Campbell 441
Ross, Margaret Clunies 441
Ross, Richard J. 187
Ross, Walter 551
Rossi, Philip J. 188
Rosslyn, Felicity 441
Rostropovich, Mstislav 642
Rotenberg-Schwartz, Michael 424–25, 445–47
Roth, Barry 15
Roth, Henry Ling 483
Roth, Randolph 188
Roth-Lochner, Barbara 188
Rothenberg, Gunther E. 561
Rothman, P. 614
Rothschild, Emma 80
Rotondò, A. 561
Rotter, Marcel 144
Rouet, D. 561
Rounce, Adam 420, 421
Round, Philip H. 188, 469
Rousseau, George S. 12, 80, 82, 188, 441
Rousseau, Jean-Jacques 15, 26, 42, 59, 69, 72, 192, 203, 214, 251, 291, 293, 294, 295, 296, 303, 304, 305, 306, 311, 312, 313, 314, 321, 356, 368, 426, 441, 450, 481, 502, 528, 535, 537, 553, 604, 613, 614, 651, 652, 654, 656, 657
Roussel, Elyette 650
Roussinova, Olga 221–23
Roux, Jean Claude 80
Roux, Pascal 80
Rowe, Elizabeth Singer 437
Rowe, Nicholas 416
Rowe, William T. 80
Rowell, E. 561
Rowland, David 248
Rowland, Herbert 319, 327, 342, 349, 350, 356, 360
Rowland, Robert 188
Rowlands, Alison 188
Rowlandson, Mary White 669, 670, 674

Index 755

Roworth, Wendy Wassyng 227
Roxburgh, Kenneth 614
Roy, G. Ross 441
Roy, Jean 614
Roy, Jeanne Helene 364
Royalton-Kisch, Martin 527, 628
Royot, Daniel 469
Rozbicki, Michal J. 80
Rozema, Patricia 454
Rozenberg, Paul 543
Rozenberg, Simone 543
Rubenstein, Artur 642
Rubin, Rehav 188
Rucker, Walter 188
Rückert, Friedrich 352
Rudd, Margaret Caroline (Mrs. Rudd) 20, 21
Rudert, Thomas 80
Rudlin, John 263
Rudolf II, Emperor 526
Rudolf, C. 227
Rudolph, J. 561
Rudwick, Martin 615
Rueda, Ana 287
Rueda Novoa, Rocío 80
Ruffing, Margit 188
Ruffner, J. A. 615
Rüger, Axel 227
Ruggiu, François-Joseph 80
Ruin, H. 615
Ruisinger, Marion M. 188
Ruiz, Roberto Gallegos 188
Rumbold, Valerie 441
Rumford, Count 592
Runge, Laura L. 441
Runge, Philip Otto 631
Rupp, Amalie von 334
Rush, Benjamin 172, 475, 562, 609
Rush, Fred L., Jr. 189
Rusi, Michela 364
Russakovsky, Lubov 249
Rüsse, Norwich 38
Russell, Alexander 51, 147

Russell, Anne 441
Russell, Daniel 476
Russell, Francis 625
Russell, Gillian 441, 561
Russell, John 521, 537
Russell, Lynette 518
Russell, Patrick 51, 147
Russell, Terence M. 227
Russett, Bruce 189
Rusterholz, Peter 322
Rutherford, John 482
Rutini, Ferdinando 645, 646
Rutz, Michael A. 189
Ruwe, Donelle 15, 441
Ryals, Kay Ferguson 673
Ryan, Vanessa L. 80, 189, 442
Ryden, David 189
Rylance, Rick 442, 444, 459
Rytting, Jenny Rebecca 442
Saage, Richard 80
Saar, Doreen Alvarez 9–10
Sabino, Robin 674
Sabor, Peter 8–9, 380, 416
Saccone, G. M. 615
Sacks, David Harris 189
Sade, Donatien Alphonse François, Marquis de 292, 295, 296, 298, 300, 304–05, 309, 311, 443, 652, 653, 654, 658, 660
Sadie, Julie Anne 647
Sadie, Stanley 647
Saeger, James Schofield 583–84
Saffin, John 471, 476
Safier, Neil 80, 189, 561
Sâgean, Mathiu (Mathieu) 562
Saggiorato, Laura 311
Sahlins, Marshal 495
Said, Edward 398, 473
Saillant, John 584, 615
Saint Amand, Pierre 311
Saint-Beuve, Charles-Augustin de 610
Saint-Cyr, Reveroni 297
Saint-Glain, Dominique de 594

Saint-Lu, André 287
Saint-Martin, Louis-Claude de 590
Saint-Pierre, Charles Irénée Castegl de, Abbé 368, 603
Saint-Simon, Louis de Rouvroy, Duc de 62, 659
Saint-Venant, Jean Claude 124
Saintsbury, George 446
Saka, Paul 189
Sakula, Alex 189
Sala Valldaura, Josep María 271, 287
Salamanca Lopez, Manuel 189
Salazar, Philippe-Joseph 659
Salber, Cecilia 442
Salem, Jean 590
Salewski, Michael 81
Salieri, Antonio 641, 645, 646
Salisbury, Earl of 260
Salisbury, Neal 674
Salls, Timothy G. X. 189
Salman, Jeroen 15
Salmon, J. H. M. 562
Salomon, Ronald 189
Saltar, Richard 94
Salter, J. 615
Salvat, Christophe 92
Salvi, Antonio 251
Salzman, Paul 370, 416, 423, 429, 442, 449, 453, 456
Salzmann, Christian Gotthilf 343
Samaniego, Félix María de 287
Sambrook, James 15, 442
Samet, Elizabeth D. 442
Sammons, Christa 615
Samper, Edgar 288
Samson, Guillemette 659
Samson, Jane 481, 483, 484, 485, 488, 491, 493
Samuelian, Kristin Flieger 442, 454
Samwell, David 514
San Pedro, Diego de 278
Sanborn, Geoffrey 406, 442, 518
Sánchez, Bertomeu 46

Sanchez, J. R. B. 615
Sánchez-Albornoz, Nicolas 190
Sánchez Barbero, Francisco 285
Sanchez Hernandez, Elena 443
Sánchez-Jáuregui, Maria Dolores 227
Sancho, Ignatius 464
Sander, Christian Levin 320
Sander, S. 562
Sanders, Arthrell D. 442
Sanderson, Nicholas 654
Sandhu, Sukhdev 442
Sandiford, Keith 442
Sandkühler, Hans Jörg 190
Sandock, Mollie 442
Sandys, George 476
Sandstrom, Alan R. 148, 152, 204
Sanfilippo, José 207
Sani, Valentino 81
Sankey, Margaret 190
Sanmartín Miguez, J. Santiago 81, 190
Santa, Ángels 288
Santesso, Aaron 615
Santiago Correa Restrepo, Juan 81
Sappho 305, 324, 368
Sarat, Austin 573, 584
Sardou, Victorien 634
Sargent, Lyman Tower 615
Sargent, Sarah E. 585
Sarjeant, William A. S. 190
Sarmant, Thierry 81
Sarmiento, Francisco Javier Puerto 190
Sarna, Jonathan D. 106, 175, 190, 196
Sarrazin, Véronique 311
Sarson, S. 585
Sarti, Giuseppe 641
Sarti, Raffaella 190
Sartori, Rodrigo Browne 434
Sashalmi, Endre 81
Sassaman, R. 585
Sasse, Günter 350
Sassi, Jonathan D. 190
Sato, Junji 311
Sauder, Gerhard 350, 351

Index

Sauer, Johann Christoph 525
Saur, Wolfgang 81
Saussure, Horace-Bénédict de 109, 114, 115, 116, 131, 140, 167, 184, 185, 186, 188, 191,195, 205, 208, 215
Sautermeister, Gert 351
Sauvage, Emmanuelle 311, 443
Savacool, J. Woodrow 212
Savage, Anne 483–84
Savonius, S.-J. 190
Sawaya, Jean-Pierre 37
Sawyer, John E. 647
Say, Jean-Baptiste 566
Sayre, Gordon M. 469, 674
Scarani, P. 615
Scarlatti, Alessandro 234, 645
Scarpa, Antonio 100
Schabas, Margaret 191
Schabio, Saskia 47, 377, 385, 394, 397, 402, 403
Schaer, Roland 615
Schafer, Daniel L. 191
Schaffeld, Norbert 505
Schakel, Peter J. 94, 185
Schama, Simon 81
Scharf, Claus 81
Scheffel, Michael 191, 291, 311, 328, 330, 333–34, 343, 351, 402, 443, 460
Scheffer, Bernd 327
Scheick, William J. 191, 443, 469
Schellenberg, Betty A. 443
Schellenberg, Renata 351
Schelling, Friedrich Wilhelm Joseph von 190, 206, 207, 615
Scheltema, Adama van 627
Schenck, David H. J. 534
Schenker, Heinrich 236
Scher-Zembitska, Lydia 81
Scherer, I. 615
Scherl, Adolf 635
Scherr, Arthur 311
Scherwatzky, Steven D. 443

Schettino, E. 616
Scheuchzer, Johann Jakob 343
Scheuermann, Mona 443, 562
Scheutz, Martin 81, 82, 191
Schick, Hartmut 249
Schickaneder, Emanuel 342
Schickore, Jutta 191
Schiera, Carlo 364
Schierholz, Stefan J. 346
Schiller, Friedrich 145, 316, 318, 324, 327, 328, 331, 332, 334, 336, 337, 340, 342, 345, 346, 351, 352, 353, 354, 356, 357, 358, 359, 360, 365
Schilling, Heinz 191
Schindler, Stephan K. 351
Schlegel, Christiane Karoline 334
Schlegel, Dorothea 360
Schlegel, Friedrich von 351, 398, 602
Schleiermacher, Friedrich Ernst Daniel 180, 199, 517
Schlichtmann, Silke 351
Schlipphacke, Heidi M. 351
Schlobach, Jochen 296, 297, 386, 422, 430
Schlomowitz, R. 600
Schløser, Jørn 69, 72, 82
Schloss, W. Andrew 234
Schlosser, Rainer 351, 364
Schlumbohm, Jürgen 191
Schlup, Michel 191
Schmal, Kerstin 191
Schmalfeldt, Janet 249
Schmedding, Robert 227
Schmeisser, Martin 616
Schmidgen, Wolfram 443
Schmidt, Benjamin 518
Schmidt, Benjamin Marius 351
Schmidt, Dennis J. 191
Schmidt, Klaus H. 585, 672, 674
Schmidt, Leigh Eric 82
Schmidt, Michael 351
Schmidt-Beste, Thomas 249
Schmidt-Biggemann, Wilhelm 149–50

Schmidt-Linsenhoff, Viktoria 339, 501, 507
Schmieder, Wolfgang 232
Schmiesing, Ann 352
Schmitt, Carl 556
Schmitz, Fried 505
Schmitz, Walter 329, 661
Schmolz-Haberlein, Michaela 82, 192
Schnabel, Johann-Gottfried 352
Schnapp, Alain 228
Schnegg, Brigitte 82
Schneider, Erich 352
Schneider, Gerhard 192
Schneider, Hans 336
Schneider, Helmut J. 340, 352
Schneider, Herbert 249
Schneider, Jürgen 82
Schneider, Konrad 82
Schneider, M. 616
Schneider, Manfred 352
Schneider, Ralf 531
Schneider, Zoe A. 562
Schneiders, Werner 352
Schnurmann, Claudia 192
Schödlbauer, Ulrich 339
Schoelcher, Victor 549
Schoenaers, Christian 311
Schoeninger, Margaret J. 162
Schoeps, Julius H. 192
Schofield, Mary Anne 529
Schofield, Peter 634–35
Schofield, Philip 122
Scholten, Frits 218
Scholz, Sally J. 192
Scholze, Dietrich 82
Schonemann, Bernd 82
Schönwälder, Karen 82
Schopenhauer, Arthur 206
Schopenhauer, Johanna 549
Schorsch, Jonathan 192
Schosler, J. 192
Schossler, Franziska 352
Schrader, Hans Jürgen 352

Schrader, Sabine 70, 82–83, 429, 436
Schraibman, José 288
Schraven, Minou 228
Schreinert, Kurt 348
Schroder, Volker 311
Schubart, Christian Friedrich Daniel 332, 355
Schubert, Franz 234, 236–37, 249, 324, 329, 636, 637–38, 643
Schubert, Gerd 352
Schubert, Venanz 377
Schuldiner, Michael 673
Schulte, Anja 192
Schulte, Rolf 83
Schulte-Tenckhoff, Isabelle 212
Schultz, Karla L. 192
Schultz, Robert 119
Schultz, Ronald 40–41
Schulz, Friedrich 352
Schulz, Georg M. 352
Schumacher, John N. 192
Schumann, Clara 642
Schürer, Norbert 397–98, 443, 533–34
Schutjer, Karin Lynn 352
Schutte, Anne Jacobson 22, 83, 193
Schuurman, Paul 192, 193
Schwab-Felisch, Oliver 249
Schwartz, Judith L. 249
Schwartz, Peter J. 353
Schwartz, Regina 469
Schwarz, Angela 83
Schwarz, Anna 83
Schwarz, Philip J. 193
Schwarzbach, Bertram Eugène 193
Schwarzchild, Edward 585
Schweitzer, Corie 443, 450
Schweitzer, Ivy 462
Schwerhoff, Gerd 83, 193
Schwieder, Gabriele 353
Schwindt, Nicole 245
Scimonello, Giovanni 353
Scinà, Domenico 610
Scott, Bill 506

Index

Scott, Clive 311, 443
Scott, D. 562
Scott, David 607, 616
Scott, Geoffrey 522
Scott, H. M. 83
Scott, Harald 391
Scott, John T. 203
Scott, Jonathan 562
Scott, Patrick 534
Scott, Sarah 323, 377, 449
Scott, Sir Walter 348–49, 376, 419
Scott of Amwell, John 435
Screech, Timon 631
Scull, Andrew 20, 83, 102
Scully, Randolph 83, 193
Seaver, Richard 658
Sebastiani, Sylvia 83, 193
Sebold, Russell P. 267, 283, 284, 288
Secada, Jorge 616
Seccombe, Joseph 476
Sedaine, Michel Jean 630
Sedgwick, Catherine 671
Seelye, John 585
Seeman, Erik R. 193, 616
Seferian, Catherine 311
Ségal, Alain 193
Segal, Gideon 616
Segal, Lore 444
Segala, Marco 83, 193
Segeberg, Harro 330
Segovia, Andrés 642
Seguin, Maria Susana 84, 193
Seidel, Michael 388–89
Seidl, Gabriele 637
Seifert, Siegfried 353, 527
Seiffert, Wolf-Dieter 248
Seillan, Jean-Marie 657, 659
Seite Salaun, Armelle 311
Seixas, Carlos 250
Seixo, Maria Alziro 505–06, 507
Self, Robert L. 585
Selig, Robert A. 585
Selkirk, Alexander 86

Sellar, Patrick 561
Sellés, Manuel A. 84, 193
Sellick, Douglas R. G. 506
Selwyn, David 444
Seneca 417
Seo, Yeong-yoon 444
Serarcangeli, Carla 194
Sergeant, John 197
Serjeantson, Richard 616
Sermain, Jean Paul 312
Sersale, Annibale (Count of Casamarciano) 259
Sertori, Girolamo 277
Sesso, Gloria 194
Seth, Catriona 562, 658, 659
Settle, Elkanah 456
Seume, Johann Gottfried 343, 353
Sewall, Jonathan Mitchell 476
Seybert, Gislinde 444
Seymour, Miranda 668
Sgard, Jean 312
Shackle, Christopher 38, 85
Shade, William G. 57, 466, 467
Shadwell, Thomas 410, 412
Shaffer, Julie 444
Shakespeare, William 181, 243, 320, 356, 360, 367, 413, 416, 458, 634
Shambar, Beth 249
Shamin, S. M. 84
Shanes, Eric 631
Shapin, S. 616
Shapin, Steven 605
Shapiro, Harry L. 502
Shapiro, Lionel Stefan 194
Sharma, Anjana 444
Sharpe, Kevin 534
Sharpe, P. 562
Sharpe, Pamela 84
Shaw, Donald 285
Shaw, Gisela 353
Shaw, John Stuart 562
Shaw, L. M. E. 562
Shcheblygina, I. V. 194

Shebbeare, John 378
Sheehan, Richard Johnson 444
Sheer, Miriam 249
Sheldon, Garrett Ward 585
Sheldon, William 261
Shelley, Mary (née Wollstonecraft) 112, 481, 664, 668, 666
Shelley, Percy Bysshe 345, 471
Shelton, Andrew Carrington 228
Shelton, Nicola 136
Shen, Jian 128
Shengtan, Jin 194
Shenstone, William 414
Shepard, A. 562
Sheppard, Jack 53
Sher, Richard B. 7, 668
Sherbo, Arthur 444
Sheridan, Frances 443
Sheridan, Geraldine 660
Sheridan, Richard Brinsley 5, 261, 390, 664, 669
Sheridan, Thomas E. 534, 586
Sherman, Sandra 12–14, 444
Sherr, David 249
Sherratt, Y. 616
Shi, Yunli 135
Shields, Carol 444
Shields, David S. 6, 51, 52, 84, 96, 461–62, 463, 464, 466, 468, 469, 477, 586
Shields, John C. 469–77
Shifflett, Andrew 444
Shiner, Larry 228
Shipton, Nathaniel N. 575
Shlomowitz, Ralph 159, 550
Shoemaker, Robert B. 84
Short, Colin C. 194
Short, John Renne 586
Showalter, English 312
Showerling, E. R. 526
Shuffleton, Frank 477, 586, 674
Shuttleton, David E. 437
Sibilla (Signiora) 242

Sickel, Lothar 228
Sicker, Martin 194
Sider, Sandra 194
Sidorsky, David 364
Sieben, Hermann-Josef 194
Sieber, Patricia 194
Siegert, Reinhart 522
Siena, Kevin P. 84, 194
Siepe, Franz 353
Siess, Jürgen 660
Sievers, Julie 194, 477
Sigmond, Peter 501
Sigot, N. 609
Sigrist, René 84, 109, 114, 115, 116, 131, 140, 167, 184, 185, 186, 188, 191, 195, 205, 208, 215
Silva, Kalina Vanderlei 84
Silver, Sean R. 445
Silverman, David 84
Silverman, Willa Z. 405, 453
Silverstone, Paul H. 85
Sim, Stuart 444, 449
Simanowski, R. 356
Simeon, Charles 182
Simmons, A. John 195
Simms, Norman 445
Simon, Anne 535, 566
Simon, Julia 195
Simon, Ralf 340
Simonelli, Maria-Rosa 182
Simonetto, Michele 85
Simonin, Suzanne 312
Simonis, Annette 353
Simonis, Linda 616
Simons, Judy 442, 444, 459
Simons, Olaf 321–22, 353
Simonutti, Luisa 195
Simpson, Matthew 85
Simpson, Robert Drew 195
Simson, John 141
Simson, John 195
Simson, Richard 502
Sinclair, Keith 494, 506

Sinclair, Shirley 491
Singerman, Alan J. 312
Singh, Arvind-pal 38, 85
Singh, G. 382, 414
Singh, Gurharpal 38, 85
Sinopoli, Franca 353
Sirgo, Henry B. 85
Siskin, Clifford 445
Sisman, Adam 16, 445
Sitter, John 373, 383, 394, 399, 400, 407, 412, 414, 415, 428, 445–47, 448
Sitwell, Edith 405
Sivils, Matthew Wynn 477
Skibitzki, Bernd 661
Skinner, A. S. 144
Skinner, John 447
Skoczylas, Anne 85, 195
Slier, Abbé 651
Sloan, David 583–84
Sloan, Herbert E. 85
Sloane, Sir Hans 577
Slomp, G. 616
Slonim, S. 586
Slonimsky, Nicolas 249
Sluijter, Eric J. 627, 632
Small, William 580
Smalls, James 228
Smallwood, Philip 196, 371, 383, 400, 409, 413, 421, 447, 448
Smart, Christopher 429, 665
Smet, Rudolf de 196
Smiles, Sam 632
Smit, H. 616
Smith, Adam 73, 80, 144, 148, 426, 550, 595, 599, 615
Smith, Barbara 393–94, 423, 437, 441, 444, 448
Smith, Benjamin 395
Smith, Bernard 483–84, 506
Smith, Bernhard 518
Smith, Carl 196
Smith, Catherine Delano 29

Smith, Charlotte 376, 389, 395–97, 419, 425, 437, 447, 528, 529
Smith, D. S. 586
Smith, David 16
Smith, David Nichol 396
Smith of Wigton, George 388
Smith, J. E. 617
Smitt, Jeffrey 7
Smith, Johanna M. 448
Smith, John Raphael 625
Smith, Jonathan Z. 196
Smith, Joseph 153
Smith, Keith Vincent 518
Smith, M. M. 586
Smith, Mark M. 196
Smith, Mary 158
Smith, Nicola 228
Smith, Peter D. 353
Smith, Samuel Stanhope 155
Smith, Sarah W. R. 396
Smith, Sir Sidney 546
Smith, S[tephenson]. Percy 491–92
Smith, Terry 518
Smith, Vanessa 502
Smith, William 212
Smither, Howard E. 647–48
Smogulecki, Nikolaus 198
Smoler, Fredric 133
Smollett, Tobias 374, 382, 420, 667, 668
Smyth, Elaine 16
Smyth, Elizabeth M. 196
Smyth, Jim 85, 105, 123, 129, 135, 138, 139, 172, 196, 202, 617
Smythe, W. R. 562
Snapp, J. Russell 85
Sneidern, Maja-Lisa von 380, 448
Snobelen, Stephen D. 196, 617
Snyder, Holly 196, 197
Snyder, L. J. 617
So'o, Asofou 518
Soane, Sir John 224
Soares, Luiz Carlos 85, 197

Soboth, Christian 354
Sobredo, James 512
Soffer, Reba N. 379
Sofka, James R. 85
Soghayroun, Ibrahim E. 197
Sohm, Philip L. 228
Sokol, David 197
Sokoloff, Kenneth L. 42
Sol, Antoinette 660
Sola, Anne de 312, 448
Sola-Corbacho, Juan Carlos 86
Solbach, Andreas 319, 321–22, 324, 335, 337, 345, 348, 354, 356, 359
Soler, José Mariá 273
Soler i Fabregat, Ramon 534
Soles, David 197
Soley, Clive 532
Sollers, Philippe 298
Solly, D. 631
Solovjova, K. 563
Sommer, Andreas Urs 197
Sommer-Mathis, Andrea 288
Sommereux, Ann 617
Sonnenberg-Stern, Karina 563
Sophocles 661
Sordet, Yann 86
Sorel, Charles 454
Sorell, Tom 617
Sørensen, Bengt Algot 354
Sørensen, Bent 228, 632
Sorensen, Janet 668
Sorkin, David 197
Sorrenson, Richard 197
Soto, Rosalba Cruz 197
Soubeyroux, Jacques 266, 270, 271–73, 276, 277, 279, 281–82, 283, 286, 287, 288, 290
Souhami, Diana 86
Soulodre-La France, Renée 86
Sousa Araújo, António de 197
Souter, Kay Torney 448
Southam, B. C. 448
Southerne, Thomas 378

Southey, Robert 514
Southgate, Beverley C. 197
Souza, Juliana Beatriz Almeida de 198
Sowerby, Robin 448
Sozzi, Lionello 312
Spaans, Joke 198
Spaas, Lieve 312
Spacks, Patricia Meyer 312, 446, 447, 448
Spaeth, Donald A. 198
Spaethling, Robert 648
Spalding, Matthew 198
Spallanzani, Lazzaro 599
Spallanzani, Mariafranca 617
Spangler, Jewel L. 198
Sparagni, Tulliola 525, 625
Sparks, John 198
Sparks, Randy J. 49
Sparrow, Elizabeth 563
Spary, E. C. 52
Speck, W. A. 12, 29
Spector, Sheila A. 198
Spedding, Patrick 312, 409, 449
Spence, George 203
Spence, Jon 449
Spence, Joseph 417
Spence, Thomas 662
Spencer, Jane 411
Spencer, John 200
Spencer, Susan 449–50
Spenser, Edmund 394, 395, 406, 446
Spicker, Friedemann 354
Spieckermann, Marie-Luise 394, 438
Spinelli, Riccardo 228
Spini, Giorgio 86, 198
Spinoza, Baruch (Benedict[us]) de 161, 195, 590, 594, 598, 604, 606, 612, 616, 617, 618, 619
Sprenger, Scott 312
Spring, Matthew 249
Springman, K. T. 586
Sprod, Dan 518
Sproule, Anna 198

Index

Spurr, John 198
Spyra, Janusz 198
Sreenivasan, Gopal
St. George, Robert Blair 586
Stabile, Susan M. 477
Stadler, Gustavus 674
Staël, Germaine, Madame de 296, 306, 394, 552, 657, 659
Stafford, J. Martin 617
Stahl, Peter 171
Stallknecht, Fabian A. 263
Staloff, Darren 586
Stammers, M. 563
Standaert, Nicolas 198
Standen, Dale 170
Staniforth, Mark 519
Stansione, Massimo 220
Stanley, Brian 86, 198
Stanley, Charlotte 101
Stanley, Glenn 250
Stanley, J. Ford 199
Stanley, John 256
Stanton, Judith Phillips 448
Stanton, Lucia 586
Stapelfeldt, Gerhard 86
Stapleton, M. L. 450
Stark, David M. 86
Stark, W. 534
Starke, Mariana 428
Starker, Janos 642
Starkey, Armstrong 199
Starkey, David J. 86
Starkey, Janet 44, 64, 78, 86
Starkey, Paul 44, 64, 78, 86
Stavinschi, Magdalena 199
Stearns, Shubal 198
Stedall, Jacqueline Anne 617
Stedman, Gesa 370, 377
Steele, Jeffrey 473
Steele, Sir Richard 667
Steele, Volney 199
Steensens, Niels 178
Stefanov, Svetoslav 86

Steggle, Matthew 450
Steigerwald, Jörn 312, 322
Stein, Charlotte von 316, 330, 331, 334
Stein, Craig C. 199
Stein, K. James 199
Stein, Louise K. 288
Steinberg, Arthur K. 87
Steinbicker, Clemens 227
Steinbrügge, Lieselotte 26
Steiner, S. A. 637
Steiner, Stefanie 250
Steller, Georg 548
Stellmacher, Wolfgang 354
Stenger, Gerhardt 617
Stenson, Marcia 494
Stepanov, V. P. 354
Stephens, Anthony 354
Stephenson, R. H. 354
Stern, Giovanni 623
Stern, Isaac 642
Stern, Julia 450
Stern, R. 618
Stern, Selma 87
Sterne, Laurence 3, 292, 296, 310, 368, 373, 374, 381, 385, 387, 389, 400, 402, 413, 418, 427, 430, 435, 439, 441, 442, 444, 449, 452, 455, 457, 459
Steuart, James 548
Stevens, D. 563
Stevens, Elizabeth C. 575
Stevens, Helen M. 144
Stevens, Jane R. 243–44, 250–51, 252–53
Stevens, Kit 501
Stevenson, C. 632
Stevenson, Christine 199
Stevenson, David 87, 450, 563
Stevenson, Gordon Park 618
Stevenson, Kay Gilliland 450, 668
Stevenson, Robert Louis 207
Stewart, A. 563
Stewart of Appin, Dougal 563

Stewart, Dugald 177, 431
Stewart, Joan Hinde 313, 450
Stewart, M. A. 129, 144, 146, 168, 172, 177, 197, 199, 202
Stewart, Philip 450, 660
Stewart, Tom 354
Stewart, Tony K. 199
Stewart, Walter K. 3, 317
Stiattesi, Pietro 220
Stibbert, Frederick 87
Stieglitz, Olaf 65
Stievermann, Jan 354
Stiffoni, Gian Giacomo 288–89
Stillingfleet, Edward (Bishop) 199
Stillman, Peter G. 451
Stillman, Robert E. 451
Stilz, Gerhard 517, 518, 519
Stinson, Russell 648
Stirk, Nigel 87, 199
Stobart, Jon 563
Stock, Barbara 618
Stock, R. D. 668
Stoddard, Solomon 103
Stolberg, Friedrich Leopold, Graf von 327
Stolberg, Michael 200, 618
Stole, Ingeborg 534
Stoler, Ann Laura 87
Stollberg-Rilinger, Barbara 87
Stone, A. 251
Stone, Daniel 87
Stone, J. C. 618
Stone, Lawrence 179
Stoomberg, Harriet J. 534–35
Storey, Geoffrey O. 200
Storrs, Christopher 563
Stoschek, Jeannette 526, 625
Stovel, Bruce 451
Stovel, Nora Foster 451
Stowell, Robin 251
Strack, Friedrich 354
Strainchamps, Edmond 645, 648
Strand, Ginger 635

Stratmann, Silke 506
Straub, Kristina 451
Strauss, D. F. M. 618
Strawson, Peter F. 613
Strayer, Brian Eugene 87, 200
Streiff, Patrick 200
Streitberger, Fritz 355
Strickland, Michael 200
Strickland, Trent 200
Strickrodt, Silke 87
Strien-Chardonneau, Madeleine van 660
Strindberg, August 317
Stroev, Alexandre 660
Stroh, Patricia 251
Strohm, Richard 251
Strong, Kathryn 14, 458–59
Stroud, Elaine Condouris 53, 95, 137–38, 148, 179, 212
Stroumsa, Guy G. 200
Struck, Bernhard 87
Struever, Nancy S. 451
Strugnell, Anthony 16, 291, 313, 535
Strunk, W. Oliver 254
Stukenbrock, Karin 88, 200
Sturgeon, Nicholas 200
Sturkenboom, Dorothée 200, 563
Sturm-Martin, Imke 82
Stuurman, Siep 563
Suarez, Michael F. 14, 16
Subramanian, Lakshmi 88, 200
Suderman, Jeffrey M. 88
Sueur, Philippe 88
Suire, Éric 88
Sullivan, Heather I. 200
Sullivan, John 355
Sullivan, Robert E. 111, 189, 200, 201
Sultan, Tipu 77
Sulzer, Caroline 615
Sulzer, Johann Georg 253
Sumi, Yoichi 313, 451
Summers, J. H. 586
Sumner, James 88, 201
Šumrada, Janez 201

Index

Sundhausen, Holm 36, 90
Supicic, I. 648
Surwillo, Lisa 271–73
Sussman, Charlotte 563
Sutcliffe, Richard 251
Sutherland, Heather 88, 201
Suzuki, Akihito 605
Svatos, Martin 88
Svitak, Zbynek 206
Swain, Shurlee 519
Swales, Martin 355
Swan, Beth 449, 451
Swanson, Heidi 331
Sward, Ellen E. 88
Swedenborg, Emanuel 107
Sweet, Daniel 583, 584
Sweet, James H. 587
Sweet, John Wood 88, 201
Sweet, R. 564
Sweet, Rosemary 88
Sweetman, John 632
Swendsen, Haagen 449
Swift, Jonathan 37, 124, 179, 299, 370, 375, 377, 378, 388, 389, 394, 409, 414, 418, 419, 421, 423, 424, 428, 429, 436, 438, 439, 441, 444, 446, 451, 452, 456, 459, 460, 523, 663, 668
Sydney, Viscount 507–08
Sylvos, Françoise 660
Symonds, Craig L. 21
Symons, John 201
Syrett, D. 564
Syrotinski, Michael 452
Szafarz, Jolanta 322
Szczekalla, M. 618
Szechi, Daniel 201
Tackett, Timothy 201, 564
Tadie, Alexis 452
Tadmor, Naomi 89
Tagge, Anne 452
Tagliani, Marianna 617
Tague, Ingrid H. 89
Taillemite, Étienne 492
Tait, L. Gordon 201, 618
Takagi, Midori 587
Talbot, Michael 251, 648
Talha, Naureen 201
Tallerud, B. 618
Tamari, Steve 89, 201
Tamer, Annette C. 477
Tammiksaar, Erki 201
Tan, Amy E. Harris 449–50
Tanck de Estrada, Dorothy 89
Tankard, Paul 668
Tanner, John 674
Tantillo, Astrida Orle 355
Tanturri, Alberto 201
Tappenbeck, Inka 335, 344
Tappert, Birgit 318, 325, 329, 340, 343, 346, 347, 352, 355
Tardieu, Jean-Pierre 289
Tarin, René 89, 313
Tarleton, Banastre (General) 579
Tarlton, Charles D. 618
Tarter, Michele Lise 164, 172, 467, 477, 478, 606, 609
Tasker, John 492
Tasman, Abel Janszoon 479, 487, 501, 508
Tassi, Agostino 220
Tassin, Guy 89
Tateo, Francesco 355
Taufferer, Franz Xavier 123
Tausch, Harald 332
Taylor, Alan 201
Taylor, Brian 506
Taylor, C. James 577
Taylor, E. Derek 202, 452
Taylor, Edward 116, 462, 469, 473, 475, 476
Taylor, Jacqueline 618
Taylor, Jacob 476
Taylor, Kay S. 89
Taylor, Kenneth L. 202
Taylor, Nancy 263

Taylor, S. 587
Taylor, William 260, 261
Tcherkezoff, Serge 492
Teeuwen, Rudolphus 415, 452, 515, 519
Teistler, Gisela 522
Teillet, Claude 202
Teja, Jesus F. de la 202
Tejada, Luis Coronas 89
Tekakwhitha, Kateri 149
Telemann, Georg Philipp 257–58, 331
Tellini, Gino 355
Teltscher, Kate 564
Temianka, Henri 642
Temple, Charlotte 669, 673
Tennenhouse, Leonard 477, 668
Terdiman, Richard 313
Termianka, Henri 642
Terquem, Olry 161
Terrasse, Jean 313
Terry, Richard 668
Tetochi, Isabella 654
Teulon, F. 202
Teute, Fredrika 618
Thale, Mary 202
Thayer, John 154
Theibault, John 561
Theobald, Mary Miley 587
Thévenot, Marie-Hélène 564
Thiel, Udo 202
Thielke, Peter 202
Thiery, Robert 303, 304, 313, 368
Thiesen, Barbara A. 202
Thiesen, John D. 175
Thiesse, Anne-Marie 89, 564
Thistlethwaite, Mark 228
Thomas, Chantal 560
Thomas, David C. 202
Thomas, Downing A. 313
Thomas, Gary C. 239
Thomas, J. P. 611
Thomas, Nicholas 478, 483, 487, 488, 489, 491, 492, 499, 502
Thomas, Philip 542, 570
Thomas, Richard F. 452
Thomas, Ruth P. 313
Thomasius, Christian 149, 150, 152, 322, 331
Thomasius, Jakob 619
Thompson, C. B. 618
Thompson, Emma 389
Thompson, Gary Richard 674
Thompson, Helen 452
Thompson, James 452
Thompson, Kevin 202
Thompson, Noel 89
Thompson, Peggy 452
Thompson, Robert 231
Thompson, Shirley 251
Thomson, Arthur S[aunders]. 506
Thomson, James 15, 380, 404, 414, 442, 447, 531, 668
Thomson, Jane 486, 491
Thomson, Peter 452
Thomson, Thomas 89
Thon, Eleonore 334
Thoreau, Henry David 473, 476
Thorn, Jennifer 452
Thorne, Christian 453
Thrale, Hester Lynch (Hester Thrale Piozzi) 369, 422, 561
Thuente, Mary Helen 202
Thuillier, Guy 69
Thums, Barbara 355
Thuret, Isaac 613
Thurlow, Lord 408
Tickell, Thomas 377
Tidcombe, Marianne 523
Tieck, Ludwig 328, 351, 400
Tieken-Boon van Ostade, Ingrid 16
Tiepolo, Giovanni Battista 623
Tierney, Brian 203
Tierney, James 16
Tietz, Manfred 89
Tighe, Janet A. 209
Tilby, Michael J. 453

Index

Tillery, Denise 444
Tilley, Joy 535
Tillot-D'Argental 293
Tillotson, John 148
Timmermanns, Benoit 656
Timms, Edward 203
Tinsley, Barbara Sher 203
Tintoretto (Jacopo Robusti) 221
Tippner, Anja 90, 313, 355
Tise, Larry E. 587
Tissot, Samuel 127
Titzenhofer, Sophie Eleonore 334
Toaff, Ariel 364
Tob, Sem 278
Tobin, Robert D. 203
Tobin, Ronald W. 313
Tocchini, Gerardo 648
Todd, Dennis 3–4, 16, 292, 369, 370, 371, 373, 391, 416, 419, 432, 438, 439, 448, 451, 453
Todd, Janet M. 411
Todd, M. 564
Todes, Samuel 203
Todorskii, Simeon 343
Todorov, Tzvetan 203, 427
Tóibín, Colm 453
Toker, Leona 453
Toland, John 118, 597
Tolbert, J. T. 619
Toledano Buendia, Carmen 314, 453
Tollet, Daniel 203
Tolley, Thomas 251
Tolron, Francine 506
Tomalin, Claire 668
Toman, Cynthia 203
Tomaselli, Sylvana 453
Tombarel-Fauconnier, Annick 535
Tomes, Nancy 203
Tomic, Sacha 203
Tomicka-Krumrey, Ewa 82
Tomlins, Christopher L. 90
Tomlinson, Charles 453
Tomlinson, Sophie 453

Tompson, Benjamin 471, 476
Tone, Theobald Wolfe 503, 560, 672
Tongiorgi, Tomasi Lucia 203
Tonnesson, Kare 90
Toohey, John 90, 507
Topazio, Virgil W. 314
Topia, André 668
Torke, Hans-Joachim 90
Torney-Parlicki, Prue 508
Torre Curiel, José Refugio de la 90
Torrente, Álvaro 266–67, 269, 270, 276, 277, 279, 280, 281, 287, 288–89
Torres, Maria Amparo Ros 204
Torres Nebrera, Gregorio 265, 266, 282, 283, 289–90
Torres Sánchez, Jaime 90
Torrey, E. Fuller 90, 204
Toscani, Claudio 251
Tosi, Laura 405, 453
Tosti, Osvaldo 204
Tóth, István György 90, 102, 117, 129, 130, 131, 151, 160, 162, 174, 175, 179, 186, 191, 203, 204, 207
Toubiana, Guy 364
Touchard, Jean 90
Toulalan, Sarah 90
Toulouse, Teresa A. 478, 674
Tournebize, Cassilde 564
Tournier, Michel 436
Tourte, François Xavier, le Jeune 240
Townley, Charles 628
Trabulse, Elías 204
Trampus, A. 564
Traninger, A. 92
Trapnell, William 213
Trappes-Lomax, John 204
Trebiliani, Maria Luisa 619
Trebitsch of Mikulov, Abraham 207
Trees, Andy 587
Treloar, John L. 204
Trench, Watkin 498
Tréogate, Joseph-Marie Loaisel de 311,

314
Treviño, Carlos Viesca 204
Trevor, William 454
Trigueros, Cándido María 284
Triller, Ursula 320
Trimmer, Sarah 15, 441, 535, 668
Trinchera, Pietro 361
Troide, Lars E. 380
Trojan, J. 64
Trollope, Anthony 465
Troost, Linda V. 91, 204, 379, 384, 389, 390, 393, 394, 411, 414, 420, 429, 430, 442, 454
Trotter, Catharine 415
Trouille, Mary Seidman 450
Trousson, Raymond 292, 314
Troy, John Thomas (Bishop) 133
Troy, Patrick 497, 503, 504, 507
Trudel, Marcel 564
Trumbull, John 465, 467
Truxes, Thomas E. 91
Tchaikovsky, Piotr Ilyitch (also: Tschaikowsky, Peter Iljitsch) 642
Tsapina, Olga A. 204
Tseëlon, Efrat 410, 454
Tubbs, William 240
Tuchman, Phyllis 619
Tuck, Richard 91
Tucker, P. 564
Tuckey, J[ames]. H[ingston]. 519
Tulard, Jean 564
Tulloch, John 386, 430
Tuma, Michael 214
Tunstall, Kate E. 314
Tuomey, Michael 204
Turenne, Comte de 592
Turgot, Anne Robert Jacques 291, 299, 556
Türk, Daniel Gottlieb 648
Turnbull, Paul 492–93, 516
Turner, Anthony 547
Turner, Caroline 516
Turner, Frederick Jackson 40
Turner, J. M. W. 632
Turner, Nat 83, 193
Turner, Stephen 493
Turner, William 631
Turra, Elisabetta Caminer 362
Turrell, Jane 471, 476
Tusa, Michael C. 251
Tüskés, Gábor 205
Tusseau, Guillaume 205
Tuyll van Serooskerken, Willem René van 660
Twagilimana, Aimable 674
Twain, Mark 8
Tweedale, G. 619
Twining, William 121
Tyerman, Daniel 501
Tyler, Natalie 454
Tyler, Royall 669, 673
Tyrsenko, Andreï Vladimirovich 205
Udovich, JoAnn 234–36, 256–257
Uerlings, Herbert 339, 501, 507
Uglow, Nathan 16
Uhalley, Stephen, Jr. 33, 43, 76, 205
Uhm, Yong-Hee 454
Uhrig, Reinhard 454
Ullmann, Helen Schatvet 205
Ulrich, Laurel Thatcher 91, 205, 587
Ultee, Maarten 91, 205
Umar, Muhammad 91
Underdown, David 91
Ungaretti, Giuseppe 361
Upton, Anthony F. 91
Urban, Hugh B. 205
Uribe Uran, Victor 91
Urstad, Tone Sundt 669
Ustinov, Peter 231
Vaccari, Ezio 205, 619
Vaget, Hans Rudolf 355
Vaggioli, Dom Felice 507
Vahtre, Sulev 91
Vaillant, Alain 659
Vainio-Korhonen, Kirsi 564
Vaj, Daniela 205

Index

Vajda, György M. 402, 416, 444
Valasek, Hubert 206
Valentin (de Boulogne), Moise 225
Valero, José Antonio 267–68, 283–86
Valestuk, Lorraine 428
Valiance, Edward 206
Valle Pavon, Guillermina del 91
Vallée, M. G. 91
Vallois, Marie Claire 314
Valmont, Madame de 309
Valois, Marguerite de 306
Valone, David A. 206
Vamboulis, Epaminondas 206
Van Beusekom, M. 587
Van Blarenberghe, L.-N. 623
Van Bunge, Wiep 619
Van Butchell, Martin 594
Van den Berg, Richard 565
Van der Kemp, Johannes 543
Van der Laan, James M. 356, 619
Van der Palm, K. 607
Van der Schueren, Eric 368, 389, 451
Van Dyke, Sir Anthony 220, 384
Van Ingen, Ferdinand 356
Van Kley, Dale K. 28, 111, 170, 176, 204, 206, 209
Van Mill, David 206
Van Sas, N. C. F. 626, 632
Van Strien Chardonneau, Madeleine 314
Van Zanden, Henry 493
Vanbrugh, Sir John 631, 639, 645
Vandenabeele, Bart 206
VandenBerg, Richard 92
VanDeusen, Nancy E. 206
Vane, Sir Henry 180
Vanhaute, Eric 92
Vanoflen, Laurence 294
Vanpée, Janie 660
Vanysacker, Dries 206
Varani, G. 619
Varenius, Bernhard 115
Varma, Lalima 206
Varney, Andrew 455

Varry, Dominique 522, 565
Vasconcelos, Sandra Guardini T. 455
Vason, George 514
Vater, Johann Severin 346
Vater, Michael 206, 207
Vaughan, M. 619
Vaughan, William 478
Vauvenargues, Luc de Clapiers, Marquis de 294
Vaux, Roberts 99
Vaux, Sieur de 55
Vavoulis, Vassilis 255–56, 640
Vázquez, Manuel E. 342
Vázquez Medel, Manuel Ángel 289, 290
Vecchi, Paola 303, 314
Veen, Henk van 623, 624, 625, 626–27, 629, 630, 632
Vega, Judith 660
Veit, Walter F. 507
Velagic, Zoran 207
Velázquez, Diego Rodríguez de Silva y 220, 625
Velasquez, E. A. 565
Velasquez, Melida 92
Velcic, Vlatka 455
Velissariou, Aspasia 669
Velkley, Richard L. 207
Ventura Rexón y Lucas, Diego 282
Venturi, Franco 55, 153
Vera, Eugenia Roldan 207
Verburch, Vranck 177
Vercruysse, Jeroom 297
Verdi, Giuseppe 220, 246
Verelst, Karin 196
Vergara, Lisa 222, 228
Verhoeven, W. M. 672, 673
Verlaine, Paul 659
Vermeer, Johannes (Jan) 218, 221–23, 224, 224, 225, 226, 227, 229
Vermeule, Blakey 619
Verpeaux, Michel 539
Verplanck, Anne 632
Verri, Alessandro 541

Verrips, Maaike 294
Versini, Laurent 314
Verwer, P. A. 607
Vescovo, Piermario 324, 361, 364
Vetter, Walther 232
Veyssière La Croze, Mathurin 308
Viano, Francesca Lidia 455
Vickers, Anita 675
Vickers, D. 587
Vickery, Amanda 92
Vico, G(i)ambattista 128, 362, 451, 454
Vicq, Pierre 92
Vieillard-Baron, Jean-Louis 381, 419
Vieira, Antonio 619
Viele, Anna 11
Vierling-Ihrig, Heike Irma Katharina 92
Vierne, Béatrice 56
Viesca, Carlos 207
Vigneau-Wilberg, Thea 526
Vigneault, Érik 657, 660
Vignolles, H. 619
Vilalta, María José 290
Vilar, Juan Bautista 273
Villacañas, Beatriz 207
Villani, P. 565
Villatoux, Marie-Catherine 92, 207
Villedieu, Marie-Catherine de Desjardins de 656
Villiers, Alan 519
Villis, Carl 619
Vincendeau, Ginette 399, 455
Vincent, David 22
Vincent, Deirdre 356
Vincent, Stephen A. 587
Virgil (Publius Vergilius Maro) 387, 431, 434, 452, 469–77, 525, 624
Visonà, Mara 229
Vittorelli, Iacopo 362
Vivaldi, Antonio 236, 248, 250, 251, 648
Vlastuin, W. van 207
Vlcek, Radomir 92
Vocelka, Karl 92
Vogel, Emil 645
Vogt, Peter 207
Vogtherr, Christope Martin 229
Voigt, Johannes 507
Volek, T. 648
Völkel, Markus 93, 207
Volkonsky, Zinaida, Princess 547
Volland, Sophie 651, 652, 658
Vollhardt, Friedrich 356
Vollmann, Ralf 356
Volpilhac Auger, Catherine 314
Volta, Alessandro 25, 106
Voltaire (François-Marie Arouet de) 13, 16, 21, 102, 146, 168, 182, 206, 290, 291, 293, 294, 297, 300, 302, 305, 306, 307, 308, 309, 310, 313, 314, 315, 344, 386, 400, 425, 599, 650, 653, 655, 657, 658, 659
Voltaire, Madame 67
Volterrano, B. Franceschini 223
Volwahsen, Andreas 207
Von Bonstetten, Karl Viktor 565
Vondraskova, Iveta 207
Voogd, Peter de 455
Voorhees, David William 208
Voros, Kati 208
Voß, Johann Heinrich 335, 344, 359
Voth, Hans-Joachim 184
Vouet, Simon 225
Vovnyanko, A. 563
Vroede, M. de 208
Vrooman, Sue Evans 527, 551
Vulpius, Christian August 356–57
Vulpius, Christiane 356
Vulpius, Ricarda 36, 90
Vuyst, Wout de 93
Wächter, Leonhard 348
Wackenroder, Wilhelm Heinrich 324, 355
Wadauer, Sigrid 93
Waddell, J. N. 408
Wade, N. J. 620
Wade, Nicholas 208

Waeber, Jacqueline 252, 314
Wägenbaur, Birgit 321, 332
Waggoner, Hyatt H. 472
Wagner, Irmgard 358
Wagner, Jacques 315, 565, 660
Wagner, Marie-France 263
Wagner, Peter 565
Wagstaff, Malcolm 93
Wahl, Volker 358
Wahrman, Dror 93, 565
Waingrow, Marshall 375
Wainwright, Jonathan 231
Wait, E. 620
Wakao, Yuji 93
Wakefield, Edith A. 101
Wakefield, Priscilla 390
Waldron, Mary 455
Wales, William 502
Walford, David 208
Walis, Ruth 620
Walk, Lori 450, 455
Walker, Anita M. 208
Walker, Brett L. 93, 565
Walker, Corinne 208
Walker, Gina Luria 139
Walker, Harlan 60
Walker, J. 565
Walker, John 42, 129
Walker, Lesley H. 93, 315
Walker, Philip L. 208
Walker, William 455
Wall, Cynthia 3–4, 16, 292, 369, 370, 371, 373, 391, 416, 419, 432, 438, 439, 448, 451, 453, 669
Wall, Richard 21, 31, 93
Wallace, Elizabeth Kowaleski 455
Wallace, Kathleen R. 368, 411
Wallace, Miriam 455
Wallen, Gerard de 229
Wallenberg, Jacob 661
Waller, Ralph 208
Walling, Karl-Friedrich 587
Wallis, John 602, 617
Wallis, Samuel 502
Wallwork, Jo 312, 370, 416, 423, 429, 449, 453, 456
Walpole, Horace 4, 371, 373, 383, 407, 427, 450, 455, 458
Walpole, Sir Robert 669
Walser-Wilhelm, Doris 565
Walser-Wilhelm, Peter 565
Walsh, John Evangelist 93
Walsh, Lorena Seebach 93, 587
Walsh, Marcus 13, 14, 17
Walsh, Patrick 93
Walsh, Sean 456
Walsh, Thomas 293, 295, 297, 302, 305, 309, 310, 311, 314, 315
Walsh, V. 587
Walsham, Alexandra 565
Walter, John 28
Walters, Robert L. 208
Walther, Johann Gottfried 252–53
Wang, Rongbin 208
Warburton, Penny 6, 387, 391, 392–93, 403, 404, 413, 415, 418, 421, 432, 453, 456, 459, 664
Ward, Andrew 208
Ward, David C. 630
Ward, Gerald W. R. 43
Ward, Seth 601
Ward, W. R. 209
Wareham, T. 565
Warminski, Andrzej 358
Warner, Christopher J. 456
Warner, Jessica 94
Warner, John Harley 209
Warren, Jack D., Jr. 588
Warren, Joyce W. 674, 675
Waron, Joseph 447
Warton, Thomas 447
Warwick, Jeff 626–27
Washington, George 29, 30, 62, 63, 66, 68, 71, 75, 77, 85, 87, 228, 378, 385, 462, 463, 467, 468, 475, 476, 568, 573, 575, 588

Washington, Lady Martha Custic 475
Wasserman, Earl 446
Wasserstein, Bernard 209
Watanabe, Koji 456
Watanabe-O'Kelly, Helen 535, 566
Watelet, C.-H. 602
Waterhouse, Henry 507–08
Waterhouse, Richard 493, 508
Waters, John 456
Waters, Peter 523
Wätjer, Jürgen 209
Watkins, E. 598, 620
Watkins, Eric 209
Watson, William C. 209
Watt, Ian 8, 666, 667
Watt, James 118, 198, 609
Watteau, Jean Antoine 221, 525
Watts, Isaac 150
Watts, Ruth 620
Watts, Sheldon 158
Waxman, Wayne 620
Wear, A. 388
Wear, Andrew 543
Weaver, John C. 209, 263
Webb, George 476
Webb, J. 229
Webb, Timothy 566
Webb, Vivienne 508, 566
Weber, Caroline 315
Weber, Christoph 209
Weber, Francis J. 209
Weber, Veit 348
Weber-Bockoldt, Petra 253
Webster, C. 620
Webster, James 253
Webster, Noah 475
Webster, T. 566
Wedde, Ian 406
Weddle, Meredith Baldwin 209
Weder, Christine 209, 358
Weekley, Carolyn J. 620
Weeks, Daniel J. 94
Weidemann, Hermann 209

Weigel, Hermine 246
Weigel, Sigrid 358
Weigelt, Horst 358
Weil, François 588
Weil, Rachel 566
Weil, Sebastien 94
Weiller, Cajetan von 92
Weimar, Klaus 358
Weinberg, Bennett Alan 209
Weinberg, Robert 210
Weinberger, Elisabeth 94
Weinbrot, Howard D. 94, 185, 456
Weiner, Howard 253
Weingrad, Michael 210
Weinman, Jaime J. 456
Weir, Judith 635
Weiss, Hermann F. 358
Weiss, Holger 210
Weiss, Otto 210
Weissberg, Liliane 358, 568, 586
Weissengruber, Erik 358
Weizsäcker, Richard von 358
Weldon, Shawn 155
Wellenreuther, Hermann 31, 126, 132, 133, 187
Welsh, Caroline 318, 344, 358
Weltman-Aron, Brigitte 94
Wendel, Thomas 243
Wender, Herbert 350
Wendors, Richard 632
Wenner, Barbara Britton 457
Went-Daoust, Yvette 660
Werkstetter, Christine 94
Werlen, Hans-Jakob 588
Wesley, Charles 210
Wesley, John 34, 110, 127, 146, 161, 380, 608
Wesley, Marilyn C. 675
Wesley, Samuel 157, 178, 243, 603, 642
Wesley, Susanna Annesley 187
Wesselius, Allen Doc 210
West, Jane 348

Index

West, Benjamin 631
West, James L. W., III 6, 373, 420, 423, 522
West, Russell 457, 478, 487
West, Shearer 622
Westerfield Tucker, Karen B. 210
Westfall, Marilyn 457
Weston, John 433
Wetering, Ernst van de 527, 628
Weyler, Karen A. 478
Wezel, Johann Karl 332
Wharam, Alan 94
Whatley, Christopher A. 566
Whatley, Janet 315
Whatmore, R. 566
Wheatley, Phillis 466, 472, 474, 476, 477, 670, 672
Wheeler, Roxann 94
Wheeler, Susan 535–36
Wheelock, Arthur K., Jr. 222, 229
Whelan, Frederick G. 94
Whelan, Timothy 210
Whewell, William 609, 617
Whitaker, John 420
White, Barbara 635
White, Charles Edward 210
White, Clare 94
White, Eryn M. 210
White, Hayden 560
White, Heather Rachelle 210
White, J. S. 620
White, William (Bishop) 151, 170, 210
Whitebread, Judith 370
Whitefield, George 116, 142
Whitelam (also: Whitlam), Sarah 490, 517
Whitman, Walt 671, 673
Whittaker, Jason 669
Whyman, Susan E. 457, 566
Whyte, Ian 566
Whytt, Robert 597
Wicke, Andrea 359
Widaman, Jean M. 232–33, 644–46, 647
Widmayer, Jan 15
Wieckenberg, Ernst-Peter 359
Wieczorrek, Michael 359
Wiegmann, A. F. A. 105
Wieland, Christoph Martin 76, 320, 324, 328, 331, 336, 353, 356
Wielema, M. R. 211
Wieniawski, Henryk 642
Wieselhuber, Franz 457
Wiesend, Reinhard 249
Wiesenfarth, Joseph 457
Wiest, Andrew A. 49, 55
Wiethölter, Waltraud 359
Wigger, John H. 211
Wiggins, Rosalind C. 211
Wigglesworth, Michael 670
Wijnekus, V. J. M. L. 537
Wilberforce, William 182
Wilcher, Robert 211
Wilcox, Lance 369–70
Wild of Littleleek, John 414
Wild, Reiner 318, 320, 321, 337, 340, 341, 342, 349
Wilde, Guillermo 211
Wilde, Oscar 430
Wilhelmina of Bayreuth 350, 440
Wilkes, John 384, 430
Wilkins, Charles 398
Wilkins, Peter 435
Wilkins, Roger W. 95
Will de Chaparro, Martina E. 211
Willan, Robert 591
Willcox, William B. 95
Willette, T. 566
William III, King 399
Williams, Alastair 253
Williams, Carolyn D. 211, 457
Williams, Christiane Kuechler 519–20
Williams, Frank 29, 30, 63, 66, 68, 71, 75, 77, 85, 87, 228, 378, 385, 462, 467, 468
Williams, G. 620

Williams, Glyndwr 493
Williams, H. G. 566
Williams, Hanbury 430
Williams, Helen Maria 95, 340, 392, 398, 415, 418, 528
Williams, Howard 211
Williams, James Homer 211
Williams, Jerry M. 17, 290
Williams, John Alexander 211
Williams, John R. 359
Williams, Peter W. 211
Williams, Robert 631
Williams, Roger L. 95
Williams, Roger 137
Williams, Sir John 533
Williams, Susan S. 673
Williams, Vernon J., Jr. 211
Williamson, Arthur 211
Williamson, Johnnie 'Notions' 121
Williamson, Karin 457
Wills, Garry 212
Wilmerding, John 588
Wilner, Arlene Fish 457
Wilputte, Earla A. 458
Wilson, Anna 212
Wilson, Brian 212
Wilson, C. 620
Wilson, Chad 405–06
Wilson, Catherine 212
Wilson, David K. 254–55
Wilson, Eric 642
Wilson, Fiona 458
Wilson, Horace Hayman 398
Wilson, Jeffrey 212
Wilson, Lisa 588
Wilson, Margaret 458
Wilson, Renate 95, 212
Wilson, Richard 95
Wilson, Stephen A. 212
Wilson, W. Daniel 212, 359
Wilson, William 489, 502
Wilton-Ely, John 458
Wiltshire, John 458–59

Wimmer, Andreas 212
Winchester, Simon 212
Winckelmann, Johann Joachim 596
Wind, Astrid 459
Wind, Barry 632
Windisch, Martin 47, 377, 385, 394, 397, 402, 403
Windle, John 536
Windler, Christian 95, 213
Wine, Humphrey 632
Winearls, Joan 536
Winer, Margot 509, 510
Winfield, Robert 194
Winiarski, Douglas L. 675
Winiger-Labuda, Anstazja 208
Winkelmann, Peter 95
Winkfield, Unca Eliza 478
Winkler, Gerhard J. 255
Winks, Robin W. 493
Winn, James Anderson 459
Winnicott, Donald 458
Winnige, Norbert 522
Winship, Michael 213, 478
Winter, Susanne 359, 365
Winterl, Jacob Joseph 154
Wintermeyer, Rolf 359
Wintermute, Alan 632
Winthrop, John 205
Wirtschafter, Elise Kimerling 566
Wiseman, Susan 392, 459
Wister, Sarah 477
Withers, Charles W. 544, 546, 555
Witherspoon, John 201, 618
Witte, Arnd 499
Wittwer, Hector 213
Woesler, Winfried 359
Wokeck, Marianne S. 588
Wokler, Robert 567, 608, 620, 621
Wolcott, Oliver, Jr. 630
Wolf, Christoph 536, 648
Wolf, Norbert Christian 359
Wolfe, James (General) 78
Wolfe, Patrick 493

Index

Wolff, Christian, Freiherr von 338
Wolff, Christoph 255
Wolff, George 110
Wolff, Larry 57, 95
Wolfgang, Aurora 315
Wolking, Henry 636
Wollersheim, Heinz-Werner 71
Wolloch, Nathaniel 621
Wollstonecraft (Godwin), Mary 144, 154, 155, 207, 211, 306, 385, 392, 399, 457, 528, 529, 536, 666
Woloch, Isser 567
Wolper, Roy S. 315
Wolterstorff, Nicolas 213
Wolzogen, Caroline von 334, 339
Wood, Craig D. 213
Wood, David 213
Wood, Dennis 660
Wood, Elizabeth 239
Wood, Houston 493
Wood, Laura Thomason 7
Wood, Marcus 533, 567
Wood, Nigel 459
Wood, Robert E. 213
Wood, Roger 588
Wood, William 153
Woodberry, Bonnie 669
Woodfield, Ian 255, 263–64
Wooding, Jonathan M. 504, 506
Woodman, Richard 95
Woodroofe, Edward 223
Woodruff, Paul 473
Woolard, Margot Ann Greenlimb 648
Wooley, David 668
Woolf, Virginia 412, 459
Woolston, Thomas 213
Wordsworth, William 454, 528
Worley, Sharon 360
Worrall, J. 621
Worth, John E. 213
Wouldenberg, R. V. 621
Wren, Sir Christopher 223
Wright, Amos J. 95

Wright, Beth S. 229
Wright, D. R. 588
Wright, E. 588
Wright, Glenn 459
Wright, Julia M. 406, 520
Wright, Robert E. 96, 588
Wright, Robert Edward 520
Wright of Derby, Joseph 565, 622
Wrigley, R. 621
Wu, Eleanor B. Morris 459
Wu, Xiaoxin 33, 43, 76, 205
Wu, Yixiong 96
Wulf, S. J. 621
Wunder, Amanda 229
Wüst, Wolfgang 39, 321
Wycherley, William 450
Wyller, Truls 213
Wyndham, Marivic 497
Wythe, George 578
Yacou, Alain 96
Yacovone, Donald 570, 579, 588
Yamanouchi, Hisaaki 459
Yang, Su-hsien 96
Yang, Wonkyung 459
Yardeni, Myriam 213
Yates, Mary Ann 264
Yates, Richard 264
Yébenes Torres, Pilar García de 102
Yelloly, John 200
Yeo, Eileen Janes 567
Yeo, Richard R. 17–18, 96, 213
Yildrum, Onur 213
Yim, Denise 315
Yoder, R. Paul 459
Yokota, Kariann 214
Yolton, John W. 214, 621
York, N. L. 589
Yoshinaka, T. 669
Young, Amy L. 214
Young, Brian 14, 18
Young, J. 621
Young, Jeffrey Robert 589
Young, Joanne 589

Young, John R.   214
Young, Sara B.   319
Young, William   439
Young-Mock, Lee   660
Youngberg, Quentin   459
Youngquist, P.   633
Youngs, Tim   512
Yousef, Nancy   214
Yovel, Yirmiyahu   621
Yrigoyen, Charles, Jr.   214
Yu, Xinzhong   214
Yukio, Mishima   652
Zach, Xaver von   113
Zacharias, Lawrence S.   578
Zafar, Rafia   675
Zafren, Herbert C.   165
Zagorin, P.   621
Zajka, Vital   96, 214
Zakatistvos, A.   118
Zall, Paul M.   96, 671
Zalyvskii, Nikolai   96
Zamboni, Lidia   365
Zamora, Andrés   290
Zamoyski, Adam   96
Zanchin, G.   607
Zaretsky, Robert D.   203
Zarka, Yves Charles   214
Zarzoso, Alfons   96, 214
Zayas, Ana de   214
Zayas, Concepción   214
Zbirkova, Viera   214
Zecchi, Lina   315
Zedelmaier, Helmut   96, 215, 301, 310
Zehm, Edith   360
Zeidlerin, Susanna Elisabeth   662
Zeiss, Laurel E.   648
Zelenski, Tadeusz   656
Zelle, Carsten   19, 360, 460
Zeno, Apostolo   233
Zenuch, Peter   215
Zhang, Guangxiang   97
Zhao, Shiyu   215
Zheng, Dedi   128
Zhou, Xun   215
Ziff, Larzer   478
Zimmermann, Johann Georg   339
Zimmerman, Robert   215
Zimpfer, Nathalie   460
Zinsser, Judith P.   215
Zinzendorf, Nikolaus Ludwig von   325
Ziolkowski, Theodore   360
Zionkowski, Linda   460
Zipes, Jack   536, 662
Ziskin, Rochelle   675
Zlatkes, Gwido   198
Zmolek, Mike   97
Znamenskij, Petr Vasilevich   215
Zoffany, Johann   624
Zook, Melinda S.   567
Zorin, Andrei   97
Zoungbo, Victorien Lavou   265, 266, 268–69, 273, 277, 279–80, 282, 286, 287, 289, 290
Zryd, Amédée   215
Zsako, Julius   254
Zubly, John Joachim   176
Zucchi, Luca   215
Zucker, Ross   621
Zückert, Hartmut   80
Zumkeller, Dominique   215
Zumsteeg, Johann Rudolf   246
Zunshine, Lisa   460
Zusman, Perla   97
Zuylen, Belle van (see: Charrière, Isabelle Agneta de)
Zweig, Arnulf   215
Zwicker, Daniel   591
Zwicker, Steven N.   380, 386, 390, 391, 397, 400, 404, 409, 412, 417, 433, 440, 456, 459
Zymner, Rüdiger   360
Zytaruk, Maria   215